MARYLAND CRIMINAL JURY INSTRUCTIONS AND COMMENTARY

Second Edition

DAVID E. AARONSON

Professor of Law

Washington College of Law
American University

THE MICHIE COMPANY
Law Publishers
CHARLOTTESVILLE, VIRGINIA

Library of Congress Catalog Card No. 88-60796
ISBN 0-87473-335-9

For my parents, Edward and May Aaronson,
With Love and Appreciation

FOREWORD

Professor David E. Aaronson was a pioneer in the publication of criminal jury instructions in this State, providing the first edition of *Maryland Criminal Jury Instructions and Commentary* in 1975. In his foreword to that edition, Judge J. Dudley Digges predicted it would prove an invaluable tool to lawyers and judges alike — an expectation that was swiftly met. But few good things last forever, and major changes that have taken place in this dynamic area of the law within the last twelve years mandate a second edition. Happily, Professor Aaronson has been willing to devote his considerable talent and experience, as well as long hours of research, drafting, and redrafting to the production of this edition.

I am confident that judges and attorneys will find this newest work of inestimable assistance in the practice of criminal law. As with any proposed form of instruction, it is essential that the user ensure that the selected instruction is appropriate to the facts of the particular case and, whenever necessary, tailor the form to fit the case. This task has been simplified greatly by the extensive commentary accompanying each instruction which includes current citations of pertinent authority. Moreover, I believe many attorneys will find this book of great assistance at the beginning of their representation in a criminal case, as a quick and easy source of information concerning the elements of each offense charged and the current Maryland law concerning those elements.

We are again indebted to Professor Aaronson for his contribution of a "nuts and bolts" tool that is so likely to help us in our daily endeavors.

John F. McAuliffe
Associate Judge of the
Court of Appeals of Maryland

July 1987

ACKNOWLEDGMENTS

I am greatly indebted to many individuals whose cooperation and help was of vital importance to the successful completion of this second edition. Judges, practicing attorneys, faculty colleagues, students, Michie Company editors, and law school support personnel made valuable contributions of their time and expertise.

A few persons deserve special acknowledgment for their important contributions to this book. My present law school dean, Fred Anderson, and former law school dean, Thomas Buergenthal, provided strong encouragement and financial support in terms of summer research grants and student research assistants. I am deeply appreciative to Hon. John F. McAuliffe for kindly consenting to author the Foreword. Robert C. Lewis, Esquire, of The Michie Company, spent a few months painstakingly editing the entire manuscript. Paul T. Stein, a former student and presently an adjunct faculty colleague, provided office space for drafting committee sessions with practicing attorneys to review instructions and provided many helpful suggestions. Hon. Deborah K. Chasanow, Hon. Howard S. Chasanow, and Hon. Irma S. Raker, a former student and adjunct faculty colleague, were always available to answer questions and made numerous helpful suggestions. Gary E. Bair, a former faculty colleague and presently Chief, Criminal Appeals Division, Maryland Attorney General's Office, also provided numerous helpful suggestions. I am intellectually indebted to Hon. Charles E. Moylan, Jr. for ideas, analysis, and grasp of legal history expressed in his scholarly opinions, publications, and continuing legal education lectures. Of the many outstanding student research assistants who worked with me on this project, I would like especially to acknowledge the contributions of Michele Cohen and Renate Staley.

ACKNOWLEDGMENTS

I am very appreciative for the generous help of many trial judges who provided copies of their own instructions, suggestions, and feedback and critique from their use of instructions in the first edition. In addition to those mentioned above, I wish especially to acknowledge the help of Hon. Elsbeth L. Bothe, Hon. Vincent J. Femia, Hon. James S. McAuliffe, Jr., Hon. William C. Miller, Hon. Joseph F. Murphy, Jr., and Hon. Calvin R. Sanders. I am also indebted to Hon. Rosalyn B. Bell of the Court of Special Appeals for her suggestions and encouragement and to Hon. Henry F. Greene, Superior Court of the District of Columbia, for providing a copy of his *Materials on Special Jury Techniques for the District of Columbia Court* (November, 1984).

The expertise of prosecutors and defense attorneys proved invaluable in drafting sessions. Also, they provided specialized knowledge in such areas as drunk driving laws and the death penalty. The following persons provided especially helpful assistance: Fred W. Bennett, Robert C. Bonsib, Reginald W. Bours, Russell F. Canan, Judith R. Catterton, Gary W. Christopher, Alan J. Goldstein, Barry H. Helfand, Martha G. Kavanaugh, Paul F. Kemp, George Lipman, Michael D. Mason, Robert E. Morin, J. Harrison Phillips III, Richard B. Rosenblatt, Andrew L. Sonner, Richard H. Sothoron, Jr., J. Theodore Wieseman, and Norman H. Yankellow.

Colleagues at the Washington College of Law, American University, have been a valuable source of information, ideas and suggestions, and assistance. I have benefited from discussions with Elliott Milstein, director of the law school's clinical program, Nancy Cook and Robert Dinerstein, co-directors of the Criminal Justice Clinic, and Paul Rice, Ira Robbins, and Herman Schwartz, colleagues sharing teaching interests in criminal law and procedure and evidence. Egon Guttman provided valuable suggestions and encouragement.

Students have made important contributions to this book. Several of them are now practicing lawyers in Maryland. Some of these students have served as my research assistants, some have contributed through independent study research projects, and others have provided feedback from their use of draft material in actual cases handled through the law school's criminal justice clinic. I am very appreciative for the assistance of the following individuals: Philip Andrews, Madeline Caliendo, Michele Cohen, Audrey Van Dyke, Roger Galvin, Abbe Gouse, Kathy Geraci, Janet Gifford, Stuart Kirsch, Jules Mermelstein, Maurice Mitts, Tom Mierswa, Sheri Orlowitz, Alain Santana, Denise Seidelman, Renate Staley, and David Thomas.

Special thanks to Mary Wason, office manager at the law school, Rosemarie Pal and Estela Scully for secretarial assistance, Iris Aberbach for editorial suggestions, Michael Benson for his helpful advice, and to Frances H. Warren and Jeff Coughter of The Michie Company.

While I am extremely fortunate to have had the assistance of the persons mentioned above, the views expressed as well as any errors in this book are solely my responsibility.

D. E. A.

INTRODUCTION

The substantive criminal laws of Maryland, and related areas of criminal procedure and evidence, have undergone many judicial and legislative changes since the first edition of this book was published in 1975. Also, some extraordinary changes have occurred in particular areas. Reflecting these changes, the six areas described below have been given special emphasis both in the instructions and commentary:

1. *Burdens of proof, presumptions, and inferences:* Major changes occurred in the burden of persuasion and the use of presumptions. In *Evans v. State,* affirmed by the Court of Appeals in 1976, Judge Charles E. Moylan, Jr., wrote a learned opinion, interpreting U.S. Supreme Court decisions, which had a major impact in such areas as homicide and criminal defenses. Numerous decisions interpreting the *Evans* case followed. Appendix V traces the impact of the *Evans* case.

2. *Rape and sexual offenses:* The General Assembly, effective July 1, 1976, enacted a comprehensive revision of the sexual offense laws. Two degrees of rape and four degrees of sexual offenses were recognized with punishment varying according to the degree of the offense. One of the objectives was to make the sexual offense laws gender neutral. A so-called "rape shield" law was enacted, limiting the evidentiary use of a sexual offense victim's prior sexual history. Effective July 1, 1987, the use of the "Lord Hale" instruction was prohibited.

3. *Theft and bad check offenses:* The General Assembly, effective July 1, 1979, enacted a comprehensive revision and consolidation of the theft and bad check offense laws. A new offense of "theft" was created in order to eliminate technical distinctions among the common law offenses of larceny, embezzlement, and false pretenses. Portions of the

legislative history, Official Commentary of the Joint Subcommittee on Theft Related Offenses, are included in the comment sections following each of the theft and bad check offense instructions.

4. *Homicide and related offenses:* Major changes in the burden of persuasion and the use of presumptions were noted earlier. The defense of imperfect self-defense, to reduce murder to manslaughter, was judicially recognized in 1983. The mental state of the crime of assault with intent to murder was clarified. The General Assembly reenacted a death penalty statute in 1978, attempting to comply with U.S. Supreme Court decisions. Recently, the U.S. Supreme Court granted certiorari to hear a Maryland case, *Mills v. State.* The Maryland Court of Appeals has authored several important opinions interpreting the Maryland death penalty statute. A revised death penalty sentencing form, conforming to these opinions, was issued, effective July 20, 1987, by the Court of Appeals' Standing Committee on Rules of Practice and Procedure. The death penalty instruction and commentary address these developments.

5. *Drunk driving offenses:* The enforcement of the drunk driving laws has been a topic of national and local importance. Extensive commentary discusses judicial decisions and legislative changes as well as issues that are likely to arise. No major legislative restructuring has occurred in this area. Questions have arisen over the definition and interrelationship of the four drunk driving offenses: driving while intoxicated; driving while under the influence of alcohol; driving while under the influence of drugs or drugs and alcohol; and, driving while under the influence of a controlled dangerous substance. Other issues include the admissibility and evidentiary significance of chemical tests of intoxication, and what police procedures are required to properly administer both chemical and non-chemical tests of intoxication.

6. *Certain criminal defenses:* The General Assembly, effective July 1, 1984, revised the insanity defense law, shifting the burden of persuasion to the defendant. The defense of necessity has received greater judicial recognition along with a clarification of the difference between this defense and the duress defense. Several cases have considered important issues in the self-defense area. Finally, as noted above, *Evans v. State,* and its progeny, have made clear that once sufficient evidence has been raised to generate a particular defense, the State must prove beyond a reasonable doubt that the defense has not been established.

Because of the extensive commentary following many of the instructions, this book should be useful to prosecutors and defense attorneys in the preparation and trial of both jury and non-jury cases. Many attorneys prepare a formal or informal checklist of potential facts-in-issue before undertaking more thorough factual investigation and legal research. The instructions together with the accompanying comment sections should be of assistance in pre-trial case preparation.

Attention is directed to the question of how pattern jury instructions should be used. Jury instructions simultaneously serve two purposes. The tension between these purposes may explain, at least in part, the challenge and difficulty of drafting understandable jury instructions. Professors Harvey S. Perlman and Stephen A. Saltzburg state:

> Improved juror comprehension is not a costless objective. A jury instruction is the medium for the message in two separate contexts. In the first instance it is the device to relate the law to the jury for application in a particular case. At the same time a jury instruction is a method for inter-lawyer exchange over what the law is and what it should be. The language of instructions frame[s] the legal issue both for the trial court and for the appellate court. Many judicial decisions use the language of jury instructions as the focal

> point for explaining the subtleties of legal doctrine. The more subtle the doctrine attempts to be, the more difficult it will be to relate it to jurors. There has always been an implicit trade-off between legal refinement and jury capability.

H. Perlman and S. Saltzburg, *Foreword* to A. Elwork, B. Sales and J. Alfini, *Making Jury Instructions Understandable* at xxiv (1982).

Many of the instructions in this book are more detailed than those appearing in other pattern jury instruction books. In general, judges prefer jury instructions that are brief and concise. In many cases, however, one or two jury instructions will be of great importance to the prosecutor and/or defense attorney. While there is, and always will be, controversy over the extent to which jurors understand, remember, and correctly apply jury instructions, some studies demonstrate that jury instructions may be a critical variable determining the outcome of trials. Judges and attorneys often desire more detailed instructions on a particular element(s) of an offense bearing directly on crucial, disputed fact issues. Jurors need and often desire more guidance from the trial judge on such disputed issues. It is easier for the judge to eliminate what is viewed as unnecessary detail than to draft additional instructions. The user will notice that sometimes part of an instruction has been placed within brackets to indicate that the language need only be given in particular circumstances. Occasionally, a choice has been given between a brief instruction and an amplified instruction. Also, suggestions for alternative or supplemental language appear in many of the comment sections.

Two extremely capable Maryland circuit court judges have independently recommended a technique that they use in instructing juries which seems to respond to the tension, noted above, between understandable jury instructions and error-free instructions that sufficiently convey the subtleties of legal doctrine. They often will, in effect, instruct the jury twice on a particularly difficult or important issue. First, they will read the formal instruction. Then, they will repeat the instruction, often with aid of an illustration, in their own words, in a more conversational tone, and with more direct eye contact with the jurors.

For the really important jury instructions in a case, pattern jury instructions should be the beginning rather than the end of the process of preparing the instructions. At a minimum there is a need to personalize the instructions by inserting the name of the defendant and, where appropriate, the names of the victim and witnesses. Also, instructions often need to be modified and adapted to the facts of each case. The comment sections should aid in the task of modifying or adapting the instructions, and they often include useful suggestions. The pattern jury instructions and commentary will be of maximum value as a basis for instructing a jury when used as a guide to what legal principles should be propounded, an aid in draftsmanship, and a source to facilitate further legal research.

The overall objective in preparing these pattern instructions was to present the applicable principles of law correctly, impartially, and understandably. Before the first edition of this book was published, a preliminary draft, containing most of the instructions, was circulated to judges, prosecutors, and defense attorneys for critical comment and field testing. Most of the instructions underwent two or three stages of re-drafting and were discussed and commented upon in small group sessions with practicing attorneys, law faculty colleagues, and law students. The practice of assembling volunteer drafting committees of prosecutors and defense attorneys was continued, for this second edition, for new instructions, such as the theft, bad check, and sexual offense instructions. Drafts of other instructions were circulated to judges, prosecutors, and defense attorneys. Improvements to the instructions also resulted from the critical comments and helpful suggestions of judges and attorneys who generously provided feedback based on experience in using the instructions in the first edition.

Three controversial issues are raised here on techniques for improving juror effectiveness in understanding, remembering, and applying jury instructions. These questions are considered in more detail in the context of Maryland law in the appendices to this book. Their importance was suggested to me during a conference, in which I participated, on "The American Jury and the Law," sponsored by The American Judicature Society, held in November, 1985, in Racine, Wisconsin. They were the subject of panel discussions at this conference.

First, should the jury be provided with written jury instructions to supplement the judge's oral instructions? Even if written jury instructions were desirable, judges face practical problems of implementation, including inadequate time to prepare a clean, typewritten copy of the instructions, as well as inadequate secretarial and photocopying services. While arguments pro and con are discussed in Appendix IV, Elwork, Sales, and Alfini, based on their own empirical research and review of the literature, conclude:

> We believe that the practice of not presenting jurors with a written copy of jury instructions to take with them into the deliberation room greatly lowers the probability that they will remember and use them....
>
> ...
>
> In conclusion, one way of increasing the probability that a juror will comprehend and remember instructions is to present them in written form as well as in the auditory mode. More specifically, we have found that the best memory and comprehension is gotten

> when jurors are allowed to follow a written version of the judge's instructions while he/she is reading them and to make check marks next to the sections that are not readily understood upon the first reading. After this initial presentation, and during the jury deliberations, jurors should be encouraged to read the instructions over several times on their own and to make especially sure that they understand the troublesome portions.

A. Elwork, B. Sales, and J. Alfini, *Making Jury Instructions Understandable* at 18, 20 (1982).

The second question is whether judges should give greater emphasis to giving preliminary and interim instructions to supplement jury instructions at the close of a case. Appendix I discusses this question and provides a suggested preliminary instruction. A federal judge, Herbert J. Stern, stated:

> To begin with, it is sheer folly to wait until the end of a trial to educate the jurors about the process over which they preside. Such a practice forces them to sit through days — if not weeks — without anything more than haphazard guidance about either the trial procedures applicable to the contest played out before their eyes, or the law which should guide their final judgment on what they are listening to.
>
> Then, but only at the very last moment of the case, all too often the trial judge routinely force-feeds the jurors more law in a one-hour dose than many law school professors administer to law students in a week. And this is done — almost as though we want to be absolutely certain that jurors have no chance to comprehend — through legal instructions crafted in technical jargon, read aloud by judges who typically keep their own heads buried in a written script.

Herbert J. Stern, *Preface* to S. Saltzburg and H. Perlman, *Federal Criminal Jury Instructions* at I-ix (1985).

The third question is whether jurors should be permitted or encouraged to take notes during all phases of the trial, including the final jury instructions. Appendix II discusses this question and provides a suggested preliminary instruction on notetaking to implement Maryland Rules of Procedure 4-326(a).

A question that may be of more interest to the litigators than to the trial judge is how a proper jury instruction request should be made and how to preserve the record for possible appeal when a requested jury instruction is denied. Appendix III discusses the proper procedure for making the record pursuant to Maryland Rules of Procedure 4-325. The large number of appellate decisions dismissing issues on appeal for failure to preserve the record evidences the fact that many trial attorneys do not know or do not properly implement the procedure for preserving the record. Appellate opinions emphasize that the procedure serves the purpose of notifying the trial judge of the specific language to which counsel objects and the specific language which counsel proposes. With this information, the judge can hear opposing counsel on the merits of the request and, in the event of error, can cure the error prior to jury deliberation. A jury instruction request by number alone may not be sufficient to preserve the record for appeal. *Holmes and Loudermill v. State* (unreported opinion #1692 of the Court of Special Appeals, February 23, 1988), *citing Belt's Wharf v. International Corporation,* 213 Md. 585, 592, 132 A.2d 588, 591 (1957) and *Sergeant Company v. Pickett,* 283 Md. 284, 289, 388 A.2d 543, 546 (1978), so suggests. The panel was divided on the question of whether the record was adequately preserved on the facts of that case.

How are the jury instructions in this book organized? The numbers used to identify jury instructions in the original edition have been retained. New numbers have been assigned for additional instructions. The material is organized into three categories. Chapters 1-3 present instructions applicable to all criminal cases — introductory instructions, those evaluating testimony and other evidence, and those on frequently used mental states. Chapter 4 presents the offense instructions. Subpart A consists of the inchoate offenses, such as attempt and conspiracy. Crimes are then grouped by type of social harm or offense category with a general category, "other offenses," as follows: subpart B — assault; subpart C — homicide; subpart D — sexual offenses; subpart E — weapons offenses; subpart F — other offenses; and, subpart G — theft and bad check offenses. Chapter 5 presents the defenses. The five appendices are then presented, followed by the Table of Cases and the Index.

For economy of expression, the pronoun reference in both the instructions and the comments is usually in the male gender, which, of course, should be modified as appropriate when instructing the jury. A few instructions have the words "suggested instruction" in parentheses after the instruction. This phrase is used where the definition of certain key terms cannot be authoritatively stated and yet the topic is sufficiently important to warrant coverage. This may occur in the following situations: where a relatively new statute introduces terms without case law history that may need clarification by the courts; where the case law is sparse or lacking on an important point; and, where there is conflict or lack of clarity in appellate decisions.

Every effort has been made to include all legislative changes and significant cases reported through September, 1987. However, the reader is cautioned to check for additional cases in the latter part of 1986 and in 1987 that may not have been included. This book is the product of several years of research and writing. The editorial process involved in publishing the book necessarily took a long time, and it was not possible to be as thorough in case coverage during this period. Your comments and suggestions for improving the instructions and/or the commentary for possible use in a later supplement or edition would be very much appreciated. My office address is: Myers Hall, Room 205, The American University Law School, 4400 Massachusetts Avenue, N.W., Washington, D.C. 20016.

Many persons question the ability of lay jurors to understand and properly apply the judge's instructions. A personal experience in serving on a jury in a criminal case has reinforced my general confidence in our jury system. When I was summoned for jury duty in Montgomery County, Maryland, a few years ago, to my surprise and delight I survived the *voir dire.* The trial was a purse snatching/robbery case. The defendant and the victim were of a different gender, race, and socio-economic group. The jury was also a diverse group based on age, gender, race, education, and occupation. The jury struggled late into the evening and the next morning to reach a verdict, sometimes with heated argument and cajoling. At one point, a juror suggested a moment of silent prayer as a means of helping to resolve an impasse. While this jury may not be representative of other juries in Montgomery County or elsewhere, it clearly made a very serious and, I believe, successful effort to apply the judge's instructions on the law to the facts of the case. This experience as a juror supports my view that, with all of its alleged imperfections, there is no better system for resolving serious, contested criminal cases. It is my hope that this book, along with other resources and materials available to judges, prosecutors, and defense counsel, may make a small contribution toward improving the administration of criminal justice in Maryland.

David E. Aaronson

March, 1988

TABLE OF CONTENTS

	Page
Foreword	v
Acknowledgments	vii
Introduction	xi

PART I

GENERAL INSTRUCTIONS

CHAPTER 1

INTRODUCTORY INSTRUCTIONS

§ 1.01.	Function of court and jury—Binding nature of instructions	3
	Comment	5
§ 1.02.	Burden of proof	9
	Comment	10
§ 1.03.	Presumption of innocence	11
	Comment	11
§ 1.04.	Reasonable doubt	12
	Comment	13
§ 1.05.	Direct and circumstantial evidence	19
	Comment	19
§ 1.06.	Evidence in the case—Judicial notice	26
	Comment	26
§ 1.07.	Evidence in the case—Stipulations	27
	(a) Stipulations of fact	27
	(b) Stipulations of testimony	27
	Comment	28
§ 1.08.	Statements of counsel—Not evidence	29
	Comment	29
§ 1.09.	Indictment [charging document]—Not evidence	32
	Comment	32
§ 1.10.	Inadmissible and stricken evidence—Court's rulings on objections to evidence	33

Page

Comment 33

§ 1.11. Publicity cautioning 34

(a) Preliminary instruction if media attention is anticipated 34

(b) Before final deliberation 34

Comment 35

§ 1.11a. Publicity cautioning (amplified instruction) 35

Comment 36

(a) In general 36

(b) Jurors reading newspaper accounts of trial 37

(c) Communications with jurors before and during trial 39

(d) Publicity before and during trial 41

§ 1.12. Admonition upon recess 43

§ 1.12a. Admonition upon recess (amplified instruction prior to first recess) 44

Comment 45

§ 1.13. When jurors cannot agree—Jury's duty to deliberate 46

Comment 46

§ 1.14. Jury's nonconcern with punishment 53

Comment 53

§ 1.15. Defendant's representation of self 54

Comment 54

CHAPTER 2

EVALUATION OF TESTIMONY AND OTHER EVIDENCE

A. Evaluation of testimony

§ 2.01. Accomplice's testimony—Corroboration 58

Comment 59

§ 2.02. Informer's testimony—Witness promised leniency .. 64

Comment 64

§ 2.03. Number of witnesses 67

Comment 67

§ 2.04. Child witness 68

		Page
	Comment	68
§ 2.05.	Expert witness	71
	Comment	71
§ 2.06.	Credibility of witnesses	75
	Comment	77
§ 2.07.	Impeachment by prior conviction(s)	81
	(a) Of the defendant	81
	(b) Of a witness other than the defendant	82
	Comment	82
§ 2.08.	Prior inconsistent and consistent statement(s)	88
	(a) Impeachment by prior inconsistent statement(s)	88
	(b) When a party seeks to impeach own witness	89
	(c) Rehabilitation by use of prior consistent statement(s)	89
	Comment	90
§ 2.09.	Defendant as witness—Impeachment by confession: confession admitted solely for impeachment purposes	95
	Comment	95
§ 2.10.	Other crimes and prior bad acts of defendant	96
	Comment	97
§ 2.11.	Court calling its own witness	105
	Comment	105

B. Evaluation of other evidence

§ 2.21.	Missing witness	107
	Comment	108
§ 2.22.	Multiple counts and multiple defendants	110
	(a) Multiple counts—One defendant	110
	(b) Lesser included offenses or inconsistent counts—One defendant	111
	(c) Multiple defendants	112
	(d) Multiple defendants—Additional instruction for different or multiple counts	113

Page
(e) Multiple defendants — Evidence applicable only to one defendant: limiting instruction 113
Comment 113
§ 2.23. Character of defendant (reputation and opinion evidence and impeachment of defendant's character witness(es)) 116
(a) Evidence of defendant's good character 116
(b) Impeachment of defendant's character witness(es): limiting instruction 116
Comment 117
§ 2.24. Flight or concealment by defendant 120
Comment 121
§ 2.25. Confession or incriminating statement of defendant 124
Comment 126
(a) Introduction and burden of proof 126
(b) Burden of proof at suppression hearing 128
(c) Permissible and impermissible uses 129
(d) Effect of unnecessary delay in initial appearance 131
(e) The judicial determination: *Miranda* 132
(1) Custody or significant deprivation of freedom and interrogation 132
(2) The *Miranda* warnings 137
(3) Waiver 138
(f) The judicial determination: voluntariness .. 144
(1) Totality of the circumstances test 144
(2) Circumstances concerning accused 145
(3) Police techniques 146
(g) Role of the jury 148
(1) Function of the jury 148
(2) Totality of the circumstances test 150
(h) Admissibility and use of defendant's silence 151
(i) Need for independent evidence corroborating defendant's confession 153
§ 2.26. *Corpus delicti*—Corroboration of defendant's confession [admission] 154

Page

Comment 155

§ 2.27. Defendant's decision not to testify (silence of defendant) 157

Comment 157

§ 2.28. Identity of defendant 159

Comment 160

§ 2.29. Identification of defendant by single eyewitness 165

Comment 165

§ 2.30. Photographic identification 166

Comment 167

§ 2.31. Fingerprint evidence 172

Comment 173

§ 2.32. Consent to blood and other chemical tests—Comment 174

(a) Criminal nontraffic offenses 174

(b) Criminal traffic offenses 178

§ 2.33. Evidence of jurisdiction 180

Comment 180

CHAPTER 3

STATES OF MIND—DEFINED

§ 3.01. General intent 183

(a) Positive act 183

(b) Failure to act where there is a duty to act .. 184

Comment 184

§ 3.02. Specific intent 186

Comment 187

§ 3.03. "Knowingly"—Defined 188

Comment 188

§ 3.04. "Willfully"—Defined 189

Comment 189

§ 3.05. "Fraudulent" (intent to defraud)—Defined 190

Comment 190

§ 3.06. "Maliciously"—Defined 190

Comment 191

§ 3.07. Proof of intent, knowledge, willfulness, etc 191

Page
Comment 192

PART II

OFFENSES

CHAPTER 4

SPECIFIC INSTRUCTIONS

A. Offenses—Generally

§ 4.01. Accessory before the fact 200
Comment 201
§ 4.02. Aiding and abetting 202
Comment 203
§ 4.03. Accessory after the fact 208
Comment 209
§ 4.04. Acts committed through innocent agents 211
Comment 211
§ 4.05. Attempt 212
Comment 213
§ 4.06. Conspiracy 216
Comment 218
(a) Classification of crime and punishment 218
(b) Elements of crime and proof 218
(c) Doctrine of merger does not apply 221
(d) "Concert of action" rule 221
(e) Effect of acquittal or prosecution of all co-conspirators 221
(f) Admissibility of co-conspirator statements as hearsay exception 222
(g) Form of indictment 226
(h) Statute of limitations 227
(i) Venue 227

B. Assault

§ 4.11. Assault 228

		Page
	Comment	228
§ 4.12.	Battery	229
	Comment	229
§ 4.13.	Assault with intent to murder	233
	Comment	235
§ 4.14.	Assault with intent to rob	239
	Comment	240
§ 4.15.	Assault with intent to commit sexual intercourse with a female under the age of fourteen where the male is four or more years older	243
	Comment	244
§ 4.16.	Assault with intent to rape or to commit a first or second degree sexual offense	246
	Comment	248

C. Homicide

§ 4.20.	Introductory instruction on grading of homicide	250
§ 4.21a.	Murder—First degree: willful, deliberate and premeditated killing	251
	Comment	252
§ 4.21b.	Murder—First degree: felony murder	255
	Comment	257
	(a) In general	257
	(b) Qualifying underlying felonies	258
	(c) Indictment on underlying felony not required	258
	(d) When act of killing is by accomplice	259
	(e) Causal nexus between underlying felony and the killing	260
	(f) When act of killing is by victim, bystander or police officer	260
	(g) Merger of underlying felony	262
§ 4.21c.	Murder—First degree: death penalty sentencing	263
	Comment	271
	(a) Introduction—Sentencing form provided by Rule 4-343	271

Page

(b) Determination of defendant's status as a principal in the first degree 284
(c) Aggravating and mitigating circumstances: statutory provisions 286
(d) Burden of proof: mitigating circumstances 290
(e) Burden of proof: balancing aggravating and mitigating circumstances 292
(f) Defining and establishing aggravating and mitigating circumstances 294
  (1) Can a single factual foundation give rise to multiple aggravating circumstances? 294
  (2) What is the meaning of "mitigating circumstances" and how are "unlisted" mitigating circumstances to be established? 296
  (3) Guidance to the jury in weighing aggravating and mitigating circumstances 301
(g) Some constitutional and definitional issues of particular aggravating and mitigating circumstances 303
  (1) Aggravating circumstance of felony murder 304
  (2) Mitigating circumstance of lack of future danger to society 306
  (3) Mitigating circumstance of youthful age of defendant 307
  (4) Mitigating circumstance of substantial impairment of defendant's mental capacity 308
  (5) Others 309
(h) Evidence that may be considered at death sentencing proceeding 309
(i) Proportionality review on appeal 312
(j) Other constitutional issues 312

§ 4.22a. Murder—Second degree 313

Page
Comment ... 316
(a) In general ... 316
(b) Malice: the mental states for murder ... 317
(c) Burdens of proof ... 323
§ 4.22b. Murder—When both first and second degree murder are in issue ... 325
§ 4.23a. Manslaughter—Voluntary: general instruction ... 326
Comment ... 328
§ 4.23b. Manslaughter—Voluntary: amplified instruction including special sources of provocation ... 328
(1) Mutual combat ... 331
(2) Battery ... 331
(3) Spousal adultery ... 332
(4) Words plus threatening conduct ... 332
Comment ... 333
(a) In general ... 333
(b) Special sources of provocation ... 337
§ 4.23c. Manslaughter—Voluntary (suggested instruction on imperfect self-defense) ... 341
Comment ... 343
§ 4.24. Manslaughter—Involuntary ... 347
(a) Which occurs as the result of doing some lawful act with gross negligence ... 347
(b) Which is caused by the grossly negligent omission to perform a legal duty ... 349
(c) Which occurs during the course of some unlawful act ... 350
Comment ... 350
§ 4.25. Manslaughter—By vehicle ... 352
Comment ... 354
§ 4.26. Homicide by motor vehicle while intoxicated (suggested instruction) ... 357
Comment ... 358

D. Sexual Offenses

1. Offenses Retained After 1976 Revision of Sexual Offense Laws

		Page
§ 4.33.	Incest	360
	Comment	362
§ 4.34.	Sodomy	368
	Comment	369
§ 4.35.	Unnatural or perverted sexual practices	371
	Comment	373

2. 1976 Revised Rape and Sexual Offense Laws

§ 4.36.	Rape offenses	378
	(a) Rape—First degree	378
	(b) Rape—Second degree	381
	(c) Rape—Second degree: victim under fourteen years and person performing act four or more years older than victim	383
	(d) Rape—Second degree: mentally defective, mentally incapacitated or physically helpless victim	385
	Comment	387
	(a) Overview	387
	(b) Age of the victim and the accused	389
	(c) Relationship of 1976 revised statutes to corresponding common law	390
	(d) Common-law background of rape offenses	391
	(e) First and second degree rape distinguished	394
	(f) Second degree rape: statutory rape	397
	(g) Second degree rape: mentally defective, mentally incapacitated or physically helpless victim	398
	(h) Rape victim's testimony need not be corroborated	399
	(i) The "Lord Hale" instruction	400

Page
(j) Defense that victim is spouse of accused 401
(k) The rape and sexual offense shield law: admissibility of evidence of victim's prior sexual conduct 402
(l) Charging document and bill of particulars 406
(m) Venue 406
§ 4.37. Sexual offenses in the first, second, third and fourth degree 407
(a) Sexual offense—First degree 407
(b) Sexual offense—Second degree 411
(c) Sexual offense—Second degree: victim under fourteen years and person performing act four or more years older than victim .. 414
(d) Sexual offense—Second degree: mentally defective, mentally incapacitated or physically helpless person 417
(e) Sexual offense—Third degree 420
(f) Sexual offense—Third degree: victim under fourteen years and person performing act four or more years older than victim 423
(g) Sexual offense—Third degree: mentally defective, mentally incapacitated or physically helpless victim 425
(h) Sexual offense—Fourth degree 428
(i) Sexual offense—Fourth degree: vaginal intercourse with person fourteen or fifteen years of age and person performing act four or more years older than victim 431
(j) Sexual offense—Fourth degree: "sexual act" with person fourteen or fifteen years of age and person performing act four or more years older than victim 432
Comment 435
(a) Overview 435
(b) First and second degree sexual offenses 437
(c) Third and fourth degree sexual offenses 441

Page

(d) Spousal immunity defense and admissibility of evidence of victim's prior sexual conduct 444

E. Weapons Offenses

§ 4.41. Carrying or wearing a concealed weapon 444
Comment 445
§ 4.42. Carrying a weapon openly with intent to injure 449
Comment 450
§ 4.43. Wearing, carrying or transporting handgun, openly or concealed 453
(a) On or about the person 453
(b) In any vehicle traveling upon public roads, highways, etc 454
Comment 456
§ 4.44. Use of handgun in the commission of a felony or crime of violence 459
Comment 461

F. Other Offenses

§ 4.51. Abortion 467
Comment 467
§ 4.52. Arson 469
Comment 470
§ 4.53. Breaking—Storehouse, etc., with intent to commit a felony or steal (Article 27, § 32) 473
Comment 475
§ 4.54. Breaking—Storehouse, etc., with intent to steal any money, goods or chattels under the value of $300 (Article 27, § 33A) 475
Comment 477
§ 4.55. Breaking—Storehouse, etc., with the taking of property (Article 27, § 33) 477
Comment 479
§ 4.56. Bribery—Obstructing justice 485
(a) Attempting to bribe 485

Page
(b) Offering a bribe 486
(c) Receiving a bribe 487
(d) Demanding a bribe 488
Comment 489
§ 4.57. Burglary 492
Comment 494
(a) Introduction 494
(b) Breaking 495
(c) Dwelling house 495
(d) Nighttime 496
(e) Intent 497
(f) Possession of stolen goods 498
§ 4.58. Child abuse 498
(a) Child abuse based on physical injury 498
(b) Child abuse based on sexual molestation or exploitation 500
Comment 500
(a) Child abuse based on physical injury 503
(b) Child abuse based on sexual molestation or exploitation 506
§ 4.59. Contempt 506
Comment 508
§ 4.60. Nonsupport 511
Comment: Desertion and nonsupport 512
§ 4.61. Disorderly conduct 515
(a) Disorderly conduct generally 515
(b) Profane cursing and swearing 515
(c) Loud and unseemly noises 516
Comment 517
(a) Disorderly conduct 517
(b) Indecent exposure 520
§ 4.62. Disorderly house 521
Comment 522
§ 4.63. Driving while intoxicated—Driving while under the influence of alcohol and/or drugs 523
Comment—Suggested instructions 523

Page

(a) "Driving while under the influence of alcohol" (suggested instruction) 523
(b) "Driving while intoxicated" (suggested instruction) 525
(c) "Driving while under the influence of drugs or drugs and alcohol" (suggested instruction) 526
(d) "Driving while under the influence of a controlled dangerous substance" (suggested instruction) 527
Comment—Discussion 528
(a) Applicable standards and definitions 528
(1) In general 528
(2) "Drive," "operate" or be in "actual physical control" 529
(3) "While intoxicated" and "under the influence" 531
(4) Drugs and controlled dangerous substances 536
(b) Proving "intoxication" and "under the influence": nonchemical evidence 537
(c) Proving "intoxication" and "under the influence": chemical evidence 540
(1) In general 540
(2) Police procedures before administering chemical tests 544
(3) Administering chemical tests: foundation requirements 551
(d) Penalties 558

§ 4.64. Embezzlement 559
Comment: Common law prior to repeal 559

§ 4.65. Escape 562
Comment 562

§ 4.66. Extortion—Verbal threat 567
Comment 567

§ 4.67. False pretenses 568
Comment: Common law prior to repeal 568

		Page
§ 4.68.	Forgery and uttering	571
	(a) Forgery	571
	(b) Uttering	573
	Comment	574
	(a) Forgery	574
	(b) Uttering	577
§ 4.69.	Housebreaking—Daytime	579
	Comment	581
§ 4.70.	Kidnapping	584
	Comment	585
	(a) Kidnapping	585
	(b) Abduction of individual under sixteen	587
	(c) Suggested instruction: abduction of an individual under sixteen	588
	(d) Abuction of child under twelve	588
§ 4.71.	Larceny	589
	Comment: Common law prior to repeal	589
§ 4.72.	Larceny after trust	593
	Comment: Common law prior to repeal	593
§ 4.73.	Larceny of use—Unauthorized use of motor vehicle, boat or livestock	596
	Comment	597
§ 4.74.	Lotteries	600
	(a) Keeping a place for selling lottery tickets	600
	(b) Owner permitting use of house or office for sale of lottery tickets	601
	Comment	602
§ 4.75.	Malicious mischief—Malicious destruction of property	604
	Comment	605
§ 4.76.	Narcotics—Possession (actual and constructive)	606
	Comment	608
§ 4.77.	Narcotics—Manufacture, distribution, dispensation or possession with intent to sell	614
	(a) Manufacture, distribute or dispense	614
	(b) Possession with intent to sell	615
	Comment	617

Page
§ 4.78. Perjury and subornation of perjury 620
(a) Perjury 620
(b) Subornation of perjury 620
Comment 621
§ 4.79. Receiving stolen goods 623
Comment: Common law prior to repeal 623
§ 4.80. Resisting arrest 628
Comment 630
§ 4.81. Riot 634
Comment 635
§ 4.82. Robbery 636
Comment 637
§ 4.83. Robbery with a deadly weapon 641
Comment 643
§ 4.84. Shoplifting 647
Comment: Common law prior to repeal 647
§ 4.85. Trespass 648
(a) Upon private land or vessel (Article 27, § 577) 649
(b) Refusal to leave public buildings (Article 27, § 577A) 649
Comment 650
§ 4.86. Unlawful use of telephone 653
Comment 653

G. Theft and Bad Check Offenses

1. Theft Offenses

Overview and Introductory Comment 654
§ 4.91. Theft—By unauthorized control 661
Official Commentary 665
Theft—In general 665
Shoplifting and receiving stolen property 665
Knowingly 666
Obtain 666

Page

Exerts control 667
Owner 667
Deprive; intent to deprive 668
Property 668
Value 669
Aggregating separate acts of theft 670
Presumptions and inferences 671
Defenses: claim of right; spousal immunity; and rightful knowledge of a trade secret 673
Grading of theft offenses: penalties ... 674
Comment 675
(a) Theft—In general 675
(b) Obtains or exerts control 678
(c) Intent 679
(d) Owner 680
(e) Value 682
(f) Aggregating separate acts of theft 683
(g) Indictments and informations 684
(h) Variance between charge and proof 686
(i) Presumptions and inferences 687
§ 4.92. Theft—By deception 688
Official Commentary 693
Comment 694
§ 4.93. Theft—By possessing stolen property 696
Official Commentary 699
Comment 702
§ 4.94. Theft—Of lost, mislaid or mistakenly delivered property 704
Official Commentary 708
Comment 709
§ 4.95. Theft—Of services 710
Official Commentary 713
Comment 714
§ 4.96. General instruction—"Rights of possession" and certain defenses applicable to theft offenses 715
Official Commentary 715

Page
Comment 718

2. Bad Checks—Obtaining Property or Services by Bad Check

Introductory Comment 718
§ 4.97a. Acts committed by a drawer or representative with knowledge of insufficient funds 722
Official Commentary 727
§ 4.97b. Acts committed by passers (payees, holders and bearers) of checks with knowledge of insufficient funds 733
Official Commentary 737
§ 4.97c. Acts committed by a drawer or representative who issues a check with intent to stop payment 739
Official Commentary 743
§ 4.97d. Acts committed by passers (payees, holders and bearers) of checks with knowledge that payment has been stopped 743
Official Commentary 746

PART III

DEFENSES

CHAPTER 5

SPECIFIC INSTRUCTIONS

§ 5.01. Voluntary drunkenness 752
Comment 753
§ 5.02. Alibi 757
Comment 758
§ 5.03. Claim of right 761
Comment 762
§ 5.04. Defense of others 765
Comment 766
§ 5.05. Duress 768
Comment 770

Page
§ 5.06. Entrapment 773
Comment 775
§ 5.07. Good character of defendant 782
Comment 782
§ 5.08. Insanity 785
Comment 788
(a) History of insanity standards 789
(b) Present standard 790
(c) Plea and verdict 795
(d) Generating jury issue, expert and lay testimony and burden of proof 797
(e) Bifurcation of trial and defendant's right against self-incrimination 800
(f) Mental retardation 802
(g) Standard of competence to stand trial distinguished 803
(h) Doctrine of diminished capacity not recognized 804
(i) Post-verdict commitment procedures 806
(j) Should the jury be instructed on the consequences of an insanity verdict? 807
§ 5.09. Mistake or ignorance of fact (suggested instruction) 810
(a) General intent element of the crime 810
(b) Specific intent element of the crime 811
Comment 812
§ 5.10. Mistaken identity 814
Comment 815
Introductory Note on Use of Self-defense Instructions, §§ 5.11 to 5.17, and Related Instructions 816
§ 5.11. Self-defense—General considerations and burden of proof 817
(a) General considerations 817
(b) Burden of proof 818
Comment 818
§ 5.12. Self-defense—Amount of force permissible 819
(a) Nondeadly force 819
(b) Deadly force 820

Page

Comment ... 821

§ 5.13. Self-defense—Where defendant is alleged aggressor 823

(a) Where there is conflicting evidence as to who is the aggressor ... 823

(b) Where defendant is aggressor using non-deadly force, victim counterattacks with deadly force, and defendant subsequently uses deadly force to defend ... 824

(c) Where defendant is aggressor using deadly force, defendant totally withdraws, and victim counterattacks using deadly force (suggested instruction) ... 824

Comment ... 825

§ 5.14. Self-defense—Where appearances are false ... 828

Comment ... 828

§ 5.15. Self-defense—Duty to retreat before using deadly force and exception for "castle doctrine" ... 830

(a) Duty to retreat before using deadly force .. 830

(b) No duty to retreat—"Castle doctrine" exception ... 830

Comment ... 831

§ 5.16. Self-defense—Prior acts, reputation (or opinion) and threats of the deceased ... 836

(a) Prior acts of violence by the deceased *known by the defendant* ... 836

(b) Reputation (or opinion) of the deceased's violent and dangerous character *known by the defendant* ... 837

(c) Reputation (or opinion) of the deceased's violent and dangerous character *not known by the defendant* ... 837

(d) Prior threats by the deceased against the defendant *known by the defendant* ... 838

(e) Prior threats by the deceased against the defendant *not known by the defendant* 838

Comment ... 839

Page

§ 5.17. Right to use nondeadly force to defend property (suggested instruction) 843
Comment 844
§ 5.18. Necessity (suggested instruction) 846
Comment 847

Appendices
I. Preliminary Instructions to the Jury 851
Suggested pre-trial introductory instruction .. 851
Comment 856
(a) Law relating to preliminary instructions .. 856
(b) Impact of preliminary instructions on jurors 858
(1) Juror responses 859
(2) Attorney responses 860
(3) Judicial responses 860
II. Notetaking by Jurors 861
Suggested additional preliminary instruction to implement Maryland Rule 4-326(a) 861
Comment 862
(a) Law relating to notetaking 862
(b) Suggested procedure for notetaking 863
(c) Impact of notetaking on juror performance 864
(1) Juror responses 866
(2) Attorney responses 867
(3) Judicial responses 867
III. How to Make Jury Instruction Requests and Procedure for Preserving the Record for Possible Appeal When a Requested Instruction Is Denied 869
(a) Rule 4-325 869
(b) Requirements for requested instructions .. 870
(c) "Some evidence" requirement 872
(d) Informal pre-charge conference 872
(e) Objections to instructions 873
(f) Appellate review of plain error 874
IV. Supplementing Oral Instructions with Written or Electronically Recorded Instructions 875

Page

(a) Existing law 875
(b) Pros and cons of permitting jurors to take instructions into the jury room 877
(c) Impact of permitting jurors to take instructions into the jury room 879
(1) Juror responses 879
(2) Attorney responses 880
(3) Judicial responses 881

V. The Impact of *Evans v. State:* Burdens of Proof, Presumptions and Inferences 883
(a) Introduction 883
(b) Situations where *Mullaney* and *Evans* will not result in unconstitutionality 885
(c) Situations where *Mullaney* and *Evans* will result in unconstitutionality 888

Table of Cases 891
Index 939

PART I
GENERAL INSTRUCTIONS

Chapter 1

INTRODUCTORY INSTRUCTIONS

§ 1.01. Function of court and jury — Binding nature of instructions.
§ 1.02. Burden of proof.
§ 1.03. Presumption of innocence.
§ 1.04. Reasonable doubt.
§ 1.05. Direct and circumstantial evidence.
§ 1.06. Evidence in the case — Judicial notice.
§ 1.07. Evidence in the case — Stipulations.
(a) Stipulations of fact.
(b) Stipulations of testimony.
§ 1.08. Statements of counsel — Not evidence.
§ 1.09. Indictment [charging document] — Not evidence.
§ 1.10. Inadmissible and stricken evidence — Court's rulings on objections to evidence.
§ 1.11. Publicity cautioning.
(a) Preliminary instruction if media attention is anticipated.
(b) Before final deliberation.
§ 1.11a. Publicity cautioning (amplified instruction).
§ 1.12. Admonition upon recess.
§ 1.12a. Admonition upon recess (amplified instruction prior to first recess).
§ 1.13. When jurors cannot agree — Jury's duty to deliberate.
§ 1.14. Jury's nonconcern with punishment.
§ 1.15. Defendant's representation of self.

§ 1.01. Function of court and jury — Binding nature of instructions.

Members of the jury, in this criminal case you, the jury, are the sole judges of the facts. You alone shall determine what the facts are — by determining the truth of the testimony presented by each witness, and giving to that testimony, as well as to any inferences which you draw from it, the weight which you feel they deserve. Your finding of facts should be made solely from the evidence introduced at trial and not from anything which you may have seen or heard elsewhere.

There are certain matters of law which are indispensable to preserving the integrity of every criminal trial and to assure a fair and impartial trial. They serve as guidelines to which every jury in a criminal trial must adhere.

[*Where no conflict exists as to the law of the crime*: Therefore, my instructions concerning the law to be applied by you in this case are binding and must be followed by you. You are not at liberty to disregard them.]

[*Where there exists conflict as to the law of the crime*: Therefore, my instructions on matters such as constitutional rights and procedural matters — the State's burden of proof, the requirement of a unanimous verdict, weighing the evidence, etc. — are binding upon you and must be followed by you. You are not at liberty to disregard them.]

There exists in this case, however, a dispute over the proper meaning of the law of the crime; that is, as to certain elements of the crime charged. Specifically, there is a conflict as to the following element(s): __________ (*Insert the disputed area of the law of the crime.*)

As to this limited area of the law, under the Maryland Constitution you, the jury, serve as the final judges of the law. My instructions on the meaning of the law of the crime, therefore, are advisory only and are not binding upon you. It is your responsibility to resolve the conflicting interpretations of the law of the crime which counsel may present to you and to decide if that law is applicable to the facts of this case as you find them to be.

Your duty, as judges of the law of the crime, is to determine what the law is, not what the law ought to be. You may not make new law or disregard existing law; rather, your duty is to resolve conflicting interpretations. You are only to determine what is the correct interpretation of the law of Maryland as it currently exists.

In your function as judge of the facts of the case, you should make a finding of the facts solely from the evidence which has been introduced at the trial, the evidence which you have seen and heard, and not from anything which you may have seen or heard elsewhere. You have the sole discretion in deciding the truth of the testimony and the weight to be given to the testimony of each witness as well as the sole discretion to decide what inferences may be drawn from the testimony.

During the course of the trial I may comment on the evidence and question the witnesses. This is not to be taken by you as any indication on the part of the court as to the truth or falsity of such evidence. Nor should you consider any statements made by the court as demonstrating a bias for either the state or the defense.

[At times during the trial, the Assistant State's Attorney or the defense attorney may make an objection to a question asked by another lawyer, or to an answer by a witness. This simply means that the lawyer is requesting that I make a decision on a particular rule of law. Do not draw any conclusion from such objections or from my rulings on the objections. These only relate to the legal questions that I must determine and should not influence your thinking.]

Your verdict, whatever it may be, must be the unanimous verdict of all twelve members of the jury.

COMMENT

For an additional suggested instruction and helpful commentary on the function of the court and jury, see Appendix I, Preliminary Instructions to the Jury, *infra.*

The instruction on this subject as it appeared in the first edition of this book has been revised completely in light of *Stevenson v. State,* 289 Md. 167, 423 A.2d 558 (1980) and its progeny.

The constitutional footing upon which the instruction rests is found in Article 23 of the Declaration of Rights in the Maryland Constitution as follows:

> In the trial of all criminal cases, the Jury shall be the Judges of law, as well as of fact, except that the Court may pass upon the sufficiency of the evidence to sustain a conviction.

Maryland Rule 4-325, in turn, implements Article 23.

This rare facet of Maryland criminal jury trials has been held not to be in conflict with the due process clause of the fourteenth amendment to the United States Constitution. *Stevenson v. State, supra; Wilkins v. Maryland,* 402 F. Supp. 76 (D. Md. 1975), *aff'd,* 538 F.2d 327 (1976); *Wyley v. Warden,* 372 F.2d 742 (4th Cir. 1967), *cert. denied,* 389 U.S. 863, *rehearing denied,* 389 U.S. 997 (1967); *Giles v. State,* 229 Md. 370, 183 A.2d 359 (1962), *appeal dismissed,* 372 U.S. 767 (1963); *Slansky v. State,* 192 Md. 94, 63 A.2d 599 (1949). In its decision upholding the constitutionality of Article 23, *Stevenson v. State, supra,* the Court of Appeals delineated the specific boundaries within which that provision applies. Any analysis of the correct application of Article 23, therefore, must be based on the *Stevenson* decision.

It is now beyond doubt that "Article 23 'does not mean precisely what it seems to say.'" *Stevenson v. State, supra* at 176 (quoting *Brady v. Maryland,* 373 U.S. 83, 89, 83 S. Ct. 1194, 1197, 10 L. Ed. 2d 215 (1963)). Although the language of Article 23 states that "the jury shall be the Judges of law, as well as of fact ...," Article 23, Maryland Declaration of Rights, the *Stevenson* decision noted that historically the role of the jury has been limited. *Stevenson v. State, supra* at 176-77. A jury never has been permitted to determine "whether a statute has been repealed, ... whether it has operative effect, ... or if it is unconstitutional ...." Likewise, a jury does not determine preliminary questions such as the court's jurisdiction, the admissibility of evidence or the competency of witnesses. *Id.* at 178-79. See also *Neal v. State,* 45 Md. App. 549, 413 A.2d 1386 (1980). Article 23 refers only to the jury's role during the trial stage and not the sentencing stage of a proceeding. *Poole v. State,* 290 Md. 114, 428 A.2d 434 (1981) (Poole I), *aff'd in part, rev'd in part, both on other grounds,* 295 Md. 167, 453 A.2d 1218 (1983) (Poole II).

As to those legal propositions upon which the integrity of the criminal jury system rests and the fairness and impartiality of each criminal trial relies, the jury plays no role in determining their application to a particular case. "Instructions on these matters ... are the guidelines of due process to which every jury is required to adhere." *Montgomery v. State,* 292 Md. 84, 91, 437 A.2d 654, 658 (1981). They include:

(1) the presumption of innocence until disproved beyond a reasonable doubt;

(2) the State's burden of persuasion as to each element of the crime;

(3) the defendant's privilege not to testify without any inferences of guilt drawn from his silence;

(4) the relevance solely to credibility of evidence used to impeach the defendant;

(5) the limitation of evidence to testimony (and reasonable inferences drawn therefrom) and exhibits admitted at trial;

(6) the exclusion from evidence of remarks by the trial judge and by counsel.

Id.; Davis v. State, 48 Md. App. 474, 427 A.2d 1085 (1981) (State's burden of proof). See *Guardino v. State,* 50 Md. App. 695, 440 A.2d 1101 (1982) (a blanket instruction made by the judge that his comments were advisory only is erroneous) and *Middleton v. State,* 49 Md. App. 286, 431 A.2d 734 (1981) (jury admonished not to speculate about the law and explained what is meant by "presumption of innocence" and "beyond a reasonable doubt").

Under Article 23, therefore, the role of the jury as "Judges of law" is limited "'to *resolv(ing) conflicting interpretations of the law (of the crime)* and to decid(ing) whether th(at) law should be applied in dubious factual situations,' *and nothing more." Stevenson v. State, supra* at 179 (*quoting Dillon v. State,* 277 Md. 571, 581, 357 A.2d 360, 367 (1976) (emphasis in the original)). In other words, this limited role is performed by the jury *only* "when an instruction culminates in a dispute as to the proper interpretation of the law of the crime for which there is a sound basis." *Montgomery v. State, supra* at 89 (emphasis in the original). Hence, "... where there is no dispute nor a sound basis for a dispute as to the law of the crime, the court's instructions are binding on the jury and counsel as well." *Id.;* see also *Randall Book Corporation v. State,* 64 Md. 589, 497 A.2d 1174 (1985), *cert. denied,* 305 Md. 176, 501 A.2d 1323 (1986); *Newman v.*

State, 65 Md. App. 85, 499 A.2d 492 (1985); *White v. State,* 66 Md. App. 100, 502 A.2d 1084 (1986).

See also *Smiley v. State,* 294 Md. 461, 450 A.2d 909 (1981); *Calhoun v. State,* 297 Md. 563, 468 A.2d 45 (1983), *cert. denied sub nom. Tichnell v. Maryland,* 466 U.S. 993, 104 S. Ct. 2374, 80 L. Ed. 2d 846 (1984); *Trimble v. State,* 300 Md. 387, 478 A.2d 1143 (1984). When conflict does arise as to the applicable law of the crime, "... counsel are granted leave to argue contrary to the court's instructions," and the court's instructions should be made expressly advisory in order to permit the jury to reach their own independent determination. *Stevenson v. State, supra* at 180. Counsel, however, may not attempt to persuade the jury, nor may the jury attempt of its own initiative, to enact new law or repeal or ignore existing law. *Id.* at 179. *Montgomery v. State, supra* at 89.

In *Neal v. State, supra,* the Court stated that Article 23 in the Maryland Constitution means that the jury's verdict is unaccountable as far as the *defendant* is concerned. The Court, however, did discuss the fact that the constitutional provision has been limited by judicial construction and statute. These limits have given the trial court certain functions: for example, the court decides, prior to a trial, whether a law is constitutional and whether a statute is free from ambiguity, and if not, whether the defendant's counsel can read the statute's preamble to the jury.

Instructions relating to Article 23 should be requested. In *Middleton v. State, supra,* the Court held that although the trial court instructed the jury that they were the judges of both law and fact, no objection was timely made, and it did not amount to plain error in violation of *Stevenson, supra.*

In Maryland, the trial judge is authorized to comment on the evidence in instructing the jury. Maryland Rule 4-325 (d), Reference to Evidence, states:

> In instructing the jury, the court may refer to or summarize the evidence in order to present clearly the issues to be decided. In that event, the court shall instruct the jury that it is the sole judge of the facts, the weight of the evidence, and the credibility of the witnesses.

Maryland opinions have spoken on other aspects of the judge's role vis-a-vis the jury. The Court has held that a trial judge should limit his comments to avoid unduly influencing the jury. This must be balanced, however, against the judge's obligation to elicit the full facts. In *Bell v. State,* 48 Md. App. 669, 429 A.2d 300, 305 (1981) the Court held that the asking of fifty-four questions by the judge was not excessive in light of the length of the trial. The Court focused on the fact that the judge did not abuse his role as an impartial arbitrator, nor did he exceed the limits of judicial discretion.

In *Spell v. State,* 49 Md. App. 323, 431 A.2d 752, 755 (1981), the trial judge commented to the jury that presence at or near the scene of a crime is a "compelling element" in the proof of criminal agency. The Court admonished the trial judge "to be more careful in using adjectives which may suggest undue weight to be given one element of consideration over another." While comment upon facts is permissible, the "area is a dangerous one and recitations must be given without suggestive emphasis."

§ 1.02. Burden of proof.

The State has the burden of proving, based upon the evidence introduced at trial, every fact necessary to convict the defendant of the crime with which he is charged. This burden remains with the State throughout the trial. The defendant does not have the burden of proving his innocence or of producing any evidence. If you are not convinced that the State has proved beyond a reasonable doubt each and every element of the offense with which the defendant is charged you must find the defendant not guilty. On the other hand, if you find from your consideration of all the evidence that the State has proved each of the elements of the offense beyond a reasonable doubt, then you should find the defendant guilty.

COMMENT

This instruction is patterned substantially after holdings in various Maryland cases. See *Mullaney v. Wilbur,* 421 U.S. 684, 95 S. Ct. 1881, 44 L. Ed. 2d 508 (1975); *Evans v. State,* 28 Md. App. 640, 349 A.2d 300 (1975), *aff'd,* 278 Md. 197, 362 A.2d 629 (1976).

In every criminal case the defendant is presumed innocent until proven guilty and the burden is on the state to prove the accused's guilt beyond a reasonable doubt. *Streat v. State,* 11 Md. App. 543, 275 A.2d 537 (1971). Every individual accused of a crime is presumed to be innocent and in order to justify a conviction, the State must affirmatively establish the defendant's guilt beyond a reasonable doubt. *McDuffie v. State,* 10 Md. App. 190, 268 A.2d 590 (1970). *Lawrence v. State,* 6 Md. App. 226, 251 A.2d 20 (1969). The Court in *Spencer v. State,* 1 Md. App. 264, 267, 229 A.2d 151, 152-53 (1967), quoted the language of the Court of Appeals in *Johnson v. State,* 227 Md. 159, 163, 175 A.2d 580, 582 (1961), as follows: "everyone accused of crime is presumed to be innocent; and in order to justify a finding of guilt, it is incumbent upon the State affirmatively to establish the defendant's guilt beyond a reasonable doubt." *Thompson v. State,* 4 Md. App. 31, 240 A.2d 780 (1968), approved the lower court's instruction to the jury which was as follows:

> In these cases, as in all other criminal cases, the burden of proof is upon the State to prove every element of a crime charged against the defendant. Therefore, I say to you that the accused is presumed innocent until proven guilty beyond a reasonable doubt. This presumption of innocence attends him throughout the trial until overcome by proof establishing his guilt beyond a reasonable doubt, and to a moral certainty. The defendant is entitled to every inference in his favor which can reasonably be drawn from the evidence. Now while the burden is upon the State of establishing proof of every fact material to the guilt of the defendant, including every circumstance that enters into the crimes charged beyond a reasonable doubt and to a moral certainty, that does not mean, however, that the State must prove the defendant guilty to an absolute or mathematical certainty. It means such evidence as you would act upon in a matter involving

> important affairs in your own life or in your own business or with regard to your own property.

Id. at 35, 240 A.2d at 783.

See Appendix V, The Impact of *Evans v. State*: Burdens of Proof, Presumptions and Inferences, *infra.*

§ 1.03. Presumption of innocence.

Every defendant in a criminal case is presumed to be innocent. You should not assume that the defendant is guilty because he is on trial. The presumption of innocence remains with the defendant throughout the trial unless and until he is proven guilty beyond a reasonable doubt.

COMMENT

A criminal defendant is presumed to be innocent. In order to warrant a finding of guilty, it is incumbent upon the State to affirmatively establish the defendant's guilt beyond a reasonable doubt. *Malcolm v. State,* 232 Md. 222, 192 A.2d 281 (1963).

The accused stands before the jury cloaked with the presumption of innocence. If the jury is not convinced beyond a reasonable doubt of his guilt, they must render a verdict of not guilty. *Holbrook v. State,* 6 Md. App. 265, 276, 250 A.2d 904, 910 (1969).

A person is innocent until he is proved guilty and there must be evidence which leads to such a result. *Wilson v. State,* 7 Md. App. 41, 55, 253 A.2d 439, 446 (1969).

The trier of facts in a criminal case is enjoined by law to give due force to the presumption of innocence, and then to proceed cautiously in weighing the evidence; but he is not commanded to be naive and to believe without scrutiny every glib suggestion or farfetched tale whether emanating from the State or defense. *Berry v. State,* 202 Md. 62, 67, 95 A.2d 319, 321 (1953).

In *Holt v. United States,* 218 U.S. 245, 253, 31 S. Ct. 2, 54 L. Ed. 1021 (1910), Justice Holmes stated:

> [The] jury is correctly instructed as to the presumption of innocence where the court states that the criminal prosecu-

> tion begins with the legal presumption that the defendant, although accused, is innocent, and that to overcome this legal presumption the evidence must be clear and convincing, and sufficiently strong to convince the jury beyond a reasonable doubt that the defendant is guilty.

See also *Agnew v. United States,* 165 U.S. 36, 49-50, 52, 17 S. Ct. 235, 240-41, 41 L. Ed. 624 (1897); *Coffin v. United States,* 156 U.S. 432, 456-60, 15 S. Ct. 394, 403-05, 39 L. Ed. 491 (1895); *United States v. Nimerick,* 118 F.2d 464, 467-68 (2d Cir.), *cert. denied,* 313 U.S. 592 (1941); Wigmore, *Evidence* § 2511 (3d ed. 1940).

The term "presumption of innocence" is, technically, an inaccurate use of the word "presumption." An instruction to the jury that a "presumption of innocence" does not exist, however, may mislead the jury into believing that the protections traditionally afforded by the presumption of innocence, for some unexplained reason, do not apply in the particular case at bar. Therefore, instructing a jury that "there is no presumption of innocence" is reversible error. *Pitts v. State,* 36 Md. App. 594, 374 A.2d 632 (1977).

§ 1.04. Reasonable doubt.

[Some of you may have served as jurors in civil cases, where you were told that it is only necessary to prove that a fact is more likely true than not true. In criminal cases, the State's proof must be more powerful than that. It must be beyond a reasonable doubt.]

The State has the burden of proving every fact necessary to constitute the offense with which the defendant is charged so that you are convinced that the defendant is guilty of this offense beyond a reasonable doubt. The State is not required to prove guilt beyond all possible doubt or to a mathematical certainty. Nor is the State required to negate every conceivable circumstance of innocence.

Reasonable doubt, as the name implies, is a doubt based on reason, a doubt for which you can give a reason. It is not a fanciful doubt, nor a whimsical doubt, nor a doubt based on conjecture. It is such a doubt as would cause a juror, after careful and impartial consideration of all of the evidence, to be so undecided that the juror cannot say that he or she has an abiding conviction of the defendant's guilt. [It is such a doubt as would cause a reasonable person to hesitate to act in the graver or more important transactions of life.]

[If you are convinced that the defendant has been proved guilty of the offense with which the defendant is charged beyond a reasonable doubt, your verdict should be "guilty"; if you are not so convinced, your verdict must be "not guilty".]

COMMENT

Because many prosecutors and defense attorneys believe that the reasonable doubt instruction is the most important general instruction in a criminal case, it is not surprising that this instruction has been the subject of controversy in every state and federal jurisdiction. In 1980, a Committee on Federal Criminal Jury Instructions of the Seventh Circuit went so far as to recommend that "no instruction be given defining 'reasonable doubt.'" The Committee argued that the phrase "reasonable doubt" is self-explanatory and is its own best definition. It felt that elaboration "tends to misleading refinements" which weaken and make imprecise the existing phrase. *United States v. Lawson,* 507 F.2d 433, 443 (7th Cir. 1974), *cert. denied,* 420 U.S. 1004 (1975). Yet, even the Seventh Circuit has refused to adopt a per se rule against defining reasonable doubt.

In Maryland and in many other jurisdictions one of the most controversial issues has been whether to include language using the words "to hesitate to act" or "without hesitation." In the above instruction, this phrase has been placed in brackets at the end of the third paragraph. It reads: "It is such a doubt as would cause a reasonable person to hesitate to act in the graver or more important transactions of life."

Another similar phrase used in defining "beyond a reasonable doubt" is as follows: "Proof beyond a reasonable doubt, therefore, is proof of such a convincing character that you would be willing to rely and act upon it without hesitation in the most important of your own affairs." Instruction #3A, *Pattern Jury Instructions,* prepared by the Committee on Pattern Jury Instructions, District Judges Association, Fifth Circuit, 1978. Some substantial arguments have been raised against using this phrase. It is argued that decisions that are commonly made in the most important affairs of our lives, such as choosing a spouse, a job, or a place to live, generally involve a very heavy element of uncertainty and risk-taking. Also, these decisions usually do not require a determination or resolution of conflicts about past events. For these reasons the Federal Judicial Center Committee on Pattern Criminal Jury Instructions felt that the analogy is misplaced and that such decisions are "wholly unlike the decisions jurors ought to make in criminal cases." Federal Judicial Center Committee to Study Criminal Jury Instructions, *Pattern Criminal Jury Instructions* (1982), Commentary to Instruction 21. It is also argued that the use of the phrase confuses the degree of certainty needed with an immediacy of acting upon that certainty.

It is possible to use "hesitate" without using the analogy to the graver or more important transactions of life. The following language has been recommended:

> Few things in life are absolutely certain. To say that you believe something beyond a reasonable doubt is to say that you are confident in your judgment. It does not require you to be absolutely certain. You may have a reasonable doubt about something if you are hesitant to accept it as true after you evaluate the evidence.

1 S. Saltzburg and H. Perlman, *Federal Criminal Jury Instructions* Instruction 3.59, "Reasonable Doubt" Defined (1985).

Despite the above considerations, many appellate opinions lend strong support to the standard formulation that a reasonable doubt is a doubt that would cause a person to hesitate to act in the most important of one's own affairs. See, e.g., *United States v. Morris,* 647 F.2d 568, 571-72 (5th Cir. 1981); *United*

States v. Fallen, 498 F.2d 172, 177 (8th Cir. 1974); *United States v. Stubin,* 446 F.2d 457, 465 (3d Cir. 1971). See also the discussion of Maryland cases *infra.*

In Maryland, a trial judge in a criminal case must give an instruction correctly explaining "reasonable doubt" if requested by the accused. *Lansdowne v. State,* 287 Md. 232, 412 A.2d 88 (1980); *Montgomery v. State,* 292 Md. 84, 437 A.2d 654 (1981). See Maryland Rule 4-325(c). The failure to instruct the jury that they have the option of finding the defendant not guilty if they have a reasonable doubt was held to be plain error in *Hutchinson v. State,* 41 Md. App. 569, 398 A.2d 451 (1979), *aff'd,* 287 Md. 198, 411 A.2d 1035 (1980). See also *Robertson v. State,* 295 Md. 688, 457 A.2d 826 (1983). But the Court held, in *Wilson v. State,* 44 Md. App. 318, 408 A.2d 1058, 1065 (1980) that it was not error to give only preliminary instructions explaining the term "beyond a reasonable doubt," though it was stated that the better approach is to repeat the instruction after all the evidence has been presented.

In order to prove the guilt of an accused beyond a reasonable doubt it is not necessary that every conceivable miraculous coincidence consistent with his innocence be negated. *Nichols v. State,* 5 Md. App. 340, 351, 247 A.2d 722 (1968). *See also Lambert v. State,* 193 Md. 551, 69 A.2d 461 (1949).

Proof of guilt beyond all doubt has never been required, even in the most serious criminal cases. *Graham v. State,* 13 Md. App. 171, 282 A.2d 162, 167 (1971), *cert. denied,* 264 Md. 748 (1972); *Pettis v. State,* 2 Md. App. 651, 653, 236 A.2d 429 (1968).

In *Brooks v. State,* 53 Md. App. 285, 452 A.2d 1285 (1982), the trial court's instruction on reasonable doubt stated that a reasonable doubt would be removed if one were to act upon a most important affair in his own life. It did not include the words "unhesitatingly" or "without hesitation." It was found not to be erroneous. See also *Poole v. State,* 295 Md. 167, 185-86, 453 A.2d 1218, 1228 (1983) (Poole II).

In *Bowers v. State,* 298 Md. 115, 468 A.2d 101 (1983), the trial judge gave the following instruction in a death sentence trial relating to the finding of aggravating circumstances beyond a reasonable doubt:

> Now, a reasonable doubt is a doubt that is founded upon reason. It is such a doubt as would cause a reasonable person to hesitate to act in the graver or more important transactions in his life.
>
> Thus, if the evidence is of a character as to persuade you of the truth of the charges against the Defendant, with the same force that would be sufficient to persuade you to act in the more important transactions in your life then you would conclude the State has proven aggravating circumstances beyond a reasonable doubt.
>
> If, on the other hand, you could not act based on that evidence in the more important transactions in your life, then you would conclude that the State had not met the burden of proof and therefore had not proven the aggravating circumstances.

Id. at 157, 468 A.2d at 122-123. The defendant objected to the court's instruction arguing that the words "without hesitation" should be added so that the jury is told that the evidence must be sufficient to persuade it to act without hesitation in the more important transactions of life. The Court of Appeals, in dictum, perceived no error in the instruction. It noted that variations of jury instructions regarding the reasonable doubt standard may be used and that, in any event, when an objection is raised to a court's instruction, attention should not be focused on a particular portion lifted out of context, but rather on the jury instruction as a whole.

The Court noted in *Bowers v. State, supra,* however, that a similar issue was before the Supreme Court of the United States in *Holland v. United States,* 348 U.S. 121, 75 S. Ct. 127, 99 L. Ed. 150 (1954). The Court there addressed the issue of whether a jury instruction using the words "would be willing to act" and "would not hesitate to act" was correct in a criminal case where the prosecution must prove the defendant's guilt beyond a reasonable doubt. The trial judge had instructed the jury that beyond a reasonable doubt is "the kind of doubt ... which you folks in the more serious and important affairs of your own lives might be willing to act upon." Relative to that instruction, the Court said:

> We think this section of the charge should have been in terms of the kind of doubt that would make a person hesitate to act, ... rather than the kind on which he would be willing

> to act. But we believe the instruction as given was not of the type that could mislead the jury into finding no reasonable doubt when in fact there was some. A definition of the doubt as something the jury would act upon would seem to create confusion rather than misapprehension. "Attempts to explain the term 'reasonable doubt' do not usually result in making it any clearer to the minds of the jury," *Miles v. United States,* 103 U.S. 304, 312, [26 L. Ed. 481 (1881),] and we feel that, taken as a whole, the instructions correctly conveyed the concept of reasonable doubt to the jury.

Id. at 140, 75 S. Ct. at 138, 99 L. Ed. at 167.

A passage from L. Hochheimer, *The Law of Crimes and Criminal Procedure* § 157 (2d ed. 1904), well-known by earlier generations of Maryland lawyers and often read to the jury by defense counsel in closing argument, is as follows:

> The burden rests upon the government of establishing by proof beyond a reasonable doubt every fact material to the guilt of the defendant, including every circumstance that enters into the grade or degree of the crime charged, and nothing is to be presumed or taken by implication against him. The law presumes every man innocent of crime. This presumption starts with the accusation and continues until the rendition of the verdict. Artificial presumptions and estoppels have no place in establishing guilt. Proof beyond a reasonable doubt means such proof as produces an abiding conviction, to a moral certainty, of the truth of the charge, and, unless the jury are thus convinced, they must acquit. If there is any reasonable doubt in which of several degrees a defendant is guilty, he can be convicted of the lowest only of those degrees. If, after consideration of the whole case, any juror should entertain a reasonable doubt of the guilt of the defendant, it is the duty of the jury so entertaining such doubt not to vote for conviction, nor to be influenced in so voting, for the sake of unanimity or to prevent a mistrial.

More recently, the Court has cited this passage as being basically in accord with that enunciated by the Supreme Court of the United States in *Jackson v. Virginia,* 443 U.S. 307, 99 S. Ct. 2781, 61 L. Ed. 2d 560 (1979). See *Bedford v. State,* 293 Md. 172, 443 A.2d 78 (1982) and *Calhoun v. State,* 297 Md. 563, 468 A.2d 45 (1983), footnotes one and four, respectively, *cert. denied sub nom. Tichnell v. Maryland,* 466 U.S. 993, 104 S. Ct. 2374, 80 L. Ed. 2d 846 (1984).

In *Cranford v. State,* 36 Md. App. 393, 395, 373 A.2d 984, 986 (1977), *cert. denied* (after having been "improvidently" granted), 282 Md. 255, 383 A.2d 687 (1978), the trial judge instructed the jury, in pertinent part, as follows:

> To be sufficient in law to justify a conviction, the admissible evidence adduced must show directly or circumstantially or support a rational inference of the facts to be proved from which you, the trier of facts, *could fairly* be convinced beyond a reasonable doubt of the Defendant's guilt of the offense charged. (Emphasis added.)

This is the legal test to be applied by a *trial judge* when ruling on a motion for a judgment of acquittal, not the legal test to be used by a jury. In this case the Court held that the error was not so plain or material to the rights of the accused as to require reversal of the conviction, because the trial judge, both before and after the offending portions of the instruction, had carefully and fully informed the jurors of the proper test for determining the sufficiency of the evidence. In addition, the appellant had failed to object to the instruction.

The burden of proof standard, as it applies to reviewing the sufficiency of the evidence, was discussed in *Streat v. State,* 11 Md. App. 543, 275 A.2d 537 (1971):

> In every criminal case the defendant is presumed innocent until proven guilty and the burden is on the State to prove the accused's guilt beyond a reasonable doubt. This Court will not disturb a jury's verdict on the evidence if the evidence adduced at trial either shows directly, or supports a rational inference of the facts to be proved from which the jury could be fairly convinced, beyond a reasonable doubt, of the accused's guilt of the offense charged.

Id. at 547, 275 A.2d at 539.

Various Maryland courts have held that in order to overturn a judgment entered on the verdict of a jury for insufficiency of evidence, it is necessary that there be no legally sufficient evidence or inferences drawable therefrom on which the jury could find a defendant guilty beyond a reasonable doubt. *Hunt v. State,*

12 Md. App. 286, 278 A.2d 637 (1971); *Dudonis v. State,* 9 Md. App. 245, 250, 263 A.2d 624 (1970); *Himmel v. State,* 9 Md. App. 395, 400, 264 A.2d 874 (1970); *Makins v. State,* 6 Md. App. 466, 472, 252 A.2d 15, 18 (1969).

The Court articulated the standard for the sufficiency of the evidence in the 1983 case of *Calhoun v. State, supra.* Quoting from *Bedford v. State, supra,* the Court stated that "the applicable standard is 'whether, after viewing the evidence in the light most favorable to the prosecution, any rational trier of fact could have found the essential elements of the crime beyond a reasonable doubt.'" *Calhoun v. State, supra,* 297 Md. at 638, 468 A.2d at 81. See also *State v. Rusk,* 289 Md. 230, 424 A.2d 720 (1981); *Tichnell v. State,* 287 Md. 695, 415 A.2d 830 (1980) (Tichnell I).

§ 1.05. Direct and circumstantial evidence.

There are two types of evidence which you may consider in this case: direct evidence and circumstantial evidence.

Direct evidence is that which is attributable to direct, actual knowledge of a fact.

Circumstantial evidence is that which proves the facts in issue indirectly; by proof of a chain of facts and circumstances from which an inference may arise as to the facts in issue.

A conviction may rest on circumstantial evidence alone or on direct evidence alone or on a combination of circumstantial and direct evidence. No greater degree of certainty is required when the evidence is circumstantial than when it is direct. Regardless of the type of evidence presented, you must be convinced of the defendant's guilt beyond a reasonable doubt by all of the facts and circumstances of the case as well as by any rational inferences which may arise.

COMMENT

There has been some uncertainty concerning the proper standard for weighing the evidence and the propriety of jury instructions where evidence on a material issue is solely circumstantial. It is clear that a conviction may be based solely upon circumstantial evidence. *Hughes v. State,* 56 Md. App. 12, 466 A.2d 533 (1983); *Pressley v. State,* 295 Md. 143, 454 A.2d 357 (1983); *Veney v. State,* 251 Md. 182, 246 A.2d 568 (1968), *cert. denied,* 394 U.S. 948 (1969) (cases cited therein); *Kelly v. State,* 14 Md. App. 287, 286 A.2d 806, *cert. denied,* 266 Md. 738 (1972).

In the past, there seemed to be a conflict between decisions of the Court of Appeals and later decisions of the Court of Special Appeals with regard to the appropriate standard for weighing the evidence when it was solely circumstantial. This apparent conflict arose in decisions reviewing both the propriety of jury instructions, *see Brown v. State,* 222 Md. 290, 159 A.2d 844 (1960); *Dove v. State,* 47 Md. App. 452, 423 A.2d 597 (1980), and decisions on the sufficiency of the evidence examining the denial of a motion for judgment of acquittal. *Veney v. State, supra; Robinson v. State,* 18 Md. App. 678, 308 A.2d 734, *cert. denied,* 296 Md. 765 (1973).

In the original edition of this book, the instruction on direct and circumstantial evidence included the following language:

> A conviction may be based solely upon circumstantial evidence. Where this occurs, the circumstances taken together must be inconsistent with, or such as to exclude, every reasonable hypothesis or theory of innocence, but proof of guilt to a mathematical certainty is not essential ....

D. Aaronson, *Maryland Criminal Jury Instructions and Commentary* § 1.05 (1st ed. 1975).

The language has been modified in this second edition as follows:

> A conviction may rest on circumstantial evidence alone or on direct evidence alone or on a combination of circumstantial and direct evidence. Regardless of the type of evidence presented, you must be convinced of the defendant's guilt beyond a reasonable doubt by all of the facts and circumstances of the case as well as by any rational inferences which may arise.

This change reflects the 1983 case of *Pressley v. State, supra,* and the case of *Metz v. State,* 9 Md. App. 15, 262 A.2d 331 (1970) as well as the numerous progeny of the latter in the Court of Special Appeals. In *Metz,* the Court emphasized that "the test for the sufficiency is the same whether the evidence be direct, circumstantial or provided by rational inferences therefrom." *Id.* at 23, 262 A.2d at 335.

The case most frequently cited as enunciating the proposition to which the Court of Appeals apparently adhered (before *Pressley v. State, supra*), and which was used as a basis for the instruction in the first edition of this work, quoted above, is *Vincent v. State,* 220 Md. 232, 151 A.2d 898 (1959). In *Vincent,* the Court of Appeals explained the history of the rule. Similar language was first found in the memorandum on a motion for reargument in *Edwards v. State,* 198 Md. 132, 81 A.2d 631 (1951).

> If we assume that circumstantial evidence, or all the evidence of any kind, must "exclude to a moral certainty every other reasonable hypothesis than that of guilt," this assumption does not change the result in the instant case — and does not furnish any "definite rule for the appraisal of circumstantial evidence." In any case, civil or criminal, to meet the test of legal sufficiency, evidence (if believed) must either show directly, or support a rational inference of, the fact to be proved. In a civil case the fact must be shown, or the inference supported, by a preponderance of probability or an opposite preponderance must be overcome. In a criminal case, the fact must be shown, or the inference supported beyond a reasonable doubt or to a moral certainty, or a reasonable doubt of an opposite fact must be created.

Id. at 157-58. In the subsequent case of *Shelton v. State,* 198 Md. 405, 84 A.2d 76 (1951), the Court of Appeals reiterated the language of *Edwards* and added the following crucial sentence:

> Before a verdict of guilty is justified, the circumstances, taken together, must be inconsistent with, or such as to exclude, every reasonable hypothesis or theory of innocence. *Bullock v. Commonwealth,* 249 Ky. 1, 60 S.W.2d 108, 94 A.L.R. 407 [1933]; 2 Wharton, *Criminal Evidence,* 11th ed., sec. 922.

Id. at 412. Finally, in *Vincent,* the Court cited *Shelton* for the proposition that:

> [w]hen guilt is based solely upon circumstantial evidence, the circumstances, taken together, must be inconsistent with, or such as to exclude, every reasonable hypothesis or theory of innocence. *Vincent v. State, supra,* 151 A.2d at 901.

Notwithstanding the frequent citation of *Vincent* as authority for the above proposition — see even *Metz v. State, supra* at 21 — the Court of Appeals in *Vincent* conceded in its opinion that the use of this language relative to its holding was pure dictum; for it found that "[t]he evidence in this case was *not* circumstantial." *Vincent v. State, supra,* 151 A.2d at 902 (emphasis added). Likewise in *Edwards v. State, supra,* the initial use of language similar to that found in *Vincent* served merely as dictum. Not only did the Court preface its discussion with "if we assume ...," it then determined that "this assumption does not change the result in this case." *Edwards v. State, supra,* 198 Md. at 157-58.

Note that, in *Shelton v. State, supra,* the first Maryland case which purports to enunciate what might be termed the "*Vincent* rule," the supporting precedents are a Kentucky case, *Bullock v. Commonwealth,* 249 Ky. 1, 60 S.W.2d 108 (1933), cited without explanation, and a legal treatise, 2 Wharton, *Criminal Evidence* § 922 (11th ed.).

In contrast, the Court of Special Appeals has emphasized continually that "the test for sufficiency is the same whether the evidence be direct, circumstantial, or provided by rational inferences therefrom." *Metz v. State, supra,* 9 Md. App. at 23. *Accord Dove v. State, supra; Holloway v. State,* 26 Md. App. 382, 339 A.2d 319 (1975), *cert. denied,* 276 Md. 745 (1975); *Williams v. State,* 22 Md. App. 714, 325 A.2d 427 (1974), *cert. denied,* 273 Md. 723 (1974); *Smith v. State,* 20 Md. App. 577, 318 A.2d 568 (1974), *cert. denied,* 272 Md. 748 (1974), *cert. denied,* 420 U.S. 909 (1975); *Robinson v. State, supra; Young v. State,* 14 Md. App. 538, 288 A.2d 198 (1972); *Kelly v. State, supra; Graham v. State,* 13 Md. App. 171, 282 A.2d 162 (1971), *cert. denied,* 264 Md. 748 (1972).

Again, in *Metz v. State, supra,* 9 Md. App. at 20, it is noted that, regardless of the type of evidence present:

> [t]he test of the sufficiency of the evidence has been established as being whether the evidence either shows directly,

> or supports a rational inference of, the facts to be proved, from which the trier of fact could fairly be convinced beyond a reasonable doubt, of the defendant's guilt of the offense charged. *Williams v. State,* 5 Md. App. 450, [247 A.2d 731 (1968)].

Subsequent decisions of the Court of Appeals have attempted to clarify the scope of the "*Vincent* rule" by emphasizing the two requirements to its application: (1) that the evidence be *solely* circumstantial and (2) that only reasonable hypotheses or theories of innocence be excluded. *Brown v. State, supra,* 222 Md. at 296, 159 A.2d at 847. *Accord Glaros v. State,* 223 Md. 272, 281, 164 A.2d 461 (1960). Nevertheless, the Court of Special Appeals, commencing with *Metz, supra,* has concluded that:

> The language [of *Vincent*] impressed upon the general test for the sufficiency of the evidence when the evidence is solely circumstantial does not, in fact, refine the general test. We believe that there is only a semantic and not a substantive distinction and that the test has the same denotative meaning with or without the additional language .... [The *Vincent* language merely paraphrases], in practical application, the statement that the evidence must show the facts to be proved from which the trier of fact could fairly be convinced beyond a reasonable doubt of the defendant's guilt of the offense charged.

Metz v. State, supra, 9 Md. App. at 22-23. Following *Metz,* the Court of Special Appeals further described the *Vincent* language as assuming "the dimensions of a litany, [which] does not accurately reflect the law." *Graham v. State, supra,* 13 Md. App. at 178.

The apparent schism between the respective positions of the Court of Appeals and the Court of Special Appeals was noted indirectly by the Court of Appeals through the use of citation form in the civil case of *Henderson v. Maryland National Bank,* 278 Md. 514, 366 A.2d 1 (1976).

> There is no requirement that to justify the inferences sought the circumstances presented by the plaintiff "negate every other positive or possible conclusion." *Board [of County Comm'rs] v. Dorcus,* 247 Md. 251, 259, 230 A.2d 656 (1967); *Pearson v. Wiltrout,* 17 Md. App. 497, 502-503, 302 A.2d 678

> (1973); *see Antonelli v. Pugh,* 231 Md. 194, 198, 189 A.2d 653 (1963). Thus, in accord with a majority of other jurisdictions, we have rejected *in civil cases* a rule analogous to that set forth in several criminal cases, that when guilt is based solely upon circumstantial evidence, the circumstances, taken together, must be inconsistent with, or such as to exclude, every reasonable hypothesis or theory of innocence. *Brown v. State,* 222 Md. 290, 296, 159 A.2d 844 (1960); *Vincent v. State,* 220 Md. 232, 237, 151 A.2d 898 (1959); *accord, Shelton v. State,* 198 Md. 405, 411-12, 84 A.2d 76 (1951); *but see Metz v. State,* 9 Md. App. 15, 20-23, 262 A.2d 311 (1970).

This controversy, however, may have been settled by the Court of Appeals in *Pressley v. State, supra.* In *Pressley,* the Court upheld the trial court's instruction which did not instruct the jury that all reasonable hypotheses or theories of innocence must be excluded and cited *Metz v. State, supra,* and 3 Wharton, *Criminal Evidence* § 980 at 477.

There appears to be a general agreement that "circumstantial evidence consists of proof of collateral facts and circumstances from which the existence of the main fact may be inferred according to reason and common experience." *Nichols v. State,* 5 Md. App. 340, 350, 247 A.2d 722 (1968). Such evidence may be used in conjunction with direct evidence. It may corroborate other testimony and may be used to prove any element of the crime, such as the *corpus delicti* or criminal agency, *Cole v. State,* 232 Md. 111, 194 A.2d 278 (1963); *Nichols v. State, supra; Coleman v. State,* 4 Md. App. 386, 243 A.2d 24 (1968); *Hines v. State,* 34 Md. App. 612, 368 A.2d 509 (1977) (identity of victim in felony murder prosecution arising out of a storehouse burning); or state of mind, *Robinson v. State,* 5 Md. App. 723, 249 A.2d 504 (1969) (guilty knowledge of an accessory may be inferred from the circumstances); *Anderson v. State,* 3 Md. App. 85, 237 A.2d 813 (1968) (state of one's mind or scienter is a question of fact and being subjective in nature, proof of wrongful intent is seldom direct but usually inferred from proven circumstances of the accused).

Any fact in issue may be established by circumstantial evidence if the circumstances, which must be proved, themselves lead to the conclusion with reasonable certainty. However, although circumstantial evidence alone may be sufficient to support a rational inference in many cases, it cannot sanction conjecture. *Morris v. Twigg,* 190 Md. 324, 58 A.2d 719 (1948).

Circumstantial evidence is admissible whenever it is relevant to a determination of guilt or innocence, and great latitude is allowed the trial court in admitting any fact or circumstance which may throw some light upon or serve as a link in a chain of evidence bearing upon the issues at trial. *Nichols v. State, supra; Corens v. State,* 185 Md. 561, 45 A.2d 340 (1946). It is not necessary that each circumstance, standing alone, be sufficient to establish guilt, but the circumstances are to be considered collectively. *Nichols v. State, supra.*

Nor does a conviction based upon circumstantial evidence require the jury to be satisfied beyond a reasonable doubt of each link in the chain of circumstances relied upon to establish the defendant's guilt. *Id.* The Court, in *Pressley v. State, supra,* also upheld the trial court's instruction that each fact in the chain of circumstances does not have to be proven beyond a reasonable doubt in order to convict the defendant. All that is required is that the jury is convinced of the defendant's guilt beyond a reasonable doubt. The Court found the instruction relating to the chain of circumstances to have been erroneously given since no chain was present in this particular case. The error, however, was found to be harmless since it did not mislead the jury into believing that the defendant could be convicted on less than a reasonable doubt standard.

There is also support for the proposition that if the inferences from the circumstantial evidence are equally consistent with innocence as well as with guilt, then the defendant is entitled to the presumption of innocence. *Robinson v. State, supra,* at 702, 308 A.2d at 747.

It is well settled that evidence need not positively be connected with the accused or the crime committed in order to render it admissible, and if there is a probability of its connection with the accused or the crime then it is admissible. *Braxton v. State,* 214 Md. 370, 135 A.2d 307 (1957); *Daniels v. State,* 213 Md. 90, 131 A.2d 267 (1957); *Watson v. State,* 208 Md. 210, 117 A.2d 549 (1955); *Berry v. State,* 202 Md. 62, 95 A.2d 319 (1953); *Jordan v.*

State, 4 Md. App. 349, 242 A.2d 829 (1968), *cert. denied,* 252 Md. 731 (1969); *Farley v. State,* 3 Md. App. 584, 240 A.2d 296 (1968); *Shelton v. State,* 3 Md. App. 394, 239 A.2d 610, *cert. denied,* 251 Md. 751 (1968); *Woodell v. State,* 2 Md. App. 433, 234 A.2d 890 (1967). A lack of positive identification affects the weight of the evidence rather than its admissibility. *Braxton v. State, supra; Daniels v. State, supra; Tomolillo v. State,* 4 Md. App. 711, 245 A.2d 94 (1968). As otherwise stated, where the connection of the proffered evidence with the accused is in doubt, probability is the only requirement. *Oden v. State,* 223 Md. 244, 164 A.2d 284 (1960); *Williams v. State,* 205 Md. 470, 109 A.2d 89 (1954); *King v. State,* 201 Md. 303, 93 A.2d 556 (1953).

§ 1.06. Evidence in the case — Judicial notice.

Judicial notice is the knowledge of certain facts or events which judges and jurors may accept as true and act upon without proof. When the court declares that it will take judicial notice of some fact or event, that fact or event becomes evidence in the case and need not be proved. In this case, the court has taken judicial notice of the following: __________ *(insert judicially noticed fact(s)).* Therefore, it should be accepted as proved.

COMMENT

This instruction is patterned substantially after holdings in various Maryland cases and should be given at the time when judicial notice is taken. In taking judicial notice, courts may avail themselves of trustworthy sources of information. *Bowser v. State,* 136 Md. 342, 110 A. 854 (1920).

The courts have judicially noticed many varied matters, including the following: that many convictions had occurred for murder in the first degree where the words "without capital punishment" were not added by the jury, and where sentence had been life imprisonment rather than death, *Veney v. State,* 251 Md. 182, 246 A.2d 568 (1968), *cert. denied,* 394 U.S. 948 (1969);

that opium is not commercially a domestic product, *United States v. Sam Chin,* 24 F. Supp. 14 (D. Md. 1938); that the sale of certain commodities without a license has been in vogue in the state for many years, *State v. Amick*, 171 Md. 536, 189 A. 817 (1937); that the manufacture of wearing apparel in improperly ventilated, unsanitary, and overcrowded apartments is likely to promote the spread of disease, *State v. Hyman,* 98 Md. 596, 57 A. 6 (1904); and the qualification of grand jurors, *Davis v. State,* 39 Md. 355 (1874).

For statutes dealing with Judicial Notice of Foreign Law, see Maryland Ann. Code, Courts and Judicial Proceedings, §§ 10-501 to 10-507.

§ 1.07. Evidence in the case — Stipulations.

In addition to the sworn testimony of witnesses and exhibits admitted into evidence, evidence includes facts and testimony which the State and the defendant agree to.

(a) Stipulations of fact

In this case, the State and the defendant agree that ___________ *(state fact(s) agreed to).* These facts are not in dispute and should be considered proven.

(b) Stipulations of testimony

___________ *(insert name of witness)* was not here to testify. The State and the defendant have agreed to what the witness would testify to if the witness were here. You are to consider the following to be the witness' testimony: ___________ *(insert agreed upon testimony).* As with any witness who testifies in this courtroom, you must decide whether or not to believe this testimony and how much weight to give it.

COMMENT

This instruction is patterned after holdings in various Maryland cases. A stipulation by the parties in open court dispenses with the need for producing evidence according to the usual formalities to prove the facts so admitted. *Murray v. State,* 226 Md. 624, 176 A.2d 794 (1961); *Beard v. State,* 216 Md. 302, 140 A.2d 672 (1958). While stipulations relating to evidence should not be extended by implication, *Wood v. State,* 185 Md. 280, 44 A.2d 859 (1945), they should be construed to ascertain and give effect to the intention of the parties. *Bresnan v. Weaver,* 151 Md. 375, 135 A. 584 (1926). Such stipulations are binding and conclusive on the parties. *Benson v. Mays,* 245 Md. 632, 227 A.2d 220 (1967), and, accordingly, where parties by stipulation admit without reservation what testimony a witness would give, if called, such stipulation may constitute evidence of the fact involved in the testimony. *Hardesty v. State,* 223 Md. 559, 165 A.2d 761 (1960). See *Gaudio v. State,* 1 Md. App. 455, 230 A.2d 700 (1967).

Two types of evidentiary stipulations may be distinguished: the parties may agree that a fact exists; the parties, not conceding that a fact exists, may agree to what a witness would say, if called to the witness stand, or to what a document or exhibit would show if introduced.

If the stipulation goes only to what the content of the testimony of a particular witness would be if the witness were to appear and testify, evidence adduced by stipulation may be in conflict with other evidence. It is then for the trier of fact to determine the facts from such conflicting evidence, based upon the credibility of the witnesses or the reliability of the testimony. *Barnes v. State,* 31 Md. App. 25, 354 A.2d 499 (1976).

When the State proffered the testimony of a nonappearing arresting officer and the defendant proffered her version of the facts without taking the stand, the result was a criminal trial based upon stipulations. It was impossible to weigh the credibility of either witness or the reliability of the evidence offered by them. The Court held that by adopting the State's version, the judge, as trier of fact, made an arbitrary choice which did not support a finding of guilt beyond a reasonable doubt. *Barnes v. State, supra.* See Comment, §2.06, Credibility of witnesses, *infra,* for further discussion of this case.

§1.08. Statements of counsel — Not evidence.

Statements and arguments of counsel are not evidence. This includes opening and closing statements as well as comments made during the course of this trial. They are only intended to aid you in interpreting and evaluating the evidence.

COMMENT

Maryland case law supports this instruction and also provides guidance to counsel of what types of statements are improper. For example, *Comi v. State,* 26 Md. App. 511, 338 A.2d 918, 926 (1975) (*quoting Wilhelm v. State,* 272 Md. 404, 411-12, 326 A.2d 707, 717 (1974)) states:

> Counsel's opening statement "should not include reference to facts which are plainly inadmissible and which he cannot or will not be permitted to prove, or which he, in good faith, does not expect to prove. An opening statement by counsel is not evidence and generally has no binding force or effect. To secure a reversal based on an opening statement the accused is usually required to establish bad faith on the part of the prosecutor in the statement of what the prosecutor expects to prove or establish substantial prejudice resulting therefrom."

In *Comi v. State, supra,* the accused was charged with receiving stolen goods and at trial the prosecutor commented that the case involved: "[T]he largest cache of stolen goods in Baltimore city." This comment was held to have been sufficiently corrected both by the judge's instruction to disregard the comment and by the prosecutor's public apology. The failure to show bad faith by the prosecutor or prejudice to the defendant, therefore, resulted in the denial of a mistrial.

In *Malekar v. State,* 26 Md. App. 498, 338 A.2d 328 (1975), the Court of Special Appeals held that there had been no judicial error, despite the failure of the trial judge to instruct the jury to disregard the impermissible comment which had been made by the prosecutor. In his opening statement, the prosecutor had made mention of a confession which had been deemed admissible in the pre-trial suppression hearing, but which later in the trial was held to be inadmissible. The defense counsel failed to ask for a curative instruction, a decision which the Court of Special Appeals considered to have been a carefully considered tactic.

In *Mouzone v. State,* 33 Md. App. 201, 364 A.2d 58 (1978), the following criteria were applied to the prosecutor's opening statement to determine if there was substantial prejudice warranting reversal: (1) the centrality of the issues affected; (2) the closeness of the case; and (3) the failure of the trial judge to take sufficient steps to mitigate the effects of the prosecutor's comments on the jury. The prosecutor made repeated remarks to the effect that the defendant "liked to kill," "was a contract killer," and was a "violent person." The outcome of the case was highly dependent upon the defendant's credibility, and none of these accusations were supported by admissible evidence. The Court reversed the defendant's conviction for second degree murder and use of a handgun in the commission of a crime since "substantial prejudice" was shown.

Counsel is also prevented from interjecting certain statements during the examination of a witness. *Meno v. State,* 117 Md. 435, 83 A. 759 (1912). Such excluded statements include commenting on facts not in evidence. In addition, counsel must adhere to the rules of evidence so that extraneous matters are not presented to the trier of fact unless they come from the witness' lips. *Day v. State,* 2 Md. App. 334, 234 A.2d 894, 899 (1967).

In closing argument, counsel may draw upon "reasonable and legitimate inferences from the facts which had been offered in evidence, from the facts which were of such general notoriety as to be matters of common knowledge and matters within the cognizance of the jury from their own observations." *Wilhelm v. State, supra,* at 445, *quoted in Perkins v. State,* 26 Md. App. 526, 541, 339 A.2d 360, 369 (1975). In other words, while it is improper for counsel in addressing the jury to base his statements on evidence which is not on the record, he may express his views as to what the evidence shows. *Shoemaker v. State,* 228 Md. 462, 180 A.2d 682 (1962); *Yopps v. State,* 228 Md. 204, 178 A.2d 879 (1962); *Cicero v. State,* 200 Md. 614, 92 A.2d 567 (1952); *Williams v. State,* 50 Md. App. 255, 437 A.2d 665 (1982); *Frazier v. State,* 3 Md. App. 470, 240 A.2d 306 (1968).

The closing arguments of counsel should be restricted to the issues involved in the case; however, since the State has the burden of proving each element of the crime charged, defense counsel should be permitted to assert that the State has failed to prove a requisite element by reference to a different offense not charged in the indictment. *Hawkins v. State,* 291 Md. 688, 436 A.2d 900 (1981). In *Eley v. State,* 288 Md. 548, 419 A.2d 384 (1980), the Court held it was error to refuse defense counsel's request to comment on the State's failure to present fingerprint evidence linking the defendant to the escape vehicle. In *Eastman v. State,* 47 Md. App. 162, 422 A.2d 41, 43 (1980), the Court held that it was not error for the prosecutor, in his closing argument, to call attention to the failure of the defendant to come forward with evidence he promised to produce in his opening statement. The Court in *Eastman v. State, supra* at 44, cited *Eley v. State, supra,* and said that since "it was not unreasonable to permit the defense to comment on the State's shortcomings in producing prosecutorial evidence, we can hardly preclude a reciprocal right for the State to call attention to the failure of the defense to come forward with that which he promised to produce."

In allowing the State to make reference in the above circumstances to the lack of the defendant's evidence, the Court dealt with the argument that these statements may indirectly be taken as a comment on the defendant's silence. The Court, in *Eastman v. State, supra* at 44, held that the statement by the State was not unreasonable since the State carefully avoided any emphasis on the defendant's failure to testify. The Court, in *Funkhouser v. State,* 51 Md. App. 16, 440 A.2d 1114, 1122 (1982), held that "[a] prosecutor should not be precluded from making a fair comment on the entire evidence; not every neutral or indirect reference that the State makes which implicitly refers to the defendant's silence is improper."

If an improper statement is made by counsel, the trial court has the discretion to grant a mistrial. *Wilhelm v. State, supra; Contee v. State,* 223 Md. 575, 165 A.2d 889 (1960). In *Thomas v. State,* 50 Md. App. 286, 437 A.2d 678 (1982), the prosecutor's closing argument was improper due to remarks about facts not admitted into evidence. The Court held that the trial judge's abuse of discretion in allowing the argument over defense counsel's objection was not reversible error because the content of the remark was information that could have been inferred from witness' testimony.

See Appendix I, Preliminary Instructions to the Jury, *infra.*

§ 1.09. Indictment [charging document] — Not evidence.

An indictment [charging document] is not to be considered evidence of the commission of a crime. It is merely a formal method of charging the defendant with the commission of a crime in order to bring him to trial. The indictment [charging document] is not evidence of guilt and no inference of guilt should be drawn because a defendant has been indicted.

COMMENT

Maryland Rule 4-326(a) provides that unless the court for good cause orders otherwise, the jury may take the charging document when they retire for their deliberations. On request of a party or in the court's own initiative, the charging document shall reflect only those charges on which the jury is to deliberate.

See Appendix I, Preliminary Instructions to the Jury, *infra.* See also Appendix II, Notetaking by Jurors, *infra.*

An indictment is not evidence, *United States v. Walker,* 313 F.2d 236 (6th Cir. 1963), and it is desirable that the court instruct the jury as to the limited nature of an indictment; however, there is no requirement that absent a request by counsel such instruction be given. *United States v. Baker,* 418 F.2d 851 (6th Cir. 1969). An indictment can be submitted to a jury as an exhibit if the jury is instructed that the indictment is not evidence. *United States v. Hephner,* 410 F.2d 930 (7th Cir. 1969). If the jury is not so instructed the verdict still stands provided it is clear beyond a reasonable doubt that neither refusal to permit juror's unlimited access to such copies, nor the offering of proper contemporaneous instruction would have altered a guilty verdict. *United States v. Baker, supra.* In *Sherman v. State,* 288 Md. 636, 421 A.2d 80 (1980), the Court of Appeals held that a five-count charging document could not be made available to the jury during deliberations where two of the five counts were "dead." *Sherman, supra,* is cited in *Coleman v. State,* 49 Md. App. 210, 431 A.2d 696, 704 (1981).

§ 1.10. Inadmissible and stricken evidence — Court's rulings on objections to evidence.

Inadmissible and stricken evidence may not be considered by you in your deliberations. You are to disregard any questions that the court has sustained an objection to. In addition, you are not to speculate as to the possible answer. If the judge rules that an answer should be stricken from the record, both the question and the answer should be disregarded. [Likewise, any exhibit to which the court has sustained an objection or which has been stricken from the record is not evidence and should be disregarded by you.]

COMMENT

This instruction is patterned substantially after holdings in Maryland cases and opinions of the Supreme Court of the United States. The issue is generally stated as to whether an instruction to disregard inadmissible and stricken evidence is sufficient to erase the strong impression improper evidence may have on the jury. The United States Supreme Court has held that, as a rule, the trial of a case should not be suspended when an error in the admission of testimony can be corrected by its withdrawal with proper instruction from the court to disregard it. *Hopt v. Utah,* 120 U.S. 430, 7 S. Ct. 614, 30 L. Ed. 708 (1887). Instances where improper evidence has made such a substantial impression on the jury, that its withdrawal will not obviate its effects, are exceptional and can be handled on appeal.

Maryland cases have followed the same reasoning. *Farrow v. Warden,* 241 Md. 724, 217 A.2d 270 (1966); *Lusby v. State,* 217 Md. 191, 141 A.2d 893 (1958); *Wilkins v. State,* 11 Md. App. 113, 273 A.2d 236, *cert. denied,* 261 Md. 730 (1971).

See Appendix I, Preliminary Instructions to the Jury, *infra.*

§ 1.11. Publicity cautioning.

(a) Preliminary instruction if media attention is anticipated

You must decide the case only on the evidence introduced at trial. Because there may be news coverage of this case, it is important that you avoid reading, listening to radio reports, or watching television reports about this case. All of the information about this case should be presented to you in the courtroom.

You should inform me if you accidentally hear news reports or other reports about the case. Please write me a note as soon as possible upon hearing such information and do not discuss it with anyone else.

(b) Before final deliberation

You must decide the case only on the evidence introduced at trial; therefore, you are to completely disregard any newspaper, television or radio reports which you may have read, seen, or heard. Such reports are not evidence.

You should strive not to be influenced in any manner by such publicity.

COMMENT

See the Comment following Instruction, § 1.11a, *infra.* See also Appendix I, Preliminary Instructions to the Jury, *infra.*

§ 1.11a. Publicity cautioning (amplified instruction).

You must decide the case only on the evidence introduced at trial; therefore, you are to completely disregard any newspaper, television or radio reports which you may have read, seen or heard.

You are also instructed not to read, observe, or listen to any news stories about this trial or about persons involved in the trial. Let me explain why you must not do so and must decide this case solely on the evidence presented in the courtroom. Due process of law requires that the evidence to be considered by you in reaching your verdict meets certain standards. All witnesses must be sworn to tell the truth and must be subject to cross-examination. News reports about this case are not subject to either of these standards, and if you read, listen to or watch these reports, you may be exposed to misleading or inaccurate information which unduly favors one side of the case, and to which the other side is unable to respond. Therefore, you must completely disregard any press, television or radio reports which you may read, see or hear. Such reports are not evidence and you should strive not be influenced in any manner whatever by such publicity.

COMMENT

(a) In general

The amplified instruction gives more emphasis to admonitions not to be influenced by out-of-court publicity. It might be a useful alternative in longer trials which have attracted media attention. It incorporates additional language suggested in the American Bar Association's Standard Relating to Fair Trial and Free Press, Sec. 3.5(e). It is partly adapted from Bar Association of the District of Columbia, *Criminal Jury Instructions for the District of Columbia* § 1.11 (3rd ed. 1978).

All persons accused of crime are entitled, as a matter of right, to be tried by a fair and impartial jury, selected according to law. About this there can be no question. But the question is constantly presented in practice of what standard or test should be applied to determine the requisite degree of fairness and impartiality of the jury. To require that jurors shall come to the trial of a crime committed in their community, no matter how notorious or atrocious it may be, with minds wholly unaffected or unimpressed by what they may have read or heard in regard to it, is to maintain a rule or standard by which most persons would be excluded from the jury. All persons, by natural instinct, are more or less biased against crime in the abstract. But natural bias, however atrocious the crime, can never be regarded as a sufficient cause for the disqualification of the juror. *Garlitz v. State,* 71 Md. 293, 299-300, 18 A. 39 (1889). All that can be required of jurors is that they shall be without bias or prejudice for or against the accused; and, that their minds are free to hear and impartially consider the evidence and to reach a verdict without regard to any former opinion or impression formed upon rumor or media reports. In other words, jurors are not required to be totally ignorant of the facts of the case prior to trial. *Simms v. State,* 49 Md. App. 515, 433 A.2d 1199 (1982). Persons cannot readily clear their minds of former impressions and leave their minds a blank. But it does not follow that such a condition of mind makes the juror incompetent. For example, mere public knowledge of a confession will not vitiate a subsequent trial and the mere fact of public statements as to matters that might or might not be admissible in evidence against an accused would not prevent a trial or vitiate a subsequent jury trial. *Baltimore Radio Show, Inc. v. State,* 193 Md. 300, 67 A.2d 497 (1949), *cert. denied,* 338 U.S. 912 (1950).

See Appendix I, Preliminary Instructions to the Jury, *infra.*

(b) Jurors reading newspaper accounts of trial

While a mistrial may be granted because of prejudicial publicity during the trial, there must be proof that some of the jurors read the offending articles. *Marshall v. United States,* 360 U.S. 310, 79 S. Ct. 1171, 3 L. Ed. 2d 1250 (1959). The general rule with respect to alleged prejudice caused by newspaper publicity, which has been clearly established in this state by judicial decision, is that the burden is upon the party alleging prejudice to show: (1) that the newspaper article is prejudicial; (2) that a juror has read the prejudicial newspaper article; and (3) that the juror's decision at the trial was influenced by the newspaper article. *Simms v. State,* 49 Md. App. 515, 433 A.2d 1199 (1982); *Barber v. State,* 16 Md. App. 235, 239, 295 A.2d 814 (1972); *Sizemore v. State,* 5 Md. App. 507, 248 A.2d 417 (1968); *Graef v. State,* 1 Md. App. 161, 228 A.2d 480 (1967); *Presley v. State,* 224 Md. 550, 555, 168 A.2d 510 (1961), *cert. denied,* 368 U.S. 957 (1962).

Where there is a lengthy hiatus between the majority of the newspaper reports and the trial, the court cannot assume that an unbiased trier of fact cannot be found. Although *voir dire* examination may not always provide sufficient protection, where "the publicity was sporadic, not inherently prejudicial and preceded the trial by several months, a trial court does not abuse its discretion by relying on *voir dire* to ascertain prejudice." *Waine v. State,* 37 Md. App. 222, 377 A.2d 509 (1977). In *Waine,* the Court reaffirmed the general rule that the party alleging prejudice has the burden of proof.

Jurors should not read newspaper accounts of the trial while it is in progress. *Holt v. United States,* 218 U.S. 245, 31 S. Ct. 2, 54 L. Ed. 1021 (1910). The danger to the defendant from a juror's reading of newspaper accounts may be greater than if the information is put in evidence, because if it were part of the evidence it would be tempered by protective procedures. *Marshall v. United States, supra.*

It appears that the Sixth and Seventh Federal Circuit Courts have adopted a rule that trial judges in those circuits must interrogate the jurors whenever prejudicial articles which may have reached the jurors have been published and this fact is called to the court's attention. See *Marson v. United States,* 203 F.2d 904 (6th Cir. 1953). Other jurisdictions do not follow this reasoning and leave the question of interrogation to the discretion of the trial judge. See *Cohen v. United States,* 297 F.2d 760, 764 (9th Cir. 1962).

Where it appears that jurors may have read a newspaper article about the crime on trial, it is the duty of the trial court to determine, so far as possible, whether the article contains improper matter, whether it was in fact read, and whether the reading could affect the verdict of the jury. The determination to be made by the trial court rests not alone on what the jury says on interrogation, but on the nature of the published material together with all other facts and circumstances in the record. This calls for the exercise of sound judicial discretion. *Marshall v. United States, supra.*

The Supreme Court has since interpreted *Marshall* as applying solely to federal courts, for that decision arose as an "'exercise of [its] supervisory power to formulate and apply proper standards for enforcement of the criminal law in the federal courts,' and not as a matter of constitutional compulsion." *Murphy v. Florida,* 421 U.S. 794, 797, 95 S. Ct. 2031, 44 L. Ed. 2d 589 (1975) (*quoting Marshall v. United States, supra,* 360 U.S. at 313).

Notwithstanding the limited application of the *Marshall* decision, as to a claim of an unfair trial in a state court, resulting from excessive or prejudicial publicity, the proper standard is whether "in the totality of the circumstances … [the] trial was not fundamentally fair." *Murphy v. Florida, supra,* 421 U.S. at 799. The burden of proof is upon the defendant to show "that the setting of the trial was inherently prejudicial or that the jury selection process of which he complains permits an inference of actual prejudice." *Id.* at 803.

Nevertheless, "extensive knowledge in the community of either the crime or the putative criminal is not sufficient by itself to render a trial constitutionally unfair." *Dobbert v. Florida,* 432 U.S. 282, 303, 97 S. Ct. 2290, 53 L. Ed. 2d 344 (1977) (*citing Murphy v. Florida, supra*). See *Prevatte v. Director, Patuxent Inst.,* 5 Md. App. 406, 248 A.2d 170 (1968). Similarly, it is not required that a prospective juror be totally ignorant of the facts and issues involved, and most well-qualified jurors will have formed some impression or opinion as to the merits of an important case. It is sufficient if the juror can lay aside his impression or opinion and render a verdict based on the evidence presented in court. *Irvin v. Dowd,* 366 U.S. 717, 81 S. Ct. 1639, 6 L. Ed. 2d 751 (1961).

Where a few members of the jury panel on *voir dire* responded affirmatively to questions concerning whether they had read anything about the case, and then briefly revealed the nature of the information they had learned from a neutral newspaper article, such cursory statements did not contaminate the entire array, and the discharge of that array, therefore, was not required. *Malekar v. State,* 26 Md. App. 498, 338 A.2d 328 (1975).

The accused in a criminal case cannot complain on appeal that he was prejudiced by virtue of a newspaper article unless he asked for a *voir dire* as to whether the jurors had read it. *Presley v. State, supra.*

Where the existence of prejudicial publicity comes to light during the trial and the judge has a chance to question the jurors and give cautionary instructions, there is no reason to assume prejudice among the jurors. *Holt v. United States, supra.*

(c) Communications with jurors before and during trial

After the trial begins, the jurors should not communicate with anyone connected with the case other than in the regular course of the trial, 53 Am. Jur. Trial § 893 (1st ed. 1945). The showing of mere communications between witnesses and jurors is not a ground for the granting of a new trial without showing that the jurors were influenced and a party was prejudiced. *Joseph F. Hughes & Co. v. Stockhausen,* 212 Md. 559, 129 A.2d 844 (1957). Generally, contact between a juror and an outsider (all persons except those connected with the trial as party, counsel, witness, or court official) is not in all cases a sufficient ground for ordering a mistrial, new trial or reversal. The misconduct must be such as to reasonably indicate that a fair and impartial trial could not be had under the circumstances. *Joseph F. Hughes & Co. v. Stockhausen, supra.*

Communications between jurors and the parties or their attorneys may be reversible error, but casual conversations not relating to the case, though improper, are usually deemed harmless. For example, the denial of a motion for mistrial was held proper and not an abuse of discretion where plaintiff's counsel had mistaken a juror in the hall of the court for a witness he was waiting for, and upon asking the juror if he was the person and finding his error, counsel walked away. *Kasten Constr. Co. v. Evans,* 260 Md. 536, 273 A.2d 90 (1971).

No person may speak to the jurors on any matter connected with the trial during an inspection of property involved in litigation; only the trial judge is permitted to make any statement to the jury during the view. Maryland Rule 2-515(b).

The guarantees of a trial by jury by the fourteenth amendment to the United States Constitution were violated where two deputy sheriffs, who were the principal witnesses for the prosecution and whose credibility inevitably determined whether the accused would be convicted, were continuously in the jurors' company during the trial, driving them to meals and to their lodging each night, and doing errands for them, even though they never discussed the case itself. *Turner v. Louisiana,* 379 U.S. 466, 85 S. Ct. 546, 13 L. Ed. 2d 424 (1965).

In one Maryland case, a bailiff advised the jury, at the request of the jury foreman, there was no legal difference between "illegal entering" and "breaking and entering." This act was held to be sufficient to require a reversal of the defendant's conviction for a daytime break-in, and a new trial was ordered. *Oliver v. State,* 25 Md. App. 647, 334 A.2d 572 (1975).

In any event, whether a mistrial should be declared is a matter within the sound discretion of the trial court. *Rent-A-Car Co. v. Globe & Rutgers Fire Ins. Co.,* 163 Md. 401, 163 A. 702 (1933).

(d) Publicity before and during trial

The problem of undue publicity before and during a trial is closely akin to that which arises when a juror, once selected, reads or hears an account of the trial which contains material which is not admissible or which has not been admitted in evidence at the trial. Maryland had held that this may constitute grounds for reversal. *Basiliko v. State,* 212 Md. 248, 129 A.2d 375 (1957).

The Maryland legislature has prohibited extended media coverage of criminal proceedings in the trial courts of this state. Maryland Ann. Code, Art. 27, § 467B(b). This partially overruled Maryland Rule of Procedure 1209 which temporarily permitted such coverage of all state judicial proceedings, subject to certain constraints. Rule 1209 still permits electronic media and photographic coverage of civil trials as well as criminal and civil appellate proceedings, subject to the discretion of the presiding judge and to court adopted guidelines governing the type, number and placement of equipment as well as the behavior of media personnel. In addition, Rule 1209 provides that the consent of all parties is required at civil trials.

As an experimental rule, Rule 1209 was effective for an eighteen-month period extending January 1, 1981 through June 30, 1982. During that period, it replaced suspended Judicial Ethics Rule 11 of Maryland Rule 1231 and Canon XXXIV. Order of the Maryland Court of Appeals, November 10, 1980. This experimental rule was extended as to civil actions until June 30, 1983. On May 26, 1983 the rule was further extended and on May 4, 1984 the Court of Appeals voted to make permanent the extended media coverage as to civil actions.

The prohibition of extended media coverage of criminal trials by the Maryland legislature should stimulate sharp debate, particularly in light of the decision of the Supreme Court of the United States in *Chandler v. Florida,* 449 U.S. 560, 101 S. Ct.

802, 66 L. Ed. 2d 740 (1981). The *Chandler* opinion initially clarified the holding of *Estes v. Texas,* 381 U.S. 532, 85 S. Ct. 1628, 14 L. Ed. 2d 543, *rehearing denied,* 382 U.S. 875 (1965) stating that, contrary to popular belief, *Estes* "did not announce a constitutional rule that all photographic or broadcast coverage of criminal trials is inherently a denial of due process...." *Chandler v. Florida, supra,* 449 U.S. at 574, 101 S. Ct. 802 at 809, 66 L. Ed. 2d at 751. It then proceeded to state the holding that Florida Canon 3A(7), which provided for electronic media and still photography coverage of public judicial proceedings, subject to the discretion of the presiding judge and to regulations promulgated by the Supreme Court of Florida, did not automatically operate to deprive of due process those criminal defendants whose trials were televised under its strictures.

The Court in *Chandler* emphasized that its decision was not based upon any supervisory jurisdiction over state courts, but rather solely upon the requirements of the federal constitution. Furthermore, it found that "[t]he risk of juror prejudice is present in any publication of a trial, but the appropriate safeguard against such prejudice is the defendant's right to demonstrate that the media's coverage of his case — be it printed or broadcast — compromised the ability of the particular jury that heard the case to adjudicate fairly." *Id.* at 575, 1101 S. Ct. at 810, 66 L. Ed. 2d at 752.

In light of *Chandler,* former Maryland Rule 1209 would seem to have a solid constitutional footing even prior to being partially overruled. Florida Canon 3A(7), which was upheld in *Chandler,* permitted media coverage of a criminal trial, even over an objection by the defendant. In notable contrast, Maryland Rule 1209 requires the written consent of all parties to a proceeding in a trial court before media coverage may be permitted.

The Supreme Court of the United States has laid down a number of other rules governing publicity as it bears upon the right of a defendant to a fair trial. Violation of these rules by a state court may be a deprivation of due process. *Sheppard v. Maxwell,* 384 U.S. 333, 86 S. Ct. 1507, 16 L. Ed. 2d 600 (1966).

There are no general restrictions on the press from reporting events that transpire in the courtroom. See *Sheppard v. Max-*

well, supra. It is now established that the first amendment extends to the public and to the press a right of access to criminal trials. *Richmond Newspapers, Inc. v. Virginia,* 448 U.S. 555, 100 S. Ct. 2814, 65 L. Ed. 2d 973 (1980). This right of access, nevertheless, is not absolute. "[A] trial judge, in the interest of the fair administration of justice, [may] impose reasonable limitations on access to a trial." *Richmond Newspapers, Inc. v. Virginia, supra,* 448 U.S. at 581, n.18. See *Patuxent Publishing Corp. v. State,* 48 Md. App. 689, 429 A.2d 554 (1981). In reaching its decision in *Richmond Newspapers,* the Court found it necessary to limit to its facts its prior decision in *Gannett Co. v. DePasquale,* 443 U.S. 368, 99 S. Ct. 2898, 61 L. Ed. 2d 608 (1979), interpreting the *Gannett* holding to be "that the sixth amendment's guarantee to the accused of a public trial gave neither the public nor the press an enforceable right of access to a pre-trial suppression hearing." *Richmond Newspapers, Inc. v. Virginia, supra,* 448 U.S. at 564 (emphasis in the original).

In *Globe Newspaper Co. v. Superior Court,* 457 U.S. 596, 102 S. Ct. 2613, 73 L. Ed. 2d 248 (1982), the Court held that a Massachusetts statute, as construed by the Massachusetts Supreme Judicial Court, requiring trial judges to exclude the press and general public from the courtroom during the testimony of victims under the age of eighteen in specified sexual offenses is unconstitutional as violative of the first amendment. While the interest of safeguarding the physical and psychological well-being of a minor is a compelling one, this interest does not justify a mandatory closure rule. A trial court can determine on a case-by-case basis whether closure is necessary to protect the welfare of a minor victim.

§ 1.12. Admonition upon recess.

[You will not be required to remain together while the court is in recess.]

You are instructed not to discuss this case with anyone or let anyone discuss this case with you or in your presence. This includes other jurors, courtroom personnel, friends and relatives, spectators and reporters. Also, you should avoid any contact with the parties, witnesses and lawyers involved in this case. If anyone tries to discuss this case with you or if anything questionable occurs, please write me a note, as soon as possible, and do not discuss it with anyone else.

You are further instructed not to form or express an opinion on the case until all of the evidence is in and the case has been submitted to you for your deliberation.

§ 1.12a. Admonition upon recess (amplified instruction prior to first recess).

[You will not be required to remain together while the court is in recess.] It is important that you follow certain rules whenever the court is in recess.

First, do not discuss the case either among yourselves or with anyone else during the course of the trial. This applies to all persons, including members of your family, friends or relatives.

Second, do not permit any other person to discuss the case in your presence. This includes courtroom spectators, witnesses, newspaper reporters and parties to this case. If anyone attempts to discuss the case with you despite your telling him or her not to, you must report that fact to me as soon as you are able. However, you should not discuss with your fellow jurors the fact that anyone tried to discuss the case with you.

Third, although it is a natural human tendency to talk with others with whom one is thrown into contact, you must not talk with any of the parties or their attorneys or any witness in this case during the course of this trial. [By this I mean that you should not only avoid discussing the case, but that you should avoid any discussion whatsoever, even to pass the time of day. If you should find yourself in a courthouse corridor or any other area where the case is being discussed by attorneys, parties or witnesses, you should leave the area as soon as possible so as to avoid hearing such discussions. In no other way can all parties be assured of the absolute impartiality that they are entitled to expect from you as jurors.]

Finally, in fairness to both the State and the defendant, you should keep an open mind throughout the trial. You are instructed not to form or express an opinion on the case until all of the evidence is in and the case has been submitted to you for your deliberation.

COMMENT

The amplified instruction is adapted from Devitt & Blackmar, *Federal Jury Practice and Instructions* § 10.14 (3rd ed. 1977), and Bar Association of the District of Columbia, *Criminal Jury Instructions for the District of Columbia* § 1.025 (3rd ed. 1978). The amplified instruction is probably most useful in longer trials.

There is no requirement that the trial judge admonish the jury upon separation of the jury. *Wilson v. State,* 4 Md. App. 192, 242 A.2d 194 (1968), *cert. denied,* 394 U.S. 975 (1969).

"The jurors sworn to try a criminal action may, at any time before the submission of the case to the jury, in the discretion of the court, be permitted to separate or may be kept in charge of proper officers." Maryland Ann. Code, Courts and Judicial Proceedings, § 8-304. See Maryland Rule 2-511(c).

In *Wilson v. State, supra* at 200, 242 A.2d at 199, the Court held that it was not prejudicial error where the trial court instructed the jury, prior to a recess, that they could discuss the case among themselves in the jury room. The Court went on to say that "[it] may be the better practice, in order to preclude any possibility of misconduct (insofar as admonition can do so) that every jury be admonished not to discuss the case among themselves, even when in the jury room, until it is finally submitted to them."

See Appendix I, Preliminary Instructions to the Jury, *infra.*

§ 1.13. When jurors cannot agree — Jury's duty to deliberate.

The verdict must represent the considered judgment of each juror. In order to return a verdict, it is necessary that each juror agree. Your verdict must be unanimous. It is your duty, as jurors, to consult with one another and to deliberate with a view toward reaching an agreement, if you can do so without violence to your individual judgments. Each of you must decide the case for yourself, but you should do so only after an impartial consideration of the evidence with your fellow jurors. In the course of your deliberation, you should not hesitate to reexamine your own views and change your opinion if you become convinced that it was erroneous. But you should not surrender your honest convictions as to the weight or effect of the evidence solely because of the opinions of your fellow jurors, or merely for the purpose of returning a verdict. You are judges of the facts as they have been presented to you through the evidence in this case. Your sole purpose should be to evaluate the evidence in the light of the law on which you have been instructed.

COMMENT

This instruction is based on the American Bar Association's recommended instruction. The ABA instruction was approved in *Kelly v. State,* 270 Md. 139, 310 A.2d 538 (1973) and *Burnette v. State,* 32 Md. App. 277, 360 A.2d 23 (1976), *rev'd,* 280 Md. 88, 371 A.2d 663 (1977). This instruction may be given either before the jury begins its deliberations or in the event that the jury becomes deadlocked. *Goodmuth v. State,* 302 Md. 613, 490 A.2d 682 (1985).

A different version of this instruction, based on the traditional "Allen" charge, has been heavily criticized as coercive. The main focus of criticism has been on the deference given to other jurors' opinions, its advice that one juror should listen to others with a "disposition to be convinced of each other's argument," and the admonition that those in the minority should reconsider their views which have made "no impression on the minds of so many equally intelligent jurors." See *Allen v. United States,* 164 U.S. 492, 17 S. Ct. 154, 41 L. Ed. 528 (1896). Conversely, instructions concerning the responsibilities of jurors in the course of their deliberations, which have been modified by deleting the coercive language of the instructions given in the *Allen* case, *supra,* have generally been approved in recent years. Such noncoercive instructions are sometimes referred to as "modified" or "Allen"-type charges. *Burnette v. State, supra.*

There has been substantial appellate litigation as to whether any circumstances exist which justify giving the traditional "Allen" charge. While the Court of Appeals seems to have definitively answered this question in the negative, a brief review of the leading cases is helpful.

There were two situations in which the traditional "Allen" charge, in the sound discretion of the judge, was formerly applied: (1) before the jury retired to first consider the case; (2) after the jury had been sequestered to deliberate as a result of an apparent deadlock.

The first case which considered the propriety of a traditional "Allen" charge and the only case which upheld use of the traditional charge was *Leupen v. Lackey,* 248 Md. 19, 234 A.2d 573 (1967). The next case to consider the matter was *Kelly v. State, supra,* which criticized the traditional charge, and would only accept a recitation of the charge as circumscribed by the American Bar Association's *Standards Relating to Trial by Jury,* quoted *infra.*

In *Kelly, supra,* the Court provided some guidance. The trial judge has greater latitude in "personalizing" an instruction when the charge is given *before* the jury retires to deliberate. The Court felt that an instruction approved in *Leupen, supra,* would be acceptable. After the jury begins its deliberations, a trial judge who decides to give an instruction because of an apparent deadlock should closely adhere to the wording of the ABA recommended instruction. Ample time for discussion of the issues should be allowed before an instruction is given or repeated.

In *Pinder v. State,* 31 Md. App. 126, 355 A.2d 489 (1976), Judge Moore stated:

> On principle, therefore, and upon the authority of *Kelly v. State, supra,* we conclude that the traditional *Allen* charge, as distinguished from an *Allen*-type charge conforming to the ABA Standards, should no longer be given in Maryland *after the jury has retired;* and we hold that its employment here accompanied by the prefatory language of the trial court previously quoted, must be held to constitute coercion and therefore reversible error.

Id. 355 A.2d at 495 (emphasis added).

While *Pinder* suggested that in appropriate circumstances the traditional "Allen" charge may still be given *before the jury has begun its deliberations,* later cases overrule this.

In *Burnette v. State, supra,* a traditional "Allen" charge was given, over the appellant's objection, four hours *after the jury had retired.* The Court of Appeals reversed the appellant's conviction, holding that the instruction constituted reversible error because it was a substantive departure from the ABA approved instruction. After discussion of *Kelly v. State, supra,* and *Leupen v. Lackey, supra,* the Court broadly condemned any substantive departures from the ABA recommended instruction, without explicitly limiting that statement to those situations where the instruction has been given after the jury has begun its deliberation and is deadlocked. Thus, the broad language in *Burnette* seems to disapprove of any use of the traditional "Allen" charge.

In *Fowlkes v. State,* 53 Md. App. 39, 451 A.2d 1270 (1982), after deliberating for less than one hour, the jury foreperson indicated that the jury was ready to give its verdict. When polled, the foreperson stated that she did not vote either way. The judge addressed the jury, before polling any of the jurors, and sent them back to deliberate. Ten minutes later they indicated a verdict of guilty. In upholding the verdict, the Court held that instruction similar in substance to the ABA instruction was not necessary since the jury was not deadlocked.

In *Oliver v. State,* 25 Md. App. 647, 334 A.2d 572 (1975), after an hour and a half of deliberation, following the presentation of all the evidence in a daytime break-in and larceny case, the judge issued an "Allen" charge to the following effect:

> I am going to send you back another half hour, ... and see what you can do, because it's difficult for me to see how on the issues of this case you can't come to some sort of agreement on it.... This case has been a day and a half .... Now it's expensive .... It means it's got to be tried all over again.

The case was reversed on the ground that the bailiff improperly gave legal advice to the foreman of the deadlocked jury, but in dicta the Court warned that language by the judge that is so coercive and intimidating as to strongly suggest agreement on a verdict by the jurors might be such an abuse of discretion as to independently warrant reversal. The decision further states that the "Allen" charge should be resorted to with care, restraint and circumspection.

The use of the traditional "Allen" charge, accompanied by prefatory language to the jury to the effect that there were reasons self-evident for the trial court not wanting to retry the rape case (i.e., to save time, expense, and spare the rape victim the traumatic reenactment of the occurrence), was held to be unduly coercive and constituted reversible error, even though the defendant had failed to object. *Pinder v. State, supra.*

A similar conclusion was reached in *Smoot v. State,* 31 Md. App. 138, 355 A.2d 495 (1976). In this case, the foreperson informed the court that the jury had reached a deadlock after approximately two hours of deliberation. The court, in response, told the jury that he "will not accept that ..." and required the jury to go back and do some more deliberating. After two more hours of deliberations, the jury again informed the court it was still deadlocked, split eight to four favoring conviction. At this time the court delivered the ABA charge. The defendant was convicted. It was held that there was an abuse of discretion for the court to order further deliberations.

But, in *Wilson v. State,* 44 Md. App. 318, 408 A.2d 1058 (1980), the trial court instructed the jury that it was absolutely necessary to return a verdict on the burglary count after it had reached guilty verdicts as to the robbery and handgun counts. This was held not to be coercive since it was clear from the jury's response to this instruction that a decision had already been reached.

In *Goodmuth v. State,* 302 Md. 613, 490 A.2d 682 (1985) and *Beach v. State,* 302 Md. 613, 490 A.2d 682 (1985) the trial judges gave traditional "Allen" charges to the juries *before* they retired. In separate appeals, Goodmuth and Beach argued that the instruction was of the type previously disapproved by the Court of Appeals as being coercive and should not have been given.

The Court pointed out that the traditional "Allen" instruction given in both these cases was expressly disapproved in *Burnette v. State, supra,* as being coercive. In rejecting the traditional "Allen" charge, the Court reiterated its approval of the ABA's suggested charge which eliminated the coercive elements of the "Allen" charge. The Court, while noting that *Burnette* involved a situation in which the coercive charge was given after the jury began deliberating, stated that the *Burnette* opinion did not distinguish between pre-deliberation and post-deliberation instructions. The Court in *Goodmuth* and *Beach* reasoned that when traditional "Allen" instructions are given before jurors retire to deliberate, the same coercion exists as when such instructions are given after deliberations had begun. Relying on *Burnette* which authorized only deviations from approved ABA instructions, which involved form and style but not substance, the Court of Appeals reversed and remanded for new trials in both cases.

Case law also suggests that the trial court should never give the instruction in such a manner as to indicate to the jury the character of the verdict to be reached. In addition, the decision as to whether to utilize an "Allen"-type charge, when to employ it, and what words should be selected, are best left to the sound discretion of the trial judge. *Cf. Oliver v. State, supra; Fletcher v. State,* 8 Md. App. 153, 258 A.2d 781 (1969), *appeal after remand, Hamilton v. State,* 12 Md. App. 91, 277 A.2d 460, *aff'd,* 265 Md.

256, 288 A.2d 885, *cert. denied,* 409 U.S. 1006 (1972); *Tyler v. United States,* 495 A.2d 1180 (D.C. 1985).

When the instruction is given because of an apparent jury deadlock after a period of deliberation, the interval from the onset of deliberation, in view of the complexity of the case, will be considered in examining whether there was an abuse of discretion in giving the instruction at the time the trial judge selected. *Smoot v. State, supra; Oliver v. State, supra; Kelly v. State, supra; Plumley v. State,* 4 Md. App. 671, 245 A.2d 111 (1968). See also *Mayfield v. State,* 302 Md. 624, 490 A.2d 687 (1985). (It was not coercive for the trial court to give an ABA approved modified "Allen" jury instruction when the jury, on becoming deadlocked, voluntarily revealed its numerical split.)

The justification for the use of an "Allen"-type instruction was stated in *Leupen v. Lackey, supra* (*quoting Allen v. United States, supra* at 501-02) as follows:

> While, undoubtedly, the verdict of the jury should represent the opinions of each individual juror, it by no means follows that opinions may not be changed by conference in the jury-room. The very object of the jury system is to secure unanimity by a comparison of views, and by arguments among the jurors themselves. It certainly cannot be the law that each juror should not listen with deference to the arguments and with a distrust of his own judgment, if he finds a large majority of the jury taking a different view of the case from what he does himself. It cannot be that each juror should go to the jury-room with a blind determination that the verdict shall represent his opinion of the case at that moment; or, that he should close his ears to the arguments of men who are equally honest and intelligent as himself.

Id. at 23, 234 A.2d at 575.

The complete text of the American Bar Association's *Standards Relating to Trial by Jury,* § 5.4 (1968), which also appears in *Kelly v. State, supra,* at note 6, is as follows:

> Length of deliberations; deadlocked jury.
>
> (a) Before the jury retires for deliberation, the court may give an instruction which informs the jury:

(i) that in order to return a verdict, each juror must agree thereto;

(ii) that jurors have a duty to consult with one another and to deliberate with a view to reaching an agreement, if it can be done without violence to individual judgment;

(iii) that each juror must decide the case for himself, but only after an impartial consideration of the evidence with his fellow jurors;

(iv) that in the course of deliberations, a juror should not hesitate to reexamine his own views and change his opinion if convinced it is erroneous; and

(v) that no juror should surrender his honest conviction as to the weight or effect of the evidence solely because of the opinion of his fellow jurors, or for the mere purpose of returning a verdict.

(b) If it appears to the court that the jury has been unable to agree, the court may require the jury to continue their deliberations and may give or repeat an instruction as provided in subsection (a). The court shall not require or threaten to require the jury to deliberate for an unreasonable length of time or for unreasonable intervals.

(c) The jury may be discharged without having agreed upon a verdict if it appears that there is no reasonable probability of agreement.

In *McKay v. State,* 32 Md. App. 451, 362 A.2d 666 (1976), *aff'd,* 280 Md. 558, 375 A.2d 228 (1977), the Court held that unanimity is an imperative of a legal verdict in a Maryland criminal prosecution before a jury, and that an accused may not waive that mandate for unanimity set forth in Article 21 of the Maryland Declaration of Rights. See, e.g., *Smith v. State,* 51 Md. App. 408, 443 A.2d 985, 996 (1982).

A trial court should not repeatedly give an "anti-deadlock instruction to a deadlocked jury." *Epperson v. United States, App. D.C.,* 495 A.2d 1170 (1985).

It is firmly established in Maryland case law that an erroneous "Allen" charge amounts to plain error under Maryland Rule 4-325(e) (formerly Rule 757(g)). Thus, an objection to the *form* of the charge may be raised for the first time on appeal. *Hutchinson v. State,* 36 Md. App. 58, 373 A.2d 50 (1977); *Pinder v. State, supra; Fletcher v. State, supra.* Worth noting is that in *Hutchin-*

son v. State, supra, the Court appeared to draw a distinction between objections based on the *form* and those based on the *timing* of the "Allen"-type charge. Thus, in *Hutchinson,* the defendant did not object to the "Allen"-type charge given after an hour and twenty minutes of jury deliberation. As a result, the Court refused to consider whether the charge was premature.

§ 1.14. Jury's nonconcern with punishment.

The question of punishment or penalty in the event of conviction is no concern of the jury and should not enter into or influence your deliberations in any way. You should not guess or speculate about the punishment. Your job will be done after finding the defendant not guilty or guilty. In the event that you do find the defendant guilty, the responsibility of punishment will be solely upon this court. You should weigh the evidence in the case and determine the guilt or innocence of the defendant solely upon the basis of such evidence, without any consideration of the matter of punishment.

COMMENT

The instruction is based upon an instruction given by the trial court in *Tripp v. State,* 36 Md. App. 459, 374 A.2d 384 (1977). In *Tripp,* the Court of Special Appeals stated:

> It is not appropriate for the State to seek a tactical advantage by indicating, in certain cases, that a defendant may receive probation or a suspended sentence if the jury brings a proper verdict of guilty in a case where it might be reluctant to do so because of the fear of inordinate punishment. Conversely, it is not appropriate for a defendant to seek a tactical advantage by indicating, in other cases (such as this one), that a defendant may still be confined and will not be "loose upon the streets" if the jury brings in a verdict of not guilty by reason of insanity. Either effort in either direction distracts the jury from the purity of its mission and is always to be discouraged.

Id. at 484, 374 A.2d at 398.

The defendant in *Tripp* was charged with murder and as the Court noted, he "wanted the jury to be assured that if they found [him] not guilty by reason of insanity, the judge could still order him confined for further mental examination." The Court stated that the penalty to be imposed upon the defendant should not be a concern of the jury.

See Comment, § 5.08, Insanity, (Subpart (j)) *Should the jury be instructed on the consequences of an insanity verdict?*, *infra*. *But see* Instruction, § 4.21c, Murder — First degree: Death penalty sentencing. The jury has a decision-making role in these cases.

See Appendix I, Preliminary Instructions to the Jury, *infra*.

§ 1.15. Defendant's representation of self.

A defendant has the right to waive counsel and to represent himself [with the help of an attorney advisor]. [A defendant who is initially represented by counsel has the right to discharge counsel and represent himself.] A defendant may have a lawyer act for him or he may act for himself. The law does not favor one choice over the other. You should not assume anything from the fact that the defendant made this choice.

COMMENT

This instruction is partially patterned after Bar Association of the District of Columbia, *Criminal Jury Instructions for the District of Columbia* § 1.14 (3rd ed. 1978). See also Devitt & Blackmar, *Federal Jury Practice and Instructions*, § 5.06 (3rd ed. 1977). *Cf. Snead v. State*, 286 Md. 122, 406 A.2d 98 (1979) (defendant's conviction reversed when trial court failed to pursue inquiry essential to a determination of defendant's right to proceed without counsel).

The instruction should be initially given at the outset of trial where a defendant chooses to represent himself. The bracketed language should be given where a defendant discharges counsel during trial and subsequently represents himself, or proceeds from the outset of trial with an attorney assisting him.

See Appendix I, Preliminary Instructions to the Jury, *infra.*

Chapter 2

EVALUATION OF TESTIMONY AND OTHER EVIDENCE

A. Evaluation of testimony

§ 2.01. Accomplice's testimony — Corroboration.
§ 2.02. Informer's testimony — Witness promised leniency.
§ 2.03. Number of witnesses.
§ 2.04. Child witness.
§ 2.05. Expert witness.
§ 2.06. Credibility of witnesses.
§ 2.07. Impeachment by prior conviction(s).
(a) Of the defendant.
(b) Of a witness other than the defendant.
§ 2.08. Prior inconsistent and consistent statement(s).
(a) Impeachment by prior inconsistent statement(s).
(b) When a party seeks to impeach own witness.
(c) Rehabilitation by use of prior consistent statement(s).
§ 2.09. Defendant as witness — Impeachment by confession: confession admitted solely for impeachment purposes.
§ 2.10. Other crimes and prior bad acts of defendant.
§ 2.11. Court calling its own witness.

B. Evaluation of other evidence

§ 2.21. Missing witness.
§ 2.22. Multiple counts and multiple defendants.
(a) Multiple counts — One defendant.
(b) Lesser included offenses or inconsistent counts — One defendant.
(c) Multiple defendants.
(d) Multiple defendants — Additional instruction for different or multiple counts.
(e) Multiple defendants — Evidence applicable only to one defendant: limiting instruction.
§ 2.23. Character of defendant (reputation and opinion evidence and impeachment of defendant's character witness(es)).
(a) Evidence of defendant's good character.
(b) Impeachment of defendant's character witnesses(es): limiting instruction.
§ 2.24. Flight or concealment by defendant.
§ 2.25. Confession or incriminating statement of defendant.
§ 2.26. *Corpus delicti* — Corroboration of defendant's confession [admission].
§ 2.27. Defendant's decision not to testify (silence of defendant).
§ 2.28. Identity of defendant.
§ 2.29. Identification of defendant by single eyewitness.
§ 2.30. Photographic identification.
§ 2.31. Fingerprint evidence.

§ 2.32. Consent to blood and other chemical tests — Comment.
§ 2.33. Evidence of jurisdiction.

A. Evaluation of testimony

§ 2.01. Accomplice's testimony — Corroboration.

You have heard testimony from __________ (*insert name of accomplice*), who was [may have been] an accomplice. An accomplice is competent to be a witness for the State. An accomplice is one who knowingly, voluntarily, and with common criminal intent aided, advised or encouraged another person in the commission of a crime either before or during the crime. Thus, the testimony of an accomplice is to be evaluated with caution.

[In this case, the State and the defendant disagree as to whether __________ (*insert name*) was an accomplice. If you are not convinced that __________ (*insert name*) was an accomplice, you should treat that testimony as you would treat the testimony of any other witness. On the other hand, if you are convinced that __________ (*insert name*) was an accomplice, you must then decide whether that testimony was corroborated.]

Before you may consider the testimony of an accomplice, you must first decide whether the testimony was corroborated. To corroborate means to strengthen. The defendant cannot be convicted solely on the uncorroborated testimony of an accomplice. The corroborating evidence does not have to prove any particular fact to which an accomplice has testified. Only slight corroboration is required. This means that there must be evidence, in addition to the testimony of __________ (*insert name*) tending to show either (1) that the defendant committed the crime charged or (2) that the defendant was with others who committed the crime, at the time and place the crime was committed.

If you find that the testimony of __________ (*insert name*) has not been corroborated, you must disregard it and may not consider it as evidence against the defendant. Remember, the defendant cannot be convicted solely on the uncorroborated testimony of an accomplice. If you find that the testimony of __________ (*insert name*) has been corroborated, it should be considered with caution and given such weight as you believe it deserves.

COMMENT

It is incumbent upon the trial judge, when requested, to give an advisory instruction to the jury on every essential point of law supported by the evidence. *Gaskins v. State,* 7 Md. App. 99, 253 A.2d 759 (1969). Failure to give an accomplice testimony jury instruction, when requested by the defendant and where appropriate, is reversible error. *Gaskins v. State, supra. Burley v. State,* 5 Md. App. 469, 248 A.2d 404 (1968); *Blizzard v. State,* 30 Md. App. 156, 351 A.2d 443, *rev'd on other grounds,* 278 Md. 556, 366 A.2d 1026 (1976). The trial court is not required to instruct the jury that accomplice testimony is to be viewed with suspicion and weighed cautiously. Adequate instructions in this area need only state that the testimony of the accomplice must be corroborated in material aspects, even though the corroboration may only be slight (i.e., not sufficient in itself to convict). *Burley v. State, supra; Blizzard v. State, supra.*

An accomplice is one who knowingly, voluntarily, and with common criminal intent unites with the principal offender in the commission of a crime either as a principal or as an accessory before the fact. *Watson v. State,* 208 Md. 210, 117 A.2d 549 (1955). *Foster v. State,* 263 Md. 388, 283 A.2d 411 (1971), *cert. denied,* 406 U.S. 908 (1972); *Burley v. State, supra.* This definition encompasses advocating, encouraging, aiding or abetting the commission of a crime. *Coleman v. State,* 209 Md. 379, 121 A.2d 254 (1956). See § 4.01, *infra,* for a discussion of accessory before the fact and see also § 4.02, *infra,* relating to aiding and abetting.

The generally accepted test to determine if a witness is an accomplice is whether he himself could be convicted for the offense either as a principal or accessory before the fact. *Sutton v. State,* 10 Md. App. 353, 270 A.2d 417 (1970). The test has otherwise been stated in terms of whether the witness could be indicted and/or punished for the crime charged against the defendant. *Watson v. State, supra.*

To hold, as a matter of law, that a person is an accomplice, the evidence must be so "clear and decisive that reasonable minds could not differ in reaching that conclusion." *Bishop v. State,* 39 Md. App. 384, 389, 385 A.2d 1206, 1210 (1978). In *Bishop,* the Court held that because the above test was not satisfied, the question of whether the government's witness was an accomplice was one of fact and not one of law. As to the test to be used in determining whether the witness is an accomplice as a matter of law, the Court wrote:

> Since the generally accepted test of whether a witness is an accomplice is whether he could be convicted for the offense charged against the defendant, either as principal or accessory before the fact, *Watson v. State, supra,* the Court must find, in effect, that the testimony was so conclusive that, were a directed verdict of guilty available in a criminal trial, and had the witness been the party charged with the crime, it would have been the witness's fate to have such entered against him.

Id. at 389-90, 385 A.2d at 1210.

See also *Burley v. State, supra,* 5 Md. App. at 472 n.2. But see *Butler v. State,* 19 Md. App. 601, 313 A.2d 554 (1974), holding that in a prosecution of unlawful possession of heroin in sufficient quantity reasonably to indicate intent to distribute, refusal of accomplice instruction with respect to testimony of witness was not improper, where witness testified that he was the landlord who had rented room to defendant and there was no testimony from any other source that any other relationship or association between them had ever existed, even though the witness had been indicted for the offense.

When evidence relating to whether or not a witness is an accomplice is capable of being determined either way and different inferences can be justified in respect thereto, the question is for the determination of the trier of fact and, in a jury case, should be submitted to the jury with proper instruction. *Christopher v. State,* 9 Md. App. 277, 263 A.2d 605 (1970); *Gaskins v. State, supra*; *Burley v. State, supra.* In *Rivenbark v. State,* 58 Md. App. 626, 473 A.2d 1329 (1984), the Court held that in a trial for murder and burglary, evidence was sufficient to support a rational inference that the witness was the accomplice of the defendant and, as such, defendant was entitled to a jury instruction on the law of accomplices and the need for sufficient corroboration of the witness's testimony. Denial of such instruction led to reversal.

An accomplice does not include an accessory after the fact. *Gardner v. State,* 6 Md. App. 483, 251 A.2d 901 (1969). (For a discussion of accessory after the fact, see Comment, § 4.03, *infra.*)

The defendant has the burden of proving by a fair preponderance of the evidence that the witness is an accomplice. *Bennett v. State,* 283 Md. 619, 392 A.2d 76 (1978). The Court held that this allocation of the burden did not violate holdings in *Mullaney v. Wilbur,* 421 U.S. 684, 95 S. Ct. 1881, 44 L. Ed. 2d 508 (1975); *In re Winship,* 397 U.S. 358, 90 S. Ct. 1068, 25 L. Ed. 2d 368 (1970); or *Evans v. State,* 28 Md. App. 640, 349 A.2d 300 (1975), *aff'd,* 278 Md. 197, 362 A.2d 629 (1976).

An accomplice does not become incompetent as a witness because of participation in the crime charged. *Price v. State,* 4 Md. App. 701, 244 A.2d 900 (1968); *Kitt v. State,* 2 Md. App. 306, 234 A.2d 621 (1967); *Lyde v. Warden,* 1 Md. App. 423, 230 A.2d 695 (1967). *See also* 23 C.J.S. *Criminal Law* § 802 (1961). Although an accomplice may be a witness, if his testimony is uncorroborated, the defendant may not be convicted. *Brown v. State,* 281 Md. 241, 378 A.2d 1104 (1977). See also *Proctor v. State,* 49 Md. App. 696, 435 A.2d 484 (1981); *Green v. State,* 49 Md. App. 1, 430 A.2d 1122, 1124 (1981), *Foster v. State, supra; Sutton v. State, supra; Gaskins v. State, supra; Burley v. State, supra.* Corroboration is required because an accomplice's testimony is from a person contaminated with guilt who admits his participation in a crime for which he particularly blames the defendant; it should be regarded with great suspicion and caution. Otherwise, the life or liberty of an innocent person might be taken away by a witness who may make the accusation to gratify his malice, to shield himself from punishment or in the hope of receiving clemency by turning state's evidence. *Gaskins v. State, supra; Watson v. State, supra.*

Corroboration need only be slight (i.e., not sufficient in itself to convict) but it cannot be general corroboration. In *Brown v. State, supra,* the Court reaffirmed its commitment to the Maryland rule which forbids the conviction of a defendant on the uncorroborated testimony of an accomplice. It must be corroborated by evidence tending to show that the accused was identified with the perpetrators of the crime or had participated in the crime itself. *Ford v. State,* 11 Md. App. 654, 276 A.2d 423 (1971); *Sutton v. State, supra; Middleton v. State,* 6 Md. App. 380, 251 A.2d 224 (1969). *See Brown v. State, supra.*

In *Jeandell v. State,* 34 Md. App. 108, 366 A.2d 79 (1976), the only evidence tending to establish the time of the alleged store break-in (as between 9:30 and 11:30 p.m. on October 5), was supplied by the accomplice's testimony. There was, however, nonaccomplice testimony identifying the defendant with the accomplices at approximately 10:30 p.m. on October 5. The Court of Special Appeals reversed the defendant's conviction on the ground that the nonaccomplice's testimony was not sufficient to corroborate the accomplice's testimony regarding the time of the alleged offense. In conclusion, the court stated that "[T]he thing rather that must be established by independent, corroborating evidence is not the identifying of the defendant with the accomplices at roughly 10:30 p.m. on Sunday night, but the identifying of the appellant with the accomplices at or near the time of the crime." 34 Md. App. at 112, 336 A.2d at 81.

In *Proctor v. State, supra,* the Court held that nonaccomplice evidence provided sufficient corroboration of accomplices' testimony under the *Brown* standard, to support defendants' convictions.

The consolidation of theft offenses in Maryland resulted in a special statute to prevent an expanded use of the accomplice testimony corroboration rule. The revised theft offenses consolidate into one crime of "theft" the act of obtaining or exerting unauthorized control over property (see Maryland Ann. Code, Art. 27, § 342(a)) and the act of receiving or possessing stolen personal property (see Art. 27, § 342(c)). The drafters of these provisions foresaw the implication that if persons who receive or possess the stolen goods are guilty of the same crime as persons who obtained or exerted unauthorized control over the goods, both could be characterized as accomplices. This might trigger the evidentiary rule that a defendant cannot be convicted on the uncorroborated testimony of an alleged accomplice. In order to maintain the relationship in which a "thief" and a "receiver" were viewed prior to the consolidation of theft offenses, Art. 27, § 342(c)(4) provides:

> A person who criminally possesses stolen property and a person who has stolen the property are not accomplices in theft for the purpose of any rule of evidence requiring corroboration of the testimony of an accomplice, unless the person who criminally possesses the property had participated in stealing.

See Instruction, § 4.91, Theft — By unauthorized control, *infra,* and Instruction, § 4.93, Theft — By possessing stolen property, *infra.*

The Court has held that, although the State's witness was the receiver of the goods allegedly stolen by the appellant, he was not necessarily an accomplice. *Trovato v. State,* 36 Md. App. 183, 373 A.2d 78 (1977). Whether the witness had also instigated and procured the theft, so as to become liable as an accomplice, was deemed a question to be decided by the finder of fact. See also *Osborne v. State,* 4 Md. App. 57, 61, 241 A.2d 171, 174 (1968). See Joint Subcommittee on Theft Related Offenses, Maryland General Assembly, *Revision of Maryland Theft Laws and Bad Check Laws (Chapter 849 of 1978)* at 40 and Comment, § 4.93, Theft — By possessing stolen property, *infra.*

For a discussion of whether a juvenile who could not be prosecuted in an adult court is subject to the accomplice corroboration rule, see Comment, § 4.33, Incest, *infra.*

§ 2.02. Informer's testimony — Witness promised leniency.

[An informer is a competent witness, and the use of informers is a recognized means of law enforcement.] The testimony of a witness who provides evidence for the State against a defendant for pay, for immunity from prosecution or punishment, or for personal advantage or vindication must be examined and weighed by you with greater care than the testimony of an ordinary witness. You must determine whether such testimony has been affected either by interest or prejudice against the defendant. You should consider such testimony with caution, because the testimony may have been colored by a desire to gain [leniency] [freedom] [a financial benefit] by testifying against the defendant.

COMMENT

An informer's instruction may not be required where there is ample corroboration of the informer's testimony. The court may be within its discretion to elect not to single out the testimony of a particular witness, but rather to permit counsel to develop factors indicating possible bias in examination and cross-examination of witnesses. No Maryland cases have been found on this point. *Cf. United States v. Lee,* 165 U.S. App. D.C. 50, 506 F.2d 111 (1974), *cert. denied,* 421 U.S. 1002 (1975). Yet, where evidence suggests that an informer acts for pay, or for immunity from punishment, or for personal advantage or vindication, it is no doubt proper for the trial court to single out the special interest of an informer and bring it to the jury's attention. See *United States v. Hill,* 152 U.S. App. D.C. 213, 470 F.2d 361 (1972). The strongest case for use of the instruction may be the situation where there is evidence that an informer is a narcotic addict with criminal charges pending against him who is being paid by the state and whose testimony is not corroborated in some material respect. See *United States v. Kinnard,* 150 U.S. App. D.C. 386, 465 F.2d 566 (1975); *United States v. Lee, supra.*

An "informer" is defined as a person used by the police as a source of information relating to criminal activities or who was a part of the illegal transaction, whose identity was unknown to the defendant but known to, or reasonably ascertainable by, the police. *Whittington v. State,* 8 Md. App. 676, 262 A.2d 75 (1970).

The United States Supreme Court has noted that the use of informers, accessories, false friends, or any of the other betrayals that are "dirty business" may raise serious questions of credibility. It has consequently held that a defendant is entitled to broad latitude in proving credibility and to have the issues submitted to the jury with "careful instructions." *On Lee v. United States,* 343 U.S. 747, 757, 72 S. Ct. 967, 973, 96 L. Ed. 1270 (1952).

The degree of caution required in the instructions varies with circumstances of each case. In *United States v. Masino,* 275 F.2d 129, 133 (2d Cir. 1960), where the government's case depended almost entirely upon the testimony of an informer, the Court held that it was error to refuse defendant's requested instruction that such testimony "must be examined with greater scrutiny than the testimony of an ordinary witness." Similarly, in *Fletcher v. United States,* 81 U.S. App. 306, 158 F.2d 321 (D.C. Cir. 1946), where the entire case against the defendant depended upon the informer's testimony, the Court held that the jury should be instructed "to scrutinize it closely for the purpose of determining whether it is colored in such a way as to place guilt upon a defendant in furtherance of the witness's own interest." Since the informer was also a drug addict, the Court added that the instruction should have required corroboration of his testimony, or stated that "it should be received with suspicion and acted upon with caution."

The Federal Judicial Center Committee to Study Criminal Jury Instructions concluded that it is important to draw attention to the testimony of witnesses who get paid for providing information about criminal activity as well as those witnesses who are testifying in exchange for immunity or other benefits. They believed that some explanation should be given to the jury since the statements by these witnesses are subject to suspicion.

They drafted a suggested instruction for each of these situations. The cautionary instruction for the testimony of a paid informer is as follows:

> You have heard the testimony of ____________. He has an arrangement with the government under which he gets paid for providing information about criminal activity. The government may present the testimony of such a person. Some people who get paid for providing information about criminal activity are entirely truthful when testifying. Still, you should consider the testimony of ____________ with more caution than the testimony of other witnesses. Since he may believe that he will continue to be paid only if he produces evidence of criminal conduct, he may have reason to make up stories or to exaggerate what others did. In deciding whether you believe ____________'s testimony, you should keep these comments in mind.

Federal Judicial Center Committee to Study Criminal Jury Instructions, *Pattern Criminal Jury Instructions* § 25 (1982). The cautionary instruction for witnesses testifying in exchange for immunity or reduced criminal liability is as follows:

> You have heard the testimony of ____________. He is providing evidence for the government in exchange for a promise from the government that (e.g.: he will not be prosecuted for the things he is testifying about; the prosecution will recommend lenient treatment in his own case). He told the government what he would testify to in exchange for this promise.
>
> The government may present the testimony of someone who has been promised favorable treatment in his own case in exchange for his testimony. Some people in this position are entirely truthful when testifying. Still, you should consider the testimony of ____________ with more caution than the testimony of other witnesses. He may have had reason to make up stories or exaggerate what others did because he wanted to strike a good bargain with the government about his own case. In deciding whether you believe ____________'s testimony, you should keep these comments in mind.

Federal Judicial Center Committee to Study Criminal Jury Instructions, *Pattern Criminal Jury Instructions* § 24 (1982).

See Comment, § 2.06, *infra,* for discussion on the credibility of witnesses.

§ 2.03. Number of witnesses.

The weight of the evidence is not necessarily determined by the number of witnesses testifying on either side. Rather, it is measured by the inherent believability, probability and persuasion of all the evidence. You should consider all the facts and circumstances in evidence to determine which of the witnesses are worthy of greater credence. You may find that the testimony of a smaller number of witnesses on one side is more worthy of belief than the testimony of a greater number of witnesses on the other side.

COMMENT

There are no reported criminal cases in Maryland on this point of law which could be located.

In *Kruszewski v. Holz,* 265 Md. 434, 290 A.2d 534 (1972), a medical malpractice case, the Court of Appeals denied the appellant's contention that it was prejudicial error for the trial court to instruct the jury that they were not to give any consideration to the number of witnesses testifying for either side. The trial court's instruction to the jury was as follows:

> You should not weigh the number of doctors who testified against one side or the other, because one witness may supply sufficient testimony to prove the facts in any particular case. So numbers is [are] not important in determining the testimony.

Id. at 443-44, 290 A.2d at 539.

In *Riffey v. Tonder,* 36 Md. App. 633, 651, 375 A.2d 1138, 1148 (1977), the Court gave the following instruction: "The weight of the evidence is not measured by the number of witnesses nor by any particular circumstances, but rather by the inherent believability, probability and persuasion of all the evidence."

§ 2.04. Child witness.

You have heard the testimony of __________ (*insert name*), who has been qualified as a witness. In evaluating the testimony of a child, you should consider each child individually. There is no precise age which determines the competency of a child to testify. This depends on the capacity and intelligence of the child, his understanding of the difference between truth and falsehood, and his appreciation of his duty to tell the truth.

As in the case of all other witnesses, you are the sole judges of the credibility of __________ (*insert name*). In weighing his testimony, you may consider not only his age, but whether he understood the seriousness of his appearance as a witness at this criminal trial, his ability to understand the questions put to him, whether he was influenced by the way the questions were asked, his capacity to observe facts and to recollect them, whether he impresses you as a truth-telling individual, and any other facts and circumstances bearing on his credibility. You should give his testimony such weight as in your judgment it is fairly entitled to receive.

COMMENT

A somewhat shorter instruction has been recommended by the Federal Judicial Center Committee to Study Criminal Jury Instructions that calls the jury's attention to the basic difficulties with the testimony of a child. It is as follows:

> You have heard the testimony of __________, and you may be wondering whether his young age should make any difference. What you must determine, as with any witness, is whether that testimony is believable. Did he understand the questions? Does he have a good memory? Is he telling the truth?
>
> Because young children may not fully understand what is happening here, it is up to you to decide whether

> ___________ understood the seriousness of his appearance as a witness at this criminal trial. In addition, young children may be influenced by the way that questions are asked. It is up to you to decide whether ___________ understood the questions asked of him. Keep this in mind when you consider ___________'s testimony.

Federal Judicial Center Committee to Study Criminal Jury Instructions, *Pattern Criminal Jury Instructions* § 28 (1982).

The capacity of children to testify is a matter which is ordinarily within the discretion of the trial court. *Robert v. State,* 220 Md. 159, 151 A.2d 737 (1959); *Brandau v. Webster,* 39 Md. App. 99, 382 A.2d 1103 (1978); *Jones v. State,* 11 Md. App. 468, 275 A.2d 508 (1971); *Watson v. State,* 6 Md. App. 134, 250 A.2d 311 (1969); *Jacobs v. State,* 6 Md. App. 238, 251 A.2d 33 (1969); *Boswell v. State,* 5 Md. App. 571, 249 A.2d 490 (1968); *Rodgers v. State,* 4 Md. App. 407, 243 A.2d 28 (1968).

The Court stated, in *Brandau v. Webster, supra,* that:

> [T]here is no rule which excludes an insane person as such or a child of any specified age from testifying but in each case the traditional test is whether the witness has intelligence enough to make it worthwhile to hear him at all and whether he feels a duty to tell the truth.

Id. at 104, 382 A.2d at 1105-1106.

The credibility and weight to be accorded their testimony is for the jury to determine. *Robert v. State, supra.*

A question that does not appear to have been addressed by the Maryland courts is at what age a cautionary instruction on evaluating the testimony of a child is no longer appropriate. It may be that this instruction should be used only in cases involving young children who appear impressionable by reason of their youth. The instruction may not be appropriate for many children at some point after the age of puberty.

In determining the competency of a child to testify, the courts have used a standard which requires that the child in question understand what it means to tell the truth and the meaning of an oath to that effect. *Saldiveri v. State,* 217 Md. 412, 143 A.2d 70 (1958); *Jones v. State, supra; Reckard v. State,* 2 Md. App. 312, 234 A.2d 630 (1967). The determination of the trial court will not be reversed on appeal unless there has been a clear abuse of discretion. *Williams v. State,* 11 Md. App. 350, 274 A.2d 403 (1971).

In *Williams, supra,* the trial court allowed an eight-year-old rape victim to testify. In addressing itself to the question of the witness's competency, the Court of Special Appeals stated:

> The victim was an 8-year-old, second grade student, who was subjected to interrogation as to her competency to testify by the trial judge, the prosecutor and the defense counsel. She stated that she knew the difference between telling the truth and telling a lie and that if one tells a lie, she will be punished. When asked by whom one would be punished, she answered: "God."
>
> The Court of Appeals and this Court have consistently held that whether a child of tender years is legally competent to testify is within the sound discretion of the trial judge and his judgment in this respect will not be disturbed on appeal unless there has been a clear abuse of that discretion. *Horsey v. State,* 225 Md. 80, 169 A.2d 457; *Saldiveri v. State,* 217 Md. 412, 143 A.2d 70 [(1958)]; *Jacobs v. State,* 6 Md. App. 238, 251 A.2d 33 [(1969)]. While the victim here was unable to give certain dates accurately, did not know the exact meaning of the words "to swear" or "to take an oath," it is evident that the trial judge found, and we cannot say he was wrong, that the victim understood the difference between telling the truth and telling a falsehood. We think under the circumstances here that there was no abuse of the trial judge's discretion in finding her legally competent to testify. *See White v. State,* 3 Md. App. 167, 170, 238 A.2d 278 [(1968)]; *Reckard v. State,* 2 Md. App. 312, 317-318, 234 A.2d 630 [(1967)].

Id. at 353, 274 A.2d at 404.

In *Johnson v. State,* 38 Md. App. 100, 379 A.2d 436 (1977), the Court held that the trial judge had not abused his discretion when he questioned an eight-year-old rape victim in order to qualify her as a competent witness. The trial judge determines the competency of a witness in Maryland. *Wyley v. Warden,* 372 F.2d 742 (4th Cir.), *cert. denied,* 389 U.S. 863, *reh'g denied,* 389 U.S. 997 (1967).

§ 2.05. Expert witness.

A person who, by education and experience, has become expert in some art, science, profession, or calling is qualified to state an opinion here about matters in that particular field in order to help you reach a conclusion about a matter in controversy. An expert witness is permitted to testify even though he did not actually witness any of the events involved in this trial.

You are not bound by the opinion of an expert. As with any other witness, it is up to you to decide whether you believe the expert's testimony and choose to rely upon it. If you should decide that the opinion of an expert witness is not based upon sufficient education and experience, or if you should conclude that the reasons, judgment and information in support of the opinion are not sound, or that the opinion is outweighed by other evidence, you may disregard the opinion in whole or in part. You are to weigh this expert testimony with all the other evidence in this case and give it as much weight as in your judgment it is fairly entitled to receive.

[If contradictory or conflicting opinion is put forth by expert witnesses, you must resolve the conflict and determine how much weight to give either opinion.]

COMMENT

The jury is to weigh all expert testimony as it does all other evidence in the case, and give to it as much consideration as the jury feels it deserves. *Snowden v. State,* 133 Md. 624, 106 A. 5 (1919). Expert opinion, therefore, must be considered along with all the other evidence in the case and must be evaluated accordingly, to determine its credibility. What must be remembered in the final analysis is that the credibility of experts, as of other witnesses, is for the jury's evaluation. *State Rds. Comm'n v. Creswell,* 235 Md. 220, 229, 201 A.2d 328, 332 (1964).

When contradictory or conflicting opinion is put forth by expert witnesses, the jury must resolve the conflict and determine which opinion it considers more credible. *Baer Bros. v. Keller,* 208 Md. 556, 119 A.2d 410 (1956); *Armour & Co. v. Leasure,* 177 Md. 393, 9 A.2d 572 (1939). If both sides present experts, the decision as to whose expert testimony would be accepted, if any, is for the jury. *Duvall v. Potomac Elec. Power Co.,* 234 Md. 42, 197 A.2d 893 (1964).

In *Sartor v. Arkansas Natural Gas Corp.,* 321 U.S. 620, 627-28, 64 S. Ct. 724, 729, 88 L. Ed. 967, 972 (1944), Justice Jackson stated for the majority:

> In considering the testimony of expert witnesses ... this Court through Mr. Justice Cardozo has said: "But plainly opinions thus offered, even if entitled to some weight, have no such conclusive force that there is error of law in refusing to follow them. This is true of opinion evidence generally whether addressed to a jury or to a judge or to a statutory board."

Dayton Power & Light Co. v. Public Util. Comm'n, 292 U.S. 290, 299, 54 S. Ct. 647, 652, 78 L. Ed. 1267, 1274 (1934).

In other words, as Justice Jackson further says in *Sartor, supra,* "The jury, even if such testimony be uncontradicted, may exercise their independent judgment."

An expert witness may testify only when the jury requires assistance in the formation of conclusions requiring special training and skill. *Empire State Ins. Co. v. Guerriero,* 193 Md. 506, 69 A.2d 269 (1949); *Langenfelder v. Thompson,* 179 Md. 502, 20 A.2d 491 (1941); *Waggaman v. Forstmann,* 217 A.2d 310 (D.C. Cir. 1966). In other words, an expert can only testify on relevant and material matters, to assist and guide the jury, where it would be difficult for the jury to form its own conclusions because its knowledge is inadequate. *Rolfes v. State,* 10 Md. App. 204, 268 A.2d 795 (1970). See also *Christ v. Wempe,* 219 Md. 627, 150 A.2d 918 (1959). On matters of common knowledge, general observation or experience, where the jurors can draw correct conclusions as well as the experts, expert testimony is not admissible. *Griffith v. Pullman Co.,* 142 Md. 514, 121 A. 362 (1923).

In *Salem v. United States Lines Co.,* 370 U.S. 31, 35, 82 S. Ct. 1119, 1122, 8 L. Ed. 2d 313 (1962), the Supreme Court held that expert testimony is not only unnecessary but may properly be excluded in the trial judge's discretion if all primary facts can be accurately and intelligibly described to the jury, and if they, as persons of common understanding, are as capable of comprehending primary facts and of drawing correct conclusions from them as are witnesses possessed of special or peculiar training, experience or observation.

There are other Maryland cases which have followed a more expansive test for the admissibility of expert testimony; this line of cases holds that the pertinent question is whether the jury can receive appreciable help from the particular witness on the subject, not whether the jury can decide the particular issue without expert help. *Terry v. State,* 34 Md. App. 99, 366 A.2d 65 (1976); *Nizer v. Phelps,* 252 Md. 185, 249 A.2d 112 (1969); *Baltimore County v. State,* 232 Md. 350, 193 A.2d 30 (1962). See McCormick, *Evidence* § 13 (2d ed. 1972).

For example, expert witnesses should be permitted to testify in mandamus proceedings regarding literary merit of a book, which had been removed from the public library on the ground that it was obscene. The witness may testify as to literary merit, contemporary community standards, and prurient interest. *Levine v. Moreland,* 229 Md. 231, 182 A.2d 484 (1962), *citing* Maryland Ann. Code, Art. 27, § 418.

The Court shall decide who, on the basis of his special knowledge, training or skill, is competent to give expert testimony, and whether this testimony would be of appreciable help to the jury in deciding the material facts in the case. *Asibem Assocs. v. Rill,* 264 Md. 272, 286 A.2d 160 (1972); *Rolfes v. State, supra; Nizer v. Phelps, supra; Pumphrey v. Tabler,* 175 Md. 498, 2 A.2d 668 (1938).

Factors in determining admissibility of any expert witness' testimony are actual experience of the witness and the likely probative value of his opinion. *Crews v. Director, Patuxent Inst.,* 245 Md. 174, 225 A.2d 436 (1967). It must be pointed out that the trial court has wide latitude in determining qualifications of expert witnesses, and it is within the sound discretion of the trial court to determine if the expert has made sufficient inquiry to justify the expression of an opinion. *Mondawmin Corp. v. Kres,* 258 Md. 307, 266 A.2d 8 (1970); *Davidson v. Miller,* 276 Md. 54, 344 A.2d 422 (1975).

In order to be an expert witness, a person must be shown to be competent on the subject on which he is to testify. *Stickell v. Mayor & City Council,* 252 Md. 464, 250 A.2d 541 (1969). He will generally be considered an expert witness, qualified to give his opinion as to the matter of his expertise, and allowed to testify if his knowledge is beyond the ken of an ordinary person and will probably appreciably aid the trier of fact in his search for truth. *Scott v. John H. Hampshire, Inc.,* 246 Md. 171, 227 A.2d 751 (1967); *Rolfes v. State, supra; Malekar v. State,* 26 Md. App. 498, 338 A.2d 328 (1975).

In *Malekar v. State, supra,* the witness was permitted to testify, though he had not been qualified by either side as an expert witness per se. The need for opinion evidence was self-evident because the witness was familiar with the dialectical foreign language spoken by the accused. The witness was thus permitted to translate statements made by the accused and to render assistance regarding interpretations of the possible connotations to be inferred from those statements.

The trial judge has broad discretion in matters of admission or exclusion of expert evidence, and his act is to be sustained unless manifestly erroneous. In *Riffey v. Tonder,* 36 Md. App. 633, 375 A.2d 1138 (1977), a civil case, the trial court had excluded the plaintiff's expert witness on the ground that his testimony would go beyond the scope of rebuttal. On appeal, that ruling was reversed because it was both "substantially injurious" to the rights of the appellant and "manifestly wrong."

A psychologist may be qualified as an expert if licensed under the "Maryland Psychologists Act." As an expert witness he may testify on such issues as insanity, competency to stand trial, and matters within the scope of that psychologist's special knowledge in any case in any court. Maryland Ann. Code, Courts and Judicial Proceedings, § 9-120. While the expert must be licensed under the "Maryland Psychologists Act," the people who perform the subordinate tasks do not need to be licensed. For example, the Court of Special Appeals held, in *Swain v. State,* 50 Md. App. 29, 435 A.2d 804, 814 (1981), that an expert witness may state an opinion that is partially based on a report prepared by a psychologist who was not certified.

Further, testimony of an expert witness should not be excluded because he bases his statement in whole or in part upon what he has read, provided his reading can be assumed to constitute part of his general knowledge adequate to enable him to form a reasonable opinion of his own. *Pennsylvania Threshermen & Farmers' Mut. Cas. Ins. Co. v. Messenger,* 181 Md. 295, 29 A.2d 653 (1943).

In addition, the Court has held that a medical expert does not have to express his opinion with absolute certainty; he may testify, based on a reasonable medical certainty, to that which could have happened, provided there is sufficient evidence of causal connection. *Wantland v. State,* 45 Md. App. 527, 413 A.2d 1376, 1385 (1980), *vacated,* 451 U.S. 1014, *aff'd on remand,* 49 Md. App. 636, 435 A.2d 102 (1981), *cert. denied,* 457 U.S. 1121 (1982).

See Instructions: § 2.03, Number of witnesses, *supra*; § 2.07, Impeachment [of defendant or witness] by prior conviction(s), *infra*; § 2.08, Prior inconsistent statements, *infra*; § 2.23, Character of defendant, *infra*; and §§ 4.36 and 4.37, Rape offenses and Sexual offenses, *infra.* (Comments following the latter two instructions contain discussions of the admissibility of evidence of prior sexual conduct of the complaining witness in rape and sexual offense cases).

§ 2.06. Credibility of witnesses.

In determining whether the government has proved the guilt of the defendant beyond a reasonable doubt, you must consider and weigh the testimony of all the witnesses who have appeared before you.

It is your job alone to determine whether to believe any witness and to what extent any witness should be believed. If there is any conflict in the testimony, it is your function to resolve the conflict and to determine where the truth lies.

In reaching a conclusion as to the credibility of any witness, you may consider any relevant circumstances that may affect the desire and capability of that witness to tell the truth. For example, you may consider the demeanor and the behavior of the witness on the witness stand and the witness' manner of testifying. In addition, I suggest that you ask yourself a few questions: Did the person impress you as honest? Did he have any particular reason not to tell the truth? Did he have a personal interest in the outcome of the case? Did he have a friendship, dislike, bias or prejudice for or against either side in this case? Did the witness seem to have a good memory? Did the witness have the opportunity and ability to observe accurately the things he testified about? Did he appear to understand the questions clearly and answer them directly?

You may consider the reasonableness or unreasonableness and the probability or improbability of the testimony of a witness in determining whether to accept it as true and accurate. You may consider whether he has been contradicted or corroborated by other credible evidence.

[There has been proof of a witness' prior criminal conviction(s). You may also consider, in weighing the evidence, the evidence of a witness' prior criminal record for the limited purpose of reflecting upon the truth or veracity of his testimony, on the theory that a person with a prior criminal record may be less apt to tell the truth than a person who does not have a criminal record.]

[In making up your mind and reaching a verdict, do not make any decisions simply because there were more witnesses on one side than on the other.]

Your job is to think about the testimony of each witness you have heard and decide how much you believe of what each witness had to say.

COMMENT

This instruction was patterned in part after: Devitt and Blackmar, *Federal Jury Practice and Instructions,* § 17.01 (3d ed. 1977); Federal Judicial Center Committee to Study Criminal Jury Instructions, *Pattern Criminal Jury Instructions* § 23 (1982); and Bar Association of the District of Columbia, *Criminal Jury Instructions for the District of Columbia* § 2.11 (3d ed. 1978).

If additional guidance is needed in evaluating inconsistencies and discrepancies in witness' testimony, Bar Association of the District of Columbia, *Criminal Jury Instructions for the District of Columbia* § 2.11 (3d ed. 1978), provides a special instruction, as follows:

> Inconsistencies or discrepancies in the testimony of a witness, or between the testimony of different witnesses, may or may not cause you to discredit such testimony. Two or more persons witnessing an incident or transaction may see or hear it differently; an innocent misrecollection, like failure of recollection, is not an uncommon experience. In weighing the effect of the discrepancy, always consider whether it pertains to a matter of important or unimportant detail, and whether the discrepancy results from innocent error or intentional falsehood.

Maryland Rule 4-325(d), Reference to Evidence, states:

> In instructing the jury, the court may refer to or summarize the evidence in order to present clearly the issues to be decided. In that event, the court shall instruct the jury that it is the sole judge of the facts, the weight of the evidence, and the credibility of the witnesses.

See, e.g., *Marshall v. State,* 291 Md. 205, 434 A.2d 555 (1981); *Perry v. State,* 234 Md. 48, 197 A.2d 833 (1964); *Duffin v. State,* 229 Md. 434, 184 A.2d 624 (1962); *Lawrence v. State,* 51 Md. App. 575, 444 A.2d 478, 483 (1982), *aff'd,* 295 Md. 557, 457 A.2d 1127 (1983); *Green v. State,* 49 Md. App. 1, 430 A.2d 1122 (1981); *Dunlap v. State,* 1 Md. App. 444, 230 A.2d 690 (1967).

Since the jury is in the favored position to evaluate and judge the attitude and demeanor of the witness, the credibility of a witness is a primary matter for the trier of facts to determine. *Brooks v. State,* 3 Md. App. 485, 512, 240 A.2d 114, 129 (1968). See also *Bryant v. State,* 49 Md. App. 272, 431 A.2d 714, 720, *cert. denied,* 291 Md. 772 (1981), *cert. denied,* 456 U.S. 949 (1982).

Inconsistencies in testimony, testimony by other witnesses, minor discrepancies, lack of positiveness in testimony and conflicting and questionable identifications relate to both the weight of evidence and credibility of witnesses. See *Logue v. State,* 37 Md. App. 41, 375 A.2d 51 (1977), *aff'd,* 282 Md. 625, 386 A.2d 780 (1978); *Hunt v. State,* 12 Md. App. 286, 278 A.2d 637 (1971); *Grey v. State,* 10 Md. App. 478, 271 A.2d 390 (1970); *Shrader v. State,* 10 Md. App. 94, 268 A.2d 257 (1970); *Dorsey v. State,* 9 Md. App. 80, 262 A.2d 591 (1970).

If a witness' testimony is so self-contradictory as to lack probative force, the trier of fact may not be allowed to speculate as to which of the versions is true. This rule is only applicable in limited circumstances. *Kucharczyk v. State,* 235 Md. 334, 201 A.2d 683 (1964) and *Bailey v. State,* 16 Md. App. 83, 294 A.2d 123 (1972).

The trier of fact needs to observe the witness to evaluate the weight of this testimony. Where the State proffered the testimony of a nonappearing arresting officer and the defendant proffered her version of the facts without taking the stand, the result was a criminal trial based on stipulations. It was impossible to weigh the credibility of either witness or the reliability of the evidence offered through them. By adopting the State's version, the court, as trier of fact, made an arbitrary choice which does not support a finding of guilt beyond a reasonable doubt. *Barnes v. State,* 31 Md. App. 25, 354 A.2d 499 (1976). See § 1.07, Comment, *supra,* for further discussion of this case.

Under Maryland Ann. Code, Courts and Judicial Proceedings, § 9-115, opinion as well as reputation evidence is admissible regarding a witness' character for truthfulness. The Court, however, has upheld the exclusion of opinion evidence when it related to the capacity of the witness to tell the truth rather than an opinion as to the witness' character for truthfulness. *Bell v. State,* 48 Md. App. 669, 429 A.2d 300, 304 (1981).

Although a witness may testify as to his opinion of a witness' character for truthfulness, there are situations where the opinion evidence would be inadmissible. In *Kelley v. State,* 288 Md. 298, 418 A.2d 217, 219 (1980), the Court held that the testimony of a prosecution witness used to impeach a defense witness' veracity was inadmissible because it created a substantial likelihood that the jury would draw an inference that the defense witness had failed a polygraph test, the results of which were inadmissible. Any opinion that the prosecution witness may have expressed would be incompetent and prejudicial; the results of the polygraph test were not competent evidence and, without these results, an opinion would be inadmissible for lack of an adequate basis.

In *Kirby v. State,* 48 Md. App. 205, 426 A.2d 423 (1981), the Court held that the trial court was within its discretion in determining the scope of cross-examining where the defense attorney was prohibited from questioning the victim about psychiatric care she had received in a case involving assault with intent to rape. The trial court had permitted defense counsel to inquire whether the victim had "ever hallucinated" and questions of that nature.

Whether a witness on the stand personally believes or disbelieves the testimony of a previous witness is irrelevant; questions to that effect are improper, either on direct or cross-examination. *Mutyambizi v. State,* 33 Md. App. 55, 363 A.2d 511 (1976).

On several occasions it has been stated:

> The rule in Maryland is that for the purpose of affecting the credibility of a witness it is impermissible to reveal that the witness has been merely accused of or arrested for a crime, but evidence that he has been convicted of a crime having some tendency to show that he is not to be believed under oath may be admissible.

Ricketts v. State, 291 Md. 701, 436 A.2d 906 (1981); *Cousins v. State,* 230 Md. 2, 185 A.2d 488 (1962); *Hurley v. State,* 6 Md. App. 348, 251 A.2d 241 (1969).

Evidence of past arrests, past criminal conduct, and other involvement with police may be introduced in certain limited situations to show bias. If there is a genuine suggestion or proffer that a witness' involvement with the police is subjecting that witness to a strong motivation to lie, that evidence may be introduced on cross-examination. Such bias impeachment is not limited to the showing of actual convictions of crime.

In *Fletcher v. State,* 50 Md. App. 349, 437 A.2d 901 (1982), the Court held that, in a prosecution which resulted in a conviction of felony and misdemeanor theft, the trial court erred in limiting cross-examination of a witness who had been charged in the case, by sustaining objections to inquiries whether the witness had received a sentence and when he would go to trial. The Court reasoned that the claim of bias which the defense sought to develop was admissible to establish the basis for an inference of undue pressure because of the witness' vulnerable status pending sentence, as well as of the witness' possible concern that his presentence investigation might cause him to be considered more culpable than he had asserted by his present and possibly past testimony.

In *Godwin v. State,* 38 Md. App. 716, 729, 382 A.2d 596, 604 (1977), *vacated,* 284 Md. 85, 403 A.2d 785 (1978), Judge Moylan, quoting the limitations set forth by Judge Lowe in *Johnson v. State,* 30 Md. App. 512, 517, 352 A.2d 371, 374 (1976) stated: "Only where there is some present possibility of coercion should such cross-examination be allowed. If it should appear that the cross-examination is directed simply at casting the witness in the suspicious light that falls upon anyone under formal accusation, the trial judge must not allow it." The trial judge should balance the probity of the conduct showing a motivation to lie against the danger that a witness may be diminished in the eyes of a jury simply by showing that he is "a bad man."

In *Scarborough v. State,* 50 Md. App. 276, 437 A.2d 672 (1982), the Court held that, where defendant's alibi defense was predicated on a witness' statements, it was within the trial court's discretion to allow the prosecution to introduce rebuttal testimony to discredit the witness and demonstrate the presence of bias.

For Maryland law supporting impeachment by prior convictions, see *Lowery v. State,* 292 Md. 2, 437 A.2d 193 (1982); *Ricketts v. State, supra; Cousins v. State, supra; Burrell v. State,*

42 Md. App. 130, 399 A.2d 1354 (1979); *Huston v. State,* 35 Md. App. 455, 371 A.2d 499, *aff'd,* 281 Md. 455, 379 A.2d 1027 (1977); *Mulligan v. State,* 18 Md. App. 588, 592-97, 308 A.2d 418, 420-23 (1973); *Kable v. State,* 17 Md. App. 16, 299 A.2d 493, *cert. denied,* 268 Md. 750 (1973) (holding that it is not proper to cross-examine a witness regarding a conviction which has been reversed on appeal); *Johnson v. State,* 4 Md. App. 648, 657-58, 244 A.2d 632 (1968), *cert. denied,* 252 Md. 731 (1969); and *Robinson v. State,* 4 Md. App. 515, 243 A.2d 879 (1968).

When the defendant is a witness, it is proper for the trial court to mildly caution him outside the jury's presence in regard to testifying truthfully. The court may also advise him of the penalties for perjury when it appears that such an instruction is necessary to prevent or terminate a commission of perjury. *Marshall v. State,* 46 Md. App. 695, 420 A.2d 1266, 1271 (1980). The Court distinguished *Webb v. Texas,* 409 U.S. 95, 93 S. Ct. 351, 34 L. Ed. 2d 330 (1972), in which the defendant's due process right was violated when the judge's threatening remarks directed only at a single witness for the defense effectively drove the witness off the stand.

§ 2.07. Impeachment by prior conviction(s).

(a) Of the defendant

You have heard evidence of the defendant's prior criminal conviction[s]. Evidence of the defendant's prior criminal conviction[s] may only be considered for the limited purpose of reflecting upon the truth and veracity of his testimony. When you weigh the defendant's testimony you may consider whether a person who would commit such [a] crime[s] would be less likely to tell the truth than a person who would not commit such [a] crime[s]. In other words, the defendant's criminal record has been admitted into evidence for the sole purpose of assisting you in evaluating his credibility, that is, his worthiness of belief. The fact that the defendant was found guilty of another [other] crime[s] is not evidence or proof of the crime charged in this case. I emphasize that you should not attempt to draw any inferences of guilt from the fact that he was convicted on [a] prior occasion[s].

(b) Of a witness other than the defendant

You have heard evidence that ________ *(insert name of witness)* has been convicted of [a] crime[s]. Evidence of a witness' prior criminal conviction[s] may only be considered for the limited purpose of reflecting upon the truth and veracity of that witness' testimony. When you weigh the testimony of ________ *(insert name of witness),* you may consider whether a person who would commit such [a] crime[s] would be less likely to tell the truth than a person who would not commit such [a] crime[s]. In other words, the witness' criminal record has been admitted into evidence for the sole purpose of assisting you in evaluating his credibility, that is, worthiness of belief. You may consider this evidence in deciding whether the witness is telling the truth, but for no other purpose.

COMMENT

As an alternative to the language of the instruction designated (a), *supra,* the Federal Judicial Center Committee to Study Criminal Jury Instructions has recommended the following language:

> You have been told that the defendant, ________, was found guilty in 19____ of (e.g.: bank robbery). This conviction has been brought to your attention only because you may wish to consider it when you decide, as with any witness, how much you will believe of his testimony in this trial. The fact that the defendant was found guilty of another crime does not mean that he committed this crime, and you must not use his guilt for the crime of ________ as proof of the crime charged in this case. You may find him guilty of

> this crime only if the government has proved beyond a reasonable doubt that he committed it.

Federal Judicial Center Committee to Study Criminal Jury Instructions, *Pattern Criminal Jury Instructions* § 41 (1982).

"It has been long and firmly established in this jurisdiction that the credibility of a witness may be impeached by evidence of his conviction of a crime." *Johnson v. State,* 9 Md. App. 166, 169, 263 A.2d 232, 235 (1970), with reference to *Smith v. State,* 64 Md. 25, 20 A. 1026 (1885). This rule applies to a defendant who takes the witness stand.

In *Braxton v. State,* 11 Md. App. 435, 274 A.2d 647 (1971), the Court summarized the standard for impeachment by prior convictions as follows:

> It has been oftentimes stated as established in this state ... that in criminal cases, where the defendant is a witness in his own behalf, he thereby puts his character in issue, and may be asked on cross-examination if he has been convicted of a crime ... [citations omitted]. This is so because it is competent for any parties to the proceedings to prove by legal evidence the conviction of any witness of an "infamous" crime. [*Citing* Maryland Ann. Code, Art. 35, § 10, which was repealed and superseded by Maryland Ann. Code, Courts and Judicial Proceedings, § 10-905].

In a footnote the Court stated that "the prior convictions need not be restricted to infamous crimes or crimes involving moral turpitude," but that they are "admissible if they involve offenses having some tendency to impeach credibility as a witness." *Braxton v. State, supra* at 438-39, 274 A.2d at 649, *citing Gunther v. State,* 4 Md. App. 181, 241 A.2d 907 (1967). See, e.g., *Duckett v. State,* 61 Md. App. 151, 485 A.2d 691 (1985), *aff'd,* 306 Md. 503, 510 A.2d 253 (1986); *Holmes v. State,* 63 Md. App. 159, 492 A.2d 351 (1985) (conviction for a "handgun violation" could not be used for impeachment since it does not qualify as a crime of moral turpitude); *Scott v. State,* 64 Md. App. 311, 494 A.2d 992 (1985) (only convictions of infamous crimes are admissible for impeachment purposes. Mere charges or arrests may not be proved as a means of past-crime punishment).

The Court, in *Braxton v. State, supra,* went on to say:

> Thus when a defendant testifies as a witness, his credibility as a witness may be attacked although he is the defendant, if he assumes the role of a witness he may be attacked as such, and cannot claim immunity from that attack on the ground that he has not put his character in evidence. 1 Wharton's Criminal Evidence, 12th Ed., § 221, 458-59. Therefore, "character" within the contemplation of the rule is confined to truth and veracity, the prior convictions going to credibility and being used to impeach, *Holbrook v. State,* 6 Md. App. 265, 250 A.2d 904 (1968), as having a tendency to show that the defendant is not to be believed. *Hurley v. State,* 6 Md. App. 348, 251 A.2d 241 (1968).

Id. at 438-39, 274 A.2d at 649.

In a second footnote the Court, in *Braxton* elaborated that when the "character of a witness-defendant is impeached by proof of prior convictions, he may be supported by evidence of good character, but it must relate to his character for truth." *Id.* at 438-39, 274 A.2d at 649 (*citing McLaughlin v. State,* 3 Md. App. 515, 240 A.2d 298 (1967)).

This longstanding impeachment rule was specifically attacked in the case of *Nance v. State,* 7 Md. App. 433, 256 A.2d 377 (1969), *cert. denied,* 398 U.S. 954 (1970). In upholding the basic rule, the Court said:

> We have, on several occasions, heard the argument that such evidence is unfair to a defendant and in some cases works a great hardship. We have some sympathy with the argument but, even so, we do not feel disposed to strike down a rule so long embedded in the law of this State.

Id. at 442, 256 A.2d at 381.

The genesis of these instructions lies in the cases of *Holbrook v. State, supra* at 273, and *Johnson v. State, supra* at 188. Both cases involved appeals based on allegedly improper instructions on impeaching the defendant by prior convictions. Though the instructions, as outlined in those cases, were upheld as proper, more emphasis should be placed on the "sole purpose" aspect of admissibility of prior convictions. The warnings regarding "limited purpose," as presented in the instructions above, set forth definitive statements of the purpose and should leave the jurors with absolutely no doubts about the use to which reference to these prior convictions may be put. By giving the jury such an absolute, emphatic statement of purpose, the "hardships to the defendant" as considered in *Nance v. State, supra,* may be mitigated.

At one time, the only crimes admitted for the purpose of impeaching were infamous crimes and crimes involving moral turpitude. This restriction is no longer the rule, for evidence need not be so restricted, "provided the violation of law may have some tendency to show that the witness is not to be believed under oath." *Ricketts v. State,* 291 Md. 701, 436 A.2d 906 (1981); *Cousins v. State,* 230 Md. 2, 185 A.2d 488 (1962); *Robinson v. State,* 4 Md. App. 515, 532-33, 243 A.2d 879, 890 (1968). See also *Lowery v. State,* 292 Md. 2, 437 A.2d 193 (1982).

It is the function of the trial judge to admit only those prior convictions which will assist the jury in assessing the credibility of the defendant. The trial judge must weigh the probative value of the convictions against the prejudice to the defendant. *Ricketts v. State, supra.*

In *Burrell v. State,* 42 Md. App. 130, 399 A.2d 1354 (1979), the Court of Special Appeals spelled out the analysis to be used under the present law to decide whether impeachment by a prior conviction is proper. If the prior conviction was for an infamous crime, impeachment by such conviction is proper regardless of how much time has passed since the conviction. See *Kirby v. State,* 48 Md. App. 205, 426 A.2d 423 (1981) (evidence that defendant had been convicted of sodomy twenty-five years earlier when he was seventeen years old was admissible).

If the prior conviction was for other than an infamous crime, the Court, in *Burrell v. State, supra,* set forth three elements which must be considered. The first element is the nature of the crime. The Court asked:

> Is [the crime] one which involves the element of deceit, or lying, or dishonesty that could lead a rational person reasonably to conclude that one who would commit such a crime would be less likely to speak the truth than one who would not commit such a crime? ... If the answer to that question is "no," the evidence is considered to be "clearly irrelevant" and simply admissible.

Id. at 140, 399 A.2d at 1359-1360.

If the answer is "yes," the Court stated that a second element must be considered — time. The Court did recognize that:

> [A]s a general rule, the farther in the past the indiscretion occurred, the weaker is its relevance to present credibility. It is somewhat akin to the law of gravity: The farther away one is from the mass, the less is its gravitational pull or influence. But, like another aspect of the law of gravity — the larger the mass, the stronger is its pull at any given distance — so it is that the more enormous the earlier crime (*i.e.* the more it embodies and therefore exudes dishonesty), the more likely will be its relevance, and thus its admissibility, even after the elapse of long intervals. With respect to other than infamous crimes, therefore, *admissibility for impeachment purposes seems to be a function of a more or less direct ratio between the degree of dishonesty inherent in the earlier crime and the time elapsed since its commission.*

Id. at 140-41, 399 A.2d 1360 (emphasis added).

The Court, in *Ricketts v. State, supra,* reiterated that these first two factors should be considered to determine the admissibility of the lesser crimes. The Court in *Ricketts,* however, did not cite *Burrell.* See also *Lowery v. State, supra,* which relied on the Court's rationale in *Ricketts.*

In *Burrell,* the third element recognized by the Court is judicial discretion, i.e., "the mechanism for weighing and blending the first two" elements. *Id.* at 141, 399 A.2d 1360. "It implies the exercise of sound judgment in the light of what is in fact before the Court," *Id.* at 145, 399 A.2d at 1364 and "should not be disturbed on appeal except in clear cases of error." *Id.* at 142, 399 A.2d at 1362 (*citing Burgess v. State,* 161 Md. 162, 155 A.2d 153 (1931)). Thus, it appears that any crime for which the defendant was convicted may be used to impeach if the judge feels that the crime has a sufficient bearing on the defendant's truth and veracity.

Nevertheless, "it is impermissible to reveal that the witness has been merely accused of or arrested for a crime ...." *Hurley v. State, supra,* 6 Md. App. at 355, 251 A.2d at 245. Similarly, "[e]vidence of conviction is not admissible if an appeal is pending, or the time for an appeal has not expired, or the conviction has been reversed, and there has been no retrial or reconviction." Maryland Ann. Code, Courts and Judicial Proceedings, § 10-905. Further, while the fact of conviction of a specific crime may be introduced, "the details of its commission cannot." *Kable v. State,* 17 Md. App. 16, 31, 299 A.2d 493, *cert. denied,* 268 Md. 750 (1973), *citing Huber v. State,* 2 Md. App. 245, 234 A.2d 264 (1967).

It is a violation of the constitutional right to counsel to use a prior conviction, obtained without assistance of counsel or a valid waiver thereof, to support guilt or enhance punishment. This principle has been applied by the Maryland courts so that evidence of a prior conviction for purposes of impeachment will be excluded "when it is established that such conviction was obtained absent representation by counsel or a valid waiver thereof." *Johnson v. State, supra* at 175; *Burgett v. Texas,* 389 U.S. 109, 88 S. Ct. 258, 19 L. Ed. 2d 319 (1967). *Accord Loper v. Beto,* 405 U.S. 473, 92 S. Ct. 1014, 31 L. Ed. 2d 374 (1972); *Von Lusch v. State,* 279 Md. 255, 368 A.2d 468 (1977).

Although the Court of Special Appeals, in *Johnson v. State, supra,* held that the admission of a constitutionally infirm conviction would be an "error of constitutional dimension," it did not foreclose the possibility that in some fact situations, such error could be found to be harmless.

> For example, that there were a number of prior convictions properly admitted, or other evidence clearly impeaching the credibility of the defendant would be of probative value in determining whether the admission of invalid convictions was harmless.

Id. at 180, 263 A.2d at 241. *See Loper v. Beto, supra,* 405 U.S. at 482 n.11, where the Court implied that an invalid conviction might properly be "used for the purpose of directly rebutting a specific false statement made from the witness stand."

The application of *Burgett v. Texas, supra,* to impeach by a prior constitutionally invalid conviction in *Johnson* did not vitiate preexisting procedural requirements. If timely objection below is not made, the question of admissibility is not preserved for appeal. *Johnson v. State, supra* at 177. If the defendant, rather than the State, introduces the conviction, he thereby waives objection. Further, "it is incumbent upon the defendant ... to state his reasons to the Court to enable it properly to determine the issue. This may be done by him out of the presence of the jury. The court shall then conduct a hearing out of the presence of the jury." *Id.* (The Court then outlined the proper procedure and respective burdens of proof at such a hearing.)

For cases delineating the procedure to be used in considering the question of the presence of counsel at any prior convictions of the defendant before sentencing, see *Johnson v. State, supra; Moore v. State,* 17 Md. App. 237, 300 A.2d 388 (1973).

The Court of Special Appeals has indicated that a change in Maryland narrowing the possibilities of impeachment by a prior conviction may be welcome. In *Burrell v. State, supra,* the Court stated:

> We, of course, are bound by those principles as enunciated by our State's highest court — we may neither ignore nor alter them; and we shall decide this case, as indeed we must, in what we hope and believe is full comformance with them. We do not think it inconsistent with our bound obeisance, however, to take account of a growing reexamination of those precepts by courts, legislatures, and commentators across the nation, and to throw open the question of whether they should be reconsidered in Maryland.

Id. at 135, 399 A.2d at 1347. Also, at the end of the decision in *Burrell v. State, supra* at 147-54, 399 A.2d at 1363-67, the Court attached an appendix tracing the state of the law around the country, indicating that the trend is to narrow impeachment of criminal defendants by prior convictions.

§ 2.08. Prior inconsistent and consistent statement(s).

(a) Impeachment by prior inconsistent statement(s)

The testimony of a witness may be discredited or impeached by showing that he has previously made statements which are inconsistent with his present trial testimony. Such prior statements are admitted into evidence solely for your consideration in evaluating the credibility, or worthiness of belief, of the witness. If you find the prior statements to be inconsistent, you may consider such statements only in your evaluation of the truth of the witness' present testimony in court. You must not consider the prior statement as establishing the truth of any fact contained in that statement.

Where an attempt has been made to impeach a witness by proof of a prior inconsistent or contradictory statement, it is for you to decide whether the attempt was successful. You may accept or reject part or all of the testimony of that witness or give it such weight as you think it deserves.

(b) When a party seeks to impeach own witness

Generally, a party will *not* be permitted to impeach the credibility of his own witness by proof of prior inconsistent statements. However, an exception to this rule is allowed where a party can satisfy the court that he has been genuinely surprised by the testimony of the witness he has called (or that hostility or deceit is involved). The proof of inconsistent statements of a party's own witness is admissible into evidence to allow the calling party to contradict the witness and demonstrate the purpose for which the witness was originally called. It is not admissible to discredit the witness, that is, to impeach the general character of the witness.

(c) Rehabilitation by use of prior consistent statement(s)

The testimony of a witness may be rehabilitated or supported by showing that the witness has previously made statements which are consistent with his present trial testimony. Such prior consistent statements are admitted into evidence solely for your consideration in evaluating the credibility of the witness. If you find that the witness said essentially the same thing on more than one occasion, it may be reason for you to believe the witness' testimony. You must not consider the prior statement as establishing the truth of any fact contained in that statement.

COMMENT

Alternative language that personalizes the instruction on prior inconsistent statements has been recommended by the Federal Judicial Center Committee to Study Criminal Jury Instructions. It is as follows:

> You will recall that ________ testified during the trial (description, if needed). You will also recall that it was brought out that before this trial he made statements about this matter. These earlier statements were brought to your attention to help you decide if you believe ________'s testimony. You cannot use these earlier statements as evidence in this case. However, if ________ said something different about this matter earlier, and the two stories were conflicting, then there may be reason for you to doubt ________'s testimony here. That's up to you to decide.

Federal Judicial Center Committee to Study Criminal Jury Instructions, *Pattern Criminal Jury Instructions* § 32 (1982).

Likewise, the Federal Judicial Center Committee recommended parallel language for rehabilitation by prior consistent statements. It is as follows:

> ________ testified in the [government's] [defense] case during the trial. You will recall that it was brought out that before this trial he made statements which were the same as, or similar to, what he said in the courtroom. These earlier statements were brought to your attention to help you decide whether you believe ________'s testimony. If ________ said essentially the same thing on more than one occasion it may be reason for you to believe ________'s testimony.

Id. § 34.

A witness may be interrogated on cross-examination as to the making of prior statements which are inconsistent with, or contradictory to, his testimony in chief. A witness whose testimony is sought to be impeached by contradictory statements, whether a party to the suit or not, may be cross-examined as to time, place and persons to whom such contradictory statements were allegedly made, and proper foundation having been laid, proof of prior contradictory statements may be submitted to the jury for their consideration in estimating the credit to be given the testimony of the witness. *Sanders v. State,* 1 Md. App. 630, 232 A.2d 555 (1967).

It is an accepted rule that any statement made by a witness prior to the trial is admissible for the purpose of impeaching the witness, but not as substantive evidence. *Eastman v. State,* 47 Md. App. 162, 422 A.2d 41, 44 (1980). In *Eastman,* the Court found no error when the State was permitted to impeach a defense witness by use of a prior contradictory statement where the statement alluded to defendant's use of drugs since the trial judge had carefully instructed the jury that the testimony was admitted only to test the credibility of the witness.

The prior contradictory statements need not have been made under oath. *Smith v. Branscome,* 251 Md. 582, 248 A.2d 455 (1968); *West v. Belle Isle Cab Co.,* 203 Md. 244, 100 A.2d 17 (1953); *Yowell v. State,* 28 Md. App. 279, 283, 344 A.2d 442, 445 (1975). See 3 Wigmore, *Evidence* § 1018 (3d ed. 1940) as support for this rule.

The policy of grand jury secrecy is not violated by impeaching a defendant by his self-contradictory testimony made before the grand jury. *Mouzone v. State,* 50 Md. App. 81, 436 A.2d 916, *rev'd on other grounds,* 294 Md. 692, 452 A.2d 661 (1981).

"Provided a proper foundation has been laid, the credit of a witness may be impeached by showing he has made statements which contradict his testimony in respect to material facts (but not in respect to facts that are collateral, irrelevant or immaterial)." *Sanders v. State, supra* at 640.

To lay the foundation for the impeachment of a witness by proof of (a) prior contradictory statement(s), the witness must be first interrogated as to time, place and person(s) to whom such contradictory statement(s) was (were) made. *Coleman v. State,* 35 Md. App. 208, 370 A.2d 174, *rev'd on other grounds,* 281 Md. 538, 380 A.2d 49 (1977); *Sanders v. State, supra.* In addition, the State is entitled to inquire of a witness whether the witness recalled testifying on a prior occasion in order to comply with the requirement for impeachment that the witness be told the time, place and to whom prior inconsistent statements were made. *Britton v. State,* 10 Md. App. 70, 267 A.2d 747 (1970). If, in laying the foundation for impeachment of a witness by proof of prior inçonsistent statements, the witness denies making the designated statement or states he does not remember whether or not he did make the statement, impeaching testimony may be offered. *Sanders v. State, supra.*

To aid the defense counsel in impeaching the testimony of the State's witnesses, the defendant's counsel has a right, at trial, to inspect prior statements of a State's witness. This right is not limited by the rules pertaining to pretrial discovery or to statements that are merely exculpatory. In *Leonard v. State,* 46 Md. App. 631, 421 A.2d 85 (1980), *aff'd,* 290 Md. 295, 429 A.2d 538 (1981), the Court noted that the defense counsel may find and use statements that are not just contradictory; according to the Court, the "more subtle aspects of potential inconsistency, intrinsically subjective, have to be viewed from the defendant's perspective, and can be properly weighed only by defense counsel." *Id.* at 638, 421 A.2d at 89.

Statements made by the defendant to a probation officer during the presentence investigation were admissible for impeachment purposes. This was not a violation of defendant's sixth amendment rights (even though counsel for the accused was not present) since the State did not contrive to separate defendant from his attorney and counsel was aware that his client was to be interviewed. *Hall v. State,* 47 Md. App. 590, 425 A.2d 227, 231 (1981), *aff'd,* 292 Md. 683, 441 A.2d 708 (1982).

As a general rule, where a witness has been discredited by proof of contradictory or inconsistent statements, his credibility may be restored by showing that the witness, at other times, made statements in accordance with his testimony, or such inconsistency may be explained. *Virginia Freight Lines, Inc. v.*

Montgomery, 256 Md. 221, 260 A.2d 59 (1969). See also *Rehabilitation of Witnesses in Maryland,* 7 Md. L. Rev. 134 (1943).

The rule governing the admissibility of a prior consistent statement was stated by Judge Moylan in *Boone v. State,* 33 Md. App. 1, 6, 363 A.2d 550 (1976), *cert. denied,* 279 Md. 281 (1976):

> The general rule is that where the credibility of a witness has been impeached in such a way as to indicate that his present testimony may be a fabrication, prior consistent statements are admissible for rehabilitative purposes if they would tend to show that such consistency was present prior to the time of probable fabrication.

The Court in *Coleman v. State,* 49 Md. App. 210, 431 A.2d 696, 706 (1981), *(citing Boone v. State, supra)* held that the prior consistent statements may be admitted for the purpose of rehabilitation since the statement existed prior to alleged prosecutorial threats of perjury charges.

As a general rule, a party who produces a witness vouches for that witness' credibility. *Poole v. State,* 290 Md. 114, 428 A.2d 434 (1981) (Poole I); *Fleming v. Prince George's County,* 277 Md. 655, 358 A.2d 892 (1976); *Patterson v. State,* 275 Md. 563, 342 A.2d 660 (1975); *Proctor Elec. Co. v. Zink,* 217 Md. 22, 141 A.2d 721 (1958). Therefore, the party who calls the witness will not be allowed to impeach his own witness by proof of contradictory statements made on other occasions, or otherwise to cross-examine the witness. *Patterson v. State, supra.* There are, however, limited exceptions to this general rule; a party may attack the witness' credibility if he can show that he has been surprised or that hostility or deceit has been involved. *Poole v. State, supra; Patterson v. State, supra; Proctor Elec. Co. v. Zink, supra.* See also *Fleming v. Prince George's County, supra; Green v. State,* 243 Md. 154, 220 A.2d 544 (1966).

The party who calls the witness must show that he has been prejudiced; it is not enough if the testimony was not beneficial or that it disappointed his expectations. *Poole v. State, supra; Fleming v. Prince George's County, supra; Green v. State, supra.* See also *Baldwin v. State,* 5 Md. App. 22, 245 A.2d 98 (1968).

The inconsistent or deceitful statements must have been made to the party who calls the witness, or to someone who communicated these statements to them. If not, the person would not have been induced to call the witness. *Patterson v. State, supra.*

If the case is tried before a jury, the trial court should go into questions of surprise and materiality out of the jury's presence. If the court finds that the party calling the witness was surprised and that he should be allowed to prove prior inconsistent statements, the trial court should specify the extent to which the prior statements may then be offered. *Poole v. State, supra; Fleming v. Prince George's County, supra.* The proof of inconsistent statements of one's own witness is allowed into evidence not to discredit the witness but to allow the calling party to contradict the witness and show the purpose for which the witness was originally called. *Poole v. State, supra; Fleming v. Prince George's County, supra; Green v. State, supra.* See also *Mondawmin Corp. v. Kres,* 258 Md. 307, 266 A.2d 8 (1970); *Hernandez v. State,* 7 Md. App. 355, 255 A.2d 449 (1969); *Sanders v. State, supra; Baldwin v. State, supra.* Moreover, the proof is not substantive evidence. *Poole v. State, supra; Patterson v. State, supra.* The person who calls the witness may, however, offer testimony of another witness which is inconsistent with the testimony of the witness. *Patterson v. State, supra.*

When neither the prosecution nor the defense is willing to vouch for the veracity of a witness and the witness appears to possess material evidence, it is within the sound discretion of the trial court to call a witness either on its own motion or at the request of either party. See Comment, § 2.11, Court calling its own witness, *infra,* for further discussion.

For impeachment of a defendant by use of a prior inconsistent statement made while undergoing custodial interrogation in violation of *Miranda v. Arizona,* 384 U.S. 436, 86 S. Ct. 1602, 16 L. Ed. 2d 694 (1966), see Instruction, § 2.09, Defendant as witness — Impeachment by confession: confession admitted solely for impeachment purposes, *infra.*

§ 2.09. Defendant as witness — Impeachment by confession: confession admitted solely for impeachment purposes.

You will recall that the defendant testified during the trial on his own behalf. You will also recall that it was brought out that he was questioned at an earlier time and made certain statements concerning the crime charged. The defendant's alleged statement[s] to the police is [are] admitted into evidence solely for your consideration in evaluating his credibility as a witness, that is, his worthiness of belief. The testimony of a defendant may be discredited or impeached by showing that he previously made statements which are inconsistent with his present testimony. If he said something different earlier, and the two stories are conflicting, then it will be up to you to decide if what he said here in court was true. You may not, however, consider what was said earlier as establishing the truth of any fact contained in it, and you must not consider it as proof or evidence of the defendant's guilt. You may consider it only in your evaluation of the truth of the defendant's present testimony in court.

COMMENT

This instruction is to be given where a defendant's statement or confession is admitted solely for the purpose of impeaching his trial testimony. Of course, in order for the statement to be used, the defendant must take the stand and testify contrary to the prior statement.

The basis for this instruction is the rule of *Harris v. New York,* 401 U.S. 222, 91 S. Ct. 643, 28 L. Ed. 2d 1 (1971) where the Supreme Court held that voluntary statements inadmissible in the prosecution's case in chief because obtained in violation of *Miranda v. Arizona,* 384 U.S. 436, 86 S. Ct. 1602, 16 L. Ed. 2d 694 (1966), may be used to impeach the credibility of the defendant if he takes the stand. In *Oregon v. Hass,* 420 U.S. 714, 95 S. Ct. 1215, 43 L. Ed. 2d 570 (1975), the Court held that voluntary statements of the defendant are also admissible to impeach him during the government's rebuttal case. The defendant's silence after receiving *Miranda* warnings cannot be used to impeach his trial testimony. *Doyle v. Ohio,* 426 U.S. 610, 96 S. Ct. 2240, 49 L. Ed. 2d 91 (1976) and *United States v. Hale,* 422 U.S. 171, 95 S. Ct. 2133, 45 L. Ed. 2d 99 (1975).

Maryland courts limit the admissibility of voluntary statements taken in violation of *Miranda* to those situations where the defendant, on direct examination, initiated the issue on which he was subsequently impeached. See *State v. Franklin,* 281 Md. 51, 375 A.2d 1116 (1977), *cert. denied,* 434 U.S. 1018 (1978); *State v. Kidd,* 281 Md. 32, 375 A.2d 1105, *cert. denied,* 434 U.S. 1002 (1977). See also *Hall v. State,* 47 Md. App. 590, 599, 425 A.2d 227, 233 (1981), *aff'd,* 292 Md. 683, 441 A.2d 708 (1982).

For further discussion on this issue, see Comment, § 2.25, Confession or incriminating statement of defendant, *infra.*

§ 2.10. Other crimes and prior bad acts of defendant.

Evidence has been introduced that the defendant ________ *(insert crimes and/or prior bad acts evidence). [If other crimes or acts are disputed:* You must decide whether you believe this evidence is accurate. If you do not believe it is accurate, you should ignore it.]

This evidence was admitted only for your consideration of whether it shows or tends to show ________ *(insert purpose for which evidence offered, e.g.)* [the defendant had the motive to commit the offense for which he is now on trial] [the defendant had the intent to commit the offense for which he is now on trial] [the defendant had a common scheme or plan to commit the offense for which he is now on trial] [the identity of the defendant as the perpetrator of the offense for which he is now on trial] [other].

In evaluating this evidence, this is the only use you may make of the evidence. You may not consider it as tending to show in any other way the defendant's guilt of the offense for which he is now on trial. The law does not allow you to convict a defendant or to punish him simply because you believe he may have done things, even bad things, not specifically charged as crimes in this case. The defendant is on trial for the crime[s] charged, and you may use the evidence of acts not charged only to help you decide __________ *(repeat the specific purpose for which the evidence is offered).* Each of the other elements of the offense[s] for which the defendant is now on trial must be proved by the State by other evidence beyond a reasonable doubt.

COMMENT

Other crimes or prior bad act evidence poses enormous problems for the court. The State is not permitted to offer evidence of bad character, except in response to evidence of good character offered by a defendant. The State is permitted, however, to offer evidence of specific acts to show something other than general bad character. There is always a danger that the jury will misuse the evidence as character evidence, rather than use it for a limited purpose. Instructing the jury is a difficult problem. It is much easier to describe the law of evidence in legal jargon than to explain it to lay persons asked to use volatile other crime and other bad act evidence. It probably is important to attempt to neutralize the potential prejudicial effect of other crime and other bad act evidence with an instruction as soon as it is offered. Otherwise, the jury may react so negatively to the evidence that no closing instruction will be able to remedy the period of the jury's thinking about what a bad person the defendant is. Therefore, a mid-trial instruction is recommended in most cases at the time the evidence is introduced. A reason for not giving such an instruction would be if defense counsel felt that the instruction would remind the jury of the evidence and unduly emphasize it and, therefore, requests that no instruction be given.

If there is more than one defendant in a case, the name of the defendant against whom the evidence is offered should be used in the instruction and the following language should be added: "You may use this evidence only in deciding whether or not ___________ *(insert name of defendant)* is guilty as charged. You may not use it in deciding whether ___________ *(insert name[s] of other defendant[s])* are guilty as charged."

A more detailed instruction has been recommended by the Federal Judicial Center Committee to Study Criminal Jury Instructions. It concluded that the best way to limit the confusion and danger of prejudice of evidence of other crimes and bad acts of the defendant is to outline the elements of the offense charged, describe the testimony, then tell the jury that after it has found the other elements beyond a reasonable doubt it can look to the prior bad acts evidence to prove the remaining element. It is as follows:

> As you know, the defendant, ___________, is on trial here for (e.g.: knowingly sending gambling materials in interstate commerce). In order for you to find the defendant guilty of this crime, the government must prove each of the following elements of the crime beyond a reasonable doubt. (First, the defendant sent gambling materials. Second, the defendant sent those materials in interstate commerce. Third, the defendant knew that these were gambling materials he was sending.)
>
> As I said, one of the things the government must prove beyond a reasonable doubt is that the defendant (knew that these were gambling materials). You have heard testimony indicating that (on prior occasions the defendant sent gambling materials between two states). That testimony is not evidence that (the defendant sent gambling materials in interstate commerce) on this particular occasion. The government must prove that from *other* evidence beyond a reasonable doubt. But if you conclude on the basis of other evidence that (the defendant did send gambling materials in interstate commerce as charged), you may consider the testimony about prior occasions in deciding whether (he knew that these were gambling materials).

> I remind you that the defendant is on trial here only for (description of charge that distinguishes it from the earlier acts). Do not convict him if the government has failed to prove this charge beyond a reasonable doubt.

Federal Judicial Center Committee to Study Criminal Jury Instructions, *Pattern Criminal Jury Instructions* § 50 (1982).

There is a long line of Maryland case law upholding the general rule that evidence which shows or tends to show that a criminal defendant has committed another crime, wholly independent of that for which he is on trial, is irrelevant and inadmissible, even though it is a crime of the same type. *Cross v. State,* 282 Md. 468, 386 A.2d 757 (1978); *McKnight v. State,* 280 Md. 604, 612, 375 A.2d 551, 556 (1977); *Ross v. State,* 276 Md. 664, 669, 350 A.2d 680, 684 (1976); *Harrison v. State,* 276 Md. 122, 345 A.2d 830 (1975); *MacEwen v. State,* 194 Md. 492, 71 A.2d 464 (1950); *Young v. State,* 152 Md. 89, 136 A. 46 (1927); *Weinsten v. State,* 146 Md. 80, 125 A. 889 (1924); *Nasim v. State,* 34 Md. App. 65, 366 A.2d 70 (1976), *cert. denied,* 434 U.S. 868 (1977); *Wethington v. State,* 3 Md. App. 237, 238 A.2d 581 (1968); *Gorski v. State,* 1 Md. App. 200, 228 A.2d 835 (1967); *Savoy v. State,* 64 Md. App. 241, 494 A.2d 957 (1985). That general rule arises from the wider prohibition against the initial introduction, by the prosecution, of evidence of the defendant's alleged bad character. Thus, evidence of other crimes or bad acts may not be introduced for the purpose of showing a probability that the defendant is a person of criminal character and, therefore, committed the crime for which he is on trial. See McCormick, *Evidence* § 190 (2d ed. 1972). The reasons for the rule were set forth by Chief Judge Murphy writing for the Court in *Straughn v. State,* 297 Md. 329, 333, 465 A.2d 1166 (1983), as follows:

> First, if a jury considers a defendant's prior criminal activity, it may decide to convict and punish him for having a criminal disposition. Second, a jury might infer that because the defendant has committed crimes in the past, he is more likely to have committed the crime for which he is being tried.... Consequently, any probative value that the evidence might have is outweighed by the potential prejudice to the defendant and is properly excluded.

There are several exceptions to the general rule above. Evidence of other crimes is admissible when it tends to establish: (1) motive; (2) intent; (3) absence of mistake; (4) a common scheme or plan; (5) the identity of the defendant as the perpetrator of the offense for which he is on trial, *Mollar v. State,* 25 Md. App. 291, 333 A.2d 625 (1975); (6) a passion or propensity for illicit sexual relations with the particular person concerned in the crime on trial; and (7) other crimes by the defendant so nearly identical in method as to earmark them as the handiwork of the defendant. See *Nasim v. State, supra; Cross v. State, supra; Ross v. State, supra; Anaweck v. State,* 63 Md. App. 239, 492 A.2d 658 (1985). Evidence of other crimes is also admissible when several offenses are so connected in point of time or circumstances that one cannot be fully shown without proving the other.

The rationale for these exceptions is simply that the evidence is offered for a purpose other than to show that the defendant is guilty because he has a criminal character. Evidence of other crimes or bad acts, however, should be subjected to "rigid scrutiny" and should be admitted only if it comes within one of the recognized exceptions. *Pulley v. State,* 38 Md. App. 682, 382 A.2d 621 (1978); *Ross v. State, supra; White v. State,* 33 Md. App. 626, 365 A.2d 605 (1976).

"Where evidence of another crime is admitted, the trial judge must instruct the jury as to the limited purpose for which it is introduced. The failure so to instruct the jury will constitute reversible error if prejudicial." *Brafman v. State,* 38 Md. App. 465, 478, 381 A.2d 687, 694 (1978) (*quoting* 1 Wharton, *Criminal Evidence,* § 264 (12th ed. 1955)). The conviction in *Brafman* was overturned because the trial judge's instruction to the jury "was not a limiting instruction, but rather was one which virtually invited the jury to consider the other crimes evidence for the very purpose for which it was not admissible: to show a probability that the defendant committed the crime for which he was on trial because he is a man of criminal character." *Id.*

In *Cross v. State, supra,* the trial court admitted evidence tending to associate the appellant with another burglary committed on the same day and in the same locality as the grand larceny for which the appellant was on trial. To explain the reason this evidence was not admissible under the common scheme or plan exception, the Court of Appeals clarified the requirements for that exception as follows:

> As a general rule, in order to gain the admission of evidence of other criminal acts under the common scheme or plan exception it is necessary that the crimes, including the crime charged, so relate to each other that proof of one tends to establish the other. *Westcoat v. State,* 231 Md. 364, 368, 190 A.2d 544, 546 (1963); *Wilson v. State,* 181 Md. 1, 3, 26 A.2d 770, 772 (1942); *see Young v. State,* 152 Md. 89, 91-92, 136 A. 46, 47 (1927). Moreover, there must be "not merely similarity in the results, but *such a concurrence of common features that the various acts are naturally to be explained as caused by a general plan of which they are the individual manifestations.*" 2 J. Wigmore, *Evidence* § 304, at 202 (3d ed. 1940). The concurrence of common features under this exception, however, must be more than simply a manner of operation, which is possessed to some extent by most criminal recidivists. A method of operation is not, by itself, a common scheme, but merely a repetitive pattern .... Thus, evidence of other crimes can be introduced under the common scheme exception only when the relationship between the time, place, circumstances or parties involved in the crimes is such that the uncharged crime or crimes "support the inference that there exists a single inseparable plan encompassing both the charged and uncharged crimes, typically, but not exclusively, embracing uncharged crimes committed in order to effect the primary crime for which the accused has been indicted."

Cross, supra, at 475, 386 A.2d at 762 (emphasis in original). See also *Wise v. State,* 47 Md. App. 656, 425 A.2d 652, 660, *cert. denied,* 454 U.S. 863 (1981).

In *State v. Werner,* 302 Md. 550, 489 A.2d 1119 (1985), the Court held that, in a prosecution of a man for incest with one of his daughters, the State is prohibited from introducing evidence to show that the defendant committed incest with another daughter. On the other hand, in a prosecution for incest between the same parties prior to the offense charged, this evidence is admissible.

The Court in *Cross* also discussed the identity exception to the rule excluding evidence of other crimes or bad acts committed by the accused. Quoting from P. Herrich, 1 *Underhill's Criminal Evidence* § 210 at 637 (6th ed. 1973), the Court stated that evidence of other offenses may be received under the identity exception if such evidence shows any of the following:

(a) the defendant's presence at the scene or in the locality of the crime on trial;

(b) that the defendant was a member of an organization whose purpose was to commit crimes similar to the one on trial;

(c) the defendant's identity from a handwriting exemplar, "mug shot," or fingerprint record from a prior arrest, or his identity through a ballistics test;

(d) the defendant's identity from a remark made by him;

(e) the defendant's prior theft of a gun, car or other object used in the offense on trial;

(f) that the defendant was found in possession of articles taken from the victim of the crime on trial;

(g) that the defendant had on another occasion used the same alias or the same confederate as was used by the perpetrator of the present crime;

(h) that a peculiar *modus operandi* used by the defendant on another occasion was used by the perpetrator of the crime on trial;

(i) that on another occasion the defendant was wearing the clothing worn by or was using certain objects used by the perpetrator of the crime at the time it was committed;

(j) that the witness' view of the defendant at the other crime enabled him to identify the defendant as the person who committed the crime on trial.

Cross, supra at 447-48, 386 A.2d at 763.

The Court held, however, that evidence of a burglary committed on the same day and in the same locality as the offense for which the appellant was on trial, was not admissible under the identity exception. The reason for this decision was the State's failure to prove to the trial judge, by clear and convincing evidence, the accused's involvement in the uncharged crime. The

Court thus reversed the appellant's conviction and remanded for a new trial.

In an unusual case, *Mollar v. State, supra,* a rape victim testified that her assailant had stated to her, during the course of the assault, that he was on parole and had been arrested before for assault, attempted murder and rape. For the purpose of establishing the identity of the assailant as that of the defendant, the State was allowed to introduce evidence that the defendant was on parole at the time of the assault and that he had been arrested in 1966 for attempted murder and subsequently convicted of assault with intent to murder. See McCormick, *Evidence* § 190 (2d ed. 1972). See also Instruction, § 5.10, Mistaken identity, *infra.*

The "handiwork" or "signature" exception was analyzed by the Court in *Brafman v. State, supra.* The Court suggested that, before admitting evidence under the above exception, the trial court consider the following:

> (1) The commonality of the facts between the "other crimes" and the immediate charges. Here, the common features must be so unusual and distinctive as to indicate that if the defendant committed the "other crimes" he committed the acts for which he is on trial.
>
> (2) The convincingness of the evidence that the other crimes were committed and that the defendant was the actor. Here, clear and convincing proof is required.
>
> (3) The probative value of the other-crimes evidence on the issue of criminal agency as weighed against the prejudicial effect of such evidence. Here, the trial judge must consider the actual need for the other-crimes evidence in the light of other evidence available to the prosecution on the issue of criminal agency. Another factor to be considered is surprise, i.e., whether the defendant has had prior notice of the proposed evidence and an opportunity to prepare a rebuttal. Also, of course, it must be clear that the defendant's criminal agency is indeed a genuine issue in the case. If, for example, consent is the only defense in a rape case, there would be no need to introduce other-crimes evidence to show the criminal agency of the defendant.

Id. at 474-75, 381 A.2d at 692.

One of the most important aspects of the exceptions to the general rule is that mere prior bad acts, as opposed to prior convictions, may trigger the application of any one of the exceptions. *Nasim v. State, supra.* Further, "the other crime, when it is found to be independently relevant and admissible, need not be established beyond a reasonable doubt, either as to its commission or as to defendant's connection therewith. . . ." McCormick, *Evidence* § 451 (2d ed. 1972); 1 Wharton, *Criminal Evidence* § 247 (12th ed. 1955). See *Cross v. State, supra* (accused's involvement in the uncharged crime must be shown by clear and convincing evidence). Whether the defendant testifies and/or calls witnesses to testify on his behalf is irrelevant to the application of the general rule of prohibition and the exceptions thereto. See Instruction, § 2.07, Impeachment by prior conviction, *supra*; and Instruction, § 2.23, Character of the defendant, *infra.*

A mechanical application of the general rule and its exceptions, however, may not always serve the cause of justice. Accordingly,

> it should be remembered that, though the evidence may fall within one or more of the exceptions, the trial judge still possesses discretion as to whether it should be received. In the judicious determination of this issue he should carefully weigh the necessity for and probativeness of the evidence concerning the collateral criminal act against the untoward prejudice which is likely to be the consequence of its admission.

Cross v. State, supra at 474, 386 A.2d at 761.

A defendant must have advance notice that evidence of a prior offense will be introduced at trial. If he is not given that information until the day of trial, he must be granted a continuance, if requested, to prepare to defend against that evidence. It is reversible error to deny a motion for a continuance under those circumstances. *Worthen v. State,* 42 Md. App. 20, 43, 399 A.2d 272, 284 (1979).

A suggestion to minimize the confusion and prejudice from the use of evidence of prior crimes and bad acts is to limit the use of the evidence to the state's rebuttal if a genuine issue is in the case as a result of the defendant's denial of intent, knowledge, etc. This would underscore the requirement that the state prove each of the other elements of the offense by *other* evidence independent of the prior crimes and bad act evidence. In its commentary to its recommended instruction on evidence of other crimes, wrongs, or acts of defendant to show intent, knowledge, etc., the Federal Judicial Center Committee to Study Criminal Jury Instructions noted: "To minimize this problem, some judges will not permit evidence of the other acts of the defendant to be introduced in the government's case in chief, but only in rebuttal if the defendant denies the intent, knowledge, etc." Federal Judicial Center Committee to Study Criminal Jury Instructions, *Pattern Criminal Jury Instructions* § 50 (1982). One problem with this suggestion, however, is that the state is entitled to use this evidence, when otherwise admissible, as counting toward its *prima facie* case to overcome a defendant's motion for judgment of acquittal at the close of the State's case in chief.

§ 2.11. Court calling its own witness.

__________ *(insert name)* was a witness called by the court. You are instructed that no greater weight is to be given a witness' testimony merely because the witness was called by the court. The witness' testimony is to be evaluated in the same manner as the testimony of any other witness.

COMMENT

The calling of a witness as the court's witness in a criminal prosecution, either for or against the accused, is a matter resting within the sound discretion of the court. The court's discretion should be exercised with great care, and some showing should be made, in the absence of the jury, to justify the court's calling a witness as its own. The majority rule is that the parties themselves have the responsibility of producing evidence and, therefore, a trial judge should call a witness as a court witness "only when the adversary system fails to produce the necessary facts and a miscarriage of justice would likely result." 9 Wigmore, *Evidence* §§ 2483-2484 (3d ed. 1940). *Patterson v. State,* 275 Md. 563, 342 A.2d 660 (1975). See also *Scarborough v. State,* 50 Md. App. 276, 437 A.2d 672 (1982).

The trial court may call a witness whose veracity and integrity will not be vouched for by either the prosecution or the defense. Witnesses who are hostile to the party calling them and who possess material evidence (usually meaning that they were present at the scene of the crime) may also be called in that fashion. *Patterson v. State, supra; Proctor Elec. Co. v. Zink,* 217 Md. 22, 141 A.2d 721 (1958). In *Scarborough v. State, supra,* the Court held that the trial court did not abuse its discretion in calling defendant's mother as a court's witness since her testimony was relevant and material and the State had established a sufficient basis for the court to view her as a hostile witness due to her relationship to defendant and the fact that she had made contradictory statements.

In *United States v. Karnes,* 531 F.2d 214, 216 (4th Cir. 1976), the Court recognized that a trial judge has "the authority, if not the duty, to call witnesses who possess relevant information affecting the outcome of the issues when the parties decline to call them." The Court noted, however, that one important check on the judge's use of such a procedure is that "the due process clause requires that a court be impartial. This impartiality is destroyed when the court assumes the role of prosecutor and undertakes to produce evidence, *essential* to overcome the defendant's presumption of innocence which the government has declined to present." *Id.* at 216-17. The Court further expressed concern over the fact that the jury had been instructed neither as to the reason the witnesses were called as "court witnesses" nor as to the fact that, as such, they were not entitled to any greater credibility. The Court concluded that the jury may have attributed greater credibility to the "court's witnesses" than it would have had they been called by the prosecution. For the above reasons, the appellant's conviction was reversed and a new trial granted.

By contrast, in *Patterson v. State, supra,* the Maryland Court of Appeals approved the court's action in calling appellant's mother, the sole eyewitness to the homicide, as a "court witness." The prosecution had requested the court to call her as the court's witness since they could not vouch for her credibility nor impeach her testimony as a State's witness. The determinative factors justifying the court's calling her as a witness were, first, that such a procedure was deemed essential to prevent a miscarriage of justice and, second, that the trial judge had scrupulously maintained his impartiality throughout the trial.

In *Coleman v. State,* 49 Md. App. 210, 431 A.2d 696, 707-08 (1981) the court's failure to instruct jury when the court called its own witnesses did not constitute reversible error in light of the instructions actually given. The jury was instructed that they were not to infer from the judge's manner or conduct that he had an opinion concerning the defendant's guilt or innocence. The judge further instructed the jury that it was their function to determine the weight and credibility of the testimony given by each witness.

B. Evaluation of other evidence

§ 2.21. Missing witness.

Evidence has been presented which indicates that __________ (*name of witness*) is an available witness who has knowledge of facts in issue and was not called to testify. You are instructed that if either the State or the defendant failed to call this witness and the witness was particularly available to it, then you may infer that his testimony would have been unfavorable to the party who did not call him. It is up to you to decide which party should have naturally called this witness. However, you should not draw such an inference where the testimony of the uncalled witness is purely cumulative and the witness is not in a better position to know the facts than those witnesses who were called. And, no inference should be drawn where the reasons for not calling the witness are reasonable and proper.

COMMENT

The missing witness rule was originally enunciated by the United States Supreme Court in *Graves v. United States,* 150 U.S. 118, 14 S. Ct. 40, 37 L. Ed. 1021 (1893). In its decision the Court authorized the use of an instruction which gave a presumption of prejudice against the party who failed to present a witness when it was "peculiarly within his power to produce [such] witnesses whose testimony would elucidate the transaction." *Id.* at 121. The *Graves* Court set up three requirements for the implementation of the rule: (1) that the witness be particularly available to the party whom the prescription is working against; (2) that the testimony concerns the basic issue in controversy; and (3) that it would be natural for the party to have called said witness in presenting his case.

Maryland law on the "missing witness" is very similar to that laid out by the Supreme Court in the *Graves* case. The missing witness rule applies where (1) there is a witness, (2) who is peculiarly available to one side and not the other, (3) whose testimony is important and noncumulative and will elucidate the transaction, and (4) who is not called to testify. *Woodland v. State,* 62 Md. App. 503, 490 A.2d 286 (1985). In addition to the above requirements, the unfavorable inference to be drawn from the failure to call a witness only arises if the relationship between the defendant and the witness is one of interest or affection. *Id.,* 490 A.2d at 290. The inference will not arise if the relationship is that of accomplice/defendant. *Id.* See also *Christensen v. State,* 274 Md. 133, 333 A.2d 45 (1975), discussed *infra; Brooks v. Daley,* 242 Md. 185, 218 A.2d 184 (1966) (it must also be within that party's power to call such witnesses); *Hoverter v. Director of Patuxent Inst.,* 231 Md. 608, 188 A.2d 696 (1963); *Wright v. Rever,* 151 Md. 558, 136 A. 61 (1926).

In *Hayes v. State,* 57 Md. App. 489, 470 A.2d 1301 (1984), involving a trial for theft over $300, the trial court erred in giving the missing witness instruction where the witness was not in control of the defendant. The giving of this instruction violated the defendant's sixth amendment right of confrontation; it was not harmless error because it was crucial and prejudicial.

In *Bing Fa Yuen v. State,* 43 Md. App. 109, 403 A.2d 819 (1979), *cert. denied,* 444 U.S. 1079 (1979), the Court of Special Appeals stated in dictum that a missing witness instruction should name the witness the judge is referring to so that the jury does not "apply the rule willy-nilly." Additionally, the Court stated that the missing witness rule creates a permissible inference and not a presumption.

When it is shown why the witness was not called upon to testify and the reasons for not calling him are reasonable and proper, no inference that his testimony would be unfavorable is permitted. *Critzer v. Shegogue,* 236 Md. 411, 204 A.2d 180 (1964). In fact, if the party to whom the witness was "peculiarly" available produces sufficient evidence to the court of the unavailability of the witness, an instruction must be given to the jury upon request that no inferences may be drawn because of the nonappearance of the witness. "The failure of a trial judge to grant the requested instruction is prejudicial error." *Bing Fa Yuen v. State, supra.*

Where there is evidence to indicate that the testimony of the uncalled witness would have been merely cumulative, the inference does not arise. *Joppy v. Hopkins,* 231 Md. 52, 188 A.2d 545 (1963). See *Nelson v. State,* 5 Md. App. 109, 245 A.2d 606 (1968); *Harris v. State,* 1 Md. App. 318, 229 A.2d 604 (1967).

In a criminal case the missing witness rule is inapplicable where the accused fails to call a co-defendant, an accomplice not presently on trial, or a person who has already been convicted of the same offense for which the defendant is being prosecuted. The violation of this rule is reversible error. The refusal to give an instruction, when requested by the defendant, that the defendant had no duty to produce such a witness and that no inference should be drawn therefrom, may also constitute reversible error. *Christensen v. State,* 274 Md. 133, 333 A.2d 45 (1975), *rev'g* 21 Md. App. 428, 320 A.2d 276 (1974).

In *Simpson v. State,* 34 Md. App. 378, 367 A.2d 66 (1977), this prohibition on the giving of the missing witness instruction was extended to a factual situation where the witnesses at issue were neither co-defendants nor accomplices in the armed robbery for which the appellant was standing trial. The Court of Special Appeals held that the rule enunciated in *Christensen, supra,* was applicable to the instant case because, under the defendant's version of the facts, those witnesses were the defendant's accomplices to the equally serious felony of selling heroin.

The rationale behind these limitations on the application of the missing witness instruction is that if such witnesses were indeed called to the stand by the defense they would probably invoke the privilege against self-incrimination, thus damaging the defendant and leaving him with a *Hobson's* choice.

The trial court has the discretion of whether to grant a continuance to locate a defense witness. In *Jackson v. State,* 288 Md. 191, 416 A.2d 278 (1980), the Court held that the trial court did not abuse its discretion in denying defense counsel's motion for a continuance to locate a missing witness. The Court noted that counsel had not made a diligent effort to locate the witness, was unable to make a proffer of the materiality of the testimony and there was no indication that the witness could be found.

§ 2.22. Multiple counts and multiple defendants.

(a) Multiple counts—One defendant

A separate offense is charged in each of the counts in the indictment. In this case the defendant has been charged with __________ *(number of counts)* offenses. Each offense, and the evidence which applies to it, should be considered separately, as if it were the only offense with which the defendant is charged. The guilt or innocence of the defendant on each individual offense should not influence your finding of guilt or innocence on any other offense.

(b) Lesser included offenses or inconsistent counts—One defendant

Separate offenses are charged in ________ *(list the inconsistent counts)* of the indictment and you should consider each of these offenses separately. In this connection, I instruct you that you may not find the defendant guilty of both of these offenses; you may only find him guilty of either one offense or the other offense, or not guilty of both offenses.

The elements of the offense of ________ as charged in count ________ of the indictment, each of which the State must prove beyond a reasonable doubt, are: ________ *(insert elements of appropriate (greater) offense instruction).*

If you should find that the State has proven beyond a reasonable doubt each and every element of the offense of ________, as charged in count ________ of the indictment, then [you should] [it is your duty to] find the defendant guilty of that count, and you should not go on to consider count ________. If you should find that the State has not proven beyond a reasonable doubt each and every element of the offense of ________, as charged in count ________ of the indictment, then you must find the defendant not guilty of that offense, and you should go on to separately consider whether the defendant is guilty of the offense of ________, as charged in count ________ of the indictment. The elements of the offense of ________ each of which the State must prove beyond a reasonable doubt, are: ________ *(insert elements of appropriate (lesser) offense instruction).*

[________ *(insert lesser offense)* is similar to ________ *(insert greater offense),* but it is not necessary for you to believe ________ *(insert element(s) that are required for greater, but not for lesser, offense)* beyond a reasonable doubt to find the defendant guilty of __________ *(insert lesser offense).* To find the defendant guilty of __________ *(insert lesser offense)* you must believe beyond a reasonable doubt: __________ *(insert elements of lesser offense).*]

If you find that the State has proven beyond a reasonable doubt each and every element of the offense of __________, as charged in count __________ of the indictment, then [you should] [it is your duty to] find the defendant guilty of that offense. If you should find that the State has not proven beyond a reasonable doubt each and every element of the offense of __________, as charged in count __________ of the indictment, then you must find the defendant not guilty of that offense.

(c) Multiple defendants

Where there is more than one defendant being tried, you should consider each defendant separately and weigh the evidence against each as if he were the only defendant. Do not think of them as a group. Each defendant is entitled to have his guilt or innocence determined from his own conduct and from the evidence which applies to him alone. You are instructed to give fair and impartial consideration to the defense of each defendant.

You are further instructed to avoid a position of prejudice against one defendant on the basis of a finding against another defendant. The guilt or innocence of any one defendant should not control or influence your verdict(s) for or against the other defendant(s).

You may find any one or more of the defendants guilty or not guilty, but your verdict must be reached in the case of each defendant on the basis of evidence applicable to him and him alone.

(d) Multiple defendants—Additional instruction for different or multiple counts

In addition to there being ________ *(insert number of defendants)* in this case, [they are not all charged with the same offense(s)] [they are charged with more than one offense]. You must consider the evidence as it relates to each defendant separately and you must consider separately each offense charged against each defendant. Each defendant is entitled to have his guilt or innocence as to each of the crimes charged determined from his own conduct and from the evidence which applies to him, as if he were being tried alone. The guilt or innocence of any one defendant of any of the crimes charged should not control or influence your verdict(s) for the other defendant(s). A separate verdict must be returned for each charge against each defendant.

(e) Multiple defendants—Evidence applicable only to one defendant: limiting instruction

Certain evidence was admitted only against [one defendant] [some defendants], and not against [the] [any] other defendant. You must consider such evidence only as it relates to the defendant(s) against whom it was admitted. You must not consider it in any way in your deliberations as to [the] [any] other defendant. Each defendant is entitled to have the case decided separately on the evidence that applies to that defendant.

COMMENT

There are no reported cases in Maryland directly on point which could be located.

Some of the language in Instruction (a), above, has been adopted from the Bar Association of the District of Columbia, *Criminal Jury Instructions for the District of Columbia* § 2.50 (3d ed. 1978).

Instruction (b) advises jurors how to return verdicts where an indictment charges lesser included offenses or inconsistent counts. This instruction is patterned after the Bar Association of the District of Columbia, *Criminal Jury Instructions for the District of Columbia* § 2.54 (3d ed. 1978).

Instruction (c) addresses the situation of multiple defendants without specific reference to whether one or more of the defendants is charged with one count or multiple counts. If there are both multiple defendants and multiple counts, it might be desirable to supplement the instruction designated as (b) to include reference to the fact that at least one of the defendants is charged with more than one count and is entitled to have each court considered separately. Instruction (d) provides such an instruction. This instruction is patterned after the Bar Association of the District of Columbia, *Criminal Jury Instructions for the District of Columbia* § 2.52 (3d ed. 1978), *citing* Devitt & Blackmar, *Federal Jury Practice and Instructions* § 17.03 (2d ed. 1970).

Another problem that may arise in a trial of multiple defendants occurs where evidence is admitted against one defendant only. In this event, it is desirable to instruct the jury that such evidence should only be considered with respect to the defendant against whom it was offered. Instruction (e) is the proper form for such a charge. This instruction is patterned after the Bar Association of the District of Columbia, *Criminal Jury Instructions for the District of Columbia* § 2.53 (2d ed. 1972), *citing* Devitt & Blackmar, *Federal Jury Practice and Instructions* § 10.06 (2d ed. 1970).

Where a case involves large amounts of evidence or numerous defendants, along with the above or similar language, the trial court might make specific mention of the defendant, or defendants, as to whom particular evidence is admissible and/or specific mention of the portion, or portions, of evidence so admissible.

Generally, admissible evidence should be considered against each defendant as it relates to that individual. In *Bruton v. United States,* 391 U.S. 123, 88 S. Ct. 1620, 20 L. Ed. 2d 476 (1968), the Court excepted confessions of a co-defendant from the general rule. In *Bruton* the confession of one defendant implicating himself and his co-defendant was admitted into evidence at a joint trial. The Court found this to be a violation of the co-defendant's sixth amendment right to cross-examine. It focused on the fact that the co-defendant would not be able to cross-examine the defendant unless he elects to testify on his own behalf. See *Bowman v. State,* 16 Md. App. 384, 297 A.2d 323 (1972); *Adam v. State,* 14 Md. App. 135, 286 A.2d 546 (1972); *Clark v. State,* 6 Md. App. 91, 250 A.2d 317 (1969).

There have been instances, however, where Maryland courts have upheld convictions when a confession of one defendant at a joint trial was admitted. In *Brooks v. State,* 32 Md. App. 116, 359 A.2d 217 (1976), the extra-judicial confession of each defendant implicating himself and his co-defendant were found to have been properly admitted at their joint trial since the defendant who made the confession testified and was subject to cross-examination. The Court recognized that it was a clear violation of *Bruton, supra,* to admit the confession of each defendant during the State's case in chief. Any violation of the confrontation clause, however, was found to have been cured when each defendant thereafter took the stand and thus made himself available for cross-examination.

In *Scott v. State,* 49 Md. App. 70, 430 A.2d 615, 619 (1981), the Court found an inculpatory extra-judicial statement made by a co-defendant to be inadmissible under the *Bruton* rule. Though found to be inadmissible, the Court of Special Appeals, relying on *Earhart v. State,* 48 Md. App. 695, 429 A.2d 557 (1981), found the error to be harmless beyond a reasonable doubt since the statements made by each defendant respectively were sufficient to sustain convictions under the felony murder rule.

The Court of Special Appeals, in discussing the use of a dual jury system, found that it did not prejudice the co-defendant where the trial judge refused to grant a severance. The Court reasoned that since defendant and co-defendant were alleged to have engaged in a single transaction constituting robbery, defendant had no vested right in shielding himself from co-defendant's cross-examination of one of the victims, and there was no problem of a confession by a nontestifying defendant as in *Bruton v. United States, supra.* Although the Court affirmed, it noted the possibility of error in the use of the multiple jury system, and that such a system is a unique and rare concept in the province of jury trials. *Scarborough v. State,* 50 Md. App. 276, 437 A.2d 672 (1982).

§ 2.23. Character of defendant (reputation and opinion evidence and impeachment of defendant's character witness(es)).

(a) Evidence of defendant's good character

The defendant has introduced evidence of his good character. This evidence consisted of testimony [that the defendant has a good reputation in the community for __________ *(insert character trait)*] [that in the witness's opinion the defendant is a __________ *(insert character trait)* person]. The defendant has a right to do this in order to show that his character is such that it would be unlikely that he would commit the crime(s) charged.

You should consider this evidence along with all the other evidence in the case in determining the guilt or innocence of the defendant and give it such weight as in your judgment it is fairly entitled to receive.

(b) Impeachment of defendant's character witness(es): limiting instruction

The defendant introduced evidence to show his good character. The State introduced evidence to impeach or rebut the defendant's character witness(es).

On cross-examination the Assistant State's Attorney asked the defendant's character witness(es) about events in the defendant's past. The prosecutor was permitted to ask these questions solely for the purpose of testing how well the witness knew the defendant [or the defendant's reputation]. You may consider those questions and answers in evaluating the reliability and weight to be given to the defendant's evidence of good character, but for no other purpose.

COMMENT

The instruction in the first edition of this book on the character and reputation of the defendant concluded with the sentence: "You are instructed that the testimony showing the good character and reputation of the defendant may be sufficient to create a reasonable doubt as to justify the acquittal of the defendant *regardless of any other evidence which has been presented.*" D. Aaronson, *Maryland Criminal Jury Instructions and Commentary* § 2.23 (1st ed. 1975) (Emphasis added). As a result of *Hennessy v. State,* 37 Md. App. 559, 378 A.2d 205 (1977), the last nine words of the original instruction have been deleted. The Court in *Hennessy* stated: "We will not permit character evidence to be isolated and considered by a jury 'regardless of any other evidence which has been presented.'" *Id.* at 566, 378 A.2d at 209. This language was also discussed in *Gooch v. State,* 34 Md. App. 331, 367 A.2d 90 (1976), where the Court held that the excision of the last sentence from the instruction as a whole and its proposed use as the sole direction to the jury was inappropriate. The original instruction, however, also included the sentence: "You should consider this evidence along with all the other evidence in the case determining the guilt or innocence of the defendant."

Regarding the weight to be given evidence of good character, the Court in *Hennessy v. State, supra,* held that such evidence "is not proof of innocence, although it may be sufficient to raise a doubt of guilt" (*quoting Edgington v. United States,* 164 U.S.

361, 367, 17 S. Ct. 72, 74, 41 L. Ed. 467, 472 (1896)). Presumably, when evidence of good character is considered along with all other evidence produced at trial, the jury is free to find the evidence sufficient to create a reasonable doubt as to the defendant's guilt; such a finding would require acquittal.

It has been long recognized in Maryland that an accused may introduce testimony of his general reputation for good character, although such testimony must be limited to "what is generally said of him by those among whom he resides." *Berger v. State,* 179 Md. 410, 20 A.2d 146 (1941). Maryland recognizes that once character evidence is introduced, the State may then offer rebuttal testimony as to a reputation to the contrary, or may cross-examine to show public report of acts inconsistent with the trait of character which the witness has asserted to be publicly attributed to the accused. *Comi v. State,* 202 Md. 472, 97 A.2d 129, *cert. denied,* 346 U.S. 898 (1953).

In a 1971 addition to the Maryland Code, the legislature created a statutory standard which enlarges the scope of proof of character evidence, permitting opinion evidence in addition to reputation evidence:

> Where character evidence is otherwise relevant to the proceeding, no person offered as a character witness who has an adequate basis for forming an opinion as to another person's character shall hereafter be excluded from giving evidence based on personal opinion to prove character, either in person or by deposition, in any suit, action, or proceeding, civil or criminal, in any court or before any judge or jury of the State.

Maryland Ann. Code, Courts and Judicial Proceedings, § 9-115. For a discussion of this statute, see *Nishchuk v. State,* 278 Md. App. 238, 362 A.2d 91 (1976). See also *Bell v. State,* 48 Md. App. 669, 429 A.2d 300 (1981).

The nature of the evidence introduced must relate to a trait involved in the crime of which the defendant is accused; e.g., community reputation for peacefulness and law abidingness is not relevant in a case dealing with a charge of incest. *Wentz v. State,* 159 Md. 161, 150 A. 278 (1930). Neither can the defendant attempt to introduce evidence of his reputation in the business community; he can only bring in evidence of his reputation in the community where he resides. *Nelson v. State,* 5 Md. App. 109, 245 A.2d 606 (1968); *Comi v. State, supra;* and *Allison v. State,* 203 Md. 1, 98 A.2d 273 (1953).

The defendant's general reputation in the community, which may tend to show that it is unlikely that the defendant committed the crime charged, is not put in issue when the defendant presents evidence relating to his community reputation. 1 Wharton, *Criminal Evidence* § 221 (12th ed. 1955). The defendant does not put his character in this frame of reference in issue merely taking the stand as a witness; it is put in issue when he states that he has good character or a good record, or offers direct evidence of good character. *Braxton v. State,* 11 Md. App. 434, 274 A.2d 647 (1971).

In *Braxton,* the Court stated:

> In *Noel v. State,* 202 Md. 247, 252 [96 A.2d 7, 10 (1953)], the Court said that the propriety of an instruction "as to the consideration and weight" to be given the testimony of character witnesses was generally recognized. It observed that under the federal practice, while failure to instruct on the point was not reversible error in the absence of a request for such an instruction where there was a request for instruction that was technically erroneous, the court should have included a correct instruction in its charge. We think that Braxton, having requested an instruction with respect to the evidence of his good character, was entitled to an instruction that the evidence should be taken into consideration by the jury in connection with all the other evidence in the case and, in arriving at their verdict of guilt or innocence, given such weight under all the facts and circumstances of the case, including the credibility, as determined by the jury, of the witness testifying as to Braxton's reputation, as it merits in the judgment of the jury.

Id. at 442, 274 A.2d at 651.

Before the defendant's character witnesses may be cross-examined regarding their knowledge of the defendant's past convictions, the prosecution, when challenged, must have available a record of convictions and have it read or proffer it. *Taylor v. State,* 278 Md. 150, 360 A.2d 430 (1976). This restriction is an extension of the rule which prohibits the cross-examination of such witnesses regarding their knowledge of the prior criminal accusations of the accused. Such a line of questioning is impermissible because it is highly prejudicial and of marginal relevance. *Id.* at 157, 360 A.2d at 435. Although the trial court violated the above-stated rule in *Taylor,* that error was harmless in view of the overwhelming evidence of the defendant's guilt.

In a prosecution for rape, the questioning of a defendant's character witness as to whether the witness had heard about a previous charge against the defendant of rape and sodomy is error, and reversible error where credibility is the crucial factor in determining guilt. *Facyson v. State,* 35 Md. App. 202, 370 A.2d 158 (1977).

There is another use of character evidence concerning the defendant which should not be confused with the use of evidence of good character by the defendant. When the defendant takes the stand on his own behalf, his character as a witness is put into question. The character of the defendant as a witness is limited to his credibility and the character evidence which is admissible is limited to the truth and veracity of the defendant. To this end prior convictions of the defendant are admissible to show that the defendant is not to be believed. *Hurley v. State,* 6 Md. App. 348, 251 A.2d 241 (1968). *See* Instruction, § 2.07, Impeachment by prior convictions, *supra. See also* Instruction, § 5.07, Good character of defendant, *infra.*

§ 2.24. Flight or concealment by defendant.

There has been evidence presented in this case which might indicate that the defendant was involved in the act of fleeing at the time of the commission of the crime, or after being accused of committing a crime.

You are instructed that the intentional flight [concealment] of a defendant immediately after the commission of a crime, or after a person is accused of a crime that has been committed, is not sufficient in itself to establish guilt. However, you may consider such evidence as tending to show a consciousness of guilt on the part of the defendant.

Flight [concealment] under these circumstances may be motivated by a variety of factors, some of which are fully consistent with innocence. You must first decide whether there is evidence of flight [concealment]. If you decide there is evidence of flight [concealment], you then must decide whether this flight [concealment] shows a consciousness of guilt.

You should consider such evidence of flight [concealment] along with all the other evidence which has been presented and give it such weight as you believe it deserves. Whether or not evidence of flight [concealment] shows a consciousness of guilt, and the significance to be attached to such evidence are matters which you alone are to decide.

COMMENT

Where, in a criminal case, there is evidence of the defendant's flight, the jury should be properly instructed as to the manner in which they should consider and weigh such evidence. As a general rule, matters occurring after the commission of the offense of which the accused is charged which are relevant to show a consciousness of guilt are admissible in evidence. "Flight from the scene of the crime is a factor that may be considered in determining guilt." *Davis v. State,* 237 Md. 97, 105, 205 A.2d 254 (1964), *cert. denied,* 382 U.S. 945 (1965); *Tasco v. State,* 223 Md. 503, 509, 165 A.2d 456 (1960), *cert. denied,* 365 U.S. 885 (1961); *Clay v. State,* 211 Md. 577, 585, 128 A.2d 634 (1957).

> Flight from justice, and its analogous conduct, have always been deemed indicative of consciousness of guilt .... It is today universally conceded that the fact of an accused's flight, *escape from custody,* resistance to arrest, concealment, assumption of a false name, and related conduct, are admissible as evidence of consciousness of guilt, and thus of guilt itself ....

Davis v. State, supra, 237 Md. at 105, 205 A.2d 259 (emphasis added). See also 7 Wigmore, *Evidence,* § 276 (3d ed. 1940). See also *Derricks v. State,* 9 Md. App. 261, 263 A.2d 597 (1970); *McLean v. State,* 6 Md. App. 366, 251 A.2d 252 (1969); *Dyson v. State,* 6 Md. App. 453, 251 A.2d 606 (1969); *Anderson v. State,* 3 Md. App. 362, 239 A.2d 579 (1968); *Williams v. State,* 3 Md. App. 58, 237 A.2d 822 (1968).

In *Pettie v. State,* 70 Md. App. 602, 522 A.2d 394 (1987), the Court held that attempted suicide is analogous to flight as evidence of consciousness of guilt and is, therefore, admissible. Where the defendant attempted to commit suicide within five and one-half hours after he was charged with assaulting the victim, the trial judge's decision to admit this evidence was not an abuse of discretion.

On the other hand, matters occurring after the offense, which are neither incriminatory nor exculpatory, and which have no bearing on the guilt or innocence of the accused, are irrelevant and inadmissible.

In *Derricks v. State, supra,* it was not shown in the record that the defendant was present at the scene when the crime was committed. The Court stated at 269-70, 263 A.2d at 601:

> His presence an hour and one half later is not the same as being present at the time the crime was committed. His flight from the proprietor, under the circumstances, although a very suspicious circumstance, was not alone sufficient to support a rational inference that he was one of the criminals.

See also *Tasco v. State, supra.*

Actions of the accused after the event may be evidence of guilty knowledge. Presence of the accused at or near the scene of a crime and flight therefrom are important elements to be considered in determining guilt. *Hernandez v. State,* 7 Md. App. 355, 255 A.2d 449 (1969). Evidence of the movements and action of the accused after the commission of the offense of which he is charged and before his arrest may be competent evidence, *Scarborough v. State,* 3 Md. App. 208, 238 A.2d 297 (1968), and this is so even though it involves another crime. *MacEwen v. State,* 194 Md. 492, 71 A.2d 464 (1950); *Cf. Tichnell v. State,* 287 Md. 695, 715, 415 A.2d 830, 841 (1980) (Tichnell I).

> Indeed, not only flight from the scene but any flight from justice, escape from custody, resistance to arrest, concealment, assumption of a false name and related conduct are admissible as evidence of consciousness of guilt and thus of guilt itself.

Hines v. State, 58 Md. App. 637, 473 A.2d 1335 (1984).

While evidence of flight or concealment by itself is insufficient to establish guilt, it may bear on the intent, purpose, or consciousness of guilt of the accused, *Westcoat v. State,* 231 Md. 364, 190 A.2d 544 (1963), and hence is admissible in evidence as a fact which may be considered by the tribunal trying the facts as bearing on guilt, *Anderson v. State, supra; Williams v. State, supra.* This is so even though the flight may constitute a criminal offense. *Clay v. State, supra.*

A lapse of time between the crime and the attempted flight goes only to the weight to be accorded the circumstance and not to the admissibility of the attempt as evidence of consciousness of guilt. *Davis v. State, supra.* In conformity with the general rule, any such instruction should have support in the record. However, an instruction as to flight of the defendant to avoid arrest may be given not only where it appears that he fled to avoid arrest after accusation of crime, but also where it may be inferred from the evidence that at the time of flight he knew he was or would be charged with the crime, or where it appears that he left the State immediately after the crime was committed. 25 A.L.R. 894-95 (1923).

In *Garrett v. State,* 59 Md. App. 97, 474 A.2d 931 (1984), evidence that defendant, while in another state six weeks after the crime, gave a fictitious name and address to a detective plus defendant's employer's testimony that defendant called employer on the date of the crime to tell him he was not returning to work were sufficient to support a jury instruction on flight or a consciousness of guilt.

A more defense-oriented instruction has been approved in the District of Columbia which specifically informs the jury of inferences that may be consistent with innocence. It is as follows:

> Flight or concealment by a person after a crime has been committed or after he has been accused of a crime may be

motivated by a variety of factors which are fully consistent with innocence. It does not create a presumption of guilt, nor does the person's flight or concealment necessarily reflect feelings of guilt. Furthermore, since innocent persons sometimes have feelings of guilt, such feelings do not necessarily reflect actual guilt. While you may consider flight or concealment as one circumstance tending to show feelings of guilt, and you may also consider feelings of guilt as evidence tending to show actual guilt, you are not required to do so. Under no circumstances may you presume a defendant's guilt from his flight or concealment.

You should consider and weight evidence of flight or concealment by the defendant in connection with all the other evidence in the case and give it such weight as in your judgment it is fairly entitled to receive.

Bar Association for the District of Columbia, *Criminal Jury Instructions for the District of Columbia* § 2.44 (3d ed. 1978). See *Austin v. United States,* 414 F.2d 1155, 1157-58 (8th Cir. 1969) and *United States v. Honesty,* 459 F.2d 1279 (D.C. Cir. 1971).

§ 2.25. Confession or incriminating statement of defendant.

Evidence has been introduced that the defendant [confessed that he committed] [made an incriminating statement about] the crime with which he is charged.

The burden is on the State to prove to you beyond a reasonable doubt that the alleged [confession] [statement] was freely and voluntarily made. A voluntary [confession] [statement] is one which, under all of the circumstances, is the product of a free and unconstrained will which has not been overborne or compelled. In determining the voluntariness of the [confession] [statement], as well as the weight which you shall give it, you should weigh any circumstances of pressure placed on the defendant against the power of resistance of the defendant.

In considering whether the alleged [confession] [statement] was free and voluntary or not, you may consider whether the defendant was specifically advised of his right to remain silent, that anything he said could be used against him in a court of law, that he had the right to the presence of an attorney during any questioning, and that if he could not afford an attorney one would be appointed for him prior to any questioning if he so desired. You may also consider whether the defendant knowingly and intelligently waived his rights, the length of time, if any, the defendant was questioned, any unnecessary delay in presenting the defendant before a judicial officer and the physical and mental condition of the defendant. You may also consider the time period which lapsed, if any, between the time of being advised of his rights and the time the alleged [confession] [statement] was made, other persons present, and all other circumstances surrounding the making of the alleged [confession] [statement], including the age, background, education, experience and intelligence of the defendant.

As I instructed you, the burden is on the State to prove to you beyond a reasonable doubt that the alleged [confession] [statement] was freely and voluntarily made. Therefore, the State must prove to you beyond a reasonable doubt that there were no threats or violence, or any direct or implied promises, however slight, or any improper influence which caused the defendant to make the alleged [confession] [statement]. [A [confession] [statement] is not voluntary if induced by promises of leniency regarding the defendant or another.]

If you find that the evidence shows beyond a reasonable doubt that the [confession] [statement] was freely and voluntarily made by the defendant, then, giving it the weight which you feel it deserves, you may consider it along with all other evidence presented in arriving at a verdict. However, if you find that the evidence does not show beyond a reasonable doubt that the [confession] [statement] was freely and voluntarily made by the defendant, then you must disregard it entirely in reaching your verdict.

COMMENT

(a) Introduction and burden of proof

The determination of whether a confession or an incriminating statement is admissible is ordinarily a matter for the trial court to decide. *Miller v. State,* 251 Md. 362, 247 A.2d 530 (1968), *modified,* 408 U.S. 934, 92 S. Ct. 2851, 33 L. Ed. 2d 747 (1972). In admitting a confession, the question of its voluntariness is initially determined by the court. If the court finds, by a preponderance of the evidence, that the confession was voluntarily made and therefore admits it, the confession is then submitted to the trier of fact. *Mulligan v. State,* 18 Md. App. 588, 308 A.2d 418 (1973) (following *Lego v. Twomey,* 404 U.S. 477, 92 S. Ct. 619, 30 L. Ed. 2d 618 (1972)); *Linkens v. State,* 202 Md. 212, 96 A.2d 246 (1953); *Price v. State,* 7 Md. App. 131, 254 A.2d 219 (1969). After being placed into evidence and before it can be utilized in determining guilt or innocence, the trier of fact must independently determine that beyond any reasonable doubt, the confession was voluntarily and freely made. *Hillard v. State,* 286 Md. 145, 406 A.2d 415 (1979).

Whenever a confession is introduced into evidence and instructions as to its voluntariness are requested, the trial judge must administer the proffered instruction regardless of his personal belief in the absence of evidence necessary to support the contention of involuntariness. *Bellamy v. State,* 50 Md. App. 65, 72-75, 435 A.2d 821, 825 (1981) (citing with approval part of Instruction, § 2.25, D. Aaronson, *Maryland Criminal Jury Instructions and Commentary* (1st ed. 1975)).

Once the trial judge has determined that the confession was voluntarily given, all of the relevant evidence on that issue is to be submitted to the jury. A trial judge may not select which circumstances relative to voluntariness may go to the jury and which may not. The jury is entitled to have before it the same evidence which the judge heard before making his decision. *Johnson v. State,* 31 Md. App. 303, 355 A.2d 504 (1976).

A trial judge may not comment to the jury that he has found the defendant's confession to be voluntary. Such a comment constitutes an inadmissible opinion upon a question of fact ultimately to be decided by the jury and is reversible error, even in the absence of objection by defense counsel. *Dempsey v. State,* 277 Md. 134, 355 A.2d 455 (1976).

If the decision of the trial judge is that a statement was made involuntarily, his finding should be announced out of the presence of the jury. The confession may not be submitted to the jury, as the jury has no function with regard to the involuntary confession. *McCarson v. State,* 8 Md. App. 20, 257 A.2d 471 (1969).

It should be clearly understood that compliance with *Miranda v. Arizona,* 384 U.S. 436, 86 S. Ct. 1602, 16 L. Ed. 2d 694 (1962) does not end the inquiry as to voluntariness. The burden of establishing compliance with *Miranda* is merely an element, albeit an important one, of establishing the question whether a confession sought to be introduced by the State was voluntarily and knowingly made. *Miranda* requirements do not supersede preexisting constitutional law on the admissibility of confessions; *Miranda* is not co-extensive with the fundamental right under the fifth and fourteenth amendments against compelled self-incrimination.

The Supreme Court of the United States has been eroding the *Miranda* requirements. See, e.g., *California v. Prysock,* 453 U.S. 355, 101 S. Ct. 2806, 69 L. Ed. 2d 696 (1981); *United States v. Mandujano,* 425 U.S. 564, 96 S. Ct. 1768, 48 L. Ed. 2d 212 (1976); *Michigan v. Mosley,* 423 U.S. 96, 96 S. Ct. 321, 46 L. Ed. 2d 313 (1975); *Oregon v. Hass,* 420 U.S. 714, 95 S. Ct. 1215, 43 L. Ed. 2d 570 (1975); *Michigan v. Tucker,* 417 U.S. 433, 94 S. Ct. 2357, 41 L. Ed. 2d 182 (1974); and *Harris v. New York,* 401 U.S. 222, 91 S. Ct. 643, 28 L. Ed. 2d 1 (1971). The Court has said that this does not mean that the fundamental constitutional right itself is being eroded. *Kidd v. State,* 33 Md. App. 445, 366 A.2d 761 (1976), *cert. denied,* 434 U.S. 1002 (1977).

This comment does not address legal issues relating to confessions obtained in violation of defendant's sixth amendment right to assistance of counsel. See, e.g., *Massiah v. United States,* 377 U.S. 201, 84 S. Ct. 1199, 12 L. Ed. 2d 246 (1964), *Brewer v. Williams,* 430 U.S. 387, 97 S. Ct. 1232, 51 L. Ed. 2d 424 (1977), *United States v. Henry,* 447 U.S. 264, 100 S. Ct. 2183, 65 L. Ed. 2d 115 (1980). Also, it does not discuss legal issues relating to suppression of confessions that are the "fruit of the poisonous tree" or other constitutional violations. For cases dealing with confessions as a poisoned fruit of fourth amendment violations, see, e.g., *Wong Sun v. United States,* 371 U.S. 471, 83 S. Ct. 407, 9 L. Ed. 2d 441 (1963), *Brown v. Illinois,* 422 U.S. 590, 95 S. Ct. 2254, 45 L. Ed. 2d 416 (1975), *Dunaway v. New York,* 442 U.S. 200, 99 S. Ct. 2248, 60 L. Ed. 2d 824 (1979), *Rawlings v. Kentucky,* 448 U.S. 98, 100 S. Ct. 2256, 65 L. Ed. 2d 633 (1980), and *Taylor v. Alabama,* 457 U.S. 687, 102 S. Ct. 2664, 73 L. Ed. 2d 314 (1982).

(b) Burden of proof at suppression hearing

Upon a general objection by the defendant to the admission of a statement made by him to the police, the State has the affirmative burden of proving to the court, by a preponderance of the evidence, that the incriminating statement was voluntary and, therefore, is admissible. *Clark v. State,* 48 Md. App. 637, 429 A.2d 287, 290 (1981); *Jones v. State,* 48 Md. App. 726, 429 A.2d 308 (1981); *Carter v. State,* 36 Md. App. 220, 373 A.2d 308 (1977); *Kidd v. State,* 33 Md. App. 445, 475-476, 366 A.2d 761, 778-79 (1976), *aff'd,* 281 Md. 32, 375 A.2d 1105 (1977), *cert. denied,* 434 U.S. 1002 (1977); *Mulligan v. State,* 18 Md. App. 588, 308 A.2d 418 (1973). See *Colorado v. Connelly,* 107 S. Ct. 515, 93 L. Ed. 2d 473 (1986).

The Court of Special Appeals in *Kidd* stated that: "Prudence would dictate that a hearing on the issue of admissibility be conducted out of the presence of the jury, but a reversal will not be called for, notwithstanding the risk, if the statement is ultimately ruled to be admissible." 33 Md. App. at 475-76. See *King v. State,* 36 Md. App. 124, 373 A.2d 292 (1977) expressing the principle that a failure to hold the suppression hearing out of the presence of the jury will not be reversible error under every circumstance. *Accord State v. Franklin,* 281 Md. 51, 375 A.2d 1116 (1977), *cert. denied,* 434 U.S. 1018 (1978) (where no issue of voluntariness or trustworthiness is presented and the record plainly reflects that the statements were freely and voluntarily given, there is not need to compel an evidentiary hearing).

Where the defendant testifies at a suppression hearing that he was coerced into confessing, the prosecution, at that time, must rebut such testimony and prove to the court the voluntariness of the confession. A failure to so do will render the confession inadmissible regardless of any evidence the prosecution may later present at trial. *Darby v. State,* 45 Md. App. 585, 414 A.2d 248 (1980).

Likewise, when the defendant testifies at a suppression hearing that he was impermissibly induced to confess, the prosecutor must call as a witness either the person alleged to have made the promise or threat or a person in whose presence it was allegedly made to refute the allegation. Unless the allegation has been refuted prior to the suppression hearing, the failure to call such a witness may require the exclusion of the confession. *Pharr v. State,* 36 Md. App. 615, 375 A.2d 1129 (1977). Nevertheless, if the asserted inducement was denied by necessary implication arising from the testimony of the interrogating officer, that may be sufficient to make a confession voluntary if all other factors warrant admission. *Ponds v. State,* 25 Md. App. 162, 335 A.2d 162 (1975).

In *Jenkins v. State,* 25 Md. App. 551, 334 A.2d 549 (1975), the defendant testified that prior to being given the *Miranda* warnings and before his confession, he had requested an attorney. The State did not put on any unequivocal evidence to rebut the accused's allegation and thus failed to meet its affirmative burden of proving the voluntariness of the confession.

(c) Permissible and impermissible uses

The Court in *Kidd v. State,* 33 Md. App. 445, 366 A.2d 761 (1976), summarized the various determinations which may be made by the judge in an admissibility hearing:

> [1] If the State has demonstrated compliance with *Miranda* as well as compliance with traditional voluntariness standards, the challenged statement will be admitted upon the merits or for any other relevant purpose;
>
> [2] If the State has failed to demonstrate compliance with *Miranda* but has demonstrated compliance with traditional voluntariness standards, the statement will not be admitted upon the merits but may, under appropriate circumstances as outlined in *Harris v. New York,* 401 U.S. 222, 91 S. Ct. 643, 28 L. Ed. 2d (1971), be admitted for the limited purpose of impeaching the credibility of a defendant who testifies in a manner contradicted by the statement.
>
> [3] If the State has failed to demonstrate compliance with traditional standards of voluntariness, the statement will not be admitted for any purpose, regardless of whether there had been compliance with *Miranda.*

Id. at 475, 366 A.2d at 778-79.

Several Maryland cases have elaborated upon the rule permitting limited use of a confession taken in violation of *Miranda* for impeachment purposes. See *State v. Kidd,* 281 Md. 32, 375 A.2d 1105 (1977), *cert. denied,* 434 U.S. 1002 (1977), in which the Court discussed the importance of strictly construing the impeachment exception to the *Miranda* rule. Quoting Weinstein and Berger, *Weinstein's Evidence* § 607 [09] (1975), the Court wrote: "If the defendant's right to take the stand and his right to have illegally obtained evidence suppressed is to have any significance at all, *Harris,* [*supra*], should be restricted to instances where the defendant on direct examination initiated the issue to which impeachment is directed." 281 Md. at 48, 375 A.2d at 1115. The Court in *State v. Kidd, supra,* held that the admission of the appellant's extra-judicial statement was not proper because the prosecutor had elicited the statement from the defendant during cross-examination. In *State v. Franklin,* 281 Md. 51, 375 A.2d 1116 (1977), *cert. denied,* 434 U.S. 1018 (1978), the introduction of a voluntary statement taken in violation of the *Miranda* requirements was proper because the appellant, on direct examination, had initiated the issue on which he was impeached.

Harris v. New York, supra, and *Oregon v. Hass,* 420 U.S. 714, 95 S. Ct. 1215, 43 L. Ed. 2d 570 (1975), have also been construed to limit the impeaching use of such statements to situations where a specific contradiction exists between the in-court testimony and the impeaching statement rather than to impeach a defendant's general credibility. In *Hall v. State,* 292 Md. 683, 441 A.2d 708 (1982), the Court of Appeals held that it was not prejudicial error when an inconsistent statement made to a probation officer without *Miranda* warnings was admitted to impeach the defendant's direct and cross-examination testimony. The court emphasized that the statement was voluntarily given, and the defendant failed to request a limiting instruction.

For further discussion, see Comment, § 2.09, Defendant as witness — Impeachment by confession: confession admitted solely for impeachment purposes, *supra.*

For applications of the rule that if the State fails to show compliance with traditional standards of voluntariness the statement will not be admitted for any purpose, see, e.g., *Mincey v. Arizona,* 437 U.S. 385, 98 S. Ct. 2408, 57 L. Ed. 2d 290 (1978) (statements coerced by police officer from a defendant as he lay in a hospital bed, nearly comatose and encumbered by tubes, needles, and breathing apparatus cannot be used in any way against the defendant at his trial); *Kidd v. State, supra,* 33 Md. App. at 475, 366 A.2d at 778-79. See *Sabatini v. State,* 14 Md. App. 431, 287 A.2d 511 (1972). *Cf. Franklin v. State,* 33 Md. App. 690, 366 A.2d 111 (1976), *rev'd,* 281 Md. 51, 375 A.2d 1116 (1977), *cert. denied,* 434 U.S. 1018 (1978); *Franklin v. State,* 6 Md. App. 572, 252 A.2d 487 (1969), *cert. denied,* 399 U.S. 912 (1970).

(d) Effect of unnecessary delay in initial appearance

Effective July 1, 1981, a confession may not be excluded from evidence solely because the defendant was not taken before a judicial officer within the appropriate time period after arrest specified by the Maryland District Rules. Maryland Ann. Code, Courts and Judicial Proceedings, § 10-912 (overruling *Johnson v. State,* 282 Md. 314, 384 A.2d 709 (1978)). A failure to comply strictly with the applicable provisions of the Maryland District Rules constitutes only one factor, among others, to be considered by the trial court in determining the voluntariness, and consequently, the admissibility of a confession. Maryland Ann. Code, Courts and Judicial Proceedings, § 10-912(b).

(e) The judicial determination: Miranda

Miranda v. Arizona, 384 U.S. 436, 86 S. Ct. 1602, 16 L. Ed. 2d 694 (1966) has produced a number of significant federal and Maryland decisions on when the warnings must be given and the adequacy of a waiver of *Miranda* rights. An analysis of *Miranda* issues falls within four areas: (1) custody or significant deprivation of freedom; (2) interrogation; (3) adequacy of warnings; (4) waiver. *Miranda* warnings are not required unless both custody or significant deprivation of freedom and police initiated questioning designed to elicit an incriminating statement or its functional equivalent are present. If *Miranda* is applicable, both adequate warnings and an adequate waiver of rights must be present in order for the *Miranda* requirements to be satisfied.

(1) Custody or significant deprivation of freedom and interrogation

The requirements of *Miranda* apply only where the suspect is undergoing custodial interrogation. *Weiner v. State,* 290 Md. 425, 430 A.2d 588 (1981); *Dixon v. State,* 1 Md. App. 623, 232 A.2d 538 (1967). Custodial interrogation means questioning initiated by a law enforcement officer after a suspect has been taken into custody or otherwise deprived of his freedom in any significant way. *Jones v. State,* 2 Md. App. 429, 234 A.2d 900 (1967). The doctrine of *Miranda,* however, does not protect an accused to the extent that all police inquiry is impermissible without prior warning. *Gaudio v. State,* 1 Md. App. 455, 230 A.2d 700 (1967). A suspect questioned on the street need not be given his *Miranda* warnings. *Morgan v. State,* 2 Md. App. 440, 234 A.2d 762 (1967). The Court's primary concern in *Miranda* was with the evils of incommunicado interrogation in a police dominated atmosphere. That decision mandates that a person about to undergo custodial interrogation be informed of his rights, but does not forbid any and all questioning prior to such warning. *Duckett v. State,* 3 Md. App. 563, 240 A.2d 332 (1968). An officer need not give the *Miranda* warnings prior to asking routine questions seeking identification. In addition, answers to such questions are admissible as evidence. *Leach v. State,* 47 Md. App. 611, 425 A.2d 234, 238 (1981); *Grimes v. State,* 44 Md. App. 580, 409 A.2d 767 (1980), *rev'd on other grounds,* 290 Md. 236, 429 A.2d 228 (1981).

Application of the *Miranda* doctrine, therefore, requires a dual analysis. There must be custody of the accused by law enforcement officers and there must be a questioning or interrogation of the accused by the officers.

The Supreme Court of the United States in *Beckwith v. United States,* 425 U.S. 341, 96 S. Ct. 1612, 48 L. Ed. 2d 1 (1976), rejected the petitioner's argument that he had been the subject of "custodial interrogation." His argument was premised on the fact that the criminal investigation has already focused on him at the time he was questioned by the government agents. The Court found that the interview (conducted at the petitioner's home by special agents of the Internal Revenue Service) was free of compulsion and thus noncustodial. The Court rejected the "focus test" for "custodial interrogation" asserted by the petitioner and held that the *Miranda* warnings were not mandated under the circumstances of the case. See also *Oregon v. Mathiason,* 429 U.S. 492, 97 S. Ct. 711, 50 L. Ed. 2d 714 (1977).

The Maryland Court of Special Appeals in *Cummings v. State,* 27 Md. App. 361, 341 A.2d 294 (1975) (prosecution for automobile manslaughter) held that the questioning of a suspect who is confined in a hospital but not under arrest is not custodial interrogation within the contemplation of *Miranda.* In a comprehensive analysis of the meaning of custodial interrogation, the Court outlined a number of practical criteria in determining whether *custody* exists: (1) place of interrogation (is it a police dominated atmosphere of psychological compulsion); (2) time of interrogation (normal or irregular hours); (3) persons present during interrogation (friends or relatives); (4) indicia of formal arrest (absence of physical restraint suggests noncustody); (5) length of interrogation and demeanor of police; and (6) lack of arrest after interrogation. In summary, the question is to be viewed from the state of mind of the suspect or, more precisely, the state of mind of a reasonable person in the suspect's circumstances, and not from the state of mind of the interrogating officer. *But cf. Orozco v. Texas,* 394 U.S. 324, 89 S. Ct. 1095, 22 L. Ed. 2d 311 (1969).

In *Berkemer v. McCarty,* 468 U.S. 420, 104 S. Ct. 3138, 82 L. Ed. 2d 317 (1984), the United States Supreme Court considered the application of *Miranda* to a stop and subsequent arrest for driving while intoxicated. A state highway patrol officer observed defendant's car weaving in and out of a lane. After following the car for two miles, the officer forced the defendant to stop and asked him to get out of the vehicle. When defendant complied, the officer noticed that he was having difficulty standing. The officer then asked defendant to perform a field sobriety test, commonly known as a "balancing test." Defendant could not do so without falling. While still at the scene of the traffic stop, the officer asked defendant whether he had been using intoxicants. Defendant replied that "he had consumed two beers and had smoked several joints of marijuana a short time before." Defendant's speech was slurred and the officer had difficulty understanding him. The defendant was then formally placed under arrest and transported to the county jail where an "intoxilyzer" test was given and further incriminating statements were taken. The Court held that while *Miranda* applies regardless of the nature or severity of the offense for which a person is suspected or arrested, the noncoercive aspects of ordinary traffic stops, including the instant case prior to the arrest, dictates that persons temporarily detained pursuant to such stops are not "in custody" for purposes of *Miranda.* The Court held, however, that the functional equivalent of arrest occurred when the suspect was formally placed under arrest after having failed one field sobriety test. The opinion implies that a suspect driven to a police station for a blood or breath test is at that point under arrest.

Goldstein, *The Growing Complexity of Trying the DWI Case,* Maryland Bar Journal 17, 18 (March, 1985) raises a question of the fairness of advising a defendant under *Miranda* of his right to remain silent and then forcing him to an election whether to take a chemical test for intoxication.

As indicated by *Berkemer, supra,* whether a suspect is "in custody" at a particular time depends on how a reasonable man in the suspect's position would have understood the situation. *Cf. Beckwith v. United States, supra.*

In *Minnesota v. Murphy,* 465 U.S. 420, 104 S. Ct. 1136, 79 L. Ed. 2d 409, *reh'g denied,* 104 S. Ct. 1932 (1984), a probationer met with his probation officer at her office pursuant to her order, and admitted in response to her questioning that he had committed rape and murder some years ago. The Court, holding *Miranda* was inapplicable because there was no custody, stated:

> [T]he coercion inherent in custodial interrogation derives in large measure from an interrogator's insinuations that the interrogation will continue until a confession is obtained.... Since Murphy was not physically restrained and could have felt from the possibility that terminating the meeting would have led to revocation of probation, [this] was not comparable to the pressure on a suspect who is painfully aware that he literally cannot escape a persistent custodial interrogator.

In a Maryland decision, *Bartram v. State,* 33 Md. App. 115, 364 A.2d 1119 (1976), *aff'd,* 280 Md. 616, 374 A.2d 1144 (1977), the Court again analyzed the meaning of the term "custodial interrogation." In *Bartram,* the defendant had been taken to a hospital emergency room following the fatal shooting of her husband, because she appeared extremely nervous and in need of medical assistance. In the emergency room, the police officer, in a nonaccusatory tone, asked the defendant what had happened. At that time the defendant was neither under arrest nor legal restraint, though the husband's death had been classified in the police report as "suspicious." The Court applied the criteria set forth in *Cummings v. State, supra,* and found that the defendant had not been in a custodial situation at the time of the officer's question. The Court stressed the following facts as having been influential in its decision: the questioning had taken place in a hospital; between 9:30 and 10:30 a.m.; in a room freely accessible to the hospital staff; the defendant had not been led to believe she was under any legal restraint; the conversation lasted about ten to fifteen minutes and was conducted in a nonaccusatory tone; and there had been no arrest immediately following the interrogation.

Voluntary statements made during routine, noncustodial identification questioning are not subject to exclusion under the rule enunciated in *Miranda. Leach v. State, supra,* 425 A.2d at 238. In *Burton v. State,* 32 Md. App. 529, 363 A.2d 243 (1976), the Court of Special Appeals held that not every questioning that takes place in a police station is a "custodial interrogation." *Carwell v. State,* 2 Md. App. 45, 232 A.2d 903 (1967), decided that a statement made by a defendant when arrested, even though he was not warned of his rights, was admissible because the statement was voluntary and not made in response to any question asked by the police. In *Cummings v. State, supra,* the Court found that the statement by the appellant, "I was only doing 40 to 45 m.p.h.," was a gratuitous or volunteered statement. Accordingly, because the statement was not made in response to any question asked by the police, it did not constitute "interrogation" within the scope of *Miranda.*

The Supreme Court of the United States defined the requirement, for purposes of applying *Miranda,* of an interrogation of the accused by police, assuming custody has been established. In *Rhode Island v. Innis,* 446 U.S. 291, 302, 100 S. Ct. 1682, 1690, 64 L. Ed. 2d 297 (1980), the Court reversed the Supreme Court of Rhode Island, which had set aside the respondent's conviction, and held that a conversation between police officers, while transporting the defendant to the police station following his arrest, did not constitute an interrogation within the meaning of *Miranda.* The "off-hand remarks" of the police officers were neither express questioning nor the "functional equivalent of questioning" and, further, it was not established that the defendant's incriminating response was the product of "words or actions on the part of police officers that they *should have known* were reasonably likely to elicit an incriminating response."

In *Graynor v. State,* 50 Md. App. 600, 440 A.2d 399, 403 (1982), the Court held that a police response to an inquiry made by the defendant does not constitute an interrogation within the meaning of *Miranda.* In *Graynor,* the defendant asked the police officer how they knew where to locate him. The police informed the defendant that they had received a phone call from his wife. Soon thereafter, the defendant made an incriminating statement. The Court held that this was not tantamount to, nor a functional equivalent of, an interrogation within the meaning of *Miranda*.

(2) The Miranda warnings

The State must show to the judge that before interrogation of a person in custody, all of the *Miranda* warnings were adequately given. *Hutchinson v. State,* 9 Md. App. 41, 262 A.2d 321, *rev'd on other grounds,* 260 Md. 227, 271 A.2d 641 (1970); *Barnhart v. State,* 5 Md. App. 222, 246 A.2d 280 (1968). According to the Court in *Miranda v. Arizona,* 384 U.S. at 444:

> Prior to any questioning, the person must be warned that he has a right to remain silent, that any statement he does make may be used as evidence against him, and that he has a right to the presence of an attorney, either retained or appointed. The defendant may waive effectuation of these rights, provided the waiver is made voluntarily, knowingly and intelligently.

See *Brown v. State,* 3 Md. App. 313, 239 A.2d 761 (1968); *Hale v. State,* 5 Md. App. 326, 247 A.2d 409 (1968); and *Robinson v. State,* 1 Md. App. 522, 231 A.2d 920 (1967). The rights must be given in clear terms, and the accused must have an opportunity to exercise those rights. *Thomas v. State,* 3 Md. App. 101, 238 A.2d 558 (1968); *Brown v. State, supra.* Advice to a prisoner that he has a right to contact a lawyer coupled with an inquiry as to whether he wants one does not comply with the requirement that the accused be told that he has the right to have counsel present. *Duckett v. State, supra.*

Also, in *Duckett, supra,* 3 Md. App. at 575, it is stated that the warnings must be applied reasonably and with common sense and "do not constitute an arid, ritualistic formula to be administered inflexibly." Thus, advising a prisoner that anything he says "can be used" against him, instead of "can and will" be used against him was adequate since the substance of the right was conveyed. *Smith v. State,* 31 Md. App. 106, 118, 355 A.2d 527

(1976); *Minor v. State,* 6 Md. App. 82, 88, 250 A.2d 113 (1969). The Supreme Court of the United States has described the flexibility with which *Miranda* should be applied as follows: "*Miranda* itself indicated that no talismanic incantation was required to satisfy its strictures." *California v. Prysock,* 453 U.S. 355, 101 S. Ct. 2806, 69 L. Ed. 2d 696 (1981). In *Prysock,* the Court reversed a finding by the California Court of Appeals that the *Miranda* warnings given to the defendant "were inadequate simply because of the order in which they were given." *Id.* at 361.

Nevertheless, "[t]he *Miranda* mandate directs absolute compliance with the prerequisite minimal standards set forth therein where the appellant is being subjected to custodial interrogation." *Brown v. State,* 4 Md. App. 261, 266, 242 A.2d 570 (1968). See also *Rock v. State,* 6 Md. App. 618, 253 A.2d 401 (1969); *Mulligan v. State,* 6 Md. App. 600, 252 A.2d 476 (1969), *appeal after remand,* 10 Md. App. 429, 271 A.2d 385 (1970). Thus, where the accused was advised of every right except the right to have a lawyer at the expense of the state, the confession was illegal. *Robinson v. State, supra.*

The *Miranda* decision also mandates that, "[N]o distinction may be drawn between inculpatory statements and statements alleged to be merely 'exculpatory.' If a statement made were in fact truly exculpatory, it would of course never be used by the prosecution." *Milhouse v. State,* 31 Md. App. 571, 358 A.2d 262 (1976) (*quoting Miranda v. Arizona,* 384 U.S. at 477).

(3) Waiver

All four warnings must be given, but the fact that the *Miranda* warnings were given does not automatically render a subsequent confession valid; the accused must knowingly and intelligently waive his rights in order to make a subsequent statement admissible in court. *Brown v. State, supra.* Such a waiver cannot occur unless the right is fully known and understood. In *Moran v. Burbine,* 475 U.S. 412, 106 S. Ct. 1135, 89 L. Ed. 2d 410 (1986), the police failed to inform a murder suspect of telephone calls from an attorney, who had been contacted by the suspect's sister with regard to an unrelated breaking and entering charge, before continuing their interrogation of the suspect. The Court held that the validity of the suspect's waiver of his *Miranda* rights was not undermined where the suspect was unaware that his sister had contacted an attorney.

The State has the burden of establishing, by a preponderance of the evidence, that the waiver was made voluntarily, knowingly and intelligently. *Leuschner v. State,* 45 Md. App. 323, 413 A.2d 227 (1980). It is presumed that a defendant does not voluntarily waive his rights to counsel and to silence and the burden upon the prosecution to reverse this presumption is great. *Tague v. Louisiana,* 444 U.S. 469, 100 S. Ct. 652, 62 L. Ed. 2d 622 (1980).

The mere recital of constitutional rights is inadequate when the circumstances surrounding the recital contradict the existence of the rights. *Walker v. State,* 12 Md. App. 684, 280 A.2d 260 (1971). The question of waiver is one of fact to be determined from the totality of the circumstances. *Leuschner v. State, supra.* In *State v. Fowler,* 259 Md. 95, 267 A.2d 228 (1970), a confession was held to be invalid after a mere "perfunctory" reading of the four rights because these rights were in fact denied. The Court stated that:

> It also goes to the heart of the voluntary quality of his actions if a right is exercised in such an atmosphere and under such conditions as to convey to the defendant, intentionally or unintentionally, a wrong impression as to what a specific right may consist of. This strikes at the core of whether he can subsequently make an intelligent waiver of a right regarding which his only knowledge is formed from an abortive and frustrating exposure to it.

Id. at 104, 267 A.2d at 234.

The Supreme Court of the United States did not find the above principle, as enunciated in *Walker* and *Fowler,* to have been violated when a petitioner was interrogated by officers approximately two hours after he first expressed his desire to remain silent. *Michigan v. Mosley,* 423 U.S. 96, 96 S. Ct. 321, 46 L. Ed. 2d 313 (1975). The defendant in *Mosley* had been arrested in connection with a number of robberies. Before interrogating him with regard to those robberies, the officers advised him of his right to remain silent. The interrogation ceased immediately when the defendant declined to discuss the robberies, and the defendant was taken to a cell. More than two hours later, another police officer took the defendant to a different place in the building. After properly advising him of his *Miranda* rights, the officer questioned the defendant concerning an unrelated holdup and murder and obtained from him an incriminating statement. The Supreme Court stated the defendant's initial desire to remain silent did not create a *per se* proscription of indefinite duration upon any resumption of the questioning. The Court, however, emphasized that the interrogation had occurred after a significant lapse of time, was conducted in a different location by another officer, was directed solely to an unrelated murder, and that the defendant's initial refusal to answer the questions concerning the robberies had been scrupulously honored.

Also, the Court of Special Appeals found the defendant in *Souffie v. State,* 50 Md. App. 547, 439 A.2d 1127, 1131-32 (1982), to have made an effective waiver although she revealed an ambivalence towards waiving her right to remain silent. The Court held that the waiver need not be expressed, but may be inferred from the evidence of the circumstances of the interrogation. Therefore, her remarks were not a "product of compulsion." The Court emphasized that the defendant indicated a desire to tell what had happened, and that if the defendant had told the officer she did not want to talk, the interview would have ended.

The Court held, in *Wantland v. State,* 45 Md. App. 527, 413 A.2d 1376, 1383 (1980), *vacated,* 451 U.S. 1121 (1981), *aff'd on remand,* 49 Md. App. 636, 435 A.2d 102 (1981), *cert. denied,* 457 U.S. 1121 (1982), that *Miranda* does not require that an accused be apprised of the evidentiary value of a statement. The duty of the police was discharged when the defendant understood he could remain silent. It was not necessary for the officer to explain that an oral statement as opposed to a written statement, could be used against him in court.

In *Latimer v. State,* 49 Md. App. 586, 433 A.2d 1234 (1981), the Court held that mere refusal to sign a *Miranda* waiver form does not invalidate statements given during a later interrogation. More than two hours after the defendant refused to sign

Miranda waiver forms, police again approached him at which time he signed the forms and made inculpatory statements. Defendant argued that the statements should be excluded as he had invoked his right to remain silent and to have assistance of counsel and had not initiated the subsequent conversation with police. Relying on *Michigan v. Mosley, supra,* the Court held that mere refusal to sign a waiver form does not preclude police interrogation at a later time. *Latimer v. State, supra* at 591, 433 A.2d at 1237. See *Connecticut v. Barrett,* 107 S. Ct. 828, 93 L. Ed. 2d 920 (1987).

Defendant in *Latimer* further argued that he was unaware that he was signing a waiver form and further that he signed under the threat of being prosecuted for contempt. The Court held that the forms were clearly marked and, as to the possibility of coercion, the trial court had properly disposed of that issue. *Id.* at 591, 433 A.2d at 1237. Not all statements made by the police which convince an accused to confess, after the accused has declined to waive his right to remain silent, constitute an impermissible inducement. In *Humphrey v. State,* 39 Md. App. 484, 386 A.2d 1238 (1978), one police officer told another, in the presence of the appellant, that they had just found the gun used in the commission of the crime. The appellant, thereupon, decided to give a confession to the officers. The Court reasoned that although the detective had hoped his statement would result in a confession, the statement did not, in the absence of deception, constitute impermissible trickery. The Court held that since the statement was absolutely true, the appellant had not been tricked but rather voluntarily waived his constitutional rights.

In *Oregon v. Elstad,* 470 U.S. 298, 105 S. Ct. 1285, 84 L. Ed. 2d 222 (1985), the Supreme Court decided whether an initial failure of police officers to administer *Miranda* warnings taints subsequent admissions made after a suspect has been fully advised of and has waived his *Miranda* rights. Defendant's initial inculpatory remark to the police who had come to the eighteen-year-old defendant's home to arrest him for burglary, was voluntary. Defendant was not in custody as neither the environment nor manner of interrogation was coercive. Failure then to administer *Miranda* warnings did not preclude the admission of a written confession obtained shortly thereafter at the station house following careful admonition of *Miranda* rights and defendant's subsequent waiver. Defendant contended that his waiver was not fully informed because he was unaware that his prior statement could not be used against him. The Court held that the *Miranda* presumption does not require that the fruits of otherwise voluntary statements be discarded as inherently tainted. It is an unwarranted extension of *Miranda* to hold that a simple failure to administer the warnings, unaccompanied by any actual coercion or other circumstances calculated to undermine the suspect's ability to exercise his free will, so taints the investigatory process that a subsequent voluntary waiver is ineffective. *Id.* 105 S. Ct. at 1291-93.

In *Edwards v. Arizona,* 451 U.S. 477, 101 S. Ct. 1880, 68 L. Ed. 2d 378 (1981), the Supreme Court held that a more stringent standard for waiver applies when, after *Miranda* warnings, an accused asserts his right to counsel in contrast to the situation in *Michigan v. Mosley, supra,* where the accused merely asserted his right to be silent. When a suspect, after *Miranda* warnings, asserts a right to counsel, the suspect is expressing a need or desire to consult with an attorney in making the decision of whether to respond to further police interrogation. Consequently, the Court adopted a *per se* rule of waiver where, after *Miranda* warnings and a suspect's invocation of the right to counsel, police officers initiate further interrogation. In such circumstances a valid waiver cannot be established merely by showing that the suspect responded to further police-initiated custodial interrogation. What is required for a valid waiver is a showing that the suspect himself initiated further communication, exchanges or conversations with the police.

As Justice Rehnquist later observed in *Oregon v. Bradshaw,* 462 U.S. 1039, 103 S. Ct. 2830, 77 L. Ed. 2d 405 (1983), *Edwards, supra,* was a prophylactic rule designed to protect an accused in police custody from being badgered by police officers. In a plurality opinion, the Court held that when Bradshaw asked a police officer, "Well, what is going to happen to me now?," there was an initiation of communication by the accused sufficient there to comply with the *Edwards* test. For applications of the *Edwards* rule, see *Smith v. Illinois,* 469 U.S. 91, 105 S. Ct. 490, 83 L. Ed. 2d 488 (1984), *Michigan v. Jackson,* 475 U.S. 625, 106 S. Ct. 1404, 89 L. Ed. 2d 631 (1986); and, *Connecticut v. Barrett,* 107 S. Ct. 828, 93 L. Ed. 2d 920 (1987).

The issue of waiver has been considered by the Court of Special Appeals on remand by the Supreme Court of the United States. *Leuschner v. Maryland,* 462 U.S. 1047, 103 S. Ct. 2836, 77 L. Ed. 2d 413 (1981). Relying on the cases of *Edwards v. Arizona, supra,* and *Rhode Island v. Innis, supra,* the Court of Special Appeals ruled that, even when the accused invokes his right to assistance of counsel, he will be deemed to have waived his right if he subsequently initiates conversation with police during which he makes an inculpatory statement. *Leuschner v. State,* 49 Md. App. 490, 433 A.2d 1195, 1196-97 (1981).

In *Leuschner,* an investigation into the disappearance of a nine-year-old boy led to the arrest of defendant. Defendant was read the *Miranda* warnings and interrogated. Sometime after interrogation had begun, defendant asserted his right to consult with an attorney. He was offered the use of a telephone, but he declined. Instead, he resumed talking. He then signed a *Miranda* waiver form and confessed to the killing. The Court held that his confession was admissible since it was not the product of interrogation but had been given voluntarily in spite of defendant's invocation of his right to assistance of counsel. Some days later defendant confessed to the killing of a second child. Since defendant had waived his rights, this statement was admissible. *Id.* 433 A.2d at 1199. See also *Swain v. State,* 50 Md. App. 29, 435 A.2d 805 (1981).

For other Maryland cases applying the *Edwards* rule, see *Radovsky v. State,* 296 Md. 386, 464 A.2d 239 (1983); *State v. Quinn,* 64 Md. App. 668, 498 A.2d 676 (1985), and *Bryant v. State,* 49 Md. App. 272, 431 A.2d 714, *cert. denied,* 291 Md. 772 (1981), *cert. denied,* 456 U.S. 949 (1982).

An accused may make a knowing, intelligent and effective waiver of his right to counsel notwithstanding that, in the presence of police, he has been advised by his attorney not to make any incriminating statements. In *Watson v. State,* 282 Md. 73, 382 A.2d 574 (1978), the appellant had agreed, upon the advice of his attorney, to take a polygraph test. The appellant was further advised by his attorney to make no statements beyond taking the test. After being informed that he had failed the test, however, the appellant made an incriminating statement to the police. The Court of Appeals found that the officers had not given the appellant the polygraph test in order to coerce or trick him into giving the confession. The Court then held that, unlike the situation in *Brewer v. Williams,* 430 U.S. 387, 97 S. Ct. 1232, 51 L. Ed. 2d 424 (1977) and *Massiah v. United States,* 377 U.S. 201, 84 S. Ct. 1199, 12 L. Ed. 2d 246 (1964), where the defendants had been tricked into giving confessions against the advice of counsel, the appellant here had effectively waived his sixth amendment rights.

(f) The judicial determination: voluntariness

(1) Totality of the circumstances test

The basic standard of admissibility is whether or not, considering the totality of the circumstances, the statement was voluntary. *McFadden v. State,* 1 Md. App. 511, 231 A.2d 910 (1967); *Murphy v. State,* 8 Md. App. 430, 260 A.2d 357 (1970). Maryland cases have placed emphasis on the free will of the accused. "[T]he proper test to be applied in determining the voluntariness of appellant's confession ... is ... whether, under all of the circumstances, it was the product of free and unconstrained will which had not been overborne or compelled...." *Robinson v. State,* 3 Md. App. 666, 672, 240 A.2d 638 (1968). "In determining whether incriminating statements, confessions, and admissions are voluntary the circumstances of pressure must be weighed against the power of resistance of the person confessing." *Hall v. Warden,* 313 F.2d 483, 490 (4th Cir.), *cert. denied,* 374 U.S. 809 (1963). See also *Walker v. State,* 12 Md. App. 684, 280 A.2d 260 (1971); *Colorado v. Connelly,* 107 S. Ct. 515, 93 L. Ed. 2d 473 (1986).

(2) Circumstances concerning accused

Circumstances concerning the accused which can and should be considered in determining the voluntariness of a confession are:

(1) The duration of the interrogation. *United States v. Thompson,* 417 F.2d 196 (4th Cir. 1969), *cert. denied,* 396 U.S. 1047 (1970); *Cooper v. State,* 1 Md. App. 190, 228 A.2d 840 (1967); *Robinson v. State, supra;*

(2) The mental ability and condition of the accused, including intelligence, education, and intoxicants which may influence such abilities and emotional condition. *United States v. Thompson, supra; Spell v. State,* 7 Md. App. 121, 253 A.2d 919 (1969); *Smallwood v. Warden,* 367 F.2d 945 (4th Cir. 1966), *cert. denied,* 386 U.S. 1022 (1967); *Cooper v. State, supra; Robinson v. State, supra; Watts v. State,* 99 Md. 30, 57 A. 542 (1904); *Wiggins v. State,* 235 Md. 97, 200 A.2d 683, *cert. denied,* 379 U.S. 861 (1964). Evidence of mental impairment from drugs or alcohol does not *per se* render a confession involuntary, but it is one factor to be considered in determining the voluntariness of a confession (i.e., whether the confession is the product of a rational intellect and a free will). *Dempsey v. State,* 277 Md. 134, 355 A.2d 455 (1976). Similarly, a confession is not *per se* inadmissible merely because the defendant is under the influence of a narcotic drug at the time the statement is made. *Johnson v. State,* 36 Md. App. 162, 373 A.2d 300 (1977), *rev'd on other grounds,* 282 Md. 314, 384 A.2d 709 (1978). In *Pharr v. State,* 36 Md. App. 615, 375 A.2d 1129 (1977), the defendant gave a confession while under the influence of both alcohol and marijuana. This statement was admissible because the Court found, by a preponderance of the evidence, that what the defendant heard and what he said during his interrogation were heard and said with understanding;

(3) Any pain or physical discomfort which the accused was undergoing. *Sabatini v. State,* 14 Md. App. 431, 287 A.2d 511 (1972); *Hadder v. State,* 238 Md. 341, 209 A.2d 70 (1965);

(4) The age of the accused. *Walker v. State, supra; McCoy v. State,* 8 Md. App. 127, 258 A.2d 611 (1969); *Robinson v. Warden,*

5 Md. App. 68, 245 A.2d 407 (1968). In *King v. State,* 36 Md. App. 124, 373 A.2d 292 (1977), the Court held that, based on the totality of the circumstances, the confession of the fourteen-year-old defendant of dull intelligence was properly admitted into evidence. The Court rejected the argument that the absence of the juvenile's parents from the interrogation room *per se* necessitated the exclusion of the confession;

(5) Detention of the accused contrary to law, *Dunaway v. New York,* 442 U.S. 200, 99 S. Ct. 2248, 60 L. Ed. 2d 824 (1979); *Blackburn v. Copinger,* 300 F. Supp. 1127 (D. Md. 1969), *aff'd,* 421 F.2d 602 (4th Cir.), *cert. denied,* 399 U.S. 910 (1970); and *Robinson v. State, supra;*

(6) The failure strictly to comply with the provisions of the Maryland District Rules pertaining to presenting a defendant before a judicial officer after arrest. Maryland Ann. Code, Courts and Judicial Proceedings, § 10-912;

(7) The background, experience and conduct of the accused, *Johnson v. Zerbst,* 304 U.S. 458, 58 S. Ct. 1019, 82 L. Ed. 1461 (1938); and *Dennis v. Warden,* 6 Md. App. 295, 251 A.2d 909 (1969);

(8) The circumstances surrounding the timing and substance of advice and warnings given the accused, *Walker v. State, supra;* and

(9) The period of time which passes between when the accused was warned of his rights and when he confessed, *Franklin v. State,* 6 Md. App. 572, 252 A.2d 487 (1969), *cert. denied,* 399 U.S. 912 (1970).

(3) Police techniques

The following types of police psychological coercions or inducements have been identified by the Court as significantly influencing its determination in finding statements involuntary:

(1) In general, any threats or violence, or any direct or implied promises, however slight, or the exertion of any improper influence. *Mincey v. Arizona,* 437 U.S. 385, 98 S. Ct. 2408, 57 L. Ed. 2d 290 (1978); *Spell v. State, supra; Hale v. State,* 5 Md. App. 326, 247 A.2d 409 (1968).

A confession was held to be voluntary when given after a statement by an officer that "there is no sense in lying." *Clark v. State,* 48 Md. App. 637, 429 A.2d 287, 291 (1981). Where the officer told the defendant that he would not be given help until he told the truth, the confession was held inadmissible. *Jones v. State,* 48 Md. App. 726, 429 A.2d 308, 313 (1981).

In *Holloway v. State,* 26 Md. App. 382, 339 A.2d 319, *cert. denied,* 276 Md. 745 (1975), the Court declared, in dictum, that a police department policy of disciplining its members for refusing to give statements that may be incriminating in investigations against police officers was coercive. Therefore, the admissions made by the officers were involuntary. This dictum is in accord with *Garrity v. New Jersey,* 385 U.S. 493, 87 S. Ct. 686, 17 L. Ed. 2d 562 (1967), which held that the threat of removal from public office for insisting on the privilege against self-incrimination rendered the resulting statements involuntary and thus inadmissible.

The confession in *Pharr v. State, supra,* was admissible because the promise made by the interrogating officer (that he would assist the appellant in getting bond if he cooperated) was made after the appellant had confessed to the crime at issue and merely before he had signed a written statement.

To the contrary, in *Hillard v. State,* 286 Md. 145, 406 A.2d 415 (1979), a statement to the defendant by a police officer that, if the defendant confessed the officer would "go to bat" for him was held to be the equivalent of a promise to speak on the defendant's behalf. The subsequent confession was held to have been induced by the officer's promise and, hence, inadmissible. See also *Bellamy v. State,* 50 Md. App. 65, 435 A.2d 821 (1981).

(2) A variety of psychological inducements used by police have been found to be so coercive as to make the subsequent statements involuntary.

(a) Accused was led to believe that the only hope of saving his life was to confess. *Blackburn v. Copinger, supra.*

(b) Accused was confronted with his brother-in-law who had disclosed what he knew. *Stevens v. Warden,* 366 F.2d 565 (4th Cir. 1966).

(c) Accused was kept in the room while his co-defendant made a self-incriminating statement. *Bryant v. State,* 49 Md. App. 272, 431 A.2d 714, *cert. denied,* 291 Md. 772 (1981), *cert. denied,* 456 U.S. 949 (1982).

(d) Accused was coerced into signing a prepared, written statement in order to have his wife, pregnant and entering labor, transported to a hospital. *Bates v. State,* 32 Md. App. 108, 359 A.2d 106 (1971).

(e) Accused was motivated to confess to assure brother's release from custody. *Jackson v. State,* 13 Md. App. 31, 280 A.2d 914 (1971).

(f) Accused was held incommunicado and not allowed to call his family. *Walker v. State, supra.*

(g) There was continual and prolonged presence of police. *State v. Fowler,* 259 Md. 95, 267 A.2d 228 (1970).

(h) Accused was told that a confession would help make things better. *Hargis v. Warden,* 3 Md. App. 76, 237 A.2d 807 (1968).

(i) Accused was told that confessing would greatly reduce his sentence. *Lyter v. State,* 2 Md. App. 654, 236 A.2d 432 (1968).

One of these inducements, standing alone, may not be enough to make a confession illegal. The degree of influence and all other circumstances must be considered in determining voluntariness.

The psychological effect of the use of polygraph devices is another factor to consider, within the totality of circumstances, in determining the voluntariness of a confession. The use of a polygraph to obtain a confession does not as a matter of law require exclusion of the confession. If such devices are used, however, the State takes a chance that the jury will consider them so coercive as to declare the confession to have been involuntary. *Johnson v. State,* 31 Md. App. 303, 355 A.2d 504 (1976). See *Watson v. State,* 282 Md. 73, 282 A.2d 574 (1978).

(g) Role of the jury

(1) Function of the jury

In Maryland, confessions are admitted into evidence through a two-step procedure. The judge initially determines the voluntariness of the confession out of the jury's presence, admitting it into evidence only if he finds it to be voluntary. Once admitted, the jury makes a final determination of voluntariness. *Gill v. State,* 265 Md. 350, 357-58, 289 A.2d 575, 579 (1972). In reaching its ultimate determination, the jury is entitled to hear "all of the evidence which affects the voluntary character of the document, and which the Court passed upon in admitting it." *Day v. State,* 196 Md. 384, 399, 76 A.2d 729, 736 (1950). The jury is not to make an independent determination on the issue of whether the *Miranda* warnings were complied with but only as to whether the alleged confession was voluntary, an element of which may be whether the defendant was properly given such warnings. The reasoning behind this, by analogy, was stated by the Court of Special Appeals in *Ehrlich v. State,* 42 Md. 730, 403 A.2d 371 (1979), when it decided that the issue of probable cause for a search is not to go to the jury. While the judge need find the confession voluntary by a preponderance of the evidence, *State v. Kidd,* 281 Md. 32, 38, 375 A.2d 1105, 1109 (*citing Lego v. Twomey,* 404 U.S. 477, 92 S. Ct. 619, 30 L. Ed. 2d 618 (1972)), *cert. denied,* 434 U.S. 1002 (1977), the jury must find it voluntary beyond a reasonable doubt. *Gill v. State, supra.*

This two-step procedure is generally known as the "Massachusetts Rule." *Jackson v. Denno,* 378 U.S. 368, 378, n.8, 84 S. Ct. 1774, 12 L. Ed. 2d 908 (1964). The procedure has been expressly adopted by the Maryland Court of Appeals as the law of Maryland (*Dempsey v. State,* 277 Md. 134, 145, 355 A.2d 455, 461 (1976)), certain decisions of the Court of Special Appeals notwithstanding. *Jacobs v. State,* 45 Md. App. 634, 655, 415 A.2d 590, 602 (1980). The respective functions of the judge and the jury in this bi-level procedure have been described as follows:

> [A]lthough the issue of voluntariness is submitted to both judge and jury, it is submitted to each for a different purpose. The judge determines voluntariness only for the purpose of deciding whether the confession is admissible as evidence — whether the jury can hear and consider it. The jury's role is to determine what, if any, weight to give the confession. If, contrary to the judge, the jury concludes that the confession is involuntary, it nevertheless remains as evidence in the case — it is not withdrawn as an exhibit, the

> testimony regarding it is not expunged; the jury simply gives it no weight. *In that sense,* a confession is not unlike other evidence: the Court determines whether it is admissible, the jury determines what weight to give it. The only real difference is the *requirement* that the jury disregard the confession if it finds the same to have been involuntarily given.

Darby v. State, 45 Md. App. 585, 594, 414 A.2d 248, 253 (1980) (emphasis in original).

As to the admission of evidence, determinations of the law are viewed as "within the sole domain of the trial judge." *Lewis v. State,* 285 Md. 705, 723-24, 404 A.2d 1073, 1083 (1979) (*citing Brady v. Maryland,* 373 U.S. 83, 89-90, 83 S. Ct. 1194, 10 L. Ed. 2d 215 (1963)). Instructions on the admissibility of a confession are "binding upon the jury." *Lewis v. State, supra,* at 724, 404 A.2d at 1083. *Accord Stevenson v. State,* 289 Md. 167, 423 A.2d 565 (1980). See Instruction, § 1.01, Function of court and jury, *supra.*

(2) Totality of the circumstances test

In reaching the ultimate determination of the voluntariness of a confession, the jury, as did the judge, must look to the totality of the circumstances surrounding the confession. *Johnson v. State,* 31 Md. App. 303, 309, 355 A.2d 504, 508 (1976), *citing Keller v. State,* 2 Md. App. 623, 626-27, 236 A.2d 313, 315 (1967). The specific evidence which the jury considers in reaching its determination is the same as that viewed by the court in making its initial determination. *Gill v. State, supra.* See discussion on "The judicial determination: voluntariness," *supra,* this section. If "the jury is not satisfied beyond a reasonable doubt that it was the free and voluntary expression of the suspect, then they must disregard it in determining his guilt or innocence." *Gill v. State, supra* at 358, 289 A.2d at 579. Jury disregard of confessions which are found by the jury to be involuntary has been termed a "*requirement.*" *Darby v. State, supra* (emphasis in original). (See the discussion above regarding *Lewis v. State, supra,* and *Stevenson v. State, supra.*)

The Supreme Court of the United States has stated that the failure of police to advise a suspect of his constitutional rights to counsel and to remain silent, as now required by *Miranda,* "is a significant factor in considering the voluntariness of statements later made." *Davis v. North Carolina,* 384 U.S. 737, 740-41, 86 S. Ct. 1761, 16 L. Ed. 2d 895 (1966); *Walker v. State,* 12 Md. App. 684, 280 A.2d 260 (1971) (dicta). Nevertheless, in advising the jury of the burden on the State to show compliance with *Miranda,* a Maryland court "is not required to set forth a specified litany." It is sufficient for the court to inform the jury that a determination of the voluntariness of statements made by the defendant includes the prerequisite that they have been made with full advice as to the constitutional rights to counsel and to remain silent. *Fried v. State,* 42 Md. App. 643, 649, 402 A.2d 101, 104 (1979).

Notwithstanding the aforementioned principle established by *Davis* and *Fried,* Judge Moylan of the Court of Special Appeals has argued by way of dicta that "the additional, latter-day dimension of constitutional voluntariness ... that looks beyond trustworthiness to the propriety of governmental behavior has no relevance to the weighing function. It is not the job of the jury to 'police the police.'" *Jacobs v. State, supra,* at 656, 415 A.2d 590.

(h) Admissibility and use of defendant's silence

The State cannot have the police testify that the accused remained silent in response to some accusatory questions and responded to others, because to admit such evidence would effectively penalize the accused for exercising his fifth amendment privilege. *Wright v. State,* 26 Md. App. 60, 336 A.2d 808 (1975). See *Doyle v. Ohio,* 426 U.S. 610, 96 S. Ct. 2240, 49 L. Ed. 2d 91 (1976). Further, the full and free exercise of the fifth amendment privilege imposes upon a state trial judge "the constitutional obligation, upon proper request, to minimize the danger that the jury will give evidentiary weight to a defendant's failure to testify." *Carter v. Kentucky,* 450 U.S. 288, 305, 101 S. Ct. 1112, 1121-22, 67 L. Ed. 2d 241 (1981). In *Carter,* the trial judge failed to fulfill his obligation by refusing to instruct the jury that "[t]he [defendant] is not compelled to testify and the fact that he does not cannot be used as an inference of guilt and should not prejudice him in any way." *Id.* at 294, 101 S. Ct. at 1113-14.

The permissible use of a defendant's silence to impeach the defendant's testimony at trial is limited. In *United States v. Hale,* 422 U.S. 171, 95 S. Ct. 2133, 45 L. Ed. 2d 99 (1975), the Court exercised its supervisory powers over the federal courts and held that evidence of the defendant's silence, following arrest and the giving of the *Miranda* warning, may not be used to impeach the testimony of the defendant on cross-examination. The Court reasoned that the probative value of such evidence was greatly outweighed by its potentially prejudicial impact on the defendant. See *State v. Raithel,* 285 Md. 478, 404 A.2d 264 (1979). In *Doyle v. Ohio, supra,* the Court granted certiorari to decide if the impeachment use of the defendant's post-arrest silence in a state criminal proceeding violated any provision of the Constitution. The Court decided that issue in the affirmative and held that the use of such evidence violates the due process clause of the fourteenth amendment.

Both *Hale* and *Doyle* have been construed as suggesting "that in some instances prosecutorial comment on post-arrest silence, although unconstitutional, might constitute a harmless error under the standard of *Chapman v. California,* 386 U.S. 18, 87 S. Ct. 824, 17 L. Ed. 2d 705 (1967)." *Morgan v. Hall,* 569 F.2d 1161, 1166 (1st Cir. 1978).

The Court of Special Appeals, however, has held that *Doyle* does not apply to cross-examination concerning pre-arrest, noncustodial silence which is designed to refute the exculpatory testimony offered by a defendant for the first time at a trial on the merits. *Robeson v. State,* 39 Md. App. 365, 386 A.2d 795 (1978), *aff'd,* 285 Md. 498, 403 A.2d 1221 (1979).

The Supreme Court of the United States failed to find a violation of the fifth amendment privilege against self incrimination by the use of a defendant's pre-arrest, pre-*Miranda* warnings silence to impeach the defendant's credibility at trial. *Jenkins v. Anderson,* 447 U.S. 231, 100 S. Ct. 2124, 65 L. Ed. 2d 86 (1980). The defendant in *Jenkins* was charged with murder. At trial, he testified that the killing occurred in self defense. On cross-examination, the prosecution attempted to impeach him with his pre-arrest silence during the two week period between the killing and his surrender to police. The Court reasoned that the reliability of the criminal process would be enhanced by such impeachment as it "follows the defendant's own decision to cast aside his cloak of silence and advance the truth function of the criminal trial." *Id.* at 238.

(i) Need for independent evidence corroborating defendant's confession

An extra-judicial confession or incriminatory admission of the accused does not warrant a conviction unless there is also independent evidence to establish the *corpus delicti,* i.e., the facts that are necessary to show that a crime has been committed. *Miller v. State,* 251 Md. 362, 247 A.2d 530 (1968); *Holland v. State,* 244 Md. 671, 224 A.2d 864 (1966); *Pierce v. State,* 227 Md. 221, 175 A.2d 743 (1961); *Burton v. State,* 7 Md. App. 671, 256 A.2d 826 (1969); *Koprivich v. State,* 1 Md. App. 147, 228 A.2d 476 (1967). Otherwise stated, an extra-judicial confession or statement by a person accused of a crime, unsupported by other evidence, is insufficient to warrant a conviction, but if there is evidence, independent of the confession, which relates to and tends to establish the *corpus delicti* the conviction may be justified. *Johnson v. State,* 238 Md. 140, 207 A.2d 643 (1965); *Bradbury v. State,* 233 Md. 421, 197 A.2d 126 (1964); *Whitmer v. State,* 1 Md. App. 127, 227 A.2d 761 (1967). The sufficiency of this independent evidence need not, by itself, establish the *corpus delicti* beyond a reasonable doubt, but any facts and circumstances that are substantial in nature and fortify the truth of the confession or statement are sufficient to support a conviction. *Miller v. State, supra. Franklin v. State,* 8 Md. App. 134, 140, 258 A.2d 767, 770 (1969). *See* Instruction, § 2.26, *Corpus Delicti* — Corroboration of defendant's confession [admission], *infra.*

§ 2.26. *Corpus delicti* — Corroboration of defendant's confession [admission].

In every criminal offense no conviction can result unless the prosecution has established the *corpus delicti*; that is, those facts that are necessary to show that a crime has been committed.

The issue of proof of the *corpus delicti* arises when the defendant has made a confession [admission]. The rule is that there must be evidence independent of the confession [admission] which relates to and establishes the *corpus delicti* in order to support a conviction.

You are instructed that any out of court statement by the defendant, unsupported by independent evidence establishing that a crime has been committed, is not sufficient to warrant conviction.

The independent evidence, by itself, need not establish the *corpus delicti* beyond a reasonable doubt. Any facts and circumstances that are substantial in nature, relate to the *corpus delicti* and fortify the truth of the statement or confession are sufficient to support a conviction. The statement of the defendant, however, when taken with these supporting facts and circumstances, must prove the *corpus delicti* beyond a reasonable doubt. [*In a homicide case* the proof of the *corpus delicti* is sufficient if it establishes the fact that the person for whose death the prosecution was instituted is dead, and that the death occurred under circumstances which indicate that it was caused criminally by someone.]

What I have just told you applies to those facts which tend to show that a crime was committed. The identity of the perpetrator of the offense may be established solely by the defendant's out of court statement, if you believe it to be true, and the identity of the defendant need not be supported by independent evidence.

COMMENT

The problem of proving the *corpus delicti* arises when the defendant has made an extra-judicial confession (a direct acknowledgment of guilt) or an admission (a statement of pertinent facts which, in connection with proof of other facts, tends to prove guilt). *Vincent v. State,* 220 Md. 232, 151 A.2d 898 (1959). In order "[t]o warrant a conviction, such a confession must be accompanied — or as the rule is typically phrased, 'corroborated' — by some independent evidence." *Lemons v. State,* 49 Md. App. 467, 468-69, 433 A.2d 1179 (1981) (providing an updated review of the origin and development of the corroboration rule).

As mentioned in the instruction, there must be evidence, independent of the confession, which relates to and tends to establish the *corpus delicti,* in order for a conviction to be justified. *Johnson v. State,* 238 Md. 140, 147, 207 A.2d 643 (1965). "[E]vidence is only 'corroborative' in the sense intended by the corroboration rule, if it touches or concerns the *corpus delicti* and — in that way — fortifies the truth of the accompanying confession. Evidence that may fortify the confession without relation to the *corpus delicti* will not be deemed 'corroborative.'" *Lemons v. State, supra* at 472, 433 A.2d at 1182.

The requirement that such evidence be "independent" of the confession has been interpreted to mean that:

> One portion of a confession cannot be used to corroborate another portion, even if the portion proposed for such use does tend to establish the *corpus delicti.* A confession simply cannot fortify its own truth. Likewise, multiple confessions of a given accused cannot be viewed as corroborative of one another, for the same danger of untruth that is present in one is present in all.

Id. at 472-73, 433 A.2d at 1183.

When direct evidence is unavailable, independent evidence may be circumstantial. *Jones v. State,* 188 Md. 263, 52 A.2d 484 (1947). Further, the independent evidence need not establish the *corpus delicti* beyond a reasonable doubt. *Cooper v. State,* 220 Md. 183, 190, 152 A.2d 120 (1959). "The *quantum* of independent proof of the *corpus delicti* is to be determined by the circumstances of each particular case." *Id.* at 191, 152 A.2d at 124. It has been held "sufficient if, when considered in connection with the confession, it satisfies the jury beyond a reasonable doubt that the crime was committed and that the defendant committed it." *Jones v. State, supra* at 271-72, 52 A.2d at 488. See *Lemons v. State, supra.* For example, in a homicide case it has been held that "the proof of the *corpus delicti* is sufficient if it establishes that fact that the person for whose death the prosecution was instituted is dead, and that the death occurred under circumstances which indicate that it was caused criminally by someone." *Jones v. State, supra,* at 272, 52 A.2d at 488. See also *Duncan v. State,* 64 Md. App. 45, 494 A.2d 235 (1985) (convictions of child abuse and second degree sexual offense reversed for failure to corroborate confession).

Proof of the identity of the accused as the offender is not a necessary element of the corroboration. *Weller v. State,* 150 Md. 278, 132 A. 624 (1926). According to the Court of Appeals:

> the sounder view of the [*corpus delicti*] rule should not include as a necessary element of the corroboration required to make admissible a confession the accused's identity or agency as a criminal. If we were to hold differently, the proof requisite for the conviction of the accused for the commission of the particular crime charged would have to be evidenced independently of the confession to make the confession admissible.

Id. at 284-85, 132 A. 624, 626. See *Foster v. State,* 230 Md. 256, 186 A.2d 619 (1962). *Accord* 7 Wigmore, *Evidence* § 2072 (Chadbourn rev. 1978) (terming a contrary position "absurd").

A question may be raised whether a determination of the existence of independent evidence of the *corpus delicti* is appropriately for the trier of fact or solely a question of law for the judge. Although authority in Maryland is sparse, it does appear that the jury makes a factual determination of whether there exists some evidence of the *corpus delicti,* independent of the confession, and, if so, whether that evidence considered with the confession is sufficient to conclude beyond a reasonable doubt that the *corpus delicti* exists and that the defendant is the perpetrator. In *Bradbury v. State,* 233 Md. 421, 197 A.2d 126 (1964), the defendant appealed a jury instruction which stated that only "slight evidence of corroboration" is needed to corroborate a confession. The defendant argued that a confession must be corroborated by independent evidence which "substantially" establishes the *corpus delicti.* Affirming the conviction, the Court of Appeals implicitly approved the role of the jury in making such a finding and held that the independent evidence necessary to support the confession need not be "full and positive" proof of the *corpus delicti* and may be small in amount if such proof, when considered with the confession, convinces the jury beyond a reasonable doubt of the guilt of the accused. *Id.* at 424, 197 A.2d at 127-128. *Accord* 7 Wigmore, *Evidence* § 2073(c) (Chadbourn rev. 1978) ("the judge's ruling is provisional only, preliminary to allowing the case to go to the jury; they in their turn must conclude, *without reference to the judge's ruling,* whether the corroboration exists to satisfy them.") (Emphasis in original). See also *Franklin v. State,* 8 Md. App. 134, 140, 258 A.2d 767 (1969).

§ 2.27. Defendant's decision not to testify (silence of defendant).

As you may have observed, the defendant did not take the stand to testify. Every defendant has an absolute constitutional right not to testify. You are instructed not to attach any significance to, or draw any inference of guilt from, the defendant's decision not to testify. It must not be considered by you in any way. A defendant is presumed innocent; he need not prove his innocence. It is the State that must prove guilt.

COMMENT

A slightly different version of this instruction was approved by the Court in *Benton v. State,* 1 Md. App. 647, 232 A.2d 541, 544 (1967), *vacated on other grounds,* 395 U.S. 784 (1969). See *Bowen v. State,* 5 Md. App. 713, 249 A.2d 499 (1969). "[T]he Fifth Amendment, in its direct application to the Federal Government, and in its bearing on the States by reason of the Fourteenth Amendment, forbids either comment by the prosecution on the accused's silence or instructions by the court that such silence is evidence of guilt." *Griffin v. California,* 380 U.S. 609, 615, 85 S. Ct. 1229, 14 L. Ed. 2d 106 (1955). See Maryland Ann. Code, Courts and Judicial Proceedings, § 9-107, for a codification of this rule.

There is a difference of opinion among practicing defense attorneys whether, and under what circumstances, to request that this instruction be given or to request that the court refrain from giving this instruction. In *Lakeside v. Oregon,* 435 U.S. 333, 98 S. Ct. 1091, 55 L. Ed. 2d 319 (1978), the Supreme Court held that a state trial judge's cautionary instruction, that the jury not draw any adverse inferences from the defendant's decision not to testify in his own behalf, which was given over the defendant's objection, did not violate the sixth or fourteenth amendments to the United States Constitution.

Prior to *Lakeside,* the Maryland Court of Special Appeals discussed this issue as follows:

> The accused is ... entitled to such an instruction if it is requested by him. We are not persuaded, however, that the giving of such an instruction by the trial judge *sua sponte,* or at the request of the prosecutor, even over the objection of the accused, constitutes reversible error in the absence of a showing that the accused suffered actual prejudice as the result of such instruction.

Pearson v. State, 28 Md. App. 196, 200, 343 A.2d 916, 920 (1975).

It is now evident that the full and free exercise of the fifth amendment privilege imposes upon a state trial judge "the constitutional obligation, upon proper request, to minimize the danger that the jury will give evidentiary weight to a defendant's failure to testify" by instructing the jury on the defendant's right to remain silent. *Carter v. Kentucky,* 450 U.S. 288, 305, 101 S. Ct. 1112, 1121-22, 67 L. Ed. 2d 241 (1981). In *Carter,* the trial judge failed to fulfill his obligation by refusing to instruct the jury that "[t]he [defendant] is not compelled to testify and the fact that he does not cannot be used as an inference of guilt and should not prejudice him in any way." *Id.* at 294, 101 S. Ct. at 1113-14.

§ 2.28. Identity of defendant.

You are instructed that the burden is on the State to prove beyond a reasonable doubt that the offense was committed and that the defendant is the person who committed it.

Whether or not any witness[es] has [have] adequately identified the defendant as the perpetrator of the crime is a question solely for you to decide. You may consider such things as: the opportunity of the witness to view the person committing the criminal acts at the time of the crime, including the length of the encounter, the distance between the various parties and the lighting conditions at the time; the witness' state of mind at the time of the offense; the witness' degree of attention to the offender during the commission of the offense; the accuracy of the witness' prior description of the criminal, if any; the certainty or lack of certainty expressed by the witness; and, any other direct or circumstantial evidence which may identify the person who committed the offense charged or which may corroborate or negate the identification of the defendant by the witness.

[You may also consider any other identification, any failure to identify or misidentification by the witness, the circumstances surrounding such identification, and the length of time between the crime and any subsequent identification.]

You must scrutinize the evidence relating to the identification of the defendant with great care. You may consider the credibility of the identifying witness, all of the circumstances surrounding a witness' identification of the defendant and any other facts and circumstances that you deem relevant bearing on the reliability of the identification. You must be satisfied beyond a reasonable doubt of the accuracy of the identification. If you are not convinced beyond a reasonable doubt of the accuracy of the identification of the defendant, you must find him not guilty.

COMMENT

Part of the language of this instruction has been adapted from The Bar Association of the District of Columbia, *Criminal Jury Instructions for the District of Columbia* § 5.06 at 338 (3d ed. 1978), which includes a discussion of the factors a jury may consider in evaluating evidence identifying a defendant. The entire instruction is as follows:

> The burden is on the Government to prove beyond a reasonable doubt, not only that the offense was committed as alleged in the indictment, but that the defendant was the person who committed it.
>
> In considering whether the Government has proved beyond a reasonable doubt that the defendant is the person who committed the offense, you may consider any one or more of the following:
>
> (1) The witness' opportunity to observe the criminal acts and the person committing them, including the length of the encounter, the distance between the various parties, the lighting conditions at the time, the witness' state of mind at the time of the offense, and other circumstances affecting the witness' opportunity to observe the person committing the offense that you deem relevant;
>
> (2) Any subsequent identification, failure to identify or misidentification by the witness, the circumstances surrounding that identification, the certainty or lack of certainty expressed by the witness, the state of mind of the witness at the time, and other circumstances bearing on the reliability of the witness' identification that you deem relevant; and
>
> (3) Any other direct or circumstantial evidence which may identify the person who committed the offense charged or corroborate or negate the identification by the witness.

> You must be satisfied beyond a reasonable doubt of the accuracy of the identification of the defendant before you may convict him. If the circumstances of the identification of the defendant are not convincing beyond a reasonable doubt, you must find the defendant not guilty.

Evidence relating to identification of the defendant often may be the most important evidence in a criminal case. Typically, cross-examination is used by the defense to probe the details of perception, memory and narration for the trier of fact. Both sides may elicit testimony concerning the lighting conditions under which the observation was made, the degree of attention on the part of the observer, the length of the observation, the observer's eyesight, the distance at which the observation was made, the length of time between the observation and the identification, the degree of certainty as to the identification, and the accuracy of the witness' prior description of the criminal.

There are generally no constitutional issues involved in the admissibility of an in-court identification in its own right that does not flow from an earlier extra-judicial (out-of-court) identification. The circumstances surrounding in-court identifications are proper subjects for probing on cross-examination. In *Green v. State,* 35 Md. App. 510, 371 A.2d 1112, *rev'd on other grounds,* 281 Md. 483, 380 A.2d 43 (1977), the Court stated that what happens in the courtroom is open for the judge and jury to see and provided some examples of how in-court identifications might be tested by cross-examination:

> An in-court identification, as any other evidence, civilly or criminally, may be tested and probed by the traditional device for such testing and probing — the use of cross-examination. ("Where would you assume a defendant would sit during the course of his trial?" "Before pointing so dramatically to my client, you had earlier testified that your assailant was a black male; I now ask you to look around this courtroom and tell us precisely how many black males are present in the room. No further questions, Your Honor!" "Before so easily picking out the defendant as he is seated here at trial table, isn't it a fact that you totally failed to pick out his photograph when it was intermingled with the photographs of other persons?" "How can you remember so

well ten months later a fact that you saw in the dark for no more than 30 seconds?", etc.)

Id. at 521, 371 A.2d at 1119.

In addition to the traditional evaluation of evidence of the identification of the defendant in the courtroom, beginning in 1967 there developed a constitutionalization of the law relating to eyewitness identification, both extra-judicial and in-court.

The United States Supreme Court in *United States v. Wade,* 388 U.S. 218, 87 S. Ct. 1926, 18 L. Ed. 2d 1149 (1967), declared that a police-arranged lineup identification is a critical stage of the prosecution at which the accused is entitled to have counsel present. A lineup held in violation of the defendant's sixth amendment right to counsel is subject to a *per se* exclusionary rule. The Court has refused to extend the right of counsel to encompass a police station show-up which takes place after arrest, but before indictment or formal charging. *Kirby v. Illinois,* 406 U.S. 682, 92 S. Ct. 1877, 32 L. Ed. 2d 411 (1972); *Moore v. Illinois,* 434 U.S. 220, 98 S. Ct. 458, 54 L. Ed. 2d 424 (1977).

The *Wade-Gilbert* rule applies only to a post-indictment lineup, a critical stage of the prosecution. *Simmons v. United States,* 390 U.S. 377, 88 S. Ct. 967, 19 L. Ed. 2d 1247 (1968). The Court held that the absence of counsel at such a pre-trial lineup also renders a subsequent courtroom identification inadmissible, unless the courtroom identification is based upon observations of the suspect other than the lineup identification. *Palmer v. State,* 5 Md. App. 691, 249 A.2d 482 (1969), ruled that the in-court identification of the accused by witnesses who viewed the lineup is to be excluded unless the prosecution established "by clear and convincing evidence that the in-court identifications were based upon observations of the suspect other than the lineup identification," that is, they had an "independent source." (*United States v. Wade, supra* at 240, 242.) Basing its holding on *Gilbert v. California,* 388 U.S. 263, 87 S. Ct. 1951, 18 L. Ed. 2d 1178 (1967), the Court further stated that evidence that the witness identified the accused at such lineup is *per se* to be excluded.

A defendant who is unable to make a *Wade-Gilbert* right to counsel argument may still establish that the identification procedure conducted in his case "was so unnecessarily suggestive and conducive to irreparable mistaken identification that he was denied due process of law." *Stovall v. Denno,* 388 U.S. 293, 302, 87 S. Ct. 1967, 1972, 18 L. Ed. 2d 1199, 1206 (1967). This determination is made by considering the "totality of the circumstances" surrounding the identification. Even where the extrajudicial identification is deemed inadmissible due to its suggestivity, if the subsequent in-court identification is not a product of the tainted identification, but is based on an independent source, such as a clear view of the suspect at the occurrence of the crime, the in-court identification may be admitted. See *Manson v. Brathwaite,* 432 U.S. 98, 97 S. Ct. 2243, 53 L. Ed. 2d 140 (1977); *Neil v. Biggers,* 409 U.S. 188, 93 S. Ct. 375, 34 L. Ed. 2d 401 (1972); *Godwin v. State,* 38 Md. App. 716, 382 A.2d 596 (1977), *vacated,* 284 Md. 85, 403 A.2d 785 (1978); *Dobson v. State,* 24 Md. App. 644, 335 A.2d 124 (1975); *Foster v. State,* 272 Md. 273, 323 A.2d 419 (1974).

The Supreme Court in *Manson v. Brathwaite, supra,* reiterated the above principle of law as follows:

> We therefore conclude that reliability is the linchpin in determining the admissibility of identification testimony for both pre- and post-*Stovall* confrontations. The factors to be considered are set out in *Biggers* ....
>
> These include the opportunity of the witness to view the criminal at the time of the crime, the witness' degree of attention, the accuracy of his prior description of the criminal, the level of certainty demonstrated at the confrontation, and the time between the crime and the confrontation. Against these factors is to be weighed the corrupting effect of the suggestive identification itself.

432 U.S. at 114, 97 S. Ct. at 2253, 53 L. Ed. 2d at 154.

The Supreme Court held in *United States v. Ash,* 413 U.S. 300, 93 S. Ct. 2568, 37 L. Ed. 2d 619 (1973), that a defendant has no sixth amendment right to counsel when a defendant's photograph is shown to an eyewitness either alone or as a part of a photographic array. The test to govern the admissibility of photographic identifications is the due process test discussed above. See *Simmons v. United States, supra.* For further discussion, see Comment, § 2.30, Photographic identification, *infra.*

In *Butler v. State,* 46 Md. App. 317, 320, 416 A.2d 773, 775 (1980), the Court held that the criteria set forth in *Biggers* were met since: (1) the victim had the opportunity to see her assailant and gave an accurate description of him to the police; (2) the witness' level of certainty was high; and (3) the length of time between the crime and the confrontation was short.

In *Rustin v. State,* 46 Md. App. 28, 32, 415 A.2d 631, 634 (1980) the Court, relying on *Manson* and *Biggers,* held that it was error to admit the extra-judicial and in-court identifications of defendant since the suggestiveness of the identification far outweighed its reliability. In this case the detective eyewitness viewed the suspect at the scene of the crime for five to ten seconds, and had previously mistakenly arrested defendant's brother. In addition, the detective testified at both the pre-trial hearing and at the trial that he could not be certain that defendant was the right person.

Admission of evidence that should be excluded under *United States v. Wade, supra,* and *Gilbert v. California, supra,* is prejudicial error unless its introduction was harmless error beyond a reasonable doubt. *Chapman v. California,* 386 U.S. 18, 87 S. Ct. 824, 17 L. Ed. 2d 705 (1967).

The admission of an in-court identification by witnesses who had previously identified an accused at a lineup, without first determining that the identifications were not tainted by an illegal lineup, was declared constitutional error in *Gilbert v. California, supra.*

In *Andrews v. State,* 291 Md. 622, 436 A.2d 1315 (1982), the Court held that where defendant changed his appearance immediately after the commission of a crime, in a deliberate attempt to avoid identification, it was not error for the court to order defendant to grow his hair and facial hair for purposes of identification.

In *State v. Collins,* 296 Md. 670, 464 A.2d 302 (1983), the Court held that where a witness has been subjected to hypnosis, the testimony may not be admitted unless he could have testified to the facts prior to being hypnotized. Hypnosis may not even be used to refresh the recollection of a witness. Further, if a witness' pre-hypnosis testimony differs significantly from his post-hypnosis testimony, he would be barred from testifying as to those conflicting recollections. See also *Simkus v. State,* 296 Md. 718, 465 A.2d 1055 (1983); *State v. Metscher,* 297 Md. 368, 464 A.2d 1052 (1983).

See also Instructions and Comments: § 1.05, Direct and circumstantial evidence, *supra;* § 2.06, Credibility of witnesses, *supra;* § 2.29, Identification of defendant by single eyewitness, *infra*; § 2.30, Photographic identification, *infra;* and § 5.10, Mistaken identity, *infra.*

§ 2.29. Identification of defendant by single eyewitness.

You are instructed that the burden is on the State to prove beyond a reasonable doubt that the offense was committed and that the defendant is the person who committed it.

You are further instructed that where the evidence raises the issue of whether the defendant was in fact the perpetrator of the crime, the identification of the defendant by a single eyewitness is sufficient evidence upon which to convict the defendant. Likewise, the identification of the defendant by the victim of the crime is sufficient evidence upon which to convict the defendant.

The weight and sufficiency to be given to identification testimony is a matter solely for your determination.

Unless you are satisfied beyond a reasonable doubt as to the defendant as the perpetrator of the crime, then you must find the defendant not guilty.

COMMENT

This instruction may be given as a supplement to Instruction, § 2.28, Identity of defendant, *supra,* where the identification of the defendant is by a single eyewitness.

There is ample Maryland precedent for the proposition that the identification by a single eyewitness of the perpetrator of the crime, if believed, is sufficient to support a conviction. See *Offutt v. State,* 44 Md. App. 670, 410 A.2d 611 (1980); *Claybrooks v. State,* 36 Md. App. 295, 374 A.2d 365 (1977); *Lightfoot v. State,* 25 Md. App. 148, 334 A.2d 152 (1975), *aff'd,* 278 Md. 231, 360 A.2d 426 (1976); *England v. State,* 21 Md. App. 412, 320 A.2d 66 (1974), *aff'd,* 274 Md. 264, 334 A.2d 98 (1975).

In *Powell v. State,* 56 Md. App. 351, 467 A.2d 1052 (1983), the Court held that a jury instruction that included the language, "I advise you that the testimony of a single eyewitness, if believed beyond a reasonable doubt, is sufficient to convict" did not improperly highlight the prosecution evidence. The trial judge gave full instructions covering the credibility of witnesses, the State's burden of proof, and reasonable doubt. The instructions ought to be viewed as a whole.

The weight and sufficiency to be given to identification testimony is a matter for the jury to determine. *Braxton v. State,* 11 Md. App. 435, 274 A.2d 647 (1971); *Watson v. State,* 7 Md. App. 225, 255 A.2d 103 (1969); *Rodgers v. State,* 4 Md. App. 407, 243 A.2d 28 (1968); *Thomas v. State,* 3 Md. App. 708, 240 A.2d 646 (1968). The suggested criteria for determining the weight and sufficiency of identification testimony are the same criteria used by the trial court to determine the admissibility of such testimony. See *Butler v. State,* 46 Md. App. 317, 416 A.2d 773 (1980); *Rustin v. State,* 46 Md. App. 28, 415 A.2d 631 (1980). See Comment, § 2.28, Identity of defendant, *supra.*

§ 2.30. Photographic identification.

You have heard evidence that prior to this trial a witness who was shown photographs of the defendant identified the defendant from those photographs. Since this identification occurred out of court, it is called an extra-judicial photographic identification. It is for you to determine the reliability of that identification and weigh it accordingly.

You may give it as much weight or as little weight as you think it is entitled to be given. In so doing you may consider such things as the opportunity of the witness to view the person committing the criminal acts at the time of the crime, the level of certainty demonstrated by the witness at the time the photograph was identified and the length of time between the crime and the photographic identification.

In addition, you may consider evidence of the circumstances of the photograph identification procedure, including the nature of the photograph itself, and any suggestiveness of the photograph or the circumstances surrounding its use that may have affected the identification. You may also consider the credibility of the identifying witness and any other facts and circumstances that you deem relevant bearing on the reliability of the photographic identification.

COMMENT

This instruction may be given as a supplement to Instruction, § 2.28, Identity of defendant, *supra,* where evidence has been introduced of an extra-judicial photographic identification.

Specific instruction as to the weight to be given photographic identification does not seem to be required so long as a general instruction is given as to the credibility and weight of all testimony generally. *Dillon v. State,* 27 Md. App. 579, 342 A.2d 677 (1975), *reviewed in* 277 Md. 571, 357 A.2d 360 (1976).

The Maryland law concerning photographic identification of the defendant stems directly from the trilogy of Supreme Court cases decided in 1967: *United States v. Wade,* 388 U.S. 218, 87 S. Ct. 1926, 18 L. Ed. 2d 1149 (1967); *Gilbert v. California,* 388 U.S. 263, 87 S. Ct. 1951, 18 L. Ed. 2d 1178 (1967); and *Stovall v. Denno,* 388 U.S. 293, 87 S. Ct. 1967, 18 L. Ed. 2d 1199 (1967). However, the Maryland Court of Appeals held that *Wade* and *Gilbert* rules do not apply to identification made from photographs; "a viewing of photographs by a witness is not rendered illegal by the absence of counsel for the accused, since there is no constitutional requirement that counsel be then present." *Smith v. State,* 6 Md. App. 59, 250 A.2d 285 (1969); *Baldwin v. State,* 5 Md. App. 22, 245 A.2d 98 (1968). The United States Supreme Court reached the same conclusion. "We hold, then, that the Sixth Amendment does not grant the right to counsel at photographic displays conducted by the Government for the purpose of allowing a witness to attempt an identification of the offender." *United States v. Ash,* 413 U.S. 300, 321, 93 S. Ct. 2568, 2579, 37 L. Ed. 2d 619, 633 (1973). The Court stated that the primary safeguard against abuses of the use of pre-trial photographic identifications is the ethical responsibility of the prosecutor and, if that safeguard fails, review remains available under the due process clause.

The validity of photographic identifications was upheld in *Simmons v. United States,* 390 U.S. 377, 88 S. Ct. 967, 19 L. Ed. 2d 1247 (1968), and adopted by Maryland in *Smith v. State, supra.* The United States Supreme Court, on this point, stated:

> Despite the hazards of initial identification by photograph, this procedure has been used widely and effectively in criminal law enforcement, from the standpoint of apprehending offenders .... We are unwilling to prohibit its employment, either in the exercise of our supervisory power or, still less, as a matter of constitutional requirement. Instead, we hold that each case must be considered on its own facts and conviction ... will be set aside only if the photographic identification procedure was so impermissibly suggestive as to give rise to a very substantial likelihood of misidentification.

Simmons v. United States, supra at 384, 88 S. Ct. at 971, 19 L. Ed. 2d at 1253. See *Bedford v. State,* 293 Md. 172, 182, 443 A.2d 78, 83 (1982) (*quoting Commonwealth v. Fitzgerald,* 376 Mass. 402, 381 N.E.2d 123 (1978)) and *Todd v. State,* 28 Md. App. 127, 343 A.2d 890 (1975), *overruled on other grounds, Douglas v. State,* 37 Md. App. 557, 378 A.2d 189 (1977), both as support for the proposition quoted in *Simmons v. United States, supra.*

The balancing test set forth in *Neil v. Biggers,* 409 U.S. 188, 93 S. Ct. 375, 34 L. Ed. 2d 401 (1972), has been expressly applied in various Maryland cases. See *Johnson v. State,* 36 Md. App. 162, 373 A.2d 300 (1977), *rev'd on other grounds,* 282 Md. 314, 384 A.2d 709 (1978); *Dobson v. State,* 24 Md. App. 644, 335 A.2d 124 (1975); *Foster v. State,* 272 Md. 273, 323 A.2d 419 (1974); *Wichter v. State,* 17 Md. App. 426, 302 A.2d 701 (1973). The Court of Special Appeals has determined that showing but one photograph is, at the least, *prima facie* impermissibly suggestive. *McGilton v. State,* 12 Md. App. 174, 278 A.2d 76 (1971).

Whether a photographic identification is unnecessarily suggestive, and whether such identification violates the due process clause of the fourteenth amendment depends on the totality of the circumstances surrounding it. *Smith v. State, supra; Billinger v. State,* 9 Md. App. 628, 267 A.2d 275 (1970); and *Coleman v. State,* 8 Md. App. 65, 258 A.2d 42 (1969). Clearly, the defendant is entitled as a matter of absolute right, under *Smith v. State, supra,* and *Perkins v. State,* 11 Md. App. 527, 275 A.2d 517 (1971), to an evidentiary hearing out of the presence of the jury, and a determination by the trial judge of whether under the circumstances the extra-judicial viewing of the photograph constituted an illegal pre-trial confrontation because it was violative of the fourteenth amendment. If the defendant can make a *prima facie* showing of illegality, the burden then shifts to the State to prove to the trial judge by clear and convincing evidence that the confrontation was legal. *Smith v. State, supra* at 291. Of course, even if the pre-trial identification procedure was found illegal, the State would still be entitled to show, if it could, by clear and convincing evidence that the in-court identification would be based on a source independent of the illegal confrontation. *Id.; Oliver v. State,* 53 Md. App. 490, 454 A.2d 856 (1983).

In *Baker v. State,* 39 Md. App. 133, 383 A.2d 698 (1978), the Court held that the in-court identification of the appellant was properly admitted into evidence because it was based upon an independent source and not upon the tainted photograph of the appellant which had been taken subsequent to his illegal arrest.

In *Jackson v. State,* 52 Md. App. 327, 499 A.2d 438 (1982), a photographic array in which defendant was the only man shown without a shirt was not impermissibly suggestive when facts of the case were analyzed in light of the five pertinent factors relating to the witness' initial observations of the culprit: (1) opportunity to observe; (2) degree of attention; (3) accuracy of prior description; (4) level of certainty; and, (5) length of time between observation and extra-judicial identification.

In *Jones v. State,* 297 Md. 7, 464 A.2d 977 (1983), the photographic identification occurred two and one half months after the shooting incident. The array, which consisted of five photographs, did not include photos of two others the witness previously stated were involved in the shooting. The defense counsel was afforded an opportunity to cross examine both the witness and the detective and the witness' and detective's testimony were substantially consistent regarding the identification procedures followed. The witness was acquainted with the defendant before the shooting incident. In these circumstances the Court held that the photographic array was not impermissibly suggestive and admission of such identification did not violate due process.

Where a victim, on the evening of the crime, identified a photo of the defendant as the man who burglarized her apartment, and a policeman responded to this identification by saying, "that's fine," and later testified that the victim had "kind of got [the] impression" that she had chosen the man police suspected of committing the crime, such comment did not make the extra-judicial photographic identification procedure impermissibly suggestive, nor did it taint the in-court identification procedure. *Martin v. State,* 51 Md. App. 142, 442 A.2d 191 (1982).

In *Kennedy v. State,* 44 Md. App. 662, 410 A.2d 1097, 1101, *aff'd,* 289 Md. 54, 421 A.2d 1376 (1980), the victim had an opportunity to view her assailant's face during the assault. As a result of being able to make a positive photographic identification of her assailant, the statements made by the police to pick someone out did not create a "substantial likelihood of irreparable misidentification."

In *Harker v. State,* 55 Md. App. 460, 463 A.2d 288 (1983), the Court held that a photographic array of defendant wearing "a plaid flannel shirt" was not impermissibly suggestive in the totality of the circumstances. These circumstances included the following: the victim prior to viewing the array made a description of the assailant's clothes on the night of the shooting similar to the clothes on the defendant in the array; there was another subject in the array similar in appearance and dress to the defendant; and, the victim's comments upon selecting defendant's photograph were directed to the facial features and the glasses, which matched the assailant's, and to the hairstyle, which did not match the assailant.

In *Straughn v. State,* 297 Md. 329, 465 A.2d 1166 (1983), the Court considered the use of mug shots in identification procedures and the danger of prejudice if the jury discovers that the defendant had a criminal record. The prime issue at the trial was the identity of the person who committed the crime. The entire photographic array from which witness chose defendant was introduced in an effort to corroborate the witness' testimony. The pictures were carefully masked to remove all explicit references to their source. At no time were they referred to as "mug shots" in the presence of the jury. Other precautions, including a relevant jury instruction, were taken. The Court recognized the need for police identification photographs. In the exercise of its discretion, the trial court must balance the probative value of the mug shots of defendant against a balancing of all factors that might prejudice defendant. The Court held that here the admission of the mug shots was not an abuse of discretion. If the jury recognized the photographs as mug shots, it might infer that the defendant had been previously arrested; that factor, standing alone, is insufficient in the circumstances of this case to constitute reversible error.

The positive identification of the accused as the perpetrator of the crime, if believed, is sufficient to justify a conviction. *Williams v. State,* 11 Md. App. 607, 275 A.2d 522 (1971); *Wilkins v. State,* 5 Md. App. 8, 245 A.2d 80 (1968). Further, the trier of fact can convict a defendant even though the witness could not identify him at trial as long as the witness made a prior, positive identification of the defendant and is available to be cross-examined at trial. *Bedford v. State, supra.* The defendant's failure to challenge the identification renders it admissible. *Bailey v. State,* 6 Md. App. 496, 252 A.2d 85 (1969). Likewise, a failure by the defendant to sustain his initial burden of proving the impermissible suggestiveness of the identification procedure will render admissible testimony of an out-of-court photographic identification. *Godwin v. State,* 38 Md. App. 716, 382 A.2d 596 (1977), *vacated,* 284 Md. 85, 403 A.2d 785 (1978).

Assuming that evidence of an identification by a pre-trial viewing of photographs was admitted as independent evidence of identification or as corroboration of the in-court identification, the rule is that such evidence is admissible, not only when adduced through the out-of-court declarant, but also when adduced through a police officer or third person observing the extra-judicial identification, if the out-of-court declarant is present at trial and available for cross-examination. *Mouzon v. State,* 9 Md. App. 57, 262 A.2d 588 (1970).

If the court does find the photographic identification to be admissible, the weight to be given to said identification is a matter for the jury to determine. *Bedford v. State, supra; Braxton v. State,* 11 Md. App. 435, 274 A.2d 647 (1971). After the identification is ruled admissible, the defendant may cross-examine the State's identifying witness and introduce evidence with regard to extra-judicial identification procedures. *McGilton v. State, supra.* Such evidence, so elicited, also goes to the weight of the in-court identification and the credibility of the identifying witness, properly matters for the trier of fact. *Miller v. State,* 7 Md. App. 344, 255 A.2d 459 (1969).

For further discussion of the constitutional procedures for evaluating the admissibility of evidence of extra-judicial and in-court identifications of the defendant, see Comment, § 2.28, Identity of defendant, *supra.*

§ 2.31. Fingerprint evidence.

The identification of the defendant as the perpetrator of the crime must be proved beyond a reasonable doubt. One means of proving this identification is by showing the correspondence between fingerprints found at the scene of the crime and the defendant's fingerprints.

You are instructed that the fingerprint evidence found at the scene of the crime must be coupled with evidence of other circumstances tending reasonably to exclude the hypothesis that the print was impressed at a time other than that of the crime, in order to prove the identification of the defendant. [You may consider circumstances such as the location of the fingerprint, the type of place or premises where it was found and the accessibility of the object upon which the print was impressed to other persons.] If you are not satisfied beyond a reasonable doubt as to the identity of the defendant as the perpetrator of the crime, then you must find the defendant not guilty.

COMMENT

The above instruction is patterned after the rule stated in *McNeil v. State,* 227 Md. 298, 176 A.2d 333 (1961); see also *McGhee v. State,* 4 Md. App. 256, 258, 243 A.2d 41, 42 (1968): "It is generally recognized that fingerprint evidence found at the scene of a crime must be coupled with evidence of other circumstances tending to reasonably exclude the hypothesis that the print was impressed at a time other than that of the crime." In commenting on the rule in *McNeil, supra,* the Maryland Court in *Edmonds v. State,* 5 Md. App. 132, 141, 245 A.2d 618, 623 (1968), stated:

> Circumstances such as will render evidence of fingerprints found at the scene sufficient to sustain conviction need not be those completely independent of the fingerprint evidence and may properly include circumstances such as location of print, character of place or premise where it was found and accessibility of general public to object upon which print was impressed.

The rationale for the rule and the instruction has been approved in other Maryland cases as well as other jurisdictions in differing fact patterns when the fingerprint of the defendant was found at the scene of the crime. The Maryland courts have held that each case involving the issue of fingerprints as a part of, or sole proof of criminal agency must be considered on its own facts. For example, in *Brunson v. State,* 9 Md. App. 1, 261 A.2d 794

(1970), the Court commented that evidence, including evidence of defendant's fingerprints on the inside of a private home to which public had no access, was sufficient to enable the jury to draw a "rational inference" that defendant was the criminal agent. The Court commented that it was not a requirement of the rule that under all circumstances the prosecution must conclusively prove that the accused could not have been there other than at the time when the crime was committed. In *Lawless v. State,* 3 Md. App. 652, 241 A.2d 155 (1968), the Court found that evidence consisting of the defendant's fingerprint impressed upon a pane of glass broken from the door where entry was gained tended to show that the defendant was at the scene of the crime and that he was there unlawfully, and was sufficient to sustain a conviction by the jury despite the defendant's contention that a *McNeil*-type instruction was error.

In *Hannah v. State,* 3 Md. App. 325, 239 A.2d 124 (1968), the Court found that fingerprints corresponding to those of the accused were found in a place where the crime was committed and under such circumstances that they could only have been impressed at the time the crime was committed. (Held to be sufficient proof of identity for jury to convict defendant).

The basic *McNeil* fingerprint rule has been sustained in situations where the evidence has been held insufficient for a conviction. *Musgrove v. State,* 3 Md. App. 54, 237 A.2d 804 (1968).

Any proven fingerprint may be received in evidence to prove the identity of the accused. *Hall v. State,* 233 Md. 878, 196 A.2d 874, *cert. denied,* 377 U.S. 982 (1964); *Breeding v. State,* 220 Md. 193, 151 A.2d 743 (1959); *Murphy v. State,* 184 Md. 70, 40 A.2d 239 (1944); *cf. United States v. Kelly,* 55 F.2d 67, 69 (2d Cir. 1939).

§ 2.32. Consent to blood and other chemical tests — Comment.

(a) Criminal nontraffic offenses

The Supreme Court of the United States has held that results of blood tests may be used as evidence at trial. *Schmerber v.*

California, 384 U.S. 757, 86 S. Ct. 1826, 16 L. Ed. 2d 908 (1966). In *Schmerber, supra,* physical evidence taken from an accused's body was distinguished from communications from his mouth or hand, the Court holding that the fifth amendment privilege against testimonial self-incrimination encompasses only the latter. See *Simms v. State,* 4 Md. App. 160, 242 A.2d 185 (1968). Thus, the results of blood tests are not self-incriminatory, and the intrusion will be permissible where the circumstances so justify.

To justify use of blood test evidence at trial, the circumstances justifying the need for the test must comply with fourth amendment requirements and the execution of the test must comply with due process.

The fourth amendment protects "[t]he right of the people to be secure in their persons ... against unreasonable search and seizures." The *Schmerber* Court deemed blood tests to be searches because they "plainly constitute searches of 'persons' and depend antecedently upon seizures of 'persons' within the meaning of" the fourth amendment. *Id.* at 761. Thus, only where the intrusions "are not justified, or ... are made in an improper manner" will they be deemed improper. *Id.* at 768.

In providing the ground rules encompassing the admissibility of such a search, the Supreme Court addressed three requirements:

> (1) the search must be made under authority of a search warrant based on probable cause or may be allowed where there is reasonable belief that an emergency exists in which delay would threaten destruction of evidence;
> (2) the test should be conducted in a scientifically reliable manner; and,
> (3) the search must be performed in a reasonable manner.

Simms v. State, supra, at 171-72, 242 A.2d at 192.

Examining the first factor, as with any other search and seizure, there must be probable cause for a warrant to be issued. Where such probable cause is not met, "the interests in human dignity and privacy which the Fourth Amendment protects forbid any such intrusion on the mere chance that desired evidence might be obtained." *Schmerber v. California, supra* at 769-70.

With respect to an emergency situation, *Schmerber* provides an example of such a case. The issue dealt with the amount of alcohol in the blood. Since alcohol in the blood diminishes shortly after drinking ceases, there was no time to find a magistrate and secure a warrant. It should be noted that tests to determine blood-type are to be distinguished from tests to determine alcohol in the blood; the "exigent circumstances" exception to the fourth amendment warrant requirement are not applicable to blood-type tests. *Mills v. State,* 28 Md. App. 300, 345 A.2d 127 (1975), *aff'd,* 278 Md. 262, 363 A.2d 491 (1976).

The second factor requires that the evidence sought (in *Schmerber* the degree to which the accused was under the influence of alcohol) should be obtained by a highly reliable and effective means (extraction of blood samples). See *Simms v. State, supra.* Thus, it is to be inferred that where the means sought to effectuate the purpose are unreliable, the intrusion would be unwarranted.

Under the third factor, as considered in Maryland case law, withdrawal of blood in a reasonable manner means the standard of safety which the Maryland legislature has required for traffic situations: A "qualified medical person," i.e., "any person permitted by law to withdraw blood from humans," shall obtain the blood for a blood test. Maryland Ann. Code, Courts and Judicial Proceedings § 10-304(a)(2) and (c). The person tested may have a physician of his own choosing administer a chemical test in addition to the one administered at the direction of the police officer. Additionally, the extraction must be performed "under clinical-like conditions." *Robinson v. State,* 18 Md. App. 678, 308 A.2d 734, 743 (1973). If no test is offered or requested by the police officer, a person may request, and the officer shall have administered, one of the chemical tests. Courts and Judicial Proceedings, § 10-304(d). In specific cases, medical personnel can take a blood test of a defendant who is unconscious if the procedure is valid. *Breithaupt v. Abram,* 352 U.S. 432, 77 S. Ct. 408, 1 L. Ed. 2d 448 (1957). The same holds true where blood is taken by subterfuge, as long as the defendant submits. *Davis v. State,* 189 Md. 640, 57 A.2d 289 (1948) (accused led to believe he was submitting to a test for medical purposes rather than criminal evidence). Also, in a traffic case, it was held that an advanced state of inebriation does not negate the capacity to consent to the test. *Mauldin v. State,* 239 Md. 592, 212 A.2d 502 (1965).

Whether the fact that the accused refused to submit to a test may be commented on at trial depends upon the circumstances surrounding the refusal. Since the right to compel the taking of the test rests on compliance with the fourth amendment and with the need for "clinical-like conditions," it would only seem natural that where authorities either have a search warrant or are confronted with an emergency situation and offer to perform the test under clinical-like conditions, refusal could be commented on at trial. In the alternative it would also seem that where refusal to submit is justified either because of lack of probable cause or because of unclinical type conditions, such refusal should not be commented on at trial. *Cf.* Courts and Judicial Proceedings, § 10-309(a), which provides, effective July 1, 1986, that the fact of a defendant's refusal to submit to any chemical test is admissible in evidence at trial for certain traffic offenses. If a person requests a chemical test and the officer refuses to administer it, a defendant can have that fact introduced into evidence. *Major v. State,* 31 Md. App. 590, 358 A.2d 609 (1976). In *South Dakota v. Neville,* 459 U.S. 553, 103 S. Ct. 916, 74 L. Ed. 748 (1983), the Supreme Court held that the admission into evidence of a defendant's refusal to submit to a blood-alcohol test does not offend the privilege against self-incrimination. The South Dakota statute permits a suspect to refuse to take a blood-alcohol test but authorizes revocation of the driver's license of a person who refuses the test and allows the refusal to be used as evidence against the defendant at trial. The Court noted that the blood-alcohol test is so safe, painless, and commonplace that the state could legitimately compel the suspect against his will to accede to the test. The action becomes no less legitimate when the state offers the option of refusing the test with penalties for making that choice.

Schmerber left open the issue of whether a search by means of a blood test is permissible where one asserts "grounds of fear, concern for health, or religious scruple." *Schmerber v. California, supra* at 771. This question remains to be decided in Maryland.

(b) Criminal traffic offenses

Article 66-1/2, Motor Vehicles, has been repealed and replaced by Maryland Ann. Code, Transportation Article. Under the statute, all drivers detained on suspicion of driving or attempting to drive while intoxicated or while under the influence of alcohol are deemed to have consented to take a chemical test to determine the alcohol content in their blood. Transportation, § 16-205.1(a).

As a result of the 1983 amendments to Maryland law, a person no longer has a right to select which of two tests, blood or breath, will be administered. The chemical test, however, will be used if (1) the defendant is unconscious or otherwise incapable of refusing to take a chemical test for alcohol; (2) injuries to the defendant require removal of the defendant to a medical facility; or (3) the equipment for administering the chemical breath test is not available. Courts and Judicial Proceedings, § 10-305(a). The urinalysis test is no longer statutorily authorized.

Although a driver is deemed to have consented, one who has not been involved in an accident which resulted in a death of another may not be compelled to take an alcohol test. A refusal, however, may result in suspension of a driver's license. One who has been involved in an accident involving a death is required to submit to a chemical test, as directed by the officer, of the person's blood or breath to determine the alcohol content. An officer may also direct a qualified medical person to withdraw blood for chemical test of an unconscious person so long as his health or well-being would not be jeopardized. See Transportation, § 16-205.1 and current supplement.

In other words, the courts have interpreted the requirement of consent very loosely; testing an unconscious person or using subterfuge to make one take the test, or testing a person so intoxicated that consent is not knowing, is of no consequence; the only issue of concern is whether there was a refusal. See *Mauldin v. State,* 239 Md. 592, 212 A.2d 502 (1965).

If legally obtained, results of a chemical test to determine blood-alcohol content may be admissible for prosecution of those charged with driving while intoxicated. For the results to be legal, the defendant may not have been compelled to submit to the analysis if no death has occurred. Effective July 1, 1986, an amendment to Courts and Judicial Proceedings, § 10-309(a), provides that while no "inference of presumption concerning either guilt or innocence arises because of refusal to submit," the "fact or refusal to submit is admissible in evidence at the trial." But if the defendant was involved in a motor vehicle accident that resulted in the death of another, results of chemical analysis are admissible regardless of whether consent was obtained. Transportation, § 16-205 (1982); Courts and Judicial Proceedings, § 10-309(a).

It has also been determined that the chemical analysis results are admissible as evidence when blood is extracted for the initial purpose of medical treatment. The Court of Appeals, in *State v. Moon,* 291 Md. 463, 436 A.2d 420 (1981) found no violation of Courts and Judicial Proceedings, § 10-309 where the accused did not affirmatively consent to a chemical test administered by or at the direction of a physician initially for the purpose of medical treatment. Therefore, the test results were admissible in subsequent prosecution for manslaughter by auto and driving while intoxicated.

An important change made in the 1978 amendment to the statute is that now a suspect may be stopped by the police while driving on any private property used by the public in general. Transportation, § 16-205.1(a) (1984).

Courts and Judicial Proceedings, § 10-307 deals with evidentiary presumptions arising from the admissibility of chemical tests measuring alcohol present in the blood or breath of the defendant. These presumptions are discussed: Instruction and Comment, § 4.63, Driving while intoxicated — Driving while under the influence, *infra.*

For further discussion of other crimes relating to driving while intoxicated, see Instructions and Comments: § 4.25, Manslaughter — By vehicle, and § 4.26, Homicide by motor vehicle while intoxicated, *infra.*

§ 2.33. Evidence of jurisdiction.

An offense against the laws of Maryland is punishable only if committed within the territorial limits of the State. You are instructed that evidence that a crime took place at a particular location within Maryland is sufficient to establish jurisdiction. Such evidence may be either direct or circumstantial.

COMMENT

The instruction appearing in the first edition of this book was titled "Evidence of Venue." In this edition, the section has been revised to refer to jurisdiction alone. Because jurisdiction and venue both relate to where the crime occurred, the terms are sometimes confused or used interchangeably. In Maryland, the distinction between jurisdiction and venue is maintained. See *State v. Jones,* 51 Md. App. 321, 443 A.2d 967 (1982), *vacated on other grounds,* 298 Md. 634, 471 A.2d 1055 (1984). While jurisdiction and venue both relate to where the crime occurred, venue presupposes the proper jurisdiction of a court. *Id.*

Jurisdiction refers to the power of the State to try the offense. A question of jurisdiction may be raised at any time, including on appeal, even though it was not raised and decided in the trial court. *Cooper v. State,* 44 Md. App. 59, 407 A.2d 756 (1979); *Miller v. State,* 44 Md. App. 587, 410 A.2d 1081 (1980), *rev'd on other grounds,* 289 Md. 443, 424 A.2d 1109 (1981). A question of jurisdiction, for example, is presented if there were an issue presented of whether the alleged crime occurred in Maryland or in the District of Columbia. See *Pennington v. State,* 308 Md. 727, 521 A.2d 1216 (1987).

It is well established in Maryland that "an offense against the laws of the State of Maryland is punishable only when committed within its territory." *Frasher v. State,* 8 Md. App. 439, 260 A.2d 656, 661, *cert. denied, McLaughlin v. Director, Patuxent Inst.,* 400 U.S. 959 (1970). See *Goodman v. State,* 237 Md. 64, 205 A.2d 53 (1964); *Breeding v. State,* 220 Md. 193, 151 A.2d 743

(1959); *Bowen v. State,* 206 Md. 368, 111 A.2d 844 (1955); *Banks v. State,* 2 Md. App. 373, 234 A.2d 798 (1967). Thus, jurisdiction would appear to be an element of the offense which the State must prove to the trier of fact beyond a reasonable doubt.

Venue, on the other hand, is not a fundamental question, but a question of policy. *State v. Batdorf,* 293 N.C. 486, 238 S.E.2d 497 (1977). It determines in which county the trial may be held; for example, whether the crime occurred in Prince George's County or Montgomery County. *McBurney v. State,* 280 Md. 21, 371 A.2d 129 (1977). Several earlier cases indicated that the issue of venue was part of the prosecution's case in chief, and, therefore, ultimately determined by the triers of fact, *Martel v. State,* 221 Md. 294, 157 A.2d 437 (1960); *Breeding v. State, supra.* This has been changed by Maryland Rule 4-252 which requires that a pretrial motion be filed as to any "defect in the institution of the prosecution" or as to any "defect on the charging document, other than its failure to show jurisdiction in the court ....", Maryland Rule 4-252(a). See *Carter v. State,* 38 Md. App. 400, 381 A.2d 309 (1978) (applying former Maryland Rule 725(b), the predecessor to former Rule 736(a)). Otherwise, unless good cause is shown, objections to such matters shall be deemed waived. *Id.* Therefore, questions of venue are usually settled before trial.

In the definition of some offenses there are provisions relating to where the crime may be tried. For example, Maryland Ann. Code, Art. 27, § 465 provides that if a person is transported by any means with the intent to violate the sexual offense statute, Art. 27, §§ 461 to 464D, the defendant may be tried in the jurisdiction where the transportation was offered, solicited, begun, continued, or ended. See *State v. Jones, supra.*

For a discussion of change in venue due to prejudicial pre-trial publicity, see *Simms v. State,* 49 Md. App. 515, 433 A.2d 1199 (1981) discussed in the Comment, § 1.11a, "Publicity cautioning," *supra.*

Chapter 3

STATES OF MIND—DEFINED

§ 3.01. General intent.
(a) Positive act.
(b) Failure to act where there is a duty to act.
§ 3.02. Specific intent.
§ 3.03. "Knowingly"—Defined.
§ 3.04. "Willfully"—Defined.
§ 3.05. "Fraudulent" (intent to defraud)—Defined.
§ 3.06. "Maliciously"—Defined.
§ 3.07. Proof of intent, knowledge, willfulness, etc.

§ 3.01. General intent.

(a) Positive act

You are instructed that intent is an essential element of the crime. Intent is a state of mind. General intent means that the defendant acted with a will to do a given act. It is a voluntary and knowing commission of an act which the law forbids. The defendant must have done the act consciously and voluntarily, and not inadvertently or accidentally.

[It has also been defined as the exercise of intelligent will, the mind being fully aware of the nature of the act which is about to be done, and with such knowledge and full liberty of action, willing and electing to do the act.]

[It is irrelevant that the defendant was ignorant of the fact that his act was a violation of the law.]

Intent ordinarily cannot be proved directly, but you may infer the defendant's intent from the surrounding circumstances. You should consider all of the facts and circumstances in evidence bearing on the defendant's state of mind. [In this regard, you may consider any statement made and act done or omitted by the defendant.]

You are instructed that you must find the element of intent before the defendant can be convicted. If the State does not prove beyond a reasonable doubt that the defendant acted with the required intent, you must find the defendant not guilty.

(b) Failure to act where there is a duty to act

You are instructed that intent is an essential element of the crime. Intent is a state of mind. General intent means that the defendant failed to act with a will not to do a given act. It is a voluntary and knowing omission to do an act required by law. The defendant's failure to do the act must have been conscious and voluntary, not inadvertent or accidental.

[It has also been defined as the exercise of intelligent will, the mind being fully aware of the omission to do an act which is required by law, and with such knowledge and full liberty of action, willing and electing not to do the act.]

[It is irrelevant that the defendant was ignorant of the fact that his omission to act was a violation of the law.]

Intent ordinarily cannot be proved directly. But you may infer the defendant's intent from the surrounding circumstances. You should consider all of the facts and circumstances in evidence bearing on the defendant's state of mind. [In this regard, you may consider any statement made and act done or omitted by the defendant.]

You are instructed that you must find the element of intent before the defendant can be convicted. If the State does not prove beyond a reasonable doubt that the defendant acted with the required intent, you must find the defendant not guilty.

COMMENT

The revised instruction deletes language which appeared in the first edition of this book as follows:

> Unless there is evidence presented to the contrary, the law presumes that a person intends the natural and probable consequences of his acts. Thus, the requisite criminal intent may be inferred from the defendant's voluntary and knowing commission of an act which is forbidden by law or from the defendant's omission to do an act required by law.

This revision was made to reflect a United States Supreme Court decision, *Sandstrom v. Montana,* 442 U.S. 510, 99 S. Ct. 2450, 61 L. Ed. 2d 4 (1979). In this case, the Court held that a jury instruction which stated "the law presumes that a person intends the ordinary consequences of his voluntary acts" unconstitutionally deprived defendant of his right to due process of law under the fourteenth amendment. The jury may have interpreted the judge's instruction as constituting a burden-shifting presumption like that in violation of *Mullaney v. Wilbur,* 421 U.S. 684, 686, 95 S. Ct. 1881, 44 L. Ed. 2d 508 (1975). Alternatively, the jury may have interpreted the judge's instruction as constituting a conclusive presumption in violation of *Morissette v. United States,* 342 U.S. 246, 72 S. Ct. 240, 96 L. Ed. 288 (1952) and *United States v. United States Gypsum,* 438 U.S. 422, 98 S. Ct. 2864, 57 L. Ed. 2d 854 (1978). Either interpretation would have deprived defendant of his right to the due process of law. The Court, in *Patterson v. New York,* 432 U.S. 197, 215, 97 S. Ct. 2319, 53 L. Ed. 2d 281 (1977), reaffirmed that "a State must prove every ingredient of an offense beyond a reasonable doubt, and ... may not shift the burden of proof to the defendant by means of such a presumption."

The Court, in *Sandstrom v. Montana, supra,* declined to characterize the questioned language as a "permissive inference" which allows but does not require the jury to draw conclusions about defendant's intent from his actions. The following language probably qualifies as a permissive inference:

> You may, but are not required, to infer that a person ordinarily intends the natural and probable consequences of acts knowingly done or knowingly omitted. However, you should consider all of the circumstances in evidence that you deem relevant in determining whether the State has proved beyond a reasonable doubt that the defendant acted with the required intent.

See Bar Association of the District of Columbia, *Criminal Jury Instructions for the District of Columbia* § 3.02 at 117 (3d ed. 1978). *Cf.* Instruction, § 3.07, Proof of intent, knowledge, willfulness, etc., *infra.* See also *Briscoe v. State,* 60 Md. App. 42, 45-46, 479 A.2d 1385, 1387 (1984); *Turner v. State,* 55 Md. App. 367, 371, 462 A.2d 70, 72-73 (1983), *modified,* 301 Md. 180, 482 A.2d 869 (1984).

Intent has been defined as the exercise of intelligent will, the mind being fully aware of the nature and consequences of the act which is about to be done with such knowledge and liberty of action, willingly and electing to do it. *Nance v. State,* 7 Md. App. 433, 256 A.2d 377 (1969), *cert. denied,* 398 U.S. 954 (1970).

Intent is a question of fact, subjective in nature and, therefore, can only be determined by a consideration of the defendant's acts and words. *Taylor v. State,* 238 Md. 424, 209 A.2d 595 (1965). See *Morissette v. United States, supra,* and *Perez v. State,* 7 Md. App. 452, 256 A.2d 369 (1969).

Gladden v. State, 20 Md. App. 492, 316 A.2d 319 (1974), a case of first impression for transferred intent, held "that the doctrine of transferred intent is the law of Maryland and that whatever *mens rea* a defendant entertains as to his intended target will carry over to any intended victim ...." *Id.* at 498, 316 A.2d at 322.

§ 3.02. Specific intent.

The defendant is charged with __________ *(specify crime),* an element of which requires specific intent. Intent is a state of mind. Specific intent requires more than a general intent to engage in certain conduct or to do certain acts. To establish specific intent, the State must prove that the defendant knowingly and willfully did an act which the law prohibits, intending a result which is prohibited by law, namely __________ *(insert particular facts of the case to which the specific intent element applies).*

Specific intent is a subjective matter which can seldom be proven directly. But you may infer the defendant's intent from the surrounding circumstances. You should consider all of the facts and circumstances in evidence bearing on the defendant's state of mind. [In this regard, you may consider any statement made and act done or omitted by the defendant.]

You are instructed that you must find the element of specific intent before the defendant can be convicted. If the State does not prove beyond a reasonable doubt that the defendant acted with the required specific intent, you must find the defendant not guilty.

COMMENT

Specific intent was originally required to prove only infamous crimes. For a concise sketch of the development of specific intent, see *Morissette v. United States,* 342 U.S. 246, 72 S. Ct. 240, 96 L. Ed. 288 (1952).

Each specific intent crime has, as one of its elements, an intent to commit the particular offense charged. Examples of this are larceny and robbery, both of which are specific intent crimes:

> [One] element of larceny is the larcenous intent; so every robbery embraces a larcenous intent. This means that every robber must intend to steal the property taken. The crucial ingredient of larcenous intent is that the intent be to deprive the owner ... permanently of his property.

Wiggins v. State, 8 Md. App. 598, 604, 261 A.2d 503, 507 (1970).

For a thorough discussion of the distinction between specific and general intent, see 21 Am. Jur. 2d *Criminal Law* §§ 129, 130 (1981).

Maryland does not recognize the doctrine of diminished capacity; therefore, it does not negate the element of specific intent. See Comment, § 5.08, subpart (h), Diminished capacity not recognized, *infra.* Voluntary intoxication, however, is a condition which can negate the element of specific intent to commit certain crimes. See Instruction, § 5.01, Voluntary drunkenness, *infra.*

§ 3.03. "Knowingly" — Defined.

"Knowingly" is generally defined as having knowledge. An act is done knowingly if done voluntarily and purposely, and not because of mistake, accident, inadvertence or other innocent reason. The purpose of the word "knowingly" is to ensure that no one would be convicted for an act done where there exists a reasonable, innocent explanation. The State has the burden of proving knowledge beyond a reasonable doubt. Knowledge can be established from all the surrounding facts and circumstances of the case. A person may be found to have knowledge where he acts with an unlawful purpose and deliberately ignores the obvious.

COMMENT

This instruction is patterned primarily after the leading case of *Greenway v. State,* 8 Md. App. 194, 259 A.2d 89 (1969). The main purpose for defining the word "knowingly" is to ensure that no person would be convicted for an act done where there is a reasonable, nonculpable explanation. *Id.* at 196.

"Knowingly" may be ascertained from evidence establishing actual or direct knowledge. *Woodruff v. State,* 11 Md. App. 202, 228, 273 A.2d 436 (1971); *Clarke v. State,* 9 Md. App. 570, 573, 266 A.2d 359 (1970). It may also be established from circumstantial evidence giving rise to an inference which is not irrational or arbitrary. See *Greenway v. State, supra* at 196. Further, as *Clarke* pointed out:

> It is a well recognized rule of law that an individual with an unlawful purpose in mind, who deliberately "shuts his eyes" to avoid knowing what would otherwise be obvious to view, acts at his peril in this regard as far as the criminal law is concerned, and is treated as having knowledge of the facts as they ultimately are discovered to be.

Clarke v. State, supra at 573. See *United States v. Squires,* 440 F.2d 859, 864 (2d Cir. 1971); R. Perkins, *Criminal Law* 771-79 (2d ed. 1969).

See Instruction, § 3.07, Proof of intent, knowledge, willfulness, etc., *infra.*

§ 3.04. "Willfully" — Defined.

"Willfully" characterizes an act which is done knowingly, with deliberate intention and for which there is no reasonable excuse. The element of deliberate intention requires that there be a full and conscious design to do an act which is a violation of the law. An act that is done merely accidentally, inadvertently, or negligently is not done willfully.

COMMENT

The word "willfully," when used as an element of a crime, means an act done knowingly and with deliberate intention. *Ewell v. State,* 207 Md. 288, 299, 114 A.2d 66, 72 (1955); *Rosenberg v. State,* 164 Md. 473, 165 A. 306 (1933); *DeBettencourt v. State,* 48 Md. App. 522, 428 A.2d 479, 481 (1981); *Duncan v. State,* 5 Md. App. 440, 445, 248 A.2d 176, 178-79 (1968). Thus, the element of "willfulness" is satisfied if the act was done "knowingly" and with a full and conscious design to breach a statute. It is not satisfied by an act that is done merely accidentally, inadvertently, or negligently. *Leatherwood v. State,* 49 Md. App. 683, 435 A.2d 477 (1981). See also *Elliot v. State,* 215 Md. 152, 160, 137 A.2d 130 (1957); *Faulcon v. State,* 211 Md. 249, 257, 126 A.2d 858 (1956). The phrase, "conscious design to do an act which is a violation of the law," relates the mental state to a requisite act, rather than to a legal standard.

"Knowingly" is used in this definition in the same way as defined in Instruction, § 3.03, "Knowingly" — Defined, *supra;* that is, to ensure that no person would be convicted for an act done where there is a reasonable, nonculpable explanation. *Greenway v. State,* 8 Md. App. 194, 196, 259 A.2d 89 (1969).

Finally, there is no requirement of a finding that willfully includes a bad purpose or evil intent to do something the law forbids. See *Ewell v. State, supra; Rosenberg v. State, supra.* To require in a case a finding of a bad purpose would be either to confuse the concept of intent with that of motive, *United States v. Moylan,* 417 F.2d 1002, 1004 (4th Cir. 1969), or to confuse the definition of willful with that of malicious and willful. See *Duncan v. State, supra* at 445. For a general discussion of "willfulness," see R. Perkins & R. Boyce, *Criminal Law* ch. 7, § 4(D) at 875-79 (3d ed. 1982). See Comment, § 3.06, "Maliciously" — Defined, *infra.*

See Instruction, § 3.07, Proof of intent, knowledge, willfulness, etc., *infra.*

§ 3.05. "Fraudulent" (intent to defraud) — Defined.

To act fraudulently or with intent to defraud means to act willfully and deliberately and with the specific intent to deceive or cheat.

COMMENT

"Fraudulent" as used in the definition of a crime means a willful and deliberate intention to defraud. *Roderick v. State,* 9 Md. App. 120, 262 A.2d 783 (1970). "Any crime which requires fraud for its perpetration is one which includes a specific 'intent' whether or not the word 'intent' is found in the definition." *Id.* at 125, 262 A.2d at 785-86.

See Instructions: § 3.02, Specific intent, *supra;* § 3.04, "Willfully" — Defined, *supra;* § 3.07, Proof of intent, knowledge, willfulness, etc., *infra.*

§ 3.06. "Maliciously" — Defined.

An act done "maliciously" is done knowingly and with deliberate intention to do harm to another, for which there is no reasonable excuse. The element of deliberate intention requires that there be a full and conscious design to do an act which is a violation of the law. An act that is done merely accidentally, inadvertently, or negligently is not done maliciously.

COMMENT

The word "maliciously," when used as an element of a crime, means an act done with the deliberate intention of causing harm to another. *Brown v. State,* 285 Md. 469, 403 A.2d 788 (1979). This harm may be physical or financial and must be proved. Thus, the fact that it was proven that the defendant willfully set fire to his own uninsured building was insufficient. *Id.* at 475, 403 A.2d at 791-93.

"Knowingly" is used in this definition in the same way as it has been previously defined; that is, to insure that no person would be convicted for an act done where there is a reasonable, nonculpable explanation. *Greenway v. State,* 8 Md. App. 194, 196, 259 A.2d 89 (1969). The element of "deliberate intention" is satisfied when there is a full and conscious design to do that which breaches a statute. See *Elliott v. State,* 215 Md. 152, 160, 137 A.2d 130 (1957); *Faulcon v. State,* 211 Md. 249, 257, 126 A.2d 858 (1956).

The term "malice" has been held to have the same meaning under the law of homicide as it does under arson law. See *DeBettencourt v. State,* 48 Md. App. 522, 428 A.2d 479, 480 (1981). In *DeBettencourt,* the Court held that the term "malice" can be defined as "the reckless doing of a dangerous act [e.g., setting a fire] with wanton indifference to the consequences [of the danger of bringing harm to others] under the law of arson." *Id.* at 532, 428 A.2d at 485.

For a discussion of arson, see Comment, § 4.52, *infra.* For a general discussion of malice as an element of murder, see Comment, § 4.22a, *infra.*

See Instruction, § 3.07 — Proof of intent, knowledge, willfulness, etc., *infra.*

§ 3.07. Proof of intent, knowledge, willfulness, etc.

__________ (*insert mens rea element*) is a state of mind. It is a subjective matter which can seldom be proven with direct evidence. But you may infer __________ (*insert mens rea element*) by drawing inferences from facts proved which reasonably indicate under all of the relevant circumstances the existence of the required state of mind. You should consider all of the facts and circumstances in evidence bearing on the defendant's state of mind. [In this regard, you may consider any statement made and act done or omitted by the defendant.]

You are instructed that you must find the element of __________ (*insert mens rea element*) before the defendant can be convicted. If the State does not prove beyond a reasonable doubt that the defendant acted with the required state of mind, namely, __________ (*insert mens rea element and relate to particular facts of case*), you must find the defendant not guilty.

COMMENT

This instruction has been substantially incorporated in Instructions, §§ 3.01 and 3.02, *supra,* and does not need to be given with those instructions.

This instruction deletes the following language which appeared in the first edition of this book: "You may presume that a person ordinarily intends the natural and probable consequences of his acts." This revision was made to reflect the decision of the Supreme Court of the United States in *Sandstrom v. Montana,* 442 U.S. 510, 99 S. Ct. 2450, 6 L. Ed. 2d 4 (1979). For a discussion of this case and its implications for proving intent, see Comment, § 3.01, General intent, *supra.*

Intent "is seldom proved directly, but is more often found by drawing inferences from facts proved which reasonably indicate under all the circumstances the existence of the required intent." *Waller v. State,* 13 Md. App. 615, 618, 284 A.2d 446, 447 (1971). "Intent, of course, is a subjective matter and may be proved by establishing facts which permit a reasonable inference that the accused intended the consequences of his acts. *Davis v. State,* 204

Md. 44, 102 A.2d 816 (1954)." *Yopps v. State,* 234 Md. 216, 220-21, 198 A.2d 264, 266 (1964); *Perez v. State,* 7 Md. App. 452, 455, 256 A.2d 369, 370 (1969). Thus, proof of intent is of necessity accomplished by circumstantial evidence where all of the facts and relevant circumstances must be considered. *Taylor v. State,* 238 Md. 424, 209 A.2d 595 (1965). See *Yopps v. State, supra.*

PART II
OFFENSES

Chapter 4

SPECIFIC INSTRUCTIONS

A. Offenses—Generally

§ 4.01. Accessory before the fact.
§ 4.02. Aiding and abetting.
§ 4.03. Accessory after the fact.
§ 4.04. Acts committed through innocent agents.
§ 4.05. Attempt.
§ 4.06. Conspiracy.

B. Assault

§ 4.11. Assault.
§ 4.12. Battery.
§ 4.13. Assault with intent to murder.
§ 4.14. Assault with intent to rob.
§ 4.15. Assault with intent to commit sexual intercourse with a female under the age of fourteen where the male is four or more years older.
§ 4.16. Assault with intent to rape or to commit a first or second degree sexual offense.

C. Homicide

§ 4.20. Introductory instruction on grading of homicide.
§ 4.21a. Murder—First degree: willful, deliberate and premeditated killing.
§ 4.21b. Murder—First degree: felony murder.
§ 4.21c. Murder—First degree: death penalty sentencing.
§ 4.22a. Murder—Second degree.
§ 4.22b. Murder—When both first and second degree murder are in issue.
§ 4.23a. Manslaughter—Voluntary: general instruction.
§ 4.23b. Manslaughter—Voluntary: amplified instruction including special sources of provocation.
(1) Mutual combat.
(2) Battery.
(3) Spousal adultery.
(4) Words plus threatening conduct.
§ 4.23c. Manslaughter—Voluntary (suggested instruction on imperfect self-defense).
§ 4.24. Manslaughter—Involuntary.
(a) Which occurs as the result of doing some lawful act with gross negligence.
(b) Which is caused by the grossly negligent omission to perform a legal duty.
(c) Which occurs during the course of some unlawful act.
§ 4.25. Manslaughter—By vehicle.
§ 4.26. Homicide by motor vehicle while intoxicated (suggested instruction).

D. Sexual Offenses

1. Offenses Retained After 1976 Revision of Sexual Offense Laws

§ 4.33. Incest.
§ 4.34. Sodomy.
§ 4.35. Unnatural or perverted sexual practices.

2. 1976 Revised Rape and Sexual Offense Laws

§ 4.36. Rape offenses.
(a) Rape—First degree.
(b) Rape—Second degree.
(c) Rape—Second degree: victim under fourteen years and person performing act four or more years older than victim.
(d) Rape—Second degree: mentally defective, mentally incapacitated or physically helpless victim.
§ 4.37. Sexual offenses in the first, second, third and fourth degree.
(a) Sexual offense—First degree.
(b) Sexual offense—Second degree.
(c) Sexual offense—Second degree: victim under fourteen years and person performing act four or more years older than victim.
(d) Sexual offense—Second degree: mentally defective, mentally incapacitated or physically helpless person.
(e) Sexual offense—Third degree.
(f) Sexual offense—Third degree: victim under fourteen years and person performing act four or more years older than victim.
(g) Sexual offense—Third degree: mentally defective, mentally incapacitated or physically helpless victim.
(h) Sexual offense—Fourth degree.
(i) Sexual offense—Fourth degree: vaginal intercourse with person fourteen or fifteen years of age and person performing act four or more years older than victim.
(j) Sexual offense—Fourth degree: "sexual act" with person fourteen or fifteen years of age and person performing act four or more years older than victim.

E. Weapons Offenses

§ 4.41. Carrying or wearing a concealed weapon.
§ 4.42. Carrying a weapon openly with intent to injure.
§ 4.43. Wearing, carrying or transporting handgun, openly or concealed.
(a) On or about the person.
(b) In any vehicle traveling upon public roads, highways, etc.
§ 4.44. Use of handgun in the commission of a felony or crime of violence.

F. Other Offenses

§ 4.51. Abortion.
§ 4.52. Arson.

§ 4.53. Breaking—Storehouse, etc., with intent to commit a felony or steal (Article 27, § 32).
§ 4.54. Breaking—Storehouse, etc., with intent to steal any money, goods or chattels under the value of $300 (Article 27, § 33A).
§ 4.55. Breaking—Storehouse, etc., with the taking of property (Article 27, § 33).
§ 4.56. Bribery—Obstructing justice.
(a) Attempting to bribe.
(b) Offering a bribe.
(c) Receiving a bribe.
(d) Demanding a bribe.
§ 4.57. Burglary.
§ 4.58. Child abuse.
(a) Child abuse based on physical injury.
(b) Child abuse based on sexual molestation or exploitation.
§ 4.59. Contempt.
§ 4.60. Nonsupport.
§ 4.61. Disorderly conduct.
(a) Disorderly conduct generally.
(b) Profane cursing and swearing.
(c) Loud and unseemly noises.
§ 4.62. Disorderly house.
§ 4.63. Driving while intoxicated—Driving while under the influence of alcohol and/or drugs.
§ 4.64. Embezzlement.
§ 4.65. Escape.
§ 4.66. Extortion—Verbal threat.
§ 4.67. False pretenses.
§ 4.68. Forgery and uttering.
(a) Forgery.
(b) Uttering.
§ 4.69. Housebreaking—Daytime.
§ 4.70. Kidnapping.
§ 4.71. Larceny.
§ 4.72. Larceny after trust.
§ 4.73. Larceny of use—Unauthorized use of motor vehicle, boat or livestock.
§ 4.74. Lotteries.
(a) Keeping a place for selling lottery tickets.
(b) Owner permitting use of house or office for sale of lottery tickets.
§ 4.75. Malicious mischief—Malicious destruction of property.
§ 4.76. Narcotics—Possession (actual and constructive).
§ 4.77. Narcotics—Manufacture, distribution, dispensation or possession with intent to sell.
(a) Manufacture, distribute or dispense.
(b) Possession with intent to sell.
§ 4.78. Perjury and subornation of perjury.
(a) Perjury.
(b) Subornation of perjury.
§ 4.79. Receiving stolen goods.
§ 4.80. Resisting arrest.

§ 4.81. Riot.
§ 4.82. Robbery.
§ 4.83. Robbery with a deadly weapon.
§ 4.84. Shoplifting.
§ 4.85. Trespass.
(a) Upon private land or vessel (Article 27, § 577).
(b) Refusal to leave public buildings (Article 27, § 577A).
§ 4.86. Unlawful use of telephone.

G. Theft and Bad Check Offenses

1. Theft Offenses

Overview and Introductory Comment

§ 4.91. Theft—By unauthorized control.
§ 4.92. Theft—By deception.
§ 4.93. Theft—By possessing stolen property.
§ 4.94. Theft—Of lost, mislaid or mistakenly delivered property.
§ 4.95. Theft—Of services.
§ 4.96. General instruction—"Rights of possession" and certain defenses applicable to theft offenses.

2. Bad Checks—Obtaining Property or Services by Bad Check

Introductory Comment

§ 4.97a. Acts committed by a drawer or representative with knowledge of insufficient funds.
§ 4.97b. Acts committed by passers (payees, holders and bearers) of checks with knowledge of insufficient funds.
§ 4.97c. Acts committed by a drawer or representative who issues a check with intent to stop payment.
§ 4.97d. Acts committed by passers (payees, holders and bearers) of checks with knowledge that payment has been stopped.

A. Offenses—Generally

§ 4.01. Accessory before the fact.

The defendant is charged with having been an accessory before the fact to the crime of __________ *(insert offense).* A person who is an accessory before the fact may be guilty of the principal offense even though he did not personally commit the acts constituting the offense.

An accessory before the fact is one who instigates, advises, encourages, or commands the commission of crime, but is not present at the time of the commission of the crime.

Presence may be actual or constructive. A person is constructively present if he is acting with the person who actually commits the crime, both pursuing a common purpose, and is aiding his associate, either by keeping watch or otherwise; or is so situated as to be able to aid him, with a view known to the other, to ensure success in the accomplishment of the common enterprise. If you find that the defendant was present at the time of the commission of the crime, either actually or constructively, then you must find that the defendant was not an accessory before the fact.

In order for a person to be convicted as an accessory before the fact, the State must prove beyond a reasonable doubt each of the elements of the underlying crime, including that the crime was committed by someone other than the defendant. [However, the principal perpetrator of an offense need not be convicted in order to convict the defendant as an accessory before the fact.]

COMMENT

At common law, parties to a felony are classified as principals in the first degree, principals in the second degree, accessories before the fact, and accessories after the fact. See Comment, §4.02, Aiding and abetting, for a discussion of the relationship of an accessory before the fact to a principal in the second degree.

An accessory before (or after) the fact can be tried regardless of whether the principal has been tried or convicted. As long as the evidence in the accessory's trial is sufficient to demonstrate that a felony has been committed, the fact that the principal has not been tried or convicted will furnish no defense to the accessory. *Lewis v. State,* 285 Md. 705, 404 A.2d 1073 (1979).

In *Jones v. State,* 302 Md. 153, 486 A.2d 184 (1985), the Court abrogated the common-law rule that an accessory may not be convicted of a greater crime than that of which his principal was convicted. The Court held on January 9, 1985, that in cases where the trial of accessories before the fact commences after the date of the opinion, an accessory before the fact may be convicted of a greater crime or greater degree of crime than that of which his principal was convicted.

An indictment in the form of the statute apparently is sufficient to sustain a charge of accessory before the fact even though the defendant was not specifically charged as an accessory. *State v. Ward,* 284 Md. 189, 396 A.2d 1041 (1978), *aff'd,* 427 A.2d 1008 (1981), *aff'd,* 447 A.2d 872 (1982). *But cf. Butina v. State,* 4 Md. App. 312, 242 A.2d 819 (1968). In *Howell v. State,* 62 Md. App. 278, 489 A.2d 55 (1985), the Court noted that *Lewis, supra,* abrogated the common-law rule that an accessory could not be tried until the principal was tried, convicted and sentenced. That change, however, does not relieve the State from establishing in the trial of an accessory that a completed felony was committed, whether the accessory's trial precedes or follows that of the principal. *Id.* 489 A.2d at 58.

A person cannot be convicted on the uncorroborated testimony of an accomplice. This includes an accessory before the fact. See Instruction, § 2.01, Accomplice's testimony — Corroboration, *supra.*

See generally *State v. Ward, supra; State v. Williamson,* 282 Md. 100, 382 A.2d 588 (1978), *aff'd,* 284 Md. 212, 395 A.2d 496 (1979); *Fabian v. State,* 235 Md. 306, 201 A.2d 511, *cert. denied,* 379 U.S. 869 (1964); *Watson v. State,* 208 Md. 210, 117 A.2d 549 (1955); *Huff v. State,* 23 Md. App. 211, 326 A.2d 198 (1974); *Butina v. State, supra;* and *Sanders v. State,* 1 Md. App. 630, 232 A.2d 555 (1967).

§ 4.02. Aiding and abetting.

A person who aids or abets the principal offender may be guilty of the principal offense even though he did not personally commit each of the acts constituting the offense and was not personally present at its commission.

To be an "aider" a person must assist, support or supplement the efforts of another. To be an "abettor" a person must instigate, advise or encourage the commission of a crime.

A person aids or abets another in the commission of a crime if he knowingly associates himself in some way with the criminal venture, or willfully participates in it as he would in something he wishes to bring about; that is to say, that he willfully seeks by some act or omission of his to make the crime succeed.

The mere physical presence by the person at the time and place of commission of such offense is not by itself sufficient to establish his guilt, but may be considered along with all the surrounding circumstances.

In order for a person to be convicted as an aider and abettor, the State must prove beyond a reasonable doubt each of the elements of the underlying crime, including that the crime was committed by someone other than the defendant. [However, the principal perpetrator of the offense need not be convicted in order to convict the defendant as an aider or abettor.]

COMMENT

This instruction is patterned substantially after holdings in various Maryland cases.

To be an aider, a person must assist, support or supplement the efforts of another; to be an abettor, a person must instigate, advise or encourage the commission of a crime and may in some instances include a person who is present at the commission of a crime without giving active assistance. *Coleman v. State,* 4 Md. App. 386, 391, 243 A.2d 24, 27 (1968). The aiding and abetting must have been done with guilty knowledge, actual or constructive. *Malloy v. State,* 4 Md. App. 420, 243 A.2d 649 (1968).

To be an aider or abettor, it is not essential that there be a prearranged concert of action. It is essential that the person accused should in some way advocate or encourage the commission of the crime. *Camphor v. State,* 233 Md. 203, 196 A.2d 75 (1963).

Under common law, persons present, actually or constructively, in aiding and abetting the commission of a crime (but not themselves committing it), are principals in the second degree. *Agresti v. State,* 2 Md. App. 278, 280, 234 A.2d 284, 285 (1967). A principal in the second degree can be found guilty of the offense that the actual perpetrator committed. *McEntire v. State,* 2 Md. App. 449, 453, 235 A.2d 311, 313 (1967). See *Pope v. State,* 284 Md. 309, 396 A.2d 1054 (1979); *State v. Ward,* 284 Md. 189, 396 A.2d 1041 (1978), *aff'd,* 290 Md. 76, 427 A.2d 1008 (1981), *aff'd,* 52 Md. App. 63, 447 A.2d 872 (1982); *McBryde v. State,* 30 Md. App. 357, 352 A.2d 324 (1976); *Butina v. State,* 4 Md. App. 312, 242 A.2d 819 (1968). One who keeps watch or guard at such convenient distance during a robbery is clearly a principal. *Thomas v. State,* 2 Md. App. 502, 507, 235 A.2d 777, 780 (1967), *cert. denied,* 392 U.S. 938 (1968). As to indictment, conviction and punishment, there is no distinction between principals in the first and second degree. *Thomas v. State,* 3 Md. App. 708, 240 A.2d 646 (1968). In Maryland there is no practical distinction between principals in the first and second degree. *Butina v. State, supra* at 318, 242 A.2d at 822. See also *Funkhouser v. State,* 51 Md. App. 16, 446 A.2d 1114 (1982).

See *Handy v. State,* 23 Md. App. 239, 326 A.2d 189 (1974), which provides a detailed summary and discussion of the law of aiding and abetting. In particular, the Court noted that:

> Maryland follows the common law that all participants in misdemeanors are principals. *Broadway v. State,* 23 Md. App. 68, 326 A.2d 212 (1974). *See Novak v. State,* 214 Md. 472, 136 A.2d 256 (1957).

Id. at 250-51, 326 A.2d at 195.

At common law there was a distinction between an accessory before the fact and a principal in the second degree for felonies. An accessory before the fact is one who is guilty of felony by reason of having aided, counseled, commanded, or encouraged the commission thereof, without having been present either actually or constructively at the moment of perpetration. Presence (or absence) at the scene of the crime thus appears to be the key factor which at common law distinguished an accessory before the fact from a principal in the second degree. *State v. Williamson,* 282 Md. 100, 105, 382 A.2d 588, 591 (1978), *aff'd,* 284 Md. 212, 395 A.2d 496 (1979). See *McBryde v. State, supra.* This presence could be constructive. R. Perkins & R. Boyce, *Criminal Law* ch. 5, § 8 at 741 (3d ed. 1982) states:

> A person is regarded as constructively present, within the rules relating to parties in criminal cases, whenever he is cooperating with the perpetrator and is so situated as to be able to aid him, with a view known to the other, to insure success in the accomplishment of the common purpose.

(*quoting Skidmore v. State,* 80 Neb. 698, 700, 115 N.W. 288, 289 (1908)).

In *Turner v. State,* 45 Md. App. 168, 175, 411 A.2d 1094, 1099 (1980), the Court held that if the jury found that the defendant was at the scene of the crime, in close proximity, or in concert with the actual perpetrator of the offense, with the purpose of assisting, watching, encouraging or preventing interference with offense at the time of its commission, then the jury may find the defendant a principal and, as such, guilty of the crime charged. In *McBryde v. State, supra,* 352 A.2d at 327, the Court stated that persons waiting in a getaway car during the commission of a felony are principals in the second degree.

With respect to the common-law rule concerning principals in the second degree, there seems to be misleading dictum in *Agresti v. State,* 2 Md. App. 278, 234 A.2d 284 (1967), later quoted in *McBryde v. State, supra.* In *Agresti,* the Court states: "Under common law, persons present, actually or constructively, aiding and abetting the commission of the crime, but not themselves committing it, are principals in the second degree, *provided there is a guilty principal in the first degree.*" *Id.* at 280, 234 A.2d at 285 (emphasis added). R. Perkins & R. Boyce, *Criminal Law* ch. 6, § 8(D) at 752-53 (3d ed. 1982) correctly states the common-law view as follows:

> With reference to trial, the principal in the second degree may be tried and convicted prior to the trial of the principal in the first degree or even after the latter has been tried and acquitted. Furthermore, a principal in the second degree may be convicted of a higher degree of guilt than the principal in the first degree.

W. LaFave & A. Scott, *Criminal Law* 500 (1972) affirms the above position with respect to the common-law approach toward principals in the second degree.

At common law, an indictment must charge a person correctly as principal or accessory according to the facts and on an indictment charging a person as principal, there could be no conviction on evidence merely showing that he was an accessory and vice versa. *McBryde v. State, supra,* 352 A.2d at 327, *citing Agresti v. State, supra.*

In *McBryde v. State, supra,* the indictment charged the appellants as accessories before the fact, but the evidence showed they were principals in the second degree. Since the appellants were incorrectly charged, the Court held that their motion for judgment of acquittal should have been granted.

The formal requirements have been relaxed in homicide cases. The Court of Appeals held, in *State v. Williamson, supra,* that a person indicted for murder in the general form prescribed by Maryland Ann. Code, Art. 27, § 616, may be convicted of murder in the first degree even if the accused was an accessory before the fact. The Court declined to decide whether or not the common-law distinctions between accessories before the fact and principals in the first and second degree continue to have validity in Maryland. The Court discussed the common law distinctions as follows:

> The distinction between accessories before the fact and principals continually grows more illusory. It certainly was one of the "technical quibbles" addressed by the General Assembly when it enacted this form of indictment in 1906. Regardless of the reasons which may have existed at common law for requiring an accessory to be indicted as such with regard to murder, it is no longer necessary to make such distinctions in an indictment in this State and has not been necessary for almost three-quarters of a century. Mrs. Williamson

> having been indicted for the murder of her husband in a form which permitted proof either that she was a principal or an accessory, and the evidence adduced having been sufficient to convict her as an accessory before the fact, there was no error.

Id. at 110, 382 A.2d at 593.

When a person aids or abets in the commission of one crime and other crimes are committed, he may be liable for all crimes which occurred in furtherance of the common design or plan to commit the crime which he aided or abetted or which were the natural or probable consequences of the crime that he aided or abetted. In *Jeter v. State,* 9 Md. App. 575, 267 A.2d 319 (1970), *aff'd,* 261 Md. 221, 274 A.2d 337 (1971) the defendant was a "lookout" for an accomplice who he knew was armed and who entered a building to commit a storehouse breaking. The defendant was arrested by police in response to a silent alarm. After he was taken into custody, his accomplice in the building shot and killed a guard. The defendant's conviction for murder as a principal in the second degree was upheld. The court noted that it made no difference that he was in custody when the murder occurred or that he did not know his accomplice intended to kill the guard. He set out to perform the storehouse breaking with an armed accomplice and was an accessory to felony murder. See also *Burko v. State,* 19 Md. App. 645, 313 A.2d 864 (1974), *cert. granted, judgment vacated & remanded,* 422 U.S. 1003, *judgment vacated & remanded,* 275 Md. 598, *judgment reinstated,* 28 Md. App. 732, 349 A.2d 355 (1975), *cert. denied,* 429 U.S. 981 (1976).

For certain crimes, such as arson and statutory burglary, the legislature has made clear in the statute that persons who would have been guilty as accessories at common law are guilty as principals in the first degree. See, e.g., Maryland Ann. Code, Art. 27, §§ 6 to 10.

An aider or abettor cannot be convicted on the uncorroborated testimony of an accomplice. See Instruction, § 2.01, Accomplice's testimony — Corroboration, *supra.* See also Instruction, § 4.01, Accessory before the fact, *supra.*

§ 4.03. Accessory after the fact.

An accessory after the fact is one who, knowing that a felony has been committed, receives, relieves or comforts the felon or gives him any other assistance in order to hinder his apprehension, trial or punishment.

In order to be guilty of this offense: (1) the defendant must have become associated with a felony after its commission; (2) the defendant must have provided assistance with knowledge that the felony has been completed; (3) the assistance must have been given to one known to be the felon; and (4) the assistance must have been given in order to hinder the felon's apprehension, trial or punishment.

The term "knowledge" means that at the time the relief or assistance was given the defendant must have had actual knowledge that the person assisted was one who had committed a felony. An act is done knowingly if done purposely, and not because of mistake, accident, inadvertence or other innocent reason. Knowledge can be inferred from all the surrounding facts and circumstances of the case. [In this regard, you may consider any statement made and act done or omitted by the defendant.]

The term "assistance" means that there must be a positive affirmative act intended to help or aid someone to escape arrest, capture or punishment. The mere failure to disclose the commission of the felony or to apprehend the felon, or mere approval of the felony is not sufficient to constitute an accessory after the fact. In order for one to be an accessory after the fact, it is essential that he was absent at the time the crime was committed.

In order for a person to be convicted as an accessory after the fact, the State must prove beyond a reasonable doubt each of the elements of the underlying crime, including that the crime was committed by someone other than the defendant. [However, the principal perpetrator of the offense need not be convicted in order to convict the defendant as an accessory after the fact.]

COMMENT

Under the common law, parties to a felony are classified as principals and accessories. An accessory after the fact "does not become connected with the offense until after its commission; he does not in any way share the guilt for the substantive crime." *McClain v. State,* 10 Md. App. 106, 268 A.2d 572 (1970). See *Howell v. State,* 62 Md. App. 278, 489 A.2d 55 (1985), for discussion of requirements for proof of this element. See also *State v. Ward,* 284 Md. 189, 396 A.2d 1041 (1978), *aff'd,* 270 Md. 76, 427 A.2d 1008 (1981), *aff'd,* 62 Md. App. 63, 447 A.2d 872 (1982).

An accessory after the fact has been defined as "one who knowing that a felony has been committed, harbors and protects the felon or renders him any other assistance to elude punishment." *Watson v. State,* 208 Md. 210, 117 A.2d 549 (1955). See also *Cooper v. State,* 44 Md. App. 59, 407 A.2d 756 (1979); *Robinson v. State,* 5 Md. App. 723, 249 A.2d 504 (1969).

It has been stated that:

> ... any assistance given to one known to be a felon in order to hinder his apprehension, trial or punishment, is sufficient to make a man an accessory after the fact; as that he concealed him in the house, or shut the door against the pursuers, until he should have an opportunity to escape; or took money from him to allow him to escape; or supplied him with money, a horse or other necessities, in order to enable him to escape; or that the principal was in prison and the jailer was bribed to let him escape; or conveyed instruments to him to enable him to break prison and escape. This and such like assistance to one known to be a felon would constitute one an accessory after the fact.

McClain v. State, supra at 115, 268 A.2d at 576, 577, *citing* R. Perkins, *Criminal Law* ch. 6, § 8 at 668 (2d ed. 1969).

It is also essential that the person accused of being an accessory after the fact was absent at the time the crime was committed. An accessory after the fact is not an accomplice — he is not connected with the crime until after its commission. *Watson v.*

State, supra. Therefore, the testimony of an accessory after the fact need not be corroborated. *Smallwood v. State,* 51 Md. App. 463, 443 A.2d 1003 (1982).

The trial of an accessory after (or before) the fact will not be precluded because the principal has not been tried or convicted. As long as the evidence in the accessory's trial is sufficient to demonstrate that a felony has been committed, the fact that the principal has not been tried or convicted will furnish no defense to the accessory. *Lewis v. State,* 285 Md. 705, 404 A.2d 1073 (1979).

If the trier of fact believes that the principal in the first degree did not commit the felony, the defendant cannot be convicted of being an accessory after the fact. In *Howell v. State,* 56 Md. App. 675, 468 A.2d 688 (1983), the defendant was charged with being an accessory after the fact to murder. The defendant's failure to receive a jury instruction on this issue was held to be fatal error where the defendant made a *prima facie* case through questioning on cross-examination of the State's witness — the alleged principal in the first degree to homicide — and getting an answer from the witness that he killed in self-defense.

Maryland Ann. Code, Art. 27, § 268F proscribes the separate offense of "harboring fugitive." Under Art. 27, § 268E, "fugitive" is defined as any individual for whose arrest a felony warrant has been issued under Maryland law. This offense has two subsections. It is an offense to knowingly harbor "... a fugitive who is avoiding prosecution, custody, or confinement after conviction of a felony ..." Art. 27, § 268F(b). It is also an offense to harbor "... any fugitive, so as to prevent his discovery and arrest, after notice or knowledge of the fact that a felony warrant has been issued for the apprehension of that fugitive, and after notice that harboring that fugitive is a punishable offense...." Art. 27, § 268F(a). "Harboring" includes offering a fugitive (1) concealment, (2) lodging, (3) care after concealment, or (4) obstruction of efforts of authorities to effect arrest of the fugitive. However, "harboring" does not include the failure to reveal the whereabouts of a fugitive by a person who did not participate in the efforts of the fugitive to elude arrest. The offense is a misdemeanor, providing for a fine of not more than $1,000 or imprisonment of not more than one year, or both. See also Maryland Ann. Code, Art. 27, § 268G, Harboring escaped prisoner.

§ 4.04. Acts committed through innocent agents.

As a general rule, whatever any person is legally capable of doing himself, he can do through another innocent person as his agent. An innocent agent is a person acting without criminal knowledge or intent.

In order for the defendant to be held responsible for acts committed through an innocent agent, the defendant: (1) must be legally capable of doing the act himself; and (2) must have willfully ordered, directed, authorized, or consented to the acts or conduct of an innocent employee or other innocent agent. The term "willfully" characterizes an act which is done knowingly, with deliberate intention and for which there is no reasonable excuse.

If you find that the defendant willfully ordered, directed, authorized, or consented to the acts or conduct of any innocent employee or other innocent agent, then the law holds him responsible for such acts or conduct as if they had been personally done by him.

COMMENT

At common law those who commit the criminal act by the hand of an innocent agent are classified as principals in the first degree as are those perpetrators who commit the act by their own hand. *Agresti v. State,* 2 Md. App. 278, 234 A.2d 284 (1967). When a crime is accomplished through the instrumentality of an innocent agent, it is not necessary that the one who has induced the act be present when the act was committed to be classified as a principal. R. Perkins & R. Boyce, *Criminal Law* ch. 6, § 8 at 723 n.10 (3d ed. 1982).

If the actor, the person who actually performs the criminal act, knows that the act is criminal and is of such capacity as to be criminally responsible, he is the principal in the first degree; and the person at whose instigation he acted, if not actually or constructively present, is an accessory before the fact. R. Perkins & R. Boyce, *Criminal Law* ch. 6, § 8 at 736-38 (3d ed. 1982). See Instruction, § 4.01, Accessory before the fact, *supra.*

§ 4.05. Attempt.

An attempt to commit a crime is, in itself, a separate crime. The defendant is charged with attempt ________ *(insert crime attempted).*

In order for a person to be guilty of this offense, the State must prove beyond a reasonable doubt that: (1) the defendant had the intent to commit the crime of ________ *(insert crime attempted);* (2) the defendant's conduct constituted a substantial step, beyond mere preparation, toward the commission of this crime; and, (3) the defendant at that time had the apparent ability to commit the crime intended.

The term "intent to commit" the crime requires that the defendant had an actual purpose or specific design to commit the intended crime. The elements of ________ *(insert crime attempted)* are ________ *(insert elements of substantive crime).* Such actual intent to commit this crime may be inferred from all of the surrounding circumstances.

An attempt to commit a crime occurs when the defendant, with criminal intent, takes a substantial step towards completing the crime which is beyond mere preparation but which may fall short of successful completion.

[If one who has intended to commit a crime freely and voluntarily abandons the idea before it has progressed beyond the state of mere preparation, he has not committed the crime of attempt.] [You may convict the defendant of an attempt to commit the crime even if the evidence shows that the offense was completed.]

COMMENT

An attempt to commit a crime is a common-law misdemeanor which is separate and distinct from the crime itself. Thus, one may be innocent of a substantive crime and guilty of an attempt to commit it. Except as provided by statute, an attempt is a common-law misdemeanor. The Court of Appeals of Maryland stated that the act must possess, "except for the failure to consummate, all the elements of the substantive crime, so that, if not prevented, it would have resulted in the full consummation of the intended crime." *Boone v. State,* 2 Md. App. 80, 233 A.2d 476 (1967). See also *Wiggins v. State,* 8 Md. App. 598, 261 A.2d 503 (1970).

The State must prove an actual, specific intent to commit the intended crime; while intent may not be inferred from the overt act alone, it may be inferred from all of the circumstances.

Difficulty arises when one tries to distinguish between "mere preparation" and the overt act which is beyond mere preparation in furtherance of the intended crime. In *Young v. State,* 303 Md. 298, 493 A.2d 352 (1985), the Court of Appeals, through an opinion by Judge Orth, provides a scholarly discussion of the *actus reus* of attempt crimes and adopts the "substantial step" test of the Model Penal Code as the criterion to determine whether an overt act is more than mere preparation. The Court noted that the Model Penal Code approach was best expressed in the slightly modified language of the State of Maryland Commission on Criminal Law, *Proposed Criminal Code* § 110.00 (1972). The Court held that it was adopting the provisions of this section, as follows:

> A person is guilty of an attempt to commit a crime when, with intent to commit a crime, he engages in conduct which constitutes a substantial step toward the commission of that crime whether or not his intention be accomplished.
>
> Conduct shall not be held to constitute a substantial step under this section unless it is strongly corroborative of the actor's criminal intention. Without negativing the sufficiency of other conduct, the following, if strongly corroborative of the actor's criminal purpose, shall not be held insufficient as a matter of law to constitute a substantial step:

(a) lying in wait, searching for or following the contemplated victim of the crime;

(b) enticing or seeking to entice the contemplated victim of the crime to go to the place contemplated for its commission;

(c) reconnoitering the place contemplated for the commission of the crime, at a time or in a manner not usual for law-abiding individuals, under circumstances that warrant alarm for the safety of persons or property in the vicinity, such as taking flight upon appearance of a police officer, refusing to identify himself, or manifestly endeavoring to conceal himself or any object;

(d) unlawful entry of a structure, vehicle or enclosure in which it is contemplated that the crime will be committed;

(e) possession of materials to be employed in the commission of the crime, which are specially designed for such unlawful use or which can serve no lawful purpose of the actor under the circumstances;

(f) possession, collection or fabrication of materials to be employed in the commission of the crime, at or near the place contemplated for its commission, where such possession, collection or fabrication serves no lawful purpose of the actor under the circumstances; or

(g) soliciting an innocent agent to engage in conduct constituting an element of the crime.

While following § 5.01(1)(c) of the Model Penal Code, the above language deletes certain subjective considerations on the part of the actor, narrows the definition of "reconnoitering" of § 5.01(2)(c) of the Model Penal Code, and, in accord with *Lightfoot v. State,* 278 Md. 231, 360 A.2d 426 (1976), eliminates failure to consummate the intended crime as one of the essential elements of a criminal attempt. Thus, the State is not required to prove beyond a reasonable doubt that the substantive crime was not in fact committed.

The Court in *Young v. State, supra,* in reviewing earlier Maryland cases dealing with the law of attempt crimes, stated that as of yet it had not indicated its approval or disapproval of an intermediate appellate court decision also dealing with the question of when an overt act is beyond mere preparation, i.e., *Frye v. State,* 62 Md. App. 310, 489 A.2d 71 (1985). In *Frye,* the Court held that the overt act by defendant of preparing to enter the back seat of an accomplice's car armed with implements necessary to carry out a kidnapping was mere preparation and did not constitute an attempt to commit a kidnapping. Between this act and the actual completion of kidnapping was a drive from Maryland into the District of Columbia to a club where the potential victim worked, finding her there, luring her outside to the car and effectively restraining and asporting her. In *Young,* the Court noted that the intermediate court apparently used a version of the so-called "proximity approach" in determining when an overt act is beyond mere preparation. Focusing on whether the defendant's acts were "dangerously proximate to success," the time and place at which the intended crime is supposed to occur take on considerable importance and the emphasis is not so much upon what the defendant has done as upon what remains to be done. In adopting the "substantial step" test of the Model Penal Code, the *Young* court specifically noted in its opinion that it eliminated from consideration the so-called "proximity approach," "the probable desistance approach," and the "equivocality approach" tests.

In *Young v. State, supra,* the Court also stated that it has not passed on two earlier intermediate court decisions dealing with the impossibility aspects of criminal attempts: *In Re Appeal No. 568, Term 1974,* 25 Md. App. 218, 220-23, 333 A.2d 649, *cert. denied,* 275 Md. 751 (1975) and *Waters v. State,* 2 Md. App. 216, 226-28, 234 A.2d 147 (1967), *cert. denied,* 259 Md. 737 (1970). The Court also cited with approval its earlier opinion dealing with the issue of abandonment, *Wiley v. State,* 237 Md. 560, 564-65, 207 A.2d 478 (1965), *overruled on other grounds, Lightfoot v. State,* 278 Md. 231, 360 A.2d 426 (1976). The *Wiley* rule is that if the requisite overt act has occurred, it is too late to renounce and abandon what has become a criminal offense. If the requisite overt act has not occurred and the renunciation occurs before the offense of attempt is completed, the attempt crime has not been committed for there is no punishable offense. In such circumstances, it does not matter whether the abandonment was motivated by increased fear of failure, detection or arrest or simply by a change of heart.

The Court held, in *Lightfoot v. State, supra* at 238, 360 A.2d at 430, that the "failure to consummate the crime is not an indispensable element of criminal attempt." In *Lightfoot* the appellant, who had been charged with both robbery and attempted robbery, was acquitted on the robbery count. The Court of Appeals affirmed the attempt conviction holding that where a defendant is charged with both the crime and the attempt to commit it, and where he is acquitted of the crime and convicted of the attempt, the attempt conviction may stand even though the evidence established that the crime was fully consummated.

The relationship of attempt and "assault with intent" crimes was discussed in *Christensen v. State,* 33 Md. App. 635, 365 A.2d 562 (1976). Attempted rape and assault with intent to rape are separate and distinct crimes; the former is a common-law misdemeanor, the latter is a felony. The crimes are distinguishable in that attempted rape may be established by proof of an overt act, or by proof of threats while assault with intent to commit rape requires more substantial acts, and cannot be established merely by proof of threats.

In *Cox v. State,* 69 Md. App. 396, 518 A.2d 132 (1986), the Court held that the crime of attempted voluntary manslaughter is committed where a person entertaining a specific intent to kill attempts to perpetrate a homicide in the heat of passion in response to legally adequate provocation.

Maryland Ann. Code, Art. 27, § 644A (limitation on sentence for attempt) provides that "(t)he sentence of a person who is convicted of an attempt to commit a crime may not exceed the maximum sentence for the crime attempted." Other provisions of the Maryland Code deal with specific attempt offenses: e.g., Art. 27, § 10 (attempt to burn building or property); Art. 27, § 450 (attempting to poison person); and, Art. 27, § 538 (attempts under sabotage prevention statutes).

§ 4.06. Conspiracy.

A conspiracy to commit a crime is, in itself, a separate crime. It exists when two or more persons enter into an agreement to accomplish a criminal or unlawful purpose [or to accomplish a lawful purpose by criminal or unlawful means].

In order for a person to be guilty of this offense, the State must prove beyond a reasonable doubt that: (1) the defendant and one or more other persons entered into an agreement; (2) the object of the agreement was criminal or unlawful [or the agreement involved achieving a lawful purpose by criminal or unlawful means]; and (3) there was a joint intent to enter into this agreement: that is, their minds met in a common design and purpose to accomplish a criminal or unlawful act [or a lawful act by criminal or unlawful means].

The gist of the offense is entering into the illegal scheme or design; it is not in doing the act, nor effecting the purpose for which the conspiracy is formed, nor in attempting to do them, nor in inciting others to do them, but in the forming of the scheme or agreement between the parties.

It is not necessary that a formal agreement be shown but there must be a meeting of the minds. The agreement does not have to be in formal words, either written or spoken. It is sufficient if the parties come to an understanding: if the minds of the parties meet understandingly so as to bring about an intelligent and deliberate agreement to do the acts contemplated. This may be shown by circumstantial evidence from which an inference of common design can be drawn. But mere similarity of conduct among various persons does not in itself establish a conspiracy. [In deciding what, if any, inferences to draw from circumstantial evidence, you may consider, among other things, the nature of the alleged acts, the relation of the parties, the interests of the alleged co-conspirators, and the totality of the surrounding circumstances leading up to and attending the alleged meeting of the minds.]

It is essential in proving the existence of a criminal conspiracy to show that two or more persons each had the criminal intent. The crime of conspiracy is committed at the moment the unlawful agreement is made. It is complete without doing any overt acts. There is no need to show any steps taken in execution of the unlawful design.

COMMENT

(a) Classification of crime and punishment

Conspiracy is a common-law crime in Maryland. As a common-law crime, conspiracy is considered a misdemeanor. See *Hammond v. Lancaster,* 194 Md. 462, 71 A.2d 474 (1950). Article 27, § 38, Maryland Ann. Code, which deals with the punishment for the crime of conspiracy, states in its entirety: "The punishment of every person convicted of the crime of conspiracy shall not exceed the maximum punishment provided for the offense he or she conspired to commit."

(b) Elements of crime and proof

The instruction is patterned substantially after holdings in leading Maryland cases. Conspiracy has been defined generally as two or more persons with joint or mutual intent entering into an agreement to accomplish an unlawful purpose, or to achieve a lawful purpose by unlawful means. *Wise v. State,* 47 Md. App. 656, 425 A.2d 652, *cert. denied,* 454 U.S. 863 (1981).

The crime of conspiracy is a combination of two or more persons to accomplish a criminal or unlawful act, or a lawful act by criminal or unlawful means. Conspiracy is the unlawful combination itself, no further overt act is required. See *Greenwald v. State,* 221 Md. 245, 157 A.2d 119 (1959), *cert. denied,* 363 U.S. 719 (1960); *Johnson v. State,* 10 Md. App. 652, 272 A.2d 422 (1971).

Because conspiracy consists of an agreement to accomplish a particular unlawful act or a lawful act by unlawful means, persons cannot be guilty of conspiracy to commit crimes which have already occurred. A conspiracy is formed to accomplish an act in the future. *Jones v. State,* 8 Md. App. 370, 259 A.2d 807 (1969). Also, it is immaterial whether the intended crime be a felony or merely a misdemeanor, and whether it be criminal at common law or by statute only. *Jones v. State, supra.*

"The 'gist' of the offense of conspiracy lies, not in doing the act, nor effecting the purpose for which the conspiracy is formed, nor in attempting to do them, nor in inciting others to do them, but in the forming of the scheme or agreement between the parties." *Regle v. State,* 9 Md. App. 346, 350, 264 A.2d 119, 122 (1970) (*citing State v. Carbone,* 10 N.J. 329, 91 A.2d 571, 574 (1952)). Therefore, a criminal conspiracy may consist of a conspiracy to do things which are not themselves criminal if done by one person. *Piracci v. State,* 207 Md. 499, 115 A.2d 262 (1955).

By its nature conspiracy is a joint or group offense requiring a concert of free wills and the union of two minds as a prerequisite to commission of the offense. If only two people were involved in a conspiracy and at a joint trial one of them was shown to be insane at the time the agreement was concluded and, therefore, was totally incapable of committing the crime, there is no punishable criminal conspiracy because there is no joint intent. *Regle v. State, supra.* If, however, the co-conspirators are tried separately, and the first, at his trial fails to establish the insanity of the second, and is found guilty, the subsequent trial and finding of insanity of the second co-conspirator will not discharge the first. *Gardner v. State,* 286 Md. 520, 408 A.2d 1317 (1979).

In *Quaglione v. State,* 15 Md. App. 571, 292 A.2d 785 (1972), the defendant was convicted of unlawfully conspiring to violate the narcotic laws. The trial judge, in his instructions to the jury at 579, 292 A.2d at 790 noted:

> You must consider whether either Quaglione (appellant) or Jones (Danny) among themselves or with others conspired and agreed upon an illegal scheme or design, or arrangement to violate the narcotics laws. In other words, if you find as a fact that on January 26, 1970, Quaglione, the defendant in this case, agreed with Jones that Jones would obtain hashish or marijuana from Quaglione for the purpose of illegally selling that drug, then this would be sufficient evi-

> dence subject to the general principles and burden of proof rules which I have outlined to you, to find him guilty of conspiring to violate the narcotic laws in the first indictment.

The Court, in *Bell v. State,* 48 Md. App. 669, 429 A.2d 300 (1981), stated that the judge, in instructing the jury as to the elements of a conspiracy to commit murder, need not instruct the jury as to the various degrees of murder; conspiracy itself constitutes premeditation which renders the underlying crime first degree murder.

A conspiracy is one offense regardless of the number of violations of the law which may have been the object of the conspiracy. In *Mason v. State,* 302 Md. 434, 488 A.2d 955 (1985), an application of these principles demonstrates that a defendant who distributes a number of controlled substances in accordance with a single unlawful agreement commits but one crime: common-law conspiracy.

The conspiracy may be shown by circumstantial evidence from which an inference of common design may be shown, it not being vital to demonstrate that the conspirators met and agreed in terms to a set design and to pursue it by common means. *See Perkins v. State,* 26 Md. App. 526, 339 A.2d 360 (1975) (which constitutes additional support for the proposition that an inference of common design may be drawn from circumstantial evidence). See also *Hill v. State,* 231 Md. 458, 190 A.2d 795 (1963); *Salzman v. State,* 49 Md. App. 25, 54, 430 A.2d 847, 864 (1981); *Jones v. State, supra; Price v. State,* 4 Md. App. 701, 704, 244 A.2d 900 (1968).

In one type of multiple conspiracy, often characterized as a wheel conspiracy, a number of persons (the spokes) are engaged in similar relationships with the same individual (the hub). In a wheel conspiracy, "the prosecution ... [is] required to prove that the existence of the other spokes was known to a particular defendant, and that the defendant did something in furtherance of a single, illegal enterprise in order that he be found to have conspired with the other spokes of the wheel." *Bolden v. State,* 44 Md. App. 643, 650, 410 A.2d 1085, 1091 (1980).

(c) Doctrine of merger does not apply

A conspiracy exists once an agreement is finalized. It is a separate and distinct offense from the substantive crime intended to be accomplished. The doctrine of merger of the conspiracy into the substantive crime does not exist. Thus, a defendant's acquittal of a particular crime does not bar a subsequent prosecution for a conspiracy to commit it. *Wilson v. State,* 8 Md. App. 653, 262 A.2d 91 (1970). Similarly, prior conviction of a specific crime does not entitle the accused to the defense of *res judicata* in a subsequent prosecution for conspiracy, even though the same evidence is introduced as a part of the proof of the conspiracy. *Rouse v. State,* 202 Md. 481, 97 A.2d 285, *cert. denied,* 346 U.S. 865 (1953); *Wilson v. State, supra.*

(d) "Concert of action" rule

Under the "concert of action" rule, an agreement by two or more persons to commit a particular crime cannot be prosecuted as a conspiracy when the crime is of such nature as necessarily to require the participation of at least two persons for its commission. *Robinson v. State,* 229 Md. 503, 184 A.2d 814 (1962). There is a limitation on this; the conspiracy must be formed prior to the commission of such a crime.

(e) Effect of acquittal or prosecution of all co-conspirators

It is not essential to the conviction of one conspirator that another shall be prosecuted or convicted. It is only where co-conspirators are tried together, and one is convicted while another or others are acquitted, resulting in repugnancy to the record, that the conviction may be discharged. *Hurwitz v. State,* 200 Md. 578, 92 A.2d 575 (1952). When co-conspirators are tried separately, however, and one is found guilty, the subsequent acquittal of the second conspirator in a separate trial will not discharge the first conspirator. A verdict in a trial of one conspirator, establishing the guilt of the conspirator on trial, also conclusively establishes the guilt of the other for purposes of that trial. *Gardner v. State,* 286 Md. 520, 408 A.2d 1317 (1979).

"It is the well-settled general rule that one defendant in a prosecution for conspiracy cannot be convicted where all of his alleged co-conspirators, be they one or more, have been acquitted or discharged under circumstances that amount to an acquittal." *Regle v. State,* 9 Md. App. 346, 351, 264 A.2d 119, 122.

In *Terrell v. State,* 34 Md. App. 418, 367 A.2d 95 (1977), the Court wrote "that the entry of a *nolle prosequi,* without the defendant's consent, and after jeopardy has attached, operates as an acquittal and precludes further prosecution for the same offense." *Id.* at 422, 367 A.2d at 98, 99 (*quoting Blondes v. State,* 273 Md. 435, 330 A.2d 169 (1975)). In *Terrell* the Court found that it could not determine from the record whether jeopardy had attached at the time the *nolle prosequi* had been entered on the conspiracy charges against the defendant's co-conspirators. Accordingly, the Court was unable to make a ruling whether the entry of the *nolle prosequi* of the defendant's co-conspirators mandated the dismissal of the indictment against the defendant. In dictum, the Court cited language from *Regle v. State, supra,* and suggested that the better reasoned view is that the entry of a *nolle prosequi,* as to one of two alleged co-conspirators, does not compel an acquittal where the *nolle prosequi* was entered with the co-conspirator's consent after the trial had begun.

(f) Admissibility of co-conspirator statements as hearsay exception

Under certain circumstances, statements of co-conspirators made out of court may be admissible at trial against another co-conspirator whether the charge is conspiracy or any other criminal offense or civil action.

Statements used against a co-conspirator which are made by a fellow conspirator to a third party should be distinguished from statements that form part of the conversation between co-conspirators. In the first case, the statements will be admissible if they were made "in the furtherance of" the conspiracy. In the second instance, the statements will be admissible if they were made at any time "during the pendency of" the conspiracy. A statement of pure history or description of criminal activity to a third party may not be in "furtherance of the conspiracy" even if made during the existence of the conspiracy.

The distinction is necessary because the admissibility of these statements may fall under different rationales. Under the so-called "verbal acts" doctrine, certain out-of-court statements are considered nonhearsay because the substantive law involved provides independent legal significance to the words and any accompanying acts. For example, in a slander action, the out-of-court alleged slanderous words may be admitted as nonhearsay under this doctrine. The declarations of one or more co-conspirators may fall within this doctrine when the declarations form part of the conversation between them; the acts of one are also admissible against the other if the acts were committed in the latter's presence and on the occasion of the alleged offense. *Haina v. State,* 30 Md. App. 295, 352 A.2d 874 (1976), *cert. denied,* 430 U.S. 906 (1977). See also *Irvin v. State,* 23 Md. App. 457, 328 A.2d 329 (1974), *aff'd,* 276 Md. 168, 344 A.2d 418 (1975); *Mason v. State,* 18 Md. App. 130, 305 A.2d 492 (1973), *cert. denied,* 416 U.S. 907 (1974). *Cf. Daugherty v. Kessler,* 264 Md. 281, 286 A.2d 95 (1972). A statement by a co-conspirator to a third person would not have independent legal significance under the "verbal acts" doctrine.

Both statements among co-conspirators and statements by a co-conspirator to a third person may be admitted under another rationale. This rationale, an outgrowth of the admission by party opponent hearsay exception, is derived from the concept of agency law in which a principal is bound by representative admissions and deeds of his agent while acting within the scope of his authority. *Irvin v. State, supra.* In effect, the analogy is that a co-conspirator acts as an agent for his fellow conspirator and as such is bound by the statements of a co-conspirator uttered while in the furtherance of the conspiracy.

These two rationales are described in E. Cleary, *McCormick on Evidence* 792 (3d ed. 1984), as follows:

> If A and B are engaged in a conspiracy the acts and declarations of B occurring while the conspiracy is actually in

> progress and in furtherance of the design are provable against A, because they are acts for which he is criminally or civilly responsible, as a matter of substantive law. But B's declarations may also be proved against A as representative admissions, to prove the truth of the matter declared, and only then are they within our present topic. The courts have seldom discriminated between declarations offered as conduct constituting part of the conspiracy and declarations offered as vicarious admissions of the facts declared....

Other theories for admitting co-conspirator statements as exceptions to the hearsay rule include: (1) a direct admission by party opponent where the out-of-court statement is made by a conspirator who is the defendant and the statement is used against himself; (2) declaration against interest exception, where the co-conspirator-declarant is not available for trial and the other requirements of the rule are met; (3) nonhearsay where the fact that the statements were made tended to prove the existence of a conspiracy, but the truth or falsity of the matter asserted in the statement is unimportant. For an example of the latter theory, see *United States v. Geaney,* 417 F.2d 1116, 1121 n.4 (2d Cir. 1969), *cert. denied sub nom. Lynch v. United States,* 397 U.S. 1028, 90 S. Ct. 1276, 25 L. Ed. 2d 539 (1970).

Notwithstanding the above distinctions, in Maryland as in other common-law jurisdictions, three elements are often said to form the foundation for the admissibility of a co-conspirator's declarations. First, the existence of the conspiracy and the connection of the co-conspirator therewith must be established. Second, a co-conspirator's declarations sought to be admitted into evidence must be made in furtherance of the conspiracy. Third, the co-conspirator's declarations must be made during the pendency of the conspiracy. *Irvin v. State, supra.*

In order to establish the first element, it is said that the State must show the existence of a conspiracy by independent evidence before hearsay declarations of a co-conspirator can be admitted into evidence. However, a distinction again needs to be drawn between statements among co-conspirators and statements of a co-conspirator to a third person. Where declarations of a conspirator are sought to be introduced through a third person, a third person cannot testify against the co-conspirator until the latter's connection with the conspiracy is proved by evidence *aliunde,* that is, by independent evidence that the conspiracy existed. This proposition is not true, however, when the witness is a conspirator who seeks to testify about statements made to him by his co-conspirator. Again, an analogy is made to the law of agency. The testimony of a third person as to what an alleged agent told him will not be received against the principal unless the agency is first established, but the agent himself may testify to relevant statements made to him by the principal. Thus, the testimony of one conspirator is admissible against a co-conspirator without the need to establish through an independent source the existence of the conspiracy. *Haina v. State, supra* at 295, 352 A.2d at 887. *Mason v. State, supra* at 136, 305 A.2d at 496, quoting 3 Underhill's *Criminal Evidence* § 861 (5th ed.).

Declarations sought to be introduced by a fellow conspirator will be received into evidence subject only to Maryland's general rule that the testimony of an accomplice be corroborated. Such corroborative evidence need only be slight and must strengthen the probative force of an accomplice's testimony; it does not have to prove any particular fact to which an accomplice has testified. Corroborative testimony must at a minimum, however, identify the defendant with the perpetrators of the crime or show the defendant's participation in the crime itself. See Comment, § 2.01 Accomplice's testimony — Corroboration, *supra.*

The second element, proof that the declaration was made in furtherance of the conspiracy, is interpreted broadly under Maryland law. *Irvin v. State, supra.* This requirement is also a product of agency law that statements made within the scope of the agency are deemed more reliable and less likely to be self-serving statements of the declarant. For examples of cases in other jurisdictions in which the furtherance requirement was held not to be met, see E. Cleary, *McCormick on Evidence* 793, n.39 (3d ed. 1984).

The third requirement, that the co-conspirator's declaration be made during the pendency of the conspiracy, is also construed broadly. *Henderson v. State,* 13 Md. App. 384, 283 A.2d 418 (1971). It has been defined to mean the duration of the unlawful agreement. *Irvin v. State, supra* at 473, 328 A.2d at 338. The duration of a conspiracy does not continue indefinitely but is restricted to the accomplishment of the "main aim" of the conspiracy. If a co-conspirator unilaterally withdraws from a conspiracy involving more than two conspirators, the conspiracy is at an end to him only. Again, the concern for reliability of the co-conspirator's declaration is at the heart of this requirement. Generally, common-law jurisdictions have concluded that while the co-conspirators are actively and secretly working toward their common aim, their statements are less likely to be self-serving and, as such, the reliability of such statements is heightened. Post-termination statements are far more likely to be self-serving and thus the reliability of such statements is diminished. Statements made during the pendency of the conspiracy are more likely to be fresh in the co-conspirator's mind and thus problems of memory and narration are lessened.

In Maryland, the above foundation requirements must be established, to the satisfaction of the judge, by a standard of *prima facie* evidence. This standard is lower than that of the preponderance of the evidence applied by a minority of common-law jurisdictions and by a growing number of federal circuits. Maryland courts have allowed flexibility in the order of proof by allowing declarations of a co-conspirator to be admitted against the defendant prior to establishing the conspiracy. *Greenwald v. State,* 221 Md. 245, 157 A.2d 119, *cert. denied,* 363 U.S. 719 (1960). See also *Johnson v. State,* 9 Md. App. 327, 264 A.2d 280 (1970). Expansion of the co-conspirator hearsay exception against the accused in criminal cases invites constitutional challenge under the confrontation clause of the sixth and fourteenth amendments. See, e.g., *Dutton v. Evans,* 400 U.S. 74, 91 S. Ct. 210, 27 L. Ed. 2d 213 (1970); *Ohio v. Roberts,* 448 U.S. 56, 100 S. Ct. 2531, 65 L. Ed. 2d 597 (1980).

(g) Form of indictment

Article 27, § 40, Maryland Ann. Code, provides that in an indictment for conspiracy it shall be sufficient to use a formula substantially to the following effect: "That A-B and C-D on the ______ day of ______ 19______ at the County

(City) aforesaid unlawfully conspired together to murder X-Y (or other conspiracy here stating briefly the object of the conspiracy), against the peace, government and dignity of the State."

The means by which the conspiracy was intended to be accomplished are only matters of evidence to prove the charge. *Lynch v. State,* 2 Md. App. 546, 236 A.2d 45 (1967), *cert. denied,* 393 U.S. 915 (1968). Counsel for defendant can seek a bill of particulars to discover more information of the means by which the conspiracy was allegedly accomplished. For other cases discussing the particularity of the indictment, see *Quaglione v. State,* 15 Md. App. 571, 292 A.2d 785 (1972); *Adams v. State,* 202 Md. 455, 97 A.2d 281 (1953), *rev'd on other grounds,* 347 U.S. 179 (1954); *Pearlman v. State,* 232 Md. 251, 192 A.2d 767 (1963), *cert. denied,* 376 U.S. 943 (1964).

(h) Statute of limitations

The Maryland statute of limitations mandates that prosecution for conspiracy be instituted within one year after the conspiracy ends. Maryland Ann. Code, Courts and Judicial Proceedings, § 5-106. In *McMorris v. State,* 26 Md. App. 660, 338 A.2d 912 (1975), *aff'd,* 277 Md. 62, 355 A.2d 438 (1976), the Court held that prosecution is commenced on the date the warrant of arrest is issued. The Court thereby rejected the defendant's assertion that the indictment for the offense also must be handed down within the one-year statutory period.

(i) Venue

In *Lievers v. State,* 3 Md. App. 597, 605, 241 A.2d 147, 152 (1968), the Court stated: "[I]t is generally held that a conspiracy may be prosecuted where the illegal agreement arose, or where an overt act in furtherance of the agreement occurred...."

B. Assault

§ 4.11. Assault.

An assault is an intentional attempt by force to inflict injury upon the person of another [or to intentionally place another in reasonable fear of an immediate injury].

In order for the defendant to be guilty of this offense, the State must prove beyond a reasonable doubt that: (1) the defendant made an attempt with force to do injury to another person [or the defendant placed another person in reasonable fear of an immediate injury]; (2) at that time, the defendant had the apparent present ability to inflict injury; and (3) the defendant intended to do the acts which constituted the assault.

Any intentional attempt or effort to apply the least amount of force to another person may be sufficient so long as violence was threatened or ordered. An assault may be committed without actually touching, striking or committing bodily harm on another. [The mere use of threatening words alone does not constitute an assault. Words may, however, give actions or accompanying conduct such a meaning as to constitute an assault.]

[*Include when an intentional attempt by force to inflict injury upon the person of another is alleged:* An intentional attempt by force to inflict injury upon another requires a present intention to injure. The intent required is the general intent to do the act which constitutes the assault. It is not necessary that there should be a specific purpose to do a particular injury.]

COMMENT

See Comment, § 4.12, Battery, *infra.*

§ 4.12. Battery.

A battery is the intentional unlawful touching or doing of bodily harm to another. The State must prove beyond a reasonable doubt that: (1) the defendant had an intent to unlawfully touch or do bodily harm to another person; and (2) there was actual contact by the defendant with that person.

The least intentional touching of the person of another is sufficient to constitute a battery. [The touching, however, must be unlawful. The word "unlawful" means that it was done without lawful authority and without the consent of the person affected.] [Where serious hurt or a breach of the public peace exists, you are to give no consideration as to whether consent was given by the person affected.]

[The touching may be done by indirect means; it includes an application of force that puts something into motion that touches another person.]

COMMENT

Assault and battery should be treated as separate crimes. "There is no single crime properly called assault and battery. When the term is used, either it refers to two crimes, or it refers to the crime of battery, and when it does the word assault is superfluous." *Woods v. State,* 14 Md. App. 627, 632, 288 A.2d 215, 218, *cert. denied,* 266 Md. 745 (1972).

Assault and battery are common-law offenses. *Yantz v. Warden,* 210 Md. 343, 123 A.2d 601, *cert. denied,* 353 U.S. 932 (1956). Assault is traditionally viewed as an attempt to injure another person by means of force. *Yantz v. Warden, supra.* Another Court stated, in distinguishing assault from battery, that the crime of assault is "the attempt or offer to beat another, without touching him" while the crime of battery is the execution of an assault or the "unlawful beating of another." *Christensen v. State,* 33 Md. App. 635, 643, 365 A.2d 562, 566-67 (1976) *(citing Woods v.*

State, supra); Anderson v. State, 61 Md. App. 436, 487 A.2d 294 (1985). In an early case, battery was described as the unlawful touching of another person. *Lamb v. State,* 67 Md. 524, 534, 10 A. 208 (1887).

In Maryland, as well as many other common-law jurisdictions, assault actually encompasses two theories. One theory involves the traditional view of an intentional attempt by force to inflict injury upon another person. Under this theory, the apprehension of impending harm by the potential victim is not an essential element in the crime, even though it may be found in most cases. *Woods v. State, supra* at 630, 288 A.2d at 216. The other theory, similar to the civil law of assault as an intentional tort, involves intentionally placing another person in reasonable apprehension or fear of an immediate injury. This theory does not require an actual present intent to commit a battery. In a 1970 case, the Court stated:

> It is true that historically some authorities held to the view that a criminal assault only occurred where the assailant was shown to have an actual present intention to inflict a battery. We agree, however with the conclusion reach by Clark & Marshall, *Law of Crimes* § 10.15 (at page 647) that "(t)he better opinion, ... is against this view, and to the effect that if a person presents a gun at another, or threatens him with a stick or other weapon, and thereby reasonably puts him in fear and causes him to act on the defensive, or to retreat, there is an assault, whether there is any actual intention to injure or not."

McGhee v. State, 9 Md. App. 526, 531, 267 A.2d 306, 309 (1970). See also *Veney v. State,* 251 Md. 159, 246 A.2d 608 (1968), *cert. denied,* 394 U.S. 948 (1969); *Hobbs v. Warden,* 223 Md. 651, 163 A.2d 331 (1960); *Kellum v. State,* 223 Md. 80, 162 A.2d 473 (1960); R. Perkins & R. Boyce, *Criminal Law* ch. 2, § 2 at 151-182 (3d ed. 1982); W. LaFave & A. Scott, *Criminal Law* 602-614 (1972).

The second element of the assault instruction, requiring that the defendant had the apparent present ability to inflict injury, is relevant to both of these theories of assault. Under the theory of an attempt to injure another person, a sometimes fine line needs to be drawn between violence merely threatened and an assault. This element ensures that there is a present intention to injure accompanied by acts that clearly go beyond mere preparation. For example, it has been said that to raise a stick at such a distance that it clearly could not injure would not be an assault. Under the theory of intentionally placing another person in reasonable apprehension of an immediate injury, if there is not apparent present ability to inflict the injury, a person could not, it would seem, be reasonable in his apprehension or fear of an immediate injury. It is the outward demonstration that constitutes the mischief which is punished as a breach of the peace under this view of assault. The outward demonstration must be reasonably sufficient to arouse fear of an immediate injury.

Under the view of assault as an intentional attempt by force to inflict injury upon another "(m)enacing acts can never amount to an assault, if it appears from accompanying words or conduct that there is no present intention to injure." Clark & Marshall, *Law of Crimes* § 10.15 at 724 (7th ed. 1967).

The traditional view is that mere words by themselves can never constitute an assault if unaccompanied by any menacing act or gesture. This view may be too broad. As one treatise writer has stated:

> Two kinds of words are included here, — informational words and threatening words. And it would seem under these circumstances that the informational words might take the place of a threatening movement or gesture and complete the assault, — wherever wrongfully placing another in apprehension of receiving an immediate battery is sufficient for this offense.

R. Perkins & R. Boyce, *Criminal Law* ch. 2, § 2 at 178 (3d ed. 1982). The example cited by the treatise writer is of one person standing in back of another and saying, "I have you covered. If you move or turn I'll shoot you." It is argued that these informational words might cause more apprehension on the part of the other person than if that person actually saw someone pointing a pistol, even though the speaker might actually be standing with his hands in his pockets.

Much more typical is the situation where words are combined with certain acts. In his classic treatise on Maryland criminal law, Hochheimer stated: "Merely rude, angry, or insolent words or actions do not constitute an assault, but words may give to actions such a meaning as to make them amount to assault." L. Hochheimer, *The Law of Crimes and Criminal Procedure* § 254 (2d ed. 1904).

A criminal assault which is not accompanied by a threat of serious harm or breach of the public peace is a crime against the person, and therefore the victim's consent is a good defense. *Taylor v. State,* 214 Md. 156, 133 A.2d 414 (1957). But such consent is no defense to an assault which tends to bring about a breach of the public peace, since such an assault is a crime against the public generally. *Taylor v. State, supra.*

The law of self-defense applies in assault cases, and a person assaulted may meet force with reasonable force. See Instructions and Comments, §§ 5.11 to 5.16, *infra,* for detailed discussions of self-defense. Also, under certain circumstances a third person has a right to go to the defense of others. See Instruction, § 5.04, Defense of others, *infra.*

Where an arrest is illegal, the person arrested may, in self-defense, use any reasonable means, including force, to effect his escape. *Williams v. State,* 204 Md. 55, 102 A.2d 714 (1954). However, a police officer may use necessary force to effectuate a legal arrest. See Instruction, § 4.80, Resisting arrest, *infra.*

A parent may also have lawful authority to use reasonable force to discipline a child. *Worthen v. State,* 42 Md. App. 20, 399 A.2d 272 (1979).

Voluntary intoxication is not a defense to assault and battery since they are general intent crimes. *Holt v. State,* 50 Md. App. 578, 580, 438 A.2d 1386, 1387 (1982) (*citing Ott v. State,* 11 Md. App. 259, 266, 273 A.2d 630, 634 (1971)). See Instruction, § 5.01, Voluntary drunkenness, *infra.*

Assault and battery are misdemeanors. No prescribed penalties exist for these crimes. One outer limit on the penalty is that it cannot constitute cruel and unusual punishment. *Roberts v. Warden,* 242 Md. 459, 219 A.2d 254, *cert. denied,* 385 U.S. 876 (1966). Another limit is that, since assault is a lesser included offense of other aggravated assaults, such as assault with intent to murder, rob, or to commit rape or a first or second degree sexual offense, the penalty cannot exceed the penalty for the more serious offense. *Simms v. State,* 288 Md. 712, 421 A.2d 957 (1980). In this case, the defendants were charged with both assault and assault with intent to rob based on the same acts. The Court held that when the defendant is convicted of only the lesser included charge, he cannot receive a sentence that exceeds the maximum sentence which could have been imposed had he been convicted of the greater charge.

§4.13. Assault with intent to murder.

The defendant is charged with assault with intent to murder. In order for the defendant to be guilty of this offense, the State must prove beyond a reasonable doubt that: (1) there was an assault on ________ *(name of victim);* (2) the defendant committed the assault; and (3) the assault was committed with the intent to kill ________ *(name of victim)* [; and (4) the assault was committed with the intent to murder; that is, it was committed without legal justification, excuse or a proper mitigating circumstance].

An assault is an intentional attempt by force or violence to inflict injury upon another person coupled with the apparent present ability to inflict such an injury.

Any intentional attempt or effort to apply the least amount of force to another person may be sufficient so long as violence was threatened or ordered. An assault may be committed without actually touching, striking or committing bodily harm on another. [The mere use of threatening words alone does not constitute an assault. Words may, however, give actions or accompanying conduct such a meaning as to make them constitute an assault.]

In order to convict the defendant of assault with intent to murder, the State must prove beyond a reasonable doubt that the defendant had the specific intent to kill ________ (*insert name of victim*). The specific intent to kill need not be shown directly but may be shown by or inferred from the circumstances. The intent to kill may be inferred from evidence showing an intent to inflict grievous bodily harm, such as firing a deadly weapon at a vital part of the victim's body. The intent cannot be inferred from the mere fact of the assault although the character of the assault and the use of a deadly weapon are factors to be considered.

[A critical element of the crime of assault with intent to murder is the term "intent to murder." "Intent to murder" means the unjustified, unexcused, and unmitigated intent to kill. The State must prove beyond a reasonable doubt that the assault was committed with such intent that, if death had resulted, it would have been murder, and not manslaughter or innocent homicide. This means that the assault must be committed without legal justification, excuse or a proper mitigating circumstance. Thus, if a death had followed from the assault, if it were merely accidental or due to simple negligence or an honest error of judgment, the intent to murder would be absent. Also, as I will instruct you, if the intent were carried out and the resulting crime was (voluntary manslaughter) (involuntary manslaughter), the intent to murder would not be present.]

[For a person to be guilty of voluntary manslaughter there must have been: (1) an intentional homicide; (2) done by the defendant; (3) in a sudden heat of passion; (4) caused by reasonable provocation; (5) before there had been a reasonable opportunity for the passion to cool; and (6) a causal connection between the provocation, the passion and the fatal act. The term "sudden heat of passion" means that the killing must have followed the provocation before there had been a reasonable opportunity for the passion to cool.]

[For a person to be guilty of involuntary manslaughter, there must be the negligent doing of some act. The amount, degree or character of the negligence to be proven is *gross* negligence. Gross negligence is defined as such negligence as amounts to a wanton or reckless disregard of human life. A person cannot be found guilty of involuntary manslaughter based on mere negligence.]

[Also, the state must prove beyond a reasonable doubt the lack of a legal justification or excuse. In this case, the defense of __________ *(include relevant defense(s), such as self-defense)* has been raised. *(Insert applicable defense instruction(s)).*]

[If you determine that the defendant is not guilty of assault with intent to murder, then it is your duty as members of the jury to consider whether the defendant is guilty of assault, which is a necessarily included lesser offense of assault with intent to murder.]

COMMENT

Maryland Ann. Code, Art. 27, § 12, provides that assault with intent to murder is a felony punishable by not less than two years and not more than thirty years. The statute does not state the elements of the crime, but the authorities and Maryland cases generally hold that the elements are as follows: (1) an assault, (2) with intent to murder, such that if death had ensued, the killing would have constituted murder in the first or second degree. *Tate v. State,* 236 Md. 312, 203 A.2d 882 (1964); *Marks v. State,* 230 Md. 108, 185 A.2d 909 (1962); *Webb v. State,* 201 Md. 158, 93 A.2d 80 (1952); Clark & Marshall, *Law of Crimes* § 10.17 (7th ed. 1967).

There must be proof of both the assault and the intent to murder. The intent cannot be inferred from the mere fact of the assault, although the character of the assault and the use of a deadly weapon are factors to be considered in determining intent. *Webb v. State, supra.*

The intent required for assault with intent to murder is the specific intent to kill. The specific intent to kill means the specific intent to bring about the death of the assault victim. *State v. Jenkins,* 307 Md. 501, 515 A.2d 465 (1986); *Glenn v. State,* 68 Md. App. 379, 511 A.2d 1110, *cert. denied,* 307 Md. 599, 516 A.2d

569 (1986). In *State v. Jenkins, supra,* the Court defined the mental state of assault with intent to kill as follows:

> In sum, the intent element of assault with intent to murder requires proof of a specific intent to kill under circumstances such that, if the victim had died, the offense would be murder. That an intent to murder may be shown by or inferred from facts showing an intent to do grievous bodily harm, does not convert the statutory offense to "assault with intent to do grievous bodily harm."

Id., 515 A.2d at 472.

The intent must be the intent to murder, not the intent to kill alone. The intent to murder requires the unjustified, unexcused, and unmitigated intent to kill. As the Court in *Glenn v. State, supra,* stated, the reason for distinguishing the intent to murder from the intent to kill is to exclude from the assault with intent to murder statute those intents to kill that would be justified, excused, or mitigated, should death result. *Id.* at 396, 511 A.2d at 1119. Thus, assault with intent to murder may be defined as "assault with intent to kill under circumstances such that if the victim should die, the crime would be murder." *Id.* at 398, 511 A.2d at 1120.

The requirement of an intent to murder is expressed in the fourth element of the first paragraph of the instruction. This element is placed in brackets because there must be an issue of justification, excuse, or mitigation generated by the evidence. This may be satisfied by evidence of voluntary or involuntary manslaughter, including imperfect self-defense, if the intent had been carried out, or a perfect defense. The language explaining mitigating circumstances in the instruction similarly has been placed in brackets.

If sufficient evidence has been introduced by either the State's or the defense's evidence, the jury must make the vital distinction between murder and manslaughter. An early case stated that the defendant is entitled to an instruction that if death had resulted, the killing must have been murder in the first or second degree and not manslaughter. *Davis v. State,* 204 Md. 44, 102 A.2d 816 (1954). See *Tate v. State, supra.*

In *State v. Faulkner,* 301 Md. 482, 483 A.2d 759 (1984), *aff'g* 54 Md. App. 113, 458 A.2d 81 (1983), the Court of Appeals held for the first time that Maryland recognizes the mitigation defense of imperfect self-defense and that this defense applies to the statutory offense of assault with intent to murder. Imperfect self-defense is a form of voluntary manslaughter. A person who kills another person while honestly, though unreasonably, believing that he is threatened with death or serious bodily harm does not act with malice. See the discussion of imperfect self-defense, Comment, § 4.23c, *infra.*

When malice is negated with respect to assault with intent to murder, the accused may be found guilty of simple assault and battery. See *Thomas v. State,* 29 Md. App. 45, 349 A.2d 384 (1975), *cert. granted,* 278 Md. 736 (1976), *cert. dismissed,* 279 Md. 604 (1977); *Finnegan v. State,* 33 Md. App. 251, 364 A.2d 124, *cert. denied,* 279 Md. 682 (1976), *cert. denied,* 433 U.S. 912 (1977). It follows that, when the evidence generates the issue of mitigation with respect to an assault with intent to murder charge, the trial court may, upon request, give an appropriate instruction to the jury. Maryland Rule 4-325(c); *Lansdowne v. State,* 287 Md. 232, 412 A.2d 88 (1980).

There are many cases which provide understanding of the meaning of the mental state of intent to kill and how this specific intent may be proven. Most of these cases arise in the procedural context of an appellate court considering the sufficiency of the evidence to support a conviction. The intent to kill is inferable from the use of a deadly weapon pointed toward a vital part of the body. *Bird v. State,* 231 Md. 432, 190 A.2d 804 (1963). Contrary to some case law that is pre-*Evans v. State,* 28 Md. App. 640, 349 A.2d 300 (1975), *aff'd,* 278 Md. 197, 362 A.2d 629 (1976), the intent to murder may not be inferred since malice must be present, and malice may not be inferred unless there is an absence of mitigating circumstances, justification, and excuse. *Finnegan v. State, supra.* But see *Woodard v. State,* 13 Md. App. 114, 282 A.2d 9 (1971). If the evidence shows that a weapon was not capable of killing the victim, e.g., a gun without a firing pin, an unloaded or toy weapon, the evidence may not be sufficient to prove assault with intent to murder; it would, however, support a charge of simple assault. *Brown v. State,* 29 Md. App. 467, 349 A.2d 267 (1975).

In *Finnegan v. State, supra,* the trial judge, in announcing the verdict in a nonjury trial, repeated several times that the pointing of a deadly weapon at a vital part of the body supports an inference of malice. The Court of Special Appeals held that the judge's statement constituted an overly broad employment of that inference because malice includes not only an intent to kill but also the absence of excuse, justification, or mitigating circumstances. The conviction of the appellant was affirmed, however, because the Court found that the statement, when viewed within the context of the total rendition of the verdict, indicated that the trial judge had not relied upon an unconstitutional presumption of malice.

Several cases considering the sufficiency of the evidence of an intent to kill have dealt with the use of firearms. In *Hall v. State,* 69 Md. App. 37, 516 A.2d 204 (1986), the Court held that mere discharge of a deadly weapon does not meet the standard of constitutional sufficiency to infer intent to murder. There is no valid inference that the shots were aimed at a person. As noted above, the intent to kill is inferable from the use of a deadly weapon pointed toward a vital part of the body. *Bird v. State, supra; Glenn v. State, supra; James v. State,* 31 Md. App. 666, 358 A.2d 595, *cert. denied,* 278 Md. 725 (1976). In *Shenberger v. State,* 234 Md. 363, 199 A.2d 233 (1964), the Court indicated that merely pointing a deadly weapon coupled with the expressed intention to kill may be sufficient. Yet, in *Brown v. State,* 64 Md. App. 324, 494 A.2d 999, *cert. denied,* 304 Md. 296 (1985), the Court indicated that merely pointing a gun is insufficient. In *Nickerson v. State,* 22 Md. App. 660, 325 A.2d 149 (1974), the Court suggested that shooting in a general direction in random fashion may be sufficient. In considering these and other earlier cases, it is useful to keep in mind that *State v. Jenkins, supra,* and *Glenn v. State, supra,* more recently underscore the Court's view that assault with intent to murder requires sufficient proof of a specific intent to kill the victim.

In *State v. Jenkins, supra,* the Court of Appeals held that the intents for assault with intent to murder and assault with intent to maim, disfigure, or disable are mutually exclusive and inconsistent. Yet, the offenses were not held to be inconsistent in the same sense that the common law crimes of larceny and receiving stolen goods were deemed inconsistent. A perpetrator of an assault may harbor both intents at the time of the assault; the intents remain mutually exclusive but they can be held disjunctively. The Court held that the conviction of assault with intent to maim, disfigure, or disable should be merged into the conviction of assault with intent to murder. The Court found that the General Assembly did not intend that separate convictions and sentences be imposed where there is but a single act of assault.

Four important changes have been made to the jury instruction since the original edition of this book. First, the intent to kill element has been revised to make clear that a specific intent to kill is required. Second, the use of the term "malice" has been replaced by an explanation of the requirement that the offense includes the element of the absence of justification, mitigation, or excuse. Third, the phrase "or a proper mitigating circumstance" has been added to the end of the phrase "without legal excuse or justification," where the latter appears in the instruction. The importance of adding the phrase "or proper mitigating circumstances" was suggested by the Maryland Court of Special Appeals in *Finnegan v. State, supra.* Fourth, the instruction has been changed to comply with the burden of proof requirements in *Evans v. State, supra,* and its progeny. *See* Appendix V, The Impact of *Evans v. State:* Burdens of Proof, Presumptions and Inferences, *infra.*

§4.14. Assault with intent to rob.

The defendant is charged with assault with intent to rob. In order for a person to be found guilty of this offense, the State must prove beyond a reasonable doubt that: (1) there was an assault on __________ *(name of victim);* (2) the defendant committed the assault; and (3) the assault was committed with the specific intent to rob.

An assault is an intentional attempt by force or violence to inflict injury upon another person coupled with the apparent present ability to inflict such an injury. [An assault is also intentionally placing another person in reasonable fear of immediate physical harm.]

Any intentional attempt or effort to apply the least amount of force to another person may be sufficient so long as violence was threatened or ordered. An assault may be committed without actually touching, striking or committing bodily harm on another. [The mere use of threatening words alone does not constitute an assault. Words may, however, give actions or accompanying conduct such a meaning as to constitute an assault.]

To establish the specific intent required, the State must prove that the defendant knowingly and willfully intended to do an act which the law prohibits, namely robbery. The intent to rob may be inferred from all the facts and circumstances, including the [words,] acts and conduct of the defendant.

Robbery is the intentional taking and carrying away of the personal property of another from the person or in his immediate presence without consent and by the use of violence or by putting another in fear with the intent to permanently deprive the owner [possessor] of his property.

[The crime of robbery is not committed if the intent is merely to use the property temporarily and then to return it.] [The crime of robbery is not committed if the intent was to take the property under a good faith claim of an ownership interest.]

In order for you to find the defendant guilty of an assault with intent to rob, it is not necessary that he accomplished his purpose to rob.

COMMENT

The crime of assault with intent to rob is an aggravated assault requiring: (1) an assault on the victim; (2) made by the accused; and (3) with the intent to rob. *Bryant v. State,* 4 Md. App. 572, 244 A.2d 446 (1967), *cert. denied,* 252 Md. 730 (1969); *Dixon v. State,* 302 Md. 447, 488 A.2d 962 (1985).

In *Offutt v. State,* 44 Md. App. 670, 410 A.2d 611, 612 (1980), testimony by victim that defendant put his hand in his pocket, pointed up and asked "Do you want to die?" was sufficient for the trier of fact to find that the victim was reasonably in fear that force would be used against her which, combined with her testimony that she was scared, constituted an assault.

Because it is not necessary to find that the defendant accomplished his purpose to rob, there is no requirement that an indictment for assault with intent to rob describe the goods and chattels. *Linkens v. State,* 202 Md. 212, 96 A.2d 246 (1953).

Where charges of assault with intent to rob and robbery arise out of the same incident and all the facts necessary to prove the assault with intent to rob are essential ingredients in proving the robbery, the assault and the robbery merge. This is only true when there have been convictions on each offense. Thus, in *Bryant v. State, supra* at 579, 244 A.2d at 451, where the facts indicated that a robbery was committed, the Court upheld the verdict of assault with intent to rob where the defendant-appellant was not convicted of robbery. Under the circumstances, the acquittal on the greater offense did not preclude conviction on the lesser offense.

If a defendant is convicted of the lesser included offense when charged with two related crimes, he may not receive a sentence that exceeds the maximum sentence possible for the greater offense. In *Simms v. State,* 288 Md. 712, 421 A.2d 957 (1980), the State charged defendants with assault with intent to rob and simple assault. Both crimes were based upon the same acts. The Court held that when jeopardy attached to-both charges, and defendants were convicted of only the lesser included charge, they could not receive a sentence that exceeded the maximum sentence which could have been imposed had they been convicted of the greater charge. Therefore, a twelve-year sentence imposed on the defendants was invalid since the maximum sentence for assault with intent to rob was ten years.

It has been said that aggravated assaults are nothing more than attempts to commit murder, rape or robbery (Clark & Marshall, *Law of Crimes* § 4.07 at 218 (6th ed. 1952)), a view apparently followed in this State. See *Farrow v. State,* 233 Md. 526, 197 A.2d 434 (1963). "Therefore the rules of law applicable to attempts are applicable to aggravated assaults." *Waters v. State,* 2 Md. App. 216, 226, 234 A.2d 147 (1967), *cert. denied,* 259 Md. 737 (1970). According to *Brooks v. State,* 2 Md. App. 291, 234 A.2d 467 (1967), assault with intent to rob may constitute attempted robbery. Therefore, for purposes of the felony-murder rule, it is within the contemplation of Maryland Ann. Code, Art. 27, § 410. *Middleton v. State,* 6 Md. App. 380, 251 A.2d 224 (1969).

In Maryland the testimony of a single eyewitness is sufficient to sustain a conviction for assault with intent to rob. *Smith v. State,* 233 Md. 430, 197 A.2d 103 (1964). See *Tillery v. State,* 2 Md. App. 142, 147-48, 233 A.2d 375 (1967). The Court in *Spencer v. State,* 1 Md. App. 264, 268, 229 A.2d 151 (1967), however, reversed a conviction of assault with intent to rob because of insufficient evidence:

> That appellant was in the company of Lipscomb before the crime, that they wanted money for wine, that he was found in the company of Lipscomb shortly after the commission of the crime breathing heavily and sweating lightly are not sufficient to support a rational inference beyond a reasonable doubt or to a moral certainty that appellant participated in the robbery or that he shared a common criminal purpose with Lipscomb to rob the driver.

Maryland Ann. Code, Art. 27, § 12, entitled "Assault with intent to murder, ravish or rob," provides that: "[e]very person convicted of assault with intent to rob, is guilty of a felony and shall be sentenced to imprisonment for not less than two years or more than ten years." The penalty for assault with intent to rob with a deadly weapon is covered by the provisions of Maryland Ann. Code, Art. 27, § 488 instead of § 12; hence, a sentence of fifteen years for such an offense was not excessive since § 488 provides for sentence of up to twenty years. *Hart v. Warden,* 213 Md. 658, 132 A.2d 592 (1957).

§ 4.15. Assault with intent to commit sexual intercourse with a female under the age of fourteen where the male is four or more years older.

In Maryland an assault upon a female under the age of fourteen, with intent to have sexual intercourse with her, where the male is four or more years older, is a crime.

In order for a person to be found guilty of this offense, the State must prove beyond a reasonable doubt that: (1) there was an assault on __________ *(name of victim);* (2) the defendant committed the assault; (3) the assault was committed with the specific intent to have sexual intercourse with __________ *(name of victim);* and (4) __________ *(name of victim),* as of the time of the assault, was a female under the age of fourteen years and the defendant at the time of the assault was at least four years older than the victim.

An assault is an intentional attempt by force or violence to inflict injury upon another person coupled with the apparent present ability to inflict such an injury. [An assault is also intentionally placing another person in reasonable fear of immediate physical harm.]

Any intentional attempt or effort to apply the least amount of force to the person of another may be sufficient so long as violence was threatened or ordered. An assault may be committed without actually touching, striking or committing bodily harm on another. [The mere use of threatening words alone does not constitute an assault. Words may, however, give actions or accompanying conduct such a meaning as to constitute an assault.]

As mentioned, the assault must be done with the specific intent to commit sexual intercourse. Sexual intercourse is defined as the actual penetration, however slight, of the male sexual organ or penis into the female sexual organ or vagina. In an assault with intent to have sexual intercourse with a female under the age of fourteen, there need not be any actual contact with or penetration of the sexual organ of the female by the sexual organ of the male. In order for you to find the defendant guilty of this offense, it is not necessary to find that the defendant accomplished his purpose to have sexual intercourse.

Force and consent are not necessary elements of this crime. A female under the age of fourteen years is deemed by the law to be incapable of consenting to sexual intercourse. The fact that the female may not have objected and may, in fact, have consented is no defense. [Where a male who is four or more years older touches or handles or takes hold a female under the age of fourteen years with the intention of having sexual intercourse with her, although without force or threats, he has committed this crime.]

As I mentioned, you must also find that __________ *(name of victim)* was under fourteen years of age and that the defendant was at least four years older than __________ *(name of victim)* at the time of the offense. [The fact that the defendant did not know that __________ *(name of victim)* was under fourteen years of age is not a defense. Such is the case, even if you find that the defendant reasonably believed __________ *(name of victim)* to be fourteen years of age or older at the time of the offense.]

COMMENT

In 1981, Maryland Ann. Code, Art. 27, § 12 was amended by eliminating the offense of assault with intent to commit vaginal intercourse with a person who is under fourteen years of age and substituting the crime of assault with intent to commit a rape in any degree or a sexual offense in the first or second degree. Article 27, § 463(a)(3) provides that a person is guilty of rape in the second degree if the person engages in vaginal intercourse with another person "(w)ho is under 14 years of age and the person performing the act is at least four years older than the victim."

When the Maryland General Assembly comprehensively revised its sexual offense laws in 1976, it recited, but did not define the elements of rape. Article 27, §464E provides that undefined words or phrases shall retain their judicially determined meaning except as expressly or by implication changed by statute. See *State v. Rusk,* 289 Md. 230, 240, 424 A.2d 720, 725 (1981). Under the common law, lack of consent is not an element of the former offense of an assault with intent to have carnal knowledge of a female child under the age of fourteen years. *Rau v. State,* 133 Md. 613, 105 A. 867 (1919). See *State v. DeLawder,* 28 Md. App. 212, 344 A.2d 446 (1975). If the complainant did not consent, the crime of assault with intent to rape — see Instruction, §4.16, *infra* — has been committed, since that crime applies equally whether the female is over or under fourteen years of age where the offense is against the will of the victim. *Weinecke v. State,* 188 Md. 172, 52 A.2d 73 (1947).

Lack of knowledge on the part of the defendant that the complainant was under the age of fourteen does not constitute a defense to the former offense of carnal knowledge, even if the defendant reasonably believed the complainant to be over fourteen years of age. *Eggleston v. State,* 4 Md. App. 124, 127, 241 A.2d 433, 434 (1968). The interpretation of the age requirements in Maryland Ann. Code, Art. 27, §463(a)(3) (cited, *supra*) was discussed in a letter dated March 11, 1976, from Maryland Assistant Attorney General George A. Nielson to Senator Steny H. Hoyer. Mr. Nielson concluded that the statute requires that the accused be four *full* years older than the victim. Thus, for example, it is not sufficient that the accused was seventeen years old while the victim was thirteen, if the accused is only three-and-a-half years older than the victim. For additional discussion of age in the grading of the sexual offense laws, see Comment, §4.36, subpart (b), Age of the victim and the accused, *infra.*

For additional common-law cases discussing the elements of the offense of assault with intent to have carnal knowledge, see *Cooper v. State,* 205 Md. 162, 106 A.2d 129, *cert. denied,* 348 U.S. 896 (1954); *Michael v. State,* 1 Md. App. 243, 229 A.2d 145 (1967), and *Weinecke v. State, supra.*

An analogous offense involves assault with intent to engage in a sexual act with another person where the victim is under fourteen years of age and the person performing the sexual act is four or more years older than the victim. This crime, entitled "Second degree sexual offense," is codified at Art. 27, § 464A(a)(3). As such, it qualifies as an aggravated sexual assault under Art. 27, § 12. As discussed in the Comment, § 4.37, Sexual offenses in the first, second, third and fourth degree, *infra,* the term "sexual act" expressly includes five types of sexual activity: cunnilingus, fellatio, anal intercourse, analingus, and the penetration, however slight, of any object into the genital or anal opening of another person's body if of such a nature as to be reasonably construed as being for the purposes of sexual arousal or gratification, or for abuse of either party.

See Comment, § 4.16, *infra,* for a discussion of assault with intent to rape or to commit a first or second degree sexual offense.

§ 4.16. Assault with intent to rape or to commit a first or second degree sexual offense.

Defendant is charged with assault with intent to commit ____________ [rape] [a first degree sexual offense] [a second degree sexual offense].

In order for the defendant to be guilty of this offense, the State must prove beyond a reasonable doubt that: (1) there was an assault on ____________ *(name of victim)*; (2) the defendant committed the assault; and (3) the assault was committed with the intent to commit ____________ [rape] [a first degree sexual offense] [a second degree sexual offense].

An assault is an intentional attempt by force or violence to inflict injury upon the person of another coupled with the apparent present ability to inflict such an injury. [An assault is also intentionally placing another person in reasonable fear of immediate physical harm.]

Any intentional attempt or effort to apply the least amount of force to the person of another may be sufficient so long as violence was threatened or ordered. An assault may be committed without actually touching, striking or committing bodily harm on another. [The mere use of threatening words alone does not constitute an assault. Words may, however, give actions or accompanying conduct such a meaning as to constitute an assault.]

(For use when defendant is charged with assault with intent to rape)

As mentioned above, the assault must be done with the specific intent to commit rape. The State must prove beyond a reasonable doubt that the defendant committed the assault with the intent to have sexual intercourse with __________ *(name of victim)* and that he had a purpose to carry into effect this intention by force or threat of force and against the consent of __________ *(name of victim)*. Sexual intercourse is defined as the actual penetration, however slight, of the male sexual organ or penis into the female sexual organ or vagina. In an assault with intent to commit rape there need not be any actual contact with or penetration of the sexual organ of the female by the sexual organ of the male. In order for you to find the defendant guilty of assault with intent to rape, it is not necessary to find that the defendant accomplished his purpose. The specific intent required is the intent to have sexual intercourse by force or threat of force and against the will or consent of the victim. The intent to rape may be inferred from all the circumstances brought out by the evidence; that is, it may be established by proven facts which permit a reasonable inference of the presence of an intent to rape.

(For use when defendant is charged with assault with intent to commit first or second degree sexual offense)

As mentioned above, the assault must be done with the specific intent to commit ________ [a first degree sexual offense] ________ [a second degree sexual offense]. ________ *(insert applicable definitions) [First degree sexual offense — See § 4.37(a), infra] [Second degree sexual offense — See § 4.37(b), § 4.37(c) or § 4.37(d), infra].*

In an assault with intent to commit ________ [a first degree sexual offense] [a second degree sexual offense] it is not necessary to find that the defendant accomplished his purpose. Therefore, there need not be any sexual act that is carried out against ________ *(name of victim).*

The intent to commit ________ [a first degree sexual offense] [a second degree sexual offense] may be inferred from all the circumstances brought out by the evidence; that is, it may be established by proven facts which permit a reasonable inference of the presence of an intent to commit ________ [a first degree sexual offense] [a second degree sexual offense].

COMMENT

In 1981, Maryland Ann. Code, Art. 27, § 12, was amended by eliminating the offense of assault with intent to commit rape and to ravish and substituting the crime of assault with intent to commit a rape in any degree or a sexual offense in the first or second degree. Therefore, an aggravated sexual assault may take any of the following forms: first degree rape, second degree rape, first degree sexual offense or second degree sexual offense.

The instruction on assault with intent to commit rape is patterned on common-law rape which is now designated as second degree rape. See Instruction and Comment, § 4.36(b), *infra*. Two other forms of second degree rape involve sexual intercourse where the victim is under fourteen years and the person performing the act is four or more years older than the victim — see Instruction, § 4.36(c), *infra* — and where the victim is mentally defective, mentally incapacitated or physically helpless — see Instruction, § 4.36(d), *infra*. Second degree rape may be elevated to first degree rape by the presence of certain aggravating circumstances occurring in the commission of the offense. See Instruction, § 4.36(a) and accompanying discussion, *infra*.

The assault with intent to commit rape instruction is patterned substantially on holdings in various Maryland cases. Most of the case law in Maryland has dealt with the common-law offense of assault with intent to rape. The essential ingredients of the crime of assault with intent to rape were established in *Middleton v. State,* 6 Md. App. 380, 251 A.2d 224 (1969), which set out the elements as: (a) an assault; (b) an intention to have carnal knowledge of a female; and (c) a purpose to carry into effect this intention with force and against the consent of the female. See also *Cooper v. State,* 220 Md. 183, 152 A.2d 120 (1959). In other words, the crime consists of an aggravated assault, that is, a specified intention is required. *Middleton v. State, supra.*

According to the Court in *Duffin v. State,* 229 Md. 434, 184 A.2d 624 (1962), a trial judge does not have to give an instruction on the defense of voluntary abandonment of purpose if there is no evidence to support it.

An aggravated assault with the intention of committing rape may also constitute an attempt to commit that crime within the purview of the felony-murder statute. See Art. 27, § 410. See also *Middleton v. State, supra.*

In *Christensen v. State,* 33 Md. App. 635, 365 A.2d 562 (1976), the Court held that, where the defendant was indicted for assault with intent to rape and attempted rape, it was not a violation of double jeopardy to acquit the defendant of assault with intent to rape and convict him of attempted rape. The Court maintained that assault with intent to rape and attempted rape are separate and distinct crimes; the former is a common-law misdemeanor, the latter is a felony. The crimes are distinguishable in that attempted rape may be established by proof of an overt act, or by proof of threats, while assault with intent to commit rape requires more substantial acts, and cannot be established merely by proof of threats. See also *Cousins v. State,* 277 Md. 383, 354 A.2d 825, *cert. denied,* 429 U.S. 1027 (1976); *Thomas v. State,* 277 Md. 257, 353 A.2d 240 (1976); *Walker v. State,* 53 Md. App. 171, 452 A.2d 1234 (1982).

Maryland Ann. Code, Art. 27, § 12, provides that every person convicted of the crime of an assault with intent to commit a rape in any degree or a sexual offense in the first or second degree is guilty of a felony and shall be sentenced to imprisonment for not less than two years nor more than fifteen years. See Instructions and Comments: §§ 4.11, 4.12, *supra,* (discussion of the crimes of assault and battery); § 4.36, *infra,* (discussion of the crime of rape); and § 4.37, *infra,* (discussion of sexual offenses).

See Comment, § 4.15, *supra,* for a discussion of assault with intent to commit sexual intercourse with a female under the age of fourteen where the male is four or more years older.

C. Homicide

§ 4.20. Introductory instruction on grading of homicide.

Homicide is the killing of one human being by another. It can be either felonious or innocent. Innocent homicide is the killing of another without criminal guilt. It occurs when the killing is committed with legal justification or excuse. Felonious homicide is the killing of another human being without legal justification or excuse.

[If you find that the defendant did commit a felonious killing, then the homicide is either murder or manslaughter.] [There are two degrees of murder: murder in the first degree and murder in the second degree.]

In this case, the defendant is charged with a felonious killing of a human being, namely __________ (*insert offense(s) charged*).

§ 4.21a. Murder — First degree: willful, deliberate and premeditated killing.

There are two degrees of murder: murder in the first degree and murder in the second degree. One distinction between first degree murder and second degree murder is based upon the elements of premeditation and deliberation. All murder which shall be perpetrated by [means of poison or lying in wait or by] any kind of willful, deliberate, and premeditated killing shall be murder in the first degree.

In order to convict the defendant of murder in the first degree, the State must prove beyond a reasonable doubt that: (1) the defendant inflicted an injury upon __________ (*name of victim*) which resulted in death; (2) at the time the injury was inflicted the defendant intended to kill __________ (*name of victim*); (3) there was no justification, excuse or a proper mitigating circumstance; and (4) the killing was willful, premeditated and deliberate.

For a homicide to be willful there must be a specific purpose and design to kill. Willful means with intentional purpose, as distinguished from accident or negligence. There must be a full and conscious knowledge of the purpose to kill. To be premeditated, the design to kill must have preceded the killing by an appreciable length of time; that is, time enough to be deliberate. Premeditation, as an element of murder, means planning or conceiving of the design or scheme to kill ahead of time, before the commission of the fatal act. Deliberation, as an element of murder, means acting in a cool state as opposed to a heated state. Deliberation implies reflection, however brief, upon the act and the consequences before committing the killing. It is a fixed and determined purpose as distinguished from a sudden impulse. Deliberation is evidenced by choice, determination, or some weighing of the pros and cons with regard to the design to kill.

[In determining whether the killing was willful, premeditated and deliberate you should consider all of the facts and circumstances, including the defendant's conduct. Three categories of evidence may be especially important: (1) any facts about how and what the defendant did before the actual killing which showed *planning activity*: that is, activity directed toward the killing; (2) any facts about the defendant's prior relationship and conduct with the victim, if any, from which *motive* may be inferred; and (3) any facts about the *manner of the killing* from which it may be inferred that the defendant must have intentionally killed according to a preconceived design.]

First degree murder, in essence, is killing in cold blood after having calculated the circumstances. You must find from the evidence the actual intent, which is the fully-formed purpose to kill. There cannot be first degree murder if the killing is the offspring of such rashness or impetuous temper that the mind had not become fully conscious of its own design.

COMMENT

This instruction on first degree premeditated murder was written to complement Instruction, § 4.22a, Murder — Second degree. Since murder in the second degree is a lesser included offense of first degree premeditated murder and the distinguishing *mens rea* element — willful, premeditated and deliberate — is almost always in dispute, it is assumed that the second degree murder instruction will also be given. A recommended sequence is to give the following instructions in such situations: § 4.20, Introductory instruction on grading of homicide; § 4.21a, Murder — First degree: willful, deliberate and premeditated killing; § 4.22a, Murder — Second degree; and § 4.22b, Murder — When both first and second degree murder are in issue. If the instruction on second degree murder is not given, this instruction can be amplified by adding relevant paragraphs from the latter form.

In Maryland, murder is divided into two degrees, first degree and second degree. First degree murder includes both premeditated murder and felony murder. See Instruction, § 4.21b, Murder — First degree: felony murder, *infra*.

Maryland Ann. Code, Art. 27, § 407, provides: "All murder which shall be perpetrated by means of poison, or lying in wait, or by any kind of wilful, deliberate and premeditated killing shall be murder in the first degree."

The essential elements of the *mens rea* of so-called premeditated murder are malice, willfulness, premeditation and deliberation. The word "malice" does not appear in this instruction but its essential components are set forth in the second, third, and fourth elements of the offense in the second paragraph. The Court has held that the judge need not employ or define the term "malice" when instructing the jury on first degree murder so long as the instruction states that the killing was "wilful, deliberate and premeditated ... without excuse, justification or mitigation." *Leach v. State,* 47 Md. App. 611, 621, 425 A.2d 234, 239 (1981).

Malice must be alleged in the indictment and proven. *Lindsay v. State,* 8 Md. App. 100, 104, 258 A.2d 760, 763 (1969); *Faulcon v. State,* 211 Md. 249, 126 A.2d 858 (1956). For a discussion of the elements of premeditated murder, see *Tichnell v. State,* 287 Md. 695, 717-18, 415 A.2d 830, 842 (1980) (Tichnell I); *Wilson v. State,* 261 Md. 551, 276 A.2d 214 (1971); *Carroll v. State,* 11 Md. App. 412, 274 A.2d 677 (1971); *DeVaughn v. State,* 232 Md. 447, 194 A.2d 109, *cert. denied,* 376 U.S. 927 (1963); *Cook v. State,* 9 Md. App. 214, 263 A.2d 33 (1970).

First degree premeditated murder has been described as follows:

> The actual intent coupled with the fully-formed malicious purpose to kill, with enough time for deliberation and premeditation to lapse so as to convince a fact finder that the slaying was not the offshoot of some intemperate conduct, rashness, or temper, but an act done under the direction of a mind that is fully conscious of its own design.

R. Gilbert & C. Moylan, Jr., *Maryland Criminal Law: Practice and Procedure* 11 (1983). See *Hyde v. State,* 228 Md. 209, 179 A.2d 421 (1962), *cert. denied,* 372 U.S. 945 (1963); *Cummings v. State,* 223 Md. 606, 165 A.2d 886 (1960), *cert. denied,* 366 U.S. 922 (1961).

In *Faulcon v. State, supra,* Judge Collins stated for the Court:

> For a homicide to be "wilful" there must be a specific purpose and design to kill. To be "deliberate" there must be a full and conscious knowledge of the purpose to kill. To be "premeditated" the design to kill must have preceded the killing by an appreciable length of time; that is, time enough to be deliberate. To justify a conviction of murder in the first degree the jury or court, sitting without a jury, must find the actual intent, the fully formed purpose to kill, with enough time for deliberation and premeditation....

Id. at 257, 126 A.2d at 862. *Accord Gladden v. State,* 273 Md. 383, 330 A.2d 176 (1974) and cases there cited.

To constitute premeditation, the intent to kill must be fully formed. The intent or design to kill must precede the act of killing by some appreciable amount of time. If the time is sufficient for some reflection and consideration, it is enough for premeditation no matter how brief the interval. *Brown v. State,* 220 Md. 29, 150 A.2d 895 (1959); *Chisley v. State,* 202 Md. 87, 95 A.2d 577 (1953); *James v. State,* 31 Md. App. 666, 358 A.2d 595 (1976). See also *Hounshell v. State,* 61 Md. App. 364, 486 A.2d 789 (1985).

Premeditation and deliberation can be proved by circumstantial as well as direct evidence. In *Tichnell v. State, supra,* the Court noted that the firing of two or more shots separated by an interval of time may be viewed as evidence of premeditation. In *Kier v. State,* 216 Md. 513, 140 A.2d 896 (1958), the Court stated:

> The brutal manner in which the victim was beaten about the face and head with these or other objects indicates a protracted period during which the assault continued. Then the assailant procured or produced a butcher knife which he plunged into her body not only once but twice. There was ample evidence to justify the trial court in its conclusion that the action of the appellant was wilful, that it was deliberate, and that it was premeditated.

Id. at 523, 140 A.2d at 900. See *Fuller v. State,* 45 Md. App. 414, 413 A.2d 277 (1980), discussing *Kier v. State, supra.*

In *Smith v. State,* 41 Md. App. 277, 398 A.2d 426 (1979), Judge Moylan observed: "There is a circular quality to the threesome [willful, deliberate, and premeditated]. They define themselves in terms of each other." *Id.* at 308, 398 A.2d at 444. In *Brown v. State,* 44 Md. App. 71, 410 A.2d 17 (1980), the Court, citing *Smith v. State, supra,* noted that "[t]he use of all three words seems to us to serve no purpose other than to shroud the intention in an aura of redundancy so as to convey the seriousness of the matter." *Id.* at 78, 410 A.2d at 22.

In *Colvin v. State,* 299 Md. 88, 472 A.2d 953, *cert. denied,* 105 S. Ct. 226 (1984), the Court held that the evidence was sufficient to prove that the killing was a premeditated act where it showed that the defendant carried the murder weapon from the kitchen to the site of assault and also showed that the victim tried to defend herself. A *prima facie* case as to this trilogy of terms is made out by proof of a specific intent to kill. *Ferrel v. State,* 60 Md. App. 459, 483 A.2d 777 (1984), *aff'd,* 304 Md. 679, 500 A.2d 1050 (1985).

For a discussion of the history of the distinction between first and second degree murder, see *Lindsay v. State, supra. See also* Comment, § 4.22a, Murder — Second degree, *infra,* for a discussion of burden of proof and inferences.

§ 4.21b. Murder — First degree: felony murder.

A person may be guilty of murder in the first degree if there was a killing in the perpetration of [or attempted perpetration] of certain felonies. The defendant has been charged with the responsibility for the death occurring in the commission of __________ (*specify applicable felony or felonies*).

In order for the defendant to be found guilty of felony murder, the State must prove beyond a reasonable doubt that: (1) the defendant [or a co-felon] inflicted an injury or injuries on __________ (*name of victim*) which resulted in death [or the defendant [or a co-felon] caused a direct lethal act against the victim by compelling the victim to occupy a position of danger]; (2) the killing occurred while the defendant [or a co-felon] was perpetrating or attempting to perpetrate the felony of __________ (*specify underlying felony*); and (3) the killing was done in furtherance of the attempted or committed felony [or in pursuit of the common purpose or objective for which the co-felons combined].

Under the felony murder rule, the State does not have to prove premeditation, deliberation and willfulness in order to prove murder in the first degree. The fact that a felony was being attempted or committed is sufficient to sustain a conviction for first degree murder if the killing resulted from and was in furtherance of the attempted or committed felony.

Any killing, even if accidental, impulsive or committed without purpose and intent to kill, is murder in the first degree if committed in the perpetration or attempted perpetration of __________ (*specify underlying felony*). However, the act of killing must be done by the defendant [or a co-felon] [unless the defendant [or a co-felon] committed an act against the victim which directly placed the victim in a position of danger. An example is where the defendant [or a co-felon] uses the victim as a shield.].

The State must prove the perpetration or attempted perpetration of the felony beyond a reasonable doubt. I will now instruct you on the elements of the felony of __________ (*specify underlying felony*): ______________________________

(*Refer to instruction on applicable underlying felony*). [The State is not required to indict and convict on the underlying felony to sustain a conviction of murder in the first degree.]

[*When there are co-felons*: If two or more persons, acting together, are perpetrating or attempting to perpetrate

__________ (*specify underlying felony*) and one of them, in the course of the felony and in furtherance of the common purpose to commit the felony, kills a human being, both the person who committed the killing and the person or persons who aided and abetted in the felony are guilty of murder in the first degree. A killing by one co-felon, even if unintentional, which is in furtherance of or pursuant to the common object or purpose for which they combined, extends criminal liability for murder in the first degree to each and every co-felon. However, there is no criminal liability on the part of the defendant if the killing was a fresh and independent product of the mind of another co-felon, outside the scope of or foreign to the common object or purpose for which they combined.]

[If you reach a verdict of guilty, you should indicate specifically whether, from all the evidence, you have found the defendant guilty of a felony murder or whether you have found the requisite intent of willfulness, premeditation and deliberation independent of the underlying felony so that the defendant would be guilty of a premeditated murder].

COMMENT

(a) In general

The felony murder rule has been codified in Maryland Ann. Code, Art. 27, §§ 408 to 410. These statutes provide that any killing committed in the perpetration or attempted perpetration of specified felonies constitutes murder in the first degree.

The elements of a willful, premeditated, deliberate act are inferred from the nexus between the homicide and the felony. Thus, it is not required that the killing be willful, deliberate and premeditated to elevate homicide to murder in the first degree. *Price v. State,* 261 Md. 573, 277 A.2d 256 (1971); *Lynch v. State,* 9 Md. App. 441, 265 A.2d 283 (1970); *Wiggins v. State,* 8 Md.

App. 598, 261 A.2d 503 (1970); *Lindsay v. State,* 8 Md. App. 100, 258 A.2d 760 (1969).

"Even an unintentional, an unplanned, an unparticipated-in death that occurs in the course of a felony is, by statutory definition, murder in the first degree." *Middleton v. State,* 6 Md. App. 380, 385, 251 A.2d 224, 227 (1969). Although there must be a causal link between the felonious act and the homicide, under the felony murder rule, harm need not be foreseeable or intentional.

(b) Qualifying underlying felonies

Pursuant to Maryland Ann. Code, felonies that qualify for the felony murder rule include arson (Art. 27, § 408), barn, stable, or warehouse burning (Art. 27, § 409), sodomy, mayhem, robbery, burglary, kidnapping, rape in any degree, sexual offense in the first or second degree, storehouse breaking, daytime housebreaking and escape (Art. 27, § 410). In the comment to the death penalty sentencing instruction, § 4.21c, *infra,* it is noted that, under Art. 27, § 413(d)(10), felony murder may be considered as an aggravating circumstance which the State can establish but only some of the preceding felonies qualify: namely, arson, robbery, and rape or sexual offense in the first degree.

In *Middleton v. State,* 6 Md. App. 380, 251 A.2d 224 (1969), the defendant was convicted of first degree murder under the felony murder rule based on the underlying crime of assault with intent to rape. The defendant argued that Art. 27, § 410 expressly applies only when there has been an attempt to perpetrate a rape. The Court held that an aggravated assault with the intention of committing rape may also constitute an attempt to commit that crime within the purview of the statute. Similarly, assault with intent to rob may also constitute an attempted robbery within the meaning of the section. See *Wright v. State,* 307 Md. 552, 515 A.2d 1157 (1986).

(c) Indictment on underlying felony not required

The State is not required to indict and convict on the underlying felony to sustain a conviction of murder in the first degree.

Adams v. State, 8 Md. App. 684, 262 A.2d 69, *cert. denied,* 400 U.S. 928 (1970); *Parker v. State,* 7 Md. App. 167, 195, 254 A.2d 381, 397 (1969), *cert. denied,* 256 Md. 747 (1970), *cert. denied,* 402 U.S. 984 (1971). In *Williams v. State,* 50 Md. App. 255, 437 A.2d 665 (1981), the Court held in a second trial, that attempted robbery could serve as the prerequisite underlying felony for felony murder even though the attempted robbery charge had been subjected to *nolle prosequi* in the first trial, which had resulted in a mistrial, since *nolle prosequi* of that charge did not amount to not guilty, acquittal, or adjudication on the merits of ultimate fact.

Also, in *Ross v. State,* 308 Md. 337, 519 A.2d 735 (1987), the Court held that the short form indictment was not unconstitutional where it identified the victim, the time, and the place of the offense and notified the defendant that he was charged with first degree murder. There is no requirement that a charging document inform the defendant of the specific theory on which the State will rely.

(d) When act of killing is by accomplice

Under the felony murder rule a participating felon is guilty of murder in the first degree when a homicide has been committed by a co-felon. *Campbell v. State,* 293 Md. 438, 444 A.2d 1034 (1982). The purpose of the felony murder rule is to deter felons from killing by holding them strictly responsible for killings they or their co-felons commit. Therefore, a co-defendant cannot assert a successful defense by asserting that the other felon did the act which resulted in the homicide. See *Mumford v. State,* 19 Md. App. 640, 313 A.2d 563 (1974).

In *Shockley v. State,* 218 Md. 491, 148 A.2d 371 (1959), the trial court was not satisfied that one of two brothers had participated in the actual killing or that he knew that the killing was to take place. The Court found, however, that he had participated in an attempt to perpetrate a robbery, and that was enough under the statute to support a finding of first degree murder. See Instructions: § 2.01, Accomplice's testimony — Corroboration, and § 4.02, Aiding and abetting, *supra.*

(e) Causal nexus between underlying felony and the killing

In *Scott v. State,* 49 Md. App. 70, 430 A.2d 615 (1981), the Court applied a "but for" test to determine whether there was a causal link between the killing and the felony. In order that conduct be actual cause of particular result, it is usually sufficient that the result would not have happened in the absence of the conduct.

In *Lipscomb v. State,* 223 Md. 599, 165 A.2d 918 (1960), a case involving rape, it was held that it made no difference as to guilt whether death occurred after the rape had been accomplished or in an attempt to perpetrate it. *Cf. Foster v. State,* 297 Md. 191, 454 A.2d 986 (1983), *cert. denied,* 464 U.S. 1073 (1984).

In *Mumford v. State,* 19 Md. App. 640, 313 A.2d 563 (1974), accomplice liability and the requirement of a causal nexus between the underlying felony and the resultant homicide are discussed. The Court ruled that the question of what is or is not a natural and probable consequence is a question for the trier of fact. In *Mumford* the trial court instructed the jury as to felony murder arising from burglary. The court refused the defendant's requested instruction to present the theory that the killing resulted from an unexpected rape committed by the defendant's companions. The appellate court reversed, stating that if the jury were properly instructed, it could have chosen not to believe that the death occurred pursuant to the burglary, but rather from rape, fresh and independent of the common design.

In *Stewart v. State,* 65 Md. App. 372, 500 A.2d 676 (1985), the Court held that the evidence was sufficient to show a causal relationship for fright-induced death of a robbery victim from heart failure approximately two hours later.

(f) When act of killing is by victim, bystander or police officer

A controversy concerning the scope of the felony murder rule exists when there is a killing done by a victim, policeman or bystander. The present trend in Maryland and elsewhere is to narrow the felony murder doctrine. See *Campbell v. State,* 293 Md. 438, 444 A.2d 1034 (1982); *Poole v. State,* 295 Md. 167, 453 A.2d 1218 (1983) (Poole II). In the past, the courts have predicated convictions of felony murder under a proximate cause analysis. For example, in *Jackson v. State,* 286 Md. 430, 408 A.2d 711 (1979), the Court held that robbers who were fleeing from an armed robbery with a hostage were responsible for the accidental killing of the hostage by a policeman who was attempting to apprehend the robbers. The Court found that the behavior of the robbers established such a causal connection with respect to the death as to make them criminally liable. In light of their criminal agency, the killing of the hostage was first degree murder with regard to the robbers.

But recently, without directly overruling *Jackson,* the Court stated that predicating a conviction under felony murder should be based on agency principles. In *Campbell,* the Court recognized that the present trend is "... to limit criminal culpability under the felony murder doctrine to lethal acts committed by felons or their accomplices and not to employ the proximate cause theory to extend criminal culpability for lethal acts of nonfelons." *Campbell, supra* at 449, 444 A.2d at 1040-1041. The Court recognized that an extension would not achieve the rule's basic purpose of deterring felons from killing by holding them strictly responsible for killings committed by persons not acting in furtherance of the felony. In *Campbell,* the defendant's murder conviction was reversed when a co-felon was killed by either a victim or a police officer. The Court did indicate, however, that a felon would still be liable for the death of a victim, regardless of who did the actual killing if the victim was used as a shield or if the defendant compelled the victim to occupy a position of danger. Their reasoning was that the above behavior constitutes a direct lethal act against the victim.

The fact that a killing was committed during perpetration of one of the felonies enumerated in the statute determines only the degree of the crime and the penalty to be imposed; the State is required to prove facts showing a felony was committed by the accused and that there was a causal link between the homicide and the felony. *Jackson v. State, supra.*

(g) Merger of underlying felony

The trial court should instruct the jury to indicate in its verdict whether the accused has been found guilty of murder under Maryland Ann. Code, Art. 27, § 410 only, or whether from all the evidence, it has found the reauisite intent of willfulness, premeditation and deliberation, independent of the underlying felony. This determination by the jury allows the court to address the question of merger as raised in *State v. Frye,* 283 Md. 709, 393 A.2d 1372 (1978). The Court in *Frye* held that if the accused is found guilty of murder under Art. 27, § 410 only, the underlying felony should be merged into the murder. Additionally, since the record was not clear as to whether the murder convictions had been premised on a finding of premeditation (Art. 27, § 407) or on the felony murder statute (Art. 27, § 410), the Court held that the doubt should be resolved in favor of the appellant and therefore in accordance with the merger doctrine.

In another felony murder case the Court reversed the appellant's conviction for the underlying felony, holding that the conviction on both charges constituted a violation of fifth amendment double jeopardy principles. *Newton v. State,* 280 Md. 260, 373 A.2d 262 (1977). Quoting the "required evidence test" enunciated by the Supreme Court in *Blockburger v. United States,* 284 U.S. 299, 304, 52 S. Ct. 180, 182, 76 L. Ed. 306, 309 (1931), the Court wrote that "the applicable rule is that where the same act or transaction constitutes a violation of two distinct statutory provisions, the test to be applied to determine whether there are two offenses or only one is whether each provision requires proof of an additional fact which the other does not." *See Pulley v. State,* 38 Md. App. 682, 382 A.2d 621 (1978); *Johnson v. State,* 38 Md. App. 306, 381 A.2d 303 (1977) (holding that simultaneous conviction for felony murder and underlying felony of attempted robbery with a deadly weapon violates the fifth amendment). In accordance with the "required evidence test," merger of a murder and the underlying felony is *not* compelled where the jury has stated that its murder verdict was based on a finding of willfulness, deliberation and premeditation beyond a reasonable doubt.

Robeson v. State, 39 Md. App. 365, 386 A.2d 795 (1978), *aff'd,* 285 Md. 498, 403 A.2d 1221 (1979); *Newton v. State, supra.*

§ 4.21c. Murder — First degree: death penalty sentencing.

The defendant has been found guilty of murder in the first degree. It is now for you, as the sentencing jury, to determine whether the proper sentence shall be imprisonment for life or the death penalty. Your determination shall be based [solely] upon the evidence presented to you during this sentencing phase [as well as the evidence presented to you during the guilt determination phase] of this trial.

My instructions concerning the law are binding on you and must be followed in determining the sentence. By your oath you are bound to determine the sentence in accordance with the law, and you must not allow any prejudice, passion or public opinion against __________ (*name of defendant*) to enter into your deliberation.

It is your recollection of the facts and your determination of the weight and credibility of any evidence or witnesses which controls. If your recollection of the testimony differs from that of counsel's or the court's, you should use your recollection of the testimony and not counsel's or mine.

[You have received copies of the verdict sheet to follow as I instruct you, but when you go to the jury room to deliberate your foreperson will carry one copy for your verdict to be delivered, and the others will be collected].

In making your determination, you shall follow the Findings and Sentencing Determination Form which [you have in your possession] [your foreperson has in his possession].

(First degree principal instruction to be given unless the defendant employed another person to commit the murder pursuant to a contract or promise of remuneration)

Under Maryland law, the defendant cannot be sentenced to death unless the State first proves beyond a reasonable doubt that the defendant was a principal in the first degree to the murder. The fact that the defendant has been convicted of first degree murder does not necessarily mean that he was the first degree principal. Your first concern will be to determine whether the defendant was a principal in the first degree to the murder.

A principal in the first degree is one who is the immediate perpetrator of the killing. He is the one who actually commits the killing by his own hand. This may include the use of a weapon or instrument, such as __________ (*list weapon or instrument(s) applicable to case: gun, knife, mechanical or chemical means, such as poison or powder, or by an animal, child, or other innocent agent acting under his direction*).

[There may be joint principals in the first degree, as where two or more cause the death of another by beating, stabbing, shooting or other means, in which both, or all, personally participate with their own hands. If, however, one holds a victim while a second inflicts a fatal injury with a knife, only the stabber is a principal in the first degree, because the stabbing caused the death and the holding was merely aiding, thus making the holder guilty as a principal in the second degree.]

[The mere physical presence by the defendant at the time and place of the killing is not by itself sufficient to establish his guilt as a principal in the first degree, but may be considered along with all the surrounding circumstances.]

As I mentioned, the State has the burden of proving that the defendant was a principal in the first degree to the murder beyond a reasonable doubt. This does not mean beyond all possible doubt or to a mathematical certainty. A reasonable doubt is a doubt founded upon reason. It is not a fanciful doubt, or a whimsical or arbitrary doubt. It is such a doubt as would cause a juror, after careful and impartial consideration of all the evidence, to be so undecided that the juror cannot say that he or she has an abiding conviction of the defendant's guilt. [It is such a doubt as would cause a reasonable person to hesitate to act in the graver or more important transactions of life.]

If you have a reasonable doubt that the defendant was a principal in the first degree to the murder, the law requires you to mark "not proven" at the end of Section I of the sentencing form. You are then to proceed to Section V and enter "life imprisonment." On the other hand, if you find beyond a reasonable doubt that the defendant was a first degree principal to the murder, you should mark "proven" at the end of Section I of the sentencing form.

If you find that the State has proven beyond a reasonable doubt that the defendant was a first degree principal to the murder, you will next answer three different, yet interrelated, questions. First, has the existence of any of the listed aggravating circumstance(s) been proven by the State beyond a reasonable doubt? [Although the statute provides for several aggravating circumstances,] the State has specified that the only aggravating circumstance(s) which you may consider in this case is (are): ____________ (*list aggravating circumstances relied upon by the State; see Section II of sentencing form or Comment, subpart (c), for a complete list*). If you unanimously find that the State has proven beyond a reasonable doubt an aggravating circumstance(s) to exist, your foreperson shall mark "proven" next to that aggravating circumstance(s) in Section II of the sentencing form. If you do not unanimously find that the State has proven beyond a reasonable doubt that a particular aggravating circumstance exists, your foreperson must mark "not proven" in the space beside that aggravating circumstance, and you may not consider that factor in determining the sentence. If the State has not proven beyond a reasonable doubt the existence of any aggravating circumstance — that is, if the listed aggravating circumstance(s) (is) (are) marked "not proven" — the sentence automatically imposed on the defendant will be life imprisonment. You must then proceed to Section V of the sentencing form and enter the words "life imprisonment." [I have instructed you on the standard of proof of beyond a reasonable doubt.] *(If first degree principal instruction was not given, instruct jury on standard of proof beyond a reasonable doubt appearing above.)*

If the State has proven beyond a reasonable doubt the existence of one or more aggravating circumstances, then you must address the second question: has the defendant proven by a preponderance of the evidence the existence of any of the listed mitigating circumstances or the existence of any other unlisted mitigating circumstance(s) which you may find appropriate in this case?

The defendant has the burden of proving the existence of any mitigating circumstance(s) by a preponderance of the evidence. The preponderance of the evidence standard which you are to apply has been defined as "more likely so than not so" or "more probable than not." This is a lesser burden of proof than the standard of "beyond a reasonable doubt." In determining whether the defendant has met this burden, you may consider any evidence presented by the defendant as well as any relevant evidence that may have been introduced by the State. A mitigating circumstance may be proven by evidence from either the State or the defense or both. The law does not require that a mitigating circumstance establish justification or excuse for the crime.

Section III of the sentencing form lists seven mitigating circumstances that must be considered in every death sentencing proceeding. In addition to those listed mitigating circumstances, you may find by a preponderance of the evidence that any additional mitigating circumstance(s) exists. Any other mitigating circumstances which you find to have been proven by a preponderance of the evidence should be specifically set forth by your foreperson in part 8 of Section III. [In addition to any other unlisted mitigating circumstances which you may find to exist, you are required to consider whether the following unlisted mitigating circumstance(s) has been established in this case: __________ *(list mitigating circumstance(s) specified by the defendant).*]

[I instruct you that the following mitigating circumstance(s) (has not been contested by the State and) has been established by a preponderance of the evidence: __________ *(list any mitigating circumstance(s) that has been established as a matter of law, such as defendant has not been previously found guilty of a crime of violence under Maryland Ann. Code, Art. 27, § 413(g)(1)).*]

In general, mitigating circumstances are any facts or factors about the defendant, his character or background, which in fairness or mercy may be considered by you during your deliberation. A mitigating circumstance is anything relating to the defendant's character or background, such as religion, education, environment, mentality, or the nature of the evidence against the defendant, which makes __________ *(insert defendant's name)* appropriately deserving of a sentence of life imprisonment rather than death. These are only examples of some of the types of mitigating circumstances you may consider. If you perceive anything relating to the defendant or the crime which causes you to believe that death may not be appropriate, you may treat such factor as a mitigating circumstance.

I will now instruct you on how to mark the sentencing form in considering whether the defendant has proven by a preponderance of the evidence the existence of any mitigating circumstance(s). See Section III of the sentencing form. For each of the listed mitigating circumstances, you are to mark one of three boxes: if you unanimously find by a preponderance of the evidence that a mitigating circumstance exists, mark the box next to the "a" letter; if you unanimously find by a preponderance of the evidence that a mitigating circumstance does not exist, mark the box next to the "b" letter; if, after a reasonable period of deliberation, one or more of you, but fewer than all 12, find by a preponderance of the evidence that a mitigating circumstance exists, mark the box next to the "c" letter. If you unanimously find by a preponderance of the evidence that one or more *unlisted* mitigating circumstances exist, you are to place a mark in the box next to the letter "a" of part 8 of Section III. You should then write in the mitigating circumstance(s) that you have found to exist. If, after a reasonable period of deliberation, one or more of you, but fewer than all 12, find by a preponderance of the evidence that one or more unlisted mitigating circumstances exist, you are to place a mark in the box next to the letter "b" of part 8 of Section III. Then, you should write in the mitigating circumstance(s) that one or more of you have found to exist.

If you unanimously find by a preponderance of the evidence that no listed or unlisted mitigating circumstance has been proven, and you have previously unanimously found that the State has proven beyond a reasonable doubt that at least one aggravating circumstance exists, the sentence automatically imposed on the defendant will be the death penalty. You should then proceed to Section V of the sentencing form and enter "death."

If one or more of you find by a preponderance of the evidence that one or more listed or unlisted mitigating circumstances have been proven, then you must address the third question: has the State proved by a preponderance of the evidence that [this] [these] aggravating circumstance(s) outweigh(s) [this] [these] mitigating circumstance(s)? Each individual juror must weigh the aggravating circumstance(s) found unanimously to have been proven against any mitigating circumstances found unanimously to have been proven, as well as against any mitigating circumstances found by that individual juror to have been proven. The burden of persuasion is upon the State with regard to the weighing of aggravating and mitigating circumstances by a preponderance of the evidence.

As I have instructed you, to prove something by a preponderance of the evidence means to produce in your minds a belief that something is "more likely so than not so" or "more probable than not" or that it is "more likely true than not true."

The weight to be given aggravating and mitigating circumstances is not necessarily determined by the number of aggravating and mitigating circumstances that you have found to exist. This is a weighing process and not a mere counting process or tallying of aggravating and mitigating circumstances. You must weigh aggravating and mitigating circumstances in terms of their substantiality and persuasiveness and not merely in terms of their relative number. You must decide how persuasive the mitigating factors are when compared to the aggravating factors. You may feel that a single mitigating circumstance is compelling enough to justify a life sentence even if you could find more than one aggravating circumstance. On the other hand, you may find that a single aggravating circumstance, when weighed against the mitigating circumstances, is sufficient to justify a death sentence.

I will now instruct you further on the process for weighing aggravating and mitigating circumstances and on the marking of the sentencing form. If you unanimously find that the State has proven by a preponderance of the evidence that the aggravating circumstance(s) marked "proven" in Section II outweigh the mitigating circumstance(s) found in Section III, the defendant will be sentenced to death. As I have instructed you, each individual juror must weigh the aggravating circumstance(s) unanimously found to have been proven by the State beyond a reasonable doubt against any mitigating circumstance(s) unanimously proven by the defendant by a preponderance of the evidence as well as against any mitigating circumstance(s) found by any individual juror or jurors to have been proven by the defendant by a preponderance of the evidence. If you were in disagreement as to the existence of a mitigating circumstance, you must proceed to the weighing process and each of you must weigh the mitigating circumstances he or she finds, if any, against the proven aggravating circumstance(s). As long as one juror adheres to the view that a mitigating circumstance(s) exists which is not outweighed by an aggravating circumstance(s), the jury cannot unanimously determine to impose a sentence of death.

If you unanimously find that the State has proven by a preponderance of the evidence that the aggravating circumstance(s) outweigh(s) the mitigating circumstance(s), the sentence shall be death. If so, you are to mark "yes" in Section IV of the sentencing form and enter "death" in Section V. If you do not unanimously find that the State has proven by a preponderance of the evidence that the aggravating circumstance(s) outweigh(s) the mitigating circumstance(s), the sentence shall be life imprisonment.

Then, you are to mark "no" in Section IV and enter "life imprisonment" in Section V.

You should carefully consider all of the facts and circumstances in evidence. Once your deliberations have ceased and you have reached your verdict, you shall each make sure that the determination and verdict written on the Findings and Sentencing Determination Form represent your own verdict and you shall then sign your name in the space provided at the end of the form.

COMMENT

(a) Introduction—Sentencing form provided by Rule 4-343

The death penalty instruction is based on the revised Findings and Sentencing Determination Form, which is reproduced at the end of this introductory section. This sentencing form was adopted by the Court of Appeals' Standing Committee on Rules of Practice and Procedure on July 20, 1987. It reflects clarifications in the death penalty law in *Foster v. State,* 304 Md. 439, 499 A.2d 1236 (1985); *Evans v. State,* 304 Md. 487, 499 A.2d 1261 (1985); and *Mills v. State,* 310 Md. 33, 527 A.2d 3 (1987). As of this writing, the U.S. Supreme Court has granted certiorari in the *Mills* case. In *Mills,* the Court distinguished between aggravating and mitigating circumstances in terms of whether unanimous jury determinations are required. The Court stated that the weighing of aggravating versus mitigating circumstances is to be performed by each juror individually.

The death penalty instruction needs to be modified in the event of either of two circumstances. The instruction assumes that the defendant is charged with being a principal in the first degree to the murder. If the defendant is charged with engaging or hiring another person to commit the murder, and the murder was committed as a result of a contract for remuneration or the promise of remuneration, the first section of the instruction must be changed. Also, this instruction assumes that the State has not given at least thirty days' notice prior to trial that it intends to seek a sentence of "imprisonment for life without the possibility of parole." Maryland Ann. Code, Art. 27, § 412(b). Additional language should refer to Section VI of the Findings and Sentencing Determination Form. If the State does not provide such notice, Section VI of the form should not be submitted to the jury. Maryland Rules of Procedure, Rule 4-343(f).

As a brief historical overview, Chapter 115, Acts of 1908 of the Maryland General Assembly provided trial courts of general jurisdiction with the discretion to sentence a person convicted of first degree murder either to death or to life imprisonment. In *Furman v. Georgia,* 408 U.S. 238, 92 S. Ct. 2726, 33 L. Ed. 2d 346 (1972), the United States Supreme Court declared in a per curiam opinion that death sentences administered under such discretionary statutes constituted cruel and unusual punishment in violation of the eighth and fourteenth amendments of the United States Constitution. Five justices supported the decision; four justices dissented. The variety of separate opinions left unclear the specific implications of the opinion. The Court, however, did enunciate the general principle that the death penalty could not be imposed under sentencing procedures that created a substantial risk that it would be inflicted in an arbitrary and capricious manner.

In *Bartholomey v. State,* 267 Md. 175, 297 A.2d 696 (1972), the Court of Appeals declared Maryland's then existing death penalty statutes unconstitutional under *Furman.* The General Assembly responded to *Furman* and *Bartholomey* by enacting a mandatory death penalty statute. Chapter 252, Acts of 1975, codified as Maryland Ann. Code, Art. 27, § 413. Under this legislation, the death penalty had to be automatically imposed upon conviction of a specifically defined and narrowly drawn class of first degree murders.

In *Woodson v. North Carolina,* 428 U.S. 280, 96 S. Ct. 2978, 49 L. Ed. 2d 444 (1976), and *Roberts v. Louisiana,* 428 U.S. 325, 96 S. Ct. 3001, 49 L. Ed. 2d 974 (1977), the Supreme Court held that mandatory death penalty statutes for first degree murder were unconstitutional because, as stated in *Woodson,* they lacked "the fundamental respect for humanity underlying the eighth amendment ... [which] requires consideration of the character and record of the individual offender and the circumstances of the particular offense as a constitutionally indispensable part of the process of inflicting the penalty of death." 428 U.S. at 304, 96 S. Ct. at 2991, 49 L. Ed. 2d at 961. In accordance with *Woodson* and *Roberts,* the Court of Appeals held that Maryland's mandatory death penalty statute was unconstitutional. *Blackwell v. State,* 278 Md. 466, 365 A.2d 545 (1976), *cert. denied,* 431 U.S. 918 (1977).

In the aftermath of *Furman,* the Supreme Court also addressed the constitutionality of "guided discretion" statutes. It upheld the death penalty statutes of Georgia, *Gregg v. Georgia,* 428 U.S. 153, 96 S. Ct. 2909, 49 L. Ed. 2d 859 (1976); Florida, *Proffitt v. Florida,* 428 U.S. 242, 96 S. Ct. 2960, 49 L. Ed. 2d 913 (1976); and Texas, *Jurek v. Texas,* 428 U.S. 262, 96 S. Ct. 2950, 49 L. Ed. 2d 929 (1976). In *Gregg,* the Court's plurality opinion approved the constitutionality of guided discretion capital sentencing statutes. The death penalty statutes upheld by the Court in *Gregg, Proffitt* and *Jurek* each contained three provisions which guarded against the concerns raised in *Furman v. Georgia, supra.* First, each of the new discretionary statutes provided for a bifurcated trial so that guilt and punishment would be separately determined. Second, imposition of the death penalty was restricted to cases in which certain aggravating circumstances were established. The sentencing authority was also required to consider the existence of mitigating circumstances. Third, the statutes provided for expedited appellate review of the death penalty statute as a check against the random or arbitrary imposition of the death penalty.

Maryland's current death penalty statute, Maryland Ann. Code, Art. 27, §§ 412 to 414, was enacted in 1978, following *Blackwell v. State, supra.* It provides for the death penalty for first degree murder under certain circumstances. With one exception, it requires that the defendant be a principal in the first degree to the killing. In Maryland, first degree murder may be based on the felony murder rule as well as premeditated murder.

The statutory scheme provides a bifurcated procedure for the adjudicatory and sentencing phases. During the sentencing phase, the imposition of the death penalty is further limited to cases in which the sentencing authority finds that the State has established at least one aggravating circumstance beyond a reasonable doubt. The defendant must be notified in advance of the State's intent to seek the death penalty and advised of each aggravating circumstance upon which the State intends to rely. The statute provides a list of ten aggravating circumstances. If the sentencing authority does not find beyond a reasonable doubt the existence of one or more of the aggravating circumstances, then the sentence shall be life imprisonment. If the sentencing authority finds the existence of one or more aggravating factors, then it must determine whether, by a preponderance of the evidence, any one of eight mitigating circumstances exist. The eighth mitigating circumstance is open-ended, providing for any additional mitigating circumstances the trier of fact finds to exist. If no mitigating factors are found to exist, the sentence to be imposed is death. The statute, later clarified by court decision, states that a sentence of life imprisonment be imposed if, by a preponderance of the evidence, the trier of fact finds that the mitigating circumstances outweigh the aggravating circumstances. Otherwise, the sentence imposed must be death.

The sentencing authority's decision must be in writing, and if the decision is made by a jury, it must be unanimous and signed by the foreperson. The trial court must impose the sentence determined by the jury. If, however, the jury is unable to agree upon a sentence within a reasonable amount of time, the court is required to dismiss the jury and impose a sentence of life imprisonment. In *Calhoun v. State,* 297 Md. 563, 468 A.2d 45 (1983), *cert. denied, Tichnell v. Maryland,* 104 S. Ct. 2374 (1984), the Court of Appeals held that this requirement (Art. 27, § 413(k)(2)) is directed to the court, not the jury, and hence, no jury instruction is required. The law (Art. 27, § 414) also provides for expedited automatic appeal of all death sentences to the Court of Appeals.

Article 27, § 413(l) provides that the Court of Appeals may adopt rules of procedure to govern the conduct of the sentencing proceeding. Pursuant to this provision, the Court of Appeals, effective January 1, 1979, adopted Rule 4-343, Sentencing —

Procedure in capital cases. This rule provided a form entitled "Findings and Sentencing Determination," which was modified, as noted above, on July 20, 1987. As formulated in the rule, the sentencing authority must specify in writing whether each aggravating or mitigating circumstance was established by the degree of proof mandated by statute (Art. 27, § 413(d) and (g)). The rule further requires the trial court to advise the defendant of his right of appeal. It also requires the trial judge to prepare an extensive report in every case where the death penalty is sought, whether or not it is imposed, to be submitted to the Court of Appeals. This report is designed to provide detailed information concerning the defendant, the offense, the victim, and the circumstances of the crime. In instances when a sentence of death is imposed, the trial judge must state his opinion whether the sentence was justified. The factual accuracy of the trial judge's report may be commented on by the parties within five days after receiving it. In addition to other considerations in the appellate review, Art. 27, § 414(e)(4) requires the Court of Appeals to conduct a proportionality review to determine "(w)hether the sentence of death is excessive or disproportionate to the penalty imposed in similar cases, considering both the crime and the defendant." Under Art. 27, § 414(f)(2), the Court of Appeals is directed to include in its decision "a reference to the similar cases which it considered."

Numerous constitutional challenges to the Maryland statute have been raised in the Court of Appeals. The most extensive constitutional analyses of the statute may be found in *Tichnell v. State,* 287 Md. 695, 415 A.2d 830 (1980) (Tichnell I), the first case to reach the appellate court under the statute, and in *Calhoun v. State, supra.* In these and numerous other cases the Court of Appeals has found that the Maryland death penalty statute is constitutional on its face under the guidelines provided by United States Supreme Court cases as well as under Articles 16 and 25 of the Maryland Declaration of Rights. The Court of Appeals has also considered numerous issues that have arisen in the application of the death penalty statute. In several cases, the Court of Appeals has reversed and remanded for a new sentencing proceeding due to an error in the application of the statute or a ruling by the trial judge. Several other issues may require litigation to clarify application of the statute. Some of these issues are discussed in this Comment.

This instruction is based upon Maryland Ann. Code, Art. 27, §§ 412 and 413, and Rule 4-343 of the Maryland Rules of Procedure. Effective July 1, 1987, Art. 27, §§ 412 and 413 were amended to authorize the State also to seek a penalty of "imprisonment for life without the possibility of parole" for first degree murder. The State may seek this penalty with or without seeking the death penalty. The penalty of "imprisonment for life without the possibility of parole" means "imprisonment for the natural life of an inmate under the custody of a correctional institution, including the Patuxent institution." Art. 27, § 413(e)(4). The State must give notice at least thirty days prior to trial that it intends to seek a sentence of "imprisonment for life without the possibility of parole." Art. 27, § 412(b). If the State does not also give notice of an intent to seek the death penalty, the Court shall determine whether to impose the penalty in a separate sentencing proceeding. Art. 27, § 413(k)(5). If the State seeks both "imprisonment for life without the possibility of parole" and the death penalty, "... and the court or jury determines that a sentence of death may not be imposed ... that court or jury shall determine whether to impose a sentence of imprisonment for life or imprisonment for life without the possibility of parole." Art. 27, § 413(k)(6). As noted above, where the State seeks both penalties this instruction will need to be modified accordingly. The penalty of "imprisonment for life without the possibility of parole" does not restrict the authority of the Governor to pardon or remit any part of a sentence. Art. 41, § 4-607(b)(3)(II). Finally, it should be noted that the statute provides no criteria or guidance to the trier of fact in determining when the penalty of "imprisonment for life without the possibility of parole" should be imposed.

Sentencing Form Provided by Rule 4-343

(CAPTION)

FINDINGS AND SENTENCING DETERMINATION

Section I

Based upon the evidence, we unanimously find that each of the following statements marked "proven" has been proved BEYOND A REASONABLE DOUBT and that each of those statements marked "not proven" has not been proven BEYOND A REASONABLE DOUBT.

1. The defendant was a principal in the first degree to the murder.

...	...
proven	not proven

2. The defendant engaged or employed another person to commit the murder and the murder was committed pursuant to an agreement or contract for remuneration or the promise of remuneration.

...	...
proven	not proven

(If one or both of the above are marked "proven," complete Section II. If both are marked "not proven," proceed to Section V and enter "Life Imprisonment.")

Section II

Based upon the evidence, we unanimously find that each of the following aggravating circumstances that is marked "proven" has been proved BEYOND A REASONABLE DOUBT and we unanimously find that each of the aggravating circumstances marked "not proven" has not been proven BEYOND A REASONABLE DOUBT.

1. The victim was a law enforcement officer who was murdered while in the performance of the officer's duties.

. . . proven . . . not proven

2. The defendant committed the murder at a time when confined in a correctional institution.

. . . proven . . . not proven

3. The defendant committed the murder in furtherance of an escape from or an attempt to escape from or evade the lawful custody, arrest, or detention of or by an officer or guard of a correctional institution or by a law enforcement officer.

. . . proven . . . not proven

4. The victim was taken or attempted to be taken in the course of a kidnapping or abduction or an attempt to kidnap or abduct.

. . . proven . . . not proven

5. The victim was a child abducted in violation of Code, Article 27, § 2.

. . . proven . . . not proven

6. The defendant committed the murder pursuant to an agreement or contract for remuneration or the promise of remuneration to commit the murder.

. . . proven . . . not proven

7. The defendant engaged or employed another person to commit the murder and the murder was committed pursuant to an

agreement or contract for remuneration or the promise of remuneration.

. . . proven . . . not proven

8. At the time of the murder, the defendant was under the sentence of death or imprisonment for life.

. . . proven . . . not proven

9. The defendant committed more than one offense of murder in the first degree arising out of the same incident.

. . . proven . . . not proven

10. The defendant committed the murder while committing or attempting to commit robbery, arson, rape in the first degree, or sexual offense in the first degree.

. . . proven . . . not proven

(If one or more of the above are marked "proven," complete Section III. If all of the above are marked "not proven," do not complete Sections III and IV and proceed to Section V and enter "Life Imprisonment.")

Section III

Based upon the evidence, we make the following determinations as to mitigating circumstances:

1. The defendant has not previously (i) been found guilty of a crime of violence; or (ii) entered a plea of guilty or nolo contendere to a charge of a crime of violence; or (iii) been granted probation on stay of entry of judgment pursuant to a charge of a crime of violence.

(As used in the preceding paragraph, "crime of violence" means abduction, arson, escape, kidnapping, mayhem, murder, robbery, rape in the first or second degree, sexual offense in the first or second degree, manslaughter other than involuntary manslaughter, an attempt to commit any of these offenses, or the use of a handgun in the commission of a felony or another crime of violence.)

(Mark only one.)

☐ (a) We unanimously find by a preponderance of the evidence that the above circumstance exists.
☐ (b) We unanimously find by a preponderance of the evidence that the above circumstance does not exist.
☐ (c) After a reasonable period of deliberation, one or more of us, but fewer than all 12, find by a preponderance of the evidence that the above circumstance exists.

2. The victim was a participant in the defendant's conduct or consented to the act which caused the victim's death.

(Mark only one.)

☐ (a) We unanimously find by a preponderance of the evidence that the above circumstance exists.
☐ (b) We unanimously find by a preponderance of the evidence that the above circumstance does not exist.
☐ (c) After a reasonable period of deliberation, one or more of us, but fewer than all 12, find by a preponderance of the evidence that the above circumstance exists.

3. The defendant acted under substantial duress, domination, or provocation of another person, even though not so substantial as to constitute a complete defense to the prosecution.

(Mark only one.)

☐ (a) We unanimously find by a preponderance of the evidence that the above circumstance exists.
☐ (b) We unanimously find by a preponderance of the evidence that the above circumstance does not exist.
☐ (c) After a reasonable period of deliberation, one or more of us, but fewer than all 12, find by a preponderance of the evidence that the above circumstance exists.

4. The murder was committed while the capacity of the defendant to appreciate the criminality of his or her conduct or to conform his or her conduct to the requirements of law was substantially impaired as a result of mental incapacity, mental disorder, or emotional disturbance.

(Mark only one.)

☐ (a) We unanimously find by a preponderance of the evidence that the above circumstance exists.
☐ (b) We unanimously find by a preponderance of the evidence that the above circumstance does not exist.
☐ (c) After a reasonable period of deliberation, one or more of us, but fewer than all 12, find by a preponderance of the evidence that the above circumstance exists.

5. The defendant was of a youthful age at the time of the crime.

(Mark only one.)

☐ (a) We unanimously find by a preponderance of the evidence that the above circumstance exists.
☐ (b) We unanimously find by a preponderance of the evidence that the above circumstance does not exist.
☐ (c) After a reasonable period of deliberation, one or more of us, but fewer than all 12, find by a preponderance of the evidence that the above circumstance exists.

6. The act of the defendant was not the sole proximate cause of the victim's death.

(Mark only one.)

☐ (a) We unanimously find by a preponderance of the evidence that the above circumstance exists.
☐ (b) We unanimously find by a preponderance of the evidence that the above circumstance does not exist.

☐ (c) After a reasonable period of deliberation, one or more of us, but fewer than all 12, find by a preponderance of the evidence that the above circumstance exists.

7. It is unlikely that the defendant will engage in further criminal activity that would constitute a continuing threat to society.

(Mark only one.)

☐ (a) We unanimously find by a preponderance of the evidence that the above circumstance exists.

☐ (b) We unanimously find by a preponderance of the evidence that the above circumstance does not exist.

☐ (c) After a reasonable period of deliberation, one or more of us, but fewer than all 12, find by a preponderance of the evidence that the above circumstance exists.

☐ 8. (a) We unanimously find by a preponderance of the evidence that the following additional mitigating circumstances exist:

....

....

....

....

(Use reverse side if necessary)

☐ (b) One or more of us, but fewer than all 12, find by a preponderance of the evidence that the following additional mitigating circumstances exist:

....

....

....

....

(Use reverse side if necessary)

(If the jury unanimously determines in Section III that no mitigating circumstances exist, do not complete Section IV. Proceed to Section V and enter "Death". If the jury or any juror determines that one or more mitigating circumstances exist, complete Section IV.)

Section IV

Each individual juror shall weigh the aggravating circumstances found unanimously to exist against any mitigating circumstances found unanimously to exist, as well as against any mitigating circumstances found by that individual juror to exist.

We unanimously find that the State has proved by A PREPONDERANCE OF THE EVIDENCE that the aggravating circumstances marked "proven" in Section II outweigh the mitigating circumstances in Section III.

. . . yes . . . no

Section V

Enter the determination of sentence either "Life Imprisonment" or "Death" according to the following instructions:

1. If both of the answers in Section I are marked "not proven," enter "Life Imprisonment."
2. If all of the answers in Section II are marked "not proven," enter "Life Imprisonment."
3. If Section III was completed and the jury unanimously determined that no mitigating circumstance exists, enter "Death."
4. If Section IV was completed and marked "no," enter "Life Imprisonment."
5. If Section IV was completed and was marked "yes," enter "Death."

We unanimously determine the sentence to be ....

Section VI

If "Life Imprisonment" is entered in Section V, answer the following question:

Based upon the evidence, does the jury unanimously determine that the sentence of life imprisonment previously entered shall be without the possibility of parole?

	. . .	. . .
	yes	no

....		....
Foreman		Juror 7
....		....
Juror 2		Juror 8
....		....
Juror 3		Juror 9
....		....
Juror 4		Juror 10
....		....
Juror 5		Juror 11
....		....
Juror 6		Juror 12
	or,	....
		JUDGE

(b) Determination of defendant's status as a principal in the first degree

With one exception, the application of the Maryland death penalty is limited to principals in the first degree by express statutory language. Maryland Ann. Code, Art. 27, § 413(e)(1). The exception is where the defendant engaged or employed another person to commit the murder and the murder was committed pursuant to an agreement or contract for remuneration or the promise of remuneration. Art. 27, § 413(d)(7). *Grandison v. State,* 305 Md. 685, 506 A.2d 580 (1986), represents the first case in which a defendant received a death sentence on conviction for a contract murder. While he was not the triggerman, the killings would not have occurred without his actions, and he is as culpable as the triggerman. The only mitigating circumstances were that he had no prior convictions for a crime of violence and he was not the sole proximate cause of the killings.

The sentencing procedure set forth by Art. 27, § 413 only applies where (1) a principal in the first degree is (2) found guilty of murder in the first degree and (3) the statutory notice by the State to the defendant is fulfilled. A conviction for the crime of first degree murder, however, does not establish the defendant's status as a principal in the first degree. The crime of first degree murder in Maryland is either "[a]ll murder which shall be perpetrated by means of poison, or lying in wait, or by any kind of wilful, deliberate and premeditated killing ..." (Art. 27, § 407) or various forms of felony murder (Art. 27, §§ 408 to 410). Before application of the statutory capital sentencing procedure, therefore, there must be not only a verdict of guilty of first degree murder, but also a determination by the trier of fact as to the degree of participation of the defendant in that murder.

Requiring the sentencing factfinder to resolve the issue of the defendant's status as a principal in the first degree presents less difficulty where the same trier of fact has already served during the adjudicatory phase of the trial. However, even if there has been a special verdict at the adjudicatory phase, the defendant may be entitled to a redetermination of this issue at the sentencing phase, given the language of Art. 27, § 413. Interview with Richard B. Rosenblatt, Assistant Attorney General, Office of the Maryland Attorney General, November 30, 1984.

Where the initial trier of fact does not subsequently serve during the sentencing phase, as provided for in Art. 27, § 413(b)(2) and (3), there would seem to be a requirement that the new sentencing trier of fact make a finding on this issue, irrespective of whether an earlier determination was made.

In *Tichnell v. State,* 290 Md. 43, 427 A.2d 991 (1981) (Tichnell II), the original death sentence was vacated on appeal and a new jury was impaneled to hear the evidence at the sentencing phase of the proceeding. The judge required that prior recorded trial testimony from the earlier proceeding be read to the sentencing jury over the defendant's objection. The Court reversed, holding that absent agreement of the parties, or a showing of unavailability of the witnesses to testify at the separate sentencing hearing, Art. 27, § 413(c) does not permit, over timely objection, the admission in evidence before a new sentencing jury of the prior recorded trial testimony to prove the existence or absence of aggravating or mitigating circumstances. This holding would seem to apply to a redetermination of the defendant's status as a principal in the first degree before a new trier of fact.

In *Stebbing v. State,* 299 Md. 331, 473 A.2d 903, *cert. denied,* 469 U.S. 900 (1984), the Court of Appeals rejected defendant's contention that Art. 27, § 413(e)(1) requires that not only the murder but also the underlying robbery, arson, rape or sexual offense in the first degree must be committed by the defendant as a principal in the first degree for the aggravating circumstances of Art. 27, § 413(d)(10) to apply. See also *Grandison v. State, supra,* 305 Md. at 766, 506 A.2d at 612.

(c) Aggravating and mitigating circumstances: statutory provisions

Maryland Ann. Code, Art. 27, § 413(d), specifies the following aggravating circumstances:

> (1) The victim was a law enforcement officer who was murdered while in the performance of his duties.
> (2) The defendant committed the murder at a time when he was confined in any correctional institution.
> (3) The defendant committed murder in furtherance of an escape or an attempt to escape from or evade the lawful custody, arrest, or detention of or by an officer or guard of a correctional institution or by a law enforcement officer.
> (4) The victim was taken or attempted to be taken in the course of a kidnapping or abduction or an attempt to kidnap or abduct.
> (5) The victim was a child abducted in violation of § 2 of this article.
> (6) The defendant committed the murder pursuant to an agreement or contract for remuneration or the promise of remuneration to commit the murder.
> (7) The defendant engaged or employed another person to commit the murder and the murder was committed pursuant to an agreement or contract for remuneration or the promise of remuneration.
> (8) At the time of the murder, the defendant was under sentence of death or imprisonment for life.

(9) The defendant committed more than one offense of murder in the first degree arising out of the same incident.

(10) The defendant committed the murder while committing or attempting to commit a robbery, arson, rape or sexual offense in the first degree.

The following mitigating circumstances are specified in Art. 27, § 413(g):

(1) The defendant has not previously (i) been found guilty of a crime of violence; (ii) entered a plea of guilty or nolo contendere to a charge of a crime of violence; or (iii) had a judgment of probation on stay of entry of judgment entered on a charge of a crime of violence. As used in this paragraph, "crime of violence" means abduction, arson, escape, kidnapping, manslaughter, except involuntary manslaughter, mayhem, murder, robbery, or rape or sexual offense in the first or second degree, or an attempt to commit any of these offenses, or the use of a handgun in the commission of a felony or another crime of violence.

(2) The victim was a participant in the defendant's conduct or consented to the act which caused the victim's death.

(3) The defendant acted under substantial duress, domination or provocation of another person, but not so substantial as to constitute a complete defense to the prosecution.

(4) The murder was committed while the capacity of the defendant to appreciate the criminality of his conduct or to conform his conduct to the requirements of law was substantially impaired as a result of mental incapacity, mental disorder or emotional disturbance.

(5) The youthful age of the defendant at the time of the crime.

(6) The act of the defendant was not the sole proximate cause of the victim's death.

(7) It is unlikely that the defendant will engage in further criminal activity that would constitute a continuing threat to society.

(8) Any other facts which the jury or the court specifically sets forth in writing that it finds as mitigating circumstances in the case.

Subsection (g)(8) was added to the list of mitigating circumstances of Art. 27, § 413 by Chapter 521, Acts of 1979, and became effective on July 1, 1979. This provision for unlisted or nonstatutory mitigating circumstances was added after the Supreme Court's decision in *Lockett v. Ohio,* 438 U.S. 586, 98 S. Ct. 2954, 57 L. Ed. 2d 973 (1978), a case in which the Ohio death penalty was invalidated because it too narrowly limited the discretion of the sentencing authority to consider mitigating circumstances. It required that the sentencing authority in all but, perhaps, the rarest kind of capital case not be precluded from considering as a mitigating factor any aspect of a defendant's character or record and any of the circumstances of the offense that the defendant proffers as a basis for a sentence less than death.

Subsection (g)(4) was changed by Chapter 296, Acts of 1983. Prior to the amendment, intoxication was specifically included in the statute as a mitigating factor. As of 1983, it was deleted. Intoxication may still be considered as a mitigating factor under subsection (g)(8) as "any other facts ... that it finds as mitigating circumstances in the case."

Subsection (d)(4), one of the aggravating circumstances, was amended by Chapter 497, Acts of 1983, deleting the words "a hostage." Prior to the amendment, the subsection read: "The victim was a hostage taken or attempted to be taken in the course of a kidnapping or abduction or an attempt to kidnap or abduct." The provision now reads: "The victim was taken or attempted to be taken in the course of a kidnapping or abduction or an attempt to kidnap or abduct." For a discussion of the definition of the words "a hostage," see *Trimble v. State,* 300 Md. 387, 478 A.2d 1143 (1984).

Effective July 1, 1987, an amendment to Art. 27, § 413(e)(3) clarifies the aggravating circumstance that the victim was a law enforcement officer who was murdered while in the performance of his duties. The definition of "law enforcement officer" is expanded to include a uniformed police officer privately employed as a security guard or special policeman. The amendment addresses the decision in *Lodowski v. State,* 302 Md. 691, 490 A.2d 1228 (1985), where the Court ruled that an off-duty police officer was not murdered while in the performance of his duties, as used in the death penalty statute, because the officer was privately employed as a security guard, even though he was wearing his police uniform and sitting in a marked police car at the time of the murder. Art. 27, § 413(e)(3)(ii)(4) provides: "If the law enforcement officer is wearing the uniform worn by the law enforcement officer while acting in an official capacity or is prominently displaying his official badge or other insignia of office, a law enforcement officer privately employed as a security officer or special policeman under the provisions of Article 41, §§ 4-901 through 4-913 of the Code."

In *Johnson v. State,* 292 Md. 405, 439 A.2d 542 (1982), the evidence presented on a particular mitigating circumstance, the lack of a prior record of a crime of violence, was not controverted by the State. The jury, however, found that there were no mitigating factors. The Court held that the sentence was in violation of the statutory scheme, although it did indicate that the weight to be given to any mitigating factor is not controlled by the Court. See also *Bowers v. State,* 298 Md. 115, 468 A.2d 101 (1983).

At least two questions have arisen in the use of the Findings and Sentencing Determination form, set forth, *supra,* this Comment at subpart (a), regarding aggravating and mitigating circumstances. First, should the jury be given a form that lists all ten aggravating circumstances where the State has specified that it intends only to rely on certain aggravating circumstances in a particular case? It can be argued that there is a potential for jury prejudice from exposing a jury to the entire list of aggravating circumstances and not just those relied upon by the State. This potential for prejudice may be compounded in light of the broad range of information about the defendant which may be presented to the jury. It would seem that this question can be dealt with simply by deleting the immaterial aggravating circumstances from the sentencing form. The July 20, 1987, revisions to the Findings and Sentencing Determination Form, Rule 4-343(f) of the Maryland Rules of Procedure, provide: "Deletions from Form. — Unless the defendant requests otherwise, Section II of the form set forth in section (e) of this Rule shall not include any aggravating circumstance that the State has not specified in the notice required under Code, Article 27, § 412(b)(1) of its intention to seek a sentence of death." A Rules Committee note states: "Omission of some aggravating circumstances from the form is not intended to preclude argument by the defendant concerning the absence of those circumstances."

Second, how should unlisted or nonstatutory mitigating circumstances be handled? Section II, item 8, of the form allows space to enter other mitigating circumstances, pursuant to Art. 27, § 413(g)(8). Should the judge add the unlisted mitigating circumstances requested by the defense prior to giving the sentencing form to the jury? Alternatively, is it the jury's responsibility to fill in that part of the sentencing form? Defense attorneys would probably prefer that the judge initially enter the defense requested "other" mitigating circumstances, leaving additional space for the jury to add still other mitigating circumstances that it might find to exist. This would focus the jury's attention during the deliberation on each of the mitigating circumstances proffered by the defense. It would also underscore for the jury the defendant's right to have particular unlisted mitigating circumstances considered.

Bowers v. State, 306 Md. 120, 507 A.2d 1072 (1986), suggests that all mitigating circumstances, those expressly mentioned under the statute, as well as other relevant circumstances proffered by the defendant, should be on equal footing before the jury. Thus, if those which are expressly mentioned are submitted in writing, those proffered by the defendant as having mitigating value which are supported by the evidence and which the jury may reasonably deem to have mitigating value must, upon defendant's timely request, also be submitted in writing.

(d) Burden of proof: mitigating circumstances

The constitutional validity of placing upon the defendant the burden of proving the existence of mitigating circumstances was firmly established in *Tichnell v. State,* 287 Md. 695, 731-733, 415 A.2d 830, 845-850 (1980) (Tichnell I) (*citing Patterson v. New York,* 432 U.S. 197, 97 S. Ct. 2319, 53 L. Ed. 2d 281 (1977), which modified *Mullaney v. Wilbur,* 421 U.S. 684, 95 S. Ct. 1881, 44 L. Ed. 2d 508 (1975) and *In re Winship,* 397 U.S. 358, 90 S. Ct. 1068, 25 L. Ed. 2d 368 (1970)). Likewise, the application of the preponderance of the evidence standard to the defendant's burden was also upheld as constitutional. Tichnell I, *supra*. See also *Johnson v. State,* 292 Md. 405, 439 A.2d 542 (1982).

A law review note, commenting on the Tichnell I holding, observed:

> Furthermore, the court's second finding seems unassailable under *Patterson v. New York,* although arguably the defendant should not be required to bear any burdens of proof in a death penalty case [citing *Lockett v. Ohio,* where the issue was raised but the plurality did not decide it. 438 U.S. 586, 600 n.16 (1978).] In *Patterson,* the Supreme Court held that once the prosecution had proved every fact necessary to constitute the offense, it was not required to disprove beyond a reasonable doubt the existence of every fact constituting a mitigating circumstance or affirmative defense.

Note, *Tichnell v. State — Maryland's Death Penalty: The Need for Reform,* 42 Maryland Law Review 875 (1983).

While there is no legislative history to explain the exact meaning of the term "preponderance of the evidence" as used in the death penalty statute, a safe assumption is that the meaning is the same as when used in the civil area. In civil cases, "preponderance of the evidence" has been defined as "more likely so than not so," "more probable than not," and "inclines more heavily to establish the existence or nonexistence of facts ... than evidence to the contrary." *Todd v. Weikle,* 36 Md. App. 663, 670, 376 A.2d 104, 108 (1977); *C & P Tel. Co. v. Hicks,* 25 Md. App. 503, 523-26, 337 A.2d 744, 756-58 (1975); *State Ins. Comm'r v. National Bureau of Cas. Underwriters,* 248 Md. 292, 305-06, 236 A.2d 282, 289 (1967); *France v. Safe Deposit & Trust Co.,* 176 Md. 306, 311, 4 A.2d 717, 719 (1939).

The jury is required to find unanimously that a mitigating circumstance has been proved by a preponderance of the evidence. Does the trier of fact also have to be unanimous as to the absence of mitigating factors? And, if a jury is in disagreement as to the existence of a mitigating factor, what should be the result? In *Mills v. State,* 310 Md. 33, 527 A.2d 3 (1987), the sentencing jury found one aggravating factor, namely that the defendant was an inmate in a correctional facility at the time of the murder, and no mitigating factors. On appeal he argued that the Maryland death penalty statute is unconstitutionally mandatory because, unless a jury can unanimously agree as to the existence of the same mitigating factor, the jury must conclude that there are no mitigating factors and, if an aggravating circumstance has been found, the statute requires a death sentence. The Court rejected this interpretation of the statute and held that the statute contemplates that the jury be unanimous both as to the existence or the absence of mitigating factors. As long as one juror adheres to the view that a mitigating factor exists which is not outweighed by an aggravating circumstance, the jury cannot unanimously determine a death sentence.

In *Mills v. State, supra,* the Court stated that when a jury is in disagreement as to the existence of a mitigating factor, the result is not a hung jury. Instead, the jury should proceed to the weighing process, each juror weighing the mitigating circumstance(s) he or she finds, if any, against the proven aggravating circumstance(s).

(e) Burden of proof: balancing aggravating and mitigating circumstances

The death penalty phase of a murder prosecution (Maryland Ann. Code, Art. 27, § 413) only places on the defendant the risk of nonpersuasion regarding mitigating factors. The burden of persuasion is on the prosecutor with respect to weighing aggravating circumstances against mitigating circumstances. It is not constitutionally required that the prosecution prove the absence of mitigating circumstances. The death penalty statute is not a mandatory death penalty law because the sentencing authority may list as a mitigating factor any factor that leads to a conclusion that death is not appropriate. *Foster, Evans, Huffington v. State,* 305 Md. 306, 503 A.2d 1326 (1986); *Foster v. State,* 304 Md. 439, 499 A.2d 1236 (1985).

The statutory language requires the trier of fact to determine whether the mitigating circumstances outweigh the aggravating circumstances when both are present. The "preponderance of the evidence" standard is to be applied. The statute states that if the mitigating circumstances do not outweigh the aggravating circumstances, the sentence is to be death. If they do outweigh the aggravating circumstances, the sentence is to be life imprisonment.

In *Tichnell v. State,* 287 Md. 695, 415 A.2d 830 (1980) (Tichnell I), the Court of Appeals recognized a lack of clarity in the language of the statute as to which party bears the burden of establishing the mitigating circumstances and whether the mitigating circumstances outweigh the aggravating circumstances: "Section 413 does not explicitly specify which party has the burden of producing evidence and the burden of persuasion." *Id.* at 730, 415 A.2d at 848. While not explicitly suggesting that it would be unconstitutional to place these burdens on the defendant, the Court in dictum, nevertheless, proposed a statutory construction that would avoid a constitutional challenge as to the balancing of aggravating and mitigating circumstances. The Court accomplished this by reversing the statutory language so that the State bears the burden of proof on this issue. It is noted that while the express statutory language is whether "the mitigating circumstances outweigh the aggravating circumstances" (Art. 27, § 413(h)), "(b)ecause the State is attempting to establish that the imposition of the death penalty is an appropriate sentence, the statute places the risk of nonpersuasion on the prosecution with respect to *whether the aggravating factors outweigh the mitigating factors.*" Tichnell I, *supra* at 730, 415 A.2d at 849 (emphasis added). Subsequent cases added to the uncertainty and confusion concerning the judicial construction of the statutory language. *Tichnell v. State,* 290 Md. 43, 427 A.2d 991 (1981) (Tichnell II); *Calhoun v. State,* 297 Md. 563, 468 A.2d 45 (1983); *Colvin v. State,* 299 Md. 88, 472 A.2d 953 (1984), *cert. denied,* 105 S. Ct. 226 (1984); *Stebbing v. State,* 299 Md. 331, 473 A.2d 903, *cert. denied,* 469 U.S. 900 (1984); *Johnson v. State,* 292 Md. 405, 439 A.2d 542 (1982). This matter appears to have been resolved in *Maziarz v. State,* 302 Md. 1, 485 A.2d 245 (1984); *Foster v. State, supra;* and *Foster, Evans, Huffington v. State, supra.*

The Court in *Foster v. State, supra,* 304 Md. at 477-78, 499 A.2d at 1256-57, held:

> With regard to the burden of proof, merely because the General Assembly in § 413(h) referred in paragraph (2) to

> whether "mitigating circumstances do not outweigh the aggravating circumstances" and in paragraph (3) to whether "mitigating circumstances outweigh the aggravating circumstances," instead of using the reverse order or some other phraseology, does not reflect a legislative intent to place any burden or risk upon the accused. If the Legislature had added a fourth paragraph to subsection (h), specifying the result if the sentencing authority found that mitigating and aggravating circumstances were in a state of even balance or if the sentencing authority was unable to determine which outweighed the other, there would have been a clear inference regarding the allocation of the burden or risk. But the Legislature added no such fourth paragraph. Instead, the Legislature in § 413(h) merely directed the sentencing authority to engage in a weighing or balancing process, without indicating which side has the burden of proof. The Legislature contemplated in § 413(h) that the sentencing authority would simply evaluate the aggravating circumstances which the prosecution had established beyond a reasonable doubt, and evaluate the mitigating circumstances which it found to exist, and determine which outweighed the other.
>
> Nevertheless, the allocation of the "burden of persuasion" for purposes of § 413(h) would become pertinent in a case where the sentencing authority found the aggravating and mitigating circumstances to be evenly balanced or was unable to determine which outweighed the other. *Consequently, because under the statute the State is the moving party, and is seeking to have the death sentence imposed, we interpreted the statute in Tichnell I to place the burden of persuasion upon the prosecution with regard to the weighing of aggravating and mitigating circumstances.* (Emphasis added).

In *Foster, Evans, Huffington v. State, supra,* 305 Md. at 309, 503 A.2d at 1328, the Court adheres to its prior holding that the burden of persuasion for purposes of Art. 27, § 413(h) is upon the prosecution.

(f) Defining and establishing aggravating and mitigating circumstances

(1) Can a single factual foundation give rise to multiple aggravating circumstances?

In *Calhoun v. State,* 297 Md. 563, 468 A.2d 45 (1983), the sentencing jury found three aggravating factors based on identical facts, namely: (1) that the victim was a law enforcement officer who was murdered while in the performance of his duties; (2) that the defendant committed the murder in furtherance of an escape from or an attempt to escape from or evade the lawful custody, arrest or detention of or by an officer or guard of a correctional institution or by a law enforcement officer; and (3) that the defendant committed the murder while committing or attempting to commit robbery. *Id.* at 589-90, 468 A.2d at 83.

The Court in the circumstances of the case rejected the defendant's argument that by permitting the pyramiding of aggravating factors based on the same act the procedure increases the chance of imposition of the death penalty without showing conduct any more dangerous or antisocial than would be present for a single aggravating factor. The Court cited *State v. Rust,* 197 Neb. 528, 250 N.W.2d 867, *cert. denied,* 434 U.S. 912 (1977) that while "it is not reasonable to construe the definitions in such a manner as to make them overlap and make the same identical facts constitute two aggravating circumstances ... at least to the extent that some added different and important element, e.g., motive or purpose, is included in each separate definition" the Legislature was entitled to make the judgment that such factors could and should be considered as aggravating factors. *Id.* at 538, 250 N.W.2d at 867.

In *Calhoun,* the Court identified different societal objectives. The protection of police officers is promoted by the first aggravating circumstance noted above. Committing a murder in furtherance of an escape could apply to murder of a civilian just as easily as to the murder of a police officer. The added element is the conduct of attempting to escape apprehension. The third aggravating factor, murder committed during the commission of a robbery, does not need a law enforcement officer as a victim. It likewise does not need to be committed during an escape from lawful custody. Its purpose is to deter a robbery.

In distinguishing *Calhoun,* the Court cited cases from other jurisdictions where the courts had disapproved of overlapping aggravating factors. See *State v. Goodman,* 298 N.C. 1, 257 S.E.2d 569 (1979); *Clark v. State,* 379 So. 2d 97 (Fla. 1979), *cert. denied,* 450 U.S. 936 (1981); *State v. Rust, supra.*

(2) What is the meaning of "mitigating circumstances" and how are "unlisted" mitigating circumstances to be established?

As to statutorily designated mitigating circumstances and unlisted or "other" mitigating circumstances, there is no statutory guidance of the definition of "mitigating." Also, there is no guidance of how unlisted mitigating circumstances are to be established.

A suggested definition of "mitigating," as recommended by the Office of the Public Defender, is as follows:

> A mitigating circumstance is simply any aspect of a person's character or background or any of the circumstances of the offense offered to you as a basis for a sentence less than death. In offering such evidence, the defendant is not in any measure suggesting that the crime was excusable or justified nor is he required to make such a showing. Rather he is seeking to show either that something about his character or upbringing calls for punishment less than death or that certain factors represent a partial explanation of how the crime came to happen — that it was in part a product of those factors.

The decisions of the United States Supreme Court in *Eddings v. Oklahoma,* 455 U.S. 104, 102 S. Ct. 869, 71 L. Ed. 2d 1 (1982), and *Lockett v. Ohio,* 438 U.S. 586, 98 S. Ct. 2954, 57 L. Ed. 2d 973 (1978), state that all relevant information about the particular offense and particular propensities of the defendant as they relate to mitigating circumstances must be reviewed at the sentencing hearing. In *Lockett,* Chief Justice Burger, writing for a plurality of the Court, stated:

> [W]e conclude that the Eighth and Fourteenth Amendments require that the sentencer ... not be precluded from considering, as a mitigating factor, any aspect of a defendant's character or record and any of the circumstances of the offense that the defendant proffers as a basis for a sentence less than death.

Id. at 604, 98 S. Ct. at 2964, 2965, 57 L. Ed. 2d at 990.

Other questions have been raised about the nature of the mitigating circumstances. Are the mitigating factors listed in Art.

27, § 413(g) matters of historical fact or are at least some of them complex matters of legal and moral judgment? Consider, for example, Art. 27, § 413(g)(3) which requires a finding that "(t)he defendant acted under substantial duress, domination or provocation of another person, but not so substantial as to constitute a complete defense to the prosecution." Similarly, Art. 27, § 413(g)(6) requires a finding that "(t)he act of the defendant was not the sole proximate cause of the victim's death." Likewise, Art. 27, § 413(g)(4) requires a finding that "(t)he murder was committed while the capacity of the defendant to appreciate the criminality of his conduct or to conform his conduct to the requirements of the law was substantially impaired as a result of mental incapacity, mental disorder or emotional disturbance."

Justice Marshall, in a dissenting opinion to a denial of a petition for a writ of certiorari in *Stebbing v. Maryland,* 469 U.S. 900, 105 S. Ct. 276, 83 L. Ed. 2d 212 (1984), observed that the Maryland "statute requires that the jury conceptualize mitigation as a historical fact to be proved, rather than as the complex legal and moral judgment that our cases require it to be." *Id.* at 904 n.3. The danger, according to Justice Marshall, is that the statutorily mandated mitigating factors rest on evidence that "easily might influence the conclusion that death is proper, even if that evidence does not conclusively *prove* the statutory mitigating factor." *Id.* at 903 (emphasis in original). If a mitigating factor is deemed by the sentencer not to be proved, the result is that the sentencer is prevented from considering any of the evidence that may be relevant to the sentence because the statute permits consideration only of the factors proved by a preponderance of the evidence. The statute denies any weight to evidence if the defendant does not convince the jury that the factor "exists" by a preponderance of the evidence. The result, in the view of Justice Marshall, is to violate *Lockett* and *Eddings* by enhancing "the risk that the death penalty will be imposed in spite of factors which may call for a less severe penalty." *Id.* (*quoting Lockett,* 438 U.S. at 605).

Justice Marshall cited the facts in *Stebbing v. Maryland, supra,* to illustrate the above problem. The defendant was nineteen years old at the time of the crime. She had previously been found to be mildly retarded and had been described as immature, impressionable, and as an abuser of a variety of drugs. The trial judge, who acted as sentencer, nevertheless found that the defendant had not borne her burden of proving, as mitigating factors, either (1) the youthful age of the defendant; or (2) that her mental incapacity, disorder, or disturbance inhibited her capacity to appreciate the criminality of her conduct or to conform to the requirements of law. Affirming the trial court on this matter, the Court of Appeals viewed the evidence in the light most favorable to the prosecution and held that a rational sentencer could have concluded that the defendant failed to prove the claimed mitigating factors. Because of that failure of proof, the sentencer could not consider the fact that the defendant was nineteen and had a certain mental history and, thus, is deprived of meaningful evidence when weighing the sentence. *Id.* at 904.

The response to Justice Marshall's argument is that such evidence may be considered by the sentencer as an unlisted mitigating circumstance under Art. 27, § 413(g)(8). For example, if the trier of fact did not find that the defendant acted under "substantial duress" under Art. 27, § 413(g)(3), it could find as an unlisted mitigating factor that the defendant acted under moderate duress. Justice Marshall, however, in a footnote, replied to this argument as follows:

> Nor does the mere fact that the sentencer may find other mitigating circumstances to include in the balance, so long as it sets them forth in writing, salvage the statute. Initially, no sentencer, who has been told he may consider certain factors only if they are proved to him, will presume he is able to consider them if they are not proved. That result would render the burden of proof provision of the statute wholly meaningless, and cannot be presumed to be what the legislature had in mind. Additionally, it is wholly plausible that jurors will "intuit perfectly legitimate mitigating circumstances which they cannot articulate," see Weisberg, *Deregulating Death,* 1983 S. Ct. Rev. 305, 373, n.262. A juror convinced that the evidence amounts to a mitigating factor "might stand mute, haunted by the defendant's look but unable to manufacture a reason for life." Ledewitz, *The Requirement of Death: Mandatory Language in the Pennsylvania Death Penalty Statute,* 21 Duquesne L. Rev. 103, 155

> (1982).... As a result, those mitigating circumstances that might be too "intangible" for a legislature to define and include in a death statute must be ignored, unless the sentencer somehow can articulate that which the legislature could not.

Id. n.3.

Despite Justice Marshall's argument that no jury which has been told that it may consider certain mitigating facts only if proved by a preponderance of the evidence will presume to be able to consider them if they are not proved, the defense should attempt to articulate any unlisted mitigating circumstances even if they are subsumed within statutorily defined mitigating factors. A major challenge for defense attorneys is to identify and endeavor to establish unlisted mitigating circumstances that may sympathetically appeal to the trier of fact. For example, it was noted earlier that intoxication was deleted from Art. 27, § 413(g)(4). Factors such as intoxication and drug addiction can be proffered as unlisted mitigating circumstances. Also, the statute requires that substantial impairment due to mental incapacity, mental disorder or emotional disturbance is necessary to qualify. If the evidence suggests less than substantial impairment, this can be proffered as an unlisted mitigating circumstance. To take another example, in a recent case the defense qualified Art. 27, § 413(g)(1) by adding that *prior to the crime* the defendant did not have a record of a crime of violence and proffered it as an unlisted mitigating circumstance.

In another case, it was argued that while "beyond a reasonable doubt" was the standard for adjudication of guilt, if there were any doubt whatsoever as to the guilt of the defendant or as to his participation in the crime as a principal in the first degree, it should be considered as a mitigating circumstance. A case cited by the Court of Appeals as "a splendid example" of the willingness of a jury to consider relevant information that may be weighed against a proven statutory aggravating circumstance is *Calhoun v. State, supra,* 297 Md. at 563, 468 A.2d at 81, where the jury determined that "a substantial mitigating factor is the defendant's background, which has been such that he has never been integrated into society. Therefore, he has been and is unable to conform with its norms and moral values." But see *Bowers v. State,* 306 Md. 120, 507 A.2d 1072 (1986), where the Court held that the murder defendant's willingness to serve the twenty-five year minimum on a life sentence before becoming eligible for parole was not a mitigating factor and not probative or relevant to the jury's determination of whether to impose the death sentence. In *Eddings v. Oklahoma, supra,* the United States Supreme Court reversed because the trial judge had declined to consider the fact of the defendant's violent background, on which evidence had been introduced, as a mitigating circumstance.

Nonstatutory and statutory mitigating factors are of equal dignity. However, there is no requirement that the jury be so instructed where the instructions as a whole do not give too much weight to the statutory factors. *Evans v. State,* 304 Md. 487, 499 A.2d 1261 (1985). Lastly, in *Skipper v. South Carolina,* 106 S. Ct. 1669, 90 L. Ed. 2d 1 (1986), the Court held that exclusion from the sentencing hearing of a jailer's testimony, and a regular visitor's testimony regarding petitioner's good behavior during the seven months he spent in jail awaiting trial deprived him of his right to place before the sentencer relevant evidence in mitigation of punishment.

Another issue not addressed in the suggested definition of mitigating circumstances is the process of determining whether an unlisted mitigating circumstance has been established. This Court of Appeals has not addressed whether this process is a one-step or two-step procedure. If the role of the sentencer is merely to find whether the proffered mitigating fact has been established by a preponderance of the evidence, its role then shifts to weighing and balancing established mitigating circumstances against aggravating circumstances. On the other hand, the State might argue that the finding of the sentencer of an unlisted mitigating circumstance is a two-step procedure: (1) does the asserted fact exist? (2) if so, does it constitute a mitigating circumstance? A case that might illustrate this procedural issue was tried in Prince George's County. The defense proffered two mitigating circumstances: (1) that the defendant is a human being; (2) that the evidence in the case was virtually all circumstantial. Do each of these factors qualify as mitigating circumstances or should the jury be instructed to make an independent finding of whether each of these facts constitute a "mitigating circumstance"?

Related to the above issue is the question of whether and under what circumstances the defendant is entitled to an instruction that an unlisted mitigating circumstance exists if the State offers no contradictory evidence. As noted earlier, in *Johnson v. State,* 292 Md. 405, 439 A.2d 542 (1982), the defense offered as a mitigating circumstance the lack of a prior record of a crime of violence pursuant to Art. 27, § 413(g)(1). This fact was not controverted by the State. The jury, however, indicated on the verdict form that it found no mitigating circumstances. The Court reversed and remanded for a new sentencing proceeding holding that where, as here, the sentencing authority fails to find the existence of a factor commanded by the legislature to be considered in mitigation of the death penalty, the death sentence was imposed in violation of the statutory design. *Id.* at 440, 439 A.2d at 561. The Court of Appeals has not yet addressed the question of whether the same result is required for unlisted as well as listed mitigating circumstances. The defense would, of course, argue that if relevant proffered facts are constitutionally required to be considered in mitigation, no distinction should be drawn as to whether the legislature recognized it or the defense asserted it.

(3) Guidance to the jury in weighing aggravating and mitigating circumstances

No statutory guidance is provided to aid the sentencer in weighing and balancing aggravating and mitigating circumstances.

The Maryland statutory scheme rejects the so-called "life option" provision. If no mitigating factors are proved by a preponderance of the evidence, the Maryland statute requires the sentencer to return a sentence of death. Maryland law in this respect differs dramatically from the statutes of the majority of states with death penalties which permit the judge or jury to return a life sentence even where no "mitigating circumstances" are found. *See* Ala. Code, §§ 13-11-1 to 13-11-9; Del. Code Ann., tit. 11, § 4209; Fla. Stat. Ann., § 921.141; Ga. Code Ann., § 27-2302; Ind. Code Ann., § 34-50-2-9; Ky. Rev. Stat., §§ 532.025 to 532.075; La. Code Crim. Proc. Ann., arts. 905-905.9; Mo. Ann. Stat., §§ 565.006 to 565.016; Neb. Rev. Stat., §§ 29-2519 to 29-2525; Nev. Rev. Stat., §§ 175.552 to 175.562; N.H. Rev. Stat. Ann., § 630.5; N.M. Stat. Ann., §§ 31-18-14, 31-20A-1 to 31-20A-6; N.C. Gen. Stat., §§ 15A-2000 to 15A-2003; Okla. Stat., tit. 21, §§ 701.10 to 701.15; S.C. Code Ann., §§ 16-3-20 to 16-3-28; S.D. Codified Laws, §§ 23A-27A-1 to 23A-27A-47; Va. Code, §§ 19.2-264.2 to 19.2-264.5; Wyo. Stat., §§ 6-4-102 to 6-4-103.

Also, Justice Marshall in his dissenting opinion to the denial of certiorari in *Stebbing v. Maryland, supra,* observed: "In addition to compressing the sentencer's wealth of information on mitigation into a rigidly compartmentalized analysis, the statute also prevents a sentencer from answering the basic question: *is death the proper sentence?*" *Id.* at 905 (emphasis added). He also stated that "much like directions to an income tax form, the instructions do not make clear precisely why a given answer in one section requires a certain response elsewhere." *Id.* n.4.

An example of a standard that includes a so-called "life option" is set forth in *State v. Wood,* 648 P.2d 71 (Utah 1982), as follows:

> After considering the totality of the aggravating and mitigating circumstances, you must be persuaded beyond a reasonable doubt that total aggravation outweighs total mitigation, and you must further be persuaded, beyond a reasonable doubt, that the imposition of the death penalty is justified and appropriate in the circumstances.

Id. at 83.

Under the Maryland statutory scheme it would seem appropriate to provide some guidance to the jury that it is not engaged in a mere mechanical task of counting aggravating and mitigating circumstances but that it is a qualitative decision to determine whether to impose the sentence of death or life imprisonment. In this balancing, is it proper to instruct the jury that the touchstone in weighing aggravating and mitigating circumstances is to determine whether the sentence should be life imprisonment or a sentence of death? For example, consider the following suggested language:

> Let me advise you as I will later in my instructions, that although this is a form with answers to be checked, you are engaged in more than a mere counting of aggravating and mitigating circumstances, or going through a checklist. It will be your duty to weigh each of the facts, the aggravating and mitigating, to determine either a sentence of life imprisonment or a sentence of death.

Office of the Public Defender of Maryland, Defendant's Proposed Instruction No. 1.

At a minimum, the judge should consider giving an instruction to the jury that weighing of aggravating and mitigating circumstances should not be based on mere numbers alone. Suppose, for example, the jury finds that one aggravating factor and three mitigating factors exist. How much weight should be given to the fact that on a numerical basis the mitigating factors may outweigh the aggravating factors, or vice versa? Counsel might consider requesting an instruction that is similar to Instruction, § 2.03, Number of witnesses, *supra.* The jury is instructed that the weight of the evidence is not necessarily determined by the number of witnesses testifying on either side. Perhaps, the jury at a minimum should be instructed along the following lines:

> The weight to be given aggravating and mitigating circumstances is not necessarily determined by the number of aggravating and mitigating circumstances that you have found to exist. This is a weighing process and not a mere tallying of aggravating and mitigating circumstances. You must weigh aggravating and mitigating circumstances in terms of their substantiality and persuasiveness and not merely in terms of their relative number. What you must decide is how compelling or persuasive are the mitigating factors when compared against the aggravating factors.

(g) Some constitutional and definitional issues of particular aggravating and mitigating circumstances

The list of aggravating and mitigating circumstances include several terms that raise constitutional and definitional issues. Some examples now follow.

(1) Aggravating circumstance of felony murder

The most frequently used aggravating circumstance is section 413(d)(10) which states: "The defendant committed the murder while committing or attempting to commit a robbery, arson, or rape or sexual offense in the first degree." This provision makes the felony murder rule an aggravating circumstance for specified felonies.

In *Stebbing v. State,* 299 Md. 331, 473 A.2d 903, *cert. denied,* 469 U.S. 900 (1984), the Court of Appeals held that Maryland Ann. Code, Art. 27, § 413(e)(1), requiring that the defendant be a principal in the first degree to the murder, does not apply to the underlying felony under Art. 27, § 413(d)(10). In this case the defendant was a principal in the second degree to the underlying rape and sexual offense in the first degree. The Court also rejected the defendant's argument that where the homicide is first degree murder solely because of the felony murder rule the underlying felonies cannot be used as aggravating factors in the capital sentencing phase. The defendant argued that the Maryland statute does not, in contrast, include first degree murder committed with premeditation and deliberation as an aggravating circumstance. Hence, a person convicted of felony murder has a disproportionately higher chance of being sentenced to death than a premeditated killer due to the "automatic" aggravating circumstance. See *State v. Cherry,* 298 N.C. 86, 257 S.E.2d 551 (1979), *cert. denied,* 446 U.S. 941 (1980).

In *Grandison v. State,* 305 Md. 685, 506 A.2d 580 (1986), the defendant contended that the act of contracting to murder was the crime itself, hence it could not also be an aggravating factor. "Maryland's capital punishment statute, Art. 27, §§ 412-414 makes plain the legislative intent that the commission of certain felonies, underlying a felony murder conviction, is to be considered an aggravating circumstance in the capital sentencing proceeding." *Stebbing v. State, supra* at 358, 473 A.2d at 917. As Art. 27, § 413(d) lists contracting for murder as an aggravating circumstance, the same rationale applies to contracting for murder. In *Grandison v. State, supra,* the defendant was the first to receive the death sentence for a contract murder conviction.

While he was not the triggerman, the murders would not have occurred without his actions, and he is as culpable as the triggerman. The only mitigating circumstances were that he had no prior conviction for a crime of violence and he was not the sole proximate cause of the killings.

In *Huffington v. State,* 304 Md. 559, 500 A.2d 272 (1985), the victim's own participation as a mitigating factor was not satisfied because, while the victim did participate in an alleged narcotics sale, the victim did not participate or consent to the carrying and concealing of a loaded pistol that the defendant fired into the victim's back.

Acts of accessories before the fact or principals in the second degree do not qualify as mitigating factors under Art. 27, § 413(g)(6) because they are not direct physical causes of death. *Evans v. State,* 304 Md. 487, 499 A.2d 1261 (1985).

Neither is a defendant's willingness to serve twenty-five years before consideration for parole a mitigating factor which the jury might consider. A defendant cannot bargain with the sentencing authority. That authority, under the statute, does not have the ultimate right to determine whether or not a defendant should be paroled. *Bowers v. State,* 306 Md. 120, 507 A.2d 1072 (1986).

In *Colvin v. State,* 299 Md. 88, 472 A.2d 953, *cert. denied,* 105 S. Ct. 226 (1984) the defendant argued that the Maryland death penalty statute is unconstitutional, *inter alia,* because it does not reserve this sanction for only "a small number of extreme cases" as required by the Supreme Court of the United States in *Godfrey v. Georgia,* 446 U.S. 420, 100 S. Ct. 1759, 64 L. Ed. 2d 398 (1980). He argued that one half of the first degree murder convictions in Maryland were based on felony murder. Also, the fact finder will automatically find the existence of the felony murder an aggravating factor at sentencing under Art. 27, § 413(d)(10). Further, the imposition of the death penalty for felony murder is disproportionate to the crime. In rejecting these arguments, the Court noted that the statute, with one exception, also requires that the defendant be a principal in the first degree to the killing. It also provides for mitigating circumstances to be weighed against aggravating circumstances. Finally, the Court noted the valid legislative goal of seeking to deter felons from murdering during the course of committing other crimes.

Similarly, the Court of Appeals in *Calhoun v. State,* 297 Md. 563, 468 A.2d 45 (1983), held that Art. 27, § 413(d)(10) is a constitutional aggravating factor. The Court distinguished *Enmund v. Florida,* 458 U.S. 782, 102 S. Ct. 3368, 73 L. Ed. 2d 1140 (1982), which held that the death penalty was excessive for an accomplice in a felony murder where the accused "neither took life, attempted to take life, nor intended to take life." See also *Bowers v. State,* 298 Md. 115, 468 A.2d 101 (1983).

(2) Mitigating circumstance of lack of future danger to society

One of the mitigating circumstances, Art. 27, § 413(g)(7) states: "It is unlikely that the defendant will engage in further criminal activity that would constitute a continuing threat to society."

In *Calhoun v. State, supra,* the Court of Appeals rejected the argument that the assessment of "future dangerousness" was so highly speculative, unreliable, and inconclusive as to violate the defendant's eighth and fourteenth amendments rights and Article 25 of the Maryland Declaration of Rights.

In applying this mitigating factor, two issues may arise. First, what is the proper time period upon which the trier of facts should focus? Does the statute mean a "continuing threat to society" as of the day of sentencing or after the defendant would have served the prison term accorded in lieu of death. If the latter is the proper interpretation, then should the jury be advised of the consequences of a life sentence in the particular case? The Court of Appeals has held that reference to future parole is improper in death penalty cases. *Bowers v. State,* 306 Md. 120, 507 A.2d 1072 (1986); *Poole v. State,* 295 Md. 167, 453 A.2d 1218 (1983) (Poole II); *Shoemaker v. State,* 228 Md. 462, 180 A.2d 682 (1962). The Court, in *Poole, supra,* feared that the jury will disregard its duty to balance the aggravating and mitigating factors against each other if the prosecutor can argue that the defendant may be paroled in the future.

A statutory provision enacted in 1986 provides that "(a) judge may not instruct the jury that the jury must assume that a sentence for life imprisonment is for the natural life of the defendant." Art. 27, §413A.

A second question involves how the jury is to define "society." Depending on how the preceding question is resolved, three definitions are possible: (1) the community surrounding the defendant both without and within prison; (2) the community surrounding the defendant excluding the prison community; or (3) the prison community in which the defendant serves his prison term excluding the surrounding community at large.

(3) Mitigating circumstance of youthful age of defendant

In 1987, Art. 27, §412 (punishment for murder) was amended to prohibit the sentence of death of certain juveniles, as follows: "If a person found guilty of murder in the first degree was less than 18 years old at the time the murder was committed, the person shall be sentenced to imprisonment for life and may not be sentenced to death." Notwithstanding this provision, it appears that under Art. 27, §413(g)(5) a youthful age, above eighteen, can be proffered as a mitigating circumstance. The latter statute states: "The youthful age of the defendant at the time of the crime."

In *Stebbing v. State,* 299 Md. 331, 473 A.2d 903, *cert. denied,* 469 U.S. 900 (1984), the defendant was nineteen years and three months old when she murdered the victim. She elected to be sentenced by the trial judge who did not find her youthful age to be a mitigating factor. The Court of Appeals stated that "youthful age" is not measured solely by chronological age. Quoting from *Eddings v. Oklahoma,* 455 U.S. 104, 102 S. Ct. 869, 71 L. Ed. 2d 1 (1982), a case involving a sixteen year old who had murdered a policeman, the Court noted that it is a time and condition of life when a person may be most susceptible to influence and to psychological damage. The Court considered prior criminal conduct, home environment, marital status, degree of maturity, and alcohol and drug abuse, among others, as factors relevant to "youthful age." The Court of Appeals held there was no error in failing to find youthful age as a mitigating factor since the defendant had been managing her own survival for much of the time since she was sixteen, had lived with at least one young man prior to her marriage and had been married for more than seven months at the time she committed the murder.

In *White v. State,* 300 Md. 719, 481 A.2d 201 (1984), the defendant was eighteen years and four months old when he committed the murder. The Court of Appeals held that under the facts of this case the jury could rationally have concluded that youthful age was not a mitigating factor. Similarly, in *Thomas v. State,* 301 Md. 294, 483 A.2d 6 (1984), despite evidence that his mental age was substantially lower than his chronological age due in part to a below normal IQ, the Court found no error in failing to find youthful age as a mitigating factor where defendant was twenty-three years old at the time of the murder.

(4) Mitigating circumstance of substantial impairment of defendant's mental capacity

Maryland Ann. Code, Art. 27, § 413(g)(4) provides as a mitigating factor a modified insanity defense. In contrast to the insanity defense applicable at the adjudicatory phase, this modified insanity defense permits the jury to take into account the defendant's diminished capacity in applying a more lenient sentence. See *Johnson v. State,* 292 Md. 405, 439 A.2d 542 (1982).

Effective July 1, 1987, the State is prohibited from executing the death sentence against an incompetent inmate and requires an incompetent inmate who otherwise would be executed to serve a sentence of life imprisonment without parole. This provision was proposed by the Governor's Task Force on Mentally Ill Offenders which concluded that Maryland law was unconstitutional in light of *Ford v. Wainwright,* 106 S. Ct. 2595, 91 L. Ed. 2d 335 (1986). Incompetency is defined as follows:

> "Incompetent" means the state of mind of an inmate who as a result of a mental disorder or mental retardation, lacks awareness (1) of the fact of his or her impending execution; and (2) he or she is to be executed for the crime of murder.

Maryland Ann. Code, Art. 27, § 75A(a)(2)(I). An inmate is not incompetent merely because his or her competence is dependent upon continuing treatment, including the use of medication. Art. 27, § 75A(a)(2)(II). Article 27, § 75A sets forth procedures for raising and determining the competency issue. This provision does not affect the power of the Governor to stay execution of a death sentence under Art. 27, § 75(c) or to commute a sentence under Art. 41, § 4-603.

See Comment at subpart (g), § 5.08, Insanity, *infra,* on standard of competence to stand trial.

(5) Others

The statute includes other aggravating and mitigating factors that may pose definitional problems, including "sole proximate cause" in Art. 27, § 413(g)(6). In *Huffington v. State,* 304 Md. 559, 500 A.2d 272 (1985), the Court rejected the defendant's argument that his act was not the sole proximate cause of the victim's death because an alleged accomplice was convicted of the felony murder of one of the victims. The alleged accomplice was a principal in the second degree or accessory before the fact and his actions were not sufficient to support the defendant's argument.

(h) Evidence that may be considered at death sentencing proceeding

Maryland Ann. Code, Art. 27, § 413(c)(1), provides for five types of evidence that may be admissible at a death sentencing proceeding:

> (i) Evidence relating to any mitigating circumstance listed in subsection (g); (ii) Evidence relating to any aggravating circumstance listed in subsection (d) of which the State had notified the defendant pursuant to § 412(b); (iii) Evidence of any prior criminal convictions, pleas of guilty or nolo contendere, or the absence of such prior convictions or pleas, to the same extent admissible in other sentencing procedures; (iv) Any presentence investigation report. However, any recommendation as to sentence contained in the report is not ad-

> missible; and (v) Any other evidence that the court deems of probative value and relevant to sentence, provided the defendant is accorded a fair opportunity to rebut any statements.

In *Calhoun v. State,* 297 Md. 563, 468 A.2d 45 (1983), the Court of Appeals rejected defendant's contention that the above provisions are so broad as to the evidence the sentencing authority is to consider in reaching its decision as to be constitutionally infirm. The Court stated that a sentencing jury's exercise of discretion is permissible as long as that exercise is conducted within the confines and in compliance with the standards of a "carefully drafted" capital sentencing statute. *Id.* at 634-635, 468 A.2d at 79.

A controversial issue interpreting the above provision is whether, and under what circumstances, the State can introduce evidence of unrelated criminal acts of the defendant which have not resulted in a criminal conviction, plea of guilty, or *nolo contendere.* In *Scott v. State,* 297 Md. 235, 465 A.2d 1126 (1983), the Court of Appeals held that subsection (c)(1)(v) of Art. 27, § 413, is qualified by subsections (c)(1)(i) and (iii) thereof, so as to preclude the admission of evidence relating to other crimes for which there has not been a conviction or a plea of guilty or *nolo contendere.* This interpretation is also supported by relating subsection (c)(1)(i) to the wording of the mitigating circumstance of Art. 27, § 413(g)(1). The Court noted that the admission of evidence of crimes for which there have been no convictions could result in the mitigating circumstances of the absence of prior convictions being outweighed or "wiped out" or eliminated. The Court stated that subsections (c)(1)(i) and (iii) serve the purpose of moderating the significantly prejudicial nature of evidence of unrelated crimes in the face of the unique severity of the death penalty. Contrary to discussion in dicta in *Johnson v. State,* 292 Md. 405, 439 A.2d 542 (1982), the Court held that these provisions collectively unambiguously restrict the type of evidence admissible in a death sentencing proceeding to something less inclusive than what generally is admissible in a nondeath penalty sentencing proceeding. *Cf. Calhoun v. State, supra,* where the Court of Appeals held that in the absence of an objection by trial counsel focusing on the point before the Court in *Scott,* evidence of defendant's conduct amounting to the common-law offense of battery is admissible under Art. 27, § 413(c)(1)(v). Judge Davidson dissented arguing that the question was properly preserved for review and, even if not, the "waiver principle" should be more liberally interpreted in death penalty cases so that a defendant will not be executed because his lawyer allegedly made a mistake in failing to properly object to the admissibility of evidence.

In *White v. State,* 300 Md. 719, 481 A.2d 201 (1984), a parole agent testified for the State at the sentencing phase that the defendant was on parole when he committed the murder for which he was being sentenced. The Court of Appeals held that this evidence was admissible under Art. 27, § 413(c)(1)(v), quoted above. The Court stated that proof that the defendant was on parole at the time of the murder is relevant to the mitigating circumstance dealing with the unlikelihood of further criminal activity that would constitute a continuing threat to society. The Court rejected defendant's argument that this mitigating circumstance had not been raised by the defendant and stated that once an aggravating factor is found the statutory scheme mandates that the jury consider each of the statutorily enumerated possible mitigating circumstances. In support of its view, the Court noted that the sentencing form presents each of the statutorily listed mitigating circumstances for consideration. Query whether there is tension between the decisions in *Scott v. State, supra,* and *White v. State, supra,* since the State could argue that evidence of unrelated crimes not resulting in conviction is always relevant to rebut the possible mitigating circumstance of the unlikelihood of further criminal activity that would constitute a continuing threat to society.

In *Tichnell v. State,* 297 Md. 432, 468 A.2d 1 (1983) (Tichnell III), the Court held that Art. 27, § 413(c) does not permit, absent agreement of the parties or a showing that the witnesses are not available to testify at a separate sentencing hearing, the admission of prior recorded testimony to prove the existence of aggravating or mitigating factors. The Court noted that the witness' demeanor and credibility were critically important.

(i) Proportionality review on appeal

In *Tichnell v. State,* 297 Md. 432, 468 A.2d 1 (1983) (Tichnell III), the Court clarified the meaning of the phrase "similar cases" as set forth in Maryland Ann. Code, Art. 27, § 414(e)(4). This provision requires the Court of Appeals to determine whether the "sentence of death is excessive or disproportionate to the penalty imposed in *similar cases*" (emphasis added). The Court of Appeals held that a case in which the defendant was sentenced to death is to be compared to other first degree murder cases in which the State sought the death penalty under Art. 27, § 413, whether it was imposed or not. The Court, however, did state that the defendant is not precluded from presenting argument, with relevant facts, that designated noncapital cases are similar.

In *Calhoun v. State,* 297 Md. 563, 468 A.2d 45 (1983), the Court rejected defendant's contention that he was denied due process of law because of the failure of the capital punishment statute on its face and in its operation to provide a means of culling those "similar cases" which the Court must consider in its proportionality review. The Court reaffirmed its holding in Tichnell III, *supra,* that the legislatively intended inventory of cases from which "similar cases" are to be culled encompasses only those first degree murder cases in which the State sought the death penalty under Art. 27, § 413, whether it was imposed or not. The defendant had argued that, in addition, it should include those cases in which the State either withdraw its intent to seek capital punishment or chose not to seek the death penalty even though a case was ostensibly "similar." The Court further held that "similar cases, in terms of a particular accused and particular crime of which he was convicted, are comprised of those involving similar aggravating and mitigating circumstances in which the State sought to have the death penalty imposed and those brought to our attention by defendants." *Id.* at 610, 468 A.2d at 67.

(j) Other constitutional issues

In *Calhoun v. State,* 297 Md. 563, 468 A.2d 45 (1983), the Court held that the capital punishment statute is not unconstitutional because of failure to provide standards to govern the exercise of prosecutorial discretion under Maryland Ann. Code, Art. 27, § 412(b) to initiate a death case. The defendant presented statistical evidence showing a wide disparity in initiating death cases by prosecutors in various Maryland counties. The Court stated that absent any specific evidence of indiscretion by prosecutors resulting in an irrational, inconsistent, or discriminatory application of the death penalty statute, the proportionality review is intended to assure that the death penalty is not imposed in a disproportionate manner. *Cf. McCleskey v. Kemp,* 107 S. Ct. 1756, 95 L. Ed. 2d 262 (1987), where the U.S. Supreme Court held that statistical evidence showing disparity in imposition of death penalty due to race of victim was insufficient to show denial of equal protection or violation of eighth amendment.

In *Calhoun v. State, supra,* the Court also rejected defendant's claim that in providing for the sentence of death by administration of lethal gas, the Maryland capital punishment scheme violates the eighth and fourteenth amendments of the United States Constitution and Articles 16 and 25 of the Maryland Declaration of Rights. The Court noted that the gallows was the method of imposing the death penalty in Maryland until the more humane method of execution by lethal gas was adopted in 1955. The defendant had argued that some states have abandoned the gas chamber in favor of lethal injection and that North Carolina allows death-row prisoners to choose between lethal injection or the gas chamber. See *Gray v. Lucas,* 710 F.2d 1048 (5th Cir.), *cert. denied,* 104 S. Ct. 211 (1983).

§ 4.22a. Murder — Second degree.

Murder in the second degree is the unlawful killing of a human being being with malice [but without premeditation and deliberation].

In order to convict the defendant of murder in the second degree, the State must prove beyond a reasonable doubt that: (1) the defendant inflicted an injury upon ________ (*name of victim*) which resulted in death; (2) and, at the time the injury was inflicted, the defendant acted with malice; [(3) and, the defendant did not kill ________ (*name of victim*) in a sudden heat of passion caused by adequate provocation]; [or with a lawful justification or excuse, namely ________ (*insert applicable defense, such as self-defense*).]

Malice is the indispensable ingredient of murder. Malice does not have its ordinary meaning of ill will or hatred but rather has its own special meanings. Malice can be found to exist in three forms. First, it exists whenever a person kills another intentionally, willfully or purposefully, unless the killing is justifiable or excusable or unless there is a proper mitigating circumstance. Second, malice also exists, in the absence of justification, legal excuse or a proper mitigating circumstance, where there is an intent to inflict great bodily harm; or third, where one does an act in wanton and willful disregard of an obvious risk of likelihood or causing death or great bodily injury.

[*To be given where further explanation of malice is needed such as in some cases involving implied malice*: To help explain the special meanings of malice, the law divides malice into express malice and implied malice or what is sometimes referred to as the equivalent of malice. Express or actual malice is something which indicates an actual intention to kill another human being, in the absence of a proper mitigating circumstance, legal excuse or justification. Even if express malice does not exist, malice may be inferred from the proof of certain facts. This implied malice or equivalent of malice historically arose from the need felt to punish, as murder, killings resulting from *life-endangering intents,* even though such intents did not involve a literal intent to kill. There are two mental states recognized as the equivalent of malice that you must consider. In the absence of justification, legal excuse or a proper mitigating circumstance, malice exists where there is an intent to inflict great bodily injury and where one does an act in wanton and willful disregard of an obvious risk or likelihood of causing death or great bodily harm.]

[This last type of equivalent of malice is sometimes referred to as "depraved-heart" murder because it involves an element of viciousness involving an extreme indifference to the value of human life. To give you an example of an act creating a grave risk of death, one can be guilty of murder for death caused by the shooting of a gun, regardless of the consequences, into a house, train, or automobile in which persons are known to be at the time where a person did this not with the intent of killing anyone but merely for his diversion.]

[If you find that the killing resulted from the use of a deadly weapon directed at a vital part of the body, an inference may be drawn that there was an intent to kill or do grievous bodily harm.]

[Homicide is manslaughter, and not murder, when a proper mitigating circumstance is present. The State must prove beyond a reasonable doubt that the defendant did not commit voluntary manslaughter, that is, did not injure __________ (*name of victim*) in a sudden heat of passion, caused by adequate provocation.]

[Voluntary manslaughter, and not murder, exists where there is: (1) an intentional killing of another person; (2) done in a sudden heat of passion; (3) caused by adequate provocation; (4) without a reasonable opportunity for the passion to cool; and (5) a causal connection exists between the provocation, the passion, and the fatal act.]

[For voluntary manslaughter to exist, there must be an intentional killing accompanied by adequate provocation. Passion without adequate provocation is not enough. The provocation must be such as might naturally cause a reasonable person in the passion of the moment to lose self-control and commit the act on impulse and without reflection. It is not the particular disposition or temperament of the defendant, but the nature of the alleged provocation, such as may be supposed to affect and influence ordinary minds that you must consider. The term "sudden heat of passion" means that the killing must have followed the provocation before there had been a reasonable opportunity for the passion to cool, that is, for a person of average disposition to regain control.]

[If you find the State has proved beyond a reasonable doubt that the defendant inflicted an injury upon __________ (*name of victim*) which resulted in death; and, that at the time the injury was inflicted, the defendant acted with malice; [and that the defendant did not injure __________ (*name of victim*) in the heat of passion caused by adequate provocation], [and, further, that the State has proved beyond a reasonable doubt the absence of __________ (*insert relevant justification or excuse, such as self-defense*)], then you should find the defendant guilty of the offense of second degree murder. On the other hand, if the State has not proved beyond a reasonable doubt that the defendant inflicted injuries that resulted in death or acted with malice [or that the defendant did *not* injure __________ (*name of victim*) in the heat of passion caused by adequate provocation,] [or that the State has not proved the absence of __________ (*insert relevant justification or excuse, such as self-defense,*)] then you must find the defendant not guilty of second degree murder. [You should then proceed further to determine whether or not the defendant is guilty of the lesser included offense of voluntary manslaughter.]

COMMENT

(a) In general

In Maryland, murder is a common-law crime which has been statutorily differentiated into degrees, each carrying differing penalties. *Lindsay v. State,* 8 Md. App. 100, 258 A.2d 760 (1969). At common law there were no degrees of murder. After defining the offenses that constitute first degree murder, the General Assembly provided in Maryland Ann. Code, Art. 27, § 411: "All other kinds of murder shall be deemed murder in the second degree." This means that if the particular crime, while containing the element of malice, is not within the scope of first degree murder, it is second degree murder. See Instructions and Comments: § 4.21a, Murder—First degree, and § 4.21b, Murder—First degree: felony murder, *supra.*

(b) Malice: the mental states for murder

Malice is the indispensable ingredient of murder. The term, "malice aforethought," which had been used in the first edition of this book, has been replaced with the word "malice." In *Godwin v. State,* 38 Md. App. 716, 382 A.2d 596 (1977), *vacated,* 284 Md. 85, 403 A.2d 785 (1978), the Court stated that the word "aforethought" need not and, perhaps, should not be included in a jury instruction. The Court stated:

> The word "aforethought" is today an absolutely useless appendage on our law. It has over the centuries been utterly drained of any meaning whatsoever. As a word of no utility but with an ever-present potential for confusion (some may innocently think that "aforethought" means aforethought), it should be struck from the lexicon of our homicide law.

Id. at 734, 382 A.2d at 606.

Malice as the *mens rea* of murder includes both a positive component — namely, an intent to kill, an intent to inflict great bodily injury, or an intent to do an act the natural tendency of which is to cause death or great bodily harm — and a negative component — namely, the absence of legally sufficient mitigating circumstances, excuse or justification. Once the defendant meets a burden of production and comes forward with sufficient evidence to generate a jury question concerning the existence of a mitigating circumstance (e.g., voluntary manslaughter) or an excuse or justification (e.g., self-defense) or such evidence is otherwise present in the State's case-in-chief, then the State has the burden of persuasion beyond a reasonable doubt to establish both the presence of the positive component *and* the absence of the negative component of malice. *Evans v. State,* 28 Md. App. 640, 349 A.2d 300 (1975), *aff'd,* 278 Md. 197, 362 A.2d 629 (1976).

Malice for second degree murder is divided into express and implied malice. The difference between express and implied malice is based on the positive component. The negative component, the absence of legally sufficient mitigating circumstances, excuse or justification, is identical. For express malice, the positive component of the mental state is the presence of an actual subjective intention to kill another human being. For implied malice, the positive component is either an actual subjective intention to inflict great bodily harm on another person or to do an act the natural tendency of which is to cause great bodily harm to another person.

In *Lindsay v. State, supra,* an often-cited case, the Court drew the basic distinctions between express and implied malice. Express malice exists whenever an accountable person kills another intentionally unless the killing is justifiable or excusable or unless there is a mitigating circumstance. According to *Lindsay,* there are two types of circumstances in which malice is implied: "where (1) there was an intent to inflict great bodily harm, and (2) conceding that there was no actual intent to injure, an act was done or duty omitted wilfully, the natural tendency of which was to cause death or great bodily harm," *Id.* at 104, 258 A.2d 763 (*citing* Clark & Marshall, *Law of Crimes* § 10.06 (6th ed. 1952)).

In *Blackwell v. State,* 34 Md. App. 547, 369 A.2d 153, *cert. denied,* 280 Md. 728 (1977), the Court more clearly identified and defined the second type of implied malice referred to in *Lindsay.* The Court stated:

> Even if express malice does not exist, malice may be inferred from proof of certain facts .... This "implied" malice arose from the need felt to punish, as murder, homicides resulting from life-endangering intents, even though such intents did not involve a literal intent to kill. As pointed out by Judge Moylan for this Court in *Evans, supra,* those additional mental states were added to the *mens rea* of murder and they are recognized today as:

1) intent-to-do-serious-bodily-injury murder;
2) felony-murder; and
3) depraved-heart murder. (Perkins gives this mental state the less emotionally charged and probably better label of "Wanton and Wilful Disregard of Unreasonable Human Risk").

Id. at 553, 369 A.2d at 157-58. The Court then quoted from R. Perkins, *Criminal Law* § 1 at 36-37 (2d ed. 1969), noting the prerequisites for so-called depraved-heart murder, as follows:

> In other words, the intent to do an act in wanton and wilful disregard of the obvious likelihood of causing death or great bodily injury is a malicious intent. The word "wanton" is the key word here. For reasons to be emphasized later a motorist who attempts to pass another car on a "blind curve" may be acting with such criminal negligence that if he causes the death of another in a resulting traffic accident he will be guilty of manslaughter. And such a motorist may be creating fully as great a human hazard as one who shoots into a house or train "just for kicks," who is guilty of murder if loss of life results. The difference is that in the act of the shooter there is an element of viciousness — an extreme indifference to the value of human life that is not found in the act of the motorist. And it is this viciousness which makes the act "wanton" as well as "wilful."

Blackwell v. State, supra at 553-554, 369 A.2d at 158.

The hypothetical motorist discussed in the above quote was qualified in the subsequent edition by adding the following sentence: "Of course, if the facts are gross enough to show extreme indifference a resulting death could be murder rather than manslaughter." R. Perkins and R. Boyce, *Criminal Law* 60 (3d ed. 1982). *Blackwell v. State, supra,* states that in enacting the manslaughter by automobile statute, (Art. 27, § 388) the General Assembly intended to preempt the subject matter of *unintended* homicides resulting from the operation of a motor vehicle. Hence, in Maryland, a conviction for murder for a death resulting from the operation of an automobile, in the absence of evidence of intentional homicide, appears not to be possible. Based on the evidence of legislative intent presented, this conclusion seems questionable.

Blackwell seems to require a subjective awareness of the grave risk to human life of the actor's conduct which is not clearly apparent in *Lindsay v. State, supra.* In their book, *Maryland Criminal Law: Practice and Procedure* (1983), Judges Richard P. Gilbert and Charles E. Moylan, Jr., citing the *Blackwell* case, concur that the perpetrator must realize the risk his behavior has created:

> A depraved heart murder is often described as a wanton and wilful killing. The term "depraved heart" means something more than conduct amounting to a high or unreasonable risk to human life. The perpetrator must realize the risk his behavior has created to the extent that his conduct may be termed wilful. Moreover, the conduct must contain an element of viciousness or contemptuous disregard for the value of human life which conduct characterizes that behavior as wanton. Thus, if A sets up a target shoot in an empty school lot on a Saturday morning and accidentally kills a child coming into the grounds, he may be guilty of manslaughter, but that irresponsible conduct does not constitute a depraved heart slaying. If A, however, sets up the target shoot on a school day when he knows children are in and about the school, such conduct establishes the wantonness necessary to demonstrate that any killing resulting therefrom is attributable to a depraved heart. Therefore, A would be guilty of murder.
>
> A classic example of the depraved heart killing is the shooting of a rifle into a passing passenger train with the result that a person on the train is slain. The same rationale would apply, of course, to shooting at vehicles on the highway.

Id. § 1.6-3 at 21.

The instruction dealing with implied malice, especially regarding so-called "depraved heart" murder, is patterned after the discussion in *Blackwell v. State, supra.* Additional amplifying language is provided in brackets to aid in the jury's understanding of the meaning of implied malice.

The Model Penal Code provides another example of an instruction requiring awareness of the risk. It first states that malice may be inferred from a homicide "committed recklessly under circumstances manifesting extreme indifference to the value of human life." Model Penal Code, § 210.2 (Proposed Official Draft, 1962). It then provides:

> A person acts recklessly with respect to a material element of an offense when he *consciously* disregards a substantial and unjustifiable risk that the material element (death) exists or will result from his conduct. The risk must be of such a nature and degree that, considering the nature and purpose of the actor's conduct and the circumstances known to him, its disregard involves a gross deviation from the standard of conduct that a law-abiding person would observe in the actor's situation.

Id. at § 2.02(2)(c) (emphasis added).

The language of an instruction on implied malice should permit a jury to distinguish, as clearly as possible, malice from reckless or criminally negligent conduct that constitutes involuntary manslaughter. It has been observed that at common law the following factors have been employed in drawing this distinction: (1) the degree of risk to human life which the actor's conduct presented; (2) the degree to which the actor was aware of the risk potential of his conduct; and (3) the degree to which the actor's conduct deviated from an objective standard of conduct. The latter factor in unusual situations permits the jury to consider the motives or social utility for the actor's risky conduct.

In *Blackwell v. State, supra,* the Court noted that so-called depraved heart murder and manslaughter by gross negligence are separated by a most narrow line. One difference between them is the absence of a need to prove willfulness in manslaughter. To be convicted of depraved heart murder, the defendant must have had knowledge or awareness of the risk to human life he was taking in the actions he was doing. Another difference is that to support a conviction for manslaughter, there must be gross negligence: that is, a wanton disregard for human life. To convict of depraved heart murder, there must be sufficient evidence showing a wanton and willful disregard of an obvious risk showing an extreme indifference to the value of human life. An optional instruction has been added to Instruction, § 4.24(a), Manslaughter — Involuntary, *infra,* to aid the jury in drawing these distinctions when both depraved heart murder and involuntary manslaughter based on gross negligence are under consideration.

Maryland adheres to the common law doctrine of transferred intent. This doctrine "transfers" the *mens rea* of the defendant from an intended victim to an unintended victim. If *A* shoots at *B,* with the intent to murder *B,* but *A*'s shot actually hits *C* and kills *C, A*'s felonious intent to kill *B* is transferred to the act of slaying *C.* A rationale for this is the so-called depraved heart murder doctrine discussed above. By his act of shooting at *B, A* creates also a high risk of death to other persons nearby and manifests an extreme indifference to the value of human life. This doctrine of "transferred intent" was recognized in *Gladden v. State,* 273 Md. 383, 330 A.2d 176, *aff'g* 20 Md. App. 492, 316 A.2d 319 (1974).

When a homicide results from the use of a deadly weapon directed at a vital part of the body, an inference may be drawn that there was an intent to kill or do grievous bodily harm. *Glenn v. State,* 68 Md. App. 379, 511 A.2d 1110 (1986); *Jones v. State,* 37 Md. App. 511, 378 A.2d 9 (1977); *Lindsay v. State, supra; Jacobs v. State,* 6 Md. App. 238, 251 A.2d 33 (1969). Malice, however, cannot be inferred since use of deadly force does not negate the absence of mitigating circumstances. *State v. Evans, supra.*

The term "malice" has been held to have the same meaning under the law of homicide as it does under arson law. See *DeBettencourt v. State,* 48 Md. App. 522, 428 A.2d 479, 480 (1981). Note, however, that this point was subject to dispute in the dissenting opinion of Judge Liss. *Id.* at 532, 428 A.2d at 485. See Instruction and Comment, § 4.52, *infra,* for discussion of arson. See also Instruction, § 3.06, "Maliciously" — Defined, *supra.*

For a general discussion of the elements of second degree murder, especially malice, see *Abney v. State,* 244 Md. 444, 223 A.2d 792 (1966), *cert. denied,* 387 U.S. 925 (1967); *Davis v. State,* 237 Md. 97, 205 A.2d 254 (1964), *cert. denied,* 382 U.S. 945 (1965); *Gunther v. State,* 228 Md. 404, 179 A.2d 880 (1962); *Faulcon v. State,* 211 Md. 249, 126 A.2d 858 (1956); *Swain v. State,* 50 Md.

App. 29, 435 A.2d 804 (1981); *Lindsay v. State, supra; Levya v. State,* 2 Md. App. 120, 233 A.2d 498 (1967).

(c) Burdens of proof

This instruction has been revised to reflect the changes mandated by *Mullaney v. Wilbur,* 421 U.S. 684, 95 S. Ct. 1881, 44 L. Ed. 2d 508 (1975), as interpreted by *Evans v. State,* 28 Md. App. 640, 349 A.2d 300 (1975), *aff'd,* 278 Md. 197, 362 A.2d 629 (1976). In *Mullaney,* the appellant challenged Maine's requirement that the defendant bear the burden of proof by a preponderance of the evidence in order to reduce the level of criminal homicide to voluntary manslaughter. The Supreme Court of the United States held that the requirement was violative of the due process standard enunciated in *In re Winship,* 397 U.S. 358, 90 S. Ct. 1068, 25 L. Ed. 2d 368 (1970), which mandates that the State prove beyond a reasonable doubt every fact necessary to constitute the crime charged.

In *Evans,* the Maryland Court of Special Appeals held that *Mullaney* requires the abrogation of the former rule in Maryland that presumed a homicide to be second degree murder. The Court further indicated that it would be unconstitutional to place the burden of persuasion on the defendant to prove any circumstance of mitigation, excuse or justification in a homicide.

Concerning the scope to be accorded the *Mullaney* decision, Judge Moylan, writing for the Court in *Evans v. State, supra* discussed the holding as follows:

> For the moment, it is enough to set out, by way of shorthand summary, that it dooms as unconstitutional any procedural device which (1) imposes upon a defendant a burden of proving, by any standard, his innocence as to any element of a crime or (2) relieves the State of its burden of ultimate persuasion beyond a reasonable doubt as to any issue fairly in the case.

Id. at 654, 349 A.2d at 318.

The Court reasoned that the Maryland presumption of second degree murder violated the due process clause because it relieved the State of its burden of establishing that the act was committed without adequate justification, excuse or circumstances of mitigation. See also *Dorsey v. State,* 278 Md. 221, 362 A.2d 642 (1976); *State v. Garland,* 29 Md. App. 27, 349 A.2d 374 (1975), *rev'd,* 278 Md. 212, 362 A.2d 638, *rev'd,* 34 Md. App. 258, 367 A.2d 30 (1976); *Edwards v. State,* 31 Md. App. 562, 358 A.2d 590 (1976).

In Maryland, however, the defendant still has the burden of going forward with sufficient evidence to generate the issue of justification, excuse or mitigation. *Tripp v. State,* 36 Md. App. 459, 374 A.2d 384 (1977). Once the defendant has met the burden of production, the State must assume the burden of persuasion beyond a reasonable doubt on the issue. See *Leach v. State,* 47 Md. App. 611, 425 A.2d 234 (1981) (there must be a legitimate issue before the judge is required to instruct the jury as to the meaning of these specific terms).

In *Patterson v. New York,* 432 U.S. 197, 97 S. Ct. 2319, 53 L. Ed. 2d 281 (1977), the Supreme Court upheld a conviction for second degree murder under a statute that required the defendant, in order to reduce the offense to manslaughter, to prove by a preponderance of the evidence that he had "acted under the influence of extreme emotional disturbance for which there was a reasonable explanation or excuse." The Court distinguished *Mullaney* on the ground that under the New York statute, unlike the Maine statute, "malice aforethought" is not an element of the offense of murder. Rather, murder is defined under the New York Law as the causing of the death of another person with the intent to do so. Also, the New York statutory standard provides more opportunity for the jury to consider mitigating circumstances than the provocation formula of voluntary manslaughter at common law. The constitutional due process limits on a statute with respect to *statutory* changes that shift the burden of proving affirmative defenses to the defendant were not clearly delineated in the *Patterson* decision.

At present in Maryland, malice is an element of the offense of murder. To prove the existence of malice, the State must establish beyond a reasonable doubt that the act which provided the homicide was (1) intentional; (2) unmitigated, and (3) committed without proper justification or excuse. *Evans v. State, supra.* It may therefore be argued that *Patterson* has little or no effect on the burden of proof in Maryland homicide cases. This view is supported by the expansive interpretation afforded the *Mullaney* decision by the Maryland Court in *Evans v. State, supra.*

For a listing of the various issues on which the Maryland courts have held that the State bears the burden of proof beyond a reasonable doubt, see Appendix V, The Impact of *Evans v. State:* Burdens of Proof, Presumptions and Inferences, *infra.*

§ 4.22b. Murder — When both first and second degree murder are in issue.

You have now been instructed on the elements both of first and second degree murder.

You should first consider whether the defendant is guilty of first degree murder as charged in the indictment. If you find that the State has proved each and every element of first degree murder beyond a reasonable doubt, then you should find the defendant guilty of first degree murder. If you so find, your deliberations should end.

[*Where premeditated murder and felony murder are in issue:* In this case, the State has presented evidence directed toward two different types of first degree murder: first degree murder based on willfulness, premeditation, and deliberation; and, first degree murder based on felony murder. If you reach a verdict of guilty, you should indicate specifically whether, from all the evidence, you have found the defendant guilty of a felony murder or whether you have found the requisite intent of willfulness, premeditation and deliberation independent of the underlying felony so that the defendant would be guilty of a premeditated murder.]

However, if you find that the State has failed to prove each and every element of the offense of first degree murder beyond a reasonable doubt, then you must find the defendant not guilty of first degree murder. You should then proceed to consider whether the defendant is guilty of second degree murder. If you find that the State has proved each and every element of the offense of second degree murder beyond a reasonable doubt, then you should find the defendant guilty of second degree murder.

(Alternative A)

[On the other hand, if the State has failed to prove beyond a reasonable doubt each and every element of the offense of second degree murder, then you must find the defendant not guilty.]

(Alternative B)

[If the State has failed to prove beyond a reasonable doubt each and every element of the offense of second degree murder, you should then proceed to consider whether the defendant is guilty of the lesser included offense of [voluntary] [involuntary] manslaughter. If you find that the State has proved each and every element of [voluntary] [involuntary] manslaughter beyond a reasonable doubt, then you should find the defendant guilty of [voluntary] [involuntary] manslaughter. On the other hand, if the State has failed to prove beyond a reasonable doubt each and every element of the offense of [voluntary] [involuntary] manslaughter, then you must find the defendant not guilty.]

§ 4.23a. Manslaughter — Voluntary: general instruction.

[If you determine that the defendant is not guilty of murder in the second degree, then you are required to consider whether the defendant is guilty of a lesser included offense known as manslaughter.] Voluntary manslaughter is defined as the intentional killing of another person without malice, justification or legal excuse.

In order for a person to be guilty of this offense, the State must prove beyond a reasonable doubt that: (1) there was an intentional killing of another person; (2) it was done by the defendant; (3) it was done in a sudden heat of passion; (4) the heat of passion was caused by adequate provocation; (5) there had not been a reasonable time for the passion to cool; and (6) there was a causal connection between the provocation, the passion and the fatal act.

For voluntary manslaughter to exist, there must be an intentional killing accompanied by provocation that must be adequate in law and, to be so, it must be so great as to reasonably excite passion and heat of blood. Passion without adequate provocation is not enough. The provocation must be such as might naturally cause a reasonable person in the passion of the moment to lose self-control and commit the act on impulse and without reflection. It is not the particular disposition or temperament of the defendant, but the nature of the alleged provocation, such as may be supposed to affect and influence ordinary minds that you must consider.

[In determining whether a person of average disposition might naturally be induced to lose self-control at the time of the fatal act and to act on impulse and without reflection, you should consider all of the facts and circumstances in evidence. You may consider the parties prior relationship, if any, the behavior of the defendant and the victim immediately before the killing, and the nature and extent of any acts of provocation. For example, a blow or other personal violence or imminent threat of violence by the deceased may, in light of all of the circumstances, constitute adequate provocation. On the other hand, a trivial or slight provocation is not adequate provocation. Mere insulting, offensive or abusive words alone, directed to the defendant by the victim, are not legally sufficient provocation.]

The term "sudden heat of passion" means that the killing must have followed the provocation before there had been a reasonable opportunity for the passion to cool; that is, for a person of average disposition to regain self-control.

To establish the crime of voluntary manslaughter you must find that the defendant inflicted the injury or injuries on the victim and that the victim died as a result of such injury or injuries.

[I have instructed you that voluntary manslaughter is the intentional killing of another person in the heat of passion caused by adequate provocation without justification or legal excuse. This means that the State must prove beyond a reasonable doubt that the killing was not an innocent homicide. In this case, the defense of ________ (*include relevant defenses, such as self-defense*) has been raised. The State must prove beyond a reasonable doubt the absence of ________ (*include relevant defenses*).]

COMMENT

See Comment after § 4.23b, *infra*.

§ 4.23b. Manslaughter — Voluntary: amplified instruction including special sources of provocation.

[If you determine that the defendant is not guilty of murder in the second degree, then you are required to consider whether the defendant is guilty of a lesser included offense known as manslaughter.] Involuntary manslaughter is defined as the intentional killing of another person without malice, justification or legal excuse.

In order for a person to be guilty of this offense, the State must prove beyond a reasonable doubt that: (1) there was an intentional killing of another person; (2) it was done by the defendant; (3) it was done in a sudden heat of passion; (4) the heat of passion was caused by adequate provocation; (5) there had not been a reasonable time for the passion to cool; and (6) there was a causal connection between the provocation, the passion and the fatal act.

For voluntary manslaughter to exist, there must be an intentional killing accompanied by provocation that must be adequate in law and, to be so, it must be so great as to reasonably excite passion and heat of blood. Passion without adequate provocation is not enough. If a person unreasonably allows passion to control judgment, that person is responsible to the full extent of the consequences of his acts. The line which distinguishes which provocations will mitigate the offense from those which will not cannot be clearly defined. Reasonableness is the test. The standard is that the provocation shall be such as might naturally induce a reasonable person in the passion of the moment to lose self-control and commit the act on impulse and without reflection.

It is not the particular disposition or temperament of the defendant, but the nature of the alleged provocation, such as may be supposed to affect and influence ordinary minds, that you must consider. [Moreover, the provocation must be such as would arouse a reasonable, sober person. If the provocation aroused the defendant simply because the defendant was intoxicated, and would not have aroused a sober person, it does not constitute adequate provocation.]

[____________ (*If applicable, insert language from:* (i) *Mutual combat;* (ii) *Battery;* (iii) *Spousal adultery;* (iv) *Words plus threatening conduct.* See under *"Special sources of adequate provocation"* immediately following this instruction)].

[In determining whether a person of average disposition might naturally be induced to lose self-control at the time of the fatal act and to act on impulse and without reflection, you should consider all of the facts and circumstances in evidence. You may consider the parties prior relationship, if any, the behavior of the defendant and the victim immediately before the killing, and the nature and extent of any acts of provocation. For example, a blow or other personal violence or imminent threat of violence by the deceased may, in light of all of the circumstances, constitute adequate provocation. On the other hand, a trivial or slight provocation is not adequate provocation. Mere insulting, offensive or abusive words alone, directed to the defendant by the victim, are not legally sufficient provocation.]

As used here the term "sudden heat of passion" means that the killing must have followed the provocation before there had been a reasonable opportunity for the passion to cool. ["Heat of passion" may include rage, resentment, anger, terror, and fear or other violent or highly wrought emotion.]

To establish the crime of voluntary manslaughter you must find that the defendant inflicted the injury or injuries on the deceased and that the deceased died as a result of such injury or injuries.

[I have instructed you that voluntary manslaughter is the intentional killing of another person in the heat of passion caused by adequate provocation without justification or legal excuse. This means that the State must prove beyond a reasonable doubt that the killing was not an innocent homicide. In this case, the defense of __________ (*include relevant defenses, such as self-defense*) has been raised. The State must prove beyond a reasonable doubt the absence of __________ (*include relevant defenses*).] [If you find that the defendant is not guilty of voluntary manslaughter, then it is your duty as members of the jury to consider whether the defendant is guilty of *involuntary* manslaughter.]

(Special sources of adequate provocation)

(1) Mutual combat.

You may consider whether mutual combat between two individuals is adequate provocation that may result in a homicide being voluntary manslaughter.

If two persons meet not intending to fight and angry words suddenly arise, and a conflict sprints up in which blows are struck on both sides, without much regard to who is the initial assailant, it is a mutual combat. It does not matter who struck the first blow if both persons intended to fight. If the occasion was unpremeditated and at the commencement of the contest the parties were on equal terms, then you may consider mutual combat as one form of adequate provocation.

You must find, however, that the actual physical contact, or the dangerous threat of serious and immediate harm was such that it caused the defendant and would have caused a reasonable person to lose self-control and to act without reflection and from passion rather than judgment.

[You are further instructed that mutual combat as a form of provocation can still be considered even if the defendant used a deadly weapon against an unarmed adversary, if the weapon was hastily snatched during the heat of passion. On the other hand, if the circumstances show that the defendant sought the victim or provoked the difficulty for the purpose of killing the deceased, the defendant would not be entitled to have an intentional homicide mitigated to voluntary manslaughter.]

(2) Battery.

A battery, or a blow struck by the victim to the person of

the defendant, may constitute adequate provocation. You must find, however, that the character of the battery was such that it caused the defendant and would have caused a reasonable person to lose self-control and to act without reflection and from passion rather than judgment. This may be shown by evidence that the defendant was struck by a painful blow or other personal violence by a fist or a weapon. A trivial or slight blow, however, is not adequate provocation.

(3) Spousal adultery.

You may consider whether discovering one's spouse in an act of adultery is adequate provocation that may result in a homicide being voluntary manslaughter. You are instructed that the availability of this form of provocation requires that the defendant discover the spouse engaged in sexual intercourse or some other significant sexual contact.

[This theory of provocation is also available to a defendant who has no previous knowledge of the spouse's adultery and who suddenly has been told of the other spouse's infidelity. In these circumstances, the sudden disclosure of this information may have the same effect on the defendant as if he has just discovered his spouse engaged in an act of adultery.]

[For the defendant to be entitled to this form of provocation you must find that the defendant acted in a heat of passion aroused by the sudden discovery of the spouse engaged in an act of adultery and that the passion of a reasonable person would have been so aroused.]

(4) Words plus threatening conduct.

You may consider whether words and deeds directed toward the defendant are adequate provocation that may result in a homicide being voluntary manslaughter. You are instructed that mere words alone directed to the defendant by the victim, no matter how insulting, offensive or abusive are not legally adequate provocation. Sufficient provocation may exist, however, if the victim's words are accompanied by conduct indicating a present intention and ability to cause the defendant bodily harm.

In considering whether the victim had the present intention and ability to cause bodily harm to the defendant, you may consider the following: (1) the height, weight, and other physical characteristics of the victim and the defendant; (2) any acts and/or deeds that would evidence the present intention and ability of the victim to cause bodily harm to the defendant; and (3) any other surrounding circumstances.

You must find, however, that the words and deeds directed toward the defendant were such that they caused the defendant, and would have caused a reasonable person, to lose self-control and act from passion rather than from judgment.

COMMENT

(a) In general

Manslaughter is a common-law offense. *Connor v. State,* 225 Md. 543, 171 A.2d 699, *cert. denied,* 368 U.S. 906 (1961). It is defined as the unlawful and felonious killing of another, without malice, either expressed or implied. *Rolfes v. State,* 10 Md. App. 204, 268 A.2d 795 (1970). The essential distinction between murder and manslaughter is the presence or absence of malice. Malice is the indispensable ingredient of murder; by its presence, homicide is murder; in its absence, homicide may be manslaughter. *Lindsay v. State,* 8 Md. App. 100, 258 A.2d 760 (1969).

Voluntary manslaughter is an intentional homicide done in a sudden heat of passion caused by reasonable provocation, and not with malice. *Gray v. State,* 6 Md. App. 677, 253 A.2d 395 (1969). The rationale of voluntary manslaughter is the assumption that, under certain circumstances, the defendant's passionate state should negate the malice essential to a murder conviction. In addition, the courts have reasoned that a murder conviction would be inappropriate in such a situation because "[t]he law does not ignore completely the weakness of human nature which surfaces in compelling circumstances." *Whitehead v. State,* 9 Md. App. 7, 14, 262 A.2d 316, 321 (1970). If, however, the circumstances show that the defendant acted from a malice which preceded the provocation, the defendant, absent some other legally adequate defense, will be guilty of murder. *Id.* at 11, 262 A.2d at 319.

In *Whitehead v. State, supra,* the Court of Appeals held that there are four requirements to be met for the "rule of provocation" to be invoked to attempt to lower murder to voluntary manslaughter: (1) there must have been adequate provocation; (2) the killing must have been in the heat of passion; (3) it must have been in a sudden heat of passion — that is, the killing must have followed the provocation before there had been a reasonable opportunity for the passion to cool; (4) there must have been a causal connection between the provocation, the passion, and the fatal act. R. Perkins & R. Boyce, *Criminal Law* 84-102 (3d ed. 1982). In *Bateman v. State,* 10 Md. App. 630, 638, 272 A.2d 64, 68 (1971), the Court commented that failure to prove any one of the necessary four elements is fatal to establishing a theory of hot-blooded provocation. See also *Cunningham v. State,* 58 Md. App. 249, 473 A.2d 40, *cert. denied,* 300 Md. 316 (1984); *Scott v. State,* 64 Md. App. 311, 494 A.2d 992 (1985).

To mitigate an intentional killing to the level of voluntary manslaughter, the provocation must have been legally adequate. "Adequate provocation" is defined as provocation which would cause a reasonable person to lose normal self-control. W. LaFave & A. Scott, *Criminal Law* § 76 at 573 (1972). The nature of the alleged provocation, such as may be supposed to affect and influence ordinary minds, and not the particular disposition or temperament of the accused may be considered in mitigation of crime. *Garlitz v. State,* 71 Md. 293, 18 A. 39 (1889). Traditionally, provocation was required to be in one of the forms which had previously been defined and recognized by the courts as "adequate provocation." W. LaFave & A. Scott, *Criminal Law* § 76 at

574 (1972). The modern trend in the courts, however, is to make a case-by-case determination as to whether the alleged provocation would have caused a reasonable person in the circumstances of the defendant to act out of an intense emotion. See *Gray v. State, supra* (by implication); W. LaFave & A. Scott, *Criminal Law* § 76 at 574 (1972); Model Penal Code, § 210.3 (1962).

What is the meaning of the phrase "heat of passion"? Commentators agree that the term is broader than intense rage or anger. Perkins and Boyce state:

> Passion does not necessarily mean rage or anger. It includes any "violent, intense, highly-wrought, or enthusiastic emotion." Terror, for example, is one of the passions which may dethrone judgment and mitigate a killing to the level of voluntary manslaughter. . . .
>
> To constitute the *heat of passion* included in this requirement it is not necessary for the passion to be so extreme that the slayer does not know what he is doing at the time; but it must be so extreme that for the moment his action is being directed by passion rather than by reason. Heat of passion, however, is not an element of the crime of manslaughter in the usual sense of that term, so that if death were caused which is a lesser degree of homicide or not homicide, the presence of passion would not make it manslaughter. Rather passion is a factor which when present with elements of murder may reduce the homicide to manslaughter.

R. Perkins & R. Boyce, *Criminal Law* 98-99 (3d ed. 1982) (emphasis in original).

LaFave and Scott equate "heat of passion" to an emotional disturbance:

> The usual type of voluntary manslaughter involves the intentional killing of another while under the influence of a reasonably-induced emotional disturbance (in earlier terminology, while in a "heat of passion" causing a temporary loss of normal self-control. Except for this reasonable emotional condition, the intentional killing would be murder. The "passion" (emotional disturbance) involved in the crime of voluntary manslaughter is generally rage (great anger); but some cases have pointed out that other intense emotions — such as fright or terror or "wild desperation" — will do. A "passion for revenge," of course, will not do.

W. LaFave & A. Scott, *Criminal Law* § 76 at 573 (1972).

Notwithstanding the broad view of "heat of passion" described above, in *State v. Faulkner,* 301 Md. 482, 483 A.2d 759 (1984), *aff'g* 54 Md. App. 113, 458 A.2d 81 (1983), the Court of Appeals distinguished imperfect self-defense from traditional voluntary manslaughter by asserting that "fear of life" is not a form of "heat of passion":

> Out of these statutes arose the mitigating defense of imperfect self-defense, which was predicated upon a "fear of life." Imperfect self-defense was applicable to a crime *without* passion so as to distinguish it from the mitigation defense founded upon heat of passion. However, because the defendant was at fault the law demanded that he bear some criminal responsibility for the homicide although he lacked the requisite *mens rea* for murder.

Id. at 487, 483 A.2d at 762 (emphasis in original). While circumstances vary, perhaps, it is possible that some persons who kill while honestly, but unreasonably, believing that they are threatened with death or serious bodily harm might act calmly under an erroneous perception that such action is needed to save their life. The doctrine of imperfect self-defense is discussed in the Comment, § 4.23c, *infra.*

Where an individual entertaining a specific intent to kill attempts to perpetrate a homicide in the heat of passion in response to legally adequate provocation, the individual may be properly convicted of attempted voluntary manslaughter. *Cox v. State,* 69 Md. App. 396, 518 A.2d 132 (1986).

There is no distinction between voluntary and involuntary manslaughter with regard to the penalty for both grades. Pursuant to Maryland Ann. Code, Art. 27, § 387, a person convicted shall be sentenced to not more than ten years in the penitentiary or fined not more than $500 or imprisoned in jail for not more than two years or both fined and imprisoned in jail.

See Comment, subpart (c), § 4.22a, *supra,* for a discussion of burdens of production and persuasion as applied to voluntary manslaughter.

(b) Special sources of provocation

The amplified instruction provides more information to the jury on the meaning of the various elements of voluntary manslaughter and on the standard to be applied in considering evidence of provocation. In addition, it provides four options for special forms of legally adequate provocation expressly recognized by the Maryland courts: (1) mutual combat; (2) battery; (3) spousal adultery; and (4) words plus threatening conduct. Other special forms of provocation are also discussed in this Comment, such as "vicarious provocation."

(1) *Mutual combat.* "A mutual encounter between parties which goes beyond mere words and onto active blows or to a manifestation of intent to use immediate and violent force, may constitute adequate provocation." R. Perkins, *Criminal Law* 57 (2d ed. 1969). See *Shuck v. State,* 29 Md. App. 33, 349 A.2d 378 (1975); *Whitehead v. State,* 9 Md. App. 7, 262 A.2d 316 (1970); *Ware v. State,* 3 Md. App. 62, 237 A.2d 526 (1968). The circumstances surrounding the affray, however, must be considered to determine whether a reasonable person in the position of the defendant would have lost control.

It should be noted that this form of provocation does not require that the blows be mutual, only the intent to fight. Thus, as long as that intent was mutual, the question of which party struck the first blow is not significant. *Whitehead v. State, supra* at 11, 252 A.2d at 319. Perkins and Boyce maintain that the combat may be mutual even where one party has not struck any blows. R. Perkins & R. Boyce, *Criminal Law* 91 (3d ed. 1982). In addition:

> The mere fact that when the quarrel began the slayer had a deadly weapon upon his person while the other was not so armed is not alone sufficient to preclude the possibility of mitigation. The question is whether or not the slayer entered the combat with the intention of using his dangerous instrument. Hence it is necessary to discriminate between the use of a deadly weapon procured beforehand for this purpose, and the sudden angry use, in the heat of combat, of a weapon which the slayer merely happened to have available at the moment.

Id. at 90-91.

As with all forms of provocation, the intent to kill must not have been formed prior to the act of provocation. *Whitehead v. State, supra.* Thus, for example, a duel between two parties cannot constitute adequate provocation. R. Perkins & R. Boyce, *Criminal Law* 91 (3d ed. 1982).

Mutual combat is well recognized in Maryland case law as a form of adequate provocation. *Shuck v. State, supra; Whitehead v. State, supra; Ware v. State, supra* (defense denied because there was adequate time for appellant's passions to have cooled).

(2) *Battery.* A battery committed upon the person of the defendant may constitute adequate provocation. R. Perkins & R. Boyce, *Criminal Law* 92 (3d ed. 1982); W. LaFave & A. Scott, *Criminal Law* § 76 at 574 (1972). The battery must be shown to have been a violent, painful blow to the defendant with a fist or weapon in order to constitute "adequate provocation." W. LaFave & A. Scott, *Criminal Law* § 76 at 574 (1972). But force which the victim was privileged by law to use is not recognized as "adequate provocation." R. Perkins & R. Boyce, *Criminal Law* 92 (3d ed. 1982).

(3) *Spousal adultery.* Finding one's spouse engaged in the act of sexual intercourse constitutes another form of adequate provocation. *Tripp v. State,* 36 Md. App. 459, 374 A.2d 384 (1977); *Bartram v. State,* 33 Md. App. 115, 364 A.2d 1119 (1976), *aff'd,* 280 Md. 616, 374 A.2d 1144 (1977); *Bateman v. State,* 10 Md. App. 630, 272 A.2d 64 (1971). In *Tripp,* Judge Moylan wrote an extensive opinion concerning the prerequisites of establishing "adequate provocation" based on spousal adultery, and, in dictum, he stated that only the *lawful spouse* of one of the parties engaged in the sexual activity is entitled to claim that he or she was "provoked" to commit the homicide. This principle was one of the factors which led to the Court's conclusion that the appellant, who had been cohabitating with the victim for two years, was not entitled to a jury instruction on voluntary manslaughter.

The second essential element of this form of the provocation defense is that the defendant must find his spouse actually engaged in, at the very least, some significant sexual contact. *Tripp v. State, supra* at 474, 374 A.2d at 394. Thus in *Bateman v. State, supra,* the Maryland Court of Special Appeals held that the defendant, who had found his wife at a party hugging another man in the presence of other guests, was not entitled to a manslaughter jury instruction. In *Tripp,* however, the Court noted that some jurisdictions have extended the theory of voluntary manslaughter to those situations where the defendant has suddenly and unexpectedly been told of his spouse's infidelity or has strong reason to believe that there has been such infidelity. *Tripp v. State, supra* at 475, 374 A.2d at 395.

The Maryland courts have not yet determined whether they would accept the above as legally adequate provocation. Consequently, the corresponding paragraph in the Instruction has been placed in brackets.

A final requirement is that the defendant commit the homicide in a sudden heat of passion. This principle is illustrated in *Bartram v. State, supra,* where the defendant was denied an instruction based on provocation because she had knowledge of her husband's adultery long before the homicide was committed. Specifically, the defendant, on numerous occasions over several years, had participated in a "menage a trois" with her husband and her husband's mistress. On the night preceding the morning in question, the defendant had been forced to sleep on the living room couch while the husband slept in the bedroom with his mistress. In the morning, after the mistress had left the house, the defendant shot and killed her husband. Concerning the adequacy of the provocation, the Court wrote: "All of this is simply not what is contemplated by the law of mitigation. [T]he law recognizes the human frailty of a sudden fury. For the long-suffering spouse, the way out of the unbearable predicament must be the divorce court and not a bullet." *Bartram v. State, supra* at 176, 364 A.2d at 1154.

(4) *Words plus threatening conduct.* Mere provoking words directed at the defendant by the victim will never be sufficient to reduce an intentional homicide to manslaughter. W. LaFave & A. Scott, *Criminal Law* § 76 at 576 (1972). Adequate provocation may be established, however, when insulting words are combined with some other circumstance which alone might not be

sufficient to establish the defense. R. Perkins & R. Boyce, *Criminal Law* 94 (3d ed. 1982). This theory was expressed by the Maryland Court of Special Appeals as follows: "[T]here is authority that sufficient provocation may consist of words accompanied by conduct indicating a present intention and ability to cause the appellant bodily harm." *Lang v. State,* 6 Md. App. 128, 132, 250 A.2d 276, 279, *cert. denied,* 396 U.S. 971 (1969). In *Lang,* however, the Court found that the appellant was not entitled to a jury instruction on the issue of provocation because there was no evidence that the victim had the intention or the ability to harm the appellant.

Comprising a distinct category of provoking words are those which convey information concerning a fact or circumstance which itself constitutes adequate provocation. See *Tripp v. State, supra* at 475, 374 A.2d at 394. It should be remembered, of course, that the requirement of suddenness will not be satisfied where the slayer had acquired the provoking information from another source much earlier in time.

(5) *Vicarious provocation.* "Vicarious provocation" may exist when the provocateur (*X*) directs provocation toward *another* person (*Y*) and the defendant (*Z*) reacts to that provocation by losing self-control and killing the provocateur (*X*). W. LaFave & A. Scott, *Criminal Law* § 76 at 577 (1972).

In *Dorsey v. State,* 29 Md. App. 97, 349 A.2d 414 (1975), *aff'd,* 278 Md. 221, 362 A.2d 642 (1976), *cert. denied, Wilson v. Maryland,* 429 U.S. 1102 (1977), the Maryland Court of Special Appeals was presented with an issue concerning the adequacy of vicarious provocation. The Court decided the case on other grounds, however, and expressly declined to decide whether vicarious provocation constitutes legally "adequate provocation" in Maryland.

Perkins and Boyce state that, in addition to spousal adultery, certain other outrageous acts may be found to constitute adequate provocation: "In this list may be mentioned, without attempting to be exhaustive, seduction of the slayer's infant daughter, rape of his close female relative, murder or serious injury of his close relative, or the act of sodomy with his young son." R. Perkins & R. Boyce, *Criminal Law* 97 (3d ed. 1982).

(6) *Killing innocent third person.* Another potential form of provocation exists where the defendant (*Z*), who has been provoked by another person (*X*), strikes out at an *innocent* person (*Y*) in blind distress. At present, the Maryland courts reject this situation as an acceptable form of adequate provocation. See *Tripp v. State, supra,* and *Bateman v. State, supra.* Perkins and Boyce state:

> If one who has received adequate provocation is so enraged that he intentionally vents his wrath upon an innocent bystander, causing his death, he will be guilty of murder; but if his deadly force was directed at the provoker and hit the other by accident, or if as a reasonable mistake of fact he thought the provocative act had been perpetrated by the deceased, he is guilty of manslaughter only, if he otherwise meets the requirements of the rule of provocation. One court has allowed a claim of manslaughter to the killing of an innocent third person where the accused may have believed the innocent person was in fact a participant in the conduct giving rise to the provocation when in fact the innocent person was not so involved.

R. Perkins & R. Boyce, *Criminal Law* 102 (3d ed. 1982).

The American Law Institute's Model Penal Code, § 201.3(1)(b), however, includes this form of provocation within its broader standard of recognizing any form of "extreme mental or emotional distress for which there is a reasonable explanation or excuse." The comment to the Code, § 201.3(1)(b), asserts that this form of provocation may "be among the strongest for the mitigation, since both the course and the intensity of the actor's emotion may be relatively less indicative of depravity of character than a homicide response to a blow."

§ 4.23c. Manslaughter — Voluntary (suggested instruction on imperfect self-defense).

I [have instructed] [will instruct] you on the law of self-defense. Now I will instruct you on a doctrine in the law known as imperfect self-defense, which is a form of manslaughter. A person who kills another person while honestly, though unreasonably, believing that he is threatened with death or serious bodily harm does not act with malice.

Complete or perfect self-defense requires not only that the defendant subjectively believed that he was in apparent, imminent or immediate danger of death or serious bodily harm from his assailant or potential assailant but that the circumstances under which the defendant acted must have been such as to produce in the mind of a reasonably prudent person, similarly situated, the reasonable belief that the other person was then about to kill him or to do to him serious bodily harm.

On the other hand, imperfect self-defense or manslaughter requires that the defendant have a subjective, honest belief that he was in apparent, imminent or immediate danger of death or serious bodily harm from his assailant or potential assailant. If a person honestly, but unreasonably, believed that he was in danger of immediate death or serious bodily injury and the act of killing was a result of that belief, such person cannot be guilty of a crime greater than manslaughter. [Also, if the defendant used greater force than a reasonable person would have used, but the defendant actually believed that the force used was necessary, the defendant's subjective and honest, though unreasonable, belief that the force used was necessary would result in a verdict of manslaughter rather than murder.]

[However, for the doctrine of imperfect self-defense to apply, it is also required that the defendant was not the initial aggressor using deadly force] [unless the defendant effectively withdrew from the encounter and the actual or potential assailant became the attacker.]

You are instructed that the burden is not on the defendant to prove either perfect or imperfect self-defense. As part of the State's burden to prove malice, the burden is on the State to prove beyond a reasonable doubt that the defendant did not act in self-defense and that there was no mitigation in the form of imperfect self-defense on the part of the defendant. If you have a reasonable doubt as to whether the defendant acted in complete self-defense (as I will more fully instruct you), you must find the defendant not guilty. If you are convinced beyond a reasonable doubt that the defendant did *not* act in complete self-defense but you do have a reasonable doubt as to whether the defendant acted in imperfect self-defense, you must find the defendant guilty of manslaughter. On the other hand, if the State has proved beyond a reasonable doubt the elements of murder in the second degree, including the absence both of perfect and imperfect self-defense, you should find the defendant guilty of murder in the second degree.

COMMENT

Since there is relatively little law on imperfect self-defense, including court discussion of appropriate jury instructions, the above instruction has been placed in this text as a *possible guide* to instructing the jury. The landmark case, discussed *infra,* is *State v. Faulkner,* 301 Md. 482, 483 A.2d 759 (1984), *aff'g* 54 Md. App. 113, 458 A.2d 81 (1983). See also *Lambert v. State,* 70 Md. App. 83, 519 A.2d 1340 (1987); *Simmons v. State,* 66 Md. App. 629, 505 A.2d 577 (1986).

LaFave and Scott state:

> A modern tendency, not yet far advanced, is to add other extenuating circumstances in the category of voluntary manslaughter, so as to include such intentional homicides as those committed in an "imperfect" right of self-defense or defense of others, or of crime-prevention, or of the defenses of coercion or necessity, in which the killing, though not justifiable, is not bad enough to be murder.

W. LaFave & A. Scott, *Criminal Law* § 77 at 583 (1972). The mitigating effect of imperfect self-defense is to negate malice and serves to reduce murder to manslaughter. *Faulkner v. State, supra.* Manslaughter is a catch-all concept, covering all homicides which are neither murder nor innocent. Imperfect self-defense also applies to assault with intent to murder. It fatally erodes this charge since there is no crime of assault with intent to manslaughter. When malice is negated with respect to assault with intent to murder, the accused may be found guilty of simple assault and battery. *Id.* See *Thomas v. State,* 29 Md. App. 45, 349 A.2d 384 (1975), *cert. granted,* 278 Md. 736 (1976), *cert. dismissed,* 279 Md. 604 (1977); *Finnegan v. State,* 33 Md. App. 251, 364 A.2d 124, *cert. denied,* 279 Md. 682 (1976), *cert. denied,* 433 U.S. 912 (1977). It follows that, when the evidence generates the issue of mitigation with respect to an assault with intent to murder charge, the trial court may, and upon request, shall give an appropriate instruction to the jury. Maryland Rule 4-325(C); *Lansdowne v. State,* 287 Md. 232, 412 A.2d 88 (1980).

In *Shuck v. State,* 29 Md. App. 33, 349 A.2d 378 (1975), the Court reversed a conviction of second degree murder and assault with intent to murder, holding that the evidence generated a jury issue as to whether the homicide might be mitigated to voluntary manslaughter. The Court stated that the defendant was entitled to intervene in defense of his companion and that he may have acted unreasonably in resorting to deadly force in what had been a nondeadly confrontation.

In *Wentworth v. State,* 29 Md. App. 110, 349 A.2d 421 (1975), the defendant and her husband kidnapped a college professor from his home and, later that evening, shot him to death. The defendant testified that she was terrified of her husband on that particular evening because he had accused her of having an adulterous relationship with the victim. The Court reversed because the burden of proof of mitigation had been improperly placed on the defendant. The Court recognized that the defense of duress does not exculpate a defendant in an unlawful homicide case but that the defendant was entitled to a jury instruction on the mitigation defense of "imperfect duress" because the defendant may have been coerced into killing the victim.

In *Law v. State,* 29 Md. App. 457, 349 A.2d 295 (1975), the Court held that the evidence presented at trial generated the issue of mitigation by way of "imperfect defense of habitation." The defendant mistakenly believed that his home was about to be burglarized and shot and killed a police officer who was trying to enter the house to investigate a suspected burglary attempt.

In *Cunningham v. State,* 58 Md. App. 249, 473 A.2d 40, *cert. denied,* 300 Md. 316 (1984), the Court discussed at length the purpose of this doctrine. The trial court refused to instruct the jury as to either perfect or imperfect self-defense and the defendant was convicted of second degree murder. The Court affirmed, holding that the defendant failed to meet his burden of production to generate a genuine jury issue as to imperfect self-defense. The Court found that even if the defendant honestly, but unreasonably, believed he shot in self-defense, the defendant was an aggressor using deadly force (a loaded gun) who made no effort to withdraw from the encounter that he initiated. In order to be entitled to a jury instruction on imperfect self-defense or, for that matter, perfect self-defense, the defendant must produce some evidence he was free from fault in bringing on the difficulty with his adversary. An initial aggressor using deadly force forfeits a right of self-defense unless there is an effective withdrawal. *Id.* at 255, 473 A.2d at 44.

In *State v. Faulkner, supra,* the Court of Appeals, in affirming the intermediate appellate court, for the first time recognized that circumstances other than hot-blooded provocation could reduce murder to voluntary manslaughter and thereby also constitute a defense to assault with intent to murder.

In its review of the doctrine of imperfect self-defense, the Court, in *Faulkner,* identified three variations of the doctrine that have been adopted in various states:

> First, some courts indicated that the doctrine would apply where the homicide would fall within the perfect self-defense doctrine but for the fault of the defendant in provoking or initiating the difficulty at the non-deadly force level.... Second, courts noted that the doctrine would apply when the defendant committed a homicide because of an honest but unreasonable belief that he was about to suffer death or serious bodily harm.... Third, other courts recognized the doctrine when the defendant used unreasonable force in defending himself and, as a result, killed his opponent ... (citations omitted).

Id. at 489, 483 A.2d at 763. The Court held that the second of the above three variations — the honest but unreasonable belief standard of imperfect self-defense — is the proper one to be followed in Maryland. A defendant who commits a homicide honestly, though unreasonably, believing that he is threatened with death or serious bodily harm, does not act with malice. Yet, because the killing was committed without justification or excuse, the defendant is not entitled to full exoneration. The intermediate ground is voluntary manslaughter based on imperfect self-defense.

And, in *Faulkner,* the Court cited with approval language from the opinion of the intermediate court that might be useful in instructing a jury:

> Perfect self-defense requires not only that the killer subjectively believed that his actions were necessary for his safety but, objectively, that a reasonable man would so consider them. Imperfect self-defense, however, requires no more than a subjective honest belief on the part of the killer that his actions were necessary for his safety, even though, on an objective appraisal by a reasonable man, they would not be found to be so. If established, the killer remains culpable and his actions are excused only to the extent that mitigation is invoked.

Id. at 500, 483 A.2d at 768-69. The Court noted that a proper jury instruction when such evidence is present would enable the jury to reach one of several verdicts: (1) if the jury concluded the defendant did not have a subjective belief that the use of deadly force was necessary, its verdict would be murder; (2) if the jury concluded that the defendant had a reasonable subjective belief, its verdict would be not guilty; and (3) if the jury concluded that the defendant honestly believed that the use of force was necessary but that this subjective belief was unreasonable under the circumstances, then its verdict would be guilty of voluntary manslaughter.

Because *State v. Faulkner, supra,* presented the sole issue of imperfect self-defense, the Court of Appeals noted that it expressed "no opinion as to the applicability of other suggested forms of 'imperfect' mitigation defenses, such as imperfect duress, imperfect defense of others, imperfect defense of property, imperfect right to prevent a felony, and imperfect necessity." *Id.* at 500 n.7, 483 A.2d at 769 n.7.

§ 4.24. Manslaughter — Involuntary.

(a) Which occurs as the result of doing some lawful act with gross negligence

Involuntary manslaughter is defined as the unlawful felonious but unintentional killing of another without malice, but without justification or legal excuse.

In order for the defendant to be found guilty of involuntary manslaughter there must be: (1) an unintentional killing of another human being; (2) by the defendant; and (3) the killing must occur as the result of doing some act in a criminally negligent manner.

To establish the crime of involuntary manslaughter, you must find that the negligence was gross or criminal. That means you must find that the negligence was of such a character as to manifest a wanton and reckless disregard of human life.

A causal connection between such gross negligence and death must exist to support a conviction, although it is not essential that the ultimate harm which resulted was foreseen or intended.

Whether the defendant's conduct constituted gross negligence must be determined on the basis of the conduct itself and not by the resultant harm. Criminal liability cannot be predicated on every careless act merely because its carelessness results in injury to another.

If the resulting death were merely accidental or the result of misadventure or due to simple negligence or an honest error of judgment in performing a lawful act, the existence of gross negligence should not be found.

[*To be given when both second degree murder based on "depraved-heart" murder and involuntary manslaughter based on gross negligence are under consideration:* In this case you must decide whether the defendant's actions constitute unlawful homicide, which could be either murder or manslaughter, or lawful or innocent homicide. If the actions which resulted in death were due merely to simple negligence, an honest error of judgment or accident, it would be lawful or innocent homicide and, if you so find, you must find the defendant not guilty. Simple negligence is not sufficient for manslaughter. Manslaughter requires a finding of gross negligence which amounts to a wanton or reckless disregard for human life. Malice is the distinguishing element which makes an unlawful killing murder rather than manslaughter.

Earlier, I instructed you on two special meanings of implied or equivalent malice: first, where there is an actual intent to inflict great bodily harm and, second, where one does an act in wanton and willful disregard of an obvious risk involving an extreme indifference to the value of human life.

In your deliberation, you will be drawing a distinction between different grades of behavior or conduct. One difference between the definitions of murder and manslaughter is the absence of a need to prove willfulness in manslaughter. To convict of depraved-heart murder the defendant must have had knowledge or awareness of the risk to human life he was taking in the actions he was doing. Another difference is the degree of risk to human life which the defendant's conduct presented. To support a conviction of manslaughter, the degree of negligence must be gross negligence: that is, it must show a wanton and reckless disregard for human life. To convict of depraved-heart murder, however, requires a wanton and willful disregard of an obvious risk showing an extreme indifference to the value of human life.

The precise line or distinction between these different grades of conduct is for you to draw. I cannot give you a precise line where one becomes the other. Somewhere in the ascending or descending scale of seriousness, recklessness, wantonness and disregard for human life cease to be manslaughter and become equivalent to malice sufficient for you to find murder. On the other hand, as I instructed you, actions due merely to simple negligence, an honest error of judgment or accident constitute lawful or innocent homicide.]

(b) Which is caused by the grossly negligent omission to perform a legal duty

Involuntary manslaughter is defined as the unlawful, felonious but unintentional killing of another without malice, but where there is no justification or legal excuse.

In order for the defendant to be found guilty of involuntary manslaughter there must be: (1) an unintentional killing of another human being; (2) by the defendant; (3) which is caused by the criminally negligent omission to perform a legal duty.

To establish the crime of involuntary manslaughter when the charge is based on negligently failing to perform a legal duty, you must find that a legal duty existed and that the negligent failure to act was gross or criminal. This means that you must find that the negligence was of such character as to manifest a wanton or reckless disregard of human life.

There must be a causal connection between such gross negligence and death, although it is not essential that the ultimate harm which resulted was foreseen or intended.

Whether the defendant's conduct constituted gross negligence must be determined on the basis of the conduct itself and not by the resultant harm. Criminal liability cannot be predicated on every careless act merely because its carelessness results in injury to another. If the resulting death were merely accidental or the result of misadventure or due to simple negligence, the existence of gross negligence cannot be found.

(c) Which occurs during the course of some unlawful act

Involuntary manslaughter is defined as the unlawful felonious but unintentional killing of another without malice but where there is no justification or legal excuse.

In order for the defendant to be found guilty of involuntary manslaughter there must be: (1) an unintentional killing of another human being; (2) by the defendant; (3) the killing must occur during the course of some unlawful act not amounting to a felony; and (4) that act itself must be dangerous to life.

If a person who causes the death of another intends to do an unlawful and wrongful act, which is punishable because it is wrong in itself, and, in so doing inflicts an unforeseen injury, he is criminally liable for that injury. A causal connection between the act committed and death must exist in order to support a conviction, although it is not essential that the ultimate harm which resulted was foreseen or intended.

To establish the crime of involuntary manslaughter when the charge is based on the commission of an unlawful act causing death, the act itself must be dangerous to life.

COMMENT

These instructions are patterned substantially after the decision in *Mills v. State,* 13 Md. App. 196, 282 A.2d 147 (1971).

Involuntary manslaughter at common law has been generally defined as the killing of another unintentionally and without malice: (1) in doing some unlawful act endangering life and not amounting to a felony; or (2) in negligently doing some act lawful in itself; or (3) by the negligent omission to perform a legal duty. To this basic definition other authorities add the qualification as to the first class of involuntary manslaughter that the unlawful act be *malum in se* and not *malum prohibitum* and, as to the second and third classes of the offense, that the person's act be criminally culpable or grossly negligent. *Allen v. State,* 39 Md. App. 686, 389 A.2d 909 (1978); *Mills v. State, supra; Rolfes v. State,* 10 Md. App. 204, 268 A.2d 795 (1970). Gross or criminal negligence, where it is used as a basis for a charge of involuntary manslaughter, has been interpreted by the Court of Appeals to mean a wanton disregard for human life. *Palmer v. State,* 223 Md. 341, 164 A.2d 467 (1960); *Mills v. State, supra.* The Court in *Mills, supra* at 200, 282 A.2d at 149 stated:

> A causal connection between such gross negligence and death must exist to support a conviction, although it is not essential that the ultimate harm which resulted was foreseen or intended.... On the other hand whether an accused's conduct constituted gross negligence must be determined by the conduct itself and not by the resultant harm.... Nor can criminal liability be predicated on every careless act merely because its carelessness results in injury to another.

Where a prosecution for involuntary manslaughter is based on the commission of an unlawful act causing death, the act must itself be dangerous to life. *State v. Gibson,* 4 Md. App. 236, 242 A.2d 575 (1968), *aff'd,* 254 Md. 399, 254 A.2d 691 (1969).

An optional additional instruction has been provided when both second degree murder based on the so-called "depraved heart" murder doctrine and involuntary manslaughter based on gross negligence are under consideration. In *Blackwell v. State,* 34 Md. App. 547, 369 A.2d 153, *cert. denied,* 280 Md. 728 (1977), the Court noted the narrow line that separates depraved heart murder and manslaughter by gross negligence. The Court stated that when the facts warrant, it is not improper to charge both crimes and, if the evidence is sufficient, to submit both to the jury for its determination which, if either, is applicable. However, a guilty verdict on both counts would be inconsistent. See the Comment, § 4.22a, Murder — Second degree, *supra,* for a discussion of the so-called depraved heart murder doctrine.

Finally, there is no distinction between voluntary and involuntary manslaughter with regard to the penalty for both grades. Pursuant to Maryland Ann. Code, Art. 27, § 387, a person convicted shall be sentenced to not more than ten years in the penitentiary or fined not more than $500, or imprisoned in jail for not more than two years or both fined and imprisoned in jail.

§ 4.25. Manslaughter — By vehicle.

Manslaughter by vehicle is the causing of the death of another as a consequence of driving, operating or controlling a vehicle in a grossly negligent manner.

In order for the defendant to be found guilty the State must prove beyond a reasonable doubt that: (1) the defendant was driving, operating or controlling a vehicle; (2) the defendant was doing so in a grossly negligent manner; (3) a death resulted; and (4) there was a causal relationship between such death and the grossly negligent driving.

Gross negligence results where the conduct of the defendant, considering all the factors of the case, was such that it amounted to a wanton or reckless disregard for human life. Intent to kill is not an element of this crime.

[In determining whether the conduct of the defendant amounted to a wanton or reckless disregard for human life, you should consider all of the facts and circumstances in evidence. You must determine what the facts are, what inferences to draw from the presence or absence of any particular factor, and the weight to give to any particular factor.

Among the factors you may consider are:

1. the nature of the area, including lighting, motor vehicle and pedestrian traffic, in which the incident occurred;

2. whether there were any violations of statutes enacted for control of motor vehicles and the nature of any such violations;

3. whether the defendant failed to maintain a proper lookout and control of the motor vehicle;

4. whether the defendant operated the motor vehicle at an excessive speed under the circumstances;

5. whether there is evidence of any unusual or erratic operation of the vehicle by the defendant prior to impact;

6. whether there is evidence of the ingestion of alcohol or other drugs, the nature, amount, time and circumstances alcohol or other drugs were taken, and their effect on the defendant's ability to control the motor vehicle;

7. the nature and degree of impact between the defendant's vehicle and the victim (or victim's vehicle);

8. the nature and extent of damage, if any, to the vehicle operated by the defendant;

9. the presence or absence of skid or centrifugal force marks leading to the point of impact;

10. whether the defendant fled the scene without making any effort to ascertain the extent of injury to the victim; and,

11. any other factors you deem applicable to the particular facts of this case.

Again, you must determine whether in the totality of the circumstances the defendant's conduct amounted to gross negligence: that is, a wanton or reckless disregard for human life. The presence or absence of any of these factors, or others found by you to be applicable, the inferences that you draw as a result, and the weight to be assigned to any particular factor are matters solely for you to determine.]

COMMENT

Manslaughter by vehicle is a statutory misdemeanor enacted to punish persons who cause the death of another as the result of the driving, operating or controlling of a vehicle in a grossly negligent manner. Maryland Ann. Code, Art. 27, § 388. The statute applies to "... an automobile, motor vehicle, motorboat, locomotive, engine, car, streetcar, train or other vehicle." It imposes a sentence of imprisonment of not more than five years, or a fine of not more that $1,000 or both a fine and imprisonment.

The statute states that the "indictment or warrant" need not specify the "manner and means" of death. A charging document is sufficient if it includes the following: "That A-B on the ____________ day of ____________ nineteen hundred and ____________ at the County (City) aforesaid, unlawfully, in a grossly negligent manner did kill and slay C-D."

An interesting question is whether an *unintended* homicide resulting from the operation of a vehicle can ever be prosecuted in Maryland as a felony of involuntary manslaughter, pursuant to Art. 27, § 387 (see Instruction, § 4.24, Manslaughter — Involuntary, *supra*), or second degree murder under the so-called depraved heart murder doctrine, pursuant to Art. 27, § 411 (see Instruction, § 4.22a, Murder — Second degree, *supra*). The appellate court has held that the General Assembly removed such a killing from the felony of common-law involuntary manslaughter and made it a statutory misdemeanor. *State v. Gibson,* 4 Md. App. 236, 242 A.2d 575 (1968), *aff'd,* 254 Md. 399, 254 A.2d 691 (1969). Further, in *Blackwell v. State,* 34 Md. App. 547, 369 A.2d 153, *cert. denied,* 280 Md. 728 (1977), the Court stated that the General Assembly intended to preempt the subject matter of *unintended* homicides so that a conviction for murder also does not seem to be possible. See the discussion in the Comment to Instruction, § 4.22a, *supra,* concerning depraved heart murder. However, an *intentional* homicide by a vehicle could be prosecuted as a felony of manslaughter or murder. In light of increased public and official concern with the protection of the public from motor vehicle homicides, especially where intoxication and speed are factors, there may be a need for the General

Assembly to reconsider the relationship of Art. 27, § 388, to other homicide offenses. The General Assembly did, however, increase the maximum penalty from three to five years effective July 1, 1982.

The legislature, in enacting the manslaughter by vehicle statute, adopted the standard of gross negligence, or a "wanton or reckless disregard of human life" as the minimum requirement to support a conviction. *State v. Gibson, supra.*

The test to be applied in gross negligence is "whether the conduct of the defendant, considering all the factors of the case, was such that it amounted to a 'wanton or reckless disregard for human life.'" *Montague v. State,* 3 Md. App. 66, 237 A.2d 816 (1968) (*citing Maryland v. Chapman,* 101 F. Supp. 335, 341 (D. Md. 1951)).

Violation of a statute enacted for control of motor vehicles may not be, by itself, sufficient to prove gross negligence. *State v. Gibson, supra* at 242 A.2d 575 n.4. Ordinarily, speed alone need not be a sufficiently negligent act to support an inference of gross negligence. *Abe v. State,* 230 Md. 439, 187 A.2d 467 (1963). However, the above two factors may, of course, be taken into consideration with other circumstances to constitute gross negligence. Factors which may be relevant are failure to keep proper lookout, failure to maintain proper control of one's automobile, and passing recklessly. *Montague v. State, supra.* In *Clay v. State,* 211 Md. 577, 128 A.2d 634 (1957), flight from a collision without effort to discover the extent of injuries or to offer aid was held to be a relevant factor. See also *Allen v. State,* 39 Md. App. 686, 696, 389 A.2d 909, 916-17 (1978). The *Clay* Court also stated that drinking, short of intoxication, may be sufficient to constitute gross negligence where the drinking "probably affects one's judgment and discretion or probably affects one's nervous system to the extent that there is a failure of normal co-ordination." *Clay v. State, supra.* But see *Thomas v. State,* 206 Md. 49, 109 A.2d 909 (1954), where the evidence of intoxication was not sufficient to prove gross negligence.

In *Blackwell v. State, supra,* the Court discussed the relationship of intoxication to the standard of "the driving ... of an automobile ... in a grossly negligent manner" under Art. 27, § 388.

The Court stated: "As we read the automobile manslaughter cases, the only reason the appellate courts of Maryland have not permitted extreme intoxication to have raised simple negligence to gross negligence by express holding, is that no case has ever been before the Court where the evidence showed a state of inebriation that would sustain a verdict of driving while intoxicated." *Id.* at 561, 369 A.2d at 162. The Court then took judicial notice that an automobile is a dangerous instrumentality and concluded, on the facts of the case: "When appellant voluntarily, if not intentionally, drank himself into a state wherein his nervous system was numbed, adversely affecting his reflexes, co-ordination, discretion and judgment, to drive an automobile thereafter itself constituted a wanton or reckless disregard for human life." *Id.* at 565, 369 A.2d at 164. See also *Willis v. State,* 55 Md. App. 65, 460 A.2d 1043 (1983), *aff'd,* 302 Md. 363, 488 A.2d 171 (1985), where the Court held that defendant's intoxication, as found by the jury, was sufficient to elevate simple negligence to gross negligence.

High speed in a congested area was held sufficient to meet the test in *Duren v. State,* 203 Md. 584, 102 A.2d 277 (1954), where the Court indicated that the environment in which speed is indulged must determine whether it does or does not show gross negligence. The Court stated:

> If there is found such lack of control, whether by reason of speed or otherwise, in a place and at a time when there is constant potentiality of injury as a result, there can be found a wanton and reckless disregard of the rights and lives of others and so, criminal indifference to consequences.

Id. at 592, 102 A.2d at 281.

For other cases discussing Maryland Ann. Code, Art. 27, § 388, see, e.g., *Johnson v. State,* 213 Md. 527, 132 A.2d 853 (1957) (evidence insufficient to support a finding of "gross negligence"); *Lilly v. State,* 212 Md. 436, 129 A.2d 839 (1957) (evidence found sufficient where intoxicated motorist drove vehicle at a high rate of speed, disobeyed a stop sign, and crashed into another vehicle, killing a passenger in his own vehicle); *Thomas v. State, supra; Floyd v. State,* 42 Md. App. 167, 399 A.2d 932 (1979) (intoxication by drugs or alcohol may give rise to a rational inference of "wanton or reckless conduct"); and *Boyd v. State*, 22 Md. App. 539, 323 A.2d 684 (1974).

For further discussion concerning driving and intoxication see Instructions and Comments: § 2.32, Consent to blood and other chemical tests, *supra;* § 4.26, Homicide by motor vehicle while intoxicated, *infra;* and § 4.63, Driving while intoxicated — Driving while under the influence of alcohol and/or drugs, *infra.*

§ 4.26. Homicide by motor vehicle while intoxicated (suggested instruction).

Homicide by vehicle while intoxicated is the causing of the death of another as a consequence of driving, operating or controlling a motor vehicle in a negligent manner while intoxicated.

In order for the defendant to be found guilty the State must prove beyond a reasonable doubt that: (1) the defendant was driving, operating or controlling a vehicle; (2) he was doing so in a negligent manner; (3) he was doing so while intoxicated; (4) a death resulted; and (5) there was a causal relationship between such death and the negligent driving while intoxicated.

The conduct of the defendant, considering all of the facts and circumstances, must amount to the negligent driving, operating or controlling of a vehicle while intoxicated. Negligent driving, operating or controlling a vehicle occurs when a person does not operate a vehicle in a manner in which an ordinarily prudent and cautious person in full possession of his faculties, using reasonable care, would operate a motor vehicle under like conditions.

The State must prove that the defendant was negligently driving while intoxicated. Proof of "intoxication" requires more than proof merely of being "under the influence of alcohol." A person is "under the influence of alcohol" when a person does not have normal use of physical and mental faculties by reason of the use of alcoholic beverages. A person is "intoxicated" when the alcohol that has been consumed has substantially impaired normal coordination.

[Intent to kill is not an element of this crime. The State is not required to prove that the defendant actually intended to harm the victim.]

COMMENT

Because of the limited case law dealing with this offense, the above instruction has been designated merely as a *suggested* form.

Maryland Ann. Code, Art. 27, § 388A, supplements the offense of manslaughter by vehicle (see Instruction, § 4.25, *supra*), and creates the statutory offense of "homicide by motor vehicle while intoxicated." The purpose of this statute is to enhance the State's chances of obtaining convictions of motorists who drive while intoxicated and kill innocent persons as a result of the imbiber's negligence. *Loscomb v. State,* 45 Md. App. 598, 416 A.2d 1276 (1980), *aff'd,* 291 Md. 424, 435 A.2d 764 (1982). Unlike manslaughter by vehicle which requires that the State prove gross negligence in order to obtain a conviction, homicide by motor vehicle while intoxicated apparently requires the State to prove only ordinary negligence. *Loscomb v. State, supra.* See also Maryland Department of Transportation (Office of the Secretary), Memo-SB 318 (March 1, 1978).

Article 27, § 388A(a) provides: "In this section 'intoxicated' has the same meaning as indicated in and is subject to the same presumptions and evidence rules of Courts and Judicial Proceedings, § 10-307 regarding intoxication under the vehicle laws of this State." See Maryland Ann. Code, Courts and Judicial Proceedings, § 10-307. See also Instructions: § 4.63, Driving while intoxicated — Driving while under the influence of alcohol and/or drugs, *infra;* § 2.32, Consent to blood and other chemical tests, *supra.* The legislature also simultaneously amended Courts and Judicial Proceedings, § 10-307, relating to the amount of alcohol in the person's "breath, blood or urine" to delete "urine." The definition of driving while intoxicated is the same as it appears in § 4.63, *infra.*

Introduction of evidence relating to alcoholic content in the body of the accused, as shown upon chemical analysis through tests, pursuant to Maryland Ann. Code, Courts and Judicial Proceedings, §§ 10-303 to 10-310, is not a prerequisite to the conviction. Conviction may be based on any competent evidence legally sufficient to establish the *corpus delicti* of the crime and the criminal agency of the accused. Similarly, the introduction of such evidence does not limit consideration of other competent evidence bearing upon whether the defendant was driving while intoxicated. See Courts and Judicial Proceedings, § 10-308; *Blackwell v. State,* 34 Md. App. 547, 369 A.2d 153, *cert. denied,* 280 Md. 728 (1977), and *Major v. State,* 31 Md. App. 590, 358 A.2d 609 (1976).

Failure to obtain express consent before administration of a chemical test to determine blood alcohol content, in violation of Maryland Ann. Code, Transportation Article, § 16-205.1, precluded admissibility of the test results through application of Courts and Judicial Proceedings, § 10-309, in a prosecution for manslaughter by motor vehicle and homicide by motor vehicle while intoxicated (Art. 27, §§ 388, 388A). *State v. Loscomb,* 291 Md. 424, 435 A.2d 464 (1981). In apparent response to *Loscomb,* the General Assembly amended the Motor Vehicle Code to provide that a person who has been involved in an accident in which a death results is required to submit to an alcohol test. An officer may also direct qualified medical personnel to withdraw blood for a chemical test of an unconscious person as long as that person's health or well-being would not be jeopardized. Transportation, § 16-205.1. See *State v. Werkheiser,* 299 Md. 529, 474 A.2d 898 (1984). When a death is not involved, a person may elect whether to take an alcohol test and to select which of two tests, blood or breath, he desires to take. See Courts and Judicial Proceedings, §§ 10-305 and 10-309.

In an indictment, information or warrant for homicide by motor vehicle while intoxicated, it is not necessary under Maryland Ann. Code, Art. 27, § 388A(b) to set forth the manner and means of death. Article 27, § 388A(c) states that: "It shall be sufficient to use a formula substantially to the following effect: That A-B on the ______ day of ______ nineteen-hundred and ______ at the County (City) aforesaid, unlawfully, while intoxicated did kill C-D, against the peace, government, and dignity of the State."

Effective July 1, 1983, the General Assembly increased the maximum penalty from imprisonment for not more than two years to imprisonment for not more than three years or a fine of not more than $1,000 or both fine and imprisonment.

For further discussion concerning driving and intoxication, see Instructions: § 2.32, Consent to blood and other chemical tests, *supra;* § 4.25, Manslaughter — By vehicle, *supra;* and § 4.63, Driving while intoxicated — Driving while under the influence of alcohol and/or drugs, *infra.*

D. Sexual Offenses

1. Offenses Retained After 1976 Revision of Sexual Offense Laws

§ 4.33. Incest.

Incest is defined as sexual intercourse between a man and a woman related to each other within a degree prohibited by law.

In order for a person to be guilty of this offense the State must prove beyond a reasonable doubt that: (1) the defendant knowingly engaged in sexual intercourse and (2) the defendant did so with a person being within the degrees of consanguinity within which marriages are prohibited in Maryland.

Sexual intercourse refers to an actual contact of the sexual organs of a man and a woman and an actual penetration into the body of the latter. Penetration is an essential element of this offense. There must be some penetration although it may be slight, of the female sexual organ, that is, the vagina, by the male sexual organ, that is, the penis. Emission is not an essential element and is not required to be proved.

Persons fall within the degree of consanguinity if they have a blood relationship within the degrees prohibited by the law of the State of Maryland. The persons in this instance are alleged to be __________ (*insert type of relationship*), a blood relationship which is within the degrees of consanguinity within which marriages are prohibited in Maryland.

Force, violence or threats of force or violence are not elements necessary to constitute the crime of incest. If a man and woman related to each other within the degree within which marriages are prohibited have sexual intercourse, however willingly, the crime of incest has been committed.

[*To be given where there is some evidence that the prosecuting witness is an accomplice:* You must determine whether the prosecuting witness in this case was a willing, consenting partner, that is, an accomplice, rather than a victim. If you find that the prosecuting witness was an accomplice rather than a victim, then that person's testimony must be corroborated. The testimony of a victim need not be corroborated. *See Instruction, § 2.01, Accomplice's testimony — Corroboration, supra, on the meaning of corroboration.*

To be an accomplice, rather than a victim, one must freely and willingly consent to the act of intercourse. Consent means a voluntary agreement by a person in the possession and exercise of sufficient mentality to make an intelligent choice, to do something proposed by another. Consent differs from assent. Consent implies some positive action and always involves submission. Assent means mere passivity or submission which does not include consent. Submission to a compelling force or as a result of being put in fear is not consent. You are instructed that the issue of consent is relevant only to determine whether the prosecuting witness is also an "accomplice," thus requiring that the testimony be corroborated. Consent is not a defense to the crime of incest.]

COMMENT

The revision and recodification in 1976 of rape and sexual offense provisions did not repeal the existing crime of incest; hence, Maryland law relating thereto remains in force. See Comment, § 4.36, *infra,* for an analysis of the 1976 legislation.

This instruction is patterned substantially after holdings in various Maryland cases, principally *Scott v. State,* 2 Md. App. 709, 237 A.2d 61 (1968). Incest is a felony in the State of Maryland and one convicted thereof shall be punished by imprisonment in the penitentiary for a term not less than one nor more than ten years. Maryland Ann. Code, Art. 27, § 335.

Under the title "Incest," the statute proscribes a person from knowingly having carnal knowledge of another person, being within the degrees of consanguinity within which marriages are prohibited by law in Maryland. Maryland Ann. Code, Art. 62, § 2 provides:

A man shall not marry:

His grandmother,
His grandfather's wife,
His wife's grandmother,
His father's sister,
His mother's sister,
His mother,
His stepmother,
His wife's mother,
His daughter,
His wife's daughter,
His son's wife,
His sister,
His son's daughter,

His daughter's daughter,
His son's son's wife,
His daughter's son's wife,
His wife's son's daughter,
His wife's daughter's daughter,
His brother's daughter,
His sister's daughter.

A woman shall not marry:

Her grandfather,
Her grandmother's husband,
Her husband's grandfather,
Her father's brother,
Her mother's brother,
Her father,
Her stepfather,
Her husband's father,
Her son,
Her daughter's son,
Her husband's son,
Her daughter's husband,
Her brother,
Her son's son,
Her son's daughter's husband,
Her daughter's daughter's husband,
Her husband's son's son,
Her husband's daughter's son,
Her brother's son,
Her sister's son.

Carnal knowledge and sexual intercourse are synonymous, Clark & Marshall, *Law of Crimes* § 11.01 at 675 (6th ed. 1952), the ancient term for the act itself being "carnal knowledge," 4 *Bl. Comm.* 210. Sexual intercourse, and thus carnal knowledge, judicially defined means "actual contact of the sexual organs of a man and woman and an actual penetration into the body of the latter." *Robert v. State,* 220 Md. 159, 151 A.2d 737 (1959) (*quoting State v. Diamond,* 264 P. 697 (Nev. 1928)). Therefore, penetration is an essential element of the crime of incest. But emission is not an essential element, as it is not embraced within the definition of sexual intercourse (carnal knowledge) and is not required to be proved to establish incest by the provisions of Art. 27, § 335.

Whether a participant in an incestuous relationship is an accomplice or victim depends on the facts of each case. *Lusby v. State,* 217 Md. 191, 141 A.2d 893 (1958). If a prosecuting witness is an accomplice or a voluntary participant in the crime, rather than a victim, adequate corroboration is needed. *Lee v. State,* 18 Md. App. 719, 308 A.2d 397 (1973). See Instruction, § 2.01, Accomplice's testimony — Corroboration, *supra.*

A woman will be an accomplice where she freely and willingly consents to the sexual union. *Lusby v. State, supra* at 199. Where a "passive participant in an incestuous relationship does not freely consent to copulation, and where the sexual union is achieved by force, threats or undue influence on the part of the aggressive participant, the passive participant is not an accomplice but a victim." *Id.* at 200.

> Consent in law means a voluntary agreement by a person in the possession and exercise of sufficient mentality to make an intelligent choice, to do something proposed by another. "Consent" differs very materially from "assent." The former implies some positive action and always involves submission. The latter means mere passivity or submission, which does not include consent.

Gregoire v. State, 211 Md. 243, 246, 128 A.2d 514, 520 (1957).

It should be emphasized that consent is not a defense to the crime of incest. The issue of consent is relevant only to determine whether the prosecuting witness is an "accomplice" rather than a "victim," thus requiring corroboration of the testimony.

Whether corroboration is needed when one partner is an ostensibly consenting juvenile presents an interesting question. Since a minor could be found only to be a juvenile delinquent, arguably corroboration may not be required. *Gregoire v. State, supra.* The Court in *Gregoire* articulated the reasons underlying the rule that a defendant may not be convicted on the uncorroborated testimony of an accomplice as follows:

> The reason for this rule is that the accomplice is a person contaminated with guilt and, therefore, his testimony should be regarded with great suspicion and caution. Otherwise the

> life or liberty of an innocent person might be taken away by a witness who makes the accusation either to gratify his malice, or to shield himself from punishment, or in the hope of receiving clemency by turning State's evidence.

Id. at 522, 128 A.2d at 247. The Court found that there was sufficient evidence to support findings of the trial judge that the two young boys were too frightened to make any resistance and, therefore, were not accomplices. The Court affirmed two convictions for unnatural and perverted sexual practice. Given the rationale of the Court, it can be argued that while a juvenile may have no motive to lie to shield himself from punishment in an adult court or in the hope of receiving clemency from prosecution in an adult court by turning State's evidence, a juvenile may have an interest in avoiding proceedings in a juvenile court and might be subject to other motives to lie that also affect adults. Complicating this issue is the fact that the generally accepted test of whether a witness is an accomplice is whether he could be "convicted" of the offense charged against the defendant either as a principal or as an accessory before the fact. See *Watson v. State,* 208 Md. 210, 117 A.2d 547 (1955) and Comment, § 2.01, Accomplice's testimony — Corroboration, *supra.* Hence, additional appellate consideration of this issue may be required.

It also has been questioned whether, in fact, corroboration is needed in incest cases where the prosecuting witness is an accomplice. In R. Gilbert and C. Moylan, Jr., *Maryland Criminal Law: Practice and Procedure* § 6.13 at 91 (1983), the authors state: "The prosecuting witness, as a matter of law, in a case of incest, is not an accomplice even though the witness may have consented to the illicit act. There are, however, decisions of other States that let the fact-finder decide whether the prosecuting witness is a victim or an accomplice." The authors cite as authority *Scott v. State, supra.* In *Scott,* the prosecutrix was the fourteen-year-old daughter of the defendant. The prosecutrix testified to a struggle and to getting slapped by her father at the time of the incident. Her younger brother, not a witness to the alleged act of intercourse, testified he was beaten by his father for telling his mother certain facts that occurred shortly after the alleged incident. Defendant was convicted in a nonjury trial of carnal knowledge, assault and battery, and incest. In affirming the conviction, the Court of Special Appeals (*citing Leek v. State, infra,* this Comment) stated: "The prosecuting witness in a rape case is not an accomplice, nor do we feel that such witness is an accomplice in an incest or carnal knowledge case. Therefore her testimony need not be corroborated." *Id.* at 714-715, 237 A.2d at 64.

In *Leek v. State,* 229 Md. 526, 184 A.2d 808 (1962), *cert. denied,* 372 U.S. 946 (1963), the defendant was convicted of rape. The Court stated: "The trial court was right in refusing a motion for judgment of acquittal. There was legally sufficient evidence from the prosecutrix (which as a matter of law need not be corroborated, *Doyal v. State* [and] *Saldiveri v. State,* [both cited and discussed, *infra,* this Comment]), which was corroborated by her mother and by the police, to enable the jury to be convinced of the guilt of the accused beyond a reasonable doubt." *Id.* at 528, 184 A.2d at 809. It is clear that the statement relating to the lack of a need for corroboration is *dictum.*

In *Doyal v. State,* 226 Md. 31, 171 A.2d 470 (1960), the Court on appeal found ample evidence that the prosecutrix in a rape case was a victim by reason of force used upon her. Therefore, the Court concluded: "The testimony of the prosecuting witness need not have been corroborated, as a matter of law, *since she was not an accomplice. Saldiveri v. State,* 217 Md. 412, 420 [full cite, *infra*]; *Lusby v. State,* 217 Md. 191, 198 [full cite, *supra*]" *Id.* at 34, 171 A.2d at 471 (emphasis added).

In *Saldiveri v. State,* 217 Md. 412, 143 A.2d 70 (1958), the Court also concluded that there was ample evidence that the eight-year-old prosecutrix in a case involving a charge of unnatural and perverted sexual practice was a victim and not an accomplice so that no corroboration was needed. Citing *Gregoire v. State, supra,* the Court emphasized that to be an accomplice a person must freely and willingly consent. The Court also cited *Lusby v. State, supra.*

In *Lusby,* the defendant was convicted of incest of his seventeen-year-old daughter. The Court of Appeals held that under the circumstances of the case, the prosecutrix was a victim and not an accomplice. The defendant's claim was that the prosecuting witness was an accomplice and that he could not be convicted on her uncorroborated testimony. The illicit relationship had begun when the daughter was thirteen years old and the defendant argued that while initially she may have been the victim, during the ensuing four-year period there came a time when she acquiesced and thereby became an accomplice. The Court, however, distinguished between mere "assent" and "consent" and held that the jury could have found that the participation of the daughter was not voluntary. The Court also held that the burden of proof that the witness is an accomplice is upon the party alleging it — namely the defendant — for the purpose of invoking the corroboration rule. The Court further held that even if the prosecuting witness was an accomplice, it has been held that evidence of a "marital vagina" may be sufficient corroboration of the testimony of the prosecuting witness.

Further, in *Lusby,* the Court discussed the paucity of authority in Maryland for the accomplice corroboration rule in incest and other sexual offense cases, as follows:

> At common law, in the trial of offenses against the chastity of women, the testimony of the prosecuting witness was sufficient evidence to support a conviction, and neither another witness nor corroborating circumstances were necessary. 7 Wigmore, *Evidence* (3d ed. 1940), Sec. 2061. There are numerous cases in other jurisdictions which do not require corroboration of an incestuous relationship even if the female participant was an accomplice [citations omitted], *but there are none in Maryland.* Compare, however, the statement in *Basoff v. State,* 208 Md. 643, 119 A.2d 917 (1956), in which we held, at p. 654, that: "(A) woman upon whom an abortion has been performed (with her consent or even on her solicitation) is regarded ... as a victim ..., rather than ... a participant ... (And) her testimony does not require corroboration where it establishes satisfactory proof of the guilt of the accused."

Id. at 199, 141 A.2d at 897 (emphasis added).

Thus, tracing the history of *Scott v. State, supra,* the Maryland Courts do appear to be applying the accomplice corroboration rule in incest and other sexual offense cases but in most cases find sufficient evidence in the record to support a finding that the prosecuting witness was a victim and not an accomplice. Arguably, the language in *Scott* itself could be interpreted as dictum because there appears to be some evidence of force. *Lusby v. State, supra,* is an incest case in which the Court of Appeals applies the corroboration rule while noting the scant Maryland authority for it. However, as *Gregoire v. State, supra,* recognizes, it is a firmly established general rule in Maryland that a person accused of crime may not be convicted on the uncorroborated testimony of an accomplice.

§ 4.34. Sodomy.

Sodomy is the sexual penetration of the anus by a man with another man or woman.

In order for the defendant to be found guilty of this offense, the State must prove beyond a reasonable doubt that the defendant knowingly [placed his penis into the anus of another person] [permitted another person to place his penis into the anus of the defendant.]

The State must prove the penetration of the penis into the anus. The slightest penetration is sufficient. Proof of emission of semen is not required.

[It is not necessary that the offense be done without the consent of the other person. Both participants in the crime of sodomy, if willing parties, are equally guilty.]

[*To be given where there is some evidence that the prosecuting witness is an accomplice:* You must determine whether the prosecuting witness in this case was a willing, consenting partner, that is, an accomplice, rather than victim. If you find that the prosecuting witness was an accomplice rather than a victim, then this person's testimony must be corroborated. The testimony of a victim need not be corroborated. *See Instruction, § 2.01, Accomplice's testimony — Corroboration, supra, on the meaning of corroboration.*

To be an accomplice, rather than a victim, one must freely and willingly consent to the sexual act. Consent means a voluntary agreement by a person in the possession and exercise of sufficient mentality to make an intelligent choice, to do something proposed by another. Consent differs from assent. Consent implies some positive action and always involves submission. Assent means mere passivity or submission which does not include consent. Submission to a compelling force, or as a result of being put in fear, is not consent. You are instructed that the issue of consent is relevant only to determine whether the prosecuting witness is also an "accomplice," thus requiring that the testimony be corroborated. Consent is not a defense to the crime of sodomy.]

COMMENT

Sodomy apparently can be prosecuted under several distinct provisions of the Maryland Ann. Code: (1) Art. 27, § 553, upon which this instruction is based; (2) Art. 27, § 554, captioned "Unnatural or perverted sexual practices," which includes sodomy within the definition of such practices (See *Cherry v. State,* 18 Md. App. 252, 306 A.2d 634 (1973) and discussion in the Comment, § 4.35, *infra*); and (3) Art. 27, §§ 464, 464A and 466C(a)(2), provisions of the 1976 revised sexual offense law which include sodomy but do not repeal the earlier sodomy statutes. See Instructions, §§ 4.37(a), 4.37(d) and 4.37(j), *infra,* relating to sodomy. See *DiBartolomeo v. State,* 61 Md. App. 302, 486 A.2d 256 (1985); *Gray v. State,* 43 Md. App. 238, 403 A.2d 853 (1979). See also Comment, § 4.36, *infra,* for an analysis of the 1976 legislation.

Under the revised sexual offense provisions, force or threat of force is an essential element for sodomy to be a sexual offense in the first or second degree. Thus, consent is a defense to a prosecution under these provisions. Under Art. 27, § 553, consensual sodomy is clearly a crime so that consent is no defense. Nonconsensual sodomy, however, can also be prosecuted under this statute.

The potential penalty under the revised sexual offense provisions is substantially greater than in the retained sodomy offense. Under Art. 27, § 553, sodomy is a felony and, upon conviction, the defendant "shall be sentenced to the penitentiary for not more than ten years." Under Art. 27, §§ 464 and 464A, however, the maximum punishment is life imprisonment for a sexual offense in the first degree and up to twenty years for a sexual offense in the second degree.

In a nonconsensual sodomy case, where no aggravating circumstances are present warranting a prosecution as a first degree sexual offense, a prosecutor apparently can proceed under either the second degree sexual offense statute or the older sodomy laws. In such a case, the same elements seem to be covered under both provisions. No guidelines are provided to guide the exercise of prosecutorial discretion in making this election. This overlap may invite a challenge on the grounds of violation of equal protection of the laws and unconstitutional delegation of legislative control over the sentencing structure as applied to a defendant charged with a second degree sexual offense amounting to unaggravated, nonconsensual sodomy.

A nonconsenting victim of an unnatural or perverted sexual practice is not an accomplice and his or her testimony need not be corroborated. *White v. State,* 3 Md. App. 167, 238 A.2d 278 (1968). However, if the prosecuting witness is a willing, consenting partner, rather than a victim, his or her testimony must be corroborated. *Bennett v. State,* 283 Md. 619, 392 A.2d 76 (1978); *Brown v. State,* 281 Md. 241, 378 A.2d 1104 (1977). When the prosecuting witness is a juvenile and could not be convicted of the offense but only found to be a juvenile delinquent, the question arises as to whether corroboration is needed because the juvenile is not, strictly speaking, an "accomplice." *Gregoire v. State,* 211 Md. 514, 128 A.2d 243 (1957). See Comment, § 4.33, Incest, *supra,* for a discussion of this question. The amount of corroboration, if needed, is only slight. See Comment, § 2.01, Accomplice's testimony — Corroboration, *supra,* for a discussion of the meaning of corroboration.

At common law, some proof of penetration is required for conviction of sodomy, although slight evidence may suffice.

Bradbury v. State, 233 Md. 421, 197 A.2d 126 (1964); *Canter v. State,* 224 Md. 483, 168 A.2d 384 (1961). On the other hand, a prosecution under Art. 27, § 554, Unnatural or perverted sexual practices (see Comment, § 4.35, *infra*) does not require proof of penetration unless an act that is specified by the prosecution involves penetration. Since the indictment need not allege the specific unnatural or perverted practice, defense counsel should request in a bill of particulars to be informed of the precise acts charged.

The crime of sodomy is based on the common-law offense. Although the word "mankind" appeared in the sixteenth-century English statutes, sodomy or buggery can be committed upon a woman. *Daniels v. State,* 237 Md. 71, 205 A.2d 295 (1964). The definition has been broadened to include other sexual acts. *DiBartolomeo v. State, supra.*

For a discussion of constitutional issues, including the right of privacy, see Comment, § 435, Unnatural or perverted sexual practices, *infra.*

§ 4.35. Unnatural or perverted sexual practices.

It is an offense for a person to commit any unnatural or perverted sexual practice.

In order for the defendant to be found guilty of this offense, the State must prove beyond a reasonable doubt:

(Alternative A)

[(1) That the defendant knowingly (2) took into his mouth (3) the sexual organ of any other person [animal].]

(Alternative B)

[(1) That the defendant knowingly (2) placed his sexual organ (3) in the mouth of any other person [animal].]

(Alternative C)

[(1) That the defendant knowingly (2) committed an unnatural or perverted sexual practice, namely, ________ (*list alleged criminal acts*), (3) with [another person] [an animal]. The term unnatural or perverted sexual practices refers to both acts of oral perversion and any other acts which, within common knowledge, are considered unnatural and perverted sexual practices. These words, then, are to be accorded the meaning naturally given them in ordinary usage.]

[*To be given where there is some evidence that the prosecuting witness is an accomplice:* You must determine whether the prosecuting witness in this case was a willing, consenting partner, that is, an accomplice, rather than a victim. If you find that the prosecuting witness was an accomplice rather than a victim, then that person's testimony must be corroborated. The testimony of a victim need not be corroborated. *See Instruction, § 2.01, Accomplice's testimony — Corroboration, supra,* on the meaning of corroboration.

To be an accomplice, rather than a victim, one must freely and willingly consent to the act of intercourse. Consent means a voluntary agreement by a person in the possession and exercise of sufficient mentality to make an intelligent choice, to do something proposed by another. Consent differs from assent. Consent implies some positive action and always involves submission. Assent means mere passivity or submission which does not include consent. Submission to a compelling force or as a result of being put in fear is not consent. You are instructed that the issue of consent is relevant only to determine whether the prosecuting witness is also an "accomplice," thus requiring that the testimony be corroborated. Consent is not a defense to the crime of unnatural or perverted sexual practices.]

COMMENT

The 1976 amendment made only stylistic changes in Maryland Ann. Code, Art. 27, § 554, prohibiting "unnatural and perverted sexual practices." See Comment, § 4.36, *infra,* for an analysis of the 1976 legislation.

It should be noted that the original sponsors of the revised sexual offense law of Maryland sought the repeal of Art. 27, §§ 553 and 554. This effort was unsuccessful, and the result has been to create a disturbing overlap of the old provisions with the revised sexual offense laws. Thus, for example, one convicted of a consensual "sexual act" (which includes sodomy, fellatio, etc.) performed with a fourteen- or fifteen-year-old child is subject to a maximum penalty of one year imprisonment or a fine of $1,000 or both. Art. 27, § 464C(a)(2). This penalty compares with a ten-year maximum penalty for consensual sodomy under Art. 27, § 553. There is no legislative guidance for prosecutors' standards relating to the exercise of their discretion in this area.

The omission of first and second degree sexual offenses (Art. 27, §§ 464 and 464A) proscribing nonconsensual acts of sodomy, fellatio, etc. from the spousal immunity provision (Art. 27, § 464D) also creates an anomaly. If a husband engages in a forcible vaginal intercourse with his wife and employs a deadly weapon during the course of that act (Art. 27, §§ 462 and 463), he is not subject to prosecution under the sexual offense statute because of the absolute spousal immunity defense incorporated in the revised law. If, however, one engages in a forcible "sexual act" with his or her spouse and employs a deadly weapon during the course of that act (Art. 27, §§ 464 and 464A), there is no spousal immunity to prosecution. Rather such person, upon conviction, is subject to the maximum penalty of life imprisonment.

Article 27, § 554, provides a fine of not more than $1000 or imprisonment for a maximum of ten years, or both, for any person convicted of the following: (1) taking into his or her mouth the sexual organ of any other person or animal; (2) placing his or her sexual organ in the mouth of any other person or animal; or

(3) committing any other unnatural or perverted sexual practice with any other person or animal. See *DiBartolomeo v. State,* 61 Md. App. 302, 486 A.2d 256 (1985).

The statute specifies that in an indictment for the offense, it is not necessary to set forth the particular unnatural or perverted sexual practice which the defendant allegedly committed, nor is it necessary to set forth the manner in which the particular unnatural or perverted sexual practice was committed.

Although the section begins with a prohibition against "oral" perversion, the words "any other unnatural or perverted sexual practice" do not refer only to acts of oral perversion. In *Blake v. State,* 210 Md. 459, 124 A.2d 273 (1956) the Court stated: "We find in the language employed a clear legislative intention to cover the whole field of unnatural and perverted sexual practices. We think it was unnecessary to describe in detail practices which are matters of common knowledge." *Id.* at 462, 124 A.2d at 274. See also *Edmonds v. State,* 18 Md. App. 55, 60, 305 A.2d 205, 208 (1973).

In the *Edmonds* case it was argued that there was no conduct which amounted to a sex act since "there was no actual contact with sexual organs of either the victim or the defendant," and that the act of inserting a mop or broom handle into the victim's rectum was not a proscribed act within the contemplation of the statute. *Id.* at 59, 305 A.2d at 207.

The Court, however, rejected this argument and held:

> We cannot agree, as the appellant argues, that the anal passage may not be classified as a sexual organ within the meaning of the statute for it is well known that it has been the source of sexual gratification, however perverted or distasteful such a method of gratification may be considered. In fact, the acts of sodomy or buggery specifically involve the penetration of the rectum. Had the appellant's penis been used to penetrate the victim's rectum there would be no question that it would have amounted to an act of sodomy or buggery. That appellant elected to use a mop or broom handle certainly takes the act out of the category of sodomy or buggery. It does not, however, in the circumstances here, take the action outside the classification of an unnatural and perverted sexual practice.

Id. at 60, 305 A.2d at 208.

In *Thomas v. State,* 301 Md. 294, 483 A.2d 6 (1984), the Court distinguished the definition of "fellatio" in a prosecution for a sexual offense in the first degree from that in unnatural or perverted sexual practices. In a first degree sexual offense prosecution, all that must be shown is some contact between the mouth and the male sexual organ. Proof of penetration is not required. See Comment, § 4.37, Sexual offenses in the first, second, third and fourth degree, *infra,* for further discussion of *Thomas.*

In *Neville v. State,* 290 Md. 364, 430 A.2d 570 (1981), the Court held that the issue of the partner's consent is irrelevant since the act itself constitutes the offense. *Id.* at 380, 430 A.2d at 578. If the prosecuting witness is an accomplice to the crime, rather than a victim, then his testimony must be corroborated. To be an accomplice one must freely and willingly consent. *Gregoire v. State,* 211 Md. 514, 128 A.2d 243 (1957).

Consent means a voluntary agreement by a person in the possession and exercise of sufficient mentality to make an intelligent choice, to do something proposed by another. "Consent" differs very materially from "assent." The former implies some positive action and always involves submission. The latter means mere passivity or submission, which does not include consent. *Id.* at 520, 128 A.2d at 246. See *Saldiveri v. State,* 217 Md. 412, 143 A.2d 70 (1958); *Winegan v. State,* 10 Md. App. 196, 268 A.2d 585 (1970); *White v. State,* 3 Md. App. 167, 238 A.2d 278 (1968). See also Instruction, § 2.01, Accomplice's testimony — Corroboration, *supra.* For a discussion of whether corroboration is needed where the prosecuting witness is a juvenile, see Comment to § 4.33, Incest, *supra.*

The constitutionality of Art. 27, § 554, was challenged in *Blake v. State, supra.* In *Blake,* the Court stated the statute was not void either for vagueness or for failing to fix an ascertainable standard of guilt. *Id.* at 461, 462, 124 A.2d at 274. In *Hughes v. State,* 14 Md. App. 497, 501, 287 A.2d 299, 302 (1972), *cert. denied,* 409 U.S. 1025 (1972), the validity of the statute was attacked on the grounds that it was unconstitutional "for overbreadth in that it punishes every person convicted of acts of sexual perversion without regard to right of privacy of (a) consenting married adults and (b) consenting unmarried adults concerning their sexual acts." The Court found the defendant had no standing to raise this issue because he was not charged with indulging in the proscribed conduct with another consenting adult but with a minor. *Id.* at 501-02, 287 A.2d at 304. The Court observed that it was conceivable that a consenting husband and wife could be convicted under this statute. However, it thought this unlikely to occur because of the need for corroboration when accomplices are involved and because of the husband-wife testimonial privilege.

In *Bowers v. Hardwick,* 106 S. Ct. 2841, 92 L. Ed. 2d 140 (1986), in a civil suit in the federal District Court respondent challenged the constitutionality of a Georgia statute criminalizing consensual sodomy and providing for a maximum sentence of twenty years' imprisonment. In a five-four decision, the United States Supreme Court held that (1) the ninth amendment and the due process clause of the fourteenth amendment of the United States Constitution do not confer a fundamental right to a homosexual to engage in sodomy because none of the fundamental rights previously asserted bear any resemblance to the right asserted in this case; (2) the result is the same even though the conduct occurs in the privacy of the home; and (3) the Court should greatly resist expanding the due process clause to cover new fundamental rights. The opinion noted that until 1961 all fifty states outlawed sodomy and, presently, twenty-four states and the District of Columbia continue to provide criminal penalties for sodomy performed in private and between consenting adults. The four dissenters noted that the Georgia statute was not, in fact, aimed at homosexual behavior and that the sex or status of the persons who engage in the act is irrelevant under the statute. They argued that, because sexual intimacy is a sensitive, key relationship of human existence and central to family life, there is a fundamental interest in sexual intimacy in private places. Justice Powell, in a separate concurring opinion, stated the view that a prison sentence for a single, private, consensual act of sodomy — and certainly a sentence of long duration — would create a serious eighth amendment issue.

In *Kelly v. State,* 45 Md. App. 212, 412 A.2d 1274 (1980), *aff'd, Neville v. State, supra,* the Court held, in a case involving a conviction for unnatural or perverted sexual practice, that the right of privacy does not protect the practice of fellatio (*citing Doe v. Commonwealth's Attorney for City of Richmond,* 403 F. Supp. 1199 (E.D. Va. 1975), *aff'd mem.* 425 U.S. 901 (1976)). The Court also rejected appellant's argument that he was denied equal protection of the law since fornication is not prohibited by Maryland law as well as the argument that any punishment for sodomy is cruel and unusual. The Court stated: "The argument is that there is no essential difference between vaginal intercourse and other sex acts .... Once again we repeat, we will not invalidate laws of such ancient vintage without clear authority from higher courts." *Kelly v. State, supra* at 217, 412 A.2d at 1277.

Article 27, § 554 was again challenged in *Neville v. State, supra,* by the defendant who argued that the statute is overly broad. Defendant also argued that the statute discriminates against unmarried persons in violation of the equal protection clause. Both arguments were rejected by the Court. Since the Court found that the acts were done in public, it did not need to determine whether enforcement of the statute violated the defendant's right to privacy. In his dissent, Judge Davidson stated that the statute is violative of the constitutionally protected right to privacy. *Id.* at 396, 430 A. 396, 430 A.2d at 586.

In *Hughes v. State, supra,* it was argued, also unsuccessfully, that the statute was unconstitutional because the means of enforcement, which allow a penal term for up to ten years, are inappropriate to effectuate the purpose of the legislation in that "punishment by incarceration would force the person convicted to engage more intensively in homosexual practices." *Id.* at 508, 287 A.2d at 306. In *Neville, supra,* the Court rejected the argument that defendant was being punished for a status offense in violation of the eighth amendment. Defendant relied on *Robinson v. California,* 370 U.S. 660, 82 S. Ct. 1417, 9 L. Ed. 2d 166 (1972). The Court rejected this argument, stating that defendant was being punished for his behavior, not for his "status."

The fact that this statute does not establish an age below which consent shall not be a bar to prosecution does not make the statute unconstitutionally vague. *Hughes v. State, supra* at 507, 287 A.2d at 305, 306.

2. 1976 Revised Rape and Sexual Offense Laws

§ 4.36. Rape offenses.

(a) Rape — First degree

The crime of rape is vaginal intercourse committed against the will and without the consent of the victim and which is accompanied by force or threat of force. In Maryland, there are two grades of rape: rape in the first degree and rape in the second degree. The distinction between rape in the first degree and rape in the second degree is the presence of [an] aggravating circumstance(s) occurring in the commission of the offense.

The defendant in this case is charged with first degree rape. The aggravating circumstance(s) which the state contends [was] [were] present in the commission of this offense [is] [are] that __________ (*insert applicable aggravating circumstance(s) below*).

[(1) the defendant allegedly employed or displayed a dangerous or deadly weapon, or an article which the victim reasonably concluded was a dangerous or deadly weapon];

[(2) the defendant allegedly inflicted [suffocation] [strangulation] [disfigurement] [serious physical injury] upon __________ [the victim] [someone other than the victim]];

[(3) the defendant allegedly threatened or placed the victim in fear that __________ [the victim] [someone known to the victim] would be imminently subjected to [death] [suffocation] [strangulation] [disfigurement] [serious physical injury] [kidnapping]];

[(4) the defendant allegedly committed the offense aided and abetted by one or more other persons].

In order for the defendant to be guilty of first degree rape, the state must prove beyond a reasonable doubt that: (1) the defendant had vaginal intercourse with the victim; (2) the act was committed without the consent and against the will of the victim; (3) the act was committed by force or threat of force, and (4) the defendant ___________ (*insert applicable aggravating circumstance(s) from above*).

Vaginal intercourse is defined as the actual penetration, however slight, of the male sexual organ or penis into the female sexual organ or vagina. Penetration is an essential element of the crime of rape. There must be some penetration, however slight, by the penis into the vagina to constitute the crime of rape. Emission of semen is not required.

Force or threat of force is an essential element of the crime. To justify a conviction, the evidence must warrant a conclusion either that the victim resisted and was overcome by force or that the victim was prevented from resisting by force or by threats to the victim's safety. No particular amount of force, either actual or constructive, is required to constitute rape. It depends on the totality of the circumstances. Force may exist without violence. If the acts and threats of the perpetrator were reasonably calculated to create a real and reasonable fear of imminent bodily harm in the victim's mind, and that fear is serious enough to impair or overcome the victim's will to resist, then such acts and threats are the equivalent of force. The fear created must be evaluated in light of the circumstances in which the victim was placed. A person is not expected to resist at the expense of life or at the risk of serious bodily injury.

Consent to the act at any time prior to penetration, however reluctantly given, deprives the subsequent intercourse of its criminal character. Consent means a voluntary agreement by a person in the possession and exercise of sufficient mentality to make an intelligent choice to do something proposed by another. Consent differs from assent. Consent implies some positive action and always involves more than mere submission. Assent means mere passivity or submission, which does not include consent. Submission to a compelling force, or as a result of being put in fear, is not consent. A person who was conscious and possessed of natural mental and physical powers when the attack took place must have resisted to the extent of her ability at the time, unless it appears that she was overcome by numbers or was so terrified by threats as to overpower the will to resist. Resistance is necessarily relative: its presence or absence depends on the facts and circumstances in each case. The real test is whether the vaginal intercourse was committed without the consent and against the will of the victim. The kind of fear in the mind of the victim which would reasonably make resistance unnecessary to support a conviction of rape includes, but is not necessarily limited to, a fear of death or serious bodily harm, or a fear so extreme as to preclude resistance, or a fear which might make the person incapable of continuing to resist.

[*To be given where some evidence has been generated that the victim is the defendant's spouse:* It is an affirmative defense that the victim was the defendant's legal spouse at the time of the commission of the alleged offense. The State must prove beyond a reasonable doubt that the victim was not the defendant's legal spouse at the time of the commission of the alleged offense [the victim and the defendant were living separate and apart pursuant to a valid court decree of divorce at the time of the offense].]

[If after a full and fair consideration of all the facts and circumstances in evidence, you are not convinced beyond a reasonable doubt that the defendant __________ (*insert applicable aggravating circumstance(s)*) in the course of committing the crime of rape, then you must find the defendant not guilty of first degree rape. On the other hand, if you find from your consideration of all of the evidence that the State has proved each of the elements of the offense beyond a reasonable doubt, then you should find the defendant guilty of first degree rape.]

[*To be given where second degree rape is a lesser included offense:* If you find that the defendant is not guilty of first degree rape, you must then proceed to consider whether the defendant is guilty of second degree rape. I will now instruct you on the elements of second degree rape.]

(b) Rape — Second degree

The crime of second degree rape is vaginal intercourse committed against the will and without the consent of the victim and accompanied by force or threat of force. In order for a person to be guilty of this offense the State must prove beyond a reasonable doubt that: (1) the defendant had vaginal intercourse with the victim; (2) the act was committed without the consent and against the will of the victim; and (3) the act was committed by force or threat of force.

Vaginal intercourse is defined as the actual penetration, however slight, of the male sexual organ or penis into the female sexual organ or vagina. Penetration is an essential element of the crime of rape. There must be some penetration, however slight, by the penis into the vagina to constitute the crime of rape. Emission of semen is not required.

Force or threat of force is an essential element of the crime. To justify a conviction, the evidence must warrant a conclusion either that the victim resisted and the victim was overcome by force or that the victim was prevented from resisting by force or by threats to the victim's safety. No particular amount of force, either actual or constructive, is required to constitute rape. It depends upon the totality of the circumstances. Force may exist without violence. If the acts and threats of the perpetrator were reasonably calculated to create a real and reasonable fear of imminent bodily harm in the victim's mind, and that fear is serious enough to impair or overcome the victim's will to resist, then such acts and threats are the equivalent of force. The fear created must be evaluated in light of the circumstances in which the victim was placed. A person is not expected to resist at the expense of life or at the risk of serious bodily injury.

Consent to the act at any time prior to penetration, however reluctantly given, deprives the subsequent intercourse of its criminal character. Consent means a voluntary agreement by a person in the possession and exercise of sufficient mentality to make an intelligent choice to do something proposed by another. Consent differs from assent. Consent implies some positive action and always involves more than mere submission. Assent means mere passivity or submission, which does not include consent. Submission to a compelling force, or as a result of being put in fear, is not consent. A person who was conscious and possessed of natural mental and physical powers when the attack took place must have resisted to the extent of her ability at the time, unless it appears that she was overcome by numbers or was so terrified by threats as to overpower the will to resist. Resistance is necessarily relative; its presence or absence depends on the facts and circumstances in each case. The real test is whether the vaginal intercourse was committed without the consent and against the will of the victim. The kind of fear in the mind of the victim which would reasonably make resistance unnecessary to support a conviction of rape includes, but is not necessarily limited to, a fear of death or serious bodily harm, or a fear so extreme as to preclude resistance, or a fear which might make the person incapable of continuing to resist.

[*To be given where some evidence has been generated that the victim is the defendant's spouse:* It is a defense that the victim was the defendant's legal spouse at the time of the commission of the alleged offense. The State must prove beyond a reasonable doubt that the victim was not the defendant's legal spouse at the time of the commission of the alleged offense [the victim and the defendant were living separate and apart pursuant to a valid court decree of divorce at the time of the offense].]

[If after full and fair consideration of all the facts and circumstances, you are not convinced beyond a reasonable doubt that the defendant engaged in an act of sexual intercourse by force or threat of force and, further, that this was against the will and without the consent of the victim, then you must find the defendant not guilty of second degree rape. On the other hand, if you find from your consideration of all of the evidence that the State has proved each of the elements of the offense beyond a reasonable doubt, then you should find the defendant guilty of second degree rape.]

(c) Rape — Second degree: victim under fourteen years and person performing act four or more years older than victim

It is unlawful for a person to engage in vaginal intercourse with one who is under fourteen years of age if the person performing the act is at least four years older than the victim. In Maryland, this offense is rape in the second degree.

In order for a person to be found guilty of this offense, the State must prove beyond a reasonable doubt that: (1) defendant engaged in vaginal intercourse with the victim; (2) the victim was less than fourteen years old at the time of the offense; and (3) the defendant was at least four years older than the victim.

Vaginal intercourse is defined as the actual penetration, however slight, of the male sexual organ or penis into the female sexual organ or vagina. Penetration is an essential element of the crime of rape. There must be some penetration, however slight, by the penis into the vagina to constitute the crime of rape. Emission of semen is not required.

The fact that the defendant did not know that the victim was under fourteen years of age is not a defense to the charge of rape in the second degree. Such is the case, even if you find that the defendant reasonably believed the victim to be fourteen years of age or older.

Finally, the basis of the charge of second degree rape is that the victim was under fourteen years of age at the time of the offense while the defendant was at least four years older than the victim. Thus, whether the victim consented to the act of sexual intercourse is immaterial. Consent is not a defense to the charge of second degree rape.

[If after a full and fair consideration of all the facts and circumstances in evidence, you are not convinced beyond a reasonable doubt that the defendant engaged in an act of sexual intercourse with the victim, who was under fourteen years of age at the time of the offense while the defendant was at least four years older than the victim, then you must find the defendant not guilty of second degree rape. On the other hand, if you find from your consideration of all of the evidence that the State has proved each of the elements of the offense beyond a reasonable doubt, then you should find the defendant guilty of second degree rape.]

(d) Rape — Second degree: mentally defective, mentally incapacitated or physically helpless victim

It is unlawful for a person to engage in vaginal intercourse with one whom the defendant knows or reasonably should know is __________ ([mentally defective] [mentally incapacitated] [physically helpless]). In Maryland, this offense is rape in the second degree.

In order for the defendant to be found guilty of this offense the State must prove beyond a reasonable doubt that: (1) the defendant engaged in vaginal intercourse with the victim; (2) the victim was __________ ([mentally defective] [mentally incapacitated] [physically helpless]); and (3) the defendant knew or reasonably should have known that the victim was __________ ([mentally defective] [mentally incapacitated] [physically helpless]).

Vaginal intercourse is defined as the actual penetration, however slight, of the male sexual organ or penis into the female sexual organ or vagina. Penetration is an essential element of the crime of rape. There must be some penetration, however slight, by the penis into the vagina to constitute the crime of rape. Emission of semen is not required.

[A person who is "mentally defective" suffers from either mental retardation or a mental disorder. The condition must be such that, at the time of the alleged offense, it rendered the victim substantially incapable of appraising the nature of the victim's or the defendant's conduct, or of resisting the act of vaginal intercourse or of communicating unwillingness to submit to the act of vaginal intercourse.]

[One who is "mentally incapacitated" is one who, due to the influence of a drug, narcotic or intoxicating substance, or due to any act committed upon the victim without the victim's consent of awareness, is rendered substantially incapable of either appraising the nature of her own or the defendant's conduct, or resisting the act of vaginal intercourse.]

[One who is "physically helpless" is one who is either (1) unconscious or (2) does not consent to an act of vaginal intercourse and is physically unable to resist an act of vaginal intercourse or (3) is physically unable to communicate unwillingness to submit to vaginal intercourse.]

To convict the defendant of second degree rape you must find beyond a reasonable doubt that the defendant knew or reasonably should have known that the victim was __________ ([mentally defective] [mentally incapacitated] [physically helpless]). An act is done knowingly if done voluntarily and purposely, and not because of mistake, accident, inadvertence or other innocent reason. In addition, the defendant reasonably should have known that the victim was __________ ([mentally defective] [mentally incapacitated] [physically helpless]), if an ordinarily prudent and cautious person in full possession of his faculties, using reasonable care, would have known that the victim was __________ ([mentally defective] [mentally incapacitated] [physically helpless]).

[*To be given where some evidence has been generated that the victim is the defendant's spouse:* It is a defense that the victim was the defendant's legal spouse at the time of the commission of the alleged offense. The State must prove beyond a reasonable doubt that the victim was not the defendant's legal spouse at the time of the commission of the alleged offense [the victim and the defendant were living separate and apart pursuant to a valid court decree of divorce at the time of the offense].]

[If after a full and fair consideration of all the facts and circumstances in evidence, you are not convinced beyond a reasonable doubt that the defendant engaged in sexual intercourse with a person who was [mentally defective] [mentally incapacitated] [physically helpless] and that the defendant knew or reasonably should have known of this condition, then you must find the defendant not guilty of second degree rape. On the other hand, if you find from your consideration of all of the evidence that the State has proved each of the elements of the offense beyond a reasonable doubt, then you should find the defendant guilty of second degree rape.]

COMMENT

(a) Overview

Acts of 1976, ch. 573, effective July 1, 1976, supplemented by amendments in 1977, 1978 and 1980, substantially revised Maryland's rape and other sexual offense laws. The newly enacted sections are codified in Maryland Ann. Code, Art. 27, §§ 461 to 465. As noted earlier, the existing crime of "incest" (Art. 27, § 335) was not repealed and, although the sponsors of the 1976 legislation sought repeal of the "sodomy" statute (Art. 27, § 553) and the statute proscribing "unnatural or perverted sexual practices" (Art. 27, § 554), these laws were preserved. See Instructions, §§ 4.33 to 4.35, *supra.*

The following chart summarizes the three categories of criminal sexual activities — vaginal intercourse, sexual acts and sexual contact — which are prohibited by the revised laws. It shows how particular aggravating circumstances affect the degree of the offense of which the defendant may be convicted. Statute section numbers and maximum penalties are indicated.

Summary of Grading Sexual Offenses

	Types of Aggravating Circumstances			
Criminal Sexual Acts:	Force, threats of force, non-consent which is aggravated by use of weapon, serious physical injury or threat thereof, or use of accomplice[1]	Force, threats of force, non-consent	Accused is 4 or more years older than the victim, whose age is indicated below	Victim is mentally defective, mentally incapacitated, or physically helpless[2]
Unlawful vaginal intercourse[3]	1° Rape (life) § 462(a)	2° Rape (20 years) § 463(a)(1)	V under 14: 2° Rape (20 years) § 463(a)(3) V 14 or 15 4° Sexual offense (1 year) § 464C(a)(3)	2° Rape (20 years) § 463(a)(2)
Unlawful sexual act[4]	1° Sexual offense (life) § 464(a)(1)	2° Sexual offense (20 years) § 464A(a)(1)	V under 14: 2° Sexual Offense (20 years) § 464A(a)(3) V 14 or 15: 4° Sexual offense (1 year) § 464C(a)(2)	2° Sexual offense (20 years) § 464A(a)(2)
Unlawful sexual contact[5]	3° Sexual offense (10 years) § 464B(a)(1)	4° Sexual offense (1 year) § 464C(a)(1)	V under 14: 3° Sexual offense (10 years) § 464B(a)(3)	3° Sexual offense (10 years) § 464B(a)(2)

1. The language is: "... with another person by force or threat of force against the will and without the consent of the other person and: (1) Employs or displays a dangerous or deadly weapon or an article which the other person reasonably concludes is a dangerous or deadly weapon; or (2) Inflicts suffocation, strangulation, disfigurement, or serious physical injury upon that person or upon anyone else in the course of committing the offense; or (3) Threatens or places the victim in fear that the victim or any person known to the victim will be imminently subjected to death, suffocation, strangulation, disfigurement, serious physical injury, or kidnapping; or (4) The person commits the offense aided and abetted by one or more other persons."

2. The three categories are defined in § 461(b), (c), and (d); the statute requires that the accused knew or should reasonably have known of the condition of the victim.

3. This has its ordinary meaning and is defined in § 461(g).

4. This is defined in § 461(e) to include: cunnilingus, fellatio, analingus, anal intercourse, and genital or anal penetration by objects in certain circumstances.

5. This is defined in § 461(f) and includes intentional touching of anal or genital areas or other intimate parts for purposes of sexual arousal or gratification or for abuse.

NOTE: § 464D bars prosecution under §§ 462, 463, 464B and 464C if the accused and victim are spouses at the time of the act unless they are living apart pursuant to a limited divorce decree; The sodomy and perverted practice sections (§ 553 and § 554) have not been expressly repealed and prohibit adult consensual acts.

(b) Age of the victim and the accused

A close reading of the statute is necessary where the victim's young age is the basis for charging the accused with rape or a sexual offense. Article 27, §§ 463(a)(3), 464A(a)(3) and 464B(a)(3) make the sexual activity at issue unlawful when the victim is under fourteen years of age and the accused is four or more years older than the "victim." Article 27, §§ 464C(2) and (3) make it unlawful to engage in either a "sexual act" or "vaginal intercourse" with anyone who is fourteen or fifteen years of age when the accused is four or more years older than the other person. A consensual "sexual contact" with one who is fourteen or fifteen years old is not proscribed by the Maryland statute. The chart reprinted below illustrates the effect of age on Maryland's sexual offense laws.

Effect of Age on Maryland's Sexual Offense Laws Where Sexual Conduct Is with Consent

Victim's Age	Defendant's Age	Sexual Act	Consent	Crime
12	15	Intercourse	yes	none
12	16[1]	Intercourse	yes	2° Rape
13	18	Intercourse	yes	2° Rape
14	17	Intercourse	yes	none
14 or 15	19	Intercourse	yes	4° Sexual Offense
13	16	Oral Sex	yes	none[2]
13	19	Oral Sex	yes	2° Sexual Offense
14 or 15	19	Oral Sex	yes	4° Sexual Offense
13	16	Sexual Contact	yes	none
13	19	Sexual Contact	yes	3° Sexual Offense
14 or 15	19	Sexual Contact	yes	none

1. The accused must have been born four *full* years earlier than the victim to be guilty of the consensual statutory sex offenses, according to a letter dated March 11, 1976, from George A. Nielson, Assistant Attorney General, to Senator Steny H. Hoyer.

2. While the accused may not be convicted under Art. 27, § 464A(a)(3), a conviction might be obtained under Art. 27, § 553 or § 554 proscribing "sodomy" and

(c) Relationship of 1976 revised statutes to corresponding common law

It is generally assumed that the earlier offenses dealing with common-law rape have been repealed. Yet, there is some ambiguity, because an amendment to the sexual offense bill that would have expressly repealed the common-law offense was deleted. A question may be raised whether striking out this language permits an inference that the legislature intended both provisions to be operative. Apparently some prosecutions for common-law rape have occurred on the assumption that common-law rape is still an offense in Maryland. No Court of Appeals interpretation, however, has addressed this question.

Persons playing a central role in the drafting of the revised statutes were interviewed. One person noted that the legislature's desire to protect against any possible loopholes is the sole reason for the amendment which deleted the language expressly repealing the common-law crime. Another argued that since the legislature did not provide any language which expressly continues the common-law crime and at the same time fully legislated on the same subject matter, the common-law crime is, *ipso facto,* repealed. This appears to be the position in the "Editor's note" of the 1979 cumulative supplement to Maryland Ann. Code, Art. 27, § 461, at page 147 which states: "Chapter 573, Acts 1976, effective July 1, 1976, repealed former §§ 461, 462, 462A, and 464 and the subheading 'Rape' and enacted present §§ 461, 462, 463, 464, 464A, 464B, 464C, 464D, and 464E, to be under the new subheading 'Sexual Offenses.'"

(d) Common-law background of rape offenses

Maryland Ann. Code, Art. 27, § 464E states that "[u]ndefined words or phrases in this subheading which describe elements of the common-law crime of rape shall retain their judicially determined meaning except to the extent expressly or by implication changed in this subheading."

Terms such as "threat of force," "without consent," "force," "against her will" and "penetration" are not defined by statute; therefore, one must look to the common law to determine their meaning. *State v. Rusk,* 289 Md. 230, 240, 424 A.2d 720, 725 (1981), *rev'g* 43 Md. App. 476, 406 A.2d 624 (1979). Pursuant to *Rusk,* the following common-law authorities may be useful in defining elements of rape offenses under the statutes.

Sexual intercourse and carnal knowledge mean actual contact of the sexual organs of a man and woman and an actual penetration into the body of the latter. These terms, sexual intercourse and carnal knowledge, are actually synonymous. *Scott v. State,* 2 Md. App. 709, 237 A.2d 61 (1968).

Penetration must be proved before there can be a conviction of rape. *Jackson v. State,* 214 Md. 454, 135 A.2d 638 (1957), *cert. denied,* 356 U.S. 940 (1958); *Smith v. State,* 224 Md. 509, 168 A.2d 356 (1961). In *Kackley v. State,* 63 Md. App. 532, 493 A.2d 364 (1985), the Court noted that penetration is a necessary element of second degree rape pursuant to Art. 27, 463(a)(3) and defined the meaning of penetration. Penetration, however slight, will sustain a conviction but the proof must show an actual entrance of the sexual organ of the male within the *labia (majora)* of the *pudendum* (the external folds of the *vulva*) of the female organ. The court reviews cases considering proof of penetration. It has never been necessary that the victim's hymen be ruptured in order that the element of penetration be proven. *Green v. State,* 243 Md. 75, 79, 220 A.2d 131 (1966). See also *Craig v. State,* 214 Md. 546, 136 A.2d 243 (1957); *Kackley v. State, supra.* Neither is emission an essential element. Emission is not embraced within the definition of sexual intercourse. *Hazel v. State,* 221 Md. 464, 468-69, 157 A.2d 922, 924 (1960). Penetration may be shown by testimony from the prosecuting witness. *Robert v. State,* 220 Md. 159, 151 A.2d 737 (1959); *McEntire v. State,* 2 Md. App. 449, 235 A.2d 311 (1967).

Where the victim's claim cannot be corroborated by wounds, bruises, or disorderly clothing, the lack of consent can be shown by fear based on reasonable apprehension. *Winegan v. State,* 10 Md. App. 196, 200-01, 268 A.2d 585 (1970). Where sexual intercourse occurs without actual force and without resistance because of fear, that fear must be a reasonable fear. *Id.*

Force is an essential element of the crime and to justify conviction, the evidence must warrant a conclusion either that the victim resisted and her resistance was overcome by force or that she was prevented from resisting by threats to her safety. But no particular amount of force, either actual or constructive, is required to constitute rape. Necessarily, the fact must depend on the prevailing circumstances. As in this case, force may exist without violence. If the acts and threats of the defendant were reasonably calculated to create in the mind of the victim — having regard to the circumstances in which she was placed — a real apprehension due to fear of imminent bodily harm serious enough to impair or overcome her will to resist, then such acts are the equivalent of force. *State v. Merchant,* 10 Md. App. 545, 556-57, 271 A.2d 752 (1970).

The rule requiring the woman's apprehension to be reasonable was set out first in *Hazel v. State, supra,* and was restated in *Winegan v. State, supra.* Submission is not the same as consent, and differs from a reluctant consent. *Walter v. State,* 9 Md. App. 385, 264 A.2d 882 (1970).

In *Robinson v. State,* 67 Md. App. 445, 508 A.2d 159 (1986), the Court stated that all that is required to prove "force" or "threat of force" is that in the mind of the victim, the victim was placed in reasonable apprehension of imminent bodily injury of such a nature as to impair or overcome his or her will to resist. The proof of force or threat of force can take any form and is demonstrated by conduct. Here, use of a screwdriver in a threatening manner is force sufficient to sustain a conviction.

Consent means a voluntary agreement by a person in the possession and exercise of sufficient mentality to make an intelligent choice to do something proposed by another. "Consent" differs materially from "assent." The former implies some positive action and always involves more than mere submission. The latter means mere passivity or submission, which does not include consent. *Gregoire v. State,* 211 Md. 514, 520, 128 A.2d 243, 246 (1957).

Force is an essential element of the crime of rape. Consent to the act at any time prior to penetration deprives the subsequent intercourse of its criminal character. *State v. Merchant, supra.* Although a woman may have consented to intercourse, if that consent is withdrawn prior to the act of penetration, then it cannot be said that she has consented to the act. *Battle v. State,* 287 Md. 675, 414 A.2d 1266, 1270 (1980). The crime of rape does not require proof of specific intent to support a conviction. *Frank v. State,* 6 Md. 332, 251 A.2d 249 (1969).

Sound public policy does not require a woman to resist an unwanted sexual relationship to the extent that she runs a substantial risk of grievous bodily harm; the sounder test is whether the act was performed with or without the consent of the prosecuting witness. *Rice v. State,* 9 Md. App. 552, 560, 267 A.2d 261, 266 (1970). The Court stated that when there is evidence of a disposition to use force and the apparent ability to do so, the question of the amount of force required becomes a matter for the trier of fact.

In *State v. Allewalt,* 308 Md. 89, 517 A.2d 741 (1986), the issue was whether the State could introduce evidence in its rebuttal that the victim suffered from post-traumatic stress disorder (PTSD) to prove lack of consent in a rape case. Dr. Spodak fulfilled the necessary qualifications to testify as an expert concerning PTSD. Evidence of the disorder is relevant insofar as any information tending to support an inference of consent or lack of consent affects the ultimate determination of whether a rape occurred. Here, Dr. Spodak testified that the victim suffered from PTSD and that in his opinion, based on the history furnished to him, the cause of the disorder was the rape complained of by the victim. If relevant, the next question is whether the PTSD testimony remains inadmissible because of the prejudicial impact it has in a rape case. The Court of Appeals reinstated the conviction vacated by the Court of Special Appeals in *Allewalt v. State,* 61 Md. App. 503, 487 A.2d 664 (1985), holding that in this case the trial court did not abuse its discretion in admitting the testimony of Dr. Spodak.

(e) First and second degree rape distinguished

The crime of second degree rape as defined in Maryland Ann. Code, Art. 27, § 463(a)(1) is elevated to rape in the first degree where certain aggravating circumstances are present. Such aggravating circumstances, set forth in Art. 27, § 462(a), include: (1) the use or display of a dangerous or deadly weapon or an article which the other person reasonably concludes is a dangerous or deadly weapon in the commission of the offense; (2) the infliction of suffocation, strangulation, disfigurement, or serious physical injury upon the victim or upon anyone else in the course of committing the rape; (3) the threatening or placing the victim in fear that the victim or any person known to the victim will be imminently subjected to death, suffocation, strangulation, disfigurement, serious physical injury, or kidnapping; and (4) commission of the rape aided and abetted by one or more other persons.

If the theory of rape in the first degree is based on the defendant's actually inflicting serious physical injury upon the other person or upon anyone else in the course of committing the offense, both the conduct of the defendant and the victim's state of mind should be considered in determining whether there was "serious physical injury." A smack in the face is not considered serious. *Mayes v. State,* 50 Md. App. 628, 440 A.2d 1093 (1982).

In *Scott v. State,* 61 Md. App. 599, 487 A.2d 1204 (1985), the Court found that there was insufficient evidence in the record to support a conviction for first degree rape. The trial court's finding that a loss of virginity is a "disfigurement" was overturned.

The Court noted that "disfigurement" is generally regarded as an externally visible blemish or scar that impairs one's appearance. Loss of virginity does nothing to impair appearance. It is not outwardly visible. A different interpretation would have the effect of automatically upgrading the rape of a virgin to first degree rape. The Court also noted that there was insufficient evidence to show that the type of vaginal lacerations suffered by the victim constituted "serious physical injury" within the meaning of Art. 27, § 462(a)(2). A two to three centimeter tear in the perineal area of the vagina does not constitute a "serious physical injury."

A thin line exists with regard to the distinction between rape in the first degree as defined in Art. 27, § 462(a)(3) and rape in the second degree as defined in Art. 27, § 463(a)(1). The latter section provides that second degree rape is vaginal intercourse by force or threat of force against the will and without the consent of the victim. The former states that rape in the first degree requires vaginal intercourse by force or threat of force against the will and without the consent of the victim along with an aggravating circumstance consisting of *threatening* the victim with death, serious bodily injury or kidnapping. See *State v. Jones,* 51 Md. App. 321, 443 A.2d 967 (1982), *vacated,* 298 Md. 634, 471 A.2d 1055 (1984). See also *Walker v. State,* 53 Md. App. 171, 452 A.2d 1234 (1982). In light of the similar aspects of the threat element in both degrees of rape, it would seem that the decision of whether to charge a person with first or second degree rape is subject to broad prosecutorial discretion. The articulateness and clarity of the language of the accused used in the course of committing the offense may be an important circumstance in the grading of this offense.

For first degree rape, actual display of a weapon is not necessary to establish the reality or the credibility of a threat that a rapist has such a weapon. *Blotkamp v. State,* 45 Md. App. 64, 411 A.2d 1068 (1980). Under the circumstances in which it was made, the rapist's reference to a knife was reasonably calculated to create in the victim's mind a real apprehension of serious bodily injury and if she had that apprehension, she was indeed threatened.

To provide assistance in the interpretation of the rape statutes, Art. 27, § 464E provides that such words not defined by the statutes retain their judicially determined meaning, except to the extent changed expressly or by implication by legislation directed to rape cases. The meaning of the terms "threat of force," "force," "without consent" and "against her will" are defined in cases involving common-law rape. *State v. Rusk,* 289 Md. 230, 424 A.2d 720 (1981), *rev'g* 43 Md. App. 476, 406 A.2d 624 (1979).

In *Sydnor v. State,* 39 Md. App. 459, 387 A.2d 297 (1978), the Court held that the term "any rape" in Art. 27, § 410 (before it was amended to include "any rape in any degree") "encompassed all rapes of various degrees." *Id.* at 465, 387 A.2d at 301. The Court's holding, in effect, bridged the gap between the effective date of the 1976 rape statute, Art. 27, § 462, and the 1977 amendment of Art. 27, § 410, thus making felony murder applicable to rapes during that period.

In *State v. Rusk, supra,* the Court, in a four-to-three decision, held that no specific amount of force is necessary to sustain a conviction of rape in the second degree. The threat of force need not be made in a particular manner in order to sustain a rape conviction as long as the victim was put in reasonable fear of death or serious bodily harm. *Id.* at 246, 424 A.2d at 728. The reasonableness of the victim's fear is a question of fact to be determined by the jury. *Id.* at 245, 424 A.2d at 727. In determining whether the fear of the victim was reasonable, weight may be given to such factors as the mental condition or the age of the victim. *Rusk v. State,* 43 Md. App. 476, 406 A.2d 624 (1979), *rev'd,* 289 Md. 230, 424 A.2d 720 (1981).

In *Blotkamp v. State, supra,* the Court affirmed convictions of first and second degree rape and approved the trial court's jury instructions. As to the definition of force, the trial judge stated: "... fear may exist without violence. If the acts and threats of the Defendant were reasonably calculated to create through fear a real apprehension of imminent bodily harm, serious enough to impair or overcome her will to resist, then such acts and threats are the equivalent of force." *Id.* at 71-72, 411 A.2d 1072. As to the standard for resistance, the trial judge stated:

> You are instructed that force is an essential element of the crime of rape, and to justify a conviction the evidence must

> convince you beyond a reasonable doubt and to a moral certainty that the prosecutrix resisted and that her resistance was overcome either by force or by her being prevented from resisting from threats to her safety. Such threats to safety, if any you should find must have been such as to have been reasonably calculated to create in her mind, having regard to the circumstances in which she was placed, a real apprehension, due to fear of imminent bodily harm, serious enough to impair or overcome her will to resist.

Id. at 72, 411 A.2d at 1072-73.

(f) Second degree rape: statutory rape

Under the revised sexual offense law, statutory rape is rape in the second degree. Maryland Ann. Code, Art. 27, § 463(a)(3). The offense is committed when the accused, who is four or more years older than the victim, engages in vaginal intercourse with the victim when the victim is less than fourteen years of age. The consent of the victim to the sexual activity is irrelevant. See *State v. DeLawder,* 28 Md. App. 212, 344 A.2d 446 (1975); *Rau v. State,* 133 Md. 613, 105 A. 867 (1919). In addition, ignorance or mistake as to the age of the complaining witness is not a defense to the charge. *Eggleston v. State,* 4 Md. App. 124, 241 A.2d 433 (1968).

The proper interpretation of the age requirements in Art. 27, §§ 463(a)(3), 464A(a)(3) and 464B(a)(3) was discussed in a letter dated March 11, 1976 from Maryland Assistant Attorney General George A. Nielson to Senator Steny H. Hoyer. Nielson concludes that, in the opinion of his office, the statute requires that the accused be four *full* years older than the victim. Thus, for example, it is not sufficient that the accused was seventeen years old while the victim was thirteen, if the accused is only three and a half years older than the victim.

In cases such as these, children are often called upon to testify. The capacity of children to testify is ordinarily a matter which is within the discretion of the trial court. However, the weight and credibility which is to be accorded their testimony is a question for the jury. *Robert v. State,* 220 Md. 159, 151 A.2d 737 (1959); *Saldiveri v. State,* 217 Md. 412, 143 A.2d 70 (1958). See Instruction, § 2.04, Child witness, *supra.*

In *Robert v. State, supra* at 163, 151 A.2d at 738, the testimony of a twelve-year-old girl that she knew what sexual intercourse was, that she knew what caused people to become pregnant, that the defendant (stepfather) had had sexual intercourse with her on several occasions at the motel of which he was the manager, and that both the defendant and the child witness' mother lived at that motel was held sufficient, if believed, to sustain the charge of statutory rape. In *Robert* there was medical testimony which showed the girl was pregnant, but there was no such evidence showing that it was due to the defendant's action. See also *Smith v. State,* 224 Md. 509, 168 A.2d 356 (1961).

(g) Second degree rape: mentally defective, mentally incapacitated or physically helpless victim

Second degree rape exists where the accused engages in vaginal intercourse with a person who is "mentally defective," "mentally incapacitated" or "physically helpless" when the accused knows or reasonably should know of the victim's mental or physical incapacity. Maryland Ann. Code, Art. 27, § 463(a)(2). "Mentally defective" means a victim who suffers from mental retardation or a mental disorder which temporarily or permanently renders the victim substantially incapable of appraising the nature of his or her conduct, or resisting the act of vaginal intercourse, a sexual act, or sexual contact, or of a communicating unwillingness to submit to the act of vaginal intercourse, a sexual act, or sexual contact. Art. 27, § 461(b). "Mentally incapacitated" means a victim who, due to the influence of a drug, narcotic or intoxicating substance, or due to any act committed upon the victim without the victim's consent or awareness, is rendered substantially incapable of either appraising the nature of his or her conduct, or resisting the act of vaginal intercourse, a sexual act, or sexual contact. Art. 27, § 461(c). "Physically helpless" means: (1) a victim who is unconscious; or (2) a victim who does not consent to an act of vaginal intercourse, a sexual act, or sexual contact, and is physically unable to resist an act of vaginal intercourse, a sexual act, or sexual contact, or communicate unwillingness to submit to an act of vaginal intercourse, a sexual act, or sexual contact. Art. 27, § 461(d).

In *Cranford v. State,* 36 Md. App. 393, 373 A.2d 984 (1977), *cert. denied* (after having been "improvidently" granted), 282 Md. 255, 383 A.2d 687 (1978), the court stated:

> It is well settled that unlawful sexual intercourse with a female person without her consent constitutes the common law felony of rape. It is also well settled that unlawful sexual intercourse with a woman who is incapable of giving or withholding consent is rape. *See* [R.] Perkins, *Criminal Law,* ch. 2, § 5 at 163 (2d ed. 1969).

Id. at 400, 373 A.2d 988. The Court in *Cranford* found that the appellant, by engaging in sexual intercourse with a woman while she was in a drunken stupor, had committed the offense of rape.

In R. Gilbert & C. Moylan, Jr., *Maryland Criminal Law: Practice and Procedure* § 5.4, at 71 (1983), the authors state: "It is difficult to conceive of the male's being unaware of the physical helplessness of the female. The same is not true, however, of mental defectiveness or incapacity which may not manifest itself to the male at the time the duo engage in sexual intercourse. Whether the male knew or reasonably should have known of the mental disability of his companion is a matter of proof for the prosecution to present and the trier of fact to weigh."

(h) Rape victim's testimony need not be corroborated

The testimony of a victim of rape need not be corroborated. Her testimony, standing alone, will constitute legally sufficient evidence to support a conviction. *Williams v. State,* 11 Md. App. 350, 274 A.2d 403 (1971). A complaint by a rape victim may be admitted as original evidence primarily to support the testimony of the victim as to the time, place, crime and name of the wrongdoer. See *Guardino v. State,* 50 Md. App. 695, 440 A.2d 1101 (1982).

In *Cantrell v. State,* 50 Md. App. 331, 437 A.2d 696 (1982), hearsay testimony by the victim's mother concerning the victim's complaint of rape made several hours after the incident was held to be admissible evidence. The Court's holding was based on *Smith v. State,* 6 Md. App. 581, 252 A.2d 277 (1968) and *Green v. State,* 161 Md. 75, 155 A. 164 (1931). *Smith v. State, supra,* held that a victim's complaint can be part of the "res gestae," and is therefore admissible as an exception to the hearsay rule. In *Green v. State, supra,* the Court of Appeals held that the evidence of the victim's complaint made within "a reasonable time under the circumstances" is original evidence, and if the victim's testimony concerning the commission of the crime can be impeached by witnesses or by cross-examination, the complaint is admissible, preferably in rebuttal, as corroborative evidence.

(i) The "Lord Hale" instruction

Effective July 1, 1987, the use of the "Lord Hale" instruction is prohibited. This jury instruction, which was previously discretionary with the judge, informs the jury that because of the nature of the charge, the testimony of the prosecuting witness should be examined with caution and that the charge is easily made and difficult to disprove.

Article 27, § 461B provides:

> In any criminal prosecution for rape, attempted rape, assault with intent to commit a rape, assault with intent to commit a sexual offense, or any other sexual offense, the jury may not be instructed: (1) To examine with caution the testimony of the prosecuting witness, solely because of the nature of the charge; (2) That the charge is easily made or difficult to disprove, solely because of the nature of the charge; or (3) As to any other similar instruction, solely because of the nature of the charge.

The "Lord Hale" instruction has been severely criticized and disapproved as improper material for jury instructions in other jurisdictions as well. Both courts and legislatures, such as in Maryland, have been persuaded by the argument that such an instruction constitutes an improper comment upon the evidence because it suggests that the victim's testimony is more likely to be false and because it arbitrarily applies a stricter test of credibility to the rape or sexual offense victim than to other witnesses. For earlier Maryland cases that had raised concern about the instruction, see *Rhoades v. State,* 56 Md. App. 601, 468 A.2d 650 (1983) and *Brooks v. State,* 53 Md. App. 285, 452 A.2d 1285 (1982).

(j) Defense that victim is spouse of accused

The revised Maryland sexual offense laws codify the common-law rule that a man cannot be convicted of rape of his wife. If the accused and victim were legally married at the time of the alleged crime, Maryland Ann. Code, Art. 27, § 464D states that the accused may not be prosecuted under Art. 27, § 462 (rape in the first degree), § 463 (rape in the second degree), § 464B (sexual offense in the third degree) and § 464C (sexual offense in the fourth degree). However, this does not mean that an attack by one spouse on another is totally excused. A spouse may still be prosecuted for assault and battery and, perhaps, for other crimes depending on the circumstances of the attack. Also, a husband may be convicted of being an accessory to the crime of rape if he aids or assists another in the rape of his wife.

Prosecutions under the above sections are not barred if the offense was committed while the husband and the wife were living separate and apart pursuant to a *valid decree* of divorce *a mensa et thoro* (bed and board divorce). Art. 27, § 464D. A husband may still assert a spousal immunity defense in situations where there is no decree of divorce such as if one spouse has deserted the other or where the husband and wife are living apart as a result of a "separation agreement" whether written or oral.

The spousal immunity defense does not apply to prosecutions for sexual offenses in the first and second degrees under Art. 27, §§ 464 and 464A which prohibit certain "sexual acts." This result is consistent with Art. 27, §§ 553 and 554 which proscribe consensual acts of "sodomy" and other "unnatural and perverted sexual practices."

As a result of *Briscoe v. State,* 40 Md. App. 120, 388 A.2d 153 (1978), it is assumed in these instructions that the State needs to prove that the victim was not the legal spouse of the accused only *after* some evidence has been generated to the contrary. In *Briscoe,* the Court of Special Appeals discussed this issue as follows: "The question of the nonspousal character of the offense is not an element of the crime, but is an affirmative defense which was never raised below. As the issue was never properly generated by the evidence, the State did not have the burden of negating it." *Briscoe v. State, supra* at 132, 388 A.2d at 160 (1978), *citing State v. Evans,* 278 Md. 197, 362 A.2d 629 (1976). *Briscoe,* however, was decided under the earlier rape statute and, therefore, is not definitive as to the proper interpretation of § 464D.

(k) The rape and sexual offense shield law: admissibility of evidence of victim's prior sexual conduct

Rape and sexual offense legislation enacted in 1976 establishes a significant evidentiary rule relating to the admissibility of the sexual offense victim's prior sexual history. In the case of a rape or sexual offense in the first or second degree, Maryland Ann. Code, Art. 27, § 461A, bars the use of evidence relating to the victim's chastity when such evidence is offered in the form of opinion or reputation testimony. Evidence relating to a victim's reputation for chastity and opinion evidence relating to a victim's chastity is limited to heterosexual contact. Testimony of victim's uncle relating to the victim's reputation for homosexuality would not be inadmissible under the section. *Lucado v. State,* 40 Md. App. 25, 389 A.2d 398 (1978).

Also, under the statute, evidence of specific instances of the rape victim's prior sexual conduct is limited to: (1) proof of the victim's past sexual conduct with the defendant; (2) proof of specific instances of sexual activity showing the source or origin of semen, pregnancy, disease or trauma; (3) proof which supports a claim that the victim had an ulterior motive in accusing the defendant of a crime; or (4) evidence offered for the purpose of impeachment when the prosecutor puts the victim's prior sexual conduct into issue. Evidence which fits into one of the enumerated exceptions is admissible, however, only if the court finds, after an *in camera* hearing, that the evidence is relevant and material to a fact in issue and that its probative value outweighs its prejudicial or inflammatory nature.

See *Joyce v. State,* 59 Md. App. 237, 474 A.2d 1369 (1984), where the Court held that the trial court did not abuse its discretion in refusing to hear the testimony of two witnesses who defense counsel said would testify that they observed and participated in consensual multiple partner sex with the victim and the defendant prior to the alleged rape. The Court observed that the proffered testimony's negligible measure of probative value was outweighed by its prejudicially subjecting the victim to public denigration.

Article 27, § 461A codifies an existing rule of evidence insofar as it excludes evidence of specific instances of a victim's prior sexual conduct. See *England v. State,* 21 Md. App. 412, 320 A.2d 66 (1974), *aff'd,* 274 Md. 264, 334 A.2d 98 (1975); *Giles v. State,* 229 Md. 370, 183 A.2d 359 (1962), *appeal dismissed,* 372 U.S. 767 (1963); *Humphreys v. State,* 227 Md. 115, 175 A.2d 777 (1961); *Cantrell v. State,* 50 Md. App. 331, 437 A.2d 696 (1981). It changes the former rule of evidence in Maryland, however, with respect to reputation and opinion evidence of the rape victim's chastity. See *Caldwell v. State,* 276 Md. 612, 349 A.2d 623 (1976); *State v. Merchant,* 10 Md. App. 545, 271 A.2d 752 (1970); *Alexander v. State,* 4 Md. App. 214, 242 A.2d 180 (1968).

Where the defense seeks to offer into evidence specific instances of the victim's prior sexual conduct, the defendant has the responsibility of raising the defense, either by written pretrial motion or by way of proffer at the time of trial. The trial court is not required *sua sponte* to hold an *in camera* hearing in order to determine whether such evidence is admissible. *Cantrell v. State, supra.* See *Souffie v. State,* 50 Md. App. 547, 439 A.2d 1127 (1982).

In *Testerman v. State,* 61 Md. App. 257, 486 A.2d 233 (1985), the victim's consent was at issue. The defense sought to admit evidence of the victim's alleged prior sexual encounters with the defendant. The Court noted that the sensitive question of the relevancy of the victim's past sexual conduct with the defendant must be decided on an *ad hoc* basis. Where, as here, the defendant contends that he and the victim engaged in a series of amicable and amorous encounters over a period of years, the evidence is relevant. Once it is decided that the evidence is relevant and material to a fact in issue, the test for admissibility under the rape "shield statute" is whether its probative value is outweighed by its inflammatory prejudicial nature. The trial court on remand must exercise its discretion to weigh its inflammatory or prejudicial nature against its probative value.

The statutory limits imposed upon cross-examination by defense counsel may invite a constitutional challenge on the grounds that the effect of the provision is violative of the defendant's sixth and fourteenth amendment rights under the confrontation and due process clauses. In *Greene v. McElroy,* 360 U.S. 474, 79 S. Ct. 1400, 3 L. Ed. 2d 1377 (1969), the Supreme Court of the United States held that the exposure of a witness' motivation in testifying is a proper and important function of the constitutionally protected right of cross-examination. In *Davis v. Alaska,* 415 U.S. 308, 94 S. Ct. 1105, 39 L. Ed. 2d 347 (1974), the Court indicated that a denial of effective cross-examination "would be constitutional error of the first magnitude and no amount of showing of want of prejudice could cure it." *Id.* at 318, 94 S. Ct. at 1111, 39 L. Ed. 2d at 355. In *Davis,* the Court held that the right of confrontation is paramount to the State's interest of protecting the privacy of a juvenile offender's criminal record. In *State v. DeLawder,* 28 Md. App. 212, 344 A.2d 446 (1975), the Maryland Court of Special Appeals discussed the effect of the *Davis* decision on the defendant's right to cross-examine the complaining witness in a rape case. An essential component of the defense in *DeLawder* was the alleged improper motive of the prosecutrix, who was under fourteen years of age, in accusing the appellant of raping her. Specifically, the appellant asserted that the prosecutrix had accused him of rape only because she believed she was pregnant by another person and was afraid to tell her mother that she had voluntarily engaged in sexual intercourse. The trial court, on the theory that consent is not a defense to statutory rape, excluded the evidence concerning the prosecutrix's prior sexual relations. The Court of Special Appeals reversed, holding that the prior sexual activity of prosecutrix was admissible to the extent it tended to prove that the prosecuting witness might have had an ulterior motive in bringing charges against the accused. The Court reasoned that "the desirability that the prosecutrix fulfill her public duty to testify free from embarrassment and with her reputation unblemished must fall before the right of an accused to seek out the truth in the process of defending himself." *Id.* at 228, 344 A.2d at 455.

In *Deinhardt v. State,* 29 Md. App. 391, 348 A.2d 286 (1976), the Maryland Court of Special Appeals again held that the trial court had erred in denying defense counsel an opportunity to cross-examine the prosecutrix concerning her alleged ulterior motive in bringing the rape charge. Unlike *DeLawder,* the evidence at issue had no relationship to the prosecuting witness' prior sexual activities. The court reversed and remanded for a new trial, stating that at the retrial the appellant should be afforded an opportunity to show bias, prejudice, or ulterior motive, if any, on the part of the principal prosecuting witness.

In compliance with the ruling, Art. 27, § 461A(a)(3) provides that evidence of specific instances of the victim's prior sexual conduct may be admitted if it supports a claim that the victim has an ulterior motive in accusing the defendant of the crime. Of course, the admissibility of that evidence is still contingent on whether the probative value of the evidence outweighs its potential for prejudice.

In *Thomas v. State,* 301 Md. 294, 483 A.2d 6 (1984), the defendant argued that the shield law, as applied to the facts in his case, violated his sixth amendment right to confront and cross-examine the witnesses against him. As part of its case-in-chief, the State called a medical doctor to testify about his examination of the victim after the assault. The medical history which was recorded in a report in the examination included information about the victim's prior sexual history. Before the doctor's testimony the State filed a motion *in limine* to preclude inquiry into whether the victim was a virgin and whether she used a birth control device. The defendant argued that the medical history was relevant to his contention that the victim consented to intercourse with him and that she "liked sex with black men." While the Court noted that rape shield laws may not be used to exclude probative evidence in violation of a defendant's constitutional rights to confrontation and due process, citing *Bell v. Harrison,* 670 F.2d 656 (6th Cir. 1982), it stated that a defendant has no constitutional right to present irrelevant evidence at trial. The Court held that evidence concerning the victim's virginity or use of a birth control device does not tend to prove or disprove that she liked sex with black men and consented to intercourse with the defendant. The Court also stated that even if there were some slight relevance, where the probative value of the evidence is outweighed by the State's interest in protecting the rape victim from harassment and humiliation at trial, its exclusion does not violate the defendant's right of confrontation, his right to present an effective defense or his right to due process of law.

(l) Charging document and bill of particulars

In any indictment, information, or warrant charging rape or a sexual offense, the statute provides that it shall be sufficient to use a form substantially to the following effect:

> That A-B on the __________ day of __________, 19__________, in the County (City) aforesaid did unlawfully commit a rape or sexual offense upon C-D, in violation of Article 27, Section (here state section violated), of the Annotated Code of Maryland; contrary to the form of the act of Assembly in such case made and provided and against the peace, government and dignity of the State.

Maryland Ann. Code, Art. 27, § 461C(a).

The statute also provides that the defendant is entitled "to a bill of particulars specifically setting forth the allegations against him." Art. 27, § 461C(b). In order to know exactly which part of the statute the defendant is alleged to have violated, defense counsel may need to file a motion for a bill of particulars.

In *Cardovi v. State,* 63 Md. App. 455, 492 A.2d 1328 (1985), the Court held that an indictment which did not specify which of the three methods in the statute were used to commit the crime was not jurisdictionally flawed, since the common parlance definition for rape is "unlawful sexual intercourse with a female without her consent," which was the very type of rape for which defendant was tried and of which he was convicted.

(m) Venue

Maryland Ann. Code, Art. 27, § 465, provides that if a person is transported by any means with the intent to violate the sexual offense statutes, Art. 27, §§ 461 to 464D, the defendant may be tried in the jurisdiction where the transportation was offered, solicited, begun, continued or ended. See *State v. Jones,* 51 Md. App. 321, 443 A.2d 967 (1982), *vacated,* 298 Md. 634, 471 A.2d 1055 (1984).

In *Lett v. State,* 51 Md. App. 668, 445 A.2d 1050 (1982), the Court held that venue was properly conferred on the county from which the victim was transported where the evidence disclosed that the defendant had the intent to commit rape when he conveyed the victim into one county from another county.

In *Copsey v. State,* 67 Md. App. 223, 507 A.2d 186 (1986), defendant was charged with a single continuing sexual offense against a minor from January 1, 1979 to November 1, 1984 so that the defendant was placed in jeopardy for any sexual offense he perpetrated upon the victim at any time during that period. The pattern was for the defendant to meet the victim in St. Mary's County, leave the county and engage in sexual behavior in Charles County, and then to return to St. Mary's County. While the defendant could have been properly charged, tried and convicted in either county, St. Mary's County moved first. Jeopardy attached to the defendant in St. Mary's County. Charles County then charged the defendant with offenses on November 26, 1980, June through August, 1983, and October 5, 1984. Since the defendant stood in jeopardy in St. Mary's County for these offenses, the motion to dismiss to prevent double jeopardy should have been granted.

§ 4.37. Sexual offenses in the first, second, third and fourth degree.

(a) Sexual offense — First degree

A sexual act is sexual activity other than vaginal intercourse which is carried out against the will and without the consent of the victim, and which is accompanied by force or threat of force. Such sexual activity constitutes the crime of sexual offense. [In Maryland, there are two grades of sexual acts for you to consider: sexual offense in the first degree and sexual offense in the second degree. The distinction between a first degree sexual offense and a second degree sexual offense is the presence of aggravating circumstances which occur in the commission of the offense.]

The defendant in this case is charged with the commission of a first degree sexual offense. The unlawful sexual act which is alleged to have been committed is ___________ ([fellatio] [cunnilingus] [anal intercourse] [analingus] [penetration of an object into the victim's anal/genital opening]). The aggravating circumstance which the State alleges was present in the commission of this offense is that the defendant ___________ (*insert applicable aggravating circumstance(s)*):

[(1) employed or displayed a dangerous or deadly weapon, or an article which the victim reasonably concluded was a dangerous or deadly weapon];

[(2) inflicted [suffocation] [strangulation] [disfigurement] or [serious physical injury] upon ___________ [the victim] [someone other than the victim]];

[(3) threatened or placed the victim in fear that ___________ [the victim] [someone known to the victim] would be imminently subjected to [death] [physical injury] [suffocation] [strangulation] [disfigurement] or [kidnapping]];

[(4) committed the offense aided and abetted by one or more other persons].

In order for the defendant to be found guilty of a first degree sexual offense, the State must prove beyond a reasonable doubt that (1) the defendant engaged in ___________ ([anal intercourse] [fellatio] [cunnilingus] [analingus] [the insertion of an object into the anal/genital opening of the victim for the purposes of sexual arousal, gratification, or abuse of either party]); (2) the act was committed without the consent and against the will of the victim; (3) the act was committed by force or threat of force; and (4) the defendant ___________ (*insert applicable aggravating circumstances from above*).

To be given in cases of cunnilingus, fellatio, analingus:

[Cunnilingus is defined as the placing of the mouth upon the female sexual organ or vagina.]

[Fellatio is defined as the placing of the mouth upon the male sexual organ or penis.]

[Analingus is defined as the placing of the mouth upon the anal opening of the victim.]

[Emission of semen is not required to be proven to establish ________ [fellatio] [analingus].]

[*To be given in cases of anal intercourse:* Anal intercourse is defined as the actual contact of the male sexual organ or penis and the victim's anal opening and an actual penetration into the body of the latter. Penetration is an essential element of the crime of anal intercourse. There must be some penetration, however slight, of the victim's anus by the defendant's sexual organ or penis, to constitute the crime of anal intercourse. Emission of semen is not an essential element required.]

[*To be given in cases of insertion of "other objects":* The insertion of any object into the genital or anal opening of the victim is unlawful if such insertion can reasonably be construed as being for the purposes of sexual gratification or arousal, or for abuse of either party and not for an accepted medical purpose. Penetration, however slight, of the victim's genital or anal opening is required to constitute an unlawful insertion.] [If the alleged insertion was for an accepted medical purpose, then such insertion does not constitute a criminal act. An accepted medical purpose would be one which is conducted so as to diagnose or treat a person in need of diagnosis or treatment.]

Force is an essential element of the crime and, to justify a conviction, the evidence must warrant a conclusion either that the victim resisted and the victim's resistance was overcome by force or that the victim was prevented from resisting by force or by threats to [her] [his] safety. No particular amount of force, either actual or constructive, is required to constitute a sexual offense. That fact must depend upon the totality of the circumstances. Force may exist without violence. If the acts and threats of the perpetrator were reasonably calculated to create a real and reasonable fear of imminent bodily harm in the victim's mind, and that fear is serious enough to impair or overcome the victim's will to resist, then such acts and threats are the equivalent of force. The fear created must be evaluated in light of the circumstances in which the victim was placed. A person is not expected to resist at the expense of life or at the risk of serious bodily injury.

Consent to the act at any time prior to the initiation of the "sexual act," however reluctantly given, deprives the subsequent sexual act of its criminal character. Consent means a voluntary agreement by a person in the possession and exercise of sufficient mentality to make an intelligent choice to do something proposed by another. Consent differs materially from assent. Consent implies some positive action and always involves more than mere submission. Assent means mere passivity or submission, which does not include consent. Submission to a compelling force, or, as a result of being put in fear, is not consent. A person who was conscious and possessed of natural mental and physical powers when the attack took place must have resisted to the extent of [her] [his] ability at the time, unless it appears that [she] [he] was overcome by numbers or was so terrified by threats as to overpower [her] [his] will to resist. Resistance is necessarily relative: its presence or absence depends on the facts and circumstances in each case. The real test is whether sexual act was committed without the consent and against the will of the victim. The kind of fear in the mind of the victim which would reasonably make resistance unnecessary to support a conviction of a sexual offense in the first degree includes, but is not necessarily limited to, a fear of death or serious bodily harm, or a fear so extreme so as to preclude resistance, or a fear which might make the person incapable of continuing to resist.

[If after a full and fair consideration of all the facts and circumstances in evidence, you are not convinced beyond a reasonable doubt that the defendant engaged in __________ ([cunnilingus] [fellatio] [anal intercourse] [analingus] [the unlawful insertion of an object into the victim's genital/anal opening for the purpose of sexual arousal, gratification, or abuse of either person]) against the will and without the consent of the victim, and that such act was accompanied by force or threat of force, and in addition that the defendant __________ (*insert applicable aggravating circumstance*) in the course of committing this offense, then you must find the defendant not guilty of first degree sexual offense. On the other hand, if you find from your consideration of all of the evidence that the state has proved each of the elements of the offense beyond a reasonable doubt, then you should find the defendant guilty of first degree sexual offense.]

[*To be given where second degree sexual offense is a lesser included offense:* If you find that the defendant is not guilty of a first degree sexual offense, you must then proceed to consider whether the defendant is guilty of a second degree sexual offense. I will now instruct you on the elements of second degree sexual offense.]

(b) Sexual offense — Second degree

The defendant in this case is charged with the commission of a second degree sexual offense. A sexual act is sexual activity other than vaginal intercourse which is carried out against the will and without the consent of the victim and which is accompanied by force or threat of force. Such sexual activity constitutes the crime of sexual offense. The unlawful sexual act which is alleged to have been committed by the defendant in this case is __________ ([cunnilingus] [fellatio] [anal intercourse] [analingus] [the insertion of an object into the victim's anal/genital opening]).

In order for the defendant to be found guilty of a second degree sexual offense, the State must prove beyond a reasonable doubt that (1) the defendant engaged in __________ ([cunnilingus] [fellatio] [anal intercourse] [analingus] [the insertion of an object into the anal/genital opening of the victim for the purpose of sexual arousal, gratification, or abuse of either party]); (2) the act was committed without the consent and against the will of the victim and (3) the act was committed by force or threat of force.

To be given in cases of cunnilingus, fellatio, analingus:

[Cunnilingus is defined as the placing of the mouth upon the female sexual organ or vagina.]

[Fellatio is defined as the placing of the mouth upon the male sexual organ or penis.]

[Analingus is defined as the placing of the mouth upon the anal opening of the victim.]

[Emission of semen is not required to be proven to establish __________ [fellatio] [analingus].]

[*To be given in cases of anal intercourse:* Anal intercourse is defined as the actual contact of the male sexual organ or penis and the victim's anal opening and an actual penetration into the body of the latter. Penetration is an essential element of the crime of anal intercourse. There must be some penetration, however slight, of the victim's anus by the defendant's sexual organ or penis to constitute the crime of anal intercourse. Emission of semen is not required.]

[*To be given in cases of insertion of "other objects":* The insertion of any object into the genital or anal opening of the victim is unlawful if such insertion can reasonably be construed as being for the purposes of sexual gratification or arousal, or for abuse of either person and not for an accepted medical purpose. Penetration, however slight, of the victim's genital or anal opening is required to constitute an unlawful insertion.] [If the alleged insertion was for an accepted medical purpose, then such insertion does not constitute a criminal act. An accepted medical purpose would be one which is conducted so as to diagnose or treat a person in need of such diagnosis or treatment.]

Force is an essential element of the crime and, to justify a conviction, the evidence must warrant a conclusion either that the victim resisted and the victim's resistance was overcome by force, or that the victim was prevented from resisting by force or by threats to [her] [his] safety. No particular amount of force, either actual or constructive, is required to constitute a sexual offense. That fact must depend upon the totality of the circumstances. Force may exist without violence. If the acts and threats of the perpetrator were reasonably calculated to create a real and reasonable fear of imminent bodily harm in the victim's mind, and that fear is serious enough to impair or overcome the victim's will to resist, then such acts and threats are the equivalent of force. The fear created must be evaluated in light of the circumstances in which the victim was placed. A person is not expected to resist at the expense of life or at the risk of serious bodily injury.

Consent to the act at any time prior to the initiation of the "sexual act," however reluctantly given, deprives the subsequent sexual act of its criminal character. Consent means a voluntary agreement by a person in the possession and exercise of sufficient mentality to make an intelligent choice to do something proposed by another. Consent differs materially from assent. Consent implies some positive action and always involves more than mere submission. Assent means mere passivity or submission, which does not include consent. Submission to a compelling force, or as a result of being put in fear, is not consent. A person who was conscious and possessed of natural mental and physical powers when the attack took place must have resisted to the extent of [her] [his] ability at the time, unless it appears that [she] [he] was overcome by numbers or was so terrified by threats as to overpower the will to resist. Resistance is necessarily relative; its presence or absence depends on the facts and circumstances in each case. The real test is whether the assault was committed without the consent and against the will of the victim. The kind of fear in the mind of the victim which would reasonably make resistance unnecessary to support a conviction of a sexual offense in the second degree includes, but is not necessarily limited to, a fear of death or serious bodily harm, or a fear so extreme as to preclude resistance, or a fear which might make the person incapable of continuing to resist.

[If after a full and fair consideration of all the facts and circumstances in evidence, you are not convinced beyond a reasonable doubt that the defendant engaged in __________ ([cunnilingus] [fellatio] [anal intercourse] [analingus] [the unlawful insertion of an object into the victim's genital/anal opening for the purpose of sexual arousal, gratification, or abuse of either person]) against the will and without the consent of the victim, and that such act was accompanied by force or threat of force, then you must find the defendant not guilty of a sexual offense in the second degree. On the other hand, if you find from your consideration of all of the evidence that the State has proved each of the elements of the offense beyond a reasonable doubt, then you should find the defendant guilty of a sexual offense in the second degree.]

(c) Sexual offense — Second degree: victim under fourteen years and person performing act four or more years older than victim

It is unlawful for a person to engage in __________ ([cunnilingus] [fellatio] [analingus] [anal intercourse]) with another person [or] [to insert any object into the vaginal or anal opening of another person for the purposes of sexual gratification, arousal, or for abuse of either person] who is under fourteen years of age if the person performing the act is at least four years older than the victim. In Maryland, this offense is considered to be a sexual offense in the second degree.

In order for a person to be found guilty of this offense, the State must prove beyond a reasonable doubt that the defendant: (1) engaged in ________ ([cunnilingus] [fellatio] [analingus] [anal intercourse]) with the victim [or] [inserted any object into the victim's anal or vaginal opening and that the insertion can reasonably be construed as being for the purposes of sexual arousal or gratification, or for abuse of either person and not for an accepted medical purpose]; (2) the victim was less than fourteen years of age at the time of the offense; and (3) the defendant was at least four years older than the victim.

[*To be given in cases of cunnilingus, fellatio, analingus:*

[Cunnilingus is defined as the placing of the mouth upon the female sexual organ or vagina.]

[Fellatio is defined as the placing of the mouth upon the male sexual organ or penis.]

[Analingus is defined as the placing of the mouth upon the anal opening of the victim.]

[Emission of semen is not required to be proven to establish [fellatio] [analingus].]]

[*To be given in cases of anal intercourse:* Anal intercourse is defined as the actual contact of the male sexual organ or penis and the victim's anal opening and an actual penetration into the body of the latter. Penetration is an essential element of the crime of anal intercourse. There must be some penetration, however slight, of the victim's anus by the defendant's sexual organ or penis, to constitute the crime of anal intercourse. Emission of semen is not required.]

[*To be given in cases of insertion of "other objects":* The insertion of any object into the genital or anal opening of the victim is unlawful if such insertion can reasonably be construed as being for the purposes of sexual gratification or arousal, or for abuse of either party and not for an accepted medical purpose. Penetration, however slight, of the victim's genital or anal opening is required to constitute an unlawful insertion.] [If the alleged insertion was for an accepted medical purpose, then such insertion does not constitute a criminal act. An accepted medical purpose would be which is conducted so as to diagnose or treat a person in need of such diagnosis or treatment.]

The fact that the defendant did not know that the victim was under fourteen years of age is not a defense to the charge of sexual offense in the second degree. Such is the case even if you find that the defendant reasonably believed the victim to be fourteen years of age or older.

Finally, the basis of the charge of sexual offense in the second degree is that the victim was under fourteen years of age at the time of the offense while the defendant was at least four years older than the victim. Thus, whether the victim consented to engage in the "sexual act" is immaterial. Consent is not a defense to this offense.

[If after a full and fair consideration of all the facts and circumstances in evidence, you are not convinced beyond a reasonable doubt that the defendant engaged in __________ ([cunnilingus] [fellatio] [anal intercourse] [analingus] [the unlawful insertion of an object into the victim's genital/anal opening for the purpose of sexual arousal, gratification, or abuse of either person]) and this act was done with the victim who was under fourteen years of age at the time of the offense while the defendant was at least four years older than the victim, then you must find the defendant not guilty of second degree sexual offense. On the other hand, if you find from your consideration of all of the evidence that the State has proved each of the elements of the offense beyond a reasonable doubt, then you should find the defendant guilty of second degree sexual offense.]

(d) Sexual offense — Second degree: mentally defective, mentally incapacitated or physically helpless person

It is a sexual offense in the second degree for a person to engage in ______ ([cunnilingus] [fellatio] [analingus] [anal intercourse]) with another person [or] [to insert any object into the vaginal or anal opening of another person for the purpose of sexual gratification or arousal or for abuse of either person] who the defendant knows or reasonably should know is ______ ([mentally defective] [mentally incapacitated] [physically helpless]).

In order for the defendant to be found guilty of this offense, the State must prove beyond a reasonable doubt that the defendant: (1) engaged in ______ ([cunnilingus] [fellatio] [analingus] [anal intercourse]) with the victim [or] [inserted any object into the victim's vaginal or anal opening and that the insertion can reasonably be construed as being for the purposes of sexual arousal or gratification, or abuse of either person and not for an accepted medical purpose]; (2) the victim was ______ ([mentally defective] [mentally incapacitated] [physically helpless]); and (3) the defendant knew or reasonably should have known that the victim was ______ ([mentally defective] [mentally incapacitated] [physically helpless]).

To be given in cases of cunnilingus, fellatio, analingus:

[Cunnilingus is defined as the placing of the mouth upon the female sexual organ or vagina.]

[Fellatio is defined as the placing of the mouth upon the male sexual organ or penis.]

[Analingus is defined as the placing of the mouth upon the anal opening of the victim.]

[Emission of semen is not required to be proven to establish ______ [fellatio] [analingus].]

[*To be given in cases of anal intercourse:* Anal intercourse is defined as the actual contact of the male sexual organ and the victim's anal opening and an actual penetration into the body of the latter. Penetration is an essential element of the crime of anal intercourse. There must be some penetration, however slight, of the victim's anus by the defendant's sexual organ or penis, to constitute the crime of anal intercourse. Emission of semen is not required.]

[*To be given in cases of insertion of "other objects":* The insertion of any object into the genital or anal opening of the victim is unlawful if such insertion can reasonably be construed as being for the purposes of sexual gratification or arousal, or for abuse of either party and not for an accepted medical purpose. Penetration, however slight, of the victim's genital or anal opening is required to constitute an unlawful insertion.] [If the alleged insertion was for an accepted medical purpose, then such insertion does not constitute a criminal act. An accepted medical purpose would be one which is conducted so as to diagnose or treat a person in need of such diagnosis or treatment.]

[A person who is "mentally defective" suffers from either mental retardation or a mental disorder. The condition must be such that, at the time of the offense, it rendered the victim substantially incapable of appraising the nature of his or her conduct, or of resisting the sexual act or of communicating unwillingness to submit to the sexual act.]

[A person who is "mentally incapacitated" is one who, due to the influence of a drug, narcotic or intoxicating substance, or due to any act committed upon the victim without the victim's consent or awareness, is rendered substantially incapable of either appraising the nature of his or her conduct, or resisting the sexual act.]

[A person who is "physically helpless" is one who either: (1) is unconscious; (2) does not consent to the sexual act and is physically unable to resist the sexual act; or (3) is physically unable to communicate unwillingness to submit to the sexual act.]

To find the defendant guilty of second degree sexual offense you must find beyond a reasonable doubt that the defendant knew or reasonably should have known that the victim was ________ ([mentally defective] [mentally incapacitated] [physically helpless]). An act is done knowingly if done voluntarily and purposely, and not because of mistake, accident, inadvertence, or other innocent reason. In addition, the defendant reasonably should have known that the victim was ________ ([mentally defective] [mentally incapacitated] [physically helpless]) if an ordinarily prudent and cautious person in full possession of [his] [her] faculties, using reasonable care, would have known that the victim was ________ ([mentally defective] [mentally incapacitated] [physically helpless]).

[If after a full and fair consideration of all the facts and circumstances in evidence, you are not convinced beyond a reasonable doubt that the defendant engaged in ________ ([cunnilingus] [fellatio] [anal intercourse] [analingus] [the unlawful insertion of an object into the victim's genital/anal opening for the purpose of sexual arousal, gratification, or abuse of either person]) and this act was done with the victim who was ________ ([mentally defective] [mentally incapacitated] [physically helpless]) and the defendant knew or reasonably should have known that victim was ________ ([mentally defective] [mentally incapacitated] [physically helpless]), then you must find the defendant not guilty of second degree sexual offense. On the other hand, if you find from your consideration of all of the evidence that the State has proved each of the elements of the offense beyond a reasonable doubt, then you should find the defendant guilty of second degree sexual offense.]

(e) Sexual offense — Third degree

It is unlawful for a person to engage in certain intentional sexual contact or touching of another person, or to cause the other person to engage in such sexual contact or touching against the will and without the consent of the other person. Unlawful sexual contact means the intentional touching of the victim's or defendant's genital, anal or other intimate areas, other than by penetration of the penis, mouth or tongue, for the purpose of sexual arousal, gratification or abuse of either person without the consent of the victim. It does not include acts commonly expressive of familiar or friendly affection, or acts done for an accepted medical purpose. In Maryland, this intentional sexual contact is a sexual offense in the third or fourth degree. The distinction between a third degree sexual offense and a fourth degree sexual offense is the presence of aggravating circumstances which occur in the commission of the unlawful sexual contact.

The defendant in this case is charged with the commission of a third degree sexual offense. The aggravating circumstance(s) which the State alleges was present in the commission of this offense is that the defendant ___________ *(insert applicable aggravating circumstance(s))*

[(1) employed or displayed a dangerous or deadly weapon or an article which the victim reasonably concluded was a dangerous or deadly weapon];

[(2) inflicted [suffocation] [strangulation] [disfigurement] or [serious physical injury] upon ___________ [the victim] [someone other than the victim]];

[(3) threatened or placed the victim in fear that ___________ [the victim] [someone known to the victim] would be imminently subjected to [death] [suffocation] [strangulation] [disfigurement] [serious physical injury] or [kidnapping]];

[(4) committed the offense aided and abetted by one or more other persons.]

In order for the defendant to be found guilty of this offense, the State must prove beyond a reasonable doubt that the defendant: (1) intentionally touched any part of the victim's __________ ([genital area] [anal area] [an intimate area of the victim's body, namely __________) other than by penetration of the penis, mouth or tongue; or, intentionally caused the victim to touch any part of the defendant's __________ ([genital area] [anal area] [an intimate area of the defendant's body, namely __________]) other than by penetration of the penis, mouth or tongue; (2) the sexual contact or touching was against the victim's will and without the victim's consent; (3) the defendant __________ *(insert applicable aggravating circumstance(s) from above);* and (4) the touching was for the purpose of sexual arousal or gratification or abuse of either person. In order to be a crime, the touching must not be an act that was commonly expressive of familial or friendly affection or for an accepted medical purpose. An accepted medical purpose would be one which is conducted so as to diagnose or treat a person in need of diagnosis or treatment.

[Sexual contact or the intentional touching of the victim's or defendant's anal or genital areas or other intimate parts for the purpose of sexual arousal, gratification or for abuse includes the penetration, however slight, by any part of a person's body, other than the penis, mouth or tongue, into the genital or anal opening of another person's body if that penetration can be reasonably construed as being for the purposes of sexual arousal or gratification, or for abuse of either person.]

The defendant must have intended to engage in the sexual contact or touching. Intent has been defined as the exercise of intelligent will, the mind being fully aware of the nature and consequences of the act which is about to be done. The defendant must have done the act consciously and voluntarily and not inadvertently or accidently.

Consent at any time prior to the intentional sexual touching, however reluctantly given, deprives the sexual contact of its criminal character. Consent means a voluntary agreement by a person in the possession and exercise of sufficient mentality to make an intelligent choice to do something proposed by another. Consent differs materially from assent. Consent implies some positive action and always involves more than mere submission. Assent means mere passivity or submission, which does not include consent. Submission to a compelling force, or as a result of being put in fear, is not consent. A person who was conscious and possessed of natural mental and physical powers when the attack took place must have resisted to the extent of [his] [her] ability at the time, unless it appears that [he] [she] was overcome by numbers or was so terrified by threats as to overpower the will to resist. Resistance is necessarily relative; its presence or absence depends on the facts and circumstances in each case. The real test is whether the sexual touching was committed without the consent and against the will of the victim. The kind of fear in the mind of the victim which would reasonably make resistance unnecessary to support a conviction of third degree sexual offense includes, but is not necessarily limited to, a fear of death or serious bodily harm, or a fear so extreme so as to preclude resistance, or a fear which might make the victim incapable of continuing to resist.

[*To be given where some evidence has been generated that the victim of a third degree sexual offense is the defendant's spouse:* It is a defense that the victim was the defendant's legal spouse at the time of the commission of the alleged offense. The State must prove beyond a reasonable doubt that the victim was not the defendant's legal spouse at the time of the commission of the alleged offense [the victim and the defendant were living separate and apart pursuant to a valid court decree of divorce at the time of the offense].]

[If after a full and fair consideration of all the facts and circumstances in evidence, you are not convinced beyond a reasonable doubt that the defendant __________ (*insert applicable aggravating circumstance(s)*) in the course of intentionally engaging in sexual contact against the will and without the consent of the victim, then you must find the defendant not guilty of third degree sexual offense. On the other hand, if you find from your consideration of all of the evidence that the State has proved each of the elements of the offense beyond a reasonable doubt, then you should find the defendant guilty of third degree sexual offense.]

(f) Sexual offense — Third degree: victim under fourteen years and person performing act four or more years older than victim

It is unlawful for a person to engage in sexual contact with one who is under fourteen years of age if the person performing the act is at least four years older than the victim. Unlawful sexual contact means the intentional touching of the victim's genital, anal or other intimate areas, other than by penetration of the penis, mouth or tongue, for the purpose of sexual arousal, gratification or abuse of either person. Sexual contact does not include acts commonly expressive of familial or friendly affection, or acts done for accepted medical purposes. In Maryland, this offense is a sexual offense in the third degree.

In order for the defendant to be found guilty of this offense, the State must prove beyond a reasonable doubt that the defendant: (1) intentionally touched any part of the victim's __________ ([genital area] [anal area] [an intimate area of the victim's body, namely __________]) other than by penetration of the penis, mouth or tongue; or, intentionally caused the victim to touch any part of the defendant's __________ ([genital area] [anal area] [an intimate area of the defendant's body, namely __________]) other than by penetration of the penis, mouth, or tongue; (2) the victim was less than fourteen years of age at the time of the offense; (3) the defendant was at least four years older than the victim at the time of the offense; and (4) the touching was for the purpose of sexual arousal, gratification, or abuse of either person. In order to be a crime, the touching must not be an act that was commonly expressive of familial or friendly affection, or for an accepted medical purpose. An accepted medical purpose would be one which is conducted so as to diagnose or treat a person in need of diagnosis or treatment.

[Sexual contact or the intentional touching of the victim's or defendant's anal or genital areas or other intimate parts for the purpose of sexual arousal, gratification or for abuse includes the penetration, however slight, by any part of a person's body, other than the penis, mouth or tongue, into the genital or anal opening of another person's body if that penetration can be reasonably construed as being for the purposes of sexual arousal, gratification or for abuse of either person.]

The defendant must have intended to engage in the sexual contact or touching. Intent has been defined as the exercise of intelligent will, the mind being fully aware of the nature and consequences of the act which is about to be done. The defendant must have done the act consciously and voluntarily and not inadvertently or accidently.

The fact that the defendant did not know that the victim was under fourteen years of age is not a defense to the charge of sexual offense in the third degree. Such is the case even if you find that the defendant reasonably believed the victim to be fourteen years of age or older.

Finally, the basis of the charge of sexual offense in the third degree is that the victim was under fourteen years of age at the time of the offense while the defendant was at least four years older than the victim. Thus, whether the victim consented to the "sexual contact" is immaterial. Consent is not a defense to this offense.

[If after a full and fair consideration of all the facts and circumstances in evidence, you are not convinced beyond a reasonable doubt that the defendant intentionally engaged in sexual contact with a victim who was under fourteen years of age at the time of the offense while the defendant was at least four years older than the victim, then you must find the defendant not guilty of third degree sexual offense. On the other hand, if you find from your consideration of all of the evidence that the State has proved each of the elements of the offense beyond a reasonable doubt, then you should find the defendant guilty of third degree sexual offense.]

(g) Sexual offense — Third degree: mentally defective, mentally incapacitated or physically helpless victim

It is unlawful for a person to engage in sexual contact with one whom the defendant knows or reasonably should know is __________ ([mentally defective] [mentally incapacitated] [physically helpless]). Unlawful sexual contact means the intentional touching of the victim's or defendant's genital, anal or other intimate areas, other than by penetration of the penis, mouth or tongue, for the purpose of sexual arousal, gratification or abuse of either person. Sexual contact does not include acts commonly expressive of familial or friendly affection, or acts done for accepted medical purposes. In Maryland, this offense is a sexual offense in the third degree.

In order for the defendant to be found guilty of this offense, the State must prove beyond a reasonable doubt that the defendant: (1) intentionally touched any part of the victim's __________ ([genital area] [anal area] [an intimate area of the victim's body, namely ________]) other than by penetration of the penis, mouth or tongue; or, intentionally caused the victim to touch any part of the defendant's ________ ([genital area] [anal area] [an intimate area of the victim's body, namely ________]) other than by penetration of the penis, mouth or tongue; (2) the victim was ________ ([mentally defective] [mentally incapacitated] [physically helpless]); (3) the defendant knew or reasonably should have known that the victim was ________ ([mentally defective] [mentally incapacitated] [physically helpless]); and (4) the touching was for the purpose of sexual arousal, gratification or abuse of either person. In order to be a crime, the touching must not be an act that was commonly expressive of familial or friendly affection, or for an accepted medical purpose. An accepted medical purpose would be one which is conducted so as to diagnose or treat a person in need of diagnosis or treatment.

[Sexual contact or the intentional touching of the victim's or defendant's anal or genital areas or other intimate parts for the purpose of sexual arousal, gratification or for abuse includes the penetration, however slight, by any part of a person's body, other than the penis, mouth or tongue, into the genital or anal opening of another person's body if that penetration can be reasonably construed as being for the purposes of sexual arousal, gratification or for abuse of either person.]

The defendant must have intended to engage in the sexual contact or touching. Intent has been defined as the exercise of intelligent will, the mind being fully aware of the nature and consequences of the act which is about to be done. The defendant must have done the act consciously and voluntarily and not inadvertently or accidently.

[A person who is "mentally defective" suffers from either mental retardation or a mental disorder. The effect of the condition must be such that, at the time of the alleged offense, it rendered the victim substantially incapable of appraising the nature of his or her conduct, or of resisting the sexual contact or of communicating unwillingness to submit to the sexual contact.]

[A person who is "mentally incapacitated" is one who, due to the influence of a drug, narcotic, or intoxicating substance, or due to any act committed upon the victim without the victim's consent or awareness, is rendered substantially incapable of either appraising the nature of his or her conduct, or resisting the sexual contact.]

[A person who is "physically helpless" is one who either (1) is unconscious; (2) does not consent to the sexual contact and is physically unable to resist the sexual contact; or (3) is physically unable to communicate unwillingness to submit to the sexual contact.]

To find the defendant guilty of third degree sexual offense you must find beyond a reasonable doubt that the defendant knew or reasonably should have known that the victim was ________ ([mentally defective] [mentally incapacitated] [physically helpless]). An act is done knowingly if done voluntarily and purposely and not because of mistake, accident, inadvertence, or other innocent reason. In addition, the defendant reasonably should have known that the victim was ________ ([mentally defective] [mentally incapacitated] [physically helpless]) if an ordinarily prudent and cautious person in full possession of [her] [his] faculties, using reasonable care, would have known that the victim was ________ ([mentally defective] [mentally incapacitated] [physically helpless]).

[*To be given where some evidence has been generated that the victim of a third degree sexual offense is the defendant's spouse:* It is a defense that the victim was the defendant's legal spouse at the time of the commission of the alleged offense. The State must prove beyond a reasonable doubt that the victim was not the defendant's legal spouse at the time of the commission of the alleged offense [the victim and the defendant were living separate and apart pursuant to a valid court decree of divorce at the time of the offense].]

[If after a full and fair consideration of all the facts and circumstances in evidence, you are not convinced beyond a reasonable doubt that the defendant intentionally engaged in sexual contact with a person who was ________ ([mentally defective] [mentally incapacitated] [physically helpless]) and that the defendant knew or reasonably should have known of this condition, then you must find the defendant not guilty of third degree sexual offense. On the other hand, if you find from your consideration of all of the evidence that the State has proved each of the elements of the offense beyond a reasonable doubt, then you should find the defendant guilty of third degree sexual offense.]

(h) Sexual offense — Fourth degree

It is unlawful for a person to engage in certain intentional sexual contact or touching of another person, or to cause the other person to engage in such sexual contact or touching against the will and without the consent of the other person. Unlawful sexual contact means the intentional touching of the victim's or defendant's genital, anal or other intimate areas, other than by penetration of the penis, mouth or tongue, for the purpose of sexual arousal, gratification or abuse of either person without the consent of the victim. It does not include acts commonly expressive of familial or friendly affection, or acts done for an accepted medical purpose. In Maryland, this intentional sexual contact is a sexual offense in the fourth degree.

In order for the defendant to be found guilty of this offense, the State must prove beyond a reasonable doubt that the defendant: (1) intentionally touched any part of the victim's ________ ([genital area] [anal area] [an intimate area of the victim's body, namely ________]) other than by penetration of the penis, mouth or tongue; or, intentionally caused the victim to touch any part of the defendant's __________ ([genital area] [anal area] [an intimate area of the defendant's body, namely __________]) other than by penetration of the penis, mouth or tongue; (2) the sexual contact or touching was against the victim's will and without the victim's consent; and, (3) the touching was for the purpose of sexual arousal or gratification or abuse of either person. In order to be a crime, the touching must not be an act that was commonly expressive of familial or friendly affection or for an accepted medical purpose. An accepted medical purpose would be one which is conducted so as to diagnose or treat a person in need of diagnosis or treatment.

[Sexual contact or the intentional touching of the victim's or defendant's anal or genital areas or other intimate parts for the purpose of sexual arousal or gratification or for abuse, includes the penetration, however slight, by any part of a person's body, other than the penis, mouth or tongue, into the genital or anal opening of another person's body if that penetration can be reasonably construed as being for the purposes of sexual arousal or gratification, or for abuse of either person.]

The defendant must have intended to engage in the sexual contact or touching. Intent has been defined as the exercise of intelligent will, the mind being fully aware of the nature and consequences of the act which is about to be done. The defendant must have done the act consciously and voluntarily and not inadvertently or accidently.

Consent at any time prior to the intentional sexual touching, however reluctantly given, deprives the sexual contact of its criminal character. Consent means a voluntary agreement by a person in the possession and exercise of sufficient mentality to make an intelligent choice to do something proposed by another. Consent differs materially from assent. Consent implies some positive action and always involves more than mere submission. Assent means mere passivity or submission, which does not include consent. Submission to a compelling force, or as a result of being put in fear, is not consent. A person who was conscious and possessed of natural mental and physical powers when the attack took place must have resisted to the extent of [his] [her] ability at the time, unless it appears that [he] [she] was overcome by numbers or was so terrified by threats as to overpower the will to resist. Resistance is necessarily relative; its presence or absence depends on the facts and circumstances in each case. The real test is whether the sexual touching was committed without the consent and against the will of the victim. The kind of fear in the mind of the victim which would reasonably make resistance unnecessary to support a conviction of a fourth degree sexual offense includes, but is not necessarily limited to, a fear of death or serious bodily harm, or a fear so extreme so as to preclude resistance, or a fear which might make the victim incapable of continuing to resist.

[*To be given where some evidence has been generated that the victim of a fourth degree sexual offense is the defendant's spouse:* It is a defense that the victim was the defendant's legal spouse at the time of the commission of the alleged offense. The State must prove beyond a reasonable doubt that the victim was not the defendant's legal spouse at the time of the commission of the alleged offense [the victim and the defendant were living separate and apart pursuant to a valid court decree of divorce at the time of the offense].]

[If after a full and fair consideration of all the facts and circumstances in evidence, you are not convinced beyond a reasonable doubt that the defendant intentionally engaged in sexual contact against the will and without the consent of the victim, then you must find the defendant not guilty of a sexual offense in the fourth degree. On the other hand, if you find from your consideration of all of the evidence that the State has proved each of the elements of the offense beyond a reasonable doubt, then you should find the defendant guilty of a sexual offense in the fourth degree.]

(i) Sexual offense — Fourth degree: vaginal intercourse with person fourteen or fifteen years of age and person performing act four or more years older than victim

It is unlawful for a person to engage in vaginal intercourse with one who is fourteen or fifteen years of age if the person performing the act is at least four years older than the victim. In Maryland, this offense is considered to be a sexual offense in the fourth degree.

In order for a person to be found guilty of this offense, the State must prove beyond a reasonable doubt that the defendant: (1) engaged in vaginal intercourse with the victim; (2) the victim was fourteen or fifteen years old at the time of the offense; and (3) the defendant was at least four years older than the victim.

Vaginal intercourse is defined as the actual penetration, however slight, of the male sexual organ or penis into the female sexual organ or vagina. Penetration is an essential element of the crime of rape. There must be some penetration, however slight, by the penis into the vagina to constitute the crime of rape. Emission of semen is not required.

The fact that the defendant did not know that the victim was [fourteen] [fifteen] years of age is not a defense to the charge of sexual offense in the fourth degree. Such is the case even if you find that the defendant reasonably believed the victim to be sixteen years of age or older.

Finally, the basis of the charge of sexual offense in the fourth degree is that the victim was [fourteen] [fifteen] years of age at the time of the offense. Thus, whether the victim consented to the act of sexual intercourse is immaterial. Consent is not a defense to this charge.

[*To be given where some evidence has been generated that the victim of a fourth degree sexual offense is the defendant's spouse:* It is a defense that the victim was the defendant's legal spouse at the time of the commission of the alleged offense. The State must prove beyond a reasonable doubt that the victim was not the defendant's legal spouse at the time of the commission of the alleged offense [the victim and the defendant were living separate and apart pursuant to a valid court decree of divorce at the time of the offense].]

[If after a full and fair consideration of all the facts and circumstances in evidence, you are not convinced beyond a reasonable doubt that the defendant engaged in an act of sexual intercourse with the victim who was [fourteen] [fifteen] years of age at the time of the offense while the defendant was at least four years older than the victim, then you must find the defendant not guilty of sexual offense in the fourth degree. On the other hand, if you find from your consideration of all of the evidence that the State has proved each of the elements of the offense beyond a reasonable doubt, then you should find the defendant guilty of sexual offense in the fourth degree.]

(j) Sexual offense — Fourth degree: "sexual act" with person fourteen or fifteen years of age and person performing act four or more years older than victim

It is unlawful for a person to engage in a "sexual act" with one who is fourteen or fifteen years of age if the person performing the act is at least four or more years older than the victim. The defendant in this case is charged with the commission of the unlawful act of __________ ([cunnilingus] [fellatio] [anal intercourse] [analingus] [the insertion of an object into the victim's genital/anal opening]). In

Maryland, this act is considered to be a sexual offense in the fourth degree.

In order for the defendant to be found guilty of a fourth degree sexual offense, the State must prove beyond a reasonable doubt that: (1) the defendant engaged in __________ ([cunnilingus] [fellatio] [anal intercourse] [analingus] [the insertion of an object into the genital/anal opening of the victim for the purposes of sexual arousal, gratification, or for abuse of either person and not for an accepted medical purpose]); (2) the victim was fourteen or fifteen years old at the time of the offense; and (3) the defendant was at least four or more years older than the victim.

To be used in cases of cunnilingus, fellatio, analingus:

[Cunnilingus is defined as the placing of the mouth upon the female sexual organ or vagina.]

[Fellatio is defined as the placing of the mouth upon the male sexual organ or penis.]

[Analingus is defined as the placing of the mouth upon the anal opening of the victim.]

[Emission of semen is not required to be proven to establish __________ [fellatio] [analingus].]

[*To be given in cases of anal intercourse:* Anal intercourse is defined as the actual contact of the male sexual organ or penis and the victim's anal opening and an actual penetration into the body of the latter. Penetration is an essential element of the crime of anal intercourse. There must be some penetration, however slight, of the victim's anus by the defendant's sexual organ to constitute the crime of anal intercourse. Emission of semen is not required.]

[*To be given in cases of insertion of "other objects":* The insertion of any object into the genital or anal opening of the victim is unlawful if such insertion can reasonably be construed as being for the purposes of sexual gratification or arousal, or for abuse of either party and not for an accepted medical purpose. Penetration, however slight, of the victim's genital or anal opening is required to constitute an unlawful insertion.] [If the alleged insertion was for an accepted medical purpose, then such insertion does not constitute a criminal act. An accepted medical purpose would be one which is conducted so as to diagnose or treat a person in need of such diagnosis or treatment.]

The fact that the defendant did not know that the victim was [fourteen] [fifteen] years of age is not a defense to the charge of sexual offense in the fourth degree. Such is the case even if you find that the defendant reasonably believed the victim to be sixteen years of age or older.

Finally, the basis of the charge of sexual offense in the fourth degree is that the victim was [fourteen] [fifteen] years of age at the time of the offense while the defendant was at least four years older than the victim. Thus, whether the victim consented to the "sexual act" is immaterial to the charge of sexual offense in the fourth degree. Consent is not a defense.

[*To be given where there is some evidence that the victim of a fourth degree sexual offense is the defendant's spouse:* It is a defense that the victim was the defendant's legal spouse at the time of the commission of the alleged offense. The state must prove beyond a reasonable doubt that the victim was not the defendant's legal spouse at the time of the commission of the alleged offense [the victim and the defendant were living separate and apart pursuant to a valid court decree of divorce at the time of the offense].]

[If after a full and fair consideration of all the facts and circumstances in evidence, you are not convinced beyond a reasonable doubt that the defendant engaged in __________ ([cunnilingus] [fellatio] [anal intercourse] [analingus] [the unlawful insertion of an object into the victim's genital/anal opening for the purposes of sexual arousal, gratification, or abuse of either person]) and this act was done with the victim who was [fourteen] [fifteen] years of age at the time of the offense while the defendant was at least four years older than the victim, then you must find the defendant not guilty of fourth degree sexual offense. On the other hand, if you find from your consideration of all of the evidence that the State has proved each of the elements of the offense beyond a reasonable doubt, then you should find the defendant guilty of fourth degree sexual offense.]

COMMENT

(a) Overview

See Comment, § 4.36, *supra,* for an analysis of the 1976 revision of Maryland's sexual offense laws.

Criminal sexual activities other than rape are now codified in Maryland Ann. Code, Art. 27, §§ 464, 464A to 464C, under the designation "sexual offense." The 1976 revised laws divide these offenses into four degrees and groups and criminal sexual activity into two major categories — "sexual acts" and "sexual contact." The legislation also proscribes certain sexual activity, regardless of consent, between any person who is fourteen or fifteen years of age or younger, and an accused who is four or more years older than the other person involved. Art. 27, § 464A(3) (sexual contact and under fourteen years of age); § 464C(2) (sexual act and fourteen or fifteen years of age), and § 464C(3) (vaginal intercourse and fourteen or fifteen years of age). In addition, it is unlawful under these statutes for a person to engage in a "sexual act" or "sexual contact" with another person who is mentally defective, mentally incapacitated or physically helpless when the accused knows or reasonably should know about the victim's mental or physical handicap. Art. 27, § 464A(2) (sexual act), and § 464B(2) (sexual contact).

The term "sexual act" expressly includes five types of sexual activity: cunnilingus, fellatio, anal intercourse, analingus, and the penetration, however slight, of any object into the genital or anal opening of another person's body. The penetration by the object must be of such a nature as to be reasonably construed as being for the purposes of sexual arousal or gratification, or for abuse of either party. Penetration of the anal or genital openings for an accepted medical purpose is not unlawful. To sustain a conviction for illegal anal intercourse, evidence of penetration, however slight, must be presented. Emission of semen is not required to constitute an unlawful sexual act. Art. 27, § 461(e).

In *Partain v. State,* 63 Md. App. 260, 492 A.2d 669 (1985), the Court considered the meaning of the term "cunnilingus." The defendant contended that the evidence was insufficient to prove a "sexual act" because cunnilingus requires penetration and the only evidence in the case was that the defendant "licked" the victim's genitals, not that he penetrated them. The Court held that cunnilingus does not require penetration of the genitals and stated that cunnilingus, while not defined in the statute, should be given its ordinary meaning of a sexual activity involving oral contact with the female genitals. The term, of Latin origin, is derived from *cunnus* meaning vulva, and *lingere* meaning to lick. The sexual offense statutes, which explicitly require penetration when it is an element of the offense, significantly omit any reference to penetration as a requirement for cunnilingus.

In *Thomas v. State,* 301 Md. 294, 483 A.2d 6 (1984), the Court, noting that the term "fellatio" is not defined in the statute, stated that the legislature intended the term to have its common, ordinary and well-accepted meaning. After citing various dictionary definitions of "fellatio," the Court held that all that must be shown is some contact between the mouth and the male sexual organ. Proof of penetration is not required. The Court rejected the defendant's argument based on *Gooch v. State,* 34 Md. App. 331, 367 A.2d 90 (1976), interpreting Art. 27, § 554, pertaining to the crime of unnatural or perverted sexual practices, that fellatio requires proof that the penis penetrated the mouth. The statute involved in *Gooch* specifically requires that a person take into "his or her mouth the sexual organ of any other person or animal," "place his or her sexual organ in the mouth of any other person or animal" or commit "any other unnatural or perverted sexual practice with any other person or animal." See Comment, § 4.35, Unnatural or perverted sexual practices, *supra.* There now appear to be two definitions of "fellatio," and, perhaps, of "cunnilingus" depending upon whether prosecution occurs under the revised sexual offense legislation or the common-law offense of unnatural or perverted sexual practice. This issue arose in *Thomas* because the evidence presented at trial indicated that the victim was forced to "kiss" defendant's penis and there was no showing that the mouth was penetrated. The defendant was prosecuted for a first degree sexual offense.

"Sexual contact" means the intentional touching of any part of the victim's or defendant's genital or anal areas, or other intimate parts, for the purpose of sexual arousal or gratification, or for the abuse of either party. Sexual contact includes the penetration, however slight, by any part of a person's body other than the penis, mouth or tongue, into the anal or genital openings of another's body if that penetration can be reasonably construed as being for the purposes of sexual arousal or gratification, or for the abuse of either party. Criminal sexual contact does not include those acts which are commonly expressive of familial or friendly affection, nor does it include acts done for accepted medical purposes. Art. 27, § 461(f).

In *Dillsworth v. State,* 66 Md. App. 263, 503 A.2d 734 (1986), *aff'd,* 308 Md. 354, 519 A.2d 1269 (1987), the Court construed the words "for abuse" in Art. 27, § 461(f), equating this phrase with a physical attack intended to inflict sexual injury with intent to cause adverse sexual effect to one or more of those parts. Here, the abuse required for conviction of a third degree sexual offense was established by the victim's testimony.

(b) First and second degree sexual offenses

For a person to be convicted of a sexual offense in the first or second degree, the underlying criminal sexual activity must have been a "sexual act." Basically, a sexual offense in the second degree is the commission of a sexual act by force or threat of force against the will and without the consent of the victim. Maryland Ann. Code, Art. 27, § 464A(a)(1). For such unlawful sexual activity to be elevated to a sexual offense in the first degree, certain aggravating circumstances must be present. A person is guilty of a sexual offense in the first degree when that person engages in a sexual act by force or threat of force against the will and without the consent of the victim, and while committing the act: (1) employs or displays a dangerous or deadly weapon or an article which the victim reasonably concludes is a dangerous or deadly weapon; or (2) inflicts suffocation, strangulation, disfigurement or serious physical injury upon the other person or upon anyone else; or (3) threatens or places the victim in fear that the victim or any person known to the victim will be imminently subjected to death, suffocation, strangulation, disfigurement, serious physical injury or kidnapping; or (4) is aided or abetted by one or more other persons. Art. 27, § 464(a)(1)(i-iv).

Any person found guilty of a sexual offense in the first degree is guilty of a felony and may be punished with up to life imprisonment. Art. 27, § 464(b).

In addition to the unlawful sexual activity proscribed by Art. 27, § 464A(a)(1), a person may be guilty of a sexual offense in the second degree in two other distinct circumstances: (1) when the defendant engaged in a sexual act with another person who is "mentally defective," "mentally incapacitated" or "physically helpless," and the defendant knows or has reason to know about the victim's mental or physical handicap (Art. 27, § 464A(a)(2)); or (2) when the defendant engaged in a sexual act with a person who is under fourteen years of age and the accused is four or more years older than the other person (Art. 27, § 464A(a)(3)). Lack of consent and the use of force or threat of force are not required to be proven to constitute the crimes charged under Art. 27, § 464A(a)(2) or 464A(a)(3).

Any person found guilty of a sexual offense in the second degree is guilty of a felony and may be imprisoned up to twenty years. Art. 27, § 464A(b).

An ambiguity exists with regard to the distinction between a sexual offense in the first degree as defined in Art. 27, § 464(a)(1)(iii) and a second degree sexual offense as defined in Art. 27, § 464A(a)(1). The latter section provides that a second degree sexual offense consists of a sexual act by force or threat of force against the will and without the consent of the victim. Article 27, § 464(a)(1)(iii) also states that a first degree sexual offense consists of a sexual act by force or threat of force against the will and without the consent of the victim, but additionally requires the aggravating circumstance that the defendant threatened the victim or someone known to the victim with death, serious bodily injury or kidnapping. In light of the similar aspects of the "threat" element in the first two degrees of sexual offenses, the decision whether to charge a person in the first or second degree is subject to broad prosecutorial discretion. The articulateness and clarity of the language of the accused used in the course of committing the offense may be an important circumstance in the grading of this offense.

A question may be raised whether "sexual acts" include both acts performed by the defendant upon the victim and acts which the defendant causes the victim to perform upon the defendant. In contrast to the definition of "sexual contact" in Art. 27, § 461(f), as the intentional touching of any part of the "victim's or actor's" anal or genital areas or other intimate parts, Art. 27, § 461(e) provides no such language. Art. 27, § 464, first degree sexual offense, and Art. 27, § 464A, second degree sexual offense, provide that a person is guilty if the person "engages" in a "sexual act." Standard dictionary definitions of "engage" ("to take part in or be employed in," "to involve oneself or become occupied") appear to be broad enough to include a case, for example, where the defendant causes the victim to perform fellatio upon the defendant as well as where the defendant is the performer. A closer scrutiny of the language of Art. 27, § 461(e) and (f) also supports this broader construction of legislative intent. Under Art. 27, § 461(f), sexual contact "includes the penetration, however slight, by any part of a person's body, *other than the penis, mouth, or tongue,* into the genital or anal opening of another person's body ..." (emphasis added). Presumably, the penetration of the penis, mouth or tongue was excluded under "sexual contact" because it was considered to be included under "sexual acts." Also, a question may be raised whether a person "engages" in an unlawful sexual act if the defendant forces a person to perform a sexual act upon a person other than the defendant.

See Instruction, § 4.35, Unnatural and perverted sexual practices, *supra,* and the accompanying Comment for a discussion of the overlap of Art. 27, §§ 553 and 554, with the first and second degree sexual offenses.

A sexual offense in the first degree parallels rape in the first degree. Both the aggravating circumstances and the penalty ("subject to imprisonment for no more than the period of his natural life") are the same. There are two critical differences. First, the prohibited sexual offense is a "sexual act" (discussed *supra,* this Comment) rather than "vaginal intercourse" as in the crime of rape.

A second difference between a sexual offense in the first or second degree and rape involves gender neutrality. While rape in the first or second degree can only be committed by a male upon a female, a male may commit a prohibited "sexual act" upon another male or upon a female and a female may commit a prohibited "sexual act" upon either a male or another female. This gender neutrality is a significant feature of the revised sexual offense laws. An exception to the rule that rape can only be committed by a male upon a female is the common-law doctrine of accessory. A female can be an accessory before the fact or a principal in the second degree to the rape of another female.

A sexual offense in the second degree parallels second degree rape. The penalties are the same ("subject to imprisonment for a period of not more than 20 years"). A second degree sexual offense involves committing a prohibited "sexual act" with another person by threatening to use force or by actually using force to compel the victim to submit against his or her will. It also includes engaging in a prohibited "sexual act" with a victim who is mentally defective, mentally incapacitated or physically helpless when the perpetrator knew or should reasonably have known of the victim's mental or physical incapacity. Finally, a second degree sexual offense is committed if the victim is under the age of fourteen years and the perpetrator is four or more years older than the victim and engages in a prohibited "sexual act." When the perpetrator is *less* than four or more years older than the victim, and the victim is under fourteen years of age and engages in a consensual "sexual act," he or she might still be guilty of sodomy or unnatural or perverted sexual practices. See Instructions: § 4.34, Sodomy and § 4.35, Unnatural or perverted sexual practices, *supra.* It should be noted that the second degree sexual offense provisions provide a potentially valuable prosecutorial tool for dealing with sexual offenses committed in institutional settings where residents are of the same sex, such as mental institutions, facilities for juveniles, and prisons.

(c) Third and fourth degree sexual offenses

For a person to be convicted of a sexual offense in the third or fourth degree, the underlying criminal sexual activity (with two exceptions) must have been a "sexual contact." The distinction between a third degree sexual offense and a fourth degree sexual offense, like that between first and second degree sexual offenses, is the presence of certain aggravating circumstances. Thus, where the defendant engages in sexual contact with another person against the will and without the consent of that person, the defendant is guilty of a sexual offense in the fourth degree, a misdemeanor. Maryland Ann. Code, Art. 27, § 464C(a)(1). However, the defendant will be guilty of a sexual offense in the third degree, a felony, if the defendant engages in "sexual contact" with another person against the will and without the consent of the other person and: (1) employs or displays a dangerous or deadly weapon or an article which the other person reasonably concludes is a dangerous or deadly weapon; or (2) inflicts suffocation, strangulation, disfigurement or serious physical injury upon the other person or upon anyone else in the course of committing the offense; or (3) threatens or places the victim in fear that the victim or any person known to the victim will be imminently subjected to death, suffocation, strangulation, disfigurement, serious physical injury or kidnapping; or (4) commits the offense aided or abetted by one or more other persons. Art. 27, § 464B(a)(1)(i-iv).

Two other types of sexual activity are codified as third degree sexual offenses: (1) if the defendant engages in "sexual contact" with another person who is "mentally defective," "mentally incapacitated" or "physically helpless" and the defendant knows or reasonably should know of the victim's handicap, the defendant is guilty of a sexual offense in the third degree; and (2) if a person engages in sexual contact with another person who is under fourteen years of age, and the defendant is four or more years older than the other party, the defendant is guilty of a third degree sexual offense. Art. 27, § 464B(a)(2) and (3). In either of these two instances, the consent of the victim is not a defense to the third degree sexual offense.

All third degree sexual offenses are felonies. Upon conviction thereof, a person is subject to imprisonment for not more than ten years. Art. 27, § 464B(b).

A third degree sexual offense is a specific intent crime, and the same elements necessary to prove the crime of assault and battery are essential ingredients to the establishment of the third degree sexual offense. *Holt v. State,* 50 Md. App. 578, 438 A.2d 1386 (1982). See also *Mayne v. State,* 45 Md. App. 483, 488, 414 A.2d 1, 4 (1980), *cert. denied,* 450 U.S. 910 (1981).

Problems of ambiguity and statutory construction arise in application of the definition of "sexual contact." Article 27, § 461(f) speaks of "the intentional touching of any part of the victim's or actor's anal or genital areas or *other intimate parts* for the purposes of sexual arousal or gratification ..." (emphasis added), but does not provide any guidance as to which parts of the body are included within the phrase, "other intimate parts." It should be noted that the Michigan sexual offense statutes, upon which Maryland's legislation is modeled, defines "intimate parts" as including "the primary genital area, groin, inner thigh, buttock, or breast of a human being." Mich. Stat. Ann., § 28.788(1)(b).

The definition of "sexual contact" in Art. 27, § 461(f) refers to the intentional touching of any part of the *"victim's or actor's* anal or genital areas or other intimate parts" (emphasis added). Article 27, § 464B(a)(3) provides, however, that a person is guilty of third degree sexual offense if the person engages in sexual contact "[w]ith another person who is under fourteen years of age and the person *performing* the sexual contact is four or more years older than the victim" (emphasis added). Does the use of the phrase, "person *performing* the sexual contact," restrict the application to cases where the defendant is the active party, or does it include situations where the defendant causes the victim to perform the sexual contact upon the defendant?

Also, suppose the defendant causes the victim to perform a sexual contact upon a third person (i.e., another victim). Is that conduct proscribed by the statute? Moreover, suppose the defendant causes the victim to touch the victim's own "anal or genital areas or other intimate parts" in the presence of the defendant. Further, suppose the defendant in the victim's presence touches the defendant's own "anal or genital area or other intimate parts." *Cf.* Instruction, § 4.61, Disorderly conduct — Comment on indecent exposure, *infra.* If situations such as those above arise, questions of statutory construction may be presented requiring the attention of the appellate courts.

As noted earlier, the definition of "sexual contact" provides "and includes the penetration, however slight, by any part of a person's body, *other than the penis, mouth, or tongue,* into the genital or anal opening of another person's body ..." (emphasis added). Presumably, a touching by the penis, mouth or tongue that does not amount to a "penetration" could be included as an unlawful "sexual contact." "Sexual contact" is defined as "the intentional touching of any part of the victim's or actor's anal or genital areas or other intimate parts for the purposes of sexual arousal or gratification or for abuse of either party ...." Art. 27, § 461(f). It is significant that the General Assembly has provided a maximum penalty for this form of prohibited "sexual contact" that is *less* than that available under a prosecution for the common-law offenses of assault and battery. In *Eccles v. State,* 59 Md. App. 554, 476 A.2d 1183 (1984), the Court held that assault and battery is not a lesser included offense of a fourth degree sexual crime. The Court noted that the fourth degree sexual offense involves sexual contact; assault does not. Assault requires an attempt to injure; fourth degree sexual offense does not. Finally, there is no prescribed penalty for common-law battery, except that it may not be constitutionally cruel or unusual. See Instructions: § 4.11, Assault, and § 4.12, Battery, *supra.*

Two additional categories of sexual activity now are fourth degree sexual offenses. If the accused engages in a "sexual act" with a person who is fourteen or fifteen years of age and the accused is four or more years older than the younger party, the accused is guilty of a fourth degree sexual offense, regardless of consent. Art. 27, § 464C(a)(2). Finally, if the accused engages in "vaginal intercourse" with another person who is either fourteen or fifteen years of age, and the accused is four or more years older than the younger party, the accused is guilty of a fourth degree sexual offense, regardless of consent. Art. 27, § 464C(a)(3). All fourth degree sexual offenses are misdemeanors and are punishable by imprisonment for not more than one year or a fine of not more than $1,000, or both. Art. 27, § 464C(b).

(d) Spousal immunity defense and admissibility of evidence of victim's prior sexual conduct

Maryland Ann. Code, Art. 27, § 464D precludes the prosecution of a person for a third or fourth degree sexual offense if the other party to the sexual activity was the accused's legal spouse at the time of the offense, unless the parties were married and living separate and apart pursuant to a valid decree of divorce *a mensa et thoro* (bed and board divorce). There is no such defense where the defendant is accused of committing a sexual offense in the first or second degree.

Article 27, § 461A of the revised sexual offense legislation also provides a significant evidentiary rule relating to the admissibility of the sexual offense victim's prior sexual history in cases where the accused is charged with a first or second degree sexual offense. At present, it is not clear what the effect of this evidentiary statute will be when the accused is jointly charged with a third or fourth degree sexual offense (where the statute has no application) along with a first or second degree sexual offense.

For a detailed discussion of these provisions, see Comment, § 4.36, subparts (i) and (j), *supra.*

E. Weapons Offenses

§ 4.41. Carrying or wearing a concealed weapon.

It is a criminal offense to carry or to wear a concealed weapon.

In order for the defendant to be guilty of this offense, the State must prove beyond a reasonable doubt that (1) the defendant was in possession of a [dirk knife] [bowie knife] [switchblade knife] [star knife] [sandclub] [metal knuckles] [razor] [nunchaku] [dangerous or deadly weapon], namely ____________ (*insert object charged as a dangerous or deadly weapon*); [(2) ____________ (*insert weapon, or object charged as the dangerous or deadly weapon*) is not a ____________, [penknife without a switchblade] [handgun]); (3) the ____________ (*insert weapon or object*) was being worn or carried on or about the defendant's person; and (4) the ___________ (*insert weapon or object*) was being carried or worn by the defendant in a concealed manner.

[A dangerous or deadly weapon is defined as an object which is likely to produce death or great bodily harm. The character of a weapon as dangerous or deadly is not necessarily determined by its design, construction or purpose. A weapon may be dangerous or deadly even though not specially designed or constructed for offensive or defensive purposes or for the destruction of life or for bodily injury. It would depend on the manner or circumstances under which the weapon is carried and/or used; that is, whether, based on the manner of circumstances under which the weapon is carried or used, it would be likely to produce death or grievous bodily harm.]

It must be shown that the defendant was either wearing or carrying the weapon or that he was in such close proximity to it as would make it available for his immediate use.

A weapon is concealed if it is worn or carried so as not to be seen by ordinary observation of an ordinary person near enough to see it if it were not concealed. Absolute invisibility is not required in order for a weapon to be considered concealed.

COMMENT

This instruction is based on Maryland Ann. Code, Art. 27, § 36. The statute proscribes two different activities: (1) carrying or wearing a concealed weapon; and (2) carrying a weapon openly with an intent or purpose of injuring another. The first part provides the basis for this instruction; the second part provides the basis for Instruction, § 4.42, *infra*.

In all criminal prosecutions, proof of the elements constituting the crime charged is essential. *Wood v. State*, 192 Md. 643, 650, 65 A.2d 316, 319 (1949). In prosecutions for carrying a concealed weapon, it is essential that the State prove that someone carried a dangerous or deadly weapon "concealed upon or about his person." *Id.;* see also *Brooks v. State,* 38 Md. App. 550, 552, 381 A.2d 718, 720 (1978), *aff'd,* 284 Md. 416, 397 A.2d 596 (1979). The *corpus delicti* of the crime may be proved by circumstantial evidence when direct evidence is not available. *Davis v. State,* 202 Md. 463, 470, 97 A.2d 303, 306 (1953).

A dangerous weapon is a weapon likely to produce death or great bodily harm. *Crawford v. State,* 174 Md. 175, 179, 197 A. 866, 867 (1938). For the purposes of the statute a dangerous or deadly weapon is any dirk knife, bowie knife, switchblade knife, star knife, sandclub, metal knuckles, razor, nunchaku, or any other dangerous or deadly weapon of any kind whatsoever (penknives without switchblade and handguns are excluded). If the State cannot show the exact type of weapon used, it must be able to show: (1) that the weapon was dangerous and deadly by the use to which it was put; and, (2) that the weapon was not a penknife without a switchblade or a handgun. *Mackall v. State,* 283 Md. 100, 111, 387 A.2d 762, 768 (1978). Many different weapons may be considered dangerous; it depends on the manner and circumstances in which they are used. See § 4.42, Comment, *infra,* for a discussion of what has been held to be a dangerous weapon, what does not constitute a dangerous weapon, and which party has the burden of proving whether the weapon fits within an exception.

The State must prove that the weapon was concealed. When the testimony of the eyewitnesses was that the defendant had no weapon in his hand when he entered the automobile, this evidence was enough to corroborate defendant's confession concerning firing the gun and convict him of the concealment charge. *Davis v. State, supra* at 471, 97 A.2d at 307.

Absolute invisibility of the weapon is not required. *Shipley v. State,* 243 Md. 262, 269, 202 A.2d 585 (1966), cited in *Crosby v. State,* 2 Md. App. 578, 203 A.2d 33 (1967). A weapon is concealed if it is so situated as not to be discernible by ordinary observation by those near enough to see it if it were not concealed. *Shipley v. State, supra* at 269, 220 A.2d 588. "Ordinary observation" is *not* an unusually thorough or detailed search stemming from the belief that contraband may be found. *Id.* at 269, 220 A.2d at 589. If the defendant attempts to conceal the weapon, and fails, the State is justified in concluding that the weapon had been concealed. *Id.* at 269, 220 A.2d at 588-589; *cf. Brookhart v. State,* 238 Md. 625, 209 A.2d 601 (1965).

Concealment may also be brought about by defendant's use of existing conditions such as darkness. In *Smith v. State,* 18 Md. App. 612, 618, 308 A.2d 442, 443 (1978), the handle of the pistol extended above the front seat of the defendant's car; but it was nighttime and the pistol was not visible until the interior lights were turned on. Since the defendant allowed the pistol to remain hidden, he was guilty of carrying a concealed weapon. *Id.* at 617, 308 A.2d at 445.

Also, where defendant's gun was tucked into his pants, and the handle was sticking out above the beltline, the trial court was justified in finding that the gun was concealed. *Crosby v. State, supra* at 580, 236 A.2d at 38-39. The officer had observed the gun protruding only because the defendant's jacket was unbuttoned. However, in *Smith v. State,* 4 Md. App. 128, 241 A.2d 437 (1968), defendant had a straight razor "protruding out" of his coat pocket, discernible in part by ordinary observation. The part that was exposed was such as to make it clearly identifiable as a straight razor, thus Art. 27, § 36(a) did not apply. *Id.* at 130, 241 A.2d at 438-439.

Also, in *Clemons v. State,* 9 Md. App. 127, 262 A.2d 786 (1970), the Court held that there was no evidence that the gun carried by defendant at the time of the robbery was in fact concealed. When the victim's testimony that "he pulled a gun from his belt" was the only evidence concerning the manner in which defendant carried the gun, this evidence was held insufficient to sustain conviction for carrying a concealed weapon. *Id.* at 130, 262 A.2d at 788.

The charging documents must be specific as to whether the weapon was carried openly or concealed. In *Pedzich v. State,* 33 Md. App. 620, 624, 365 A.2d 567, 569 (1976), the charging documents of the prosecution did not specify whether the shotgun was concealed or carried openly by defendant with intent to injure. Thus, the Court held that the documents were insufficient to charge defendant with either offense. *Id.* Where the warrant was captioned as a concealed weapon warrant specifically setting forth that the defendant was charged with unlawfully carrying two dangerous and deadly weapons, an amendment to the warrant adding "concealed upon and about his person" did not change the basic description of the offense. *Gray v. State,* 216 Md. 410, 414-415, 140 A.2d 643, 646 (1958), *overruled, Thanos v. State,* 282 Md. 709, 387 A.2d 286 (1978).

In addition, the weapon need not actually be on or about the person of the defendant. As long as it was in such proximity to the defendant as would make it available for his immediate use, the charge is valid. *Corbin v. State,* 237 Md. 486, 206 A.2d 809 (1965). *Webster v. State,* 228 Md. 481, 180 A.2d 493 (1963); *Veney v. State,* 227 Md. 608, 177 A.2d 883 (1961); *Evans v. State,* 11 Md. App. 451, 274 A.2d 653 (1971).

There are exceptions as to who may be found guilty under this statute. The exceptions include officers of the state and other conservators of the peace. Article 27, § 36(d) also includes an exception for:

> Any person who shall carry such weapon as a reasonable precaution against apprehended danger, but the tribunal before which any case arising under the provisions of this section may be tried, shall have the right to judge of the reasonableness of the carrying of any such weapon, and the proper occasion therefor, under the evidence in the case.

The burden of proof is on the defendant to show that he falls within one of the exceptions. *Spurrier v. State,* 229 Md. 110, 182 A.2d 358 (1962); *Roos v. State,* 45 Md. App. 21, 410 A.2d 1113 (1980); *Jordan v. State,* 24 Md. App. 267, 330 A.2d 496 (1975).

The section on which this instruction is based does not specify a *mens rea* term. In light of the serious, potential penalty provided for the offense, a question may arise whether the courts will read in a *mens rea* term, such as "knowingly" to cover an unusual circumstance, e.g., where a person may have carried or worn a weapon without knowledge.

The doctrine of merger did not preclude the state from charging defendant with carrying a concealed weapon under Art. 27, § 36(a), and with carrying a weapon while traveling on the public roads and highways, Art. 27, § 36B(b). *Pinkett v. State,* 30 Md. App. 458, 472, 352 A.2d 358, 367 (1976). The Court held that the legislative intent of the two statutes was to make a person wearing, carrying or transporting more than one gun (here one handgun and one shotgun) guilty of more than one crime. *Id.* at 473, 352 A.2d 368.

A "star knife," defined in Art. 27, § 36(b), "is a device used as a throwing weapon, consisting of several sharp or pointed blades arrayed as radially disposed arms about a central disk."

A "nunchaku," defined in Art. 27, § 36(c), "is a device consisting of two pieces of wood, metal, plastic, or other like substance connected by any chain, rope, leather or other flexible material not exceeding 24 inches in length."

A person convicted of this offense is guilty of a misdemeanor and shall be fined not more than $1,000 or imprisoned in jail for not more than three years. Article 27, § 36(a) also provides that ". . . in case of conviction, if it shall appear from the evidence that such weapon was carried, concealed or openly, with the deliberate purpose of injuring the person or destroying the life of another, the court shall impose the highest sentence of imprisonment prescribed."

For a related offense, see Art. 27, § 36A, carrying or possessing deadly weapon upon school property.

§ 4.42. Carrying a weapon openly with intent to injure.

It is a criminal offense to wear or carry a dangerous or deadly weapon openly with the intent or purpose of injuring another person.

In order for the defendant to be guilty of this offense, the State must prove beyond a reasonable doubt that: (1) the defendant was in possession of a [dirk knife] [bowie knife] [switchblade knife] [star knife] [sandclub] [metal knuckles] [razor] [nunchaku] [chemical mace] [tear gas] [dangerous or deadly weapon], namely ________ (*insert object charged as a dangerous or deadly weapon*); (2) ________ (*insert weapon or object charged as dangerous or deadly weapon*) was not a ________ ([penknife without a switchblade] [handgun]); (3) the ________ (*insert weapon or object*) was being carried or worn openly by the defendant; and (4) the __________ (*insert weapon or object*) was carried or worn openly with the intent or purpose of injuring another.

[A dangerous or deadly weapon is defined as an object which is likely to produce death or great bodily harm. The character of a weapon as dangerous or deadly is not necessarily determined by its design, construction or purpose. A weapon may be dangerous or deadly even though not especially designed or constructed for offensive or defensive purposes or for the destruction of life or for bodily injury. It would depend on the manner or circumstances under which the weapon is carried and/or used; that is, whether, based on the manner or circumstances that the weapon is carried or used, it would be likely to produce death or grievous bodily harm.]

The State must prove beyond a reasonable doubt that the defendant carried the deadly or dangerous weapon expressly intending to cause injury to another.

COMMENT

This instruction is based upon Maryland Ann. Code, Art. 27, § 36. The statute proscribes two different activities: (1) carrying or wearing a concealed weapon; and (2) carrying a weapon openly with an intent or purpose of injuring another. The first part provides the basis for Instruction, § 4.41; the second part provides the basis for this instruction.

There is little, if any, case law pertaining only to the latter offense. However, where the two offenses overlap (for example, the definition of a dangerous weapon), the case law is applicable to both offenses.

To obtain a conviction for the offense of carrying a weapon openly with intent to injure, the State must prove (1) the carrying of a dangerous weapon; (2) openly; (3) with the intent of injuring any person in any unlawful manner. *Brooks v. State,* 38 Md. App. 550, 381 A.2d 718 (1978), *aff'd,* 284 Md. 416, 397 A.2d 596 (1979).

A dangerous weapon is one likely to produce death or great bodily harm. *Crawford v. State,* 174 Md. 175, 179, 197 A. 866, 867 (1938). For the purposes of the statute a dangerous or deadly weapon is any dirk knife, bowie knife, switchblade knife, star knife, sandclub, metal knuckles, razor, nunchaku, chemical mace, tear gas or any other dangerous or deadly weapon of any kind whatsoever (penknives without switchblade and handguns are excluded).

Many different items may be considered dangerous weapons depending on the manner and circumstances in which they are used. In *Jackson v. State,* 231 Md. 591, 191 A.2d 432 (1963), a starter's pistol, incapable of discharging a projectile, was held to be a dangerous weapon. An unloaded pistol has also been held to be a dangerous weapon since it was used as an agent of intimidation and could have been used as a bludgeon. *Wallace v. Warden,* 226 Md. 670, 671-672, 174 A.2d 435, 436 (1961); *Hayes v. State,* 211 Md. 111, 126 A.2d 576 (1956). When a microphone cord on a taxi radio was used as a garrote, it was found to be a dangerous weapon. *Shipley v. State,* 243 Md. 262, 220 A.2d 585 (1966); *Bennett v. State,* 237 Md. 212, 205 A.2d 393 (1964). A gravity knife not in good working order (but capable of being used) was held to be a dangerous and deadly weapon. *Savoy v. State,* 236 Md. 36, 39, 202 A.2d 324, 325-326 (1964).

A loaded pistol is a dangerous and deadly weapon, *Crawford v. State, supra,* but the offense of wearing or carrying a handgun is punished under Art. 27, § 36B, a separate statute, and not under Art. 27, § 36(a). Article 27, § 36B prohibits the wearing, carrying or transporting of any handgun, concealed or openly, without a permit. Permits are issued pursuant to the provisions of Art. 27, § 36E.

The failure of a witness to refer to the weapon as a knife in her initial police statement goes to the weight of the evidence and not the admissibility. *Wantland v. State,* 45 Md. App. 527, 413 A.2d 1376 (1980), *vacated,* 451 U.S. 1014 (1981), *aff'd on remand,* 49 Md. App. 636, 435 A.2d 102 (1981), *cert. denied,* 457 U.S. 1121 (1982). In *Wantland* the Court held that the jury was free to infer, based on the testimony of the witness as well as the fact that the victim was stabbed, that the defendant carried a weapon with the requisite intent to injure. *Id.* at 542, 413 A.2d at 1385.

In *Mackall v. State,* 283 Md. 100, 111, 387 A.2d 762, 768 (1978), the Court held that it was incumbent on the State to prove beyond a reasonable doubt that the weapon carried was one which the statute expressly specified shall not be carried. The Court stated that the weapons excepted in the statute are as necessary to the description of the offense as are the weapons proscribed. In this case, the State had to prove that the weapon was not a penknife without a switchblade. Since the State was only able to show that the weapon was a knife and that it was used in a dangerous and deadly manner, and could not show that the knife was not a penknife without a switchblade, the Court of Appeals reversed the defendant's conviction because of insufficient evidence. *Mackall* was distinguished from *Spurrier v. State,* 229 Md. 110, 182 A.2d 358 (1962). In *Spurrier* the exceptions did not constitute an element of the offense charged. See also *Howes v. State,* 141 Md. 532, 119 A. 297 (1922).

When a penal act contains an exception so incorporated with the substance of the clause defining the offense as to constitute a material part of the description of the ingredients which constitute the offense, the burden is on the State to prove beyond a reasonable doubt, that the offense charged is not within the exception. *Mackall v. State, supra* at 100, 387 A.2d at 768. If the exception is part of the offense the State must negate the exception to prove its case. *Id.* See also *Roos v. State,* 45 Md. App. 21, 26, 410 A.2d 1113, 1116 (1980). In *Spurrier* the Court held that the exceptions [formerly specified in Art. 27, § 36(c), now § 36(d)] are not an element of the offense charged. Therefore, the burden of proof was on the defendant to establish that he fell within one or more of the exceptions. *Spurrier v. State, supra.*

It is not necessary for the State to prove an assault to sustain a conviction for carrying a weapon openly with intent to injure. The offenses of assault with intent to murder and carrying a weapon openly with intent to injure each require proof of a fact which the other does not; the two offenses are not the same and do not merge. *Brooks v. State,* 284 Md. 416, 423, 397 A.2d 596, 599 (1979). Such offenses are not the same for double jeopardy purposes either. *Cousins v. State,* 277 Md. 383, 354 A.2d 825, 834 (1976), *cert. denied,* 429 U.S. 1027 (1976).

Under the statute "if it shall appear from the evidence that such weapon was carried, concealed or openly, with the deliberate purpose of injuring the person or destroying the life of another, the court shall impose the highest sentence of imprisonment prescribed." Art. 27, § 36(a).

See Comment, § 4.41, Carrying or wearing a concealed weapon, *supra,* for a discussion of other aspects of the statute, including certain definitions, and the exception for a person "who shall carry such weapon as a reasonable precaution against apprehended danger."

§ 4.43. Wearing, carrying or transporting handgun, openly or concealed.

(a) On or about the person

It is unlawful for any person to wear, carry or transport a handgun, whether concealed or openly, on or about his person. The defendant is charged with wearing, carrying, or transporting a __________ (*insert applicable weapon*).

In order for the defendant to be guilty of this offense, the State must prove beyond a reasonable doubt that the defendant: (1) [knowingly] wore, carried or transported a __________ (*insert weapon*) on or about his person; and (2) that it constitutes a handgun under Maryland law.

A handgun is any pistol, revolver, or other firearm designed to (fire a bullet) (expel a projectile) by the action of an explosive and is capable of being concealed on or about the person. [It includes a short-barreled shotgun and a short-barreled rifle.] [It does not include a shotgun, rifle or antique firearm.]

[A short-barreled shotgun is defined as a shotgun having one or more barrels less than eighteen inches in length or is a weapon made from a shotgun if such weapon, as modified, has an overall length of less than twenty-six inches.]

[A short-barreled rifle is defined as a rifle having one or more barrels less than sixteen inches in length or a weapon made from a rifle if such weapon, as modified, has an overall length of less than twenty-six inches.]

[A shotgun is defined as a weapon designed and intended to be fired from the shoulder and to use an explosive in a fixed shotgun shell to fire through a smooth bore either a number of ball shot or a single projectile for each single pull of the trigger.]

[A rifle is defined as a weapon designed and intended to be fired from the shoulder and to use an explosive in a fixed metallic cartridge to fire only a single projectile through a rifled bore for each single pull of the trigger.]

[An antique firearm is defined as any firearm (including any firearm with a matchlock, flintlock, percussion cap, or similar type of ignition system) manufactured in or before 1898. It also includes any replica of such a firearm if such replica is not designed for using rimfire or conventional centerfire fixed ammunition or uses rimfire or conventional centerfire fixed ammunition which is no longer manufactured in the United States and which is not readily available in the ordinary channels of commercial trade.]

(b) In any vehicle traveling upon public roads, highways, etc.

It is unlawful for any person to wear, carry or knowingly transport any handgun, whether concealed or openly, in any vehicle traveling upon the (public roads) (highways) (waterways) (airways) (upon roads or parking lots generally used by the public). The defendant is charged with wearing, carrying, or knowingly transporting a ___________ (*insert applicable weapon*).

In order for the defendant to be guilty of this offense, the State must prove beyond a reasonable doubt that the defendant: (1) wore, carried or knowingly transported a ___________ (*insert weapon*) in a vehicle traveling upon the (public roads) (highways) (waterways) (airways) (upon roads or parking lots generally used by the public) and (2) that the object or weapon constitutes a handgun under Maryland law.

[The word "knowingly" is generally defined as having knowledge. An act is done knowingly if done voluntarily and purposely, and not because of mistake, accident, inadvertence or other innocent reason. Knowledge can be established directly or can be inferred from all of the surrounding facts and circumstances of the case. The State has the burden to prove knowledge beyond a reasonable doubt.]

A handgun is any pistol, revolver, or other firearm designed to (fire a bullet) (expel a projectile) by the action of an explosive and is capable of being concealed on or about the person. [It includes a short-barreled shotgun and a short-barreled rifle.] It does not include a shotgun, rifle or antique firearm.]

[A short-barreled shotgun is defined as a shotgun having one or more barrels less than eighteen inches in length or is a weapon made from a shotgun if such weapon, as modified, has an overall length of less than twenty-six inches.]

[A short-barreled rifle is defined as a rifle having one or more barrels less than sixteen inches in length or a weapon made from a rifle if such weapon, as modified, has an overall length of less than twenty-six inches.]

[A shotgun is defined as a weapon designed and intended to be fired from the shoulder and to use an explosive in a fixed shotgun shell to fire through a smooth bore either a number of ball shot or a single projectile for each single pull of the trigger.]

[A rifle is defined as a weapon designed and intended to be fired from the shoulder and to use an explosive in a fixed metallic cartridge to fire only a single projectile through a rifled bore for each single pull of the trigger.]

[An antique firearm is defined as any firearm (including any firearm with a matchlock, flintlock, percussion cap, or similar type of ignition system) manufactured in or before

1898. It also includes any replica of such a firearm if such replica is not designed for using rimfire or conventional centerfire fixed ammunition or uses rimfire or conventional centerfire fixed ammunition which is no longer manufactured in the United States and which is not readily available in the ordinary channels of commercial trade.]

COMMENT

There are a number of different activities proscribed by Maryland Ann. Code, Article 27, § 36B. The first two are found in Art. 27, § 36B(b). First, no person can "wear, carry, or transport" a handgun upon or about his person. This law applies whether the handgun is concealed or openly carried. Second, no person can "wear, carry or knowingly transport any handgun, whether concealed or open, in a vehicle traveling upon the public roads, highways, waterways, or airways, or upon roads or parking lots generally used by the public." This criminal act is not conditioned on operation or ownership of the vehicle but upon the physical act of wearing, carrying or knowingly transporting the handgun in the vehicle. 57 Op. Att'y Gen. 288 (1972).

The first part of Art. 27, § 36B(b) on which Instruction, § 4.43(a), *supra,* is based does not specify a *mens rea* term before "wear, carry or transport any handgun." In contrast, the second part of Art. 27, § 36B(b) on which Instruction, § 4.43(b), *supra,* is based requires that the defendant "wear, carry or *knowingly* transport a handgun" in any vehicle (emphasis added). In light of the serious penalty provided for this offense, a question may arise as to whether the courts will read in a *mens rea* term in cases where the defendant (in an unusual case certainly) "wore, carried or transported" a handgun on his person without knowledge or intent. For this reason, the word "knowingly" is placed in brackets in Instruction (a). Also, after the above quoted provision, the statute states: "and it shall be a rebuttable presumption that the person is knowingly transporting the handgun." *Evans v. State,* 28 Md. App. 640, 349 A.2d 300 (1975), *aff'd,* 278 Md. 197, 362 A.2d 629 (1976), and its progeny suggest that such a rebuttable presumption would be unconstitutional if it is interpreted as shifting the burden of persuasion to the defendant on an essential element of the crime. See Appendix V, The Impact of *Evans v. State:* Burdens of Proof, Presumptions and Inferences, *infra.* For this reason, this reference to the rebuttable presumption has not been included in Instruction (b), *supra.* Instead, the definition of "knowingly," placed within brackets, instructs the jury that knowledge can be inferred from all of the surrounding facts and circumstances of the case.

In Art. 27, § 36F(a), "handgun" is defined as including any pistol, revolver or other firearm which is capable of being concealed on the person. This includes short-barreled shotguns and rifles. In *Tisdale v. State,* 30 Md. App. 334, 353 A.2d 653 (1976), the Court held that the definition of "pistol or revolver" in Art. 27, § 441, relating to the registration and sale of firearms, has a different objective from the handgun law and does not apply to Art. 27, § 36F.

The term handgun does not include just any hand weapon that resembles or simulates the appearance of a pistol or revolver and is capable of discharging a missile by any method of propulsion. For a device to be a handgun it must be a firearm or must be readily or easily convertible into a firearm that propels its missiles by gunpowder or a similar explosive. See *Douglas v. State,* 37 Md. App. 557, 378 A.2d 189, 190 (1977), *overruling Todd v. State,* 28 Md. App. 127, 343 A.2d 890 (1975).

In *Pharr v. State,* 36 Md. App. 615, 375 A.2d 1129 (1977), the appellant's conviction for the use of a handgun in the commission of a crime of violence was reversed on the grounds that there was no showing that the weapon at issue fit within the statutory definition of a handgun. In this case, no gun had been introduced into evidence and the appellant, in his confession, had stated that the gun which he had used was merely a "blank gun." *Cf. Johnson v. State,* 44 Md. App. 515, 411 A.2d 118 (1980).

In *Howell v. State,* 278 Md. 389, 364 A.2d 797 (1976), the Court held that a tear gas pistol is not a handgun within the meaning of Art. 27, § 36F. The Court noted that penal statutes are to be strictly construed and that to be a firearm it must propel a missile by gunpowder or some such similar explosive. Tear gas is not a missile within the natural and ordinary meaning of the term. Also, an expert witness had testified that this device could not be readily or easily converted into a gun which would be explosive of projectiles.

It is interesting to note, here, that a 1980 amendment of Art. 27, § 36(a) inserted "chemical mace or tear gas device" in the description of weapons prohibited from being worn or carried "openly with the intent or purpose of injuring any person in any unlawful manner."

For discussion of the question whether a firearm must be *usable* to constitute a handgun and the nature of the offense under Art. 27, § 36B(d), see Comment, § 4.44, *infra*.

Article 27, § 36F is the source of the definitions used in these instructions, i.e., "short-barreled shotgun," "short-barreled rifle," "shotgun," "rifle" and "antique firearm." The section provides that the term, "vehicle," includes any motor vehicle, as defined in Title 11 of the Transportation Article, trains, aircraft, and vessels.

Law-enforcement personnel and various other persons are exempt from the limitations on carrying handguns. See Art. 27, § 36B(c)(1) to (5) for all of the exceptions.

Article 27, § 36B(b)(i) to (iv) provides penalties for violations of the statute. One convicted of an offense for the first time shall be fined not less than $250, nor more than $2,500 or be imprisoned for not less than thirty days nor more than three years. The statute also provides harsher penalties for those who have been convicted of certain offenses once before and those that have been convicted a number of times.

Violations are misdemeanors. Sentencing is determined according to the offender's previous record of convictions and the place where the handgun was found. If the defendant carried, wore or transported the handgun with the deliberate purpose of injuring or killing another, the court must look to a separate sentencing provision. Art. 27, § 36B(b)(iv).

Other related offenses include: Art. 27, § 481C (possession of short-barreled rifles and short-barreled shotguns); Art. 27, § 36G (restrictions on possession of firearms at demonstrations in public places).

§ 4.44. Use of handgun in the commission of a felony or crime of violence.

The use of a handgun [an antique firearm capable of being concealed on the person] in the commission of any felony or any crime of violence is a separate crime in and of itself.

In order for the defendant to be guilty of this offense, the State must prove beyond a reasonable doubt that the defendant: (1) [knowingly] used a __________ (*insert weapon used*); (2) the weapon or object used constitutes a handgun under Maryland law [an antique firearm capable of being concealed on the person]; and (3) at the time the defendant used a __________ (*insert weapon used*), the defendant was committing a felony or crime of violence, namely __________ (*insert alleged felony or crime of violence*).

If the State proves beyond a reasonable doubt that the defendant used a __________ (*insert weapon used*), you must determine whether __________ (*insert weapon used*) is a handgun as defined by law [an antique firearm capable of being concealed on the person]. A handgun is any pistol, revolver or other firearm designed to [fire a bullet] [expel a projectile] by the action of an explosive and is capable of being concealed on or about the person. [It includes a short-barreled shotgun and a short-barreled rifle.] [It shall not include a shotgun, rifle or antique firearm.]

[A short-barreled shotgun is defined as a shotgun having one or more barrels less than eighteen inches in length or is a weapon made from a shotgun if such weapon, as modified, has an overall length of less than twenty-six inches.]

[A short-barreled rifle is defined as a rifle having one or more barrels less than sixteen inches in length or a weapon made from a rifle if such weapon, as modified, has an overall length of less than twenty-six inches.]

[A shotgun is defined as a weapon designed and intended to be fired from a shoulder and to use an explosive in a fixed shotgun shell to fire through a smooth bore either a number of ball shot or a single projectile for each single pull of the trigger.]

[A rifle is defined as a weapon designed and intended to be fired from the shoulder and to use an explosive in a fixed metallic cartridge to fire only a single projectile through a rifled bore for each single pull of the trigger.]

[An antique firearm is defined as any firearm (including any firearm with a matchlock, flintlock, percussion cap, or similar type of ignition system) manufactured in or before 1898. It also includes any replica of such a firearm if such replica is not designed for using rimfire or conventional centerfire fixed ammunition or uses rimfire or conventional centerfire fixed ammunition which is no longer manufactured in the United States and which is not readily available in the ordinary channels of commercial trade.]

To be used where underlying crime is designated in the statute as a "crime of violence": The defendant is charged with unlawful use of a handgun [antique firearm capable of being concealed on the person] in the commission of ___________ (*insert underlying crime of violence*). I instruct you that ___________ (*insert underlying crime of violence*) is a crime of violence under Maryland law. [*See list of applicable crimes of violence in Comment.*] The State must prove beyond a reasonable doubt that the defendant either attempted or committed the crime of ___________ (*insert underlying crime of violence*) and used a handgun in the attempt or commission of the crime.

I will now instruct you on the elements of the crime of ___________ (*insert underlying crime of violence*). [*See Instruction, § 4.05, supra, attempted commission of a crime.*]

To be used where underlying crime is a felony: The defendant is charged with unlawful use of a handgun [antique firearm capable of being concealed on the person] in the commission of ___________ (*insert underlying felony*). I instruct you that ___________ (*insert underlying felony*) is a felony under Maryland law. The State must prove beyond a reasonable doubt that the defendant committed __________ (*insert underlying felony*) and used a handgun in the commission of the offense.

[*To be used where Court determines that assault with intent to commit the felony is statutorily applicable:* If you do not find beyond a reasonable doubt that the defendant completed the crime of __________ (*insert underlying felony*), you should then proceed to consider whether the State has proved beyond a reasonable doubt that the defendant committed assault with intent to commit __________ (*insert applicable felony*) and used a handgun in the commission of this offense.]

I will now instruct you on the elements of the felony of __________ (*insert applicable felony*). [*See, if applicable, Instructions, §§ 4.13 to 4.16, supra, for instructions on certain aggravated assaults.*]

COMMENT

The crime of use of a handgun in the commission of any felony or crime of violence was created with passage of the Handgun Control Act of 1972 (codified in Maryland Ann. Code, Art. 27, §§ 36B to 36F). *Whack v. State,* 283 Md. 137, 416 A.2d 265 (1980), *appeal dismissed,* 450 U.S. 990 (1981); *State ex rel. Sonner v. Shearin,* 272 Md. 502, 325 A.2d 573 (1974).

Article 27, § 36B(d) was amended in 1983 to include the use of an "antique firearm" capable of being concealed on the person. It is unclear whether a *mens rea* element must be established before a defendant can be convicted of unlawful use of a handgun in the commission of a felony or crime of violence. The statute itself does not specify that an intent to use a handgun is required, but the term "use," the purpose of the statute and the penalty provided suggest that the element of knowledge or intent is required. Though the precise definition of "use" is unclear, it is difficult to imagine how one would use a handgun without knowing or intending to do so. Further, the legislative purpose in enacting this statute was to curb the more frequent use of handguns in perpetrating crimes of violence. See Art. 27, § 36B(a) (the declaration of policy); *Wright v. State,* 24 Md. App. 309, 330 A.2d 482 (1975). Convicting those that do not have knowledge or intent, arguably, does not further this purpose. Lastly, the penalty range for first offenders is five to twenty years imprisonment. This would be a severe sentence for one who did not have knowledge or intent to commit a crime. For these reasons the word "knowingly" is placed in the instruction in brackets.

If a *mens rea* term is required, it must then be determined whether this requirement of knowledge or intent goes to the use of the handgun or to the use of the handgun with the knowledge or intent that it be used in a felony or crime of violence. Since most underlying felonies will have an independent *mens rea* term, a finding of knowing use of the handgun and intentional commission of an act, which is a felony or crime of violence, will probably suffice. Since this crime is not limited to underlying crimes requiring an independent *mens rea*, a case may arise that presents this issue. By looking at the purpose of the statute, it could be argued that the defendant must intend to use the handgun in the commission of a felony or crime of violence, that is, knowingly use the handgun in a knowing commission of a felony or crime of violence.

The jury must answer two questions in the affirmative to convict the defendant: (1) was the weapon a handgun as defined in Art. 27, § 36(F)(a); and (2) was it used to commit a felony or crime of violence?

As defined by the statute, "handgun" includes a pistol, revolver, or other firearm designed to expel a projectile by the action of an explosive, and which is capable of being concealed on the person. This includes a short-barreled shotgun and a short-barreled rifle. It does not include a shotgun, rifle, or CO_2 pellet gun nor does it include just any hand weapon simulating the appearance of a pistol or revolver that is capable of discharging a missile by any method of propulsion. For a device to be a handgun it must be a firearm or must be readily convertible into a firearm that propels its missiles by gunpowder or a similar explosive. See Comment, § 4.33, Wearing, carrying or transporting handgun, openly or concealed, *supra,* for a discussion of cases applying the statutory definition of "handgun."

The State must prove, beyond a reasonable doubt, that the defendant used a handgun during the commission of either a felony or a crime of violence as a prerequisite to being convicted of a violation of Art. 27, § 36B(d). *Beard v. State,* 47 Md. App. 410, 413-414, 423 A.2d 275, 276-277 (1980); *Raley v. State,* 32 Md. App. 515, 363 A.2d 261 (1976), *cert. denied,* 278 Md. 731 (1978), *cert. denied,* 431 U.S. 965 (1977); *Ford v. State,* 274 Md. 546, 337 A.2d 81 (1975). The State may use circumstantial evidence to support a conviction. *Dove v. State,* 47 Md. App. 452, 456, 423 A.2d 597, 599 (1980).

Article 27, § 441, provides:

> The term 'crime of violence' means abduction; arson; burglary, including common-law and all statutory and storehouse forms of burglary offenses; escape; housebreaking; kidnapping; manslaughter, excepting involuntary manslaughter; mayhem; murder; rape; robbery; robbery with a deadly weapon; sexual offense in the first degree; and sodomy; or an attempt to commit any of the aforesaid offenses; or assault with intent to commit any other offense punishable by imprisonment for more than one year.

(This definition differs from that set forth in Art. 27, § 643B, relating to mandatory sentences for crimes of violence.)

Note that the definition of a crime of violence in Art. 27, § 441, includes attempts to commit any of the stated crimes. Therefore, the commission of the actual crime need not be completed to be included as a crime of violence.

Also, Art. 27, § 441, presents an interesting and difficult question of statutory interpretation in requiring determination of the crimes to which the phrase, "or an assault with intent to commit any other offense punishable by imprisonment for more than one year" is applicable. It should be observed that the definition of crimes of violence in Art. 27, § 441(e), relating to regulation of the sale or transfer of pistols and revolvers, is incorporated by reference in Art. 27, § 36(B)(d). The phrase was no doubt drafted to take into consideration crimes committed in Maryland or in any other state. See Art. 27, § 442. Further, Art. 27, § 12, governs the penalties for aggravated assaults. The only aggravated assaults statutorily recognized are assault with intent to rob, murder, and to commit a rape in any degree or a sexual offense in the first or second degree. It is worth noting that Art. 27, § 643(B)(a), requiring mandatory sentences for crimes of violence, limits aggravated assaults to assault with intent to murder and assault with intent to rape in the definition of "crime of violence." If this statutory context were to be ignored, it could be argued that "an assault with intent to commit any other offense punishable by more than one year" applies not only to all felonies but to those misdemeanors which authorize punishment by imprisonment for more than one year.

Since the offense delineated in Art. 27, § 36B(d), is separate and distinct from the underlying felony or crime of violence, an individual on trial for the handgun charge does not have to be separately accused of a felony or crime of violence. *Ford v. State, supra,* at 551, 337 A.2d at 85 (1975). Also, conviction on a handgun count can be sustained even if defendant is found not guilty on a separate felony count. When a jury determines that the accused did not commit a felony or crime of violence but is guilty of the use of a handgun in the commission of such felony or crime of violence, the jury has rendered inconsistent verdicts. Yet, prior cases have repudiated the assertion that jury verdicts must be consistent. *Id.* In *Shell v. State,* 307 Md. 46, 512 A.2d 358 (1986), the question of inconsistent verdicts that arose in the *Ford* case occurred in a nonjury trial. The Court noted that commission of a felony or crime of violence is an essential ingredient of the Art. 27, § 36B(d) handgun offense and, thus, limited the *Ford* holding to jury trials.

"In order to avoid this deleterious result the possibility of inconsistent verdicts must be minimized." *Mack v. State,* 300 Md. 583, 595, 479 A.2d 1344, 1350 (1984). When there is a multicount indictment charging a crime of violence and use of a handgun in the commission of a crime of violence, the trial court is required to instruct the jury, upon defendant's request, that defendant could not be found guilty of use of a handgun in the commission of a violent crime, if he was found not guilty of charged crimes of violence. *Id.* at 596, 479 A.2d 1350. However, if the jury returns inconsistent verdicts, both jury verdicts will be allowed to stand. Similarly, a finding of guilty under each can both stand.

A violation of Art. 27, § 36B(d) does not depend upon the actual carrying or physical use of a handgun (or an antique firearm) on the streets or in public. The statute is violated if the use of the handgun was on a private street. *Elchin v. State,* 47 Md. App. 358, 363, 424 A.2d 155, 158 (1980). A defendant need not have personally used the handgun. A person who gives a handgun to another, or obtains one for him to use in the commission of the crime, abets the crime and, therefore, the abettor is a principal subject to the provisions of the statute. *Broadway v. State,* 23 Md. App. 68, 79, 326 A.2d 212, 219 (1974). In addition, one who hires or importunes another to commit a crime with a handgun is also subject to the statute.

The statute does not require that the weapon actually be fired. *Couplin v. State,* 37 Md. App. 567, 578, 378 A.2d 197, 202-203 (1977).

The Court in *Brown v. State,* 29 Md. App. 467, 349 A.2d 267 (1975), held that a failure to show that the gun was loaded would not preclude a conviction for the unlawful use of a handgun in the commission of a felony. The court in *White v. State,* 23 Md. App. 151, 165, 326 A.2d 219, 227 (1974), held that the gun does not have to be operable to require proof that a handgun was used in the commission of a crime. In *York v. State,* 56 Md. App. 222, 467 A.2d 552 (1983), the Court made clear that the statute only applies to a firearm in workable condition that is usable as a handgun (explosive of projectiles) or a firearm readily convertible to that purpose. However, where a Titan and Tiger revolver had a minor mechanical defect that prevented its cylinder from revolving and it could be made to fire if unusual human strength or possibly two hands with force were exerted against its trigger and the defect was correctable in about one minute by the use of simple tools, the weapon was a handgun for purposes of Art. 27, § 36B(d).

The court has also held that the handgun need not be produced in court as evidence. *Couplin v. State, supra.* This decision may still be in effect as long as there is another way for the Court to determine that the handgun was capable of "expelling projectiles." See *York v. State, supra.*

It is a valid exercise of judicial discretion to incorporate into the handgun instruction the legislative purpose of enacting the statute. *Dillon v. State,* 27 Md. App. 579, 588, 342 A.2d 677, 683 (1975), *reviewed in* 277 Md. 571, 357 A.2d 360, 369 (1976). However, despite there being no prejudicial effect in doing so, it is not mandatory to read the purpose to the jury. *Elchin v. State, supra.*

Use of a handgun in the commission of a felony or crime of violence constitutes a separate crime, independent of the underlying felony or crime of violence, and mandates a separate minimum sentence. *Dillon v. State,* 277 Md. 571, 584, 357 A.2d 360, 369 (1976); *Wright v. State, supra; State ex rel. Sonner v. Shearin, supra.* The statute forbids the doctrine of merger of sentences. *Couplin v. State, supra.*

There is no legislative history indicating that Art. 27, § 36B(d) was not intended to apply to robbery cases already covered by Art. 27, § 488 (robbery with a deadly weapon). The handgun penalties were intended to be imposed *in addition* to the penalties under other applicable statutes. *Whack v. State, supra.* The use of a weapon to intimidate the victim of a robbery is viewed as an aggravating factor. The use of a handgun is also an aggravating factor which requires an additional penalty under Art. 27, § 36B(d). *Id.* Therefore, a conviction under Art. 27, § 36B(d) is different than a conviction for robbery with a deadly weapon. The latter requires proof of both a robbery and the use of a deadly weapon (not necessarily a handgun) in its perpetration. A conviction under Art. 27, § 36B(d) requires proof that a handgun was used as well as proof that it was used in commission of a felony or crime of violence. *Couplin v. State, supra.*

In *Stevenson v. State,* 43 Md. App. 120, 403 A.2d 812 (1972), *aff'd,* 287 Md. 504, 413 A.2d 1340 (1980), the Court held that the imposition of separate sentences for robbery with a deadly weapon and the use of a handgun in commission of a felony does not violate double jeopardy principles.

The sentence for a person convicted of using a handgun in the commission of a felony or crime of violence cannot be less than five years nor more than twenty years. The sentence for a second offense cannot be less than five years nor more than twenty years, and it is mandatory that the court impose no less than "a minimum consecutive sentence of five years which shall be served consecutively and not concurrently to any other sentence imposed by virtue of the commission of said felony or misdemeanor." Art. 27, § 36B(d)(2).

F. Other Offenses

§ 4.51. Abortion.

COMMENT

Maryland repealed and reenacted its abortion laws in 1982, transferring them from Maryland Ann. Code, Art. 43, to the Health-General Article, §§ 20-201 to 20-214.

The revised laws are divided into three parts. Part I, entitled "Abortion Referral Service," makes it a misdemeanor (1) to engage in or advertise an abortion referral service (Maryland Ann. Code, Health-General, § 20-201); (2) to operate an abortion referral service unless it is registered with the Department (Health-General, § 20-203); or (3) for a person who operates an abortion referral service to split the fee received by the facility or person who performs the abortion (Health-General, § 20-204). A violation carries a maximum fine of $1,000 or one year imprisonment. Health-General, § 20-206.

Part II, entitled "Abortion Restrictions," makes it a misdemeanor for a person (1) to sell any type of drug or instrumentality that may be used in an abortion except an abortion performed by a licensed physician in an accredited hospital; or (2) to give any advice, counsel or assistance for the purpose of obtaining an abortion except for an abortion by a licensed physician in an accredited hospital. Health-General, § 20-210.

Part III, entitled "Information," states that if an abortion is not necessary to save the life of the woman, certain information must be provided. The information to be provided includes financial and other material assistance available to the woman in order to carry the pregnancy and raise and support the child, or the availability of adoption. A "willful" violation of this section is a misdemeanor and carries a maximum fine of $500. Health-General, § 20-210.

The revisions were necessitated by the United States Supreme Court decisions in *Roe v. Wade,* 410 U.S. 113, 93 S. Ct. 705, 35 L.

Ed. 2d 147 (1973) and *Doe v. Bolton,* 410 U.S. 179, 93 S. Ct. 739, 35 L. Ed. 2d 201 (1973) which restricted the application of state abortion laws from and after the first trimester of pregnancy. In *Roe v. Wade, supra,* it was held that a state criminal abortion statute violated the due process clause of the fourteenth amendment in that such statute exempted from criminality only a life-saving procedure on behalf of the mother without regard to the stage of the pregnancy or without recognition of other interests. Under *Roe* (1) an abortion prior to approximately the first trimester of pregnancy can be performed by the attending physician in consultation with his patient. The physician and patient are free to determine without regulation the desirability and necessity of the abortion. (2) For the stage subsequent to approximately the end of the first trimester the state may, if it chooses, regulate the abortion procedure in ways that are reasonably related to maternal health. (3) For the stage subsequent to viability, the state, if it chooses, may regulate or even proscribe abortion except where it is necessary in appropriate medical judgment for the preservation of the life or health of the mother.

In *State v. Ingel,* 18 Md. App. 514, 308 A.2d 223 (1973), the Court of Special Appeals discussed Art. 43, § 139 (now Health-General, § 20-210) in light of *Roe v. Wade, supra,* and *Doe v. Bolton, supra.*

The Court held that: (1) the provision that certain acts are crimes if done other than by a "licensed physician" was constitutional; (2) the provision that the acts are crimes if done "other than in a hospital accredited and licensed by the State Board of Health and Mental Hygiene" was unconstitutional on its face; and (3) the dictates of *Roe v. Wade, supra,* and *Doe v. Bolton, supra,* are fully retroactive with respect to Art. 43, § 139.

In *Connecticut v. Menillo,* 423 U.S. 9, 96 S. Ct. 170, 46 L. Ed. 2d 152 (1975), the Supreme Court stated that a state statute unconstitutionally restricts a woman's right to an abortion if it permits the termination of pregnancy only when it is necessary to save the life of the expectant mother. The Court held, however, that a state statute of a similar nature, which makes criminal an attempted abortion by any person, is constitutional and thus fully effective against the performance of abortions by non-physicians. The state interest in maternal health provides the additional justification for prosecutions against nonphysicians who conduct abortions during even the first trimester.

See also *Planned Parenthood v. Danforth,* 428 U.S. 52, 96 S. Ct. 2831, 49 L. Ed. 2d 788 (1976); *Colautti v. Franklin,* 439 U.S. 379, 99 S. Ct. 675, 58 L. Ed. 2d 596 (1979); *Planned Parenthood Ass'n v. Ashcroft,* 462 U.S. 476, 103 S. Ct. 2517, 76 L. Ed. 2d 733 (1983); *Simopoulos v. Virginia,* 462 U.S. 506, 103 S. Ct. 2532, 76 L. Ed. 2d 755 (1983); *Akron v. Akron Center for Reprod. Health,* 462 U.S. 416, 103 S. Ct. 2481, 76 L. Ed. 2d 687 (1983).

§4.52. Arson.

A person commits arson if he willfully and maliciously either sets fire to or causes to be burned a dwelling house or other property designated by statute [or if he aids, counsels or procures the burning].

The defendant is charged with ________ ([setting fire to] [causing to be burned] [aiding, counselling, or procuring the burning of]) ________ (*specify property*). You are instructed that ________ (*specify property*) is property designated by statute.

In order for a person to be found guilty of this offense, the State must prove beyond a reasonable doubt that: (1) the fire did occur to ________ (*specify property*); (2) the defendant actually set the fire [or aided, counseled or procured the burning]; and (3) the defendant's acts were done willfully and maliciously.

The burden is on the State to show that the burning was with a criminal design. Where nothing except the burning appears, the law presumes it to be accidental or from natural causes. The term "willfully" characterizes an act done with deliberate intention for which there is no reasonable excuse. The term "maliciously" describes an act done with the deliberate intention of harming another person. The State may prove intent by the circumstances surrounding the burning. If the State proves that the burning was willful and malicious, the slightest burning makes the offense complete. There is no requirement that the structure be destroyed.

In order for a person to be found guilty of a charge that he willfully and maliciously set fire to or burned or caused to be burned the property, such person must have actually set the fire, either by his own hand or by the hand of an agent [or such person must have aided, counseled or procured the setting of the fire or the burning or the causing to be burned, even though he did not commit the crime himself].

COMMENT

This instruction is patterned substantially after the case law in Maryland. Arson as a common-law crime was the malicious burning of the dwelling house of another. *Butina v. State,* 4 Md. App. 312, 242 A.2d 819 (1968). Maryland Ann. Code, Art. 27, § 6 enlarges the scope of the common law to encompass "any dwelling house or any kitchen, shop, barn, stable or other outhouse that is parcel thereof, or belonging to or adjoining thereto, whether the property of himself, or of another." The penalty for a violation of Art. 27, § 6, is not more than thirty years in the penitentiary.

The scope of the crime of arson is further enlarged by Art. 27, §§ 7 and 8. Art. 27, § 7, includes "any barn, stable, garage or other building or pier, wharf, boathouse, or any facility attached to a pier or wharf, whether the property of himself or of another, not a parcel of a dwelling house; or any shop, storehouse, warehouse, factory, mill or other building, whether the property of himself or of another; or any church, meetinghouse, courthouse, workhouse, school, jail, or other public building or any public bridge." The sentence for an Art. 27, § 7, offense is not more than twenty years in the penitentiary. Art. 27, § 8, which was repealed and reenacted by Acts 1981, ch. 768, extends the crime of arson to include the "personal property of another person." If the damage to the property is less than $1000, a person who violates the section is guilty of a misdemeanor and may be fined up to $500 or incarcerated for not more than eighteen months or both.

If damage to the property is $1000 or more, a person who violates the provisions of Art. 27, § 8 is guilty of a felony and may be sentenced to a term of incarceration of not more than five years or fined up to $5000 or both.

Arson is a specific intent crime and requires a person to act willfully and maliciously. Where nothing but the burning appears, the law presumes it to have been accidental or from natural causes. *Hughes v. State,* 6 Md. App. 389, 251 A.2d 373 (1969). See Instructions, §§ 3.04 and 3.06 for definitions of "willfully" and "maliciously."

To prove a fire was maliciously and willfully set, the State can show the fire was incendiary in nature. *Hughes v. State, supra.* However, since "maliciously" means having the intention to do harm to another, the fact that it was shown that the defendant willfully set fire to his own uninsured building was not enough to infer that it was done maliciously. *Brown v. State,* 285 Md. 469, 403 A.2d 788 (1979).

In *DeBettencourt v. State,* 48 Md. App. 522, 531-32, 428 A.2d 479, 485 (1981), however, the Court held that proof of the "setting of a dangerous fire with reckless and wanton disregard of the consequences in terms of bringing harm to others" satisfies the requirements of "willful" and "malicious" under the law of arson. This interpretation was challenged in Judge Liss' dissenting opinion. *Id.* at 532-33, 428 A.2d at 485.

Incendiarism may be shown by:

> [T]he manner in which the fire was burned, by the presence of an odor of flammable liquid, by the fact that combustible materials or flammable liquids or their containers were found on the burned premises, by demonstrating the improbability that the fire had resulted from accidental or natural causes, by evidence of threats to destroy the property, by the isolation of the premises, by the absence of any natural cause for the fire, by precautions taken to avoid a fire or other facts of similar import tending to show that the fire had an incendiary origin.

Hughes v. State, supra at 394, 251 A.2d at 376.

Arson may be proved by circumstantial evidence and the inferences which may reasonably be drawn therefrom. *McDowell v. State,* 231 Md. 205, 189 A.2d 611 (1963); *Smith v. State,* 20 Md.

App. 577, 318 A.2d 568 (1974), *cert. denied,* 272 Md. 748 (1974), *cert. denied,* 420 U.S. 909 (1975). The presence of the defendant in the vicinity of the fire, whether before or after its occurrence is always relevant. *McDowell v. State, supra.* See also *Nasim v. State,* 34 Md. App. 65, 366 A.2d 70 (1976), *cert. denied,* 434 U.S. 868 (1977).

One who aids, counsels or procures is to be treated as a principal. *Abrams v. Warden,* 333 F. Supp. 612 (D. Md. 1971). To be guilty of counseling, the burning must have occurred. *Butina v. State, supra.*

Butina v. State, supra, at 317-18, 242 A.2d at 822, states:

> Since under the statute two separate substantive offenses of arson are defined, it follows that to be validly convicted a person must be properly charged with the offense of arson which the evidence shows he committed. So if he, in fact, set fire to or burned or caused to be burned a dwelling house, he cannot be convicted on a charge that he aided, counseled or procured the burning, and vice versa. But in considering the offense which he in fact committed, consideration must be given to the distinction at common law between principals and accessories, for even though the statute makes a person a principal who at common law would be an accessory before the fact to arson, we think that a person may be convicted of setting a fire to or burning or causing to burn a dwelling house only if he would have been a principal at common law and that he may be convicted of arson only if he would have been an accessory before the fact at common law.

In *Hines v. State,* 34 Md. App. 612, 368 A.2d 509 (1977), evidence that the building at issue was merely full of smoke, even when coupled with the appellant's extrajudicial statement that the building was burning when he left, was not sufficient to prove the *corpus delicti* of the crime of arson as codified in Art. 27, § 7. To sustain a conviction for arson it is essential that the State prove the fire was in a part of the structure itself and did not merely damage items within the building. See *Ellerba v. State,* 41 Md. App. 712, 398 A.2d 1250 (1979).

For a discussion of the offense of arson for the purpose of defrauding an insurance company (prohibited by Art. 27, § 9), see *Borza v. State,* 25 Md. App. 391, 335 A.2d 142 (1975).

A special provision governs the burning of trash containers, such as dumpsters used for trash and refuse collection at shopping malls and apartment and office buildings. Art. 27, § 9A. A special provision also proscribes the burning of a cross or other religious symbol. Art. 27, § 10A. A "person, who, while perpetrating, or attempting to perpetrate a crime, shall set fire to or burn any of the buildings specified in this subtitle" is guilty of a separate crime. Art. 27, § 11. Finally, any person who willfully and maliciously *attempts* to set fire to enumerated buildings or property or who commits "any act preliminary thereto, or in furtherance thereof" is punished under a separate provision. Art. 27, § 10. A separate subsection specifies what constitutes an "attempt" under this section. Art. 27, § 10(c).

§ 4.53. Breaking — Storehouse, etc., with intent to commit a felony or steal (Article 27, § 32).

Breaking in or out of a premise with the intent to __________ ([murder] [commit a felony] [steal goods, money or personal property]) is a crime.

In order for the defendant to be guilty of this offense, the State must prove beyond a reasonable doubt that: (1) there was a breaking; (2) the breaking was of a __________, ([storehouse] [filling station] [garage] [trailer] [cabin] [diner] [warehouse] [outhouse], [boat]); (3) the defendant was the person who did the breaking; and (4) the defendant had the intent at the time of the breaking to __________ ([murder] [commit a felony] [steal, take or carry away the money, goods or personal property of another of the value of $300 or more]).

It is essential to prove a breaking. The breaking may be into or out of a premise. [The breaking may be actual or constructive.] A[n actual] breaking may be made by unloosening, removing or displacing any covering or fastening of the premises. A[n actual] breaking must include some overt act, such as raising a window, opening a door, lifting a latch, drawing a bolt or removing a screen. A breaking occurs if the slightest force is used to open the premises. The breaking must be of some part of the structure. [A constructive breaking occurs when a person gains entrance by trick, fraud, artifice or other similar means. There is no breaking if a person has a right to enter or if he enters with the consent of the owner, unless trick, fraud, or artifice is used to obtain that consent.] It is not necessary to prove an actual entry into the premises.

[The breaking is not limited to an outside door or window. If the outside door is open but there is an entrance into a part of the structure which is closed, there is a breaking. Some part of the building itself must be opened, such as an inner door. The opening of a trunk, box or piece of furniture within the building will not meet the requirement.]

It is also essential that the defendant at the time of the breaking had the intent to __________ ([murder] [commit the crime of __________, which I instruct you is a felony under Maryland law] [steal, take or carry away money or the personal goods of another of the value of $300 or more]). It is not necessary that the defendant did in fact __________ ([commit murder] [commit the felony] [steal, take or carry away the personal goods of another]). You need only find that the defendant intended to do so. Felonious intent can be inferred from the circumstances. However, there must be some fact or circumstance, in addition to proof of the breaking, from which you can reasonably determine that the defendant did intend to __________ ([murder] [commit a felony] [steal, take or carry away money or the personal goods of another of the value of $300 or more]).

[In determining whether the State has proved beyond a reasonable doubt that the defendant intended to steal the money, goods or personal property of another of the value of $300 or more, you should consider all of the facts and circumstances in evidence. [In this regard, you may consider the value of the contents of the structure where the breaking occurred as well as any facts, circumstances or inferences of whether the defendant was aware of the value of this property and had a design to steal it.] [In this regard, you may consider the value of the goods actually stolen. If the value of the goods actually stolen was less than $300 but all of the facts and circumstances in evidence give rise to a rational inference that the defendant actually intended to take goods valued at $300 or more, you may find that the defendant intended to steal goods of the value of $300 or more, even though the value of the goods actually reduced to the defendant's possession was less than $300. On the other hand, if the evidence merely shows that the goods taken were valued at less than $300, the defendant may not be found guilty of this offense.]]

[If the defendant has been found in exclusive possession of goods which have been identified as being identical with goods taken in a recent breaking, and if there is no reasonable explanation of such possession, then you may draw an inference of fact that the defendant was the burglar, sufficient to justify a conviction, if you also find that there was in fact a breaking and that the value of the goods intended to be stolen was $300 or more.]

COMMENT

See Comment, § 4.55, Breaking, storehouse, etc., with the taking of property, *infra.*

§ 4.54. Breaking — Storehouse, etc., with intent to steal any money, goods or chattels under the value of $300 (Article 27, § 33A).

Breaking into certain designated premises and __________ ([intending to steal] [stealing goods, money or chattel]) is a crime.

In order for the defendant to be guilty of this offense, the State must prove beyond a reasonable doubt that: (1) there was a breaking into; (2) the breaking into was of a ____________ ([shop] [storehouse] [tobacco house] [warehouse] [building] [boat] [craft] [vessel]); (3) the defendant was the person who did the breaking; and (*Alternative A:* the defendant had an *intent to steal* money, goods or chattel valued at *less* than $300) (*Alternative B:* the defendant *stole* money, goods or chattel of a value *less* than $5).

It is essential to prove a breaking. [The breaking may be actual or constructive.] A[n actual] breaking may be made by unloosening, removing or displacing any covering or fastening of the premises. A[n actual] breaking must include some overt act, such as raising a window, opening a door, lifting a latch, drawing a bolt or removing a screen. A breaking occurs if the slightest force is used to open the premises. The breaking must be of some part of the structure. [A constructive breaking occurs when a person gains entrance by trick, fraud, artifice or other similar means. There is no breaking if a person has a right to enter or if he enters with the consent of the owner, unless trick, fraud, or artifice is used to obtain that consent.] It is not necessary to prove an actual entry into the premises.

[The breaking is not limited to an outside door or window. If the outside door is open but there is an entrance into a part of the structure which is closed, there is a breaking. Some part of the building itself must be opened, such as an inner door. The opening of a trunk, box or piece of furniture within the building will not meet the requirement.]

If charged with Alternative A

It is not necessary that the defendant did in fact steal any money, goods or chattels. You need only find that he intended to do so. Intent may be inferred from the circumstances. This intent, however, must be some fact or circumstance, in addition to proof of the breaking, from which you can reasonably determine that the defendant did intend to steal money, goods or chattels under the value of $300.

[If the defendant has been found in exclusive possession of goods which have been identified as being identical with goods taken in a recent breaking, and if there is no reasonable explanation of such possession, then you may draw an inference of fact that the defendant was the burglar, sufficient to justify a conviction, if you also find that there was in fact a breaking.]

If charged with Alternative B

The State must prove that the defendant did in fact steal the goods, chattels or money in question. Stealing is defined as the taking and carrying away of the money, goods or chattels of another with the intent to permanently deprive the other of his property.

[If the defendant has been found in exclusive possession of goods which have been identified as being identical with goods taken in a recent breaking, and if there is no reasonable explanation of such possession, then you may draw an inference of fact that the defendant was the burglar, sufficient to justify a conviction, if you also find that there was in fact a breaking.]

COMMENT

See Comment, § 4.55, Breaking — Storehouse, etc., with the taking of property, *infra*.

§ 4.55. Breaking — Storehouse, etc., with the taking of property (Article 27, § 33).

Breaking into certain designated premises and stealing goods, money or chattels is a crime.

In order for the defendant to be guilty of this offense, the State must prove beyond a reasonable doubt that: (1) there was a breaking into; (2) the breaking into was of a __________ ([shop] [storeroom] [filling station] [garage] [trailer] [boat] [cabin] [diner] [tobacco house] [warehouse]); (3) the defendant was the person who did the breaking into; (4) money, goods, or personal property were stolen by the defendant of a value equal to or greater than $5.

It is essential to prove a breaking. [The breaking may be actual or constructive.] A[n actual] breaking may be made by unloosening, removing or displacing any covering or fastening of the premises. A[n actual] breaking must include some overt act, such as raising a window, opening a door, lifting a latch, drawing a bolt or removing a screen. A breaking occurs if the slightest force is used to open the premises. The breaking must be of some part of the structure. [A constructive breaking occurs when a person gains entrance by trick, fraud, artifice or other similar means. There is no breaking if a person has a right to enter or if he enters with the consent of the owner, unless trick, fraud or artifice is used to obtain the consent.]

[The breaking is not limited to an outside door or window. If the outside door is open but there is an entrance into a part of the structure which is closed, there is a breaking. Some part of the building itself must be opened, such as an inner door. The opening of a trunk, box or piece of furniture within the building will not meet the requirement.]

The State must prove that the defendant did in fact steal the goods, chattels or money in question. Stealing is defined as the taking and carrying away of the money, goods or chattels of another with the intent to permanently deprive the other of his property.

[If the defendant has been found in exclusive possession of goods which have been identified as being identical with goods taken in a recent breaking, and if there is not reasonable explanation of such possession, then you may draw an inference of fact that the defendant was the burglar, sufficient to justify a conviction, if you also find that there was in fact a breaking.]

COMMENT

These instructions are taken from case law in Maryland dealing with storehouse breaking and with three separate provisions of the Maryland Ann. Code, namely: Art. 27, §§ 32, 33 and 33A. Section 33A of Article 27 was formerly § 342, which was renumbered by Acts 1978, ch. 849. The following chart illustrates the differences between the statutes:

*Comparison of Breaking Statutes**

	§ 32	§ 33	§ 33A Alternative "A"	§ 33A Alternative "B"
Nature of breaking	in or out	into	into	into
Activity prohibited	intent to steal or commit felony	actually steals	intent to steal	actually steals
Required value	greater than or equal to $300	greater than or equal to $5	less than $300	less than $5
Status of offense	felony	felony	misdemeanor	misdemeanor
Punishment	sentenced to penitentiary for not more than 10 years	restore goods or pay value; sentenced to penitentiary for not more than 10 years	restore goods or pay value; sentence** of not more than 18 months	restore goods or pay value; sentence** of not more than 18 months

*In addition to these differences, there is a slight difference in the type of designated premises specified under these statutes.

**The convicted misdemeanant "shall ... be further sentenced to the penitentiary or house of correction, or to the jail of the county in which the offense may have been committed, or of the City of Baltimore, if the offense be committed in said city."

These provisions set forth three separate statutory crimes of storehouse breaking. *Turner v. State,* 242 Md. 408, 219 A.2d 39 (1966). The statutes require a "breaking." However, none of the sections explicitly requires that an entry be made. *Ball v. State,* 7 Md. App. 219, 254 A.2d 367 (1969). Therefore, no proof of an entry is required. *Jennings v. State,* 8 Md. App. 312, 259 A.2d 543 (1969). Yet, it should be noted that the statutes proscribe two different types of activities. Art. 27, § 32 and the first alternative (designated "A" herein) set forth in Art. 27, § 33A require merely an intent to engage in the proscribed acts. On the other hand, Art. 27, § 33 and the second alternative of Art. 27, § 33A (designated "B" herein) require that the defendant actually steal. Where the goods stolen are located within the structure, an entry is implied from the act of taking and carrying away the personal property of another.

The element of breaking, essential to prove the offense of storehouse breaking as codified in Art. 27, § 32, is met even if the intruder breaks *out* of the building, as opposed to only *into* the building. *Sample v. State,* 33 Md. App. 398, 365 A.2d 773 (1976). In this regard, a close reading of the three statutes is instructive. Article 27, § 32 refers to the crime of "breaking a storehouse," etc., while Art. 27, §§ 33 and 33A proscribe "breaking *into* any shop" and "break *into* any shop." The word "into" does not appear after the word "breaking" in Art. 27, § 32.

"Breaking" has the same meaning as an element of the statutory offenses of burglary as it has as an element of common-law burglary. *Sizemore v. State,* 10 Md. App. 682, 272 A.2d 824 (1971). "Breaking" is given its common-law meaning. *Brooks v. State,* 25 Md. App. 194, 333 A.2d 352 (1975), *aff'd,* 277 Md. 155, 353 A.2d 217 (1976). It requires either an actual or constructive breaking of a storehouse, etc., by a criminal trespass. A constructive breaking includes an entry gained by artifice, by fraud, by conspiracy with those within, or by threats. An accused's failure to leave the premises when the store closed for business made his original entrance a constructive, illegal breaking and entering *ab initio. Brooks v. State, supra.*

An actual breaking may be made by unloosening, removing or displacing any covering or fastening of the premises, such as lifting a latch, drawing a bolt, raising an unfastened window, or pushing open a door kept closed by its own weight. *Sparkman v. State,* 3 Md. App. 527, 240 A.2d 328 (1968). See also *Jones v. State,* 2 Md. App. 356, 234 A.2d 625 (1967); *Reagan v. State,* 2 Md. App. 262, 234 A.2d 278 (1967). Turning a doorknob and opening a closed door or merely further opening a door left ajar involves sufficient force to constitute an actual breaking, provided it is a trespassory act. There is no breaking, however, if a person has a right to enter or if he enters with the consent of the owner. *Martin v. State,* 10 Md. App. 274, 269 A.2d 182 (1970). See also *Finke v. State,* 56 Md. App. 450, 468 A.2d 353 (1983).

If one breaks the inner door to a room in the building he may be guilty of storehouse breaking; to be convicted one need not break an outer door to a building. One is not guilty of storehouse breaking, however, if he only breaks into a storage chest since it forms no part of the real estate. *Arnold v. State,* 7 Md. App. 1, 252 A.2d 878 (1969). See *Sizemore v. State, supra.*

For the purpose of the three statutory provisions, all buildings other than a dwelling house are within the meaning of the structures enumerated in the sections. (These enumerations contain numerous structures including storehouses.) *Hackley v. State,* 237 Md. 566, 207 A.2d 475 (1965); *Buckley v. State,* 2 Md. App. 508, 235 A.2d 754 (1967).

Certain structures have been specifically found to be storehouses: storerooms, *Hardison v. State,* 226 Md. 53, 172 A.2d 407 (1961); supermarkets, *Id.*; schoolhouses, *Springfield v. State,* 238 Md. 611, 208 A.2d 603 (1965); fraternity houses, *Poff v. State,* 4 Md. App. 186, 241 A.2d 898 (1968); vacant apartments, *Arnold v. State, supra*; motion picture theaters, *Hackley v. State, supra*; and churches, *Sizemore v. State, supra.*

Article 27, § 33A has been amended to include any boat, craft or vessels.

Intent is an element of felonious storehouse breaking under Art. 27, § 32 and an element of the misdemeanor of storehouse breaking under Art. 27, § 33A. The difference between the two sections is that under the former it must be proven that the property which the defendant intended to take was valued over $300. The actual intention at the time of the breaking is controlling, not whether any goods of value were actually stolen, *Ridley v. State,* 228 Md. 281, 179 A.2d 710 (1962); *Sparkman v. State, supra; Pearre v. State,* 237 Md. 622, 206 A.2d 249 (1965); *Brown v. State,* 50 Md. App. 651, 441 A.2d 354 (1982); *O'Brien v. State,* 1 Md. App. 94, 227 A.2d 362 (1967): Felonious intent can be inferred from the circumstances where the defendant was interrupted shortly after breaking into the storehouse. *Pearre v. State, supra.* It is necessary, however, in proving intent that there be proof of some fact, circumstance, act or declaration of the defendant in addition to the proof of the mere breaking from which the trier of facts can find the intent. *Felkner v. State,* 218 Md. 300, 146 A.2d 424 (1958); *Benton v. State,* 8 Md. App. 388, 260 A.2d 86 (1969).

It is a well accepted principle that the intention may be inferred from the circumstances. *O'Brien v. State, supra; Sparkman v. State, supra; Robinson v. State,* 4 Md. App. 515, 243 A.2d 879 (1968); *Johnson v. State,* 5 Md. App. 540, 248 A.2d 663 (1968). Even when dealing with Art. 27, § 32, which requires that the value of the goods be over $300, felonious intent may be shown circumstantially although articles of small or no value are taken. *Tyner v. Warden,* 232 Md. 666, 194 A.2d 793 (1963); *Johnson v. State, supra; Barnett v. State,* 5 Md. App. 5, 245 A.2d 104 (1968). It is also permissible for the trier of fact to infer an intent to steal goods worth more than the actual value of the article stolen so as to establish an intent to commit a felony. *Wallace v. State,* 231 Md. 517, 191 A.2d 221 (1963).

A method of proving the accused's intent to steal goods of the value of $300 or more is to establish the value of the goods actually stolen. Another method is to establish by appropriate testimony the value of the contents of the building where the breaking occurred. *Johnson v. State, supra.*

In one case it was found that: "The attempt by the appellants to enter a storehouse (which they knew carried a substantial inventory) in the nighttime, with an axe, was sufficient to support a rational inference that they intended to steal everything of value that they could find and carry away." *Hebb v. State,* 10 Md. App. 145, 149, 268 A.2d 578, 581 (1970). See also *Howard v. State,* 240 Md. 699, 213 A.2d 288 (1965); *Mercer v. State,* 237 Md. 479, 206 A.2d 797 (1965).

To support a felony conviction under Art. 27, § 33, it must be shown that: (a) there was a breaking; and (b) there was a larceny amounting in value of $5 or more. *Hyman v. State,* 4 Md. App. 636, 244 A.2d 616 (1968); *Turner v. State, supra.* A defendant will be found guilty of the misdemeanor of storehouse breaking if the value of the goods is under $5.

If the defendant is found in exclusive possession of recently stolen goods, he may be convicted of storehouse breaking unless he has a satisfactory explanation of how he acquired those goods.

Ponder v. State, 227 Md. 570, 177 A.2d 839 (1962); *Pointer v. State,* 238 Md. 23, 207 A.2d 611 (1965); *Lambiotte v. State,* 17 Md. App. 545, 303 A.2d 163 (1973). (See Comment, § 4.57, Burglary, for a related application of this evidentiary rule.) While possession of recently stolen articles from a burglarized dwelling may be sufficient to permit a rational inference that the possessor was the burglar, *Boggs v. State,* 228 Md. 168, 179 A.2d 338 (1962), mere possession of recently stolen articles is not sufficient to permit a rational inference that there was a breaking of a dwelling from which they were stolen in the absence of any evidence that there was an actual or constructive breaking of the dwelling. *Reagan v. State, supra.*

Article 27, §§ 32, 33 and 33A are complementary and mutually exclusive. See *Wersten v. State,* 232 Md. 164, 192 A.2d 286 (1963); *Fields v. State,* 50 Md. App. 717, 439 A.2d 1121 (1982), for a discussion of the relationship between Art. 27, §§ 32 and 33A. Also, there are no inconsistencies between Art. 27, §§ 33 and 33A; the two offenses have separate elements, the intent in one and the stealing in the other, and are, therefore, distinct crimes. *Fields v. State, supra; Fabian v. State,* 235 Md. 306, 201 A.2d 511, *cert. denied,* 379 U.S. 869 (1964). Hence, Art. 27, § 33A is not considered a lesser included offense or a lesser degree of § 32. *Grimes v. State,* 290 Md. 236, 429 A.2d 228 (1981), *rev'd on other grounds,* 290 Md. 236, 429 A.2d 228 (1981).

Storehouse breaking as described in Art. 27, §§ 32 and 33 is a felony and under the statutes carries a maximum penalty of ten years in the penitentiary in addition to restitution of any goods, money or chattel actually taken. Storehouse breaking as defined by Art. 27, § 33A is a misdemeanor and provides a maximum penalty of eighteen months of incarceration in addition to restitution of any goods, money or chattel actually taken.

A separate misdemeanor exists for merely breaking and entering a storehouse, etc., punishable by a fine of not more than $500, or imprisonment for not more than six months, or both. There is no requirement of an intent to steal or commit a felony or to take anything of value. Art. 27, § 31B.

The General Assembly has provided a separate offense called "burglary with explosives." The crime consists of breaking and entering, either by day or by night, any building, whether inhabited or not, and opening or attempting to open any vault, safe or other secure place by the use of nitroglycerine, gunpowder or other explosive and it is a felony punishable in the penitentiary for not more than forty years. Art. 27, §§ 34 and 35.

See § 4.57, Instructions, Burglary, and § 4.69, Housebreaking — Daytime, *infra*.

§ 4.56. Bribery — Obstructing justice.

(a) Attempting to bribe

The defendant in this case has been charged with attempted bribery. Bribery, as used here, means the voluntary giving or offering to any public official of any sum of money or thing of value to influence him in the performance of his official duties. An attempt to commit a crime is defined as an endeavor to commit that crime or an act done with the intent to commit that crime, beyond mere preparation, but which may fall short of successful completion.

In order for the defendant to be guilty of this offense the State must prove beyond a reasonable doubt that: (1) there was an offer; (2) the offer was made by the defendant; (3) the offer was of something of value; (4) the offer was made to a public officer or official; (5) the defendant knew the offeree was a public officer or official; and (6) the offer was made with the intent that this thing of value would influence the public official in the performance of his duties.

The defendant must have had an actual purpose or specific design to bribe the official. Such actual intent may be inferred from the circumstances. The intent must have been to influence the public official's actions, vote, opinion, decision or judgment on any matter, question, cause or proceeding which is then before him or which might come or be brought before him in his official capacity. Official duties may include those implicitly authorized by custom and circumstance which amount to an official practice, as well as those prescribed by statute or written rules and regulations. The thing of value may be anything of value including, but not limited to, a gift or gratuity or sum of money.

The State need not prove that there was an actual tender of a bribe. That is, there need not be any actual passing of the money nor the attempt to pass money. Any expression of the ability to produce the amount or thing of value offered is sufficient.

An attempt to commit a crime occurs when the defendant does some act with criminal intent beyond mere preparation but which falls short of a successful completion of the crime. It is required that the defendant perform some act in the nature of a direct movement toward the commission of the offense. There must be an effort towards consummation of the crime, an act done in pursuance of a criminal act but falling short of commission of the crime.

(b) Offering a bribe.

The defendant in this case is charged with offering a bribe. Bribery as used here means the voluntary giving or offering to any public official of any sum of money or thing of value to influence him in the performance of his official duties.

In order for a person to be guilty of this offense the State must prove beyond a reasonable doubt that: (1) there was an offer; (2) the offer was made by the defendant; (3) the offer was of something of value; (4) the offer was made to a public officer or official; (5) the defendant knew the offeree was a public officer or official; (6) the offer was made with the intent that this thing of value would influence the public official in the performance of his public duties; and (7) there was a passing of a thing of value to the public officer or official.

The essence of this offense is the passing of a thing of value to a public officer or official in the performance of his official duties.

It is essential that the gift or offering be made with the intent to influence the public official's actions, vote, opinion, decision or judgment on any matter, question, cause or proceeding which is then before him or which might come or be brought before him in his official capacity. Official duties may include those implicitly authorized by custom and circumstance which amount to an official practice, as well as those prescribed by statute or written rules and regulations. The thing of value may be anything of value including, but not limited to, a gift or gratuity or sum of money.

(c) Receiving a bribe

The defendant in this case has been charged with receiving a bribe. Bribery, as used here, means the giving or offering to, and receipt by a public official of any sum of money or thing of value for the purpose of influencing him in the performance of his official duties, or for neglecting or failing to perform these duties.

In order for the defendant to be found guilty of this offense, the State must prove beyond a reasonable doubt that: (1) there was an offer of something of value; (2) this offer was made to a public official or officer with the intention that this thing of value would influence him in the performance of his official duties; (3) the defendant is a public officer or official; (4) the defendant received this thing of value; and (5) he received it with the intention that by receiving it he would be influenced in the performance or discharge of his official duties.

It is essential that the gift or offering was received by the public official with the intent that he would be influenced thereby in performing or discharging his official duties, or for neglecting or failing to perform his official duties.

Official duties may include those implicitly authorized by custom and circumstance which amount to an official practice, as well as those prescribed by statute or written rules and regulations.

The thing of value may be anything of value including, but not limited to, a gift, gratuity, fee, testimonial or sum of money.

You must determine whether the defendant was a public officer and if he was offered and accepted something of value. If you find that the defendant was a public officer who was offered and who accepted something of value, you must then determine whether he accepted this thing of value with the understanding between himself and the giver that by reason of his accepting this thing of value he would be influenced in the discharge of his official duties. Such intent may be inferred from all the circumstances in evidence.

It is immaterial whether or not the defendant was in fact influenced in the performance of his official duties; it is the intent at the time he accepted the thing of value which is material in determining his guilt or innocence.

(d) Demanding a bribe

The defendant in this case has been charged with demanding a bribe. Bribery, as used here, means the giving or offering to, and demand or receipt by, a public official of any sum of money or thing of value for the purpose of influencing him in the performance of his official duties, or for neglecting or failing to perform those duties.

In order for the defendant to be found guilty of this offense, the State must prove beyond a reasonable doubt that: (1) there was a demand; (2) the demand was made by the defendant; (3) the defendant is a public official or officer; (4) the demand was for something of value; and (5) the demand was made with the intention that by receiving the thing of value the defendant would be influenced in the performance or discharge of his official duties.

It is essential that the demand was made by the public official with the intent that he would be influenced thereby in performing or discharging his official duties, or for neglecting or failing to perform his official duties.

Official duties may include those implicitly authorized by custom and circumstance which amount to an official practice, as well as those prescribed by statute or written rules and regulations.

The thing of value may be anything of value including, but not limited to, a gift, gratuity, fee, testimonial or sum of money.

You must determine whether the defendant was a public officer and if he demanded something of value. If you find that the defendant was a public officer and that he did demand something of value, you must then determine if he did so with the understanding between himself and the giver that he would then be influenced in the discharge of his official duties. Such intent may be inferred from all the circumstances in evidence.

It is immaterial whether or not the defendant was in fact influenced in the performance of his official duties; it is the intent at the time he made the demand which is material in determining his guilt or innocence.

COMMENT

Bribery is a common-law as well as a statutory crime. It is codified in Maryland Ann. Code, Art. 27, § 23. The penalty for the crime is a fine of not less than $100 nor more than $5,000, or not less than two years nor more than twelve years in the penitentiary, or both.

The definition of the crime of bribery in this instruction is based on the decisions in *Raimondi v. State,* 12 Md. App. 322,

278 A.2d 664 (1971), *aff'd,* 265 Md. 229, 288 A.2d 882, *cert. denied,* 409 U.S. 948 (1972); and *Kable v. State,* 17 Md. App. 16, 299 A.2d 493, *cert. denied,* 268 Md. 750 (1973). *Kable* involved receiving a bribe.

The essence of the crime of bribery is the passing of money to the public officer to influence the officer in the performance of his official duties. *Cunningham v. State,* 190 Md. 578, 59 A.2d 337 (1948). For a case on the corrupt intent, see *Raimondi v. State, supra.*

The interpretation of the words "official duties" is discussed in *Kable v. State, supra* at 21. In that case the right of a police officer in Prince George's County to recommend *nol pros* of traffic cases in which he brought the original charges was found by the Court to be a "responsibility implicitly authorized by custom and circumstance, amounting to an official practice and, consequently one of his 'official duties.'" The Court cited *United States v. Birdsall,* 233 U.S. 223, 34 S. Ct. 512, 58 L. Ed. 930 (1914):

> To constitute it official action, it was not necessary that it should be prescribed by statute; it was sufficient that it was governed by a lawful requirement of the Department under whose authority the officer was acting .... Nor was it necessary that the requirement should be prescribed by a written rule or regulation. It might also be found in an established usage which constituted the common law of the Department and fixed the duties of those engaged in its activities .... In numerous instances duties not completely defined by written rules are clearly established by settled practice, and action taken in the course of their performance must be regarded as within provisions of the above mentioned statutes against bribery.

Id. at 230-31, 34 S. Ct. at 514, 58 L. Ed. at 934.

The court in *Kable* also cited a New York case, *People v. Lafaro,* 250 N.Y. 336, 165 N.E. 518 (1929), which construed the definition of bribery to extend to those situations where an officer "accepted a bribe to act corruptly in a matter to which he bears some official relation, though the act itself may be technically beyond his duties."

A person would not be guilty of bribery if he bribed or attempted to bribe an officer while the officer was making an illegal arrest. *Sugarman v. State,* 173 Md. 52, 195 A. 324 (1937). In

Sugarman, no bribery conviction was under review. The term "official duties" therefore does not include an officer while making an illegal arrest. However, it should be noted that in *Soles v. State,* 16 Md. App. 656, 299 A.2d 502 (1973), *cert. denied,* 415 U.S. 950 (1974), which involved a lawful arrest, the Court referred to the *Sugarman* decision as a "treasure chest of now discarded principle" stating that it "was from a time when close constitutional calculations would not nullify an apparently good arrest procedure." *Id.* at 513 n.8, 299 A.2d 674 n.8.

For a case on attempted bribery, see *Raimondi v. State, supra.* Under the statute, a person who attempts to bribe a public official is subject to the same penalty as a person who actually completes the offense. A question can be raised of whether a defendant can be convicted of attempting to bribe if the evidence shows that there was an actual tender of a bribe and a passing of a thing of value to the public officer. In *Lightfoot v. State,* 278 Md. 231, 238, 360 A.2d 426, 430 (1976), the Court held that the failure to consummate the crime is not an indispensable element of criminal attempt. See Comment, § 4.05, Attempt, *supra,* for a discussion of this case.

Under the statute, anyone not entirely without criminal capacity may be a briber. With respect to the bribe-taker, the statute designates classes, and only a person within one of these classes is a potential bribee. It is possible, however, that by the breadth of the classes of bribees specified, the legislature intended to include all public officers and employees with respect to the performance of their official duties. *State v. Canova,* 278 Md. 483, 365 A.2d 988 (1976).

The fact that a public official may demand money to influence the performance of his official duties, and thus be guilty of bribery, does not mean that he may not also be guilty of extortion, if the demand for money is accompanied by a threat that, unless it is paid, he will do injury to the person or property of the party upon whom the demand is made. *Carey v. State,* 43 Md. App. 246, 405 A.2d 293 (1979), *cert. denied,* 445 U.S. 967 (1980).

In the case of *Spector v. State,* 289 Md. 407, 425 A.2d 197, *cert. denied,* 452 U.S. 906 (1981), the Court sought to distinguish the state statutory definition from the standard enunciated in the federal cases. The federal cases require that the gift be offered or accepted in exchange for a *quid pro quo* on the part of the public official. This is to distinguish the crime of bribery from the offense delineated in 18 U.S.C. § 201(g) known as receiving an illegal gratuity. In Maryland, since there is no crime known as acceptance of an illegal gratuity, there is no requirement of a *quid pro quo.* Hence, the prosecution need only prove intent to influence official conduct.

Maryland courts have jurisdiction over this offense where the actual bribery attempt occurred in the District of Columbia because the gravamen of the offense is to influence the performance of a person's official duties in Maryland. *Grindstaff v. State,* 57 Md. App. 812, 470 A.2d 809 (1984). Bribery and attempted bribery are excluded from those misdemeanors that must be prosecuted within a year. *State v. Canova, supra.*

There are several related bribery offenses. The General Assembly has declared that it is a crime to bribe or attempt to bribe any official, participant, or person connected in any way with any athletic contest. Art. 27, § 24. Any amateur or professional athlete or other person participating or connected with any athletic contest who accepts a bribe to alter the outcome of the contest is also guilty of a misdemeanor. Art. 27, § 25. A separate statute proscribes procuring a juror who is bribed or accepting a bribe by a juror for gain or profit in exchange for a verdict. Art. 27, § 26. Closely related is a statute punishing anyone who threatens or forces or endeavors to intimidate or impede any juror, witness or court officer in the discharge of his duty. Art. 27, § 27. Finally, it is illegal in any election for public office or referendum to promise any gift or reward to secure any person's vote or ballot. Art. 27, § 28.

§ 4.57. Burglary.

Burglary is the breaking and entering of the dwelling house of another, in the nighttime, with the intent to commit a felony [or with the intent to steal, take or carry away and permanently deprive another of the possession of personal goods].

In order for a person to be found guilty of this offense the State must prove beyond a reasonable doubt that: (1) there was a breaking and an entering (2) by the defendant; (3) the building broken into was the dwelling house of another; (4) the breaking and entering was at night; and (5) the perpetrator's intent was to commit a felony [or steal, take or carry away and permanently deprive another of the possession of personal goods].

The requirement of a breaking and entering is met if the slightest force is used in entering a dwelling house. Breaking may be actual or constructive. Actual breaking means loosening, removing or displacing any covering or fastening of the premises. It may consist of lifting a latch, drawing a bolt, raising and unfastening a window, turning a key or knob, or pushing open a door kept closed by its own weight. There can be no actual breaking if there is no evidence to show that there had been any tampering. If a person had permission to enter the premises there is no actual breaking. There may be a constructive breaking, as where entrance is obtained by intimidation or trickery.

The term "dwelling house" refers to a building which is used regularly as a place to sleep.

It is not necessary that the perpetrator did in fact take anything or commit a felony. However, it is essential that he had the intent to do so. Proof of intent may be inferred from the circumstances of each case. There must be proof of some fact, circumstance, act or declaration of the defendant in addition to proof of mere breaking and entering from which you can find the requisite intent.

[If the State proves that the defendant was in exclusive possession of goods recently stolen in a burglary, and if there is not a reasonable explanation of how he came into the possession of the goods, then you may infer that the possessor was the perpetrator of the burglary. In order for possession to be exclusive, there must be personal possession by the defendant which involves a distinct and conscious assertion of possession by the exercise of complete dominion and right of disposal.]

[Mere possession of recently stolen articles is not sufficient to permit a rational inference that there was a breaking of the dwelling from which they were stolen, in the absence of any evidence that there was an actual or constructive breaking.]

COMMENT

(a) Introduction

This instruction follows the Maryland case law as well as the statutory provisions (Maryland Ann. Code, Art. 27, §§ 29, 30(a), 31) governing the crime of burglary. In Maryland, burglary is a common-law as well as a statutory offense and both are recognized. *Martin v. State,* 10 Md. App. 274, 269 A.2d 182 (1970). Under common law, the felony of burglary is the breaking and entering of the dwelling house of another in the nighttime with an intent to commit a felony. *Reagan v. State,* 4 Md. App. 590, 244 A.2d 623 (1968); *Benton v. State,* 8 Md. App. 388, 260 A.2d 86 (1969); *Hall v. State,* 1 Md. App. 392, 230 A.2d 473 (1967); *Sizemore v. State,* 10 Md. App. 682, 272 A.2d 824 (1971).

Article 27, § 30(a) defines burglary as follows:

> Every person, his aiders, abettors, and counsellors, who shall break and enter any dwelling house in the nighttime with the intent to steal, take or carry away the personal goods of another of any value therefrom shall be deemed a felon, and shall be guilty of the crime of burglary.

This statute was added to the Code of Maryland in order to include petit larceny of a dwelling house in the nighttime as a burglary. *Randolph v. State,* 10 Md. App. 89, 267 A.2d 767 (1970); *Bever v. State,* 4 Md. App. 436, 243 A.2d 634 (1968); *Martin v. State, supra.* Whoever violates the statute or the common law is a felon. *Drouin v. State,* 222 Md. 271, 160 A.2d 85 (1960). Article 27, § 29 states that the penalty for burglary shall be the restoration of the thing taken or payment for the full value thereof and not more than twenty years in prison. This penalty applies to both the common-law and statutory burglary. *Reagan v. State, supra.*

(b) Breaking

Both at common law and by statute it is essential to show a breaking. *Jones v. State,* 2 Md. App. 356, 234 A.2d 625 (1967); *Sizemore v. State,* 10 Md. App. 682, 272 A.2d 824 (1971). Breaking should be interpreted in a common sense manner, i.e., it would not be a breaking if one entered an open window. *Reagan v. State,* 2 Md. App. 262, 234 A.2d 278 (1967). The breaking must actually be in some part of the house and it will not suffice if an outside fence was broken or if an open door of the house was the point of entry. *Arnold v. State,* 7 Md. App. 1, 252 A.2d 878 (1969). Actual breaking means loosening, removing or displacing any covering or fastening of the premises. It may consist of lifting a latch, drawing a bolt, raising and unfastening a window, turning a key or knob, or pushing open a door kept closed by its own weight. *Jones v. State, supra; Reagan v. State* (1967), *supra.* There can be no breaking if there is no evidence to show that there had been any tampering nor any evidence to show the house had been secured prior to entry. *Reagan v. State,* 6 Md. App. 477, 251 A.2d 615 (1969). Furthermore, if a person had permission to enter the premises, there is no breaking. *Martin v. State,* 10 Md. App. 274, 269 A.2d 182 (1970). See *Finke v. State,* 56 Md. App. 450, 468 A.2d 353 (1983).

If entry into a dwelling is gained by deceit, fraud, trick or artifice, the element of "fraud" is equated to "force" by the courts and a "constructive" breaking is sufficient to satisfy the element of breaking. *Brooks v. State,* 277 Md. 155, 353 A.2d 217 (1976), *aff'g* 25 Md. App. 194, 333 A.2d 352 (1975).

(c) Dwelling house

It is essential in establishing that a burglary was committed to show that the building broken into was a dwelling house. The test as to whether or not a building is a dwelling house is whether or not it is used regularly as a place to sleep. An empty apartment is not a dwelling house. *Poff v. State,* 4 Md. App. 186, 241 A.2d 898 (1968). A house is not a "dwelling" where the owner or tenant did not live there and did not intend to do so. A building does not become a dwelling house by the reason that someone may sleep there on rare occasions or take an occasional nap there. *Marston v. State,* 9 Md. App. 360, 264 A.2d 127 (1970). However, if a building is owned by a corporation and lived in by its servants it may be properly known as a dwelling house of the corporation. *Jones v. State,* 2 Md. App. 356, 234 A.2d 625 (1967). In *Herbert v. State,* 31 Md. App. 48, 354 A.2d 449 (1976), the Court held that a motel complex utilized for overnight sleeping accommodations by paying guests constitutes a "dwelling house" within the meaning of the burglary statute. In *Kanaras v. State,* 54 Md. App. 568, 460 A.2d 61 (1983), the Court held that there was sufficient evidence produced at trial to find that a recreation vehicle or mini-motor home was a "dwelling house" within the meaning of the daytime burglary statute, Art. 27, § 30(b). In *Wallace v. State,* 63 Md. App. 399, 492 A.2d 970 (1985), the Court held that the evidence failed to show that the structure was a "dwelling house" where at the time of the breaking the tenants had permanently vacated their apartment.

An exception to the requirement that the breaking and entering must be of a dwelling house is that a church may be the subject of common-law burglary. *McGraw v. State,* 234 Md. 273, 199 A.2d 229, *cert. denied,* 379 U.S. 862 (1964); *Hannah v. State,* 3 Md. App. 325, 239 A.2d 124 (1968). This offense could also be prosecuted as storehouse burglary. See *Sizemore v. State,* 10 Md. App. 682, 272 A.2d 824 (1971) and Instructions, §§ 4.53 to 4.55, *supra. Cf. Holtman v. State,* 12 Md. App. 168, 278 A.2d 82 (1971).

(d) Nighttime

Proof that the breaking and entering was at night is essential to the crime of burglary. *Jung v. State,* 9 Md. App. 300, 263 A.2d 618 (1970); *Reagan v. State,* 4 Md. App. 590, 244 A.2d 623 (1968); *Reagan v. State,* 2 Md. App. 262, 234 A.2d 278 (1967).

Nighttime is not defined by statute in Maryland. However, the time when the moon or sun rises or sets on a particular day is judicially known. Therefore, at a certain hour on a certain date it was or was not daylight. This is a proper subject of judicial knowledge and the judge may inform himself in any way which may seem best in his discretion, and act accordingly. *Bowser v. State,* 136 Md. 342, 110 A. 854 (1920); *Wiggins v. State,* 4 Md.

App. 95, 241 A.2d 424 (1968). In Maryland, neither common-law nor statutory burglary covered the crime of breaking and entering a dwelling house in the daytime. This, however, is covered by Art. 27, § 30(b). If a person has been charged with burglary and there is no evidence that the crime was committed in the nighttime, he may still be convicted of daytime housebreaking. *Jung v. State, supra.* For additional information on daytime housebreaking as distinguished from burglary, see *St. Clair v. State,* 1 Md. App. 605, 232 A.2d 565 (1967); *Gazaille v. State,* 2 Md. App. 462, 235 A.2d 306 (1967); *Reagan v. State* (1968), *supra.* See Instruction, § 4.69, Housebreaking — Daytime, *infra.*

(e) Intent

The final element which is essential to the crime of burglary is intent. *Robinson v. State,* 53 Md. 151, 36 Am. R. 399 (1880). This felonious intent is an element of both statutory and common-law burglary. *Benton v. State,* 8 Md. App. 388, 260 A.2d 86 (1969). Proof of intent need not be direct but may be inferred from the circumstances of each case. *Benton v. State, supra.* However, it is generally held that to prove the requisite intent there must be proof of some fact, circumstance, act or declaration of the accused, in addition to proof of a mere breaking and entering from which the trier of fact can find intent. *Felkner v. State,* 218 Md. 300, 146 A.2d 424 (1958); *Clemons v. State,* 228 Md. 237, 179 A.2d 418 (1962); *Benton v. State, supra.*

To prove the requisite intent to steal, it is not necessary that goods actually be taken. Felonious intent may be proven by the surrounding circumstances. Thus, in *Herbert v. State,* 31 Md. App. 48, 354 A.2d 449 (1976), there was sufficient proof of felonious intent when the appellant was discovered trying surreptitiously to open several motel doors at night while in possession of a number of motel keys. See also *Makins v. State,* 6 Md. App. 466, 252 A.2d 15 (1969); *Robinson v. State,* 4 Md. App. 515, 243 A.2d 879 (1968). The trier of fact can only draw reasonable inferences in an effort to discover the real intent of the person who broke and entered a dwelling house. *Read v. State,* 7 Md. App. 200, 253 A.2d 774 (1969).

(f) Possession of stolen goods

Finally, and in addition to proving a person had committed the elements discussed above, there is one other means by which a person can be found guilty of the crime of burglary. Possession of goods recently stolen in a burglary can give rise to an inference that the possessor was the burglar. See *Allen v. State,* 2 Md. App. 740, 237 A.2d 90 (1968); *Hickman v. State,* 1 Md. App. 578, 232 A.2d 282 (1967); *Anglin v. State,* 244 Md. 652, 224 A.2d 668 (1966), *cert. denied,* 386 U.S. 947 (1967). It has not been conclusively determined what will constitute "recent" for these circumstances. *Anglin v. State, supra.* Unless the possessor can explain his possession of the goods in a manner which reasonably shows innocence, the possession may be controlling as to guilt of burglary. *Butz v. State,* 221 Md. 68, 156 A.2d 423 (1959). The State must show that the defendant had exclusive possession of the goods. *Hickman v. State, supra,* and if the possessor presents evidence that he was not the burglar, he then becomes the possessor of stolen goods. *Anglin v. State,* 1 Md. App. 85, 227 A.2d 364 (1967).

While possession of recently stolen articles from a burglarized dwelling may be sufficient to permit a rational inference that the possessor was the burglar, *Boggs v. State,* 228 Md. 168, 179 A.2d 338 (1962), mere possession of recently stolen articles is not sufficient to permit a rational inference that there was a breaking of a dwelling from which they were stolen, in the absence of any evidence that there was an actual or constructive breaking of the dwelling. *Reagan v. State,* 2 Md. App. 262, 234 A.2d 278 (1967).

See Instructions, §§ 4.53 to 4.55, Breaking — Storehouse, etc., *supra;* and Instruction, § 4.69, Housebreaking — Daytime, *infra.* The reader may refer to the Comments of these sections for a discussion of some similar elements of these offenses.

§ 4.58. Child abuse.

(a) Child abuse based on physical injury

The offense of child abuse based on physical injury is committed when any parent or other person who has the permanent or temporary care or custody or responsibility for the supervision of a minor child, uses cruel or inhumane treatment, or maliciously acts, to cause a physical injury or injuries to such child.

In order for a person to be guilty of this offense the State must prove beyond a reasonable doubt that: (1) the victim was a child under the age of eighteen; (2) the defendant is either the parent or other person having the permanent or temporary care or custody or responsibility for the supervision of the child; (3) there was a physical injury or injuries sustained by the child; (4) the physical injury or injuries resulted from cruel or inhumane treatment, or from a malicious act or acts by the defendant, under circumstances that indicate that the child's health or welfare was harmed or threatened.

[Cruel or inhumane treatment includes, but is not necessarily limited to, acts, conduct or force designed to cause or known to create a substantial risk of causing death, serious bodily harm or disfigurement to the child and which, in fact, resulted in physical injury under circumstances that indicate that the child's health or welfare was harmed or threatened by the injury.]

[You are also instructed that cruel or inhumane treatment includes the failure to obtain some form of medical assistance or treatment for a child where the parent or custodian has reason to know that the child is injured and in need of medical assistance and where the failure to act led to (a worsening of the child's condition) (additional physical injury) under circumstances that indicate that the child's health or welfare was harmed or threatened.]

You are instructed that "malicious acts" are those acts, conduct or force done with the deliberate intention of causing physical injury to the child.

A defendant is not guilty of this offense if the defendant had good intentions but merely exercised bad judgment. If the child was injured consistent with reasonable norms of parental control, then the defendant is not guilty of child abuse.

(b) Child abuse based on sexual molestation or exploitation

The offense of child abuse based on sexual molestation or exploitation is committed when any parent or other person who has the permanent or temporary care or custody or responsibility for the supervision of a minor child, sexually molests or exploits such child, whether physical injuries are sustained or not.

In order for a person to be guilty of this offense, the State must prove beyond a reasonable doubt that: (1) the victim was a child under the age of eighteen; (2) the defendant is either the parent or other person having the permanent or temporary care or custody or responsibility for the supervision of the child; (3) the child was sexually molested or exploited by the defendant, by __________ *(list act(s) or method of sexual molestation or exploitation).*

You are instructed that sexual molestation or exploitation includes, but is not limited to __________ (incest) (rape) (sexual offense in any degree) (sodomy) (unnatural or perverted sexual practices).

COMMENT

This instruction includes the basic holdings under Maryland law regarding the unlawful and criminal mistreatment of minor children. It should be noted initially that inherent in the child abuse law (Maryland Ann. Code, Art. 27, § 35A, as repealed and reenacted by Acts 1984, ch. 296, effective October 1, 1984) is the fact that Maryland makes the abuse of a child a felony and that conviction for this distinct offense carries a maximum penalty of fifteen years in the State penitentiary. When the former child abuse statute was amended (Acts 1970, ch. 385, effective July 1, 1973) the General Assembly indicated that the purpose and intent of the law is to protect children "... who have been the subject of abuse by mandating the reporting of suspected abuse, by extending immunity to those who report in good faith, by requiring prompt investigations of such reports and by causing immediate, cooperative efforts by the responsible agencies on behalf of such children." Reporting provisions are contained in Family Law Article, §§ 5-901 to 5-912.

Thus, although assault and battery are common-law misdemeanors, the perpetuating of assault and battery on a minor child under particular circumstances has evolved into a statutory felony in Maryland. Where the child abuse statute and the common-law crime of assault and battery overlap, such as where one in *loco parentis* is guilty of using immoderate force in the course of exercising authority over a child, the child abuse statutory crime does not repeal the common-law crime. *Anderson v. State,* 61 Md. App. 436, 487 A.2d 294 (1985).

Historically, under Roman law, a father had absolute power of life and death over his children. Blackstone notes, however, that under English law the father could lawfully correct the child as a minor in a reasonable manner, this being for the benefit of the child's "education." 4 *Blackstone's Commentaries* 452. It is an intriguing historical irony that when the common law sought to protect the unreasonably beaten child, it did so under the Roman law concept of *parens patriae,* the higher interest of the State in the child, superior to even that of its parents. It would thus seem, in the evolution of the law, that the parents or those acting in *loco parentis* are not the sole and final arbiters of proper corporal punishment for the child. This evidently is embodied in the spirit of the Maryland statutes regarding the felony of child abuse. See *Smith v. State,* 62 Md. App. 670, 491 A.2d 587 (1985) for a review of the evolution of Maryland's child abuse law.

In the area of evidence, there are two important aspects of the evolution of criminal proceedings under the Maryland Child Abuse Law. First, under Maryland Code Ann., Courts and Judicial Proceedings, § 9-106, a wife can be forced to testify against her husband, and vice versa, when there is a prosecution in a criminal court arising from child abuse. This was clearly expressed by the Court in *James v. State,* 5 Md. App. 647, 248 A.2d 910 (1969). Also, the attending and/or reporting physician's diagnosis and report may be important evidence relevant to the factual manifestation of the assault and battery. The following are seven indices of suspicion that a physician uses to diagnose a battery or a minor child:

1. The child's age is usually less than three.
2. Characteristic distribution of fractures.
3. Disproportionate amount of soft tissue injury.
4. Evidence that the injuries occurred at different times and are in different stages of repair.
5. Cause of recent trauma doubtful.
6. Suspicious family history.
7. Previous similar episodes.

James v. State, supra at 650, 248 A.2d at 912.

Additionally, evidence of prior beatings is admissible as evidence of other offenses having a "natural tendency to establish or offer a[n] inference as to a principal fact at issue or matter in dispute." *Fabian v. State,* 235 Md. 306, 318, 201 A.2d 511, 518 (1964), *cert. denied,* 379 U.S. 869 (1964). See also *Worthen v. State,* 42 Md. App. 20, 399 A.2d 22 (1979); *Duley v. State,* 56 Md. App. 275, 467 A.2d 776 (1983).

A final note with regard to the force which may be applied to a minor child. The Model Penal Code states that the use of force upon or toward the person of another is justifiable if:

> 1. The actor is the parent or guardian or other person similarly responsible for the general care and supervision of a minor or a person acting at the request of such parent, guardian or other responsible person; and
>
> > a. The force is used for the purpose of safeguarding or promoting the welfare of the minor, including the prevention or punishment of his conduct; and
> > b. The force used is not designed to cause or known to create a substantial risk of causing death, serious bodily harm, disfigurement, extreme pain or mental distress or gross degradation. *See* Model Penal Code § 3.08.

Someone who has the "responsibility" for the supervision of a minor child can be held liable under the statute. In such a case, the State must show that such supervision was obtained upon the mutual consent, expressed or implied, by the one legally charged with the care of the child and by the one assuming the "responsibility." *Pope v. State,* 284 Md. 309, 396 A.2d 1054, 1063 (1979). Parental punishment must therefore remain within the bounds of moderation. *Bowers v. State,* 38 Md. App. 21, 379 A.2d 748 (1977), *aff'd,* 283 Md. 115, 389 A.2d 341 (1978). "So long as the chastisement was moderate and reasonable, in light of the age, condition and disposition of the child, and other surrounding circumstances, the parent or custodian would not incur criminal liability for assault or battery or a similar offense." *Anderson v. State, supra* at 446, 487 A.2d at 299.

In *Smith v. State, supra,* the Court held that failure of the information to state the age of the victim rendered it void as not stating an offense. For cases considering the relationship between child abuse prosecutions and juvenile proceedings involving Child in Need of Assistance petitions, see *In re Neil C,* 308 Md. App. 591, 521 A.2d 329 (1987) and *Lee v. State,* 62 Md. App. 341, 489 A.2d 87 (1985).

The former child abuse statute was amended (Acts 1974, ch. 372) to eliminate the need to prove a physical injury if the crime involves a sexually abused child. For ease of understanding and discussion, the instruction and the remainder of this comment have each been divided into two sections dealing with the two bases for prosecution under the statute.

(a) Child abuse based on physical injury

Under the Maryland child abuse statute, a parent or other person who has permanent or temporary care or custody or responsibility for supervision of a child is criminally liable for causing physical injury to be sustained by the child "as a result of cruel or inhumane treatment or as a result of a malicious act." Maryland Ann. Code Art. 27, § 35A. In *State v. Fabritz,* 276 Md. 416, 348 A.2d 275 (1975), *cert. denied,* 425 U.S. 942 (1976), the Court held that "cruel or inhumane treatment" does not require that the injury result from a physical assault upon the child or from any physical force initially applied by the accused. Thus, the Court sustained the mother's conviction when she failed to obtain medical assistance for her daughter for eight hours after having reason to know the daughter was in need of assistance. The Court reasoned that the mother's failure to act caused the child to sustain bodily injuries additional to those resulting from the original beating, thus causing a worsening of the injuries and leading to the child's death. *Cf. Fabritz v. Traurig,* 583 F.2d 697 (4th Cir. 1978), *cert. denied,* 443 U.S. 915 (1979). See also *Pope v. State,* 284 Md. 309, 396 A.2d 1054 (1970).

An alternative theory, not explicitly addressed by the Court, is that a parent has a duty to act based on the reasonable foreseeability of the harm to the child. Under this theory, criminal liability would arise when the harm was foreseeable and when the failure to act led to a worsening of the child's condition.

In *Robey v. State,* 54 Md. App. 60, 456 A.2d 953 (1983), the question presented was whether a parent who was temporarily insane when she beat her child may be held criminally responsible for failure to seek medical care for the child during lucid intervals. The Court held that the defense of insanity has never been extended to negative responsibility for actions taken during lucid intervals. The Court affirmed defendant's convictions for child abuse and involuntary manslaughter.

In another child abuse case, the Court held that the mother's mere presence at the scene of her child's brutal beating (by the mother's paramour) is not sufficient evidence of aiding and abetting on which to base the mother's conviction for child abuse. *Bowers v. State,* 38 Md. App. 21, 379 A.2d 748 (1977), *aff'd,* 283 Md. 115, 389 A.2d 341 (1978).

The Court of Appeals has held that the Maryland child abuse statute, which defined "abuse" as being "cruel or inhumane treatment," was not unconstitutionally vague. *Bowers v. State, supra.*

"Malicious" was defined by the Court of Appeals in an arson setting as "the intention to cause harm to another." *Brown v. State,* 285 Md. 469, 474, 403 A.2d 788, 791 (1979). There would appear to be no reason to define it differently in a child abuse prosecution.

There has been no specification of the *mens rea* required for "cruel or inhumane treatment." However, the Court of Special Appeals apparently has assumed that there is a *mens rea* required. In *Worthen v. State,* 42 Md. App. 20, 399 A.2d 22 (1979), the Court reversed the conviction of a defendant whose request for the complete child abuse instruction from the first edition of this book was denied. The trial court had omitted the last two paragraphs of the instruction. Those paragraphs were as follows:

> The defendant must have knowingly and willfully caused injuries and these injuries must have required the care and treatment of a physician.
>
> A person is not guilty of this offense if he had good intentions but exercised bad judgment. If the child was injured in a fashion consistent with reasonable norms of parental control then the defendant is not guilty. Unless you find that the defendant substituted a willful and malicious desire to inflict harm and pain in place of a genuine effort to correct the child by acceptable means, you must find the defendant not guilty.

Since the defendant's entire defense was that his actions "had not exceeded the bounds of parental propriety," the Court of Special Appeals held that the refusal to grant the requested instruction was error. *Id.* at 46, 399 A.2d at 280, 286. The Court specifically stated:

> In a child abuse case, by virtue of its application only to those in *loco parentis,* see *Pope v. State, supra,* an accused begins with a permissible degree of corporal punishment of a child for which he or she as a parent figure cannot be held accountable. Beyond that even, the person is not guilty if his intentions were good, but his judgment bad, in exercising his right to punish.

Id. at 40, 399 A.2d at 283.

An interesting point is that, although the defendant was acquitted of child abuse and convicted of assault and battery, the Court of Special Appeals still held that it was error not to give the complete child abuse instruction. The *Worthen* prosecution was based on physical injury and the Court made no distinction between "malicious acts" and "cruel or inhumane treatment." A *mens rea* element therefore appears to be required for any conviction relating to child abuse based on physical injuries.

In *Duley v. State,* 56 Md. App. 275, 467 A.2d 776 (1983), the Court held that evidence that the defendant hit his infant baby hard enough to break her ribs and shook her hard enough to rupture the blood vessels in her brain was sufficient to convict for child abuse and manslaughter.

(b) Child abuse based on sexual molestation or exploitation

As stated earlier, Maryland's child abuse statute (Maryland Ann. Code, Art. 27, § 35A) was amended in 1974 to allow a prosecution based on sexual abuse, even with no physical injury. Sexual abuse was defined as:

> [A]ny act or acts involving sexual molestation or exploitation, including but not limited to incest, rape, carnal knowledge, sodomy or unnatural or perverted sexual practices on a child by any parent, adoptive parent or other person who has the permanent or temporary care or custody or responsibility for supervision of a minor child.

The statute was amended again (Acts 1977, ch. 290) to replace the term "carnal knowledge" with the phrase "or sexual offense in any degree." Minor technical amendments were made in 1979, 1980 and 1981 and now, as reenacted in 1984, the section provides:

> (4)(i) *"Sexual abuse"* means any act that involves sexual molestation or exploitation of a child by a parent or other person who has permanent or temporary care or custody or responsibility for supervision of a child.
>
> (ii) "Sexual abuse" includes, but is not limited to:
>
> a. Incest, rape, or sexual offense in any degree;
> b. Sodomy; and
> c. Unnatural or perverted sexual practices.

See Instructions and Comments: § 4.33, Incest; § 4.34, Sodomy; § 4.35, Unnatural and perverted sexual practices; § 4.36, Rape offenses; § 4.37, Sexual offenses in the first, second, third and fourth degrees.

§ 4.59. Contempt.

Contempt is conduct which tends to bring the authority and administration of the law into disrespect or disregard. It is conduct, either actions or words, which tends to impede, embarrass or obstruct the court in the discharge of its duties. Such conduct despises or scorns the authority, justice and dignity of the court.

Contemptuous conduct may consist of *(use relevant description or add other relevant language):*

[1. Misbehavior in the presence of the court or so near the presence of the court that an obstruction of justice results];

[2. Misbehavior of the officers of the court in official transactions];

[3. Disobedience to any lawful command of the court. Before a person may be held in contempt for violating a court order, that person must have had knowledge of the court order and the terms or import of that order must be reasonably definite and specific];

[4. Intentional interference with a witness or party to an action. Such interference must unlawfully detain or prevent or disable the witness or party from attending or testifying at a hearing scheduled by the court or a commissioner. Such interference can occur when the witness is going to, remaining at or returning from a hearing];

[5. Intentional removal, concealment, or destruction of a book, paper or document which was to be produced for evidentiary purposes at a trial or before a commissioner. Notice that the item was to be produced for evidentiary purposes must have been given];

[6. Aiding any person to escape or removing any property from the possession of any officer who holds that person or property by order of a court of competent jurisdiction];

[7. Impersonation of an attorney or other officer of the court without authority to do so].

In order for the defendant to be found guilty of this offense, the State must prove beyond a reasonable doubt that the defendant intentionally conducted himself with a calculated purpose to accomplish a contempt of court. The State must prove beyond a reasonable doubt that the defendant did not act in good faith, that the defendant did not mean his conduct to be other than contemptuous.

COMMENT

The statutory provision for contempt of court, Maryland Ann. Code, Courts and Judicial Proceedings, § 1-202, is augmented by Maryland Rules P1 to P5 which describe both direct and constructive civil and criminal contempts. The statutory authorization for appeals in contempt cases is set forth in Courts and Judicial Proceedings, §§ 12-304(a) and 12-304(b). *Cf. Chambers v. State,* 3 Md. App. 642, 240 A.2d 644 (1968).

The instruction begins with a general description of contempt as in *Goldsborough v. State,* 12 Md. App. 346, 355, 278 A.2d 623, 628 (1971). Illustrative grounds are included and should be selected or supplemented as required. The statutory grounds of Maryland Ann. Code, Art. 26, § 4 (now repealed) are included as suggestive descriptions of relevant conduct. The list of punishable acts in the former statute was not binding on the court's inherent power to punish for contempt. The criminal contempt power is inherent in all courts. *Ex parte Maulsby,* 13 Md. 625 (1859). See *Muskus v. State,* 14 Md. App. 348, 286 A.2d 783 (1972); *Goldsborough v. State, supra.* For this reason, the statute (Art. 26, § 4) was replaced by Courts and Judicial Proceedings, § 1-202, which provides a simple statement of the court's contempt power and a reference to the Maryland Rules. However, "while trial judges must be given wide latitude to punish contemptuous conduct they must ever be on guard against confusing offenses to their sensibilities with obstructions to the administration of justice." *Muskus v. State, supra.* See also *Jones v. State,* 32 Md. App. 490, 362 A.2d 660 (1976), discussed *infra,* this Comment.

In *Goldsborough v. State, supra,* the Maryland cases on contempt are grouped as follows: (a) contempt by attorney or advocate; (b) improper publicity; (c) violation of orders not to construct or maintain; (d) failure to appear or produce records; (e) exercise of improper influence upon the administration of justice; and (f) failure to obey other court orders.

The "beyond a reasonable doubt" standard was approved in *Goldsborough v. State, supra* at 358, 278 A.2d at 630. See *A.V. Laurins & Co. v. Prince George's County,* 46 Md. App. 548, 420 A.2d 982 (1980). The "good faith" negation of intent is also derived from *Goldsborough v. State, supra* at 357, 278 A.2d at 629, and is included to define the jury's fact-finding role relating to intent.

A jury trial is required in criminal contempt cases, both direct and constructive, if the sentence imposed is six months or more. *Wilkins v. State,* 293 Md. 335, 444 A.2d 445 (1982); *Roll v. State,* 15 Md. App. 31, 228 A.2d 605 (1972), *aff'd in part and modified in part,* 267 Md. 714, 298 A.2d 867 (1973).

The United States Supreme Court has ruled that a defendant in a criminal contempt case should be tried by a judge other than one "reviled by the contemnor." The Court based its conclusion on the fourteenth amendment to the United States Constitution. *Mayberry v. Pennsylvania,* 400 U.S. 455, 91 S. Ct. 499, 27 L. Ed. 2d 532 (1971).

In *Kober v. State,* 41 Md. App. 174, 395 A.2d 1228 (1979), the Court discussed the procedure a trial judge should follow before finding a witness in contempt for refusal to testify. Because of the critical role which the right against compulsory self-incrimination plays in our legal system, before finding a witness in contempt, the trial judge must ascertain, by inquiry when necessary, whether a refusal to testify is privileged. Only after determining that the refusal to testify is not privileged, may the judge find that witness in contempt of court.

In *State v. Roll,* 267 Md. 714, 298 A.2d 867 (1973), the appellants refused to testify before a grand jury in a narcotics case because they feared reprisals. Under the facts and circumstances of this case, this refusal did not constitute direct contempt. The use of contempt power demands care and discretion so as to avoid arbitrary, capricious or oppressive application of this power. *Liner v. State,* 62 Md. App. 381, 489 A.2d 553 (1985).

In *Cohen v. State,* 19 Md. App. 85, 309 A.2d 294 (1973), it was decided that the appellant was not guilty of direct criminal contempt by filing a written and oral motion that the judge disqualify himself on grounds of bias and prejudice.

An example of constructive contempt is found in *Pearson v. State,* 28 Md. App. 464, 347 A.2d 239 (1975), wherein the improper conduct consisted of the appellant's voluntary failure to return to court following a recess for lunch. Because this behavior did not take place in the actual presence of the court and did not prevent the court from continuing the proceedings in the appellant's absence, the appellant's actions constituted constructive, rather than direct, contempt.

But in *Murphy v. State,* 46 Md. App. 138, 416 A.2d 748 (1980), the Court stated that one must look at the nature of the contemptuous acts to determine whether they occurred in the presence of the court. In this case an attorney failed to appear in court or give reasonable notice thereof. He was held to be in direct contempt. The court's reasoning was based on the fact that an attorney plays such an integral role in the judicial process that without his presence the "wheels of justice grind to a halt." Therefore, the attorney's absence from the courtroom was seen to intrude upon the operation and dignity of the court and was immediately cognizable to the judge. *Cf. Jones v. State,* 61 Md. App. 94, 484 A.2d 1050 (1984).

In *Dorsey v. State,* 295 Md. 217, 454 A.2d 353 (1983), the defendants in a cell area adjacent to courtroom made so much noise that court proceedings were disrupted. Defendants were initially cited with constructive contempt. At the hearing, the citation was amended to direct contempt but procedures for constructive contempt followed. Even if the court mistakenly labels constructive contempt as direct, the court has jurisdiction and, if procedural safeguards for constructive contempt are followed, a conviction will stand.

Under Maryland Rule P3.b an order for contempt must recite facts; it cannot be limited to conclusions of the court or characterizations concerning the contemnor's behavior. *Robinson v. State,* 19 Md. App. 20, 308 A.2d 712 (1973).

In *Dorsey v. State,* 56 Md. App. 54, 466 A.2d 546 (1983), the Court considered Maryland Rule P4.b.1(c) and held that contempt proceedings were properly commenced despite the fact that a signed show cause order was not served upon the defendant. The defendant appeared as a party in the action in which the contempt was charged by entering a plea of not guilty. The original show cause order was signed by a judge and an unsigned copy was served on the defendant by delivery in open court.

In *Jones v. State, supra,* the Court noted that to facilitate appellate review of a criminal contempt order, Maryland Rule P3 requires that the court's order of contempt recite the facts upon which the contempt is based. On appeal, the function of the Court is to assess the legal sufficiency of the facts recited in the contempt order based on a review of the contempt order and on the trial transcript. See *Kandel v. State,* 252 Md. 668, 250 A.2d 853 (1968). In *Jones,* the Court concluded that there was nothing in the transcript to indicate that appellant's single act of slamming his hands on the bench before him "beyond a reasonable doubt" was "in direct defiance of the dignity and authority of the tribunal or interfered with the due and proper administration of justice." *Jones v. State, supra* (*citing In re Lee,* 170 Md. 43, 47, 183 A. 560 (1935), *cert. denied,* 298 U.S. 680 (1936)).

For a discussion of the differences between civil and criminal contempt, see *Pearson v. State, supra; Myers v. State,* 23 Md. App. 275, 326 A.2d 773 (1974).

§4.60. Nonsupport.

Nonsupport is the willful failure of a [spouse] [parent] to provide for the [other spouse] [child] [without just cause].

To be found guilty of the offense of nonsupport the State must prove beyond a reasonable doubt that: (1) the defendant is a [husband] [wife] [parent]; (2) in that capacity he willfully failed to provide support for his [spouse] [child]; [and (3) he did so without just cause].

The word "willfully" means an act done with deliberate intention for which there is no reasonable excuse. In other words, the defendant must have had the means of support or the ability to obtain the means of support and his failure to provide support must have been done with deliberate intention for which there is no reasonable excuse. Unless there has been evidence from which you can determine that the defendant intentionally refused to support his [spouse] [child], although he had the capacity to do so, you must find the defendant not guilty. In reaching this determination you may consider earning power as well as actual earnings.

COMMENT: DESERTION AND NONSUPPORT

Maryland Ann. Code, Art. 27, § 88, prior to amendment in 1978, was declared unconstitutional in *Coleman v. State,* 37 Md. App. 322, 277 A.2d 553 (1977). In *Coleman,* the Court held that the statute established a distinction solely upon the basis of sex, and that such a distinction was violative of Article 46 of the Maryland Declaration of Rights. The constitutional infirmity was corrected by an amendment which made the law applicable to either of the spouses. Acts 1978, ch. 921, effective July 1, 1978.

Article 27, § 88 was repealed by Acts 1984, ch. 296, § 1, effective October 1, 1984, and reenacted under Maryland Ann. Code, Family Law, §§ 10-201 to 10-219. Currently, there are three criminal offenses dealing with desertion and nonsupport: (1) desertion; (2) nonsupport of a child; and (3) nonsupport of a spouse. See Family Law, §§ 10-201 and 10-203.

Family Law, § 10-201(a) provides: "A spouse may not willfully fail to provide for the support of the other spouse, without just cause." Family Law, § 10-203 provides: "A parent may not willfully fail to provide for the support of his or her minor child." It should be noted that "without just cause" appears in § 10-201, desertion of a spouse, but not in § 10-203, desertion of a child. Therefore, brackets appear around the third element of proof in the instruction. Query, if the court will allow a defendant charged with nonsupport of a child to use a defense of just cause. Since the statute states the parent must "willfully" fail to provide for support, this may allow the defendant to argue just cause as a defense.

The purposes of these sections are: to assist spouses and children in directly procuring support and thereby prevent them from becoming public burdens; to punish the offenders for failing to provide support; and, by the fear of punishment, to prevent the commission of such an offense. *State v. Berry,* 287 Md. 491, 413 A.2d 557 (1980); *Ewell v. State,* 207 Md. 288, 114 A.2d 66 (1955).

These provisions cannot be limited or nullified by custom or administrative practice. *Ewell v. State, supra.* Therefore, a husband's offer to show that the practice of the State Attorney's office was not to institute prosecution for nonsupport where there was an equity proceeding pending between the parties, or where the wife had funds of her own, was properly rejected by the trial court. *Ewell v. State, supra.* Query whether there are some circumstances which would permit the defendant to raise a constitutional defense of lack of equal protection in the enforcement of the statute.

The term "child" as used in Family Law, § 10-203 refers to both legitimate and illegitimate children. See *State v. Rawlings,* 38 Md. App. 479, 381 A.2d 708 (1978). In addition, in *Rawlings* the Court stated that unless there have been prior acts or declarations establishing, under the requirements of the inheritance statute, the paternity of an illegitimate child, paternity must be established under the Paternity Act before criminal charges can be instituted. *But cf. Dayhoff v. State,* 206 Md. 25, 109 A.2d 760 (1954). Judgment of conviction was justified under the Lord Mansfield rule that a child born during wedlock is presumed to be legitimate and that the mother's testimony is not admissible to show that the child was illegitimate. The due process clause requires, however, that in criminal cases the burden of proof be placed on the State to prove each element of the crime beyond a reasonable doubt. See Appendix V, The Impact of *Evans v. State:* Burdens of Proof, Presumptions and Inferences, *infra.*

The defendant must willfully fail to provide for his or her spouse without just cause to be guilty under Family Law, § 10-201. *Ewell v. State, supra.* The term "willfully" in criminal statutes characterizes an act done with deliberate intention for which there is no reasonable excuse. *Ewell v. State, supra.*

Willful failure to support presupposes the existence of, or the ability to obtain, the means of support by the defendant. The spouse must have the means or the capacity to obtain them. *Ewell v. State, supra.*

To sustain a conviction under Family Law, § 10-201 there must have been testimony from which the trier of facts could have determined that the spouse intentionally refused support although he had the capacity to do so. *Ewell v. State, supra.* Earning power as well as actual earnings may be considered. *Rosenberg v. State,* 164 Md. 473, 165 A. 306 (1933).

The possession of funds by a wife, which she denied having, did not bar the right of the state to convict her husband under this section for her ultimate benefit; thus, the husband was not prejudiced by the failure to permit him to cross-examine his wife with regard to her undoubtedly false statements in regard to her financial means. *Ewell v. State, supra.*

The obligation of the father to support his minor children under Family Law, § 10-203, is not affected by a divorce and the custody of the children being given to the mother. *Boggs v. Boggs,* 138 Md. 422, 114 A. 474 (1921); *Alvey v. Hartwig,* 106 Md. 254, 67 A. 132 (1907). Moreover, a husband's obligation to support his wife cannot be qualified so as to require support only if the wife divorced him. *Ewell v. State, supra.*

As to separate maintenance or alimony decrees not barring criminal prosecution for nonsupport, see *Ewell v. State, supra.*

A state has legislative power to make a resident subject to criminal prosecution for failure to support a dependent who lives outside the state. *State v. James,* 203 Md. 113, 100 A.2d 12 (1953).

The failure to support, if the father is domiciled here, regardless of the location of the children, is the act of omission at which the finger of the statute points. *State v. James, supra.*

Discussing revocation of probation on a conviction of willful failure to provide support, the Court held in *State v. Berry, supra* at 493-494, 413 A.2d at 559, that a defendant's probation may be revoked for failure to support his wife and children as ordered, and defendant may be sentenced under the original conviction when the period of probation had expired. Therefore, the State may issue the warrant within or without the probationary period so long as the actual hearing on the merits is timely held.

A sentence of eighteen months may be lawfully given a petitioner under a writ of *habeas corpus* for nonsupport (to which he admittedly pleaded guilty) as well as for desertion (to which he claimed he pleaded not guilty). *Pritchard v. Warden,* 209 Md. 662, 121 A.2d 696 (1956).

See *Hall v. Warden,* 214 Md. 652, 135 A.2d 895 (1957); *Hands v. Warden,* 205 Md. 642, 109 A.2d 51 (1954); *Bethlehem-Fairfield Shipyard, Inc. v. Rosenthal,* 185 Md. 416, 45 A.2d 79 (1945); *Dougherty v. Dougherty,* 189 Md. 316, 55 A.2d 787 (1947); *Borchert v. Borchert,* 185 Md. 586, 45 A.2d 463 (1946); *Walker v. Walker,* 125 Md. 649, 94 A. 346 (1915); *Sanders v. State,* 8 Md. App. 17, 257 A.2d 442 (1969).

§ 4.61. Disorderly conduct.

(a) Disorderly conduct generally

It is an offense to act in a disorderly manner to the disturbance of the public peace in certain designated places.

In order for the defendant to be found guilty of this offense the State must prove beyond a reasonable doubt that: (1) the defendant willfully acted in a disorderly manner to the disturbance of the public peace; (2) he did so in the actual presence of other persons; (3) those other persons may have been disturbed or provoked to resentment thereby; and (4) the defendant did so in __________, which is one of the locations specified in the statute.

The gist of the crime of disorderly conduct is the doing and/or saying of that which offends, disturbs, incites or tends to incite other persons gathered in the same area to the disturbance of the public peace.

[Implicit in the disorderly conduct statute is a prohibition against a person willfully acting in a disorderly manner by making loud and unseemly noises or by profanely cursing and swearing.]

(b) Profane cursing and swearing

When a charge of disorderly conduct is based on profane cursing and swearing, it must be shown that those words were fighting words. Fighting words are those which tend to incite an immediate breach of the peace. Fighting words are those which have a direct tendency to cause acts of violence by a person(s) to whom individually the remark is addressed. The test is what persons of common intelligence would understand to be likely to cause an average listener to fight. Derisive or annoying words would be fighting words once they have the characteristic of plainly tending to excite the listeners to a breach of peace. Profanity per se would not amount to disorderly conduct. The words used would have to be fighting words to be punishable. Other persons must have been within hearing of this language.

I emphasize that the State does not have the power to punish acts or words which, although vulgar and offensive, are not fighting words as I have defined them.

I suggest that you first determine from the nature and contents of the facts and circumstances in evidence whether the acts or words complained of were of the kind that the State may punish. If so, you must then determine whether the conduct complained of was in the actual presence of other persons who might have been disturbed or provoked to cause acts of violence.

(c) Loud and unseemly noises

The State must prove that the defendant made loud and unseemly noises or performed some other physical acts to the disturbance of the public peace.

To be loud means that it is characterized by a high volume and intensity of sound, clamorous and insistent. Unseemly means in violation of accepted standards of what is right or proper. You must determine whether the defendant was making loud and unseemly noises. The act complained of must have been of such a nature as to affect the peace and quiet of persons, actually present, who may have witnessed it and who may have been disturbed or provoked to resentment.

I suggest that you first determine from the nature and contents of the facts and circumstances in evidence whether the acts or words complained of were loud and unseemly noises as I have defined these terms. If so, you must then determine whether the conduct complained of was in the actual presence of other persons who might have been disturbed or provoked to resentment.

COMMENT

(a) Disorderly conduct

There are a number of statutory provisions which concern disorderly conduct or disturbance of the public peace. This instruction was formulated from Maryland Ann. Code, Art. 27, § 123(a) which states that a "person may not act in a disorderly manner to the disturbance of the public peace" in designated places. It also is based on Art. 27, § 122 which provides similar language and also proscribes wilfully acting "in a disorderly manner by making loud and unseemly noises or by profanely cursing, swearing or using obscene language" in designated places. Article 27, § 121 incorporates similar language and also proscribes wilfully obstructing or hindering the free passage of persons along any public street, etc.

Also, the following statutory provisions come under the headings of disturbance of the public peace and drunkenness and disorderly conduct:

> Maryland Ann. Code, Education, § 26-103, Drinking or possessing intoxicating beverages on school premises.
>
> Art. 27, § 121A, Harassment.
>
> Art. 27, § 124, Disorderly conduct on land of another.
>
> Art. 27, § 125, Keeping disorderly house. (See Instruction, § 4.62, *infra*.)

Although there was no crime of disorderly conduct at common law, nevertheless,

> [I]t was a crime at common law to do many of the things that constitute disorderly conduct under present day statutes, such as making loud noises so as to disturb the peace of the neighborhood, collecting a crowd in a public place by means of loud or unseemly noises or language, or disturbing a meeting assembled for religious worship or any other unlawful purpose.

Drews v. State, 224 Md. 186, 192, 167 A.2d 341, 343 (1961).

The Court of Appeals held in *Harris v. State,* 237 Md. 299, 206 A.2d 254 (1965), that "a failure to obey a reasonable and lawful request by a police officer fairly made to prevent a disturbance to the public peace constitutes disorderly conduct." See also *Sharpe v. State,* 231 Md. 401, 190 A.2d 628 (1963), *cert. denied,* 375 U.S. 946 (1963); *Drews v. State, supra; McIntyre v. State,* 1 Md. App. 586, 232 A.2d 279 (1967).

Refusal to obey a proper order of an officer may constitute an offense justifying arrest particularly where there is profanity in the presence of others that may threaten a breach of the peace. *Sharpe v. State, supra.* In that case the Court never reached the issue of whether the disorderly conduct charge could be justified and there were very strong dissents. *Heinze v. Murphy,* 180 Md. 423, 428-29, 24 A.2d 917, 920 (1942).

> The gist of the crime of disorderly conduct under § 123 of Art. 27, as it was in the cases of common law predecessor crimes, is the doing or saying, or both, of that which offends, disturbs, incites, or tends to incite a number of people gathered in the same area.

Drews v. State, supra.

> Disorderly conduct requires actual presence of other persons who may witness the conduct or hear the language and who may be disturbed or provoked to resentment thereby ... [It] would not be necessary that the state prove such other persons in fact heard the noises; it would be sufficient if they were passing by or along the [area] so that reasonably they may have heard them.

In re Nawrocki, 15 Md. App. 252, 258, 289 A.2d 846, 850 (1972). In *Luthardt v. State,* 6 Md. App. 251, 251 A.2d 40 (1969), the defendant was arrested during the course of an interracial demonstration. A conviction of disorderly conduct did not violate the defendant's first and fourteenth amendment rights:

> The state may, therefore, prevent and punish some classes of speech, among which are the "lewd and obscene, the profane, the libelous, and the insulting or 'fighting' words — those which by their very utterance inflict injury or tend to incite an immediate breach of the peace [since] such utterances are no essential part of any exposition of ideas, and are of such slight social value as a step to truth that any benefit that may be derived from them is clearly outweighed by the social interest in order and morality." *Chaplinsky v. New Hampshire,* 315 U.S. 568 at page 572, 62 S. Ct. 766, 86 L. Ed. 1031 (1942). See also *Cantwell v. Connecticut,* 310 U.S. 296 at page 308, to the effect that the right of free speech

> does not sanction incitement to riot or the right to exhort others to physical attack upon those belonging to another sect. And as we recognized in *Lynch v. State,* 2 Md. App. 546, 557, the resort to epithets or personal abuse is not in any sense communication of information or opinion safeguarded by the Constitution. See also *Feiner v. New York,* 340 U.S. 315, 71 S. Ct. 303, 95 L. Ed. 295 (1951); *Terminiello v. Chicago,* 337 U.S. 1, 69 S. Ct. 894, 93 L. Ed. 1131 (1949). *Id.* at 258, 251 A.2d at 44.

In *Cohen v. California,* 403 U.S. 15, 91 S. Ct. 1780, 291 L. Ed. 2d 284, *reh'g denied,* 404 U.S. 876 (1971), the defendant appeared in a corridor of Los Angeles County Courthouse wearing a jacket plainly showing the words "Fuck the Draft." "The State may not consistently with the First and Fourteenth Amendments, make the simple public display here involved of this single four-letter expletive a criminal offense." *Id.* at 26.

An important Maryland case is *Reese v. State,* 17 Md. App. 73, 299 A.2d 848 (1973). The part of the instruction on fighting words is from this case which cites *Chaplinsky v. New Hampshire, supra; Cohen v. California, supra; Terminiello v. Chicago, supra;* and *Gooding v. Wilson,* 405 U.S. 518, 92 S. Ct. 1103, 31 L. Ed. 2d 408 (1972).

The Court of Appeals has held that the expression "the fucking niggers in this country are no better than the goddamned policemen," though spoken in a restaurant with a racially mixed crowd, was not "fighting words" within the facts of the case. *Downs v. State,* 278 Md. 610, 366 A.2d 41 (1976), *cert. denied,* 431 U.S. 974 (1977) (*citing Bachelar v. Maryland,* 397 U.S. 564, 90 S. Ct. 1312, 25 L. Ed. 2d 570 (1970)). The Court reasoned as follows:

> This remark was made by Downs during a conversation with friends. There was no direct evidence that it was spoken to anyone other than the persons sitting at the booth with Downs. Even if there were, no evidence was adduced that anyone else, besides Trooper Taylor, heard this statement. Even if someone else did, there was no evidence that he or she was offended by it. And, even if someone were offended by it, there was no evidence that any person was so aroused as to respond in a violent manner. Thus, Downs' remarks were not the kind of personally abusive epithets which fall outside of the protection of the First Amendment under the

> rubric of "fighting" words. He engaged in protected speech. That his views might be offensive to someone who overheard him does not warrant a conviction for disorderly conduct.

Id. at 618, 366 A.2d at 46.

In *Diehl v. State,* 294 Md. App. 466, 451 A.2d 115 (1982), the Court held that it was not disorderly conduct in violation of Art. 27, § 121, for a passenger in a car, stopped for a traffic violation, to loudly assert that he had a right to leave the scene, underscoring the statements with the expletive, "fuck you," after being told by the police to get back into the car. The passenger's words were held not be "fighting words" designed to provoke violence in the officer, and they were not obscene or profane. The passenger did not willfully intend to disturb the peace but only intended to communicate his outrage to the officer. His speech, therefore, was within the protection of the first amendment.

(b) Indecent exposure

The common-law crime of indecent exposure, as interpreted in *Dill v. State,* 24 Md. App. 695, 332 A.2d 690 (1975), was effectively repealed by the 1967 amendment to Maryland Ann. Code, Art. 27, § 122. Subsequently, however, the Maryland legislature amended this section by eliminating from it any references to the crime of indecent exposure and in its place, adopted Art. 27, § 335A, which reads as follows: "Every person convicted of the common-law crime of indecent exposure is guilty of a misdemeanor and shall be punished by imprisonment for not more than three years or a fine of not more than $1,000, or both."

In *Neal v. State,* 45 Md. App. 549, 413 A.2d 1386 (1980), the Court, reviewing the legislative history of the indecent exposure laws, stated that when a statute abrogating a principle of the common law is repealed, the common-law principle is revived. Hence, the Court held that the common-law crime of indecent exposure was revived, making proof of the crime less difficult without the added element of intent.

The common-law elements of the offense of indecent exposure remain intact and they include: (1) willful and intentional exposure of the private parts of one's body; (2) a public place in which it is performed; and (3) the presence of other person(s). As a further explanation of the term "public," the Court in *Messina v. State,* 212 Md. 602, 606, 130 A.2d 578, 580 (1957), wrote, "it is immaterial that the exposure is seen by only one person if it occurs at a place open or exposed to the view of the public and where anyone who happened to have been nearby could have seen it if he had looked."

In *Ricketts v. State,* 291 Md. 701, 436 A.2d 906 (1981) the Court discussed a defendant's prior conviction for indecent exposure and its admissibility for purposes of impeachment. The Court stated that indecent exposure is not an infamous crime, a crime of moral turpitude, a felony, nor a crime involving dishonesty or deceit, but rather, is a lesser crime which includes a wide range of behavior. Therefore, a factfinder would not be able to judge whether the offense affects the defendant's credibility.

§ 4.62. Disorderly house.

In order for the defendant to be guilty of this offense, the State must prove beyond a reasonable doubt that: (1) the defendant kept or maintained a house; (2) the house was disorderly, that is, the house constituted a common nuisance; and (3) the defendant knowingly created, maintained, promoted, or continued the common nuisance.

[To constitute this offense, a house need not be a home; it may be a room, a tent, a boat or a place of business. It is not necessary to be the owner or manager of the property in order to be guilty of this offense. The charge relates not to ownership but to the conduct of the place in creating, maintaining, promoting, or continuing a common nuisance.]

A house may be disorderly either from the purpose for which it is used or from the way in which it is kept.

The State must prove that a common nuisance has been created or permitted. A common nuisance exists when there is the maintenance, promotion or continuance of that which is noisome and offensive, or annoying and vexatious, or that which is plainly hurtful to the public, or that which is a public outrage against common decency or common morality, or that which tends plainly and directly to the corruption of the morals, honesty and good habits of the people.

It must appear that the acts injurious or offensive to the public which constitute the nuisance are recurrent. There is no particular extent of time prescribed during which the improper practices must continue or recur. The commission of a single or isolated act on the premises would not cause a place to be a disorderly house.

A place may be disorderly even though it is quietly kept, no conspicuous improprieties are permitted, and the activities are not open to public observation.

COMMENT

This instruction is based on case law in Maryland, especially *Ward v. State,* 9 Md. App. 583, 267 A.2d 255 (1970) and *Curley v. State,* 215 Md. 382, 137 A.2d 640 (1958).

The offense of keeping a disorderly house is a common-law misdemeanor in the state of Maryland, although punishment for the offense is fixed by statute, Maryland Ann. Code, Art. 27, § 125. *Jackson v. State,* 176 Md. 399, 5 A.2d 282 (1939). Since the crime is not defined by statute, it has been afforded its common-law meaning in this State. *Lutz v. State,* 167 Md. 12, 172 A. 354 (1934); *Beard v. State,* 71 Md. 275, 17 A. 1044 (1889); *Ward v. State, supra.*

The definition in *Beard v. State, supra,* is in general agreement with the authorities. See 24 Am. Jur. 2d, *Disorderly Houses* § 1; Wharton's *Criminal Law,* §§ 309-312 (2d ed. 1852); R. Perkins and R. Boyce, *Criminal Law* 487 (3d ed. 1982). Underlying the common law definition is the concept that the disorderly house is a nuisance, habitually kept. The classification of a disorderly house as a nuisance was well established at common law. In *Lutz v. State, supra,* the Court of Appeals described a disorderly house as a "kind of offensive nuisance"; and *Jackson v. State, supra,* gave approval to charging the crime in terms of its being an offense, "to the common nuisance of all the people." It was held a nuisance at common law because it drew together "dissolute persons engaged in unlawful and injurious practices ... thereby [to] endanger the public peace and corrupt good morals." 24 Am. Jur. 2d, *Disorderly Houses* § 10.

In *Everhart v. State,* 20 Md. App. 71, 97-102, 315 A.2d 80, 97-99 (1974), *rev'd,* 274 Md. 459, 337 A.2d 100 (1975), the Court provides a lengthy discussion of the definition of a common law nuisance. In *Tucker v. State,* 19 Md. App. 39, 45-48, 308 A.2d 696, 699-700 (1973), common nuisance is discussed and applied to the illicit storing or selling of controlled dangerous substances in a room.

In *Hunt v. State,* 20 Md. App. 164, 168, 314 A.2d 743, 745 (1974), the Court discussed the sufficiency of the evidence for establishing a common nuisance. The Court stated that the evidence may be deemed sufficient "when *the character of the culpable acts and the circumstances under which they were committed* are taken into account, it appears they were repeated often enough to warrant an inference that the house was kept for the indulgence of such [improper] practices." (Emphasis in original.)

In a case based upon the statute, the Court of Appeals assumed that knowledge or scienter must be shown. *Kolker v. State,* 230 Md. 157, 186 A.2d 212 (1962).

§ 4.63. Driving while intoxicated — Driving while under the influence of alcohol and/or drugs.

COMMENT—SUGGESTED INSTRUCTIONS

(a) "Driving while under the influence of alcohol" (suggested instruction)

It is unlawful for any person to drive or attempt to drive any vehicle while under the influence of alcohol. Under Maryland law, "drive" means to drive, operate, move, or be in actual physical control of a vehicle.

In order for the defendant to be found guilty of this offense, the State must prove, beyond a reasonable doubt, that the defendant attempted to or did drive, operate, move, or was in actual physical control of a vehicle while under the influence of alcohol.

A person is under the influence of alcohol when such person does not have normal use of his physical and mental faculties by reason of the use of alcoholic beverages: that is, a person's judgment and nervous system are affected from the use of alcohol to the extent that there is a failure of normal coordination. [In relation to driving or operating a motor vehicle, a failure of normal coordination exists when, as a result of the use of alcoholic beverages, a person is incapable of operating a vehicle in a manner in which an ordinarily prudent and cautious person in full possession of his faculties, using reasonable care, would operate a vehicle under like conditions.]

["Driving" a vehicle means the steering and controlling of a vehicle while in motion. "Operating" a vehicle includes driving a vehicle but also includes starting the engine of a standing vehicle for the purpose of putting the vehicle into motion. "Actual physical control" of a vehicle means that a person has existing or present bodily restraint, directing influence, domination or regulation of a vehicle. A person could have actual physical control while merely parking or standing still so long as the person was keeping the vehicle in restraint or was in a position to regulate its movement. A person need not actually move the vehicle to be in actual physical control.]

[In this case you have heard evidence that a chemical breath [blood] test was administered to the defendant and that the defendant had ____________ per cent of alcohol in his breath [blood] at the time of the administration of the test. Under Maryland law if the test results show that the defendant had 0.08 per cent or more of alcohol in the breath [blood], you may, but need not, infer that the defendant was driving while under the influence of alcohol. In your deliberation to determine whether the defendant was driving while under the influence of alcohol at the time in question, you should consider all of the facts and circumstances in evidence.]

(b) "Driving while intoxicated" (suggested instruction)

It is unlawful for any person to drive or attempt to drive any vehicle while intoxicated. Under Maryland law, "drive" means to drive, operate, move, or be in actual physical control of a vehicle.

In order for the defendant to be found guilty of this offense, the State must prove, beyond a reasonable doubt, that the defendant attempted to or did drive, operate, move, or was in actual physical control of a vehicle while intoxicated.

Under Maryland law, intoxication requires a greater degree of mental and physical impairment than being under the influence of alcohol.

[I earlier instructed you that a person is under the influence of alcohol when such person does not have *normal* use of his physical and mental faculties by reason of the use of alcoholic beverages: that is, a person's judgment and nervous system are affected from the use of alcohol to the extent that there is a failure of *normal coordination*.]

A person is intoxicated when a person's mental and physical faculties are impaired to a *substantial degree* from the use of alcoholic beverages: that is, a person's judgment and nervous system are affected from the use of alcohol to the extent that there is a substantial or significant impairment of coordination. [In relation to driving or operating a motor vehicle, a substantial or significant impairment of coordination exists when, as a result of the use of alcoholic beverages, a person lacks substantial capability to operate a vehicle in a manner that an ordinarily prudent and cautious person in full possession of his faculties, using reasonable care, would operate a vehicle under like conditions.]

["Driving" a vehicle means the steering and controlling of a vehicle while in motion. "Operating" a vehicle includes driving a vehicle but also includes starting the engine of a standing vehicle for the purpose of putting the vehicle into motion. "Actual physical control" of a vehicle means that a person has existing or present bodily restraint, directing influence, domination or regulation of a vehicle. A person could have actual physical control while merely parking or standing still so long as the person was keeping the vehicle in restraint or was in a position to regulate its movement. A person need not actually move the vehicle to be in actual physical control.]

[In this case you have heard evidence that a chemical breath [blood] test was administered to the defendant and that the defendant had __________ per cent of alcohol in his breath [blood] at the time of the administration of the test. Under Maryland law if the test results show that the defendant had 0.13 per cent or more of alcohol in the breath [blood], you may, but need not, infer that the defendant was driving while intoxicated. In your deliberation to determine whether the defendant was driving while intoxicated at the time in question, you should consider all of the facts and circumstances in evidence.]

(c) "Driving while under the influence of drugs or drugs and alcohol" (suggested instruction)

It is unlawful for any person to drive or attempt to drive any vehicle while such person is so far under the influence of any drug, any combination of drugs, or a combination of one or more drugs and alcohol that he cannot drive a vehicle safely. Under Maryland law, "drive" means to drive, operate, move, or be in actual physical control of a vehicle.

In order for the defendant to be found guilty of this offense, the State must prove, beyond a reasonable doubt, that the defendant attempted to or did drive, operate, move, or was in actual physical control of a vehicle while being so far under the influence of any drug, any combination of drugs, or a combination of one or more drugs and alcohol that he could not drive the vehicle safely.

A person is under the influence of a drug, combination of drugs or a combination of one or more drugs and alcohol when such person does not have normal use of his physical and mental faculties by reason of the use of such drugs and/or alcohol: that is, a person's judgment and nervous system are affected from the use of drugs and/or alcohol to the extent that there is a failure of normal coordination. [In relation to driving or operating a motor vehicle, a failure of normal coordination exists when, as a result of the use of drugs and/or alcoholic beverages, a person is incapable of operating a vehicle in a manner in which an ordinarily prudent and cautious person in full possession of his faculties, using reasonable care, would operate a vehicle under like conditions.]

["Driving" a vehicle means the steering and controlling of a vehicle while in motion. "Operating" a vehicle includes driving a vehicle but also includes starting the engine of a standing vehicle for the purpose of putting the vehicle into motion. "Actual physical control" of a vehicle means that a person has existing or present bodily restraint, directing influence, domination or regulation of a vehicle. A person could have actual physical control while merely parking or standing still so long as the person was keeping the vehicle in restraint or was in a position to regulate its movement. A person need not actually move the vehicle to be in actual physical control.]

[It is not a defense that the defendant was entitled to use the drug, combination of drugs, or combination of one or more drugs and alcohol, unless he was *unaware* that the drug or combination of drugs and/or alcohol would make him incapable of safely driving a motor vehicle.]

(d) "Driving while under the influence of a controlled dangerous substance" (suggested instruction)

It is unlawful for a person to drive or attempt to drive any vehicle while under the influence of any controlled dangerous substance, as that term is defined under Maryland law [unless the person is legally entitled to use the controlled dangerous substance]. Under Maryland law, "drive" means to drive, operate, move, or be in actual physical control of a vehicle.

In order for the defendant to be found guilty of this offense, the State must prove beyond a reasonable doubt that: (1) the defendant attempted to or did drive, operate, move, or was in actual physical control of a motor vehicle on or about __________ *(insert date of alleged offense);* (2) while so doing, the defendant was under the influence of __________, which is a controlled dangerous substance under Maryland law; [and (3) the defendant was not legally entitled to use __________ *(insert alleged controlled dangerous substance)* at the time of the alleged offense].

A person is under the influence of a drug when a person does not have normal use of his physical and mental faculties by reason of the use of such drug: that is, a person's judgment and nervous system are affected from the use of such drug to the extent that there is a failure of normal coordination. [In relation to driving or operating a motor vehicle, a failure of normal coordination exists when, as a result of the use of a drug, in this instance __________ *(insert alleged controlled dangerous substance),* a person is incapable of operating a vehicle in a manner that an ordinarily prudent and cautious person in full possession of his faculties, using reasonable care, would operate a vehicle under like conditions.]

["Driving" a vehicle means the steering and controlling of a vehicle while in motion. "Operating" a vehicle includes driving a vehicle but also includes starting the engine of a standing vehicle for the purpose of putting the vehicle into motion. "Actual physical control" of a vehicle means that a person has existing or present bodily restraint, directing influence, domination or regulation of a vehicle. A person could have actual physical control while merely parking or standing still so long as the person was keeping the vehicle in restraint or was in a position to regulate its movement. A person need not actually move the vehicle to be in actual physical control.]

COMMENT—DISCUSSION

(a) Applicable standards and definitions

(1) In general

Maryland Ann. Code, Art. 66½, § 11-902, has been superseded by Maryland Ann. Code, Transportation Article, § 21-902. The substance of the statutory prohibition against driving while intoxicated, however, has not been affected by this change.

Transportation, § 21-902 enumerates four separate offenses: (a) Driving while intoxicated; (b) Driving while under the influence of alcohol; (c) Driving while under the influence of drugs or drugs and alcohol; and (d) Driving while under the influence of a controlled dangerous substance. Some ambiguity exists in this statute, however, because of the failure of the courts and the General Assembly to give the definitions of, and the distinctions among, these four offenses. For this reason, the instructions, marked as "suggested," are set forth in this Comment. Additional guidance may especially be needed on the definition of "intoxicated." If chemical analysis of the percentage of alcohol in the blood or breath is available, a statutory presumption provides "prima facie" evidence of intoxication. Alcohol testing is discussed, *infra*.

In 1985, the General Assembly enacted a prohibition to supplement existing statutes. Transportation, § 21-903, Consumption of alcoholic beverages while driving on highway, states: "A person may not consume an alcoholic beverage while driving a motor vehicle on a highway of this State."

For a general discussion of Maryland's drunk driving laws, see Note, *Maryland's Drunk Driving Laws: An Overview,* 11 U. Balt. L. Rev. 357 (1982).

(2) "Drive," "operate" or be in "actual physical control"

Maryland Ann. Code, Transportation, § 21-902 makes it unlawful to "drive or attempt to drive while intoxicated, etc." This section must be read in light of Transportation, § 11-114, which states that "'Drive' means to drive, operate, move or be in actual physical control of a vehicle, including the exercise of control over or the steering of a vehicle being towed by a motor vehicle."

The term, "motor vehicle," is defined in Transportation, § 11-135.

The Court, prior to the repeal of Art. 66½, § 11-902, distinguished between the terms "drive" and "actual physical control of a vehicle." The former statute made it "unlawful for any person to drive or attempt to drive or to be in actual physical control of any vehicle within this State while his driving ability is impaired by the consumption of alcohol." In *Thomas v. State,* 277 Md. 314, 353 A.2d 256 (1976), the Court avoided the question of whether appellant's behavior constituted "actual physical control of a vehicle" by holding that failure to specifically charge the defendant with being "in actual physical control," limited the State to proving that the defendant drove or attempted to drive a vehicle (vehicle in motion) while his driving ability was impaired by alcohol. By defining "drive" to include drive, operate, move or be in actual physical control of a vehicle in the present statute, the General Assembly appears to have effectively responded to the procedural problem of the *Thomas* case.

The facts of *Thomas* present a type of case that no doubt will face the courts in applying the standard of "actual physical control" of a vehicle. The general question is whether a person found asleep behind the wheel of a vehicle has actual physical control of the vehicle. How the appellate courts will treat this case may depend on other facts, such as whether the key to the ignition is on, whether the motor is running, etc. By using the word "actual," the General Assembly arguably requires more than constructive control.

In *Thomas,* a police officer observed a vehicle with lights on standing on the left paved shoulder of a lighted ramp leading from a highway to a parkway. The officer testified that as he "approached the vehicle [he] observed that [Thomas] was either asleep or passed out on the driver's side of the vehicle.... [T]he windows were up. The keys were in the ignition. The motor was off." The officer tapped on the window and asked Thomas to step out of his vehicle. The officer smelled alcohol and Thomas "was staggering." His speech was slurred. He was "disoriented." The officer had no knowledge of whether the vehicle was in operating condition nor did he make any investigation which would reveal to him how recently the vehicle had been operated. The officer said that Thomas made no explanation to him as to how the vehicle reached the location at which it was found. The officer's testimony was the sole evidence offered by the State. *Id.* at 315-16, 353 A.2d at 257.

The Court in *Thomas* held that it was incumbent upon the prosecution to prove beyond a reasonable doubt that the defendant drove a vehicle (in motion) while in an intoxicated condition. The defendant was not compelled to take the stand to explain the circumstances in which he was found in a vehicle by the side of the road in a possibly intoxicated state. The Court reasoned that the conviction could not stand on the mere suspicion that the defendant had driven his car to that location. There was no evidence of how long Thomas had been at that location.

Also left to conjecture was whether the vehicle was operable. In its opinion the Court reviewed cases from other jurisdictions that defined terms such as "driving" and "operating" a motor vehicle.

While there are no Maryland cases defining the term "actual physical control" of a vehicle, the Court in *State v. Ruona,* 133 Mont. 243, 321 P.2d 615, 618 (1958), held that "if a person has existing or present bodily restraint, directing influence, domination or regulation of an automobile," then he is considered to be in actual physical control thereof. Further, one "could have actual physical control while merely parking or standing still, so long as he was keeping the car in restraint or in a position to regulate its movements." *State v. Ruona, supra; Parker v. State,* 424 P.2d 997 (Okla. Crim. App. 1967). However, if this is interpreted as not requiring an *actus reus* there may be a question of whether a sentence for such a criminal offense is cruel and unusual punishment. *Robinson v. California,* 370 U.S. 660, 82 S. Ct. 1417, 8 L. Ed. 2d 758 (1962). Case law gathered from other jurisdictions indicates that one need not move the vehicle to be in actual physical control, whereas such motion would be necessary to constitute driving or attempting to drive.

With respect to any potential issue concerning vagueness, the term "actual physical control" has been held not to be so vague and indefinite that one so charged is deprived of due process. *Parker v. State, supra.*

(3) "While intoxicated" and "under the influence"

In *United States v. Channell,* 423 F. Supp. 1017 (D. Md. 1976) the Court rejected a challenge that the term "intoxicated" as used in Maryland Ann. Code, Art. 66½, § 11-902(a), was unconstitutionally vague. The court stated that "[w]hile it is seemingly true that the standard 'intoxicated' is capable of more precise definition, the failure of the Maryland legislature and courts to define the term is not a denial of due process in this case in which the evidence discloses beyond a reasonable doubt that the defendant was highly intoxicated, according to the generally accepted meaning of those words." *Id.* at 1026.

Brooks v. State, 41 Md. App. 123, 395 A.2d 1224 (1979), provides some guidance in attempting to distinguish between "intoxicated" and "under the influence." The case arose under an earlier statutory scheme. Defendant was charged with speeding and "driving while intoxicated or *impaired* by alcohol." The jury determined that the evidence was insufficient to sustain a driving while intoxicated charge, but returned a conviction of driving while impaired under the then Maryland Ann. Code, Transportation, § 21-902(b). The defendant argued on appeal that the terms "intoxicated" and "impaired by the consumption of alcohol" are unconstitutionally vague in violation of the due process clause, and that no case law exists to rectify the absence of definitional specificity. The Court, *inter alia,* cited *United States v. Channell, supra,* in denying appellant's claim. The Court noted that the words involved must be "accorded the meaning naturally given them in ordinary usage," *citing Blake v. State,* 210 Md. 459, 462, 124 A.2d 273, 274 (1956). The Court discussed cases from other jurisdictions to demonstrate there are "common meanings" to these terms.

In its opinion in *Brooks v. State, supra,* the Court in a footnote stated that "the case law seems to indicate that the phrases 'under the influence of alcohol' and 'ability impaired by alcohol' are synonymous." 41 Md. App. at 128, n.2, 395 A.2d at 1227, n.2. As support, the Court cited *Croom v. Fiedler,* 341 F.2d 909, 911 (6th Cir. 1965) and *City of Farmington v. Joseph,* 91 N.M. 414, 575 P.2d 104, 107 (Ct. App. 1978). The Court, ascribing to the word "impaired" its common meaning stated: "*we believe it is generally viewed as a state less than intoxication where consumption of alcohol has affected one's normal coordination*" (citing *Clay v. State,* 211 Md. 577, 128 A.2d 634 (1957)). 41 Md. App. at 128, 395 A.2d at 1224 (emphasis added).

In *Clay v. State, supra,* the Court of Appeals examined the gross negligence standard of the manslaughter automobile statutes in relating to appellant's drinking. The Court provided some guidance for defining the term "under the influence" as "probably affecting one's judgment and discretion or probably affecting one's nervous system to the extent that there is a failure of normal coordination, although not amounting to intoxication ...." *Id.,* 128 A.2d at 638. The Court's use of the term "probably," raises a possible constitutional issue of vagueness.

The Supreme Court of Louisiana in *State v. Hightower,* 238 La. 876, 116 So. 2d 699, 702 (1959) provided a definition of intoxication that may be useful in Maryland in articulating the meaning of "under the influence" in terms of a failure of normal coordination:

> A person is intoxicated [under the influence] ... when such person does not have normal use of his physical and mental faculties by reason of the use of alcoholic beverages [or narcotics], thus rendering such person incapable of operating an automobile in a manner in which an ordinarily prudent and cautious man in full possession of his faculties, using reasonable care, would operate a motor vehicle under like conditions.

A problem with the above standard is that it may be tantamount to requiring that the prosecutor prove the driver was operating a vehicle unsafely and that such unsafe operation was caused by the driver's consumption of alcohol. An opinion of the Maryland Attorney General concludes that proof of unsafe operation is not a necessary element of the offenses of driving while intoxicated and driving while under the influence of alcohol. 68 Op. Att'y Gen. 551 (1983).

In support of his conclusion the Attorney General notes that proof of unsafe operation is clearly an element of the State's case in a prosecution for violation of Transportation, §21-902(c) (1), driving under the influence of drugs or a combination of drugs and alcohol. The presence of the restrictive clause "that he cannot drive a vehicle safely" and the absence of that or a similar clause from § 21-902 (a) and (b) — driving while intoxicated and driving while under the influence of alcohol — arguably shows that the General Assembly did not intend to require proof of unsafe operation. The opinion, in further explanation of the differing standards, distinguishes between alcohol and drugs, as follows:

> All forms of alcohol have similar, harmful effects on coordination and other driving skills, and these harmful effects can be accurately inferred from a blood alcohol test. Behavioral evidence, such as evidence of unsafe operation, is therefore unnecessary to the proof of the offenses under § 21-902 (a) or (b). By contrast, the wide variety of drugs and their widely varying effects mean that a scientific measure like

> blood alcohol testing is not feasible. Only behavioral evidence — proof that the driver "cannot drive a vehicle safely" — can establish the harmful effects of a given drug.

Id. at 444.

A weakness in this argument, as acknowledged in a footnote in the opinion, is that the results of a chemical test are not needed to sustain a conviction under Transportation, § 21-902(a) or (b) and are not available when a person refuses to take the test or the test is not otherwise administered.

The instruction above on "under the influence" draws upon the Court's guidance in *Brooks v. State, supra,* and *Clay v. State, supra.* Language based on *State v. Hightower, supra* is used and placed in brackets. It is used, however, not as describing an additional element of the offense, but instead provides additional guidance on the meaning of a "failure of normal coordination" by relating it to driving or operating a motor vehicle. In light of the Attorney General's opinion, however, it may be argued that this additional language implicitly places a burden on the prosecutor not required by the General Assembly.

Since driving "under the influence" is defined in terms of a failure of "normal coordination," a question not addressed by the Maryland Courts is whether normal coordination is judged from the standpoint of a reasonable person, an objective test, or from the viewpoint of the defendant, a subjective test. If the latter, the defendant's "normal coordination" would probably be the coordination of the defendant prior to the alleged drinking or when sober. It may be argued that it is unfair to judge the coordination of a large, middle-aged, rotund person by a standard of coordination of a high school or college athlete. A subjective-objective test could be used to judge the defendant's coordination in reference to a sober person of similar age, physical stature, condition, and health. While perhaps closer to a subjective test than an objective test, this formulation compares the defendant's coordination with reference to a class of persons sharing similar characteristics. The instructions do not elaborate on the meaning of "normal coordination."

The problem of defining "intoxicated" remains. No reported cases interpreting this term have been found, with Maryland apparently leaving the problem of definition and application to the trier of fact in accordance with the "common meaning" of the term. *Singleton v. Roman,* 195 Md. 241, 72 A.2d 705 (1950). Yet, some guidance to the trier of fact seems necessary. As quoted above, *Brooks v. State, supra,* makes it clear that "intoxication" is a state greater than "under the influence." Hence, it seems to be a reasonable inference that something more than a mere failure of normal coordination as a result of the use of alcoholic beverages is required. While clarification is needed by the appellate courts, it seems reasonable to suppose that "intoxication" requires a substantial impairment of coordination. The instruction on "driving while intoxicated," accordingly, is framed along these lines.

A question that may need clarification by the courts is whether "driving under the influence of alcohol" is a lesser included offense of "driving while intoxicated." Alan J. Goldstein, in *The Growing Complexity of Trying the DWI Case,* Maryland Bar Journal 17 (March 1985) observes:

> In the area of charging documents the current status of the law is in flux due to a number of inconsistent decisions from the Court of Appeals and the Court of Special Appeals. The Court of Appeals decision in *Ayre v. State,* 291 Md. 155, 433 A.2d 1150 (1981) indicates that unless every material element of a given offense is expressly alleged on a district court citation, the citation must be dismissed for failure to state an offense. Some courts have dismissed citations for failing to allege jurisdiction. ("Md.") and/or venue (e.g., "P.G.").
>
> While the Court of Special Appeals held in *Insley v. State,* 32 Md. App. 46, 358 A.2d 246 (1976) that a charge of "driving in an intoxicated condition" did not charge what many lawyers believed was a lesser included offense of "driving while ability impaired," courts are unable to agree whether "driving while intoxicated" includes "driving under the influence of alcohol." Thus, some courts will acquit a defendant on both charges if only "intoxicated" is alleged while others will convict for "under the influence" when the evidence is insufficient for a conviction under the more serious offense prescribed of "driving while intoxicated."

Id. at 18. See Transportation, § 26-405. There is tension between the language of *Insley v. State, supra,* and § 26-405. In *Vonoppenfeld v. State,* 53 Md. App. 462, 454 A.2d 402 (1983) there is a suggestion that *Insley v. State, supra,* preceded the codification of § 26-405, but it has also been noted that § 26-405 merely recodified an earlier provision.

Finally, the phrase "driving while intoxicated" in Transportation, § 21-902(a) does not specifically require that the intoxication result from the use of alcohol. In contrast, § 21-902(b) specifically refers to "driving while under the influence of alcohol." Because the General Assembly provided separate offenses in § 21-902(c) and (d) where the use of drugs and a combination of drugs and alcohol are involved, it could be argued that driving while intoxicated means driving while intoxicated from alcohol. This interpretation is consistent with the view that the Assembly has provided two degrees of offenses involving the use of alcohol: driving while intoxicated and driving while under the influence. On the other hand, the two drug related driving offenses involve "merely" driving under the influence and the Legislature has provided for potentially higher penalties for driving while intoxicated. Transportation, § 27-101. Also, the Assembly could easily have restricted the definition of "intoxication" to alcoholic substances and it did not. It could therefore be argued that the Assembly intended the term "intoxication" to have a broader meaning. One problem with this interpretation is that the present art of chemical drug testing permits gradations in the degree of intoxication from alcohol. Recognizing this the General Assembly has consequently provided statutory evidentiary standards. No such standards are provided for intoxication from substances other than alcohol. The appellate courts may need to resolve this question of interpretation. If a broader definition applies, the suggested instruction, "Driving while intoxicated," *supra,* will have to be modified where intoxicating substances other than alcohol are involved and the State seeks a conviction on the more serious offense.

(4) Drugs and controlled dangerous substances

As noted, the General Assembly has provided two offenses for driving while under the influence of drugs. Maryland Ann. Code, Transportation, § 21-902(c) proscribes driving under the influence of any drug, any combination of drugs, or a combination of one or more drugs and alcohol to the degree that the person cannot drive a vehicle safely. A defense can be based on lack of awareness that the drug or combination would make the person incapable of safely driving a vehicle. Transportation, § 21-902(d) proscribes driving any vehicle while under the influence of a controlled dangerous substance, as that term is defined in Art. 27, § 279, unless the person is entitled to use the controlled dangerous substance.

In *Cook v. State,* 62 Md. App. 634, 490 A.2d 1311 (1985), the Court held that nothing in the statute or its underlying intent precludes the State from proceeding under § 21-902(c) merely because a drug may be classifiable as a controlled dangerous substance, provided the State is prepared to prove the additional statutory element of unsafe operation. While § 21-902(c) may have been primarily aimed at the misuse of over-the-counter and prescription drugs, it does not follow that the Assembly intended to exclude those driving offenses involving the use of more dangerous and heavily controlled drugs.

(b) Proving "intoxication" and "under the influence": nonchemical evidence

Introduction of evidence of the alcoholic content in an accused's body, as shown upon chemical analysis through tests made pursuant to Maryland Ann. Code, Courts and Judicial Proceedings, §§ 10-302 to 10-309, is not a prerequisite to conviction for the crimes of driving while intoxicated or driving while impaired. A conviction may be based on any competent evidence legally sufficient to establish the *corpus delicti* of the crimes and the criminal agency of the accused. For example, in *Major v. State,* 31 Md. App. 590, 358 A.2d 609 (1976), the prosecutor introduced into evidence the defendant's driving record which indicated that the defendant's driver's license had been revoked on six different occasions. The remainder of the evidence consisted of the arresting officer's testimony that, at the time he was arrested, the defendant had alcohol on his breath, his clothes were messy, his attitude indifferent, and he staggered when he walked. The Court held that this evidence was sufficient to support defendant's conviction of driving while intoxicated, in the absence of scientific evidence of intoxication. See also *United States v. Channell,* 423 F. Supp. 1017, 1021 (D. Md. 1976).

In *Brooks v. State,* 41 Md. App. 123, 395 A.2d 1224 (1979), a police officer was the State's sole witness. A chemical analysis of defendant's alcohol blood count was not performed. In addition to the officer's observations, three empty twelve-ounce beer bottles were found by the officer in defendant's car. The defendant himself took the stand and admitted drinking three beers shortly before being stopped by the police officer. Another defense witness testified that the defendant appeared to have been drinking prior to his consumption of the three bottles of beer. The Court noted that chemical evidence of alcohol consumption is unnecessary for conviction.

Medical technology has not advanced as far with respect to drug use as it has for alcohol use in being able to determine, for example, the amount of marijuana present in the body. For this reason, all drug induced offenses which produce diminished capacity to drive are lumped into the same generic category of "under the influence." The State needs to produce evidence of the defendant's failure of normal coordination.

If being under the influence of alcohol is defined as a failure of normal coordination, the state of the defendant's coordination prior to drinking may be very important. Obviously, the state of one's health and the use of any medications may affect a person's "normal coordination" as well as appearance. The wearing of contact lenses may affect the degree of redness of the eyes.

The defendant's behavior from the time he or she was stopped by the police officer may be highly relevant. Was the defendant able to get out of the car unassisted? How did the defendant walk when he or she got out of the car? If taken to the police station, was the defendant able to walk up or down any steps unassisted? It has been observed that intoxicated persons generally have greater difficulty walking down steps then walking up steps. Was the defendant handcuffed at the time of any of the observations?

The suspect may be given a variety of coordination "tests" by police officers after being stopped on suspicion of intoxication. Both the prosecutor and defense attorney need to consider the significance of the test results. It has been suggested that coordination tests are a measure of one's ability to understand and follow directions as well as a measure of coordination. Defense attorneys are sometimes advised to consider recreating the "test" in the courtroom and to request that the police officer demonstrate how the test was given, and the defendant's responses. For some tests, such as the "alphabet test," the police officer may be asked to demonstrate the test in the courtroom. Factors such as education level and whether English is a defendant's primary language may be relevant to performance on this test. If the police officer testifies that the defendant's speech was slurred, defense counsel may consider asking the officer to demonstrate how the defendant actually recited the alphabet or spoke when making other statements.

An infrequently explored question is whether certain "field sobriety" tests administered by the police officer should be subjected to the standards of scientific evidence. Are the tests a valid and reliable measure of "normal coordination" and, if so, under what circumstances? Can the court take judicial notice of the validity of the principles underlying the tests and, if not, does the police officer have sufficient understanding of the underlying principles to qualify as an expert witness? Should the police officer actually be qualified on the stand as an expert witness as a prerequisite to being allowed to testify to the results and interpretation of certain field tests? Are there commonly understood guidelines to interpret the results of particular tests? Were the tests properly administered and the results accurately recorded in the instant case? While evidence of field sobriety tests may not formally be treated as scientific evidence, defense counsel can often effectively enhance his presentation and cross-examination if he approaches the evidence as if it were scientific in nature.

In response to the argument that field sobriety tests constitute scientific evidence, the State can argue that any lay witness can give opinions on certain matters under the so-called "collective facts" rule, including whether the defendant appeared to be drunk or under the influence of alcohol. In explaining such an opinion the witness can give the basis for the opinion or the "primary" facts upon which the opinion is based. This may include not only the defendant's appearance but a descriptive statement of the defendant's behavior in response to field sobriety "tests." If this is the theory for admitting evidence of field sobriety tests, the police officer testifying as a lay witness should not be allowed to give an opinion specifically as to the significance of the defendant's performance on any particular test. In other words, the officer probably cannot grade the defendant and testify as to whether the defendant passed or flunked a particular test. Also, under this theory, the defense may argue that the lay opinion violates the so-called "ultimate issue" rule. Since an ultimate issue in the case is whether the defendant was under the influence of alcohol at the time when he was driving a motor vehicle, the officer's opinion may be phrased in a way that goes directly to the ultimate issue. Under the Federal Rules of Evidence, Rule 704, the ultimate issue rule has been abolished; witnesses, however, may still not testify to lay opinions if phrased in terms of inadequately explored legal criteria.

In *McAvoy v. State,* 70 Md. App. 661, 523 A.2d 618 (1987), the Court held that the defendant's performance on the field sobriety tests was properly admitted. *Miranda* warnings were held to be inapplicable to any evidence provided by the defendant prior to his arrest. Also, the defendant's inability to perform the field sobriety test did not reveal any of his subjective knowledge or thought processes and was, therefore, neither testimony nor communication.

(c) Proving "intoxication" and "under the influence": chemical evidence

(1) In general

The evidentiary use of chemical tests for blood alcohol content is provided for in Maryland Ann. Code, Courts and Judicial Proceedings, Title 10, Subtitle 3.

Chemical tests are admitted into evidence pursuant to §§ 10-302 to 10-309. Section 10-307 applies to alcohol present in the blood or breath and gives rise to the following presumptions:

(1) 0.05% or less alcohol in blood or breath: it is presumed that the defendant was not intoxicated and that the defendant was not driving under the influence of alcohol;

(2) More than 0.05% but less than 0.08% of alcohol in the blood or breath: there are no presumptions in either direction;

(3) 0.08% of alcohol in the blood or breath: there is *prima facie* evidence that the defendant was driving under the influence of alcohol;

(4) 0.13% of alcohol in the blood or breath: this is considered *prima facie* evidence that the defendant was intoxicated.

Effective, July 1, 1986, the General Assembly added subsection (f) to § 10-307, to provide an additional statutory "prima facie" evidence rule as follows: "If at the time of testing there was in the person's blood 0.01 percent or more by weight of alcohol, as determined by an analysis of the person's blood or breath, it shall be prima facie evidence that the defendant was driving with alcohol in the defendant's blood."

These presumptions or inferences are applicable in all cases where the defendant is facing criminal charges for driving while intoxicated or under the influence. *State v. Loscomb,* 291 Md. 424, 435 A.2d 764 (1981). For a discussion of the applicability of these statutory presumptions in civil cases, see *Fouche v. Masters,* 47 Md. App. 11, 420 A.2d 1279 (1980). In light of *Briscoe v. State,* 60 Md. App. 42, 479 A.2d 1385 (1984), discussed *infra,* and the constitutional law relating to presumptions in criminal cases, a jury instruction relating to the statutory evidentiary standards of items (3) and (4) above should probably state that the jury "may but need not infer," for example, from a level of 0.13% or more of alcohol in the blood or breath that the defendant was intoxicated. Alternatively, the jury could be instructed that they "may infer, but are not required to infer" that the defendant was intoxicated. A major benefit of the above statute to the State is that the statute relieves the State from the burden of calling an expert witness to interpret the significance of the test findings to the jury. Further, the legislative standards tell the judge that if certain evidence has been introduced there is a sufficient case to go to the jury.

In a prosecution for driving while intoxicated or driving while under the influence, Courts and Judicial Proceedings, § 10-309(a) requires that test results be excluded from evidence if they are obtained "contrary to" the statutory requirements:

> Except as provided in § 16-205.1(c) of the Transportation Article [relating to accidents that result in the death of another person], a person may not be compelled to submit to a chemical analysis provided for in this subtitle. Evidence of chemical analysis is not admissible in a prosecution for a violation of § 21-902 of the Transportation Article if obtained contrary to its provisions. No inference or presumption concerning either guilt or innocence arises because of refusal to submit. The fact of refusal to submit is not admissible in evidence at the trial.

See also 68 Op. Att'y Gen. 432 (Opinion No. 83-014) (April 14, 1983).

In *State v. Loscomb, supra,* the Court construed the scope of the exclusionary rule requiring that alcohol test results be excluded from evidence if obtained contrary to statutory requirements as applied to prosecutions charging violations of Art. 27, § 388 (manslaughter by automobile, etc.) and § 388A (homicide by motor vehicle while intoxicated). A chemical test was administered to the accused without obtaining the affirmative consent required by § 16-205.1(c) of the Transportation Article. The Court held that because there was a failure to comply with this procedural requirement, the exclusionary rule of § 10-309 applied.

An exception to the defendant's right to refuse to submit to a chemical test is where a person is involved in an accident involving a death. In this situation a person is required to submit to a chemical test. Transportation, § 16-205.1(c). Also, the exclusionary rule of Courts and Judicial Proceedings, § 10-309(a), quoted *supra,* was modified effective July 1, 1982, to assure that chemical test results would be available in prosecutions for crimes involving the death of a person. Section 10-309(c) provides that "[n]othing in this section precludes or limits the admissibility of evidence of chemical analysis in any prosecution other than for a violation of § 21-902 of the Transportation Article." The General Assembly effectively overruled *State v. Loscomb,* 291 Md. 424, 435 A.2d 764 (1981), which had interpreted the language of § 10-309(a) (which then did not have the words "in a prosecution for a violation of § 21-902") to mean that the exclusionary rule was applicable in a prosecution for manslaughter by automobile, and homicide by motor vehicle while intoxicated.

In *Briscoe v. State, supra,* the defendant was charged with manslaughter by motor vehicle, homicide by motor vehicle while intoxicated, driving while intoxicated, and driving while license revoked, and was convicted of the first, third, and fourth count (the jury having merged count two into count one). The defendant was given a blood test that was the result of standard medical procedures but which was not administered in compliance with the required procedures of Transportation, §§ 10-302 to 10-306. At the trial the judge admitted evidence of the blood test results showing alcohol content of .27. A doctor testified that a person with that much alcohol in his blood would be "pretty drunk." There was other evidence tending to show the defendant's intoxication. Over a timely objection, the trial judge read to the jury § 10-307, including subsection (e) which provides: "If at the time of testing there was in the person's blood 0.13 percent or more by weight of alcohol, as determined by an analysis of the person's blood or breath, it shall be prima facie evidence that the defendant was intoxicated." The Court of Special Appeals reversed the convictions of manslaughter and driving while intoxicated. The Court held:

> This instruction, which the State concedes should not have been given, plainly told the jury that they could indulge in a prima facie inference that Briscoe was intoxicated. The statutory "prima facie evidence" language is, of course, addressed to the trial judge. It tells him, in effect, that if certain evidence has been introduced (after compliance with the statutory preconditions) there is a case sufficient to go the jury — a case in which the jury may but is not required to find intoxication. In the case before us, we cannot hold that the "prima facie evidence" instruction was not prejudicial so far as the driving while intoxicated charge is concerned. Use of the "prima facie evidence" wording of § 10-307(e) might have incorrectly persuaded the jury that this was a statutory presumption, thus requiring Briscoe to rebut it.

Id. at 45-46, 479 A.2d at 1387.

In *Briscoe,* the Court also stated that the results of a chemical test not performed pursuant to the statutory requirements of

Transportation, §§ 10-302 to 10-306 may be admitted into evidence but that the statutory inferences of intoxication contained in § 10-307 are not available under these circumstances. In support of its statement, the Court cited *State v. Moon,* 291 Md. 463, 436 A.2d 420 (1981), discussed *infra,* this Comment. In that case the Court held that the exclusionary rules apply only to chemical tests administered for purposes of prosecution.

Another exception to the defendant's right to refuse to submit to a chemical test is that a police officer may direct a qualified medical person to withdraw blood for a chemical test from an unconscious person, so long as his or her health or well-being would not be jeopardized. See Transportation, § 16-105.1; Comment, § 2.32, Consent to blood and other chemical tests, *supra.*

(2) Police procedures before administering chemical tests

When a driver is stopped on suspicion of driving while intoxicated or under the influence, the police officer may first request that the motorist take a preliminary breath test. The police officer shall advise the person to be tested that "neither a refusal to take the test nor the taking of the test shall prevent or require a subsequent chemical test pursuant to § 16-205.1 of this article" [relating to suspension of driver's license for refusal to submit to chemical test for intoxication]. Maryland Ann. Code, Transportation, § 16-205.2. The statute also provides:

> The results of the preliminary breath test shall be used as a guide for the police officer in deciding whether an arrest should be made and may not be used as evidence by the State in any court action. The results of the preliminary breath test may be used as evidence by a defendant in a court action. The taking of or refusal to submit to a preliminary breath test is not admissible in any court action. Any evidence pertaining to a preliminary breath test may not be used in a civil action.

Transportation, § 16-205.2(c). Query whether the State could, nevertheless, use such evidence for impeachment purposes. *Cf. United States v. Havens,* 446 U.S. 620, 100 S. Ct. 1912, 64 L. Ed. 2d 559 (1980); Note, *Maryland's Drunk Driving Laws: An Overview,* 11 U. Balt. L. Rev. 357, 359 n.15 (1982). Also, since the evidentiary limitations relate to court action, query whether either the State or the defendant could use the preliminary breath test results at a hearing before the Motor Vehicle Administration.

Refusal to submit to the preliminary breath test does not carry with it the administrative penalties incurred upon refusal to take a chemical test under Transportation, § 16-205.

A police officer seeking a chemical test pursuant to § 16-205.1 must follow certain procedures. The police officer must advise the motorist of the consequences of a refusal to take the test. The officer "shall advise him that, on receipt of a sworn statement from the officer that the driver was so charged and refused to take a chemical test for alcohol, the [Motor Vehicle] Administration shall ... suspend his driver's license for a period of not less than 60 days nor more than 6 months for a first offense and not less than 120 days nor more than 1 year for a second or subsequent offense." Transportation, § 16-205.1(b)(1). The statute requires:

> ... [I]f a police officer stops or detains any individual who the police officer has reasonable grounds to believe is or has been driving or attempting to drive a motor vehicle while intoxicated or while under the influence of alcohol and who is not unconscious or otherwise incapable of refusing to take a chemical test for alcohol, the police officer shall:
>
> (i) Detain the individual;
>
> (ii) Request that the individual permit a chemical test to be taken of the individual's blood or breath to determine the alcoholic content of the individual's blood;
>
> (iii) Advise the individual of the administrative penalties that shall be imposed for refusal to take the test; and
>
> (iv) If the individual refuses to take the test, send a sworn report to the [Motor Vehicle] Administration within 72 hours after detention ....

Transportation, § 16-205.1(b)(2). The officer's report to the Motor Vehicle Administration must recite the reasonable grounds for the officer's belief that the driver was driving or attempting to drive a motor vehicle while intoxicated or while under the influence of alcohol and the fact of the driver's refusal to take the test "after being informed of the administrative penalties that shall be imposed for refusal." Transportation, § 16-205.1(b)(2)(iv).

A question has arisen as to what constitutes adequate notice to the driver regarding the "administrative penalties" for refusal to take the chemical test. The Maryland State Police and other law enforcement agencies have used a standard form — Form DR-15, "Advice of Rights and Administrative Penalties for Refusal to Submit to a Chemical Test," to inform the detained driver. In pertinent part, Form DR-15 reads as follows:

> [Y]ou have the right to refuse to submit to any such tests, and on your refusal, no test shall be administered ... [Y]our refusal to submit to a chemical test shall result in the suspension of your driver's license and/or driving privilege for not less than 60 days nor more than 6 months.

68 Op. Att'y Gen. 432 (Opinion No. 83-014) (April 14, 1983).

In fact, a driver who refuses to take the test may appear at a hearing within thirty days to "show cause why the driver's license or privilege to drive should not be suspended." Transportation, § 16-205.1(f)(1). "At the hearing, the driver may present evidence about the driver's refusal to take the test and may be represented by an attorney." Transportation, § 16-205.1(f)(3). The statute provides that after the hearing the Motor Vehicle Administration shall suspend the driver's license or privilege to drive for not less than sixty days nor more than six months for a first offense and not less than 120 days nor more than one year for a second or subsequent offense, if the Administration determines that the driver was charged as set forth in the statute above and refused to take a chemical test for alcohol. Transportation, § 16-205.1(f)(4). The statute continues:

> The [Motor Vehicle] Administration may modify this suspension or issue a restrictive license if:
>
> (i) The licensee is required to drive a motor vehicle in the course of employment;
>
> (ii) The license is required for the purpose of attending an alcoholic prevention of treatment program; or
>
> (iii) It finds that the licensee has no alternative means of transportation available and without the license, the licensee's ability to earn a living would be severely impaired.

Transportation, § 16-205.1(f)(5). A suspension is reviewable on appeal to the Circuit Court. Transportation, §§ 16-205.1(g) and 12-209.

Is Form DR-15, *supra,* sufficient statutory notice in light of the fact that it does not contain advice about the driver's right to a hearing and to appeal an adverse decision? In addition, it does not advise of the circumstances under which the Motor Vehicle Administration may modify a suspension or issue a restructive license instead of ordering a complete suspension. Further, is the advice sufficient if it does not inform the driver that the fact of refusal is not admissible in a prosecution for driving while intoxicated or while under the influence of alcohol?

The Attorney General issued an opinion which concluded that Form DR-15 complies with the statutory requirement that the police officer shall "(a)dvise the individual of the administrative penalties that shall be imposed for refusal to take the test" under Transportation, § 16-205.1(b)(2)(iii). 68 Op. Att'y Gen. 432 (Opinion No. 83-014) (April 14, 1983). It is argued that the phrase "administrative penalties" merely refers to the mandatory suspension referred to in § 16-205.1(b)(1). The contrary argument is that the phrase more broadly refers to procedural rights, mitigating circumstances, or evidentiary exclusions. No Maryland decision has addressed the level of detail to be disclosed by the police officer in § 16-205.1. The Attorney General's opinion reviews case law from other jurisdictions considering similar issues.

As a result of the 1983 amendments to Maryland law, a person no longer has a right to select which of two tests, blood or breath, will be administered. The breath test will be administered. The chemical test, however, will be used if (1) the defendant is unconscious or otherwise incapable of refusing to take a chemical test for alcohol; (2) injuries to the defendant require removal of the defendant to a medical facility; or (3) the equipment for administering the chemical breath test is not available. Courts and Judicial Proceedings, § 10-305(a). The urinalysis test is no longer statutorily authorized.

The specimen of breath or blood must be taken within two hours after a person is apprehended. Courts and Judicial Proceedings, § 10-303. See *Hasselhoff v. State,* 67 Md. App. 645, 508 A.2d 1030 (1986). The term "apprehended" as it appears in the statute is ambiguous. However, the Court of Appeals explained in *Willis v. State,* 302 Md. 363, 488 A.2d 171 (1985), that an accused is "apprehended when a police officer has reasonable grounds to believe that the person is or has been driving a motor vehicle while intoxicated or while under the influence of alcohol and the police officer reasonably acts upon that information by stopping or detaining the person." *Id.* at 376, 488 A.2d at 178. *Cf. State v. Moon,* 291 Md. 463, 436 A.2d 420 (1981) where the blood sample was obtained not for the purpose of prosecution but for the purpose of treatment as a result of a drug screening test ordered by his physician. The Court held that the evidence was admissible despite the fact that the blood sample was taken more than two hours after the incident. The statutory exclusionary rules apply only to chemical tests administered for purposes of prosecution.

Except as provided in Transportation, § 16-205.1(c), a person may not be compelled to submit to a chemical analysis. No inference or presumption concerning either guilt or innocence arises because of refusal to submit. However, the fact of refusal to submit is admissible in evidence at the trial. Courts and Judicial Proceedings, § 10-309(a). Also, if a person requests a chemical test and the officer refuses to administer it, a defendant can have that fact introduced into evidence. *Major v. State,* 31 Md. App. 590, 603, 358 A.2d 609, 617 (1976) (dictum). In *State v. Werkheiser,* 299 Md. 529, 474 A.2d 898 (1984), the police officer failed to obtain a blood sample from defendant while he was unconscious. The trial judge dismissed the case involving driving while intoxicated. The Court held that dismissal was not an appropriate remedy. The trial judge should have permitted an inference that had the test been administered, the result would have been favorable to the defendant and the jury could have weighed this evidence along with other evidence in determining defendant's guilt or innocence. *Cf.* Instruction, § 2.21, Missing witness, *supra.*

In *Berkemer v. McCarty,* 468 U.S. 420, 104 S. Ct. 3138, 82 L. Ed. 317 (1984), the United States Supreme Court discussed the application of the *Miranda* rules to stops and arrests for driving while intoxicated. Prior to arrest, persons temporarily detained at roadside pursuant to a stop (even where there is brief questioning and a field sobriety "balancing test" for intoxication) are usually not "in custody" and no *Miranda* warnings are required. The Court held, however, that the functional equivalent of arrest occurred when the suspect was formally placed under arrest after having failed one field sobriety test. The opinion implies that a suspect driven to a police station for a blood or breath test is at that point under arrest. See Instruction, § 2.25, Confession or incriminating state of defendant, *supra.*

In *McAvoy v. State,* 70 Md. App. 661, 523 A.2d 618 (1987), the defendant contended that the results of his breathalyzer test should have been suppressed because he was not advised of his *Miranda* rights. The Court held that the fifth amendment, however, only protects an accused from being compelled to provide evidence of a testimonial or communicative nature. No testimony or communication is compelled when the accused is a donor of blood or breath for determining the percentage of ethyl alcohol in his blood. A person who is arrested for driving while intoxicated or driving while under the influence of alcohol is not entitled to *Miranda* warnings prior to being given the option to submit to the blood-alcohol tests. The Court held that the results of the breathalyzer test were, thus, properly admitted.

In *Sites v. State,* 300 Md. 702, 481 A.2d 192 (1984), the Court held that a defendant has a due process right upon request and within a reasonable time, to consult counsel before being forced to choose whether or not to take a breathalyzer test to determine blood alcohol content, so long as it does not interfere with the testing process or the ability to administer the test. In *Brosan v. Cochran,* 307 Md. 662, 516 A.2d 970 (1986), the Court held that administration of a breathalyzer test by counsel is effective communication with counsel prior to a decision whether to submit to the State test where timely administered and where it will not substantially interfere with the State testing process. Alan J. Goldstein in his article, Maryland Bar Journal, *supra,* at 18, referring to *Berkemer v. McCarthy, supra,* and *Sites v. State, supra,* observes: "These cases read together raise difficult and interesting questions regarding the obligation of the police to advise a defendant about his right to counsel, whether that obligation is different depending upon whether it is a Fifth, Sixth or Fourteenth Amendment right to counsel, and when in the course of a driving while intoxicated case these various rights attach."

In *Little v. State,* 300 Md. 485, 479 A.2d 903 (1984), the Court upheld the use of sobriety checkpoints as consistent with fourth amendment requirements so long as the following conditions are met: (1) the discretion of the officers in the field is carefully circumscribed by clear objective regulations established by high level administrative officials; (2) approaching drivers are given adequate warning that there is a roadblock ahead; (3) the likelihood of apprehension, fear or surprise is reduced by a display of legitimate police authority at the roadblock; and (4) vehicles are stopped on a systematic, nonrandom basis that shows drivers that they are not being singled out for arbitrary reasons. Each checkpoint must be evaluated by applying the above criteria. Questions that may arise in the application of these criteria include: how large a warning sign must be posted?; is one warning sign sufficient?; if the checkpoint is used after dark, what lighting of the sign(s), if any, is required?; where must the sign(s) be posted in relationship to the checkpoint?; and, what opportunity, if any, must be provided for motorists to change their course and avoid stopping at the checkpoint? At least one trial judge has taken the position that, because local traffic regulations require a motorist to give a turn signal at least 100 feet before an intersection, the warning sign must be posted at least 100 feet before a turn-off to give the motorist an opportunity to make a legal turn before passing the checkpoint. It also has been suggested that one adequately lighted, four-by-five foot sign (i.e., twenty square feet) may be sufficient notice if properly placed.

In conclusion, Maryland statutes provide protections for the suspected drunk driver beyond that deemed required by the United States Constitution. See *Schmerber v. California,* 384 U.S. 757, 86 S. Ct. 1826, 16 L. Ed. 2d 908 (1966); *South Dakota v. Neville,* 459 U.S. 553, 103 S. Ct. 916, 74 L. Ed. 2d 748 (1983); Instruction, § 2.32, Consent to blood and other chemical tests, *supra.* In *State v. Moon, supra,* the Court noted that these statutes are primarily concerned with the protection of the public rather than protection of the accused. In recent years, the General Assembly has attempted to increase the deterrent effect of drunk driving laws by limiting certain protections formerly extended to suspected drunk drivers, such as no longer permitting the driver to select the chemical test of his or her choice, and compelling the use of chemical tests in all cases where a person is involved in an accident in which a death results. Yet, under the current law, it may well be in a suspect's best interest to refuse a chemical test since the penalty for refusal is only civil in nature (usually involving license suspension). A person consenting to the administration of a chemical test may run a greater risk of being successfully prosecuted on criminal charges which may involve not only suspension or revocation of a driving license, but fines and possible imprisonment as well. For these reasons, the Maryland Legislature might consider compelling the use of chemical tests in all cases where drunk driving is reasonably suspected. As a practical matter, such a proposal might increase the risk of dangerous officer-citizen confrontations involving its enforcement. A more modest proposal would require chemical tests when an accident involves personal injury or at least personal injury serious enough to require immediate medical attention.

(3) Administering chemical tests: foundation requirements

Foundation evidence is important to establish the accuracy of chemical tests for intoxication, because results based on faulty equipment or procedures are of little value:

> The proponent of a chemical or scientific test must establish that the test itself is reliable and that its administration in the particular instance conformed to the procedure necessary to insure reliability.... Without a foundation guaranteeing the test's reliability, the test result is not probative as a measurement and hence is irrelevant.

State v. Dille, 258 N.W.2d 565, 567 (Minn. 1977). In Maryland Ann. Code, Courts and Judicial Proceedings, Title 10, Subtitle 3, requires that certain safeguards be followed to assure the accuracy of the tests. The State Toxicologist has issued detailed regulations concerning personnel and equipment with the purpose of assuring accurate chemical test results. Regulations of the Toxicologist, Office of the Chief Medical Examiner, Postmortem Examiners Commission, State of Maryland, Regarding Tests of Breath and Blood for Alcohol (1983). Further guidance is provided in an opinion of the Attorney General at 68 Op. Att'y Gen. 446 (Opinion No. 83-022) (June 1, 1983). Thus, the results of a chemical test are not admissible if the State fails to show that it complied substantially with the statutory requirements *and* the defendant objects to the introduction of the test results. In addition, unless the statutes are interpreted to repeal the common law, it would appear that common-law requirements for the admissibility of scientific evidence must be complied with also.

The State must first establish that a chemical test was administered or conducted by a "qualified person" defined as "a person who has received training in the use of the equipment in a training program approved by the toxicologist under the Postmortem Examiners Commission and who is either a police officer, a police employee, or an employee of the Chief Medical Examiner." Courts and Judicial Proceedings, § 10-304(a)(3). The officer arresting the individual may not administer the chemical breath test. § 10-304(b). A "qualified medical person" — i.e., "any person permitted by law to withdraw blood from humans" — shall obtain the blood for a blood test. § 10-304(a)(2) and (c). The person tested may have a physician of his own choosing administer a chemical test in addition to the one administered at the direction of the police officer. If no test is offered or requested by the police officer, a person may request, and the officer shall have administered, one of the chemical tests. § 10-304(d).

The qualifications of the technician can, of course, be established through the testimony of the technician who ran the test, with supporting evidence. Also,

> [I]n any criminal trial in which intoxication due to the consumption of alcohol, or being under the influence of alcohol, is an issue, a copy of a report of the results of a chemical test of breath or blood signed by the technician or analyst who performed the test, is admissible as substantive evidence without the presence or testimony of the technician or analyst who performed the test.

Courts and Judicial Proceedings, § 10-306(a). To do so, however, the State "shall at least 20 days before trial, notify the defendant or his attorney in writing of its intention and delivery to the defendant or his attorney a copy of the test results to be offered." § 10-306(b)(1). The defendant then has the right on timely and proper notice — i.e. to "notify the court and the State in writing no later than 10 days before trial" to insist that the technician appear and testify at the trial. § 10-306(b)(2). The defendant's failure to give timely and proper notice constitutes a waiver of the defendant's right to the presence and testimony of the technician. § 10-306(b)(3). This discussion assumes that the phrase, "the results of a chemical test of breath or blood," in § 10-306(a) is not limited simply to the outcome of the tests but may be construed to include other information such as proof of the technician's qualifications. This question has not yet been litigated.

The next foundation requirement is that certain safeguards have been used to assure the accuracy of the tests. As noted above, the specimen of breath or blood must be taken within two hours after the person is apprehended. § 10-303. The evidence required to make this showing would ordinarily consist of the testimony of the detaining officer as to the time of apprehension, and the testimony of the person who took the sample as to the time of its taking. In a breath test where the taking of the sample and the administration of the test are essentially simultaneous, the time of the sample taking can probably be included in the report of test results that may be admitted pursuant to the provisions of § 10-306, discussed *supra*. Arguably in a blood test, if the "qualified medical person" who draws the blood sample states the time in a hospital or similar record, this record may qualify under the business record exception to the hearsay rule, pursuant to § 10-101. See 68 Op. Att'y Gen. 446 (Opinion No. 83-022) (June 1, 1983) (mimeographed opinions at 9). However, there may be a question in a criminal case as to whether use of the business record exception to the hearsay rule violates a defendant's constitutional right to confrontation.

The breath test must also use equipment "approved by the toxicologist under the Postmortem Examiners Commission at the direction of a police officer." § 10-304(b). The blood test must use "equipment approved by the toxicologist under the Postmortem Examiners Commission in a laboratory approved by the toxicologist." § 10-304(c). The statute specifies the form of proof to establish these facts:

> For the purpose of establishing that the test was administered with equipment approved by the toxicologist under the Postmortem Examiners Commission, a statement signed by the toxicologist certifying that the equipment used in the test has been approved by him shall be prima facie evidence

> of the approval, and the statement is admissible in evidence without the necessity of the toxicologist personally appearing in court.

§ 10-304(e). Query whether in a criminal case such a method of proof violates the defendant's rights to constitutional confrontation. See discussion in *Casper v. State,* 70 Md. App. 576, 521 A.2d 1281 (1987).

The statute discussed above provides that the report of the technician or analyst who performed the test be admitted into evidence upon notice to the defendant. Absent a request for the presence of the technician, there is a provision requiring that the technician's report include the following: "State that the test was performed with equipment approved by the toxicologist under the Postmortem Examiners Commission at the direction of a police officer." § 10-306(a)(2)(ii). If the State does not submit the toxicologist's certification of the equipment, pursuant to § 10-304(c), *supra,* but instead relies on the technician's report, is this sufficient evidence to establish that the equipment was properly certified? It can be argued that the defendant has waived his right to the presence of the technician, and hence the entire report is admissible. It can also be argued, however, that if the technician were present, the technician's testimony that the toxicologist had certified the equipment does not meet the statutory requirement of § 10-304(c) quoted *supra.* Such testimony by the technician could also be subject to a hearsay objection. Since the technician could not so testify if he appeared personally, arguably the technician's report, without the toxicologist's certification, is insufficient to meet statutory requirements.

Also, under the statute the testing equipment apparently need only be approved once by the toxicologist irrespective of its age, usage, and condition. Common-law evidentiary standards suggest that the foundation should be sufficient to permit a conclusion that the testing equipment was in proper operating condition at the time of the test. Query whether a one-time certification, if that is the practice, is sufficient. Assuming that the State satisfies the statutory certification requirement, if additional foundation evidence is needed, perhaps the technician can provide evidence of the maintenance and current condition of the breathalyzer equipment.

In addition to foundation evidence relating to the qualifications of the tester, the timeliness of the sample, and the equipment used, a question may arise as to whether the ampoules containing the chemical solution used in a breathalyzer test are an integral element of the test equipment, thus requiring approval of the toxicologist pursuant to § 10-304(b). If the chemical solution is incorrectly formulated, the test results will be inaccurate. An opinion of the Attorney General concludes that the ampoules are an integral element of the test equipment and, hence, must be approved by the toxicologist. 68 Op. Att'y Gen. 446 (Opinion No. 83-022) (June 1, 1983) (mimeographed opinion at 10); *Casper v. State,* 70 Md. App. 576, 521 A.2d 1281 (1987). This raises a practical problem since checking the formulation of the chemical solution requires breaking a sealed ampoule. Therefore, not every ampoule can be checked. It has been suggested that the toxicologist's approval can be based on a spot check within a large batch or, perhaps, on a manufacturer's certification. 68 Op. Att'y Gen. 446 (Opinion No. 83-022) (June 1, 1983) (mimeographed opinion at 10, n.9). the latter approach, however, may raise evidentiary questions as to the admissibility of the manufacturer's certification pursuant to the hearsay rule, and the confrontation rights of the defendant.

In addition to the above, there are questions of what other solutions are integral elements of chemical test equipment such that the State is required by statute to introduce a toxicologist's certification, pursuant to § 10-304. In addition to the chemical ampoules, discussed above, there is a simulator stock solution which is prepared by the toxicologist. The technician mixes this solution by adding water so that it is precisely calibrated to permit comparison with the suspect's sample. If the prepared solution is considered to be an essential component of the breathalyzer equipment, it is obvious that the toxicologist has not and cannot certify to the validity of the final stock solution. For an explanation of how the breath test works, see e.g., R. Erwin, *Defense of Drunk Driving Cases* § 15.01 (3d ed. 1980); Bellotti, *The Preparation and Trial of a Drunken Driving Case Involving a Breathalyzer,* 1 Nat'l J. Crim. Def. 131 (1975). Similarly, there are several solutions used in blood testing that are not certified by the toxicologist. If the statute is strictly construed by the courts, there may be a need to revise the statute to permit certification by the technician rather than by the toxicologist of certain solutions used in the test equipment or to delegate the certification to other qualified persons.

Also, must the State preserve breath or blood samples so that the defense may examine them? Under *Brady v. Maryland,* 373 U.S. 83, 83 S. Ct. 1194, 10 L. Ed. 2d 215 (1963), upon request, certain exculpatory evidence is discoverable as a matter of constitutional law under both the due process clause of the fourteenth amendment and pursuant to any statutory or court rules of discovery. The United States Supreme Court has specifically held, however, that there is no constitutional right to require that the State preserve breath samples so that the defendant may examine them. *California v. Trombetta,* 467 U.S. 479, 104 S. Ct. 2528, 81 L. Ed. 2d 413 (1984).

Further, the blood or breath samples must be shown to be genuine; authentication is typically shown through proof of chain of custody. If it is not the defendant's blood or breath that is the subject of the test results, obviously the results are not relevant to whether the defendant was intoxicated or under the influence of alcohol on a particular occasion. The chain of custody may be more complicated for blood tests than breath tests, since in breath tests the taking of the sample and the administration of the test occur at the same time.

A controversy has arisen as to whether some breathalyzer test results may be distorted by radio frequency interference (RFI). In the early 1980's the manufacturer of the breathalyzer machines used in Maryland and in other states notified their customers that radio transmitting devices, including "walkie-talkies" and other devices that may be present in police stations, could under certain circumstances affect test results. Periodic testing of each machine was recommended. In response, Maryland tested its machines and concluded that no machine was affected to the point that rendered test results inaccurate. The greatest danger was where a radio transmitting device was operated within a few feet of the machine. Some questions have been raised concerning the testing procedure and, apparently, no follow-up periodic testing has occurred. Some defense counsel have filed discovery motions, pursuant to *Brady v. Maryland, supra,* requesting the results of any tests on the specific machine at issue in the case. One defense counsel has commented as follows:

> Even though the State originally tested the machines to determine their susceptibility to RFI, it has not implemented a program of periodic checks to determine RFI vulnerability. Some judges have held that the failure of the State to respond to defense discovery efforts in the RFI testing area requires the sanction of suppression of the test results.

Alan J. Goldstein, *The Growing Complexity of Trying the DWI Case,* Maryland Bar Journal 17, 18 (March 1985). A question has been raised as to whether the State has any burden in terms of the common-law foundation requirements for scientific evidence, to make some showing of the absence of radio frequency interference in the particular case. Any evidence proffered by the defense concerning the use of radio transmitting devices in close proximity to the breathalyzer machine at issue, would support the need for such an evidentiary foundation. *Cf. Fitzwater v. State,* 57 Md. App. 274, 469 A.2d 909 (1984). The cost of defense expert witnesses often precludes the litigation of the radio frequency interference issue at trial. There is some case law in other jurisdictions on the issue of radio frequency interference with breathalyzer test results.

Finally, special problems exist with interpreting breath and blood test results. In both of these tests, the time at which the test is administered is crucial to a valid result. The test results will be completely valid only if performed after the alcohol has been completely absorbed, in other words, after it has passed from the body's stomach and intestines to its blood and tissues. Absorption does not occur immediately, but rather on an average of one hour after consumption has begun. Once the point of absorption has been reached, the body begins to eliminate the alcohol. Thus, it is possible for a person to be found under the influence or intoxicated when he was in fact sober at the time of the occurrence if his body had not reached the point of absorption. 1 R. Erwin, *Defense of Drunk Driving Cases* §§ 15-11, 15-12, 16-22 (1982). It has been suggested that the results of the breath test may also be affected by stress. Further, the breath sample may be contaminated by such factors as an anesthetic for toothache relief, the inhalation of industrial vapors, or a chronic breathing disorder. Results of a blood test may be affected by a contaminated blood sample, a decomposed sample due to delayed analysis or instruments that are not sterile. 1 R. Erwin, *Defense of Drunk Driving Cases* §§ 16-22, 17-65, 17-68, 17-74, 18-17, 18-18.4, 18-18.5 (1982).

(d) Penalties

The penalties for a violation of the various drunk driving offenses are set forth in Maryland Ann. Code, Transportation Article, § 27-101.

The penalties for a person who is convicted of driving while intoxicated, Transportation, § 21-902(a), are as follows:

1. For a first offense, a fine of not more than $1,000, or imprisonment for not more than one year, or both; and,
2. For a second offense, a fine of not more than $1,000, or imprisonment for not more than two years, or both. Also, a person who is convicted of driving while intoxicated within three years of a prior conviction under § 21-902(a) is subject to mandatory minimum penalty of imprisonment for not less than forty-eight hours or community service for not less than eighty hours; and,
3. For a third or subsequent offense, a fine of not more than $2,000, or imprisonment for not more than three years, or both.

The penalties for a person who is convicted of driving while under the influence of alcohol and/or drugs, § 21-902(b), (c) and (d), are as follows:

1. A fine of not more than $500 or imprisonment for not more than two months or both; and,
2. For a second or subsequent violation of driving while under the influence of alcohol, § 21-902(b), a fine of not more than $500 or imprisonment for not more than one year or both.

In *Blackwell v. State,* 34 Md. App. 547, 369 A.2d 153, *cert. denied,* 280 Md. 728 (1977), the Court held that to be convicted as a second offender for driving while intoxicated, an accused must be charged as a second offender. A prior conviction pursuant to § 21-902(b) (formerly driving while impaired) is not sufficient. In *Tereshuk v. State,* 66 Md. App. 193, 503 A.2d 254 (1986), the Court held that a person convicted of driving while under the influence of alcohol, § 21-902(b), can be sentenced as a second or subsequent offender when the earlier convictions were for "driving while ability impaired by alcohol" (former § 21-902(b)). In 1981 the law was changed from stating that a person may not drive "while his driving ability is impaired by the consumption of alcohol" to a person may not drive "while under the influence of alcohol."

In *Kursch v. State,* 55 Md. App. 103, 460 A.2d 639 (1983), the Court held that a certified copy of defendant's driving record from the Motor Vehicle Administration, showing that on two previous occasions the defendant had points assessed against him for driving while his ability was impaired by alcohol, is admissible to show prior motor vehicle convictions since under Transportation, § 16-402 points are assessed against an individual only after conviction.

§ 4.64. Embezzlement.

COMMENT: COMMON LAW PRIOR TO REPEAL

The crime of embezzlement has been repealed. This Comment, which followed the former instruction, has been retained to give guidance to possible statutory interpretations of the legislation as to the prior common law.

As part of the revision (Acts 1978, ch. 849) of the laws of Maryland relating to bad check offenses and various theft crimes, Maryland Ann. Code, §§ 128 to 131, 133, 137 and 138 of Article 27 were repealed. The crime of embezzlement, formerly prosecuted under these provisions, has been replaced by Art. 27, § 342(a) and (b) under the consolidation of theft-related offenses. Article 27, § 132, captioned "Fraudulent misappropriation by fiduciaries," was retained unchanged and is independent of the general theft statutes.

See Instructions: § 4.91 Theft — By unauthorized control, and § 4.92, Theft — By deception, *infra,* which are patterned upon the revised theft offenses.

The following code sections proscribe related crimes: Art. 27, § 132 applies to fiduciaries; Art. 27, § 134 relates to the fraudulent receipt of consigned property without the owner's consent; Art. 27, § 135 deals with the wrongful disposal of cargo of a vessel and the refusal to pay over consideration for sale of cargo; Art. 27, § 126 covers the embezzlement of wills, patents, deeds, records, etc.; and, Art. 27, § 127 relates to destroying or secreting wills.

The embezzlement instruction in the first edition of this book was based on a narrowly drawn statute: Art. 27, § 129, enacted by the Maryland General Assembly of 1886, which borrowed it almost verbatim from the earlier English embezzlement statutes. *Nolan v. State,* 213 Md. 298, 312, 131 A.2d 851, 858 (1957). Unlike other more general embezzlement statutes enacted in some states, the section was limited to the conversion of only such property as "... shall be delivered to or received, or taken into possession by him, for or in the name or on account of his master or employer...." The statute applies only to property intercepted by the agent or employee while it was on its way to, and had not yet reached, the master's possession. It did not apply where the master handed over property to the agent or employee, either directly or indirectly, through the hands of someone else, for example, of another servant. This latter situation was one of the reasons for the subsequent enactment (Acts 1945, ch. 831) of the separate crime of "larceny after trust" codified in Art. 27, § 353, also repealed in 1978. See Comment, § 4.72, Larceny after trust, *infra.* A thoughtful discussion of the differences between embezzlement and larceny after trust is provided in *Urciolo v. State,* 272 Md. 607, 325 A.2d 878 (1974).

Gordon v. State, 5 Md. App. 291, 246 A.2d 623 (1968), held that embezzlement is a statutory offense penalizing fraudulent conversions of personal property and money which could not be prosecuted at common law as larceny as there was no trespassory taking. Article 29, § 129 was held to require proof that the accused was: (1) employed as a cashier, servant, agent, clerk, or officer by a person or corporate body; (2) in such a capacity that he received personal property for or in the name or on account of his master or employer; (3) thereafter fraudulently embezzled such property.

The *Gordon* case further held that although an attorney may be an agent within the statute, to prove the criminal agency of the accused in fraudulent embezzlement of funds in an escrow account, it was necessary to show that it was the accused's activities, not another's, which caused the deficiency in the escrow account. See also *Tabbs v. State,* 10 Md. App. 177, 268 A.2d 598 (1970); *Waldrop v. State,* 12 Md. App. 371, 278 A.2d 619 (1971).

Loker v. State, 250 Md. 677, 245 A.2d 814 (1968), *cert. denied,* 393 U.S. 1082 (1969), held that although embezzlement by elected or appointed public officers is covered under Art. 27, § 138, such persons could also be charged under Art. 27, § 129.

The difference between larceny and embezzlement is that in larceny the taking is by trespass while in embezzlement the original taking was lawful. Trespass is not required because its place is supplied by the relation of trust and confidence between the parties. Larceny and embezzlement are distinguished in *Nolan v. State, supra,* and *Farlow v. State,* 9 Md. App. 515, 265 A.2d 578 (1970). Further, where an embezzlement statute such as Art. 27, § 129, refers only to designated persons occupying particular relationships, it is essential in proving the offense to show the existence of the relationship. Finally, it is necessary to show that the defendant had actual possession of the funds at the time of the alleged appropriation.

Denton v. State, 77 Md. 527, 26 A. 1022 (1893), held that it is not necessary to show that the defendant received the money by virtue of his employment nor that he had authority to receive it, but only that it was received in the name or on the account of the employer. In embezzlement, property appropriated is not obtained by fraud but is received by the culprit lawfully. *MacEwen v. State,* 194 Md. 492, 71 A.2d 464 (1950).

In *Peddersen v. State,* 223 Md. 329, 164 A.2d 539 (1960), the Court held that an intent to appropriate is a vital element, and the offense is complete when a person entrusted with the money forms an intent to convert it to his own use and has possession with such intent. This case also discusses venue.

Finally, *Tabbs v. State, supra,* reaffirmed *Gordon v. State, supra,* in the three elements necessary to prove the offense. It also stated that the employer did not have to own the money but merely have a legal or property interest in it.

§ 4.65. Escape.

Escape is defined as the unauthorized departure from lawful custody from any place of confinement.

In order for the accused to be guilty of this offense, the State must prove beyond a reasonable doubt that: (1) the defendant was detained; (2) the detainment was under color of law; (3) the defendant was confined in a jail or other place of confinement; and (4) the defendant departed without authorization from lawful custody.

The use of force is not a requisite of an escape. An escape may occur with or without the use of force.

The departure must be from the limits within which the accused was required by law to remain at the time of the alleged departure.

Where imprisonment is under color of law, a person is not entitled to self-help but must apply for release through regular legal channels.

If after a full and fair consideration of all the facts and circumstances in evidence, unless you are convinced beyond a reasonable doubt that the defendant committed the crime of escape, then you must find the defendant not guilty.

COMMENT

This instruction is based upon the Maryland Ann. Code, Art. 27, § 139, which codifies both the common-law offenses of "simple escape" and "breach of prison," and decisions of the Court of Appeals on the subject of escape. Article 27, § 139 is a broadly based statute encompassing all escapes from confinement.

Chapter 21, Acts of 1982, which enacted the Health-General Article repealed former Art. 27, § 139 and reenacted it. The revision incorporates in subsection (a) the substance of former Art. 43B, § 17 and former Art. 52A, § 10(b), which made escape from the Drug Abuse Administration or certain juvenile institutions a felony. Subsection (c) was also revised to make the aider of an escapee guilty of a felony. The use of the word, "person," in subsection (c) reflects the legislative intent to consolidate in one statutory provision the Maryland law concerning all aiders and abettors of escape. See *Watkins v. State,* 42 Md. App. 349, 400 A.2d 464 (1979). Subsequent amendments in 1983 and 1984 involve changes that were largely technical.

At common law, "simple escape" meant the unauthorized departure of a prisoner from legal custody without the use of force. "Prison breach" was the unauthorized departure of a prisoner from legal custody accomplished by the use of force. *Fabian v. State,* 3 Md. App. 270, 239 A.2d 100 (1968); 3 Wharton, *Criminal Law and Procedure* §§ 1367, 1368 (Anderson ed. 1957). As early as 1810, the General Assembly of Maryland sought to proscribe the common law of escape and has several times revised such a statute.

In *State v. Magliano,* 7 Md. App. 286, 255 A.2d 470 (1969), the Court held that it was the legislative intent under Art. 27, § 139 to create a new crime of escape, although analogous to the common-law crime, and that the statutory crime of escape encompasses both the common-law "simple escape" and "breach of prison." Hence, the use of force is not a requisite of an escape, *Meadows v. State,* 3 Md. App. 441, 239 A.2d 767 (1968), and there is no distinction between departure by force and departure without force. *Fabian v. State, supra.*

See *Hutchinson v. State,* 36 Md. App. 58, 373 A.2d 50 (1977), in which the Court affirmed appellant's conviction for escape. The Court held that the elements of that offense did not require the State to prove the means by which the escape had taken place. In *State v. Morton,* 295 Md. 487, 456 A.2d 909 (1983), the Court held that the indictment sufficiently characterized the crime and informed the inmates of the accusation against them where it specified the fact of their lawful confinement, their willful departure from custody, the location of the escapes and the dates on which the escapes allegedly occurred. The State is not required to set out the details concerning the manner in which the accused escaped. A bill of particulars may be sought for that purpose.

Also, there is no distinction between an escape from within prison walls and one effected when the prisoner, while still in legal custody, is physically outside the prison area. *Ford v. State,* 237 Md. 266, 205 A.2d 809 (1965); *Shifflet v. State,* 4 Md. App. 227, 242 A.2d 182 (1968). In discussing the physical act of escape, R. Perkins & R. Boyce, *Criminal Law,* ch. 5, § 3 at 564 (3d ed. 1982) states:

> [A] prisoner may be guilty of an escape from his cell although unable to get beyond the prison walls. In other words, the limits within which a prisoner may be required by law to remain, at a certain time, may be the walls of his cell, the walls of his prison, the boundaries of the prison farm, the immediate presence of his guard on the street or elsewhere, the general area of a project on which he is working, such as a road job, or some other. Whatever the limits may be for him at the time of departure therefrom is a physical act of an escape.

In *Fabian v. State, supra* at 107, the Court found the provisions of the Maryland statute on escape consistent with this statement, and held that where the defendant had been required to remain within the maximum security area of the jail and escaped therefrom, he had violated Art. 27, § 139, whether or not he had left the jail building itself.

A defendant who was serving time was taken to court for trial on subsequent charges and escaped from the courtroom. Such escape was held to be an escape from the correctional institution. Although he was outside the prison area in a physical sense, he had remained in legal custody. *Slagle v. State,* 243 Md. 435, 221 A.2d 641 (1966) *(citing Ford v. State, supra). Robinson v. State,* 18 Md. App. 438, 306 A.2d 624 (1973), involves an escape from a work release program.

In *Fleeger v. State,* 301 Md. 155, 482 A.2d 490 (1984), the Court held that because the consecutive sentencing provision presupposes a sentence based on a valid criminal conviction, Art. 27, § 139 (a) is not applicable to a defendant who, at the time of his escape from the county jail, had not been convicted, but was awaiting trial.

Article 27, § 139 includes not only unlawful escape by "an offender" but by "any person legally detained and confined" in the places enumerated, regardless of the cause of detention. *Baker v. State,* 205 Md. 42, 106 A.2d 692 (1954). And it has been held that where the imprisonment is under color of law, the prisoner is not entitled to resort to self-help but must apply for his release through regular legal channels, even though he might be able to show such defects in the procedures by which he was arrested and imprisoned as would justify his release. *Jennings v. State,* 8 Md. App. 321, 259 A.2d 547 (1969). See also *Vucci v. State,* 18 Md. App. 157, 305 A.2d 483 (1973).

The statute has been interpreted to mean that "the crime of escape takes place either: (1) in the county where the physical departure actually occurs; or (2) in the county where the institution is located, which is the prisoner's "place of confinement" and from which his "constructive" departure occurs. "[T]he gravamen of the offense prohibited by Art. 27, § 139 is the physical departure by an inmate from the 'place of confinement,' and although the prohibited act may physically take place in a separate geographical area, the effects of that act occur at the place of confinement," which is also a proper place of venue. *Stewart v. State,* 275 Md. 258, 340 A.2d 290 (1975), *aff'g* 21 Md. App. 346, 319 A.2d 621 (1974). The above decision is premised on the rationale that to limit venue to the place where the escape occurred would impose an impractical impediment in the administration of criminal justice, as it would require the attendance of witnesses and the production of documents at a place far removed from the situs of the institution to which the inmate had been committed.

This offense applies to any individual legally detained "in the State penitentiary or a jail, house of correction, reformatory, station house, or other place of confinement in this State or who is committed to the Drug Abuse Administration for examination or inpatient treatment." Art. 27, § 139(a)(1). It should be noted that Patuxent Institution is a place of confinement within the meaning of Art. 27, § 139, *Caparella v. State,* 214 Md. 355, 135 A.2d 311 (1957), as is Clifton T. Perkins State Hospital, *Slagle v. State, supra.*

The penalty for violation of Art. 27, § 139 is confinement in the penitentiary, jail or house of correction for such additional period, not exceeding ten years, as the court may adjudge. The 1972 amendment specifies that a sentence so imposed shall be consecutive to the sentence imposed upon original confinement and shall not be suspended. However, Art. 27, § 139(a) formerly stated that for escapes from the Maryland Correctional Training Center in Hagerstown which have not involved an assault, the sentence shall not exceed confinement for three years. By amending Art. 27, § 139(a), the General Assembly abolished the distinction in penalties between the Training Center and other institutions. See Art. 27, § 139(a) as amended in 1978. It is interesting to note that in two cases, the statute, before amendment, was held not to violate the equal protection clause. *Clark v. State,* 284 Md. 260, 396 A.2d 243, *cert. denied,* 444 U.S. 858 (1979); *State v. Rogers,* 40 Md. App. 573, 392 A.2d 1186 (1978).

In *Craddock v. State,* 47 Md. App. 513, 424 A.2d 168 (1981), the Court of Appeals held that a prisoner charged with escape can defend on the grounds of necessity and duress (terms which were used interchangeably in this case) when the five requirements articulated by the Court in *Robinson v. State,* 42 Md. App. 617, 402 A.2d 115 (1979) are met.

In order to prevail the escapee must show:

1. He was faced with a specific threat of imminent serious bodily harm or death;
2. There was no opportunity to alert prison officials or to have done so would have been futile;
3. There was no time to request relief from the Courts;
4. No force or violence was used against other persons during the escape;
5. The prisoner contacts prison officials immediately upon reaching a safe place.

The Court, relying on *United States v. Bailey,* 444 U.S. 394, 412-13, 100 S. Ct. 624, 636, 62 L. Ed. 2d 575, 592 (1980), held that the judge need not instruct the jury as to the defense of necessity or duress unless the defendant proffered "testimony of a *bona fide* effort to surrender or return to custody as soon as the claimed duress or necessity had lost its coercive force." *Craddock v. State, supra* at 516, 424 A.2d at 170.

See Instructions: § 5.05, Duress, and § 5.18, Necessity, *infra.*

§ 4.66. Extortion — Verbal threat.

In order for the defendant to be found guilty of this offense, the State must prove beyond a reasonable doubt that: (1) there was a threat; (2) the threat was verbal; (3) the subject of the threat was to do any injury to the person or property of another; and (4) the threat was made with a view towards extorting or gaining anything of value.

The threat to the victim need not be made directly; it can be made to the victim's agents or employees. [The threat may be to accuse another person of any crime of an indictable nature under the laws of this state, which, if true, would bring such person into contempt or disrepute, or the threat may be to do injury to the person or property of anyone.] The threat need not be in precise words. It may be by suggestion or innuendo. The existence of a threat may be determined and ascertained by you from the circumstances under which it is uttered and the relations between the parties.

It is not essential that anything of value actually be received but it is essential that the threat was made with a view to extort or to gain any goods, money, chattel or any other valuable thing.

COMMENT

This instruction is patterned largely on the holding in the case of *Iozzi v. State,* 5 Md. App. 415, 247 A.2d 758 (1968).

Extortive threat is a felony proscribed in Maryland Ann. Code, Art. 27, § 562. It is punishable by a term in the penitentiary of not less than two nor more than ten years. The three requirements of the crime are: (1) that a verbal threat be made; (2) the subject of the threat be injury to the person or property of anyone, such injury to the person including threats to accuse another of indictable, disreputable crimes; and (3) the making of the threat is with a view to extort or gain anything of value. *Iozzi v. State, supra* at 760.

The Maryland statute places emphasis on the actual threat and does not require that anything of value actually be obtained. *Id.* It also does not require that precise words of threat be uttered. An innuendo or suggestion giving rise to an inference of a threat to person or property is sufficient. The jury is permitted to consider the circumstances under which it is uttered and the relationships of the parties to determine whether an extortive threat was made. *Id.* The threat need not be made directly. *Lenoir v. State,* 197 Md. 495, 80 A.2d 3 (1951).

Bribery and extortion are separate offenses; therefore, one may be convicted of both. For example, a public official who demands money to influence the performance of his official duties and accompanies that demand with a threat that, unless it is paid, he will do injury to the person or property of the party may be guilty of both bribery and extortion. See *Carey v. State,* 43 Md. App. 246, 405 A.2d 293 (1979), *cert. denied,* 445 U.S. 967 (1980).

In addition to Art. 27, § 562, there are four related sections in Article 27: § 562A, Coercing or intimidating another to contribute or donate; § 562B, Extortion generally; § 562C, Extortion by State or local officer or employee generally; and, § 562D, Extortion by State or local officer or employee against another employee.

Other related provisions are: Art. 27, § 561, Sending, delivering, etc., threatening letter, etc., and Art. 27, § 563, Extorting by false accusation.

§ 4.67. False pretenses.

COMMENT: COMMON LAW PRIOR TO REPEAL

The crime of false pretenses, has been repealed. This Comment which followed the former instruction has been retained to give guidance to possible statutory interpretations of the legislation as to the prior common law.

As part of the revision (Acts 1978, ch. 849) of the laws of Maryland related to bad check offenses and various theft crimes, Maryland Ann. Code, § 140 of Article 27 was repealed as it related to false pretenses and the crime formerly prosecuted under the section, has been replaced under the consolidation of theft-related offenses by Art. 27, § 342(b).

See Instruction, § 4.92, Theft — By deception, *infra,* which is patterned upon the revised theft offenses.

In *Willis v. State,* 205 Md. 118, 119-120, 106 A.2d 85, 87 (1954), the Court held that the State must prove that there was a "... representation of an existing fact made with intent to defraud, and that the operation of such representation [acted] as a deception, induced a transfer and the obtaining of the money or property by the person committing the fraud to the loss of another." In *Smith v. State,* 237 Md. 573, 207 A.2d 493 (1965), the Court based its decision on the three elements stated in *Willis v. State, supra.* For other statements of the law, see *Harris v. State,* 27 Md. App. 547, 342 A.2d 305 (1975); *Baumgartner v. State,* 21 Md. App. 251, 319 A.2d 549 (1974); *Sinclair v. State,* 21 Md. App. 477, 319 A.2d 549, *aff'd,* 274 Md. 646, 337 A.2d 703 (1975); *Polisher v. State,* 11 Md. App. 555, 276 A.2d 102, *cert. denied,* 262 Md. 749, *cert. denied,* 404 U.S. 984 (1971); *Bosley v. State,* 14 Md. App. 83, 286 A.2d 203 (1972); and *Davis v. State,* 18 Md. App. 378, 306 A.2d 620 (1973).

Article 27, § 140 formerly stated that a mere promise for future payment not intended to be performed was not sufficient to sustain a conviction and, thus, it was essential that the representations made were of a past or existing fact. *Smith v. State, supra.* In *Polisher v. State, supra,* the Court, commenting on the manner in which a false pretense could be made, stated: "... it may be words, or conduct that has the effect of misrepresenting existing facts to the victim .... The false pretense may be made in writing, orally, or by telephone ...." *Id.* at 580, 276 A.2d at 114. It is immaterial that the false representation was ambiguous when the intent and reasonable effect of the defendant's conduct was to mislead the victim. The holder of equitable title to land may describe himself as the "owner" of the land without liability of criminal prosecution for false pretenses. *Burroughs v. State,* 21 Md. App. 648, 320 A.2d 587 (1974).

In *Davis v. State, supra,* the appellant had made statements concerning the existence of a certain organization which would perform certain services. The Court held that it was incumbent on the State to prove that the organization did not exist and did not perform these functions.

When the organization was an ongoing business, the representations made by an employee of the company concerning certain travel franchises had to be promises of future acts. *Berman v. State,* 35 Md. App. 193, 370 A.2d 580 (1977). Standing alone, these promises did not violate the false pretense statute, despite the fact that the organization's weakened financial condition probably precluded it from delivering on some of those promises. "Whether there is implied in the false representation an ability or capacity to perform *vel non* is not the test." *Id.* at 201, 370 A.2d at 584.

The State had to prove that the representation was made with the intent to defraud. Again the Court in *Willis v. State, supra* at 127, 106 A.2d at 89, spoke to this point: "... the State had the burden of proving that the defendant was motivated by a fraudulent intent in inducing the vendor to part with its property...." In *Smith v. State, supra,* the Court stated intent could be inferred by looking at the representation in light of all the circumstances. The case of *Waye v. State,* 231 Md. 510, 191 A.2d 428 (1963), emphasized this point. Intentionally imposing an obvious and unreasonable risk of loss without the knowledge or consent of the victim by reason of the deceit might have satisfied the requirement of intent to defraud. There was no doctrine of *lucri causa* in false pretenses. The defendant was responsible for his false pretense although he did not personally gain any benefit from the money or property which had been obtained thereby. The money received from another need not be applied to the taker's benefit. The defendant may be guilty although he may have intended to repay the money or to restore the property in the future. *Polisher v. State, supra* at 580-81. *Baskerville v. State,* 23 Md. App. 439, 444-47, 327 A.2d 918 (1974).

Carey v. State, 19 Md. App. 695, 696-97, 313 A.2d 696, 697 (1974), reiterated another element which the State had to establish: "Maryland Code, Art. 27, sec. 140, defining the crime of false pretenses, requires proof of the fraudulent acquisition of ownership, not mere possession. *Farlow v. State,* 9 Md. App. 515, 517-518, 265 A.2d 578 (1970). This requirement, which necessitates a showing of the intention of the owner as well as the accused, was clearly set forth in Clark and Marshall, *Crimes* § 12.23 at 925 (7th ed.)."

The last element to be proven was that the victim relied on the representation to his detriment. *Davis v. State,* 229 Md. 139, 182 A.2d 49, *cert. denied,* 371 U.S. 898 (1962). The case of *Levy v. State,* 225 Md. 201, 170 A.2d 216, *cert. denied,* 368 U.S. 865 (1961), stood for this proposition. In *Levy,* the Court reversed a conviction where the testimony showed that the victim knew the defendant and did not rely on any representation made by the defendant in parting with his money. See also *Franczkowski v. State,* 239 Md. 126, 210 A.2d 504 (1965), *overruled, Lightfoot v. State,* 278 Md. 231, 360 A.2d 426 (1976). A further illustration of this point can be found in *Dolan v. State,* 1 Md. App. 292, 229 A.2d 443 (1967). The Court in *Dolan* reversed a conviction of an unlicensed insurance agent on the grounds that the investigator who brought insurance and subsequently played a part in the arrest knew of the defendant's lack of authority to sell and therefore did not rely on the defendant's representations.

A victim may have relied on a false representation to his detriment, although no financial loss was incurred, where he exposed himself to a risk or hazard which he would not have assumed but for that reliance. The gravamen of the offense was the making of the false pretense with intent to defraud and thereby obtain another's property. It was not essential that the victim actually suffer pecuniary loss. *Baskerville v. State, supra* at 442-44.

§ 4.68. Forgery and uttering.

(a) Forgery

Forgery is the fraudulent making of a false writing [or the material alteration of a writing] having apparent legal significance.

In order for the defendant to be found guilty of this offense, the State must prove beyond a reasonable doubt

that: (1) there was a writing, namely a __________ *(insert type of writing specified in statute — see list in Comment (a) to this instruction — or otherwise accepted at common law);* (2) such writing was [falsely made] [forged] [materially altered] [counterfeited]; (3) the defendant [falsely made] [forged] [materially altered] [counterfeited] such instrument [or willingly aided or assisted in forging, falsely making or counterfeiting such instrument]; (4) it was [falsely made] [forged] [materially altered] [counterfeited] with the intent to defraud; (5) the writing was in such form as to be of apparent legal significance and hence capable of deceiving or defrauding.

Intent to defraud means to act willfully and deliberately, and with the specific intent to deceive or cheat. [The writing required is not limited to a handwriting. It includes typewriting, printing or engraving.] [The terms "falsely made" and "forged" both describe a fictitious making relating to the genuineness of execution of an instrument.] [Counterfeiting an instrument means falsely making it, that is, the making of a copy without authority or right and with a view to deceive or defraud by passing the copy as original or genuine.]

[The possession and uttering of a forged instrument are circumstances you may take into consideration along with all of the other facts in evidence in determining whether the possessor was the forger. Uttering is the offering or publishing of a false instrument with fraudulent intent.]

[An instrument which is entirely valueless on its face and of no binding force or effect for any purpose of harm or liability or injury to anyone cannot be the subject of forgery.]

[The offense of forgery may exist even though the name used was assumed or fictitious when it is shown that it was used with the intent to defraud.]

(b) Uttering

It is a crime to utter or publish as true any false, forged, materially altered, or counterfeited instrument. Uttering is the offering of a false instrument with intent to defraud.

In order for the defendant to be found guilty of this offense, the State must prove beyond a reasonable doubt that: (1) there was a writing, namely a ________ *(insert type of writing specified in statute — see list in Comment (b) to this instruction — or otherwise accepted at common law);* (2) the writing was offered by the defendant as true or genuine; (3) it was known by the defendant to be [false] [forged] [materially altered] [a counterfeit writing]; and (4) it was offered with the intent to defraud another person.

Intent to defraud means willfully and deliberately and with specific intent to deceive or cheat.

The offering of a false instrument with fraudulent intent constitutes an uttering regardless of whether it is acted upon or not. It is not necessary that the person accused of uttering be the actual forger. It is essential that the defendant had prior knowledge of the fact that the instrument was false, forged, materially altered or counterfeited. Such knowledge may be shown by direct evidence or it may be inferred from the facts and circumstances of the particular transaction. Evidence of possession of a forged instrument and evidence of uttering it are circumstances you may take into consideration, along with all of the other facts in evidence, in determining whether the defendant knew of the instrument's falsity.

[In proving uttering, forgery is not necessarily proven. In forgery the writing must be falsely made with the intent to defraud. In uttering, although the writing must be offered with the intent to defraud, the writing need not be falsely made with this same intent. If the writing was in fact false and was offered or published as genuine with knowledge of its falsity and with intent to defraud, the crime of uttering is committed.]

COMMENT

(a) Forgery

This instruction is based on Maryland case law and Maryland Ann. Code, Art. 27, § 44(a), which states: "(a)ny person who shall falsely make, forge or counterfeit, or cause or procure to be falsely made, forged or counterfeited, or willingly aid or assist in falsely making, forging, altering, or counterfeiting any [see list of instruments, below], with intention to defraud any person whomsoever has committed forgery."

In *Smith v. State,* 7 Md. App. 457, 461, 256 A.2d 357, 360 (1969), the Court discussed the terms "falsely make," "forge" and "counterfeit" as follows: "... we think the terms 'falsely make' and 'forge' are synonymous, both describing a spurious or fictitious making relating to the genuineness of execution of an instrument ... the term 'counterfeit' ... signifies the fabrication of a ... representation."

The following instruments are designated in Art. 27, § 44(a) to be the subject of forgery: (1) deed; (2) document or affidavit of waiver or release of mechanics' lien; (3) will, testament or codicil; (4) power of attorney; (5) bond; (6) writing obligatory; (7) bill of exchange; (8) promissory note for the payment of money or property; (9) endorsement or assignment of any bond, writing obligatory, bill of exchange, or promissory note for the payment of money or property; (10) acquittance or receipt for money or property or any acquisition or receipt for money or property; and (11) any entries in a book or account or ledger.

The Maryland Court of Special Appeals has discussed the important distinction between the execution of false statements in a genuine document and the making of a spurious document, only the latter of which constitutes forgery. *Reese v. State,* 37 Md. App. 450, 378 A.2d 4 (1977), *aff'd,* 283 Md. 86, 388 A.2d 122 (1978). As to the distinction between these two acts, the Court in *Reese* states: "Though a forgery, like false pretenses, requires a lie, it must be a lie about the document itself. The lie must relate to the genuineness of the document." *Id.* at 455, 378 A.2d at 7 (quoting W. LaFave and A. Scott, *Criminal Law* § 90 at 671 (1972)).

Common-law forgery is applicable whenever the statute does not govern. Thus, the fact that a particular document is not specified in Art. 27, § 44(a) does not preclude prosecution for forgery of an unenumerated type of instrument if fraudulent falsification of the writing in question would have been an indictable offense at common law. *State v. Reese,* 283 Md. 86, 388 A.2d 122 (1978); *Reddick v. State,* 219 Md. 95, 148 A.2d 384, *cert. denied,* 360 U.S. 930 (1959); *Green v. State,* 32 Md. App. 567, 363 A.2d 530 (1976).

In *State v. Reese, supra,* the Court held that false entries in books of account or ledgers were not within the list of the then statute or the applicable common law. The statute has been amended (Acts 1980, ch. 326) to extend the coverage.

Forgery is defined at common law as "a false making or material alteration, with intent to defraud, of any writing which if genuine might apparently be of legal efficacy or the foundation of a legal liability." *Reddick v. State, supra* at 98, 148 A.2d at 386; *Smith v. State, supra; Nelson v. State,* 224 Md. 374, 377-378, 167 A.2d 871, 873 (1961) (*citing* R. Perkins, *Criminal Law,* ch. 4, § 8 (2d ed. 1969)). Therefore, the writing or instrument must have the capability to defraud or deceive. *Smith v. State, supra* at 461, 256 A.2d at 360. For an instrument to be capable of defrauding or deceiving, it must have "some value or purpose other than its own." *State v. Reese, supra* at 93, 388 A.2d at 127, (*citing* R. Perkins, *Criminal Law* § 342 (2d ed. 1969)).

In *Smith v. State, supra,* the defendant was convicted of forgery. The Court held that a blank check which did not contain a name of the payee, a signature of a payer, and had no date or amount was insufficient to convict the defendant of forgery since the check had no legal efficacy and, therefore, was not capable of defrauding.

At common law, the "counterfeiting of any writing with fraudulent intent, whereby another might be prejudiced is forgery." *State v. Reese, supra* at 92, 388 A.2d at 127. The writing had to be proved. To meet the requirement that "another might be prejudiced" the falsity had to go to the "genuineness of the execution of the document." *Id.* Counterfeiting is included in forgery since it "means the making of a copy without authority or right and with a view towards deceiving or defrauding by passing the copy as an original or genuine." *Smith v. State, supra* at 461, 256 A.2d at 360.

Forgery of an instrument was held in *Green v. State, supra,* to differ from forgery of an endorsement. The Court held that, although they are both common-law offenses, the latter is not included in what Art. 27, § 44(a) proscribes. In *Green,* the Court held that an indictment for forgery of a check is at variance with a conviction for forgery of an endorsement under Art. 27, § 44. However, if the forgery goes to a material part of the instrument, it is considered a forgery of the instrument.

The instrument must actually be falsely made or materially altered with the intention to defraud. *Harding v. Ja Laur Corp.,* 20 Md. App. 209, 212, 315 A.2d 132, 134 (1974); *Bieber v. State,* 8 Md. App. 522, 261 A.2d 202 (1970).

It is not necessary to prove that the intent was to defraud any certain person. *Reddick v. State, supra.* The writing of one's own name with intent to defraud can constitute forgery. *Nelson v. State, supra.* For further discussion of the meaning of intent to defraud, see Instruction, § 3.05, Fraudulent (intent to defraud) — Defined, *supra.*

A "material alteration" was defined in *Harding v. Ja Laur Corp., supra* at 212, 315 A.2d at 134 (*citing* R. Perkins, *Criminal Law* § 8 (2d ed. 1969)) as follows:

> A material alteration may be in the form of (1) an addition to the writing, (2) *a substitution of something different in the place of what originally appeared,* or (3) the removal of part of the original. The removal may be by erasure or in some other manner, such as by cutting off a qualifying clause appearing after the signature. (Emphasis in original.)

The criminal agent of the forgery need not be the criminal agent in the uttering and it is "obvious that proof that a person committed uttering is not per se proof that he forged the uttered instrument." *Bieber v. State, supra* at 529, 261 A.2d at 205. As to any inference regarding the identity of the forger, the Court in *Bieber* stated:

> We think it clear that the rule this State has adopted is that, absent a credible nonculpable explanation, the possession

> and uttering of a forged instrument by one claiming under it raises an inference which provides evidence sufficient to sustain a conviction that the possessor was the forger. In other words, the inference makes out a *prima facie* case which is rebuttable by the showing of circumstances to the contrary.
>
> The rule ... is to be distinguished from the presumption in the absence of evidence to the contrary, that a forgery was committed where the forged instrument was first uttered by the defendant or found in his possession. Such presumption goes to jurisdiction or venue, not to guilt.

Id. at 529-30, 261 A.2d 206. See also *Green v. State, supra; Turner v. State,* 6 Md. App. 337, 251 A.2d 383 (1969). *Cf.*, Appendix V, The Impact of *Evans v. State:* Burdens of Proof, Presumptions, and Inferences, *infra.*

Separate statutory offenses proscribing particular types of forgery include the following: (1) Public documents generally, Art. 27, § 45; (2) Public seals, Art. 27, § 46; (3) Stamp of Comptroller, Art. 27, § 47; (4) Orders, etc., for money or goods, Art. 27, § 48; and (5) Physicians' prescriptions, orders, etc., Art. 27, § 55.

One convicted of forgery may be sentenced to imprisonment for not more than ten years and/or fined not more than $1,000. Art. 27, § 44(a).

(b) Uttering

As with forgery, uttering is both a statutory and a common-law crime in Maryland. Maryland Ann. Code, Art. 27, § 44(b). The instruction on uttering is based on Maryland case law, particularly *Levy v. State,* 225 Md. 201, 170 A.2d 216, *cert. denied,* 368 U.S. 865 (1961); *Bieber v. State,* 8 Md. App. 522, 261 A.2d 202 (1970); and *Pearson v. State,* 8 Md. App. 79, 258 A.2d 917 (1969).

Article 27, § 44(b) proscribes the uttering of the following instruments: (1) deed; (2) will, testament or codicil; (3) power of attorney; (4) bond; (5) writing obligatory; (6) bill of exchange; (7) promissory note for the payment of money or property; (8) endorsement or assignment of any bond, writing obligatory, bill of exchange or promissory note for the payment of money or property; (9) acquittance or receipt for money or property; (10) document of waiver or release of mechanics' lien; and, (11) entries in a book of account or ledger.

The facts to be proved to establish the *corpus delicti* of uttering a forged instrument are: (1) the instrument must be uttered or published as true or genuine; (2) it must be known by the party uttering that it was false, altered, forged or counterfeited; and (3) it must be uttered with intent to defraud another person. *Bieber v. State, supra; Banks v. State,* 8 Md. App. 182, 258 A.2d 924 (1969); *Pearson v. State, supra.*

The mere offer of a false instrument with fraudulent intent constitutes an uttering, regardless of its successful consummation. *Draper v. State,* 231 Md. 423, 190 A.2d 643 (1963), *cert. denied,* 381 U.S. 952 (1965); *Levy v. State, supra; Beard v. State,* 4 Md. App. 685, 244 A.2d 906 (1968). Thus, the offering of a false instrument with fraudulent intent constitutes an uttering regardless of whether it is acted upon or not. Further, it is not necessary that the defendant be the actual forger. *Levy v. State, supra; Bieber v. State, supra; Pearson v. State, supra.*

Article 27, § 44(b), if read literally, does not require an intent to defraud or knowledge that the instrument is false, forged, altered or counterfeited. The Court in *Pearson v. State, supra,* stated:

> While Section 44, in its present form, does not contain any requirement of prior knowledge of the instrument's falsity, or of an intention to defraud, we think it plain that by making it unlawful to utter or publish as true a forged instrument, the legislature thereby intended to encompass all elements of the offense....

Id. at 84, 258 A.2d at 920. See also Instruction, § 3.05, "Fraudulent" (intent to defraud) — Defined, *supra,* for discussion of the meaning of intent to defraud.

As to intent, in uttering a forged instrument, although the instrument must be falsely made, it need not be so made with the intent to defraud, if in fact it was false and published as genuine with knowledge of its falsity. The intent to defraud is only required with respect to the utterance. In other words, the crime is committed by the publishing with intent to defraud. *Bieber v. State, supra.*

As to knowledge of the crime *Pearson v. State, supra,* states that knowledge that the instrument is a forgery is essential to the conviction of the crime of uttering, this state of mind is generally to be inferred from a person's conduct when viewed in the light of all the accompanying circumstances; it is always a question of fact, and proof is seldom direct, but can be inferred from the circumstances. See also *Bieber v. State, supra.*

As to burden of proof, to obtain a conviction for uttering a forged instrument, the State must adduce sufficient evidence that the uttered instrument was in fact forged. *Banks v. State, supra.* With respect to evidence in a forgery trial, a jury cannot convict one of forgery merely because it was convinced beyond a reasonable doubt that the defendant uttered the instrument. *Bieber v. State, supra.* However, the fact that the defendant uttered the instrument may be taken into consideration with other facts and circumstances in determining guilty knowledge.

With regard to liability of persons, the criminal agent in the forgery is not necessarily the criminal agent in the uttering; one person may forge the instrument, the other may utter it. *Bieber v. State, supra.* In proving the crime of uttering a forged instrument, forgery is not necessarily proved. *Id.*

Uttering a forged instrument and obtaining money by false pretense are separate and distinct crimes, even though they may be merged. *Beard v. State, supra.*

One convicted under Art. 27, § 44(b) shall be imprisoned for not more than ten years and/or fined not more than $1,000.

§ 4.69. Housebreaking — Daytime.

It is an offense to break into a dwelling house with intent to [commit murder] [commit a felony] [steal, take or carry away the goods of another of any value therefrom].

In order for the defendant to be found guilty of this offense the State must prove beyond a reasonable doubt that: (1) there was a breaking; (2) by the defendant; (3) the dwelling broken into was a dwelling house of another; and (4) the defendant's intent was to [commit murder] [commit a felony] [steal, take or carry away the goods of another of any value therefrom].

Breaking may be actual or constructive. Actual breaking means the unloosening, removing or displacing of any covering or fastening of the premises. It may consist of lifting a latch, drawing a bolt, raising an unfastened window, turning a key, turning a knob, or pushing open a door kept closed merely by its own weight. There is a breaking if the intruder, by force, removes an obstacle which, if left untouched, would prevent entrance. There can be no actual breaking if there is no evidence to show that there had been any tampering. If a person had permission to enter the premises, there is no actual breaking. There may be a constructive breaking as where entrance is obtained by intimidation or trickery.

The breaking must be of a dwelling house. A building is a dwelling house if it is used regularly as a place to sleep.

It is not necessary that the defendant did in fact [take anything] [commit a felony] [commit murder]. However, it is essential that he had the intent to do so. Proof of intent may be inferred from the circumstances of the case. There must be proof of some fact, circumstance, act or declaration of the defendant in addition to proof of mere breaking from which you can find the requisite intent.

[If the State proves that the defendant was in exclusive possession of goods recently stolen in a housebreaking, and if there is not a reasonable explanation of how he came into the possession of the goods, then you may infer that the possessor was the perpetrator of the housebreaking. In order for possession to be exclusive there must be personal possession by the defendant which involves a distinct and conscious assertion of possession by the exercise of complete dominion and right of disposal. Mere possession of recently stolen articles is not sufficient to permit a rational inference that there was a breaking of the dwelling from which they were stolen, in the absence of any evidence that there was an actual or constructive breaking].

COMMENT

Maryland recognizes six separate and distinct crimes related to the breaking of structures. Three of these relate to breaking of structures other than dwelling houses. (See Instructions, §§ 4.53, 4.54 and 4.55, Breaking — Storehouse, etc., *supra*.) Of the three concerning dwelling houses two are burglary, one under the common law and the other by statutory definition. (See Instruction, § 4.57, Burglary, *supra*). The remaining offense pertains to daytime housebreaking. The offense of daytime housebreaking and the three offenses as to the breaking of structures other than dwelling houses (which, for convenience are referred to as storehouse breakings) are not burglary at all. *Sizemore v. State,* 10 Md. App. 682, 684-85, 272 A.2d 824 (1971).

The statutory provision regarding daytime housebreaking, Maryland Ann. Code, Art. 27, § 30(b), proscribes the breaking of a dwelling house in the daytime with intent to commit murder or to commit a felony therein or steal, take or carry away the goods of another of any value therefrom.

Reagan v. State, 4 Md. App. 590, 244 A.2d 623 (1968), states:

> [A]lthough not designated as burglary, the offense proscribed by § 30(b) includes the essential elements of both burglary and statutory burglary with two exceptions: (1) the breaking need not be in the nighttime, and (2) merely a breaking is required rather than a breaking and entering.

Id. at 594, 244 A.2d at 626.

A related statutory provision is Art. 27, § 31A, Breaking and entering the dwelling house of another. This misdemeanor offense requires no intent to commit a felony or steal but does require the breaking and entering of the dwelling house of another. In *Hawkins v. State,* 291 Md. 688, 436 A.2d 900 (1981), the Court held that this misdemeanor offense is not a lesser included offense of daytime housebreaking under Art. 27, § 30(b) because each requires proof of an element not required by the other. However, at the trial for daytime housebreaking, defense counsel should have been permitted to refer to the misdemeanor offense in his closing argument.

The statutory offense of daytime housebreaking must be construed in light of the common law even though the definition and analysis of burglary at common law does not necessarily apply. *Reagan v. State,* 2 Md. App. 262, 267, 234 A.2d 278 (1967).

In *Reagan v. State* (1967), *supra,* the Court also stated:

> At common law, the breaking, actual or constructive, requires a break of the dwelling by trespass, but this is distinguished from an entrance by a mere trespass. Actual breaking means the unloosening, removing, or displacing of any covering or fastening of the premises. It may consist of the lifting of a latch or drawing of a bolt; the raising of an unfastened window; the turning of a key; the turning of a knob; or the pushing open of a closed door, so kept merely by its own weight. Constructive breaking occurs, whenever an entrance is obtained by intimidation or artifice....

Id. at 267-68, 234 A.2d at 281 (*citing* L. Hochheimer, *Laws of Crimes and Criminal Procedure,* § 549 at 320 (1st ed.)). In *Jones v. State,* 2 Md. App. 356, 234 A.2d 625 (1967), the Court further explained:

> [T]here is a breaking if the intruder, by force, removes an obstacle which if left untouched would prevent entrance. So, while the further pushing open of a door or window left partly open, is a breaking, entry through a door or window already open is not, for leaving a door or window open shows such negligence as to forfeit all claim to the peculiar protection extended to dwelling houses.

Id. at 360, 234 A.2d at 628 (*citing* Clark & Marshall, *Law of Crimes,* § 13.03 at 877-79 (6th ed. 1952)). See *Finke v. State,* 56 Md. App. 450, 468 A.2d 353 (1983).

If entry into a dwelling is gained by deceit, fraud, trick or artifice, the element of "fraud" is equated to "force" by the courts and a "constructive" breaking is sufficient to satisfy the element of breaking. *Brooks v. State,* 277 Md. 155, 353 A.2d 217 (1976), *aff'g* 25 Md. App. 194, 333 A.2d 352 (1975).

While possession of recently stolen articles from a burglarized dwelling may be sufficient to permit a rational inference that the possessor was the burglar, *Boggs v. State,* 228 Md. 168, 179 A.2d 338 (1962), mere possession of recently stolen articles is not sufficient to permit a rational inference that there was a breaking of the dwelling from which they were stolen, in the absence of any evidence that there was an actual or constructive breaking of the dwelling. *Reagan v. State* (1967), *supra.*

The breaking must be of a dwelling house. "The test as to whether or not a building is a 'dwelling house' is whether or not it is used regularly as a place to sleep. No building becomes a 'dwelling' by reason of the fact that someone may sleep there on rare occasions or take an occasional nap there." *Poff v. State,* 4 Md. App. 186, 189, 241 A.2d 898 (1968). A person who breaks into a church is not guilty of statutory housebreaking because a church is not a dwelling house. *Sizemore v. State, supra* at 689. In *Herbert v. State,* 31 Md. App. 48, 354 A.2d 449 (1976), the Court held that a motel complex used for overnight sleeping accommodations by paying guests was a "dwelling house." In *Kanaras v. State,* 54 Md. App. 568, 460 A.2d 61 (1983), the Court held that sufficient evidence was produced at trial to sustain a finding that a recreation vehicle or mini-motor home was a "dwelling house." The Court noted, however, that generally a vehicle-type structure used primarily for transportation purposes should not be regarded as a "dwelling house" even if occasionally used for sleeping. For a detailed discussion of the meaning of "dwelling house," see *Wallace v. State,* 63 Md. App. 399, 492 A.2d 970 (1985). In *Wallace,* the Court held that the evidence failed to show that the structure was a "dwelling house" where at the time of the breaking the tenants had permanently vacated their apartment and no new tenants had yet moved in.

"[T]he time of the offense, 'in the daytime,' is not an essential element of the crime, and is not used in the statute to define or characterize the offense but merely to distinguish it from burglary which must be committed in the nighttime." *Reagan v. State* (1968), *supra* at 594, 244 A.2d at 626.

Where it cannot be determined from the evidence presented whether the breaking and entering occurred in the daytime or the nighttime, it has been held "that when all other elements of the crime are present, a conviction of daytime housebreaking, if properly charged in the indictment, is permissible as the lesser crime." *Jung v. State,* 9 Md. App. 300, 302, 263 A.2d 618 (1970). See also *Gazaille v. State,* 2 Md. App. 462, 235 A.2d 306 (1967); *St. Clair v. State,* 1 Md. App. 605, 232 A.2d 565 (1967).

Felonious intent is an essential element of burglary at common law. Proof of it need not be direct, and may be inferred from the circumstances. *Benton v. State,* 8 Md. App. 388, 260 A.2d 86,

88 (1969). An inference of intent does not arise, however, where the accused voluntarily leaves the premises he had unlawfully broken into, having stolen nothing. *In re John A.*, 44 Md. App. 476, 409 A.2d 744 (1980).

For a discussion of similar elements of this offense, see Comments, §§ 4.53 to 4.55, Breaking — Storehouse, etc., *supra;* and Comment, § 4.57, Burglary, *supra.*

§ 4.70. Kidnapping.

Kidnapping is the detaining of a person against his will and the carrying of that person from the place where he was seized to some other place [either within or without the State], with the intent to carry to another place [or with the intent to conceal within or without the State].

In order for the defendant to be found guilty of this offense, the State must prove beyond a reasonable doubt that: (1) the victim was detained against his will; (2) the victim was carried from the place he was detained to some other place against his will [either within or without the State]; (3) the defendant intended to have the victim carried to some other place against his will [or, had the intent to conceal such person against his will]; (4) the defendant was the person who carried the victim against his will [the defendant was the person who counseled, aided or abetted the detaining or carrying]; [(5) the detaining was done without authority of law].

It is essential that there was a transporting of the victim from the place where the victim was seized or detained to some other place [either out of or within this State].

The victim must have been unlawfully removed against his will. The unlawful removal must have been accomplished through force, coercion, trickery or fraud. [It is enough to find force if it can be shown that the defendant intended to injure the victim or actually used physical force or some other form of violence.]

COMMENT

(a) Kidnapping

The instruction as set forth in the first edition of this book has been revised for two reasons: (1) to reflect the Court's focus on the relationship between kidnapping and false imprisonment; (2) to accentuate the difference between common-law kidnapping and Maryland Ann. Code, Art. 27, § 337. Kidnapping today has been held to be false imprisonment aggravated by transportation of the victim. *Johnson v. State,* 292 Md. 405, 439 A.2d 542 (1982); *Midgett v. State,* 216 Md. 26, 139 A.2d 209 (1958); *Tate v. State,* 32 Md. App. 613, 616-17, 363 A.2d 622, 625 (1976). False imprisonment is the restraint of one's freedom against his will without authority of law. *Hunt v. State,* 12 Md. App. 286, 278 A.2d 637 (1971).

Under Art. 27, § 337, forcible carrying is not necessary, it can be fraudulent. In other words, the common-law requirement that there be an assaultive taking is no longer present. In *Tate v. State, supra,* the victim was raped after entering a taxi that she had requested to pick her up. The Court held that this fraudulent carrying was enough to constitute kidnapping. In *Dean v. State,* 46 Md. App. 536, 420 A.2d 288 (1980), four girls agreed to ride in the truck with the defendant. The Court held that this voluntary joy ride became a nonconsensual and unlawful carrying away when the defendant would not let the girls leave the truck unless they had intercourse. See also *Watkins v. State,* 59 Md. App. 705, 478 A.2d 326 (1984).

At common law the defendant had to carry the person kidnapped into another country to be guilty of kidnapping. Article 27, § 337 provides that both intrastate as well as interstate kidnapping are felonies. *Tate v. State, supra; Lester v. State,* 9 Md. App. 542, 266 A.2d 361 (1970); *Shrader v. State,* 10 Md. App. 94, 268 A.2d 257 (1970). Also, it does not matter that the victim was carried away only a short distance. *Carey v. State,* 54 Md. App. 448, 458 A.2d 90 (1983), *aff'd,* 299 Md. 17, 472 A.2d 444 (1984).

The statute also specifies that there must be an intent to carry such person to such other place or, in the alternative, an intent to conceal such person in or out of the State. *Midgett v. State, su-*

pra. Thus, kidnapping is the unlawful forcible or fraudulent carrying out of or within this State of any person, with the intent to have such person carried out of or within this State or concealed within or without this State. It seems clear that the intent to conceal is an intent to conceal after the victim has been transported.

Proof of intent is necessary, *Laws v. State,* 6 Md. App. 243, 251 A.2d 237 (1969), but the alternative intents should not be charged in the same jury instruction. To use the alternatives in the same jury instruction may make those instructions misleading, confusing and clearly prejudicial by diverting the minds of the jurors. *Midgett v. State, supra.* In *Midgett,* the instruction did not distinguish false imprisonment from kidnapping and the instruction referred to the word "concealed" even though the indictment did not charge the defendant with the intent to conceal. The Court seemed to indicate that even if the indictment had charged concealment, it would be better not to use the alternatives in the same jury instruction.

One may be convicted of kidnapping without actually seizing the victim. All that is required is that the seizer and the defendant were acting with a joint purpose. See *Carpenter v. United States,* 264 F.2d 565, 572 (4th Cir.), *cert. denied,* 360 U.S. 936 (1959). In *Johnson v. State, supra,* the defendant did not actually seize the victim, though he did transport her. The Court of Appeals held that this was sufficient to support a conviction for kidnapping. *Id.* at 432-33, 439 A.2d at 558.

As mentioned above, false imprisonment is a lesser included offense of kidnapping. *Hunt v. State, supra.*

An exclusion from the kidnapping statute (Art. 27, § 337) is provided "in the case of a person under eighteen years of age, by a parent thereof." Thus, if one parent takes away a child from the other parent with intent to carry the child to some other place or conceal the child, the offense of "kidnapping" has not been committed.

A related kidnapping statute, which appears to have been rarely used, proscribes kidnapping of a child under sixteen. Art. 27, § 338. While it authorizes the same penalty as the general kidnapping statute, the provision has raised some problems of interpretation. See *Moore v. State,* 23 Md. App. 540, 329 A.2d 48

(1974). The statute merely proscribes "forcibly or fraudulently stealing, taking or carrying away any child under the age of sixteen years, except by a parent thereof...." It does not specify whether the child had to be carried away outside of the State. Also, it does not proscribe concealment of the child within the State.

A person convicted of kidnapping is guilty of a felony and shall be sentenced to the penitentiary for not more than thirty years. Although the kidnapping statute contains no provision for a fine, the lesser included common-law offense of false imprisonment may be punishable by a fine. *Street v. State,* 60 Md. App. 573, 483 A.2d 1316 (1984), *aff'd,* 307 Md. 262, 513 A.2d 870 (1986).

(b) Abduction of individual under sixteen

Maryland Ann. Code, Art. 27, § 1 was amended (Acts 1978, ch. 1019) so as to make abduction a misdemeanor applicable to the abduction of an individual (male or female) under the age of sixteen. The former statute applied to females under the age of eighteen and the offense was a felony.

There has been very little case law governing this area. The leading case is *Brown v. State,* 72 Md. 468, 20 A. 186 (1890), which held that if a female went on her own accord and without any prompting or inducement on the part of the defendant, the defendant could not be found guilty.

The essential elements of the crime of abduction are the specific purposes statutorily set forth. Thus, the abduction of an individual under the age of sixteen years for purposes of "prostitution, fornication or concubinage" is prohibited. However, if the purpose is for marriage, an essential element is missing. Therefore, a conviction under an abduction statute requires evidence clearly showing not only a taking but a taking for a specified purpose. Note, 26 Md. L. Rev. 198 (1966).

This misdemeanor offense carries a penalty of imprisonment for not more than eight years. There appears to have been few prosecutions under this statute. A likely reason is that many situations that could be prosecuted under this statute are prosecuted under the felony kidnapping statute. The abduction of a child by force or fraud is kidnapping.

Because of the dearth of case law interpreting this statute, the following instruction is placed herein merely as a guide in formulating an instruction.

(c) Suggested instruction: abduction of an individual under sixteen

The enticement, persuasion or forcible abduction of any person under the age of sixteen years for the purposes of prostitution, fornication or concubinage is an offense under the statutory laws of Maryland.

In order for a person to be guilty of this offense the State must prove beyond a reasonable doubt that: (1) a person was enticed, persuaded or forcibly abducted; (2) the person was under the age of sixteen years; (3) the defendant was the person who either enticed, persuaded or forcibly abducted the person, or the defendant was an accessory thereto [or the defendant knowingly harbored or knowingly secreted the person]; (4) the person was taken from the custody and control of his parent or parents [or guardians]; (5) the person was so abducted, persuaded or enticed without the consent of his parent(s) [or guardian, or the person(s) having temporary care or custody]; and (6) the enticement, persuasion or abduction was carried out for the specific purpose of either prostitution, fornication or concubinage.

The law requires evidence clearly showing that there was a taking and that taking must be shown to have been for one of the purposes specified in the statute, that is, prostitution, fornication or concubinage.

To entice or persuade a person is to prompt or induce them to do a thing. Concubinage is the act or practice of cohabitation without marriage.

[An accessory is one who aids and abets the principal offender in the commission of the crimes.] [For jury instruction on this point, see § 4.02, Aiding and abetting, *supra*.]

(d) Abduction of child under twelve

A separate statute, Maryland Ann. Code, Art. 27, § 2, proscribes the acts of abducting, persuading or enticing a child under twelve from the custody and control of the parent(s) or lawful guardian(s) or knowingly secreting or harboring a child with intent to deprive the parent(s) or lawful guardian(s) of the custody, care and control of the child. The penalty for an offender or an accessory for this felony is imprisonment in the penitentiary for not more than twenty years.

Until its repeal, effective October 1, 1984, unlawful abduction or detention of a child under twelve by a parent or relative from a lawful custodian was separately punished under Art. 27, § 2A. For present provisions concerning child abduction, see Family Law, §§ 9-301 to 9-307.

Similar to abduction of an individual under sixteen, there is a dearth of case law interpreting Art. 27, § 2. Again, the most probable explanation is that such conduct would be prosecuted under the general kidnapping statute.

§ 4.71. Larceny.

COMMENT: COMMON LAW PRIOR TO REPEAL

The crime of larceny as covered by this section in the first edition of this book has been repealed. See Instruction, § 4.91, Theft by unauthorized control, *infra*. This Comment has been retained to give guidance to possible statutory interpretations of the legislation as to the prior common law.

As part of the revision (Acts 1978, ch. 849) of the laws of Maryland relating to bad check offenses and various theft crimes, Maryland Ann. Code, Art. 27, §§ 340, 341, 343A, 344, 345, 346, 347, 348, 350, 351, 352 and 353 were repealed. These statutory provisions, set forth under the former subheading "Larceny" have been replaced by Art. 27, §§ 340 to 344, under the subheading "Theft." (Former §§ 342 and 343 of Article 27 were renumbered to be §§ 33A and 486A respectively.)

Instruction, § 4.91, Theft by unauthorized control, has been patterned on Art. 27, § 342(a) of the revised theft offenses.

Certain offenses were not repealed by the 1978 Act. These include: Art. 27, § 349; Art. 27, § 349A (renumbered to be Transportation, § 14-103); and Art. 27, § 353A (renumbered to be Art. 27, § 207).

In the former instruction, the definition of larceny was derived from *Robinson v. State,* 4 Md. App. 515, 532, 243 A.2d 879, 890 (1968); and *Farlow v. State,* 9 Md. App. 515, 516-17, 265 A.2d 578, 580 (1970): "Thus, it must be a trespassory taking and trespass against possession is the matrix of the common law larceny concept." The value was supplied by Art. 27, §§ 340 and 341, with the test of value cited from *Mason v. State,* 9 Md. App. 61, 63, 262 A.2d 576-77 (1970); and *Jewell v. State,* 216 Md. 110, 113, 139 A.2d 707-08 (1958). See also *Mercer v. State,* 237 Md. 479, 206 A.2d 797 (1965); and *Jones v. State,* 6 Md. App. 344, 251 A.2d 46 (1969). The owner of personal property is qualified to give an opinion on its worth as he is usually the purchaser and intimately familiar with the property. *Cofflin v. State,* 230 Md. 139, 142, 186 A.2d 216, 218 (1962).

The ownership interest test was approved by *Richardson v. State,* 221 Md. 85, 88, 156 A.2d 436, 438 (1959). When the owner is other than a natural person "corporate existence may be proved orally and by general reputation," but the ownership must be alleged and proven. *Richardson, supra* at 88, 156 A.2d at 438; *Paesch v. State,* 2 Md. App. 746, 749, 237 A.2d 83, 85 (1968); *Sippio v. State,* 227 Md. 449, 177 A.2d 261 (1962). The good faith defense was adopted from dicta in *Saunders v. Mullinix,* 195 Md. 235, 240, 72 A.2d 720, 722 (1950).

Asportation may be, as described in *McCord v. State,* 15 Md. App. 63, 71, 289 A.2d 7, 11 (1972), "removal to the distance of a 'hair's breadth.'"

Appropriation must be with the intent to steal from one who has lawful possession and deprive the owner of such property permanently. See *Halcomb v. State,* 6 Md. App. 32, 250 A.2d 119 (1969). If, however, one takes another's property without his consent and abandons it at a place from which it is not likely to be returned to the owner or recaptured by him, it may be inferred that he intended to deprive the owner of it permanently, though he may testify that he only intended to use it temporarily. *Sizemore v. State,* 5 Md. App. 507, 248 A.2d 417 (1968). One who takes or returns the property of another without the latter's consent, for a debt which he in good faith claims the owner of the property owes him, is not guilty of larceny, since the existence of the debt or the bona fide belief in its existence shows a lack of wrongful and fraudulent intent in the taking or detention of the property. *Saunders v. Mullinix, supra.* Also, for an owner committing larceny of his own goods, see *Richardson v. State, supra; Wersten v. State,* 228 Md. 226, 179 A.2d 364 (1962) (distinction between general interest and special interest); see also R. Perkins & R. Boyce, *Criminal Law* ch. 4, § 1 at 331 (3d ed. 1982); *Melia v. State,* 5 Md. App. 354, 247 A.2d 554 (1968).

The "taking" refers to the taking possession of the property from one who is in lawful possession of said property. Thus, it must be a trespassory taking. *Farlow v. State, supra.*

When the defendant's intent arose was of critical importance in determining whether a trespassory taking was present. In *Ricketts v. State,* 46 Md. App. 410, 417 A.2d 465 (1980), *aff'd,* 290 Md. 287, 429 A.2d 1025 (1981), a vehicle was discovered soon after the appellant rented it under an assumed name. The motor had been removed. In addition, there was evidence of an attempt to secure a second vehicle under an assumed name. The Court found that the jury could reasonably infer that the appellant possessed a fraudulent intent at the time he acquired the vehicle, and, thus, there was a trespassory taking.

Asportation of the stolen property is also an essential element of larceny. *Gardner v. State,* 6 Md. App. 483, 251 A.2d 901 (1969). It is not necessary that the property be carried any particular distance or that possession and control be retained for any particular length of time by the thief. The slightest asportation is sufficient. The trespassor must acquire complete control over the property, but the slightest entire removal of it from the place it occupies, even for a moment, is enough. *Wiggins v. State,* 8 Md. App. 598, 261 A.2d 503 (1970).

In general, the taking of possession from another is always a trespass unless done with the consent of the other. *Farlow v. State, supra.*

A person who is found in possession of recently stolen goods is required to produce a reasonable explanation of such possession or face an inference that he is the one who has stolen them. *Cason v. State,* 230 Md. 356, 187 A.2d 103 (1963). *Cf.* Appendix V, The Impact of *Evans v. State:* Burdens of Proof, Presumptions, and Inferences, *infra.* It is clear, however, that a mere showing of legal title to the place where the stolen property was discovered will not, standing alone, permit an inference of guilt to be drawn. *Cross v. State,* 282 Md. 468, 386 A.2d 757, 765 (1978).

The possession of recently stolen goods raises an inference of fact, not a presumption of law. *Brooks v. State,* 235 Md. 23, 200 A.2d 177 (1964). The inference from possession of recently stolen goods was considered in *Zimmerman v. State,* 9 Md. App. 488, 265 A.2d 764, 770 (1970), *rev'd on other grounds,* 261 Md. 11, 273 A.2d 156 (1971), which dismissed any fifth amendment challenge to requiring an accused to provide a reasonable explanation of how he acquired possession. The inference "ordinarily cannot be imputed to a companion of the possessor without other supporting evidence; even though both may be observed committing a similar crime at a different time or place." *Matthews v. State,* 237 Md. 384, 389, 206 A.2d 714, 717 (1965).

Generally, the market value of stolen property, and not its cost or worth to the owner, is the proper basis for determining value in order to establish the grade of offense. *Jewell v. State, supra.*

Market value of goods determines grade of offense, and the owner of the personal property in common use may express an opinion as to its value without qualification as an expert. *Mason v. State, supra.*

The test for value is market value and particularly retail value. *Lauder v. State,* 233 Md. 142, 195 A.2d 610 (1963).

Larceny is a specific intent crime. *State v. Gover,* 267 Md. 602, 298 A.2d 378 (1973). This case discusses the defense of voluntary intoxication.

Where the person who actually takes the property is guilty, he who procured him to commit the larceny is, if present, guilty as the principal, and if absent, is guilty as an accessory before the fact. There are no accessories at common law in petit larceny, but all participants are principals. *Anello v. State,* 201 Md. 164, 93 A.2d 71 (1952); *Canton Nat'l Bank v. American Bonding & Trust Co.,* 111 Md. 41, 73 A. 684 (1909). See Instruction: § 4.02, Aiding and abetting, *supra.*

According to the *former* statutes, larceny was a misdemeanor if the value of the property taken was less than $100 (Art. 27, § 341) and a felony if the value of the property taken was $100 or more (Art. 27, § 340). Restitution of the property itself or the full value thereof, plus a sentence of a fine of not more than $100 for a misdemeanor and not more than $1,000 for a felony and/or imprisonment for not more than eighteen months in the house of correction or jail for a misdemeanor, and fifteen years for a felony could be imposed.

Other statutory provisions relating to larceny are as follows: Art. 27, § 33A, Breaking into building or boat with intent to steal (see Instruction, § 4.55, Breaking — Storehouse, etc., with taking of property, *supra*); Art. 27, § 486A — Bonds, notes, checks, etc.; wills; Art. 27, § 349 — Unauthorized use of livestock, boat or vehicle (see Instruction, § 4.73 — Larceny of use — Unauthorized use of motor vehicle, boat or livestock); Transportation, § 14-103, Possession of motor vehicle master key; Art. 27, § 207, Conversion of leased or rented goods.

§ 4.72. Larceny after trust.

COMMENT: COMMON LAW PRIOR TO REPEAL

As part of the revision (Acts 1978, ch. 849) of the laws of Maryland, relating to bad check offenses and various theft crimes, Maryland Ann. Code, Art. 27, § 353 was repealed. The crime of "larceny by trust," heretofore prosecuted under this section, has been replaced by § 342(a) of Article 27. See Instructions and Comments, §§ 4.91 to 4.97d, *infra,* relating to theft and bad check offenses. Note particularly the Official Commentary under Instruction, § 4.91 which is patterned after Art. 27, § 342(a). The instruction is also followed by limited commentary drawn partly from case law of other jurisdictions that have undertaken similar revisions of their theft laws; this Comment on the former "larceny after trust" instruction, based upon the common-law crime, has been preserved to give guidance to possible statutory interpretations of the legislation as to the prior common law.

The former instruction was based on Art. 27, § 353. The history of this section, which was patterned after a Georgia statute, is reviewed in *Van v. State,* 1 Md. App. 347, 230 A.2d 109 (1967). The Maryland statute encompassed the conversion of property by any person lawfully entrusted with the possession of goods or property "for the purposes of applying the same for the use and benefit of the owner or person who delivered the goods...." After considering the express language of the statute and reviewing Georgia cases, the Court in *Van* concluded that although a defendant might be guilty of embezzlement, that in itself is no reason why he could not, in the alternative, be guilty of larceny after trust.

In *Spillers v. State,* 10 Md. App. 643, 272 A.2d 49 (1971), the defendant contended that, since she was a mere servant of the firm for which she worked, the theft by her made her guilty of larceny and not larceny after trust. Citing *Van v. State, supra,* the Court held that whether as agent or servant, she was entrusted with the property for the purpose of applying the same for the benefit of the owner and that she fraudulently converted such property to her own use. In affirming the conviction for larceny after trust, the Court stated that the larceny after trust statute was designed to cover those troublesome cases where it is difficult to decide whether the crime involved was larceny or embezzlement. The Court noted that the statute provided the prosecutor with a crime which overlaps both larceny and embezzlement when the facts involved an entrustment of a thing of value fraudulently converted by the defendant. *Spillers v. State, supra; Urciolo v. State,* 272 Md. 607, 325 A.2d 878 (1974); *Pachmayr v. State,* 1 Md. App. 270, 229 A.2d 434 (1967).

A description of the crime is contained in *Connor v. State,* 6 Md. App. 261, 262-63, 250 A.2d 915, 916 (1969). "The essential element in the crime of larceny after trust is conversion." *Bowen v. State,* 206 Md. 368, 375, 111 A.2d 844, 847 (1955). Specific intent is required. *Roderick v. State,* 9 Md. App. 120, 262 A.2d 783, 786 (1970).

The language describing intent in the former instruction was found in *Roderick v. State, supra* at 125, 262 A.2d at 785. For the definition of "entrust" see *Spillers v. State, supra* at 650, 272 A.2d at 53.

Any crime which requires fraud for its perpetration is one which includes a specific intent whether or not the word "intent" is found in the definition. *Roderick v. State, supra.*

Before an individual charged with larceny after trust could be legally convicted it must have been shown, beyond a reasonable doubt, that there was a willful, deliberate conversion of the items entrusted to the accused and that there was a purposeful refusal, accompanied by a fraudulent intent, to return them to the rightful owner. *Roderick v. State, supra.* Ownership of the depository by the master is not conclusive of possession in him, but access to and control of it are indicia of possession, the ultimate fact of which is determined by the circumstances in each case. By the servant placing the property in a depository in the possession of the master, the servant's exclusive possession of the property is terminated, and the subsequent taking is a trespass. *Connor v. State, supra.* The term entrust does not require that legal title be held by the person entrusted. It is sufficient if it is shown that the thing of value was committed to the accused. *Spillers v. State, supra.* The entrustment can be for very simple and single purposes. *Van v. State, supra.* It is larceny after trust if a person entrusted with the possession of goods for the purpose of applying them for the use and benefit of the owner or person who delivered them, fraudulently converts them to his own use. *Farlow v. State,* 9 Md. App. 515, 265 A.2d 578 (1970).

The owner of personal property is qualified to give an opinion on its worth as he is usually the purchaser and intimately familiar with the property. *Cofflin v. State,* 230 Md. 139, 142, 186 A.2d 216, 218 (1962). When the owner is other than a natural person, "corporate existence may be proved orally and by general reputation" and the ownership must be alleged and proven. *Richardson v. State,* 221 Md. 85, 88, 156 A.2d 436, 438 (1959); *Paesch v. State,* 2 Md. App. 746, 749, 237 A.2d 83, 85 (1968).

The good faith defense was adopted from dicta in *Saunders v. Mullinix,* 195 Md. 235, 240, 72 A.2d 720, 722 (1950).

It is not necessary that the property be carried any particular distance or that possession and control be retained for any particular length of time. *Wiggins v. State,* 8 Md. App. 598, 261 A.2d 503 (1970).

Excluded from the former instruction was the evidentiary rule inviting the inference of criminal agency to be drawn from an unexplained possession of recently stolen property. As larceny after trust concerned not possession — which was acquired legally — but conversion, the unexplained possession of property characterized as stolen did not justify the inference of conversion without more evidence. An accused would naturally be in possession, even though his continued possession past conversion was unlawful; the inference without a foundation of conversion was untenable.

"[T]he term entrust does not require that legal title be held by the person entrusted. It is sufficient if it is shown that the check or thing of value was committed to the accused. (Webster's New International Dictionary)." *Spillers v. State, supra* at 650.

According to the former statute, the crime was a misdemeanor if the value of the property converted was less than $100 and a felony if the value of the property converted was $100 or more. Restitution of the property itself or the full value thereof, plus a sentence of a fine of not more than $500 and/or imprisonment for not more than one year in the house of correction or jail for a misdemeanor, and a fine of not more than $1,000 and/or imprisonment for not more than five years for a felony, could be imposed.

See also Art. 27, § 207, Conversion of leased or rented goods, and Comment, § 4.64, Embezzlement, *supra.*

§ 4.73. Larceny of use —Unauthorized use of motor vehicle, boat or livestock.

Larceny of use involves the taking and carrying away [or the aiding or abetting of such taking and carrying away] of property of another with the intent to temporarily deprive the owner of its possession, custody or use.

In order for the defendant to be guilty of this offense, the State must prove beyond a reasonable doubt that: (1) there was a taking; (2) there was a carrying away; (3) the taking and the carrying away were of the property of another; (4) the taking and the carrying were by the defendant [or the defendant aided and abetted in the taking and the carrying away]; and (5) the taking and the carrying away were done with the intent to temporarily deprive the owner of its custody, possession or use.

The property must be taken and carried away with the intent to temporarily deprive the owner of its possession, custody or use, and not with the intent to steal the property permanently.

The property could have been taken from any place where it was found, whether on or off the owner's premises. To be an owner, a person must have a legal interest or special property interest in that which is taken. The owner may be any person, body corporate or body politic in the State.

In order to constitute larceny of the use, the taking and carrying away must be against the will and consent of the owner. In order for a person to be guilty of this offense, a person does not have to be the actual taker, but may be one who participated with criminal intent in the continued use of the property after the original taking. Such person must have "guilty knowledge." Guilty knowledge may be inferred from facts and circumstances which would cause a reasonable person of ordinary intelligence, observation and caution to believe, in light of the facts and circumstances, that the property had been unlawfully taken.

[In the absence of a reasonable explanation, the possession of property recently taken allows you to infer that the defendant did take such property.]

[If the property is taken under a good faith claim of an ownership interest, the taker could not have the required intent to take the property of another.]

COMMENT

Despite the revision and general consolidation of the laws of Maryland relating to various theft offenses (Acts 1978, ch. 849), Maryland Ann. Code, Art. 27, § 349, was retained. As of July 1, 1979, "boat, craft, vessel" were added to the coverage of the section.

The offense may be roughly characterized as larceny of the use of the designated objects, including motor vehicles. *Wright v. Sas,* 187 Md. 507, 50 A.2d 809 (1947).

The distinction between the larceny of a motor vehicle (proscribed under the former statute, Art. 27, § 348, and presently by Art. 27, § 342(a)) and the larceny of its use (commonly referred to as unauthorized use of a motor vehicle, Art. 27, § 349) is that in the larceny of the motor vehicle there must be an intent to deprive the owner permanently of his property, while in larceny of the use the intent is to deprive the owner temporarily. *Sizemore v. State,* 5 Md. App. 507, 515-16, 248 A.2d 417, 422 (1968).

Article 27, § 349 originated in 1880 when the legislature created the misdemeanor of larceny of the use of any horse or other animal, or any carriage or other vehicle, though taken for present use, and not with intent of appropriating or converting the same. *Johnson v. State,* 2 Md. App. 486, 236 A.2d 41 (1967); *Robinson v. State,* 17 Md. App. 451, 455-56, 302 A.2d 659 (1973).

The intent inference in this instruction is adapted from *Anello v. State,* 201 Md. 164, 167-68, 93 A.2d 71, 72-3 (1952). The statute "makes aiders or abettors equally guilty with the principal perpetrator of the crime." *Id.* at 168, 93 A.2d at 73. Therefore, there can be no accessories in larceny of the use property. *Banks v. State,* 2 Md. App. 373, 234 A.2d 798 (1967).

An allegation of the ownership of the property taken is required and must be proven to show that the property was of another; however, the ownership need only be a legal interest or special property interest. *Richardson v. State,* 221 Md. 85, 88, 156 A.2d 436, 438 (1959).

In *Jones v. State,* 304 Md. 216, 498 A.2d 622 (1985), the Court affirmed a conviction for unauthorized use of a motor vehicle holding that a bailment relationship between vehicle owner and defendant as repairman came to an end once the defendant used the vehicle after being told to stop work and leave it where it was. While the bailee initially received possession, but not title, to the bailed goods, when the bailment was terminated, the possession vested constructively in the owner. Any appropriation after that time constituted a trespass. A bailment at common law could be terminated in several ways: a countermand of the bailee's authority; a completion of the purpose for the bailment; an act of the bailee such as "breaking the bulk" or taking a portion of the goods in the bail; and exceeding the scope of the owner's consent to part with his property. Here, once the defendant used the vehicle after being told to stop work and leave the vehicle where it was, the bailment relationship came to an end and the use of the vehicle thereafter by defendant was against the will and consent of the owner.

Taking the property of another under a good faith claim that the property represents a debt owed indicates that the perpetrator did not have the intent to deprive the other person of property owned by the other person. *Saunders v. Mullinix,* 195 Md. 235, 240, 72 A.2d 720, 722 (1950). No one can violate this statute unless he has criminal intent. *Anello v. State, supra.*

Intent to deprive an owner of his possession includes future possession. Therefore, participation in the continued use of the car after the original taking would manifest an intent to deprive the owner of his possession during such participation. *Johnson v. State, supra* (*citing Anello v. State, supra* at 167). It is the State's burden to show that the defendant possessed the requisite criminal intent under this section. *Hale v. State,* 5 Md. App. 326, 247 A.2d 409 (1968). While guilty knowledge is essential to the conviction of a person accused of larceny of use, such knowledge may be inferred from facts and circumstances such as would cause a reasonable man of ordinary intelligence, observation and caution to believe that the property had been unlawfully taken. *Johnson v. State, supra* at 490-91; *Banks v. State, supra; Anello v. State, supra.* In order to convict for larceny of use, it is not essential to prove that the accused took the property from the owner. Participation alone in the continued use of the vehicle by a passenger with the requisite criminal intent is sufficient to sustain a conviction. *Johnson v. State, supra* at 490. This section does not cover cases involving intent to deprive the owner of his property permanently, as in larceny, but is designed to embrace only cases involving intent to deprive the owner of his custody or use of such property temporarily without intent to steal it. *Fletcher v. State,* 231 Md. 190, 189 A.2d 641 (1963).

The mere fact that the car was abandoned shortly after it was taken does not preclude the possibility that the taker had a larcenous intent. *Gibson v. State,* 8 Md. App. 1, 256 A.2d 890 (1969). The identity of the property may be established by circumstantial evidence. *Spence v. State,* 224 Md. 17, 165 A.2d 917 (1960).

Recent possession of stolen goods is evidence of guilt of the possessor and casts the burden on the possessor of such stolen goods to give a reasonable explanation of how he came into possession thereof. *Sizemore v. State, supra. Cf.* Appendix V, The Impact of *Evans v. State:* Burdens of Proof, Presumptions, and Inferences, *infra.* If, however, one takes another's property without his consent and abandons it at a place from which it is not likely to be returned to the owner, or recaptured by him, it may be inferred that he intended to deprive the owner of it permanently, though he may testify that he only intended to use it temporarily. *Sizemore v. State, supra.*

The offense is a misdemeanor. A person convicted is required to restore the property or pay to the owner(s) its full value and be fined not less than $50.00 nor more than $100.00 or be imprisoned in the house of correction or jail for not less than six months nor more than four years or be both fined and imprisoned.

§ 4.74. Lotteries.

(a) Keeping a place for selling lottery tickets

The keeping of a place for the sale or exchange of lottery tickets, not part of the State lottery system or other exempted gambling activity, is an offense.

In order for a person to be guilty of this offense, the State must prove beyond a reasonable doubt that: (1) the defendant kept a place for the purpose of the sale or exchange of lottery tickets; (2) the place was used for the sale or exchange of lottery tickets [policy, certificate, or anything by which the vendor or other person promises or guarantees that any particular number, character, ticket or certificate shall in any event, or on the happening of any contingency in the nature of a lottery, entitle the purchaser or holder to receive money, property or evidence of debt].

The place used may be any house, office or other place which is maintained for the purpose of selling lottery tickets. It makes no difference whether or not the defendant owns the place. All that has to be shown is that he is keeping the place for the purpose of the sale or exchange of lottery tickets.

A lottery is defined as the offering of a prize and, in return, the giving of a consideration for an opportunity to win the prize and, finally, the awarding of the prize by chance. The essential elements of lottery are consideration, chance and prize. The element of consideration requires the payment of money or other thing of value by the purchaser to the lottery sponsor for the opportunity to win a prize awarded by chance.

A lottery ticket represents anything tangible or intangible by which sale of a chance or share in the lottery is manifested. It makes no difference whether the bets are committed to paper or not. A lottery ticket may constitute a mere exchange of words between the lottery operator and the bettor by which they agree upon the terms under which a chance or share in the lottery is being acquired.

(b) Owner permitting use of house or office for sale of lottery tickets

It is an offense for an owner to permit his house or office to be used as a place for selling lottery tickets not part of the State lottery system or other exempted gambling activity.

In order for the defendant to be found guilty of this offense, the State must prove beyond a reasonable doubt that: (1) the defendant is the owner of a [house] [office]; (2) the defendant permitted that [house] [office] to be used [was aware that the house or office was being used] as a place for selling lottery tickets [any policy, certificate, or a thing by which the vendor or other person promises or guarantees that any particular number, ticket, character or certificate shall, in any event or on the happening of any contingency in the nature of a lottery, entitle the purchaser or holder to receive money, property, or evidence of debt].

The place used must be a house or office. [These terms have been construed to include an automobile.] The term "owner" means that the defendant must have a proprietary interest in the premises. Interest in the property as a lessee is sufficient ownership. Mere occupancy of or presence in a house or office does not satisfy the requirement of ownership.

It is essential that the defendant had knowledge that the premises were being used for the illegal purpose. It must be shown that the defendant was aware of or permitted the unlawful use. Any person who knows that his house or office is used for such purpose is considered as permitting such use. There need not be proof of direct participation by the defendant in the lottery.

A lottery is defined as the offering of a prize and, in return, the giving of a consideration for an opportunity to win the prize, and finally the awarding of the prize by chance. The essential elements of lottery are consideration, chance and prize. The element of consideration requires the payment of money or other thing of value by the purchaser to the lottery sponsor for the opportunity to win a prize awarded by chance.

A lottery ticket represents anything tangible or intangible by which sale of a chance or share in the lottery is manifested. It makes no difference whether the bets are committed to paper or not. A lottery ticket may constitute a mere exchange of words between the lottery operator and the bettor by which they agree upon the terms under which a chance or share in the lottery is being acquired.

COMMENT

Sections 356 through 371B of Article 27, Maryland Ann. Code, deal with lotteries. Pursuant to Art. 27, § 371A, the provisions relating to lotteries do not apply to the State lottery system established in Article 88D, State Government. Also, in *American Legion, Clopper Michael Post No. 10, Inc. v. State,* 294 Md. 1, 447 A.2d 842 (1982), the Court held that the legislature intended that bingo gambling activities authorized under Art. 27, § 255 not be held to be lotteries even though they possess elements of a lottery. See *State v. Adams,* 293 Md. 665, 447 A.2d 833 (1982).

Article 27, § 356 prohibits any person from drawing any lottery or selling any lottery ticket, policies or certificates or anything by which the vendor or other person promises or guarantees that any particular number, character, ticket or certificate shall, on the happening of a contingency, entitle the purchaser or holder to receive money, property or evidence of debt.

Article 27, § 362 proscribes possession of any book, list, slip or record of the numbers drawn in any lottery or any book, list, slip or record of any lottery ticket or of any money received or to be received from or for the sale of any such lottery ticket. Thus, mere possession of lottery tickets is unlawful. See *Williams v. State,* 7 Md. App. 5, 252 A.2d 880 (1969). See also *Ford v. State,* 85 Md. 465, 37 A. 172 (1897); *Rucker v. State,* 196 Md. 334, 76 A.2d 572 (1950). This section does not apply, however, to any person in possession of a lottery ticket or slip issued "by this State or any other government."

The first instruction, designated (a), is based on Art. 27, § 360, which proscribes keeping a place for selling, etc., of lottery tickets. This includes keeping a place in Maryland for sale or barter of out-of-state lottery tickets, even if the lottery in question may be legal under the laws of a sister state. 57 Op. Att'y Gen. 346 (1972). Ownership is not an element of the crime of keeping a place for the purpose of selling lottery tickets. *Williams v. State, supra.* Such a house, office, or place includes automobiles. *Williams v. State, supra. See also Dawson v. State,* 11 Md. App. 694, 276 A.2d 680 (1971); *Robinson v. State,* 229 Md. 503, 184 A.2d 814 (1962); *Moore v. State,* 199 Md. 676, 87 A.2d 577 (1952).

In a lottery there is the offering of a prize, the giving of a consideration for an opportunity to win the prize, and the awarding of the prize by chance. *Silbert v. State,* 12 Md. App. 516, 280 A.2d 55 (1971). In *Mid-Atlantic Coca-Cola Bottling Co. v. Chen, Walsh & Tecler,* 296 Md. 99, 460 A.2d 44 (1983), the Court noted that the essential elements of lottery are consideration, chance and prize. The element of consideration requires the payment of money or other thing of value by the purchaser to the lottery sponsor for the opportunity to win a prize awarded by chance. A lottery's essential element of consideration is absent when there is no money or other thing of value given or required to be given for the opportunity to receive an award determined by chance.

A lottery ticket represents anything tangible or intangible by which sale of a chance or share in the lottery is manifested. This may constitute a mere exchange of words between lottery operators and bettors by which they agree upon terms under which a chance or share in the lottery is acquired. It makes no difference whether the bets are committed to paper or not. *Silbert v. State, supra.*

The second instruction, (b), is based on Art. 27, § 361, which makes it an offense for an owner of a house to permit the use of the house for the sale of lottery tickets. Any person who knows that his house or office is used for such purpose shall be considered as permitting the same. The owner of the house is considered to be one vested with title of property in fee or one who has title to the leasehold interest under a ninety-nine year lease. Mere occupancy of or presence in a house or office does not satisfy the requirement of ownership. There must be some proprietary interest. *Williams v. State, supra.* Knowledge of the illegal purpose is required. *Propst v. State,* 5 Md. App. 36, 44, 245 A.2d 88 (1968).

§ 4.75. Malicious mischief — Malicious destruction of property.

Malicious mischief is committed by any person who willfully and maliciously destroys, injures, defaces or molests any real or personal property of another.

In order for the defendant to be guilty of this offense the State must prove beyond a reasonable doubt that: (1) the act must have been done willfully and maliciously; (2) the act must have been done to the real or personal property of another; (3) the property must have been injured, defaced, destroyed or molested; and (4) the defendant must have done the act.

The requirement of maliciously and willfully means either the defendant specifically intended to cause destruction or injury to another's property, or the act was done without any justification, excuse or mitigation, in wanton and willful disregard of the plain and strong likelihood of such harm.

COMMENT

The elements of the offense under Maryland Ann. Code, Art. 27, § 111 are: (1) as to the property, it may be real or personal property but must be that of another; (2) as to the mischief, the property must be destroyed, injured, defaced or molested; (3) as to the *mens rea*, the mischief must be willful and malicious. *Duncan v. State,* 5 Md. App. 440, 248 A.2d 176 (1968).

Malice is a term of art, implying wickedness and excluding a just cause or excuse. It is implied from an unlawful act willfully done. *Duncan v. State, supra.*

The *mens rea* requirement of malicious mischief is a property-endangering state of mind, without justification, excuse, or mitigation. *Duncan v. State, supra.*

The special element of *mens rea* in malicious mischief, designated in the statute as "willfully and maliciously," requires either a specific intent to cause the destruction, injury, defacement or molestation of the property of another, or an act done in wanton and willful disregard of the plain and strong likelihood of such harm, without any justification, excuse or substantial mitigation. *Duncan v. State, supra.*

Without evidence of a specific intent to cause the destruction or evidence of an act done in wanton and willful disregard of the likelihood of such harm, a conviction under Art. 27, § 111 cannot be sustained. *Spears v. State,* 38 Md. App. 700, 382 A.2d 616 (1978). In *Spears* the Court reiterated the elements of the crime of malicious mischief, *citing Duncan v. State, supra.*

There is no practical distinction between "willful" and "malicious" as used in the section proscribing malicious mischief, as malice includes any wrongful act done willfully or purposely. *Duncan v. State, supra.*

There is no requirement that the indictment place ownership of the property destroyed in another individual or individuals. Thus, where the property destroyed was property of the penitentiary, an indictment alleging ownership in the State was drawn in conformance with the statute. *McLaughlin v. State,* 3 Md. App. 515, 240 A.2d 298 (1968).

In an indictment for malicious mischief, it is not necessary to show personal ill will against the owner of the property. *Duncan v. State, supra.*

The offense of malicious destruction of property is a misdemeanor. Pursuant to an amendment effective July 1, 1985, the legislature altered the penalty as follows: If the property defaced, destroyed, injured, or molested has a value of less than $300, a fine not exceeding $500 or imprisonment not exceeding sixty days or both may be imposed. If the property has a value of $300 or more, a fine not exceeding $2,500 or imprisonment not exceeding three years or both may be imposed.

See, generally, *Gibson v. State,* 238 Md. 414, 209 A.2d 242 (1965); *Seward v. State,* 208 Md. 341, 118 A.2d 505 (1955); *Picone v. Talbott,* 29 Md. App. 536, 349 A.2d 615 (1975); *Winebrenner v. State,* 6 Md. App. 440, 251 A.2d 610 (1969); *Fisher v. State,* 5 Md. App. 155, 245 A.2d 624 (1968); *Williams v. State,* 3 Md. App. 58, 237 A.2d 822 (1968).

§ 4.76. Narcotics — Possession (actual and constructive).

It is an offense to possess certain specifically designated controlled dangerous substances unless [possession is authorized by law] [such substance was obtained directly from a practitioner or by a valid prescription or order from a practitioner while acting in the course of his professional practice].

In order for the defendant to be found guilty of this offense, the State must prove beyond a reasonable doubt that the defendant had possession of __________ *(insert applicable narcotic(s) designated by statute to be a controlled substance(s)).*

You must determine whether or not the substance in question was __________ *(insert applicable narcotic(s) designated by statute).* In so doing you may consider all the evidence in the case which may aid the determination of this issue, including the testimony of any expert or other witness who may have testified either to support or to dispute the allegation that the substance in question was __________ *(insert applicable narcotic(s) designated by statute).*

[Possession of __________ *(insert applicable narcotic(s) designated by statute)* is not a crime if authorized by law. Thus, it is not unlawful to possess a controlled dangerous substance if such substance was obtained directly from a practitioner or by a valid prescription or order from a practitioner while acting in the course of his professional practice.]

Possession means the conscious act or condition of having on one's person or taking into one's control. Holding at one's disposal or control means to exercise a restraining or directing influence over something. The State must prove that the defendant exercised a restraining or directing influence over an object or article which is, in fact, __________ *(insert applicable narcotic(s)).* [It is no excuse that a person does not know that what he or she controls is a prohibited narcotic drug.]

[Possession need not be immediate and direct. There may be constructive possession. Constructive possession exists when an article is taken into a person's control or he holds it at his disposal but it is not on his person. Possession may be by one person or there may be joint possession by several persons. The duration of the possession and the quantity possessed are not material, nor is it necessary to prove ownership in the sense of title.]

[When a charge is based on joint possession, you may wish to consider some of the following factors as relevant to your determination of whether the defendant in fact was guilty of such possession: (1) the nearness or distance between the defendant and the alleged narcotic(s); (2) whether the alleged narcotic(s) was within the view of the defendant or otherwise within his knowledge; (3) whether the alleged narcotic(s) was hidden in a place(s) not shown to be within defendant's view or knowledge or under his control; (4) whether the defendant had an ownership or possessory right in the place where the alleged narcotic(s) was found; and (5) lack of or presence of evidence from which a reasonable inference could be drawn that the defendant was participating with others in the mutual use and enjoyment of the alleged narcotic(s).]

[Where one has exclusive possession of a home or apartment in which prohibited narcotics are found, you may, but are not required to, infer that such person knew of the presence of the narcotics and had control of them. Where the defendant has not been in such exclusive possession, it may not be inferred that he knew of the presence of the narcotics and had control of them, unless other incriminating circumstances are shown which tend to support such an inference. You should consider all of the facts and surrounding circumstances in evidence in making your determination.]

COMMENT

The Controlled Dangerous Substances Act, Art. 27, §§ 276 through 302, Maryland Ann. Code, makes it illegal to possess specifically designated substances except as authorized by law. A variety of related offenses are also proscribed. Article 27, § 287(a) specifically prohibits the possession of any controlled dangerous substance, unless such substance was obtained directly, or pursuant to a valid prescription or order from a practitioner, while acting in the course of his professional practice. Article 27, § 277(t)(1) defines "practitioner" to mean one of the following: "A physician, dentist, veterinarian, scientific investigator, or other person licensed, registered or otherwise permitted to distribute, dispense, conduct research with respect to or administer a controlled dangerous substance in the course of professional practice or research in this State."

Pursuant to Art. 27, § 281, a person who manufactures, distributes, or dispenses any controlled dangerous substance within the State shall obtain annually a registration issued by the Maryland Department of Health and Mental Hygiene. Persons so registered are authorized to possess, manufacture, distribute or dispense such substances to the extent authorized by their registration and in conformity with other regulations. Certain persons are exempt from registration and while acting in the course of their business or profession may lawfully possess a controlled dangerous substance. Included within this category are: (1) agents of any registered manufacturer, distributor or dispenser of a controlled dangerous substance if such agent is acting in the usual course of his business or employment; (2) a common or contract carrier or warehouseman, or an employee, whose possession is in the usual course of his business or employment; and (3) an ultimate user or a person in possession of a controlled dangerous substance pursuant to a lawful order of a practitioner while acting in good faith and in the ordinary course of business or professional practice.

Article 27, § 298(a) on the burden of proof provides as follows:

> It shall not be necessary for the State to negate any exemption, proviso or exception set forth in this subheading ... and the burden of proof of any such exemption, proviso or exception shall be upon the person claiming its benefit. In the absence of proof that a person is the duly authorized holder of an appropriate registration or order form issued under this subheading, he shall be presumed not to be the holder of such registration or form, and the burden of proof shall be upon him to rebut such presumption.

See *Mills v. State,* 12 Md. App. 449, 279 A.2d 473 (1971), *cert. denied,* 406 U.S. 967 (1972). Query whether the burden referred to in this statute is the burden of producing sufficient evidence to generate an issue and/or the ultimate burden of persuasion. *Cf.* Appendix V, The Impact of *Evans v. State:* Burdens of Proof, Presumptions and Inferences, *infra.*

The list of controlled dangerous substances is set forth in schedules in Art. 27, § 279. Five different schedules are used depending on the potential for abuse, whether there is an accepted medical use for the substance, and the likelihood that abuse may lead to physical or psychological dependence. Art. 27, § 287(a), proscribes the possession of "any controlled dangerous substance." "Controlled dangerous substance" is defined by Art. 27, § 277(f) to mean any "drug, substance or immediate precursor in Schedules I through V" set forth in Art. 27, § 279. In *State v. Ciccarelli,* 55 Md. App. 150, 461 A.2d 550 (1983), the Court stated that the statute makes clear that Schedules I through V are not fixed, finite and all inclusive. The Court held that the legislature is under no obligation to include a particular new substance in the section in order for it to be controlled. The federal law's inclusion of phendimetrazine as a controlled dangerous substance (21 CFR §§ 1308 to 1313) resulted in automatic inclusion of such substance as a proscribed drug under Maryland's Controlled Dangerous Substance Act, despite the fact that at that time the substance was not listed in the Maryland Register as such. *Samson v. State,* 27 Md. App. 326, 341 A.2d 817 (1975).

Article 27, § 277(s) defines possession as meaning "the exercise of actual or constructive dominion or control over a thing by one or more persons." In a prosecution for possession and control of a narcotic drug, it is not necessary for the State to allege or prove scienter to obtain a conviction. *Jenkins v. State,* 215 Md. 70, 74-76, 137 A.2d 115 (1957); *Hunt v. State,* 2 Md. App. 443, 234 A.2d 785 (1967).

> [T]he State is not required to show that the accused's control of the narcotic drug was knowing and willful; it is no excuse that the accused does not know that what he controls is a prohibited narcotic drug. But before the State may obtain a conviction, it must adduce evidence to meet the test of legal sufficiency; such evidence must show directly, or support a rational inference, that the accused did in fact control the drug in the sense contemplated by the statute, namely that he exercised restraining or directing influence over it.

Davis v. State, 9 Md. App. 48, 52, 262 A.2d 578, 581 (1970). See *State v. Leach,* 296 Md. 591, 463 A.2d 872 (1983).

Query, where the evidence shows that the defendant was in unwitting or unconscious possession of an article or object which turns out to be a narcotic drug, whether a conviction raises constitutional questions based on lack of an *actus reus*. See *Dugdale v. Regina,* 1 El. and Bl. 435, 118 Eng. Rep. 499 (1853); *Baender v. Barnett,* 255 U.S. 224, 41 S. Ct. 271, 65 L. Ed. 597 (1921); also *cf. Robinson v. California,* 370 U.S. 660, 82 S. Ct. 1417, 8 L. Ed. 2d 758 (1962); *Lambert v. California,* 355 U.S. 225, 78 S. Ct. 240, 2 L. Ed. 228 (1957). An example would be the situation where one person plants a narcotic drug on another person. Can possession exist when a person is not aware that an article is taken into a person's control or is held at his disposal?

Possession need not be immediate and direct; there may be constructive possession. See *Hill v. State,* 237 Md. 630, 206 A.2d 677 (1965); *Bryant v. State,* 229 Md. 531, 185 A.2d 190 (1962); *Folk v. State,* 11 Md. App. 508, 275 A.2d 184 (1971); *Middleton v. State,* 10 Md. App. 18, 267 A.2d 759 (1970); *Anderson v. State,* 9 Md. App. 639, 267 A.2d 302 (1970); *Franklin v. State,* 8 Md. App. 134, 258 A.2d 767 (1969); *Haley v. State,* 7 Md. App. 18, 253 A.2d 424 (1969).

The definition of constructive possession in this instruction is taken from *Jason v. State,* 9 Md. App. 102, 262 A.2d 774 (1970). If a person is in physical possession of a narcotic then he also has it under his control. But a person may be in control of a narcotic without being in the physical possession of it. *Jason v. State, supra* at 113.

If physical possession includes control, then the conviction of a person for possession of narcotics on evidence that he physically possessed the narcotic would make it duplicitous to convict that person for having the narcotic under his control based on the same possession. *Haley v. State, supra.* This concept was extended in *Jason:* "A conviction of possession of narcotic based on possession and conviction of having the narcotic under one's control, based on the same constructive possession, would be duplicitous and the conviction for control precluded." *Jason v. State, supra* at 116. See also *Henderson v. State,* 13 Md. App. 384, 283 A.2d 418 (1971); *Graybeal v. State,* 13 Md. App. 557, 284 A.2d 37 (1971); *Nutt v. State,* 9 Md. App. 102, 262 A.2d 774 (1970).

> It has been held that where one has exclusive possession of a home or apartment in which prohibited narcotics are found, it may be inferred even in the absence of other incriminating evidence, that such person knew of the presence

> of the narcotics and had control of them; but where the accused has not been in such exclusive possession, it may not be inferred that he knew of the presence of the narcotics and had control of them, unless other incriminating circumstances are shown which tend to buttress such an inference.

Davis v. State, supra at 52-53, 262 A.2d at 581.

Jason v. State, supra at 111, supports the portion of the charge dealing with possession by one or more persons by saying that there may be joint possession in several persons. See also *Rucker v. State,* 196 Md. 334, 76 A.2d 572 (1950); and *Haley v. State, supra.* A survey of cases on joint possession is found in *Folk v. State, supra,* at 512-18, 275 A.2d at 187-89. Reviewing these cases, the Court observed:

> The common thread running through all of these cases negating joint possession is 1) the lack of proximity between the defendant and the contraband, 2) the fact that the contraband was secreted away in hidden places not shown to be within his gaze or knowledge or in any way under his control, and 3) the lack of evidence from which a reasonable inference could be drawn that the defendant was participating with others in the mutual use of the contraband.
>
> The common thread running through all of these cases affirming joint possession is 1) proximity between the defendant and the contraband, 2) the fact that the contraband was within the view or otherwise within the knowledge of the defendant, 3) ownership or some possessory right in the premises or the automobile in which the contraband is found or 4) the presence of circumstances from which a reasonable inference could be drawn that the defendant was participating with others in the mutual use and enjoyment of the contraband.

The above quotation from *Folk v. State* is cited with approval in *Ford v. State,* 37 Md. App. 373, 377 A.2d 577 (1977).

Applying the standards outlined in *Folk v. State, supra,* the Court in *Cain v. State,* 34 Md. App. 446, 367 A.2d 47 (1977) reversed the defendant's conviction of possession and intent to distribute drugs on the ground that the evidence was insufficient to support the conviction. The evidence showed that appellant was one of a number of persons in the general vicinity of a bus which had been under the surveillance of narcotics agents. The contraband was found in the refrigerator located in the rear of the bus, although some marihuana and a pipe were in plain view on a dresser.

A closely related crime, possession of drug related paraphernalia, is proscribed by Art. 27, § 287(d). The specific types of paraphernalia are enumerated in the statute. For an interpretation of § 287(d)(i), see *Doswell v. State*, 53 Md. App. 647, 455 A.2d 995 (1983). See also *Russell v. State*, 69 Md. App. 554, 518 A.2d 1081 (1987). It is a misdemeanor to keep or maintain a "common nuisance" which means "any dwelling house, apartment, building, vessel, aircraft, or any place whatever which is resorted to by drug abusers for purposes of illegally administering controlled dangerous substances or which is used for the illegal manufacture, distribution, dispensing, storage or concealment of controlled dangerous substances or controlled paraphernalia...." Art. 27, § 286(a)(5).

A person convicted of possession of a controlled dangerous substance or controlled paraphernalia is guilty of a misdemeanor and may be sentenced to imprisonment for not more than four years, a fine of not more than $25,000, or both. A lesser penalty is provided, however, where the possession involves marihuana. Imprisonment may not exceed one year and a fine may not exceed $1,000 or both. Art. 27, § 287(e). Under certain circumstances a first offender may have a stay of the entering of the judgment of guilt, may be placed on probation and may be required to undergo inpatient or outpatient treatment for drug abuse. Upon fulfillment of the terms and conditions, the public criminal record can be expunged. Art. 27, § 292. A person who is convicted a second or subsequent time may be sentenced to twice the term of imprisonment or twice the fine, or both, provided for in the statute for the first offense. Art. 27, § 293. In addition to these penalties, Art. 27, § 297 provides broad forfeiture authority for all controlled dangerous substances, related materials and equipment, any property used as a container for such substances, all conveyances used for transport, including aircraft, vehicles or vessels, all drug paraphernalia, and all money, coin, or currency used or intended for use in connection with the illegal manufacture, distribution, dispensing or possession of controlled dangerous substances.

§ 4.77. Narcotics — Manufacture, distribution, dispensation or possession with intent to sell.

(a) Manufacture, distribute or dispense

It is an offense to manufacture, distribute or dispense a controlled dangerous substance.

In order for the defendant to be found guilty of this offense, the State must prove beyond a reasonable doubt that the defendant knowingly either manufactured, distributed, or dispensed ________ *(insert applicable narcotic(s) designated by statute to be (a) controlled substance(s)).* [You are instructed that a sale of a substance is included within the meaning of the term distribute. A sale includes not only an exchange of something for money but also includes barter and exchange.]

________ *(insert applicable substance)* has been designated by statute to be a controlled substance(s). You must determine whether or not the material(s) in question [was] [were] ________ *(insert applicable narcotic(s) designated by statute).* In so doing you may consider all the evidence in the case which may aid the determination of that issue, including the testimony of any expert or other witness who may have testified either to support or to dispute the allegation that the substance in question was ________ *(insert applicable narcotic(s) designated by statute).*

[Manufacture is the production, preparation, propagation, compounding, conversion or processing of a substance, either directly or indirectly, by extraction from a substance of natural origin, or independently by means of chemical synthesis. This term includes any packaging or repackaging of the substance or labeling or relabeling of its containers. This term does not include the preparation or compounding of such substance: (1) by a practitioner as an incident to his administering or dispensing of a controlled dangerous substance in the course of his professional practice; or (2) by a practitioner, or by his authorized agent under his supervision for the purpose of, or as an incident to, research, teaching, or chemical synthesis and not for sale.]

[Distribution, as used here, means to deliver other than by dispensing a controlled dangerous substance. As I instructed you, a sale is included in the term distribution.]

[Dispense means to deliver a controlled dangerous substance to the ultimate user or the human research subject by or pursuant to the lawful order of a practitioner, including the prescribing, administering, packaging, labeling or compounding necessary to the preparation of the substance for delivery.]

(b) Possession with intent to sell

It is an offense to possess a controlled dangerous substance in sufficient quantity reasonably to indicate, under all the circumstances, an intent to manufacture, distribute or dispense a controlled dangerous substance.

In order for the defendant to be found guilty of this offense, the State must prove beyond a reasonable doubt that the defendant possessed __________ *(insert applicable narcotic(s) designated by statute to be (a) controlled substance(s))* in sufficient quantity to reasonably indicate under all the circumstances an intent to manufacture, distribute or dispense this substance(s).

[A sale is included in the term distribute. An intent to sell includes not only an intent to exchange something for money but also includes barter, exchange or offer.]

__________ *(insert applicable substance)* has been designated by statute to be a controlled substance(s). You must determine whether or not the material(s) in question [was] [were] __________ *(insert applicable narcotic(s) designated by statute)*. In so doing you may consider all the evidence in the case which may aid the determination of that issue, including the testimony of any expert or other witness who may have testified either to support or to dispute the allegation that the substance in question was __________ *(insert applicable narcotic(s) designated by statute).*

[Possession means the act or condition of having in or taking into one's control or holding at one's disposal. Holding at one's disposal or control means to exercise a restraining or directing influence over something.]

[For instructions on constructive and joint possession, see Instruction, § 4.76, Narcotics — Possession (actual and constructive), *supra.*]

An intent to manufacture, distribute, or dispense is required. Intent may be inferred from the facts proven and the surrounding circumstances.

[Manufacture is the production, preparation, propagation, compounding, conversion or processing of a substance, either directly or indirectly, by extraction from a substance of natural origin, or independently by means of chemical synthesis. This term includes any packaging or repackaging of the substance or labeling or relabeling of its containers. This term does not include the preparation or compounding of such substance: (1) by a practitioner as an incident to his administering or dispensing of a controlled dangerous substance in the course of his professional practice; or (2) by a practitioner, or by his authorized agent under his supervision for the purpose of, or as an incident to, research, teaching, or chemical synthesis and not for sale.]

[Distribution, as used here, means to deliver, other than by dispensing, a controlled dangerous substance. As I instructed you, a sale is included in the term distribution.]

[Dispense means to deliver a controlled dangerous substance to the ultimate user or the human research subject by or pursuant to the lawful order of a practitioner, including the prescribing, administering, packaging, labeling or compounding necessary to the preparation of the substance for delivery.]

COMMENT

This instruction is based on Maryland Ann. Code, Art. 27, § 286(a)(1). This section provides that, except as authorized by this subheading, it is unlawful for any person: "To manufacture, distribute, or dispense, or to possess a controlled dangerous substance in sufficient quantity to reasonably indicate under all circumstances an intent to manufacture, distribute, or dispense, a controlled dangerous substance." In *Killie v. State,* 14 Md. App. 465, 287 A.2d 310 (1972), the Court held that the qualifying phrase in subsection (a)(1) setting out the additional element that the controlled dangerous substance shall be "in sufficient quantity to reasonably indicate ..." modifies only the act of possessing and not the alternatively proscribed acts of manufacturing, distributing or dispensing. Pursuant to this construction of the statute, the instruction has been divided into two parts, designated (a) and (b).

Definitions of the words "manufacture," "distribute" and "dispense" are set forth in Art. 27, § 277. Many of these definitions have been accepted by the courts as correct statements of the law. *Berlin v. State,* 12 Md. App. 48, 277 A.2d 468 (1971); *Rosenberg v. State,* 12 Md. App. 20, 22-23, 276 A.2d 708 (1971); *Moore v. State,* 13 Md. App. 711, 284 A.2d 614 (1971). Note that the first two cases were decided upon the language of the previous statute; many of the definitions have been rewritten and supplemented. The definition of "possession" in Instruction (b) is as set forth in *Williams v. State,* 7 Md. App. 5, 252 A.2d 880 (1969).

Sale has been held to be included in the term distribution. *Rosenberg v. State, supra.* Sale also includes barter, exchange, or offer and each transaction made by any person, whether as a principal, proprietor, agent, servant or employer. See Art. 27, § 277(l), quoted in *Rosenberg v. State, supra.*

Growing marihuana plants has been held to be manufacture under Art. 27, § 286(a)(1). *Puckett v. State,* 13 Md. App. 584, 284 A.2d 257 (1971).

The law specifically exempts legitimate medical purposes in the definitions. Art. 27, § 277(k), (p).

It was held in *Johnson v. State,* 221 Md. 177, 156 A.2d 441 (1959), that in a prosecution for sale, the weight of the evidence and the credibility of the witnesses are for the determination of the trier of fact.

What is a sufficient quantity to sustain a conviction is determined on a case-by-case basis. In *Waller v. State,* 13 Md. App. 615, 618, 284 A.2d 446 (1971), the Court held that the legislature in using the words "in sufficient quantity to reasonably indicate under all circumstances an intent" meant no more and no less than with intent and, the intent is more often found by drawing inferences from the facts proven and the surrounding circumstances. See *Yopps v. State,* 234 Md. 216, 198 A.2d 264 (1964); *Salzman v. State,* 49 Md. App. 25, 430 A.2d 847, 864 (1981). The *Waller* case also held that the lack of a specific quantity did not make the statute unconstitutionally vague.

In *Williams v. State,* 14 Md. App. 619, 287 A.2d 803 (1972), the Court held that possession of 131 capsules of heroin and forty glassine bags of heroin was a sufficient quantity to justify a reasonable inference of possession with intent to distribute. In *Graybeal v. State,* 13 Md. App. 557, 284 A.2d 37 (1971), seventy marihuana plants were found sufficient to justify a reasonable inference of intent to distribute or disburse marihuana. See also *Byrd v. State,* 16 Md. App. 391, 297 A.2d 312 (1972).

The intent to commit the crime in Maryland is inferred from the surrounding facts and circumstances but that there has to be intent was upheld in *Waller v. State, supra* at 618. See *Toyer v. State,* 234 Md. 324, 199 A.2d 233 (1964); *Stewart v. State,* 232 Md. 318, 193 A.2d 40 (1963); *Knight v. State,* 229 Md. 460, 184 A.2d 709 (1962); *Whyte v. State,* 229 Md. 459, 184 A.2d 738 (1962). See *Ricks v. State,* 70 Md. App. 287, 520 A.2d 1136 (1987).

There is some authority in Maryland that if the appropriate case presented itself the Court would accept the principle announced in *United States v. Prince,* 264 F.2d 850 (3d Cir. 1959), that if the defendant acted only as an agent for a narcotics officer in purchasing the drugs from a third person with whom he was not associated, he may not be convicted as a seller and he is entitled to an instruction to that effect. See *Snead v. State,* 234 Md. 63, 197 A.2d 920 (1964); *Owens v. State,* 236 Md. 626, 204 A.2d 70 (1964).

Article 27, § 286 proscribes several related crimes including creating, distributing or possessing with intent to distribute a counterfeit controlled dangerous substance and manufacturing, distributing, or possessing any machine, equipment, instrument or device which is adopted for production of controlled dangerous substances. Also, under Art. 27, § 286(a)(5), it is an offense to:

> Keep or maintain any common nuisance, which shall mean any dwelling house, apartment, building, vehicle, vessel, aircraft, or any place whatever which is resorted to by drug abusers for purposes of illegally administering controlled dangerous substances or which is used for the illegal manufacture, distribution, dispensing, storage or concealment of controlled dangerous substances or controlled paraphernalia, as defined in subsection (d) of § 287 of this subheading.

See *Hunt v. State,* 20 Md. App. 164, 314 A.2d 743 (1974); *Tucker v. State,* 19 Md. App. 39, 308 A.2d 696 (1973); *Nutt v. State,* 16 Md. App. 695, 299 A.2d 468 (1973); and, *Skinner v. State,* 16 Md. App. 116, 293 A.2d 828 (1972).

Article 27, § 286C, effective July 1, 1986, creates the separate offense of "(u)sing minors for distribution of controlled dangerous substances." This offense is a felony with an authorized sentence of imprisonment for up to ten years or a fine up to $10,000 or both.

The penalties for conviction under Art. 27, § 286 are as follows: if the substance is classified in Schedule I or II and is a narcotic drug, it is a felony punishable by imprisonment for not more than twenty years, a fine of not more than $25,000, or both (one who has been previously convicted shall be sentenced to imprisonment for not less than ten years); if the substance is phencyclidine, and certain other substances, classified in Schedule II, it is a felony punishable by imprisonment for not more than twenty years, or a fine not more than $20,000, or both (one who has been previously convicted shall be sentenced to imprisonment for not less than ten years); any other substance in Schedule I, II, III, IV or V is also a felony punishable by not more than five years, a fine of not more than $15,000, or both (one who has been previously convicted shall be sentenced to imprisonment for not less than two years).

§ 4.78. Perjury and subornation of perjury.

(a) Perjury

Perjury is the willful making of a false statement material to the issue, under oath, in a judicial proceeding or by affidavit. Perjury has also been defined as the swearing willfully, falsely and corruptly without probable cause of belief.

In order for a person to be guilty of this offense the State must prove beyond a reasonable doubt that: (1) a false statement was made by the defendant; (2) such statement was willfully made; (3) such statement was made under oath; (4) such statement was made in ____________, which is a proceeding specifically designated by statute; and (5) such false statement was material to the issue or point in question.

To be willful the statement must be deliberately willful and not the result of surprise, confusion or bona fide mistake.

(b) Subornation of perjury

Subornation of perjury is the procurement of another to make a false oath or affirmation.

In order for the defendant to be found guilty of this offense the state must prove beyond a reasonable doubt that: (1) there was a material false statement made willfully by another under oath in a judicial proceeding or affidavit; (2) this false statement was procured by the defendant; and (3) the defendant knew that the statement was false.

To procure and to suborn means to contrive, to cause, to induce, to instigate. To constitute subornation of perjury, you must find beyond a reasonable doubt that the defendant procured the commission of the perjury by inciting, instigating or persuading another to commit the crime of perjury, and the crime of perjury must actually have been committed.

COMMENT

If made willfully and falsely, perjury may be committed in the following circumstances: (1) in all cases where false swearing would be perjury at common law; (2) in all affidavits required to be taken by law; and (3) any account, report or testimony to be made to the government, in court or pursuant to the Maryland Rules. Maryland Ann. Code, Art. 27, § 435, defines perjury to include common-law perjury as well as other acts which at common law constituted the lesser crime of false swearing. *Gatewood v. State,* 15 Md. App. 314, 290 A.2d 551 (1972). The essential features of perjury at common law are the willful making, when under oath in a judicial proceeding or court of justice, of a false statement material to the issue or point in question. See *Smith v. State,* 51 Md. App. 408, 443 A.2d 985 (1982); *State v. Mercer,* 101 Md. 535, 61 A. 220 (1905); *Deckard v. State,* 38 Md. 186, 201 (1873). See *Hourie v. State,* 53 Md. App. 62, 452 A.2d 440 (1982), *aff'd,* 298 Md. 50, 467 A.2d 1016 (1983), for a discussion of the history of the Maryland law of perjury.

The offense of perjury consists of swearing falsely and corruptly without probable cause of belief. To be willful, the false oath must be deliberate and not the result of surprise, confusion or bona fide mistake. *Brown v. State,* 225 Md. 610, 171 A.2d 456 (1961); 3 Wharton, *Criminal Law and Procedure,* §§ 1290-91 (Anderson ed. 1957).

However, an essential element of the crime of perjury is that the false testimony on which the charge is based must have been material to the issues or matter in connection with which it was given. *Weinstein v. State,* 146 Md. 80, 125 A. 889 (1924); *Gatewood v. State, supra.*

Article 27, § 438 specifies that any person who procures another to make a false oath or affirmation in any cases embraced in § 435 (perjury) or § 437 (contradictory statements) shall be deemed guilty of subornation of perjury. To procure and to suborn means to contrive, to cause, to induce, to instigate. *United States v. Petite,* 147 F. Supp. 791, 793 (D. Md. 1957), *aff'd,* 262 F.2d 788 (4th Cir. 1959), *rev'd on other grounds,* 361 U.S. 529, 80 S. Ct. 450, 4 L. Ed. 2d 490 (1960). To constitute subornation of perjury, the party charged must procure the commission of the perjury by inciting, instigating or persuading the witness to commit the crime, and perjury must have been actually committed. *United States v. Petite, supra* (*citing* Wharton's *Criminal Law* § 1595, at 1844-1845 (12th ed. 1955)). An attorney who knowingly presents perjured testimony on his client's behalf is subject to criminal prosecution for subornation of perjury. *State v. Lloyd,* 48 Md. App. 535, 429 A.2d 244 (1981).

The common law required that perjury be established by the direct testimony of two witnesses. Maryland does not subscribe to this rule. The court in 1971 relaxed the rule by holding that perjury may be established by the testimony of one witness and other independent corroborative evidence equal in weight to that of a second witness. *State v. Devers,* 260 Md. 360, 272 A.2d 794, 800, *cert. denied,* 404 U.S. 824 (1971). The Court of Appeals has more recently held that the two witness rule is not applicable, thereby allowing perjury to be established solely by circumstantial evidence. *Smith v. State, supra.* Since subornation is, in substance, the same as perjury, the same proof of the perjured statement is required together with the proof that the statement was procured by the accused. *State v. Devers, supra* at 372, 272 A.2d at 800; *Hammer v. United States,* 271 U.S. 620, 628, 46 S. Ct. 603, 70 L. Ed. 1118 (1926). See also *Hourie v. State, supra.*

"[A]n attempt by an accused to suborn a witness is relevant and may be introduced as an admission by conduct, tending to show guilt. *Saunders v. State,* 28 Md. App. 455, 346 A.2d 448 (1975), *citing State v. Graves,* 301 So. 2d 864, 866 (La. 1974); *People v. Hooper,* 50 Mich. App. 186, 212 N.W.2d 786 (1973); *People v. Perez,* 169 Cal. App. 2d 473, 337 P.2d 539 (1959); 1 Wharton's *Criminal Evidence* § 462 (13th ed. 1972); 29 Am. Jur. 2d *Evidence,* §§ 292, 293 (1967). An attempt by a third person, on behalf of the defendant, to suborn a witness is likewise admissible. Before evidence of such third party's attempt can be introduced, however, the State must establish that the actions of the third party were authorized by the defendant. *Saunders v. State, supra (citing State v. Graves, supra); People v. Terry,* 57 Cal. 2d 538, 370 P.2d 985 (1962), *cert. denied,* 375 U.S. 960 (1963); 29 Am. Jur. 2d *Evidence* § 293.

Finally, it is sufficient to allege and prove that one of two contradictory statements made under oath or affirmation is or must be false and willful without specifying which one. One making such material contradictory statements shall be guilty of perjury. Art. 27, § 437. Every person who is convicted of perjury or subornation of perjury shall be sentenced to imprisonment for not more than ten years. Art. 27, § 439. *Cf. State v. Levitt,* 42 Md. App. 1, 426 A.2d 383, 388 (1981) (dealing with false statements under the Alcoholic Beverages Law).

§ 4.79. Receiving stolen goods.

COMMENT: COMMON LAW PRIOR TO REPEAL

The crime termed receiving stolen goods under Maryland Ann. Code, Art. 27, §§ 466 and 467 has been repealed and incorporated into the consolidated theft crimes enacted by Acts 1978, ch. 849. This Comment to the instruction on "Receiving stolen goods," contained in this first edition of this book has been retained to give guidance to possible statutory interpretations of the legislation as to the prior common law.

There are two offenses in the consolidated theft crimes subheading under which receiving stolen property could probably be prosecuted. Under Art. 27, § 342(a) (see Instruction, § 4.91, Theft — By unauthorized control *infra*), the general language used merely requires that the offender receive possession and have the purpose of depriving. The language makes no distinction concerning the way the property was obtained.

Under Art. 27, § 342(c) (see Instruction, § 4.93, Theft — By possessing stolen property, *infra*), the more narrow language requires that: (1) the property be personal property; (2) the property be stolen property; and (3) the offender have knowledge that the property was stolen property. This provision is broader than the crime of receiving stolen goods, which it encompasses.

Under the prior statute, Art. 27, § 466, receiving stolen goods, etc., to the value of $100 or more, was a felony and punishable by a sentence of ten years or less, or a fine of not more than $1,000 or both. Under Art. 27, § 467, receiving stolen goods, etc., under the value of $100, was a misdemeanor. Under the revised theft offenses, theft of goods of the value of $300 or more is a felony punishable by imprisonment for not more than fifteen years or a fine of not more than $1,000, or both. Theft of goods of the value of less than $300 is a misdemeanor. See Art. 27, § 342(f).

Under the prior law, the value of the goods was not an element necessary to constitute the offense. It did not have to be alleged nor proved as alleged. The State had to prove the value of the goods received to establish the punishment authorized and the classification of the offense. *Jackson v. State,* 10 Md. App. 337, 348, 270 A.2d 322 (1970).

The four elements which had to be present to constitute the offense were: (1) the property must have been received; (2) it must, at the time of its receipt, have been stolen property; (3) the receiver must have had guilty knowledge that it was stolen property; and (4) his intent in receiving it must have been fraudulent. *Jordan v. State,* 219 Md. 36, 43, 148 A.2d 292 (1959); *McGlothlin v. State,* 1 Md. App. 256, 261-262, 229 A.2d 428 (1967); *Cobb v. State,* 2 Md. App. 230, 233, 234 A.2d 155 (1967); *Kincer v. State,* 5 Md. App. 80, 245 A.2d 411 (1968); *Carter v. State,* 10 Md. App. 50, 53, 267 A.2d 743 (1970); *Jackson v. State, supra* at 345.

The fraudulent intent of the receiver need not have been *lucri causa,* but it was sufficient where merely hostile to the title of the real owner. *Jordan v. State, supra* at 43; *State v. Hodges,* 55 Md. 127 (1880); *McGlothlin v. State, supra* at 262; *Kincer v. State, supra* at 87-88; *Jackson v. State, supra* at 352. In *Jordan v. State, supra* at 43, the defendant denied any connection with the stolen property, and the Court held that where there was a connection and such connection supported the presence of the remaining elements of the offense, there could be no doubt as to the intention of the accused with regard thereto. In *McGlothlin v. State, supra* at 262, where the appellant had at least attempted to pawn the stolen article, the act was clearly hostile to the title of the true owner and, therefore, permitted an inference of fraudulent intent.

In *Jordan v. State, supra* at 43, the victim clearly testified that his vehicle had been stolen and there was no denial of the same; therefore, a finding that the property was stolen was amply justified. In *McGlothlin v. State, supra* at 262, the prosecuting witness testified his home had been broken into and the articles received in evidence were his property and those stolen from his home. Therefore the finding that such property was stolen was amply justified.

Manual possession was not necessary to constitute receiving. However, one was guilty of receiving as soon as he obtained a measure of control or dominion over the custody of the goods. Such receiving could be by an agent or through the instrumentality of another. It was not necessary that the accused should have actually seen the goods.

In *Polansky v. State,* 205 Md. 362, 366, 109 A.2d 52, 54 (1954), it was held sufficient evidence of possession when the facts showed defendant, though never in proximity to stolen property, had directed its distribution to different people. The issue of receipt of stolen goods was determined from the circumstances as to whether dominion and control of the goods were transferred to the person alleged to be the receiver. *Jordan v. State, supra* at 44.

The identity of property received with that allegedly stolen must have been established beyond a reasonable doubt; and while such identity could be established by circumstantial evidence where such evidence was sufficient to exclude every reasonable hypothesis save that of the guilt of the accused. *Cobb v. State, supra* at 235, 234 A.2d at 158. See also *Bell v. State,* 220 Md. 75, 150 A.2d 908 (1959).

Guilty knowledge that the property was stolen was one of the essential elements of receiving stolen property. It was not necessary, however, that such knowledge was direct or actual. Such knowledge could be found in a rational inference deducted from circumstantial evidence when such proof indicated that the receiver knew or could reasonably have suspected that the property in his possession was stolen. *McGlothlin v. State, supra* at 262, 229 A.2d at 431.

Conflicting statements made by the receiver regarding the ownership of the stolen property have been the basis for a finding of guilty knowledge. *Marini v. State,* 30 Md. App. 19, 351 A.2d 463 (1976). In *Marini* the defendant, at the time of his arrest, denied ownership of the stolen vehicle, but later testified that he had been an innocent purchaser of the car without knowledge that it had been stolen. A jury finding of guilty knowledge based on disbelief of the defendant's conflicting statements was upheld on the grounds that although either of the defendant's explanations could have been true, both could not be. Thus the defendant's change of statements regarding ownership indicated an attempt to conceal his guilty knowledge.

The determination of who had possession of the stolen property was a major circumstance in ascertaining that the goods were stolen. *Jordan v. State, supra* at 49; *Kincer v. State, supra* at 86.

In a 1968 case, the Court said:

> [When] an accused is found in unexplained and exculpatory possession of recently stolen goods, an inference of fact may be drawn which, if the circumstances revealed by the testimony so indicate, will support a conviction of receiving stolen goods. *Anglin v. State,* 244 Md. 652 [, 227 A.2d 364 (1967)]. Before such an inference can arise, however, the possession of the goods must be accompanied by three essential ingredients upon which the rule is based. The evidence must demonstrate (1) that the goods were recently stolen, (2) that their possession is unexplained, and (3) that the possession is exclusive.

Mills v. State, 3 Md. App. 693, 698, 241 A.2d 166, 169 (1968).

In *Mills,* a car theft conviction was reversed because the record did not stipulate the date the vehicle was stolen and, therefore, element (1), the requirement that the goods were recently stolen, was not sufficiently proven. See also *Lambiotte v. State,* 17 Md. App. 545, 303 A.2d 163 (1973).

"Absent a reasonable explanation, exclusive possession of recently stolen property authorizes the trier of fact to draw an inference of guilt sufficient to sustain the conviction of the possessor as either the thief or a receiver of stolen goods, *e.g., Brewer v. Mele,* 267 Md. 437, 449, 298 A.2d 156, 164 (1972) (citation of authorities) …." *Cross v. State,* 282 Md. 468, 480, 386 A.2d 757, 765 (1978). In *Cross,* the jury had been instructed that they could infer from the discovery of the stolen ring in Cross's automobile that he was the thief. The Court of Appeals reversed the petitioner's conviction for grand larceny holding that where there was no evidence placing him at any time in the vehicle in question, the mere showing that he held legal title to the automobile did not permit an inference of guilt to be drawn.

In *Osborne v. State,* 4 Md. App. 57, 241 A.2d 171 (1968), the Court said:

> When one accused of receiving stolen property is a mere aider or abettor in the commission of the robbery, other than an accessory before or after the fact, the decisions are in conflict as to whether the circumstances can ever be such that he can be convicted of receiving the property stolen. The inquiry in such cases would appear to be whether the participation in the robbery by one accused of receiving the goods is of such character and extent as to make the receiving a part of the theft itself, or whether the receiving is, under the circumstances, so distinct as to constitute the separate offense of receiving stolen property.

Id. at 60, 241 A.2d at 173.

In *Osborne v. State, supra* at 69, the sole evidence against Osborne was that given by an accomplice. The conviction of receiving stolen property was reversed. The rule is generally that the receiver and the thief are not accomplices and, therefore, the testimony of the latter is not usually required to be corroborative to convict the former. But, "an exception to that rule is recognized when the thief and receiver of stolen property conspire together, or enter into a pre-arranged plan, for one to steal and deliver the property to the other; and pursuant to such plan, one does steal and deliver to the other." *Osborne v. State, supra* at 61-62. "It is firmly established that a person who is a principal thief cannot be found guilty of criminally receiving the goods stolen, for the reason that he cannot receive from himself." *Osborne v. State, supra* at 60; *Jackson v. State,* 5 Md. App. 425, 427, 247 A.2d 743 (1968).

"Thus in receiving, unlike larceny, the ownership of the goods is not an essential element of the offense, although the fact that they were stolen is. Thus, it is not necessary that, the ownership of the goods received be proved precisely as alleged; proof that they were stolen goods is sufficient." *Jackson v. State* (1970), *supra* at 348-49, 270 A.2d at 328; *Peaper v. State,* 14 Md. App. 201, 210, 286 A.2d 176 (1972).

§ 4.80. Resisting arrest.

Resistance to a lawful arrest is a criminal offense.

In order for the defendant to be found guilty of this offense the State must prove beyond a reasonable doubt that: (1) there was an arrest of the defendant; (2) the arrest was lawful; (3) there was a refusal to submit to that arrest by the defendant; (4) the resistance was to an officer of the law in the performance of his duties; and (5) the officer had identified himself as an officer.

An arrest is the detention of a known or suspected offender for the purpose of prosecuting him for a crime. The act of arresting includes the taking, seizing, or detaining of the person of another, touching or putting hands upon him, or any act indicating an intention to arrest. When a person is approached by a police officer and merely questioned as to his identity and actions, this contact between an officer and the person is not an arrest.

[A person is not permitted to resist an arrest that is based on an arrest warrant even if the warrant is defective unless the defect is so glaring that a person of ordinary intelligence would pronounce it null and void by merely looking at it.]

[A police officer may lawfully arrest without a warrant any person for any crime: (1) which the arrestee commits or attempts to commit in the officer's presence or within his view; or (2) which the officer has probable cause to believe is being committed in his presence or within his view and may reasonably believe that arrestee is committing.]

[A police officer may lawfully arrest without a warrant for a felony which the officer has probable cause to believe has been committed or attempted by the arrestee whether or not in the officer's presence or within his view.]

[A police officer may lawfully arrest one who [attempts] [commits] certain designated offenses even though he does not have a warrant. One of these [attempted] offenses is

__________ *(insert designated offense(s) listed in Art. 27, § 594B(f)).* An officer may make a lawful arrest when he has probable cause to believe: (1) that the arrestee has committed or attempted to commit such offense; and (2) that unless immediately arrested the arrestee may not be apprehended, or may cause injury to the person or property of one or more persons, or may tamper with, dispose of, or destroy evidence.]

[The substance of all definitions of probable cause is a reasonable ground for believing that the person about to be arrested is guilty. Reasonable grounds or probable cause for an arrest exists when the facts and circumstances within the knowledge of the officer, of which he has reasonably trustworthy information, are sufficient in themselves to warrant a person of reasonable caution in the belief that an offense has been committed or is being committed. The existence of probable cause justifying an arrest without a warrant is determined by factual and practical considerations of everyday life on which reasonable and prudent persons, not legal technicians act. It is a pragmatic question to be determined in each case in the light of the particular circumstances. The rule of probable cause requires less evidence for such belief than would justify a conviction, but more evidence than that which would arouse a mere suspicion. Only a probability and not a prima facie showing of criminal activity is the standard for probable cause.]

[It is the existence of probable cause at the time of the arrest which is the measure of the legality of the arrest.]

[Probable cause may be based on information collectively within the knowledge of the police team. When an officer acting on the direction to arrest was personally without probable cause to justify the arrest, it may be shown that information within the knowledge of the police team constituted probable cause. Under these circumstances the state must produce the evidence on which the officers initiating the arrest acted.]

You must determine from the facts and circumstances in this case whether the defendant was lawfully arrested.

[If you determine that the defendant was not lawfully arrested and no arrest warrant was used, then the defendant had a right to resist that arrest.] [If you determine that the defendant was not lawfully arrested, and an arrest warrant was used, the defendant has a right to resist only if the arrest warrant was so defective that a person of ordinary intelligence would pronounce it null and void by looking at it.] One who is illegally arrested may use reasonable force to effectuate his escape.

If you find that the defendant was lawfully arrested, you must then proceed to determine whether he refused to submit to that arrest, whether that resistance was to an officer of the law in the performance of his legal duties, and whether the officer had identified himself as such.

To sustain a conviction, there must have been an actual resistance to a lawful arrest. Mere flight is not resistance. There is a distinction between avoidance and resistance. Generally, some overt act is necessary to constitute resistance. Words alone may suffice if spoken under circumstances affording the officer reasonable grounds to believe that he could not proceed without incurring evident risk of injury. Mere impertinence is not enough; it is essential that the defendant interfered with the officer's duties.

The police officer must have made known his identity before making the arrest.

COMMENT

The instruction is patterned on Maryland case law. Resisting arrest is a common-law offense in Maryland, generally classified as a type of obstruction of justice. *McGee v. State,* 1 Md. App. 239, 229 A.2d 432 (1967). A related offense of resisting, hindering, or obstructing an officer of the law in the performance of his duties was also recognized at common law. This offense can occur even before there is an arrest. *Cover v. State,* 297 Md. 398, 466 A.2d 1276 (1983); *Busch v. State,* 289 Md. 669, 426 A.2d 954 (1981); *Roddy v. Finnegan,* 43 Md. 490, 505 (1876).

The offense of resisting arrest consists of the refusal to submit to a lawful arrest and resistance to an officer of the law in the performance of his duties. *Preston v. Warden,* 225 Md. 628, 169 A.2d 407 (1961); *In re Nawrocki,* 15 Md. App. 252, 289 A.2d 846 (1972); *Streeter v. State,* 5 Md. App. 435, 248 A.2d 119 (1968); *Carwell v. State,* 2 Md. App. 45, 232 A.2d 903 (1967).

There must be actual resistance. There is a distinction between avoidance and resistance. Mere flight is not resistance. Jerking away from an officer is resistance, but cursing him is not. *In re Nawrocki, supra.*

The force must be willfully employed to resist arrest. Thus, if the arrestee, while being taken to the police station, strikes the officer for the sole purpose of venting his spleen, this may be an assault, but it is not resisting arrest. Generally some overt act is necessary. Words alone may constitute the offense, but only if spoken under circumstances affording the officer reasonable grounds to believe he cannot proceed with the arrest without incurring evident risk of serious injury. Mere impertinence is not enough; it is essential that the arrestee interfere with the officer's duties. R. Perkins, *Criminal Law,* ch. 5, § 3 at 496-97, (2d ed. 1969), *cited with approval* in *In re Nawrocki, supra* at 263-64, 289 A.2d at 853.

Resisting an unlawful arrest is not a crime in Maryland. If an arrest is illegal, the arrestee may use any reasonable means even force, to effect his escape. *Jenkins v. State,* 232 Md. 529, 194 A.2d 618 (1963); *Sharpe v. State,* 231 Md. 401, 190 A.2d 628 (1963); *Williams v. State,* 204 Md. 55, 102 A.2d 714 (1954); *Sugarman v. State,* 173 Md. 52, 195 A. 321 (1937); *In re Nawrocki, supra.*

In *Rodgers v. State,* 280 Md. 406, 373 A.2d 944 (1977), *cert. denied,* 434 U.S. 928 (1978), the Court reviewed the historical development of the common-law right to resist an unlawful arrest. The Court reaffirmed the principle that an illegal arrest, not based upon a warrant, may be resisted by reasonable means. The Court held, however, that because the arrest at issue was based on a warrant, the appellant did not act lawfully in resisting the arrest, even though that warrant was defective. An individual may properly resist an arrest based on a warrant only where the warrant is defective and "the defect must be so glaring and palpable that any person of ordinary intelligence by merely looking at and reading it, will at once pronounce it null and void, and of no effect as a warrant." *Id.* at 417, 373 A.2d at 950 (*quoting Lewin v. Uzuber,* 65 Md. 341, 349, 4 A. 285, 289 (1886)).

However, one threatened with an illegal arrest may not use excessive force to resist. If excessive force is used the "arrestee" may be charged with an unlawful assault. *Jenkins v. State, supra; Sharpe v. State, supra; Kellum v. State,* 223 Md. 80, 162 A.2d 473 (1960).

A "conditional" arrest for the purpose of executing a warrant is not an unlawful arrest and may not be resisted. The act of arresting includes the "taking, seizing or detaining of the person of another, touching or putting hands upon him in the execution of process, or any act indicating an intention to arrest." *McGee v. State, supra* at 242.

An arrest has been defined as the detention of a known or suspected offender for the purpose of prosecuting him for a crime. *Cornish v. State,* 215 Md. 64, 67, 137 A.2d 170, 172 (1957).

"There is detention only when there is a touching, by the arrestor or when the arrestee is told that he is under arrest and submits. Where there is no touching, the intention of the arrestor and the understanding of the arrestee are determinative for, in order for there to be an arrest in such case, there must always be an intent on the part of one to arrest the other and an intent on the part of such other to submit. When one is approached by a police officer and merely questioned as to his identity and actions, this is only an accosting and not an arrest." *McChan v. State,* 238 Md. 149, 157, 207 A.2d 632 (1965).

Arrests may be made with or without an arrest warrant under certain circumstances. "In *Aguilar v. Texas,* 378 U.S. 108, 845 S. Ct. 1509, 12 L. Ed. 2d 723 (1964), the Supreme Court pointed out that the preference for warrants is so marked, that less persuasive evidence will justify the issuance of a warrant than would justify a warrantless search or warrantless arrest." *Hignut v. State,* 17 Md. App. 399, 409, 303 A.2d 173 (1973).

Maryland Ann. Code, Art. 27, §§ 594B and 594C, provide statutory authority for police officers and persons other than police officers to arrest without warrant.

The definition of probable cause is taken from *Graham v. State,* 239 Md. 521, 525-26, 212 A.2d 287 (1965), *citing in part* 5 Am. Jur. 2d, *Arrest,* § 48 (1962). See also *McChan v. State, supra;* and *Rife v. State,* 9 Md. App. 658, 267 A.2d 326 (1970) (discussing the authority of a police officer to arrest without a warrant).

It is the existence of probable cause at the time of arrest which is the measure of legality of the arrest. *Collins v. State,* 17 Md. App. 376, 383, 302 A.2d 693 (1973); *Evans v. State,* 11 Md. App. 451, 274 A.2d 653 (1971); *Hebron v. State,* 13 Md. App. 134, 281 A.2d 547 (1971).

"Probable cause may be based on information collectively within the knowledge of the police team." *Hebron v. State, supra.* So even when an officer acting on a direction to arrest was personally without sufficient probable cause to justify the arrest, it may be shown that information within the knowledge of the police team constituted probable cause. *Thompson v. State,* 15 Md. App. 335, 290 A.2d 565 (1972). In such case, of course, the State is required to produce the evidence on which the officers initiating the arrest acted. *Id.; Collins v. State, supra* at 383.

When a civil rights action against a police officer is filed pursuant to 42 U.S.C.A. § 1983, there is a defense of good faith and probable cause which is available to the police officer. *Richardson v. Snow,* 340 F. Supp. 1261, 1263 (D. Md. 1972) (*citing Pierson v. Ray,* 386 U.S. 547, 557, 87 S. Ct. 1213, 18 L. Ed. 2d 288 (1967)). Under the circumstances a different standard of probable cause is applied. The probable cause needed to establish the defense of the police officer under *Pierson v. Ray, supra,* is not probable cause in the constitutional sense, but is instead a reasonable belief on the part of the defendant police officer that his conduct was lawful in attempting to carry out an arrest. *Richardson v. Snow, supra* at 1264.

In *Richardson,* a case involving a Prince George's County Police Department detective and the former Police Chief, the Court cited with approval the decision in *Bivens v. Six Unknown*

Named Agents of Fed. Bureau of Narcotics, 456 F.2d 1339, 1348 (2d Cir. 1972):

> Therefore, to prevail the police officer need not allege and prove probable cause in the constitutional sense. The standard governing police conduct is composed of two elements. The first is subjective and the second is objective. Thus, the officer must allege and prove not only that he believed, in good faith, that his conduct was lawful, but also that his belief was reasonable. And so we hold that it is a defense to hold and prove good faith and reasonable belief in the validity of the arrest and search and in the necessity for carrying out the arrest and search in the way the arrest was made and the search was conducted.

The jury decides whether an arrest was legal. *Williams v. State, supra.*

The State has the burden of establishing beyond a reasonable doubt that at the time of the arrest the individual making the arrest was in fact a police officer. *Lyles v. State,* 10 Md. App. 265, 269 A.2d 178 (1970). To come within the protection of the law, police officers must make known their identity before exercising the prerogative of arrest. "Upon thus making themselves known, they then come within the protection of the law, and a citizen is thereupon bound to submit at least to the point of ascertaining the character of the charge and the extent of the officer's authority." *Jordan v. State,* 17 Md. App. 201, 300 A.2d 701 (1973) (*citing Daniel v. State,* 132 So. 2d 312, 314 (Fla. 1961)).

The testimony of a single witness, even the police officer, is sufficient to support a conviction for resisting arrest. *McGee v. State, supra.*

The fact that the defendant was never charged with the offense for which he was being arrested is immaterial. *Sharpe v. State, supra; Price v. State,* 227 Md. 28, 175 A.2d 11 (1961).

There is no fixed penalty for resisting arrest. A ten year sentence for resisting arrest and assaulting a police officer is neither illegal, nor excessive. *Preston v. Warden, supra.*

§ 4.81. Riot.

Riot is a disturbance of the peace by three or more unlawfully assembled persons who carry out a common purpose in such a violent and turbulent manner as to terrify others.

In order for the defendant to be found guilty of this offense the State must prove beyond a reasonable doubt that: (1) there was an unlawful assembly, namely __________ (*insert type of unlawful assembly*); (2) three or more persons participated in that unlawful assembly; (3) the defendant was one of those three or more persons; and (4) the participation was with common intent to carry out a common purpose, in a violent or turbulent manner calculated to terrify others.

COMMENT

Riot is a common-law crime in Maryland. It is not frequently prosecuted, and consequently there is little case law on the subject.

One individual may be guilty of rioting as long as it is proven that he acted in concert with at least two other persons.

The most authoritative treatment by the Maryland Court of Appeals on the crime of riot appears in *Cohen v. State,* 173 Md. 216, 195 A. 532 (1937). In that case the defendant attacked the indictment charging him with riot, stating that the indictment named only the defendant and no others. The defendant correctly stated that at common law there must be at least three people for a riot, but he argued that since he was the only named individual the indictment must be nullified. The Court stated: "One person can be charged with rioting provided he is alleged to have been so engaged with at least two other persons.... If unknown, it is essential that the indictment so state." *Id.* at 234.

"At common law it was necessary that three or more persons be unlawfully assembled to carry out a common purpose in such violent or turbulent manner as to terrify others, and assault or destruction of property may or may not be incident to the execution of the riot. The assembly must be unlawful, or else there is no riot, and the unlawful assembly must be charged in the indictment. [L.] Hochheimer, *Criminal Law* §§ 429-431," *Cohen v. State, supra* at 221. See also *Gibson v. State,* 17 Md. App. 246,

300 A.2d 692 (1973); *Briscoe v. State,* 3 Md. App. 462, 466-67, 240 A.2d 109 (1968).

§ 4.82. Robbery.

Robbery is the taking and carrying away of personal property of another from his person or in his immediate presence, by violence or by putting him in fear with the intent to permanently deprive him of the property.

In order for the defendant to be guilty of this offense, the State must prove beyond a reasonable doubt that: (1) there was a trespassory taking by the defendant; (2) there was a carrying away by the defendant; (3) this taking and carrying away was of the personal property of another; (4) the personal property was taken from the person of the victim or in his immediate presence; (5) it was taken without consent; (6) it was taken with the intent to permanently deprive the possessor of it; and (7) it was taken by force or violence or by putting the possessor in fear.

Robbery is a specific intent crime. There must have been an intent to permanently deprive the lawful possessor of his property. This means that the State must prove that the accused knowingly, deliberately, intentionally did take and carry away the property with the intent to steal. The intent may be inferred from all the facts and circumstances, including the words, acts and conduct of the defendant. The intent must have been present at the time of the taking.

[The word "taking" refers to the taking of possession. In general, the taking of possession from another is always a trespass unless it is done with the consent of the owner. If the property was taken under a good faith claim of an ownership interest, then the defendant could not have the required intent.]

It is necessary that the property was both taken and carried away. In order to constitute an asportation or carrying away, the robber must acquire complete control of the property at least for an instant. The slightest asportation is sufficient, even though the property might immediately be abandoned or returned to its rightful owner.

[The property need not be owned by the person robbed. The property may be taken from someone who had custody over the property and who had legal or special interest in it.]

The violence may be actual, as by application of physical force, or constructive, as by putting a person in fear. The violence must accompany or come before the robbery. It is only in the absence of actual violence that a putting in fear is required. The element of fear does not have to be shown; it is sufficient if the means employed were of such as to excite reasonable fear of danger and reasonably cause the possessor to surrender his property.

COMMENT

This instruction is patterned substantially after holdings in various Maryland cases. Robbery is a crime in Maryland under the common law. *Darby v. State,* 3 Md. App. 407, 413, 239 A.2d 584 (1968). Robbery has been defined as the felonious taking and carrying away of the personal property of another (or of which he has possession or custody) from his person or in his presence, by violence, or by putting him in fear. *Phenious v. State,* 11 Md. App. 385, 274 A.2d 658 (1971); *Gray v. State,* 10 Md. App. 478, 271 A.2d 390 (1970); *McClain v. State,* 10 Md. App. 106, 268 A.2d 572 (1970); *Wiggins v. State,* 8 Md. App. 598, 261 A.2d 503 (1970); *Williams v. State,* 7 Md. App. 683, 256 A.2d 776 (1969); *Hartley v. State,* 4 Md. App. 450, 243 A.2d 665 (1968); *Tender v. State,* 2 Md. App. 692, 237 A.2d 65 (1968). The penalty is fixed by Maryland Ann. Code, Art. 27, § 486, as restoration of the property taken or payment of its full value, and three to ten years in the penitentiary.

Robbery is a specific intent crime. *State v. Gover,* 267 Md. 602, 298 A.2d 378 (1973). Larcenous intent is an essential ingredient of robbery. *Leeson v. State,* 293 Md. 425, 445 A.2d 21, 26 (1982); *Hadder v. State,* 238 Md. 341, 209 A.2d 70 (1965). Its crucial element, however, is the intent to permanently deprive the owner of his property. *Id.* Every robber embraces a larcenous intent, and this means that every robber must intend to steal the property taken. *Cates v. State,* 21 Md. App. 363, 320 A.2d 75 (1974). The need for a larcenous intent was reiterated in *Leeson v. State, supra.* In this case, the defendants alleged that they did not have the necessary intent to be convicted of robbery since the owners, in a scheme to defraud an insurance company, consented to the taking of their possessions. The Court remanded the case to determine whether consent actually existed. The intent must be to deprive the owner permanently of his property. *Wiggins v. State, supra.*

Intent to steal is subjective, it need not be directly and objectively demonstrated, but may be inferred from a totality of the circumstances. *Id.*

In *Halcomb v. State,* 6 Md. App. 32, 250 A.2d 119 (1969), the defendant was charged with robbing an officer of his revolver and espantoon. The Court gave an instruction to the jury that they could find the requisite intent to rob if they concluded that, at the time the property was taken, the accused had the intent to deprive the owner of the items. The Court of Special Appeals held that it was error to give this instruction since the jury had to find that at the time the accused took the officer's property he had a specific intent to deprive the officer of these items permanently, and that if they were taken for a purpose other than to steal, or were taken solely to disarm the officer, or to prevent him from striking or shooting the accused, the accused was then not guilty.

Intent has been further defined as the exercise of intelligent will, the mind being fully aware of the nature and consequences of the act which is about to be done, with such knowledge and full liberty of action, willing and electing to do it. *Nance v. State,* 7 Md. App. 433, 256 A.2d 377 (1969), *cert. denied,* 398 U.S. 954 (1970).

The amount of money stolen is not an essential element of the offense of robbery, so long as the proof shows that something of value was taken. It is sufficient to prove only the taking of a greater or lesser sum of money than that alleged in the indictment. *Johnson v. State,* 227 Md. 159, 175 A.2d 580 (1961); *Oliver v. State,* 8 Md. App. 610, 261 A.2d 498 (1970); *Love v. State,* 6 Md. App. 639, 252 A.2d 493 (1969). All elements necessary to constitute larceny are necessary to constitute robbery. *Wiggins v. State, supra.*

Actual or constructive violence must precede or accompany the taking to constitute robbery. If the force precedes the taking, the intent to steal need not coincide with the force since it is sufficient if there be force followed by a taking with intent to steal as part of the same general occurrence or episode. Even if the force results in death, a taking and asportation after death is nevertheless robbery. *Stebbing v. State,* 299 Md. 331, 473 A.2d 903, *cert. denied,* 469 U.S. 900 (1984). See *Giles v. State,* 8 Md. App. 721, 261 A.2d 806 (1970).

Robbery has been described as the larceny from the person of another by violence. The violence may be actual, as by the application of physical force, or constructive, as by the putting of one in fear. *Wiggins v. State, supra.* If the property, which is the subject of the robbery, is taken in the victim's presence, it is taken constructively from his person. *Williams v. State, supra.* It must be noted that the element of fear need not be shown. It is enough that the person assailed was: (1) actually put in fear if the means employed are calculated to instill fear in the heart or mind of a reasonable person. *Hayes v. State,* 211 Md. 111, 126 A.2d 576 (1956); *Holtman v. State,* 12 Md. App. 168, 278 A.2d 82 (1971); *Giles v. State, supra; Harrison v. State,* 3 Md. App. 148, 238 A.2d 153 (1968); and (2) reasonably cause the owner to surrender his property. *Spence v. State,* 51 Md. App. 359, 443 A.2d 648, 649 (1982), *rev'd on other grounds,* 296 Md. 416, 463 A.2d 808 (1983). In *Spence,* the Court held that the element of intimidation was satisfied when the defendant walked around the victim's apartment with one hand in a canvas bag.

In *Foster v. State,* 297 Md. 191, 454 A.2d 986 (1983), *cert. denied,* 464 U.S. 1073 (1984), the defendant argued on appeal that the evidence was insufficient to establish that the property taken was taken from the victim's "presence." There was evidence to show that the victim's property was taken from a room in a motel other than the one in which the victim was present at the time of the related murder. Citing cases from other jurisdictions, the Court noted that the scope of the term "presence" involves proximity and control. The property taken must have been close enough to the victim and sufficiently under the victim's control that, had the victim not been subject to violence or intimidation by the robber, the victim could have prevented the taking. The Court held that the above evidence, if believed, was sufficient to show that the property was taken from the victim's presence and, therefore, a robbery had been committed.

In a robbery, if the assailant acquires complete possession and control of the property, even for an instant, the offense is complete, though he immediately afterwards drops or abandons it or returns it to the person robbed. *Wiggins v. State, supra.* Attempted robbery may be predicated upon a finding of intent to steal goods from the person of another by violence, but without the consummation of the larceny. *Id.* It is not necessary to allege ownership of money stolen in a robbery. A charge of robbery may be sustained by proof that the property was forcibly taken from the care, custody, control, management or possession of one having a right superior to that of the robber. *Oliver v. State, supra.*

In *Holmes v. State,* 10 Md. App. 253, 269 A.2d 175 (1970), it was held that there was sufficient evidence to establish appellant's criminal agency in connection with a robbery, where he had been identified by the robbery victim at a preliminary hearing. The victim testified at appellant's trial that a police photograph of appellant taken shortly after his arrest, and admitted into evidence, was that of one of the robbers. The presence of the accused at the scene of the robbery is an important element that may be considered in determining his guilt or innocence. But presence alone at the scene of the robbery is not sufficient to establish participation in the perpetration of the crime. *Johnson v. State, supra.*

> [I]t is not robbery to obtain property from the person of another by a mere trick, and without force, or to pick another's pocket without using more force than is necessary to lift the property from the pocket; nor is it robbery to suddenly snatch property from another when there is no resistance and no more force, therefore, than is necessary to the mere act of snatching. Clark and Marshall Crimes (6th Edi-

> tion) Section 12.13; Annotation 8 A.L.R. 359. Conversely, it has been held robbery, "for a person to seize another's watch or purse, and use sufficient force to break a chain or guard by which it is attached to his person, or to run against another, or rudely push him about, for the purpose of diverting his attention and robbing him, and thus take a purse from his pocket." Clark and Marshall Crimes, Section 12.13. And as that preeminent text authority further notes in the same Section, the fact that surprise aids the force employed to accomplish the taking will not prevent the force from aggravating the offense, so as to make it robbery, it not mattering that the victim does not know that he is being robbed. Within these rules, it has been held robbery to put an arm around one's neck, ostensibly to whisper to him, and then pick his pocket; or to pick one's pockets while scuffling with him; or while jostling him; or while running against him; or while pushing him; or while crowding and putting one's arms around him. 8 A.L.R. at 360-361.

Cooper v. State, 9 Md. App. 478, 480-81, 265 A.2d 569, 571 (1970). See also *Williams v. State, supra.*

Article 27, § 486 provides a statutory penalty for the common-law offense of robbery. It states: "Every person convicted of the crime of robbery, or as accessory thereto before the fact, shall restore the thing robbed or taken to the owner, or shall pay to him the full value thereof, and be sentenced to the penitentiary for not less than three nor more than ten years." Article 27, § 486A, Bonds, notes, checks, etc.; wills, provides for a crime of statutory robbery. The common-law crime of robbery applies only to the forcible taking of tangible personal property. This provision expands the scope of the offense to include enumerated items of intangible property. The punishment is the same as for the common-law offense.

§ 4.83. Robbery with a deadly weapon.

Robbery with a deadly or dangerous weapon consists of the crime of robbery coupled with both the use of a weapon to produce intimidation and the apparent ability to use the weapon.

In order for the defendant to be found guilty of this offense, the State must prove beyond a reasonable doubt

that: (1) there was a trespassory taking by the defendant; (2) there was a carrying away by the defendant; (3) this taking and carrying away was of the personal property of another; (4) the personal property was taken from the person of the victim or in his immediate presence; (5) it was taken without consent; (6) it was taken with the intent to permanently deprive the possessor of it; and (7) it was committed with the use of a deadly or dangerous weapon with intent to produce intimidation and the apparent ability to use the weapon.

Robbery is a specific intent crime. There must have been an intent to permanently deprive the lawful possessor of his property. This means that the State must prove that the defendant knowingly, deliberately, intentionally did take and carry away the property with the intent to steal. The intent may be determined from the words, acts and conduct of the defendant. The intent must have been present at the time of the taking.

[The word "taking" refers to the taking of possession. In general, the taking of possession from another is always a trespass unless it is done with the consent of the owner. If the property was taken under a good faith claim of an ownership interest, then the defendant could not have the requisite intent.]

It is necessary that the property was both taken and carried away. In order to constitute an asportation or carrying away, the robber must acquire complete control of the property at least for an instant. The slightest asportation is sufficient, even though the property might immediately be abandoned or returned to its rightful owner.

[The property need not be owned by the person robbed. The property may be taken from someone who had custody over the property and who had legal or special interest in it.]

A weapon is generally defined as anything used or designed to be used in destroying, defeating or injuring an enemy, or an instrument of offensive or defensive combat.

It is necessary for you to find that the weapon used was either dangerous or deadly. A weapon is either dangerous or deadly when used in such a way which is likely to produce death or grievous bodily harm. [Whether an object or instrument is a dangerous or deadly weapon is not necessarily determined by its design, construction, or purpose. If a weapon is in fact used in such a way as is likely to produce death or grievous bodily harm, it may be properly regarded as a dangerous or deadly weapon. For example, an object not deadly in itself, such as a club, may not be a dangerous or deadly weapon unless used in a threatening manner.]

Robbery with a deadly or dangerous weapon is predicated upon a finding of intent to rob by means of intimidation produced by the use of a weapon, coupled with the apparent ability to execute the implied threat to use the weapon if resistance is offered. As long as there is an intent to rob by means of a dangerous or deadly weapon, it is unnecessary to find an intent or ability to execute the implied threat in the event of resistance. It need not be shown that the person assailed was actually put in fear if the means employed were calculated to instill fear in the heart or mind of a reasonable person.

COMMENT

This instruction is patterned substantially after holdings in various Maryland cases. Robbery is a common-law crime in Maryland. It has been defined as the felonious taking and carrying away of the personal property of another (or of which he has possession or custody) from the person or in his presence, by violence or by putting him in fear. See Comment, § 4.82, Robbery, *supra*. See also *Spence v. State*, 51 Md. App. 359, 443 A.2d 648 (1982), *rev'd on other grounds*, 296 Md. 416, 463 A.2d 808

(1983); Clark & Marshall, Law of Crimes §§ 12.09, 12.11 (6th ed. 1958). To constitute robbery the property must, as in larceny, be both taken and carried away, so that an asportation of the stolen property as well as a trespass would appear to be indispensable elements of the offense. *McCord v. State,* 15 Md. App. 63, 289 A.2d 7 (1972). It is necessary that the accused had a larcenous intent to permanently deprive the owner of his property. *Halcomb v. State,* 6 Md. App. 32, 250 A.2d 119 (1969).

There can be no robbery without a larcenous intent. This intent may be ascertained and determined from the words, acts and conduct of the accused. An intent formed subsequent to the taking is immaterial, but subsequent appropriation is a circumstance to be considered, along with all other relevant facts, in determining the existence of and intent to steal at the time of the initial taking. *Midgett v. State,* 216 Md. 26, 139 A.2d 209 (1958).

Armed robbery is the commission of a robbery with a deadly weapon. *Bell v. State,* 5 Md. App. 276, 246 A.2d 286 (1968). It is necessary that the robbery was committed with a dangerous or deadly weapon carried either by the defendant or by another robber who was aided and abetted by the defendant.

Robbery with a deadly weapon is predicated upon a finding of intent to rob by means of intimidation produced by the use of a weapon, coupled with the apparent ability to execute the implied threat to use the weapon if resistance is offered. *Jackson v. State,* 231 Md. 591, 191 A.2d 432 (1963). See also *Claybrooks v. State,* 36 Md. App. 295, 374 A.2d 365 (1977).

A weapon is generally defined as anything used or designed to be used in destroying, defeating or injuring an enemy, or an instrument of offensive or defensive combat. *Bennett v. State,* 237 Md. 212, 205 A.2d 393 (1964). It is necessary under the statute for the state to show that the weapon used was, in reality, either dangerous or deadly. *Vincent v. State,* 220 Md. 232, 151 A.2d 898 (1959); *Bell v. State, supra.* The character of a weapon as a dangerous or deadly weapon is not necessarily determined by its design, construction, or purpose. *Bennett v. State, supra.* When a weapon is in fact used in such a way as is likely to produce death or grievous bodily harm, it may be properly regarded as a dangerous or deadly weapon. *Id.* A weapon not deadly per se, such as a club, may not be dangerous within the meaning of the statute unless utilized in a threatening manner. *Hobbs v. Pepersack,* 301 F.2d 875 (4th Cir. 1962). Where a taxicab driver was put in fear by a cord twisted about his neck, the cord being an effective instrument of strangulation, although used only to restrain the driver, a finding that the manner of use of the cord in the robbery constituted it a dangerous weapon was fully supported by the evidence. *Bennett v. State, supra.* A knife may be either a deadly weapon or only a dangerous one, depending on the size of the blade and the manner of its use. *Hobbs v. Pepersack, supra; Bell v. State, supra.*

A starter's pistol used by the accused in two robberies was a deadly weapon within the meaning of the statute. *Jackson v. State, supra.* An unloaded pistol, used in an attempt to rob, is a dangerous weapon within the meaning of this section. *Hayes v. State,* 211 Md. 111, 126 A.2d 576 (1956); *Jackson v. State, supra.* It is unnecessary for the state to prove the gun or weapon used in committing the robbery was loaded. *Vincent v. State, supra; Davis v. State,* 225 Md. 45, 168 A.2d 884 (1961); *Hobbs v. Pepersack,* 206 F. Supp. 301 (D. Md. 1962).

As long as there is an intent to rob by means of a dangerous or deadly weapon, it is unnecessary to find an intent or ability to execute the implied threat in the event of resistance. It need not be shown that the person assailed was actually put in fear if the means employed were calculated to instill fear in the heart or mind of a reasonable person. *Graham v. State,* 13 Md. App. 171, 282 A.2d 162 (1971); *Gardner v. State,* 8 Md. App. 694, 261 A.2d 799 (1970); *Thompson v. State,* 5 Md. App. 191, 245 A.2d 903 (1968); *Bell v. State, supra.*

Identification of the accused by one eyewitness is sufficient to sustain a conviction of robbery with a deadly weapon. *Shrader v. State,* 10 Md. App. 94, 268 A.2d 257 (1970); *Gardner v. State, supra; Price v. State,* 3 Md. App. 155, 238 A.2d 275 (1968); *Britton v. State,* 2 Md. App. 285, 234 A.2d 274 (1967); *Crumb v. State,* 1 Md. App. 98, 227 A.2d 369 (1967).

Maryland Ann. Code, Art. 27, § 488 does not create a new substantive crime of "robbery with a deadly weapon," it merely provides a greater penalty for a robbery when it is committed with a deadly weapon. *Phenious v. State,* 11 Md. App. 385, 274 A.2d 658 (1971); *Gray v. State,* 10 Md. App. 478, 271 A.2d 390

(1970); *McChan v. State,* 9 Md. App. 311, 264 A.2d 130 (1970); *Parker v. State,* 7 Md. App. 167, 254 A.2d 381 (1969), *cert. denied,* 256 Md. 747 (1970), *cert. denied,* 402 U.S. 984 (1971); *Frazier v. State,* 5 Md. App. 88, 245 A.2d 614 (1968); *Barnes v. State,* 5 Md. App. 144, 245 A.2d 626 (1968); *Darby v. State,* 3 Md. App. 407, 239 A.2d 584 (1968).

Article 27, §§ 488 and 486 do not define the crime of robbery but merely provide a statutory penalty for common law robbery. Included in the sections are the penalty for the accessory before the fact to the crime of robbery and a statutory penalty more severe when the robbery or attempted robbery is committed with a dangerous or deadly weapon. *Butina v. State,* 4 Md. App. 312, 242 A.2d 819 (1968); *Gray v. State, supra; Phenious v. State, supra.*

In *Whack v. State,* 288 Md. 137, 416 A.2d 265 (1980), *appeal dismissed,* 450 U.S. 990 (1981), the Court held that separate sentences may be imposed for robbery with a deadly weapon (Art. 27, § 488) and use of a handgun in the commission of a felony (Art. 27, § 36B(d)) when both convictions were based upon a single act of robbery with a handgun. Reviewing the legislative history, the Court stated that the legislature would have specifically excepted "handguns" from Art. 27, § 488 if such weapons were not intended to be included. Therefore, when the weapon used in a robbery is a handgun, it is viewed as a further aggravating factor authorizing the additional penalty under § 36B(d).

In light of *Whack v. State, supra,* the Court has held that there was no error in the imposition of consecutive sentences for the robbery with a deadly weapon and using a handgun in commission of a crime of violence. *Calhoun v. State,* 46 Md. App. 478, 418 A.2d 1241, 1245 (1980).

Also, consecutive sentences are permitted for assault with intent to murder and attempted armed robbery arising from the same transaction. *Johnson v. No. 1872,* 56 Md. App. 205, 467 A.2d 544 (1983). See also *Loud v. State,* 63 Md. App. 702, 493 A.2d 1092 (1985). In *Thomas v. Warden,* 683 F.2d 83 (4th Cir.), *cert. denied,* 459 U.S. 1042 (1982), the Court held that the Maryland legislature intended to allow multiple prosecution and sentencing in armed robbery cases involving property owned by a single entity where property is taken from the lawful possession of multiple custodians of discrete portions of the property and where each custodian is put under individual armed threat in the course of the taking.

The Court has stated that it is not always necessary that tangible evidence be physically admitted at a trial. In *Holle v. State,* 26 Md. App. 267, 337 A.2d 163, 166 (1975), the Court interposed the following hypothetical to illustrate this principle:

> For example, if a felon commits a robbery with a deadly weapon, disposes of it before being apprehended, and it is not recovered, the *corpus delicti* of the crime may be proved on the testimony of the victim or an eyewitness that the robber used such a weapon. Even when evidence is available it need not be physically offered .... In such instances, the description of the tangible evidence is the equivalent of the physical production of the evidence, and the failure to produce it goes at most to the weight of the evidence and the credibility of the witness describing it.

Simple robbery is treated as the lesser included offense of armed robbery when both offenses are charged and based on the same acts. *Sweetwine v. State,* 288 Md. 199, 421 A.2d 60, *cert. denied,* 101 S. Ct. 579 (1980).

It would not be prejudicial error for a judge to dismiss assault, robbery and attempt counts for an indictment after finding the defendant guilty of robbery with a deadly weapon because of the doctrine of merger as applied to lesser included offenses. *McDuffie v. State,* 12 Md. App. 264, 278 A.2d 307 (1971). See also *Tender v. State,* 2 Md. App. 692, 237 A.2d 65 (1968).

Pursuant to Art. 27, § 488, a person convicted of robbery or attempt to rob with a dangerous or deadly weapon, or accessory thereto, shall restore to the owner the thing robbed or taken, or pay full value, and be sentenced to imprisonment for not more than twenty years.

See Instruction, § 4.82, Robbery, *supra.*

§ 4.84. Shoplifting.

COMMENT: COMMON LAW PRIOR TO REPEAL

The crime termed "shoplifting" under Maryland Ann. Code, Art. 27, § 551A has been repealed and incorporated into the consolidated theft crimes enacted by Acts 1978, ch. 849. The revision consists of a single consolidated offense designated as "Theft."

The crime now is covered by Art. 27, § 342(a) and (b). See Instructions: § 4.91, Theft — By unauthorized control, and § 4.92, Theft — By deception, *infra*. These two instructions, patterned after the revised theft offenses, include limited commentary drawn upon case law of other jurisdictions that have undertaken similar revisions of their theft laws. This Comment, based upon the former crime of shoplifting, has been retained to give guidance to possible statutory interpretations of the legislation as to the prior common law.

Former Art. 27, § 551A(d) set forth the penalties for persons convicted of the crime of shoplifting. A violation of subsection (a) or (b) of the section with goods valued at $100 or more was a felony punishable by restitution and a fine of not more than $1,000, or a prison term of not more than three years. If the violation occurred with goods valued at less than $100, the defendant was guilty of a misdemeanor; he still had to make restitution, but he might not be fined more than $100 and imprisoned for more than eighteen months.

Subsection (g) of Art. 27, § 551A did not repeal the larceny laws; thus, there was no inconsistency in allowing either a conviction for larceny or one under § 551A for theft of goods from a mercantile establishment. *Saunders v. State,* 8 Md. App. 143, 258 A.2d 776 (1969).

Though it might be that concealing goods in a mercantile establishment would, under certain circumstances, support the rational inference that a person concealing goods intended to appropriate them, to support such an inference it was necessary that the fact of concealment by the accused be first established. *Barnes v. State,* 31 Md. App. 25, 354 A.2d 499 (1976). In *Barnes,* the conviction of the appellant was reversed due to the insufficiency of the evidence concerning the concealment of the merchandise.

§ 4.85. Trespass.

Trespass, in general, is the presence upon the property of another after being notified by the owner or one under his authority to keep off the premises where there is no *bona fide* claim of right to remain.

(a) Upon private land or vessel (Article 27, § 577)

Wanton trespass upon private land or vessel is a criminal offense.

In order for a person to be guilty of this offense, the State must prove beyond a reasonable doubt: (a) a wanton trespass by the defendant on the private property of another person, namely, __________ (*specify the nature of the property, such as land, premises or private property, boat or other marine vessel*); and, (b) the defendant remained upon, entered upon or crossed over the property after notice to leave the property was given by a person in possession or by his duly authorized agent.

A wanton trespass is extreme recklessness and utter disregard for the property rights of another. You are instructed that if the defendant had a *bona fide* claim of right to remain on the property, there is no wanton trespass to the property rights of another. In the absence of a *bona fide* claim of right to remain on the property, remaining on the premises after due notice has been received may constitute a wanton trespass.

In order to constitute the offense of trespass after warning, it is necessary for the State to prove that a warning to leave the premises was given by a person in possession or by his duly authorized agent.

(b) Refusal to leave public buildings (Article 27, § 577A)

It is an offense to refuse to leave a public building or grounds on request to do so.

In order for a defendant to be guilty of this offense the State must prove beyond a reasonable doubt that: (1) the defendant refused or failed to leave; (2) a public building or grounds or a specific part of the property; (3) after being directed to do so by a regularly employed guard, watchman or other authorized employee of the public agency or institution owning, operating or maintaining the building or property; and (4) the building, grounds, or a specific part of the property was regularly closed to the public during this time and the defendant had no lawful business to pursue at such place [or *if during normal business hours* the defendant was acting in a manner disruptive of and disturbing to the conduct of normal business by such agency or institution].

The term "lawful business" means any constitutionally protected activity and not the more restricted meaning often given to the word "business." Guilt must be based on the actual lack of lawful business, not on the apparent lack of lawful business.

COMMENT

Maryland Ann. Code, Art. 27, §§ 576 to 577B, 579A, 579B and 580 deal with the offense of trespass.

Article 27, § 576, trespass on posted property, is a misdemeanor and punishable by a fine not exceeding $500 or imprisonment not exceeding three months or both. Under this section the notice, *i.e.,* the posting must have been made in a conspicuous manner. The proceedings must be initiated by the landowner or tenant of the property unlawfully entered.

Article 27, § 577, wanton trespass upon private land or vessel, is a misdemeanor and punishable by a fine of not more than $500. The word "wanton" means "characterized by extreme recklessness and utter disregard for the rights of others." *Dennis v. Baltimore Transit Co.,* 189 Md. 610, 56 A.2d 813, 817 (1948). It is not a violation if the entry upon or crossing over the land is done under a *bona fide* claim or right of ownership of such land. See *Krauss v. State,* 216 Md. 369, 140 A.2d 653 (1958).

When the Legislature passed the State public accommodations act (Art. 49B, § 11), it brought about a fundamental change in

Article 27, § 577, because it made lawful a variety of situations which would have been unlawful before its enactment. *Bell v. State,* 236 Md. 356, 204 A.2d 54 (1964).

Article 27, § 577A, refusing to leave public buildings or grounds upon request, is a misdemeanor and punishable by a fine of $1000 and/or imprisonment for up to six months. The language of this section which permits the request to be made "if a reasonable man can say that the other has no apparent lawful business to pursue at such place" has withstood a constitutional attack on due process grounds. *Anderson v. State,* 12 Md. App. 186, 278 A.2d 439 (1971).

In *Anderson v. State, supra* at 192-93, 278 A.2d at 442-43, the Court construed the meaning of the phrase in § 577A, "if the surrounding circumstances are such as to indicate to a reasonable man that such person has no apparent lawful business to pursue at such place," as follows:

> As we construe the statute, an authorized employee may properly request a person to leave a public building during those hours of the day or night when it is regularly closed to the public if the surrounding circumstances are such as to indicate to a reasonable man that the person has no apparent lawful business to pursue. This "lawful business" clause is a requirement for the notice rather than for the guilt of the offense. In other words, although an effective notice may be given if the surrounding circumstances are such as to indicate to a reasonable man that the person notified had no apparent lawful business to pursue, the criterion for guilt upon failure to obey the notice is that the person, in fact, had no lawful business to pursue. This construction obviates the absurd result that a person shown to have actual business to pursue could be convicted of the offense because the surrounding circumstances at the time of the notice were such as to indicate to a reasonable man that he apparently did not. We find the clear legislative intent to be that guilt be predicated not on apparent but actual lack of lawful business.

Article 27, § 577B, trespass upon grounds of University of Maryland, State colleges, community colleges or any public school, was repealed in 1978. Violation was a misdemeanor punishable by a fine of up to $1000 and/or imprisonment of up to six months. Under the section, administrative personnel and staff were deemed competent to deny access to the buildings or grounds of the institution to persons who were not *bona fide,* currently registered students, staff or faculty at the institution and who had no lawful business to pursue at the institution, or who were acting in a manner disruptive or disturbing to the normal educational functions of the school. *Kirstel v. State,* 13 Md. App. 482, 284 A.2d 12 (1971). Currently, a similar provision is found at Maryland Ann. Code, Education, § 26-102.

Article 27, § 579A, (entering or remaining in stable area of race track after notice) is a misdemeanor punishable by a fine of up to $1,000 and/or imprisonment of not more than six months. Article 27, § 579B proscribes entering upon the cultivated land of another without permission of the owner or agent of the owner. "Cultivated land" means land which has been cleared of its natural vegetation and is presently planted with a crop or orchard. This provision requires a "wanton entry" and, hence, does not apply to persons who enter the land seeking to provide a lawful service or to persons entering the land under color of law or title. This offense is a misdemeanor punishable by a fine of not more than $500.00.

Article 27, § 580 (trespass in order to look into windows, etc.) is a misdemeanor punishable by a fine of not more than $50 and/or imprisonment for not more than thirty days.

In *State v. Schuller,* 280 Md. 305, 372 A.2d 1076 (1977), the issue presented to the Court was the constitutionality of Art. 27, § 580A, which prohibits picketing "before or about the residence or dwelling place of any individual." There was an exemption from this prohibition for picketing in connection with labor disputes. The Court held the statute unconstitutionally overbroad because of its blanket prohibition on residential picketing. As an alternative ground for the decision, the Court held the statute violative of the equal protection clause. That decision was based on the Court's finding that the exemption for labor disputes constituted the creation of an impermissible distinction based on the content of the expression.

§ 4.86. Unlawful use of telephone.

Misuse of telephone facilities or equipment can be a criminal offense. It is a crime where a person makes repeated telephone calls with the intent to annoy, abuse, torment, harass or embarrass one or more persons.

In order for the defendant to be found guilty of this offense, the State must prove beyond a reasonable doubt that: (1) the defendant did make repeated telephone calls to ____________ (*name of victim(s)*) and (2) the defendant did so with the specific intent to annoy, abuse, torment, harass or embarrass.

In determining whether repeated calls were made with the necessary specific intent, possible factors to consider are: (1) the number of telephone calls made by the defendant; (2) whether the telephone calls were made anonymously; (3) whether the defendant made any threats of bodily harm; (4) whether the telephone calls were made at regular hours; and (5) any evidence of the motivation of the defendant, as well as other factors. The weight to be given to any factor, if present, is solely for your determination in relation to all of the evidence in the case.

COMMENT

In *Caldwell v. State,* 26 Md. App. 94, 337 A.2d 476 (1975), the Court held that the evidence was insufficient to sustain a conviction for unlawful use of a telephone under Maryland Ann. Code, Art. 27, § 555A since specific intent "to annoy, abuse, torment, harass or embarrass" could not be determined. The appellant had displayed no desire to remain anonymous, had made a total of two calls each during regular hours and had made no threats of bodily harm.

In addition to the above, the appellant in *Caldwell* argued that the statute was unconstitutionally vague, a violation of his right to due process under the fourteenth amendment to the United States Constitution and Article 23 of the Maryland Declaration of Rights. The Court rejected that argument, holding that Art. 27, § 555A falls within the "specific intent exception" to the vagueness doctrine. The Court cited *Papachristou v. City of Jacksonville,* 405 U.S. 156, 92 S. Ct. 839, 31 L. Ed. 2d 110 (1972) and *Screws v. United States,* 425 U.S. 91, 65 S. Ct. 1031, 89 L. Ed. 1496 (1945). The constitutionality of the statute was again attacked, this time on first amendment grounds, in *Von Lusch v. State,* 39 Md. App. 517, 387 A.2d 306 (1978). The Court rejected the appellant's argument, stating:

> The Maryland statute does not prohibit speech or communication as such. It simply protects one from the harassment and annoyance of having his own telephone used in an abusive fashion by an unwanted intruder upon his privacy. Citizens have a right to speak. Citizens also have a right not to be forced to listen. Freedom of speech does not encompass the right to abuse the telephone with the specific intent to annoy and to harass the recipient of the call.

Id. at 525, 387 A.2d at 310. There are two other theories of telephone misuse not included in the above instruction. Article 27, § 555A (1) provides that it is unlawful to use a telephone "for an anonymous call or calls if in a manner reasonably to be expected to annoy, abuse, torment, harass, or embarrass one or more persons." Article 27, § 555A (3) provides that it is unlawful to use a telephone "for any comment, request, suggestion or proposal which is obscene, lewd, lascivious, filthy, or indecent."

Unlawful use of a telephone is a misdemeanor. The penalty is a fine of not more than $500 or imprisonment for not more than three years or both.

G. Theft and Bad Check Offenses

(1) Theft Offenses

Overview and Introductory Comment

Effective July 1, 1979, the Maryland General Assembly enacted a substantive revision of the laws relating to bad check offenses and various theft crimes. See 1978 Acts, ch. 849 and Maryland Ann. Code, Art. 27, §§ 140 to 145, 340 to 344.

As a result of the enactment, a number of the instructions carried in the first edition of this book have been superseded. However, to provide guidance for possible statutory interpretations of the legislation as related to prior common law, the Comments under the former instructions have been retained. The subjects of the Comments and sections where they appear are as follows: Embezzlement, § 4.64; False pretenses, § 4.67; Larceny, § 4.71; Larceny after trust, § 4.72; Receiving stolen goods, § 4.79; and Shoplifting, § 4.84.

The theft crimes covered by the revised laws are offenses which may be described as "larceny related" and do not involve elements of coercion. Crimes such as burglary, robbery and extortion were not within the scope of the 1978 Act.

The crimes revised by the 1978 Act have been consolidated and placed under a new subheading entitled "Theft." The laws proscribe certain acts pertaining to theft of property, labor, and services; provide certain defenses and presumptions; and specify applicable penalties.

The concept of consolidation has been characterized by Herbert Wechsler as the effort "to draw a clear and rational line between forbidden and permitted acquisition and to end acquittals that are based on minor technicalities." Wechsler, *Codification of Criminal Law in the United States: The Model Penal Code,* 68 Colum. L. Rev. 1425, 1448 (1968). Consolidation has been the natural response of states to the undisciplined proliferation of theft-type offenses. For example, Maryland statutes contained a plethora of special sections dealing with narrowly defined instances of conduct. This resulted in difficulties in discovering the applicable law on which to base criminal charges as well as confusion due to the numerous parallel statutes. The 1978 Act seeks to eliminate those technical distinctions contained in the larceny related offenses.

Some of the highlights of the consolidated theft offenses include:

1. Theft by unauthorized control *does not* require an intent to *permanently* deprive a person of property in order for the offense of theft to be committed since the word "deprive" as defined in the statute does not require permanent taking.

(See Instruction, § 4.91, Theft — By unauthorized control, *infra.*)

2. "Criminal possession" has been merged with the single crime of "theft" as a broad replacement for the crime of "receiving stolen property." (See Instruction, § 4.93, Theft — By possessing stolen property, *infra.*)

3. A special section designed to be of assistance in prosecuting "professional fences." The revised statute provides that the requisite mental element may be inferred from the existence of certain enumerated facts. (See Instruction, § 4.93, Theft — By possessing stolen property, *infra.*)

4. A subsection which provides that wrongfully obtaining services is an aspect of the consolidated crime of theft. (See Instruction, § 4.95, Theft — Of services, *infra.*)

5. The term "obtain" is used in relation to property and services thereby eliminating what formerly was the distinction between larceny (a trespassory taking in which mere possession was obtained) and false pretenses (obtaining title as well as possession). (See Instruction, § 4.91, Theft — By unauthorized control, *infra.*)

6. The broad definition of the term "exerts control" not only includes asportation (taking, carrying away), but also covers instances where the perpetrator rightfully has possession and unlawfully takes or transfers some interest held by another (e.g., acts formerly constituting embezzlement and larceny after trust). (See Instruction, § 4.91, Theft — By unauthorized control, *infra.*)

A significant Maryland opinion, *Craddock v. State,* 64 Md. App. 269, 494 A.2d 971 (1985), defining the purpose of the revised theft offense, is discussed in the comments following Instruction, § 4.91, Theft — By unauthorized control, *infra.*

The Maryland General Assembly intended the law (Acts 1978, ch. 849) to be construed and applied prospectively. The provisions of the Act apply to offenses committed on or after the effective date of July 1, 1979. This prospective application was necessary to avoid the constitutional prohibition against *ex post facto* laws.

Moreover, the repeal or amendment by the Act of crimes and offenses existing prior to its effective date does not preclude the prosecution of persons who, prior to such date, committed crimes and offenses as those crimes and offenses then existed. Thus, instructions that have been superseded continue to have limited application.

The following Table shows the relationship between theft offenses that have been repealed (first column of citations) and the consolidated theft provisions (second column of citations) revised and enacted in 1978.

Comparative Table

Consolidation of Maryland Theft-Related Offenses*

Citation Art./Sec. Repealed	Description	Citation Art./Sec. Revised	Notes and Comments
27/128	Embezzlement by bank president or director	27/342(a) & (b)	See definition of "obtain" (27/340(f)) & "exerts control" (27/340(d))
27/129	Embezzlement by cashier, servant, etc.	27/342(a) & (b)	See definition of "obtain" (27/340(f)) & "exerts control" (27/340(d))
27/131	Embezzlement by insurance agent	27/342(a) & (b)	See definition of "obtain" (27/340(f)) & "exerts control" (27/340(d))
27/138	Embezzlement by public official	27/342(a) & (b)	
27/140	False pretenses	27/342(b)	See definition of "deception" (27/340(b))
27/141	Obtaining goods based on false credit rating	27/342(b)	See definition of "deception" (27/340(b))

*Source: Joint Subcommittee on Theft Related Offenses, Maryland General Assembly, Revision of Maryland Theft Laws and Bad Check Laws, ch. 849 (1978), Appendix, Pages 128-31. Some items of limited applicability (*e.g.*, "horse stealing," "master of vessel neglecting or refusing to pay share of cargo profits to vessel's owner") were deleted.

Citation Art./Sec. Repealed	Description	Citation Art./Sec. Revised	Notes and Comments
27/143	Theft of services	27/342(a) & (b)	See definition of "obtain" (27/340(f)) & "deception" (27/340(b)). Note definition of "property" (27/340(h)) includes "services"
27/145	Restitution for embezzled goods	27/342(e)	See 27/342(f) which provides for restoring the property taken to the owner
27/146	Obtaining registration of animal by false pretense	27/342(b)	Note definition of "deception" (27/340(b)). Definition of "property" (27/340(h)) includes written instruments representing something of value to the owner
27/147	Obtaining loan of money by misrepresentation of pecuniary responsibility	27/342(b)	
27/149A	Obtaining registration of animal or false pedigree by false pretense	27/342(b)	
27/161	Obtaining lodging by false pretense	27/342(a) & (b)	Note definition of "property" (27/340(h)) includes services
27/162	Obtaining food, beverage, or accommodations by false pretense	27/342(a) & (b)	
27/162A	Obtaining food, lodging, etc., in Charles County	27/342(a) & (b)	
27/205	Theft of motor vehicle by false representation	27/342(b)	See definition of "deception" (27/340(b))

Citation Art./Sec. Repealed	Description	Citation Art./Sec. Revised	Notes and Comments
27/210	Failure to return leased property	27/342(a)	
27/340	Larceny of $100 or greater	27/342(a)	See penalty (27/342(f)(1))
27/341	Larceny—less than $100	27/342(a)	See penalty (27/342(f)(2))
27/343A	Stealing from coin-operated machine	27/342(a) & (b)	See definition of "coin machine" (27/340(a)) & also definition of "deception" (27/340(b)(1)(v) & also definition of "slug" (27/340(j))
27/344	Stealing agricultural products	27/342(a)	Note definition of "property" (27/340(h)) includes, by way of illustration, "things growing on or affixed to, or found on land"
27/345	Stealing dog or cat	27/342(a)	Note definition of "property" (27/340(h)) includes, by way of illustration, "animals ... which ordinarily are kept in a state of confinement"
27/347	Receiving or purchase of stolen merchandise	27/342(c)	
27/351	Stealing pipes, water fixtures or gas fixtures or other articles or other articles of value attached to a warehouse, dwelling house, etc.	27/342(a)	
27/353	Larceny after trust	27/342(a)	

Citation Art./Sec. Repealed	Description	Citation Art./Sec. Revised	Notes and Comments
27/466	Receiving stolen goods, money, etc., having a value of $100 or greater	27/342(c)	See penalty (27/342(f)(1))
27/467	Receiving stolen goods, money, etc., having a value of less than $100	27/342(c)	See penalty (27/342(f)(2))
27/551A	Shoplifting	27/342(a) & (b)	Note "deception" includes alteration of price tag or label (27/340(b)(1)(vi)). See that merchant & employee immunity as contained in ... 27/551A(c) is repealed
27/555	Refusing to pay transportation fare	27/342(a) & (b)	Definition of "property" includes, by way of illustration, "transportation services" (27/340(i)(2))

The following instructions, §§ 4.91 to 4.96, use the basic language and format of the statutory offenses. The Comments thereunder are divided into two parts. The first part reproduces with minor modifications relevant parts of Official Commentary of the Joint Subcommittee on Theft Related Offenses of the Maryland General Assembly. This valuable work is available in pamphlet form: Joint Subcommittee on Theft Related Offenses, *Revision of the Maryland Theft Laws and Bad Check Laws,* Chapter 849, (1978). Published by the Maryland General Assembly, Department of Legislative Reference, 90 State Circle, Annapolis, Maryland 21401, the pamphlet includes some information that has not been reproduced here. A second printing was issued in April, 1979. Additional materials and cross-references added by the author of this book are contained in brackets.

The Maryland theft offenses draw heavily upon Illinois statutory provisions in effect since January 1, 1962. The Comments following the official commentary portions offer discussions of Illinois cases decided prior to the date of the Maryland revision with the thought that they present a useful guide to understanding the statutes and serve to supplement the notes on Maryland decisions written since 1979.

Note that the selections from the office commentary and the Comment following Instruction, § 4.91, Theft — By unauthorized control, include extensive discussion of elements of the general theft offense which are not repeated in the Comments following the other instructions in this subpart.

§ 4.91. Theft — By unauthorized control.

The defendant has been charged with theft of [$300 or more] [less than $300].

In order for the defendant to be guilty of this offense the State must prove beyond a reasonable doubt that: (1) __________ (*insert name of owner*) was the owner of certain property, namely __________ (*list item(s) of property*); (2) the defendant willfully or knowingly obtained control, or exerted control, which is unauthorized, over the property; and (3) [the defendant had the purpose of depriving the owner of the property] [the defendant willfully or knowingly used, concealed or abandoned the property in such a manner as to deprive the owner of the property] [the defendant used, concealed or abandoned the property knowing the use, concealment or abandonment probably would deprive the owner of the property].

[The State must also prove beyond a reasonable doubt that the value of the property (or services) was $300 or more. If the State does not prove beyond a reasonable doubt that the value of the property (or services) was $300 or more, but that the property (or services) had some value, you must then find that the property (or services) had a value of less than $300.] *or*

[The defendant has been charged with theft of less than $300. You do not have to determine the exact value of the property (or services) but the State must prove beyond a reasonable doubt that the property (or services) had some value.]

The term "owner" means a person, *other than the offender,* who has any interest in the property, including mere possession, without whose consent the defendant has no authority to exert control over the property. [The owner's interest in the property may be lawful or unlawful; even a person who unlawfully possesses property may occupy the position of owner.]

The term "willfully" means an act done with deliberate intention for which there is no reasonable excuse.

The term "knowingly" means that a person is aware of his conduct or the existing circumstances. A person acts knowingly when such person is practically certain of the results of his conduct. A person has knowledge of the existence of a fact when he is practically certain of its existence. The term "knowingly" does not include accident, mistake, negligence or recklessness.

The term "obtain" means [in relation to property, to bring about a transfer of interest or possession, whether to the defendant or to another] [in relation to services, to secure the performance of the services].

The phrase "exerts control" includes, but is not limited to, the taking, carrying away, appropriating to one's own use, or sale, conveyance, transfer of title to, interest in, or possession of property. [Thus, someone other than the person who initiates the wrongful taking or acquisition of property may be guilty of theft.] ["Exerts control" does not include trespassing on the land of another or occupying without authorization the land of another.]

The word "deprive" means the withholding of property of another (permanently) (for such a period as to appropriate a portion of its value) (with the purpose to restore it only upon payment of reward or other compensation) (to dispose of the property and use or deal with the property as to make it unlikely that the owner will recover it).

The term "property" means anything of value. It includes but is not limited to __________ *(insert relevant categories from list of items appearing in Official Commentary, this section, infra).*

[The term "services" includes, but is not limited to (labor services) (professional services) (telecommunications) (public utilities) (toll facilities) (transportation services) (lodging) (entertainment) (restaurant services) (the use of equipment, including, but not limited to, computers and other data processing equipment).]

[In the absence of a reasonable explanation of such possession the exclusive possession of property recently stolen allows you to infer that the person in possession [did steal such property] [was a receiver of stolen property]. Thus, if the property was found in possession of the defendant and if the evidence demonstrates that: (1) the property was recently stolen; (2) the possession is unexplained; and (3) the possession was exclusive, then an inference of fact may arise that the defendant [did steal such property] [was a receiver of stolen property].]

The term "value" means the market value of the property (or services) at the time and place of the crime, [or if the market value cannot be satisfactorily ascertained, the cost of the replacement of the property within a reasonable time after the crime].

[The term "value" in the case of certain written instruments that do not have a readily ascertainable market value, whether or not they have been issued or delivered, shall be measured as follows: [The value of an instrument constituting evidence of debt such as a check, draft, or promissory note shall be determined as the amount due or collectible. This figure ordinarily is the face amount of the indebtedness less any portion which has been satisfied.] [The value of an instrument which creates, releases, discharges or otherwise affects any valuable legal right, privilege or obligation shall be determined as the amount of economic loss which the owner of the instrument might reasonably suffer by virtue of the loss of the instrument.] [If the property of the theft is a trade secret, which does not have a readily ascertainable market value, its value shall be deemed any reasonable value representing the damage to the owner suffered by reason of losing an advantage over those who do not know of or use the trade secret].]

[If you find that the theft has been committed as one scheme or continuing course of conduct, whether from the same or several sources, you may consider the conduct as one offense and total the value of the property or services in determining whether the theft is more or less than $300.]

[In a prosecution for the offense of theft, it is a defense that: __________ [the defendant acted under a good faith claim of right to the property involved] [the defendant acted in honest belief that he had the right to obtain or exert control over the property as he did] [the property involved was that of the defendant's spouse, unless the defendant and the defendant's spouse were not living together as husband and wife and were living in separate abodes at the time of the alleged theft] [the defendant rightfully knew the trade secret or that it was available to him from a source other than the owner of the trade secret].]

[*Where the offense charge is felony theft and there is some evidence of misdemeanor theft:* Your verdict must take one of three forms. If you conclude beyond a reasonable doubt that the State has proved each of the elements of the offense, and you also find beyond a reasonable doubt that the value of the property (or services) was $300 or more, your verdict should be "guilty of theft of $300 or more". If you conclude beyond a reasonable doubt that the State has proved each of the elements of the offense of theft and you are unable to determine, beyond a reasonable doubt, whether the value of property (or services) was more or less than $300 or if you determine that the value of the property (or services) was some value less than $300, your verdict should be "guilty of theft of less than $300." If you are not convinced beyond a reasonable doubt that the State has proved each and every element of the offense, you must find the defendant not guilty.]

OFFICIAL COMMENTARY

Joint Subcommittee on Theft Related Offenses, Maryland General Assembly, *Revision of Maryland Theft Laws and Bad Check Laws,* ch. 849 (1978)

Theft — In general.

This subsection [Art. 27, § 342(a)] presents one set of circumstances which constitutes the offense of "theft." Two elements are required by this subsection. They are (1) a "knowing" or willful exertion of control or the obtaining of control (inadvertent or negligent exertion or obtainment of control is not punishable), and (2) a purpose to "deprive" (the mental element prevalent in most thefts).

The required mental state (having a purpose to deprive) is usually proven by the offender's disposition of the property. However, to cover those instances where the purpose to deprive is more difficult to prove (*e.g.*, taking and abandonment of an automobile) paragraphs (2) and (3) have been provided.

Shoplifting and receiving stolen property.

Most of the activities which previously constituted shoplifting will now be a theft offense through a violation of this subsection [Art. 27, § 342(c)]. The Subcommittee was of the opinion that shoplifting had become a crime that was not regarded seriously by many persons and was achieving an almost socially acceptable status. It was therefore decided that the sterile label of shoplifting would be purged from the Code and that the activities constituting shoplifting would be denominated as "theft." A perpetrator of these activities would then be known as a "thief" — a designation which properly reflects the character of this crime and the class of offender with whom he should be categorized.

In addition, because this subsection makes no distinction concerning the way the property was obtained, it could be used to prosecute instances of "receiving stolen property." However, a receiving stolen property offense would be more appropriately prosecuted under the criminal possession provision. [See Instruction, § 4.93, Theft—By possessing stolen property, *infra.*]

Knowingly.

All instances of the offense of theft require that the perpetrator obtains, exerts control over, or possesses the property, or obtains services "knowingly." The offense of theft cannot be committed inadvertently or negligently.

The words used in this subsection [Art. 27, § 340(e)] to describe "knowingly" preclude imputing negligent or reckless meaning to that term. It is required that, in order for a person to act "knowingly," he must be "practically certain" that the result will be caused by his conduct. The use of the words "practically certain" were chosen since these words connote a high degree of certainty. The words are used in Model Penal Code § 2.02 (2) (b) (Official Draft 1962). The Comment to this Section in Model Penal Code § 2.02, Comment at 125 (Tent. Draft No. 4, 1955) points out the distinction between acting knowingly and acting recklessly. It is the intent of this subsection that the meaning be conveyed that to act "knowingly" requires something more than reckless conduct. Therefore, one who acts recklessly with regard to property may be guilty of some crime, but he is not guilty of theft by virtue of his reckless conduct.

In keeping with this intent that to act "knowingly" requires a high degree of certainty (or at least more than reckless or negligent conduct), and to achieve uniformity of meaning, the phrase "aware of a high probability" should be changed to "practically certain."

Obtain.

The word "obtain" [Art. 27, § 340(f)] describes a manner in which a person can steal property or services. It applies to instances where there is a constructive acquisition of the property. Asportation, or the carrying away of property, is not within the meaning of "obtain." Therefore, this term does not require the perpetrator to personally make the transfer, he need only effect the transfer or cause it to happen.

The most common use of this word will be in cases where the theft is accomplished by deception. The thief does not actually take the property, he merely accepts its transfer to him (or some third person); the transfer having been made as a result of some misrepresentation.

This definition also eliminates what formerly was the distinction between larceny (a trespassory taking in which mere possession was obtained) and false pretenses (obtaining title as well as possession). Under the terms of this definition it makes no difference whether mere possession or some interest (*e.g.,* title) is obtained.

Exerts control.

This subsection [Art. 27, § 340(d)] is not a strict definition of the words "exerts control." It is an illustration of what the phrase "includes, but is not limited to." It is, therefore, a guide to assist in providing meaning to these words.

As the text of this subsection illustrates, asportation ("taking, carrying away") is within the meaning of these words. Also covered are instances where the perpetrator rightfully has possession and unlawfully takes or transfers some interest held by another (*e.g.,* acts formerly constituting embezzlement and larceny after trust). Therefore, these words embrace the broad scope of situations in which the offender personally engages in the taking or transfer of (1) possession or (2) some interest in the property.

Owner.

The term "owner" [Art. 27, § 340(g)] has an important definition. When used in the text of Art. 27, § 342, it indicates whose property a person may not obtain or exert control over. As stated by this definition, even a person who unlawfully possesses property (*e.g.,* a thief) occupies the status of an "owner" as against another person who has no authority to exert control over the property without the consent of the person who has the status of an "owner." Briefly stated, this gives ownership rights in property to a thief as against another thief who would deprive him of the property. This concept is amplified in the defenses provided where it is made clear that it is not a defense to the offense of theft that the property was taken from a person who had also obtained possession of the property by illegal means.

Deprive; intent to deprive.

The definition of "deprive" [Art. 27, § 340(c)] does not require that there be an intention to withhold the property permanently. The property need only be withheld from the owner "for such a period as to appropriate a portion of its value." Because this language does not require a permanent or prolonged period of deprivation, this definition is applicable to what is known as "unauthorized use" offenses.

The requisite mental state of having an intent to deprive is most frequently proved by the defendant's handling of the property. To enhance the prospect of proving this mental state when the purpose to deprive is more difficult to prove, part (4) ["to dispose of the property and use or deal with the property so as to make it unlikely that the owner will recover it"] has been added to the definition.

Property.

The term "property" [Art. 27, § 340(h)] when used in these instructions means anything of value. "Property" includes, but is not limited to, the following:

(1) Real estate;

(2) Money;

(3) Commercial instruments;

(4) Admission or transportation tickets;

(5) Written instruments representing or embodying rights concerning anything of value, or services, or anything otherwise of value to the owner;

(6) Things growing on or affixed to, or found on land, or part of or affixed to any building;

(7) Electricity, gas, and water;

(8) Birds, animals, and fish which ordinarily are kept in a state of confinement;

(9) Food and drink;

(10) Samples, cultures, micro-organisms, specimens;

(11) Records, recordings, documents, blueprints, drawings, maps, and whole or partial copies, descriptions, photographs, prototypes or models thereof; or any other articles, materials, devices, substances, and whole or partial copies, descriptions, photographs, prototypes, or models thereof which represent evidence, reflect or record secret scientific, technical, merchandising production or management information, design process, procedure, formula, invention, trade secret, or improvement;

(12) Financial instruments, information, electronically produced data, computer software and programs in either machine or human readable form, and other tangible or intangible items of value.

This subsection brings acts in relation to real property within the offense of theft. This is accomplished because "real estate" is included in the meaning of "property." Because of the broad language of this subsection it was thought possible that it could be interpreted to prosecute trespassers and squatters as thieves. In order to avoid this result, the disclaimer [Art. 27, § 340(d), definition of "exerts control"] was added to exclude trespassers and squatters from its meaning. This exclusion was in keeping with the policy recommended by the Maryland Commission on Criminal Law and is similar to a Texas statutory provision.

Value.

[Article 27, § 340(l) includes criteria for determining the value of stolen property or service where the property does not have a readily ascertainable market value.] The basic formula for determining value is by reference to the market value of the property or services. Using market value as an index of value is in keeping with the present basis of determining value. As was stated in *Jewell v. State,* 216 Md. 110, 113, 139 A.2d 707, 708 (1958), "Generally, the market value ... and not its cost or its worth to the owner, is the proper basis of comparison to use in determining value in order to establish the grade of the offense."

Under the terms of this subsection, if the market value cannot be readily determined, the replacement cost will be the index for ascribing value. Special provisions are also provided for cases of written instruments and trade secrets when a readily ascertainable market value cannot be assigned. The method of determining the value of written instruments which constitute a debt (e.g., a check or promissory note) is the amount due or collectible (face amount). This basis of value is in conformity with the holding in *State v. Cassel,* 2 H & G 407, 410-11 (1828). Therein the Court stated, "By an express decision of this Court in *Towson v. The Havre de Grace Bank,* 6 H. & J. 53, bank notes are considered and treated as money; and it would, therefore, seem to be strange that no rule or principle is held to exist, by which a jury could not ascertain their value for the purpose of graduating the offense charged in the indictment. We think the true rule is to look for that purpose to the sum which upon the face of them they promise to pay." For further discussion of ascribing value to written instruments see *Felkner v. State,* 218 Md. 300, 308-11, 146 A.2d 424, 430-31 (1958).

Finally, if value cannot be determined to be an amount of $300 or greater (felony offense) or less than $300 (misdemeanor offense), the value shall be determined to be less than $300. This gives assurances that in borderline cases where it is difficult to impute the value as less than $300, or $300 or greater, the defendant will be subject, upon conviction, to the lesser penalty.

Aggregating separate acts of theft.

Article 27, § 340(l)(5), in a departure from the common law, provides that under certain circumstances the value of property may be aggregated for the purposes of determining the potential penalty, as follows: "When theft is committed in violation of this subheading pursuant to one scheme or continuing course of conduct, whether from the same or several sources, the conduct may be considered as one offense and the value of the property or services aggregated in determining whether the theft is a felony or a misdemeanor."

This paragraph allows aggregation of the value of stolen property or services in order to determine whether theft is a felony or a misdemeanor. In this manner, the total value of the property or services which are stolen in any one scheme or continuing course of conduct may be considered to decide if the cumulative amount taken warrants a misdemeanor or felony penalty. Although the value of property may be aggregated for the purposes of determining the potential penalty, the prosecution must still allege and prove each separate incident that is part of the aggregated offense.

The paragraph on aggregation was inserted on the basis that a person who steals property at different times from several persons and places, as part of a continuing scheme, has engaged in activity which is just as reprehensible as a person who steals an equal amount from a single person and place at one time. It is a marked departure from the common law which requires that the property be stolen from a single person at a single time and place. For a general discussion of this provision see Model Penal Code, § 206.15 (3), Comment (Tent. Draft No. 2, 1954).

Maine and Texas are among the states that have adopted aggregation provisions. In his article in the *Maine Law Review,* 28 Maine L. Rev. 13, 18-19 (1976), Peter G. Ballou refers to a number of "unsettled or unclear" points in these provisions. Below is an example of such points:

> 1. Does failure to prove one of the component criminal acts require acquittal on the whole count or should the fact-finder simply reduce the aggregated total?
> 2. Is the question of whether the crimes are sufficiently related to allow aggregation a question of law or fact?
> 3. Does a finding or ruling that the crimes are too unrelated to allow aggregation nevertheless permit conviction of one of the component crimes of the count or is dismissal or acquittal required?
> 4. To what does jeopardy attach?
> 5. Is failure to aggregate where there is one scheme fatal to any or all of the crimes charged separately?
> 6. Can a court, absent undue prejudice to the defendant, order that a single count be treated as separate crimes, or vice versa?

Presumptions and inferences.

[Article 27, § 343(d) provides: "All common law and evidentiary presumptions applicable on July 1, 1979 to offenses which are consolidated under the provisions of this subheading are also applicable to the offense of theft, unless specifically repealed or modified by the provisions of this subheading, or unless modified by court decisions rendered after July 1, 1979." Pursuant to this section, the instruction includes in brackets the inference that exclusive and unexplained possession of recently stolen property may give rise to an inference that the defendant did steal or receive stolen property. Query whether the word "inferences" should have been used in the statute rather than the word "presumptions." See Appendix V, The Impact of *Evans v. State:* Burdens of Proof, Presumptions and Inferences, *infra.*]

This subsection was inserted to ensure the common law and evidentiary presumptions which are applicable to offenses merged into the single offense of theft by this statute are continued in effect and are applicable to the newly created offense of theft. An example of one such presumption sought to be preserved by the language of this subsection is the presumption that possession of recently stolen property gives rise to the inference that the possessor is the thief or a receiver of stolen goods. The constitutionality of this particular presumption was upheld in *Dinkins v. State,* 29 Md. App. 577, 583, 349 A.2d 676, 681, *aff'd,* 278 Md. 238, 362 A.2d 91 (1976).

By merging the acts of receiving stolen goods and the acts constituting the actual stealing into a single offense (*i.e.,* theft) some confusion has been eliminated. Under Maryland case law, either of two inferences could arise if a person was found in possession of recently stolen goods. One inference was that the possessor was the thief, and the other inference was that the possessor was the receiver of stolen goods (see *Richardson v. State,* 398 F. Supp. 425 (D. Md. 1975)). [See also Comment, § 4.79, Receiving stolen goods, *supra,* and cases cited therein.] In some instances, courts were confounded by the dilemma of which inference to draw. However, now that the act of stealing and the act of receiving constitute a single offense (*i.e.,* theft), the confusion is eliminated.

In order to allow a measure of flexibility and to recognize changes made in presumptions, it is expressly provided that these common law and evidentiary presumptions may be modified by the provisions of this subheading or by court decisions rendered after July 1, 1979 (the effective date of the theft offense consolidation statute).

Defenses: claim of right; spousal immunity; and rightful knowledge of a trade secret.

As noted above, there are three types of defenses to the offense of theft. These defenses are: (1) claim of right, (2) spousal immunity, and (3) rightful knowledge or alternative availability of a trade secret.

Subparts (1) and (2) [Art. 27, § 343(c)] present the "claim of right defenses." As presently drafted, these defenses are only applicable to the offense of theft when "property" is involved. Some consideration will have to be given to extending these "claim of right" defenses to make them applicable to instances when a theft is committed involving services.

The claim of right defense springs from the notion that in cases of common-law larceny, the defendant must have had an intent to permanently deprive the owner of the property. If the defendant acted under a mistake as to his right to deal with the property, he could not be guilty of larceny. Similarly, if the defendant can produce evidence that he was acting under an honest belief he had a "claim of right," this will be weighed by the trier of the facts in resolving the issue of whether the defendant possessed the requisite *mens rea* to commit the offense of theft. The claim of right defense was referred to in dicta by the Court of Appeals in the case of *Saunders v. Mullinix,* 195 Md. 235, 72 A.2d 720 (1950). Therein, the Court stated, "It is a generally accepted rule in criminal prosecutions that one who either takes or retains the property of another without the latter's consent for a debt which he in good faith claims to be due him by the owner of the property is not guilty of larceny, because the existence of the debt or the *bona fide* belief of its existence shows a lack of felonious intent in the taking or detention of the property." *Id.* at 240, 72 A.2d at 722. [In *Sibert v. State,* 301 Md. 141, 482 A.2d 483 (1984), the Court noted that Art. 27, § 343(c)(1) does not define the phrase "claim of right," but this defense usually arises when a person asserts a right to the property on demand in satisfaction of a claim. An instruction that merely delineates the mental elements of theft by possession under Art. 27, 342(c) does not fairly cover the honest belief defense.]

The interspousal theft defense perpetuates the common-law concept that because a husband and wife are a unit they cannot steal from one another. By perpetuating this notion through this defense, it is hoped that the criminal law will not be used by spouses as a punitive tool against each other in domestic disputes. However, in cases where the spouses are not living together as man and wife, it was believed the attendant circumstances that often arise or accompany these situations warrant the adoption of a policy denying the availability of the interspousal defense.

A defense to the theft of trade secrets is also a part of this section. The basis of this defense is that the trade secret was not really a secret to the defendant. That is to say that the defendant either rightfully knew the secret or that it was available from some source other than the owner. [See § 4.96 — General instruction — "Rights of possession" and certain defenses applicable to theft offenses, *infra.* See also Comment, § 5.03, Claim of right, *infra.*]

[Under Article 27, § 343(c)(1)(2)(3), the defenses to the offense of theft refer to property and not to services. However, Article 27, § 340(h) defines property as "anything of value," which would seem to include services. Also, it is clear from the statutory scheme that theft of services is not a separate crime but merely one of the ways in which the crime of theft can be committed. For these reasons, Instruction, § 4.95, Theft — Of services, *infra,* includes these defenses as possible defenses to theft of services.]

Grading of theft offenses: penalties.

[Article 27, § 342(f) provides:

> (1) A person convicted of theft where the property or services that was the subject of the theft has a value of $300 or greater is guilty of a felony and shall restore the property taken to the owner or pay him the value of the property or services, and be fined not more than $1,000, or be imprisoned for not more than 15 years, or be both fined and imprisoned in the discretion of the court.

(2) A person convicted of theft where the property or services that was the subject of the theft has a value of less than $300 is guilty of a misdemeanor and shall restore the property taken to the owner to pay him the value of the property or services, and be fined not more than $500, or be imprisoned for not more than 18 months, or be both fined and imprisoned in the discretion of the court; however, all actions or prosecutions for theft where the property or services that was the subject of the theft has a value of less than $300 shall be commenced within 2 years after the commission of the offense.]

This subsection provides the penalties for theft. The penalties are applicable to thefts committed by taking property or services, and no variation in the penalty is provided on the basis of whether the object of the theft is property or services. The only criteria for determining the penalty is the value of the property or services that is the subject of the theft. However, the value of the stolen property, which is the factor determining whether the offense is a felony or a misdemeanor and consequently subjects the offender to a greater or lesser penalty, has been modified. Previously, it was a felony to steal *property* having a value of $100 or greater and a misdemeanor to steal *property* having a value of less than $100. Under this subsection, it is a felony to steal *property or services* having a value of $300 or greater and a misdemeanor to steal *property or services* having a value of less than $300.

The decisions to set the line between a felony and a misdemeanor at $300 was largely arbitrary and arrived at after a discussion of inflation and other factors which have increased the dollar value of both property and services. The same penalties and dollar value demarcating between a felony and a misdemeanor were established for bad check offenses.

COMMENT

(a) Theft — In General

As noted in the introductory comment to this subpart, the Maryland consolidated theft offenses draw upon the Illinois statutes. Many of the key provisions are identical. Consequently, a rich experience in terms of fairly well-developed case law is available and on the assumption that the Illinois decisions provide a useful guide to issues that have and may arise in Maryland, this Comment includes discussion of numerous Illinois cases along with notes on Maryland decisions.

In Illinois, a person commits the crime of theft when he knowingly obtains or exerts unauthorized control over the property of the owner and intends to deprive the owner permanently of the use or benefit of the property; or knowingly uses, conceals or abandons the property in such a manner as to deprive the owner permanently of such use or benefit; or uses, conceals, or abandons the property knowing such use, concealment or abandonment probably will deprive the owner permanently of such use or benefit. Ill. Ann. Stat. ch. 38, § 16-1 (Smith-Hurd 1977). See also *People v. Joy,* 44 Ill. App. 3d 349, 358 N.E.2d 101 (1976); *People v. Shoemaker,* 31 Ill. App. 3d 724, 334 N.E.2d 347 (1975); *People v. Dickerson,* 21 Ill. App. 3d 977, 316 N.E.2d 519 (1974), *rev'd on other grounds,* 61 Ill. 2d 580, 338 N.E.2d 184 (1975); *People v. Smith,* 90 Ill. App. 2d 388, 234 N.E.2d 161 (1967). Note that in Maryland the definition of "deprive" does not require an intent to withhold the property permanently. See Maryland Ann. Code, Art. 27, § 340(c).

The phrase "unauthorized control" means control exercised over property of another without the consent of the owner. *People v. Hoy,* 12 Ill. App. 3d 524, 299 N.E.2d 502 (1973). To establish the crime of theft, it must be shown that there was unauthorized control over the object of the theft and that the taking and conversion of the property were without consent of the owner. For the purposes of the statute, the concept of "unauthorized control" is broad, even though the word "control" has no legal or technical meaning distinct from its popular acceptance. *People v. Bullock,* 123 Ill. App. 2d 30, 259 N.E.2d 641 (1970).

In *Craddock v. State,* 64 Md. App. 269, 494 A.2d 971 (1985), the trial judge instructed the jury that it could find defendant guilty of theft even if the jurors could not agree as to what form of theft had been proven. The Court affirmed the conviction, noting that the revised theft offense combines the offenses of larceny, embezzlement, false pretenses and receiving stolen property. Its purpose is to avoid the subtle distinctions that had to be alleged and proved to establish the separate crimes under the former law. The Court quoted from Article 27, § 341, as follows:

> An accusation of theft may be proved by evidence that it was committed in any manner that would be theft under this subheading, notwithstanding the specification of a different manner in the information ..., subject only to the power of the Court to ensure a fair trial by granting a continuance or other appropriate relief if the conduct of the defense would be prejudiced by lack of fair notice or surprise.

Here, defendant was charged with unlawfully stealing personal property, including sterling silver and jewelry, having the value of $300 or greater, pursuant to one scheme and continuing course of conduct. The Court held that the indictment charged an offense under Article 27, § 342. The particular method used by the wrongdoer is not material. The gravamen of the offense of theft is the depriving of the owner of his rightful possession of his property. The law requires unanimity only in the verdict. The jury was not required to agree as to what form of theft had been proven as long as jurors unanimously agreed that theft in some form was committed.

In *Lee v. State,* 59 Md. App. 28, 474 A.2d 537 (1984), a decision of first impression in Maryland, the Court held that a defendant can be convicted of theft when shopping in a self-service store, without removing the goods from the store's premises. The Court held that shoplifting in a self-service store constitutes theft by virtue of Art. 27, § 342(a). In *Lee,* the defendant removed two bottles of cognac from the shelves of a self-service liquor store, concealing one bottle in his pants and holding the other in his hand. When approached by an employee, the defendant returned both bottles to the shelf and fled the store. The conviction was affirmed because the defendant knowingly obtained unauthorized control over the property of another when he consciously picked up the bottle of cognac and concealed the bottle in his pants. The Court noted that the intent to deprive the owner of his property can be inferred from his furtive handling of the property. Once a customer goes beyond the mere removal of goods from a shelf and crosses the threshold into the realm of behavior inconsistent with the owner's expectations, the circumstances may be such that a larcenous intent can be inferred.

(b) Obtains or exerts control

The phrase "obtains or exerts control," in the Illinois law providing that a person commits the offense of theft when he knowingly obtains or exerts control over property of the owner, includes not only the taking of property but also the carrying away, sale, or possession of the property. Thus, a person other than the actor who initiates the wrongful asportation may be guilty of theft. *People v. Dziak,* 30 Ill. App. 3d 859, 333 N.E.2d 582 (1975).

In *Offutt v. State,* 55 Md. App. 261, 463 A.2d 876 (1983), evidence was held sufficient to sustain a conviction for theft when recently stolen goods were recovered from a closet in a master bedroom which defendant shared with lessee of the apartment and where the defendant had keys to the apartment and listed that address with the Department of Transportation. The Court held the evidence could sustain a conviction of theft either under Art. 27, § 342(a) (obtaining or exerting unauthorized control) or § 342(c) (possession of stolen property).

In *Lane v. State,* 60 Md. App. 412, 483 A.2d 369 (1984), appellant who was in the real estate business, was convicted of theft based on a scheme to procure mortgage loans for purchasers of properties through the use of "straw buyers" and falsified employment and loan documents. The Court held that theft is committed when, with the intention to deprive the owner of the property, the defendant obtains or exerts unauthorized control of the property of another or obtains control over the property of another by deception. Appellant was prosecuted under Art. 27, § 342(a) and (b) and convicted of a felony (theft in excess of $300). The Court held that the crime was complete upon the making of the loan, rejecting appellant's argument that because the loans were secured by a deed of trust on the real estate there was no evidence that appellant intended to deprive the mortgage company of the money. The determination of whether a crime is a felony or a misdemeanor depends on the value of the property that was the subject of the offense, regardless of the amount of repayment.

In a prosecution for the offense of theft in Illinois, the term "obtain" means: (a) in relation to property, to bring about a transfer of interest or possession, whether to the offender or to another; and (b) in relation to services, to secure the performance thereof. Ill. Ann. Stat., ch. 38, § 15-7 (Smith-Hurd 1977).

The phrase "obtains or exerts control" over property includes, but is not limited to, the taking, carrying away, or the sale, conveyance or transfer of title to, or interest in or possession of property. Ill. Crim. Code of 1961, § 15-8; Ill. Ann. Stat., ch. 38, § 15-8 (Smith-Hurd 1977). Under Illinois law, the terms "exerts control" and "obtains control" are interchangeable; substitution of the phrase "exerts control" for the statutory words "obtains control" in the instructions relating to the offense of theft did not amount to reversible error. *People v. Collins,* 48 Ill. App. 3d 643, 362 N.E.2d 1118 (1977).

It has been held that the "obtaining of unauthorized control" includes, but is not limited to the initial taking or carrying away, *People v. Helm,* 10 Ill. App. 3d 643, 295 N.E.2d 78 (1973). Therefore, the unauthorized possession need not begin at the time of the original taking. *People v. Snow,* 21 Ill. App. 3d 873, 316 N.E.2d 216 (1974); *People v. Quick,* 15 Ill. App. 3d 300, 304 N.E.2d 143 (1973). Thus, one is a thief when he knowingly exerts unauthorized control through mere possession of the property, intending permanently to deprive the owner of its use. This point is illustrated by the decision in *People v. Nunn,* 63 Ill. App. 2d 465, 212 N.E.2d 342 (1965). The defendant argued that the evidence did not show that he had taken the car from the place where it had been parked by the owner. The Court held that the defendant's alibi as to the time the car was taken was immaterial because the unauthorized possession need not begin on the day of the original theft, but may be shown by possession at the time of arrest.

(c) Intent

In Illinois, the element of intent in the crime of theft, an essential element, is the intent to deprive the owner permanently of the use or benefit of his property. *People v. Hargrave,* 29 Ill. App. 3d 89, 329 N.E.2d 814 (1975); *People v. Debartalo,* 24 Ill. App. 3d 1000, 322 N.E.2d 251 (1975); *People v. Wilson,* 23 Ill. App. 3d 457, 318 N.E.2d 767 (1974); *People v. Woods,* 17 Ill. App. 3d 835,

308 N.E.2d 856 (1974). Note that the Maryland Code does not require an intent to permanently deprive for the offense of theft because the word "deprive," as defined in the statute, does not require a permanent taking. Art. 27, § 340 (c). In a trial for theft, intent may and often must be proved by facts and circumstances surrounding the alleged criminal act. *People v. Sims,* 29 Ill. App. 3d 815, 331 N.E.2d 178 (1975); *People v. Bell,* 9 Ill. App. 3d 465, 292 N.E.2d 219 (1972). For example, circumstances at the time of the defendant's apprehension, including the fact that the defendant had only one dollar on his person and had been stuffing store merchandise worth $30.54 in his trousers, signified the defendant's intent to steal. *People v. Sims, supra.*

The taking of articles and concealment, if determined to be done with the intention of stealing or depriving the owner of the use or benefit of the property, however brief, may constitute theft. Thus, the circumstance that a defendant had not yet reached the checkout counter where articles would have to be paid for, did not prevent a conviction of theft. *City of Joliet v. Gregorec,* 12 Ill. App. 2d 998, 299 N.E.2d 356 (1973).

In *Lee v. State,* 59 Md. App. 28, 474 A.2d 537 (1984), the Court noted that the intent to deprive the owner of his property can be inferred from the furtive handling of property. See discussion of *Lee, supra,* this Comment.

An instruction that merely delineates the mental elements of theft by possession does not fairly cover the honest belief or claim of right defense. *Sibert v. State,* 301 Md. 141, 482 A.2d 483 (1984).

(d) Owner

Under the Illinois theft scheme, "owner" means a person, other than the offender, who has possession of or any interest in the property involved, even though such interest or possession is unlawful, and without whose consent the offender has no authority to exert control over the property. Ill. Crim. Code of 1961, § 15-2; Ill. Ann. Stat., ch. 88, § 15-2 (Smith-Hurd 1977). In a prosecution for the offense of theft, an essential element that must be shown is that a person other than the accused either owns or has a superior possessory interest in the property allegedly stolen. *People v. Cowan,* 49 Ill. App. 3d 367, 364 N.E.2d 362 (1977); *People v. Cassman,* 32 Ill. App. 3d 456, 336 N.E.2d 85 (1975); *People v. Drake,* 20 Ill. App. 3d 762, 314 N.E.2d 532 (1974).

Theft is an offense against possession and not necessarily legal title. *People v. Woods,* 15 Ill. App. 3d 221, 303 N.E.2d 562 (1973); *People v. Smith,* 90 Ill. App. 2d 388, 234 N.E.2d 161 (1967). Therefore, it is sufficient to demonstrate some possessory interest in the property at the time of the offense, such as agency or bailment. *People v. Demos,* 3 Ill. App. 3d 284, 278 N.E.2d 89 (1971).

If it is contended that the owner of allegedly stolen property is a corporation, the legal existence of that corporation must be proved. *People v. Bell,* 18 Ill. App. 3d 130, 309 N.E.2d 344 (1974). However, in *People v. Lewis,* 13 Ill. App. 3d 688, 301 N.E.2d 159 (1973), the Court held that a theft complaint which alleged that the defendant stole property of a certain "company" adequately averred that the complainant was a corporate entity capable of owning property. See also *People v. Cicchetti,* 2 Ill. App. 3d 535, 275 N.E.2d 661 (1971).

Illinois courts have given an expansive interpretation to the term "owner." It has been held that "owner" or "person" from whom the theft of property is proscribed includes an unincorporated business association. *People v. Woods* (1973), *supra.* In *People v. Decker,* 19 Ill. App. 3d 86, 311 N.E.2d 228 (1974), the Court held that co-trustees of a premium trust had sufficient possessory interest in funds represented by the defendant to qualify as owners at the time of the theft. Similarly, a discount store licensed to do business in the state was a legal entity capable of owning alleged stolen property. *People v. McAllister,* 31 Ill. App. 3d 825, 334 N.E.2d 885 (1975). Thus, in that case the Court found that a store security officer's testimony that the defendant took items belonging to the store was sufficient to prove the store's ownership of the items for purposes of establishing the offense of theft. Also, testimony of possession by a salesman for the legal owners thereof was sufficient proof of ownership as against one who had stolen the property. *People v. Tomaszek,* 54 Ill. App. 2d 254, 204 N.E.2d 30, *cert. denied,* 382 U.S. 827 (1964).

In *People v. Smith, supra,* it was held that while the resident manager of a hotel who signed a complaint charging theft of certain hotel property was not the owner thereof, as resident manager he did have authorized control over the hotel's property and in that capacity was an "owner" within the statutory definition.

In *People v. Jones,* 123 Ill. App. 2d 389, 259 N.E.2d 393 (1970), the Court held that the payee of an alleged stolen check had sufficient interest in the check and the proceeds thereof to meet the definition of "owner."

The purpose of requiring that ownership of stolen property be proved is to assure that it was neither abandoned nor owned by the accused, and that it was taken from one who is the owner. *People v. McAllister, supra.* More importantly, the requirement that the ownership of property alleged to have been stolen be proved safeguards the accused against double jeopardy. *People v. Cassman, supra.*

(e) Value

In Maryland, the value of the property alleged to have been stolen is not an element of the offense; rather it is only relevant to the penalty which may be imposed. *Proctor v. State,* 49 Md. App. 696, 704, 435 A.2d 484, 488 (1981). If the crime charged is theft of $300 or more and the value of the object is not proved to be greater than $300, then the defendant may be found guilty of theft of less than $300. See *Ward v. State,* 52 Md. App. 664, 451 A.2d 1243 (1983); *People v. Price,* 81 Ill. App. 2d 111, 225 N.E.2d 453 (1967). In order to sustain a felony conviction, the value of the stolen property must be proven beyond a reasonable doubt to be in excess of $300. Art. 27, § 342(f)(1) and (2).

Even though value is not an element of the offense of theft, to be convicted of theft, the object taken must have some value. See definition of "property." Art. 27, § 340(h). In *Stackowitz v. State,* 68 Md. App. 368, 511 A.2d 1105 (1986), the Court held that a person cannot be convicted of the crime of theft for taking or assuming control over something that has no value whatever.

In *State v. Hunt,* 49 Md. App. 355, 432 A.2d 479 (1981), the Court held that Article 27, § 340(l)(5) permits the State to aggregate the value of all property stolen pursuant to one scheme or continuing course of conduct to determine whether the theft is a misdemeanor or a felony.

The exact amount of the object of the theft need not be in evidence; an estimation is sufficient. In *Proctor v. State, supra,* the owner's grandson testified that the value of guns stolen was $1200. The Court held that the grandson's estimation was sufficient since the value of the property obviously exceeded $300.

See the discussion of *Lane v. State,* 60 Md. App. 412, 483 A.2d 369 (1984), *supra,* this Comment, where the Court held that determination of whether a crime is a felony or a misdemeanor depends on the value of the property that was the subject of the offense, irregardless of the amount of repayment.

(f) Aggregating separate acts of theft

Article 27, § 340(l)(5) allows theft offenses to be aggregated if they are committed as a common scheme or continuing course of conduct for purposes of determining whether the crime is a felony or misdemeanor. There is no definition of what constitutes a "common scheme or continuing course of conduct."

In a different context, the Maryland courts have interpreted the phrase, "common scheme or plan," for purposes of determining when the State will be permitted to introduce evidence of other crimes and prior bad acts of defendant. Because there is a similarity of language and both involve holding the defendant accountable for his behavior at different times and places, the Court's interpretation may be helpful. In *Cross v. State,* 282 Md. 468, 386 A.2d 757 (1978), the trial court admitted evidence tending to associate the defendant with another burglary committed on the same day and in the same locality as the grand larceny for which the defendant was on trial. The Court noted:

> Moreover, there must be "not merely a similarity in the results, but such a concurrence of common features that the various acts are naturally to be explained as caused by a general plan of which they are the individual manifestations...." The concurrence of common features under this exception, however, must be more than simply a manner of operation, which is possessed to some extent by most crimi-

> nal recidivists. A method of operation is not, by itself, a common scheme, but merely a repetitive pattern.... Thus, evidence of other crimes can be introduced under the common scheme exception only when the relationship between the time, place, circumstances or parties involved in the crimes is such that the uncharged crime or crimes "support the inference that there exists a single inseparable plan encompassing both the charged and uncharged crimes, typically, but not exclusively, embracing uncharged crimes committed in order to effect the primary crime for which the accused has been indicted."

Id. at 475-76, 386 A.2d at 762. See Comment, § 2.10, Other crimes and prior bad acts of defendant, *supra,* for a discussion of *Cross v. State, supra,* and related cases. A complementary approach to an aggregation provision is for the General Assembly to provide increased penalties for habitual offenders or criminal recidivists where the unrelated acts are not considered to constitute "one offense." See Comment § 4.96, General instruction — "Rights of possession" and certain defenses applicable to theft offenses, *infra.*

(g) Indictments and informations

Generally, a complaint alleging that defendants committed the offense of theft in that they obtained unauthorized control over property with intent to deprive the owner of the use and benefit of the property, would not be fatally defective for failure to use the word "knowingly." *People v. Reese,* 11 Ill. App. 3d 817, 298 N.E.2d 315 (1973). See also *People v. Betts,* 17 Ill. App. 3d 22, 307 N.E.2d 672 (1974) (complaint alleging theft with intent to deprive the owner permanently of the use and benefit of the property is sufficient to describe requisite mental state despite the absence of the words "knowingly" or "unauthorized"). But an information which alleges that the defendant "knowingly obtained or exerted unauthorized control" over the described property of another, and fails to allege the intent to deprive the owner permanently of the use and benefit of the property is insufficient in Illinois to charge the offense of theft. *People v. Diming,* 13 Ill. App. 3d 1092, 302 N.E.2d 712 (1973). Moreover, any information charging theft, but failing to refer to any act indicating mental state or to the mental state of the defendant is insufficient. *People v. Smith,* 7 Ill. App. 3d 350, 287 N.E.2d 509 (1972); *People v. Haynes,* 132 Ill. App. 2d 1031, 270 N.E.2d 63 (1971).

In *State v. Hunt,* 49 Md. App. 355, 432 A.2d 479 (1981), the Court held that where the charging document alleges a series of thefts but fails to allege that they were committed pursuant to one scheme or continuing course of conduct, the charging document merely alleges separate and distinct crimes in a single count and is, therefore, duplicitous, and dismissal on that basis is appropriate.

In *Whitehead v. State,* 54 Md. App. 428, 458 A.2d 905 (1983), an indictment charging the defendant with unlawful stealing was held sufficient by "implied scienter" to allege the necessary specific intent. It is sufficient to give the defendant information necessary to enable him to prepare a defense and to protect him from further prosecution for the same offense.

The Maryland Annotated Code provides that in any indictment, information, warrant or other charging document for theft, it is sufficient to use a formula substantially to the following effect:

> [T]hat A-B on the __________ day of __________, 19__________, in the County (City) aforesaid, did steal (here specifying the property or services stolen) of C-D, having a value of (less than $300 or $300 or greater) in violation of Article 27, § 342, of the Annotated Code of Maryland; contrary to the form of the Act of Assembly in such case made and provided, and against the peace, government and dignity of the State.

Art. 27, § 344(a).

In *Jones v. State,* 303 Md. 323, 493 A.2d 1062 (1985), the Court rejected a constitutional challenge to the legal sufficiency of the statutory form of charging document for the crime of theft. The Court held that there is no requirement for an express recital of the manner or means of committing the offense. This information, if not otherwise provided by the prosecutor, is available through a bill of particulars. Where such a bill of particulars is requested, even where prosecutors use open file discovery methods, the trial judge should grant the request in view of the statute's history.

(h) Variance between charge and proof

Illinois courts have liberally treated variances between theft indictments charging the violation of the statute and the ultimate proof at trial. On the question of the ownership, in *People v. Tomaszek,* 54 Ill. App. 2d 254, 204 N.E.2d 30, *cert. denied,* 382 U.S. 827 (1964), the Court held that there was no fatal variance between proof that the legal owner of stolen property was the office supply and typewriter companies, and the charge in the indictment indicating that the property belonged to the complainant who was a salesman for the legal owners. Proof of specific ownership of the property, in the person named in the indictment is unnecessary if it is shown that the named person has some possessory interest in the property at the time of the offense. *People v. Decker,* 19 Ill. App. 3d 86, 311 N.E.2d 228 (1974). Similarly, a slight variance between the name of the corporate owner of the property as alleged in the indictment and its actual name is immaterial. See *People v. Kaye,* 112 Ill. App. 2d 141, 251 N.E.2d 306 (1969) (corporate name of victim was changed prior to date of the theft but the corporate entity remained the owner of merchandise in question; variance between the name of victim in complaint and the evidence was not fatal).

In Illinois, it has been held that if a theft indictment alleges the value to be in excess of $150, but the proof shows value to be less than $150, there is no fatal variance, but the court imposing sentence is limited to a misdemeanor sentence. *People v. Edwards,* 21 Ill. App. 3d 354, 315 N.E.2d 91 (1974). Similarly, when a defendant was indicted for having stolen an automobile having a value of more than $100 and convicted of having stolen an automobile exceeding $150 in value, the crime for which the defendant was indicted was theft and the value of the property went only to the penalty which might be imposed; thus, the defendant was not convicted of a crime for which he had not been indicted. *People v. Price,* 81 Ill. App. 2d 111, 225 N.E.2d 453 (1967). As noted earlier in this comment in the discussion of value, it has been held in Maryland that the value of the property alleged to have been stolen is not an element of the offense but is only relevant to the penalty which may be imposed. See *Proctor v. State,* 49 Md. App. 696, 435 A.2d 484 (1981).

(i) Presumptions and inferences

Pursuant to Art. 27, § 343(d), all common-law and evidentiary presumptions applicable on July 1, 1979 to offenses consolidated under the theft provisions are also applicable to the offense of theft, unless specifically repealed or modified by statute or court decision.

Under Maryland common law, either of two inferences can arise when a person is found in possession of recently stolen goods. One inference is that the possessor was the thief, and the other inference is that the possessor was the receiver of stolen goods. See *Richardson v. State,* 398 F. Supp. 425, 433 (1975); Comment, § 4.79, Receiving stolen goods, *supra.*

Before either such inference can arise, however, the possession of the goods must be accompanied by the three essential ingredients upon which the rule is based. The evidence must demonstrate: (1) that the goods were recently stolen, (2) that their possession is unexplained, and (3) that the possession is exclusive. *Mills v. State,* 3 Md. App. 693, 698, 41 A.2d 166, 169 (1968). See also *Anglin v. State,* 244 Md. 652, 224 A.2d 668 (1966); *Dinkins v. State,* 29 Md. App. 577, 586, 349 A.2d 676, 680 *aff'd,* 278 Md. 238, 362 A.2d 91 (1976); *Jones v. State,* 42 Md. App. 209, 400 A.2d 1 (1979); *Fowler v. State,* 18 Md. App. 37, 305 A.2d 200 (1973); *Wynn v. State,* 69 Md. App. 536, 518 A.2d 1072 (1987).

The possession cannot be constructive possession but it may involve joint possession, as the Court observed:

> ... to support the inference the possession must be personal and with a distinct, implied, or express assertion of property by the exercise of complete dominion and right of disposal. A mere constructive possession is not enough; the accused will not be presumed to have stolen articles which he does not know he possesses. It is in the sense of a personal possession ... that the possession is exclusive .... [T]he possession to be exclusive, need not necessarily be in one person and may be a joint possession.

Boswell v. State, 5 Md. App. 571, 578-79, 249 A.2d 490, 496-97 (1968).

Therefore, joint exclusive possession, which may mean possession that is exclusive of all persons except those who were parties to the crime, may also give rise to an inference of fact that the defendant was a receiver of stolen goods.

This inference has withstood an attack grounded upon the fifth amendment privilege against self-incrimination. *Evans v. State,* 28 Md. App. 640, 349 A.2d 300 (1975), *aff'd,* 278 Md. 197, 362 A.2d 629 (1976). The Court of Special Appeals held that "[s]ince an inference does not shift a burden either of persuasion or of going forward with evidence to a defendant, it does not come under the scrutiny of *Mullaney v. Wilbur* [421 U.S. 684, 95 S. Ct. 1881, 44 L. Ed. 2d 508 (1975)] in that regard." For additional support for the above proposition, see *Horn v. State,* 29 Md. App. 23, 349 A.2d 372 (1975). For further discussion of presumptions and inferences, see Appendix V, The Impact of *Evans v. State:* Burdens of Proof, Presumptions and Inferences, *infra.*

§ 4.92. Theft — By deception.

The defendant has been charged with theft of [$300 or more] [less than $300] by use of deception.

In order for the defendant to be guilty of this offense, the State must prove beyond a reasonable doubt that: (1) ____________ *(insert name of owner)* was the owner of certain property, namely ____________ *(list item(s) of property)*; (2) the defendant willfully or knowingly used deception to obtain control and did obtain control over the property; and (3) (the defendant had the purpose of depriving the owner of the property) (the defendant willfully or knowingly used, concealed, or abandoned the property in such a manner as to deprive the owner of the property) (the defendant used, concealed or abandoned the property knowing the use, concealment or abandonment probably would deprive the owner of the property).

[The State must also prove beyond a reasonable doubt that the value of the property (or services) was $300 or more. If the State does not prove beyond a reasonable doubt that the value of the property (or services) was $300 or more, but that the property (or services) had some value, you must then find that the property (or services) had a value of less than $300.] *or*

[The defendant has been charged with theft of less than $300. You do not have to determine the exact value of the property (or services) but the State must prove beyond a reasonable doubt that the property (or services) had some value.]

The term "owner" means a person, other than the offender, who has any interest in the property, including mere possession, without whose consent the defendant has no authority to obtain or exert control over the property. [The owner's interest in the property may be lawful or unlawful; even a person who unlawfully possesses property may occupy the position of owner.]

The term "willfully" means an act done with deliberate intention for which there is no reasonable excuse.

The term "knowingly" means that a person is aware of his conduct or the existing circumstances. A person acts knowingly when such person is practically certain of the results of his conduct. A person has knowledge of the existence of a fact when he is practically certain of its existence. The term "knowingly" does not include accident, mistake, negligence or recklessness.

You must also find that the defendant obtained unauthorized control over property. The term "obtain" means [in relation to property, to bring about a transfer of interest or possession, whether to the defendant or to another] [in relation to services, to secure the performance of the services].

The word "deception" means to knowingly __________ (*insert relevant categories from the following list*): (create or confirm in another an impression which is false and which the defendant does not believe to be true); (fail to correct a false impression which the defendant previously has created or confirmed); (prevent another from acquiring information pertinent to the disposition of the property involved); (sell or otherwise transfer or encumber property, failing to disclose a lien, adverse claim, or other legal impediment to the enjoyment of the property, whether the impediment is or is not of value or the impediment is not a matter of official record); (insert or deposit a slug in a coin machine) [the term "slug" means an object or article which, by virtue of its size, shape or any other quality, is capable of being inserted or deposited in a coin machine as an improper substitute for a coin, bill or token required for the operation of the machine. The term "coin machine" means a coin box, turnstile, vending machine, or other mechanical or electrical device or receptacle designed to receive a coin, bill, or a token made to be received by the machine, and in return for the insertion or deposit thereof, automatically to offer, to provide, to assist in providing, or to permit the acquisition of some property or service]; (remove, alter or otherwise disfigure any label or price tag); (promise performance which the defendant does not intend to perform or knows will not be performed. You may not infer or establish the defendant's knowledge or intention from the fact alone that the promise was not performed); (misrepresent the value of a motor vehicle offered for sale by tampering with, interfering with, resetting or altering the odometer with intent to change the number of miles indicated).

The word "deception," when used in these instructions, does *not* include puffing or false statements of immaterial facts and exaggerated representations unlikely to deceive ordinary persons.

The word "deprive" means the withholding of property of another (permanently) (for such a period as to appropriate a portion of its value) (with the purpose to restore it only upon payment of reward or other compensation) (to dispose of the property and use or deal with the property as to make it unlikely that the owner will recover it).

The term "property" means anything of value. It includes but is not limited to __________ (*insert relevant categories from list of items appearing in Official Commentary, § 4.91, supra*).

[The term "services" includes, but is not limited to (labor services) (professional services) (telecommunications) (public utilities) (toll facilities) (transportation services) (lodging) (entertainment) (restaurant services) (the use of equipment, including, but not limited to, computers and other data processing equipment).]

The term "value" means the market value of the property (or service(s)) at the time and place of the crime [or if the market value cannot be satisfactorily found, the cost of the replacement of the property within a reasonable time after the crime].

[The term "value" in the case of certain written instruments that do not have a readily ascertainable market value, whether or not they have been issued or delivered, shall be measured as follows: [The value of an instrument constituting evidence of debt such as a check, draft, or promissory note shall be determined as the amount due or collectible. This figure ordinarily is the face amount of the indebtedness less any portion which has been satisfied.] [The value of an instrument which creates, releases, discharges or otherwise affects any valuable legal right, privilege or obligation shall be determined as the amount of economic loss which the owner of the instrument might reasonably suffer by virtue of the loss of the instrument.] [If the property of the theft is a trade secret, which does not have a readily ascertainable market value, its value shall be deemed any reasonable value representing the damage to the owner suffered by reason of losing an advantage over those who do not know of or use the trade secret].]

[If you find that the theft has been committed as one scheme or continuing course of conduct, whether from the same or several sources, you may consider the conduct as one offense and total the value of the property or services in determining whether the theft is more or less than $300.]

[In the absence of a reasonable explanation of such possession, the exclusive possession of property recently stolen allows you to infer that the person in possession [did steal such property] [was a receiver of stolen property]. Thus, if the property was found in possession of the defendant and if the evidence demonstrates that: (1) the property was recently stolen; (2) the possession is unexplained; and (3) the possession was exclusive, then an inference of fact may arise that the defendant [did steal such property] [was a receiver of stolen property].]

[In a prosecution for the offense of theft, it is a defense that: __________ [the defendant acted under a good faith claim of right to the property involved] [the defendant acted in honest belief that he had the right to obtain or exert control over the property as he did] [the property involved was that of the defendant's spouse, unless the defendant and the defendant's spouse were not living together as husband and wife and were living in separate abodes at the time of the alleged theft] [the defendant rightfully knew the trade secret or that it was available to him from a source other than the owner of the trade secret].]

[*Where the offense charged is felony theft and there is some evidence of misdemeanor theft:* Your verdict must take one of three forms. If you conclude beyond a reasonable doubt that the State has proved each of the elements of the offense, and you also find beyond a reasonable doubt that the value of the property (or services) was $300 or more, your verdict should be "guilty of theft of $300 or more." If you conclude beyond a reasonable doubt that the State has proved each of the elements of the offense of theft and you are unable to determine, beyond a reasonable doubt, whether the value of the property (or services) was more or less than $300 or if you determine that the value of the property (or service) was some value less than $300 your verdict should be "guilty of theft of less than $300." If you are not convinced beyond a reasonable doubt that the State has proved each and every element of the offense, you must find the defendant not guilty.]

OFFICIAL COMMENTARY

Joint Subcommittee on Theft Related Offenses, Maryland General Assembly, *Revision of Maryland Theft Laws and Bad Check Laws,* ch. 849 (1978)

This subsection [Art. 27, §342(b)] specifically treats the offense of theft when deception is an element of the offense. The elements embraced by an offense committed under the specific terms of this subsection are also adequately covered in a more general manner by Art. 27, § 342(a). [See Official Commentary, § 4.91, *supra.*] It was decided to include this subsection containing more explicit elements of theft by deception to be in conformity with the decision made by commissions that revised criminal codes in states such as Illinois and Montana.

As used in these instructions, the word "deception" [see Art. 27, § 340(b)] forms the nucleus around which the offense of theft is delineated in situations where property or services are wrongfully taken by means of the perpetrator making some misrepresentation.

The scope of this definition covers situations in which statements, assertions, promises and acts will be viewed as deceptive. The language of the text which prescribes these situations is self-explanatory.

The basic elements of this definition are derived from similar definitions in states that have enacted statutes consolidating their theft offenses. In addition to the basic definition derived from the laws of other states, language has been inserted pertaining to the use of slugs and altering price tags and labels. The language concerning the alteration of price tags and labels insures that this activity which was previously classified as shoplifting will now be categorized as theft, by virtue of its "deceptive" nature.

Among the acts which qualify as deception is promising performance which the offender does not *intend* to perform or *knows* will not be performed. However, the requisite knowledge of intention may not be inferred from the mere fact that the promise was not performed. The prohibition which requires more than nonperformance to prove the requisite intent was thought desirable as a matter of trial tactics and is in keeping with similar provisions in Oregon (Or. Rev. Stat., sec. 164.085(3)), Maine (Me. Rev. Stat. Ann., tit. 17-A, sec. 354(2)(A) (West 1977 Pamphlet)), and Texas (Tex. Penal Code Ann., tit. 7, sec. 31.03(2)(E) (Vernon 1974)).

An exception has also been made to exclude puffing, exaggerations and false statements of immaterial facts from the broad language of this definition.

The term "property" when used in these instructions means anything of value.... [See Official Commentary, § 4.91, *supra,* for list. See also § 4.96, General instruction — "Rights of possession" and certain defenses applicable to theft offenses.]

COMMENT

As in the case of other instructions in this subpart on theft offenses, this Comment is based partly on the similar Illinois law.

Under the Illinois theft offense scheme, a person commits theft when he knowingly obtains by deception control over property of the owner, and intends to deprive the owner permanently of the use or benefit of the property; or knowingly uses, conceals or abandons the property in such manner as to deprive the owner permanently of such use or benefit; or uses, conceals or abandons the property knowing such use, concealment or abandonment will deprive the owner permanently of such use or benefit. Ill. Crim. Code of 1961, § 16-1(b)(1)(2)(3); Ill. Ann. Stat. ch. 38, § 16-1(b)(1)(2)(3) (Smith-Hurd 1977). In Maryland, however, the definition of "deprive" does not require an intent to withhold the property permanently. Maryland Ann. Code, Art. 27, § 340(c).

In a prosecution for the offense of theft by deception, the essential elements that must be proved are: that a named person was the owner of the specified property; that the defendant knowingly obtained by deception control over the property; and that the defendant acted with the intent to permanently deprive the named owner of the use and benefit of the property. *People v. Decker,* 19 Ill. App. 3d 86, 311 N.E.2d 228 (1974).

The intent of the defendant is the essence of the offense of theft by deception. In a prosecution for the offense of theft by deception, evidence that the defendant tendered a check knowingly without having funds on deposit in and of itself supported the inference and existence of the required felonious intent. *People v. Reons,* 20 Ill. App. 3d 1005, 313 N.E.2d 184 (1974). Similarly, state's evidence consisting of testimony of a food store security guard that the defendant, after removing smoked hams from shelf, placed them in his wife's purse, then picked up and placed in his shopping cart a carton of pop and wheeled the cart to the checkout line to pay for the pop, while his wife left the store with the hams in her purse, was sufficient evidence to sustain a conviction for theft by deception. *People v. Johnson,* 59 Ill. App. 3d 115, 376 N.E.2d 8 (1978).

In a Maryland case, *Franklin v. State,* 60 Md. App. 277, 482 A.2d 168 (1984), the defendant was convicted of theft by deception as a result of an undercover investigation by the Immigration & Naturalization Service (INS) into the unlawful issuing of alien work permits. The defendant asserted that because the INS agent/"victim" knew that defendant could not procure a valid INS work permit, the INS agent/"victim" could not have relied on defendant's representations to produce one. Although the INS official knew the defendant could not furnish a valid work permit, the agent bargained for a counterfeit permit. The INS agent was, therefore, defrauded of $175 in attempting to receive a bogus work permit.

See the discussion of *Lane v. State,* 60 Md. App. 412, 483 A.2d 369 (1984) in Comment, § 4.91, *supra.* Appellant, in the real estate business, was convicted of theft based on a scheme to procure mortgage loans for purchasers of properties through the use of "straw buyers" and falsified employment and loan documents.

§ 4.93. Theft—By possessing stolen property.

The defendant has been charged with theft of [$300 or more] [less than $300] by possession of stolen property.

In order for the defendant to be guilty of this offense, the State must prove beyond a reasonable doubt that: (1) the defendant was in possession of certain personal property, namely ____________ (*list item(s) of property*); (2) this personal property had been stolen; (3) the defendant [knew the property had been stolen] [believed that it probably had been stolen]; and (4) [the defendant had the purpose of depriving the owner of the property] [the defendant willfully or knowingly used, concealed or abandoned the property in such a manner as to deprive the owner of the property] [the defendant used, concealed or abandoned the property knowing the use, concealment or abandonment probably would deprive the owner of the property].

[The State must also prove beyond a reasonable doubt that the value of the property was $300 or more. If the State does not prove beyond a reasonable doubt that the value of the property was $300 or more, but that the property had some value, you must then find that the property had a value of less than $300.] *or*

[The defendant has been charged with theft of less than $300. You do not have to determine the exact value of the property but the State must prove beyond a reasonable doubt that the property had some value.]

The term "owner" means a person, other than the offender, who has any interest in the property, including mere possession, without whose consent the defendant has no authority to obtain or exert control over the property. [The owner's interest in the property may be lawful or unlawful; even a person who unlawfully possesses property may occupy the position of owner.]

The term "willfully" means an act done with deliberate intention for which there is no reasonable excuse.

The term "knowingly" means that a person is aware of his conduct or the existing circumstances. A person acts knowingly when such person is practically certain of the results of his conduct. A person has knowledge of the existence of a fact when he is practically certain of its existence. The term "knowingly" does not include accident, mistake, negligence or recklessness.

[If the defendant is in the business of buying or selling goods, you may, but are not required to, infer that the defendant knew that the property had been stolen if [the defendant has been found in possession or control of property stolen from two or more persons on separate occasions] [the defendant has acquired stolen property in a separate transaction during the year before this criminal possession charge] [the defendant acquired the property for a value which he knew was far below its reasonable value and the defendant is in the business of buying or selling property of the sort possessed]. You should consider all of the facts and circumstances in evidence in determining whether to infer that the defendant had knowledge that the property had been stolen.]

The word "deprive" means the withholding of property of another [permanently] [for such a period as to appropriate a portion of its value] [with the purpose to restore it only upon payment of reward or other compensation] [to dispose of the property and use or deal with the property as to make it unlikely that the owner will recover it].

The term "property" means any personal property of value. It includes but is not limited to ________ *(insert relevant categories from list of items appearing in Official Commentary, § 4.91, supra).*

The term "value" means the market value of the property at the time and place of the crime [or if the market value cannot be satisfactorily found, the cost of the replacement of the property within a reasonable time after the crime].

[The term "value" in the case of certain written instruments that do not have a readily ascertainable market value, whether or not they have been issued or delivered, shall be measured as follows: [The value of an instrument constituting evidence of debt such as a check, draft, or promissory note shall be determined as the amount due or collectible. This figure ordinarily is the face amount of the indebtedness less any portion which has been satisfied.] [The value of an instrument which creates, releases, discharges or otherwise affects any valuable legal right, privilege or obligation shall be determined as the amount of economic loss which the owner of the instrument might reasonably suffer by virtue of the loss of the instrument.] [If the property of the theft is a trade secret, which does not have a readily ascertainable market value, its value shall be deemed any reasonable value representing the damage to the owner suffered by reason of losing an advantage over those who do not know of or use the trade secret].]

[If you find that the theft has been committed as one scheme or continuing course of conduct, whether from the same or several sources, you may consider the conduct as one offense and total the value of the property or services in determining whether the theft is more or less than $300.]

[In a prosecution for theft by possession of stolen property it is *not* a defense that [the person who stole the property has not been convicted, apprehended or identified] [the defendant stole or participated in the stealing of the property] [the stealing of the property did not occur in this State].]

[In a prosecution for the offense of theft, it is a defense that: [the defendant acted under a good faith claim of right to the property involved] [the defendant acted in honest belief that he had the right to obtain or exert control over the property as he did] [the property involved was that of the defendant's spouse, unless the defendant and the defendant's spouse were not living together as husband and wife and were living in separate abodes at the time of the alleged theft] [the defendant rightfully knew the trade secret or that it was available to him from a source other than the owner of the trade secret].]

[*Where the offense charged is felony theft and there is some evidence of misdemeanor theft:* Your verdict must take one of three forms. If you conclude beyond a reasonable doubt that the State has proved each of the elements of the offense, and you also find beyond a reasonable doubt that the value of the property was $300 or more, your verdict should be "guilty of theft of $300 or more." If you conclude beyond a reasonable doubt that the State has proved each of the elements of the offense of theft and you are unable to determine, beyond a reasonable doubt, whether the value of the property was more or less than $300 or if you determine that the value of the property was some value less than $300, your verdict should be "guilty of theft of less than $300." If you are not convinced beyond a reasonable doubt that the State has proved each and every element of the offense, you must find the defendant not guilty.]

OFFICIAL COMMENTARY

Joint Subcommittee on Theft Related Offenses, Maryland General Assembly, *Revision of Maryland Theft Laws and Bad Check Laws,* ch. 849 (1978)

This subsection [Art. 27, § 342(c)] melds acts of "criminal possession" to the offense of theft. This criminal possession concept is new to Maryland law. Its scope is broader than the crime of "receiving stolen goods" which it encompasses.

By merging the acts of receiving stolen goods and the acts constituting the actual stealing into a single offense (*i.e.,* theft) some confusion has been eliminated. Under Maryland case law, either of two inferences could arise if a person was found in possession of recently stolen goods. One inference was that the possessor was the thief, and the other inference was that the possessor was the receiver of stolen goods. (See *Richardson v. State,* 398 F. Supp. 425 at 433 (D. Md. 1975)). In some instances, courts were confounded by the dilemma of which inference to draw. However, now that the act of stealing and the act of receiving constitute a single offense (*i.e.,* theft), the confusion is eliminated.

This subsection contains a certain amount of duplicity of the provisions of subsection (a) [of Art. 27, § 342] [See Official Commentary, § 4.91, Theft—By unauthorized control, *supra*]. It was inserted as a more precise and definitive statement of the unlawful conduct constituting criminal possession. Whereas subsection (a) is very broad, this section is somewhat narrower. The generalized language used in Art. 27, § 342(a) merely requires that the offender receive possession and have the purpose of depriving. But the limited language of this subsection [Art. 27, § 342(c)] is restricted by the requirements that (1) the property be personal property, (2) the property be stolen property, and (3) the offender have knowledge that the property was stolen property.

Several aspects of this subsection present issues that warrant discussion and possible modifications and clarification. These issues include the following:

(1) Is the phrase "believing that it has probably been stolen" surplus language? The phrase "*knowing* that it has been stolen" is used. The word "knowing" which is used in this phrase is a term adequately illustrated by subsection 340(e) to include "practically certain that the result will be caused."

(2) Is clarification needed as to the meaning of the word "possesses"? This is not a defined term in the statute and some questions have been raised as to whether clarifying language is necessary to make it clear that the word possesses includes not only actual physical possession, but also constructive possession. Under Maryland case law, "[t]o convict an accused of receiving stolen property, it is not necessary to show that he came into actual, manual possession of stolen property; constructive or potential possession is sufficient." *Polansky v. State,* 205 Md. 362, 366, 109 A.2d 52, 54 (1954). If the interpretation of *Polansky* is judicially applied to this subsection, no further clarification would be nec-

essary. However, all doubt and confusion could probably be avoided by substituting the term "obtains" for "possesses" in line 459. The term "obtains" has a definite meaning which includes constructive acts. [See Instruction, § 4.91, *supra* and commentary.]

(3) Is clarification needed for the word "stolen"? Some concern has been expressed that "stolen property" might be interpreted by the courts to restrict this subsection to only property acquired by common-law larceny.

(4) Is it desirable to insert a provision to allow for the lawful handling of stolen property? Oregon has provided such language (*i.e.,* "In a prosecution for theft by receiving, it is a defense that the defendant received, retained, concealed or disposed of the property with the intent of restoring it to the owner." — Or. Rev. Stat., § 164.035(3) (1977 Replacement Part)). The purpose of this type of defense would be to prevent misinterpretation or abuse of this subsection on "criminal possession." Such an example of potential abuse would be strictly applying the meaning of "deprive" (withholding the property for such a period as to appropriate a portion of its value) in some cases.

The paragraph [defining the inference of the requisite knowledge] was specifically included to be of assistance in prosecuting "professional fences." It accomplishes this purpose by providing that the requisite mental element may be inferred from the existence of certain enumerated facts. This inference does not, however, relieve the State of its obligation to prove beyond a reasonable doubt that the defendant possessed the required knowledge.

[Article 27, § 342(c)(4) provides as follows: "A person who criminally possesses stolen property and a person who has stolen the property are not accomplices in theft for the purpose of any rule of evidence requiring corroboration of the testimony of an accomplice, unless the person who criminally possesses the property had participated in the stealing." The official commentary which follows explains that this provision maintains the separate relationship in which a thief and receiver were viewed prior to the consolidation of theft offenses for purpose of avoiding the evidentiary requirement of corroboration for "accomplice" testimony.]

[The paragraph eliminating the requirement of corroboration of the testimony of an accomplice] is necessary because the offense of theft consolidates into that one crime the act of obtaining or exerting unauthorized control over property [Art. 27, § 342(a) and (b); Instructions §§ 4.91 and 4.92, *supra*], and the act of receiving or possessing stolen property [Art. 27, § 342(c)]. As a result of this consolidation, persons who obtain or exert unauthorized control, and persons who receive or possess the stolen goods are guilty of the same crime (*i.e.,* theft) and could be characterized as accomplices. Therefore, the evidentiary rule requiring an accomplice's testimony in a criminal case to be corroborated could be applied. This would mean that if either the culprit who was the "receiver" or the defendant who actually stole the property were to testify against each other, the testimony would have to be corroborated. [See Instruction, § 2.01, Accomplice's testimony — Corroboration, *supra.*]

Maryland has recognized "that a thief and a receiver are not accomplices." *Osborne v. State,* 4 Md. App. 57, 61, 241 A.2d 171, 174 (1968). This subsection [Art. 27, § 342(c)], therefore, preserves this rule and maintains the relationship in which a thief and receiver are viewed under current Maryland law even though the separate acts of both offenders are merged into the single crime of theft.

[See § 4.96, General instruction — "Rights of possession" and certain defenses applicable to theft offenses, *infra.*]

COMMENT

In Maryland, there are two offenses under which receiving stolen property could seemingly be prosecuted. See Instruction, § 4.91, Theft — By unauthorized control, *supra;* and this Instruction, § 4.93, Theft — By possessing stolen property. Theft by unauthorized control makes no distinction concerning the way the property was obtained. Theft by possessing stolen property is broader than the crime of receiving stolen goods which it encompasses. See *Sibert v. State,* 301 Md. 141, 482 A.2d 483 (1984).

The concept of possessing stolen property in Illinois is a wholly distinct form of the crime of theft. In Illinois, a person commits theft when he knowingly obtains control over stolen property, knowing the property to have been stolen by another or under such circumstances as would reasonably induce him to believe that the property was stolen, and: (1) intends to deprive the owner permanently of the use or benefit of the property; (2) knowingly uses, conceals or abandons the property in such manner as to deprive the owner permanently of such use or benefit; or (3) uses, conceals or abandons the property knowing such use, concealment or abandonment probably will deprive the owner permanently of such use or benefit. See Ill. Crim. Code of 1961, § 16-1; Ill. Ann. Stat., ch. 38, § 16-1(d) (Smith-Hurd 1977).

Thus, the essential elements of the crime of theft by possession in Illinois are that: (1) the property has, in fact, been stolen by a person other than the one charged; (2) the one charged has actually received the property stolen or aided in concealing it; and (3) the receiver knew the property was stolen and and that he received the property for his own gain or to prevent the owner from repossessing it. *People v. Weiss,* 34 Ill. App. 3d 840, 341 N.E.2d 79 (1976).

In Illinois, recent, exclusive, unexplained possession of stolen property is evidence that the possessor is guilty of wrongful taking. It is not, however, evidence that the possessor is guilty of the crime of possessing stolen property knowing it to have been stolen by another. *People v. Rosochacki,* 21 Ill. App. 3d 477, 315 N.E.2d 633 (1974); *People v. Malone,* 1 Ill. App. 3d 160, 275 N.E.2d 236 (1971).

In both Maryland and Illinois, to sustain a conviction, it must be proved that the defendant knew that the property was stolen at the time he received or possessed it. Possession of stolen property may be proved by circumstantial evidence. In *Offutt v. State,* 55 Md. App. 261, 463 A.2d 876 (1983), evidence was held sufficient to sustain a conviction for theft when recently stolen goods were recovered from a closet in a master bedroom which defendant shared with lessee of the apartment and where the defendant had keys to the apartment and listed that address with the Department of Transportation. The Court held the evidence legally sufficient to warrant a conviction of theft under Article 27, § 342(a) (obtaining or exerting unauthorized control) or § 342(c) (possession of stolen property).

In Illinois, such knowledge may be established by proof of circumstances which would induce belief in a reasonable mind that the property had been stolen and by the receipt of such property by the accused without inquiry as to its source or the title of the one from whom it was received. *People v. LaValley,* 7 Ill. App. 3d 1051, 289 N.E.2d 45, 47 (1972). Thus, a conviction for theft was sufficiently supported by circumstantial evidence which included the fact that a camper truck in which stolen articles were found was owned by the defendant and was being driven by him when he and his two companions were stopped by the police. *People v. Street,* 11 Ill. App. 3d 243, 296 N.E.2d 606, 607 (1973). This evidence, and the testimony of witnesses who saw defendant's companions pry open the door of a jewelry store and flee in the defendant's truck, was sufficient to support a conviction. *Cf. People v. Watts,* 55 Ill. App. 3d 66, 370 N.E.2d 583 (1977) (evidence of guns previously stolen found concealed in defendant's station wagon in which defendant was a passenger was insufficient to prove that defendant was a receiver of stolen goods and a conviction could not be based on the jury's inference that the two other people in defendant's car were the ones who had stolen the guns since they and not defendant were in charge of the car while defendant was only a passenger).

Maryland Ann. Code, Art. 27, § 342(c)(3)(ii) states that it is not a defense that the "defendant stole or participated in the stealing." Therefore, a defendant may be prosecuted for the crime of possessing stolen property even if he was the thief. This differs from the Illinois statute. In Illinois, proof that the property was stolen by a person other than the defendant is an indispensable condition for a conviction of theft.

§ 4.94. Theft—Of lost, mislaid or mistakenly delivered property.

The defendant has been charged with theft of [$300 or more] [less than $300] of [lost or mislaid] [mistakenly delivered] property.

In order for the defendant to be guilty of this offense, the State must prove beyond a reasonable doubt that: (1) __________ (*insert name of owner*) was the owner of certain property, namely __________ (*list item(s) of property*); (2) the defendant obtained control over this property; (3)

the defendant knew the property had been [lost or mislaid] [delivered under a mistake as to the identity of the recipient or nature or amount of the property]; (4) the defendant [knew or learned of the identity of the owner] [knew, or was aware of, or learned of a reasonable method of identifying the owner]; (5) the defendant failed to take reasonable measures to restore the property to the owner; and, (6) the defendant had the purpose of permanently depriving the owner of the use or benefit of the property when he obtained the property or at any later time.

[The State must also prove beyond a reasonable doubt that the value of the property was $300 or more. If the State does not beyond prove beyond a reasonable doubt that the value of the property was $300 or more, but that the property had some value, you must then find that the property had a value of less than $300.] *or*

[The defendant has been charged with theft of less than $300. You do not have to determine the exact value of the property but the State must prove beyond a reasonable doubt that the property had some value.]

The term "owner" means a person other than the offender who has any interest in the property, including mere possession, without whose consent the defendant has no authority to exert control over the property. [The owner's interest in the property may be lawful or unlawful; even a person who unlawfully possesses property may occupy the position of owner.]

The term "obtained" in the phrase "obtain control" means to bring about a transfer of interest or possession in the property.

The term "knowingly" means that a person is aware of his conduct or the existing circumstances. A person acts knowingly when such person is practically certain of the results of his conduct. A person has knowledge of the existence of a fact when he is practically certain of its existence. The term "knowingly" does not include accident, mistake, negligence or recklessness.

The term "property" means anything of value. It includes but is not limited to ________ *(insert relevant categories from list of items appearing in Official Commentary, § 4.91, supra).*

The term "value" means the market value of the property at the time and place of the crime [or if the market value cannot be satisfactorily found, the cost of the replacement of the property within a reasonable time after the crime].

[The term "value" in the case of certain written instruments that do not have a readily ascertainable market value, whether or not they have been issued or delivered, shall be measured as follows: [The value of an instrument constituting evidence of debt such as a check, draft, or promissory note shall be determined as the amount due or collectible. This figure ordinarily is the face amount of the indebtedness less any portion which has been satisfied.] [The value of an instrument which creates, releases, discharges or otherwise affects any valuable legal right, privilege or obligation shall be determined as the amount of economic loss which the owner of the instrument might reasonably suffer by virtue of the loss of the instrument.] [If the property of the theft is a trade secret, which does not have a readily ascertainable market value, its value shall be deemed any reasonable value representing the damage to the owner suffered by reason of losing an advantage over those who do not know of or use the trade secret].]

[If you find that the theft has been committed as one scheme or continuing course of conduct, whether from the same or several sources, you may consider the conduct as one offense and total the value of the property or services in determining whether the theft is more or less than $300.]

[In a prosecution for the offense of theft, it is a defense that: __________ [the defendant acted under a good faith claim of right to the property involved] [the defendant acted in honest belief that he had the right to obtain or exert control over the property as he did] [the property involved was that of the defendant's spouse, unless the defendant and the defendant's spouse were not living together as husband and wife and were living in separate abodes at the time of the alleged theft] [the defendant rightfully knew the trade secret or that it was available to him from a source other than the owner of the trade secret].]

[*Where the offense charge is felony theft and there is some evidence of misdemeanor theft:* Your verdict must take one of three forms. If you conclude beyond a reasonable doubt that the State has proved each of the elements of the offense, and you also find beyond a reasonable doubt that the value of the property was $300 or more, your verdict should be "guilty of theft of $300 or more." If you conclude beyond a reasonable doubt that the State has proved each of the elements of the offense of theft and you are unable to determine, beyond a reasonable doubt, whether the value of the property was more or less than $300 or if you determine that the value of the property was some value less than $300, your verdict should be "guilty of theft of less than $300." If you are not convinced beyond a reasonable doubt that the State has proved each and every element of the offense, you must find the defendant not guilty.]

OFFICIAL COMMENTARY

Joint Subcommittee on Theft Related Offenses, Maryland General Assembly, *Revision of Maryland Theft Laws and Bad Check Laws,* ch. 849 (1978)

This subsection [Art. 27, § 342(d)] pertains to instances when a person, acting in a certain manner, "obtains control" over "property of another" (see definition [Art. 27, § 340(i)]) which has been (1) lost, (2) mislaid, or (3) delivered by mistake. The manner in which the person must act is outlined by paragraphs (1), (2) and (3) of this subsection. The circumstances outlined in these paragraphs are expressed conjunctively, and therefore *all three* of these elements must exist in order for there to be a conviction of theft of lost, mislaid or misdelivered property under this subsection.

It was a crime at common law to deprive the owner of lost property or possession of that property if the finder of the lost property formulated the intent to deprive at the time he found the property. It was reasoned that in order for there to be a larceny at common law, there must be a trespassory taking. The trespass could only occur if the intent to deprive was formulated at the time the property was found. A person who came into possession of lost property without having an intent to deprive the rightful owner of possession was regarded not to have committed a trespass, since he lacked the *mens rea* necessary to be guilty of larceny and was therefore in lawful possession of the lost property.

This requirement that the intent to deprive be formulated when the lost property is discovered has been viewed as a fiction of the common law. The purpose of this requirement was to induce the finder to take appropriate measures to discover the identity of the rightful owner. By taking these measures, the finder provided proof of his innocence through evidence of a lack of *mens rea* necessary to constitute larceny. For a discussion of common-law larceny of lost property, see Model Penal Code sec. 223.5, Comment (Proposed Official Draft, 1962), and Model Penal Code sec. 206.5, Comment (Tent. Draft No. 2, 1954). A Maryland view of larceny by the finder of goods is found in *Brown v. State,* 236 Md. 505, 204 A.2d 532 (1964).

In order to avoid this fiction of the common law which requires a nebulous determination of whether there was an intent to deprive at the time the property was found, it was decided that an intent which is formulated at any time with a purpose of depriving the rightful owner of lost, mislaid or misdelivered property is sufficient to constitute the crime of theft. However, in addition to this intent to deprive, the finder must know the identity of the owner or be aware of a reasonable method of identifying the owner *and* fail to take reasonable measures to restore the property to the owner.

The term "property" when used in these instructions means anything of value .... [See Official Commentary, § 4.91, *supra,* for list.]

COMMENT

Since the Illinois law is similar to the Maryland provision and Illinois court decisions interpreting its statute may be a useful guide to issues arising in Maryland, this Comment is based on Illinois cases.

A person who obtains control over lost or mislaid property commits theft when he (1) knows or learns the identity of the owner, or knows, or is aware of, or learns of a reasonable method of identifying the owner; and (2) fails to take reasonable measures to restore the property to the owner; and (3) intends to deprive the owner permanently of the use or benefit of the property. The failure to take reasonable measures to restore the property to the owner is an essential element of the offense of theft of lost or mislaid property. *People v. Hines,* 12 Ill. App. 3d 582, 299 N.E.2d 581 (1973). See Ill. Ann. Stat., ch. 38, § 16-2 (Smith-Hurd 1977).

The Illinois statute codifies the common law and case law of the crime of larceny of lost or mislaid property. In *People v. Waggoner,* 388 Ill. 468, 58 N.E.2d 553, *cert. denied,* 329 U.S. 768 (1945), the Court held that where the finder of lost goods knows or has a reasonable clue as to the identity of the owner, and intends to deprive the owner permanently of his property, the finder is guilty of larceny (theft). Similarly, in *People v. Betts,* 367 Ill. 499, 11 N.E.2d 942 (1938), the Court held that, generally, in a case involving lost goods, if the finder at the time of the finding intends to deprive the owner permanently of his property and knows or has a reasonable clue as to who the owner is, the finder is guilty of larceny (theft).

It is important to note that all three subsections outlined above are in the conjunctive, and therefore, the requirements of all three subsections must coincide before the offense is committed.

§ 4.95. Theft—Of services.

The defendant has been charged with theft of [$300 or more] [less than $300] of services.

In order for the defendant to be guilty of this offense, the State must prove beyond a reasonable doubt that: (1) __________ *(insert name of owner)* was the provider of certain services, namely, __________ *(list nature or type of services);* (2) the defendant obtained these services which were available only for compensation; and (3) the defendant obtained the services [by deception] [knowing the services were provided without the consent of the person providing them].

[The State must also prove beyond a reasonable doubt that the value of the services was $300 or more. If the State does not prove beyond a reasonable doubt that the value of the services was $300 or more, but that the services had some value, you must then find that the services had a value of less than $300.] *or*

[The defendant has been charged with theft of less than $300. You do not have to determine the exact value of the services but the State must prove beyond a reasonable doubt that the services had some value.]

The term "owner" means a person, other than the offender, who has any interest in the service, including mere possession, without whose consent the defendant has no authority to obtain the service. [The owner's interest in the service may be lawful or unlawful; even a person who unlawfully provides services may occupy the position of owner.]

The term "services" includes, but is not limited to, (labor services) (professional services) (telecommunications) (public utilities) (toll facilities) (transportation services) (lodging) (entertainment) (restaurant services) (the use of equipment, including, but not limited to, computers and other data processing equipment).

The term "obtain," in relation to services, means to secure the performance of the services.

The word "deception" means to knowingly ________ (*insert relevant categories from the following list*): (create or confirm in another an impression which is false and which the defendant does not believe to be true); (fail to correct a false impression which the defendant previously has created or confirmed); (prevent another from acquiring information pertinent to the disposition of the property involved); (sell or otherwise transfer or encumber property, failing to disclose a lien, adverse claim, or other legal impediment to the enjoyment of the property, whether the impediment is or is not of value or the impediment is not a matter of official record); (insert or deposit a slug in a coin machine) [the term "slug" means an object or article which, by virtue of its size, shape or any other quality, is capable of being inserted or deposited in a coin machine as an improper substitute for a coin, bill or token required for the operation of the machine. The term "coin machine" means a coin box, turnstile, vending machine, or other mechanical or electrical device or receptacle designed to receive a coin, bill, or a token made to be received by the machine, and in return for the insertion or deposit thereof, automatically to offer, to provide, to assist in providing, or to permit the acquisition of some property or service]; (remove, alter or otherwise disfigure any label or price tag); (promise performance which the defendant does not intend to perform or knows will not be performed. You may not infer or establish the defendant's knowledge or intention from the fact alone that the promise was not performed); (misrepresent the value of a motor vehicle offered for sale by tampering with, interfering with, resetting or altering the odometer with intent to change the number of miles indicated).

The word "deception," when used in these instructions, does *not* include puffing or false statements of immaterial facts and exaggerated representations unlikely to deceive ordinary persons.

The term "knowingly" means that a person is aware of his conduct or the existing circumstances. A person acts knowingly when such person is practically certain of the results of his conduct. A person has knowledge of the existence of a fact when he is practically certain of its existence. The term "knowingly" does not include accident, mistake, negligence or recklessness.

The term "value" means the market value of the services at the time and place of the crime, [or if the market value cannot be satisfactorily ascertained, the cost of the replacement of the services within a reasonable time after the crime].

[If you find that the theft has been committed as one scheme or continuing course of conduct, whether from the same or several sources, you may consider the conduct as one offense and total the value of the services in determining whether the theft is more or less than $300.]

[In a prosecution for the offense of theft, it is a defense that: [the defendant acted under a good faith claim of right to the services involved] [the defendant acted in honest belief that he had the right to obtain or exert control over the services as he did] [the services involved were those of the defendant's spouse, unless the defendant and the defendant's spouse were not living together as husband and wife and were living in separate abodes at the time of the alleged theft].]

[*Where the offense charged is felony theft and there is some evidence of misdemeanor theft:* Your verdict must take one of three forms. If you conclude beyond a reasonable doubt that the State has proved each of the elements of the offense, and you also find beyond a reasonable doubt that the value of the services was $300 or more, your verdict should be "guilty of theft of $300 or more." If you conclude beyond a reasonable doubt that the State has proved each of the elements of the offense of theft and you are unable to determine, beyond a reasonable doubt, whether the value of the services was more or less than $300 or if you determine that the value of the services was some value less than $300, your verdict should be "guilty of theft of less than $300." If you are not convinced beyond a reasonable doubt that the State has proved each and every element of the offense, you must find the defendant not guilty.]

OFFICIAL COMMENTARY

Joint Subcommittee on Theft Related Offenses, Maryland General Assembly, *Revision of Maryland Theft Laws and Bad Check Laws,* ch. 849 (1978)

This subsection [Art. 27, § 342(e)] provides that wrongfully obtaining services is an aspect of the consolidated crime of theft. Some consideration was given to delineating "theft of services" as a separate crime. However, it was finally concluded that there was no compelling or logical reason to treat theft involving the wrongful appropriation of services differently from stealing property.

This subsection provides an "illustration" of the meaning of services. It is not an all inclusive definition, but rather provides examples of what services "includes, but is not limited to." These examples are a guide to assist the reader and supplement the ordinary and plain meaning of the word "services."

The term "services" is used primarily in subsection 342(e). Subsection 342(e) delineates the aspects of unlawfully obtaining services which constitute the crime of "theft." Therefore, theft of services is *not* a separate crime under the provisions of this statute, but rather is one of the ways in which the crime of theft can be committed.

[This instruction is based on Art. 27, § 342(e), obtaining services by deception. However, since Art. 27, § 340(h) defines property as "anything of value," theft of services apparently also could be prosecuted under other provisions of the Consolidated Theft Offenses. See Instructions: § 4.91, Theft — By unauthorized control, *supra,* and § 4.92, Theft — By deception, *supra.*]

[See also § 4.96, General instruction — "Rights of possession" and certain defenses applicable to theft offenses, *infra.*]

COMMENT

Again, this comment is based on cases decided under Illinois law which is similar to the Maryland enactment.

A person commits the offense of theft when he obtains the use of services of another which are available only for compensation by deception or knowing that the services are provided without the consent of the person providing them. See Ill. Ann. Stat., ch. 38, § 16-3(a) (Smith-Hurd 1977).

This section was to protect all types of business from the unscrupulous practices of prospective customers. *People v. Dillon,* 93 Ill. App. 2d 151, 236 N.E.2d 411 (1968).

An important element in a prosecution under this section is the requirement that the defendant "obtain" or secure the performance of the labor or services. It has been held that a defendant who allegedly had moved around a ticket agent and entered a transit authority train platform without paying his fare could not be convicted of *theft of services* where he had been apprehended prior to boarding the train. *People v. Davis,* 5 Ill. App. 3d 95, 283 N.E.2d 317 (1972). See Ill. Ann. Stat., ch. 38, § 15-7 (Smith-Hurd 1977).

§ 4.96. General instruction — "Rights of possession" and certain defenses applicable to theft offenses.

[It is *not* a defense to the offense of theft that the defendant had an interest in the property which was the subject of the theft if another person also had an interest or *right of (continued) possession* in the property which the defendant was not entitled to infringe. [A joint or common owner of property does *not* have a right of possession of the property greater than that of any joint or common owner.] [In the absence of an agreement to the contrary, a person in lawful possession of property has a greater right of possession than a person only having a security interest in the property, even if legal title to the property lies with the holder of the security interest pursuant to a conditional sales contract or other security agreement].]

[It is not a defense to theft that the property was taken, obtained, or withheld from a person who had obtained possession of the property by illegal means.]

OFFICIAL COMMENTARY

Joint Subcommittee on Theft Related Offenses, Maryland General Assembly, *Revision of Maryland Theft Laws and Bad Check Laws,* ch. 849 (1978)

In some instances, more than one person has a legally recognized interest in property. If there is a dispute as to the right of possession, these legal interests may be in conflict when offered by each of the parties as justification to their acts in securing possession of the property. This subsection attempts to delineate the right of possession in such a situation where there is a dispute as to who has the right of possession.

[Art. 27, § 343(a)(1)] is a general statement which recognizes that a person who currently has a possessory interest in property has a right to continued possession when that right is threatened by the claim of a person with a non-possessory interest. In other words, a bare interest in property does not entitle one to possession. This paragraph is also a reiteration and amplification of an analogous concept which is expressed in the definition of "owner" [Art. 27, § 340(g)] . That concept recognizes the person with possessory rights as the owner. It forbids the infringement of these rights by characterizing an owner as a person "... who has possession of or any other interest in the property ... and without whose consent the offender has no authority to exert control over the property." Similarly, [Art. 27, § 343(a)(1)] is an ancillary statement to the definition of "property of another" [Art. 27, § 340(i)]. The definition of "property of another" echoes the concept that some interests are superior to others by stating that property is "property in which a person ... has an interest which the offender does not have authority to defeat or impair, even though the offender himself may have an interest in the property."

In summary, this paragraph, supplemented by the definitions of "owner" and "property of another," recognizes the superiority of certain interests. It should therefore be clear that merely because a person has an interest in property, that does not entitle them to deprive another person of the property if that other person also has an interest coupled with an exclusive or superior right of possession.

It will be a matter for the courts to determine in instances where there is more than one person with an interest in the property whether the provisions of [Art. 27, § 343(a)(1)] are applicable and specifically whether there exists an interest or right of possession in the property that the defendant "is not entitled to infringe." So as not to leave this determination one exclusively to judicial discretion and to give the courts guidance in particular factual situations, (additional) provisions [Art. 27, § 340(a)(2)(i) and (ii)] were added to this subsection.

These deal with two specific instances where more than one person may assert a legitimate claim to the possession of property. In these instances, it seeks to clarify the right of possession as that "right of possession" is delineated by the provisions of [Art. 27, § 343(a)(1)]. A provision was inserted for the purpose of preserving the common-law bar to prosecution in instances where joint or common owners appropriate mutually held property. This subparagraph precludes a successful prosecution under the provisions of [Art. 27, § 343(a)(1)], claiming rights of possession. The problem posed by such instances is resolved by declaring "A joint or common owner of property does not have a right of possession of the property superior to that of any other joint or common owner of the property." Therefore, for the purposes of [Art. 27, § 343(a)(1)] joint and common owners cannot have an interest or right of possession in the property that the other joint or common owners cannot infringe.

Subparagraph (a)(2)(ii) [Art. 27, § 343] protects lawful possession by the creditor [sic] in instances where the property is the subject of a security agreement and both the secured party and the creditor [sic] claim rights of possession. The problem posed by such instances is resolved by providing "... in the absence of specific [word "specific" deleted by amendment, Acts 1980, ch. 348] agreements to the contrary, a person in lawful possession of property has a right of possession superior to that of a person having only a security interest in the property...." In this manner the secured party is precluded from taking property *solely* on the basis of his security interest in the property. As a practical matter, it is expected that most conditional sales agreements will be written to provide a right of repossession for the secured party. In these instances, the provisions of this subparagraph will be circumvented by providing "a specific agreement to the contrary."

The principle that even a person who has obtained property by illegal means has a right to possession of the property as against another who unlawfully deprives him of the property is noted above. The provisions of the subsection [Art. 27, § 343(b)] are a reiteration of the same principle expressed in the definition of "owner."

No Maryland appellate case can be found which speaks to the issue of a thief's interest in stolen property as against another thief who would steal it from him. However, the Court of Appeals has addressed the ownership requirement as it pertains to larceny and other larceny-related offenses. In *Richardson v. State*, 221 Md. 85 at 88, 156 A.2d 436 at 438 (1959) the Court stated, "It is fundamental ... that in a prosecution for larceny one of the essential elements to be proved is the ownership of the stolen property...." In clarifying the meaning of "ownership" the Court said, "... [I]t is generally held that in a prosecution for larceny, an allegation of the ownership of stolen goods is supported by proof of any legal interest or special property in goods, as, for instance, where the person named in the indictment is in lawful possession as a bailee or common carrier." Therefore, to the extent it can be argued that a thief does not have a legal interest or special property in the goods he has stolen, it may be concluded that this subsection is a departure from current Maryland law.

For further analysis of the ownership and property interests required in larceny cases see Ferttilla, *Larceny in Maryland—A Crime Against Ownership or Possession,* 24 Md. L. Rev. 181 (1964). A brief discussion of a thief's ownership interests in stolen property may be found in 52A C.J.S. *Larceny* § 13 (1968).

COMMENT

Pursuant to Maryland Ann. Code, Art. 27, § 343(a)(2)(ii), the Court in *Borgen v. State,* 56 Md. App. 529, 468 A.2d 394 (1983), held that a *prima facie* case of theft was not proved by the State, when an auto abandoned by its true owner was taken into possession by the defendant. The defendant's possession was upheld although a bank maintained a security lien on the vehicle.

For a discussion of other defenses relating to theft offenses, see Official Commentary following Instruction, § 4.91, Theft—By unauthorized control, particularly under the heading: Defenses: claim of right; spousal immunity; and rightful knowledge of a trade secret.

(2) Bad checks — Obtaining Property or Services by Bad Check

INTRODUCTORY COMMENT

Section 4, ch. 849, Acts 1978, effective July 1, 1979, repealed the former bad check provisions of Maryland Ann. Code, Art. 27, §§ 140 to 142 and 143 to 149A and the former subheading "False

Pretenses, Bad Checks, etc." New provisions [Art. 27, §§ 140 to 144] were enacted under the subheading "Bad Checks."

Article 27, § 141 proscribes four different types of behavior as constituting acts of obtaining property or services by bad check. Each is a subsection of Art. 27, § 141 and covered herein by a separate jury instruction. The relationship of these four offenses may be better understood by the use of the following chart which also serves as a guide to the applicable jury instruction.

Obtaining property or services by bad check

	Utter (delivery by a drawer)	Pass (delivery of a previously uttered check by a payee, holder or bearer)
Insufficient funds to cover a check (no funds to cover a check; less funds than needed; no account upon which check is written)	Instruction, § 4.97a Art. 27, § 141(a) Drawer utters check with knowledge of insufficient funds	Instruction, § 4.97b Art. 27, § 141(b) Payee, holder or bearer passes check knowing that drawer of check has insufficient funds
Stopped payment of the check	Instruction, § 4.97c Art. 27, § 141(c) Drawer intends to stop payment at time of uttering a check and causes drawee to refuse to recognize check	Instruction, § 4.97d Art. 27, § 141(d) Payee, holder or bearer passes check knowing that payment of the check has been stopped

As the above chart shows, there are two bad check offenses involving insufficient funds: (1) Instruction 4.97a is applicable where the drawer or representative drawer (such as an officer signing a check on behalf of a corporation) obtains property or services by delivery of a check — referred to as "uttering" — knowing that he or his principal has insufficient funds with the drawee to cover the check and other outstanding checks; (2) Instruction 4.97b is applicable where a payee, holder or bearer of a check obtains property or services by delivery of a previously uttered check — referred to as "passing" — knowing that the drawer of the check has insufficient funds with the drawee to cover the check and other outstanding checks. In both situations an intent or belief must exist at the time of delivery of the check that payment will be refused by the drawee upon presentation of the check and, in fact, payment is refused by the drawee upon presentation.

Also, as shown in the above chart, two other bad check offenses involve situations where payment is stopped or countermanded. Instruction 4.97c applies where a drawer or representative drawer obtains property or services by delivery (uttering) of a check knowing that he or his principal at the time of delivery intends, without the consent of the payee, to stop or countermand the payment of the check. Instruction 4.97d applies where a payee, holder or bearer of a check obtains property or services by delivery of a previously uttered check (passing) knowing that payment of the check has been stopped or countermanded. In both situations, payment is, in fact, refused by the drawee upon presentation.

The above chart and explanation show that the "bad check" offenses are based on an important distinction between the acts committed by a drawer who "utters" a check and acts by a payee, holder, or bearer who "passes" a check.

An area of possible court challenge is the use of several "presumptions" stated in Art. 27, § 142. The former Code provision contained the "presumption" that giving a worthless check was *prima facie* evidence of an intent to cheat or defraud. "Presumptions" now apply only to a drawer or representative drawer who "utters" a check and not to a payee, holder or bearer who takes from the drawer and subsequently "passes" the check. The argument was accepted that since the passer of the check may not even know the drawer, it cannot be fairly "presumed" that a payee, holder or bearer is familiar with the drawer's bank account. Article 27, § 142(c), providing for a simplified method of proof of dishonor of a check by the drawee and insufficiency of drawer's funds, also uses the phrase "shall constitute presumptive evidence" and would seem to be applicable in cases involving a payee, holder or bearer, as well as a drawer or representative drawer.

The use of the ambiguous term "presumption" invites court challenge in light of *Evans v. State,* 28 Md. App. 640, 349 A.2d 300 (1975), *aff'd,* 278 Md. 197, 362 A.2d 629 (1976). See Appendix V, The Impact of *Evans v. State:* Burdens of Proof, Presumptions, and Inferences, *infra.* In the following instructions the term "presumption" has been placed in brackets and the term "inference" is offered as an alternative. Also, the phrase, "shall constitute presumptive evidence" from Art. 27, § 142(c) has been placed in brackets and the instruction is phrased in terms of an inference.

Article 27, § 140 provides definitions of terms. The definitions of the terms "obtain" and "value" explicitly incorporate the definitions used in the consolidated theft offense provisions, Art. 27, § 340. The felony-misdemeanor distinction and penalties for obtaining property or services of $300 or more or of some value less than $300 used in the theft offense provisions, are also used in the bad check offense sections.

The definitions adopted in Art. 27, § 140 were intended to be consistent with modern usage under the Uniform Commercial Code. The term "funds" has been restricted to mean "money or credit." The definition of "check" specifically provides that an instrument does not qualify as a check if it is postdated; hence, a bad check offense cannot be prosecuted on the basis of an instrument that is postdated. No definition is provided for the term "presentation," although this term appears in each of the four acts constituting bad check offenses. The term has been defined elsewhere as the "act of delivering the instrument (check) for acceptance or payment" and, perhaps, this or similar language should be added to the instructions if amplification is needed.

Article 27, § 144(a) provides for a limitation on prosecution if the offender makes the check good within ten days after its dishonor. While the former Art. 27, § 142 extended this ten-day "grace period" only to Maryland residents, this section extends it to all persons. Language is included both in Art. 27, §§ 144(a) and 342(b) of the consolidated theft offense provisions to ensure that the ten-day "grace period" is not circumvented by prosecution for another offense, such as theft by deception, unless there has been some misrepresentation other than a misrepresentation as to the sufficiency of the funds to cover the check. Article 27, § 144(b) does allow for immediate prosecution if the person uttering the check was the drawer and did not have an account with the drawee at the time of the utterance.

The materials labeled "Official Commentary," which follow the instructions in this subpart, are products of the Joint Subcommittee on Theft Related Offenses of the Maryland General Assembly, *Revision of the Maryland Theft Laws and Bad Check Laws,* ch. 849 (1978). Details from this Commentary covering various definitions appear only after Instruction, § 4.97a and are not repeated following the subsequent instructions. Additional information by the author of this book supplementary to the Official Commentary is shown in brackets.

§ 4.97a. Acts committed by a drawer or representative with knowledge of insufficient funds.

The defendant has been charged with obtaining property or services by bad check of [$300 or more] [less than $300].

In order for the defendant to be found guilty of this offense, the State must prove beyond a reasonable doubt that: (1) ___________ *(insert name of defendant)* was a drawer [representative drawer] of a check; (2) ___________ *(name of the defendant)* obtained ___________ *(insert property or services)* by uttering the check knowing that he [or his principal] had [insufficient funds with ___________ *(insert name of drawee)* to cover the check and other outstanding checks] [no account with ___________ *(insert name of drawee)*]; (3) ___________ *(name of defendant)* intended or believed at the time of utterance that payment would be refused by the drawee upon presentation; and (4) payment was refused by ___________ *(name of drawee)* upon presentation.

[The State must also prove beyond a reasonable doubt that the value of the property (or services) was $300 or more. If the State does not prove beyond a reasonable doubt that the value of the property (or services) was $300 or more, but that the property (or services) had some value, you must then find that the property (or services) had a value of less than $300.] *or*

[The defendant has been charged with obtaining less than $300. You do not have to determine the exact value of the property (or services) but the State must prove beyond a reasonable doubt that the property (or services) had some value.]

The term "obtain" means [in relation to property, to bring about a transfer of interest or possession, whether to the defendant or to another] [in relation to services, to secure the performance of the services].

__________ *(insert definition of property or services from one of the following two paragraphs.)*

[The term "property" means anything of value. Property includes __________ *(insert appropriate item from the list appearing in Official Commentary following this Instruction, § 4.97a).*]

[The term "services" includes __________ *(insert appropriate item from the following list or an additional item pursuant to definition that the term "services" includes, but is not limited to: (1) labor or professional service; (2) telecommunication, public utility, toll facilities, or transportation service; or (3) lodging, entertainment or restaurant service).*]

The term "drawer" in relation to the phrase "drawer of a check" means a person whose name appears as the primary obligor [whether the actual signature be his own or of a person purportedly authorized to draw the check in his behalf].

[*Use only in cases where person who is the primary obligor has signed the check:* The primary obligor, in the usual case, is the person whose signature appears in the lower right hand corner on the face of the check.]

[The phrase "representative drawer" means a person who signs a check as drawer in a representative capacity or as agent of the person whose name appears as the principal drawer or obligor. Examples of situations in which a representative drawer is most likely to sign a check are: an officer signing on behalf of a corporation; a trustee signing on behalf of the trust; and a personal representative signing on behalf of the estate.]

The term "uttering" a check essentially means the delivery of the check. The delivery must be by a drawer [representative drawer] who delivers it or causes it to be delivered to another person who acquires a right against the drawer. [A person who draws a check with the intent that it be delivered is deemed to have uttered the check if the delivery occurs.]

[The term "check" means any check, draft or other negotiable instrument of any kind which is not postdated as to the time of utterance.]

The term "funds" means money or credit. A drawer has "insufficient funds" with __________ *(name of drawee)* when the drawer has no funds or account whatever or funds in an amount less than that needed to cover the check and other outstanding checks. [A check dishonored for "no account" shall also be deemed to have been dishonored for "insufficient funds."] Thus, three situations in which a drawer is regarded to have "insufficient funds" are: (1) there are no funds to cover the check; (2) there are less funds than needed to cover the check and other outstanding checks; and (3) no account exists upon which the check is written.

Inferences; presumptions

[When the drawer of a check has insufficient funds with the drawee to cover the check and other outstanding checks at the time of utterance, [you may, but are not required, to infer] [it is presumed] that the subscribing drawer [representative drawer] knows of the insufficiency.]

[[You are allowed, but not required, to infer] [It is presumed] that a subscribing drawer [or representative drawer] of an ultimately dishonored check intended or believed that the check would be dishonored upon presentation when: (the drawer had no account with the drawee at the time of the utterance) (the drawer had insufficient funds with the drawee at the time of utterance to cover the check and other outstanding checks; and the check was presented to the drawee for payment not more than thirty days after the date of utterance; and the drawer had insufficient funds with the drawee at the time of presentation).]

[Presentation may be defined as the act of delivering the check for [acceptance] [payment].]

Method of proof of dishonor of a check by the drawee, lack of account with the drawee at the time of the utterance and insufficiency of drawer's funds at the time of presentation:

[Notice of protest of the check [may permit you to infer] [is presumptive evidence] that the check has been dishonored by the drawee.]

[A certificate under oath of an authorized representative of the drawee declaring (the dishonor) (lack of account at the time of the presentation) (insufficiency of funds at the time of presentation and utterance) [may permit you to infer] [is presumptive evidence of] __________ *(insert a dishonor, a lack of account and/or an insufficiency of funds.)*]

The term "value" means the market value of the property or services at the time and place of the crime [or if the market value cannot be satisfactorily determined, the cost of the replacement of the property within a reasonable time after the crime].

["Value" in the case of certain written instruments, whether or not they have been issued or delivered, may not have a readily ascertainable market value, and shall be measured as follows: [The value of an instrument constituting evidence of debt, such as a check, draft or promissory note, shall be determined as the amount due or collectible. This figure ordinarily is the face amount of the indebtedness less any portion which has been satisfied.] [The value of an instrument which creates, releases, discharges, or otherwise affects any valuable legal right, privilege, or obligation shall be determined as the amount of economic loss which the owner of the instrument might reasonably suffer by virtue of the loss of the instrument.] [If the property obtained by a bad check is a trade secret, which does not have a readily ascertainable market value, its value shall be deemed as any reasonable value representing the damage to the owner suffered by reason of losing an advantage over those who do not know of or use the trade secret.]]

[If you find that the offense has been committed as one scheme or continuing course of conduct, whether from the same or several sources, you may consider the conduct as one offense and total the value of the property or services in determining whether the offense of obtaining property or services by bad check is more or less than $300.]

[*Where the offense charged is a felony and there is some evidence of a misdemeanor:* Your verdict must take one of three forms. If you conclude beyond a reasonable doubt that the State has proved each of the elements of the offense, and you also find beyond a reasonable doubt that the value of the property (or services) was $300 or more, your verdict should be "guilty of obtaining $300 or more." If you conclude beyond a reasonable doubt that the State has proved each of the elements of the offense and you are unable to determine, beyond a reasonable doubt, whether the value of the property (or services) was more or less than $300 or if you determine that the value of the property (or services) was some value less than $300, your verdict should be "guilty of obtaining less than $300." If you are not convinced beyond a reasonable doubt that the State has proved each and every element of the offense, you must find the defendant not guilty.]

OFFICIAL COMMENTARY

Joint Subcommittee on Theft Related Offenses, Maryland General Assembly, *Revision of Maryland Theft Laws and Bad Check Laws,* ch. 849 (1978)

[Maryland Ann. Code, Art. 27, § 141(a)] pertains to acts committed by a drawer or representative drawer. A corresponding provision pertains to payees, holders and bearers.

Mere issuance of a [bad] check by a drawer or representative drawer is not sufficient to violate the provisions of this subsection. Property or services must be obtained by the uttering of the check. The requirement that goods or services be obtained is consistent with the provisions of the Maryland Code which this section replaces. [Former Art. 27, § 142.]

It is also required that the drawer or representative drawer know of the insufficiency of funds at the time he utters the check. For provisions and commentary on knowledge of insufficiency of funds by the drawer, see [Art. 27, § 142(a)].

In addition, the drawer must intend or believe that payment will be refused by the drawee. Presumptions as to the intent and belief of the drawer that the check would be dishonored are dealt with in Art. 27, § 142(b).

Finally, the drawee must refuse payment upon presentation. There can be no completed offense until the drawee actually refuses payment upon presentation. Proof constituting presumptive evidence of dishonor and insufficiency may be had in the manner provided in Art. 27, § 142(c).

The use of the word "obtain" is appropriate to describe the acquisition of property or services by bad check, since it is through the "uttering" or "passing" of the check that the perpetrator *"brings about a transfer"* of the property or services to him.

[Article 27, § 140(g) refers to the definition of "property" in Art. 27, § 340(h). "Property" means anything of value, including but not limited to:

(1) Real estate;

(2) Money;

(3) Commercial instruments;

(4) Admission or transportation tickets;

(5) Written instruments representing or embodying rights concerning anything of value, or services, or anything otherwise of value to the owner;

(6) Things growing on or affixed to, or found on land, or part of or affixed to any building;

(7) Electricity, gas, and water;

(8) Birds, animals, and fish which ordinarily are kept in a state of confinement;

(9) Food and drink;

(10) Samples, cultures, micro-organisms, specimens;

(11) Records, recordings, documents, blueprints, drawings, maps, and whole or partial copies, descriptions, photographs, prototypes[,] or models thereof; or any other articles, materials, devices, substances, and whole or partial copies, descriptions, photographs, prototypes, or models thereof which represent evidence, reflect or record secret scientific, technical, merchandising[,] production or management information, designed [sic] process, procedure, formula, invention, trade secret, or improvement;

(12) Financial instruments, information, electronically produced data, computer software and programs in either machine or human readable form, and other tangible or intangible items of value.]

[The definition of "services," unlike the definition of "property" is contained in Art. 27, § 140, in subsection (i). The definition, however, uses the same language that is used in the theft definition of "service," Art. 27, § 340(j), except a subpart (4) of the latter is omitted. Article 27, § 140(i) provides: "'Services' includes, but is not limited to:

(1) Labor or professional service;

(2) Telecommunication, public utility, toll facilities, or transportation service; or

(3) Lodging, entertainment, or restaurant service."

Article 27, § 340(j), which relates to theft offenses, also includes the following item: "The use of equipment (including, but not limited to, computers and other data processing equipment)."]

The term "drawer" is not specifically defined by the Uniform Commercial Code or the correlative Title 3 of the Commercial Law Article of the Annotated Code of Maryland (Maryland Uniform Commercial Code — Commercial Paper). However, this definition has been inserted for the purpose of clarity and generally corresponds to the meaning of the term "drawer" as employed in the Uniform Commercial Code and commercial usage.

This definition makes it clear that the "drawer" is the person who is "the primary obligor" and not the person whose signature appears on the check as "a person purportedly authorized to draw the check in his behalf." For the Maryland Uniform Commercial Code treatment of signatures on commercial instruments and signatures by authorized representatives, see [Maryland Ann. Code, Commercial Law, §§ 3-401 and 3-403].

The phrase "representative drawer" describes instances in which a drawer is an agent of the principal obligor of the instrument. Examples of situations in which a representative drawer is most likely to sign a check are: an officer signing on behalf of a corporation, a trustee signing on behalf of the trust, and a personal representative signing on behalf of the estate. In these examples, the corporation, trust and estate would be the drawers and the officer, trustee and personal representative would be acting in the capacity of "representative drawer."

The signature of a representative is dealt with in the commercial sphere by [Commercial Law, § 3-403]. The term "representative" is defined in the context of the Maryland Uniform Commercial Code by [Commercial Law, § 1-201(35)].

The essence of uttering a check is the delivery of the check. The delivery must be by a drawer or representative drawer, or one of them must cause its delivery. This delivery must be made to some person who acquires rights against the drawer with respect to the check. Unless the delivery is accomplished in this manner, uttering does not take place.

The use of the term "utter" as it applies to drawers and representative drawers should be compared to the use of the term "pass" as that term applies to payees, holders and bearers.

In conformity with the draft of the Proposed Criminal Code prepared by the Maryland Commission on Criminal Law, the definitions in this section were adopted to be consistent with modern commercial usage under the Uniform Commercial Code.

The definition of "check" [Art. 27, § 140(a)] specifically provides that an instrument does not qualify as a check if it is postdated. Therefore, a bad check offense cannot be prosecuted on the basis of an instrument that is postdated.

The meaning of "check" and other words used in this definition of "check" may be found in the Maryland [Ann. Code,] Commercial Law [Article]. Citations to these words are as follows:

1. check—[Commercial Law], § 3-104(2)(b).
2. draft—[Commercial Law], § 3-104(2)(a).
3. negotiable instrument—[Commercial Law], § 3-104(1).
4. instrument—[Commercial Law], § 3-102(1)(e).

The term "funds" [Art. 27, § 140(c)] has been restricted to mean "money or credit." This meaning is consistent with § 3-104(1)(b) of the Maryland Uniform Commercial Code which requires that a negotiable instrument (*e.g.*, check) "contain an unconditional promise or order to pay a sum certain in money." For a definition of money see ... Commercial Law, § 1-201(24).

The use of the word "credit" in the definition [of "funds"] serves two purposes. First, it recognizes that technically a bank does not ordinarily actually hold the money of a person who has an account with it. In reality it is a relationship where the bank extends credit on the basis of accumulated deposits. Secondly, by including the word "credit," legal sanction is given to the now common arrangement in which the drawer provides monetary resources to satisfy a check through an automatic loan that has been pre-arranged by an agreement between the drawer and drawee which is implemented in the eventuality of an overdraft.

This subsection [Art. 27, § 140(d)] also outlines three instances in which a drawer is regarded to have insufficient funds. These are: (1) no funds to cover a check, (2) less funds than needed to cover a check, and (3) no account upon which the check is written.

Dishonor is treated by the Maryland Uniform Commercial Code in ..., Commercial Law, § 3-507. This section states that an instrument is dishonored when "... presentment is duly made and due acceptance or payment is refused or cannot be obtained." [Commercial Law, § 3-507(a)].

This Section [Art. 27, § 142] contains a number of presumptions that will be useful in prosecuting "bad check" cases.

[Former] Section 142 of Article 27 of the Annotated Code of Maryland contained the presumption that giving a worthless check was prima facie evidence of an intent to cheat or defraud. The presumption provided by subsection (a) is more restrictive in its application than the presumption in the repealed [Art. 27, § 142]. The presumption provided by subsection (a) [in the new law] applies only to drawers and representative drawers who utter the check. It does not apply to a payee, holder or bearer who takes from the drawer and subsequently passes the check. This policy of not making the presumption applicable to one who passes the check was adopted on the basis of the reasoning stated in the Report of the Commission on Criminal Law that "... the passer of the check may not even know the drawer, and cannot fairly be presumed to be familiar with his bank account."

Under the terms of [Art. 27, § 142(b)], conditions are set forth by which the intent or belief on the part of the defendant that is required by [Art. 27, § 141(a)(2)] (an intent or belief that the check would be dishonored) may be presumed from the establishment of certain facts. Two factual situations are outlined under which the presumption will arise. The first is when the drawer had no account with the drawee. The second is when the drawer had insufficient funds at the time of utterance and presentation of the check, if the time of presentment was not more than thirty days after the date of utterance.

[Although Art. 27, § 142 sets forth "presumptions," its real effect is to create "inferences." This is supported by the statement in the Official Commentary that: "the existence of this presumption does not, however, relieve the State of its obligation to prove conclusively the requisite intent on the part of the defendant. See Appendix V, Impact of *Evans v. State:* Burdens of Proof, Presumptions, and Inferences, *infra.*]

[Article 27, §142(c)] sets forth a simplified manner in which presumptive evidence constituting proof of dishonor of a check [proof of a lack of account with the drawee at the time of the utterance] and insufficiency of funds may be presented. The two methods specified are: (1) a certificate under oath of an authorized representative of the drawee declaring the dishonor, [lack of account] and insufficiency; and (2) a notice of protest of the check. For statutory information on commercial usage and manner of protest see [Commercial Law], § 3-509 .... [Query whether this "simplified" manner of proof raises substantial evidentiary issues involving the hearsay rule and the confrontation clause of the sixth amendment of the United States Constitution.]

Article 27, § 144 perpetuates [former] Art. 27, § 142, [barring] prosecution of a bad check offense if the offender makes the check good within ten days after its dishonor [provided the uttering or passing was not accompanied by a false representation other than a false representation that there were sufficient funds with the drawee to cover the check. A drawer who utters a check and does not have an account with the drawee at the time of the utterance may be immediately prosecuted under the theft subheading or a section of this subheading]. Although the former [Art. 27, § 142] extends this ten-day "grace period" only to Maryland residents, this section extends the ten-day period to all persons.

Language is also contained in this section [Art. 27, § 144] to ensure that the ten-day period is not circumvented through prosecution of the offense under another provision of the Code (e.g., theft (by deception) [Art. 27, § 342(b)]), unless there has been some misrepresentation other than a misrepresentation as to the sufficiency of the funds to cover the check. A complementary provision is [Art. 277, § 344(b)] of the subheading "Theft."

This subsection [Art. 27, § 143(a)] provides a penalty for passing a bad check. The penalty that a person is subject to is based on the value of the property or services obtained by the bad check.

The penalty for obtaining property or services having a value of $300 or greater is the same as the penalty for theft of property of $300 or greater. This penalty is a change from the former law. Before the new bad check offenses were enacted the penalty was based upon whether the goods and services obtained by a bad check had a value of $500 or greater, or less than $500. In the case of goods and services having a value of $500 or more, the penalty prescribed was punishment "by fine and imprisonment, or by confinement in the penitentiary for not less than two nor more than ten years, as the court shall award" [Former Art. 27, §§ 142 and 140]. [Art. 27, § 143(a) now provides that the felony of obtaining property or services by a bad check when the property or services has a value of $300 or greater can result in a fine of not more than $1,000, or imprisonment for not more than fifteen years or both fine and imprisonment.]

[Art. 27, § 143(b)] specifies the penalty for persons convicted of obtaining property or services having a value of less than $300 [as a fine of not more than $100, or imprisonment for not more than eighteen months, or both fine and imprisonment. This penalty is the same as the penalty provided for theft of property or services having a value of less than $300].

The penalty prescribed by this section [Art. 27, § 143(b)] differs from the penalty specified for a misdemeanor bad check offense under former [Art. 27, § 142]. [The repealed law stated] that the penalty in such misdemeanor cases (instances where the property or services obtained had a value of less than $500) shall be a fine of not more than $500 and imprisonment for not more than eighteen months.

[Art. 27, § 143(c)] provides for restoration of property and restitution for the value of property and services obtained by a bad check. The provisions are consistent with the analogous provisions of [former Art. 27, § 145] which is repealed by this statute. [Former Art. 27, 142A, credit card offenses, has been renumbered as Art. 27, § 145.]

§ 4.97b. Acts committed by passers (payees, holders and bearers) of checks with knowledge of insufficient funds.

The defendant has been charged with obtaining property or services by bad check of [$300 or more] [less than $300].

In order for the defendant to be found guilty of this offense, the State must prove beyond a reasonable doubt that: (1) ____________ *(insert name of defendant)* was the (payee) (holder) (bearer) of a check; (2) ____________ *(name of defendant)* obtained ______ *(insert property or services)* by passing the check knowing that the drawer of the check had (insufficient funds with ______ *(name of drawee)* to cover the check and other outstanding checks) (no account with ______ *(name of drawee));* (3) ______ *(name of defendant)* intended or believed at the time the check was passed that payment would be refused by ______ *(name of drawee)* upon presentation; and, (4) payment was refused by ______ *(name of drawee)* upon presentation.

[The State must also prove beyond a reasonable doubt that the value of the property (or services) was $300 or more. If the State does not prove beyond a reasonable doubt that the value of the property (or services) was $300 or more, but that the property (or services) had some value, you must then find that the property (or services) had a value of less than $300.] *or*

[The defendant has been charged with obtaining less than $300. You do not have to determine the exact value of the property (or services) but the State must prove beyond a reasonable doubt that the property (or services) had some value.]

The term "obtain" means [in relation to property, to bring about a transfer of interest or possession, whether to the defendant or to another] [in relation to services, to secure the performance of the services].

______ *(insert definition of property or services from one of the following two paragraphs.)*

[The term "property" means anything of value. Property includes ______ *(insert appropriate item from the list appearing in Official Commentary, § 4.97a, supra).*]

[The term "services" includes ______ *(insert appropriate item from the following list or an additional item pursuant to definition that the term "services" includes, but is not limited to: (1) labor or professional services; (2) telecommunication, public utility, toll facilities or trans-*

portation service; or (3) lodging, entertainment or restaurant service).]

The term "drawer" in relation to the phrase "drawer of a check" means the person whose name appears as the primary obligor [whether the actual signature be that of himself or of a person purportedly authorized to draw the check in his behalf].

[*Use only in cases where person that is the primary obligor has signed the check:* The primary obligor, in the usual case, is the person whose signature appears in the lower right hand corner on the face of the check.]

[The term "check" means any check, draft or other negotiable instrument of any kind which is not postdated as to the time of utterance.]

The term "pass" essentially means the delivery of a check, for a purpose other than collection, to a third person who acquires a right relating to the check. The check must have been initially drawn, that is, written or made by another person at an earlier time who delivered it or caused it to be delivered to the defendant who, as a payee, holder or bearer, was the "passer."

The term "funds" means money or credit. A drawer has "insufficient funds" with __________ *(name of drawee)* when the drawer has no funds or account whatever or funds in an amount less than that needed to cover the check and other outstanding checks. [A check dishonored for "no account" shall also be deemed to have been dishonored for "insufficient funds."] Thus, three situations in which a drawer is regarded to have "insufficient funds" are: (1) there are no funds to cover the check; (2) there are less funds than needed to cover the check and other outstanding checks; and (3) no account exists upon which the check is written.

[Presentation may be defined as the act of delivering the check for [acceptance] [payment].]

Method of proof of dishonor of a check by a drawee, lack of account with the drawee at the time of utterance, and insufficiency of drawer's funds at the time of presentation:

[Notice of protest of the check [may permit you to infer] [is presumptive evidence] that the check has been dishonored by the drawee.]

[A certificate under oath of an authorized representative of the drawee declaring (the dishonor) (lack of account at the time of the presentation) (insufficiency of funds at the time of presentation and utterance) [may permit you to infer] [is presumptive evidence of] __________ *(insert a dishonor, a lack of account and/or an insufficiency of funds.)*]

The term "value" means the market value of the property or services at the time of the crime [or if the market value cannot be satisfactorily determined, the cost of the replacement of the property within a reasonable time after the crime].

["Value" in the case of certain written instruments, whether or not they have been issued or delivered, may not have a readily ascertainable market value, and shall be measured as follows: [The value of an instrument constituting evidence of debt, such as a check, draft or promissory note, shall be determined as the amount due or collectible. This figure ordinarily is the face amount of the indebtedness less any portion which has been satisfied.] [The value of an instrument which creates, releases, discharges, or otherwise affects any valuable legal right, privilege or obligation shall be determined as the amount of economic loss which the owner of the instrument might reasonably suffer by virtue of the loss of the instrument.] [If the property obtained by a bad check is a trade secret, which does not have a readily ascertainable market value, its value shall be deemed as any reasonable value representing the damage to the owner suffered by reason of losing an advantage over those who do not know of or use the trade secret.]]

[If you find that the offense has been committed as one scheme or continuing course of conduct, whether from the same or several sources, you may consider the conduct as one offense and total the value of the property or services in determining whether the offense of obtaining property or services by bad check is more or less than $300.]

[*Where the offense charged is a felony and there is some evidence of a misdemeanor:* Your verdict must take one of three forms. If you conclude beyond a reasonable doubt that the State has proved each of the elements of the offense, and you also find beyond a reasonable doubt that the value of the property (or services) was $300 or more, your verdict should be "guilty of obtaining $300 or more." If you conclude beyond a reasonable doubt that the State has proved each of the elements of the offense and you are unable to determine, beyond a reasonable doubt, whether the value of the property (or services) was more or less than $300 or if you determine that the value of the property (or services) was some value less than $300, your verdict should be "guilty of obtaining less than $300." If you are not convinced beyond a reasonable doubt that the State has proved each and every element of the offense, you must find the defendant not guilty.]

OFFICIAL COMMENTARY

Joint Subcommittee on Theft Related Offenses, Maryland General Assembly, *Revision of Maryland Theft Laws and Bad Check Laws,* ch. 849 (1978)

Maryland Ann. Code [Art. 27, § 141(b)] pertains to the acts of payees, holders and bearers of checks since only these persons can "pass" a check.

Just as is required by subsection (a) of [Art. 27, § 141] (which pertains to drawers and representative drawers) this subsection [(b)] also requires that some property or service be obtained. Mere delivery of the check by a payee, holder or bearer is not sufficient to constitute a bad check charge, unless some property or service is obtained in response to the delivery. This requirement that property or services be obtained was required by [former Art. 27, § 142] which was repealed and replaced by this [Art. 27, § 141].

[Article 27, § 141(b)] also requires that the person passing the check intend or believe that payment of the check will be refused upon presentation. This requirement is similar to the required "intent to cheat or defraud another" in the ... bad check provision repealed.... However, this intent or belief is not in itself sufficient to complete a bad check offense. There must be in addition to this intent or belief a refusal by the drawee to pay the check upon presentation....

The accepted commercial meaning of "holder" is found in [Maryland Ann. Code, Commercial Law Article, § 1-201(20) ...], and "bearer" is in [Commercial Law, § 1-201(5) ...].

[The presumptions applicable to Art. 27, § 141(a) embodied in Instruction and Official Commentary, § 4.97(a), Acts committed by a drawer or representative with knowledge of insufficient funds, *supra,* are not applicable to this instruction.]

[Former Art. 27, § 142] contained the presumption that giving a worthless check was prima facie evidence of an intent to cheat or defraud. The presumption provided by subsection (a) [Art. 27, § 141(a)] is more restrictive in its application than the presumption in the repealed [section]. The presumption provided by subsection (a) applies only to drawers and representative drawers who utter the check. It does not apply to a payee, holder or bearer who takes from the drawer and subsequently passes check. This policy to not make the presumption applicable to one who passes the check was adopted on the basis of the reasoning stated in the Report of the Commission on Criminal Law that "... the passer of the check may not ever know the drawer, and cannot fairly be presumed to be familiar with his bank account."

[For a definition of "property" and discussion of "value," "insufficient funds," and other terms as well as penalties and limitations on prosecution, see the Instruction and Official Commentary, § 4.97(a), Acts committed by a drawer or representative with knowledge of insufficient funds, *supra*.]

§ 4.97c. Acts committed by a drawer or representative who issues a check with intent to stop payment.

The defendant has been charged with obtaining property or services by bad check of [$300 or more] [less than $300].

In order for the defendant to be found guilty of this offense, the State must prove beyond a reasonable doubt that: (1) __________ *(insert name of defendant)* was a drawer [representative drawer] of a check; (2) __________ *(name of defendant)* obtained __________ *(insert property or services)* by uttering a check; (3) __________ *(name of defendant)* knew, at the time the check was uttered, that he [or his principal] intended to stop or countermand the payment of the check [or intended to cause the drawee to disregard or dishonor or refuse to recognize the check] without the consent of the payee; and, (4) payment was refused by __________ *(name of drawee)* upon presentation.

[The State must also prove beyond a reasonable doubt that the value of the property (or services) was $300 or more. If the State does not prove beyond a reasonable doubt that the value of the property (or services) was $300 or more, but that the property (or services) had some value, you must then find that the property (or services) had a value of less than $300.] *or*

[The defendant has been charged with theft of less than $300. You do not have to determine the exact value of the property (or services) but the State must prove beyond a reasonable doubt that the property (or services) had some value.]

The term "obtain" means [in relation to property, to bring about a transfer of interest or possession, whether to the defendant or to another] [in relation to services, to secure the performance of the services].

__________ *(insert definition of property or services from one of the following two paragraphs).*

[The term "property," means anything of value. Property includes __________ *(insert appropriate item from the list appearing in Official Commentary, § 4.97a, supra).*]

[The term "services" includes __________ *(insert appropriate item from the following list or an additional item pursuant to definition that the term "services" includes, but is not limited to: (1) labor or professional service; (2) telecommunication, public utility, toll facilities or transportation service, or (3) lodging, entertainment or restaurant service).*]

The term "drawer" in relation to the phrase "drawer of a check" means the person whose name appears as the primary obligor [whether the actual signature be that of himself or of a person purportedly authorized to draw the check in his behalf].

[*Use only cases where person that is the primary obligor has signed the check*: The primary obligor, in the usual case, is the person whose signature appears in the lower right hand corner on the face of a check.]

[The phrase "representative drawer" means a person who signs a check as drawer in a representative capacity or as agent of the person whose name appears as the principal drawer or obligor. Examples of situations in which a representative drawer is most likely to sign a check are: an officer signing on behalf of a corporation, a trustee signing on behalf of the trust, and a personal representative signing on behalf of the estate.]

The term "uttering" a check essentially means the delivery of the check. The delivery must be by a drawer [representative drawer] who delivers it or causes it to be delivered to another person who acquires a right against the drawer. [A person who draws a check with the intent that it be delivered is deemed to have uttered the check if the delivery occurs.]

[The term "check" means any check, draft or other negotiable instrument of any kind which is not postdated as to the time of utterance.]

The fact that a drawer [representative drawer] without the consent of the payee, stopped or countermanded the check [or otherwise caused the drawee to disregard or dishonor or refuse to recognize the check] without returning or tendering the return of property obtained [is a basis from which you may, but are not required to, infer] [constitutes presumptive evidence] that the drawer [representative drawer] had the intent to stop or countermand payment [or otherwise causes the drawee to disregard or dishonor or refuse to recognize the check] at the time of uttering.

[Presentation may be defined as the act of delivering the check for [acceptance] [payment].]

The term "value" means the market value of the property or service at the time and place of the crime [or if the market value cannot be satisfactorily determined, the cost of the replacement of the property within a reasonable time after the crime].

["Value" in the case of certain written instruments, whether or not they have been issued or delivered, may not have a readily ascertainable market value, and shall be measured as follows: [The value of an instrument constituting evidence of debt, such as a check, draft or promissory note, shall be determined as the amount due or collectible. This figure ordinarily is the face amount of the indebtedness less any portion which has been satisfied.] [The value of an instrument which creates, releases, discharges or otherwise affects any valuable legal right, privilege or obligation shall be determined as the amount of economic loss which the owner of the instrument might reasonably suffer by virtue of the loss of the instrument.] [If the property obtained by a bad check is a trade secret, which does not have a readily ascertainable market value, its value shall be deemed as any reasonable value representing the damage to the owner suffered by reason of losing an advantage over those who do not know of or use the trade secret.]]

[If you find that the offense has been committed as one scheme or continuing course of conduct, whether from the same or several sources, you may consider the conduct as one offense and total the value of the property or services in determining whether the offense of obtaining property or services by bad check is more or less than $300.]

[*Where the offense charged is a felony and there is some evidence of a misdemeanor:* Your verdict must take one of three forms. If you conclude beyond a reasonable doubt that the State has proved each of the elements of the offense, and you also find beyond a reasonable doubt that the value of the property (or services) was $300 or more, your verdict should be "guilty of obtaining $300 or more." If you conclude beyond a reasonable doubt that the State has proved each of the elements of the offense and you are unable to determine, beyond a reasonable doubt, whether the value of the property (or services) was more or less than $300 or if you determine that the value of the property (or services) was some value less than $300, your verdict should be "guilty of obtaining less than $300." If you are not convinced beyond a reasonable doubt that the State has proved each and every element of the offense, you must find the defendant not guilty.]

OFFICIAL COMMENTARY

Joint Subcommittee on Theft Related Offenses, Maryland General Assembly, *Revision of Maryland Theft Laws and Bad Check Laws,* ch. 849 (1978)

Maryland Ann. Code, Art. 27, § 141(c) covers situations in which a drawer or representative drawer issues a check with the intent to stop payment on the check at the time it was issued. Of course, the stop payment order must be made without consent of the payee and the check must ultimately be dishonored in order for the offense to be committed. The provisions of this subsection, in conjunction with corresponding subsection (d), replace [Art. 27, § 144]. The language of this subsection is largely taken from the section that it replaces.

The presumption pertaining to instances where the drawer or representative drawer stops or countermands payment of a check without the consent of the payee and without tendering or returning the property obtained is provided in [Art. 27, § 142(d)].

This subsection [Art. 27, § 142(d)] was inserted to preserve the presumption applicable to instances where the drawer stops payment on a check or otherwise caused the check to be dishonored without the consent of the payee and without returning or tendering the return of the property obtained. This presumption was codified in [Art. 27, § 144] which is repealed by this bill.

[See Official Commentary, § 4.97a, Acts committed by a drawer or representative with knowledge of insufficient funds, *supra,* for definition of "property," "value" and related terms as well as the penalty and limitation on prosecution.]

§ 4.97d. Acts committed by passers (payees, holders and bearers) of checks with knowledge that payment has been stopped.

The defendant has been charged with obtaining property or services by bad check of [$300 or more] [less than $300].

In order for the defendant to be found guilty of this offense, the State must prove beyond a reasonable doubt

that: (1) ____________ *(insert name of defendant)* was the (payee) (holder) (bearer) of a check; (2) ____________ *(name of defendant)* obtained ____________ *(insert property or services)* by passing the check; (3) ____________ *(name of defendant)* knew that (payment of the check had been stopped or countermanded) (the drawee of the check would disregard or dishonor or refuse to recognize the check); and (4) payment was refused by ____________ *(name of drawee)* upon presentation.

[The State must also prove beyond a reasonable doubt that the value of the property (or services) was $300 or more. If the State does not prove beyond a reasonable doubt that the value of the property (or services) was $300 or more, but that the property (or services) had some value, you must then find that the property (or services) had a value of less than $300.] *or*

[The defendant has been charged with obtaining less than $300. You do not have to determine the exact value of the property (or services) but the State must prove beyond a reasonable doubt that the property (or services) had some value.]

The term "obtain" means [in relation to property, to bring about a transfer of interest or possession, whether to the defendant or to another] [in relation to services, to secure the performance of the services].

____________ *(insert definition of property or services from one of the following two paragraphs).*

[The term "property" means anything of value. Property includes ____________ *(insert appropriate item from the list appearing in Official Commentary, § 4.97a, supra).*]

[The term "services" includes ____________ *(insert appropriate item from the following list or an additional item pursuant to definition that the term "services" includes, but is not limited to: (1) labor or professional service; (2) telecommunication, public utility, toll facilities or trans-*

portation service; or (3) lodging, entertainment or restaurant service).]

The term "check" means any check, draft or other negotiable instrument of any kind which is not postdated as to the time of utterance.

The term "pass" essentially means the delivery of a check, for a purpose other than collection, to a third person who acquires a right relating to the check. The check must have been initially drawn, that is, written or made by another person at an earlier time who delivered it or caused it to be delivered to the defendant who, as a payee, holder or bearer, was the "passer."

[Presentation may be defined as the act of delivering the check for [acceptance] [payment].]

The term "value" means the market value of the property or services at the time and place of the crime [or if the market value cannot be satisfactorily ascertained, the cost of the replacement of the property within a reasonable time after the crime].

["Value" in the case of certain written instruments, whether or not they have been issued or delivered, may not have a readily ascertainable market value, and shall be measured as follows: [The value of an instrument constituting evidence of debt, such as a check, draft or promissory note, shall be determined as the amount due or collectible. This figure ordinarily is the face amount of the indebtedness less any portion which has been satisfied.] [The value of an instrument which creates, releases, discharges or otherwise affects any valuable legal right, privilege or obligation shall be determined as the amount of economic loss which the owner of the instrument might reasonably suffer by virtue of the loss of the instrument.] [If the property obtained by a bad check is a trade secret, which does not have a readily ascertainable market value, its value shall be deemed as any reasonable value representing the damage to the owner suffered by reason of losing an advantage over those who do not know of or use the trade secret.]]

[If you find that the offense has been committed as one scheme or continuing course of conduct, whether from the same or several sources, you may consider the conduct as one offense and total the value of the property or services in determining whether the offense of obtaining property or services by bad check is more or less than $300.]

[*Where the offense charged is a felony and there is some evidence of a misdemeanor:* Your verdict must take one of three forms. If you conclude beyond a reasonable doubt that the State has proved each of the elements of the offense, and you also find beyond a reasonable doubt that the value of the property (or services) was $300 or more, your verdict should be "guilty of obtaining $300 or more." If you conclude beyond a reasonable doubt that the State has proved each of the elements of the offense and you are unable to determine, beyond a reasonable doubt, whether the value of the property (or services) was more or less than $300 or if you determine that the value of the property (or services) was some value less than $300, your verdict should be "guilty of obtaining less than $300." If you are not convinced beyond a reasonable doubt that the State has proved each and every element of the offense, you must find the defendant not guilty.]

OFFICIAL COMMENTARY

Joint Subcommittee on Theft Related Offenses, Maryland General Assembly, *Revision of Maryland Theft Laws and Bad Check Laws,* ch. 849 (1978)

This subsection [Art. 27, § 141(d)] applies to a payee, holder, or bearer who delivers a check knowing that payment of the check has been stopped or countermanded. The corresponding subsection that applies to drawers and representative drawers is subsection (c) [Art. 27, § 141(c); see, Instruction, § 4.97c, Acts committed by a drawer or representative who issues a check with intent to stop payment, *supra.*] In order for the offense to be completed, payment of the check must be refused upon presentation.

[For a discussion of the distinction between "utter" and "pass," see Official Commentary, § 4.97b, Acts committed by passers (payees, holders and bearers) of checks with knowledge of insufficient funds, *supra.* See also Official Commentary, § 4.97a, Acts committed by a drawer or representative with knowledge of insufficient funds, *supra,* for a definition of "property," "value" and related terms as well as the penalty and limitation on prosecution.]

PART III
DEFENSES

Chapter 5

SPECIFIC INSTRUCTIONS

§ 5.01. Voluntary drunkenness.
§ 5.02. Alibi.
§ 5.03. Claim of right.
§ 5.04. Defense of others.
§ 5.05. Duress.
§ 5.06. Entrapment.
§ 5.07. Good character of defendant.
§ 5.08. Insanity.
§ 5.09. Mistake or ignorance of fact (suggested instruction).
(a) General intent element of the crime.
(b) Specific intent element of the crime.
§ 5.10. Mistaken identity.
§ 5.11. Self-defense — General considerations and burden of proof.
(a) General considerations.
(b) Burden of proof.
§ 5.12. Self-defense — Amount of force permissible.
(a) Nondeadly force.
(b) Deadly force.
§ 5.13. Self-defense — Where defendant is alleged aggressor.
(a) Where there is conflicting evidence as to who is the aggressor.
(b) Where defendant is aggressor using nondeadly force, victim counterattacks with deadly force, and defendant subsequently uses deadly force to defend.
(c) Where defendant is aggressor using deadly force, defendant totally withdraws, and victim counterattacks using deadly force (suggested instruction).
§ 5.14. Self-defense — Where appearances are false.
§ 5.15. Self-defense — Duty to retreat before using deadly force and exception for "castle doctrine."
(a) Duty to retreat before using deadly force.
(b) No duty to retreat — "Castle doctrine" exception.
§ 5.16. Self-defense — Prior acts, reputation (or opinion) and threats of the deceased.
(a) Prior acts of violence by the deceased *known* by the defendant.
(b) Reputation (or opinion) of the deceased's violent and dangerous character *known* by the defendant.
(c) Reputation (or opinion) of the deceased's violent and dangerous character *not known* by the defendant.
(d) Prior threats by the deceased against the defendant *known* by the defendant.
(e) Prior threats by the deceased against the defendant *not known* by the defendant.
§ 5.17. Right to use nondeadly force to defend property (suggested instruction).
§ 5.18. Necessity (suggested instruction).

§ 5.01. Voluntary drunkenness.

I have already instructed you that in order for a person to be found guilty of an offense, the State must prove each and every element of the offense charged beyond a reasonable doubt. The defendant has been charged with __________ *(insert crime charged).* Therefore, one of the elements which the State must prove is that the defendant acted with the specific intent to __________ *(insert crime charged).*

There is evidence in this case tending to show that the defendant may have been intoxicated prior to, and at the time of, the alleged commission of the offense with which he is charged. Generally, voluntary drunkenness is no defense to a criminal charge. An exception occurs when a defendant is charged with a crime requiring specific intent. If the defendant was so intoxicated that he was unable to formulate the specific intent required to commit the crime, then an essential element of the crime has not been established. The fact that the defendant may have been intoxicated at the time of the commission of the alleged offense may be considered by you as bearing upon this specific intent.

For drunkenness to be a defense to the crime requiring specific intent, the intent to commit the crime must arise after the person became intoxicated.

An issue in this case is not whether the defendant was drunk at the time of the commission of the alleged crime; it is whether the defendant was so intoxicated at the time the act was committed as to be incapable of forming the specific intent to __________ *(insert crime charged),* which is a necessary element of the offense charged.

If after a full and fair consideration of all of the facts and circumstances in evidence, you have a reasonable doubt as to whether the defendant [had the capacity] [was sober enough] to form the specific intent, which is a necessary element of this offense, then you must find the defendant not guilty. On the other hand, if the State has convinced you beyond a reasonable doubt that the defendant did [have the capacity] [was sober enough] to commit the specific intent crime of __________ *(insert crime charged),* then you [should] [must] conclude that voluntary intoxication does not excuse the defendant of criminal responsibility.

COMMENT

This instruction is based on Maryland appellate decisions, especially *State v. Gover,* 267 Md. 602, 298 A.2d 378 (1973). See also *Shell v. State,* 307 Md. 46, 512 A.2d 358 (1986) and *Smith v. State,* 69 Md. App. 115, 516 A.2d 985 (1986).

Maryland decisions have held that voluntary drunkenness is not a defense to a crime, but where a crime required a specific intent, motive or purpose, voluntary drunkenness may be considered in determining whether the accused lacked the mental capacity to commit the crime. *State v. Gover, supra* at 606, 298 A.2d at 381; *Avey v. State,* 249 Md. 385, 240 A.2d 107 (1968); *Smith v. State,* 41 Md. App. 277, 398 A.2d 426 (1979); *Frank v. State,* 6 Md. App. 332, 251 A.2d 249 (1969); *Parker v. State,* 7 Md. App. 167, 254 A.2d 381 (1969), *cert. denied,* 256 Md. 747, (1970), *cert. denied,* 402 U.S. 984 (1971); *Brown v. State,* 6 Md. App. 631, 252 A.2d 887 (1969); *Clarke v. State,* 3 Md. App. 447, 240 A.2d 291 (1968); *Biggs v. State, supra.*

In *Frank v. State, supra* at 333, 251 A.2d at 250, the Court instructed the jury in part:

> [W]here a particular motive, intent or purpose is an essential element of a crime, drunkenness may be considered in determining whether or not the accused lacked the mental capacity to form the requisite motive, intent or purpose and if a sufficient mental incapacity is found to exist, drunkenness may constitute a defense to the particular offense charged.

The above instruction was given with reference to the charges of assault with intent to commit murder and assault with intent to commit rape. In *Michael v. State,* 1 Md. App. 243, 229 A.2d 145 (1967), the Court considered the alleged drunkenness of a defendant charged with assault with intent to have carnal knowledge of a female under the age of fourteen in determining the extent of his criminal intent. This approach was extended to the charges of robbery and larceny in *State v. Gover, supra.*

In *Shell v. State, supra,* the Court reviewed the distinction between so-called "specific intent" and "general intent" crimes in the context of Maryland cases providing for a defense of involuntary intoxication. The Court held that the defendant could not be convicted of using a handgun in the commission of a felony or crime of violence in a nonjury trial where he had been found unable, due to voluntary drug-induced intoxication, to form the intent necessary to be found guilty of the underlying felony or crime of violence. The Court also held, over a dissenting opinion by Judge McAuliffe, that willfully and maliciously destroying property of another is a specific intent crime and the intent was negated by the defendant's voluntary drug-induced intoxication. Finally, the Court held that knowingly transporting a handgun in a vehicle is not a specific intent crime and, therefore, the defendant's voluntary drug-induced intoxication did not preclude a conviction. *Cf. Biggs v. State,* 56 Md. App. 638, 468 A.2d 669 (1983).

In *Holt v. State,* 50 Md. App. 578, 438 A.2d 1386 (1982), the Court reversed convictions for the specific intent crimes of third degree sexual offense and attempted third degree sexual offense because the trial court failed to give a requested instruction on voluntary intoxication when it was supported by the evidence.

Intoxication, if proven, will not always be a defense to a specific intent crime; it must be shown that the degree of intoxication was great. Judge Digges stated in *Gover:*

> We hold that voluntary drunkenness can be a defense to a specific intent crime, but the degree of intoxication which must be demonstrated to exonerate a defendant is great. Evidence of drunkenness which falls short of a proven incapacity in the accused to form the intent necessary to constitute the crime merely establishes that the mind was affected by drink so that he more readily gave way to some violent passion and does not rebut the presumption that a man intends the natural consequences of his act.

State v. Gover, supra at 608, 298 A.2d at 381. The last sentence of Judge Digges' statement requires a careful distinction between requiring the defendant to produce sufficient evidence to generate an issue for the trier of fact and shifting the burden of persuasion, as noted below. In *Sandstrom v. Montana,* 442 U.S. 510, 99 S. Ct. 2450, 61 L. Ed. 2d 4 (1979), the Supreme Court held that a jury instruction that "the law presumes that a person intends the ordinary consequences of his voluntary acts" may violate the due process clause of the fourteenth amendment requiring that the State prove every *fact* necessary to constitute the crime charged.

In *Myers v. State,* 58 Md. App. 211, 472 A.2d 1027 (1984), the Court held that the evidence of intoxication did not satisfy the *Gover* test. See also *Johnson v. State,* 292 Md. 405, 439 A.2d 542 (1982). A defendant cannot use intoxication as a defense when he drinks merely to bolster his courage.

In *Smith v. State, supra,* the Court reviewed Maryland cases dealing with the sufficiency of the evidence to generate a jury instruction on voluntary intoxication, stating that the *Gover* rule still governs. The Court held that the defendant was entitled to a jury instruction on voluntary intoxication as a defense to the specific intent crimes of assault with intent to murder, shooting with intent to disable, and use of handgun in the commission of a crime of violence which was based on a specific intent crime. The defendant had consumed a large quantity of alcohol and drugs during the afternoon and evening prior to the shooting, which occurred around 2:00 a.m. The Court found the evidence sufficient to raise the defense despite the State's argument that there was no direct testimony that the defendant consumed inebriants after the early evening hours and the evidence showed that the defendant had successfully traveled a quarter mile to his girl friend's house after the shooting.

Mullaney v. Wilbur, 421 U.S. 684, 95 S. Ct. 1881, 44 L. Ed. 2d 508 (1975) and *Evans v. State,* 28 Md. App. 640, 349 A.2d 300 (1975), *aff'd,* 278 Md. 197, 362 A.2d 629 (1976) compel the conclusion that once evidence of the defendant's intoxication is in issue, the State bears the burden of proving beyond a reasonable doubt that the defendant was not so intoxicated as to be incapable of forming the specific intent to commit the crime alleged. See Appendix V, The Impact of *Evans v. State:* Burdens of Proof, Presumptions and Inferences, *infra.*

In *Teves v. State,* 33 Md. App. 195, 364 A.2d 593 (1976), the defendant complained that the court's instruction on intoxication unconstitutionally placed the burden of persuasion on him to prove that he was intoxicated, and therefore, could not have formed the requisite specific intent to commit first degree murder. The Court, in upholding the defendant's conviction, reasoned that when the State proved beyond a reasonable doubt the killing was willful, deliberate and premeditated, it negated the defense of voluntary intoxication. A "state of mind fully conscious of its own design cannot coexist with one which is incapable of forming, because of intoxication, the specific intent to kill." *Id.* at 200-201, 364 A.2d at 596. It further stated that "instructions must not be judged in artificial isolation, but must be viewed in the context of the overall charge in determining whether the principles of *Mullaney* were violated." *Id.* at 198, 364 A.2d at 594. Therefore, even if the intoxication instruction were erroneous, it was harmless beyond a reasonable doubt. *Id.* at 201, 364 A.2d at 596. *Cf. Mayne v. State,* 45 Md. App. 483, 414 A.2d 1 (1980), *cert. denied,* 450 U.S. 910 (1981).

Chronic alcoholism *per se* is not a defense where no factual showing has been made that the accused was so drunk at the time of the crime as to be incapable of forming the requisite criminal intent. *Prather v. Warden,* 1 Md. App. 478, 481, 231 A.2d 726, 728 (1967), *cert. denied,* 389 U.S. 1056 (1968).

Voluntary intoxication (or voluntary drug abuse) and its relationship to the insanity defense is discussed in *Porreca v. State,* 49 Md. App. 522, 433 A.2d 1204 (1981). The Court distinguished between the mental effect of voluntary intoxication or drug abuse which is the immediate result of a particular alcoholic bout or drug abuse and a "fixed insanity" (which may be temporary), where sustained drug abuse has caused a mental disorder and where the effects of the disorder exist even after the drugs have worn off. The former cannot be used in an insanity defense but the latter can. The testimony showed that the defendant's disorder was of the latter variety. The trial court's holding that defendant had not put his sanity in issue was erroneously based on the finding that defendant's psychosis was caused by voluntary drug abuse. See also *Parker v. State, supra,* and Comment, § 5.08, Insanity, *infra,* for a discussion of *Parker* and of "diminished capacity."

§ 5.02. Alibi.

__________ *(name of defendant)* has offered testimony to establish an alibi. An alibi is a defense which is based on evidence that the defendant was not present at the time when, or at the place where, he is alleged to have committed the offense charged.

The claim of alibi is a legitimate, legal and proper defense. The presence of the defendant at the time and place of the criminal act is not to be presumed or assumed. In every case where the presence of the defendant at the commission of the crime is essential to his conviction, the State must establish his presence beyond a reasonable doubt.

You are not to weigh the evidence relating to the alibi and determine from that alone whether you have a reasonable doubt of guilt. You should consider such evidence along with all of the other evidence. In this connection you should consider whether the alibi testimony covered the entire period of time during which the crime may have been committed.

If after a full and fair consideration of all the facts and circumstances in evidence, you have a reasonable doubt as to whether the defendant was present at the time the crime was committed, then you must find him not guilty. On the other hand, if the State has convinced you beyond a reasonable doubt that the defendant was present at the time of the commission of the crime, then you [should] [must] conclude that the alibi defense does not excuse the defendant of criminal liability.

COMMENT

This instruction is patterned substantially after the leading Maryland case in this area, *Floyd v. State,* 205 Md. 573, 109 A.2d 729 (1954). An alibi is proof that the accused did not and could not commit the crime charged because he was not at the scene of the crime at the time it was committed, having been at another place at that time.

To warrant a conviction the State must prove the charge beyond a reasonable doubt. *Floyd v. State, supra, citing Wood v. State,* 192 Md. 643, 65 A.2d 316 (1949). A thoroughly established alibi of the defendant, proceeding as it does upon the idea that he was elsewhere at the time of the commission of the crime, precludes the possibility of guilt. *Basoff v. State,* 208 Md. 643, 655, 119 A.2d 917, 923 (1956); *Floyd v. State, supra.*

The Court has provided a test for determining when an alibi instruction should be given. It states:

> Sufficient evidence to raise an alibi issue exists when the defendant's evidence, if believed, reasonably excludes the possibility of his presence at the time and place of the alleged offense; the defendant's evidence must tend to prove that it was impossible or highly improbable that he was at the scene of the crime when it was alleged to have occurred.

Pulley v. State, 38 Md. App. 682, 689, 382 A.2d 621, 625 (1978), *quoting Ferguson v. State,* 488 P.2d 1032, 1039 (Alaska 1971). When the evidence in a case generates the issue of alibi, and when the defendant requests an instruction, the defendant is entitled to a specific alibi instruction. The defendant's uncorroborated testimony that he was at some other place at the time of the crime is sufficient to generate the issue. *Smith v. State,* 302 Md. 175, 486 A.2d 196 (1985).

All of the evidence in a criminal trial is to be considered together. In other words, the trier of fact does not merely weigh the evidence relating to the alibi and determine from that alone whether there is reasonable doubt of guilt. *Basoff v. State, supra.* The trier of fact in a criminal prosecution may weigh alibi testimony but is not required to accept its truthfulness. *Duffy v. State,* 243 Md. 425, 221 A.2d 653 (1966); *Fletcher v. State,* 6 Md. App. 219, 251 A.2d 35 (1969); *Melia v. State,* 5 Md. App. 354, 247

A.2d 554 (1968); *Marshall v. State,* 3 Md. App. 715, 240 A.2d 767 (1968); *Logan v. State,* 1 Md. App. 213, 228 A.2d 837 (1967).

Maryland Rule 4-263(d)(3) relates to discovery of witnesses and their statements and, under the rule, a defendant is required to notify the court, prior to trial, of an intention to have an alibi witness testify. In *Middleton v. State,* 49 Md. App. 286, 431 A.2d 734 (1981), the defendant failed to so notify the court. At trial it was discovered that the alibi witness and a juror were friends. The Court held that, since the defendant had violated the rule, the trial judge did not abuse his discretion when, pursuant to [Rule 4-263(i)], he refused to allow the witness to testify. In *Taliaferro v. State,* 295 Md. 376, 456 A.2d 29 (1983), the Court held that the trial court acted within the bounds of its discretion in excluding an alibi witness' testimony where defendant, without any justifying excuse, did not disclose his alibi witness until the close of the State's case in a jury trial.

The Court in *Taliaferro* observed that, in the context of a notice of alibi rule, the United States Supreme Court has not yet passed upon the constitutionality of exclusion as the sanction for violation by a defendant, although state and lower federal courts have held that the exclusion does not offend the sixth amendment right to have compulsory process for obtaining witnesses. The trial court has discretion to fashion an appropriate order when there is a failure to comply with the alibi notice rule. A court may grant a reasonable continuance, prohibit a party from introducing in evidence the matter not disclosed or enter any other appropriate order. The Maryland rule does not mandate exclusion as the sanction for violation. Whether exclusion of alibi witness testimony constitutes an abuse of discretion depends on such factors as whether the disclosure violation was technical or substantial, the timing of the ultimate disclosure, the reason, if any, for the violation, the degree of prejudice to the parties, whether any resulting prejudice might be cured by a postponement and, if so, the overall desirability of a continuance.

Although Rule 4-263(d)(3) allows discovery of a witness' name, the State does not have to disclose those witnesses it plans to use to impeach a defense witness' credibility. In *Williams v. State,* 50 Md. App. 255, 437 A.2d 665 (1981), the Court held the rule was not applicable and disclosure not necessary, since the witness did not rebut the alibi, but merely impeached the credibility of the witness.

The alibi defense has been the subject of substantial appellate litigation and learned discussion by the Court. See *Grady v. State,* 24 Md. App. 85, 329 A.2d 726 (1974), *aff'd,* 276 Md. 178, 345 A.2d 436 (1975); *Daniels v. State,* 24 Md. App. 1, 329 A.2d 712 (1974); *Robinson v. State,* 20 Md. App. 450, 316 A.2d 268 (1974).

An alibi defense is not an affirmative defense. An affirmative defense is one that concedes the basic position of the State, but nevertheless, asserts that the defendant is not guilty, *e.g.,* self defense.

In *Jackson v. State,* 22 Md. App. 257, 322 A.2d 574 (1974), the Court quotes with approval the following statement of Judge Moylan in *Robinson v. State, supra:*

> We think the sound view to be that an alibi is not an affirmative defense, placing any burden upon a defendant beyond the self-evident one of attempting to erode the State's proof to a point where it no longer convinces the fact finder beyond a reasonable doubt. Proof of an alibi, like any other defense testimony, is simply a means of controverting the State's effort to establish criminal agency.

Id. at 260, 322 A.2d at 576. In *Brooks v. State,* 53 Md. App. 285, 452 A.2d 1285 (1982), the Court held that when a alibi defense is raised, the State is not obligated to prove the defendant was not where he says he was. Rather, the State is obligated to prove beyond a reasonable doubt that the defendant was present at the scene and time of the crime.

In *Beckette v. State,* 31 Md. App. 85, 355 A.2d 515 (1976), the Court reversed the conviction of the appellant on the ground that the judge had instructed the jury to the effect that once the State has introduced evidence placing the defendant at the scene of the crime, the defendant had the "burden" of going forward with evidence sufficient to persuade the jury that a reasonable doubt exists as to whether or not he was present. The Court found that such an instruction was prejudicial as being likely to mislead the jury into believing that the defendant carries a burden of proving his alibi beyond a reasonable doubt. Once the issue of the accused's presence at the scene of the crime has been raised, by either the State's or defendant's evidence, the State bears the burden of proving beyond a reasonable doubt the presence of the defendant at the scene of the crime. See *Mullaney v. Wilbur,* 421 U.S. 684, 95 S. Ct. 1881, 44 L. Ed. 2d 508 (1975); *Evans v. State,* 28 Md. App. 640, 349 A.2d 300 (1975), *aff'd,* 278 Md. 197, 362 A.2d 629 (1976); *Beckette v. State, supra; Grady v. State, supra; Brooks v. State, supra.* See also Appendix V, The Impact of *Evans v. State:* Burdens of Proof, Presumptions and Inferences, *infra.*

§ 5.03. Claim of right.

You have already been instructed that in order for a person to be found guilty of an offense, the State must prove each and every element of the offense charged beyond a reasonable doubt. The defendant has been charged with __________ *(insert crime charged).* Therefore, one of the elements which the State must prove is that the defendant acted with the specific intent to __________ *(insert element of offense)* which is required for the crime of __________ *(insert crime charged).*

Evidence has been introduced that the defendant believed that he had a *bona fide* right to take the property he is alleged to have stolen: that is, a good faith belief in the right to take the property.

If one takes property of another which he believes, in good faith, to be his and to which he believed he had a right to possession, or which he honestly believed he had a right to take, then the specific intent to __________ *(insert element of offense)* which is required for the crime of __________ *(insert crime charged),* has not been established. This is true even if the defendant was mistaken or careless in arriving at such a belief.

If after a full and fair consideration of all the facts and circumstances in evidence, you have a reasonable doubt as to whether the defendant did act in the good faith belief that he had a right to the property, then you must find the defendant not guilty of the offense charged. On the other hand, if the State has convinced you beyond a reasonable doubt that the defendant did *not* act with a good faith belief that he had the right to the property, then you [should] [must] conclude that the claim of right defense does not excuse the defendant of criminal responsibility.

COMMENT

Maryland Ann. Code, Art. 27, § 343(c)(1) and (2) provides:

> (c) It is a defense to the offense of theft that:
> (1) The defendant acted under a good faith claim of right to the property involved;
> (2) The defendant acted in the honest belief that he had the right to obtain or exert control over the property as he did....

For a discussion of the statute and the leading Maryland case of *Saunders v. Mullinix,* 195 Md. 235, 72 A.2d 720 (1950), see Official Commentary, § 4.91, *supra.*

In *Saunders, supra* at 240, 72 A.2d at 722, the Court stated:

> It is a generally accepted rule in criminal prosecutions that one who either takes or retains the property of another without the latter's consent for a debt which he in good faith claims to be due him by the owner of the property is not guilty of larceny, because the existence of the debt or the *bona fide* belief in its existence shows a lack of felonious intent in the taking or detention of the property.

"Defendant is not guilty of larceny if he has taken possession of the property with the reasonable and actual belief that it had been abandoned." *Szewczyk v. State,* 7 Md. App. 597, 601, 256 A.2d 713, 715 (1969), *citing* 2 Wharton, Criminal Law & Procedure § 493 at 161 (Anderson ed. 1957).

Defendant lacks the specific intent required if he honestly believes that he has a claim of right to the property in question. This belief may be greatly mistaken, careless and perhaps even negligent. See *Rex v. Knight,* 2 East P.C. 510 (1982) (there is no such thing as larceny by negligence); *Szewczyk v. State, supra* at 601, 256 A.2d at 715; *First Nat'l Bank & Trust v. State,* 141 Ga.

App. 471, 233 S.E.2d 861 (1977). The openness with which one takes the property is relevant to the question of the good faith of the taker. *State v. Heyes,* 44 Wash. 2d 579, 269 P.2d 577, 584 (1954). The more unreasonable the defendant's belief, however, the more difficult it is to show that he took the property in good faith.

A few states have revised their penal codes "to create a category of negligent theft. The Model Penal Code proceeds on the contrary view that theft has been and should be regarded as a crime of purposeful appropriation of the property interests of others." ALI, Model Penal Code and Commentaries, Part II, Vol. 2, page 152 (1980).

In *Cates v. State,* 21 Md. App. 363, 320 A.2d 75 (1974), the defendant was convicted of robbery for forcibly trying to recover money "lost in a crap game." In determining whether there had been a robbery, the Court ascertained whether the accused had a legally recognizable right which could be asserted in court. The Court stated: "... the question is ultimately one of basic public policy, which unequivocally dictates that the proper forum for resolving debt disputes is a court of law; pursuant to legal process — not the street, at the business end of a lethal weapon." [Citing dissenting opinion in *People v. Butler,* 55 Cal. Rptr. 511, 421 P.2d 703 (1967)]. Based on the premise that the Court cannot countenance illegal transactions, it is against public policy generally to allow one who loses at gambling the help of the court to recover his losses. *Id.* at 370, 320 A.2d at 80. One who undertakes to recover such losses by force of arms is guilty of robbery. *Id.* The Court noted that there is an exclusive statutory remedy. One who loses at gambling can recover his losses as a common law debt under Maryland Ann. Code, Art. 27, § 243. *Id.* at 371 and 374, 320 A.2d at 80 and 82.

The Court in *Cates v. State, supra,* also cited *Nichols v. State,* 231 Md. 313, 190 A.2d 645 (1963) with approval. The Court noted that in *Nichols,* the defendant bought an automobile using the name of another person and was convicted of false pretenses arising out of the conditional sales contract. The defendant's representation that he was another person was material to the seller's extension of credit to him. The seller repossessed the car when the defendant failed to make the required payments. The defendant then took the car back without the seller's authority. The defendant asserted that the car was his since the seller failed to comply with a statute which required that he give the buyer notice of the amount due and five days to redeem. The Court rejected this defense by inferring the defendant's intent to defraud, and found the defendant guilty of larceny.

> The phrase *claim of right* and the phrase *honestly believes himself to be entitled,* when applied to an intentional taking of property, must be given a limited and not a broad interpretation. They must be taken to require a legally recognizable right which can be successfully asserted in our courts. The *intent to steal,* the element of larceny which makes it and robbery specific intent crimes, must be evaluated objectively and not subjectively, and within the framework of rights and obligations given and imposed by the law.

Cates v. State, supra at 369, 320 A.2d at 79 (emphasis in original).

Compare Richardson v. United States, 403 F.2d 574 (D.C. Cir. 1968), in which the Court held that one who believes, in good faith, that he is entitled to the money he has taken, does not have the requisite specific intent to commit robbery. The government argued that no instruction on a claim of right defense was necessary unless defendant had a legally enforceable right to the property. The Court found the government's argument unpersuasive and declared that: "specific intent depends upon a state of mind, not upon a legal fact." *Id.* at 576. It noted that people will be deterred from self-help since there are other criminal statutes prohibiting this behavior which do not require a specific intent.

Perkins and Boyce apparently take a broader view of the claim of right defense than *Cates* and state:

> It has been held that it is not robbery to collect money that is legally and presently due, or *bona fide* believed to be due, by force or intimidation — even at pistol point. This position is sound because as pointed out in the discussion of larceny, an intent to collect a debt is not an intent to steal. But some courts reached the other conclusion, apparently assuming that, however illogical it may be, it is necessary to hold that such conduct is robbery because otherwise any creditor would be free to collect his claim by threat of violence. Obviously this is not the law. Collecting a debt in that manner

> would constitute statutory extortion (blackmail) and would usually involve other offenses, particularly if a weapon is employed.

R. Perkins & R. Boyce, *Criminal Law* Ch. 4, § 2A at 344-45 (3d ed. 1982). As the Court in *State v. Goldsberry,* 160 Kan. 138, 160 P.2d 690, 696 (1945) stated: "An intent to steal property and a bona fide claim of right to take it are incompatible.... The fact that the taker employs force or a trick to obtain what he thinks he owns or has the right to take does not necessarily alter the rule that one cannot intend to steal what he thinks is his."

Whether the defendant had the necessary intent to steal is a question for the trier of fact to determine. *Cates v. State, supra* at 366, 320 A.2d at 78; *Szewczyk v. State, supra* at 601, 256 A.2d at 715.

§ 5.04. Defense of others.

A person has a right to go to the defense of another person. You have heard evidence that the defendant witnessed a violent assault on another person.

In order to justify or excuse the actions of the defendant, it is necessary that: (1) the defendant witnessed a violent assault upon __________ *(name of other person defendant alleged to have defended);* (2) the defendant honestly and reasonably believed that his actions were necessary to protect the life or person of another; and (3) the force used by the defendant was not unreasonable or excessive; that is, the defendant used the same degree of force that the person attacked could reasonably have used to repel the attack. [A person would not be entitled to use any greater force than he had reasonable grounds to believe, and actually did believe, to be necessary under the circumstances to save life or avert serious bodily harm.]

You must determine whether the defendant was justified in meeting force with force; that is, you must determine under the circumstances as they appeared to the defendant at the time of the incident whether the defendant actually and reasonably believed that the person he was defending was in imminent danger of serious bodily harm or death.

The State has the burden to prove beyond a reasonable doubt that the defense of others has not been established.

If after a full and fair consideration of all the facts and circumstances in evidence, you have a reasonable doubt as to whether or not the defense of others has been established, you must find the defendant not guilty. On the other hand, if the State has convinced you beyond a reasonable doubt that the defense has *not* been established, then the defense of others will not excuse the defendant of criminal liability.

COMMENT

The Court, in *Alexander v. State,* 52 Md. App. 171, 447 A.2d 880, *aff'd,* 294 Md. 600, 451 A.2d 664 (1982), traced the defense of others from its common-law origin. This defense of others evolved from the right to protect one's property. It only allowed a third person to defend those "closely related to, or associated with, the intervenor." *Id.* at 172, 447 A.2d at 882. Since the 1960's this defense has changed, especially since the enactment of Maryland Ann. Code, Art. 27, § 12A (1982) which states:

> Any person witnessing a violent assault upon the person of another may lawfully aid the person being assaulted by assisting in that person's defense. The force exerted upon the attacker or attackers by the person witnessing the assault may be that degree of force which the assaulted person is allowed to assert in defending himself.

It is not clear whether this statute replaces or merely modifies the common law.

The statute makes it clear that any person has a right to use the defense of any other person whether or not closely associated with the defendant. It is not clear, however, whether use of the term "witnessing" would narrow the common-law doctrine to certain persons having a right to go to the defense of another if they had reasonably "believed" another was in danger. If the person hearing of an assault comes upon the encounter when the fighting has ceased, it can be argued there is no right to defend another. On the other hand, if the person hearing of the encounter did not actually see who initiated the assault but arrived before the encounter ended, the person would still be a "witness" under the statute. Thus, the statute and the common-law positions, perhaps, can be reconciled.

The Court, in *Alexander,* also addressed the issue of whether the defendant stands in the shoes of the victim or whether the defendant's actions are based on his reasonable beliefs. Prior to *Gray v. State,* 6 Md. App. 677, 253 A.2d 395 (1969), the courts emphasized what the third party victim could have done in evaluating whether the defendant's actions were reasonable; in other words, the defendant stood in the shoes of the one attacked. See *Guerriero v. State,* 213 Md. 545, 132 A.2d 466 (1957) and *Tipton v. State,* 1 Md. App. 556, 232 A.2d 289 (1967). In *Gray v. State, supra,* however, the Court focused on the reasonable beliefs of the defendant, not the beliefs of the attacked party. In *Gray* the defendant was charged with the killing of his father. The defendant claimed that he was coming to the aid of his mother since his father was violently assaulting her. In this context, the Court approved the following instruction:

> [I]n order to justify or excuse the killing of another on the ground of self-defense, it is necessary to establish that the defendant ... believed at the time he was, or a person close to him or some close relative was in immediate danger of losing his or her life, or suffering serious bodily harm and believed it necessary in the protection of that life of another to save that person, that the circumstances were such as to warrant reasonable grounds for such belief in a mind of ordinary reason.

Id. at 685, 253 A.2d at 400.

This view was defended in *Alexander v. State, supra,* in which the Court recognized that this position "[b]etter fulfills our contemporary social needs by merging the encouragement of crime prevention with the privilege of defending others." *Id.* at 175, 447 A.2d at 883. See also *Shuck v. State,* 29 Md. App. 33, 349 A.2d 378 (1975).

Despite *Alexander's* holding that the defense is to be measured from the reasonable beliefs of the defendant, and not the person alleged to have been attacked, the Maryland statute states the following standard: "The force exerted upon the attacker or attackers by the person witnessing the assault may be that degree of force which the assaulted person is allowed to assert in defending himself." Art. 27, § 12A (1982).

There may be some tension between this provision of the statute and the holding in *Alexander.* The holding in *Alexander* goes more to whether the person he was defending was in imminent danger of serious bodily harm. The provision of the statute seems to go to the amount of force the defendant may use once involved in the encounter. Even here, however, a case may arise in which the facts known or reasonably believed by the defendant are different from the facts known by the person attacked. For example, a situation where the person attacked knows the aggressor's gun is unloaded, but the defendant does not. Under *Alexander,* it would seem that the amount of force to be used should also be judged from the viewpoint of the defendant. Under the statute, however, if could reasonably be argued that the language requires that the facts and circumstances be judged from the standpoint of the person attacked in determining the reasonableness of the amount of force used by the defendant. See also *Guerriero v. State, supra.*

The Court in *Alexander* also recognized that a prisoner may use this defense since the laws "apply to all persons equally." *Alexander v. State, supra* at 181, 447 A.2d at 886. It stated that a prisoner's actions and the reasonableness of his perceptions are elements to be considered by the fact finder. *Id.* at 183, 447 A.2d at 887.

See Instructions, §§ 5.11 to 5.17, *infra,* for further discussion relating to self-defense.

§ 5.05. Duress.

Since it is essential to a crime that the defendant voluntarily committed a criminal act, it is a defense that the defendant did not act voluntarily but acted as a result of compelling force or coercion exerted on him.

For duress or coercion to excuse the commission of a criminal act, three elements must be present: (1) the duress or coercion must be present, imminent and impending; (2) the coercion must be such as to cause a well-grounded fear of death or serious bodily injury if the criminal act is not done; and (3) the coercion must be of such a nature as to leave no reasonable opportunity to escape the danger without committing the crime. This means that if the defendant had a reasonable opportunity to avoid doing the criminal act without undue exposure to risk of death or serious bodily harm, then you [should] [must] find that the defense of duress has not been established.

I have just instructed you that duress or coercion must be present, imminent and impending. The defense of duress is not established by proof that the defendant had been threatened with violence at some prior time, if the defendant was not under any personal constraint at the time of the actual commission of the crime charged. Mere fear or threat by another is not sufficient to constitute a defense, unless it is such as to cause a reasonable fear of death or serious bodily injury if the criminal act is not done.

[The defense cannot be established if the threat or harm is only of future, but not present, personal injury.] [It also cannot be established if the threat or harm is only property damage.] [Further, the defense cannot be claimed if the defendant by his own fault or misconduct created the emergency or necessity which confronted him.]

Since the burden of proof is on the State, the State must prove beyond a reasonable doubt that the defendant did not act under duress. Therefore, if after a full and fair consideration of all the facts and circumstances in evidence, you have a reasonable doubt as to whether the defendant committed the crime with which he is charged under duress as it has been defined, you must find him not guilty. On the other hand, if the State convinces you beyond a reasonable doubt that the defendant did *not* act under duress, then you [should] [must] conclude that the defense of duress does not excuse the defendant of criminal liability.

COMMENT

Duress arises when one is coerced by another person, while necessity usually arises when one is coerced by the existing circumstances. *Robinson v. State,* 42 Md. App. 617, 619, 402 A.2d 115, 116 (1979), *citing Frasher v. State,* 8 Md. App. 439, 447-48, 260 A.2d 656, 661, *cert. denied, McLaughlin v. Director, Patuxent Inst.* (1970). See Instruction, § 5.18, Necessity, *infra.*

When the pressure causing a person to commit a criminal act is caused by human beings, the defense will usually be "duress" rather than "necessity." See *Sigma Reproductive Health Center v. State,* 297 Md. 660, 675, 467 A.2d 483, 490 (1983). However, in *State v. Crawford,* 308 Md. 683, 521 A.2d 1193 (1987), quoting W. LaFave & A. Scott, Criminal Law, § 50 at 381-82 n.2 (1972), the Court distinguished the typical duress case in which one person orders another person to engage in certain conduct prohibited by the criminal law or else suffer certain consequences. When a person acts to avoid a greater harm from a person who has not given such an order, the situation ought to be dealt with as a form of necessity rather than duress. For example, in *Crawford,* which was treated as a case of "necessity," the defendant allegedly was severely attacked by another person and picked up a handgun which was originally possessed by the assailant and only became available to him after he had disarmed the assailant and was again attacked. The Court noted that the defendant was entitled to a jury instruction on necessity as a defense to a charge of illegal possession of a handgun under Maryland Ann. Code, Art. 27, § 36B(b).

The general rationale for the defense of duress is based on the principle that the conduct which violates the law is justified because a greater harm is avoided. *Wentworth v. State,* 29 Md. App. 110, 117-18, 349 A.2d 421, 426 (1975).

Duress may be used as a defense to all crimes other than the taking of the life of an innocent person. *Frasher v. State, supra* at 447-48, 260 A.2d at 661, *citing* 1 Wharton, *Criminal Law & Procedure* (§ 123 at 261 Anderson ed. 1957). See also *Robinson v. State supra; Wentworth v. State, supra.* This principle has its roots in social policy. *Wentworth v. State, supra* at 118, 349 A.2d at 426.

The elements of duress are set forth in *Wentworth v. State, supra; Frasher v. State, supra; Darby v. State,* 3 Md. App. 407, 239 A.2d 584 (1968), *cert. denied,* 393 U.S. 1105 (1969).

In *Frasher,* upon which this instruction is primarily based, the Court of Special Appeals held that the following lower court instruction to the jury on duress was proper:

> If the Defendant did not commit the criminal act with which he was charged willfully or voluntarily but as a result of coercion exerted on him, he is not criminally responsible. Not every form of duress or compulsion, however, relieves a defendant of responsibility for a criminal act. Coercion which will ... excuse ... the commission of a criminal act must be immediate and of such a nature as to induce in the Defendant's mind the well-grounded apprehension of death or serious bodily injury if the act is not done. There must be no reasonable opportunity for the Defendant to escape the danger without committing the crime. If you have a reasonable doubt whether or not the defendant committed the act with which he is charged under duress as it has been defined, you must find him not guilty.

Id. at 450, 260 A.2d at 663.

Prior to *Frasher,* in *Darby v. State, supra* at 420-21, 239 A.2d at 592-93, the Court of Special Appeals had approved the use of the following instruction in its entirety (again based largely upon Wharton's *Criminal Law*), while holding that use of the first paragraph alone would be incorrect especially in light of the fact that the defendant could have avoided the act and that he was not under personal constraint:

> Since it is essential to a crime that the defendant committed a voluntary act, it is a defense as to all crimes other than the taking of the life of an innocent person, that the defendant did not act voluntarily but acted under a compelling force of coercion or duress. In order to constitute a defense, the coercion or duress must be present, imminent and impending, and of such a nature as to induce a well-grounded apprehension of death or serious bodily injury if the act is not done. Mere fear or threat by another is not sufficient to constitute a defense.
>
> The defense of duress is not established by proof that the defendant had been threatened with violence at some prior time, if he was not under any personal constraint at the time of the actual commission of the crime charged. The defense

> cannot be raised if the apprehended harm is only that of property damage, or future but not present personal injury.
>
> The compulsion must be of such a character as to have no opportunity to the accused for escape. The doctrine of coercion or duress cannot be invoked as an excuse by one who had a reasonable opportunity to avoid doing the act without undue exposure to death or serious bodily harm.
>
> The defense cannot be claimed if the defendant by his own fault or misconduct created the emergency or necessity which confronted him.

While, as of this writing, there are no Maryland cases on Point, *Mullaney v. Wilbur,* 421 U.S. 684, 95 S. Ct. 1881, 44 L. Ed. 2d 508 (1975) and *Evans v. State,* 28 Md. App. 640, 349 A.2d 300 (1975), *aff'd,* 278 Md. 197, 362 A.2d 629 (1976), support the proposition that once the issue of duress has been raised, by either the State's or defendant's evidence, the burden is on the State to prove the absence of duress in the context of the case.

Further support for this proposition may be drawn from *Wentworth v. State, supra.* In *Wentworth,* the defendant's claim of duress was insufficient to exculpate her from the crime charged, murder. Nevertheless, as an imperfect defense, a finding of duress could have supplied sufficient mitigation to diminish the degree of guilt from murder to manslaughter. The issue of duress, therefore, presented a genuine issue for the jury. As a result, the jury instruction which improperly placed upon her the burden of proving mitigation and which improperly relieved the State of its burden of proving the element of nonmitigation beyond a reasonable doubt required a reversal under *Mullaney v. Wilbur, supra,* as analyzed in *Evans v. State, supra* at 658, 349 A.2d at 316-17. See Appendix V, The Impact of *Evans v. State:* Burdens of Proof, Presumptions and Inferences, *infra.*

As to the crime of escape, the Supreme Court of the United States has held that a defendant is not entitled to an instruction on the theory of duress unless the defendant first proffers "testimony of a *bona fide* effort to surrender or return to custody as soon as the claimed duress or necessity has lost its coercive force." *United States v. Bailey,* 444 U.S. 394, 412-13, 100 S. Ct. 624, 636, 62 L. Ed. 2d 575, 592 (1980), *cert. denied,* 459 U.S. 853 (1982); *Craddock v. State,* 47 Md. App. 513, 516, 424 A.2d 168, 170 (1981). The Court reasserted that "one principle remains constant: if there was a reasonable, legal alternative to violating the law, 'a chance both to refuse to do the criminal act and also to avoid the threatened harm,' the defenses will fail." *United States v. Bailey, supra* at 410, 100 S. Ct. at 635, 62 L. Ed. 2d at 591 (*citing* W. LaFave and A. Scott, *Handbook on Criminal Law* § 28 (1972)). See Comment, § 4.65, Escape, *supra,* for further discussion on the relationship between duress and escape.

§ 5.06. Entrapment.

Evidence has been introduced which indicates that law enforcement officials may have induced the defendant to commit an unlawful act with which the defendant is charged. Where a person did not have an intent or purpose to violate the law, but is induced or persuaded by law enforcement officers (or their agents) to commit a crime, that person is a victim of entrapment and he cannot be convicted of that crime.

You must determine whether the defendant has been entrapped. You must first consider whether the police (directly or through their agents) induced or persuaded the defendant to commit the offense charged. The burden is on the State to prove beyond a reasonable doubt that the defendant was not induced or persuaded by a police officer (or a State agent) to commit the offense charged. In making this determination, you should consider all of the facts and circumstances in evidence. In considering the behavior of the police (or their agents), you should ask yourself whether an officer of the law (or an agent) by any plan or contrivance induced the defendant to commit the crime charged.

[Inducement by law enforcement officers may take many different forms, including, for example, persuasion in the form of repeated and persistent solicitations to overcome a person's reluctance to commit a crime, fraudulent representations, threats, coercive tactics, harassment, promises or reward, or pleas based on need, sympathy or friendship.] [Law enforcement officers are permitted, however, to use artifice, stealth and stratagem that provide a person with the opportunity to commit a crime. This includes the use of undercover agents and operations in which false names and false appearances are used]

If the State proves beyond a reasonable doubt that the police (or other State agents) did *not* induce or persuade the defendant to commit the crime charged, then you should find that the defense of entrapment has not been established.

However, if you find that the State has not met this burden, that is, you have a reasonable doubt whether the police (or other State agents) induced or persuaded the defendant to commit the offense charged, then the State must prove beyond a reasonable doubt that the defendant was ready and willing without persuasion to commit the offense. In other words, the State must prove beyond a reasonable doubt that the defendant had a predisposition to commit the offense. Again, you should consider all of the facts and circumstances in evidence in making your determination. In so doing, you should ask yourself whether the defendant was awaiting any favorable opportunity to commit the crime charged. Was the defendant's criminal conduct due to his own readiness and not to the persuasion of the police?

[A defendant's predisposition or willingness to commit the crime charged may be shown, for example, by evidence of his prior conduct of a similar nature or by evidence, direct or circumstantial, that the defendant was ready and willing to engage in the illegal conduct in question, such as, ready acquiescence to a police officer's solicitation, ready access to similar contraband, the possession of paraphernalia generally associated with criminal activity of the type charged, or any statements made in the course of the transaction by a defendant, including displays of expert knowledge and boasts about previous similar criminal activity.]

[The fact, if it is a fact, that the defendant may have committed prior offenses of a similar nature does not by itself require you to conclude that he had the predisposition or readiness to commit the offense(s) with which he is now charged. In evaluating this matter of predisposition, you should look to the totality of the circumstances involved in the offense(s) with which the defendant is charged.]

When a person already has the readiness and willingness to break the law, the mere fact that State agents provide what appears to be a favorable opportunity for commission of the offense is not entrapment. On the other hand, if the defendant would not have committed the criminal act but for the inducement or persuasion of law enforcement officers (or their agents), the defendant is a victim of entrapment and cannot be convicted of the crime.

COMMENT

Bowser v. State, 50 Md. App. 363, 439 A.2d 1 (1981) appears to have settled the uncertainty which existed in Maryland as to which party has the burden of persuasion on each of the elements of entrapment. The instruction of the trial judge was summarized with approval by the Court, as follows:

> The trial judge instructed the jury on the issue of entrapment and further instructed to the effect that where the defense of entrapment is raised, the State has the burden of proving beyond any reasonable doubt that the defendant was not induced by a state agent to violate the law. If the State fails to prove the defendant was not induced, then in order to convict, the jury would have to find beyond any reasonable doubt that the defendant was ready and willing to commit the crime charged.

Id. at 367, 439 A.2d at 3. In footnote 4, the Court noted that the State had conceded at the trial level that the State had the burden of proving beyond any reasonable doubt that the defendant was not entrapped pursuant to language by the Court of Appeals in *State v. Evans,* 278 Md. 197, 362 A.2d 629 (1976), which referred to *Evans v. State,* 28 Md. App. 640, 349 A.2d 300 (1975), *aff'd,* 278 Md. 197, 362 A.2d 629 (1976), and adopted the analysis that: "[with] any defense theory of justification, excuse or mitigation, including...*entrapment*...a jury instruction...which cast upon the defendant the burden of persuasion by a preponderance of the evidence...was constitutionally defective...since it shifted the burden to the defendant to prove justification or excuse...." *State v. Evans, supra* at 207, 362 A.2d at 632-33 (emphasis added). See also *Mullaney v. Wilbur,* 421 U.S. 684, 94 S. Ct. 1881, 44 L. Ed. 2d 508 (1975); R. Gilbert and C. Moylan, Jr., *Maryland Criminal Law: Practice and Procedure* Ch. 22 at 237 n.2 (1983); Park, *The Entrapment Controversy,* 60 Minn. L. Rev. 163, 262-63 (1971); Appendix V, The Impact of *Evans v. State:* Burdens of Proof, Presumptions and Inferences, *infra.*

The earlier view on the burden of persuasion was set forth in *Simmons v. State,* 8 Md. App. 355, 259 A.2d 814 (1969) which placed the burden on the defendant to establish by a preponderance of the evidence that the police or their agents induced the defendant to commit the offense. Then, the State had the burden of proving beyond a reasonable doubt that the defendant's conduct was due to the defendant's own predisposition. See also *United States v. Russell,* 411 U.S. 423, 93 S. Ct. 1637, 36 L. Ed. 2d 36 (1973); *Dravo v. State,* 46 Md. App. 622, 626, 420 A.2d 1012, 1015 (1980); *Fisher v. State,* 28 Md. App. 243, 248-49, 345 A.2d 110, 113-14 (1975), *cert. denied,* 276 Md. 743 (1976). The earlier view of the burden of persuasion in *Simmons v. State, supra,* was quoted in dictum in *Kenney v. State,* 62 Md. App. 555, 490 A.2d 738 (1985) in the context of a general discussion of the history of the entrapment defense in Maryland without reference to the more recent developments.

If the defendant makes a proper request, the trial judge must instruct the jury on the defense of entrapment as long as there is sufficient evidence that the defendant was induced by a government official. *Bowser v. State, supra* at 367 n.4, 439 A.2d at 3 n.4; *Byrd v. State,* 16 Md. App. 391, 297 A.2d 312 (1972). The burden of production is on the defendant to raise the issue. Note, however, that this burden is not one of persuasion; therefore, the defendant need only produce some evidence that State agents induced the defendant to commit the offense.

In *Adcock v. State,* 66 Md. App. 454, 504 A.2d 1160 (1986), the Court held that the defendant failed to make out a *prima facie* case of entrapment so as to generate an issue for the trier of fact. Instead of testifying that she was induced to commit a crime, the defendant swore she committed no crime and had no idea a crime was about to be committed. In his opinion, Judge Moylan reasons that alternative defenses of entrapment and denial of the offense are not possible. The defendant has a burden of production as to both (1) improper inducing behavior on the part of the State and (2) the actual succumbing to that inducement on the part of the defendant. The testimony "I did not do it" is no *prima facie* predicate for the proposition "I did do it but only because I was induced to do it." But see *Hansford v. United States,* 112 U.S. App. D.C. 359, 303 F.2d 219 (1962) (en banc), permitting alternative defenses of entrapment and denial of the offense.

The Supreme Court of the United States first recognized the entrapment defense in *Sorrells v. United States,* 287 U.S. 435, 53 S. Ct. 210, 77 L. Ed. 413 (1932), and enunciated the "origin of interest" test. *Simmons v. State, supra.* The defense of entrapment is made available to preclude the government from contending that the accused is guilty where the government officers are the instigators of the criminal conduct. The courts have stated, however, that the purpose of the entrapment defense is not to permit guilty parties to go free. Stealth and strategy by law enforcement officers is permissible, but not where a criminal design originates with them and they implant in an innocent mind the disposition to commit crime and induce its commission. Law enforcement agents do not commit entrapment by merely affording opportunities or facilities for the commission of an offense; entrapment occurs where the criminal conduct is the product of the creative activity of law enforcement officers. *Bowser v. State, supra; Dravo v. State, supra; Simmons v. State, supra; Schuman v. State,* 19 Md. App. 400, 311 A.2d 460 (1973); *Poff v. State,* 4 Md. App. 186, 241 A.2d 898 (1968). The defense of entrapment is not available when a private person who is not an agent or instrumentality of the State makes the inducement.

Since its decision in *Sorrells,* the United States Supreme Court has decided several cases dealing with the entrapment defense. See, e.g., *United States v. Russell, supra; Sherman v. United States,* 356 U.S. 369, 78 S. Ct. 819, 2 L. Ed. 2d 848 (1958). In *Russell, supra,* Justice Rehnquist stated: "*Sorrells* is a precedent of long standing that has already been once re-examined in *Sherman* and implicitly there reaffirmed. Since the defense is not of constitutional dimension, Congress may address itself to the question and adopt any substantive definition of the defense that it may find desirable." *United States v. Russell, supra* at 433, 93 S. Ct. at 1643, 36 L. Ed. 2d at 374.

Because the United States Supreme Court decisions are not constitutionally based, Maryland is not bound by these decisions. It was not until 1952, in *Ferraro v. State,* 200 Md. 274, 89 A.2d 628 (1952), that the entrapment defense was formally judicially recognized in Maryland. The test adopted in Maryland in 1969 is that of the majority in *Sorrells v. United States, supra.* In adopting this so-called "origin of interest" test in *Simmons v. State, supra,* the Court discussed and rejected a so-called "objective test" (focusing on the behavior of law enforcement agents) which did not also focus on whether the defendant was nonetheless predisposed to commit the crime. The *Simmons* test was approved in *Groham v. State,* 258 Md. 552, 267 A.2d 193 (1970), *cert. denied,* 401 U.S. 982 (1971) where two questions were stated: (1) whether there was an inducement on the part of the government officials or their agents, and if so (2) whether the defendant showed any predisposition to commit the offense. Judicial decisions have further explicated the *Simmons* holding in *Fisher v. State, supra,* and *Dravo v. State, supra.* In *Bowser v. State, supra,* the Court approved the two questions posed above in *Groham.* For a discussion of the history of the entrapment defense, *see Kenney v. State, supra.*

The State must prove that government officials did not induce the accused to commit the crime. In doing so, it seems that the State must show that its agents did not repeatedly and persistently solicit a law abiding citizen to commit a crime he would not otherwise have committed. *Dravo v. State, supra; Perkins v. State,* 26 Md. App. 526, 339 A.2d 360 (1975).

In *Poff v. State, supra,* it was held that entrapment by the police presupposes that police officers solicited or procured the commission of a crime. The mere fact that the police officers laid a trap and provided the defendant with the opportunity to commit burglary did not constitute entrapment. See also *Byrd v. State, supra.*

In *Perkins v. State, supra,* the appellant, convicted of unlawful distribution of marijuana, argued entrapment in that the arresting officer simulated smoking marijuana in his presence and beguiled him into believing that the officer, like himself, had acquired the smoking habit in Vietnam. The Court rejected this argument holding that appellant failed to meet his initial burden of proving police inducement because he was unable to show a "repeated and persistent solicitation of a previously law abiding citizen in order to overcome his reluctance to commit a crime." *Perkins v. State, supra* at 537, 339 A.2d at 367 (*quoting Stewart v. State,* 232 Md. 318, 321, 193 A.2d 40, 42 (1963)). In addition, the Court found that, when the appellant testified as to his use of marijuana and his sale of that substance to friends prior to his encounter with the officer, he clearly illustrated his predisposition to commit the offense at issue.

Even if the State fails to prove that the defendant did not commit the offense because of police inducement, the issue is still submitted to the jury if there is sufficient evidence from which the jury could find that the criminal conduct resulted from the defendant's own readiness or predisposition to commit the offense, not the inducement. *Bowser v. State, supra* at 370, 439 A.2d at 5. To determine whether the defendant was "ready and willing without persuasion" to commit the offense, the totality of the circumstances must be examined. Therefore, a reasonable suspicion that the accused is about to engage in the commission of an offense may be relevant, though not essential. *Simmons v. State, supra* at 363, 259 A.2d at 819. The State, however, has the burden of proving beyond a reasonable doubt that the defendant's conduct was the result of his own predisposition. *Byrd v. State, supra* at 401-02, 297 A.2d 312, 318 (1972) (*quoting Simmons v. State, supra* at 364, 259 A.2d at 819); *Bowser v. State, supra.* See *Reimsnider v. State,* 60 Md. App. 589, 483 A.2d 1324 (1984).

In *Hampton v. United States,* 425 U.S. 484, 96 S. Ct. 1646, 48 L. Ed. 2d 113 (1976), the drug itself that constituted the *corpus delicti* of the federal narcotics offense was supplied by a government informant. The Supreme Court, however, declined to accept the defense of entrapment, emphasizing as in *Russell, supra,* that this defense focuses predominantly on the intent or predisposition of the defendant to commit the crime, rather than upon the conduct of government agents. The Court reiterated that it is only when the government's deception actually implants the criminal design in the mind of the defendant that the defense of entrapment is available. Where the defendant concedes his predisposition to the particular crime, the defense does not come into play.

In *Hardiman v. State,* 50 Md. App. 98, 436 A.2d 923 (1981), the Court, relying on *Roviaro v. United States,* 353 U.S. 53, 77 S. Ct. 623, 1 L. Ed. 2d 639 (1957), held that where defendant, who was convicted of possession and distribution of methamphetamine, raised the defense of entrapment, refusal to compel disclosure of the identity of the government's informant was prejudicial error requiring reversal due to the fact that the informant had arranged and participated in the criminal act, and that he was the only witness who might have testified to defendant's possible lack of knowledge of the contents of the package involved in the criminal transaction. The Court's ruling was further justified since disclosure was necessary and relevant to a fair defense on the merits, and there was no evidence that disclosure of the informant's identity would jeopardize his personal safety.

Once the defendant raises the defense of entrapment, the State may inquire into the defendant's conduct and predisposition to commit the crime. *Sherman v. United States, supra; Bowser v. State, supra* at 371, 439 A.2d at 6; *Simmons v. State, supra.* The Court, in *Bowser,* recognized that:

> The State may use various permissible methods to rebut an entrapment claim. Among the most common, are proof of prior convictions for similar offenses and evidence of similar criminal acts committed by the accused. In addition, a defendant's ready acquiescence to a police officer's solicitation may itself indicate predisposition, as might the ready access to contraband, the possession of paraphernalia generally as-

> sociated with criminal activity, or any statements made in the course of the transaction, including displays of expert knowledge and boasts about previous similar criminal activity.

Bowser v. State, supra at 372, 439 A.2d at 6.

The defendant need not have been convicted or arrested for the other offenses. It is also permissible to introduce evidence of subsequent crimes if they are similar in nature to the offense in issue. See *Berlin v. State,* 12 Md. App. 48, 277 A.2d 468 (1971); *Bowser v. State, supra* at 372, 439 A.2d at 6. Even though this evidence may be admitted, secondhand reputation evidence, and other unreliable hearsay may not be used to establish predisposition. *Id.* at 375, 439 A.2d at 7-8. See also *United States v. Webster,* 649 F.2d 346, 350 (5th Cir. 1980).

In *Kenney v. State, supra,* the Court discussed procedural questions concerning raising the entrapment defense and the role of the judge and jury. Since entrapment is not a constitutional defense, neither a pre-trial motion to dismiss the indictment nor a motion to suppress the evidence lies. Once the defense has been raised, the question is for the trier of fact to decide. To seek acquittal based on entrapment as a matter of law, the defendant first makes his motion for acquittal at the close of the State's case. The court considers the motion for acquittal viewing the evidence in the light most favorable to the State. In *Fisher v. State, supra,* the Court set forth the circumstances in which the defense of entrapment is established as a matter of law:

> The initial test of the evidence, within the framework of the substantive law of entrapment, is always a matter of law for the court. The question to be decided depends upon how the question is raised. A motion for judgment of acquittal based upon that defense requires the court to decide whether there is undisputed evidence, so clear and decisive that reasonable minds, applying the correct law, could not differ in finding that the defendant was induced by the police to commit the offense, and that his criminal conduct was due to the persuasion of the police, and not to his own readiness or predisposition to commit the offense. Only when such is the state of the evidence is there entrapment as a matter of law.

Id. at 250, 345 A.2d at 114-15.

If the court denies the motion for judgment of acquittal, the defendant may choose whether to offer evidence or not. The presentation of any additional evidence by the defense after the close of the State's case effectively withdraws the motion. See Maryland Rule 4-324, effective July 1, 1984, superseding without significant change former Rule 756. To preserve the entrapment issue in a jury case, the defendant must make or renew the motion for acquittal at the end of the case. This time the court considers the issue based on the evidence presented by both the State and the defendant. The defendant's failure to move for judgment of acquittal at the close of all the evidence precludes appellate review of the sufficiency of the evidence.

§ 5.07. Good character of defendant.

During the course of this trial you have heard testimony concerning the good character of the defendant. Evidence of good character involving the trait(s) of __________ *(insert applicable trait)* is relevant to the question of whether the defendant is innocent or guilty of __________ *(insert crime(s) charged).*

Although the existence of good character is not in itself a defense to a crime, you may consider it along with all the other evidence in the case, and give it such weight as you feel it deserves. You may decide that it is improbable that a person possessing this (these) trait(s) of good character would have committed the crime(s) charged. In other words, this evidence, along with all the other evidence in the case, may be sufficient to create a reasonable doubt of the defendant's guilt so as to require the acquittal of the defendant.

COMMENT

This instruction is based largely on *Braxton v. State,* 11 Md. App. 435, 274 A.2d 647 (1971), which refers to 1 Wharton *Criminal Evidence* § 221 at 458-59 (12th ed. 1955).

According to *Braxton, supra* at 439, 274 A.2d at 649-50:

> As distinguished from the limited concept of character within the impeachment rule as relating only to credibility, a defendant may always offer evidence of his good character and to prove that his character was such as to make it unlikely that he would have committed the act charged against him. The defendant does not put his "character" in this frame of reference in issue by merely taking the stand as a witness. It is put in issue, however, when he states that he has good character or a good record, or offers direct evidence of good character.

See *Gooch v. State,* 34 Md. App. 331, 367 A.2d 90, 92 (1976) to support the proposition that an accused has a right to present evidence of good character.

"To be relevant, it is necessary that the character be confined to an attribute or trait the existence or nonexistence of which would be involved in the noncommission or commission of the particular crime charged." *Braxton v. State, supra* at 440, 274 A.2d at 650, *citing* Wharton, *Criminal Evidence, supra* at 456-63. *See also Hallengren v. State,* 14 Md. App. 43, 286 A.2d 213 (1972). In *Braxton v. State, supra,* defendant offered evidence of his good character to show that it was unlikely that he would commit armed robbery. The Court held that the good character evidence was admissible in a prosecution for robbery. In *Hallengren v. State, supra* at 49, 286 A.2d 216-17, however, the Court did not find that the failure to give a good character evidence instruction was an error where defendant was charged with violating Maryland Ann. Code, Art. 27, §§ 121, 123 (disturbing the neighborhood and acting in a disorderly manner). The Court distinguished the case from *Braxton* holding that the defendant was merely offering the evidence to bolster his own credibility.

Where a crime of violence is at issue, evidence of peaceable character is relevant. In *Hurley v. State,* 60 Md. App. 539, 483 A.2d 1298 (1984), the Court held that because manslaughter involves an intentional killing of a human being, testimony concerning the defendant's nonassaultive nature meets the relevancy standard. See also *Grant v. State,* 55 Md. App. 1, 461 A.2d 524 (1983). In *Pierce v. State,* 62 Md. App. 453, 490 A.2d 261

(1985), the Court held that although two witnesses were allowed to testify as to appellant's general good character and law-abiding nature, the court's refusal to allow the witnesses to respond to questions regarding her peaceable or nonassaultive nature was reversible error.

Evidence of good character of the defendant should be considered along with all the other evidence in determining the guilt or innocence of the defendant. This issue was addressed in *Hennessy v. State,* 37 Md. 559, 378 A.2d 205 (1977). As a result of *Hennessy,* the words, "of itself," referring to evidence of good character, in the last sentence of the instruction in the first edition of this book have been deleted. The Court stated that if the evidence of good character and reputation *alone* might create a reasonable doubt, then this evidence would, in effect, be raised "to a position superior to any other evidence and, in effect, preempt the jury's prerogative in weighing all the evidence together." *Id.* at 565, 378 A.2d at 208. See Comment, § 2.23, Character of defendant, *supra,* for a discussion of *Hennessy v. State.*

In *Gooch v. State, supra,* defense counsel requested an instruction on character evidence. The request was made after the Court had concluded its advisory instructions to the jury. Because of the trial court's refusal to supplement its advisory instructions, the Court of Special Appeals reversed, holding that, notwithstanding the untimeliness in requesting the instruction, the trial court had the duty to give an independent instruction on character evidence. The trial court's general instruction as to the weight and credibility to be given various witnesses' testimony was found insufficient to properly instruct the jury on appellant's good character defense. *See also Noel v. State,* 202 Md. 247, 96 A.2d 7 (1953).

Maryland Ann. Code, Courts and Judicial Proceedings, § 9-115 has modified the common law. Character may now be proved by opinion evidence. See *Waine v. State,* 37 Md. App. 222, 247, 377 A.2d 509, 522-23 (1977); *Beckette v. State,* 31 Md. App. 85, 93, 355 A.2d 515, 521 (1976). The statute is set forth in the Comment, § 2.23, Character of defendant, *supra.* In *Durkin v. State,* 284 Md. 445, 397 A.2d 600 (1979), the Court held that the extent of the basis of the personal opinion character testimony relates to admissibility and not just to the weight given to the testimony by the trier of fact. The trial judge has the threshold task of determining that the personal opinion of the character witness is relevant and that it has an adequate basis. This determination will be overturned on appeal only if there is a clear abuse of discretion.

A character witness cannot be cross-examined about previous accusations, just convictions. *Facyson v. State,* 35 Md. App. 202, 370 A.2d 158 (1977).

Although the State cannot impeach defendant's credibility on the basis of a conviction which has a constitutional infirmity, they can impeach the defendant's character witness with such a conviction. The trial judge must protect against the misuse of such evidence. The Court has noted that the purpose of cross-examination of a character witness is to discredit the witness, not the accused. *Taylor v. State,* 28 Md. App. 560, 563-69, 346 A.2d 718, 719-23 (1975), *aff'd,* 278 Md. 150, 360 A.2d 430 (1976).

Cases on the concept of character within the impeachment rule include *Avery v. State,* 15 Md. App. 520, 292 A.2d 728 (1972); *Raimondi v. State,* 12 Md. App. 322, 278 A.2d 664 (1971), *aff'd,* 265 Md. 229, 288 A.2d 882, *cert. denied,* 409 U.S. 948 (1972); *Braxton v. State, supra.*

The defendant's failure to call character witnesses in his behalf may not be commented upon by the State. *Blizzard v. State,* 30 Md. App. 156, 351 A.2d 443 (1976), *rev'd on other grounds,* 278 Md. 556, 366 A.2d 1026 (1976); *Taylor v. State, supra; Braxton v. State, supra* at 439, 274 A.2d at 650.

§ 5.08. Insanity.

The law presumes that all persons, including those accused of crime, are responsible for their conduct. When the issue of insanity is raised, the defendant is required to prove his lack of criminal responsibility by a preponderance of the evidence. The preponderance of the evidence standard which you are to apply has been defined as "more likely so than not so" or "more probable than not."

It is a fundamental principle of criminal law that a person is not criminally responsible for an act if he was insane at the time he committed it. A defendant is not responsible for his criminal conduct and must be found insane at the time of the commission of the alleged crime if, at the time of such conduct, as a result of mental disorder (or mental retardation) he lacked substantial capacity either to appreciate the criminality of his conduct or to conform his conduct to the requirements of the law.

The term mental disorder, as used here, means a behavioral or emotional illness resulting from a psychiatric or neurological disorder. [It includes a mental illness that so substantially impairs the mental or emotional functioning of the individual as to make care and treatment necessary or advisable for the welfare of the individual or for the safety of the person or property of another.] It does not include an abnormality manifested only by repeated criminal or otherwise antisocial conduct.

[The term mental retardation means a significantly subaverage intellectual functioning and impairment in the adaptive behavior of an individual that originates during the developmental period of the individual.]

The fact that at the time of the alleged crime a person was suffering from a mental disorder [or mental retardation] does not, by itself, exempt him from criminal responsibility; he is exempt from criminal responsibility only if, as a result of mental disorder [or mental retardation], he lacks substantial capacity either to appreciate the criminality of his conduct or to conform his conduct to the requirements of the law.

The expression "substantial capacity" means power or ability to a material or substantial degree. The expression "to appreciate the criminality of his conduct" means to realize that his conduct is criminally wrong, to understand that it is criminally wrong as a matter of importance and reality, and not as merely a bare abstraction put into words. The expression "to conform his conduct to the requirements of law" means to act as the law requires a person to act under the circumstances. The law recognizes that will power or behavior control, like reason, may be seriously impaired or destroyed by a mental disorder (or mental retardation) so that the person so affected loses his capacity or ability to exercise control over himself.

In summary, there are three threshold questions. First, was the defendant suffering from any behavioral or emotional illness [or mental retardation] at the time of the alleged crime? Second, if so, was it the result of any psychiatric or neurological disorder rather than an abnormality manifested only by repeated criminal or other antisocial conduct? Third, if so, did such mental disorder (or mental retardation) induce or cause a substantial lack of the defendant's capacity either to appreciate the criminality of his conduct or to conform his conduct to the requirements of the law?

Before considering the question of the defendant's criminal responsibility, you should first determine whether the State has established by proof beyond a reasonable doubt that the defendant did, in fact, commit the crime(s) with which he is charged. If you are not convinced beyond a reasonable doubt that he did commit the crime(s), then you should go no further but simply bring in a verdict of not guilty. If, on the other hand, you are convinced beyond a reasonable doubt that the defendant did, in fact, commit the crime(s), then you should determine whether or not he was criminally responsible at the time he did so.

I suggest that you approach the question of criminal responsibility in this way. You should first determine whether the defendant, at the time of the commission of the alleged crime, was suffering from a mental disorder (or mental retardation). The defendant must prove by a preponderance of the evidence that he was suffering from a mental disorder (or mental retardation). If you are not convinced that the defendant was suffering from a mental disorder (or mental retardation), then you should find him criminally responsible at the time of the alleged crime, and if you have found beyond a reasonable doubt that he did commit the crime(s) alleged, you should bring in a verdict of guilty.

If a preponderance of the evidence supports a finding that the defendant was suffering from a mental disorder [or mental retardation], then you should next determine, by a preponderance of the evidence, whether, as a result of this mental disorder [or mental retardation], the defendant lacked substantial capacity either to appreciate the criminality of his conduct or to conform his conduct to the requirements of the law. If you *are* convinced that the defendant was suffering from a mental disorder (or mental retardation) but are *not* convinced by a preponderance of the evidence that he lacked substantial capacity *either* to appreciate the criminality of his conduct *or* to conform his conduct to the requirements of law, then you should find him criminally responsible at the time the alleged crime was committed. If you find beyond a reasonable doubt that the defendant did commit the crime(s) alleged, then you should bring in a verdict of guilty.

If you are convinced beyond a reasonable doubt that the defendant did commit the crime(s) as alleged and you are convinced by a preponderance of the evidence that the defendant lacked substantial capacity either to appreciate the criminality of his conduct or to conform his conduct to the requirements of the law as the result of a mental disorder (or mental retardation), then you must find him not criminally responsible at the time of the alleged crime(s). Then your verdict should be not criminally responsible by reason of insanity.

COMMENT

This instruction is based on Maryland Ann. Code, Health-General Article, Title 12. It relies heavily on the Court's decisions in

Pouncey v. State, 297 Md. 264, 465 A.2d 475 (1983); *Langworthy v. State,* 284 Md. 588, 399 A.2d 578 (1979), *cert. denied,* 450 U.S. 960 (1981); *Young v. State,* 14 Md. App. 538, 288 A.2d 198 (1972); *Sherrill v. State,* 14 Md. App. 146, 286 A.2d 528 (1972); *Love v. State,* 16 Md. App. 364, 297 A.2d 309 (1972); *Truesdale v. State,* 16 Md. App. 260, 295 A.2d 808 (1972).

The new insanity defense law (Acts 1984, ch. 501) became effective July 1, 1984. Its significant changes include: (1) shifting the burden of proof to the defendant on the insanity issue; (2) requiring automatic commitment to a mental institution upon adjudication of insanity; and (3) shifting the burden of proof to the defendant after commitment to establish entitlement to release. For a discussion of the revised law, see *Anderson v. Department of Health & Mental Hygiene,* 64 Md. App. 674, 498 A.2d 679 (1985).

(a) History of insanity standards

A review of the insanity standards used in Maryland prior to and including the present standard appears in *Young v. State,* 14 Md. App. 538, 288 A.2d 198 (1972). The Colonial Constitution of Maryland contains in its Declaration of Rights the following statement: "An inhabitant of the State of Maryland, as a part of the legacy of the common law of England bequeathed him by the People, is not responsible for his criminal conduct if he was insane at the time he committed the crime." *Id.* at 540, 288 A.2d at 200. This reference is the first formal recognition given by the State to the longstanding English practice which dates back to the time of Henry III.

The General Assembly adopted the first insanity defense statute in 1826 with the passage of Chapter 197, § 1 of the 1826 Maryland Acts. At the time, the standard was not specifically set out but was developed as common law by the courts.

The Maryland Court of Appeals in 1888 recognized the rule in *M'Naghten's Case,* 8 Eng. Rep. 718 (1843), in *Spencer v. State,* 69 Md. 28, 13 A. 809 (1888). The "M'Naghten-Spencer" test of criminal responsibility, relying upon whether an individual had sufficient mental capacity to distinguish right from wrong, remained virtually intact until 1967 when the American Law Institute (ALI) standard was adopted to quell the confusion which had developed over this vague and undefined standard. The present statute differs from the 1967 version only slightly. The terms "mental disease or defect," which appeared in the earlier version, and in the American Law Institute's (ALI) 1962 Model Penal Code, § 4.01, were first adopted by the State in 1967, but the section was changed to read "mental disorder" in 1970. As discussed in subpart (f), Mental retardation, *infra* this Comment, legislative changes have occurred regarding mental retardation.

In 1984 the Maryland General Assembly revised the insanity defense. This legislation resulted from a report issued by the Governor's Task Force to Review the Defense of Insanity established in 1982. The ALI standard remains intact while the primary statutory changes can be grouped into three categories discussed, *infra,* in this Comment as follows: subpart (c), Plea and verdict; subpart (d), Generating jury issue, expert and lay testimony and burden of proof; and subpart (i), Post-verdict commitment procedures. For an overview of the legislative changes, see Aaronson, *Maryland Responds to the Hinckley Case: Changes in the Insanity Defense,* 35 Md. B.J. 84 (January 1985).

(b) Present standard

Maryland Ann. Code, Health-General Article, § 12-108 provides the statutory authority for the insanity test currently in use. It should be noted that the test appears in the "Health" title of the Code, not under "Criminal Law." This procedural distinction reflects the General Assembly's intent to resolve the issues involving mental disability and criminal responsibility on a medical and social level rather than on a penal level.

Health-General, § 12-108 reads as follows:

> (a) *Test — In general.* — A defendant is not criminally responsible for criminal conduct if, at the time of that conduct, the defendant, because of a mental disorder or mental retardation, lacks substantial capacity:
>
> (1) To appreciate the criminality of that conduct; or
>
> (2) To conform that conduct to the requirements of law.
>
> (b) *Same — Exclusion.* — For purposes of this section, "mental disorder" does not include an abnormality that is

manifested only by repeated criminal or otherwise antisocial conduct.

The definition of "mental disorder" is set forth in General-Health, § 12-101(f). It states that "'Mental disorder' means a behavioral or emotional illness that results from a psychiatric or neurological disorder." It "includes a mental illness that so substantially impairs the mental or emotional functioning of an individual as to make care or treatment necessary or advisable for the welfare of the individual or for the safety of the person or property of another." General-Health, § 12-101(f)(3) states that "'mental disorder' does not include 'mental retardation.'" (Note that mental retardation may relieve one from criminal responsibility. For further explanation, see subpart (f), Mental retardation, *infra* this Comment.)

The threshold question to be answered in any discussion of Maryland's insanity standard concerns the meaning and application of *mental disorder.* As previously mentioned, the Maryland criminal responsibility test closely mirrors the ALI test with one exception. The ALI test defines its standard in the following manner: "A person is not responsible for criminal conduct if, at the time of such conduct, as a result of *mental disease or defect* he lacks substantial capacity either to appreciate the criminality of his conduct or to conform his conduct to the requirements of the law." (Model Penal Code, § 4.01 (1962)). The ALI Penal Code drafters did not provide a definition of "mental disease or defect." The Maryland General Assembly substituted "mental disorder" for "mental disease or defect" since the courts had considerable difficulty in defining the term "mental disease or defect."

In *Sherrill v. State,* 14 Md. App. 146, 286 A.2d 528 (1972), the Court discussed the adoption of the use of the term "mental disorder" in place of "mental disease or defect" and inclusion in the statute of a definition of "mental disorder" to provide the courts with guidance. The Court recognized that use of the phrase "mental disease or defect" created considerable confusion among psychiatrists testifying on behalf of the defendant. The same Court, in *Young v. State,* 14 Md. App. 538, 288 A.2d 198 (1972) discussed how the term "mental disorder" was defined. It set forth a definition of mental disorder as follows:

> (1) any mental disorder which so substantially impaired his mental or emotional functioning as to make it necessary or advisable for his welfare or for the safety of the persons or property of others that he receive care and treatment; or (2) a degree of subnormality of intellectual development expected to be of life duration which reduced his capability to manage himself or his affairs; [*but see* subpart (f), Mental retardation, *infra,* this Comment]; or
> (3) any other form of behavioral or emotional illness, which as to any of the three, were the result of any psychiatric or neurological disorder other than an abnormality manifested only by repeated criminal or otherwise antisocial conduct.

Id. at 546, 288 A.2d at 203.

As noted by the Court in *Sherrill,* and later in *Young,* the change in the test was one of "substance and not just form." The legislature's awareness of the conflict of opinion created by the use of the former term, "mental disease or defect," resulted in the adoption of the more concrete standard which could be understood and uniformly applied by the courts.

Analysis of the *Sherrill* opinion reveals, however, that the use of a defined term like mental disorder may do little to ease the difficulty which exists when the legal profession becomes closely involved with medical terms.

The defendant, Kyle Sherrill, was convicted in a nonjury trial for kidnapping and committing unnatural and perverted sex upon a child. His behavior was defined by several certified psychiatrists as pedophilia. The question was whether pedophilia could be classified as a mental disease, defect or disorder, and whether it was a psychiatric or neurological disorder rather than a sexual deviance. The result of extensive cross-examination was a plethora of medical terms. No two psychiatrists used the same language when classifying the defendant's condition. The Court sought to clarify this problem by setting forth the following questions which, in conjunction with the procedural sections, were to provide a clear path through the bramble bush. According to the *Sherrill* decision, the testifying psychiatrist should first be asked the threshold question of whether the defendant was suffering from any mental disorder. Second, the psychiatrist should be asked whether the disorder is the result of any psychiatric or neurological disorder. The final question is whether such disorder induced or caused a substantial lack of the defendant's capacity to appreciate the wrongfulness of his conduct or to conform his conduct to the requirements of the law.

In both *Young* and *Sherrill,* deference was paid to the *Diagnostic and Statistical Manual,* published by the American Psychiatric Association. The Court clearly implied that any mental disorder categorized in the Manual places one at least past the point of the initial threshold question. This approach may be criticized as giving too great a role to the psychiatric profession. The concern that medical terminology should not control legal outcomes is reflected in the landmark District of Columbia case, *McDonald v. United States,* 312 F.2d 847 (D.C. Cir. 1962), which provides a legal standard rather than a medical standard for "mental disease or defect." This legal standard is as follows: "A mental disease or defect includes any abnormal condition of the mind which substantially affects mental or emotional processes and substantially impairs behavior controls." 312 F.2d at 851. This standard was incorporated into the District of Columbia's version of the ALI test in *United States v. Brawner,* 471 F.2d 969 (D.C. Cir. 1972).

For a discussion of whether the presence of a genetic defect, i.e., an extra "y" chromosome, can qualify as a "mental disorder" and whether a geneticist can provide "with reasonable medical certainty" an expert opinion of the defendant's alleged insanity, see *Millard v. State,* 8 Md. App. 419, 261 A.2d 227 (1970).

In *Parker v. State,* 7 Md. App. 167, 254 A.2d 381 (1969), *cert. denied,* 256 Md. 747 (1970), *cert. denied,* 402 U.S. 984 (1971), the Court discussed the circumstances under which drunkenness might qualify for an insanity defense. Note that the new test was not yet in effect ("mental disorder" had not been substituted for "mental disease or defect"). The Court distinguished between "temporary" insanity, (that is, insanity caused by a particular alcoholic bout) and "permanent" or "settled" insanity (that is, insanity which is an alcoholic psychosis resulting from long continued habits of excessive drinking). It stated that one suffering from "temporary" insanity is one that is sane prior to drinking and again after the influences of the intoxication have worn off. Temporary insanity, as defined, will not excuse the defendant of criminal liability even if he meets the requirements of the insanity test. On the other hand, one suffering from "permanent" or "settled" insanity may be excused from criminal responsibility. The Court, however, recognized that such terms may be oversimplified since one suffering from delirium tremens or alcoholic hallucinosis may be excused of criminal responsibility even if the condition was temporary. It further noted that the real distinction is between "the direct results of drinking, which are voluntarily sought after, and its remote and undesired consequences." *Id.* at 179, 254 A.2d at 388. The Court also recognized that voluntary drunkenness may still be taken into consideration whenever a particular motive, purpose, or intent is an element of the crime charged. E.g., *Springer v. Collins,* 586 F.2d 329, *cert. denied,* 440 U.S. 923 (1978). See Comment, § 5.01, Voluntary drunkenness, *supra,* for further discussion.

In *Porreca v. State,* 49 Md. App. 522, 433 A.2d 1204 (1981), the defendant was sane before using PCP (phencyclidine), a controlled dangerous substance, and sane again after the effects of the drug wore off. The defendant suffered from a psychosis which was the product of habitual drug abuse rather than ingestion on a single occasion. This psychosis lingered for several months after drug use had ceased, thus raising a legal question as to defendant's sanity. The Court found that the defendant demonstrated enough evidence of "permanent" or "fixed" insanity, since he was sane again only after the effects of the psychosis dissipated. The trial court's holding that defendant had not put his sanity in issue was erroneously based on the finding that defendant's psychosis was caused by voluntary drug abuse.

In *Robey v. State,* 54 Md. App. 60, 456 A.2d 953 (1983), medical and psychiatric testimony established that a parent beat her child over the course of several months, resulting in the child's death. Between the beatings the defendant recognized what she had done, became depressed, felt guilty, and cried; she did not, however, seek medical care for the injury she inflicted on her child. The Court held that under any definition, the insanity defense has never been extended to negate responsibility for actions taken during lucid intervals. Finding that the failure to obtain medical care necessary to her child's health occurred during such periods, the Court affirmed defendant's conviction for involuntary manslaughter and child abuse.

(c) Plea and verdict

A person accused of a crime in Maryland may plead: "not guilty, guilty, or, with the consent of the court, nolo contendere. In addition to any of these pleas, the defendant may interpose the defense of insanity as permitted by law." Maryland Rule 4-242(a). The traditional "not guilty by reason of insanity" plea and verdict apparently does not technically exist as such under Maryland law. See *Riggleman v. State,* 33 Md. App. 344, 364 A.2d 1159 (1976).

Once a written plea of "not criminally responsible by reason of insanity" has been filed, the trier of fact shall find, by separate verdict, whether the defendant was criminally responsible when the crime was committed. Maryland Ann. Code, Health-General Article, § 12-109(a) and (c). The written plea must be filed at the time provided for initial pleading, unless, for good cause shown, the court allows the plea to be filed later. Health-General, § 12-109(a)(2). In *Grandison v. State,* 305 Md. 685, 506 A.2d 580 (1986), the Court held that there was no error in refusing to grant defendant's request to file a plea the day before trial was to begin because the defendant failed to show good cause for the late filing.

The jury must first make a determination as to whether the defendant committed the criminal act(s) charged. The term "criminal act(s) charged" is used to indicate that the trier of fact first determines whether the State proved beyond a reasonable doubt all the elements of the crime. This determination is made before considering the plea of not criminally responsible. General-Health, Task Force Comment to § 12-109.

There are three possible outcomes when in addition to a general plea of not guilty, an insanity plea is interposed:

> 1. If the verdict on the general plea is not guilty, the plea of insanity becomes moot. Patently, a person, whether sane or insane, may not be held criminally responsible for an offense of which he has been acquitted....
>
> 2. If the verdict on the general plea is guilty and the special verdict on the additional plea is that the defendant was sane at the time of the commission of the offense, the court shall impose sentence....
>
> 3. If the verdict on the general plea is guilty and the special verdict on the additional plea is that the accused was

> insane at the time of the commission of the offense ... he shall not be held responsible for his criminal conduct.

Langworthy v. State, 284 Md. 588, 593-94, 399 A.2d 578, 584 (1979), *cert. denied,* 450 U.S. 960 (1981).

In *Langworthy,* the defendant was convicted of rape but was found insane at the time the crime was committed. The Court of Appeals upheld the statutory scheme. It emphasized that "the clear legislative intent regarding the successful interposition of a plea of insanity is not that an accused is to be found not guilty of the criminal act it was proved he committed, but that he shall not be punished therefor." *Id.* at 598, 399 A.2d at 584. The Court further held that a finding of "guilty and insane" was a final judgment; therefore, the defendant was entitled to appellate review.

Pouncey v. State, 297 Md. 264, 465 A.2d 475 (1983) adds further support that guilty and insane verdicts are not inconsistent. In *Pouncey,* the defendant was found guilty of murder in the first degree when she drowned her son. She was also found insane. The Court of Appeals upheld "the guilty and insane" verdict. It also specifically addressed the question of whether one found insane can have the necessary *mens rea* to commit a general intent crime by stating that "insanity is not tantamount to an absence of *mens rea." Id.* at 269, 465 A.2d at 478. See also *Langworthy v. State, supra* at 599, 399 A.2d at 584 n.12 ("neither of these (insanity) tests is necessarily at variance with a general intent to commit a crime"). Further, the Court recognized that, although the defendant may never be sentenced as a criminal, the legislature has not removed all noncriminal collateral consequences of committing a criminal act, such as being held in a mental institution until it is determined that release would not constitute a danger to the individual or to the person or property of others.

The statutory change provides a needed clarification in the verdict form. Prior to the change in 1984, Health-General, § 12-108, stated the verdict as "the defendant was insane when the alleged crime was committed." Both the plea and verdict are now stated as "not criminally responsible" and "not criminally responsible by reason of insanity." Health-General, § 12-109. The Task Force felt that the term "not criminally responsible" makes clear that the defendant remains morally and personally responsible even though the defendant meets the standard and should be relieved of criminal responsibility and criminal sanctions. Thus, the Task Force recommends avoiding the terms "insane" and "insanity" to the greatest extent possible. These terms convey a mental image that may unfairly prejudice the credibility of the plea when the defendant seems reliably normal by contrast. The terms also tend to perpetuate stigmatizing images of all mentally ill persons in the public mind, including those who have committed no crime.

Prior to the statutory change, the Court in *Langworthy v. State, supra,* and *Pouncey v. State, supra,* while discussing the separate factual findings to be made by the trier of fact, noted that findings of "guilty" and "insane" were not inconsistent. The Court noted that the reason for this is that insane persons can still form the general *mens rea* to commit a crime. Query whether in cases where the defendant lacks the capacity to form the required specific intent *mens rea,* guilty and insane verdicts may be inherently inconsistent. The Court in *Langworthy* was careful to state the outcome as "... he shall not be held responsible for his criminal conduct." 284 Md. at 588, 399 A.2d at 581. In this regard it should be noted that diminished capacity is not a recognized defense in Maryland. See *Johnson v. State,* 292 Md. 405, 439 A.2d 542 (1982), and the discussion of diminished capacity, subpart (h), this Comment, *infra.*

(d) Generating jury issue, expert and lay testimony and burden of proof

The defendant is presumed criminally responsible. If a defendant wants to assert a defense of insanity, evidence sufficient to raise an issue of lack of criminal responsibility must be adduced. The insanity plea itself, without more, does not generate a jury issue as to the defendant's insanity. *Hawkins v. State,* 34 Md. App. 82, 366 A.2d 421 (1976). See also *Van Meter v. State,* 30 Md. App. 406, 352 A.2d 850 (1976). Once some evidence is presented, the Court will determine preliminarily whether in the minds of reasonable jurors there is sufficient proof, if believed, to raise a question as to the accused's criminal responsibility. If sufficient proof exists, the issue will go to the jury. See *Van Meter v. State, supra; Evans v. State,* 28 Md. App. 640, 349 A.2d 300 (1975), *aff'd,* 278 Md. 197, 362 A.2d 629 (1976). These cases clearly indicate that the issue of insanity may be generated by either the defendant's or the State's evidence. In a jury trial such proof may be presented out of the jury's presence. *Saul v. State,* 6 Md. App. 540, 252 A.2d 282 (1969), *aff'd,* 258 Md. 100, 265 A.2d 178 (1970); *Dubs v. State,* 2 Md. App. 524, 235 A.2d 764 (1967). Since the General Assembly, effective July 1, 1984, shifted the burden of persuasion to the defendant by a preponderance of the evidence, query whether the defendant's preliminary burden of going forward with sufficient evidence to generate a jury issue also has increased.

Expert testimony in support of settled or fixed insanity is sufficient evidence to raise the insanity defense. *Porreca v. State,* 49 Md. App. 522, 529, 433 A.2d 1204, 1208 (1981). In *Ake v. Oklahoma,* 470 U.S. 68, 105 S. Ct. 1087, 84 L. Ed. 2d 53 (1985), the defendant in a capital case was initially found incompetent to stand trial. During his three-month stay at the state hospital, no inquiry had been made into his sanity at the time of the offense, and, as an indigent, the defendant could not afford to pay for a psychiatrist. Counsel asked the trial court either to arrange to have a psychiatrist perform the examination or provide funds so that the defense could arrange for a private psychiatrist. The trial judge rejected this request. The Supreme Court held that when a defendant has made a preliminary showing that his sanity at the time of the offense is likely to be a significant factor at trial, the Constitution of the United States requires that a State provide access to a psychiatrist's assistance on this issue, if the defendant cannot otherwise afford one. The Court stated that the decision on how to implement this right is left to the states.

In *Johnson v. State,* 292 Md. 405, 439 A.2d 542 (1982), the Court held that it is not a violation of defendant's due process or equal protection rights for the trial court to deny the request of defendant, who pleaded not guilty by reason of insanity, that the court appoint a private independent psychiatrist to examine him at state expense where the court had already arranged for defendant to be examined by psychiatrists at the state mental hospital. A psychiatrist at the state hospital is "independent," even though compensated by the state, just as counsel assigned to an indigent defendant is "independent," although he too is compensated by the state. The defendant produced no evidence of the state psychiatrist's partiality or incompetence.

For a discussion of the admissibility of expert opinion of defendant's sanity as part of a hospital record, see *Gregory v. State,* 40 Md. App. 297, 391 A.2d 437 (1978). The Court discusses the hearsay rule and the business and public record exceptions and the constitutional issue of whether admitting expert opinion in hospital records against a defendant violates the right of confrontation of witnesses.

In *State v. Conn,* 286 Md. 406, 408 A.2d 700 (1979), the Court held that a lay witness, based upon his personal observation, may express his conclusion or impression that an individual seemed to be mentally normal or abnormal when an insanity defense has been raised. The lower court erred in concluding that the testimony constituted an impermissible opinion by a lay witness on the ultimate issue of sanity. Normal conduct and abnormal conduct are matters of common knowledge, and lay persons may conclude from observation that certain observed conduct is abnormal.

Once the issue of insanity is generated, the defendant has the burden to establish by a preponderance of the evidence the defense of being not criminally responsible. Maryland Ann. Code, Health-General Article, § 12-109(b).

Query whether the statutory change, which places the burden of proof upon the defendant by a preponderance of the evidence, violates the constitutional due process standards of *Evans v. State, supra,* and its progeny. See Appendix V, The Impact of *Evans v. State:* Burdens of Proof, Presumptions and Inferences, *infra.* If being not criminally responsible, arguably, is an exculpatory fact related to punishment only, due process may not preclude placing the burden of proof upon the defendant. Similar provisions have been impliedly ratified by the United States Supreme Court. See *Jones v. United States,* 463 U.S. 354, 103 S. Ct. 3043, 77 L. Ed. 2d 694 (1983).

(e) Bifurcation of trial and defendant's right against self-incrimination

A leading case on whether the defendant can obtain a separate trial on the issue of criminal responsibility is *Tull v. State,* 230 Md. 596, 188 A.2d 150 (1963). At trial, the defense counsel filed a motion for a separate trial on the issue of insanity, asserting that the testimony would tend to confuse the jury and create prejudice toward the defendant in the minds of the jury. The trial court denied the motion. On appeal, the Court held that bifurcation of the issues of guilt and criminal responsibility is not a requirement, but remained silent as to whether the court had discretion to grant bifurcation and whether any set of circumstances would be persuasive upon such a motion.

The next criminal appeal reviewing a denial of defendant's motion for bifurcated trial was *Sweeney v. State,* 6 Md. App. 431, 252 A.2d 9 (1969). In *Sweeney,* the Court recognized that an essential element of guilt is at issue when the defendant asserts an insanity defense. Therefore, if the defendant were entitled to two separate trials, he would, in effect, be given two separate trials on the merits. The Court held that this was not required by due process.

The Court in *Sweeney,* not only upheld the language of *Tull v. State, supra,* but went several steps further. It stated that a denial of the bifurcation motion was not error in the case even though the State did not oppose the motion. Moreover, the Court added that it did not find any requirement compelling a bifurcated trial, "... and on the contrary, think(s) it clear that the legislative intent was to the contrary." *Id.* at 439, 252 A.2d at 14. But see *Holmes v. United States,* 363 F.2d 281 (D.C. Cir. 1966) and *Contee v. United States,* 410 F.2d 249 (D.C. Cir. 1969). These two appellate cases from the District of Columbia were cited in *Sweeney v. State, supra,* as contrary authority but without weight in Maryland. The *Holmes* court recognized that substantial prejudice may result from the simultaneous trial on the insanity and not guilty pleas. Subsequent decisions in Maryland have upheld *Sweeney v. State, supra.* See *Bremer v. State,* 18 Md. App. 291, 307 A.2d 503, *cert. denied,* 415 U.S. 930 (1973); *Morris v. State,* 11 Md. App. 18, 272 A.2d 663 (1971); *Avey v.*

State, 9 Md. App. 227, 263 A.2d 609 (1970). *Cf. United States v. King,* 582 F.2d 888 (4th Cir. 1978).

In *Sweeney v. State, supra,* the Court gave little consideration to the alleged violations of the defendant's right against self-incrimination and the related right to due process from Maryland's single trial procedure. In *Bartholomey v. State,* 260 Md. 504, 273 A.2d 164 (1971), *modified,* 408 U.S. 938, 92 S. Ct. 2870, 33 L. Ed. 2d 759 (1973), the Court held the defendant's privilege against self-incrimination was not violated and the defendant's choice to testify on his own behalf was a strategic decision that was not mandated by the State's procedural rules. Death sentences imposed on Bartholomey were vacated. *Bartholomey v. Maryland,* 408 U.S. 938, 92 S. Ct. 2870, 33 L. Ed. 2d 759 (1971), *reh'g denied,* 409 U.S. 901 (1972).

On remand, the Court of Appeals held that the legality of the murder convictions was unaffected by the invalidity of the death sentences. *Bartholomey v. State,* 267 Md. 175, 297 A.2d 696 (1972).

In *Bremer v. State, supra,* the Court held that denial of a bifurcated trial presented no fifth amendment problem. The Court held that requiring a defendant who asserts the insanity defense to submit to a psychiatric evaluation could not be attacked on constitutional grounds. The Court rejected the argument that the defendant would be subjecting himself to a substantial risk of self-incrimination by cooperating with the State's psychiatrist and making statements which would later be disclosed to a jury deciding his guilt or innocence. The Court held that "where the defendant has pleaded insanity as a defense and presented evidence to meet the threshold question, the maintenance of a fair state-individual balance requires that the State be permitted to have him examined. If the State is to shoulder the responsibility of establishing sanity beyond a reasonable doubt, it must have the means to do so." *Id.* at 341, 307 A.2d at 519. *Accord Williamson v. State,* 36 Md. App. 405, 374 A.2d 909 (1977), *rev'd on other grounds,* 282 Md. 100, 382 A.2d 588 (1978). *But cf. Estelle v. Smith,* 451 U.S. 454, 101 S. Ct. 1866, 68 L. Ed. 2d 359 (1981) (where psychiatrist's evaluation was for the limited, neutral purpose of determining competency to stand trial, and results were used at a capital sentencing for the broader purpose of establishing defendant's future dangerousness, admission of testimony was held violative of the fifth amendment). If the insanity defense under existing law is now viewed an as exculpatory fact related solely to punishment with the burden of persuasion on the defendant, query whether the Court would consider the question of bifurcation in a different light.

(f) Mental retardation

After a period of uncertainty, it is now clear that the test of responsibility for criminal conduct is applicable to a defendant suffering from a mental disorder or mental retardation.

Prior to 1972, mental disorder was defined in Art. 59, § 3(f) of the Maryland Annotated Code as follows:

> Mental disorder means mental illness or *mental retardation* or any other form of behavioral or emotional illness resulting from any psychiatric or neurological disorder (emphasis added).

Under this statutory formulation, the mentally retarded defendant was clearly able to invoke the insanity defense. *Love v. State,* 16 Md. App. 364, 297 A.2d 309 (1972).

In 1972, the definition of mental disorder in Art. 59, § 3(f) was amended expressly to exclude mental retardation. The 1972 change seemed to be a recognition that mental retardation is not synonymous with mental defect, that is, not all mentally retarded persons suffer from a "mental illness." While affording such persons an improved status, the General Assembly apparently did not foresee the impact of this change on the availability of the insanity defense to the retarded defendant. In 1981, the definition of mental disorder was again amended, this time to include mental retardation. See *Johnson v. State,* 50 Md. App. 584, 439 A.2d 607 (1982). In the 1982 revision and, currently, pursuant to the 1984 repeal and reenactment of the Health-General Article, Title 12, the definition of "mental disorder," § 12-101(f), excludes mental retardation. The comment following the section states that the 1984 Task Force advised against defining "mental retardation" for purposes of Title 12. However, as noted above, in connection with the test for criminal responsibility, § 12-108, there is reference to the term and it appears in other sections of the title, *e.g.*, § 12-104, Examination as to competence.

There is no specific definition of "mental retardation" in the Maryland criminal laws but reference may be made to Title 7, Developmental Disabilities Law. The definition therein, Health-General, § 7-102(l) is:

> "Mental retardation" means a developmental disability that is evidenced by significantly subaverage intellectual functioning and impairment in the adaptive behavior of an individual.

For a helpful analysis of the present test for criminal responsibility, see the Task Force Comment to § 12-107, Maryland Ann. Code, Health-General Article.

(g) Standard of competence to stand trial distinguished

The insanity defense is based on the defendant's lack of criminal responsibility at the time of the alleged crime. The defendant's competency to stand trial relates to the defendant's mental condition at the time of trial. Unlike the inquiry for criminal responsibility, the issue of a defendant's competency to stand trial should always be determined by the court and never presented to the jury. See *Raithel v. State,* 280 Md. 291, 372 A.2d 1069 (1977), for a discussion of the burden of proof in competency determinations.

The primary statutory authority, replacing all prior common law, is Maryland Ann. Code, Health-General, § 12-103, Court determination of competency. The competency standard seeks to determine whether the defendant is able to understand the nature or the object of the criminal proceedings against him, and whether he is able to assist in his own defense. For a discussion of this standard, see *Jolley v. State,* 282 Md. 353, 384 A.2d 91 (1978). See also Health-General, § 12-101(d) Defining "incompetent to stand trial."

One interrelationship between competency to stand trial and insanity as a complete defense, arises where a possibly incompetent defendant seeks to prevent counsel from raising an insanity defense or, where once raised, requests counsel to withdraw an insanity defense. In *Langworthy v. State,* 46 Md. App. 116, 416 A.2d 1287 (1980), *cert. denied,* 450 U.S. 960 (1981), the Court stated that once an insanity plea is filed, defendant's counsel has a responsibility to see that it is not improvidently withdrawn, even at the defendant's request. See also *Riggleman v. State,* 33 Md. App. 344, 364 A.2d 1159, 1163 (1976). Trial counsel has a duty and the court a responsibility to prevent withdrawal of the insanity plea by an obviously incompetent defendant. *White v. State,* 17 Md. App. 58, 299 A.2d 873, 876 (1973).

See Comment at subpart (g), § 4.21.c, Murder — First degree: Death penalty sentencing, *supra.* The State is prohibited from executing an incompetent inmate.

(h) Doctrine of diminished capacity not recognized

Evidence that demonstrates lack of mental capacity which is insufficient to establish legal insanity may not be introduced to negate the requisite intent to commit a crime (including specific intent crimes). *Johnson v. State,* 303 Md. 487, 495 A.2d 1 (1985); *Johnson v. State,* 292 Md. 405, 439 A.2d 542 (1982); *Simmons v. State,* 292 Md. 478, 439 A.2d 581 (1982); *Allen v. State,* 230 Md. 533, 188 A.2d 159 (1963); *Holt v. State,* 50 Md. App. 578, 438 A.2d 1386 (1982). See also *Armstead v. State,* 227 Md. 73, 175 A.2d 24 (1961); *Cole v. State,* 212 Md. 55, 128 A.2d 437 (1957). In *Johnson* (1982), *supra* at 420, 439 A.2d at 551, the Court noted that the doctrine of diminished capacity was not recognized at common law (*citing Fisher v. United States,* 328 U.S. 463, 476, 66 S. Ct. 1318, 1325, 90 L. Ed. 1382 (1945)) and that it "conflicts with the governing principle of criminal law that all legally sane individuals are equally capable of forming and possessing the same types and degrees of intent." In other words, if the law did not hold all persons responsible for their actions regardless of their particular mental strengths or weaknesses, it would not serve as a means of social control. The Court also recognized that any change should come from the General Assembly since it is the legislature's duty to balance the community's interests with the interests of those accused of crimes. *Id.* at 425, 439 A.2d at 554. See *Cole v. State, supra.* Evidence of diminished capacity, however, may be considered at sentencing. *Johnson v. State, supra; Logan v. State,* 289 Md. 460, 425 A.2d 632 (1981). See also *Scott v. State,* 297 Md. 235, 465 A.2d 1126 (1983); Maryland Ann. Code, Art. 27, § 413(c); and Instruction, § 4.21c, Murder — First degree: Death penalty sentencing, *supra.*

In *Swain v. State,* 50 Md. App. 29, 435 A.2d 805 (1981), the Court held that because Maryland does not recognize the diminished capacity defense, evidence which supported this defense does not raise a legitimate jury issue on the question of justification, excuse, or mitigation. The Court, *citing Evans v. State,* 28 Md. App. 640, 349 A.2d 300 (1975), *aff'd,* 278 Md. 197, 362 A.2d 629 (1976), determined that trial judges need not instruct juries on excuse and mitigation unless there is sufficient evidence to generate a jury question. See also *Holt v. State, supra.* In *Simmons v. State,* 66 Md. 629, 505 A.2d 577 (1986), the Court held that the use of psychiatric testimony to negate *mens rea* is prohibited except where the insanity defense is pled. Psychiatric or psychological testimony is not admissible to mitigate *mens rea* when offered to support the defense of imperfect self-defense.

While Maryland does not recognize the doctrine of diminished capacity or responsibility, it has recognized that voluntary intoxication is a condition which can negate the specific intent to commit certain crimes. *State v. Gover,* 267 Md. 602, 298 A.2d 378 (1973); *Avey v. State,* 249 Md. 385, 240 A.2d 107 (1968); *Stansbury v. State,* 218 Md. 255, 146 A.2d 17 (1958); *Chisley v. State,* 202 Md. 87, 95 A.2d 577 (1953); *Michael v. State,* 1 Md. App. 243, 229 A.2d 145 (1967). See Comment, § 5.01, Voluntary drunkenness, *supra,* and the cases therein discussed. Query whether it is inconsistent to hold that voluntary drunkenness can negate a defendant's capacity to form the specific intent while diminished mental capacity, no matter how substantial, cannot negate a defendant's capacity to form a specific intent. Circuit Judge Leventhal writing for the United States Court of Appeals for the District of Columbia *en banc* stated:

> Neither logic nor justice can tolerate a jurisprudence that defines the elements of an offense as requiring a mental state such that one defendant can properly argue that his voluntary drunkenness removed his capacity to form the specific intent but another defendant is inhibited from a sub-

> mission of his contention that an abnormal mental condition, for which he was in no way responsible, negated his capacity to form a particular specific intent....

United States v. Brawner, 471 F.2d 969, 999 (D.C. Cir. 1972).

Note, however, that the degree of intoxication necessary to negate the defendant's capacity to form the specific intent is great. See *Johnson v. State, supra* at 425 n.10, 439 A.2d at 554 n.10, and *State v. Gover, supra.*

(i) Post-verdict commitment procedures

If the defendant is found not criminally responsible, the Court will automatically commit him to a maximum security psychiatric institution for an indeterminate length of time. See Maryland Ann. Code, Health-General, § 12-111. See also *Langworthy v. State,* 284 Md. 588, 594, 399 A.2d 578, 581 (1979), *cert. denied,* 450 U.S. 960 (1981). The automatic commitment procedures rely heavily for their constitutional support on *Jones v. United States,* 463 U.S. 354, 103 S. Ct. 3043, 77 L. Ed. 694 (1983). The underlying rationale that permits the State to authorize automatic commitment is based on the nature of the verdict of not criminally responsible. The verdict itself establishes the two essential criteria for commitment: mental disorder or retardation and dangerousness. Dangerousness is rationally inferred from the proof at trial, beyond a reasonable doubt, that the defendant committed a criminal act. Continuing mental disorder or mental retardation is rationally inferred by defendant's plea and proof at trial by a preponderance of the evidence that at the time the criminal act was committed, the defendant was suffering from a mental disorder or mental retardation.

An individual found not criminally responsible is automatically committed for an indeterminate period to confinement in a psychiatric institution until such time as the individual proves eligibility for release. At release hearings the burden is on the committed individual to prove by a preponderance of the evidence that he or she is no longer, as a result of mental disorder or retardation, dangerous to self or the persons or property of others. This clearly places these individuals in a different position from civilly committed mental patients and also makes clear that the State's policy is the protection of the public as well as treatment of the individual. The substantive standard is unchanged — dangerousness as a result of mental disorder or mental retardation — and the Constitutional protections remain in place — a mandatory judicial hearing with notice and assistance of counsel.

A release hearing is mandated fifty days after commitment, unless waived, and yearly thereafter. The hearing is an administrative hearing, followed by the court's review or, when requested, a hearing before the court and/or a jury. Provision is made for exception to the hearing officer's report and for appeal.

Changes were made in the terms and conditions governing conditional release. The psychiatric institution and the individual's counsel both can make specific recommendations to the hearing officer of the conditions to be imposed. The hearing officer reports the recommendations of the terms to the court. The court then imposes its conditions by order.

In *Anderson v. Department of Health & Mental Hygiene*, 64 Md. App. 674, 498 A.2d 668 (1985), the Court held that the revised insanity defense law, effective July 1, 1984, applies to persons who were "under commitment" on the effective date of the statute. The *ex post facto* prohibition is not applicable because it applies only to penal laws. Committing an insane defendant is not punishment but protection of both the individual and society.

(j) Should the jury be instructed on the consequences of an insanity verdict?

Jurisdictions differ on the question of whether the jury should be told of the consequences of a verdict of not criminally responsible by reason of insanity. The Maryland Governor's Task Force to Review the Defense of Insanity debated this issue and considered adding the following as a third section to Maryland Ann. Code, Health-General Article, § 12-109:

> (c) *Jury instruction.* — The Court shall instruct the jury that if the defendant is found not criminally responsible by reason of insanity, the Court has the authority to commit the defendant to the Department of Health and Mental Hygiene for institutional, inpatient care and treatment.

After thorough discussion, the Task Force voted not to include this provision but noted that it was a closely divided question.

Some courts have held that the jury should not be told since those consequences are not relevant to whether the defendant met or did not meet the test of legal insanity. An instruction on this question is based on the belief that jurors, in common with the general population, are aware of the meanings and consequences of guilty and not guilty verdicts, but a verdict of not criminally responsible by reason of insanity may not have such a commonly understood meaning. It has been argued that juries may feel that the burden of preventing future violence is upon them even though that is not the issue before them. An instruction informing them that society has available other procedures to deal with this serious concern should help the jury to focus its attention on the narrower question of criminal responsibility. At least eleven states presently require or permit such an instruction.

While Maryland courts have not addressed this issue, they have discussed in other contexts the propriety of an attorney's comment in closing argument regarding appellate review and the possibility of parole. In *Poole v. State,* 295 Md. 167, 453 A.2d 1218 (1983) (a death penalty case), the Court held that comments to the jury concerning appellate review have no relevance and merely encourage the jury to shift their responsibility to another body. Comments made with respect to possibility of future parole were also held improper. For a detailed discussion of the propriety of attorney's comments regarding the possibility of parole in closing argument, see *Shoemaker v. State,* 228 Md. 462, 180 A.2d 682 (1962). *Compare* Comment, § 1.14, Jury's nonconcern with punishment, *supra.*

Among the jurisdictions which have approved an instruction, see, e.g., *Commonwealth v. Mulgrew,* 475 Pa. 271, 380 A.2d 349 (1977); *Commonwealth v. Mutina,* 366 Mass. 810, 323 N.E.2d 294 (1975). In *Mutina,* the court stated:

> On balance then, we believe it is best to entrust jurors with a knowledge of the consequences of a verdict of not guilty by reason of insanity. If jurors can be entrusted with responsibility for a defendant's life and liberty in such cases as this, they are entitled to know what protection they and their

> fellow citizens will have if they conscientiously apply the law to the evidence and arrive at a verdict of not guilty by reason of insanity — a verdict which necessarily requires the chilling determination that the defendant is an insane killer not legally responsible for his acts.

Id., 323 N.E.2d at 301.

If an instruction on the consequences of an insanity verdict is permitted, the difficult question of how to word this instruction remains. Prosecutors and defense counsel may disagree on the specificity with which the consequences of an insanity verdict should be described. As quoted above, the Governor's Task Force recommended fairly general language, which does not completely track the mandatory commitment provision enacted by the General Assembly. As noted in a previous section, if the defendant is found not criminally responsible, the Court will automatically commit the defendant to a maximum security psychiatric institution for an indeterminate length of time.

On the other hand, the judge or counsel may prefer more specific language which informs the jury of post-commitment procedures governing custody. An example of a fairly detailed instruction appears in Bar Association of the District of Columbia, *Criminal Jury Instructions: District of Columbia* (3d ed. 1978), § 5.11, "Effect of a Finding of Not Guilty by Reason of Insanity," which states:

> If the defendant is found not guilty by reason of insanity, it becomes the duty of the court to commit him to St. Elizabeth's Hospital. There will be a hearing within 50 days to determine whether the defendant is entitled to release. In that hearing the defendant has the burden of proof. The defendant will remain in custody, and will be entitled to release from custody only if the Court finds by a preponderance of the evidence that he is not likely to injure himself or other persons due to mental illness.

Id. at 350. In the District of Columbia, it is still within the court's discretion to give this instruction, even if the defendant requests that it not be given. *United States v. Brawner,* 471 F.2d 969, 992 (D.C. Cir. 1972). The current Maryland post-commitment procedure appears to be very similar to the procedure described in the above District of Columbia instruction.

§ 5.09. Mistake or ignorance of fact (suggested instruction).

(a) General intent element of the crime

Evidence has been introduced that the defendant's acts arose from a mistake or ignorance of fact.

In order to convict a person of __________ *(insert crime charged),* the State must prove beyond a reasonable doubt that the defendant had the __________ *(insert applicable mens rea, such as knowledge or intent)* to commit __________ *(insert the specific element of the crime to which the mens rea applies)* as well as every other element of the crime. If the actions of the defendant arose from a reasonable mistake or ignorance of fact, then the defendant did not have the __________ *(insert applicable general intent mens rea)* which is a necessary element of the crime. Therefore, this mistake or ignorance of fact will excuse the defendant from criminal responsibility.

In order for this defense to apply, the defendant must have had an honest and reasonable belief in the existence of circumstances, which, if true, would make the act for which the defendant is charged an innocent act. In other words, the mistaken belief must have been based on reasonable grounds and have been of such a nature that the conduct would have been lawful and proper had the facts been as the defendant honestly and reasonably supposed them to be. It is not reasonable if the mistake or ignorance of fact arose as a result of the defendant's negligence or his failure to exercise proper care.

If after a full and fair consideration of all the facts and circumstances in evidence, you have a reasonable doubt as to whether the defendant's acts arose from a reasonable mistake or ignorance of fact, then you must find the defendant not guilty of __________ *(insert crime charged).* On the other hand, if the State has convinced you beyond a reasonable doubt that the defendant's acts did *not* arise from a reasonable mistake or ignorance of fact, then you [should] [must] find that such mistake of fact or ignorance will not excuse the defendant of criminal responsibility.

(b) Specific intent element of the crime

Evidence has been introduced that the defendant's acts arose from a mistake or ignorance of fact.

In order to convict a person of __________ *(insert crime charged),* the State must prove beyond a reasonable doubt that the defendant had the __________ *(insert applicable specific intent mens rea, such as purpose or willfulness)* to commit the __________ *(insert element of crime to which the mens rea applies)* and to prove every other element of the crime.

If the actions of the defendant arose from a mistake or ignorance of fact, then the defendant did not have the __________ *(insert applicable specific intent mens rea such as purpose or willfulness)* which is a necessary element of this crime. Therefore, this mistake or ignorance of fact will excuse the defendant from criminal responsibility.

In order for this defense to apply, the defendant must have had an honest and good faith belief in the existence of circumstances which, if true, would make the act for which the defendant is charged an innocent act. In other words, the mistaken belief must be of such a nature that the conduct would have been lawful and proper had the facts been as the defendant honestly supposed them to be.

If after a full and fair consideration of all the facts and circumstances in evidence, you have a reasonable doubt as to whether the defendant's acts arose from a reasonable mistake or ignorance of fact, then you must find the defendant not guilty of __________ *(insert crime charged).* On the other hand, if the State has convinced you beyond a reasonable doubt that the defendant's acts did *not* arise from a reasonable mistake or ignorance of fact, then you [should] [must] find that such mistake or ignorance of fact will not excuse the defendant of criminal responsibility.

COMMENT

There appears to be no Maryland case law on mistake of fact.

Ignorance or mistake of fact in the commission of an act which, but for such mistake, would be a crime may result in the absence of the malice or criminal intention which may be an essential element of the crime. The general rule is that such ignorance or mistake of fact will exempt one from criminal responsibility. *United States v. Byrd,* 352 F.2d 570, 572 (2d Cir. 1965); *United States v. Cianciulli,* 482 F. Supp. 585, 620 (E.D. Pa. 1979).

A person will be excused from criminal liability when charged with a general intent crime as long as the mistaken belief is (a) honestly entertained, (b) based on reasonable grounds and (c) of such a nature that the conduct would have been lawful and proper had the facts been as they were reasonably supposed to be. R. Perkins & R. Boyce, *Criminal Law* 1045 (3d ed. 1982). See also *Davis v. State,* 265 Ind. 476, 355 N.E.2d 836 (1976); *Townsend v. United States,* 68 App. D.C. 223, 95 F.2d 352 (D.C. Cir. 1938). In other words, an honest and reasonable belief in the existence of circumstances which, if true, would make an act for which a person is indicted an innocent act, is a good defense, both at common law and in cases of statutory offenses, unless excluded expressly or by necessary implication. *Commonwealth v. Bollinger,* 197 Pa. Super. 492, 179 A.2d 253 (1962); *People v. Vogel,* 46 Cal. 2d 798, 299 P.2d 850 (1956). It is not a defense to a general intent crime if the mistake arises from lack of proper care on the part of the accused. In other words, one may not close his eyes to what is obvious. *United States v. Squires,* 440 F.2d 859, 864 (2d Cir. 1971); *United States v. Cianciulli, supra* at 621; *Green v. State,* 153 Tex. Crim. App. 442, 221 S.W.2d 612 (1949).

The textwriters, Perkins and Boyce, distinguish those cases requiring a general *mens rea* from those requiring a "special mental element." They state that even an unreasonable mistake, if entertained in good faith, is inconsistent with guilt if it negates some special element required for guilt of the offense:

> One, for example, who kills another because of a mistaken belief that his own life is in imminent peril at the hands of the other, is not excused if there is no reasonable ground for this belief. If a specific intent or other special mental element is required for guilt of the offense charged, the possibility of excuse due to a mistake of fact not based on reasonable grounds is obvious. The ultimate question in any prosecution is whether or not all the essential elements of guilt are established. If any such element is found to be wanting, guilt has not been substantiated; and hence if proof of a mistake of fact even without the support of reasonable grounds, negatives the existence of such an element, it also disproves the charge itself.

R. Perkins & R. Boyce, *Criminal Law* 1045-46 (3d ed. 1982).

The rationale for the difference in standards for general and specific intent crimes is seldom expressed. Again, Perkins and Boyce suggest that where a general *mens rea* is required the mistake excuses the behavior. Where there is a "special mental element" required, the defendant is not acquitted because the mistake excuses the behavior, but because an essential element is missing. If the mistake results in an essential element being absent, the mistake does not have to be reasonable. *Id.* at 1035, 1046.

In other words, when a person is charged with a specific intent crime, a subjective standard is applied; that is, a mistaken belief will excuse him of criminal liability as long as the mistake is entertained in good faith and it negates the necessary *mens rea* in the crime charged. *People v. Navarro,* 99 Cal. App. 3d Supp. 1, 160 Cal. Rptr. 692 (1979); R. Perkins & R. Boyce, *Criminal Law* 1046 (3d ed. 1982). See W. LaFave & A. Scott, *Criminal Law* 356 (1972).

Ignorance or mistake of fact is not, however, an excuse for violating a statute enacted in the exercise of the police power, which has as its purpose the punishment of a prohibited act without regard to the existence of criminal intent. *United States v. Weiler,* 458 F.2d 474 (3d Cir. 1972); *People v. Treen,* 33 Misc. 2d 571, 225 N.Y.S.2d 787 (1962). *Cf. United v. Squires, supra.*

Mistake of fact is different from factual impossibility. For a discussion of factual impossibility, see Comment, § 4.05, Attempt, *supra.*

§ 5.10. Mistaken identity.

Evidence has been introduced that ________ *(insert name(s) of witness(es))* [is] [are] mistaken in identifying the defendant as the perpetrator of the crime.

Whether or not a witness has adequately identified the defendant as the perpetrator of the crime is a question solely for you to decide. In other words, the credibility of the witness is a matter for your consideration and determination. In reaching your determination, you may consider such factors as any mistake, hesitancy or inconsistency on the part of the identifying witness.

Specifically, you may consider the opportunity of the witness to view the person committing the criminal acts at the time of the crime, including: (1) how long the encounter lasted; (2) the distance between the various persons; (3) the lighting conditions at the time; (4) the witness' state of mind at the time of the offense; and (5) the witness' degree of attention to the offender during the commission of the offense.

Also, you may consider the accuracy of the witness' prior description of the criminal, if any; the certainty or lack of certainty expressed by the witness; the demeanor and conduct of the witness making the identification; and any other direct or circumstantial evidence which may identify the person who committed the offense charged or which corroborates — that is, strengthens — or negates the identification of the defendant by the witness.

[You may also consider any other identification by the witness; any failure to identify or misidentification by the witness; the circumstances surrounding the identification procedure; the length of time between the crime and any subsequent identification; and any other circumstances bearing on the reliability of the witness' identification that you deem relevant.]

[The identification of the defendant as the perpetrator of the crime by a single eyewitness, if believed, is sufficient to support a conviction.]

Before you may find the defendant guilty of the crime, you must be satisfied beyond a reasonable doubt of the accuracy of the identification.

COMMENT

Under Maryland law, identification of the accused as perpetrator of the crime by a single eyewitness, if believed by the trier of fact, is sufficient to support conviction. See *Jones v. State,* 11 Md. App. 468, 275 A.2d 508 (1971); *Metallo v. State,* 10 Md. App. 76, 267 A.2d 804 (1970); *Johnson v. State,* 9 Md. App. 143, 262 A.2d 792 (1970).

The weight of the evidence, as well as the credibility of the witnesses, is for the trier of fact to determine. *Jones v. State,* 10 Md. App. 420, 424, 270 A.2d 827, 831 (1971); *Smith v. State,* 6 Md. App. 59, 64, 250 A.2d 285, 288 (1969); *Carroll v. State,* 3 Md. App. 50, 53, 237 A.2d 535, 537 (1968).

It is well settled in Maryland that the lack of positiveness in identifying the defendant as the person who committed the crime by a witness goes to the weight of the evidence, not its admissibility. *Robinson v. State,* 5 Md. App. 723, 249 A.2d 504 (1969); *Gibson v. State,* 4 Md. App. 222, 242 A.2d 204 (1968).

In *Hammond v. State,* 241 Md. 733, 217 A.2d 569, *cert. denied,* 385 U.S. 918 (1966), a slight variance in the prosecution witness' testimony as to the color of the defendant's shirt was held insufficient to overcome the conviction of larceny where testimony of another witness to the effect that the defendant was the thief, was clear and unequivocal.

The in-court identification may flow either from a proper pretrial identification or an independent source. *Jordan v. State,* 19 Md. App. 283, 310 A.2d 575, 576 (1973). The lack of identification or initial equivocation in identifying the defendant in a pretrial line-up or photo array also goes to the weight of the evidence, not its admissibility. *Corbin v. State,* 237 Md. 486, 206 A.2d 809 (1965); *Franklin v. State,* 18 Md. App. 651, 308 A.2d 752 (1973); *Carroll v. State, supra.*

The defendant may challenge the legality of a pre-trial identification out of the jury's presence. If the defendant does object, he has the burden of making a *prima facie* case that the pre-trial identification was illegal. The State then has the burden of proving that the pre-trial identification was legal. If the court finds the pre-trial identification to be legal, it is admissible as substantive evidence. If the court finds it to be illegal, the evidence is not admissible. If the pre-trial identification is excluded, the State has the burden of proving by clear and convincing evidence, that the in-court identification is not a product of the impermissibly suggestive pre-trial identification but is instead based on an independent source. *Smith v. State, supra* at 65, 250 A.2d at 291. See also *Cousins v. State,* 18 Md. App. 552, 556, 308 A.2d 692, 694 (1973); *Jones v. State, supra* at 423, 270 A.2d at 831.

The defendant, of course, may bring out circumstances surrounding the pre-trial identification which shed light on the weight of the evidence. *Perkins v. State,* 11 Md. App. 527, 533-34, 275 A.2d 517, 522 (1971).

The part of the instruction which relates to the circumstances surrounding an identification is based in part on the Bar Association of the District of Columbia, *Criminal Jury Instructions for the District of Columbia* § 5.06 (3d ed. 1978).

See Instructions: § 2.28, Identity of defendant; § 2.29, Identification of defendant by single eyewitness; and § 2.30, Photographic identification, all *supra.*

Introductory Note on Use of Self-defense Instructions, §§ 5.11 to 5.17, and Related Instructions

Where the defendant is charged with criminal homicide and asserts a defense of self-defense, the following instructions should be considered, where applicable, perhaps in the following order: § 5.11(a), Self-defense: General considerations; § 5.12(b), Self-defense — Amount of force permissible: Deadly force; § 5.13, Self-defense — Where defendant is alleged agressor; § 5.15, Duty to retreat before using deadly force and exception for "castle doctrine"; § 5.11(b), Self-defense: Burden of proof; § 5.16, Prior acts, reputation (or opinion) and threats of the deceased; § 5.04,

Defense of others; and § 5.14, Self-defense — Where appearances are false.

If imperfect self-defense is a consideration, see Comment, § 4.23c, Manslaughter — Voluntary: Suggested instruction on imperfect self-defense, *supra*.

Where the defendant asserts a defense of self-defense based on the use of nondeadly force, the following instructions should be considered, where applicable: § 5.11(a), Self-defense: General considerations; § 5.12(a), Self-defense — Amount of force permissible: Nondeadly force; § 5.04, Defense of others; § 5.17, Right to use nondeadly force to defend property; § 5.11(b), Self-defense: Burden of proof. Instruction, § 5.16, Prior acts, reputation (or opinion) and threats of deceased, should be modified, where appropriate, to nondeadly force situations.

§ 5.11. Self-defense — General considerations and burden of proof.

(a) General considerations

Evidence has been presented that the defendant acted in self-defense. Under certain circumstances a person has the right to use a reasonable amount of force in self-defense.

In order to justify __________ *(specify crime(s) to which the defense applies)* on the basis of self-defense, the defendant must have (1) actually believed that he was in imminent or immediate danger of [bodily harm] [serious bodily harm or death] from his assailant or potential assailant and (2) must have had reasonable grounds for that belief.

In considering the evidence relating to self-defense, the question is *not* whether you believe, looking backward in time, that the use of force was necessary. The question is whether the defendant, under the circumstances as they appeared to him at the time of the incident, actually believed he was in imminent danger of [bodily harm] [serious bodily harm or death] and had reasonable grounds for that belief. [In considering the reasonableness of the defendant's belief, you should consider whether the circumstances under which the defendant acted were such as would produce in the mind of a reasonably prudent person, similarly situated, the belief that he was in imminent danger of [bodily harm] [serious bodily harm or death].]

(b) Burden of proof

Since the burden of proof is on the State, the State must prove beyond a reasonable doubt that the defendant was *not* justified in using [deadly] [nondeadly] force to defend himself. Therefore, if after a full and fair consideration of all the facts and circumstances in evidence, you have a reasonable doubt as to whether the defendant was justified in using such force to defend himself, you must find the defendant not guilty of the offense charged. On the other hand, if you find that the State has proven beyond a reasonable doubt that the defendant was *not* justified in using such force to defend himself, then you [should] [must] find that the defense of self-defense does not excuse the defendant of criminal liability.

COMMENT

This instruction should be used in conjunction with Instructions, §§ 5.12 to 5.17, *infra,* as applicable. For a discussion of imperfect self-defense, see Comment, § 4.23c, Manslaughter — Voluntary: Suggested instruction on imperfect self-defense, *supra.*

Homicide committed in valid self-defense is either justifiable or excusable. If a feloniously assaulted person, being without fault himself, necessarily kills his assailant to save himself from death or a serious bodily harm, there is justifiable self-defense. *Whitehead v. State,* 9 Md. App. 7, 262 A.2d 316 (1970). Excusable self-defense occurs when a person becomes engaged in a sudden affray or combat and in the course of the affray or combat necessarily, or under reasonably apparent necessity, kills his adversary to save himself from death or great bodily harm after retreating as far as he can with safety. *Whitehead v. State, supra.*

The burden of proof has been substantially modified by *Mullaney v. Wilbur,* 421 U.S. 684, 95 S. Ct. 1881, 44 L. Ed. 2d 508 (1975), and *Evans v. State,* 28 Md. App. 640, 349 A.2d 300 (1975), *aff'd,* 278 Md. 197, 362 A.2d 629 (1976). A jury issue of self-defense may be generated by either the defendant's or State's evidence. Once generated, the burden is on the State to prove beyond a reasonable doubt that the defendant did not act in justifiable self-defense. *Finnegan v. State,* 33 Md. App. 251, 364 A.2d 124, *cert. denied,* 279 Md. 682 (1976), *cert. denied,* 433 U.S. 912 (1977); *Jacobs v. State,* 32 Md. App. 509, 363 A.2d 257 (1976).

The Court of Appeals in *State v. Evans,* 278 Md. 197, 362 A.2d 629 (1976) stated that the burden of producing "some evidence" on the issue of self-defense so as to give rise to a jury issue may be properly placed on a defendant. Once the issue is raised, however, the State carries the ultimate burden of persuasion and must prove every element of the offense beyond a reasonable doubt. *Id.* at 207, 362 A.2d at 635. See also *Tichnell v. State,* 287 Md. 695, 415 A.2d 830 (1980); Appendix V, The Impact of *Evans v. State:* Burdens of Proof, Presumptions and Inferences, *infra.*

Force may not be used to vindicate an act, only to repel one. Thus, where defendant claimed that she killed the victim after he raped her, she was not entitled to a jury instruction on self-defense as there could be no self-defense after the rape. *Souffie v. State,* 50 Md. App. 547, 439 A.2d 1127 (1982).

When an illegal arrest is warrantless, the individual may resist with reasonable force. *Rodgers v. State,* 32 Md. App. 90, 359 A.2d 122 (1976), *aff'd,* 280 Md. 406, 373 A.2d 944 (1977). For further discussion, see Comment, § 4.80, Resisting arrest, *supra.*

§ 5.12. Self-defense — Amount of force permissible.

(a) Nondeadly force

A person may use nondeadly force against another person if he honestly and reasonably believes the other person is immediately about to inflict unlawful bodily harm upon him. The amount of force used to defend against an assailant may not, however, be unreasonable or excessive: that is, a person is not justified in using any greater force than he had reasonable grounds to believe, and actually did believe, was necessary under the circumstances. In determining whether the defendant was justified in using force and whether the amount of force used was reasonable, you should consider all of the facts and circumstances in evidence.

[In determining whether the defendant used excessive force in defending himself, you may consider all the circumstances under which he acted. The claim of self-defense is not necessarily defeated if greater force than would have seemed necessary to a calm mind was used by the defendant in the heat of passion resulting from an assault upon him. A belief which may be unreasonable to a calm mind may be actually and reasonably held under the circumstances as they appeared to the defendant at the time of the incident.]

(b) Deadly force

If the defendant was justified in using force in self-defense, he would not be entitled to use any greater force than he had reasonable grounds to believe, and actually did believe, to be necessary under the circumstances to save his life or avert serious bodily harm.

You must determine whether the defendant was justified in the amount of force used. The amount of force a person may use to defend against an assailant may not be unreasonable or excessive; that is, a person is not justified in using any greater force than he had reasonable grounds to believe, and actually did believe, was necessary under the circumstances. Deadly force means force which is intended to cause, or is likely to cause, death or great bodily harm.

Deadly force is unreasonable if nondeadly force is obviously sufficient to avert the threatened harm.

If the defendant actually believed and had reasonable grounds to believe that he was in imminent danger of death or serious bodily harm and that deadly force was necessary to repel such danger, then he had the right to use deadly force to defend himself.

[In determining whether the defendant used excessive force in defending himself, you may consider all the circumstances under which he acted. The claim of self-defense is not necessarily defeated if greater force than would have seemed necessary to a calm mind was used by the defendant in the heat of passion resulting from an assault upon him. A belief which may be unreasonable to a calm mind may be actually and reasonably held under the circumstances as they appeared to the defendant at the time of the incident.]

COMMENT

This instruction is to be read in conjunction with § 5.11, Self-defense — General considerations and burden of proof, *supra,* and other self-defense instructions. See also Comment, § 4.23c, Manslaughter — Voluntary: Suggested instruction on imperfect self-defense, *supra.*

The force used to repel the harm must not be unreasonable or excessive; the force can be no greater than the exigency demanded. *Tichnell v. State,* 287 Md. 695, 415 A.2d 830 (1980); *Brown v. State,* 4 Md. App. 261, 268, 242 A.2d 570, 574 (1968); *Tipton v. State,* 1 Md. App. 556, 232 A.2d 289 (1967). See also *Ware v. State,* 3 Md. App. 62, 65, 237 A.2d 526, 528 (1968). In other words, the amount of force must "reasonably relate to the threatened harm which he seeks to avoid." *Shuck v. State,* 29 Md. App. 33, 38, 349 A.2d 378, 381 (1975). It is for the trier of fact to determine whether the accused was justified in meeting force with force. *Brown v. State,* 6 Md. App. 631, 252 A.2d 887 (1969); *Gray v. State,* 4 Md. App. 175, 241 A.2d 909 (1968).

The law of self-defense and defense of others (see Instruction, § 5.04, *supra*) makes a distinction between "deadly" force — that which is intended or likely to cause death or great bodily harm — and "nondeadly" force — that which is neither intended nor likely to do so — just as there is a distinction between force which is reasonable and force which is unreasonable.

> Deadly force and reasonable force are neither mutually exclusive nor collectively exhaustive. Deadly force is unreasonable if nondeadly force is obviously sufficient to avert the threatened harm, but may be entirely reasonable under other circumstances. And even nondeadly force is unreasonable if it is obviously and substantially in excess of what is needed for the particular defense.

R. Perkins, *Criminal Law* 993 (2d ed. 1969). See also *Thomas v. State,* 9 Md. App. 94, 262 A.2d 797 (1970); *Cummings v. State,* 7 Md. App. 687, 256 A.2d 894 (1969).

Thus, where the force is deadly and the trier of fact finds that nondeadly force would have been sufficient to avert the threatened harm, the force used by the defendant is unreasonable and the homicide is not excusable. *Thomas v. State, supra* at 99, 262 A.2d at 800. See *Shuck v. State, supra.*

One may use nondeadly force if he reasonably believes another is about to inflict unlawful bodily harm. If, however, one believes that his attacker is about to inflict death or serious bodily injury and deadly force is necessary to prevent it, deadly force may be used. *Shuck v. State, supra. See also Guerriero v. State,* 213 Md. 545, 132 A.2d 466 (1957); *Perry v. State,* 234 Md. 48, 197 A.2d 833 (1964); *Jones v. State,* 13 Md. App. 677, 284 A.2d 635 (1971).

The killing of a human being in necessary self-defense is justifiable homicide. *Nixon v. State,* 204 Md. 475, 105 A.2d 243 (1954). The provocation must be great and the violence extreme to justify the use of a deadly weapon, and the character and extent of the assault are important considerations in determining whether the use of a deadly weapon was justified in repelling the attack. *Nixon v. State, supra.* Although a person may defend himself by taking the life of the aggressor, he cannot use more force than was necessary. *Tipton v. State, supra; Guerriero v. State, supra.*

When dealing with deadly force, the defendant must have reasonable grounds to believe, and must in fact believe himself to be in apparent, imminent or immediate danger of death or serious bodily harm from his assailant or potential assailant. This belief must be the same as the belief of a reasonably prudent person acting in similar circumstances. The defendant's need to resort to self-defense should be judged by the facts as they appeared to him, whatever they truly were. See, e.g., *Winner v. State,* 144 Md. 682, 125 A. 397 (1924), *Jones v. State, supra;* Instruction, § 5.14, Self-defense — Where appearances are false, *infra.*

§ 5.13. Self-defense — Where defendant is alleged aggressor.

(a) Where there is conflicting evidence as to who is the aggressor

There has been testimony both that the __________ *(insert victim's name)* was the aggressor and that __________ *(insert defendant's name)* was the aggressor. You must first determine from the evidence who, in fact, was the aggressor. By "aggressor," I mean the person who initiated the conflict and attack.

[You are instructed that mere words by the [defendant] [victim] without more do not make one the aggressor or initiator of the attack.]

If you find that __________ *(insert victim's name)* was the initial aggressor, then the defendant has the right of self-defense which must be exercised according to the law of self-defense as I have instructed you.

[If you find that the defendant initiated the conflict and attacked __________ *(insert victim's name)* using (or threatening the use of) deadly force, the defendant cannot rely upon the right of self-defense to justify his use of force. It is a general principle of law that where a person attacks another in a manner calculated to kill or to do serious bodily harm, the person has forfeited his privilege of self-defense.]

(b) Where defendant is aggressor using nondeadly force, victim counterattacks with deadly force, and defendant subsequently uses deadly force to defend

If you find that the defendant was the aggressor, that is, he initiated the conflict and attacked __________ *(insert name of victim)* using *nondeadly* force, and __________ *(insert name of victim)* counterattacked using *deadly* force, then the defendant becomes the defender and, under certain circumstances, may be excused on the ground of self-defense. "Deadly force" means force which is calculated to cause serious bodily harm or death. "Nondeadly force" means force which is *not* calculated to cause serious bodily harm or death.

Before a defendant who is an initial aggressor using nondeadly force can be excused on the grounds of self-defense, the defendant has a duty to retreat to avoid the danger if he can do so consistent with his safety. If there is no safe place available, the defendant is entitled to use whatever force is reasonably necessary to repel the counterattack in order to save himself from imminent danger of serious bodily harm or death.

(c) Where defendant is aggressor using deadly force, defendant totally withdraws, and victim counterattacks using deadly force (suggested instruction)

If you find that the defendant was the aggressor, that is, he initiated the conflict and attacked the other party using (or threatening the use of) deadly force (force which is calculated to cause serious bodily harm or death), I instructed you that the defendant forfeits his privilege of self-defense. There is, however, one exception to this rule. A total "withdrawal" will restore this privilege of self-defense. This means that the defendant must bring his attack to an end. The defendant must withdraw from the conflict in good faith and communicate this withdrawal by words or actions. If a person is unable to get entirely away from the other, he must in some manner convey to the other person the information that the fight is over. The withdrawal must be communicated to the original victim such that further fear of danger would not be reasonable. If the circumstances do not permit the defendant to do so, this is his own misfortune for bringing such a predicament upon himself.

If you find that the defendant did withdraw from the conflict, and he is thereafter pursued, he is justified in using deadly force to save himself from imminent danger of death or serious bodily harm.

COMMENT

This instruction should be given in conjunction with Instructions: § 5.11, Self-defense — General considerations and burden of proof, *supra;* § 5.12, Self-defense — Amount of force permissible, *supra;* and §§ 5.14 to 5.17, *infra,* as applicable. See also Comment, § 4.23(c), Manslaughter — Voluntary: Suggested instruction on imperfect self-defense, *supra.*

It is for the trier of fact to determine who was the aggressor, the defendant or the victim, where the evidence conflicts. *Gainer v. State,* 40 Md. App. 382, 381 A.2d 856 (1978), *cert. denied,* 284 Md. 743 (1978). For a discussion of methods of proving who was the aggressor, see Comment, § 5.16, Prior acts, reputation (or opinion) and threats of the deceased, *infra.*

If the defendant was the aggressor and used or threatened deadly force, the general principle is that a murderous assailant forfeits the right of self-defense. In *Cunningham v. State,* 58 Md. App. 249, 473 A.2d 40, *cert. denied,* 300 Md. 316 (1984), the defendant, resentful of having his Moped taken earlier in the day by the ultimate victim, armed himself and went looking for the victim. As he approached the victim, the defendant drew the gun, and the victim, who was leaning on the Moped, "put his hands in his pants." From this the defendant concluded that the victim "was grabbing for something" and consequently shot him. The Court held that an aggressor (threatening deadly force), faced even with the reasonable belief in the necessity to kill, cannot have the defense of self-defense because that requires both freedom from fault in bringing on the difficulty with the adversary, and the entertainment of beliefs which are reasonable both (a) that his adversary will, unless forcibly prevented, immediately inflict a fatal or serious injury; and, (b) that he must use deadly force to prevent the infliction of such an injury.

On the other hand, if the defendant was the aggressor using nondeadly force and the victim counterattacks and escalates the encounter by using deadly force, the defendant has a right of self-defense but must first attempt to retreat if a safe retreat is available. Part (b) of this instruction reflects this situation and is patterned after *Tipton v. State,* 1 Md. App. 556, 232 A.2d 289 (1967). In *Tipton,* the Court stated:

> [W]e think reason and logic would support the proposition that where one attacks another in a manner not calculated to kill or to do serious bodily harm, and the defender counterattacks, using excessive and unreasonable force in a manner reasonably calculated to cause death or great bodily harm, then the original attacker becomes the defender. If the original assailant is unable to retreat to a place of safety or there is no place of safety available, then he may use whatever force is necessary to repel the counterattack of the original defender.

Id. at 562, 232 A.2d at 292.

The Court, in *Dawson v. State,* 40 Md. App. 640, 395 A.2d 160 (1978), stressed that when the defendant initiates the combat using nondeadly force, the defendant has a duty to retreat as far as he can with safety before repelling with deadly force. See also *Thomas v. State,* 9 Md. App. 94, 262 A.2d 797 (1970); and *Whitehead v. State,* 9 Md. App. 7, 262 A.2d 316 (1970). See Instruction, § 5.15, Duty to retreat before using deadly force and exception for "castle doctrine," *infra.*

A question not addressed by the Maryland courts is whether a defendant who is an aggressor using or threatening deadly force can regain the right of self-defense if he brings his attack to an end by totally withdrawing from the encounter. Part (c) of this instruction addresses this situation and is designated as "suggested" because of the absence of Maryland case law. In discussing self-defense, Perkins and Boyce state that not even "retreat to the wall" is available to one who starts, or willingly engages in an encounter with malice aforethought. Although he retreats as far as he can and then kills the other as the only possible means of saving his own life, he is guilty of murder. However:

> [E]ven the murderous assailant has not forfeited his privilege of self-defense forever. He has forfeited it for the moment. He cannot reacquire it by "retreat to the wall." Nothing short of "withdrawal" will restore this privilege .... This means he must bring his attack to an end ... (I)f he is unable to get entirely away from the other, he must in some manner convey to him the information that the fight is over. If the circumstances do not permit him to do so, this is his own misfortune for bringing such a predicament upon himself .... Unless withdrawal has been manifested and communicated to the original victim such that apprehension of further danger would not be reasonable, a claim of self-defense is not valid.

R. Perkins & R. Boyce, *Criminal Law* 1130 (3d ed. 1982).

Perkins and Boyce add that someone holding a deadly weapon in his hand, available for instant use, may frequently find it impossible to convey this information to an adversary. "Even a plain statement in words may reasonably be interpreted by the other to be merely a ruse, intended for no purpose other than to gain an advantage in the fight." *Id.* See also W. LaFave & A. Scott, *Criminal Law* 395 (1972).

The Courts have recognized that a person not seeking to fight may arm himself in anticipation of an assault. See *Bruce v. State,* 218 Md. 87, 145 A.2d 428 (1958); *Gainer v. State, supra; Law v. State,* 21 Md. App. 13, 318 A.2d 859 (1974); and, *Crawford v. State,* 231 Md. 354, 190 A.2d 538 (1963). In *Gunther v. State,* 228 Md. 404, 179 A.2d 880 (1962), the Court noted that a person may not carry a weapon in contravention of a statutory provision but that a person does not necessarily forfeit his privilege of self-defense because he has previously armed himself in anticipation of an attack. In *Crawford v. State,* 61 Md. App. 620, 487 A.2d

1214 (1985), *aff'd,* 308 Md. 683, 521 A.2d 1193 (1987), the Court distinguished between arming oneself in anticipation of an attack and defending oneself from an actual, ongoing attack. In the latter situation, a defense of duress or necessity may be available to a statutory charge of unlawfully carrying a handgun. *Cf. Medley v. State,* 52 Md. App. 225, 448 A.2d 363, *cert. denied,* 294 Md. 544 (1982).

§ 5.14. Self-defense — Where appearances are false.

The right of self-defense is based on whether the facts, as they appeared to the defendant, reasonably justified the use of force.

The defendant would be justified in using force in self-defense, even though it may afterwards have turned out that the appearances were false, if he had reasonable grounds to believe, and in fact believed himself in apparent, imminent or immediate danger of [bodily harm] [serious bodily harm or death].

[If the defendant actually believed and had reasonable grounds to believe that he was in imminent danger of death or serious bodily harm and that deadly force was necessary to repel such danger, he had the right to use deadly force to defend himself even if afterwards the facts turned out to be that there was neither the purpose on the part of the other person to kill him or do him serious bodily harm, nor imminent danger that it would be done, nor actual necessity that deadly force be used in self-defense.]

In evaluating all of the facts and circumstances in evidence, you must consider the circumstances as they appeared to the defendant at the time of the incident.

COMMENT

This instruction should be given in conjunction with § 5.11, Self-defense — General considerations and burden of proof, *supra,* and other self-defense instructions, as applicable. See also Instruction, § 5.04, Defense of others, *supra.*

The right to defend one's self when appearances are false seems to be well established in Maryland.

The defendant must have had reasonable grounds to believe, and in fact have believed, that he was about to be assaulted. *Tichnell v. State,* 287 Md. 695, 415 A.2d 830 (1980); *Finnegan v. State,* 33 Md. App. 251, 255, 364 A.2d 124, 128, *cert. denied,* 279 Md. 682 (1976), *cert. denied,* 433 U.S. 912 (1977); *Morris v. State,* 4 Md. App. 328, 242 A.2d 582 (1968); *Brown v. State,* 4 Md. App. 261, 242 A.2d 570 (1968). The defendant's necessity for resorting to self-defense should be judged by the facts as they appeared to him. *Winner v. State,* 144 Md. 682, 125 A. 397 (1924).

In *Bennett v. State,* 230 Md. 562, 567, 188 A.2d 142, 144 (1963), the defendant had asked the trial court to instruct the jury that "it is not necessary that the danger be actual or real or about to transpire but that one may act in self-defense on appearance alone." The appellate court stated that the trial court had given the "substance" of the requested instruction.

The Court has discussed the admissibility of evidence relating to character of the victim or deceased. In *Jones v. State,* 13 Md. App. 677, 684-685, 284 A.2d 635, 639 (1971), the Court stated:

> Where the defendant claims that he acted in self-defense, and there is some testimony of an overt act on the part of the deceased and some testimony tending to support the theory of self-defense, *where the necessity for the defendant's resorting to it should be judged by the facts as they appeared to him, whatever they truly were,* he may give in evidence whatever he knew of the character, prior conduct, threats or other utterances of the person with whom he was contending, which is admitted in evidence, not to show that the deceased was bad, but in this special instance was dangerous. (Emphasis added.)

In both *Armstrong v. State,* 51 Md. App. 508, 511, 444 A.2d 1049, 1050 (1982) and *Williamson v. State,* 25 Md. App. 338, 333 A.2d 653 (1975), the Court reiterated this rule. It stated that the defendant may offer evidence of specific acts which he is aware of at the time of the incident since this evidence bears upon the reasonableness of the defendant's actions. See Instruction, § 5.16, Prior acts, reputation (or opinion) and threats of the deceased, *infra.*

§ 5.15. Self-defense — Duty to retreat before using deadly force and exception for "castle doctrine."

(a) Duty to retreat before using deadly force

Before a defendant can be excused for the use of deadly force on the grounds of self-defense, the defendant has a duty to retreat or to avoid the danger if such means were within his power and consistent with his safety. If there is no safe place available, the defendant is not required to retreat before resorting to the use of deadly force. You should consider all of the facts and circumstances in evidence in determining whether the defendant did retreat or attempted to retreat as far as he could with safety and, if not, whether under the circumstances the defendant could have safely retreated before resorting to the use of deadly force.

(b) No duty to retreat — "Castle doctrine" exception

[There is an exception to the general rule that a person has a duty to retreat before using deadly force.] A person who is attacked in his own home has no duty to retreat before resorting to deadly force. If the defendant was an occupant of the dwelling in which he was attacked, and he is without fault, he is entitled to stand his ground and repel an attack in his own dwelling [or its immediate surrounding area], even if he could have retreated with safety. However, the occupant still must abide by the other requirements of the law of self-defense, as I have instructed you.

[To be an occupant of a dwelling, the person need not be the head of the household nor have an ownership or leasehold interest. This right extends to all members of the household, whether the person is residing there temporarily or permanently. [An occupant of the dwelling need not retreat even if attacked by another occupant.]]

COMMENT

A controversy exists among the states as to whether an innocent person — that is, a person who was not the initial aggressor — has a general duty to retreat, if a safe place is available, before resorting to deadly force. How this question has been resolved has depended upon the balancing of two competing principles: the unnecessary taking of human life and a person's liberty interest in remaining where he has a right to be.

While it is not absolutely clear that Maryland has resolved this issue, it appears that an innocent person has a general duty to retreat before resorting to deadly force if he can do so with safety and there is a safe place to retreat. See *Barton v. State,* 46 Md. App. 616, 420 A.2d 1009 (1980); *Jackson v. State,* 31 Md. App. 518, 357 A.2d 845 (1976); *Law v. State,* 21 Md. App. 13, 318 A.2d 859 (1974); *Tipton v. State,* 1 Md. App. 556, 232 A.2d 289 (1967). See also *Bruce v. State,* 218 Md. 87, 145 A.2d 428 (1958); *DeVaughn v. State,* 232 Md. 447, 194 A.2d 109 (1963), *cert. denied,* 376 U.S. 927 (1963).

The Court in *Barton v. State, supra,* citing *Bruce v. State, supra,* and *DeVaughn v. State, supra,* stated that there is a duty "to retreat or avoid danger if such means are within [a person's] power and consistent with his safety." The Court added in dicta that "ordinarily, to invoke the defense successfully, the defendant must show that it was not possible to retreat safely, either at all or any farther than he had." *Id.* at 618, 420 A.2d at 1010. The Court, in *Law v. State, supra,* specifically stated that "[t]he distinction between the defense of home [discussed *infra* this Comment] and the defense of person is primarily that in the former there is no duty to retreat." *Id.* at 26, 318 A.2d at 867.

The Courts seem to make a troubling distinction between those cases in which the peril is imminent and those in which it is not. If the peril is not imminent, the person attacked must retreat if he can do so with safety and there is a safe place to retreat. If the peril is imminent, the person attacked need not retreat, but may stand his ground and defend himself. *Barton v.*

State, supra; Gainer v. State, 40 Md. App. 382, 391 A.2d 856, *cert. denied,* 284 Md. 743 (1978); *DeVaughn v. State, supra; Bruce v. State, supra.* In *DeVaughn,* the Court stated:

> The law on the subject of self-defense was fully set forth by this Court in the comparatively recent case of *Bruce v. State,* 218 Md. 87, 96-97, 145 A.2d 428, 433 (1958), where we said in approving the trial court's instructions to the jury: ... [I]n order to justify or excuse the killing of another on the ground of self-defense, it was necessary to establish that the defendant was not the aggressor and did not provoke the conflict; that the defendant believed at the time he was in such immediate danger of losing his own life or suffering serious bodily harm as made it necessary to take the life of the deceased to save himself; that the circumstances were such as to warrant reasonable grounds for such belief in the mind of a man of ordinary reason; that, if the peril of the defendant was imminent, *he did not have to retreat but had a right to stand his ground and to defend and protect himself;* that an attempted battery may be met by resisting force with force provided no unnecessary violence was used and proper measures were taken to avoid the conflict and escape from shedding blood; and that *it was the duty of the defendant to retreat or avoid danger if such means were within his power and consistent with his safety.*

Id. at 112 (emphasis added).

The above language in *DeVaughn v. State, supra,* quoting *Bruce v. State, supra,* is disturbingly ambiguous. There is no duty to retreat when the peril is imminent and in the same paragraph a duty to retreat whenever possible. The ambiguity can be resolved by interpreting the statement that there is no duty to retreat when the peril is imminent as merely a tautology, describing situations where it is impossible to find a safe retreat due to imminent harm. If so, these cases can be read to support the proposition that there is a general duty to retreat before resorting to deadly force whenever the defendant is able to retreat in safety. Otherwise, if the peril is really *not* imminent, the question may be raised as to whether there is a right in any circumstances to resort to deadly force in self-defense, including the circumstance when one first attempts retreat. Unfortunately, no elaboration is provided of what is an "imminent" as contrasted with a "less than imminent" peril.

Whether the peril is imminent is judged by the defendant's reasonable belief. *Tichnell v. State,* 287 Md. 695, 415 A.2d 830 (1980); *Finnegan v. State,* 33 Md. App. 251, 364 A.2d 124, *cert. denied,* 279 Md. 682 (1976), *cert. denied,* 433 U.S. 912 (1977); *Brown v. State,* 4 Md. App. 261, 242 A.2d 570 (1968).

Moreover, there is case law which adds further uncertainty to this rule by distinguishing between those cases in which one is assaulted through no fault of his own and those in which the defendant and the victim are engaged in mutual combat. *Whitehead v. State,* 9 Md. App. 7, 262 A.2d 316 (1970). See also *Bruce v. State, supra,* and *Thomas v. State,* 9 Md. App. 94, 262 A.2d 797 (1970). In *Whitehead,* the Court stated:

> Justifiable self-defense is where a person is feloniously assaulted, being without fault himself, and necessarily kills his assailant to save himself from death or great bodily harm .... Excusable self-defense is where a person becomes engaged in a sudden affray or combat, and in the course of the affray or combat, necessarily, or under reasonably apparent necessity, kills his adversary to save himself from death or great bodily harm *after retreating as far as he can with safety.* The force used must not be unreasonable or excessive.

Id. at 10, 262 A.2d 319 (emphasis added). The Court stated that "the combat is mutual if the intent to fight is mutual." *Id.* at 11, 262 A.2d at 319. It further stated that in combats that are mutual, it does not matter who strikes the first blow. *Id.* (Note that the Court, in *Law v. State, supra,* n.3, provides other definitions for justified and excusable homicide.) These cases imply that one must retreat if engaged in mutual combat, but that in justifiable self-defense there is no duty to retreat. See *Thomas v. State, supra.* See also *Dawson v. State,* 40 Md. App. 640, 395 A.2d 160 (1978).

The strongest recognition in Maryland of a general duty to retreat before resorting to deadly force, if one can do so in safety, is implicitly found in cases which discuss an "exception" to this rule termed the "castle doctrine." *Barton v. State, supra* at 618, 420 A.2d at 1010; *Law v. State, supra; DeVaughn v. State, supra.* See also *Bruce v. State, supra.* The rule is that an occupant of a dwelling does not have to retreat when he is attacked within his dwelling, or its curtilage, if he is without fault, even if he could have retreated with safety. *Barton v. State, supra; Gainer v. State, supra; Jackson v. State, supra; Law v. State, supra.* The Court of Appeals has recognized that "a man faced with the danger of an attack upon his dwelling need not retreat from his home to escape the danger, but instead may stand his ground and, if necessary to repel the attack, may kill the attacker." *Crawford v. State,* 231 Md. 354, 361, 190 A.2d 538, 541 (1963). In *Jackson v. State, supra* at 522-23, 357 A.2d 845, the Court, citing *Crawford v. State, supra,* held: "a man assaulted in his dwelling 'may use such means as are absolutely necessary to repel the assailant from his house, or *to prevent his forcible entry,* even to the taking of life'."

Further, the Court in *Barton v. State, supra* at 46 Md. App. at 617, 420 A.2d at 1010, stated: "[one] is not bound to flee and become a fugitive from his home, for if that were required, there would, theoretically, be no refuge for him anywhere in the world."

This exception applies to members of the household as well as to the head of the household. *Gainer v. State, supra* at 388, 391 A.2d at 861; *Jackson v. State, supra.* In other words, one does not need a proprietary or leasehold interest in the property. *Barton v. State, supra* at 619, 420 A.2d at 1009. See *Crawford v. State, supra* at 361, 190 A.2d at 542, in which the Court of Appeals notes, in dicta, that his right extends to a lodger in the home.

In *Barton v. State, supra,* The Court held that it was error not to give the "castle" doctrine instruction in the case where defendant had recently moved into his girlfriend's apartment and the victim was a stranger. The Court held any member of the household who is temporarily or permanently residing there, whether or not he has a proprietary or leasehold interest in the property, may be considered to be in his own dwelling place.

In *DeVaughn v. State, supra,* however, the defendant was living in the residence where the incident occurred. The Court found that this residence was not the defendant's "castle" since he admitted to having another home.

In *Jackson v. State, supra* at 524, 357 A.2d at 848, the Court held that the trial court had acted erroneously in instructing the jury that the defendant had a duty to flee her residence in the face of an assault by an intruder. In addition, it held that the lower court acted erroneously in refusing to comply with the defense counsel's request that the jury be affirmatively instructed that one attacked in his own home has no duty to retreat. Though the alleged assailant had been residing at the home of the appellant during the time in question, the Court found that he occupied the status of intruder since he had previously been requested to leave the dwelling. For this reason, the Court found it unnecessary to determine whether Maryland should follow the rule that "joint occupancy of a dwelling activates the rule of retreat or escape ...."

The Court in *Gainer v. State, supra* at 390, 391 A.2d at 861, did address the question of joint occupancy and held that "when an attack occurs in one's home by an assailant who is not an intruder but who has a right to be on the premises, an assailed person who is without fault, need not 'retreat to the wall' before defending himself."

Despite this exception to the general retreat rule, a person attacked in his home is not given a license to kill anyone who unlawfully enters; the occupant is still subject to the prerequisites of self-defense such as the apprehension of harm must be reasonable and the use of force must not be more than is necessary. *Gainer v. State, supra* at 392, 391 A.2d at 862. See also *DeVaughn v. State, supra; Bruce v. State, supra; Law v. State, supra; Crawford v. State, supra.* In *DeVaughn,* the Court held that one may not use excessive force, even in his own home. In *Law v. State, supra* at 27, 318 A.2d at 867, the Court held that an occupant may take an intruder's life only if he is assaulted in his dwelling and he had a reasonable apprehension that the intruder was going to commit a felony or inflict injury.

The Court of Special Appeals, in *Dawson v. State, supra,* has settled any confusion regarding the duty to retreat when one is the initial aggressor using *nondeadly* force. The Court held that if the defendant was the original aggressor, using nondeadly force, and the victim responded with deadly force, the defendant may use deadly force in self-defense if there is no available opportunity to retreat. *Dawson v. State, supra,* quoting R. Perkins, *Criminal Law* § 4 at 1005-06 (2d ed. 1969); *Tipton v. State, supra.* See Instruction, § 5.13(b) — Where defendant is aggressor using nondeadly force, victim counterattacks with deadly force, and defendant subsequently uses deadly force to defend, *supra*.

The issue of whether an *innocent* person has a duty to retreat before resorting to nondeadly force, if he can do so consistent with his safety, does not seem to have been addressed in Maryland. The text writers, however, seem to be in agreement that there is no duty to retreat if an innocent person is attacked in a place where he has the right to be. R. Perkins & R. Boyce, *Criminal Law* § 1116 (3d ed. 1982), and W. LaFave & A. Scott, *Criminal Law* § 53 at 395 (1972). Perkins and Boyce state:

> One who is himself free from fault is privileged to use nondeadly force in self-defense ... [if he] reasonably believes the other intends to commit a battery upon him ... the defensive force is not unreasonable ... and ... the defender reasonably believes he cannot avoid the threatened harm without either using force or giving up some right or privilege.

Id. at 1116. LaFave and Scott state that "[i]t seems everywhere agreed that one who can safely retreat need not do so before using nondeadly force." *Id.* at 395. This view seems logical in light of the policy considerations justifying the use of self-defense: that is, the preservation of life need not be balanced against the liberty interest of the person attacked. On the other hand, it could be argued that a safe retreat should be taken if the use of any force could be avoided. A strong tradition of individualism has supported the view that innocent persons should not be required to run or flee before resorting to reasonable nondeadly force if they are at a place where they have a right to be.

§ 5.16. Self-defense — Prior acts, reputation (or opinion) and threats of the deceased.

(a) Prior acts of violence by the deceased known by the defendant

Evidence has been presented of alleged past acts of violence by ____________ *(insert name of deceased)* which were known by the defendant.

When a defendant is charged with homicide, and asserts that he killed in self-defense, an important factor in determining his justification is his belief in an impending attack by the deceased. Where there is evidence of past acts of violence by the deceased that were *known* by the defendant, you may consider such evidence in determining who was the aggressor, that is, on the likelihood that __________ *(insert name of deceased)* threatened the defendant with imminent bodily harm. You may also consider such evidence in determining the reasonableness of the defendant's fear of danger to his safety.

(b) Reputation (or opinion) of the deceased's violent and dangerous character known by the defendant

Evidence has been presented of the alleged violent and dangerous character of __________ *(insert name of deceased)* which was known by the defendant.

When a defendant is charged with homicide, and asserts that he killed in self-defense, an important factor in determining his justification is his belief in an impending attack by the deceased. Where there is reputation [opinion] evidence of the violent and dangerous character of deceased that was *known* by the defendant, you may consider such evidence in determining who was the aggressor, that is, on the likelihood that __________ *(insert name of deceased)* threatened the defendant with imminent bodily harm. You may also consider such evidence in determining the reasonableness of the defendant's fear of danger to his safety.

(c) Reputation (or opinion) of the deceased's violent and dangerous character not known by the defendant

Evidence has been presented of the alleged violent and dangerous character of __________ (*insert name of deceased*) which was *not* known by the defendant.

When a defendant is charged with homicide, and asserts that he killed in self-defense, it is important to determine who was the aggressor, that is, the likelihood that __________ (*insert name of deceased*) threatened the defendant with imminent bodily harm. Where there is reputation [opinion] evidence of the violent and dangerous character of the deceased that was *not known* by the defendant at the time of the alleged crime, you may consider whether such evidence of the deceased's violent and dangerous character corroborates or strengthens the defendant's account of who was the aggressor.

(d) Prior threats by the deceased against the defendant known by the defendant

Evidence has been presented of alleged past threats against the defendant by __________ (*insert name of deceased*).

When a defendant is charged with homicide, and asserts that he killed in self-defense, an important factor in determining his justification is her belief in an impending attack by the deceased. When evidence of past threats are *known* by the defendant at the time of the alleged crime, you may consider such evidence in determining who was the aggressor, that is, on the likelihood that __________ *(insert name of deceased)* threatened the defendant with imminent bodily harm. You may also consider such evidence in determining the reasonableness of the defendant's fear of danger to his safety.

(e) Prior threats by the deceased against the defendant not known by the defendant

Evidence has been presented of alleged past threats against the defendant by __________ (*insert name of deceased*).

When a defendant is charged with homicide, and asserts that he killed in self-defense, it is important to determine who was the aggressor, that is, the likelihood that __________ *insert name of deceased)* threatened the defendant with imminent bodily harm. Where there is evidence of past threats against the defendant by the deceased that were *not known* by the defendant at the time of the alleged crime, you may consider such evidence in determining who was the aggressor.

COMMENT

This instruction may be adapted to self-defense situations other than homicide cases. If the instruction is used for other cases, "victim" should be substituted for "deceased."

There is a general rule that character and reputation of the victim is not in issue. This rule, however, may not be applicable when there is a claim of self-defense. *Nixon v. State,* 204 Md. 475, 105 A.2d 243 (1954).

Evidence of the defendant's knowledge of the deceased's character as a violent and dangerous person is relevant for two reasons: first, the violent and dangerous character of the victim is relevant in determining who was the aggressor. *Gunther v. State,* 228 Md. 404, 179 A.2d 880 (1962); *Thomas v. State,* 301 Md. 294, 483 A.2d 6 (1984). Further, if the evidence is to corroborate testimony of the defendant as to the circumstances of the encounter, the evidence is admissible regardless of whether the accused has prior knowledge of the victim's violent character. *Williamson v. State,* 25 Md. App. 338, 333 A.2d 653 (1975). See Wharton, *Criminal Evidence* § 236 (13th ed. 1972).

Second, "[i]t is competent for [the defendant] to prove his knowledge of facts which would have a reasonable tendency to justify his asserted belief as to the existence of a deadly purpose in the overt acts of the deceased." *Jones v. State,* 182 Md. 653, 659, 35 A.2d 916, 919 (1944). See *Armstrong v. State,* 51 Md. App. 508, 444 A.2d 1049 (1982). The defendant's state of mind is very important since it aids the jury in determining the reasonableness of the defendant's apprehension. *Thomas v. State, su-*

pra; Gunther v. State, supra; Jones v. State, supra; Winner v. State, 144 Md. 682, 125 A. 397 (1924). See also *Richards v. State,* 65 Md. App. 141, 499 A.2d 965 (1985).

In *Jones v. State,* 13 Md. App. 677, 284 A.2d 635 (1971), the Court stated:

> The general rule concerning the admissibility of an accused's testimony as to his prior knowledge of deceased's reputation and prior conduct was stated by the Court of Appeals of Maryland in *Jones v. State,* 182 Md. 653, 660, 35 A.2d 916, 919 (1944). "Where the defendant claims that he acted in self-defense, and there is some testimony of an overt act on the part of the deceased and some testimony tending to support the theory of self-defense, where the necessity for the defendant's resorting to it should be judged by the facts as they appeared to him, whatever they truly were, he may give in evidence whatever he knew of the character, prior conduct, threats or other utterances of the person with whom he was contending, which is admitted in evidence, not to show that the deceased was bad, but in this special instance was dangerous."

Id. at 684-85, 284 A.2d at 639.

It should be noted that character evidence will only be admitted for the purpose of determining the defendant's state of mind if the defendant knew the victim's reputation. The defendant's conduct could not be influenced by the victim's reputation if the defendant did not know of this reputation. *Williamson v. State, supra; Thomas v. State, supra.* However, evidence of the victim's reputation may be admissible to determine who was the aggressor even if the defendant did not know of the victim's reputation.

There are three methods of proving the character of the deceased: reputation evidence, opinion evidence, and specific acts evidence, that is, evidence of past acts of violence by the deceased. Maryland has enacted the following statute which now allows opinion evidence to be introduced:

> Where character evidence is otherwise relevant to the proceeding, no person offered as a character witness who has an adequate basis for forming an opinion as to another person's character shall hereafter be excluded from giving evidence based on personal opinion to prove character, either in person or by deposition, in any suit, action or proceeding, civil or criminal, in any court or before any judge or jury of the state.

Maryland Ann. Code, Courts and Judicial Proceedings, § 9-115. This statute provides that opinion evidence will be admissible to the same extent as reputation evidence.

Prior to this statute, when the method of proof was reputation and not opinion evidence, the Court of Special Appeals held in *Long v. State,* 7 Md. App. 256, 254 A.2d 707 (1969), that the reputation must be the general reputation of the person, not his reputation in the police department.

The relevance of specific acts of the deceased is also two-fold. First, evidence of specific acts of violence, whether known by the defendant or not, may be considered by the jury in determining who was the aggressor. *Barger v. State,* 2 Md. App. 565, 235 A.2d 751 (1967); *Bowyer v. State,* 2 Md. App. 454, 235 A.2d 317 (1967); *Gunther v. State, supra.*

Second, a defendant asserting a self-defense claim may also offer evidence of specific acts of which he was aware at the time of the killing since this evidence relates to the reasonableness of his actions. *Williamson v. State, supra.* The Court, in *Williamson* (*citing Jones v. State, supra* at 659, 35 A.2d at 919), stated that "previous acts of violence by the deceased, especially if committed recently, known to the defendant, might have an even stronger influence on his mind than would be produced by knowledge of the reputation of the deceased for violence." *Williamson v. State, supra* at 344, 333 A.2d at 656. See also *Armstrong v. State, supra.*

The courts have also addressed the more specific situation of prior threats which is encompassed within the category of evidence of prior specific acts. In *Bowyer v. State, supra,* the Court stated:

> Maryland has permitted threats against the accused, as opposed to threats against others, to be introduced into evidence whether the accused knew of them at the time of the homicide or not, *Turpin v. State,* 55 Md. 462 [(1881)]; *Winner v. State,* [*supra*]. Maryland has also permitted the use of threats against others where the accused was aware of them at the time of the homicide. *Jones v. State,* [*supra*] .... We know of no authority that permits the use of threats against others when such threats are not known to the accused at the time of the affray.

Id. at 459, 235 A.2d at 320.

Thus, threats directed at the defendant, whether he knew of them or not, are admissible, while threats or specific acts of violence directed at others are only admissible if the defendant had knowledge of them. Threats unknown to the defendant are obviously not related to the defendant's state of mind. Yet, threats unknown to, but directed against, the defendant are relevant as tending to show which party was the aggressor. *Barger v. State, supra.* See also *Magness v. State,* 2 Md. App. 320, 234 A.2d 481 (1967) and Wharton, *Criminal Law* § 199 (12th ed. 1932).

A foundation is required before evidence of the character of the deceased will be admitted. If the character evidence is introduced to prove the defendant's state of mind when the victim was killed to show that the defendant had reasonable grounds to believe that he was in danger, the defendant first must prove: (1) his knowledge of the victim's prior acts of violence; and (2) an overt act demonstrating the victim's deadly intent toward the defendant. *Thomas v. State, supra; Gunther v. State, supra.* If the character evidence is used to corroborate evidence that the victim was the initial aggressor, the defendant first must establish an evidentiary foundation tending to support the self-defense claim and testimony of an overt act on the part of the deceased or some question as to who was the aggressor. *Thomas v. State, supra; Williamson v. State, supra; Nixon v. State, supra.*

Knowledge that someone is dangerous does not require one to avoid contact with this person; the right of the defendant to go wherever he legally has a right to go is not abridged by the fact that he might be attacked. *Gunther v. State, supra* at 409, 179 A.2d at 883. See also *Perry v. State,* 234 Md. 48, 197 A.2d 833, 837 (1964), in which the Court stated a man may proceed with his legitimate business despite apprehension, provided he does not in any sense seek an encounter and is not the aggressor.

Moreover, if one is not seeking an encounter but is merely apprehensive that he may be attacked by someone, then he has a right to arm himself in anticipation of the assault without forfeiting his privilege of self-defense. *Gunther v. State, supra* at 408, 179 A.2d at 882. See also *Bruce v. State,* 218 Md. 87, 145 A.2d 428 (1958); *Gainer v. State,* 40 Md. App. 382, 391 A.2d 856, *cert. denied,* 284 Md. 743 (1978); *Law v. State,* 21 Md. App. 13, 318 A.2d 859 (1974); R. Perkins and R. Boyce, *Criminal Law* ch.

10, § 4, p. 1131 (3d ed. 1982); L. Hochheimer, *Crimes and Criminal Procedure,* § 344 (2d ed. 1904). This right, however, has been modified by the enactment of Maryland Ann. Code, Art. 27, §§ 36, 36A, and 36B, proscribing carrying or wearing concealed weapons and related weapons offenses. The Court, in *Medley v. State,* 52 Md. App. 225, 448 A.2d 363 (1982), stated that *Gunther, supra,* can now be read as recognizing "that one does not necessarily forfeit his privilege of self-defense because he has previously armed himself in anticipation of an attack." *Id.* at 234, 448 A.2d at 368. A person may not carry a weapon in contravention of a statutory provision. An exception may be the defense of duress or necessity. In *Crawford v. State,* 61 Md. App. 620, 487 A.2d 1214 (1985), *aff'd,* 308 Md. 683, 521 A.2d 1193 (1987), the Court recognized the applicability of these defenses to a handgun charge under Art. 27, § 36B where the defendant armed himself during the course of a repeated and lengthy ongoing attack from armed intruders. The Court distinguished this situation from the case of a person arming himself in anticipation of an attack.

§ 5.17. Right to use nondeadly force to defend property (suggested instruction).

[You have been instructed that to convict the defendant of battery, the State must prove beyond a reasonable doubt that the bodily contact was without lawful authority.]

A person is justified in using reasonable nondeadly force to protect his property from [trespass] [theft] if he honestly and reasonably believes that his property is in immediate danger of an unlawful [trespass] [taking] and that the use of force is necessary to avoid that danger.

The intentional infliction upon another of a harmful or offensive contact by a means not intended to cause death or serious bodily harm is *privileged* for the purpose of ending another's intrusion upon one's [land] [personal property], if: (1) the alleged intruder had no legal right to intrude; (2) the defendant honestly and reasonably believed that the intrusion could be ended only by immediate bodily contact;

(3) the type of contact the defendant used was reasonable and not excessive; (4) [the defendant first requested the alleged intruder to stop the intrusion and this request was disregarded] [the defendant reasonably believed that a request to stop the intrusion would be useless] [the defendant reasonably believed that it would be dangerous to make a request to stop the intrusion] [the defendant reasonably believed that substantial harm would be done to the [land] [personal property] before a request to stop the intrusion could be made]; (5) and the intrusion was ended in such a manner that there was no danger to innocent people or their property.

[The defendant may be justified in using nondeadly force to remove an alleged intruder even if the alleged intruder reasonably believed he had a right to intrude on the defendant's [land] [personal property].]

Since the burden of proof is on the State, the State must prove beyond a reasonable doubt that the defendant was *not* justified in the use of nondeadly force to defend property. Therefore, if after a full and fair consideration of all the facts and circumstances in evidence, you have a reasonable doubt as to whether the defendant was justified in using such force to defend property, you must find the defendant not guilty of the offense charged. On the other hand, if you find that the State has proved beyond a reasonable doubt that the defendant was *not* justified in using such nondeadly force in the defense of property, then you [should] [must] find that the defense of property does not excuse the defendant of criminal liability.

COMMENT

This suggested jury instruction is based substantially on *Maddran v. Mullendore,* 206 Md. 291, 111 A.2d 608 (1955). The Court held that:

> [T]he intentional infliction upon another of a harmful or offensive contact or other bodily harm by a means not in-

> tended to cause death or serious bodily harm is privileged for the purpose of preventing or terminating another's intrusion upon the actor's possession of land or chattels, if (1) such intrusion is not privileged, and (2) the actor reasonably believes that the intrusion can be prevented or terminated only by the immediate infliction of the bodily harm, and (3) the means he uses are reasonable, and (4) he has first requested the other to desist from the intrusion and the other has disregarded the request, or he reasonably believes that a request will be useless, or it will be dangerous to make a request, or substantial harm will be done to the land or chattel before a request can be made.

Id. at 300, 111 A.2d at 612. See *Vancherie v. Siperly,* 243 Md. 366, 221 A.2d 356 (1966).

The Court in *Maddran* did state, however, that persons may remove the obstruction when it interferes with their rights only as long as they do not disturb the public peace or put innocent persons in peril. See also *Fedder v. Component Structures Corp.,* 23 Md. App. 375, 329 A.2d 56 (1974).

The Court further noted, in *Maddran,* that the privilege exists even if the intruder reasonably, but mistakenly believed he had a right or privilege to intrude, unless the actor intentionally and negligently caused the intruder's mistake.

While this ruling was made in the context of a civil case, the same rule has been applied to the criminal law:

> [O]ne in lawful possession of real or personal property is privileged to use reasonable nondeadly force if this is necessary or is reasonably believed to be necessary to prevent or terminate an unprivileged intrusion upon his right of possession ....
>
> In the case of an ordinary trespasser Hale said the owner "may not beat him, but may gently lay his hands upon him to put him out," but at the present time no force is privileged if a mere request will suffice, and hence even mild force should not be used until a request has first been made and disregarded unless there is reason to believe that a request would be either useless, dangerous or not in time to prevent substantial harm.

R. Perkins, *Criminal Law* ch. 10, § 7 at 1027-28 (2d ed. 1969).

Note that, according to Perkins, the use of force intended or likely to cause death or great bodily injury is never authorized for the defense of property.

This defense would most likely be used for the crime of battery. Since battery is an intentional touching of another *without lawful authority,* this defense would negate an element of the crime of battery. Since the State must prove all of the elements of a crime beyond a reasonable doubt, it would appear that once evidence of this defense is introduced the State would have to disprove it beyond a reasonable doubt. *Mullaney v. Wilbur,* 421 U.S. 684, 95 S. Ct. 1881, 44 L. Ed. 2d 508 (1975); *Evans v. State,* 28 Md. App. 640, 349 A.2d 300 (1975), *aff'd,* 278 Md. 197, 362 A.2d 629 (1976). See Appendix V, The Impact of *Evans v. State:* Burdens of Proof, Presumptions and Inferences, *infra.*

§ 5.18. Necessity (suggested instruction).

The defense of necessity is available when a person is forced to choose between two evils, one of which is committing a crime, and the other is a greater evil or harm, and the defendant acted to avoid the greater harm.

In order for the defense of necessity to excuse criminal conduct, (1) the defendant or another person must be in present and immediate danger of death or serious bodily injury (or threat to life, limb, or health), namely __________ (*insert threat or danger*), or reasonably believed himself or others to be in such danger; (2) the defendant must not have intentionally or recklessly placed himself in a situation in which it was probable that he would be forced to choose the criminal conduct; (3) the defendant must not have had a reasonable, legal alternative to committing the criminal conduct of __________ (*insert alleged crime*); (4) the defendant must have stopped or discontinued doing the criminal conduct as soon as the danger or apparent danger ended; and, (5) the emergency or other dangerous circumstance was not created by the wrongful act of the defendant.

Since the burden of proof is on the State, the State must prove beyond a reasonable doubt that the defendant did not act under necessity. Therefore, if after a full and fair consideration of all the facts and circumstances in evidence, you have a reasonable doubt as to whether the defendant committed the crime charged under necessity as it has been defined, you must find him not guilty. On the other hand, if the State convinces you beyond a reasonable doubt that the defendant did *not* act under necessity, then you [should] [must] conclude that the defense of necessity does not excuse the defendant for committing the crime(s) charged.

COMMENT

This instruction is adapted from *State v. Crawford,* 308 Md. 683, 521 A.2d 1193 (1987). See *Sigma Reproductive Health Center v. State,* 297 Md. 660, 467 A.2d 483 (1983); *Robinson v. State,* 42 Md. App. 617, 402 A.2d 115 (1979); *Wentworth v. State,* 29 Md. App. 110, 349 A.2d 421 (1975); *Frasher v. State,* 8 Md. App. 439, 260 A.2d 656 (1970), *cert. denied sub nom. McLaughlin v. Director, Patuxent Inst.,* 400 U.S. 959, 91 S. Ct. 360, 27 L. Ed. 2d 269 (1970). See also Instruction, § 5.05 — Duress, *supra.*

Necessity is usually distinguished from duress in that the circumstances of compulsion do not arise from force of another person. See *Robinson v. State, supra; Frasher v. State, supra.* Duress arises when a person is coerced by another person, while necessity usually arises when a person is coerced by the existing circumstances. An often cited example of necessity arises when the defendant has committed a traffic violation because of an existing emergency. The justification for the necessity defense is not that a person faced with a choice of two evils lacks the *mens rea* for the crime but that the law promotes the achievement of high values at the expense of lower ones and that sometimes the greater good for society will be accomplished by violating the literal language of the criminal law. *State v. Crawford, supra.*

The necessity defense may be applicable where the compulsion did arise from a situation created by another person. In *State v. Crawford, supra,* the Court held that necessity could be a defense to a charge of illegal possession of a handgun under Maryland Ann. Code, Art. 27, § 36(B)(b). The Court stated:

> The typical duress case, however, has involved a situation in which A has ordered B to engage in certain conduct prohibited by the criminal law or else suffer certain consequences. It might well be argued that when an individual acts to avoid a greater harm from a person who has not given such an order ... the situation ought to be dealt with as a form of necessity rather than duress.

State v. Crawford, supra at 691, 521 A.2d at 1197 n.1, *quoting* W. LaFave & A. Scott, *Criminal Law* § 50 at 381-82 n.2 (1972).

For a discussion of necessity as a defense to the crime of escape, see *United States v. Bailey,* 444 U.S. 394, 100 S. Ct. 624, 62 L. Ed. 2d 575 (1980), *cert. denied,* 459 U.S. 853 (1982); *Craddock v. State,* 47 Md. App. 513, 424 A.2d 168 (1981); *Robinson v. State, supra. See also* Instruction, § 4.65, Escape, *supra.*

The courts have held that duress, coercion or compulsion is ordinarily a valid defense to a charge of a crime if all of the relevant criteria are met. *Wentworth v. State, supra* at 117, 349 A.2d at 426 (1975). According to W. LaFave and A. Scott, *Criminal Law* 374-75 (1972), the justification of the defense of necessity is that a harm of greater magnitude is avoided.

The Court, in *Frasher v. State, supra* (*citing* R. Perkins, *Criminal Law* 847 (1957)), stated: "If a choice exists but only between two evils, one of which is the commission of a wrongful act, and the emergency was not created by the wrongful act of another person, it is spoken of as an act done in the case of necessity." The *Frasher* court went on to explain that:

> [T]his doctrine applies not only to the obvious situation when the act done was necessary, or reasonably seemed to be necessary, to save life, limb, or health, as for example, self-defense, defense of other persons, or defense of habitation, but also where the act done was not of particular gravity and the danger or apparent danger to be avoided was less serious in its nature.

Id. at 448, 260 A.2d at 662.

Stephens, *Digest of the Criminal Law,* Art. 32 states:

> An act which would otherwise be a crime may be excused if the person accused can show it was done only in order to avoid consequences which could not otherwise be avoided, and which if they had followed, would have inflicted upon him, or upon others whom he was bound to protect, inevita-

> ble and irreparable evil; that no more was done than was reasonably necessary for that purpose; and that evil inflicted by it was not disproportionate to the evil avoided.

In *Crawford v. State,* 61 Md. App. 620, 487 A.2d 1214 (1985), *aff'd,* 308 Md. 683, 521 A.2d 1193 (1987), a case arose which the Court termed one of necessity or "duress of the circumstances." The defendant appealed from denial of a requested jury instruction giving his theory of the defense to a charge of unlawfully carrying a handgun. The defendant had testified that he armed himself during the course of a repeated and lengthy ongoing attack from armed intruders. The Court reversed. While the statute provides no such defense, the Court felt, on the facts of this case, that such a defense was valid, based on the primary law of nature of self-defense and common sense. It distinguished between arming oneself in anticipation of an attack and defending oneself from an actual, ongoing attack.

Affirming *Crawford v. State, supra,* the Court in its 1987 holding in *State v. Crawford, supra,* held that five elements must be present for necessity to be a valid defense to the crime of unlawful possession of a handgun: (1) the defendant must be in present, imminent, and impending peril of death or serious bodily injury, or reasonably believe himself or others to be in such danger; (2) the defendant must not have intentionally or recklessly placed himself in a situation in which it was probable that he would be forced to choose the criminal conduct; (3) the defendant must not have any reasonable, legal alternative to possessing the handgun; (4) the handgun must be made available to the defendant without preconceived design; and (5) the defendant must give up possession of the handgun as soon as the necessity or apparent necessity ends. The Court stated that if the threatened harm is property damage or future personal injury, the defense of necessity will not be viable. The gun control legislation passed by the General Assembly in 1972 eliminated any right to carry a handgun in anticipation of future harm. Also, the defense of necessity cannot be asserted if the compulsion to possess the handgun arose directly from the defendant's own misconduct.

In *Frasher v. State, supra,* the Court held that the necessity defense had no application to a defendant charged with control of heroin and possession of narcotic paraphernalia, who was brought into the State with such items by a bail bondsman after the defendant had failed to appear on another matter. It noted that the necessity defense is not available when there is a prosecution for an offense not requiring intent, at least where the defendant could have avoided the emergency by taking advance precautions. *Id.* at 448, 260 A.2d at 662.

Although the burden of proof has not been discussed in cases that involved the necessity defense, there appears to be no reason why the burden of proof relating to the necessity defense is any different than the burden of proof in other defenses. Therefore, once sufficient evidence has been introduced to generate the defense, the State has the burden of proving beyond a reasonable doubt that the defendant was not compelled by necessity to do the criminal act. See *Mullaney v. Wilbur,* 421 U.S. 684, 95 S. Ct. 1881, 44 L. Ed. 2d 508 (1975), and *Evans v. State,* 278 Md. 197, 362 A.2d 629 (1976). See also Appendix V, The Impact of *Evans v. State:* Burdens of Proof, Presumptions and Inferences, *infra.*

The necessity defense is not available when a person takes the life of an innocent person. *Robinson v. State, supra; Frasher v. State, supra* at 447-48, 260 A.2d at 661. See also *Wentworth v. State, supra* at 118, 349 A.2d at 427. The necessity defense applies only where the apparent danger to be avoided is less serious than the defendant's acts. The defense, thus, is not available where the choice is either the defendant's or the victim's life because the defendant may not be allowed to choose between two *innocent* lives. See Comment, § 5.05, Duress, *supra,* which notes that the defense of duress may be used as a defense to all crimes *other* than the taking of life of an innocent person. In contrast, self-defense involves merely a choice between the defendant's life and the assailant's, a *noninnocent,* life. If the defendant's act involved saving two or more innocent lives at the expense of taking another innocent life, a more difficult situation is created. Although such a situation is unlikely to arise, legislative clarification of the defense of necessity may be desirable. *Cf.* the American Law Institute's Model Penal Code § 3.02, Justification Generally: Choice of Evils (1962).

Appendix I
PRELIMINARY INSTRUCTIONS TO THE JURY

Suggested pre-trial introductory instruction

Members of the Jury:

Before we begin the trial, I would like to tell you about what will be happening. I want to describe how the trial will be conducted and explain what we will be doing — you, the lawyers for both sides, and I. At the end of the trial I will give you more detailed guidance on how you are to go about reaching your decision. Now I simply want to explain how the trial will proceed.

This criminal case has been brought by the State. I will sometimes refer to the State as the prosecution. The State is represented at this trial by an Assistant State's Attorney, __________ *(insert attorney's name).* The defendant, __________ *(insert defendant's name),* is represented by his lawyer, __________ *(insert attorney's name).* [*Alternative:* The defendant, __________ *(insert defendant's name),* has decided to represent himself and not use the services of a lawyer. He has a perfect right to do this. His decision has no bearing on whether he is guilty or not guilty, and it should have no effect on your consideration of the case.] [See Instruction, § 1.15, Defendant's representation of self, *supra.*]

The defendant has been charged by the State with violation of a state law. He is charged with __________ *(insert crime(s) charged).* The charge(s) against the defendant (is) (are) contained in the indictment. The indictment is simply the description of the charge made by the State against the defendant; it is not evidence of anything. [See Instruction, § 1.09, Indictment — Not evidence, *supra.*] The defendant pleaded not guilty to the charge. He is presumed innocent and may not be found guilty by you unless all twelve of you unanimously find that the State has proved his guilt beyond a reasonable doubt. [See Instructions, § 1.03, Presumption of innocence, and § 1.04, Reasonable doubt, *supra.*] [*Addition for multi-defendant cases:* The defendants are being tried together because the State has charged that they worked together to commit the crime(s) of __________ *(insert crime(s) charged).* But you will have to give separate consideration to the case against each defendant. Each is entitled to your separate consideration. Do not think of them as a group.]

The first step in the trial will be the opening statement. The prosecution in its opening statement will tell you about the evidence which it intends to put before you, in order to give you an idea of what the prosecution's case will be about.

Just as the indictment is not evidence, neither is the opening statement evidence. Its purpose is only to help you understand what the evidence will be and what the State will try to prove. [See Instruction, § 1.08, Statements of counsel — Not evidence, *supra.*]

[*To be given where the defense does not reserve opening statement:* After the State's opening statement, the defendant's attorney will make an opening statement. At this point in the trial, no evidence has been offered by either side.]

Next, the State will offer evidence that it says will support the charges against the defendant. The State's evidence in this case will consist of the testimony of witnesses as well as documents and exhibits.

After presentation of the State's evidence, the defendant's lawyer may [make an opening statement and] present evidence on the defendant's behalf, but he is not required to do so. I remind you that the defendant is presumed innocent and the State must prove the guilt of the defendant beyond a reasonable doubt. The defendant does not have to prove his innocence.

After you have heard all the evidence on both sides, each side will be given time for their final arguments. I just told you that the opening statements by the lawyers are not evidence. The same applies to the closing arguments. They are not evidence either. In their closing arguments the lawyers for the prosecution and the defendant will summarize their cases to help you understand the evidence that was presented.

The final part of the trial occurs when I instruct you about the rules of law which you are to use in reaching your verdict. After hearing my instructions, you will leave the courtroom together and make your decision. Your deliberations will be secret. You will never have to explain your verdict to anyone.

Now that I have described the trial itself, let me explain the jobs that you and I are going to perform during the trial. My job is to conduct the trial of this case in an orderly, fair, and efficient manner, to rule on questions of law which come up during the trial, and to instruct you on the law which applies to this case. I will make rulings on legal questions in response to questions raised by the attorneys as we go along. I will give you final instructions after the evidence and arguments are completed. It is your duty to accept the law as I state it to you. [See Instruction, § 1.01, Function of court and jury — Binding nature of instructions, *supra.*]

[*Where conflict exists as to the law of the crime:* In this case, there is a limited exception in which you will have a role in resolving the correct interpretation of one aspect of the crime charged. My instructions in this area will be advisory only. I will provide you with detailed instructions at the conclusion of the trial.]

You will decide whether the state has proved, beyond a reasonable doubt, that the defendant has committed the crime(s) of ____________ *(insert crime(s) charged).* You must base that decision only on the evidence in the case and my instructions about the law.

[*Insert discussion of the elements of the offense(s) here if they are to be mentioned in the preliminary instruction:* ____________.]

[*Insert the following considerations for evaluating witnesses' testimony, if desired:* You must consider and weigh all of the evidence in this case, including the testimony of all witnesses who appear before you, and you alone are to decide whether to believe any witnesses, and the extent to which any witness should be believed. It is your job to resolve any conflicts in the evidence which may occur during the trial and to decide where the truth lies.]

[*Insert the following statement that the jury should not consider punishment, if desired:* If you find the defendant guilty, it will then be my job to decide what punishment should be imposed. You should not guess or speculate about the punishment. It should not enter into your consideration or discussion at any time.] [See Instruction, § 1.14, Jury's nonconcern with punishment, *supra.*]

During the course of the trial, you should not talk with any witness, or with the defendant, or with any of the lawyers in the case. Please don't talk with them about any subject at all. In addition, during the course of the trial you should not talk about the trial with anyone else — not your family, not your friends, not the people you work with. Also, you should not discuss this case among yourselves until I have instructed you on the law and you have gone to the jury room to make your decision at the end of the trial. [See Instructions, §§ 1.12, 1.12a, Admonition upon recess, *supra.*] It is important that you wait until all the evidence is received and you have heard my instructions on rules of law before you deliberate among yourselves. Let me add that during the course of the trial you will receive all the evidence you properly may consider to decide the case. Because of this, you should not attempt to gather any information on your own which you think might be helpful. Do not engage in any outside reading on this case, do not attempt to visit any places mentioned in the case, and do not in any other way try to learn about the case outside the courtroom. If at any time during the trial anyone should attempt to discuss the case with you, you should refuse to do so and should advise me immediately. Please write me a note as soon as possible and do not discuss it with anyone else.

Now that the trial has begun, you must not read about it in the newspapers or watch or listen to television or radio reports of what is happening here. [See Instructions, §§ 1.11, 1.11a, Publicity cautioning, *supra.*]

The reason for these rules, as I am certain you will understand, is that your decision in this case must be made solely on the evidence presented at the trial.

At times during the trial, a lawyer may make an objection to a question asked by another lawyer, or to an answer by a witness. This simply means that the lawyer is requesting that I make a decision on a particular rule of law. Do not draw any conclusion from such objections or from my rulings on the objections. These only relate to the legal questions that I must determine and should not influence your thinking. If I sustain an objection to a question, the witness may not answer it. You are to disregard the question, and you must not speculate or guess as to what answer might have been given had I allowed the question to be answered. Similarly, if I tell you not to consider a particular statement, you should put that statement out of your mind and you may not refer to that statement in your later deliberations.

During the course of the trial I may ask a question of a witness. If I do, that does not indicate I have any opinion about the facts in the case. What the verdict shall be in this case is your sole and exclusive responsibility.

Finally, let me clarify something you may wonder about later. During the course of the trial I may have to interrupt the proceedings to confer with the attorneys about the rules of law which should apply here. Sometimes we will talk here at the bench. But some of these conferences may take time so, as a convenience to you, I may excuse you from the courtroom. I will try to avoid these interruptions as much as possible, but please be patient even if the trial seems to be moving slowly, because conferences often save time for all of us.

Ladies and gentlemen, it is important that you keep an open mind and that you not decide any issue in this case until the entire case has been submitted to you with my final instructions.

[Insert Instruction, Appendix II, Notetaking by Jurors.]

Thank you for your attention.

COMMENT

(a) Law relating to preliminary instructions

The above instruction is an example of a standard preliminary instruction to be used before or at the beginning of the trial. It has been based in part on the instruction prepared by the Federal Judicial Center's *Pattern Criminal Jury Instructions* (Report of the Federal Judicial Center Committee to Study Criminal Jury Instructions, June 1982). Where there is a conflict as to the law of the crime, see also Instruction, § 1.01, Function of the court and jury — Binding nature of instructions, and the accompanying Comment.

Preliminary instructions can be helpful in "setting the stage"; that is, to inform jurors as to what rules and procedures will be followed. In addition they might include a statement of the legal standards to be applied. These preliminary statements should not, however, be a substitute for requested final instructions.

The American Bar Association encourages the use of preliminary instructions to inform the jury of the following:

> (a) the function of the indictment, (b) the function of the jury as sole judges of the facts, (c) the restriction of their consideration to the evidence, (d) the presumption of innocence of the accused, (e) the burden of proof beyond a reasonable doubt, (f) matters concerning credibility, (g) the functions of courts and counsel, (h) the elements of the crimes charged, (i) a glossary of some of the terms to be used, (j) admonition as to outside conversation, newspaper accounts, etc., (k) explanation of the verdict and how it is reached — all the explanatory data which will put jurymen in the best possible position to perform the responsible task assigned to them.

3 ABA Standards for Criminal Justice § 3.6(e) at 108 (2d ed. 1980).

Maryland Rule 4-325(c) authorizes the judge to instruct the jury as to the applicable law and the extent to which the instructions are binding. While the giving of final instructions after the close of evidence under Rule 4-325(a) is mandatory when requested by one of the parties, the giving of preliminary instructions is totally within the discretion of the trial judge. *Elchin v. State,* 47 Md. App. 358, 424 A.2d 155, 159 (1980).

Rule 4-325(c) states, however, that the trial court need not give any requested instruction if the content of that instruction is "fairly covered by the instructions actually given." Generally, a preliminary instruction without a final instruction will not be deemed to have fairly covered the content of the requested instruction. This is because the intervening time period and introduction of evidence tends to lessen the impact of a preliminary remark on the jury. A preliminary remark may be misunderstood since it is not given in the context of the actual evidence adduced at trial; moreover, a preliminary remark may well have been forgotten at the time of deliberation. *Lansdowne v. State,* 287 Md. 232, 412 A.2d 88 (1980).

Where preliminary remarks defining "reasonable doubt" were made prior to opening statements, the introduction of evidence, and six hours prior to deliberation, the Court held that the requested instruction (re-definition of "reasonable doubt") was not "fairly covered" by the preliminary instructions. The preliminary remark did not constitute an instruction within the meaning of former Maryland Rules 757(b) (now Rule 4-325(c)) and

757(d) (now Rule 4-325(a)). The judge's subsequent admonition to the jury to recall the remark was insufficient to convert the preliminary remark into an instruction. Therefore, the judge erred in failing to instruct the jury concerning the meaning of "reasonable doubt." The instruction should have been made at the close of evidence. *Lansdowne v. State, supra* at 95-96.

In a similar case the trial judge defined "beyond reasonable doubt" in his preliminary remarks to the jury just after it had been impaneled. Although the judge did not repeat the definition of the term, the Court found no error on appeal. This case can be distinguished from *Lansdowne* in that here, the Court held that the final instructions were quite detailed and made reference to the term "reasonable doubt" (which had been defined in his preliminary remarks) at least *ten times.* The preliminary remarks, together with the final instructions, "fairly covered" the requested instruction. *Wilson v. State,* 44 Md. App. 318, 408 A.2d 1058 (1980). In a footnote, however, the Court stated that "... the better practice is to repeat the instruction." *Id.* at 324, 424 A.2d at 1063 n.3. Rule 4-325(c) provides that "[t]he Court need not grant a requested instruction if the matter is fairly covered by instructions actually given." In the case of *Wilson v. State, supra,* the Court found that the matter of reasonable doubt had been fairly covered. The Court is not compelled to repeat the explanation of a term. *Jones v. State,* 38 Md. App. 288, 380 A.2d 659 (1977), *rev'd on other grounds,* 283 Md. 709, 393 A.2d 1372 (1978); *Raley v. State,* 32 Md. App. 515, 363 A.2d 261 (1976); *cert. denied,* 278 Md. 731 (1978), *cert. denied,* 431 U.S. 965 (1977).

(b) Impact of preliminary instructions on jurors

In 1983, an empirical study was undertaken for the Committee on Improving Jury Communications of the Judicial Council of Wisconsin. Half of the ninety-six trials studied were criminal. At the conclusion of each trial, questionnaires were distributed to the trial judge, counsel and all jurors. One aspect of the study dealt with preliminary jury instructions. It addressed such questions as whether pre-trial instructions improve juror comprehension of the instructions, affect the ease or speed of jury deliberations, increase or reduce the perceived fairness of the trial, disrupt the trial process, or benefit one side or the other. See also Goldberg, *Memory, Magic, and Myth: The Timing of Jury Instructions,* 59 Or. L. Rev. 451 (1981). In half of the trials, jurors were given preliminary instructions, and in the other half preliminary instructions were not provided. The Wisconsin study[1] is the most thorough empirical study available, and the results are presented in part as follows:

(1) Juror responses

In half the test trials, the judge was asked to give as many instructions as possible before the evidence was presented, in addition to his final charge to the jury.

This was the only communication technique that produced a statistically significant difference in the jurors' overall satisfaction with the way the trial was conducted. Jurors not given preliminary instructions rated their satisfaction level at 7 (9 = very satisfied), while those given pre-instructions rated it at 7.5.

Jurors not given pre-instructions estimated the helpfulness of that technique at 5.9 to 6.7 (9 = very helpful) in deciding the importance of various pieces of evidence, remembering evidence during deliberations, evaluating the importance of evidence, reinforcing the judge's final charge, understanding the law, applying the law to the facts, and organizing the information presented during the trial. Jurors given pre-instructions rated the technique even more helpful than it was estimated by the other jurors to be. Their responses on those questions ranged from 7.2 to 7.9 (9 = very helpful).

[1] The Wisconsin study was undertaken by Professor Steven D. Penrod, Department of Psychology, University of Wisconsin-Madison. It was sponsored by the Wisconsin Judicial Council, Madison, Wisconsin, through its Executive Secretary, James L. Fullin, Jr. The results of the study were presented in mimeograph form at a conference attended by the author. Sponsored by The American Judicature Society, the conference on "The American Jury and the Law" was held on November 18-20, 1985, at the Wingspread Conference Center, Racine, Wisconsin.

(2) Attorney responses

Regardless of whether or not the jury was given preliminary instructions in their trial, attorneys agreed that the technique had a slightly positive effect on the overall fairness of the trial and did not significantly disrupt the trial process or adversely affect the ability of the jury to perform its duty adequately. Attorneys in cases where no pre-instructions were given estimated that that technique would slightly help the prosecuting attorney and slightly hurt the defense. However, the opposite result was reported by attorneys in cases where preliminary instructions were actually given. That is, the preliminary instructions helped the defense and hurt the prosecution slightly. This effect was not to be exaggerated; the mean response was always close to five on the nine-point scale.

(3) Judicial responses

Regardless of whether preliminary instructions were given in their trial, judges disagreed strongly with statements that the technique detracts from the fairness of the trial, adversely affects the jury's ability to perform its duty, and disrupts the trial process. Judges agreed that the technique has a slightly favorable impact on the overall fairness of the trial and does not systematically favor or hurt the prosecution or defense.

Appendix II

NOTETAKING BY JURORS

Suggested additional preliminary instruction to implement Maryland Rule 4-326(a)

If you want to take notes during the course of the trial, you may do so. However, it is difficult to take detailed notes and pay attention to what the witnesses are saying at the same time. If you do take notes, be sure that it does not interfere with your listening to and consideration of all the evidence. Your notes are not evidence and should not take precedence over your independent recollection of the evidence. If you do take notes, do not discuss them with anyone before you begin your deliberations. [Do not take your notes with you at the end of the day. Be sure to leave them in the jury room.] You may not use notes taken by anyone else.

Notebooks [will be] [have been] made available to you merely as a convenience in the event that you wish to take notes. You are not required to take notes and should not do so if it will distract you from giving full time and attention to the testimony and evidence in this case. Jurors who do not take notes should rely on their own memories and not be influenced by the fact that other jurors have taken notes.

If you choose not to take notes, remember it is your own individual responsibility to listen carefully to the evidence. You cannot give this responsibility to someone who is taking notes. We depend on the judgment of all members of the jury; you must all remember the evidence in this case.

[You will notice that we are making an official record of the trial. You will not, however, have typewritten transcripts of this record available for use in reaching your decision.]

COMMENT

(a) Law relating to notetaking

Maryland Rule of Procedure 4-326(a) provides:

> (a) **Items Taken to Jury Room.** — Jurors may take notes regarding the evidence, and they may keep the notes with them when they retire for their deliberations. Unless the court for good cause orders otherwise, the jury may also take the charging documents and exhibits which have been admitted into evidence, except that a deposition may not be taken into the jury room without the agreement of all parties and the consent of the court. Electronically recorded instructions or oral instructions reduced to writing may be taken into the jury room only with the permission of the court. On request of a party or on the court's own initiative, the charging documents shall reflect only those charges on which the jury is to deliberate. The court may impose safeguards for the preservation of the exhibits and the safety of the jurors.

Based on this provision, it appears that jurors are granted a right to take notes on the evidence presented.

Under prior Rule 558(b), the judge had discretion in deciding whether notetaking should be permitted. In *Dillon v. State,* 27 Md. App. 579, 342 A.2d 677 (1955), *reviewed in* 277 Md. 571, 357 A.2d 360 (1976), the Court of Appeals held: "We do not interpret the quoted portion of Rule 558 as intending a departure from the holding in *Cahill,* ... that the question whether the jurors will be permitted to take notes is within the discretion of the trial judge." *Id.* at 581, 342 A.2d at 679. See *Cahill v. Mayor of Baltimore,* 129 Md. 17, 26-27, 98 A. 235, 238 (1916). See also *Raimondi v. State,* 265 Md. 229, 231, 288 A.2d 882, 884 (1972).

Maryland Rule 4-326(a) very closely parallels the American Bar Association Standards, *Trial By Jury* 4.2 that: "Jurors may take notes regarding the evidence presented to them and keep these notes with them when they retire for deliberations. Such notes should be treated as confidential between the juror making them and his fellow jurors."

A question may be raised concerning the scope of Rule 4-326(a) in relation to the phrase "regarding the evidence." Do jurors have the right to take notes not only during the presentation of evidence but during the opening and closing arguments and the judge's instructions as well? Assuming generally that the rule does not permit a trial judge to exercise discretion against notetaking, the rule seems unclear as to whether a judge can exercise discretion to prohibit notetaking during opening and closing arguments and while the judge is instructing the jury.

The great majority of the states and the federal courts have allowed notetaking at least in the trial judge's discretion. See Petroff, *The Practice of Jury Notetaking — Misconduct, Right, or Privilege?,* 18 Okla. L. Rev. 125 (1965); *The Jury System in the Federal Courts,* 26 F.R.D. 409, 457-58 (1961); *Report of the Judicial Conference Committee on the Operation of the Jury System,* 26 F.R.D. 424 (1960); Bar Association of the District of Columbia, *Criminal Jury Instructions* Note 1.015 (3d ed. 1978); Annotation, 154 A.L.R. 878 *et seq.;* Annotation, 14 A.L.R.3d 833 *et seq.* See also *United States v. Campbell,* 138 F. Supp. 344, 348 *et seq.* (N.D. Iowa 1956); *People v. DiLuca,* 31 Cr. L. Rptr. 2028 (N.Y. Sup. Ct., App. Div. 1982).

In *United States v. Polowichak,* 783 F.2d 410 (4th Cir. 1986), the Court of Appeals held that if jurors are permitted to take notes, they should be instructed that their notes are not evidence and should not take precedence over their independent recollection of the proceeding.

(b) Suggested procedure for notetaking

The following is adapted from *Materials on Special Jury Techniques,* prepared by Judge Henry F. Greene, November 1984, for the District of Columbia Superior Court.

During the trial, jurors will be permitted to take notes in notebooks which, along with pencils, will be made available to them by the court. During short recesses the notebooks may be left on the jurors' chairs, and the courtroom will be protected. Before overnight recesses, unless the jury deliberation room is secured, the notebooks will be collected by the bailiff or the clerk and delivered to the judge, who will retain them and have them distributed to the jurors when the trial resumes.

At the end of the trial the jurors will be permitted to take their notebooks to the jury room during their deliberations. At the end of their deliberations, they will be told to tear out any notes from the notebooks and to deliver the notes to the foreperson. The foreperson then will deliver the notes to the judge, who will destroy them. Alternatively, jurors can be told to leave their notes in the deliberation room for collection by the court. The judge will instruct the jurors that at no time during or after the trial will he or anyone else examine the notes.

The jurors also will be instructed that: (1) the notebooks are made available to them merely as a convenience in the event they wish to take notes; (2) jurors are not required to take notes; (3) they should not do so if notetaking would distract them from giving full time and attention to the testimony and evidence in the case; and (4) jurors who do not take notes should rely on their own memories and not be influenced by the fact that other jurors have taken notes.

If jurors are permitted to take notes, some explanation during the preliminary instruction as to why notebooks and pencils are being provided to them is appropriate. Similarly, remarks with reference to the proper use and disposition of their notes bear repeating in the final instruction.

(c) Impact of notetaking on juror performance

The question of whether jurors should be allowed to take notes and, if so, the impact on the trial process, has been the subject of long-standing debate.

Arguments against juror notetaking often proceed along the following lines. A juror armed with notes may dominate others. A case might turn on an imperfectly written note. One feature of the case may receive emphasis over others as a result of allowing notetaking. A dishonest juror may even falsify his notes. Notetaking will distract jurors because it is extremely difficult to take careful notes and at the same time to carefully observe witnesses. Finally, it is argued that allowing notes into the jury room could cause disagreement as to who took the most accurate notes and could consequently prolong trials.

In *United States v. Chiarella,* 184 F.2d 903, 907 (2d Cir. 1950), *rev'd,* 341 U.S. 946, 71 S. Ct. 1004, 95 L. Ed. 1370 (issue of juror notetaking not addressed by Supreme Court), *modified,* 187 F.2d 12 (1951), Judge Learned Hand labeled objections to juror notetaking as "far fetched" and "imaginary." To the above arguments, the following replies are made. Certain jurors are likely to be more influential than others whether or not notetaking is allowed. Conflicts of memory exist irrespective of notetaking and, yet, jurors resolve these disagreements and achieve unanimity. Undue influence is much less likely at present when the vast majority of jurors are literate. If a case could turn on an imperfectly written note, it also could turn on an imperfect memory. That one feature of a case might receive emphasis over others is a danger inherent in the jury system; this danger is not increased by the fact that a juror takes a note. Falsification by a dishonest juror is equally feasible, whether it is done by means of a written memo or a spoken word. As to the argument that notetaking will distract a juror, it is argued that taking notes actually concentrates one's attention on the testimony. Finally, it is argued that memory is fallible and that notes are a valuable aid in recollecting evidence. It is an archaic practice to expect jurors to rely solely on their memories.

Little empirical data evaluating the impact of notetaking on juror performance exists. In 1983, the Committee on Improving Jury Communications of the Judicial Council of Wisconsin studied notetaking by jurors. Of ninety-six trials studied, one-half were criminal trials. The trials were divided into two groups. In one group no notetaking was permitted. In the other group, jurors were allowed to take notes not only during the presentation of evidence but during the opening and closing arguments of counsel and the judge's instructions. Questionnaires were distributed to the trial judge, counsel, and all jurors after each trial. The Wisconsin study [see Comment, subpart (b), note 1, Appendix I, *supra*] may be the most thorough empirical study available. Its results are presented in part as follows:

(1) Juror responses

In one-half of the trials, jurors were allowed to take notes, not only during the presentation of evidence but during the opening and closing arguments of counsel and the judge's instructions. Of the jurors allowed to take notes, approximately 66 percent reported that they did so. Of those taking notes, 70 percent took four or fewer pages. Virtually all the jurors responded that they took fewer than two pages each of notes during opening statements, closing statements, and judicial instructions. However, about 20 percent took more than three pages of notes during presentation of each party's evidence. The mean amount of notes taken during the prosecutor's case was the same as during the defense case. About 10 percent of the jurors reported that parts of the trial happened too fast to take accurate notes. On a nine-point scale, jurors responded in the middle of the scale (5.6) when asked how much they relied on their notes during deliberations. They found their notes moderately valuable (6.6).

Seventeen percent of the jurors reported that there were times when jurors' notes disagreed. Ninety percent said that this happened three or fewer times. Most frequently (16), this disagreement was resolved by checking the notes, refreshing their memory, or discovering an error in the notes. Four jurors reported that differences in the notes were resolved by a vote of the jurors.

Some jurors not allowed to take notes estimated that they would be distracted by their own (4.9) or others' (3.5) notetaking (9 = very distracted). Jurors allowed to take notes reported that they were not at all distracted (1.7) by the procedure.

Jurors agreed that jurors who took notes should not have more influence during deliberation than non-notetakers (3.1; 1 = not at all). Notetaking jurors did not have more influence during deliberations (3.6; 1 = not at all). When asked what advice they would give future jurors about taking notes, the most frequent (40) comment was that such notes are helpful. Thirty-two jurors recommended that notes be used for numbers and small details. Thirty-seven recommended that notes be kept brief and concise. Twenty-four recommended that jurors not allow themselves to be distracted by notetaking, while fifteen said that notes are important for only certain parts of the trial. Of the total responding,

193 said that allowing jurors to take notes was a good idea, while thirty-seven said it was not. Fifty-three felt that notetaking could be distracting, while fifty-six said it might be useful in some situations. Thirty-seven said that notetaking is especially helpful in lengthy trials.

(2) Attorney responses

Regardless of whether the jurors in their trial were permitted to take notes, attorneys disagreed fairly strongly with statements that notetaking disrupts the trial process, interferes with the presentation of their case, is costly in time or effort, or detracts from the fairness of the trial. They also indicated slight disagreement with the statement that jurors cannot be trusted to take notes accurately. Attorneys rated the procedure neutral from the standpoint of favoring or hurting the prosecution or defense.

Attorneys in trials where jurors were allowed to take notes disagreed strongly with their counterparts in trials where jurors were not allowed to take notes on whether juror notetaking distracted the notetaker, other jurors, the attorneys, or the witnesses. Where notetaking was permitted, attorneys reported that it was far less distracting to all participants than it was estimated to be by attorneys in trials where the procedure was not used.

(3) Judicial responses

Judges reported that jurors allowed to take notes were much more attentive. They found that the evidence and the issues in the case were presented more clearly. Judges reported significantly greater satisfaction with the performance of the prosecuting attorney in these trials. Judges agreed with the attorneys that the procedure had no systematic bias in favor of or against the prosecution or defense.

Judges in trials where notetaking was not permitted disagreed only slightly with statements that it would distract the jurors, attorneys and witnesses, focus attention on irrelevant issues, add costs in time and effort, and detract from the fairness of the trial.

However, judges in trials where notetaking was permitted disagreed very strongly with statements of these alleged disadvantages.

The Wisconsin study described above provides support for the view that there may be no legitimate basis upon which a trial judge should be permitted to exercise his discretion against notetaking. Maryland Rule of Procedure 4-326(a), set forth above, appears to reflect this position.

Appendix III

HOW TO MAKE JURY INSTRUCTION REQUESTS AND PROCEDURE FOR PRESERVING THE RECORD FOR POSSIBLE APPEAL WHEN A REQUESTED INSTRUCTION IS DENIED

(a) Rule 4-325

The basis for understanding how to make jury instruction requests and how to preserve the record for possible appeal is Maryland Rule of Procedure 4-325. Because of the importance of this rule, it is reprinted in its entirety as follows:

(a) When Given. — The court shall give instructions to the jury at the conclusion of all the evidence and before closing arguments and may supplement them at a later time when appropriate. In its discretion the court may also give opening and interim instructions.

(b) Written Requests. — The parties may file written requests for instructions at or before the close of the evidence and shall do so at any time fixed by the court.

(c) How Given. — The court may, and at the request of any party shall, instruct the jury as to the applicable law and the extent to which the instructions are binding. The court may give its instructions orally or, with the consent of the parties, in writing instead of orally. The court need not grant a requested instruction if the matter is fairly covered by instructions actually given.

(d) Reference to Evidence. — In instructing the jury, the court may refer to or summarize the evidence in order to present clearly the issues to be decided. In that event, the court shall instruct the jury that it is the sole judge of the facts, the weight of the evidence, and the credibility of the witnesses.

(e) Objection. — No party may assign as error the giving or the failure to give an instruction unless the party objects on the record promptly after the court instructs the jury, stating distinctly the matter to which the party objects and the grounds of the objection. Upon request of any party, the court shall receive objections out of the hearing of the jury. An appellate court, on its own initiative or on the suggestion of a party, may however take cognizance of any plain error in the instructions, material to the rights of the defendant, despite a failure to object.

(f) Argument. — Nothing in this Rule precludes any party from arguing that the law applicable to the case is different from the law described in the instructions of the court stated not to be binding.

(b) Requirements for requested instructions

As stated in the last sentence of Rule 4-325(c) the judge need not grant any requested instruction if the matter is fairly covered by instructions actually given. As the Court stated in *Leatherwood v. State,* 49 Md. App. 683, 435 A.2d 477 (1981), "the law is satisfied if the trial court's instructions read as a whole adequately and clearly state the law applicable to the case." *Nizer v. Phelps,* 252 Md. 185, 249 A.2d 112 (1969); *Alston v. Forsythe,* 226 Md. 121, 172 A.2d 474 (1961); *Kable v. State,* 17 Md. App. 16, 299 A.2d 493, *cert. denied,* 268 Md. 750 (1973); *Shotkosky v. State,* 8 Md. App. 492, 261 A.2d 171 (1970).

The giving of an erroneous jury instruction is not grounds for reversal if the defendant is not prejudiced by the instruction. *Lindsay v. State,* 8 Md. App. 100, 258 A.2d 760 (1969) ("harmless error" doctrine). Further, if counsel did not properly object to instructions under Rule 4-325(e), and there was an error of omission which could have been readily cured, no appeal will be heard absent plain error. *Cooper v. State,* 44 Md. App. 59, 407 A.2d 756 (1979).

The Court in *Jackson v. State,* 46 Md. App. 325, 416 A.2d 1353 (1980) held that the refusal to give instructions because the requested instruction was not submitted in writing was reversible error. The Court stated that while requests for jury instructions may be in writing, written requests are not a prerequisite for instructions. The court must give instructions on any issue of law fairly covered by the evidence whenever it is asked by a party or counsel to do so. Failure to give such instruction is fatal error. *Jackson v. State,* supra at 329, 416 A.2d at 1356. See *Johnson v. State,* 303 Md. 487, 495 A.2d 1 (1985); *Smith v. State,* 302 Md. 175, 486 A.2d 196 (1985); *Mack v. State,* 300 Md. 583, 479 A.2d 1344 (1984); *Ghassemien v. Schafer,* 52 Md. App. 31, 447 A.2d 84

(1982); *Morrow v. State,* 293 Md. 247, 443 A.2d 108 (1982); *Funkhouser v. State,* 51 Md. App. 16, 440 A.2d 1114 (1982); *Leatherwood v. State, supra; Prokopis v. State,* 49 Md. App. 531, 433 A.2d 1191 (1981); *Wilson v. State,* 44 Md. App. 318, 408 A.2d 1058 (1979).

The above decisions are reflected in Rule 4-325(c). When requested by counsel, Rule 4-325(c) is mandatory. A trial judge must give a requested instruction that correctly states the applicable law which has not been fairly covered in instructions actually given if there is some evidence in the case which supports giving the instruction. A party is generally entitled to have his theory of the case presented to the jury through a requested instruction if that theory is a correct exposition of the law. Thus, three requirements must be met: (1) the instruction must correctly state the law; (2) it is not fairly covered by other instructions; and, (3) the law is applicable in light of the evidence before the jury. See *Johnson v. State, supra; Smith v. State, supra.* In certain circumstances the "last" requirement may be relaxed. In *Bellamy v. State,* 50 Md. App. 65, 435 A.2d 821 (1981), the Court held that whenever a confession is introduced into evidence and instructions as to its voluntariness are requested, the trial judge must give the proffered instructions regardless of his personal belief in the absence of evidence necessary to support the contention of involuntariness.

The Court apparently is not required to give instructions to the jury, even as to presumption of innocence and burden of proof, where one of the attorneys does not request the instruction. See *Hall v. State,* 292 Md. 683, 441 A.2d 708 (1982). Tension exists, however, between the language of Rule 4-325(a): "When Given. — The court *shall* give instructions to the jury at the conclusion of all the evidence ..." and Rule 4-325(c): "How Given. — The court *may,* and at the request of any party shall, instruct the jury as to the applicable law ..." (emphases added). Rule 4-325(a) assumes that the Court shall give some instruction to the jury which is not conditioned upon an attorney's request.

(c) "Some evidence" requirement

As noted above, "some evidence" must exist to justify giving a requested jury instruction. The trial judge and the appellate court may conclude that a particular instruction is "superfluous" if there is lacking "some evidence" to permit reasonable jurors to arrive at the determination that counsel seeks. In making this determination on appeal, the Court is bound by the "cold record," as reflected in the written trial transcript. Counsel's judgment at the moment of trial and appellate court's judgment on review of the record may differ as to whether the "some evidence" test has been met. If counsel desires to adequately preserve the record for appeal, special diligence is needed throughout the trial to ensure that the trial transcript will clearly demonstrate that "some evidence" was presented to justify giving a jury instruction. A surprising number of appellate decisions hold that an otherwise erroneous instruction actually given or an otherwise valid requested instruction that is denied by the trial judge is "harmless error" or "superfluous" since the "some evidence" requirement was not met.

(d) Informal pre-charge conference

Requests for jury instructions are frequently made in an informal conference that takes place "off the record." The discussion between the judge and counsel about jury instruction requests has been described as "charge bargaining." Counsel may attempt to persuade the judge to give one or more of its requested instructions. The judge may attempt to convince counsel that the court's instructions fairly cover the issue. It is the author's opinion that this conference or informal discussion is a critical stage of the trial that often is entirely overlooked or approached with inadequate preparation by counsel. It is surprising how few counsel present the judge with proposed written instructions that adapt form instructions to the facts of the case. Some experienced counsel prefer to present just one or two written instructions that relate to the basic theory of their case. They may be willing to rely on the judge's standard instructions to cover the other topics or they may request particular patterned instructions. This pre-instruction conference may be counsel's only opportunity to present their theory of the law as applied to the particular facts of the case and, if granted, may provide a basis upon which closing argument is structured. Counsel's concurrence with the judge's proposed instructions implies a decision to forego preserving the record for appeal based on erroneous jury instructions.

(e) Objections to instructions

Some counsel erroneously believe that voicing their objections to a proposed instruction at an informal pre-charge conference is sufficient to preserve the record for an appeal. If counsel desires to preserve the record in the event of a subsequent appeal, objections to the trial judge's instructions *and* proffering the specific language of counsel's requested instructions must be placed "on the record". Rule 4-325(e) provides: "No party may assign as error the giving or the failure to give an instruction unless the party objects on the record promptly *after the court instructs the jury,* stating distinctly the matter to which the party objects and the grounds of the objection" (emphasis added). It is clear from Rule 4-325(e) that a formal objection must be made after the trial judge has formally instructed the jury. Failure to initially request an instruction at an informal pre-charge conference, however, will not preclude counsel from requesting the instruction after the court has completed giving its instructions to the jury. *Gooch v. State,* 34 Md. App. 331, 367 A.2d 90 (1976); *Noel v. State,* 202 Md. 247, 96 A.2d 7 (1952).

In order to make the record, counsel should request to "approach the bench" or have the jury excused and repeat "for the record" (*i.e.,* transcribed by the court reporter or otherwise recorded) exceptions to the instructions given, the grounds therefor, and the exact language of the requested instructions. A portion of the trial transcript showing that an adequate record has been made must be appended to the brief in the event of an appeal.

Some judges follow the practice of asking counsel if there are any objections to the instructions in open court in the presence of the jury immediately after the instructions are given. Counsel may hesitate to voice any objection in front of the jury. The solution to this problem is to request a bench conference and, perhaps, at the bench, if the objections are lengthy, a request should be made that there should be a brief recess so that the jury can be excused while objections are made.

Objections immediately following the instruction of the jury perform the additional function of providing notice to the judge and an opportunity for the judge to make any corrections and additions to the instructions. Counsel must listen very carefully to the instructions to the jury to make sure that the language agreed upon in the pre-charge conference is actually given. An advantage of written instructions is that counsel can examine the text of the instruction while the judge is reading the instruction to the jury.

(f) Appellate review of plain error

Rule 4-325(e) provides that an appellate court may, in its discretion, take cognizance of and correct any plain error in the instructions that is material to the rights of the defendant, even though the error was not objected to at the trial. The appellate court should take cognizance of error that was not objected to in instances that are compelling, extraordinary, exceptional, or fundamental to assure the defendant a fair trial. *State v. Hutchinson,* 287 Md. 198, 411 A.2d 1035 (1980). See *Souffie v. State,* 50 Md. App. 547, 439 A.2d 1127 (1982). In *Hutchinson, supra,* the jury was not instructed that the defendant could be found not guilty, although the verdict sheet contained all possible verdicts, and the defendant did not object. The Court found error and granted a new trial. Absent extreme circumstances, appellate review of plain error in instructions is discretionary. See *Booth v. State,* 62 Md. App. 26, 488 A.2d 195 (1985), *aff'd,* 306 Md. 313, 508 A.2d 976 (1986).

Appendix IV

SUPPLEMENTING ORAL INSTRUCTIONS WITH WRITTEN OR ELECTRONICALLY RECORDED INSTRUCTIONS

(a) Existing law

A question frequently asked is how well jurors are actually able to follow the trial judge's oral instructions. Would the administration of justice be improved if the trial judge's oral instructions were supplemented by written (or possibly tape-recorded) instructions? While some trial judges do submit written jury instructions, the prevailing practice in Maryland has been *not* to provide written jury instructions. This comment offers a brief examination of legal authority and reviews arguments pro and con for supplementing oral instructions with written or electronically recorded jury instructions.

In Maryland, the question of whether jurors may bring instructions with them into the jury room has been one of discretion for the trial judge, although consent of the parties may be required. Rule 4-326(a) of the Maryland Rules of Procedure speaks directly to this issue:

> **(a) Items Taken to Jury Room.** — Jurors may take notes regarding the evidence, and they may keep the notes with them when they retire for their deliberations. Unless the court for good cause orders otherwise, the jury may also take the charging document and exhibits which have been admitted into evidence, except that a deposition may not be taken into the jury room without the agreement of all parties and the consent of the court. *Electronically recorded instructions or oral instructions reduced to writing may be taken into the jury room only with the permission of the court.* On request of a party or on the court's own initiative, the charging documents shall reflect only those charges on which the jury is to deliberate. The court may impose safeguards for the preservation of the exhibits and the safety of the jurors (emphasis added).

Note that the rule requiring the permission of the court for instructions to be taken into the jury room does not address the question of providing access to such instructions in open court.

A question may be raised as to whether consent of counsel is also required before written or recorded instructions can be taken into the jury room. No mention of consent of counsel appears in Rule 4-326(a). However, Rule 4-325(c) provides: "The court may give its instructions orally, or, *with the consent of the parties,* in writing" (emphasis added). It can be argued that the language of Rule 4-325(c) applies only to the initial jury instructions and that consent of both parties is not required to supplement oral instructions with written or electronically recorded copies of the instructions. Further, the predecessor to Rule 4-326(a), Rule 757(e), also made no mention of consent of counsel. It provided that the jury could take into the jury room certain items, including written instructions, "as the court may deem necessary for proper consideration of the case." In *Mack v. State,* 69 Md. App. 245, 517 A.2d 108 (1986), the Court held that under Rule 4-325(c) consent of the defendant is not required where both oral and written instructions are provided. Only where instructions are to be given in writing *instead of* orally must consent be obtained.

Of some interest is the fact that older civil case authority in Maryland seems to support the idea of sending written instructions into the jury room for use during deliberations. In *Mutual Life Ins. Co. v. Rain,* 108 Md. 353, 356, 70 A. 87, 89 (1908), the Court states: "[W]e do not commend the giving of verbal instructions, deeming it much better practice to carefully reduce all instructions to writing, and in this form to submit them to the jury." See also *Winslow v. Atz,* 168 Md. 230, 177 A. 272 (1935); M.L.E. *Trial* §§ 162, 254; *Md. Digest Trial* § 223. Poe, in his treatise, indicates that it was a regular practice for the jury to take written instructions into the jury room: "At the end of the discussion the jury retired to consider the verdict, taking with them the pleadings and the court's instructions, but no other papers whatsoever, except by consent of counsel." 2 *Poe's Pleading and Practice* § 328 (5th ed. 1925). See also *Cahill v. Mayor and City Council of Baltimore,* 129 Md. 17, 25-26, 98 A. 235, 239 (1916).

In *Thomas v. State,* 50 Md. App. 286, 437 A.2d 678 (1982), the Court of Special Appeals, relying on former Rule 757(e) (now 4-326(a)), held that it was not an abuse of discretion for the trial court to limit written instructions provided to jurors during deliberations to those concerning the law of substantive crimes, and to refuse to permit the jury to use during deliberation instructions concerning burden of proof and presumption of innocence. The Court reasoned that the latter instructions were more readily understood when delivered orally. *Accord GMC v. Wernsing,* 54 Md. App. 19, 456 A.2d 939 (1983) (a civil case before the same court), *aff'd,* 298 Md. 406, 470 A.2d 802 (1984).

(b) Pros and cons of permitting jurors to take instructions into the jury room

Many arguments have been raised for encouraging trial judges to permit the jury to carry written instructions into the jury room. First, jurors are likely to forget oral instructions that are long and complex. Second, individual jurors may be prevented from placing undue regard upon a particular instruction which they remember in isolation from other instructions, or in imposing their recollections upon other jurors. Third, a verdict may be reached more quickly if time need not be spent in attempting to recall specific instructions. Fourth, the necessity for notetaking, where permitted by the trial judge during the giving of instructions, would be eliminated resulting in a possibility of greater attentiveness to the instructions as a whole. Cunningham, *Should Instructions Go Into the Jury Room?* 33 Cal. S.B.J. 278, 285 (1958).

Critics of the practice, however, fear prolongation of the trial caused by rereading of the instructions by jurors; the possibility of undue emphasis being given particular instructions; an increased likelihood of one juror's interpretation being imposed upon others; and a greater difficulty in interpretation which might be posed by the existence of a document setting forth the instructions. Cunningham, *supra* at 286.

Discussions with several judges suggest that many judges are willing to submit written instructions in at least some criminal cases, but that serious practical obstacles interfere. In a criminal case the final determination of the language to be given to a jury generally occurs during a short period of time after the close of the evidence and before final argument begins. During this period the trial judge usually provides a final opportunity for counsel on both sides to request particular instructions. The final instructions may consist of a hodgepodge of instructions the judge has given in previous cases, submissions of counsel, form instructions, and language suggested from recent appellate decisions. Inadequate time and resources often exist for these instructions to be fully assembled in a form for submission to the jury. There may be a need for the finally assembled instructions to be retyped. If one copy is available in written form, ready access to photocopying or reproduction facilities may not be available. A recess of some length following closing arguments might be necessary for the preparation of written instructions. Additional demands would be placed on limited support services available to many trial judges (paper for duplicating instructions, typists to prepare the instructions for the jury, quick access to photocopying equipment, etc.). If there is an increasing recognition of the desirability of supplementing oral instructions in at least some criminal cases, additional attention needs to be given to the practical problems of implementation.

One suggestion that may deserve consideration is submitting electronically recorded instructions into the jury room or making these instructions available in open court. Tape recording the trial judge's oral instructions and making the recording available to the jury would avoid the administrative problems of preparing written instructions discussed above. A frequent objection to the practice of taping instructions is that it may encourage the jury to overemphasize certain portions of the charge. This danger exists whether copies are provided in writing or electronically recorded. Several courts have addressed this concern. Some courts hold that the jury charge must be considered as a whole. See, e.g., *United States v. Holmes,* 680 F.2d 1340, 1354 (11th Cir. 1982). Other courts have held that any likelihood that jurors will take an unbalanced view of the charge can be overcome by a careful instruction, which stresses the importance of considering the charge as a whole. See *United States v. Watson,* 669 F.2d 1374, 1386 (11th Cir. 1982). See also Katz, *Reinstructing the Jury by Tape Recording,* 41 J. Am. Jud. Soc. 148 (1958); Hansel, *Should the Jury Have Tape Recorded Instructions?,* Ariz. St. L.J. 599 (1983).

Judge Henry Greene in *Materials on Special Jury Techniques* for the District of Columbia Court, November 1984, suggests that where the trial judge decides to tape record final jury instructions and send them to the jury, it is appropriate to advise counsel of the procedure in advance and to instruct the jury about the procedure at the end of the instructions. The jurors will be advised that the tape has been "punched" so that it cannot be erased or recorded over. They will be further advised that they are not required to listen to the instructions again, and if they choose to listen to the tape, they need not listen to it in its entirety. Their access to the recorded instructions does not mean that they may give special emphasis to any one instruction. [Alternatively, they may be advised that should they choose to listen to the tape, they must listen to it in its entirety.] They should not be discouraged from sending questions to the court if they feel it is necessary during their deliberations. It is probably also desirable to preserve the tape recording of the instructions and file it in its case jacket, pending appeal, or until the time for filing notice of appeal has elapsed.

(c) Impact of permitting jurors to take instructions into the jury room

In 1983, the Committee on Improving Jury Communications of the Judicial Council of Wisconsin attempted to evaluate the impact of sending written instructions into the jury room for use during deliberations. Under the experimental procedure, it was recommended that copies of all instructions be given to the jury. Ninety-six actual trials were studied, half of which were criminal trials. At the end of each trial, questionnaires were distributed to the trial judge, counsel, and all jurors. Some of the results of the Wisconsin study [see Comment, subpart (b), note 1, Appendix I, *supra*] are as follows:

(1) Juror responses

Jurors given written instructions made various uses of them. Eighty-three percent reported that the instructions were read aloud during deliberations. The most frequent (mode) response was that the jury looked at the written instructions three times during deliberations and spent ten minutes looking at them and discussing them. However, the mean response was that the jury looked at the written instruction 5.8 times and spent 25 minutes looking at and discussing them. This difference may be explained by the hypothesis that in certain trials the jurors spent much more than ten minutes discussing the instructions.

Jurors not given written instructions estimated the helpfulness of that technique at 6 (9 = very helpful) in understanding the trial proceedings, reaching a proper verdict, and understanding the judge's instructions completely and properly. Jurors given written instructions rated the helpfulness of that technique even higher, at 7 (9 = very helpful). Jurors not given written instructions estimated that they would rely on them more heavily (6.4) than was reported (5.9) by jurors given written instructions. Both groups responded with the same frequency (6.6), that written instructions would help settle disagreement among jurors about the meaning and application of the judge's instructions.

In an open-ended question asking for reactions and comments to the written instruction procedure, the most frequent response (208) was that this technique was a good idea and helpful to the jury. Almost 60 percent of the jurors responded with positive comments. Forty-three jurors thought the technique was not helpful or necessary.

(2) Attorney responses

Responses from attorneys who participated in trials where written instructions were used usually showed no significant difference from those where written instructions were not used. Attorneys rated the technique neutral in terms of favoring or hurting the plaintiff/prosecution or defense. Most felt the technique had no significant adverse effect on the jury's ability to perform its duty. Although they did report that it delayed the trial somewhat, most attorneys agreed that allowing the jury to have written instructions did not detract from the fairness of the trial. Attorneys in trials where that technique was used more emphatically responded that it did not detract from the fairness of the trial.

(3) Judicial responses

Judges tended to be somewhat more critical of the technique than jurors and attorneys. Judges required to submit written instructions felt more strongly that that technique disrupted the trial process than judges who did not submit written instructions. Judges agreed with attorneys that this technique did not categorically help or hurt the prosecution or defendant. They also rated the technique as having a positive effect on the fairness of the trial and on the jury's ability to perform its job adequately.

Appendix V

THE IMPACT OF *EVANS v. STATE:* BURDENS OF PROOF, PRESUMPTIONS AND INFERENCES

(a) Introduction

The complex and learned opinion of Judge Moylan in *Evans v. State,* 28 Md. App. 640, 349 A.2d 300 (1975), *aff'd,* 278 Md. 197, 362 A.2d 629 (1976), provided the impetus for a major revision of Maryland's criminal law, particularly the law of homicide, in the areas of burdens of proof, presumptions, and inferences. Judge Moylan set forth a schematic summary of the holding of *Mullaney v. Wilbur,* 421 U.S. 684, 95 S. Ct. 1881, 44 L. Ed. 2d 508 (1975) in the beginning of his opinion in *Evans.* This schematic summary is used as a basis for organizing the discussion of Maryland case law. What follows is an attempt to "flesh out" in abbreviated fashion the impact of *Mullaney* and *Evans* on Maryland case law.

In *Mullaney,* the appellant challenged Maine's requirement that the defendant bear the burden of proof by a preponderance of the evidence in order to reduce second degree murder to voluntary manslaughter. The Supreme Court held that the requirements violated the due process standard enunciated in *In re Winship,* 397 U.S. 358, 90 S. Ct. 1068, 25 L. Ed. 2d 368 (1970), which mandates that the state prove beyond a reasonable doubt every fact necessary to constitute the crime charged.

In *Evans v. State, supra,* the Court of Special Appeals held that *Mullaney* requires abrogation of the former rule in Maryland which presumed a homicide to be second degree murder. The Court further indicated that it would be unconstitutional to place the burden of persuasion on the defendant to prove any circumstance of mitigation, excuse, or justification in a homicide case. Judge Moylan discussed the scope to be accorded the *Mullaney* decision:

> For the moment, it is enough to set out, by way of shorthand summary, that it dooms as unconstitutional any procedural device which (1) imposes upon a defendant a burden of

> proving, by any standards, his innocence as to any element of a crime or (2) relieves the State of its burden of ultimate persuasion beyond a reasonable doubt as to any issue fairly in the case.

Id. at 654, 349 A.2d at 318. See also *Swain v. State,* 50 Md. App. 29, 435 A.2d 805 (1981); *Dorsey v. State,* 278 Md. 221, 362 A.2d 642 (1976); *State v. Garland,* 278 Md. 212, 362 A.2d 638, *rev'd,* 34 Md. App. 258, 367 A.2d 30 (1976); *Finnegan v. State,* 33 Md. App. 251, 364 A.2d 124, *cert. denied,* 279 Md. 682 (1976), *cert. denied,* 433 U.S. 912 (1977); *Edwards v. State,* 31 Md. App. 562, 358 A.2d 590 (1976). As noted below, the defendant still may be required to carry the burden of going forward with sufficient evidence to generate the issue of justification, excuse, or mitigation. *Tripp v. State,* 36 Md. App. 459, 374 A.2d 384 (1977). Once the defendant has met the burden of production, the State must assume the burden of persuasion beyond a reasonable doubt on the issue. *Evans v. State, supra.*

In *Patterson v. New York,* 432 U.S. 197, 97 S. Ct. 2319, 53 L. Ed. 2d 281 (1977), the Supreme Court upheld a conviction for second degree murder where the defendant was seeking to reduce the offense to manslaughter. The statute required the defendant to prove by a preponderance of the evidence that he had acted "under the influence of an extreme emotional disturbance for which there was a reasonable explanation or excuse." The Court distinguished *Mullaney* on the ground that under the New York statute, unlike the Maine statute, "malice aforethought" is not an element of the offense of murder. Rather, murder is defined under New York law as the causing of the death of another person with the intent to do so. Also, the New York statutory standard provided more opportunity for the jury to consider mitigating circumstances than provided by the common-law provocation standard. The constitutional restrictions on a state regarding *statutory* changes that shift the burden of proving affirmative defenses to the defendant were not clearly delineated in *Patterson.*

At present in Maryland, malice is an element of the offense of murder. One may, therefore, argue that *Patterson* has little or no effect on the burden of proof in Maryland homicide cases. This view is supported by the expansive interpretation afforded the

Mullaney decision by the Maryland Court in *Evans v. State, supra.*

Applying *Evans,* generally, the Court in *Finnegan v. State, supra,* held that a trial judge's verdict will bear the same scrutiny as a trial by jury if the judge indicates that he relied upon an unconstitutional burden of proof. In another case the Court held that the trial court's instruction that "(m)alice is something done intentionally and without lawful excuse," properly viewed in the context of the overall charge, did not constitute reversible error. The instructions, when considered in their entirety, did not unconstitutionally relieve the State of its burden of proving beyond a reasonable doubt the absence of provocation or other mitigating circumstances. *State v. Garland,* 29 Md. App. 27, 349 A.2d 374 (1975), *rev'd,* 278 Md. 212, 362 A.2d 638, *rev'd,* 34 Md. App. 258, 367 A.2d 30 (1976).

The impact of *Mullaney* and *Evans* is most clearly understood by organizing the cases into two categories: (1) situations where *Mullaney* and *Evans* will not result in unconstitutionality; and (2) situations where *Mullaney* and *Evans* will result in unconstitutionality. The following discussion merely attempts to highlight some of the principal cases and does not purport to be definitive.

(b) Situations where Mullaney and Evans will not result in unconstitutionality

1. An innocuous statement as to burden of proof such as "all murder is presumed to be murder in the second degree." This is simply a circular way of saying that the State must prove every element of the crime beyond a reasonable doubt. Therefore, for semantic rather than constitutional reasons such usage should be discontinued. See *Evans v. State, supra.*

2. Any rule of substantive law. *Mullaney* does not affect substantive law but, rather, just procedure. Therefore, a state may define murder as not including a special *mens rea.* If it does, it is not affected by *Mullaney.* See *Evans v. State, supra.*

a. Various forms of first degree murder are not affected by *Mullaney.* It is "well settled that murder in the second degree and manslaughter are lesser included offenses (of murder in the first degree)." *Blackwell v. State,* 278 Md. 466, 365 A.2d 545 (1976), *cert. denied,* 431 U.S. 918 (1977).

b. The doctrine of transferred intent is not modified by *Mullaney.* See *Evans v. State, supra.*

c. *Mullaney* does not affect any substantive law pertaining to implied malice, such as the felony murder doctrine. See *Evans v. State, supra.* In *McDowell v. State,* 31 Md. App. 652, 358 A.2d 624 (1976), the Court noted that felony murder statutes are not affected by *Mullaney.* The *mens rea* of the underlying felony supplies the malice by definition. See *Warren v. State,* 29 Md. App. 560, 350 A.2d 173 (1976).

3. A permissible inference in which the jury may, but is not required, to infer one fact from the existence of another fact or circumstance is not affected by *Mullaney* and *Evans.* A permissible inference does not shift the burden of persuasion. For example, the jury may infer an intent to do grievous bodily harm from the use of a deadly weapon. Only an intent to do grievous bodily harm may be inferred; malice may not be inferred. Inferences, however, must pass constitutional muster. The State must show a rational connection between the basic fact and the inferred fact by a preponderance of the evidence on the basis of the particular facts of each case. In other words, fact A must rationally lead to fact B in the context in which it was proven. See, e.g., *Ulster County Court v. Allen,* 442 U.S. 140, 99 S. Ct. 2213, 60 L. Ed. 2d 777 (1979); *Sandstrom v. Montana,* 442 U.S. 510, 99 S. Ct. 2450, 61 L. Ed. 2d 39 (1979); *Leary v. United States,* 395 U.S. 6, 89 S. Ct. 1532, 23 L. Ed. 2d 57 (1969); *United States v. Tot,* 319 U.S. 463, 63 S. Ct. 1241, 87 L. Ed. 2d 1519 (1943).

In *Horn v. State,* 29 Md. App. 23, 349 A.2d 372 (1975), the Court considered the permissible inference relating to exclusive possession of recently stolen goods. In the absence of satisfactory explanation, exclusive possession of recently stolen goods permits an inference of fact that the possessor broke into a storehouse. This rule creates no "presumption" but merely permits an inference of fact. It does not shift the burden of persuasion nor the burden of going forward with evidence. The Court held that on the facts presented, the inference was applied properly and was not within the scrutiny of *Mullaney.* Also, see *Tipton v.*

State, 39 Md. App. 578, 387 A.2d 628 (1978) (drinking while driving leads to a permissible inference of the defendant's wanton and reckless disregard for human life); *Dinkins v. State,* 29 Md. App. 577, 349 A.2d 676, *aff'd,* 278 Md. 238, 362 A.2d 91 (1976); *McCree v. State,* 33 Md. App. 82, 363 A.2d 647 (1976).

But malice must be proved by the state beyond a reasonable doubt. See *Morris v. State,* 33 Md. App. 185, 364 A.2d 588 (1976) (while it may be proper to infer an intention to kill or to do grievous bodily harm from the directing of a deadly weapon at a vital part of the human anatomy, it is improper to infer *malice,* since the use of force does not itself negate the absence of mitigating circumstances). See also *Finnegan v. State,* 33 Md. App. 251, 364 A.2d 124, *cert. denied,* 279 Md. 682 (1976), *cert. denied,* 433 U.S. 912 (1977); *James v. State,* 31 Md. App. 666, 358 A.2d 595 (1976); *Gilbert v. State,* 36 Md. App. 196, 373 A.2d 311 (1977); *Thompson v. State,* 38 Md. App. 499, 381 A.2d 704 (1978); *Kashansky v. State,* 39 Md. App. 313, 385 A.2d 811 (1978).

An important question is how to word a jury instruction so that jurors will understand that they may or may not draw a permissible inference, depending on their findings of the preliminary facts. There is a danger that merely using the word "may" rather than "must" or "should" will not adequately convey that the inference is indeed permissible. A suggested approach is to instruct the jury that "they may, but need not, infer" the particular fact.

4. A presumption in the Thayer-Wigmore tradition simply places upon the defendant the onus of producing evidence, or of relying at his risk upon evidence produced by the State, sufficient to generate a jury issue with respect to a particular defense. Once the issue is generated by evidence, the presumption totally dissipates and the State assumes the burden of persuasion on that issue beyond a reasonable doubt. Since the presumption has totally served its purpose once a jury issue has been created, the jury never hears of the presumption. *Evans v. State, supra.* See also *Mullaney, supra* nn.28 and 31 at 703, 95 S. Ct. at 1891, 44 L. Ed. 2d at 522; *Jones v. State,* 37 Md. App. 511, 378 A.2d 9 (1977); *Tripp v. State,* 36 Md. App. 459, 374 A.2d 384 (1977).

5. *Mullaney* and *Evans* do not affect the rule placing the burden of proving by a fair preponderance of the evidence on the

defendant that a particular State's witness was an accomplice, thereby raising the rule of corroboration. Proof by a defendant that a State's witness is an accomplice involves no shifting of the burden to the defendant to disprove any fact essential to the offenses charged. Whether or not the witness was an accomplice bears no direct relationship to any element of robbery with a deadly weapon or the use of a handgun in the commission of a felony. *Bennett v. State,* 283 Md. 619, 623, 392 A.2d 76, 80 (1978).

(c) Situations where Mullaney and Evans will result in unconstitutionality

1. The most immediate and direct impact of *Mullaney* is to outlaw in a criminal trial the shifting of the ultimate burden of persuasion onto a defendant, by any standard of proof on any issue. *Evans v. State, supra* at 706, 349 A.2d at 351. One application of this rule is to outlaw any presumption in the "Morgan" tradition that operates to shift the burden of persuasion, as contrasted to merely shifting the burden of going forward to produce evidence. This ruling applies, by way of a partial list of examples, to such defenses as:

a. Any theory of justification (including self-defense in some forms). See *Gunther v. State,* 228 Md. 404, 179 A.2d 880 (1961); *DeVaughn v. State,* 232 Md. 447, 194 A.2d 1091, *cert. denied,* 376 U.S. 927 (1963); *Tichnell v. State,* 287 Md. 695, 415 A.2d 530 (1980). *Cf. Squire v. State,* 32 Md. App. 307, 363 A.2d 520 (1976) (jury instruction which violated the principles of *Mullaney* in placing burden on defendant to prove self-defense is not "plain error").

b. Any theory of excuse (including self-defense in other forms and including accident or misadventure). See *Wilson v. State,* 28 Md. App. 168, 343 A.2d 537 (1975); *Wright v. State,* 29 Md. App. 110, 349 A.2d 421 (1975); *Stambaugh v. State,* 30 Md. App. 707, 353 A.2d 638 (1976); *Jacobs v. State,* 32 Md. App. 509, 363 A.2d 257 (1976); *Milhouse v. State,* 31 Md. App. 571, 358 A.2d 262 (1976); *Hunter v. Williams,* 570 F.2d 510 (4th Cir. 1978).

c. Insanity. A possible exception to the rule prohibiting shifting the burden of persuasion to the defendant is the insanity defense. The insanity defense allegedly is an exculpatory fact related to criminal punishment, as opposed to negating one of the essential elements of the crime. Once the issue of insanity is generated, the defendant has the burden to establish by a preponderance of the evidence the defense of no criminal responsibility. Maryland Ann. Code, Health — General Article, § 12-109(b). Query whether it can be argued that this statutory change violates the constitutional due process standards of *Evans v. State, supra,* and its progeny. While *Evans* may extend the bounds of constitutionality, similar provisions have been impliedly ratified by the United States Supreme Court. See *Jones v. United States,* 463 U.S. 354, 103 S. Ct. 3043, 77 L. Ed. 2d 694 (1983).

d. Any theory of mitigation (including hot-blooded response to legally adequate provocation). See *Evans v. State, supra.* See also *Wentworth v. State,* 29 Md. App. 110, 349 A.2d 421 (1975); *Law v. State,* 29 Md. App. 457, 349 A.2d 295 (1975).

e. Intoxication. Once evidence of the defendant's intoxication is in issue, the State bears the burden of proving beyond a reasonable doubt that the defendant was not so intoxicated as to be incapable of forming the specific intent to commit the crime. *Evans v. State, supra;* but see *Teves v. State,* 33 Md. App. 195, 364 A.2d 503 (1976) (when the State proved beyond a reasonable doubt that a killing was willful, deliberate and premeditated, this negated the defense of voluntary intoxication).

f. Entrapment. The burden of production is on the defendant to generate the issue for the trier of fact. Once the defense of entrapment is raised, the State has the burden of proving beyond any reasonable doubt that the defendant was not induced by a state agent to violate the law. If the State fails to prove the defendant was not induced, then in order to convict, the trier of fact would have to find beyond any reasonable doubt that the defendant was ready and willing to commit the crime charged. In other words, it was the defendant's predisposition rather than any inducement which caused the criminal conduct. *Bowser v. State,* 50 Md. App. 363, 367, 439 A.2d 1, 3 (1981).

g. Duress or coercion. While, as of this writing, there are no Maryland cases on point, *Evans v. State, supra,* supports the proposition that once the issue of duress has been raised by either the State's or the defendant's evidence, the burden is on the State to prove the absence of duress. See also *Wentworth v. State, supra.*

h. Necessity. There are no Maryland cases on point, but there appears to be no reason why the burden of proof relating to the necessity defense is any different than the burden of proof in other defenses. It appears that once sufficient evidence has been introduced to generate the defense, the State has the burden of proving beyond a reasonable doubt that the defendant was not compelled by necessity to do the criminal act.

i. Alibi. Once the issue of the accused's presence at the scene of the crime has been raised by either the State's or the defendant's evidence, the State bears the burden of proving beyond a reasonable doubt the presence of the defendant at the scene of the crime. See *Evans v. State, supra; Grady v. State,* 24 Md. App. 85, 329 A.2d 726 (1974), *aff'd,* 276 Md. 178, 345 A.2d 436 (1975); *Beckette v. State,* 31 Md. App. 85, 355 A.2d 515 (1976).

Table of Cases

A

Abe v. State, 230 Md. 439, 187 A.2d 467 (1963) — § 4.25.
Abney v. State, 244 Md. 444, 223 A.2d 792 (1966) — § 4.22a.
Abrams v. Warden, 333 F. Supp. 612 (D. Md. 1971) — § 4.52.
Adam v. State, 14 Md. App. 135, 286 A.2d 546 (1972) — § 2.22.
Adams v. State, 202 Md. 455, 97 A.2d 281 (1953) — § 4.06.
Adams v. State, 8 Md. App. 684, 262 A.2d 69 (1970) — § 4.21b.
Adcock v. State, 66 Md. App. 454, 504 A.2d 1160 (1986) — § 5.06.
Agnew v. United States, 165 U.S. 36, 17 S. Ct. 235, 41 L. Ed. 624 (1897) — § 1.03.
Agresti v. State, 2 Md. App. 278, 234 A.2d 284 (1967) — §§ 4.02, 4.04.
Aguilar v. Texas, 378 U.S. 108, 84 S. Ct. 1509, 12 L. Ed. 2d 723 (1964) — § 4.80.
Ake v. Oklahoma, 470 U.S. 68, 105 S. Ct. 1087, 84 L. Ed. 2d 53 (1985) — § 5.08.
Akron v. Akron Center for Reprod. Health, 462 U.S. 416, 103 S. Ct. 2481, 76 L. Ed. 2d 687 (1983) — § 4.51.
Alexander v. State, 4 Md. App. 214, 242 A.2d 180 (1968) — § 4.36.
Allen v. State, 230 Md. 533, 188 A.2d 159 (1963) — § 5.08.
Allen v. State, 2 Md. App. 740, 237 A.2d 90 (1968) — § 4.57.
Allen v. State, 39 Md. App. 686, 389 A.2d 909 (1978) — §§ 4.24, 4.25.
Allen v. United States, 164 U.S. 492, 17 S. Ct. 154, 41 L. Ed. 528 (1896) — § 1.13.
Allewalt v. State, 61 Md. App. 503, 487 A.2d 664 (1985) — § 4.36.
Allison v. State, 203 Md. 1, 98 A.2d 273 (1953) — § 2.23.
Alston v. Forsythe, 226 Md. 121, 172 A.2d 474 (1961) — Appx. III.
Alvey v. Hartwig, 106 Md. 254, 67 A. 132 (1907) — § 4.60.
American Legion, Clopper Michael Post No. 10, Inc. v. State, 294 Md. 1, 447 A.2d 842 (1982) — § 4.74.
Anaweck v. State, 63 Md. App. 239, 492 A.2d 658 (1985) — § 2.10.
Anderson v. Department of Health & Mental Hygiene, 64 Md. App. 674, 498 A.2d 679 (1985) — § 5.08.
Anderson v. State, 3 Md. App. 85, 237 A.2d 813 (1968) — § 1.05.
Anderson v. State, 3 Md. App. 362, 239 A.2d 579 (1968) — § 2.24.
Anderson v. State, 9 Md. App. 639, 267 A.2d 302 (1970) — § 4.76.
Anderson v. State, 12 Md. App. 186, 278 A.2d 439 (1971) — § 4.85.
Anderson v. State, 61 Md. App. 436, 487 A.2d 294 (1985) — §§ 4.12, 4.58.
Andrews v. State, 291 Md. 622, 436 A.2d 1315 (1982) — § 2.28.
Anello v. State, 201 Md. 164, 93 A.2d 71 (1952) — §§ 4.71, 4.73.
Anglin v. State, 244 Md. 652, 224 A.2d 668 (1966) — §§ 4.57, 4.91.

Anglin v. State, 1 Md. App. 85, 227 A.2d 364 (1967) — §§ 4.57, 4.79.
Antonelli v. Pugh, 231 Md. 194, 189 A.2d 653 (1963) — § 1.05.
Armour & Co. v. Leasure, 177 Md. 393, 9 A.2d 572 (1939) — § 2.05.
Armstead v. State, 227 Md. 73, 175 A.2d 24 (1961) — § 5.08.
Armstrong v. State, 51 Md. App. 508, 444 A.2d 1049 (1982) — §§ 5.14, 5.16.
Arnold v. State, 7 Md. App. 1, 252 A.2d 878 (1969) — §§ 4.55, 4.57.
Asibem Assoc's v. Rill, 264 Md. 272, 286 A.2d 160 (1972) — § 2.05.
Austin v. United States, 414 F.2d 1155 (8th Cir. 1969) — § 2.24.
Avery v. State, 15 Md. App. 520, 292 A.2d 728 (1972) — § 5.07.
Avery v. State, 249 Md. 385, 240 A.2d 107 (1968) — §§ 5.01, 508.
Avery v. State, 9 Md. App. 227, 263 A.2d 609 (1970) — § 5.08.
A.V. Laurins & Co. v. Prince George's County, 46 Md. App. 548, 420 A.2d 982 (1980) — § 4.59.
Ayre v. State, 291 Md. 155, 433 A.2d 1150 (1981) — § 4.63.

B

Bachellar v. Maryland, 397 U.S. 564, 90 S. Ct. 1312, 25 L. Ed. 2d 570 (1970) — § 4.61.
Baender v. Barnett, 255 U.S. 224, 41 S. Ct. 271, 65 L. Ed. 597 (1921) — § 4.76.
Baer Bros. v. Keller, 208 Md. 556, 119 A.2d 410 (1956) — § 2.05.
Bailey v. State, 6 Md. App. 496, 252 A.2d 85 (1969) — § 2.30.
Bailey v. State, 16 Md. App. 83, 294 A.2d 123 (1972) — § 2.06.
Baker v. State, 205 Md. 42, 106 A.2d 692 (1954) — § 4.65.
Baker v. State, 39 Md. App. 133, 383 A.2d 698 (1978) — § 2.30.
Baldwin v. State, 5 Md. App. 22, 245 A.2d 98 (1968) — §§ 2.08, 2.30.
Ball v. State, 7 Md. App. 219, 254 A.2d 367 (1969) — § 4.55.
Baltimore County v. State, 232 Md. 350, 193 A.2d 30 (1962) — § 2.05.
Baltimore Radio Show, Inc. v. State, 193 Md. 300, 67 A.2d 497 (1949) — § 1.11a.
Banks v. State, 2 Md. App. 373, 234 A.2d 798 (1967) — §§ 2.33, 4.73.
Banks v. State, 8 Md. App. 182, 258 A.2d 924 (1969) — § 4.68.
Barber v. State, 16 Md. App. 235, 295 A.2d 814 (1972) — § 1.11a.
Barger v. State, 2 Md. App. 565, 235 A.2d 751 (1967) — § 5.16.
Barnes v. State, 5 Md. App. 144, 245 A.2d 626 (1968) — § 4.83.
Barnes v. State, 31 Md. App. 25, 354 A.2d 499 (1976) — §§ 1.07, 2.06, 4.84.
Barnett v. State, 5 Md. App. 5, 245 A.2d 104 (1968) — § 4.55.
Barnhart v. State, 5 Md. App. 222, 246 A.2d 280 (1968) — § 2.25.
Bartholomey v. Maryland, 408 U.S. 938, 92 S. Ct. 2870, 33 L. Ed. 2d 759 (1971) — § 5.08.
Bartholomey v. State, 260 Md. 504, 273 A.2d 164 (1971) — § 5.08.

Bartholomey v. State, 267 Md. 175, 297 A.2d 696 (1972) — §§ 4.21c, 5.08.
Barton v. State, 46 Md. App. 616, 420 A.2d 1009 (1980) — § 5.15.
Bartram v. State, 33 Md. App. 115, 364 A.2d 1119 (1976) — §§ 2.25, 4.23b.
Basiliko v. State, 212 Md. 248, 129 A.2d 375 (1957) — § 1.11a.
Baskerville v. State, 23 Md. App. 439, 327 A.2d 918 (1974) — § 4.67.
Basoff v. State, 208 Md. 643, 119 A.2d 917 (1956) — §§ 4.33, 5.02.
Bateman v. State, 10 Md. App. 630, 272 A.2d 64 (1971) — § 4.23b.
Bates v. State, 32 Md. App. 108, 359 A.2d 106 (1976) — § 2.25.
Battle v. State, 287 Md. 675, 414 A.2d 1266 (1980) — § 4.36.
Baumgartner v. State, 21 Md. App. 251, 319 A.2d 592 (1974) — § 4.67.
Beach v. State, 302 Md. 613, 490 A.2d 682 (1985) — § 1.13.
Beard v. State, 71 Md. 275, 17 A. 1044 (1889) — § 4.62.
Beard v. State, 216 Md. 302, 140 A.2d 672 (1958) — § 1.07.
Beard v. State, 4 Md. App. 685, 244 A.2d 906 (1968) — § 4.68.
Beard v. State, 47 Md. App. 410, 423 A.2d 275 (1980) — § 4.44.
Beckette v. State, 31 Md. App. 85, 355 A.2d 515 (1976) — §§ 5.02, 507, Appx. V.
Beckwith v. United States, 425 U.S. 341, 96 S. Ct. 1612, 48 L. Ed. 2d 1 (1976) — § 2.25.
Bedford v. State, 293 Md. 172, 443 A.2d 78 (1982) — §§ 1.04, 2.30.
Bell v. Harrison, 670 F.2d 656 (6th Cir. 1982) — § 4.36.
Bell v. State, 220 Md. 75, 150 A.2d 908 (1959) — § 4.79.
Bell v. State, 236 Md. 356, 204 A.2d 54 (1964) — § 4.85.
Bell v. State, 5 Md. App. 276, 246 A.2d 286 (1968) — § 4.83.
Bell v. State, 48 Md. App. 669, 429 A.2d 300 (1981) — §§ 1.01, 2.06, 2.23, 4.06.
Bellamy v. State, 50 Md. App. 65, 435 A.2d 821 (1981) — § 2.25, Appx. III.
Bennett v. State, 230 Md. 562, 188 A.2d 142 (1963) — § 5.14.
Bennett v. State, 237 Md. 212, 205 A.2d 393 (1964) — §§ 4.42, 4.83.
Bennett v. State, 283 Md. 619, 392 A.2d 76 (1978) — §§ 2.01, 4.34, Appx. V.
Benson v. Mays, 245 Md. 632, 227 A.2d 220 (1967) — § 1.07.
Benton v. State, 1 Md. App. 647, 232 A.2d 541 (1967) — § 2.27.
Benton v. State, 8 Md. App. 388, 260 A.2d 86 (1969) — §§ 4.55, 4.57, 4.69.
Berger v. State, 179 Md. 410, 20 A.2d 146 (1941) — § 2.23.
Berkemer v. McCarty, 468 U.S. 420, 104 S. Ct. 3138, 82 L. Ed. 2d 317 (1984) — §§ 2.25, 4.63.
Berlin v. State, 12 Md. App. 48, 277 A.2d 468 (1971) — §§ 4.77, 5.06.
Berman v. State, 35 Md. App. 193, 370 A.2d 580 (1977) — § 4.67.
Berry v. State, 202 Md. 62, 95 A.2d 319 (1953) — §§ 1.03, 1.05.

Bethlehem-Fairfield Shipyard, Inc. v. Rosenthal, 185 Md. 416, 45 A.2d 79 (1945) — § 4.60.
Bever v. State, 4 Md. App. 436, 243 A.2d 634 (1968) — § 4.57.
Bieber v. State, 8 Md. App. 522, 261 A.2d 202 (1970) — § 4.68.
Biggs v. State, 56 Md. App. 638, 468 A.2d 669 (1983) — § 5.01.
Billinger v. State, 9 Md. App. 628, 267 A.2d 275 (1970) — § 2.30.
Bing Fa Yuen v. State, 43 Md. App. 109, 403 A.2d 819 (1979) — § 2.21.
Bird v. State, 231 Md. 432, 190 A.2d 804 (1963) — § 4.13.
Bishop v. State, 39 Md. App. 384, 385 A.2d 1206 (1978) — § 2.01.
Bivens v. Six Unknown Named Agents of Fed. Bureau of Narcotics, 456 F.2d 1339 (2d Cir. 1972) — § 4.80.
Blackburn v. Copinger, 300 F. Supp. 1127 (D. Md. 1969) — § 2.25.
Blackwell v. State, 278 Md. 466, 365 A.2d 545 (1976) — § 4.21c, Appx. V.
Blackwell v. State, 34 Md. App. 547, 369 A.2d 153 (1977) — §§ 4.22a, 4.24, 4.25, 4.26, 4.63.
Blake v. State, 210 Md. 459, 124 A.2d 273 (1956) — §§ 4.35, 4.63.
Blizzard v. State, 30 Md. App. 156, 351 A.2d 443 (1976) — §§ 2.01, 5.07.
Blockburger v. United States, 284 U.S. 299, 52 S. Ct. 180, 76 L. Ed. 306 (1932) — § 4.21b.
Blondes v. State, 273 Md. 435, 330 A.2d 169 (1975) — § 4.06.
Blotkamp v. State, 45 Md. App. 64, 411 A.2d 1068 (1980) — § 4.36.
Board of County Comm'rs v. Dorcus, 247 Md. 251, 230 A.2d 656 (1967) — § 1.05.
Boggs v. Boggs, 138 Md. 422, 114 A. 474 (1921) — § 4.60.
Boggs v. State, 228 Md. 168, 179 A.2d 338 (1962) — §§ 4.55, 4.57, 4.69.
Bolden v. State, 44 Md. App. 643, 410 A.2d 1085 (1980) — § 4.06.
Boone v. State, 2 Md. App. 80, 233 A.2d 476 (1967) — § 4.05.
Boone v. State, 33 Md. App. 1, 363 A.2d 550 (1976) — § 2.08.
Booth v. State, 62 Md. App. 26, 488 A.2d 195 (1985) — Appx. III.
Borchert v. Borchert, 185 Md. 586, 45 A.2d 463 (1946) — § 4.60.
Borgen v. State, 56 Md. App. 529, 468 A.2d 394 (1983) — § 4.96.
Borza v. State, 25 Md. App. 391, 335 A.2d 142 (1975) — § 4.52.
Bosley v. State, 14 Md. App. 83, 286 A.2d 203 (1972) — § 4.67.
Boswell v. State, 5 Md. App. 571, 249 A.2d 490 (1968) — §§ 2.04, 4.91.
Bowen v. State, 206 Md. 368, 111 A.2d 844 (1955) — §§ 2.33, 472.
Bowen v. State, 5 Md. App. 713, 249 A.2d 499 (1969) — § 2.27.
Bowers v. Hardwick, — U.S. —, 106 S. Ct. 2841, 92 L. Ed. 2d 140 (1986) — § 4.35.
Bowers v. State, 283 Md. 115, 389 A.2d 341 (1978) — § 4.58.
Bowers v. State, 298 Md. 115, 468 A.2d 101 (1983) — §§ 1.04, 4.21c.
Bowers v. State, 306 Md. 120, 507 A.2d 1072 (1986) — § 4.21c.
Bowers v. State, 38 Md. App. 21, 379 A.2d 748 (1977) — § 4.58.
Bowman v. State, 16 Md. App. 384, 297 A.2d 323 (1972) — § 2.22.
Bowser v. State, 136 Md. 342, 110 A. 854 (1920) — §§ 1.06, 4.57.
Bowser v. State, 50 Md. App. 363, 439 A.2d 1 (1981) — § 5.06, Appx. V.

Bowyer v. State, 2 Md. App. 454, 235 A.2d 317 (1967) — § 5.16.
Boyd v. State, 22 Md. App. 539, 323 A.2d 684 (1974) — § 4.25.
Bradbury v. State, 233 Md. 421, 197 A.2d 126 (1964) — §§ 2.25, 2.26, 4.34.
Brady v. Maryland, 373 U.S. 83, 83 S. Ct. 1194, 10 L. Ed. 2d 215 (1963) — §§ 1.01, 2.25, 4.63.
Brafman v. State, 38 Md. App. 465, 381 A.2d 687 (1978) — § 2.10.
Brandau v. Webster, 39 Md. App. 99, 382 A.2d 1103 (1978) — § 2.04.
Braxton v. State, 214 Md. 370, 135 A.2d 307 (1975) — § 1.05.
Braxton v. State, 11 Md. App. 435, 274 A.2d 647 (1971) — §§ 2.07, 2.23, 2.29, 2.30, 5.07.
Breeding v. State, 220 Md. 193, 151 A.2d 743 (1959) — §§ 2.31, 2.33.
Breithaupt v. Abram, 352 U.S. 432, 77 S. Ct. 408, 1 L. Ed. 2d 448 (1957) — § 2.32.
Bremer v. State, 18 Md. App. 291, 307 A.2d 503 (1973) — § 5.08.
Bresnan v. Weaver, 151 Md. 375, 135 A. 584 (1926) — § 1.07.
Brewer v. Mele, 267 Md. 437, 298 A.2d 156 (1972) — § 4.79.
Brewer v. Williams, 430 U.S. 387, 97 S. Ct. 1232, 51 L. Ed. 2d 424 (1977) — § 2.25.
Briscoe v. State, 3 Md. App. 462, 240 A.2d 109 (1968) — § 4.81.
Briscoe v. State, 40 Md. App. 120, 388 A.2d 153 (1978) — § 4.36.
Briscoe v. State, 60 Md. App. 42, 479 A.2d 1385 (1984) — §§ 3.01, 4.63.
Britton v. State, 2 Md. App. 285, 234 A.2d 274 (1967) — § 4.83.
Britton v. State, 10 Md. App. 70, 267 A.2d 747 (1970) — § 2.08.
Broadway v. State, 23 Md. App. 68, 326 A.2d 212 (1974) — §§ 4.02, 4.44.
Brookhart v. State, 238 Md. 625, 209 A.2d 601 (1965) — § 4.41.
Brooks v. Daley, 242 Md. 185, 218 A.2d 184 (1966) — § 2.21.
Brooks v. State, 235 Md. 23, 200 A.2d 177 (1964) — § 4.71.
Brooks v. State, 277 Md. 155, 353 A.2d 217 (1976) — §§ 4.57, 4.69.
Brooks v. State, 284 Md. 416, 397 A.2d 596 (1979) — § 4.42.
Brooks v. State, 2 Md. App. 291, 234 A.2d 467 (1967) — § 4.14.
Brooks v. State, 3 Md. App. 485, 240 A.2d 114 (1968) — § 2.06.
Brooks v. State, 25 Md. App. 194, 333 A.2d 352 (1975) — § 4.55.
Brooks v. State, 32 Md. App. 116, 359 A.2d 217 (1976) — § 2.22.
Brooks v. State, 38 Md. App. 550, 381 A.2d 718 (1978) — §§ 4.41, 4.42.
Brooks v. State, 41 Md. App. 123, 395 A.2d 1224 (1979) — § 4.63.
Brooks v. State, 53 Md. App. 285, 452 A.2d 1285 (1982) — §§ 1.04, 4.36, 5.02.
Brosan v. Cochran, 307 Md. 662, 516 A.2d 970 (1986) — § 4.63.
Brown v. Illinois, 422 U.S. 590, 95 S. Ct. 2254, 45 L. Ed. 2d 416 (1975) — § 2.25.
Brown v. State, 72 Md. 468, 20 A. 186 (1890) — § 4.70.
Brown v. State, 220 Md. 29, 150 A.2d 895 (1959) — § 4.21a.
Brown v. State, 222 Md. 290, 159 A.2d 844 (1960) — § 1.05.
Brown v. State, 225 Md. 610, 171 A.2d 456 (1961) — § 4.78.

Brown v. State, 236 Md. 505, 204 A.2d 532 (1964) — § 4.94.
Brown v. State, 281 Md. 241, 378 A.2d 1104 (1977) — §§ 2.01, 4.34.
Brown v. State, 285 Md. 469, 403 A.2d 788 (1979) — §§ 3.06, 4.52, 4.58.
Brown v. State, 3 Md. App. 313, 239 A.2d 761 (1968) — § 2.25.
Brown v. State, 4 Md. App. 261, 242 A.2d 570 (1968) — §§ 2.25, 5.12, 5.14, 5.15.
Brown v. State, 6 Md. App. 631, 252 A.2d 887 (1969) — §§ 5.01, 5.12.
Brown v. State, 29 Md. App. 467, 349 A.2d 267 (1975) — §§ 4.13, 4.44.
Brown v. State, 44 Md. App. 71, 410 A.2d 17 (1980) — § 4.21a.
Brown v. State, 50 Md. App. 651, 441 A.2d 354 (1982) — § 4.55.
Brown v. State, 64 Md. App. 324, 494 A.2d 999 (1985) — § 4.13.
Bruce v. State, 218 Md. 87, 145 A.2d 428 (1958) — §§ 5.13, 5.15, 5.16.
Brunson v. State, 9 Md. App. 1, 261 A.2d 794 (1970) — § 2.31.
Bruton v. United States, 391 U.S. 123, 88 S. Ct. 1620, 20 L. Ed. 2d 476 (1968) — § 2.22.
Bryant v. State, 229 Md. 531, 185 A.2d 190 (1962) — § 4.76.
Bryant v. State, 4 Md. App. 572, 244 A.2d 446 (1968) — § 4.14.
Bryant v. State, 49 Md. App. 272, 431 A.2d 714 (1981) — §§ 2.06, 2.25.
Buckley v. State, 2 Md. App. 508, 234 A.2d 754 (1967) — § 4.55.
Bullock v. Commonwealth, 249 Ky. 1, 60 S.W.2d 108 (1933) — § 1.05.
Burgess v. State, 161 Md. 162, 155 A. 153 (1931) — § 2.07.
Burgett v. Texas, 389 U.S. 109, 88 S. Ct. 258, 19 L. Ed. 2d 319 (1967) — § 2.07.
Burko v. State, 19 Md. App. 645, 313 A.2d 864 (1974) — § 4.02.
Burley v. State, 5 Md. App. 469, 248 A.2d 404 (1968) — § 2.01.
Burnette v. State, 280 Md. 88, 371 A.2d 663 (1977) — § 1.13.
Burrell v. State, 42 Md. App. 130, 399 A.2d 1354 (1979) — §§ 2.06, 207.
Burroughs v. State, 21 Md. App. 648, 320 A.2d 587 (1974) — § 4.67.
Burton v. State, 7 Md. App. 671, 256 A.2d 826 (1969) — § 2.25.
Burton v. State, 32 Md. App. 529, 363 A.2d 243 (1976) — § 2.25.
Busch v. State, 289 Md. 669, 426 A.2d 954 (1981) — § 4.80.
Butina v. State, 4 Md. App. 312, 242 A.2d 819 (1968) — §§ 4.01, 402, 4.52, 4.83.
Butler v. State, 19 Md. App. 601, 313 A.2d 554 (1974) — § 2.01.
Butler v. State, 46 Md. App. 317, 416 A.2d 773 (1980) — §§ 2.28, 2.29.
Butz v. State, 221 Md. 68, 156 A.2d 423 (1959) — § 4.57.
Byrd v. State, 16 Md. App. 391, 297 A.2d 312 (1972) — §§ 4.77, 5.06.

C

Cahill v. Mayor of Baltimore, 129 Md. 17, 98 A. 235 (1916) — Appxs. II, IV.
Cain v. State, 34 Md. App. 446, 367 A.2d 47 (1977) — § 4.76.
Caldwell v. State, 276 Md. 612, 349 A.2d 623 (1976) — § 4.36.
Caldwell v. State, 26 Md. App. 94, 337 A.2d 476 (1975) — § 4.86.

Calhoun v. State, 297 Md. 563, 468 A.2d 45 (1983) — §§ 1.01, 1.04, 4.21c.
Calhoun v. State, 46 Md. App. 478, 418 A.2d 1241 (1980) — § 4.83.
California v. Prysock, 453 U.S. 355, 101 S. Ct. 2806, 69 L. Ed. 2d 696 (1981) — § 2.25.
California v. Trombetta, 467 U.S. 479, 104 S. Ct. 2528, 81 L. Ed. 2d 413 (1984) — § 4.63.
Campbell v. State, 293 Md. 438, 444 A.2d 1034 (1982) — § 4.21b.
Camphor v. State, 233 Md. 203, 196 A.2d 75 (1963) — § 4.02.
C & P Tel. Co. v. Hicks, 25 Md. App. 503, 337 A.2d 744 (1975) — § 4.21c.
Canter v. State, 224 Md. 483, 168 A.2d 384 (1961) — § 4.34.
Canton Nat'l Bank v. American Bonding & Trust Co., 111 Md. 41, 73 A. 684 (1909) — § 4.71.
Cantrell v. State, 50 Md. App. 331, 437 A.2d 696 (1982) — § 4.36.
Cantwell v. Connecticut, 310 U.S. 296, 60 S. Ct. 900, 84 L. Ed. 1213 (1940) — § 4.61.
Caparella v. State, 214 Md. 355, 135 A.2d 311 (1957) — § 4.65.
Cardovi v. State, 63 Md. App. 455, 492 A.2d 1328 (1985) — § 4.36.
Carey v. State, 19 Md. App. 695, 313 A.2d 696 (1974) — § 4.67.
Carey v. State, 43 Md. App. 246, 405 A.2d 293 (1979) — §§ 4.56, 4.66.
Carey v. State, 54 Md. App. 448, 458 A.2d 90 (1983) — § 4.70.
Carpenter v. United States, 264 F.2d 565 (4th Cir. 1959) — § 4.70.
Carroll v. State, 3 Md. App. 50, 237 A.2d 535 (1968) — § 5.10.
Carroll v. State, 11 Md. App. 412, 274 A.2d 677 (1971) — § 4.21a.
Carter v. Kentucky, 450 U.S. 288, 101 S. Ct. 1112, 67 L. Ed. 2d 241 (1981) — §§ 2.25, 2.27.
Carter v. State, 10 Md. App. 50, 267 A.2d 743 (1970) — § 4.79.
Carter v. State, 36 Md. App. 220, 373 A.2d 308 (1977) — § 2.25.
Carter v. State, 38 Md. App. 400, 381 A.2d 309 (1978) — § 2.33.
Carwell v. State, 2 Md. App. 45, 232 A.2d 903 (1967) — §§ 2.25, 4.80.
Cason v. State, 230 Md. 356, 187 A.2d 103 (1963) — § 4.71.
Casper v. State, 70 Md. App. 576, 521 A.2d 1281 (1987) — § 4.63.
Cates v. State, 21 Md. App. 363, 320 A.2d 75 (1974) — §§ 4.82, 5.03.
Chambers v. State, 3 Md. App. 642, 240 A.2d 644 (1968) — § 4.59.
Chandler v. Florida, 449 U.S. 560, 101 S. Ct. 802, 66 L. Ed. 2d 740 (1981) — § 1.11a.
Chaplinsky v. New Hampshire, 315 U.S. 568, 62 S. Ct. 766, 86 L. Ed. 1031 (1942) — § 4.61.
Chapman v. California, 386 U.S. 18, 87 S. Ct. 824, 17 L. Ed. 2d 705 (1967) — §§ 2.25, 2.28.
Cherry v. State, 18 Md. App. 252, 306 A.2d 634 (1973) — § 4.34.
Chisley v. State, 202 Md. 87, 95 A.2d 577 (1953) — §§ 4.21a, 5.08.
Christ v. Wempe, 219 Md. 627, 150 A.2d 918 (1959) — § 2.05.
Christensen v. State, 274 Md. 133, 333 A.2d 45 (1975) — § 2.21.
Christensen v. State, 33 Md. App. 635, 365 A.2d 562 (1976) — §§ 4.05, 4.12, 4.16.

Christopher v. State, 9 Md. App. 277, 263 A.2d 605 (1970) — § 2.01.
Cicero v. State, 200 Md. 614, 92 A.2d 567 (1952) — § 1.08.
City of Farmington v. Joseph, 91 N.M. 414, 575 P.2d 104 (Ct. App. 1978) — § 4.63.
City of Joliet v. Gregorec, 12 Ill. App. 3d 998, 299 N.E.2d 356 (1973) — § 4.91.
Clark v. State, 379 So. 2d 97 (Fla. 1979) — § 4.21c.
Clark v. State, 284 Md. 260, 396 A.2d 243 (1979) — § 4.65.
Clark v. State, 6 Md. App. 91, 250 A.2d 317 (1969) — § 2.22.
Clark v. State, 48 Md. App. 637, 429 A.2d 287 (1981) — § 2.25.
Clarke v. State, 3 Md. App. 447, 240 A.2d 291 (1968) — § 5.01.
Clarke v. State, 9 Md. App. 570, 266 A.2d 259 (1970) — § 3.03.
Clay v. State, 211 Md. 577, 128 A.2d 634 (1957) — §§ 2.24, 4.25, 4.63.
Claybrooks v. State, 36 Md. App. 295, 374 A.2d 365 (1977) — §§ 2.29, 4.83.
Clemons v. State, 228 Md. 237, 179 A.2d 418 (1962) — § 4.57.
Clemons v. State, 9 Md. App. 127, 262 A.2d 786 (1970) — § 4.41.
Cobb v. State, 2 Md. App. 230, 234 A.2d 155 (1967) — § 4.79.
Coffin v. United States, 156 U.S. 432, 15 S. Ct. 394, 39 L. Ed. 481 (1895) — § 1.03.
Cofflin v. State, 230 Md. 139, 186 A.2d 216 (1962) — §§ 4.71, 4.72.
Cohen v. California, 403 U.S. 15, 91 S. Ct. 1780, 29 L. Ed. 2d 284 (1971) — § 4.61.
Cohen v. State, 173 Md. 216, 195 A. 532 (1937) — § 4.81.
Cohen v. State, 19 Md. App. 85, 309 A.2d 294 (1973) — § 4.59.
Cohen v. United States, 297 F.2d 760 (9th Cir. 1962) — § 1.11a.
Colautti v. Franklin, 439 U.S. 379, 99 S. Ct. 675, 58 L. Ed. 2d 596 (1979) — § 4.51.
Cole v. State, 212 Md. 55, 128 A.2d 437 (1957) — § 5.08.
Cole v. State, 232 Md. 111, 194 A.2d 278 (1963) — § 1.05.
Coleman v. State, 209 Md. 379, 121 A.2d 254 (1956) — § 2.01.
Coleman v. State, 4 Md. App. 386, 243 A.2d 24 (1968) — §§ 1.05, 4.02.
Coleman v. State, 8 Md. App. 65, 258 A.2d 42 (1969) — § 2.30.
Coleman v. State, 35 Md. App. 208, 370 A.2d 174 (1977) — § 2.08.
Coleman v. State, 37 Md. App. 322, 377 A.2d 553 (1977) — § 4.60.
Coleman v. State, 49 Md. App. 210, 431 A.2d 696 (1981) — §§ 1.09, 2.08, 2.11.
Collins v. State, 17 Md. App. 376, 302 A.2d 693 (1973) — § 4.80.
Colorado v. Connelly, 107 S. Ct. 515, 93 L. Ed. 2d 473 (1986) — § 2.25.
Colvin v. State, 299 Md. 88, 472 A.2d 953 (1984) — §§ 4.21a, 4.21c.
Comi v. State, 202 Md. 472, 97 A.2d 129 (1953) — § 2.23.
Comi v. State, 26 Md. App. 511, 338 A.2d 918 (1975) — § 1.08.
Commonwealth v. Bollinger, 197 Pa. Super. 492, 179 A.2d 253 (1962) — § 5.09.

Commonwealth v. Fitzgerald, 376 Mass. 402, 381 N.E.2d 123 (1978) — § 2.30.
Commonwealth v. Mulgrew, 475 Pa. 271, 380 A.2d 349 (1977) — § 5.08.
Commonwealth v. Mutina, 366 Mass. 810, 323 N.E.2d 294 (1975) — § 5.08.
Connecticut v. Barrett, 107 S. Ct. 828, 93 L. Ed. 2d 920 (1987) — § 2.25.
Connecticut v. Menillo, 423 U.S. 9, 96 S. Ct. 170, 46 L. Ed. 2d 152 (1975) — § 4.51.
Connor v. State, 225 Md. 543, 171 A.2d 699 (1961) — § 4.23b.
Connor v. State, 6 Md. App. 261, 250 A.2d 915 (1969) — § 4.72.
Contee v. State, 223 Md. 575, 165 A.2d 889 (1960) — § 1.08.
Contee v. United States, 410 F.2d 249 (D.C. Cir. 1969) — § 5.08.
Cook v. State, 9 Md. App. 214, 263 A.2d 33 (1970) — § 4.21a.
Cook v. State, 62 Md. App. 634, 490 A.2d 1311 (1985) — § 4.63.
Cooper v. State, 205 Md. 162, 106 A.2d 129 (1954) — § 4.15.
Cooper v. State, 220 Md. 183, 152 A.2d 120 (1959) — §§ 2.26, 4.16.
Cooper v. State, 1 Md. App. 190, 228 A.2d 840 (1967) — § 2.25.
Cooper v. State, 9 Md. App. 478, 265 A.2d 569 (1970) — § 4.82.
Cooper v. State, 44 Md. App. 59, 407 A.2d 756 (1979) — §§ 2.33, 4.03, Appx. III.
Copsey v. State, 67 Md. App. 223, 507 A.2d 186 (1986) — § 4.36.
Corbin v. State, 237 Md. 486, 206 A.2d 809 (1965) — §§ 4.41, 5.10.
Corens v. State, 185 Md. 561, 45 A.2d 340 (1946) — § 1.05.
Cornish v. State, 215 Md. 64, 137 A.2d 170 (1957) — § 4.80.
Couplin v. State, 37 Md. App. 567, 378 A.2d 197 (1977) — § 4.44.
Cousins v. State, 230 Md. 2, 185 A.2d 488 (1962) — §§ 2.06, 2.07.
Cousins v. State, 277 Md. 338, 354 A.2d 825 (1976) — §§ 4.16, 4.42.
Cousins v. State, 18 Md. App. 552, 308 A.2d 692 (1973) — § 5.10.
Cover v. State, 297 Md. 398, 466 A.2d 1276 (1983) — § 4.80.
Cox v. State, 69 Md. App. 396, 518 A.2d 132 (1986) — §§ 4.05, 4.23b.
Craddock v. State, 47 Md. App. 513, 424 A.2d 168 (1981) — §§ 4.65, 5.05, 5.18.
Craddock v. State, 64 Md. App. 269, 494 A.2d 971 (1985) — § 4.91.
Craig v. State, 214 Md. 546, 136 A.2d 243 (1957) — § 4.36.
Cranford v. State, 36 Md. App. 393, 373 A.2d 984 (1977) — §§ 1.04, 4.36.
Crawford v. State, 174 Md. 175, 197 A. 866 (1938) — §§ 4.41, 4.42.
Crawford v. State, 231 Md. 354, 190 A.2d 538 (1963) — §§ 5.13, 5.15.
Crawford v. State, 61 Md. App. 620, 487 A.2d 1214 (1985) — §§ 5.13, 5.16, 5.18.
Crews v. Director of Patuxent Inst., 245 Md. 174, 225 A.2d 436 (1967) — § 2.05.
Critzer v. Shegogue, 236 Md. 411, 204 A.2d 180 (1964) — § 2.21.
Croom v. Fiedler, 341 F.2d 909 (6th Cir. 1965) — § 4.63.
Crosby v. State, 2 Md. App. 578, 236 A.2d 33 (1967) — § 4.41.

Cross v. State, 282 Md. 468, 386 A.2d 757 (1978) — §§ 2.10, 4.71, 4.79, 4.91.
Crumb v. State, 1 Md. App. 98, 227 A.2d 369 (1967) — § 4.83.
Cummings v. State, 223 Md. 606, 165 A.2d 886 (1960) — § 4.21a.
Cummings v. State, 7 Md. App. 687, 256 A.2d 894 (1969) — § 5.12.
Cummings v. State, 27 Md. App. 361, 341 A.2d 294 (1975) — § 2.25.
Cunningham v. State, 190 Md. 578, 59 A.2d 337 (1948) — § 4.56.
Cunningham v. State, 58 Md. App. 249, 473 A.2d 40 (1984) — §§ 4.23b, 4.23c, 5.13.
Curley v. State, 215 Md. 382, 137 A.2d 640 (1958) — § 4.62.

D

Daniel v. State, 132 So. 2d 312 (Fla. 1961) — § 4.80.
Daniels v. State, 213 Md. 90, 131 A.2d 267 (1957) — § 1.05.
Daniels v. State, 237 Md. 71, 205 A.2d 295 (1964) — § 4.34.
Daniels v. State, 24 Md. App. 1, 329 A.2d 712 (1974) — § 5.02.
Darby v. State, 3 Md. App. 407, 239 A.2d 584 (1968) — §§ 4.82, 4.83, 5.05.
Darby v. State, 45 Md. App. 585, 414 A.2d 248 (1980) — § 2.25.
Daugherty v. Kessler, 264 Md. 281, 286 A.2d 95 (1972) — § 4.06.
Davidson v. Miller, 276 Md. 54, 344 A.2d 422 (1975) — § 2.05.
Davis v. Alaska, 415 U.S. 308, 94 S. Ct. 1105, 39 L. Ed. 2d 347 (1974) — § 4.36.
Davis v. North Carolina, 384 U.S. 737, 86 S. Ct. 1761, 16 L. Ed. 2d 895 (1966) — § 2.25.
Davis v. State, 39 Md. 355 (1874) — § 1.06.
Davis v. State, 189 Md. 640, 57 A.2d 289 (1948) — § 2.32.
Davis v. State, 202 Md. 463, 97 A.2d 303 (1953) — § 4.41.
Davis v. State, 204 Md. 44, 102 A.2d 816 (1954) — §§ 3.07, 4.13.
Davis v. State, 225 Md. 45, 168 A.2d 884 (1961) — § 4.83.
Davis v. State, 229 Md. 139, 182 A.2d 49 (1962) — § 4.67.
Davis v. State, 237 Md. 97, 205 A.2d 254 (1964) — §§ 2.24, 4.22a.
Davis v. State, 9 Md. App. 48, 262 A.2d 578 (1970) — § 4.76.
Davis v. State, 18 Md. App. 378, 306 A.2d 620 (1973) — § 4.67.
Davis v. State, 48 Md. App. 474, 427 A.2d 1085 (1981) — § 1.01.
Davis v. State, 265 Ind. 476, 355 N.E.2d 836 (1976) — § 5.09.
Dawson v. State, 11 Md. App. 694, 276 A.2d 680 (1971) — § 4.74.
Dawson v. State, 40 Md. App. 640, 395 A.2d 160 (1978) — §§ 5.13, 5.15.
Day v. State, 196 Md. 384, 76 A.2d 729 (1950) — § 2.25.
Day v. State, 2 Md. App. 334, 234 A.2d 894 (1967) — § 1.08.
Dayhoff v. State, 206 Md. 25, 109 A.2d 760 (1954) — § 4.60.
Dayton Power & Light Co. v. Public Util. Comm'n, 292 U.S. 290, 54 S. Ct. 647, 78 L. Ed. 1267 (1934) — § 2.05.
Dean v. State, 46 Md. App. 536, 420 A.2d 288 (1980) — § 4.70.

DeBettencourt v. State, 48 Md. App. 522, 428 A.2d 479 (1981) — §§ 3.04, 3.06, 4.22a, 4.52.
Deinhardt v. State, 29 Md. App. 391, 348 A.2d 286 (1976) — § 4.36.
Dempsey v. State, 277 Md. 134, 355 A.2d 455 (1976) — § 2.25.
Dennis v. Baltimore Transit Co., 189 Md. 610, 56 A.2d 813 (1948) — § 4.85.
Dennis v. Warden, 6 Md. App. 295, 251 A.2d 909 (1969) — § 2.25.
Denton v. State, 77 Md. 527, 26 A. 1022 (1893) — § 4.64.
Derricks v. State, 9 Md. App. 261, 263 A.2d 597 (1970) — § 2.24.
DeVaughn v. State, 232 Md. 447, 194 A.2d 109 (1963) — §§ 4.21a, 5.15, Appx. V.
DiBartolomeo v. State, 61 Md. App. 302, 486 A.2d 256 (1985) — §§ 4.34, 4.35.
Diehl v. State, 294 Md. App. 466, 451 A.2d 115 (1982) — § 4.61.
Dill v. State, 24 Md. App. 695, 332 A.2d 690 (1975) — § 4.61.
Dillon v. State, 277 Md. 571, 357 A.2d 360 (1976) — §§ 1.01, 4.44.
Dillon v. State, 27 Md. App. 579, 342 A.2d 677 (1975) — §§ 2.30, 4.44, Appx. II.
Dillsworth v. State, 66 Md. App. 263, 503 A.2d 734 (1986) — § 4.37.
Dinkins v. State, 29 Md. App. 577, 349 A.2d 676 (1976) — § 4.91, Appx. V.
Dixon v. State, 302 Md. 447, 488 A.2d 962 (1985) — § 4.14.
Dixon v. State, 1 Md. App. 623, 232 A.2d 538 (1967) — § 2.25.
Dobbert v. Florida, 432 U.S. 282, 97 S. Ct. 2290, 53 L. Ed. 2d 344 (1977) — § 1.11a.
Dobson v. State, 24 Md. App. 644, 335 A.2d 124 (1975) — §§ 2.28, 2.30.
Doe v. Bolton, 410 U.S. 179, 93 S. Ct. 739, 35 L. Ed. 2d 201 (1973) — § 4.51.
John Doe v. Commonwealth's Att'y, 403 F. Supp. 1199 (E.D. Va. 1975) — § 4.35.
Dolan v. State, 1 Md. App. 292, 229 A.2d 443 (1967) — § 4.67.
Dorsey v. State, 278 Md. 221, 362 A.2d 642 (1976) — § 4.22a, Appx. V.
Dorsey v. State, 295 Md. 217, 454 A.2d 353 (1983) — § 4.59.
Dorsey v. State, 9 Md. App. 80, 262 A.2d 591 (1970) — § 2.06.
Dorsey v. State, 29 Md. App. 97, 349 A.2d 414 (1975) — § 4.23b.
Dorsey v. State, 56 Md. App. 54, 466 A.2d 546 (1983) — § 4.59.
Doswell v. State, 53 Md. App. 647, 455 A.2d 995 (1983) — § 4.76.
Dougherty v. Dougherty, 189 Md. 316, 55 A.2d 787 (1947) — § 4.60.
Douglas v. State, 37 Md. App. 557, 378 A.2d 189 (1977) — §§ 2.30, 4.43.
Dove v. State, 47 Md. App. 452, 423 A.2d 597 (1980) — §§ 1.05, 4.44.
Downs v. State, 278 Md. 610, 366 A.2d 41 (1976) — § 4.61.
Doyal v. State, 226 Md. 31, 171 A.2d 470 (1960) — § 4.33.
Doyle v. Ohio, 426 U.S. 610, 96 S. Ct. 2240, 49 L. Ed. 2d 91 (1976) — §§ 2.09, 2.25.
Draper v. State, 231 Md. 423, 190 A.2d 643 (1963) — § 4.68.

Dravo v. State, 46 Md. App. 622, 420 A.2d 1012 (1980) — § 5.06.
Drews v. State, 224 Md. 186, 167 A.2d 341 (1961) — § 4.61.
Drouin v. State, 222 Md. 271, 160 A.2d 85 (1960) — § 4.57.
Dubs v. State, 2 Md. App. 524, 235 A.2d 764 (1967) — § 5.08.
Duckett v. State, 3 Md. App. 563, 240 A.2d 332 (1968) — § 2.25.
Duckett v. State, 61 Md. App. 151, 485 A.2d 691 (1985) — § 2.07.
Dudonis v. State, 9 Md. App. 245, 263 A.2d 624 (1970) — § 1.04.
Duffin v. State, 229 Md. 434, 184 A.2d 624 (1962) — §§ 2.06, 4.16.
Duffy v. State, 243 Md. 425, 221 A.2d 653 (1966) — § 5.02.
Dugdale v. Regina, 1 El. and Bl. 435, 118 Eng. Rep. 499 (1853) — § 4.76.
Duley v. State, 56 Md. App. 275, 467 A.2d 776 (1983) — § 4.58.
Dunaway v. New York, 442 U.S. 200, 99 S. Ct. 2248, 60 L. Ed. 2d 824 (1979) — § 2.25.
Duncan v. State, 5 Md. App. 440, 248 A.2d 176 (1968) — §§ 3.04, 4.75.
Duncan v. State, 64 Md. App. 45, 494 A.2d 235 (1985) — § 2.26.
Dunlap v. State, 1 Md. App. 444, 230 A.2d 690 (1967) — § 2.06.
Duren v. State, 203 Md. 584, 102 A.2d 277 (1954) — § 4.25.
Durkin v. State, 284 Md. 445, 397 A.2d 600 (1979) — § 5.07.
Dutton v. Evans, 400 U.S. 74, 91 S. Ct. 210, 27 L. Ed. 2d 213 (1970) — § 4.06.
Duvall v. Potomac Elec. Power Co., 234 Md. 42, 197 A.2d 893 (1964) — § 2.05.
Dyson v. State, 6 Md. App. 453, 251 A.2d 606 (1969) — § 2.24.

E

Earhart v. State, 48 Md. App. 695, 429 A.2d 557 (1981) — § 2.22.
Eastman v. State, 47 Md. App. 162, 422 A.2d 41 (1980) — § 1.08.
Eccles v. State, 59 Md. App. 554, 476 A.2d 1183 (1984) — § 4.37.
Eddings v. Oklahoma, 455 U.S. 104, 102 S. Ct. 869, 71 L. Ed. 2d 1 (1982) — § 4.21c.
Edington v. United States, 164 U.S. 361, 17 S. Ct. 72, 41 L. Ed. 467 (1896) — § 2.23.
Edmonds v. State, 5 Md. App. 132, 245 A.2d 618 (1968) — § 2.31.
Edmonds v. State, 18 Md. App. 55, 305 A.2d 205 (1973) — § 4.35.
Edwards v. Arizona, 451 U.S. 477, 101 S. Ct. 1880, 68 L. Ed. 2d 378 (1981) — § 2.25.
Edwards v. State, 198 Md. 132, 81 A.2d 631 (1951) — § 1.05.
Edwards v. State, 31 Md. App. 562, 358 A.2d 590 (1976) — § 4.22a, Appx. V.
Eggleston v. State, 4 Md. App. 124, 241 A.2d 433 (1968) — §§ 4.15, 4.36.
Ehrlich v. State, 42 Md. 730, 403 A.2d 371 (1979) — § 2.25.
Elchin v. State, 47 Md. App. 358, 424 A.2d 155 (1980) — § 4.44, Appx. I.
Eley v. State, 288 Md. 548, 419 A.2d 384 (1980) — § 1.08.
Ellerba v. State, 41 Md. App. 712, 398 A.2d 1250 (1979) — § 4.52.

Elliott v. State, 215 Md. 152, 137 A.2d 130 (1957) — §§ 3.04, 3.06.
Empire State Ins. Co. v. Guerriero, 193 Md. 506, 69 A.2d 259 (1949) — § 2.05.
England v. State, 21 Md. App. 412, 320 A.2d 66 (1974) — §§ 2.29, 4.36.
Enmond v. Florida, 458 U.S. 782, 102 S. Ct. 3368, 73 L. Ed. 2d 1140 (1982) — § 4.21c.
Epperson v. United States, App. D.C., 495 A.2d 1170 (1985) — § 1.13.
Estelle v. Smith, 451 U.S. 454, 101 S. Ct. 1866, 68 L. Ed. 2d 359 (1981) — § 5.08.
Estes v. Texas, 381 U.S. 532, 85 S. Ct. 1628, 14 L. Ed. 2d 543 (1965) — § 1.11a.
Evans v. State, 278 Md. 197, 362 A.2d 629 (1976) — § 5.18.
Evans v. State, 304 Md. 487, 499 A.2d 1261 (1985) — § 4.21c.
Evans v. State, 11 Md. App. 451, 274 A.2d 653 (1971) — §§ 4.41, 4.80.
Evans v. State, 28 Md. App. 640, 349 A.2d 300 (1975) — §§ 1.02, 2.01, 4.13, 4.22a, 4.43, 4.91, 4.97 (Intro. Comment), 5.01, 5.02, 5.05, 5.06, 5.08, 5.11, 5.17, Appx. V.
Everhart v. State, 20 Md. App. 71, 315 A.2d 80 (1974) — § 4.62.
Ewell v. State, 207 Md. 288, 114 A.2d 66 (1955) — §§ 3.04, 4.60.
Ex parte Maulsby, 13 Md. 625 (1859) — § 4.59.

F

Fabian v. State, 235 Md. 306, 201 A.2d 511 (1964) — §§ 4.01, 4.55, 4.58.
Fabian v. State, 3 Md. App. 270, 239 A.2d 100 (1968) — § 4.65.
Fabritz v. Traurig, 583 F.2d 697 (4th Cir. 1978) — § 4.58.
Facyson v. State, 35 Md. App. 202, 370 A.2d 158 (1977) — §§ 2.23, 5.07.
Farley v. State, 3 Md. App. 584, 240 A.2d 296 (1968) — § 1.05.
Farlow v. State, 9 Md. App. 515, 265 A.2d 578 (1970) — §§ 4.64, 4.67, 4.71, 4.72.
Farrow v. State, 233 Md. 526, 197 A.2d 434 (1963) — § 4.14.
Farrow v. Warden, Md. Penitentiary, 241 Md. 724, 217 A.2d 270 (1966) — § 1.10.
Faulcon v. State, 211 Md. 249, 126 A.2d 858 (1956) — §§ 3.04, 3.06, 4.21a, 4.22a.
Fedder v. Component Structures Corp., 23 Md. App. 375, 329 A.2d 56 (1974) — § 5.17.
Feiner v. New York, 340 U.S. 315, 71 S. Ct. 303, 95 L. Ed. 295 (1951) — § 4.61.
Felkner v. State, 218 Md. 300, 146 A.2d 424 (1958) — §§ 4.55, 4.57, 4.91.
Ferguson v. State, 488 P.2d 1032 (Alaska 1971) — § 5.02.
Ferraro v. State, 200 Md. 274, 89 A.2d 628 (1952) — § 5.06.
Ferrel v. State, 60 Md. App. 459, 483 A.2d 777 (1984) — § 4.21a.
Fields v. State, 50 Md. App. 717, 439 A.2d 1121 (1982) — § 4.55.

Finke v. State, 56 Md. App. 450, 468, A.2d 353 (1983) — §§ 4.55, 4.57, 4.69.
Finnegan v. State, 33 Md. App. 251, 364 A.2d 124 (1976) — §§ 4.13, 4.23c, 5.11, 5.14, 5.15, Appx. V.
First Nat'l Bank & Trust v. State, 141 Ga. App. 471, 233 S.E.2d 861 (1977) — § 5.03.
Fisher v. State, 5 Md. App. 155, 245 A.2d 624 (1968) — § 4.75.
Fisher v. State, 28 Md. App. 243, 345 A.2d 110 (1975) — § 5.06.
Fisher v. United States, 328 U.S. 463, 66 S. Ct. 1318, 90 L. Ed. 1382 (1945) — § 5.08.
Fitzwater v. State, 57 Md. App. 274, 469 A.2d 909 (1984) — § 4.63.
Fleeger v. State, 301 Md. 155, 482 A.2d 490 (1984) — § 4.65.
Fleming v. Prince George's County, 277 Md. 655, 358 A.2d 892 (1976) — § 2.08.
Fletcher v. State, 231 Md. 190, 189 A.2d 641 (1963) — § 4.73.
Fletcher v. State, 8 Md. App. 153, 258 A.2d 781 (1969) — § 1.13.
Fletcher v. State, 6 Md. App. 219, 251 A.2d 35 (1969) — § 5.02.
Fletcher v. State, 50 Md. App. 349, 437 A.2d 901 (1982) — § 2.06.
Fletcher v. United States, 158 F.2d 321 (D.C. Cir. 1946) — § 2.02.
Floyd v. State, 205 Md. 573, 109 A.2d 729 (1954) — § 5.02.
Floyd v. State, 42 Md. App. 167, 399 A.2d 932 (1979) — § 4.25.
Folk v. State, 11 Md. App. 508, 275 A.2d 184 (1971) — § 4.76.
Ford v. State, 85 Md. 465, 37 A. 172 (1897) — § 4.74.
Ford v. State, 237 Md. 266, 205 A.2d 809 (1965) — § 4.65.
Ford v. State, 274 Md. 546, 337 A.2d 81 (1975) — § 4.44.
Ford v. State, 11 Md. App. 654, 276 A.2d 423 (1971) — § 2.01.
Ford v. State, 37 Md. App. 373, 377 A.2d 577 (1977) — § 4.76.
Ford v. Wainwright, 477 U.S. —, 106 S. Ct. 2595, 91 L. Ed. 2d 335 (1986) — § 4.21c.
Foster v. State, 230 Md. 256, 186 A.2d 619 (1962) — § 2.26.
Foster v. State, 263 Md. 388, 283 A.2d 411 (1971) — § 2.01.
Foster v. State, 272 Md. 273, 323 A.2d 419 (1974) — §§ 2.28, 2.30.
Foster v. State, 297 Md. 191, 464 A.2d 986 (1983) — §§ 4.21b, 4.82.
Foster v. State, 304 Md. 439, 499 A.2d 1236 (1985) — § 4.21c.
Foster, Evans, Huffington v. State, 305 Md. 306, 503 A.2d 1326 (1986) — § 4.21c.
Fouche v. Masters, 47 Md. App. 11, 420 A.2d 1279 (1980) — § 4.63.
Fowler v. State, 18 Md. App. 37, 305 A.2d 200 (1973) — § 4.91.
Fowlkes v. State, 53 Md. App. 39, 451 A.2d 1270 (1982) — § 1.13.
France v. Safe Deposit & Trust Co., 176 Md. 306, 4 A.2d 717 (1939) — § 4.21c.
Franczkowski v. State, 239 Md. 126, 210 A.2d 504 (1965) — § 4.67.
Frank v. State, 6 Md. App. 332, 251 A.2d 249 (1969) — §§ 4.36, 5.01.
Franklin v. State, 6 Md. App. 572, 252 A.2d 487 (1969) — § 2.25.

Franklin v. State, 8 Md. App. 134, 258 A.2d 767 (1969) — §§ 2.25, 2.26, 4.76.
Franklin v. State, 18 Md. App. 651, 308 A.2d 752 (1973) — § 5.10.
Franklin v. State, 33 Md. App. 690, 366 A.2d 111 (1976) — § 2.25.
Franklin v. State, 60 Md. App. 277, 482 A.2d 168 (1984) — § 4.92.
Frasher v. State, 8 Md. App. 439, 260 A.2d 656 (1970) — §§ 2.33, 5.05, 5.18.
Frazier v. State, 3 Md. App. 470, 240 A.2d 306 (1968) — § 1.08.
Frazier v. State, 5 Md. App. 88, 245 A.2d 614 (1968) — § 4.83.
Fried v. State, 42 Md. App. 643, 402 A.2d 101 (1979) — § 2.25.
Frye v. State, 62 Md. App. 310, 489 A.2d 71 (1985) — § 4.05.
Fuller v. State, 45 Md. App. 414, 413 A.2d 277 (1980) — § 4.21a.
Funkhouser v. State, 51 Md. App. 16, 440 A.2d 1114 (1982) — §§ 1.08, 4.02, Appx. III.
Furman v. Georgia, 408 U.S. 238, 92 S. Ct. 2726, 33 L. Ed. 2d 346 (1972) — § 4.21c.

G

Gainer v. State, 40 Md. App. 382, 391 A.2d 856 (1978) — §§ 5.13, 5.15, 5.16.
Gannett Co. v. DePasquale, 443 U.S. 368, 99 S. Ct. 2898, 61 L. Ed. 2d 608 (1979) — § 1.11a.
Gardner v. State, 286 Md. 520, 408 A.2d 1317 (1979) — § 4.06.
Gardner v. State, 6 Md. App. 483, 251 A.2d 901 (1969) — §§ 2.01, 4.71.
Gardner v. State, 8 Md. App. 694, 261 A.2d 799 (1970) — § 4.83.
Garlitz v. State, 71 Md. 293, 18 A. 39 (1889) — §§ 1.11a, 4.23b.
Garrett v. State, 59 Md. App. 97, 474 A.2d 931 (1984) — § 2.24.
Garrity v. New Jersey, 385 U.S. 493, 87 S. Ct. 616, 17 L. Ed. 2d 562 (1967) — § 2.25.
Gaskins v. State, 7 Md. App. 99, 253 A.2d 759 (1969) — § 2.01.
Gatewood v. State, 15 Md. App. 314, 290 A.2d 551 (1972) — § 4.78.
Gaudio v. State, 1 Md. App. 455, 230 A.2d 700 (1967) — §§ 1.07, 2.25.
Gazaille v. State, 2 Md. App. 462, 235 A.2d 306 (1967) — §§ 4.57, 4.69.
Ghassemien v. Schafer, 52 Md. App. 31, 447 A.2d 84 (1982) — Appx. III.
Gibson v. State, 238 Md. 414, 209 A.2d 242 (1965) — § 4.75.
Gibson v. State, 4 Md. App. 222, 242 A.2d 204 (1968) — § 5.10.
Gibson v. State, 8 Md. App. 1, 256 A.2d 890 (1969) — § 4.73.
Gibson v. State, 17 Md. App. 246, 300 A.2d 692 (1973) — § 4.81.
Gilbert v. California, 388 U.S. 263, 87 S. Ct. 1951, 18 L. Ed. 2d 1178 (1967) — §§ 2.28, 2.30.
Gilbert v. State, 36 Md. App. 196, 373 A.2d 311 (1977) — Appx. V.
Giles v. State, 229 Md. 370, 183 A.2d 359 (1962) — §§ 1.01, 4.36.
Giles v. State, 8 Md. App. 721, 261 A.2d 806 (1970) — § 4.82.
Gill v. State, 11 Md. App. 378, 274 A.2d 667 (1971) — § 2.25.

Gladden v. State, 273 Md. 383, 330 A.2d 176 (1974) — §§ 4.21a, 4.22a.
Gladden v. State, 20 Md. App. 492, 316 A.2d 319 (1974) — § 3.01.
Glaros v. State, 223 Md. 272, 164 A.2d 461 (1960) — § 1.05.
Glenn v. State, 68 Md. App. 379, 511 A.2d 1110 (1986) — §§ 4.13, 4.22a.
Globe Newspaper Co. v. Superior Court, 457 U.S. 596, 102 S. Ct. 2613, 73 L. Ed. 2d 248 (1982) — § 1.11a.
GMC v. Wernsing, 54 Md. App. 19, 456 A.2d 939 (1983) — Appx. IV.
Godfrey v. Georgia, 446 U.S. 420, 100 S. Ct. 1759, 64 L. Ed. 2d 398 (1980) — § 4.21c.
Godwin v. State, 38 Md. App. 716, 382 A.2d 596 (1977) — §§ 2.06, 2.28, 2.30, 4.22a.
Goldsborough v. State, 12 Md. App. 346, 278 A.2d 623 (1971) — § 4.59.
Gooch v. State, 34 Md. App. 331, 367 A.2d 90 (1976) — §§ 2.23, 4.37, 5.07, Appx. III.
Gooding v. Wilson, 405 U.S. 518, 92 S. Ct. 1103, 31 L. Ed. 2d 408 (1972) — § 4.61.
Goodman v. State, 237 Md. 64, 205 A.2d 53 (1964) — § 2.33.
Goodmuth v. State, 302 Md. 613, 490 A.2d 682 (1985) — § 1.13.
Gordon v. State, 5 Md. App. 291, 246 A.2d 623 (1968) — § 4.64.
Gorski v. State, 1 Md. App. 200, 228 A.2d 835 (1967) — § 2.10.
Grady v. State, 24 Md. App. 85, 329 A.2d 726 (1974) — § 5.02, Appx. V.
Graef v. State, 1 Md. App. 161, 228 A.2d 480 (1967) — § 1.11a.
Graham v. State, 239 Md. 521, 212 A.2d 287 (1965) — § 4.80.
Graham v. State, 13 Md. App. 171, 282 A.2d 162 (1971) — §§ 1.04, 1.05, 4.83.
Grandison v. State, 305 Md. 685, 506 A.2d 580 (1986) — §§ 4.21c, 5.08.
Grant v. State, 55 Md. App. 1, 461 A.2d 524 (1983) — § 5.07.
Graves v. United States, 150 U.S. 118, 14 S. Ct. 40, 37 L. Ed. 1021 (1893) — § 2.21.
Gray v. Lucas, 710 F.2d 1048 (5th Cir. 1983) — § 4.21c.
Gray v. State, 216 Md. 410, 140 A.2d 643 (1958) — § 4.41.
Gray v. State, 4 Md. App. 175, 241 A.2d 909 (1968) — § 5.12.
Gray v. State, 6 Md. App. 677, 253 A.2d 395 (1969) — §§ 4.23b, 5.04.
Gray v. State, 10 Md. App. 478, 271 A.2d 390 (1970) — §§ 2.06, 4.82, 4.83.
Gray v. State, 43 Md. App. 238, 403 A.2d 853 (1979) — § 4.34.
Graybeal v. State, 13 Md. App. 557, 284 A.2d 37 (1971) — §§ 4.76, 4.77.
Graynor v. State, 50 Md. App. 600, 440 A.2d 399 (1982) — § 2.25.
Green v. State, 161 Md. 75, 155 A.2d 164 (1931) — § 4.36.
Green v. State, 243 Md. 75, 220 A.2d 131 (1966) — § 4.36.
Green v. State, 243 Md. 154, 220 A.2d 544 (1966) — § 2.08.
Green v. State, 32 Md. App. 567, 363 A.2d 530 (1976) — § 4.68.
Green v. State, 35 Md. App. 510, 371 A.2d 1112 (1977) — 2.28.
Green v. State, 49 Md. App. 1, 430 A.2d 1122 (1981) — §§ 2.01, 2.06.

Green v. State, 153 Tex. Crim. App. 442, 221 S.W.2d 612 (1949) — § 5.09.
Greene v. McElroy, 360 U.S. 474, 79 S. Ct. 1400, 3 L. Ed. 2d 1377 (1969) — § 4.36.
Greenwald v. State, 221 Md. 245, 157 A.2d 119 (1959) — § 4.06.
Greenway v. State, 8 Md. App. 194, 259 A.2d 89 (1969) — §§ 3.03, 3.04, 3.06.
Gregg v. Georgia, 428 U.S. 153, 96 S. Ct. 2909, 49 L. Ed. 2d 859 (1976) — § 4.21c.
Gregoire v. State, 211 Md. 514, 128 A.2d 243 (1957) — §§ 4.33, 4.34, 4.35, 4.36.
Gregory v. State, 40 Md. App. 297, 391 A.2d 437 (1978) — § 5.08.
Griffin v. California, 380 U.S. 609, 85 S. Ct. 1229, 14 L. Ed. 2d 106 (1965) — § 2.27.
Griffith v. Pullman Co., 142 Md. 514, 121 A. 362 (1923) — § 2.05.
Grimes v. State, 290 Md. 236, 429 A.2d 228 (1981) — § 4.55.
Grimes v. State, 44 Md. App. 580, 409 A.2d 767 (1980) — § 2.25.
Grindstaff v. State, 57 Md. App. 812, 470 A.2d 809 (1984) — § 4.56.
Groham v. State, 258 Md. 552, 267 A.2d 193 (1970) — § 5.06.
Guardino v. State, 50 Md. App. 695, 440 A.2d 1101 (1982) — §§ 1.01, 4.36.
Guerriero v. State, 213 Md. 545, 132 A.2d 466 (1957) — §§ 5.04, 5.12.
Gunther v. State, 228 Md. 404, 179 A.2d 880 (1962) — §§ 4.22a, 5.13, 5.16, Appx. V.
Gunther v. State, 4 Md. App. 181, 241 A.2d 907 (1967) — § 2.07.

H

Hackley v. State, 237 Md. 566, 207 A.2d 475 (1965) — § 4.55.
Hadder v. State, 238 Md. 341, 209 A.2d 70 (1965) — §§ 2.25, 4.82.
Haina v. State, 30 Md. App. 295, 352 A.2d 874 (1976) — § 4.06.
Halcomb v. State, 6 Md. App. 32, 250 A.2d 119 (1969) — §§ 4.71, 4.82, 4.83.
Hale v. State, 5 Md. App. 326, 247 A.2d 409 (1968) — §§ 2.25, 4.73.
Haley v. State, 7 Md. App. 18, 253 A.2d 424 (1969) — § 4.76.
Hall v. State, 233 Md. 378, 196 A.2d 874 (1964) — § 2.31.
Hall v. State, 292 Md. 683, 441 A.2d 708 (1982) — § 2.25, Appx. III.
Hall v. State, 1 Md. App. 392, 230 A.2d 473 (1967) — § 4.57.
Hall v. State, 47 Md. App. 590, 425 A.2d 227 (1981) — §§ 2.08, 2.09.
Hall v. State, 69 Md. App. 37, 516 A.2d 204 (1986) — § 4.13.
Hall v. Warden, 214 Md. 652, 135 A.2d 895 (1957) — § 4.60.
Hall v. Warden, 313 F.2d 483 (4th Cir. 1963) — § 2.25.
Hallengren v. State, 14 Md. App. 43, 286 A.2d 213 (1972) — § 5.07.
Hamilton v. State, 12 Md. App. 91, 277 A.2d 460 (1972) — § 1.13.

Hammer v. United States, 271 U.S. 620, 46 S. Ct. 603, 70 L. Ed. 1118 (1926) — § 4.78.
Hammond v. Lancaster, 194 Md. 462, 71 A.2d 474 (1950) — § 4.06.
Hammond v. State, 241 Md. 733, 217 A.2d 569 (1966) — § 5.10.
Hampton v. United States, 425 U.S. 484, 96 S. Ct. 1646, 48 L. Ed. 2d 113 (1976) — § 5.06.
Hands v. Warden, 205 Md. 642, 109 A.2d 51 (1954) — § 4.60.
Handy v. State, 23 Md. App. 239, 326 A.2d 189 (1974) — § 4.02.
Hannah v. State, 3 Md. App. 325, 239 A.2d 124 (1968) — §§ 2.31, 4.57.
Hansford v. United States, 112 U.S. App. D.C. 359, 303 F.2d 219 (1962) — § 5.06.
Hardesty v. State, 223 Md. 559, 165 A.2d 761 (1960) — § 1.07.
Hardiman v. State, 50 Md. App. 98, 436 A.2d 923 (1981) — § 5.06.
Harding v. Ja Laur Corp., 20 Md. App. 209, 315 A.2d 132 (1974) — § 4.68.
Hardison v. State, 226 Md. 53, 172 A.2d 407 (1961) — § 4.55.
Hargis v. Warden, 3 Md. App. 76, 237 A.2d 807 (1968) — § 2.25.
Harker v. State, 55 Md. App. 460, 463 A.2d 288 (1983) — § 2.30.
Harris v. New York, 401 U.S. 222, 91 S. Ct. 643, 28 L. Ed. 2d 1 (1971) — §§ 2.09, 2.25.
Harris v. State, 237 Md. 299, 206 A.2d 254 (1965) — § 4.61.
Harris v. State, 1 Md. App. 318, 229 A.2d 604 (1967) — § 2.21.
Harris v. State, 27 Md. App. 547, 342 A.2d 305 (1975) — § 4.67.
Harrison v. State, 276 Md. 122, 345 A.2d 830 (1975) — § 2.10.
Harrison v. State, 3 Md. App. 148, 238 A.2d 153 (1968) — § 4.82.
Hart v. Warden, 213 Md. 658, 132 A.2d 592 (1957) — § 4.14.
Hartley v. State, 4 Md. App. 450, 243 A.2d 665 (1968) — § 4.82.
Hasselhoff v. State, 67 Md. App. 645, 508 A.2d 1030 (1986) — § 4.63.
Hawkins v. State, 291 Md. 688, 436 A.2d 900 (1981) — §§ 1.08, 4.69.
Hawkins v. State, 34 Md. App. 82, 366 A.2d 421 (1976) — § 5.08.
Hayes v. State, 211 Md. 111, 126 A.2d 576 (1956) — §§ 4.42, 4.82, 4.83.
Hayes v. State, 57 Md. App. 489, 470 A.2d 1301 (1984) — § 2.21.
Hazel v. State, 221 Md. 464, 157 A.2d 922 (1960) — § 4.36.
Hebb v. State, 10 Md. App. 145, 268 A.2d 578 (1970) — § 4.55.
Hebron v. State, 13 Md. App. 134, 281 A.2d 547 (1971) — § 4.80.
Heinze v. Murphy, 180 Md. 423, 24 A.2d 917 (1942) — § 4.61.
Henderson v. Maryland Nat'l Bank, 278 Md. 514, 366 A.2d 1 (1976) — § 1.05.
Henderson v. State, 13 Md. App. 384, 283 A.2d 418 (1971) — §§ 4.06, 4.76.
Hennessy v. State, 37 Md. App. 559, 378 A.2d 205 (1977) — §§ 2.23, 5.07.
Herbert v. State, 31 Md. App. 48, 354 A.2d 449 (1976) — §§ 4.57, 4.69.
Hernandez v. State, 7 Md. App. 355, 255 A.2d 449 (1969) — §§ 2.08, 2.24.
Hickman v. State, 1 Md. App. 578, 232 A.2d 282 (1967) — § 4.57.
Hignut v. State, 17 Md. App. 399, 303 A.2d 173 (1973) — § 4.80.

Hill v. State, 231 Md. 458, 190 A.2d 795 (1963) — § 4.06.
Hill v. State, 237 Md. 630, 206 A.2d 677 (1965) — § 4.76.
Hillard v. State, 286 Md. 145, 406 A.2d 415 (1979) — § 2.25.
Himmel v. State, 9 Md. App. 395, 264 A.2d 874 (1970) — § 1.04.
Hines v. State, 34 Md. App. 612, 368 A.2d 509 (1977) — §§ 1.05, 4.52.
Hines v. State, 58 Md. App. 637, 473 A.2d 1335 (1984) — § 2.24.
Hobbs v. Pepersack, 301 F.2d 875 (4th Cir. 1962) — § 4.83.
Hobbs v. Pepersack, 206 F. Supp. 301 (D. Md. 1962) — § 4.83.
Hobbs v. Warden, 223 Md. 651, 163 A.2d 331 (1960) — § 4.12.
Holbrook v. State, 6 Md. App. 265, 250 A.2d 904 (1969) — §§ 1.03, 207.
Holland v. State, 244 Md. 671, 224 A.2d 864 (1966) — § 2.25.
Holland v. United States, 348 U.S. 121, 75 S. Ct. 127, 99 L. Ed. 150 (1954) — § 1.04.
Holle v. State, 26 Md. App. 267, 337 A.2d 163 (1975) — § 4.83.
Holloway v. State, 26 Md. App. 382, 339 A.2d 319 (1975) — §§ 1.05, 2.25.
Holmes v. State, 10 Md. App. 253, 269 A.2d 175 (1970) — § 4.82.
Holmes v. State, 63 Md. App. 159, 492 A.2d 351 (1985) — § 2.07.
Holmes v. United States, 363 F.2d 281 (D.C. Cir. 1966) — § 5.08.
Holt v. State, 50 Md. App. 578, 438 A.2d 1386 (1982) — §§ 4.12, 4.37, 5.01, 5.08.
Holt v. United States, 218 U.S. 245, 31 S. Ct. 2, 54 L. Ed. 1021 (1910) — §§ 1.03, 1.11a.
Holtman v. State, 12 Md. App. 168, 278 A.2d 82 (1971) — §§ 4.57, 4.82.
Hopt v. Utah, 120 U.S. 430, 7 S. Ct. 614, 30 L. Ed. 708 (1887) — § 1.10.
Horn v. State, 29 Md. App. 23, 349 A.2d 372 (1975) — § 4.91, Appx. V.
Hounshell v. State, 61 Md. App. 364, 486 A.2d 789 (1985) — § 4.21a.
Hourie v. State, 53 Md. App. 62, 452 A.2d 440 (1982) — § 4.78.
Hoverter v. Director of Patuxent Inst., 231 Md. 608, 188 A.2d 696 (1963) — § 2.21.
Howard v. State, 240 Md. 699, 213 A.2d 288 (1965) — § 4.55.
Howell v. State, 278 Md. 389, 364 A.2d 797 (1976) — § 4.43.
Howell v. State, 56 Md. App. 675, 468 A.2d 688 (1983) — § 4.03.
Howell v. State, 62 Md. App. 278, 489 A.2d 55 (1985) — §§ 4.01, 4.03.
Howes v. State, 141 Md. 532, 119 A. 297 (1922) — § 4.42.
Huber v. State, 2 Md. App. 245, 234 A.2d 264 (1967) — § 2.07.
Huff v. State, 23 Md. App. 211, 326 A.2d 198 (1974) — § 4.01.
Huffington v. State, 304 Md. 559, 500 A.2d 272 (1985) — § 4.21c.
Hughes v. State, 6 Md. App. 389, 251 A.2d 373 (1969) — § 4.52.
Hughes v. State, 14 Md. App. 497, 287 A.2d 299 (1972) — § 4.35.
Hughes v. State, 56 Md. App. 12, 466 A.2d 533 (1983) — § 1.05.
Humphrey v. State, 39 Md. App. 484, 386 A.2d 1238 (1978) — § 2.25.
Humphreys v. State, 227 Md. 115, 175 A.2d 777 (1961) — § 4.36.
Hunt v. State, 2 Md. App. 443, 234 A.2d 785 (1967) — § 4.76.
Hunt v. State, 12 Md. App. 286, 278 A.2d 637 (1971) — §§ 1.04, 2.06, 4.70.

Hunt v. State, 20 Md. App. 164, 314 A.2d 743 (1974) — §§ 4.62, 4.77.
Hunter v. Williams, 570 F.2d 510 (4th Cir. 1978) — Appx. V.
Hurley v. State, 6 Md. App. 348, 251 A.2d 241 (1969) — §§ 2.06, 2.07, 2.23.
Hurley v. State, 60 Md. App. 539, 483 A.2d 1298 (1984) — § 5.07.
Hurwitz v. State, 200 Md. 578, 92 A.2d 575 (1952) — § 4.06.
Huston v. State, 35 Md. App. 455, 371 A.2d 449 (1977) — § 2.06.
Hutchinson v. State, 9 Md. App. 41, 262 A.2d 321 (1970) — § 2.25.
Hutchinson v. State, 36 Md. App. 58, 373 A.2d 50 (1977) — §§ 1.13, 4.65.
Hutchinson v. State, 41 Md. App. 569, 398 A.2d 451 (1979) — § 1.04.
Hyde v. State, 228 Md. 209, 179 A.2d 421 (1961) — § 4.21a.
Hyman v. State, 4 Md. App. 636, 244 A.2d 616 (1968) — § 4.55.

I

In re Appeal No. 568, Term 1974, 25 Md. App. 218, 333 A.2d 649 (1975) — § 4.05.
In re John A., 44 Md. App. 476, 409 A.2d 744 (1980) — § 4.69.
In re Lee, 170 Md. 43, 183 A. 560 (1935) — § 4.59.
In re Nawrocki, 15 Md. App. 252, 289 A.2d 846 (1972) — §§ 4.61, 4.80.
In re Neil C., 308 Md. App. 591, 521 A.2d 329 (1987) — § 4.58.
In re Winship, 397 U.S. 358, 90 S. Ct. 1068, 25 L. Ed. 2d 368 (1970) — §§ 2.01, 4.21c, 4.22a, Appx. V.
Insley v. State, 32 Md. App. 46, 358 A.2d 246 (1976) — § 4.63.
Iozzi v. State, 5 Md. App. 415, 247 A.2d 758 (1968) — § 4.66.
Irvin v. Dowd, 366 U.S. 717, 81 S. Ct. 1639, 6 L. Ed. 2d 751 (1961) — § 1.11a.
Irvin v. State, 23 Md. App. 457, 328 A.2d 329 (1974) — § 4.06.

J

Jackson v. Denno, 378 U.S. 368, 84 S. Ct. 1774, 12 L. Ed. 2d 908 (1964) — § 2.25.
Jackson v. State, 176 Md. 399, 5 A.2d 282 (1939) — § 4.62.
Jackson v. State, 214 Md. 454, 135 A.2d 638 (1957) — § 4.36.
Jackson v. State, 231 Md. 591, 191 A.2d 432 (1963) — §§ 4.42, 4.83.
Jackson v. State, 286 Md. 430, 408 A.2d 711 (1979) — § 4.21b.
Jackson v. State, 288 Md. 191, 416 A.2d 278 (1980) — § 2.21.
Jackson v. State, 5 Md. App. 425, 247 A.2d 743 (1968) — § 4.79.
Jackson v. State, 10 Md. App. 337, 270 A.2d 322 (1970) — § 4.79.
Jackson v. State, 13 Md. App. 31, 280 A.2d 914 (1971) — § 2.25.
Jackson v. State, 22 Md. App. 257, 322 A.2d 574 (1974) — § 5.02.
Jackson v. State, 31 Md. App. 518, 357 A.2d 845 (1976) — § 5.15.
Jackson v. State, 46 Md. App. 325, 416 A.2d 1353 (1980) — Appx. III.
Jackson v. State, 52 Md. App. 327, 499 A.2d 438 (1982) — § 2.30.

Jackson v. Virginia, 443 U.S. 307, 99 S. Ct. 2781, 61 L. Ed. 2d 560 (1979) — § 1.04.
Jacobs v. State, 6 Md. App. 238, 251 A.2d 33 (1969) — §§ 2.04, 4.22a.
Jacobs v. State, 32 Md. App. 509, 363 A.2d 257 (1976) — § 5.11, Appx. V.
Jacobs v. State, 45 Md. App. 634, 415 A.2d 590 (1980) — § 2.25.
James v. State, 5 Md. App. 647, 248 A.2d 910 (1969) — § 4.58.
James v. State, 31 Md. App. 666, 358 A.2d 595 (1976) — §§ 4.13, 4.21a, Appx. V.
Jason v. State, 9 Md. App. 102, 262 A.2d 774 (1970) — § 4.76.
Jeandell v. State, 34 Md. App. 108, 366 A.2d 79 (1976) — § 2.01.
Jenkins v. Anderson, 447 U.S. 231, 100 S. Ct. 2124, 65 L. Ed. 2d 86 (1980) — § 2.25.
Jenkins v. State, 215 Md. 70, 137 A.2d 115 (1957) — § 4.76.
Jenkins v. State, 232 Md. 529, 194 A.2d 618 (1963) — § 4.80.
Jenkins v. State, 25 Md. App. 551, 334 A.2d 549 (1975) — § 2.25.
Jennings v. State, 8 Md. App. 312, 259 A.2d 543 (1969) — § 4.55.
Jennings v. State, 8 Md. App. 321, 259 A.2d 547 (1969) — § 4.65.
Jeter v. State, 9 Md. App. 575, 267 A.2d 319 (1970) — § 4.02.
Jewell v. State, 216 Md. 110, 139 A.2d 707 (1958) — §§ 4.71, 4.91.
Johnson v. No. 1872, 56 Md. App. 205, 467 A.2d 544 (1983) — § 4.83.
Johnson v. State, 213 Md. 527, 132 A.2d 853 (1957) — § 4.25.
Johnson v. State, 221 Md. 177, 156 A.2d 441 (1959) — § 4.77.
Johnson v. State, 227 Md. 159, 175 A.2d 580 (1961) — §§ 1.02, 4.82.
Johnson v. State, 238 Md. 140, 207 A.2d 643 (1965) — §§ 2.25, 2.26.
Johnson v. State, 282 Md. 314, 384 A.2d 709 (1978) — § 2.25.
Johnson v. State, 292 Md. 405, 439 A.2d 542 (1982) — §§ 4.21c, 4.70, 5.01, 5.08.
Johnson v. State, 303 Md. 487, 495 A.2d 1 (1985) — Appx. III.
Johnson v. State, 303 Md. 487, 495 A.2d 1 (1985) — § 5.08.
Johnson v. State, 2 Md. App. 486, 236 A.2d 41 (1967) — § 4.73.
Johnson v. State, 4 Md. App. 648, 244 A.2d 632 (1968) — § 2.06.
Johnson v. State, 5 Md. App. 540, 248 A.2d 663 (1968) — § 4.55.
Johnson v. State, 9 Md. App. 143, 262 A.2d 792 (1970) — § 5.10.
Johnson v. State, 9 Md. App. 166, 263 A.2d 232 (1970) — § 2.07.
Johnson v. State, 9 Md. App. 327, 264 A.2d 280 (1970) — § 4.06.
Johnson v. State, 10 Md. App. 652, 272 A.2d 422 (1971) — § 4.06.
Johnson v. State, 30 Md. App. 512, 352 A.2d 371 (1976) — § 2.06.
Johnson v. State, 31 Md. App. 303, 355 A.2d 504 (1976) — § 2.25.
Johnson v. State, 36 Md. App. 162, 373 A.2d 300 (1977) — §§ 2.25, 2.30.
Johnson v. State, 38 Md. App. 100, 379 A.2d 436 (1977) — § 2.04.
Johnson v. State, 38 Md. App. 306, 381 A.2d 303 (1977) — § 4.21b.
Johnson v. State, 44 Md. App. 515, 411 A.2d 118 (1980) — § 4.43.
Johnson v. State, 50 Md. App. 584, 439 A.2d 607 (1982) — § 5.08.
Johnson v. Zerbst, 304 U.S. 458, 58 S. Ct. 1019, 82 L. Ed. 1461 (1938) — § 2.25.

Jolley v. State, 282 Md. 353, 384 A.2d 91 (1978) — § 5.08.
Jones v. State, 182 Md. 653, 35 A.2d 916 (1944) — § 5.16.
Jones v. State, 188 Md. 263, 52 A.2d 484 (1947) — § 2.26.
Jones v. State, 297 Md. 7, 464 A.2d 977 (1983) — § 2.30.
Jones v. State, 302 Md. 153, 486 A.2d 184 (1985) — § 4.01.
Jones v. State, 303 Md. 323, 493 A.2d 1062 (1985) — § 4.91.
Jones v. State, 304 Md. 216, 498 A.2d 622 (1985) — § 4.73.
Jones v. State, 2 Md. App. 356, 234 A.2d 625 (1967) — §§ 4.55, 4.57, 4.69.
Jones v. State, 2 Md. App. 429, 234 A.2d 900 (1967) — § 2.25.
Jones v. State, 6 Md. App. 344, 251 A.2d 46 (1969) — § 4.71.
Jones v. State, 8 Md. App. 370, 259 A.2d 807 (1969) — § 4.06.
Jones v. State, 10 Md. App. 420, 270 A.2d 827 (1971) — § 5.10.
Jones v. State, 11 Md. App. 468, 275 A.2d 508 (1971) — §§ 2.04, 5.10.
Jones v. State, 13 Md. App. 677, 284 A.2d 635 (1971) — §§ 5.12, 5.14, 5.16.
Jones v. State, 32 Md. App. 490, 362 A.2d 660 (1977) — § 4.59.
Jones v. State, 37 Md. App. 511, 378 A.2d 9 (1977) — § 4.22a, Appx. V.
Jones v. State, 38 Md. App. 288, 380 A.2d 659 (1977) — Appx. I.
Jones v. State, 42 Md. App. 209, 400 A.2d 1 (1979) — § 4.91.
Jones v. State, 48 Md. App. 726, 429 A.2d 308 (1981) — § 2.25.
Jones v. State, 61 Md. App. 94, 484 A.2d 1050 (1984) — § 4.59.
Jones v. United States, 463 U.S. 354, 103 S. Ct. 3043, 77 L. Ed. 2d 694 (1983) — § 5.08, Appx. V.
Joppy v. Hopkins, 231 Md. 52, 188 A.2d 545 (1963) — § 2.21.
Jordan v. State, 219 Md. 36, 148 A.2d 292 (1959) — § 4.79.
Jordan v. State, 4 Md. App. 349, 242 A.2d 829 (1968) — § 1.05.
Jordan v. State, 17 Md. App. 201, 300 A.2d 701 (1973) — § 4.80.
Jordan v. State, 19 Md. App. 283, 310 A.2d 575 (1973) — § 5.10.
Jordan v. State, 24 Md. App. 267, 330 A.2d 496 (1975) — § 4.41.
Joseph F. Hughes & Co. v. Stockhausen, 212 Md. 559, 129 A.2d 844 (1957) — § 1.11a.
Joyce v. State, 59 Md. App. 237, 474 A.2d 1369 (1984) — § 4.36.
Jung v. State, 9 Md. App. 300, 263 A.2d 618 (1970) — §§ 4.57, 4.69.
Jurek v. Texas, 428 U.S. 262, 96 S. Ct. 2950, 49 L. Ed. 2d 929 (1976) — § 4.21c.

K

Kable v. State, 17 Md. App. 16, 299 A.2d 493 (1973) — §§ 2.06, 2.07, 4.56, Appx. III.
Kackley v. State, 63 Md. App. 532, 493 A.2d 364 (1985) — § 4.36.
Kanaras v. State, 54 Md. App. 568, 460 A.2d 61 (1983) — §§ 4.57, 4.69.
Kandel v. State, 252 Md. 668, 250 A.2d 853 (1969) — § 4.59.
Kashansky v. State, 39 Md. App. 313, 385 A.2d 811 (1978) — Appx. V.
Kasten Constr. Co. v. Evans, 260 Md. 536, 273 A.2d 90 (1971) — § 1.11a.

Keller v. State, 2 Md. App. 623, 236 A.2d 313 (1967) — § 2.25.
Kelley v. State, 288 Md. 298, 418 A.2d 217 (1980) — § 2.06.
Kellum v. State, 223 Md. 80, 162 A.2d 473 (1960) — §§ 4.12, 4.80.
Kelly v. State, 270 Md. 139, 310 A.2d 538 (1973) — § 1.13.
Kelly v. State, 14 Md. App. 287, 286 A.2d 806 (1972) — § 1.05.
Kelly v. State, 45 Md. App. 212, 412 A.2d 1274 (1980) — § 4.35.
Kennedy v. State, 44 Md. App. 662, 410 A.2d 1097 (1980) — § 2.30.
Kenney v. State, 62 Md. App. 555, 490 A.2d 738 (1985) — § 5.06.
Kidd v. State, 33 Md. App. 445, 366 A.2d 761 (1976) — § 2.25.
Kier v. State, 216 Md. 513, 140 A.2d 896 (1958) — § 4.21a.
Killie v. State, 14 Md. App. 465, 287 A.2d 310 (1972) — § 4.77.
Kincer v. State, 5 Md. App. 80, 245 A.2d 411 (1968) — § 4.79.
King v. State, 201 Md. 303, 93 A.2d 556 (1953) — § 1.05.
King v. State, 36 Md. App. 124, 373 A.2d 292 (1977) — § 2.25.
Kirby v. Illinois, 406 U.S. 682, 92 S. Ct. 1877, 32 L. Ed. 2d 411 (1972) — § 2.28.
Kirby v. State, 48 Md. App. 205, 426 A.2d 423 (1981) — §§ 2.06, 2.07.
Kirstel v. State, 13 Md. App. App. 482, 284 A.2d 12 (1971) — § 4.85.
Kitt v. State, 2d Md. App. 306, 234 A.2d 621 (1967) — § 2.01.
Knight v. State, 229 Md. 460, 184 A.2d 709 (1962) — § 4.77.
Kober v. State, 41 Md. App. 174, 395 A.2d 1228 (1979) — § 4.59.
Kolker v. State, 230 Md. 157, 186 A.2d 212 (1962) — § 4.62.
Koprivich v. State, 1 Md. App. 147, 228 A.2d 476 (1967) — § 2.25.
Krauss v. State, 216 Md. 369, 140 A.2d 653 (1958) — § 4.85.
Kruszewski v. Holz, 265 Md. 434, 290 A.2d 534 (1972) — § 2.03.
Kucharczyk v. State, 235 Md. 334, 201 A.2d 683 (1964) — § 2.06.
Kursch v. State, 55 Md. App. 103, 460 A.2d 639 (1983) — § 4.63.

L

Lakeside v. Oregon, 435 U.S. 333, 98 S. Ct. 1091, 55 L. Ed. 2d 319 (1978) — § 2.27.
Lamb v. State, 67 Md. 524, 10 A. 208 (1887) — § 4.12.
Lambert v. California, 355 U.S. 225, 78 S. Ct. 240, 2 L. Ed. 2d 228 (1957) — § 4.76.
Lambert v. State, 193 Md. 551, 69 A.2d 461 (1949) — § 1.04.
Lambert v. State, 70 Md. App. 83, 519 A.2d 1340 (1987) — § 4.23c.
Lambiotte v. State, 17 Md. App. 545, 303 A.2d 163 (1973) — §§ 455, 4.79.
Lansdowne v. State, 287 Md. 232, 412 A.2d 88 (1980) — §§ 1.04, 4.13, 4.23c, Appx. I.
Lane v. State, 60 Md. App. 412, 483 A.2d 369 (1984) — §§ 4.91, 4.92.
Lang v. State, 6 Md. App. 128, 250 A.2d 276 (1969) — § 4.23b.
Langenfelder v. Thompson, 179 Md. 502, 20 A.2d 491 (1941) — § 2.05.
Langworthy v. State, 284 Md. 588, 399 A.2d 578 (1979) — § 5.08.
Langworthy v. State, 46 Md. App. 116, 416 A.2d 1287 (1980) — § 5.08.

Latimer v. State, 49 Md. App. 586, 433 A.2d 1234 (1981) — § 2.25.
Lauder v. State, 233 Md. 142, 195 A.2d 610 (1963) — § 4.71.
Law v. State, 21 Md. App. 13, 318 A.2d 859 (1974) — §§ 5.13, 5.15, 5.16.
Law v. State, 29 Md. App. 457, 349 A.2d 295 (1975) — § 4.23c, Appx. V.
Lawless v. State, 3 Md. App. 652, 241 A.2d 155 (1968) — § 2.31.
Lawrence v. State, 6 Md. App. 226, 251 A.2d 20 (1969) — § 1.02.
Lawrence v. State, 51 Md. App. 575, 444 A.2d 478 (1982) — § 2.06.
Laws v. State, 6 Md. App. 243, 251 A.2d 237 (1969) — § 4.70.
Leach v. State, 47 Md. App. 611, 425 A.2d 234 (1981) — §§ 2.25, 4.21a, 4.22a.
Leary v. United States, 395 U.S. 6, 89 S. Ct. 1532, 23 L. Ed. 2d 57 (1969) — Appx. V.
Leatherwood v. State, 49 Md. App. 683, 435 A.2d 477 (1981) — § 3.04, Appx. III.
Lee v. State, 18 Md. App. 719, 308 A.2d 397 (1973) — § 4.33.
Lee v. State, 59 Md. App. 28, 474 A.2d 537 (1984) — § 4.91.
Lee v. State, 62 Md. App. 341, 489 A.2d 87 (1985) — § 4.58.
Leek v. State, 229 Md. 526, 184 A.2d 808 (1962) — § 4.33.
Leeson v. State, 293 Md. 425, 445 A.2d 21 (1982) — § 4.82.
Lego v. Twomey, 404 U.S. 477, 92 S. Ct. 619, 30 L. Ed. 2d 618 (1972) — § 2.25.
Lemons v. State, 49 Md. App. 467, 433 A.2d 1179 (1981) — § 2.26.
Lenoir v. State, 197 Md. 495, 80 A.2d 3 (1951) — § 4.66.
Leonard v. State, 46 Md. App. 631, 421 A.2d 85 (1980) — § 2.08.
Lester v. State, 9 Md. App. 542, 266 A.2d 361 (1970) — § 4.70.
Lett v. State, 51 Md. App. 668, 445 A.2d 1050 (1982) — § 4.36.
Leupen v. Lackey, 248 Md. 19, 234 A.2d 573 (1967) — § 1.13.
Leuschner v. Maryland, 462 U.S. 1047, 103 S. Ct. 2836, 77 L. Ed. 2d 413 (1981) — § 2.25.
Leuschener v. State, 45 Md. App. 323, 413 A.2d 227 (1980) — § 2.25.
Leuschener v. State, 49 Md. App. 490, 433 A.2d 1195 (1981) — § 2.25.
Levine v. Moreland, 229 Md. 231, 182 A.2d 484 (1962) — § 2.05.
Levy v. State, 225 Md. 201, 170 A.2d 216 (1961) — §§ 4.67, 4.68.
Levya v. State, 2 Md. App. 120, 233 A.2d 498 (1967) — § 4.22a.
Lewin v. Uzuber, 65 Md. 341, 4 A. 285 (1886) — § 4.80.
Lewis v. State, 285 Md. 705, 404 A.2d 1073 (1979) — §§ 2.25, 4.01, 4.03.
Lievers v. State, 3 Md. App. 597, 241 A.2d 147 (1968) — § 4.06.
Lightfoot v. State, 278 Md. 231, 360 A.2d 426 (1976) — §§ 4.05, 4.56, 4.67.
Lightfoot v. State, 25 Md. App. 148, 334 A.2d 152 (1975) — § 2.29.
Lilly v. State, 212 Md. 436, 129 A.2d 839 (1957) — § 4.25.
Lindsay v. State, 8 Md. App. 100, 258 A.2d 760 (1969) — §§ 4.21a, 4.21b, 4.22a, 4.23b, Appx. III.
Liner v. State, 62 Md. App. 381, 489 A.2d 553 (1985) — § 4.59.
Linkens v. State, 202 Md. 212, 96 A.2d 246 (1953) — §§ 2.25, 4.14.

Lipscomb v. State, 223 Md. 599, 165 A.2d 918 (1960) — § 4.21b.
Little v. State, 300 Md. 485, 479 A.2d 903 (1984) — § 4.63.
Lockett v. Ohio, 438 U.S. 586, 98 S. Ct. 2954, 57 L. Ed. 2d 973 (1978) — § 4.21c.
Lodowski v. State, 302 Md. 691, 490 A.2d 1228 (1985) — § 4.21c.
Logan v. State, 289 Md. 460, 425 A.2d 632 (1981) — § 5.08.
Logan v. State, 1 Md. App. 213, 228 A.2d 837 (1967) — § 5.02.
Logue v. State, 37 Md. App. 41, 375 A.2d 51 (1977) — § 2.06.
Loker v. State, 250 Md. 677, 245 A.2d 814 (1968) — § 4.64.
Loug v. State, 7 Md. App. 256, 254 A.2d 707 (1969) — § 5.16.
Loper v. Beto, 405 U.S. 473, 92 S. Ct. 1014, 31 L. Ed. 2d 374 (1972) — § 2.07.
Loscomb v. State, 45 Md. App. 598, 416 A.2d 1276 (1980) — § 4.26.
Loud v. State, 63 Md. App. 702, 493 A.2d 1092 (1985) — § 4.83.
Love v. State, 6 Md. App. 639, 252 A.2d 493 (1969) — § 4.82.
Love v. State, 16 Md. App. 364, 297 A.2d 309 (1972) — § 5.08.
Lowery v. State, 292 Md. 2, 437 A.2d 193 (1982) — §§ 2.06, 2.07.
Lucado v. State, 40 Md. App. 25, 389 A.2d 398 (1978) — § 4.36.
Lusby v. State, 217 Md. 191, 141 A.2d 893 (1958) — §§ 1.10, 4.33.
Luthardt v. State, 6 Md. App. 251, 251 A.2d 40 (1969) — § 4.61.
Lutz v. State, 167 Md. 12, 172 A. 354 (1934) — § 4.62.
Lyde v. Warden, 1 Md. App. 423, 230 A.2d 695 (1967) — § 2.01.
Lyles v. State, 10 Md. App. 265, 269 A.2d 178 (1970) — § 4.80.
Lynch v. State, 2 Md. App. 546, 236 A.2d 45 (1967) — § 4.06.
Lynch v. State, 9 Md. App. 441, 265 A.2d 283 (1970) — § 4.21b.
Lynch v. United States, 397 U.S. 1028, 90 S. Ct. 1276, 25 L. Ed. 2d 539 (1970) — § 4.06.
Lyter v. State, 2 Md. App. 654, 236 A.2d 432 (1968) — § 2.25.

M

MacEwen v. State, 194 Md. 492, 71 A.2d 464 (1950) — §§ 2.10, 2.24, 4.64.
Mack v. State, 300 Md. 583, 479 A.2d 1344 (1984) — § 4.44, Appx. III.
Mack v. State, 69 Md. App. 245, 517 A.2d 108 (1986) — Appx. IV.
Mackall v. State, 283 Md. 100, 387 A.2d 762 (1978) — §§ 4.41, 4.42.
Maddran v. Mullendore, 206 Md. 291, 111 A.2d 608 (1955) — § 5.17.
Magness v. State, 2 Md. App. 320, 234 A.2d 481 (1967) — § 5.16.
Major v. State, 31 Md. App. 590, 358 A.2d 609 (1976) — §§ 2.32, 4.26, 4.63.
Makins v. State, 6 Md. App. 466, 252 A.2d 15 (1969) — §§ 1.04, 4.57.
Malcolm v. State, 232 Md. 222, 192 A.2d 281 (1963) — § 1.03.
Malekar v. State, 26 Md. App. 498, 338 A.2d 328 (1975) — §§ 1.08, 1.11a, 2.05.
Malloy v. State, 4 Md. App. 420, 243 A.2d 649 (1968) — § 4.02.

Manson v. Brathwaite, 432 U.S. 98, 97 S. Ct. 2243, 53 L. Ed. 2d 140 (1977) — § 2.28.
Marini v. State, 30 Md. App. 19, 351 A.2d 463 (1976) — § 4.79.
Marks v. State, 230 Md. 108, 185 A.2d 909 (1962) — § 4.13.
Marshall v. State, 291 Md. 205, 434 A.2d 555 (1981) — § 2.06.
Marshall v. State, 3 Md. App. 715, 240 A.2d 767 (1968) — § 5.02.
Marshall v. State, 46 Md. App. 695, 420 A.2d 1266 (1980) — § 2.06.
Marshall v. United States, 360 U.S. 310, 79 S. Ct. 1171, 3 L. Ed. 2d 1250 (1959) — § 1.11a.
Marson v. United States, 203 F.2d 904 (6th Cir. 1953) — § 1.11a.
Marston v. State, 9 Md. App. 360, 264 A.2d 127 (1970) — § 4.57.
Martel v. State, 221 Md. 294, 157 A.2d 437 (1960) — § 2.33.
Martin v. State, 10 Md. App. 274, 269 A.2d 182 (1970) — §§ 4.55, 4.57.
Martin v. State, 51 Md. App. 142, 442 A.2d 191 (1982) — § 2.30.
Maryland v. Chapman, 101 F. Supp. 335, 341 (D. Md. 1951) — § 4.25.
Mason v. State, 302 Md. 434, 488 A.2d 955 (1985) — § 4.06.
Mason v. State, 9 Md. App. 61, 262 A.2d 576 (1970) — § 4.71.
Mason v. State, 18 Md. App. 130, 305 A.2d 492 (1973) — § 4.06.
Massiah v. United States, 377 U.S. 201, 84 S. Ct. 1199, 12 L. Ed. 2d 246 (1964) — § 2.25.
Matthews v. State, 237 Md. 384, 206 A.2d 714 (1965) — § 4.71.
Mauldin v. State, 239 Md. 592, 212 A.2d 502 (1965) — § 2.32.
Mayherry v. Pennsylvania, 400 U.S. 455, 91 S. Ct. 499, 27 L. Ed. 2d 532 (1971) — § 4.59.
Mayes v. State, 50 Md. App. 628, 440 A.2d 1093 (1982) — § 4.36.
Mayfield v. State, 302 Md. 624, 490 A.2d 687 (1985) — § 1.13.
Mayne v. State, 45 Md. App. 483, 414 A.2d 1 (1980) — §§ 4.37, 5.01.
Maziarz v. State, 302 Md. 1, 485 A.2d 245 (1984) — § 4.21c.
McAvoy v. State, 70 Md. App. 661, 523 A.2d 618 (1987) — § 4.63.
McBryde v. State, 30 Md. App. 357, 352 A.2d 324 (1976) — § 4.02.
McBurney v. State, 280 Md. 21, 371 A.2d 129 (1977) — § 2.33.
McCarson v. State, 8 Md. App. 20, 257 A.2d 471 (1969) — § 2.25.
McChan v. State, 238 Md. 149, 207 A.2d 632 (1965) — § 4.80.
McChan v. State, 9 Md. App. 311, 264 A.2d 130 (1970) — § 4.83.
McClain v. State, 10 Md. App. 106, 268 A.2d 572 (1970) — §§ 4.03, 4.82.
McCleskey v. Kemp, 107 S. Ct. 1756, 95 L. Ed. 2d 262 (1987) — § 4.21c.
McCord v. State, 15 Md. App. 63, 289 A.2d 7 (1972) — §§ 4.71, 4.83.
McCoy v. State, 8 Md. App. 127, 258 A.2d 611 (1969) — § 2.25.
McCree v. State, 33 Md. App. 82, 363 A.2d 647 (1976) — Appx. V.
McDonald v. United States, 312 F.2d 847 (D.C. Cir. 1962) — § 5.08.
McDowell v. State, 231 Md. 205, 189 A.2d 611 (1963) — § 4.52.
McDowell v. State, 31 Md. App. 652, 358 A.2d 624 (1976) — Appx. V.
McDuffie v. State, 10 Md. App. 190, 268 A.2d 590 (1970) — § 1.02.
McDuffie v. State, 12 Md. App. 264, 278 A.2d 307 (1971) — § 4.83.
McEntire v. State, 2 Md. App. 449, 235 A.2d 311 (1967) — §§ 4.02, 4.36.

McFadden v. State, 1 Md. App. 511, 231 A.2d 910 (1967) — § 2.25.
McGee v. State, 1 Md. App. 239, 229 A.2d 432 (1967) — § 4.80.
McGhee v. State, 4 Md. App. 256, 243 A.2d 41 (1968) — § 2.31.
McGhee v. State, 9 Md. App. 526, 267 A.2d 306 (1970) — § 4.12.
McGilton v. State, 12 Md. App. 174, 278 A.2d 76 (1971) — § 2.30.
McGlothlin v. State, 1 Md. App. 256, 229 A.2d 428 (1967) — § 4.79.
McGraw v. State, 234 Md. 273, 199 A.2d 229 (1964) — § 4.57.
McIntyre v. State, 1 Md. App. 586, 232 A.2d 279 (1967) — § 4.61.
McKay v. State, 32 Md. App. 451, 362 A.2d 666 (1976) — § 1.13.
McKnight v. State, 280 Md. 604, 375 A.2d 551 (1977) — § 2.10.
McLaughlin v. State, 3 Md. App. 515, 240 A.2d 298 (1968) — §§ 2.07, 4.75.
McLean v. State, 6 Md. App. 366, 251 A.2d 252 (1969) — § 2.24.
McMorris v. State, 26 Md. App. 660, 338 A.2d 912 (1975) — § 4.06.
McNeil v. State, 227 Md. 298, 176 A.2d 338 (1961) — § 2.31.
Meadows v. State, 3 Md. App. 441, 239 A.2d 767 (1968) — § 4.65.
Medley v. State, 52 Md. App. 225, 448 A.2d 363 (1982) — §§ 5.13, 5.16.
Melia v. State, 5 Md. App. 354, 247 A.2d 554 (1968) — §§ 4.71, 5.02.
Meno v. State, 117 Md. 435, 83 A. 759 (1912) — § 1.08.
Mercer v. State, 237 Md. 479, 206 A.2d 797 (1965) — §§ 4.55, 4.71.
Messina v. State, 212 Md. 602, 130 A.2d 578 (1957) — § 4.61.
Metallo v. State, 10 Md. App. 76, 267 A.2d 804 (1970) — § 5.10.
Metz v. State, 9 Md. App. 15, 262 A.2d 331 (1970) — § 1.05.
Michael v. State, 1 Md. App. 243, 229 A.2d 145 (1967) — §§ 4.15, 5.01, 5.08.
Michigan v. Jackson, 475 U.S. 625, 106 S. Ct. 1404, 89 L. Ed. 2d 631 (1986) — § 2.25.
Michigan v. Mosely, 423 U.S. 96, 96 S. Ct. 321, 46 L. Ed. 2d 313 (1975) — § 2.25.
Michigan v. Tucker, 417 U.S. 433, 94 S. Ct. 2357, 41 L. Ed. 2d 182 (1974) — § 2.25.
Mid-Atlantic Coca-Cola Bottling Co. v. Chen, Walsh & Tecker, 296 Md. 99, 460 A.2d 44 (1983) — § 4.74.
Middleton v. State, 6 Md. App. 380, 251 A.2d 224 (1969) — §§ 2.01, 4.14, 4.16, 4.21b.
Middleton v. State, 10 Md. App. 18, 267 A.2d 759 (1970) — § 4.76.
Middleton v. State, 49 Md. App. 286, 431 A.2d 734 (1981) — §§ 1.01, 5.02.
Midgett v. State, 216 Md. 26, 139 A.2d 209 (1958) — §§ 4.70, 4.83.
Miles v. United States, 103 U.S. 304, 26 L. Ed. 481 (1881) — § 1.04.
Milhouse v. State, 31 Md. App. 571, 358 A.2d 262 (1976) — § 2.25, Appx. V.
Millard v. State, 8 Md. App. 419, 261 A.2d 227 (1970) — § 5.08.
Miller v. State, 251 Md. 362, 247 A.2d 530 (1968) — § 2.25.
Miller v. State, 7 Md. App. 344, 255 A.2d 459 (1969) — § 2.30.

Miller v. State, 44 Md. App. 5.87, 410 A.2d 1081 (1980) — § 2.33.
Mills v. State, 310 Md. 33, 527 A.2d 3 (1987) — § 4.21c.
Mills v. State, 3 Md. App. 693, 241 A.2d 166 (1968) — §§ 4.79, 4.91.
Mills v. State, 12 Md. App. 449, 279 A.2d 473 (1971) — § 4.76.
Mills v. State, 13 Md. App. 196, 282 A.2d 147 (1971) — § 4.24.
Mills v. State, 28 Md. App. 300, 345 A.2d 127 (1975) — § 2.32.
Mincey v. Arizona, 437 U.S. 385, 98 S. Ct. 2408, 57 L. Ed. 2d 290 (1978) — § 2.25.
Minnesota v. Murphy, 465 U.S. 420, 104 S. Ct. 1136, 79 L. Ed. 2d 409 (1984) — § 2.25.
Minor v. State, 6 Md. App. 82, 250 A.2d 113 (1969) — § 2.25.
Miranda v. Arizona, 384 U.S. 436, 86 S. Ct. 1602, 16 L. Ed. 2d 694 (1966) — §§ 2.08, 2.09, 2.25, 4.63.
M'Naghten's Case, 8 Eng. Rep. 718 (1843) — § 5.08.
Mollar v. State, 25 Md. App. 291, 333 A.2d 625 (1975) — § 2.10.
Mondawmin Corp. v. Kres, 258 Md. 307, 266 A.2d 8 (1970) — §§ 2.05, 2.08.
Montague v. State, 3 Md. App. 66, 237 A.2d 816 (1968) — § 4.25.
Montgomery v. State, 292 Md. 84, 437 A.2d 654 (1981) — §§ 1.01, 1.04.
Moore v. Illinois, 434 U.S. 220, 98 S. Ct. 458, 54 L. Ed. 2d 424 (1977) — § 2.28.
Moore v. State, 199 Md. 676, 87 A.2d 577 (1952) — § 4.74.
Moore v. State, 13 Md. App. 711, 284 A.2d 614 (1971) — § 4.77.
Moore v. State, 17 Md. App. 237, 300 A.2d 388 (1973) — § 2.07.
Moore v. State, 23 Md. App. 540, 329 A.29 48 (1974) — § 4.70.
Moran v. Burbine, 475 U.S. 412, 106 S. Ct. 1135, 89 L. Ed. 2d 410 (1986) — § 2.25.
Morgan v. Hall, 569 F.2d 1161 (1st Cir. 1978) — § 2.25.
Morgan v. State, 2 Md. App. 440, 234 A.2d 762 (1967) — § 2.25.
Morissette v. United States, 342 U.S. 246, 72 S. Ct. 240, 96 L. Ed. 288 (1952) — §§ 3.01, 3.02.
Morris v. State, 4 Md. App. 328, 242 A.2d 582 (1968) — § 5.14.
Morris v. State, 11 Md. App. 18, 272 A.2d 663 (1971) — § 5.08.
Morris v. State, 33 Md. App. 185, 364 A.2d 588 (1976) — Appx. V.
Morris v. Twigg, 190 Md. 324, 58 A.2d 719 (1948) — § 1.05.
Morrow v. State, 293 Md. 247, 443 A.2d 108, (1982) — Appx. III.
Mousone v. State, 33 Md. App. 201, 364 A.2d 58 (1978) — § 1.08.
Mouzon v. State, 9 Md. App. 57, 262 A.2d 588 (1970) — § 2.30.
Mouzone v. State, 50 Md. App. 81, 436 A.2d 916 (1981) — § 2.08.
Mullaney v. Wilbur, 421 U.S. 684, 95 S. Ct. 1881, 44 L. Ed. 2d 508 (1975) — §§ 1.02, 2.01, 3.01, 4.21c, 4.22a, 4.91, 5.01, 5.02, 5.05, 5.06, 5.11, 5.17, 5.18, Appx. V.
Mulligan v. State, 6 Md. App. 600, 252 A.2d 476 (1969) — § 2.25.
Mulligan v. State, 18 Md. App. 588, 308 A.2d 418 (1973) — §§ 2.06, 2.25.
Mumford v. State, 19 Md. App. 640, 313 A.2d 563 (1974) — § 4.21b.

Murphy v. Florida, 421 U.S. 794, 95 S. Ct. 2031, 44 L. Ed. 2d 589 (1975) — § 1.11a.
Murphy v. State, 184 Md. 70, 40 A.2d 239 (1944) — § 2.31.
Murphy v. State, 8 Md. App. 430, 260 A.2d 357 (1970) — § 2.25.
Murphy v. State, 46 Md. App. 138, 416 A.2d 748 (1980) — § 4.59.
Murray v. State, 226 Md. 624, 174 A.2d 794 (1961) — § 1.07.
Musgrove v. State, 3 Md. App. 54, 237 A.2d 804 (1968) — § 2.31.
Muskus v. State, 14 Md. App. 348, 286 A.2d 783 (1972) — § 4.59.
Mutual Life Ins. Co. v. Rain, 108 Md. 353, 70 A. 87 (1908) — Appx. IV.
Mutyambizi v. State, 33 Md. App. 55, 363 A.2d 511 (1976) — § 2.06.
Myers v. State, 23 Md. App. 275, 326 A.2d 773 (1974) — § 4.59.
Myers v. State, 58 Md. App. 211, 472 A.2d 1027 (1984) — § 5.01.

N

Nance v. State, 7 Md. App. 433, 256 A.2d 377 (1969) — §§ 2.07, 3.02, 4.82.
Nasim v. State, 34 Md. App. 65, 366 A.2d 70 (1976) — §§ 2.10, 4.52.
Neal v. State, 45 Md. App. 549, 413 A.2d 1386 (1980) — §§ 1.01, 4.61.
Neil v. Biggers, 409 U.S. 188, 93 S. Ct. 375, 34 L. Ed. 2d 401 (1972) — §§ 2.28, 2.30.
Nelson v. State, 224 Md. 374, 167 A.2d 871 (1961) — § 4.68.
Nelson v. State, 5 Md. App. 109, 245 A.2d 606 (1968) — §§ 2.21, 2.23.
Neville v. State, 290 Md. 364, 430 A.2d 570 (1981) — § 4.35.
Newman v. State, 65 Md. App. 85, 499 A.2d 492 (1985) — § 1.01.
Newton v. State, 280 Md. 260, 373 A.2d 262 (1977) — § 4.21b.
Nichols v. State, 231 Md. 313, 190 A.2d 645 (1963) — § 5.03.
Nichols v. State, 5 Md. App. 340, 247 A.2d 722 (1968) — §§ 1.04, 1.05.
Nickerson v. State, 22 Md. App. 660, 325 A.2d 149 (1974) — §4.13.
Nischuk v. State, 278 Md. App. 238, 362 A.2d 91 (1976) — § 2.23.
Nixon v. State, 204 Md. 475, 105 A.2d 243 (1954) — §§ 5.12, 5.16.
Nizer v. Phelps, 252 Md. 185, 249 A.2d 112 (1967) — § 2.05, Appx. III.
Noel v. State, 202 Md. 247, 96 A.2d 7 (1953) — §§2.23, 5.07, Appx. III.
Nolan v. State, 213 Md. 298, 131 A.2d 851 (1957) — § 4.64.
Novak v. State, 214 Md. 472, 136 A.2d 256 (1957) — § 4.02.
Nutt v. State, 9 Md. App. 102, 262 A.2d 774 (1970) — §§ 4.76, 4.77.

O

O'Brien v. State, 1 Md. App. 94, 227 A.2d 362 (1967) — § 4.55.
Oden v. State, 223 Md. 244, 164 A.2d 284 (1960) — § 1.05.
Offutt v. State, 44 Md. App. 670, 410 A.2d 611 (1980) — §§ 2.29, 4.14.
Offutt v. State, 55 Md. App. 261, 463 A.2d 876 (1983) — §§ 4.91, 4.93.
Ohio v. Roberts, 448 U.S. 56, 100 S. Ct. 2531, 65 L. Ed. 2d 597 (1980) — § 4.06.
Oliver v. State, 8 Md. App. 610, 261 A.2d 498 (1970) — § 4.82.

Oliver v. State, 25 Md. App. 647, 334 A.2d 572 (1975) — §§ 1.11a, 1.13.
Oliver v. State, 53 Md. App. 490, 454 A.2d 856 (1983) — § 2.30.
On lee v. United States, 343 U.S. 747, 72 S. Ct. 967, 96 L. Ed. 1270 (1952) — § 2.02.
Oregon v. Bradshaw, 462 U.S. 1039, 103 S. Ct. 2830, 77 L. Ed. 2d 405 (1983) — § 2.25.
Oregon v. Elstad, 470 U.S. 298, 105 S. Ct. 1285, 84 L. Ed. 2d 222 (1985) — § 2.25.
Oregon v. Hass, 420 U.S. 714, 95 S. Ct. 1215, 43 L. Ed. 2d 570 (1975) — §§ 2.09, 2.25.
Oregon v. Mathiason, 429 U.S. 492, 97 S. Ct. 711, 50 L. Ed. 2d 714 (1977) — § 2.25.
Orozco v. Texas, 394 U.S. 324, 89 S. Ct. 1095, 22 L. Ed. 2d 311 (1969) — § 2.25.
Osborne v. State, 4 Md. App. 57, 241 A.2d 171 (1968) — §§ 2.01, 4.79, 4.93.
Ott v. State, 11 Md. App. 259, 273 A.2d 630 (1971) — § 4.12.
Owens v. State, 236 Md. 626, 204 A.2d 70 (1964) — § 4.77.

P

Pachmayr v. State, 1 Md. App. 270, 229 A.2d 434 (1967) — § 4.72.
Paesch v. State, 2 Md. App. 746, 237 A.2d 83 (1968) — §§ 4.71, 4.72.
Palmer v. State, 223 Md. 341, 164 A.2d 467 (1960) — § 4.24.
Palmer v. State, 5 Md. App. 691, 249 A.2d 482 (1969) — § 2.28.
Papachristou v. City of Jacksonville, 405 U.S. 156, 92 S. Ct. 839, 31 L. Ed. 2d 110 (1972) — § 4.86.
Parker v. State, 424 P.2d 997 (Okla. Crim. App. 1967) — § 4.63.
Parker v. State, 7 Md. App. 167, 254 A.2d 381 (1969) — §§ 4.21b, 4.83, 5.01, 5.08.
Partain v. State, 63 Md. App. 260, 492 A.2d 669 (1985) — § 4.37.
Patterson v. New York, 432 U.S. 197, 97 S. Ct. 2319, 53 L. Ed. 2d 281 (1977) — §§ 3.01, 4.21c, 4.22a, Appx. V.
Patterson v. State, 275 Md. 563, 342 A.2d 660 (1975) — §§ 2.08, 2.11.
Patuxent Publishing Corp. v. State, 48 Md. App. 689, 429 A.2d 554 (1981) — § 1.11a.
Peaper v. State, 14 Md. App. 201, 286 A.2d 176 (1972) — § 4.79.
Pearlman v. State, 232 Md. 251, 192 A.2d 767 (1963) — § 4.06.
Pearre v. State, 237 Md. 622, 206 A.2d 249 (1965) — § 4.55.
Pearson v. State, 8 Md. App. 79, 258 A.2d 917 (1969) — § 4.68.
Pearson v. State, 28 Md. App. 196, 343 A.2d 916 (1975) — § 2.27.
Pearson v. State, 28 Md. App. 464, 347 A.2d 239 (1975) — § 4.59.
Pearson v. Wiltrout, 17 Md. App. 497, 302 A.2d 678 (1973) — § 1.05.
Peddersen v. State, 223 Md. 329, 164 A.2d 539 (1960) — § 4.64.
Pedzich v. State, 33 Md. App. 620, 365 A.2d 567 (1976) — § 4.41.

Pennington v. State, 308 Md. 727, 521 A.2d 1216 (1987) — § 2.33.
Pennsylvania Threshermen & Farmers' Mut. Cas. Ins. Co. v. Messenger, 181 Md. 295, 29 A.2d 653 (1943) — § 2.05.
People v. Bell, 9 Ill. App. 3d 465, 292 N.E.2d 219 (1972) — § 4.91.
People v. Bell, 18 Ill. App. 3d 130, 309 N.E.2d 344 (1974) — § 4.91.
People v. Betts, 367 Ill. 499, 11 N.E.2d 942 (1937) — § 4.94.
People v. Betts, 17 Ill. App. 3d 22, 307 N.E.2d 672 (1974) — § 4.91.
People v. Bullock, 123 Ill. App. 2d 30, 259 N.E.2d 641 (1970) — § 4.91.
People v. Cassman, 32 Ill. App. 3d 456, 336 N.E.2d 85 (1975) — § 4.91.
People v. Cicchetti, 2 Ill. App. 3d 535, 275 N.E.2d 661 (1971) — § 4.91.
People v. Collins, 48 Ill. App. 3d 643, 362 N.E.2d 1118 (1977) — § 4.91.
People v. Cowan, 49 Ill. App. 3d 367, 364 N.E.2d 362 (1977) — § 4.91.
People v. Davis, 5 Ill. App. 3d 95, 283 N.E.2d 317 (1972) — § 4.95.
People v. Debartolo, 24 Ill. App. 3d 1000, 322 N.E.2d 251 (1975) — § 4.91.
People v. Decker, 19 Ill. App. 3d 86, 311 N.E.2d 228 (1974) — §§ 4.91, 4.92.
People v. Demos, 3 Ill. App. 3d 284, 278 N.E.2d 89 (1971) — § 4.91.
People v. Dickerson, 21 Ill. App. 3d 977, 316 N.E.2d 519 (1974) — § 4.91.
People v. Dillon, 93 Ill. App. 2d 151, 236 N.E.2d 411 (1968) — § 4.95.
People v. DiLuca, 31 Cr. L. Rpt. 2028 (N.Y. Sup. Ct. App. Div. 1982) — Appx. II.
People v. Diming, 13 Ill. App. 3d 1092, 302 N.E.2d 712 (1973) — § 4.91.
People v. Drake, 20 Ill. App. 3d 762, 314 N.E.2d 532 (1974) — § 4.91.
People v. Dziak, 30 Ill. App. 3d 859, 333 N.E.2d 582 (1975) — § 4.91.
People v. Edwards, 21 Ill. App. 3d 354, 315 N.E.2d 91 (1974) — § 4.91.
People v. Hargrave, 29 Ill. App. 3d 89, 329 N.E.2d 814 (1975) — § 4.91.
People v. Haynes, 132 Ill. App. 2d 1031, 270 N.E.2d 63 (1971) — § 4.91.
People v. Helm, 10 Ill. App. 3d 643, 295 N.E.2d 78 (1973) — § 4.91.
People v. Hines, 12 Ill. App. 3d 582, 299 N.E.2d 581 (1973) — § 4.94.
People v. Hooper, 50 Mich. App. 186, 212 N.W.2d 786 (1973) — § 4.78.
People v. Hoy, 12 Ill. App. 3d 524, 299 N.E.2d 502 (1973) — § 4.91.
People v. Johnson, 59 Ill. App. 3d 115, 376 N.E.2d 8 (1978) — § 4.92.
People v. Jones, 123 Ill. App. 2d 389, 259 N.E.2d 393 (1970) — § 4.91.
People v. Joy, 44 Ill. App. 3d 349, 358 N.E.2d 101 (1976) — § 4.91.
People v. Kaye, 112 Ill. App. 2d 141, 251 N.E.2d 306 (1969) — § 4.91.
People v. Lafaro, 250 N.Y. 356, 165 N.E. 518 (1929) — § 4.56.
People v. La Valley, 7 Ill. App. 3d 1051, 289 N.E.2d 45 (1972) — § 4.93.
People v. Lewis, 13 Ill. App. 3d 688, 301 N.E.2d 159 (1973) — § 4.91.
People v. Malone, 1 Ill. App. 3d 860, 275 N.E.2d 236 (1971) — § 4.93.
People v. McAllister, 31 Ill. App. 3d 825, 334 N.E.2d 885 (1975) — § 4.91.
People v. Navorro, 99 Cal. App. 3d Supp. 1, 160 Cal. Rptr. 692 (1979) — § 5.09.
People v. Nunn, 63 Ill. App. 2d 465, 212 N.E.2d 342 (1965) — § 4.91.

People v. Perez, 169 Cal. App. 2d 473, 337 P.2d 539 (1959) — § 4.78.
People v. Price, 81 Ill. App. 2d 111, 225 N.E.2d 453 (1967) — § 4.91.
People v. Quick, 15 Ill. App. 3d 300, 304 N.E.2d 143 (1973) — § 4.91.
People v. Reese, 11 Ill. App. 3d 817, 298 N.E.2d 315 (1973) — § 4.91.
People v. Reons, 20 Ill. App. 3d 1005, 313 N.E.2d 184 (1974) — § 4.92.
People v. Rosochacki, 21 Ill. App. 3d 477, 315 N.E.2d 633 (1974) — § 4.93.
People v. Shoemaker, 31 Ill. App. 3d 724, 334 N.E.2d 347 (1975) — § 4.91.
People v. Sims, 29 Ill. App. 3d 815, 331 N.E.2d 178 (1975) — § 4.91.
People v. Smith, 90 Ill. App. 2d 388, 234 N.E.2d 161 (1967) — § 4.91.
People v. Smith, 7 Ill. App. 3d 350, 287 N.E.2d 509 (1972) — § 4.91.
People v. Snow, 21 Ill. App. 3d 873, 316 N.E.2d 216 (1974) — § 4.91.
People v. Street, 11 Ill. App. 3d 243, 296 N.E.2d 606 (1973) — § 4.93.
People v. Terry, 57 Cal. 2d 538, 21 Cal. Rptr. 185, 370 P.2d 985 (1962) — § 4.78.
People v. Tomaszek, 54 Ill. App. 2d 254, 204 N.E.2d 30 (1964) — § 4.91.
People v. Treen, 33 Misc. 2d 571, 225 N.Y.S.2d 787 (1962) — § 5.09.
People v. Vogel, 46 Cal. 2d 798, 299 P.2d 850 (1956) — § 5.09.
People v. Waggoner, 388 Ill. 468, 58 N.E.2d 553 (1945) — § 4.94.
People v. Watts, 55 Ill. App. 3d 66, 370 N.E.2d 583 (1977) — § 4.93.
People v. Weiss, 34 Ill. App. 3d 840, 341 N.E.2d 79 (1976) — § 4.93.
People v. Wilson, 23 Ill. App. 3d 457, 318 N.E.2d 767 (1974) — § 4.91.
People v. Woods, 15 Ill. App. 3d 221, 303 N.E.2d 562 (1973) — § 4.91.
People v. Woods, 17 Ill. App. 3d 835, 308 N.E.2d 856 (1974) — § 4.91.
Perez v. State, 7 Md. App. 452, 256 A.2d 369 (1969) — §§ 3.01, 3.07.
Perkins v. State, 11 Md. App. 527, 275 A.2d 517 (1971) — §§ 2.30, 5.10.
Perkins v. State, 26 Md. App. 526, 339 A.2d 360 (1975) — §§ 1.08, 4.06, 5.06.
Perry v. State, 234 Md. 48, 197 A.2d 833 (1964) — §§ 2.06, 5.12, 5.16.
Pettie v. State, 70 Md. App. 602, 522 A.2d 394 (1987) — § 2.24.
Pettis v. State, 2 Md. App. 651, 236 A.2d 429 (1968) — § 1.04.
Pharr v. State, 36 Md. App. 615, 375 A.2d 1129 (1977) — §§ 2.25, 4.43.
Phenious v. State, 11 Md. App. 385, 274 A.2d 658 (1971) — §§ 4.82, 4.83.
Picone v. Talbott, 29 Md. App. 536, 349 A.2d 615 (1975) — § 4.75.
Pierce v. State, 227 Md. 221, 175 A.2d 743 (1961) — § 2.25.
Pierce v. State, 62 Md. App. 453, 490 A.2d 261 (1985) — § 5.07.
Pierson v. Ray, 386 U.S. 547, 87 S. Ct. 1213, 18 L. Ed. 2d 288 (1967) — § 4.80.
Pinder v. State, 31 Md. App. 126, 355 A.2d 489 (1976) — § 1.13.
Pinkett v. State, 30 Md. App. 458, 352 A.2d 358 (1976) — § 4.41.
Piracci v. State, 207 Md. 499, 115 A.2d 262 (1955) — § 4.06.
Pitts v. State, 36 Md. App. 594, 374 A.2d 632 (1977) — § 1.03.
Planned Parenthood Ass'n v. Ashcroft, 462 U.S. 476, 103 S. Ct. 2517, 76 L. Ed. 2d 733 (1983) — § 4.51.

Planned Parenthood v. Danforth, 428 U.S. 52, 96 S. Ct. 2831, 49 L. Ed. 2d 788 (1976) — § 4.51.
Plumley v. State, 4 Md. App. 671, 245 A.2d 111 (1968) — § 1.13.
Poff v. State, 4 Md. App. 186, 241 A.2d 898 (1968) — §§ 4.55, 4.57, 4.69, 5.06.
Pointer v. State, 238 Md. 23, 207 A.2d 611 (1965) — § 4.55.
Polansky v. State, 205 Md. 362, 109 A.2d 52 (1954) — §§ 4.79, 4.93.
Polisher v. State, 11 Md. App. 555, 276 A.2d 102 (1971) — § 4.67.
Ponder v. State, 227 Md. 570, 177 A.2d 839 (1962) — § 4.55.
Ponds v. State, 25 Md. App. 162, 335 A.2d 162 (1975) — § 2.25.
Poole v. State, 290 Md. 114, 428 A.2d 434 (1981) — §§ 1.01, 2.08.
Poole v. State, 295 Md. 167, 453 A.2d 1218 (1983) — §§ 1.04, 4.21b, 4.21c, 5.08.
Pope v. State, 284 Md. 309, 396 A.2d 1054 (1979) — §§ 4.02, 4.58.
Porreca v. State, 49 Md. App. 522, 433 A.2d 1204 (1981) — §§ 5.01, 5.08.
Pouncey v. State, 297 Md. 264, 465 A.2d 475 (1983) — § 5.08.
Powell v. State, 56 Md. App. 351, 467 A.2d 1052 (1983) — § 2.29.
Prather v. Warden, 1 Md. App. 478, 231 A.2d 726 (1967) — § 5.01.
Presley v. State, 224 Md. 550, 168 A.2d 510 (1961) — § 1.11a.
Pressley v. State, 295 Md. 143, 454 A.2d 347 (1983) — § 1.05.
Preston v. Warden, 225 Md. 628, 169 A.2d 407 (1961) — § 4.80.
Prevatte v. Director, Patuxent Inst., 5 Md. App. 406, 248 A.2d 170 (1968) — § 1.11a.
Price v. State, 227 Md. 28, 175 A.2d 11 (1961) — § 4.80.
Price v. State, 261 Md. 573, 277 A.2d 256 (1971) — § 4.21b.
Price v. State, 3 Md. App. 155, 238 A.2d 275 (1968) — § 4.83.
Price v. State, 4 Md. App. 701, 244 A.2d 900 (1968) — §§ 2.01, 4.06.
Price v. State, 7 Md. App. 131, 254 A.2d 219 (1969) — § 2.25.
Pritchard v. Warden, 209 Md. 662, 121 A.2d 696 (1956) — § 4.60.
Proctor v. State, 49 Md. App. 696, 435 A.2d 484 (1981) — §§ 2.01, 4.91.
Proctor Elec. Co. v. Zink, 217 Md. 22, 141 A.2d 721 (1958) — §§ 2.08, 2.11.
Proffitt v. Florida, 428 U.S. 242, 96 S. Ct. 2960, 49 L. Ed. 2d 913 (1976) — § 4.21c.
Prokopis v. State, 49 Md. App. 531, 433 A.2d 1191 (1981) — Appx. III.
Propst v. State, 5 Md. App. 36, 245 A.2d 88 (1968) — § 4.74.
Puckett v. State, 13 Md. App. 584, 284 A.2d 252 (1971) — § 4.77.
Pulley v. State, 38 Md. App. 682, 382 A.2d 621 (1978) — §§ 2.10, 4.21b, 5.02.
Pumphrey v. Tabler, 175 Md. 498, 2 A.2d 668 (1938) — § 2.05.

Q

Quaglione v. State, 15 Md. App. 571, 292 A.2d 785 (1972) — § 4.06.

R

Radovsky v. State, 296 Md. 386, 464 A.2d 239 (1983) — § 2.25.
Raimondi v. State, 265 Md. 229, 288 A.2d 882 (1972) — Appx. II.
Raimondi v. State, 12 Md. App. 322, 278 A.2d 664 (1971) — §§ 4.56, 5.07.
Raithel v. State, 280 Md. 291, 372 A.2d 1069 (1977) — § 5.08.
Raley v. State, 32 Md. App. 515, 363 A.2d 261 (1976) — § 4.44, Appx. I.
Randell Book Corporation v. State, 64 Md. 589, 497 A.2d 1174 (1985) — § 1.01.
Randolph v. State, 10 Md. App. 89, 267 A.2d 767 (1970) — § 4.57.
Rau v. State, 133 Md. 613, 105 A. 867 (1919) — §§ 4.15, 4.36.
Rawlings v. Kentucky, 448 U.S. 98, 100 S. Ct. 2556, 65 L. Ed. 2d 633 (1980) — § 2.25.
Read v. State, 7 Md. App. 200, 253 A.2d 774 (1969) — § 4.57.
Reagan v. State, 2 Md. App. 262, 234 A.2d 278 (1967) — §§ 4.55, 4.57, 4.69.
Reagan v. State, 4 Md. App. 590, 244 A.2d 623 (1968) — §§ 4.57, 4.69.
Reagan v. State, 6 Md. App. 477, 251 A.2d 615 (1969) — § 4.57.
Reckard v. State, 2 Md. App. 312, 234 A.2d 630 (1967) — § 2.04.
Reddick v. State, 219 Md. 95, 148 A.2d 384 (1959) — § 4.68.
Reese v. State, 17 Md. App. 73, 299 A.2d 848 (1973) — § 4.61.
Reese v. State, 37 Md. App. 450, 378 A.2d 4 (1977) — § 4.68.
Regle v. State, 9 Md. App. 346, 264 A.2d 119 (1970) — § 4.06.
Reinsnider v. State, 60 Md. App. 589, 483 A.2d 1324 (1984) — § 5.06.
Rent-A-Car Co. v. Globe & Rutgers Fire Ins. Co., 163 Md. 401, 163 A. 702 (1933) — § 1.11a.
Rex v. Knight, 2 East D.C. 510 (1782) — § 5.03.
Rhoades v. State, 56 Md. App. 601, 468 A.2d 650 (1983) — § 4.36.
Rhodes Island v. Innis, 446 U.S. 291, 100 S. Ct. 1682, 64 L. Ed. 2d 297 (1980) — § 2.25.
Rice v. State, 9 Md. App. 552, 267 A.2d 261 (1970) — § 4.36.
Richards v. State, 65 Md. App. 141, 499 A.2d 965 (1985) — § 5.16.
Richardson v. Snow, 340 F. Supp. 1261 (D. Md. 1972) — § 4.80.
Richards v. State, 221 Md. 85, 156 A.2d 436 (1959) — §§ 4.71, 4.72, 4.73, 4.96.
Richardson v. State, 398 F. Supp. 425 (1975) — §§ 4.91, 4.93.
Richardson v. United States, 403 F.2d 574 (D.C. Cir. 1968) — § 5.03.
Richmond Newspapers, Inc. v. Virginia, 448 U.S. 555, 100 S. Ct. 2814, 65 L. Ed. 2d 973 (1980) — § 1.11a.
Ricketts v. State, 291 Md. 701, 436 A.2d 906 (1981) — §§ 2.06, 207, 4.61.
Ricketts v. State, 46 Md. App. 410, 417 A.2d 465 (1980) — § 4.71.
Ricks v. State, 70 Md. App. 287, 520 A.2d 1136 (1987) — § 4.77.
Ridley v. State, 228 Md. 281, 179 A.2d 710 (1962) — § 4.55.
Rife v. State, 9 Md. App. 658, 267 A.2d 326 (1970) — § 4.80.
Riffey v. Tonder, 36 Md. App. 633, 375 A.2d 1138 (1977) — §§ 2.03, 2.05.
Riggleman v. State, 33 Md. App. 344, 364 A.2d 1159 (1976) — § 5.08.

Rivenback v. State, 58 Md. App. 626, 473 A.2d 1329 (1984) — § 2.01.
Robert v. State, 220 Md. 159, 151 A.2d 737 (1959) — §§ 2.04, 4.33, 4.36.
Roberts v. Louisiana, 431 U.S. 633, 97 S. Ct. 1993, 52 L. Ed. 2d 637 (1977) — § 4.21c.
Roberts v. Warden, 242 Md. 459, 219 A.2d 254 (1966) — § 4.12.
Robertson v. State, 295 Md. 688, 457 A.2d 826 (1983) — § 1.04.
Robeson v. State, 39 Md. App. 365, 386 A.2d 795 (1978) — §§ 2.25, 4.21b.
Robey v. State, 54 Md. App. 60, 456 A.2d 953 (1983) — §§ 4.58, 5.08.
Robinson v. California, 370 U.S. 660, 82 S. Ct. 1417, 8 L. Ed. 2d 758 (1962) — §§ 4.35, 4.63, 4.76.
Robinson v. State, 53 Md. 151, 36 Am. R. 399 (1880) — § 4.57.
Robinson v. State, 229 Md. 503, 184 A.2d 814 (1962) — §§ 4.06, 4.74.
Robinson v. State, 1 Md. App. 522, 231 A.2d 920 (1967) — § 2.25.
Robinson v. State, 3 Md. App. 666, 240 A.2d 638 (1968) — § 2.25.
Robinson v. State, 4 Md. App. 515, 243 A.2d 879 (1968) — §§ 2.06, 2.07, 4.55, 4.57, 4.71.
Robinson v. State, 5 Md. App. 723, 249 A.2d 504 (1969) — §§ 1.05, 4.01, 5.10.
Robinson v. State, 17 Md. App. 451, 302 A.2d 659 (1973) — § 4.73.
Robinson v. State, 18 Md. App. 438, 306 A.2d 624 (1973) — § 4.65.
Robinson v. State, 18 Md. App. 678, 308 A.2d 734 (1973) — §§ 1.05, 2.32.
Robinson v. State, 19 Md. App. 20, 308 A.2d 712 (1973) — § 4.59.
Robinson v. State, 20 Md. App. 450, 316 A.2d 268 (1974) — § 5.02.
Robinson v. State, 42 Md. App. 617, 402 A.2d 115 (1979) — §§ 4.65, 5.05, 5.18.
Robinson v. State, 67 Md. App. 445, 508 A.2d 159 (1986) — § 4.36.
Robinson v. Warden, 5 Md. App. 68, 245 A.2d 407 (1968) — § 2.25.
Rock v. State, 6 Md. App. 618, 253 A.2d 401 (1969) — § 2.25.
Roddy v. Finnegan, 43 Md. 490 (1876) — § 4.80.
Roderick v. State, 9 Md. App. 120, 262 A.2d 783 (1970) — §§ 3.05, 4.72.
Rodgers v. State, 280 Md. 406, 373 A.2d 944 (1977) — § 4.80.
Rodgers v. State, 4 Md. App. 407, 243 A.2d 28 (1968) — §§ 2.04, 2.29.
Rodgers v. State, 32 Md. App. 90, 359 A.2d 122 (1976) — § 5.11.
Roe v. Wade, 410 U.S. 113, 93 S. Ct. 705, 35 L. Ed. 2d 147 (1973) — § 4.51.
Rolfes v. State, 10 Md. App. 204, 268 A.2d 795 (1970) — §§ 2.05, 4.23b, 4.24.
Roll v. State, 15 Md. App. 31, 288 A.2d 605 (1972) — § 4.59.
Roos v. State, 45 Md. App. 21, 410 A.2d 1113 (1980) — §§ 4.41, 4.42.
Rosenberg v. State, 164 Md. 473, 165 A. 306 (1933) — §§ 3.04, 4.60.
Rosenberg v. State, 12 Md. App. 20, 276 A.2d 708 (1971) — § 4.77.
Ross v. State, 276 Md. 664, 350 A.2d 680 (1976) — § 2.10.
Ross v. State, 308 Md. 337, 519 A.2d 735 (1987) — § 4.21b.
Rouse v. State, 202 Md. 481, 97 A.2d 285 (1953) — § 4.06.

Roviaro v. United States, 353 U.S. 53, 77 S. Ct. 623 1 L. Ed. 2d 639 (1957) — § 5.06.
Rucker v. State, 196 Md. 334, 76 A.2d 572 (1950) — §§ 4.74, 4.76.
Rusk v. State, 43 Md. App. 476, 406 A.2d 624 (1979) — § 4.36.
Russell v. State, 69 Md. App. 554, 518 A.2d 1081 (1987) — § 4.76.
Rustin v. State, 46 Md. App. 28, 415 A.2d 631 (1980) — §§ 2.28, 2.29.

S

Sabatini v. State, 14 Md. App. 431, 287 A.2d 511 (1972) — § 2.25.
St. Clair v. State, 1 Md. App. 605, 232 A.2d 565 (1967) — §§ 4.57, 4.69.
Saldiveri v. State, 217 Md. 412, 143 A.2d 70 (1958) — §§ 2.04, 4.33, 4.35, 4.36.
Salem v. United States Lines Co., 370 U.S. 31, 82 S. Ct. 1119, 8 L. Ed. 2d 313 (1962) — § 2.05.
Salzman v. State, 49 Md. App. 25, 430 A.2d 847 (1981) — §§ 4.06, 4.77.
Sample v. State, 33 Md. App. 398, 365 A.2d 773 (1976) — § 4.55.
Samson v. State, 27 Md. App. 326, 341 A.2d 817 (1975) — § 4.76.
Sanders v. State, 1 Md. App. 630, 232 A.2d 555 (1967) — §§ 2.08, 4.01.
Sanders v. State, 8 Md. App. 17, 257 A.2d 442 (1969) — § 4.60.
Sandstrom v. Montana, 442 U.S. 510, 99 S. Ct. 2450, 61 L. Ed. 2d 4 (1979) — §§ 3.01, 3.07, 5.01, Appx. V.
Sartor v. Arkansas Natural Gas Corp., 321 U.S. 620, 64 S. Ct. 724, 88 L. Ed. 2d 967 (1944) — § 2.05.
Saul v. State, 6 Md. App. 540, 252 A.2d 282 (1969) — § 5.08.
Saunders v. Mullinix, 195 Md. 235, 72 A.2d 720 (1950) — §§ 4.71, 4.72, 4.73, 4.91, 5.03.
Saunders v. State, 8 Md. App. 143, 258 A.2d 776 (1969) — § 4.84.
Saunders v. State, 28 Md. App. 455, 346 A.2d 448 (1975) — § 4.78.
Savoy v. State, 236 Md. 36, 202 A.2d 324 (1964) — § 4.42.
Savoy v. State, 64 Md. App. 241, 494 A.2d 957 (1985) — § 2.10.
Scarborough v. State, 3 Md. App. 208, 238 A.2d 297 (1968) — § 2.24.
Scarborough v. State, 50 Md. App. 276, 437 A.2d 672 (1982) — §§ 2.06, 2.11, 2.22.
Schmerber v. California, 384 U.S. 757, 86 S. Ct. 1826, 16 L. Ed. 2d 908 (1966) — §§ 2.32, 4.63.
Schuman v. State, 19 Md. App. 400, 311 A.2d 460 (1973) — § 5.06.
Scott v. John H. Hampshire, Inc., 246 Md. 171, 227 A.2d 751 (1967) — § 2.05.
Scott v. State, 29 Md. 235, 465 A.2d 1126 (1983) — §§ 4.21c, 5.08.
Scott v. State, 2 Md. App. 709, 237 A.2d 61 (1968) — §§ 4.33, 4.36.
Scott v. State, 49 Md. App. 70, 430 A.2d 615 (1981) — §§ 2.22, 4.21b.
Scott v. State, 61 Md. App. 599, 487 A.2d 1204 (1985) — § 4.36.
Scott v. State, 64 Md. App. 311, 494 A.2d 992 (1985) — §§ 2.07, 4.23b.

Screws v. United States, 325 U.S. 91, 65 S. Ct. 1031, 89 L. Ed. 2d 1495 (1945) — § 4.86.
Seward v. State, 208 Md. 341, 118 A.2d 505 (1955) — § 4.75.
Sharpe v. State, 231 Md. 401, 190 A.2d 628 (1963) — §§ 4.61, 4.80.
Shell v. State, 307 Md. 46, 512 A.2d 358 (1986) — §§ 4.44, 5.01.
Shelton v. State, 198 Md. 405, 84 A.2d 76 (1951) — § 1.05.
Shelton v. State, 3 Md. App. 394, 239 A.2d 610 (1968) — § 1.05.
Shenberger v. State, 234 Md. 363, 199 A.2d 233 (1964) — § 4.13.
Sheppard v. Maxwell, 384 U.S. 333, 86 S. Ct. 1507, 16 L. Ed. 2d 600 (1966) — § 1.11a.
Sherman v. State, 288 Md. 636, 421 A.2d 80 (1980) — § 1.09.
Sherman v. United States, 356 U.S. 369, 78 S. Ct. 819, 2 L. Ed. 2d 848 (1958) — § 5.06.
Sherrill v. State, 14 Md. App. 146, 286 A.2d 528 (1972) — § 5.08.
Shifflet v. State, 4 Md. App. 227, 242 A.2d 182 (1968) — § 4.65.
Shipley v. State, 243 Md. 262, 220 A.2d 585 (1966) — §§ 4.41, 4.42.
Shockley v. State, 218 Md. 491, 148 A.2d 371 (1959) — § 4.21b.
Shoemaker v. State, 228 Md. 462, 180 A.2d 682 (1962) — §§ 1.08, 4.21c, 5.08.
Shotkosky v. State, 8 Md. App. 492, 261 A.2d 171 (1970) — Appx. III.
Shrader v. State, 10 Md. App. 268 A.2d 257 (1970) — §§ 2.06, 4.70, 4.83.
Shuck v. State, 29 Md. App. 33, 349 A.2d 378 (1975) — §§ 4.23b, 4.23c, 5.04, 5.12.
Sibert v. State, 301 Md. 141, 482 A.2d 483 (1984) — §§ 4.91, 4.93.
Sigma Reproductive Health Center v. State, 297 Md. 660, 467 A.2d 483 (1983) — §§ 5.05, 5.18.
Silbert v. State, 12 Md. App. 516, 280 A.2d 55 (1971) — § 4.74.
Simkus v. State, 296 Md. 718, 464 A.2d 1055 (1983) — § 2.28.
Simmons v. State, 292 Md. 478, 439 A.2d 581 (1982) — § 5.08.
Simmons v. State, 8 Md. App. 355, 259 A.2d 814 (1969) — § 5.06.
Simmons v. State, 66 Md. App. 629, 505 A.2d 577 (1986) — §§ 4.23c, 5.08.
Simmons v. United States, 390 U.S. 377, 88 S. Ct. 967, 19 L. Ed. 2d 1247 (1968) — §§ 2.28, 2.30.
Simms v. State, 288 Md. 712, 421 A.2d 957 (1980) — §§ 4.12, 4.14.
Simms v. State, 4 Md. App. 160, 242 A.2d 185 (1968) — § 2.32.
Simms v. State, 49 Md. App. 515, 433 A.2d 1199 (1982) — §§ 1.11a, 2.33.
Simopoulos v. Virginia, 462 U.S. 506, 103 S. Ct. 232, 76 L. Ed. 2d 755 (1983) — § 4.51.
Simpson v. State, 34 Md. App. 378, 367 A.2d 66 (1977) — § 2.21.
Sinclair v. State, 21 Md. App. 477, 319 A.2d 549 (1975) — § 4.67.
Singleton v. Roman, 195 Md. 241, 72 A.2d 705 (1950) — § 4.63.
Sippio v. State, 227 Md. 449, 177 A.2d 261 (1962) — § 4.71.
Sites v. State, 300 Md. 702, 481 A.2d 192 (1984) — § 4.63.

Sizemore v. State, 5 Md. App. 507, 248 A.2d 417 (1968) — §§ 1.11a, 4.71, 4.73.
Sizemore v. State, 10 Md. App. 682, 272 A.2d 824 (1971) — §§ 4.55, 4.57, 4.69.
Skidmore v. State, 80 Neb. 698, 115 N.W. 288 (1908) — § 4.02.
Skinner v. State, 16 Md. App. 116, 293 A.2d 828 (1972) — § 4.77.
Skipper v. South Carolina — U.S. —, 106 S. Ct. 1669, 90 L. Ed. 2d 1 (1986) — § 4.21c.
Slagle v. State, 243 Md. 435, 221 A.2d 641 (1966) — § 4.65.
Slansky v. State, 192 Md. 94, 63 A.2d 599 (1949) — § 1.01.
Smallwood v. State, 51 Md. App. 463, 443 A.2d 1003 (1982) — § 4.03.
Smallwood v. Warden, 367 F.2d 945 (4th Cir. 1966) — § 2.25.
Smiley v. State, 294 Md. 461, 450 A.2d 909 (1981) — § 1.01.
Smith v. Branscome, 251 Md. 582, 248 A.2d 455 (1968) — § 2.08.
Smith v. Illinois, 469 U.S. 91, 105 S. Ct. 490, 83 L. Ed. 2d 488 (1984) — § 2.25.
Smith v. State, 64 Md. 25, 20 A. 1026 (1885) — § 2.07.
Smith v. State, 224 Md. 509, 168 A.2d 356 (1961) — § 4.36.
Smith v. State, 233 Md. 430, 197 A.2d 103 (1964) — § 4.14.
Smith v. State, 237 Md. 573, 207 A.2d 493 (1965) — § 4.67.
Smith v. State, 302 Md. 175, 486 A.2d 196 (1985) — § 5.02, Appx. III.
Smith v. State, 4 Md. App. 128, 241 A.2d 437 (1968) — § 4.41.
Smith v. State, 6 Md. App. 59, 250 A.2d 285 (1969) — §§ 2.30, 5.10.
Smith v. State, 6 Md. App. 581, 252 A.2d 277 (1968) — § 4.36.
Smith v. State, 7 Md. App. 457, 256 A.2d 357 (1969) — § 4.68.
Smith v. State, 18 Md. App. 612, 308 A.2d 442 (1973) — § 4.41.
Smith v. State, 20 Md. App. 577, 318 A.2d 568 (1974) — §§ 1.05, 4.52.
Smith v. State, 31 Md. App. 106, 355 A.2d 527 (1976) — § 2.25.
Smith v. State, 41 Md. App. 277, 398 A.2d 426 (1979) — §§ 4.21a, 5.01.
Smith v. State, 51 Md. App. 408, 443 A.2d 985 (1982) — §§ 1.13, 4.78.
Smith v. State, 62 Md. App. 670, 491 A.2d 587 (1985) — § 4.58.
Smith v. State, 69 Md. App. 115, 516 A.2d 985 (1986) — § 5.01.
Smoot v. State, 31 Md. App. 138, 355 A.2d 495 (1976) — § 1.13.
Snead v. State, 234 Md. 63, 197 A.2d 920 (1964) — § 4.77.
Snead v. State, 286 Md. 122, 406 A.2d 98 (1976) — § 1.15.
Snowden v. State, 133 Md. 624, 106 A. 5 (1919) — § 2.05.
Soles v. State, 16 Md. App. 656, 299 A.2d 502 (1973) — § 4.56.
Sorrells v. United States, 287 U.S. 435, 53 S. Ct. 210, 77 L. Ed. 2d 413 (1932) — § 5.06.
Souffie v. State, 50 Md. App. 547, 439 A.2d 1127 (1982) — §§ 2.25, 4.36, 5.11, Appx. III.
South Dakota v. Neville, 459 U.S. 553, 103 S. Ct. 916, 74 L. Ed. 2d 748 (1983) — §§ 2.32, 4.63.
Sparkman v. State, 3 Md. App. 527, 240 A.2d 328 (1968) — § 4.55.
Spears v. State, 38 Md. App. 700, 382 A.2d 616 (1978) — § 4.75.

Spector v. State, 289 Md. 407, 425 A.2d 197 (1981) — § 4.56.
Spell v. State, 7 Md. App. 121, 253 A.2d 919 (1969) — § 2.25.
Spell v. State, 49 Md. App. 323, 431 A.2d 752 (1981) — § 1.01.
Spence v. State, 224 Md. 17, 165 A.2d 917 (1960) — § 4.73.
Spence v. State, 51 Md. App. 359, 443 A.2d 648 (1982) — §§ 4.82, 4.83.
Spencer v. State, 69 Md. 28, 13 A. 809 (1888) — § 5.08.
Spencer v. State, 1 Md. App. 264, 229 A.2d 151 (1967) — §§ 1.02, 4.14.
Spillers v. State, 10 Md. App. 643, 272 A.2d 49 (1971) — § 4.72.
Spinger v. Collins, 586 F.2d 329 (4th Cir. 1978) — § 5.08.
Springfield v. State, 238 Md. 611, 208 A.2d 603 (1965) — § 4.55.
Spurrier v. State, 229 Md. 110, 182 A.2d 358 (1962) — §§ 4.41, 4.42.
Squire v. State, 32 Md. App. 307, 363 A.2d 520 (1976) — Appx. V.
Stockowitz v. State, 68 Md. App. 368, 511 A.2d 1105 (1986) — § 4.91.
Stambaugh v. State, 30 Md. App. 707, 353 A.2d 638 (1976) — Appx. V.
Stansbury v. State, 218 Md. 255, 146 A.2d 17 (1958) — § 5.08.
State v. Adams, 293 Md. 665, 447 A.2d 833 (1982) — § 4.74.
State v. Allewalt, 308 Md. 89, 517 A.2d 741 (1986) — § 4.36.
State v. Amick, 171 Md. 536, 189 A. 817 (1937) — § 1.06.
State v. Batdort, 293 N.C. 486, 238 S.E.2d 497 (1977) — § 2.33.
State v. Berry, 287 Md. 491, 413 A.2d 557 (1980) — § 4.60.
State v. Canova, 278 Md. 483, 365 A.2d 988 (1976) — § 4.56.
State v. Carbone, 10 N.J. 329, 91 A.2d 571 (1952) — § 4.06.
State v. Cassel, 2 Harris & G. 407 (1828) — § 4.91.
State v. Cherry, 298 N.C. 86, 257 L. Ed. 2d 551 (1979) — § 4.21c.
State v. Ciccarelli, 55 Md. App. 150, 461 A.2d 550 (1983) — § 4.76.
State v. Collins, 296 Md. 670, 464 A.2d 1038 (1983) — § 2.28.
State v. Conn, 286 Md. 406, 408 A.2d 700 (1979) — § 5.08.
State v. Crawford, 308 Md. 683, 521 A.2d 1193 (1987) — §§ 5.05, 5.18.
State v. DeLawder, 28 Md. App. 212, 344 A.2d 446 (1975) — §§ 4.15, 4.36.
State v. Devers, 260 Md. 360, 272 A.2d 794 (1971) — § 4.78.
State v. Diamond, 264 P. 697 (Nev. 1928) — § 4.33.
State v. Dille, 258 N.W.2d 565 (Minn. 1977) — § 4.63.
State v. Evans, 278 Md. 197, 362 A.2d 629 (1976) — §§ 4.36, 5.06, 5.11.
State v. Fabritz, 276 Md. 416, 348 A.2d 275 (1975) — § 4.58.
State v. Faulkner, 301 Md. 482, 483 A.2d 759 (1984) — §§ 4.13, 4.23b, 4.23c.
State v. Fowler, 259 Md. 95, 267 A.2d 228 (1970) — § 2.25.
State v. Franklin, 281 Md. 51, 375 A.2d 1116 (1977) — §§ 2.09, 2.25.
State v. Frye, 283 Md. 709, 393 A.2d 1372 (1978) — § 4.21b.
State v. Garland, 29 Md. App. 27, 349 A.2d 734 (1975) — § 4.22a, Appx. V.
State v. Gibson, 4 Md. App. 236, 242 A.2d 575 (1968) — §§ 4.24, 4.25.
State v. Goldsberry, 160 Kan. 138, 160 P.2d 690 (1945) — § 5.03.
State v. Goodman, 298 N.C. 1, 257 S.E.2d 569 (1979) — § 4.21c.

State v. Gover, 267 Md. 602, 298 A.2d 378 (1973) — §§ 4.71, 4.82, 5.01, 5.08.
State v. Graves, — La. —, 301 So. 2d 864 (1974) — § 4.78.
State v. Heyes, 44 Wash. 2d 579, 269 P.2d 577 (1954) — § 5.03.
State v. Hightower, 238 La. 876, 116 So. 2d 699 (1959) — § 4.63.
State v. Hodges, 55 Md. 127 (1880) — § 4.79.
State v. Hunt, 49 Md. App. 355, 432 A.2d 479 (1981) — § 4.91.
State v. Hutchinson, 287 Md. 198, 411 A.2d 1035 (1980) — Appx. III.
State v. Hyman, 98 Md. 596, 57 A. 6 (1904) — § 1.06.
State v. Ingel, 18 Md. App. 514, 308 A.2d 223 (1973) — § 4.51.
State v. James, 203 Md. 113, 100 A.2d 12 (1953) — § 4.60.
State v. Jenkins, 307 Md. 501, 515 A.2d 465 (1986) — § 4.13.
State v. Jones, 51 Md. App. 321, 443 A.2d 967 (1982) — §§ 2.33, 4.36.
State v. Kidd, 281 Md. 32, 375 A.2d 1105 (1977) — §§ 2.09, 2.25.
State v. Leach, 296 Md. 591, 463 A.2d 872 (1983) — § 4.76.
State v. Levitt, 42 Md. App. 1, 426 A.2d 383 (1981) — § 4.78.
State v. Lloyd, 48 Md. App. 535, 429 A.2d 244 (1981) — § 4.78.
State v. Loscomb, 291 Md. 424, 435 A.2d 464 (1981) — §§ 4.26, 4.63.
State v. Magliano, 7 Md. App. 286, 255 A.2d 470 (1969) — § 4.65.
State v. Mercer, 101 Md. 535, 61 A. 220 (1905) — § 4.78.
State v. Merchant, 10 Md. App. 545, 271 A.2d 752 (1970) — § 4.36.
State v. Metscher, 297 Md. 368, 464 A.2d 1052 (1983) — § 2.28.
State v. Moon, 291 Md. 463, 436 A.2d 420 (1981) — §§ 2.32, 4.63.
State v. Morton, 295 Md. 487, 456 A.2d 909 (1983) — § 4.65.
State v. Quinn, 64 Md. App. 668, 498 A.2d 676 (1985) — § 2.25.
State v. Raithel, 285 Md. 478, 404 A.2d 264 (1979) — § 2.25.
State v. Rawlings, 38 Md. App. 479, 381 A.2d 708 (1978) — § 4.60.
State v. Reese, 283 Md. 86, 388 A.2d 122 (1978) — § 4.68.
State v. Rogers, 40 Md. App. 573, 392 A.2d 1186 (1978) — § 4.65.
State v. Roll, 267 Md. 714, 298 A.2d 867 (1973) — § 4.59.
State v. Ruona, 133 Mont. 243, 321 P.2d 615 (1958) — § 4.63.
State v. Rusk, 289 Md. 230, 424 A.2d 720 (1981) — §§ 1.04, 4.15, 4.36.
State v. Rust, 197 Neb. 528, 250 N.W.2d 867 (1977) — § 4.21c.
State v. Schuller, 280 Md. 305, 372 A.2d 1076 (1977) — § 4.85.
State v. Ward, 284 Md. 189, 396 A.2d 1041 (1978) — §§ 4.01, 4.02, 4.03.
State v. Werner, 302 Md. 550, 489 A.2d 1119 (1985) — § 2.10.
State v. Williamson, 282 Md. 100, 382 A.2d 588 (1978) — §§ 4.01, 4.02.
State v. Werkheiser, 299 Md. 529, 474 A.2d 898 (1984) — §§ 4.26, 4.63.
State v. Wood, 648 P.2d 71 (Utah 1982) — § 4.21c.
State ex rel. Sonner v. Shearin, 272 Md. 502, 325 A.2d 573 (1974) — § 4.44.
State Ins. Comm'r v. National Bureau of Cas. Underwriters, 248 Md. 292, 305, 236 A.2d 282 (1967) — § 4.21c.
State Rds. Comm'n v. Creswell, 235 Md. 220, 201 A.2d 328 (1964) — § 2.05.

Stebbing v. Maryland, 469 U.S. 900, 105 S. Ct. 276, 83 L. Ed. 2d 212 (1984) — § 4.21c.
Stebbing v. State, 299 Md. 331, 473 A.2d 903 (1984) — §§ 4.21c, 4.82.
Stevens v. Warden, 366 F.2d 565 (4th Cir. 1966) — § 2.25.
Stevenson v. State, 289 Md. 167, 423 A.2d 558 (1980) — §§ 1.01, 2.25.
Stevenson v. State, 43 Md. App. 120, 403 A.2d 812 (1972) — § 4.44.
Stewart v. State, 232 Md. 318, 193 A.2d 40 (1963) — §§ 4.77, 5.06.
Stewart v. State, 275 Md. 258, 340 A.2d 290 (1975) — § 4.65.
Stewart v. State, 65 Md. App. 372, 500 A.2d 676 (1985) — § 4.21b.
Stickell v. Mayor of Baltimore, 252 Md. 464, 250 A.2d 541 (1969) — § 2.05.
Stovall v. Denno, 388 U.S. 293, 87 S. Ct. 1967, 18 L. Ed. 2d 1199 (1967) — §§ 2.28, 2.30.
Straughn v. State, 297 Md. 329, 465 A.2d 1166 (1983) — §§ 2.10, 2.30.
Streat v. State, 11 Md. App. 543, 275 A.2d 537 (1971) — §§ 1.02, 1.04.
Street v. State, 60 Md. App. 573, 483 A.2d 1316 (1984) — § 4.70.
Streeter v. State, 5 Md. App. 435, 248 A.2d 119 (1968) — § 4.80.
Sugarman v. State, 173 Md. 52, 195 A. 324 (1937) — §§ 4.56, 4.80.
Sutton v. State, 10 Md. App. 353, 270 A.2d 497 (1970) — § 2.01.
Swain v. State, 50 Md. App. 29, 435 A.2d 804 (1981) — §§ 2.05, 2.25, 4.22a, 5.08, Appx. V.
Sweeney v. State, 6 Md. App. 431, 252 A.2d 9 (1969) — § 5.08.
Sweetwine v. State, 288 Md. 199, 421 A.2d 60 (1980) — § 4.83.
Sydnor v. State, 39 Md. App. 459, 387 A.2d 297 (1978) — § 4.36.
Szewczyk v. State, 7 Md. App. 597, 256 A.2d 713 (1969) — § 5.03.

T

Tabbs v. State, 10 Md. App. 177, 268 A.2d 598 (1970) — § 4.64.
Tague v. Louisiana, 444 U.S. 469, 100 S. Ct. 652, 62 L. Ed. 2d 622 (1980) — § 2.25.
Tasco v. State, 223 Md. 503, 165 A.2d 456 (1960) — § 2.24.
Taliaferro v. State, 295 Md. 376, 456 A.2d 29 (1983) — § 5.02.
Tate v. State, 236 Md. 312, 203 A.2d 882 (1964) — § 4.13.
Tate v. State, 32 Md. App. 613, 363 A.2d 622 (1976) — § 4.70.
Taylor v. Alabama, 457 U.S. 687, 102 S. Ct. 2664, 73 L. Ed. 2d 314 (1982) — § 2.25.
Taylor v. State, 214 Md. 156, 133 A.2d 414 (1957) — § 4.12.
Taylor v. State, 238 Md. 424, 209 A.2d 595 (1965) — §§ 3.01. 3.07.
Taylor v. State, 278 Md. 150, 360 A.2d 430 (1976) — § 2.23.
Taylor v. State, 28 Md. App. 560, 346 A.2d 718 (1975) — § 5.07.
Tender v. State, 2 Md. App. 692, 237 A.2d 65 (1968) — §§ 4.82, 4.83.
Tereshuk v. State, 66 Md. App. 193, 503 A.2d 254 (1986) — § 4.63.
Terminiello v. Chicago, 337 U.S. 1, 69 S. Ct. 894, 93 L. Ed. 2d 1131 (1949) — § 4.61.

Terrell v. State, 34 Md. App. 418, 367 A.2d 95 (1977) — § 4.06.
Testerman v. State, 61 Md. App. 257, 486 A.2d 233 (1985) — § 4.36.
Teves v. State, 33 Md. App. 195, 364 A.2d 593 (1976) — § 5.01, Appx. V.
Thanos v. State, 282 Md. 709, 387 A.2d 286 (1978) — § 4.41.
Thomas v. State, 206 Md. 49, 109 A.2d 909 (1954) — § 4.25.
Thomas v. State, 277 Md. 257, 353 A.2d 240 (1976) — § 4.16.
Thomas v. State, 277 Md. 314, 353 A.2d 256 (1976) — § 4.63.
Thomas v. State, 301 Md. 294, 483 A.2d 6 (1984) — §§ 4.21c, 4.35, 4.36, 4.37, 5.16.
Thomas v. State, 2 Md. App. 502, 235 A.2d 777 (1967) — § 4.02.
Thomas v. State, 3 Md. App. 101, 238 A.2d 558 (1968) — § 2.25.
Thomas v. State, 3 Md. App. 708, 240 A.2d 646 (1968) — §§ 2.29, 4.02.
Thomas v. State, 9 Md. App. 94, 262 A.2d 797 (1970) — §§ 5.12, 5.13, 5.15.
Thomas v. State, 29 Md. App. 45, 349 A.2d 384 (1975) — §§ 4.13, 4.23c.
Thomas v. State, 50 Md. App. 286, 437 A.2d 678 (1982) — § 1.08, Appx. IV.
Thomas v. Warden, 683 F.2d 83 (4th Cir. 1982) — § 4.83.
Thompson v. State, 4 Md. App. 31, 240 A.2d 780 (1968) — § 1.02.
Thompson v. State, 5 Md. App. 191, 245 A.2d 903 (1968) — § 4.83.
Thompson v. State, 15 Md. App. 335, 290 A.2d 565 (1972) — § 4.80.
Thompson v. State, 38 Md. App. 499, 381 A.2d 704 (1978) — Appx. V.
Tichnell v. Maryland, 466 U.S. 993, 104 S. Ct. 2374, 80 L. Ed. 2d 846 (1984) — §§ 1.01, 1.04, 4.21c.
Tichnell v. State, 287 Md. 695, 415 A.2d 830 (1980) — §§ 1.04, 2.24, 4.21a, 4.21c, 5.11, 5.12, 5.14, 5.15, Appx. V.
Tichnell v. State, 290 Md. 43, 427 A.2d 991 (1981) — § 4.21c.
Tichnell v. State, 297 Md. 432, 468 A.2d 1 (1983) — § 4.21c.
Tillery v. State, 2 Md. App. 142, 233 A.2d 375 (1967) — § 4.14.
Tipton v. State, 1 Md. App. 556, 232 A.2d 289 (1967) — §§ 5.04, 5.12, 5.13, 5.15.
Tipton v. State, 39 Md. App. 578, 387 A.2d 628 (1978) — Appx. V.
Tisdale v. State, 30 Md. App. 334, 353 A.2d 658 (1976) — § 4.43.
Todd v. State, 28 Md. App. 127, 343 A.2d 890 (1975) — §§ 2.30, 4.43.
Todd v. Weikle, 36 Md. App. 663, 376 A.2d 104 (1977) — § 4.21c.
Tomolillo v. State, 4 Md. App. 711, 245 A.2d 94 (1968) — § 1.05.
Townsend v. United States, 95 F.2d 352 (D.C. Cir. 1938) — § 5.09.
Toyer v. State, 234 Md. 324, 199 A.2d 233 (1964) — § 4.77.
Trimble v. State, 300 Md. 387, 478 A.2d 1143 (1984) — §§ 1.01, 4.21c.
Tripp v. State, 36 Md. App. 459, 374 A.2d 384 (1977) — §§ 1.14, 4.22a, 4.23b, Appx. V.
Trovoto v. State, 36 Md. App. 183, 373 A.2d 78 (1977) — § 2.01.
Truesdale v. State, 16 Md. App. 260, 295 A.2d 808 (1972) — § 5.08.
Tucker v. State, 19 Md. App. 39, 308 A.2d 696 (1973) — §§ 4.62, 4.77.
Tull v. State, 230 Md. 596, 188 A.2d 150 (1963) — § 5.08.

Turner v. Louisiana, 379 U.S. 466, 85 S. Ct. 546, 13 L. Ed. 2d 424 (1965) — § 1.11a.
Turner v. State, 242 Md. 408, 219 A.2d 39 (1966) — § 4.55.
Turner v. State, 6 Md. App. 337, 251 A.2d 383 (1969) — § 4.68.
Turner v. State, 45 Md. App. 168, 411 A.2d 1094 (1980) — § 4.02.
Turner v. State, 55 Md. App. 367, 462 A.2d 70 (1983) — § 3.01.
Turpin v. State, 55 Md. 462 (1881) — § 5.16.
Tyler v. United States, App. D.C. 495 A.2d 1180 (1985) — § 1.13.
Tyner v. Warden, 232 Md. 666, 194 A.2d 793 (1963) — § 4.55.

U

Ulster County Court v. Allen, 442 U.S. 140, 99 S. Ct. 2213, 60 L. Ed. 2d 777 (1979) — Appx. V.
United States v. Ash, 413 U.S. 300, 93 S. Ct. 2568, 37 L. Ed. 2d 153 (1973) — §§ 2.28, 2.30.
United States v. Bailey, 444 U.S. 394, 100 S. Ct. 624, 62 L. Ed. 2d 575 (1980) — §§ 4.65, 5.05, 5.18.
United States v. Baker, 418 F.2d 851 (6th Cir. 1969) — § 1.09.
United States v. Birdsall, 233 U.S. 223, 34 S. Ct. 512, 58 L. Ed. 930 (1914) — § 4.56.
United States v. Brawner, 471 F.2d 969 (D.C. Cir. 1972) — § 5.08.
United States v. Byrd, 352 F.2d 570 (2d Cir. 1965) — § 5.09.
United States v. Campbell, 138 F. Supp. 344 (N.D. Iowa 1956) — Appx. II.
United States v. Channel, 423 F. Supp. 1017 (D. Md. 1976) — § 4.63.
United States v. Chiarella, 184 F.2d 903 (2d Cir. 1950) — Appx. II.
United States v. Cianciulli, 482 F. Supp. 585 (E.D. Pa. 1979) — § 5.09.
United States v. Fallen, 498 F.2d 172 (8th Cir. 1974) — § 1.04.
United States v. Geaney, 417 F.2d 1116 (2d Cir. 1969) — § 4.06.
United States v. Hale, 422 U.S. 171, 95 S. Ct. 2133, 45 L. Ed. 2d 99 (1975) — §§ 2.09, 2.25.
United States v. Havens, 446 U.S. 620, 100 S. Ct. 1912, 64 L. Ed. 2d 559 (1980) — § 4.63.
United States v. Henry, 447 U.S. 264, 100 S. Ct. 2183, 65 L. Ed. 2d 115 (1980) — § 2.25.
United States v. Hephner, 410 F.2d 930 (7th Cir. 1969) — § 1.09.
United States v. Hill, 152 U.S. App. D.C. 213, 470 F.2d 361 (1972) — § 2.02.
United States v. Honesty, 459 F.2d 1279 (D.C. Cir. 1971) — § 2.24.
United States v. Holmes, 680 F.2d 1340 (11th Cir. 1982) — Appx. IV.
United States v. Karnes, 531 F.2d 214 (4th Cir. 1976) — § 2.11.
United States v. Kelly, 55 F.2d 67 (2d Cir. 1932) — § 2.31.
United States v. King, 582 F.2d 888 (4th Cir. 1978) — § 5.08.

United States v. Kinnard, 150 U.S. App. D.C. 386, 465 F.2d 566 (1975) — § 2.02.
United States v. Lawson, 507 F.2d 433 (7th Cir. 1974) — § 1.04.
United States v. Lee, 165 U.S. App. D.C. 50, 506 F.2d 111 (1974) — § 2.02.
United States v. Mandujano, 425 U.S. 564, 96 S. Ct. 1768, 48 L. Ed. 2d 212 (1976) — § 2.25.
United States v. Masino, 275 F.2d 129 (2d Cir. 1960) — § 2.02.
United States v. Morris, 647 F.2d 568 (5th Cir. 1981) — § 1.04.
United States v. Moylan, 417 F.2d 1002 (4th Cir. 1969) — § 3.04.
United States v. Nimerick, 118 F.2d 464 (2d Cir. 1941) — § 1.03.
United States v. Petite, 147 F. Supp. 791 (D. Md. 1957) — § 4.78.
United States v. Polowichak, 783 F.2d 410 (4th Cir. 1926) — Appx. II.
United States v. Prince, 264 F.2d 850 (3d Cir. 1959) — § 4.77.
United States v. Russell, 411 U.S. 423, 93 S. Ct. 1637, 36 L. Ed. 2d 366 (1973) — § 5.06.
United States v. Sam Chin, 24 F. Supp. 14 (D. Md. 1938) — § 1.06.
United States v. Squires, 440 F.2d 859 (2d Cir. 1971) — §§ 3.03, 5.09.
United States v. Stubin, 446 F.2d 457 (3d Cir. 1971) — § 1.04.
United States v. Thompson, 417 F.2d 196 (4th Cir. 1969) — § 2.25.
United States v. Tot, 319 U.S. 463, 63 S. Ct. 1241, 87 L. Ed. 2d 1519 (1943) — Appx. V.
United States v. United States Gypsum, 438 U.S. 422, 98 S. Ct. 2864, 57 L. Ed. 2d 854 (1978) — § 3.01.
United States v. Wade, 388 U.S. 218, 87 S. Ct. 1926, 18 L. Ed. 2d 1149 (1967) — §§ 2.28, 2.30.
United States v. Walker, 313 F.2d 236 (6th Cir. 1963) — § 1.09.
United States v. Watson, 669 F.2d 1374 (11th Cir. 1982) — Appx. IV.
United States v. Webster, 649 F.2d 346 (5th Cir. 1980) — § 5.06.
United States v. Weiler, 458 F.2d 474 (3d Cir. 1972) — § 5.09.
Urciolo v. State, 272 Md. 607, 325 A.2d 878 (1974) — §§ 4.64, 4.72.

V

Van v. State, 1 Md. App. 347, 230 A.2d 109 (1967) — § 4.72.
Vancherie v. Siperly, 243 Md. 366, 221 A.2d 356 (1966) — § 5.17.
Van Meter v. State, 30 Md. App. 406, 352 A.2d 850 (1976) — § 5.08.
Veney v. State, 227 Md. 608, 177 A.2d 883 (1961) — § 4.41.
Veney v. State, 251 Md. 159, 246 A.2d 608 (1968) — § 4.12.
Veney v. State, 251 Md. 182, 246 A.2d 568 (1968) — §§ 1.05, 1.06.
Vincent v. State, 220 Md. 232, 151 A.2d 898 (1959) — §§ 1.05, 2.26, 4.83.
Virginia Freight Lines, Inc. v. Montgomery, 256 Md. 221, 260 A.2d 59 (1969) — § 2.08.
Von Lusch v. State, 279 Md. 255, 368 A.2d 468 (1977) — § 2.07.
Von Lusch v. State, 39 Md. App. 517, 387 A.2d 306 (1978) — § 4.86.

Vonoppenfeld v. State, 53 Md. App. 462, 454 A.2d 402 (1983) — § 4.63.
Vucci v. State, 18 Md. App. 157, 305 A.2d 483 (1973) — § 4.65.

W

Waggaman v. Forstmann, App. D.C., 217 A.2d 310 (1966) — § 2.05.
Waine v. State, 37 Md. App. 222, 377 A.2d 509 (1977) — §§ 1.11a, 5.07.
Waldrop v. State, 12 Md. App. 371, 278 A.2d 619 (1971) — § 4.64.
Walker v. State, 12 Md. App. 684, 280 A.2d 260 (1971) — § 2.25.
Walker v. State, 53 Md. App. 171, 452 A.2d 1234 (1982) — §§ 4.16, 4.36.
Walker v. Walker, 125 Md. 649, 94 A.2d 346 (1915) — § 4.60.
Wallace v. State, 231 Md. 517, 191 A.2d 221 (1963) — § 4.55.
Wallace v. State, 63 Md. App. 399, 492 A.2d 970 (1985) — §§ 4.57, 4.69.
Wallace v. Warden, 226 Md. 670, 174 A.2d 435 (1961) — § 4.42.
Waller v. State, 13 Md. App. 615, 284 A.2d 446 (1971) — §§ 3.07, 4.77.
Walter v. State, 9 Md. App. 385, 264 A.2d 882 (1970) — § 4.36.
Wantland v. State, 45 Md. App. 527, 413 A.2d 1376 (1980) — §§ 2.05, 2.25, 4.42.
Ward v. State, 9 Md. App. 583, 267 A.2d 255 (1970) — § 4.62.
Ward v. State, 52 Md. App. 664, 451 A.2d 1243 (1983) — § 4.91.
Ware v. State, 3 Md. App. 62, 237 A.2d 526 (1968) — §§ 4.23b, 5.11.
Warren v. State, 29 Md. App. 560, 350 A.2d 173 (1976) — Appx. V.
Waters v. State, 2 Md. App. 216, 234 A.2d 147 (1967) — §§ 4.05, 4.14.
Watkins v. State, 42 Md. App. 349, 400 A.2d 464 (1979) — § 4.65.
Watson v. State, 208 Md. 210, 117 A.2d 549 (1955) — §§ 1.05, 2.01, 4.01, 4.03, 4.33.
Watson v. State, 282 Md. 73, 382 A.2d 574 (1978) — § 2.25.
Watson v. State, 6 Md. App. 134, 250 A.2d 311 (1969) — § 2.04.
Watson v. State, 7 Md. App. 225, 255 A.2d 103 (1969) — § 2.29.
Watkins v. State, 59 Md. App. 705, 478 A.2d 326 (1984) — § 4.70.
Watts v. State, 99 Md. 30, 57 A. 542 (1904) — § 2.25.
Waye v. State, 231 Md. 510, 191 A.2d 428 (1963) — § 4.67.
Webb v. State, 201 Md. 158, 93 A.2d 80 (1952) — § 4.13.
Webb v. Texas, 409 U.S. 95, 93 S. Ct. 351, 34 L. Ed. 2d 330 (1972) — § 2.06.
Webster v. State, 228 Md. 481, 180 A.2d 493 (1963) — § 4.41.
Weinecke v. State, 188 Md. 172, 52 A.2d 73 (1947) — § 4.15.
Weiner v. State, 290 Md. App. 425, 430 A.2d 588 (1981) — § 2.25.
Weinstein v. State, 146 Md. 80, 125 A. 899 (1924) — §§ 2.10, 4.78.
Weller v. State, 150 Md. 278, 132 A. 624 (1926) — § 2.26.
Wentworth v. State, 29 Md. App. 110, 349 A.2d 421 (1975) — §§ 4.23c, 5.05, 5.18, Appx. V.
Wentz v. State, 159 Md. 161, 15 A. 278 (1930) — § 2.23.
Wersten v. State, 228 Md. 226, 179 A.2d 364 (1962) — § 4.71.
Wersten v. State, 232 Md. 164, 192 A.2d 286 (1963) — § 4.55.

West v. Belle Isle Cab Co., 203 Md. 244, 100 A.2d 17 (1953) — § 2.08.
Westcoat v. State, 231 Md. 364, 190 A.2d 544 (1963) — §§ 2.10, 2.24.
Wethington v. State, 3 Md. App. 237, 238 A.2d 581 (1968) — § 2.10.
Whack v. State, 283 Md. 137, 416 A.2d 265 (1980) — §§ 4.44, 4.83.
White v. State, 300 Md. 719, 481 A.2d 201 (1984) — § 4.21c.
White v. State, 3 Md. App. 167, 238 A.2d 278 (1968) — §§ 2.04, 4.34, 4.35.
White v. State, 17 Md. App. 58, 299 A.2d 873 (1973) — § 5.08.
White v. State, 23 Md. App. 151, 326 A.2d 219 (1974) — § 4.44.
White v. State, 33 Md. App. 626, 365 A.2d 605 (1976) — § 2.10.
White v. State, 66 Md. App. 100, 502 A.2d 1084 (1986) — § 1.01.
Whitehead v. State, 9 Md. App. 7, 262 A.2d 316 (1970) — §§ 4.23b, 5.11, 5.13, 5.15.
Whitehead v. State, 54 Md. App. 428, 458 A.2d 905 (1983) — § 4.91.
Whitmer v. State, 1 Md. App. 127, 227 A.2d 761 (1967) — § 2.25.
Whittington v. State, 8 Md. App. 676, 262 A.2d 75 (1970) — § 2.02.
Whyte v. State, 229 Md. 459, 184 A.2d 783 (1962) — § 4.77.
Wichter v. State, 17 Md. App. 426, 302 A.2d 701 (1973) — § 2.30.
Wiggins v. State, 235 Md. 97, 200 A.2d 683 (1964) — § 2.25.
Wiggins v. State, 4 Md. App. 95, 241 A.2d 424 (1968) — § 4.57.
Wiggins v. State, 8 Md. App. 598, 261 A.2d 503 (1970) — §§ 3.02, 4.05, 4.21b, 4.71, 4.72, 4.82.
Wiley v. State, 237 Md. 560, 207 A.2d 478 (1965) — § 4.05.
Wilhelm v. State, 272 Md. 404, 326 A.2d 707 (1974) — § 1.08.
Wilkins v. Maryland, 402 F. Supp. 76 (D. Md. 1975) — § 1.01.
Wilkins v. State, 293 Md. 335, 444 A.2d 445 (1982) — § 4.59.
Wilkins v. State, 5 Md. App. 8, 245 A.2d 80 (1968) — § 2.30.
Wilkins v. State, 11 Md. App. 113, 273 A.2d 236 (1971) — § 1.10.
Williams v. State, 204 Md. 55, 102 A.2d 714 (1954) — §§ 4.12, 4.80.
Williams v. State, 205 Md. 470, 109 A.2d 89 (1954) — § 1.05.
Williams v. State, 3 Md. App. 58, 237 A.2d 822 (1968) — §§ 2.24, 4.75.
Williams v. State, 5 Md. App. 450, 247 A.2d 731 (1968) — § 1.05.
Williams v. State, 7 Md. App. 5, 252 A.2d 880 (1969) — §§ 4.74, 4.77.
Williams v. State, 7 Md. App. 683, 256 A.2d 776 (1969) — § 4.82.
Williams v. State, 11 Md. App. 350, 274 A.2d 403 (1971) — §§ 2.04, 4.36.
Williams v. State, 11 Md. App. 607, 275 A.2d 522 (1971) — § 2.30.
Williams v. State, 14 Md. App. 619, 287 A.2d 803 (1972) — § 4.77.
Williams v. State, 22 Md. App. 714, 325 A.2d 427 (1974) — § 1.05.
Williams v. State, 50 Md. App. 255, 437 A.2d 665 (1982) — §§ 1.08, 4.21b, 5.02.
Williamson v. State, 25 Md. App. 338, 333 A.2d 653 (1975) — §§ 5.14, 5.16.
Williamson v. State, 36 Md. App. 405, 374 A.2d 909 (1977) — § 5.08.
Willis v. State, 205 Md. 118, 106 A.2d 85 (1954) — § 4.67.
Willis v. State, 302 Md. 363, 488 A.2d 171 (1985) — § 4.63.

Willis v. State, 55 Md. App. 65, 460 A.2d 1043 (1983) — § 4.25.
Wilson v. State, 181 Md. 1, 26 A.2d 770 (1942) — § 2.10.
Wilson v. State, 261 Md. 551, 276 A.2d 214 (1971) — § 4.21a.
Wilson v. State, 4 Md. App. 192, 242 A.2d 194 (1968) — § 1.12a.
Wilson v. State, 7 Md. App. 41, 253 A.2d 439 (1969) — § 1.03.
Wilson v. State, 8 Md. App. 653, 262 A.2d 91 (1970) — § 4.06.
Wilson v. State, 28 Md. App. 168, 343 A.2d 537 (1975) — Appx. V.
Wilson v. State, 44 Md. App. 318, 408 A.2d 1058 (1980) — §§ 1.04, 1.13, Apps. I, III.
Winebrenner v. State, 6 Md. App. 440, 251 A.2d 610 (1969) — § 4.75.
Winegan v. State, 10 Md. App. 196, 268 A.2d 585 (1970) — §§ 4.35, 4.36.
Winner v. State, 144 Md. 682, 125 A. 397 (1924) — §§ 5.12, 5.14, 5.16.
Winslow v. Atz, 168 Md. 230, 177 A. 272 (1935) — Appx. IV.
Wise v. State, 47 Md. App. 656, 425 A.2d 652 (1981) — §§ 2.10, 4.06.
Wong Sun v. United States, 371 U.S. 471, 83 S. Ct. 407, 9 L. Ed. 2d 441 (1963) — § 2.25.
Wood v. State, 185 Md. 280, 44 A.2d 859 (1945) — § 1.07.
Wood v. State, 192 Md. 643, 65 A.2d 316 (1949) — §§ 4.41, 5.02.
Woodard v. State, 13 Md. App. 114, 282 A.2d 9 (1971) — § 4.13.
Woodell v. State, 2 Md. App. 433, 234 A.2d 890 (1967) — § 1.05.
Woodland v. State, 62 Md. App. 503, 490 A.2d 286 (1985) — § 2.21.
Woodruff v. State, 11 Md. App. 202, 273 A.2d 436 (1971) — § 3.03.
Woods v. State, 14 Md. App. 627, 288 A.2d 215 (1972) — § 4.12.
Woodson v. North Carolina, 428 U.S. 280, 96 S. Ct. 2987, 49 L. Ed. 2d 944 (1976) — § 4.21c.
Worthen v. State, 42 Md. App. 20, 399 A.2d 272 (1979) — §§ 2.10, 4.12, 4.58.
Wright v. Rever, 151 Md. 558, 136 A. 61 (1926) — § 2.21.
Wright v. Sas, 187 Md. 507, 50 A.2d 809 (1947) — § 4.73.
Wright v. State, 307 Md. 552, 515 A.2d 1157 (1986) — § 4.21b.
Wright v. State, 24 Md. App. 309, 330 A.2d 482 (1975) — § 4.44.
Wright v. State, 26 Md. App. 60, 336 A.2d 808 (1975) — § 2.25.
Wright v. State, 29 Md. App. 110, 349 A.2d 421 (1975) — Appx. V.
Wyley v. Warden, 372 F.2d 742 (4th Cir. 1967) — §§ 1.01, 2.04.
Wynn v. State, 69 Md. App. 536, 518 A.2d 1072 (1987) — § 4.91.

Y

Yantz v. Warden, 210 Md. 343, 123 A.2d 601 (1956) — § 4.12.
Yopps v. State, 228 Md. 204, 178 A.2d 879 (1962) — § 1.08.
Yopps v. State, 234 Md. 216, 198 A.2d 264 (1964) — §§ 3.07, 4.77.
York v. State, 56 Md. App. 222, 467 A.2d 552 (1983) — § 4.44.
Young v. State, 152 Md. 89, 136 A. 46 (1927) — § 2.10.
Young v. State, 303 Md. 298, 493 A.2d 352 (1985) — § 4.05.
Young v. State, 14 Md. App. 538, 288 A.2d 198 (1972) — §§ 1.05, 5.08.

Yowell v. State, 28 Md. App. 279, 344 A.2d 442 (1975) — § 2.08.
Yuen v. State, 43 Md. App. 109, 403 A.2d 819 (1979) — § 2.21.

Z

Zimmerman v. State, 9 Md. App. 488, 265 A.2d 764 (1970) — § 4.71.

Index

A

ABDUCTION.
Kidnapping.
Individual under sixteen, §4.70.
ABORTIONS.
General provisions, §4.51.
ABUSE.
Child abuse, §4.58.
ACCOMPLICES AND ACCESSORIES.
Accessory after the fact.
Generally, §4.03.
Accessory before the fact.
Generally, §4.01.
Aiding and abetting.
Generally, §4.02.
Corroboration of accomplice's testimony, §2.01.
Incest, §4.33.
Sodomy, §4.34.
Testimony.
Corroboration of accomplice's testimony, §2.01.
Unnatural or perverted sexual practices, §4.35.
Witnesses.
Corroboration of accomplice's testimony, §2.01.
AFFIRMATIONS.
Perjury, §4.78.
Subornation of perjury, §4.78.
AGENCY.
Innocent agents.
Acts committed through innocent agents, §4.04.
Receiving stolen goods, §4.79.
AIDING AND ABETTING.
Generally, §4.02.
ALCOHOLIC BEVERAGES.
Drunkenness.
Voluntary drunkenness.
Defense to crime requiring specific intent, §5.01.

ALCOHOLIC BEVERAGES—Cont'd
Motor vehicles.
Driving while intoxicated or impaired, §4.63.
Homicide by motor vehicle while intoxicated, §4.26.

ALIBI.
Generally, §5.02.

ANNOYING PHONE CALLS, §4.86.

ARREST.
Defined, §4.80.
Felony.
When arrest lawful, §4.80.
Lawful arrest.
When arrest lawful, §4.80.
Probable cause.
Defined, §4.80.
Resisting arrest.
Generally, §4.80.

ARSON.
Burden of proof, §4.52.
Defined, §4.52.
Elements of crime, §4.52.

ASSAULT.
Defined, §4.11.
Generally, §4.11.
Intent.
Assault with intent to commit sexual intercourse.
Female under age fourteen where male is four or more years older, §4.15.
Assault with intent to murder, §4.13.
Assault with intent to rape or commit first or second degree sexual offense, §4.16.
Assault with intent to rob, §4.14.
Required intent for crime, §4.11.
Murder.
Assault with intent to murder, §4.13.
Rape.
Assault with intent to rape or commit first or second degree sexual offense, §4.16.
Robbery.
Assault with intent to rob, §4.14.

ATTEMPT.
Bribery, §4.56.
Generally, §4.05.

ATTORNEYS AT LAW.
Defendant's representation of self, §1.15.
Evidence.
Statements of counsel.
Not evidence, §1.08.
Statements of counsel.
Not evidence, §1.08.

AUTOMOBILES.
General provisions.
See MOTOR VEHICLES.

B

BATTERY.
Defined, §4.12.
Elements of crime, §4.12.
Generally, §4.12.
Intent.
Required intent of crime, §4.12.

BINDING NATURE OF INSTRUCTION, §1.01.

BLOOD TESTS.
Consent to blood tests, §2.32.

BOATS.
Larceny.
Unauthorized use, §4.73.
Trespass, §4.85.

BREAKING.
Actual breaking.
Defined, §4.69.
Burglary, §4.57.
Constructive breaking.
Defined, §4.69.
Definitions, §§4.53 to 4.55.
Elements of crime, §§4.53 to 4.55.
Housebreaking.
Daytime housebreaking, §4.69.
Storehouse, etc., with intent to commit felony or steal, §4.53.
Storehouse, etc., with intent to steal any money, goods or chattels under the value of $300, §4.54.
Storehouse, etc., with the taking of property, §4.55.

BRIBERY.
Attempt, §4.56.
Defined, §4.56.
Demanding of bribe, §4.56.

BRIBERY—Cont'd
Elements of crime, §4.56.
Generally, §4.56.
Intent.
Attempting to bribe, §4.56.
Offering of bribe, §4.56.
Receiving of bribe, §4.56.

BUILDINGS.
Public buildings.
Refusal to leave, §4.85.
Trespass, §4.85.

BURDEN OF PROOF.
Arson, §4.52.
Confessions.
Free involuntary confession, §2-25.
Defendant.
Identity of defendant, §2.28.
Defenses.
Self-defense, §5.11.
Entrapment, §5.06.
Evans v. State.
Impact on burden of proof, Appendix V.
Generally, §1.02.
Murder.
First degree murder, §4.21 (a).
Self-defense, §5.11.

BURGLARY.
Breaking and entering, §4.57.
Defenses.
Claim of right.
Use as defense, §5.03.
Defined, §4.57.
Dwelling house.
Defined, §4.57.
Elements of crime, §4.57.

C

CAPITAL PUNISHMENT.
Death penalty sentencing.
First degree murder, §4.21 (c).

CARNAL KNOWLEDGE.
General provisions.
See SEXUAL OFFENSES.

CHARACTER.
Defendant, §2.23.
Reputation, §2.23.
Defenses.
Good character.
Use of evidence of good character as a defense, §§2.23, 5.07.
Good character.
Use of evidence of good character as a defense, §§2.23, 5.07.

CHARGING DOCUMENT.
Evidence.
Not evidence, §1.09.

CHECKS.
Theft.
Insufficient funds.
Acts committed by passers, §4.97 (b).
Issuance with intent to stop payment, §4.97 (c).
Knowledge of insufficient funds, §4.97 (a).
Knowledge that payment has been stopped.
Acts committed by passers, §4.97 (d).

CHEMICAL TESTS.
Consent, §2.32.

CHILD ABUSE, §4.58.

CHILDREN.
Abuse.
Child abuse, §4.58.
Nonsupport.
Generally, §5.60.
Sexual intercourse.
Assault with intent to commit sexual intercourse.
Female under age of fourteen.
Male four or more years older, §4.15.
Witnesses.
Evaluation of testimony, §2.04.

CIRCUMSTANTIAL EVIDENCE, §1.05.

CONCEALED WEAPONS.
See WEAPONS.

CONCEALMENT.
Defendant, §2.24.

CONFESSIONS.
Admission solely for impeachment purposes, §2.09.
Burden of proof.
Free involuntary confession, §2.25.

CONFESSIONS—Cont'd
Corpus delicti.
Corroboration of defendant's confession, §2.26.
Defendant, §2.25.
Corroboration of defendant's confession.
Corpus delicti, §2.26.
Defendant as witness.
Impeachment by confession, §2.09.
Generally, §2.25.

CONSENT.
Blood and other chemical tests, §2.32.
Incest, §4.33.
Sodomy, §4.34.

CONSPIRACY.
Generally, §4.06.

CONTEMPT.
Generally, §4.59.

CONTROLLED SUBSTANCES.
Narcotics.
See NARCOTICS.

CONVERSION.
Larceny.
General provisions.
See LARCENY.

CONVICTIONS.
Impeachment by prior convictions, §2.07.

CORPUS DELICTI.
Corroboration of defendant's confession, §2.26.

CORROBORATION.
Accomplice's testimony, §2.01.
Confessions.
Corpus delicti.
Corroboration of defendant's confession, §2.26.

COUNTS.
Multiple counts, §2.22.

COURT.
Advice to jury.
Function of court, §1.01.
Function of court, §1.01.
Witness.
Court calling own witness, §2.11.

CREDIBILITY OF WITNESSES, §2.06.

D

DEATH PENALTY SENTENCING.
First degree murder, §4.21 (c).
DECEASED.
Prior acts of violence.
Use as a defense, §5.16.
Reputation.
Prior acts of violence and reputation for violence of the deceased.
Use as a defense, §5.16.
Threats.
Prior threats of the deceased.
Use as a defense, §5.16.
DEFENDANT.
Attorneys at law.
Self-representation, §1.15.
Burden of proof.
Identity of defendant, §2.28.
Character, §2.23.
Concealment, §2.24.
Confessions.
General provisions.
See CONFESSIONS.
Eyewitness identification, §2.29.
Fingerprints.
Identification of defendant by fingerprints, §2.31.
Flight, §2.24.
Identity of defendant, §2.28.
Eyewitness identification, §2.29.
Fingerprint evidence, §2.31.
Photographic identification, §2.30.
Incriminating statements, §2.25.
Multiple defendants, §2.22.
Other crimes of defendant, §2.10.
Photographic identification, §2.30.
Prior bad acts of defendant, §2.10.
Prior convictions.
Impeachment by prior convictions, §2.07.
Self-representation, §1.15.
Silence of defendant, §2.27.
Witness.
Defendant as witness.
Decision not to testify, §2.27.
Impeachment by confession, §2.09.
Impeachment by prior convictions, §2.07.

DEFENSE OF OTHERS.
Use as a defense, §5.04.

DEFENSES.
Alibi.
Generally, §5.02.
Burglary.
Claim of right.
Use as defense, §5.03.
Character.
Good character.
Use of evidence of good character as a defense, §§2.23, 5.07.
Claim of right, §5.03.
Defense of others, §5.04.
Drunkenness.
Voluntary drunkenness, §5.01.
Duress, §5.05.
Embezzlement.
Claim of right, §5.03.
Entrapment, §5.06.
Homicide.
Defense of others, §5.04.
Prior acts of violence and reputation for violence of the deceased, §5.16.
Prior threats of the deceased, §5.16.
Identity.
Mistaken identity, §5.10.
Ignorance of fact, §5.09.
Insanity.
Generally, §5.08.
Intent.
Specific intent.
Claim of right.
Use as defense in crime requiring specific intent to steal, §5.03.
Intoxication.
Voluntary intoxication.
Defense to crime requiring specific intent, §5.01.
Larceny.
Claim of right, §5.03.
Manslaughter.
Defense of others, §5.04.
Prior acts of violence and reputation for violence of the deceased, §5.16.
Prior threats of the deceased, §5.16.

DEFENSES—Cont'd
Manslaughter—Cont'd
Self-defense.
Imperfect self-defense, §4.23 (c).
Mistaken identity, §5.10.
Mistake of fact, §5.09.
Murder.
Defense of others, §5.04.
Prior acts of violence and reputation of violence for the deceased, §5.16.
Prior threats of the deceased, §5.16.
Necessity, §5.18.
Reputation.
Good character.
Use of evidence of good character as a defense, §§2.23, 5.07.
Robbery.
Claim of right, §5.03.
Self-defense.
Amount of force permissible.
Deadly force, §5.12.
Non-deadly force, §5.12.
Burden of proof, §5.11.
Deadly force.
When permissible, §5.12.
Defendant.
Where defendant is alleged aggressor, §5.13.
Defense of others, §5.04.
Duty to retreat, §5.15.
False appearances.
Where appearances are false, §5.14.
General consideration, §5.11.
Manslaughter.
Imperfect self-defense, §4.23 (c).
Non-deadly force.
Use to defend property, §5.17.
When permissible, §5.12.
Prior acts of violence and reputation for violence of the deceased, §5.16.
Retreat.
Duty to retreat, §5.15.
Specific intent.
Voluntary intoxication.
Use as defense in crime requiring specific intent, §5.01.
Stolen goods.
Claim of right, §5.03.

DEFENSES—Cont'd
Theft.
Claim of right, §5.03.
General provisions, §4.96.
Rights of possession, §4.96.
Threats.
Prior threats of the deceased, §5.16.
Violence.
Prior acts of violence of the deceased, §5.16.

DEFINITIONS.
Arrest, §4.80.
Arson, §4.52.
Assault, §4.11.
Battery, §4.12.
Breaking, §§4.53 to 4.55.
Actual breaking, §4.69.
Constructive breaking, §4.69.
Bribery, §4.56.
Burglary, §4.57.
Dwelling house, §4.57.
Drugs.
Narcotics.
Possession, §4.76.
Escape, §4.65.
Forgery, §4.68.
Fraudulent, §3.05.
Incest, §4.33.
Intent.
General intent, §3.01.
Intent to defraud, §3.05.
Specific intent, §3.02.
Kidnapping, §4.70.
Knowingly, §3.03.
Maliciously, §3.06.
Manslaughter, §4.23 (a).
Involuntary manslaughter, §4.24.
Mental disorder, §5.08.
Mental illness, §5.08.
Mental retardation, §5.08.
Narcotics.
Possession, §4.76.
Perjury, §4.78.
Rape, §§4.16, 4.36.
Robbery, §§4.14, 4.82.
Sexual offenses, §4.37.

DEFINITIONS—Cont'd
Sodomy, §4.34.
Substantial capacity, §5.08.
Theft.
By deception, §4.92.
Lost, mislaid or mistakenly delivered property, §4.94.
Possession of stolen property, §4.93.
Services, §4.95.
Unauthorized control, §4.91.
Unnatural or perverted sexual practices, §4.35.
Uttering, §4.68.
Weapons.
Concealed weapons, §4.41.
Willfully, §3.04.

DENIAL OF REQUESTED INSTRUCTION.
Perserving record for possible appeal, Appendix III.

DESERTION AND NONSUPPORT.
Generally, §4.60.

DESTRUCTION OF PROPERTY.
Malicious mischief, §4.75.

DIRECT EVIDENCE, §1.05.

DISORDERLY CONDUCT.
Generally, §4.61.

DISORDERLY HOUSE.
Keeping a disorderly house.
Generally, §4.62.

DOUBT.
Reasonable doubt, §1.04.

DRUGS.
Motor vehicles.
Driving while under the influence, §4.63.
Narcotics.
Constructive possession, §4.76.
Definitions.
Possession, §4.76.
Distribution, §4.77.
Intent.
Manufacture, possession, etc., with intent to sell, §4.77.
Manufacture, §4.77.
Possession.
Actual possession, §4.76.
Constructive possession, §4.76.
Defined, §4.76.

DRUGS—Cont'd
Narcotics—Cont'd
Possession—Cont'd
Elements of crime, §4.76.
Intent to sell, §4.77.
Sales.
Possession with intent to sell, §4.77.
Sales.
Possession with intent to sell, §4.77.

DRUNKENNESS.
Defenses.
Voluntary drunkenness, §5.01.
Motor vehicles.
Driving while intoxicated or impaired, §4.63.
Homicide by motor vehicle while intoxicated, §4.26.
Voluntary drunkenness.
Defense to crime requiring specific intent, §5.01.

DURESS.
Generally, §5.05.

E

ELECTRONICALLY RECORDED INSTRUCTIONS.
Supplementing oral instructions, Appendix IV.

EMBEZZLEMENT.
Defenses.
Claim of right, §5.03.
General provisions, §4.64.

ENTRAPMENT.
Burden of proof, §5.06.
Generally, §5.06.

ESCAPE.
Defined, §4.65.
Elements of crime, §4.65.
Generally, §4.65.

EVANS V. STATE.
Impact, Appendix V.

EVIDENCE.
Attorneys at law.
Statements of counsel.
Not evidence, §1.08.
Burden of proof.
See BURDEN OF PROOF.

EVIDENCE—Cont'd
Charging document.
Not evidence, §1.09.
Circumstantial evidence, §1.05.
Defenses.
See DEFENSES.
Direct evidence, §1.05.
Fingerprint evidence, §2.31.
Inadmissible evidence.
Not to be considered, §1.10.
Indictments.
Not evidence, §1.09.
Judicial notice, §1.06.
Jurisdiction, §2.33.
Objections to evidence.
Rulings of court, §1.10.
Stipulations, §1.07.
Stricken evidence.
Not to be considered, §1.10.
Witnesses.
See WITNESSES.

EXPERT WITNESSES.
Generally, §2.05.

EXTORTION.
Elements of crime, §4.66.
Verbal threats, §4.66.

F

FACT.
Mistake of fact.
Use as a defense, §5.09.

FALSE IMPRISONMENT.
Kidnapping, §4.70.

FALSE PRETENSES.
Generally, §4.67.

FELONIES.
Weapons.
Handguns.
Use in commision of felony or crime of violence, §4.44.

FELONY MURDER.
Generally, §4.21 (b).

FINGERPRINTS.
Defendant.
Identification of defendant by fingerprints, §2.31.
FIREARMS.
Weapons.
See WEAPONS.
FLIGHT.
Defendant, §2.24.
FORGERY.
Defined, §4.68.
Elements of crime, §4.68.
Intent to defraud, §4.68.
Uttering.
Distinction between uttering and forgery, §4.68.
FRAUD AND DECEIT.
Definition of fraudulent, §3.05.
Intent.
Intent to defraud.
Defined, §3.05.

G

GUNS.
Weapons.
See WEAPONS.

H

HANDGUNS.
Weapons.
See WEAPONS.
HOMICIDE.
Defenses.
Defense of others, §5.04.
Prior acts of violence and reputation for violence of the deceased, §5.16.
Prior threats of the deceased, §5.16.
Introductory instruction on grading of homicide, §4.20.
Manslaughter.
See MANSLAUGHTER.
Motor vehicles.
Homicide while intoxicated, §4.26.
Murder.
See MURDER.

HOUSEBREAKING.
Daytime housebreaking.
Generally, §4.69.

HOW TO MAKE INSTRUCTION REQUESTS, Appendix III.

HUSBAND AND WIFE.
Desertion and nonsupport, §4.60.

I

IDENTITY.
Defendant, §2.28.
Eyewitness identification, §2.29.
Fingerprint identification, §2.31.
Photographic identification, §2.30.
Single eyewitness, §2.29.
Mistaken identity.
Use as a defense, §5.10.

IMPEACHMENT.
Convictions.
Impeachment by prior convictions, §2.07.
Defendant.
Character witnesses, §2.23.
Confession, §2.09.
Prior convictions, §2.07.
Prior inconsistent statements, §2.08.

INCEST.
Accomplices and accessories, §4.33.
Consent, §4.33.
Defined, §4.33.
Elements of crime, §4.33.

INCRIMINATING STATEMENTS.
Defendant, §2.25.

INDECENT EXPOSURE.
General provisions, §4.61.

INDICTMENTS.
Evidence.
Not evidence, §1.09.
Multiple counts, §2.22.

INFANTS.
Children.
See CHILDREN.

INFORMERS.
Testimony, §2.02.
Witnesses.
Testimony of informer, §2.02.

INJURIES.
Weapons.
Carrying a weapon openly with intent to injure, §4.42.

INNOCENCE.
Presumption of innocence, §1.03.

INSANITY.
Defenses.
Use of insanity as defense, §5.08.
Mental disorder.
Defined, §5.08.
Mental illness.
Defined, §5.08.
Mental retardation.
Defined, §5.08.
Substantial capacity.
Defined, §5.08.

INTENT.
Assault.
Assault with intent to murder, §4.13.
Assault with intent to rape or commit first or second degree sexual offense, §4.16.
Assault with intent to rob, §4.14.
Required intent for crime, §4.11.
Sexual intercourse.
Assault with intent to commit sexual intercourse.
Female under age fourteen where male is four or more years older, §4.15.
Battery.
Required intent for crime, §4.12.
Bribery.
Attempting to bribe, §4.56.
Defenses.
Specific intent.
Claim of right.
Use as defense in crime requiring specific intent to steal, §5.03.
Voluntary intoxication.
Use as defense in crime requiring specific intent, §5.01.
Definitions.
General intent, §3.01.

INTENT—Cont'd
Definitions—Cont'd
Intent to defraud, §3.05.
Specific intent, §3.02.
Drugs.
Narcotics.
Manufacture, possession, etc., with intent to sell, §4.77.
Elements of crime, §4.11.
Forgery.
Intent to defraud, §4.68.
Fraud and deceit.
Intent to defraud.
Defined, §3.05.
General intent.
Defined, §3.01.
Kidnapping, §4.70.
Malicious mischief.
Specific intent required, §4.75.
Murder.
Assault with intent to murder, §4.13.
Narcotics.
Manufacture, possession, etc., with intent to sell, §4.77.
Proof of intent, §3.07.
Rape.
Assault with intent to rape, §4.16.
Robbery.
Assault with intent to rob, §4.14.
Specific intent crime, §4.82.
Specific intent.
Claim of right.
Use as defense in crime requiring specific intent to steal, §5.03.
Defined, §3.02.
Voluntary drunkenness.
Defense to crime requiring specific intent, §5.01.
Theft, §4.91.
Uttering.
Intent to defraud, §4.68.
Weapons.
Carrying a weapon openly with intent to injure, §4.42.

INTOXICATING LIQUORS.
General provisions.
See ALCOHOLIC BEVERAGES.

INTOXICATION.
Defenses.
Use as defense in crime requiring specific intent, §5.01.

INTOXICATION—Cont'd
Motor vehicles.
Driving while intoxicated or impaired, §4.63.
Homicide by motor vehicle while intoxicated, §4.26.

J

JUDICIAL NOTICE, §1.06.
JURISDICTION.
Evidence of jurisdiction, §2.33.
JURY.
Agreement.
When jurors cannot agree, §1.13.
Communications with jurors, §1.11.
Admonition during recess, §1.12.
Amplified instruction.
Prior to first recess, §1.12 (a).
Amplified instruction, §1.11.
Determination of law.
Function of jury, §1.01.
Duty to deliberate, §1.13.
Function of jury, §1.01.
Judge of facts.
Function of jury, §1.01.
Punishment.
Nonconcern with punishment, §1.14.

K

KIDNAPPING.
Abduction.
Individual under sixteen, §4.70.
Defined, §4.70.
Elements of crime, §4.70.
False imprisonment, §4.70.
Intent, §4.70.
KNIVES.
Weapons generally.
See WEAPONS.
KNOWINGLY.
Defined, §3.03.
KNOWLEDGE.
Proof, §3.07.

L

LAND.
Trespass, §4.85.
LARCENY.
After trust, §4.72.
Boats.
Unauthorized use, §4.73.
Defenses.
Claim of right, §5.03.
General provisions, §4.71.
Livestock.
Unauthorized use, §4.73.
Motor vehicles.
Unauthorized use, §4.73.
Use.
Larceny of use.
Unauthorized use of motor vehicle, boat or livestock, §4.73.
LAW ENFORCEMENT OFFICIALS.
Entrapment.
Defense of entrapment, §5.06.
LENIENCY.
Witness promised leniency.
Testimony, §2.02.
LESSER INCLUDED OFFENSES, §2.22
LIVESTOCK.
Larceny.
Unauthorized use, §4.73.
LOTTERIES.
Keeping a place for selling lottery tickets.
Elements of crime, §4.74.
Place of use, §4.74.
Owner permitting use of office or house for sale of lottery tickets.
Elements of crime, §4.74.

M

MALICE.
Murder.
Second degree murder, §4.22 (a).
MALICIOUSLY.
Defined, §3.06.

MALICIOUS MISCHIEF.
Elements of crime, §4.75.
Intent.
Specific intent required, §4.75.

MANSLAUGHTER.
Defenses.
Defense of others, §5.04.
Prior acts of violence and reputation for violence of the deceased, §5.16.
Prior threats of the deceased, §5.16.
Self-defense.
Imperfect self-defense, §4.23 (c).
Definitions.
Involuntary manslaughter, §4.24.
Sudden heat of passion, §4.23 (a).
Voluntary manslaughter, §4.23 (a).
Involuntary manslaughter.
Defined, §4.24.
Elements of crime, §4.24.
Motor vehicles.
Manslaughter by vehicle, §4.25.
Negligence.
Involuntary manslaughter, §4.24.
Self-defense.
Imperfect self-defense, §4.23 (c).
Vehicles, §4.25.
Voluntary manslaughter.
Amplified instruction including special sources of provocation, §4.23 (b).
Defined, §4.23 (a).
Elements of crime, §4.23 (a).
General instruction, §4.23 (a).
Imperfect self-defense, §4.23 (c).
Special sources of provocation, §4.23 (b).
Sudden heat of passion.
Defined, §4.23 (a).

MENTAL ILLNESS.
Insanity.
See INSANITY.

MINORS.
Children.
See CHILDREN.

MISTAKE.
Defenses.
Mistaken identity, §5.10.
Mistake of fact, §5.09.
Fact.
Mistake of fact.
Use as a defense, §5.09.
Identity.
Mistaken identity.
Use as a defense, §5.10.

MOTOR VEHICLES.
Alcoholic beverages.
Driving while intoxicated, §4.63.
Driving while under the influence, §4.63.
Drugs.
Driving while under the influence, §4.63.
Drunkenness.
Driving while intoxicated, §4.63.
Driving while under the influence, §4.63.
Homicide by motor vehicle while intoxicated, §4.26.
Manslaughter by vehicle, §4.25.
Narcotics.
Driving while under the influence, §4.63.
Unauthorized use, §4.73.

MURDER.
Assault.
Assault with intent to murder, §4.13.
Burden of proof.
First degree murder, §4.21 (a).
Death penalty sentencing, §4.21 (c).
Defenses.
Defense of others, §5.04.
Prior acts of violence and reputation for violence of the deceased, §5.16.
Prior threats of the deceased, §5.16.
Defined, §4.21 (a).
Deliberation, §4.21 (a).
Felony murder, §4.21 (b).
First degree murder.
Burden of proof, §4.21 (a).
Death penalty sentencing, §4.21 (c).
Deliberation, §4.21 (a).
Distinction between first degree and second degree murder, §4.21 (a).

MURDER—Cont'd
First degree murder—Cont'd
Felony murder, §4.21 (b).
Premeditation, §4.21 (a).
When both first and second degree murder are in issue, §4.22 (b).
Intent.
Assault with intent to murder, §4.13.
Malice.
Second degree murder, §4.22 (a).
Premeditation, §4.21 (a).
Second degree murder, §4.22 (a).
When both first and second degree murder are in issue, §4.22 (b).
Sentencing.
Death penalty sentencing, §4.21 (c).

N

NARCOTICS.
Constructive possession, §4.76.
Definitions.
Possession, §4.76.
Distribution, §4.77.
Intent.
Manufacture, possession, etc., with intent to sell, §4.77.
Manufacture, §4.77.
Motor vehicles.
Driving while under the influence, §4.63.
Possession.
Actual possession, §4.76.
Constructive possession, §4.76.
Defined, §4.76.
Elements of crime, §4.76.
Intent.
Possession with intent to sell, §4.77.
Sales.
Possession with intent to sell, §4.77.
Sales.
Possession with intent to sell, §4.77.

NECESSITY.
Use as a defense, §5.18.

NEGLECT.
Desertion and nonsupport, §4.60.

NEGLIGENCE.
Manslaughter.
Involuntary manslaughter, §4.24.

NEWSPAPERS.
Publicity.
Cautioning on publicity, §1.11.
Amplified instruction, §1.11 (a).

NOISE.
Disorderly conduct, §4.61.

NONSUPPORT.
General provisions, §4.60.

NUISANCES.
Disorderly house.
Keeping a disorderly house, §4.62.

O

OATHS.
Perjury, §5.78.
Subornation of perjury, §4.78.

OBSCENITY.
Use of obscene language.
Disorderly conduct, §4.61.

OBSTRUCTION OF JUSTICE, §4.56.

ORDERS OF COURT.
Violation of court order.
Contempt, §4.59.

P

PARENT AND CHILD.
Nonsupport, §4.60.

PERJURY.
Defined, §4.78.
Elements of crime, §4.78.
Generally, §4.78.
Subornation of perjury.
Generally, §4.78.

PERVERTED SEXUAL PRACTICES, §4.35.

PHOTOGRAPHS.
Identification of defendant, §2.30.

POLICE.
Entrapment.
Defense of entrapment, §5.06.

POSSESSION.
Narcotics, §4.76.

PRELIMINARY INSTRUCTIONS, Appendix I.
Note taking by jurors, Appendix II.

PRESUMPTIONS.
Evans v. State.
Impact on presumptions, Appendix V.
Innocence.
Presumption of innocence, §1.03.
Witnesses.
Missing witness.
Presumption of unfavorable testimony, §2.21.

PROFANITY.
Disorderly conduct, §4.61.

PROPERTY.
Trespass, §4.85.

PUBLIC BUILDINGS.
Refusal to leave, §4.85.

PUBLICITY.
Cautioning on publicity, §1.11.
Amplified instruction, §1.11 (a).

PUNISHMENT.
Death penalty sentencing.
First degree murder, §4.21 (c).
Jury.
Nonconcern with punishment, §1.14.

R

RADIO AND TELEVISION.
Publicity.
Cautioning on publicity, §1.11.
Amplified instruction, §1.11 (a).

RAPE.
Assault.
Assault with intent to rape, §4.16.
Defined, §§4.16, 4.36.
First degree rape, §4.36.
Intent.
Assault with intent to rape, §4.16.
Second degree rape, §4.36.
Mentally defective, mentally incapacitated or physically helpless victims, §4.36.

RAPE—Cont'd
Second degree rape—Cont'd
Victim under fourteen years of age.
Person performing act four years or more older than victim, §4.36.

REASONABLE DOUBT, §1.04.

RECEIVING STOLEN GOODS.
Generally, §4.78.

RECESS.
Admonition upon recess, §1.12.
Amplified instruction prior to first recess, §1.12 (a).

RECORD.
Perserving record for possible appeal, Appendix III.

REHABILITATION.
Witnesses.
Prior consistent statements, §2.08.

REPUTATION.
Deceased.
Prior acts of violence and reputation for violence of the deceased.
Use as a defense, §5.16.
Defenses.
Generally, §2.23.
Good character.
Use of evidence of good character as a defense, §5.07.
Reputation of deceased for prior acts of violence, §5.16.
Prior reputation of the deceased.
Use as a defense, §5.16.
Self-defense.
Prior acts of violence and reputation for violence of the deceased.
Use as a defense, §5.16.

RESISTING ARREST.
Generally, §4.80.

RETREAT.
Duty to retreat, §5.15.

RIOT.
Generally, §4.81.

ROBBERY.
Assault.
Assault with intent to rob, §4.14.
Deadly weapon.
Robbery with a deadly weapon, §4.83.

ROBBERY—Cont'd
Defenses.
Claim of right, §5.03.
Defined, §§4.14, 4.82.
Elements of crime, §4.82.
Intent.
Assault with intent to rob, §4.14.
Specific intent crime, §4.82.
Robbery with a deadly weapon, §4.83.
Weapons.
Robbery with a deadly weapon, §4.83.

S

SALES.
Lotteries.
See LOTTERIES.
Narcotics.
Possession with intent to sell, §4.77.

SELF-DEFENSE.
Amount of force permissible.
Deadly force, §5.12.
Non-deadly force, §5.12.
Burden of proof, §5.11.
Deadly force.
When permissible, §5.12.
Defendant.
Where defendant is alleged aggressor, §5.13.
Defense of others, §5.04.
Duty to retreat, §5.15.
False appearances.
Where appearances are false, §5.14.
General consideration, §5.11.
Manslaughter.
Imperfect self-defense, §4.23 (c).
Non-deadly force.
Use to defend property, §5.17.
When permissible, §5.12.
Prior acts of violence and reputation for violence of the deceased, §5.16.
Retreat.
Duty to retreat, §5.15.

SEXUAL INTERCOURSE.
Assault.
Assault with intent to commit sexual intercourse.
Female under age fourteen where male is four or more years older, §4.15.
Children.
Assault with intent to commit sexual intercourse.
Female under age of fourteen.
Male four or more years older, §4.15.

SEXUAL OFFENSES.
Defined, §4.37.
First degree, §4.37.
Fourth degree, §4.37.
Incest, §4.33.
Rape.
See RAPE.
Second degree, §4.37.
Sodomy, §4.34.
Third degree, §4.37.
Unnatural or perverted sexual practices, §4.35.

SHOPLIFTING.
Generally, §4.84.

SILENCE OF DEFENDANT.
Decision not to testify, §2.27.

SODOMY.
Accomplices and accessories, §4.34.
Consent, §4.34.
Defined, §4.34.
Elements of crime, §4.34.

SPOUSES.
Nonsupport, §4.60.

STIPULATIONS.
Generally, §1.07.

STOLEN GOODS.
Defenses.
Claim of right, §5.03.
Possession of stolen property.
Theft, §4.93.
Receiving stolen goods.
Generally, §4.79.

STOREHOUSES.
Breaking, §4.54.

STOREHOUSES—Cont'd
Breaking—Cont'd
With intent to commit a felony or steal, §4.53.
With intent to steal any money, goods or chattels under the value of $300, §4.54.
With the taking of property, §4.55.

SUBORNATION OF PERJURY.
Generally, §4.78.

SUPPORT.
Nonsupport.
Generally, §4.60.

T

TELEPHONES.
Unlawful use, §4.86.

THEFT.
Breaking.
See BREAKING.
By deception, §4.92.
Checks.
Issuance with intent to stop payment, §4.97 (c).
Knowledge of insufficient funds, §4.97 (a).
Passers of checks, §4.97 (b).
Knowledge that payment has been stopped.
Acts committed by passers, §4.97 (d).
Defenses.
Claim of right, §5.03.
Rights of possession, §4.96.
Definitions.
By deception, §4.92.
Lost, mislaid or mistakenly delivered property, §4.94.
Possession of stolen property, §4.93.
Services, §4.95.
Unauthorized control, §4.91.
Embezzlement, §4.64.
False pretenses, §4.67.
Intent, §4.91.
Larceny, §§4.71 to 4.73.
See LARCENY.
Lost, mislaid or mistakenly delivered property, §4.94.
Possession of stolen property, §4.93.
Receiving stolen goods, §4.79.
Rights of possession, §4.96.

THEFT—Cont'd
Robbery.
See ROBBERY.
Services, §4.95.
Shoplifting, §4.84.
Stolen goods.
See STOLEN GOODS.
Unauthorized control, §4.91.
Definitions, §4.91.

THREATS.
Defenses.
Prior threats of the deceased, §5.16.
Extortion.
Verbal threats, §4.66.
Verbal threats.
Extortion, §4.66.

TICKETS.
Lottery tickets.
See LOTTERIES.

TRESPASS.
Generally, §4.85.

U

UNNATURAL OR PERVERTED SEXUAL PRACTICES.
Accomplices and accessories, §4.35.
Defined, §4.35.
Elements of crime, §4.35.

UTTERING.
Defined, §4.68.
Elements of crime, §4.68.
Forgery.
Distinction between uttering and forgery, §4.68.
Intent to defraud, §4.68.

W

WEAPONS.
Carrying.
Carrying a weapon openly with intent to injure, §4.42.
Concealed weapons, §4.41.
Handguns, §4.43.
Concealed weapons.
Carrying or wearing, §4.41.

WEAPONS—Cont'd
Concealed weapons—Cont'd
Defined, §4.41.
Handgun, §4.43.
Definitions.
Concealed weapons, §4.41.
Dangerous or deadly weapons, §§4.41, 4.42.
Felonies.
Handguns.
Use in commission of felony or crime of violence, §4.44.
Handguns.
Use in commission of felony or crime of violence, §4.44.
Wearing, carrying or transporting openly or concealed, §4.43.
Injury.
Carrying a weapon openly with intent to injure, §4.42.
Intent.
Carrying a weapon openly with intent to injure, §4.42.
Robbery.
Robbery with a deadly weapon, §4.83.
Wearing.
Concealed weapons, §4.41.
Handgun, §4.43.

WILLFULLY.
Defined, §3.04.

WILLFULNESS.
Proof, §3.07.

WITNESSES.
Accomplices and accessories.
Corroboration of accomplice's testimony, §2.01.
Character witnesses.
Impeachment, §2.23.
Children.
Evaluation of testimony, §2.04.
Confessions.
Defendant as witness.
Impeachment by confession, §2.09.
Court.
Calling its own witness, §2.11.
Credibility, §2.06.
Defendant as witness.
Decision not to testify, §2.27.
Impeachment by confession, §2.09.
Impeachment by prior convictions, §2.07.
Expert witnesses, §2.05.

WITNESSES—Cont'd
Impeachment.
Character witnesses, §2.23.
Defendant as witness.
Impeachment by confession, §2.09.
Prior convictions, §2.07.
Prior inconsistent statements, §2.08.
Informers.
Testimony of informer, §2.02.
Leniency.
Witness promised leniency, §2.02.
Missing witness.
Presumption of unfavorable testimony, §2.21.
Number of witnesses, §2.03.
Presumptions.
Missing witness.
Presumption of unfavorable testimony, §2.21.
Prior inconsistent statements, §2.08.
Rehabilitation.
Prior consistent statements, §2.08.

WRITING.
Forgery, §4.68.
Uttering, §4.68.

WRITTEN INSTRUCTIONS.
Supplementing oral instructions, Appendix IV.